Contemporary
Literary Criticism
Yearbook 1987

Guide to Gale Literary Criticism Series

When you need to review criticism of literary works, these are the Gale series to use:

If the author's death date is: **You should turn to:**

After Dec. 31, 1959
(or author is still living)

CONTEMPORARY LITERARY CRITICISM

for example: Jorge Luis Borges, Anthony Burgess,
William Faulkner, Mary Gordon,
Ernest Hemingway, Iris Murdoch

1900 through 1959

TWENTIETH-CENTURY LITERARY CRITICISM

for example: Willa Cather, F. Scott Fitzgerald,
Henry James, Mark Twain, Virginia Woolf

1800 through 1899

NINETEENTH-CENTURY LITERATURE CRITICISM

for example: Fedor Dostoevski, Nathaniel Hawthorne,
George Sand, William Wordsworth

1400 through 1799

LITERATURE CRITICISM FROM 1400 TO 1800
(excluding Shakespeare)

for example: Anne Bradstreet, Daniel Defoe,
Alexander Pope, François Rabelais,
Jonathan Swift, Phillis Wheatley

SHAKESPEAREAN CRITICISM

Shakespeare's plays and poetry

Antiquity through 1399

CLASSICAL AND MEDIEVAL LITERATURE CRITICISM

for example: Dante, Homer, Plato, Sophocles, Vergil,
the Beowulf Poet

Gale also publishes related criticism series:

CHILDREN'S LITERATURE REVIEW

This series covers authors and illustrators of all eras who write for
the preschool through high school audience.

SHORT STORY CRITICISM

This series covers the major short fiction writers of all nationalities
and periods of literary history.

ISSN 0091-3421

Volume 50

Contemporary Literary Criticism

Yearbook 1987

The Year in Fiction, Poetry, Drama,
and World Literature and the Year's
New Authors, Prizewinners, Obituaries,
and Works of Literary Biography

Sharon K. Hall

EDITOR

 Gale Research Inc.

Book Tower • Detroit, Michigan 48226

STAFF

Sharon K. Hall, *Editor*

Anne Sharp, *Senior Assistant Editor*

Derek T. Bell, Ruth P. Feingold, *Assistant Editors*
Joyce A. Davis, *Research Assistant*

Roger Matuz, *Contributing Editor*

Jeanne A. Gough, *Production & Permissions Manager*
Lizbeth A. Purdy, *Production Supervisor*
Kathleen M. Cook, *Production Coordinator*
Cathy Beranek, Suzanne Powers, Kristine E. Tipton, Lee Ann Welsh, *Editorial Assistants*
Linda M. Pugliese, *Manuscript Coordinator*
Maureen A. Puhl, *Senior Manuscript Assistant*
Donna Craft, Jennifer E. Gale, Rosetta Irene Simms, *Manuscript Assistants*

Victoria B. Cariappa, *Research Supervisor*
Maureen R. Richards, *Research Coordinator*
Mary D. Wise, *Senior Research Assistant*
Joyce E. Doyle, Kevin B. Hillstrom, Karen D. Kaus, Eric Priehs,
Filomena Sgambati, Laura B. Standley, *Research Assistants*

Janice M. Mach, *Text Permissions Supervisor*
Kathy Grell, *Text Permissions Coordinator*
Mabel E. Gurney, *Research Permissions Coordinator*
Josephine M. Keene, *Senior Permissions Assistant*
Eileen H. Baehr, H. Diane Cooper, Anita L. Ransom, Kimberly F. Smilay,
Permissions Assistants
Melissa A. Kamuyu, Martha A. Mulder, Lisa M. Wimmer, *Permissions Clerks*

Patricia A. Seefelt, *Picture Permissions Supervisor*
Margaret A. Chamberlain, *Picture Permissions Coordinator*
Pamela A. Hayes, Lillian Tyus, *Permissions Clerks*

Mary Beth Trimper, *Production Manager*
Anthony J. Scolaro, *External Production Assistant*

Arthur Chartow, *Art Director*
Linda A. Davis, *External Production Assistant*

Laura Bryant, *Production Supervisor*
Louise Gagné, *Internal Production Associate*
Jean Rushlow, *Internal Production Assistant*

Library of Congress Catalog Card Number 76-38938
ISBN 0-8103-4424-6
ISSN 0091-3421

Printed in the United States of America

Contents

Preface vii

Authors Forthcoming in *CLC* xi

Appendix 451

Literary Criticism Series Cumulative Author Index 463

CLC Cumulative Nationality Index 525

CLC-50 Title Index 535

Literary Biography

Preface

Every year, an overwhelming number of new publications and significant literary events confront the reader interested in contemporary literature. Who are the year's notable new authors? What dramas have been introduced on the New York stage? Who won the literary world's most prestigious awards? Which authors have been the subjects of significant new literary biographies, and what approach did the biographer take—factual, interpretive, psychological, critical? Finally, who among our best-known contemporary writers died during the year, and what is the reaction of the literary world?

To answer such questions and assist students, teachers, librarians, researchers, and general readers in keeping abreast of current literary activities and trends, the *Contemporary Literary Criticism Yearbook* is being published as part of the *Contemporary Literary Criticism (CLC)* series.

Standard *CLC* volumes provide readers with a comprehensive view of modern literature by presenting excerpted criticism on the works of novelists, poets, playwrights, short story writers, scriptwriters, and other creative writers who are now living or who died after December 31, 1959. Works covered in regular *CLC* volumes are those that have generated significant critical commentary within recent years, with a strong emphasis on works by established authors who frequently appear on the syllabuses of high school and college literature courses.

To complement this broad coverage, the *Yearbook* focuses in depth on a given year's literary activity and highlights a larger number of currently noteworthy authors and books than is possible in standard *CLC* volumes. The *Yearbook* provides critical overviews of the past year's works in various genres, supplies up-to-date critical commentary on new authors and prizewinning writers whose publications have made recent news, and notes the deaths of major contemporary literary figures. In addition, the *Yearbook* expands the scope of regular *CLC* volumes by presenting excerpted criticism on the works of literary biographers, whose growing importance in the literary world warrants increased attention. The *Yearbook* is, in short, a valuable supplement to the regular *CLC* volumes in its comprehensive treatment of the year's activity in literature. Since the majority of the authors covered in the *Yearbook* and regular *CLC* volumes are living writers who continue to publish, an author frequently appears more than once in the series. There is, of course, no duplication of reprinted criticism.

Scope of the Work

CLC Yearbook 1987 includes excerpted criticism on over 50 authors and provides comprehensive coverage of the year's significant literary events. As with the regular volumes of *CLC,* the authors covered include those who are now living or who died after December 31, 1959. In addition, the *Yearbook* also includes essays commissioned exclusively for this publication. The *Yearbook* is divided into five sections: "The Year in Review," "New Authors," "Prizewinners," "Obituaries," and "Literary Biography."

The Year in Review—This section includes specially commissioned essays by prominent literary figures who survey the year's new works in their respective fields. In *CLC Yearbook 1987* we have the advantage of viewing "The Year in Fiction" from the perspective of Robert Wilson, book critic for *USA Today.* Wilson is a member of the National Book Critics Circle and serves on NBCC's Board of Directors. "The Year in Poetry" is presented by Sidney Burris, who is a poet, critic, and assistant professor of English at the University of Arkansas. Burris's poetry has appeared in the *Atlantic Monthly, Poetry, Prairie Schooner, Missouri Review,* and *New Virginia Review,* and both a collection of his poems and a critical study of Irish poet Seamus Heaney are in press. "The Year in Drama" is reviewed by Robert Cohen, author of numerous books on the theater, including *Giraudoux: Three Faces of Destiny* (1969), *Creative Play Direction* (1974), and *Theatre* (1982). Cohen is also chair of the drama department at the University of California, Irvine. Finally, "The Year in World Literature" is discussed by William Riggan, who as associate editor of the quarterly *World Literature Today* is in a unique position to comment on important international literature; Riggan specializes in Third World, Slavic, and Anglo-American literatures. These annual survey essays on fiction, poetry, drama, and world literature are a special feature of the *Yearbook,* and provide a focus that is outside the scope of our regular *CLC* volumes.

New Authors—*CLC Yearbook 1987* introduces fifteen writers whose first book, or first book in English-language translation, was published during 1987. Authors were selected for inclusion if their work was reviewed in several sources and garnered significant criticism. Although the regular *CLC* volumes often cover new writers, the *Yearbook* provides more timely and more extensive coverage of authors just coming into prominence. This expanded coverage includes writers of poetry, short stories, and novels. *CLC Yearbook 1987,* for example, presents short story writer David Michael Kaplan and the novelists Valerie Sayers, whose novel *Due East* offers a touching father-daughter portrait, and Bruce Duffy, whose novel *The World as I Found It* explores the lives of Ludwig Wittgenstein, Bertrand Russell, and G. E. Moore.

Prizewinners—This section of *Yearbook* begins with a list of literary prizes and honors announced in 1987, citing the award, its recipient, and the title of the prize-winning work. *CLC Yearbook 1987* then highlights fifteen major prizewinners who will be featured in the *Yearbook*. A "Prize Commentary" follows, discussing each award featured in the *Yearbook* and indicating the year the award was established, the reason it was established, the awarding body, how the winner is chosen, and the nature of the prize (money, trophy, etc.). After the "Prize Commentary," entries on individual award winners are presented. Recipients of established literary honors, such as the Pulitzer Prize, are included as well as authors who have won less established but increasingly important prizes, such as the PEN/Faulkner Award for Fiction, the only award given to writers by writers. In addition to the winners of major American awards, recipients of several outstanding international prizes are also covered. Thus we include England's distinguished Booker-McConnell Prize, awarded to Penelope Lively, and Canada's Governor General's Literary Awards, presented to Alice Munro for fiction, Sharon Pollock for drama, and Al Purdy for poetry. We have, of course, also featured the literary world's most prestigious award, the Nobel Prize in literature, bestowed on Russian-born American poet Joseph Brodsky.

Obituaries—This section begins with a necrology of *CLC* authors. Following the necrology, individual author entries are included for the more prominent writers whose influence on contemporary literature is reflected in the obituaries, reminiscences, tributes, or retrospective essays included in their entries. *CLC Yearbook 1987,* for example, presents entries on Jean Anouilh, James Baldwin, Erskine Caldwell, Margaret Laurence, and Primo Levi, among others.

Literary Biography—Since literary biographies are outside the scope of works covered in regular *CLC* volumes, the *Yearbook* provides an opportunity to offer comprehensive commentary on these prominent and popular works. This part of the *Yearbook,* then, is devoted to criticism on literary biographies of authors who are within the *CLC* time period. We do not, therefore, include biographies of authors of the early twentieth century or of previous centuries. Besides giving a personal perspective on the authors who are the subjects of the literary biographies, this section also introduces readers to today's biographers and their methods, styles, and approaches to the genre. *CLC Yearbook 1987* discusses six literary biographies, including the first full-length biography of the colorful Rebecca west, by Victoria Glendinning, and *Sylvia Plath: A Biography,* by Linda Wagner-Martin, which was limited by the refusal of the Hughes estate (Plath was married to Ted Hughes) to grant permission to quote the poet's work.

Format of the Book

With the exception of the essays in "The Year in Review" section, which are written specifically for this publication, the *Yearbook* is comprised of excerpted criticism. There are approximately 400 individual excerpts in *CLC Yearbook 1987* drawn from hundreds of literary reviews, general magazines, distinguished newspapers, and scholarly journals. The excerpts included reflect the attention the authors and their works have received by critics writing in English and by critics from other nations whose work has been translated; critical books and articles not translated into English have been excluded.

Since the *Yearbook* is designed to complement other *CLC* volumes, *Yearbook* entries generally follow the same format with some variations and additional features. *Yearbook* entries variously contain the following elements:

- The **author heading,** which is included in entries in the "New Authors," "Prizewinners," and "Obituaries" sections, cites the author's full name. The portion of the name outside the parentheses denotes the form under which the author has most commonly published. If an author has written consistently under a pseudonym, the pseudonym will be listed in the author heading and the real name given on the first line of the author entry. Also located at the beginning of the author entry are any important name variations under which an author has written. For new authors and obituaries, the author's name is followed by the birth date and, in the case of an obituary, the death date. Uncertainty as to a birth or death date is indicated by question marks. For prizewinners, the author's name is followed by the title of the prizewinning work and the award received.

● The **book heading,** which is included in entries in the "Literary Biography" section, cites the complete title of the book followed by the biographer's name.

● A brief **biographical and critical introduction** to the author and his or her work precedes the excerpted criticism in entries in the "New Authors" and "Prizewinners" sections.

● **Cross-references** have been included in all sections, except "The Year in Review," to direct the reader to other useful sources published by Gale Research: *Contemporary Authors,* which includes detailed biographical and bibliographical sketches on more than 90,000 authors; *Children's Literature Review,* which presents excerpted criticism on the works of authors of children's books; *Something about the Author,* which contains heavily illustrated biographical sketches on writers and illustrators who create books for children and young adults; *Contemporary Issues Criticism,* which presents excerpted commentary on the nonfiction works of authors who influence contemporary thought; *Dictionary of Literary Biography,* which provides original evaluations of authors important to literary history; *Contemporary Authors Autobiography Series,* which offers autobiographical essays by prominent writers; and *Something about the Author Autobiographical Series,* which presents autobiographical essays by authors of interest to young readers. Previous volumes of *CLC* in which the author has been featured are also listed. Cross-references are provided for both the authors and subjects of literary biographies. In *CLC Yearbook 1987,* for example, the entry on Victoria Glendinning's *Rebecca West: A Life* cites additional sources of information on both Glendinning and West.

● A list of **principal works,** including the author's first and last published work and other important works, is provided in entries in the "Obituaries" section in order to reflect the author's entire literary career. The list is chronological by date of first book publication and identifies the genre of each work. In the case of foreign authors where there are both foreign language publications and English translations, the title and date of the first English-language edition are given in brackets. Unless otherwise indicated, dramas are dated by first performance, not first publication.

● A **portrait** of the author is included, when available, in entries in the "New Authors," "Prizewinners," and "Obituaries" sections.

● An **excerpt** from the author's work is included, when available, in entries in the "New Authors," "Prizewinners," and "Literary Biography" sections, in order to provide the reader with a sampling of the author's thematic approach and style.

● The **excerpted criticism,** included in all entries except those in "The Year in Review" section, represents essays selected by editors to reflect the spectrum of opinion about a specific work or about an author's writing in general. The excerpts are presented chronologically, adding a useful perspective to the entry. All titles featured in the entry are printed in boldface type, which enables the reader to easily identify the works being discussed.

● Selected critical excerpts are prefaced by **explanatory notes** that give important information regarding critics and their work and also provide a summary of the criticism.

● A complete **bibliographical citation**, designed to help the user find the original essay or book, follows each excerpt.

Other Features

● A list of **Authors Forthcoming in *CLC*** previews the authors to be researched for future volumes.

● An **Appendix** lists the sources from which material in the volume has been reprinted. Many other sources have also been consulted during the preparation of the volume.

● A **Cumulative Index to Authors** lists all the authors who have appeared in *Contemporary Literary Criticism* (including authors who are the subject of works of literary biography covered in the *Yearbook*); *Twentieth-Century Literary Criticism, Nineteenth-Century Literature Criticism, Literature Criticism from*

1400-1800, and *Classical and Medieval Literature Criticism* along with cross-references to other Gale series: *Short Story Criticism, Children's Literature Review, Authors in the News, Contemporary Authors, Contemporary Authors Autobiography Series, Contemporary Authors Bibliographical Series, Dictionary of Literary Biography, Something about the Author, Something about the Author Autobiography Series,* and *Yesterday's Authors of Books for Children.* Users will welcome this cumulated author index as a useful tool for locating an author within the various series. The index, which lists birth and death dates when available, will be particularly valuable for those authors who are identified with a certain period but whose death date causes them to be placed in another, or for those authors whose careers span two periods. For example, F. Scott Fitzgerald is found in *Twentieth-Century Literary Criticism,* yet a writer often associated with him, Ernest Hemingway, is found in *Contemporary Literary Criticism.*

● A **Cumulative Nationality Index** alphabetically lists all authors featured in *CLC* by nationality, followed by numbers corresponding to the volumes in which they appear.

● A **Title Index** alphabetically lists all titles reviewed in the current volume of *CLC.* Titles are followed by the corresponding page numbers where they may be located. In cases where the same title is used by different authors, the authors' surnames are given in parentheses after the title; for example, *Collected Poems* (Berryman) and *Collected Poems* (Eliot). For foreign titles, a cross-reference is given to the translated English title. Titles of novels, novellas, dramas, films, record albums, and poetry, short story, essay collections are printed in italics, while all individual poems, short stories, essays are printed in roman type within quotation marks; when published separately (e.g., T. S. Eliot's poem *The Waste Land*), the title will also be printed in italics.

● In response to numerous suggestions from librarians, Gale has also produced a special paperbound edition of the *CLC* title index. This annual cumulation, which alphabetically lists all titles reviewed in the series, is available to all customers and will be published with the first volume of *CLC* issued in each calendar year. Additional copies of the index are available upon request. Librarians and patrons will welcome this separate index: it saves shelf space, is easily disposable upon receipt of the following year's cumulation, and is more portable and thus easier to use than was previously possible.

Acknowledgments

No work of this scope can be accomplished without the cooperation of many people. The editors especially wish to thank the copyright holders of the excerpted criticism and photographs included in this volume, the permissions managers of many book and magazine publishing companies for assisting us in securing reprint rights, and Anthony Bogucki for assistance with copyright research. We are also grateful to the staffs of the Detroit Public Library, the Library of Congress, the University of Detroit Library, the University of Michigan Library, and the Wayne State University Library for making their resources available to us.

Suggestions Are Welcome

The editors welcome the comments and suggestions of readers to expand the coverage and enhance the usefulness of the series.

Authors Forthcoming in *CLC*

Contemporary Literary Criticism, Volumes 51 and 52 will feature criticism on a number of authors not previously covered in this series as well as excerpted reviews of newer works by authors included in earlier volumes.

To Be Included in Volume 51

Chinua Achebe (Nigerian novelist, short story writer, poet, and essayist)—One of Africa's most important contemporary writers, Achebe chronicles the cultural and psychological effects of European colonization on the Ibo, a native Nigerian tribe. His entry will include reviews of his recent novel, *Anthills of the Savannah.*

Anita Brookner (English novelist, nonfiction writer, and critic)—Best known as the author of *Hotel du Lac,* for which she received the Booker McConnell Prize for fiction, Brookner writes novels that focus upon well-educated, affluent women whose lives are often disrupted by unfaithful husbands and lovers. Recent works to be covered in her entry include *Family and Friends* and *The Misalliance.*

Noël Coward (English dramatist, lyricist, novelist, short story writer, scriptwriter, and autobiographer)—A prolific and versatile playwright, Coward is best remembered for whimsical social comedies that display his talent for creating imaginative plots and witty, acerbic dialogue. Recent revivals of such popular Coward plays as *Private Lives, Blithe Spirit,* and *Design for Living* have renewed interest in his work.

Kenneth Fearing (American poet, novelist, and editor)— Best known for the thriller novel *The Big Clock,* from which the recent film *No Way Out* was adapted, Fearing also distinguished himself during the Depression era as a poet whose verse attacked the dehumanizing effects of a capitalistic industrialized society.

Nadine Gordimer (South African novelist, short story writer, critic, and editor)—Gordimer is respected for examining the effects of the South African apartheid system on both ruling whites and oppressed blacks. Criticism in Gordimer's entry will focus upon her recent novel, *A Sport of Nature.*

Katherine Govier (Canadian novelist, short story writer, and journalist)—In her fiction, Govier often depicts female characters who must confront elements of their past in order to live contentedly in the present. Govier's interest in history is reflected in her recent novel, *Between Man,* which intertwines the stories of a contemporary history professor and an Indian woman who died mysteriously in the 1880s.

Patrick Hamilton (English dramatist, novelist, and scriptwriter)—Best known for his psychological plays *Rope* and *Angel Street,* Hamilton also wrote several novels during the 1930s and 1940s set in and around English pubs that portray the disordered lives of criminals, outcasts, and misfits.

Lisel Mueller (German-born American poet and critic)—Using such traditional techniques as metaphor, simile, and personification, Mueller concentrates on discovering the extraordinary aspects of ordinary objects and events. Collections of verse to be covered in her entry include *The Private Life* and *Second Language.*

Tom Wolfe (American essayist, journalist, editor, critic, and novelist)—Regarded as one of the most original stylists in contemporary literature, Wolfe figured prominently in the development of New Journalism, a form of expository writing that blends reporting with such techniques of fiction as stream of consciousness, extended dialogue, shifting points of view, and detailed scenarios. This entry will focus upon Wolfe's recent first novel, *The Bonfire of the Vanities.*

Yevgeny Yevtushenko (Russian poet and novelist)—Among the most outspoken and controversial poets to emerge in the Soviet Union since the death of Stalin, Yevtushenko has written two recent novels, *Wild Berries,* and *Ardabiola,* in which he expands on the personal themes of his poetry.

Peter Ackroyd (English novelist, biographer, and critic)—An acclaimed biographer of such esteemed writers as T.S. Eliot and Ezra Pound, Ackroyd has also elicited significant praise for his novels focusing upon prominent literary figures. Among the works to be covered in his entry are *The Last Testament of Oscar Wilde, Hawksmoor,* and *Chatterton.*

Conrad Aiken (American poet, novelist, short story writer, critic, dramatist, memoirist, and autobiographer)—A major figure in twentieth-century American literature who was awarded the Pulitzer Prize in Poetry in 1930, Aiken employed formal stylistic techniques and an often somber tone in his verse to examine themes related to such topics as spirituality, philosophy, psychology, and science.

Woody Allen (American dramatist, short story writer, scriptwriter, and director)—Best known for his work as a comedian, actor, and filmmaker, Allen is also a noted author of fiction and drama. Criticism in his entry will focus upon the short story collections *Getting Even, Without Feathers,* and *Side Effects* and such plays as *Don't Drink the Water* and *Play It Again, Sam.*

Gregory Benford (American novelist and short story writer)—Benford has written several works of speculative science fiction in which he contrasts the negative and positive aspects of such phenomena as alien contact and technological advancement.

Maryse Conde (Guadeloupean-born French novelist, short story writer, and dramatist)—Conde's novels often portray the lives of contemporary Caribbean and African women. Included in her entry will be criticism of *Moi, Tituba, sorcière, Noire de Salem,* a fictionalized biography of Tituba, a Barbadian slave who was tried for witchcraft in colonial Massachusetts.

William Faulkner (American novelist, short story writer, poet, and scriptwriter)—A seminal figure in modern literature, Faulkner was best known for novels and short stories set in his fictional locale of Yoknapatawpha County. Criticism in this volume will focus upon *Absalom, Absalom!,* one of Faulkner's most frequently analyzed works.

Christopher Hope (South African novelist, poet, short story writer, and dramatist)—In his novels *A Separate Development* and *Kruger's Alp,* Hope employs black humor, surrealism, allegory, and satire to explore the implications of racial discrimination in South Africa under the apartheid system.

Louis MacNeice (Irish-born English poet, critic, translator, dramatist, scriptwriter, and novelist)—A member of the "Oxford Group" of poets of the 1930s that included W.H. Auden, C. Day Lewis, and Stephen Spender, MacNeice is best known for verse in which he examines social concerns and the vagaries of the human condition.

Gloria Naylor (American novelist and short story writer)—Recognized as the author of *The Women of Brewster Place,* for which she received the American Book Award for best first novel, Naylor often examines the experiences of black American women in her fiction. Criticism in Naylor's entry will focus upon her novels *Linden Hills* and *Mama Day.*

Erika Ritter (Canadian dramatist, essayist, and short story writer)—Ritter's plays follow the plight of intelligent contemporary women who attempt to balance love and careers in the wake of the feminist movement. Ritter's entry will also include criticism of her collection of satirical essays, *Urban Scrawls.*

The Year in Review

The Year in Fiction
by Robert Wilson

Few fiction writers are satisfied with the amount of critical attention their books receive. Many suspect conspiracies to repress their work, conspiracies including, at the very least, that superannuated book reviewer at a certain news magazine, the entire editorial staff of a major newspaper, the owner of an important literary journal, and several members of their own publisher's publicity department. The truth is that most reviewers and editors are too busy or too disorganized to participate in conspiracies. Many books get less attention than they deserve simply because there are too many books published each year. Sometimes a few books do get more than their share of what little critical attention there is to go around. But it's rare, a lot rarer than most writers believe, for a newspaper of the importance of *The New York Times* to mount a campaign on behalf of a particular book. It's rarer still—in fact, it's never happened before, in my memory—for a number of writers to band together to complain that a particular novel, lavishly reviewed from sea to shining sea, has not yet won a major prize.

Both happened in 1987 with the game book, Toni Morrison's fifth novel, *Beloved. The New York Times* gave an unusual if not unheard-of amount of space to the book. On August 26, it ran a 1,200-word interview with Morrison. On September 2, staff reviewer Michiko Kakutani called the book "extraordinary," and mentioned Morrison's "magisterial yet sensuous prose," comparing its characters to those of opera or Greek drama. On the front page of the September 13 *New York Times Book Review,* reviewer Margaret Atwood called the novel "another triumph." *Beloved* was nominated for a National Book Award, a National Book Critics Circle Award, and the $50,000 Ritz Paris Hemingway prize.

When, in November, *Beloved* did not win the National Book Award, *The New York Times* ran several news stories commenting upon how surprised certain unspecified members of the New York literati were. Then on November 16, Kakutani wrote a controversial 1,400-word "Critic's Notebook" column unfavorably comparing *Paco's Story*, the 1986 novel by Larry Heinemann that won the award, with *Beloved,* which Kakutani then proceeded to review again. In January, after *Beloved* did not win the National Book Critics Circle Fiction award (which Morrison had won for her previous novel, *Song of Solomon*), *The New York Times* gave more than half a page of space in its January 24 *Book Review* to a letter and a statement signed by forty-eight writers protesting that Morrison "has yet to receive the keystone honors of the National Book Award or the Pulitzer Prize"—an obvious attempt to intimidate the Pulitzer Prize jury, which would announce its winners at the end of March. It also ran a 500-word news story about the protest and yet another "Critic's Notebook," this time by Walter Goodman, speculating on whether the lobbying on Morrison's behalf for the Pulitzer would have any effect. One hopes and assumes that the Pulitzer board is above such pressure. In any event, Morrison did win the prize.

Dust jacket of Beloved, *by Toni Morrison. Alfred A. Knopf, 1987. Jacket design by R. D. Scudellari. Courtesy of Alfred A. Knopf, Inc.*

Beloved, which tells the heartwrenching story of an escaped slave woman who murders her baby rather than allow her to grow up enslaved, has been widely recognized as one of the most significant novels of the year. Most reviewers admired the book, and most review publications gave their reviews prominent display. It has been reported that the letter and statement in *The New York Times* were not written at Morrison's request, but in response to a friend's observation that Morrison was dispirited at not winning an award. Which takes me back to where I began.

Prominent Contemporaries

This was a year when others of our most prominent fiction writers might also have been less than satisfied with the critical reception of their books. Novels published this year by Saul Bellow (*More Die of Heartbreak*), John Barth (*The Tidewater Tales*), James Dickey (*Alnilam*), Stanley Elkin (*The Rabbi of Lud*), Gail Godwin (*A Southern Family*), Joyce Carol Oates (*You Must Remember This*), Cynthia Ozick (*The Messiah of*

Stockholm), Walker Percy (*The Thanatos Syndrome*), Wallace Stegner (*Crossing to Safety*) and Kurt Vonnegut (*Bluebeard*) were generally judged not to be up to the best work their authors have done, although many of them were favorably reviewed anyway.

Bellow's narrator is a chatterbox named Kenneth Trachtenberg, who spends his time studying his uncle, Benn Crader, a botanist with a genius for plants and a typically Bellovian incompetence with women and the world at large. Although *More Die of Heartbreak* is both brilliant and funny at times, it can also be too digressive and occasionally even somewhat boring.

Barth's compendium of tales, like his earlier novel *Sabbatical*, features a couple sailing the Chesapeake Bay. On this trip they happen across Odysseus and Scheherazade, and also find themselves involved in CIA and Mafia business. Despite the abundance of plot, *The Tidewater Tales* is "ponderous and long-winded," according to critic Tom LeClair.

Dickey's massive novel, several time the length of his *Deliverance,* has to do with a blind man in search of information about the death of his son, a flier at an Air Corps training camp during World War II. *Alnilam*'s story is melodramatic and the writing often windy, but occasionally, especially when Dickey has the blind man imagining scenes of aerial combat, the prose soars.

In *The Rabbi of Lud* Elkin offers up another of his novels that are short on plot and long on verbal firepower and black humor; it is the story of a rabbi graduate of an "offshore yeshiva" who conducts burial services in a New Jersey town named Lud that is almost wholly devoted to the business of death.

Godwin's generic title—*A Southern Family*—is at least descriptive of her novel about a Southern family whose reunion explodes in violence with the supposed murder-suicide of a son and his companion, leaving the other family members to piece together what has happened.

You Must Remember This, Oates's major effort of the year (she is nothing if not productive), is set in upstate New York during the '50s, and it is rife with details of the period: the Rosenberg execution, bomb shelters, McCarthyism. The texture of her characters' lives is typically, for Oates, gray and gritty, and its energy, also typically, comes from the violence bubbling beneath the surface of such lives.

Ozick's new novel, *The Messiah of Stockholm*—a nominee for the 1988 PEN/Faulkner award—features a Swedish book reviewer who becomes convinced that he is the illegitimate son of the real-life writer Bruno Schulz, a Polish jew murdered by the Nazis in 1942. Amid various questions of authenticity and forgery, a manuscript emerges that is purported to be Schulz's last, lost work, "The Messiah." Ozick is so concerned with such big questions as the idolatry of art that she occasionally slips from the profound into the abstruse.

Percy brings back Dr. Tom More from *Love in the Ruins* to track down a medical mystery featuring social engineering on the lower Mississippi, against a backdrop of this death-loving century, which is in its last decade in the book. Percy's speculative novels are not quite his best, but *The Thanatos Syndrome* is nonetheless a dazzling, thoughtful book.

Stegner's *Crossing to Safety* follows the lives of two bright academic couples who are devoted to each other and to a pond house they visit together each summer in Vermont. In the present tense of the book, the couples are old, and one of the

Dust jacket of Crossing to Safety, *by Wallace Stegner. Random House, 1987. Jacket design and illustration by Wendell Minor. Courtesy of Random House, Inc.*

four is near death, which casts a melancholy shadow over lives that have been lived thoughtfully and well. Enduring friendship, dignity in age, the human and finally hopeless need to make order out of chaos, all are themes in a book that, although small in scale compared to his award-winning earlier novels, is one of the most satisfying novels of 1987.

In *Bluebeard* Vonnegut casts his story in the form of an autobiography, that of a failed abstract-expressionist painter named Rebo Karabekian (a minor character in his 1973 novel, *Breakfast of Champions*) who has grown rich by having fortuitously collected the works of such artist friends as Rothko and Pollock before they were worth anything. The book features familiar Vonnegut mannerisms and uncommon, even for Vonnegut, high spirits.

One writer who belongs close to the head of this class did produce a work that many reviewers judged the best of a distinguished career. Philip Roth's *The Counterlife* once again features the writer's alter ego, Nathan Zuckerman, in a fractured narrative in which Zuckerman dies and then doesn't die, and in which Roth's old subjects of sexuality and Jewish identity are taken up in writing of impressive virtuosity. The novel won the National Book Critics Circle Award for Fiction. Other nominees for the award, besides Morrison, included Stegner, Tom Wolfe for *The Bonfire of the Vanities* and Jane Smiley for a story collection called *The Age of Grief*.

Among other works published in 1987 by serious writers who are household names, at least in bookish households, was the posthumous appearance of what is apparently the only surviving fragment (or perhaps all that was ever written) of *Answered*

Dust jacket of The Age of Grief, *by Jane Smiley. Alfred A. Knopf, 1987. Jacket painting by Guy Gladwell. Jacket design by Sue Keston. Courtesy of Alfred A. Knopf, Inc.*

Prayers, which Truman Capote claimed would be his masterwork. Most reviewers agreed that publishing what amounted to salacious gossip about the rich or the fashionable was a large mistake, besmirching a career at its most lustrous in *In Cold Blood.*

Speaking of writers who live among the wealthy and the powerful, and who are almost as famous as television personalities as they are as novelists, Gore Vidal published the latest in his series of American historical chronicles. This one, *Empire,* moves to the turn-of-the century administrations of McKinley and Roosevelt, to illustrate themes of greed and imperialism. As usual, Vidal was praised in the reviews both as novelist and historian.

Finally, among our literary heavy-weights, John Updike published *Trust Me,* a collection of short stories. As ever, these stories are sparklingly written, concerning themselves with the achy yearnings and sweet sorrows of upper-middle-class life in these times.

First Novelists

Those are fifteen writers, then, who didn't need to go begging for critical attention. Did they displace writers less well known whose works also deserved recognition? Probably. It is an odd truth about the reviewing of fiction in this country, however, that a novelist who is completely unknown is more likely to get attention than one who has published a book or more but has not yet won the gold. Perhaps because of the general cultural tendency to celebrate what is young or new, reviewers seem hungry to discover first-time novelists. So here are fifteen novelists who weren't novelist before 1987 rolled around.

Unfortunately for my scheme, *all* of them weren't unknown. Most prominent among the year's first novelists was Tom Wolfe, a literary celebrity for two decades for his energetic and carefully observed journalism. *The Bonfire of the Vanities* was not just a critical success and an award nominee, it was an immediate best-seller. The story of the downfall of Sherman McCoy, a Wall Street high roller who thinks of himself as a "Master of the Universe" is distinguished by Wolfe's reportorial gifts, his attention to the details of class and culture that only the great novelists have. Yet the novel devolves into a kind of police procedural, and Wolfe's lack of feeling for any of his characters finally flaws the book.

Another first novel to ride high on the best-seller lists in some ways resembled *Bonfire,* as critic Jonathan Yardley pointed out. But Scott Turow's *Presumed Innocent* is much more deliberately a crime story, a courtroom drama set in Chicago whose ending left many readers feeling manipulated.

Far down the best-seller lists from these two, and yet a local best-seller in Washington, D.C., in whose suburbs its author lives, *The World as I found It* by Bruce Duffy takes as its unlikely protagonist the philosopher Ludwig Wittgenstein.

Critic Bruce Allen's choice for best novel of the year was a first effort by Maria Thomas, called *Antonia Saw the Oryx First.* Set in East Africa, it tells the story of a white woman doctor who must compete with a native healer, but who nonetheless bemoans the passage of the old ways, and looks with bemusement at Africa in transition.

A nominee for the National Book Award, Howard Norman's *The Northern Lights* tells about a small town in the Canadian

Dust jacket of The Bonfire of the Vanities, *by Tom Wolfe. Farrar, Straus and Giroux, 1987. Jacket design © 1987 by Fred Marcellino. Reproduced by permission of Farrar, Straus and Giroux, Inc.*

north isolated from the world except for what it can hear on shortwave radio.

Two other widely admired first novels included *First Light*, by Charles Baxter, a book with an imploding structure that takes its title from the first atomic explosion at Los Alamos, and *Imagining Argentina*, by Lawrence Thornton, a brilliant, night-marish story of a husband whose wife has been disappeared by the Argentine military, written by a writer who has never been to that country. The latter was nominated for a PEN/Faulkner award.

One of my favorite first novels of the year was *Renifleur's Daughter*, a book by Candida Fraze that is both sensual and sensuous, about a young woman growing up in a wonderful Georgetown house that has an odiferous garden. Renifleur is a Freudian term for a person sexually stimulated by odors. The title is no doubt meant to echo that of Hawthorne's tale, also set largely in a garden, "Rappaccini's Daughter."

A novel that got some of its attention because of the attention paid to the novels of his wife, Louise Erdrich—which she says he collaborated on —Michael Dorris's *A Yellow Raft in Blue Water* is said by him to be a collaboration with her. Like her *Love Medicine*, and somewhat less like her *The Beet Queen*, it is a saga of an American Indian family, involving three generations of women on a Montana reservation.

Among other first novels singled out for attention in 1987; *The Automotive History of Lucky Kellerman*, by Steve Heller, about an older man ruminating on his life as he restores a car in rural Oklahoma; *The Broom of the System*, by David Foster Wallace, a verbally exuberant, Pynchonesque story set in Cleveland in 1990; *Crooked Hearts*, by Robert Boswell, a story about family love featuring an eccentric Midwestern family starting over in Yuma, Arizona; *Ellen Foster*, by Kaye Gibbons, the tale of a Southern, female David Copperfield; *Mama*, by Terry Mc-Millan, a comic novel about a poor black family in Point Haven, Michigan, and eventually in Southern California; and *The Object of My Affection*, by Stephen McCauley, a funny novel about life in New York City in the '80s featuring the unlikely duo of an unwed mother and her live-in male homosexual friend.

Contemporaries

And what of those novelists in the middle, neither new and shiny nor literary superstars? Here in brief are two dozen of dozens in this category that I might mention:

In *An Adultery*, Alexander Theroux (brother of Paul) writes and sometimes overwrites the story of an artist-in-residence at a New England prep school who falls passionately in love with another man's wife.

AEgypt is John Crowley's story of an upstate New York his-torian who turns to "ancient theologies, old magic systems" to find meanings in life beyond those conventionally accepted.

Age, by Hortense Calisher, is a short novel about an aging couple who decide to face up to the fact that one will die before the other by each keeping a journal for the surviving spouse to take comfort in.

The American Ambassador, by Ward Just, an international thriller featuring a U.S. diplomat and his terrorist son, is often well-written but has a preposterous plot involving the son's plan to assassinate his father.

Cigarettes, by Harry Mathews, is a complex but ingeniously designed experimental novel in which thirteen characters in Saratoga Springs and Greenwich Village all have in common a woman named Elizabeth.

Dancing at the Rascal Fair, the second novel in Ivan Doig's Montana trilogy, features two young Scotsmen who homestead in Montana in hopes of striking it rich in silver.

In *Five Hundred Scorpions*, Shelby Hearon's tenth novel, a middle-aged lawyer finds new ways of seeing the world on a visit to Mexico.

Poet and novelist Marge Piercy, in *Gone to Soldiers*, intertwines the stories of ten characters as different as a WAF pilot and a teenager in the French underground, struggling to live through World War II.

A decade after the publication of her novel *The Women's Room*, Marilyn French brought out *Her Mother's Daughter* in 1987. It tells about four generations of women who pass their anger and frustrations on to their daughters.

In the Country of Last Things, Paul Auster tells the story of a woman looking for her brother in a future world that has suf-fered large-scale destruction. One reviewer described the book as Orwell written by Kafka.

Life during Wartime, by Lucius Shepard, is a futuristic novel about war in Central America, seen through the eyes of a young U.S. soldier.

Mother Love, by Candace Flynt, the author of a fine first novel called *Chasing Dad*, tells the story of three sisters in Greens-

Dust jacket of Five Hundred Scorpions, *by Shelby Hearon. Atheneum, 1987. Jacket design copyright © 1987 by James Steinberg. Reproduced by permission of James Steinberg.*

boro, North Carolina, trying to cope with the death of their mother, and perhaps even harder, with their memories of her.

In *Persian Nights,* Diane Johnson's first novel in nine years, a wealthy doctor's wife finds herself alone in Shiraz, Iran, just before the fall of the Shah. There she learns that she has lived her life too carelessly, and that her actions do have consequences.

Susan Richards Shreve, in *Queen of Hearts,* tells the story of a woman rumored to be a witch in a town near Salem, Massachusetts, where many strange things happen. In spite of the spookiness, it is a novel filled with strong, compelling characters.

The Red White and Blue is John Gregory Dunne's story of a journalist and screenwriter (like Dunne himself) who is well-placed to observe much of what has happened in contemporary history, but whose own moral ambivalence makes it hard to care about his observations.

John Edgar Wideman in his new novel *Reuben* writes again about the impoverished Homewood section of Pittsburgh that was the subject of his Homewood Trilogy, one volume of which won the PEN/Faulkner award. The title character in this novel is a fixer, a man who can make certain things right in the ghetto, but who suffers himself from the burden of living in his surroundings.

Rich in Love is the second novel by Josephine Humphreys, whose first, *Dreams of Sleep,* won a PEN award for first fiction. Both books are set in her native Charleston, and although the reviews most often unfavorably compared her new book with her old one, I found *Rich in Love* simpler, more appealing, and more filled with heart's wisdom.

Tending to Virginia, Jill McCorkle's third novel, tells of three generations of women in a North Carolina family tending to the pregnant Ginny Sue, who has temporarily left her husband. All the women are talkers, and numerous family stories give way, on an afternoon of a great storm, to confessions and realizations that affect all the women.

Larry McMurty's first novel after his Pulitzer-winning *Lonesome Dove* is called *Texasville.* It returns years later to Thalia, Texas, the scene of his novel *The Last Picture Show,* and shows what has become of some of its characters. Most reviewers found the book uneven, and it had little of the commercial success of *Lonesome Dove.*

That Night, by Alice McDermott, a PEN/Faulkner award nominee, tells and retells the story of a confrontation in a middle-class suburban neighborhood between a hoody boy and his hoody friends and the family of a girl he has impregnated, who has been shipped off to an aunt's house to have the baby.

William McPherson's second novel, *To the Sargasso Sea,* takes the action forward some thirty years from his acclaimed first book, *Testing the Current.* The year is now 1971, and the young boy through whose eyes we saw the earlier book is now a playwright who, at forty, feels that his life might be falling apart, and knows that he must change it.

Set in 1932 in Wabash, Illinois, a steel town feeling the hardships of the Depression, Robert Olen Butler's *Wabash* tells the story of an angry, silent steelworker and his goodhearted wife, whose marriage has been frozen by the death of their daughter.

A nominee for the PEN/Faulkner award, *World's End,* by T. Coraghessan Boyle, weaves the past with the present as it follows three families in the valley of the Hudson River over three centuries, with climactic moments coming in the late seventeenth century, the late 1940s, and 1968. One critic called it "one of the most ambitious American novels of recent years."

The Year of Silence, the fifth book of fiction by Madison Smartt Bell, explores the suicide by overdose of a young woman in a grim and seamy New York City, through the stories of people who knew her, and, in one chapter, through her own eyes.

Short Story Collections

It is always being said lately that we are living in a renaissance of the short story—a cliche that threatens to reach the proportions of the one about the death of the novel a decade or so ago. The following selection among 1987's collections of short stories certainly has its bright spots, including especially such relatively unknown writers as Jane Smiley, Steve Stern, and Richard Bausch, but we are hardly talking about anything to compare with the days when Hemingway, Faulkner, Fitzgerald, Katherine Anne Porter, and others were all writing stories, nor are we even approaching, it seems to me, a more recent golden age, when one could find the stories of Eudora Welty, Flannery O'Connor, Peter Taylor, and John Cheever appearing in the magazines. Writing programs are cranking out more short-story writers, and more publishers seem willing to publish them than they were a decade ago in the seventies, but an age is judged by how many great or near-great writers it produces, not by how many practitioners it can claim.

That said, I should also say that one of the most impressive long stories I have read since, say, Peter Taylor's "In the Miro District," is the title story in Jane Smiley's *The Age of Grief,* which was nominated for a National Book Critics Circle award. Working with subjects that are almost absurdly banal—two Midwest dentists who are married to each other—she creates a world that is exciting in the wisdom about love, marriage, and jealousy that her narrator, the husband, is able to bring to it. None of the other stories in the collection approaches the richness of this one, but then no other stories that I read this year approach it, either.

The only other book of stories nominated for a major award this year is Richard Bausch's *Spirits,* a PEN/Faulkner nominee. These nine stories, which mostly deal with domestic situations, confront both the specter of loss and the dark corners of the spirit. Novelist Robb Forman Dew wrote about the book, "again and again Bausch's characters hunger after and struggle toward a morality that will embrace any bit of goodness, or kindness, or decency in the world."

Another story collection having to do with domestic life is Elizabeth Tallent's *Time with Children.* In these stories, however, what the characters hunger for is love outside the domestic situations in which they find themselves.

Novelist Mary Gordon's first collection of stories, *Temporary Shelter,* deals persistently with the dangers life has to offer: all the best things imaginable in life, love, work, friendship, and, of course, childhood, offer only temporary shelter from those dangers.

Robert Coover's *A Night at the Movies; or, You Must Remember This* offers a breviary of cinematic legends, as Edmund White called it, including Chaplin, Bogart, Astaire, and Valentino, using the "syntax of films," as Coover himself described it.

Poet Donald Hall published a short volume of twelve elegantly written stories called *The Ideal Bakery.* Several are satirical, and three are elegiac, including "Christmas Snow," a memory of a childhood Christmas in New Hampshire filled with lovely detail. Novelist John Casey wrote, "Of the 12 I found three resonantly brilliant and enormously moving. Most of the other nine are almost as good, always admirably wrought, pleasures to reread."

Maria Thomas may be the only American writer to publish two good books of fiction in 1987. I've mentioned her first novel, *Antonia Saw the Oryx First*. *Come to Africa and Save your Marriage* is a first book of stories dealing mostly with non-Africans who confront Africa and find out something about themselves.

Steve Sterns' *Lazar Malkin Enters Heaven* is also a much-praised first collection, mostly set in a Jewish neighborhood in Memphis called the Pinch. Many of his characters have an I.B. Singeresque fascination with dybbuks and the occult. Another much-praised first book was Pinckney Benedict's *Town Smokes*, stories of his native West Virginia in the mold of Breece D'J Pancake. Another first collection, this one by a well-regarded non-fiction writer, is Bill Barich's *Hard to Be Good*. Most of the stories have to do with boys or men settling for limitations in their lives.

Richard Ford's *Rock Springs* is also a collection of stories about men, but these men are all youngish, all are somehow concerned with manhood, and the stories are filled with violence, hunting, sports. Most of the stories are told in the first person, and all are set in the West.

Jayne Anne Phillips's new collection, *Fast Lanes,* at times reminds one of her first collection, the often glib and self-consciously shocking *Black Tickets,* and at others of her novel, *Machine Dreams,* the story of a family, set in West Virginia.

Strangers in Paradise is Lee K. Abbott's third collection of short stories, and as in the two earlier books, most of his characters come from the small town of Deming, New Mexico. His stories deal both with the ordinary pressures of life there and with the extraordinary pressures of life under combat in Vietnam.

So there is a baker's dozen of short story collections for 1987. If all of them cannot be said to be from Donald Hall's ideal bakery, consider that my fictional ideal and yours are likely to be quite different. In fact, for all the books noted above it is best to remember that (with apologies to Henry James) the bakery of fiction has many ovens. It is just this diversity of things made that makes fiction both tasty and nutritious.

The Year in Poetry

by Sidney Burris

In a recent number of *The Times Literary Supplement* (March 11-17, 1988), the English poet Alan Jenkins described his visit to the Bread Loaf Writer's Conference, held during the month of August in Vermont:

> Everyone agrees that there's a Bread Loaf sound, but it means different things to different people. If you've dutifully attended all the readings (formal and informal), workshops and lectures on offer through the two-week Writer's Conference, it might be the two-or-three-beat, unrhymed and aggressively irregular poetic line—not so much turned as hobbled, the breaks always against the grain of sense and speech—delivered with a peculiar rising inflection: the Bread Loaf line, the style and the voice . . . adopted by very nearly all the young poets, published, soon-to-be-published or without-a-hope-in-hell, I heard as a guest there last summer.

Bread Loaf rises loftily among the American writing conferences, and Jenkins's response to this gathering of post-colonial luminaries—he mentions the conference's "all-American feel"—falls neatly in line with the long and august tradition of polite disparagement that is often invoked when English poets confront the American poetic line, "unrhymed and aggressively irregular." Many of our lines rhyme, in fact, and many are regular, even aggressively, monotonously so. Although generalities like Jenkins's invite the debunking detail that renders them useless, generalities often exercise the aphoristic truth, the truth of the single observation that, when indiscriminately scrutinized, seems indiscriminately applicable. Whitman originated the American obsession with experimentation in poetic form, and unlike our English counterparts, many of our poets have written under its aegis. But the capable poet's experimentation, emphasizing individuality and revision, often becomes the incapable poet's incoherence, emphasizing narcissism and novelty. Most of the poetry written during any given year, decade, or century neither compels nor endures; that is the harsh lesson of literary history. But a glance through the forgotten poems and books published in America and England during the twentieth century encourages another generality: much of the innocuous verse written in America seems blithely unaware of the traditional patterns of rhyme and meter, while the similarly uncompelling poetry written in England is often suffocated by them. Jenkins's censures are most obviously appropriate when directed toward the lower levels of poetic accomplishment.

Younger American Poets

Much has been written recently concerning the rise of a new formalism—capital letters are very nearly required—among American poets, particularly those under the age of forty. Its apologists, often decrying the sad state of letters that surrounds them, hastily summon the great names of the tradition to support their indictments so that the invoked tradition naively accommodates such dissimilar spirits, for example, as Petrarch,

Wyatt, Sidney, Spenser, Shakespeare, Donne, and Milton. These poets knew how to write a sonnet, it is solemnly proclaimed, and so do we, and so should you—that is the stern implication. Literary nostalgia often serves the whimsical desire for literary authority because it allows censorious writers to justify their preferences by claiming as kindred spirits various writers from the past that have been conscripted into an amorphous tradition. Wyatt's importation in the early sixteenth century of the sonnet form from the Italian model must be recognized as an attempt, among other things, to stabilize the English line, still in its infancy. His was a program of renovation, and it was informed with an invigorating dissatisfaction with the native English tradition as it then existed. The bold, far-ranging license exhibited by Wyatt's sense of poetic form would find no place in many of the camps that would currently claim him as a founding father.

Poetic forms often become associated with various subject matters, and in T. R. Hummer's latest collection, **Lower Class Heresy** (Illinois), the long lines of its essentially narrative poems recall, in order to revise, the ornately discursive techniques popularized in this century by Robert Penn Warren: "Light scatters / Over that ragged western edge of sky he knows / Is trees, hedgerow, wheatfield's boundary, the end of the family / Farm, a border taking on in this moment's illumination / The look of a black raw rip / In the tissue of the air. . . ." The poem had begun with the admission that "maybe this has been done before," and several poems later in "Dogma: Pigmeat and Whiskey," when Hummer pauses to proclaim that he knows he sounds "like just another Southern storyteller telling / Another Southern story," his narrative line, and the poems that depend on them, are slowly but convincingly transformed into critical revisions of the tradition that he has inherited. Hummer, while confronting the Southern obsessions with "the war, that Dark and Bloody Ground, / Family, memory, history, old men, [and] time," has begun in this collection to question his relation to these concerns and, what is most important, to examine the techniques of narrative poetry so often used to develop them. It is a rare accomplishment when the revision of the poet's syntax *really* instigates the revision of the poet's intellect, but Hummer is moving in this direction with force and clarity.

The Squanicook Eclogues (Norton) by Melissa Green continues this exploration between regional polemics and poetic form. The title poem is divided into four sections that correspond to the four seasons, and the lines, as far as the pentameter measure is concerned, are hypermetrical, each one extending to six and, on occasion, seven beats. The writing is densely textured, even in the simplest vignettes: "August has shriven the grass," Green writes in "August," "the green sargassos of June / And summer's alfalfa is lusterless gold in a nimbus of heat / Waiting the baler." The poem takes place in Massachusetts, and the focus is consciously regional, fiercely territorial: "New Hampshire, north of us, was broad / And diffident as France." The collection begins with the poet walking in April "beside the crooked stone fence bordering two states,'' and the fence here has been "heaved by frost." Perhaps the allusion to Frost's "Mending Wall," where the "frozen-ground-swell . . . spills the upper boulders," is obvious, but Green's poetry insists on the provincial vision urbanely rendered, and that is a pastoral commonplace. Rather than labor after significance, contorting her lines to support her ideas, Green allows her exuberant descriptions ("the maples khaki undersides lift in a brisk salute") to develop line by line, unfettered by self-indulgent explanation. Confidence, joy, enthusiasm, pleasure, even innocence—these qualities abound here, and often they are sustaining ones. Green debuts here in a winning fashion.

The Yale Series of Younger Poets, currently judged by James Merrill, now includes Julie Agoos's *Above the Land* (Yale), the eighty-second volume admitted to its fatted shelf. As in Green's volume, New England represents the American landscape of the collection, but unlike Green's volume, New England is continually countered by Italy, or in "At Ponte a Mensola," by the city of Florence: "A stone plaque on the stone wall / of the Via Vincigliata lists / artists whose inspiration once added / a solemn, foreign appeal to the stillness. / Shelley lived on the Via D'Annunzio." This "foreign appeal," filtered through the American sensibility, results in the peculiar combination of envy, attraction, and resentment that accompanies the American writer who visits Florence and confronts the long history of a cosmopolitan literary culture. If contemporary American culture is essentially peripatetic—the last poem of the volume is entitled "Preparing to Move"—then the assemblage of Agoos's poems honestly represents this restlessness; but if our culture is essentially expansive, as Whitman wished to believe, then these poems are continually examining its expanding regional persuasions.

Perhaps more so than with most collections, Jorie Graham's *The End of Beauty* (Ecco) suffers from excerpted quotations because the arguments of her poems are accretive, eschewing entirely the vignette, the series of short set-pieces that often provide the memorable sections of long poems. Her ambitious lines are very long, and their organizational music often evades the attentive ear, even on the fifth and sixth reading. But the conceptual maneuvers of the poetry, which often involve introspective faculty. The poems argue, rebut, brood, assert, retract, meditate, and stop, only to suggest their continuance—many of the poems close with dashes or no punctuation at all. Adversaries of her poetry will find gimmickry in abundance, while her advocates are discovering bold innovation; as in all innovative writing, however, fashionable novelties and enduring refinements are initially difficult to separate because they both share an overriding concern for originality. The poems in this collection, however, are founded on thoroughgoing, intellectually seductive revisions of several important myths and archetypes, and their deft manipulation of this weighty material, along with their inoffensive insistence on autobiography, fetches them early laurels.

In "Dogma: Whiskey and Pigmeat," Hummer included Pound's terse remark that the "narrative impulse is a product of the village mentality," and with characteristic honesty and critical acumen, agreed with him and then continued his story, a story made stronger by its formal awareness. David Bottoms, since his first collection won the Walt Whitman Award in 1980, has written in a similarly narrative vein, but it lacks the technical investigations that would simultaneously advance his plot while exposing the underpinnings of his methods. The poems collected in *Under the Vulture Tree* (Quill/Morrow), his third

Dust jacket of The End of Beauty: Poems, *by Jorie Graham. Ecco, 1987. Jacket painting by Eric Fischl, detail from "Untitled" (Two Women in Bedroom). Dust jacket design by Cynthia Krupat. By permission of The Echo Press.*

volume, have elevated the various conventions of the storyteller's art to a level of arresting abstraction that imbues the experience it organizes with the kind of efficient elegance found in stained glass windows that embody, for example, Christian parables. "In the Ice Pasture," the poem that opens the collection, recounts the story of the poet's attempt to ride a horse, who has fallen through the ice on a pond, back to the shore. The transitional passages of the story—How *did* he get on that horse's back?—are subsumed by the iconographic concision of its major sections. The poem ends with the "night / cracked like an egg shattered in the storm / of two beasts becoming one, or one beast being born." The image of horse and rider erupting from the ice reflects the heraldic quality of Bottoms's writing, but the individual elements of his heraldry—his vultures, guitars, banjos, snakes, and swamps—provide the luminous detail of his narratives.

While Bottoms's verse concentrates on stories from the South, David Wojahn's *Glassworks* (Pittsburgh) is trained on the north-central United States. His cities are St. Paul and Minneapolis, and the relentless fluency of his poems, often relying on stanza patterns typically associated with syllabic verse, often causes his poems to end with the kind of nonchalance that belies the typographical precision of his work. Nancy Schoenberger's *Girl on a White Porch* (Missouri), a book similarly relaxed in its cadences, returns to the Deep South of Louisiana, and in a poem such as "By Certain Rivers," the undulations of the verse ("The cottonwood / full of pollen, swollen waters") accurately mimic the motions of the meandering river. Her version of the South is gentile, yet not elitist, and her best poems reclaim the graceful intonations and images that have most often been represented in the distinguished tradition of Southern fiction.

The flexible forms of Charles Martin's *Steal the Bacon* (Johns Hopkins)—from nonce forms to rhyming quatrains that employ eighteenth-century diction—are as flexible as his nimble subject matters: from a playful treatment of "sensual mouselife" that doubles as a serious meditation on ambition, avarice, and derring-do to a narration by Crusoe's man Friday, Martin's book offers delight while avoiding foppishness, deals in traditional form while eschewing claustrophobia, and engages the intellect while spurning didacticism. Derek Walcott chose *Cities in Motion* by Sylvia Moss (Illinois) as one of the winners of The National Poetry Series, and although its poems, considered individually, are not as formally ambitious as those of Martin's collection, the book's value resides in Moss's insistence on carefully directing each of the short poems toward the governing idea of the book, an investigation of the personal life in terms of its relation to the culture which spawns and nourishes it. But personal lives assume various shapes and guises, and in Karen Fish's *The Cedar Canoe* (Georgia), the narcissistic satisfactions of autobiography are countered by a free verse that generally seems etched and inevitable, and that alone, according to W. H. Auden, who proclaimed himself incapable of meeting free verse's special demands, is an accomplishment.

Just when narrative poetry seemed to have settled comfortably into the formulaic pattern of chronicling mundane actions that lead indirectly, but predictably, to the kind of transcendence that has become diluted by its ubiquity in contemporary writing, Robert McDowell's *Quiet Money* (Henry Holt) combines the skeletal rhythms of blank verse with the fleshy stories of mysteries, pot-boilers, and documentaries. The tone that McDowell orchestrates is off-hand, self-deprecating, and conversational, but his bag of tricks bulges with understatement and subversion—it is a book of many, occasionally insidious talents, all of which have been carefully marshaled to reform the wary reader of contemporary verse. The reformation is thorough and welcome. In *Customs* (Georgia), Joseph Duemer manipulates a similarly conversational line, but its effect differs radically from McDowell's line because Duemer's forms, particularly his stanzas, more obviously call attention to themselves. And Duemer's subjects, from baseball to the death of Delmore Schwartz—or rather, the matriculation of Schwartz into Heaven—take a signal pleasure in intellection, in placing a procession of imagery in its proper conceptual order. Duemer is a poet of implication, and his verse, often approaching the casually meditational tones associated with Lowell's generation, typically juxtaposes the quotidian, unruly reality and the ordering intellect, a tradition in American verse that begins, as most do, with Whitman. That such a tradition should be carried on by a poet as unlike Whitman as Duemer testifies to Duemer's strength as well as the tradition's longevity.

RECOMMENDED: Debra Bruce, *Sudden Hunger* (Arkansas); Susan Stewart, *The Hive* (Georgia); Ronald Wallace, *People and Dog in the Sun* (Pittsburgh); Mark Doty, *Turtle, Swan* (Godine); Jon Veinberg, *An Owl's Landscape* (Vanderbilt); Francis Blessington, *Lantskip* (William L. Bauhan); Mark Irwin, *The Halo of Desire*, (Galileo); Judith Skillman, *Worship of the Visible Spectrum* (Breitenbush); Barbara Chase-Riboud, *Portrait of a Nude Woman as Cleopatra* (Quill/Morrow); Laurence Goldstein, *The Three Gardens* (Copper Beech Press); Peter Cooley, *The Van Gogh Notebook* (Carnegie-Mellon); Bill Meissner, *The Sleepwalker's Son* (Ohio); Jane Miller, *American Odalisque* (Copper Canyon Press); Barbara Anderson, *Junk City* (Persea Books).

Contemporaries

W. D. Snodgrass has been publishing poetry now for over thirty years, and his new *Selected Poems, 1957-1987* (Soho) deserves only superlatives. In 1959, he won the Pulitzer Prize for *Heart's Needle,* and although his work is often associated indiscriminately with the poetry of Lowell, Berryman, Plath, and Sexton, the various confessions of his inaugural prize-winning volume seem far less self-indulgent in their tenor than those of his contemporaries. Snodgrass has remained throughout his career a poet obsessed with stanzaic organization, and just as his stanzas provide the structural boundaries of his language, so these structural boundaries intensify his diction. No other American poet is as enlivened by such a wide array of stanza forms, and no other poet better exemplifies the technical control of conversational rhythms. David Wagoner's *Through the Forest: New and Selected Poems* (Atlantic Monthly) gathers together two decades of writing that bear the mark of the sustained poetic intelligence—an enduring concern with several, and several only, subject matters. The natural world, desire, and love, in varying degrees of prominence, order most of the memorable poems in this volume, and the spirits invoked by his verse—Frost, Roethke, Wright—never dwarf or lessen its accomplishment. He is a poet of natural fluency and seduction, two qualities that have survived throughout his career unabated by fashion or trend.

Amplitude: New and Selected Poems by Tess Gallagher (Graywolf) draws on her three previous volumes and concludes with a copious gathering of new work. Gallagher is a poet of presence—her poems most always begin in the present tense, and their narration is meant to sustain a kind of heightened testimonial. When she succeeds, as in "Amplitude," the title poem of her new work, her observations will often seem randomly ordered, but that is not the case. Gallagher delights in the illusion of diversity, and her verse will go to inventive ends to insure its survival. Marvin Bell's *New and Selected Poems* (Atheneum), culled from eight volumes and twenty years of writing, provides an eloquent testimony to a career that has been steadily but quietly gaining momentum—neither a poet of flashy form not sensational confession, Bell has insisted that, at one level, ideas must govern his poems, and so this collection is full of the memorable surprises that attend the discovery of the well ordered, concisely rendered moment. The only four-line poem in the volume, "An Elm We Lost," reveals the quixotic grace and unusual perspective that characterizes his best work: "On it we wrote a little easy / about who loved who. / Shade moves in the grass, never still, / and they still do."

When the subject of formal verse arises, Auden's name does too, and among living American writers, Howard Nemerov might suitably head the list. He shares with Auden as no one else does—not Hecht, not Wilbur, not Merrill—a notably comfortable relation with poetic form, a relation that Auden would call "comfy." But in his latest volume, *War Stories: Poems about Long Ago and Now* (Chicago), Nemerov confronts his experiences as a pilot in the Second World War, and never a maudlin note is sounded. "The War in the Air" begins, "For a saving grace, we didn't see our dead, / Who rarely bothered coming home to die / But simply stayed away out there / In the clean war, the war in the air." Simple eloquence, the plain but ordered statement, and an enduring capacity for invention—Nemerov's verse always earns its keep by its rich and varied tonality. Illinois has combined and reissued James Whitehead's two full-length collections of verse, *Domains* and *Local Men,*

Dust jacket of Amplitude: New and Selected Poems, *by Tess Gallagher. Graywolf Press, 1987. Jacket illustration "Laguna Azul" copyright © 1987 by Alfredo Arreguin. Reprinted by permission of Graywolf Press.*

and they arrive at an auspicious time, providing an exemplary rejoinder to those who speak with prophetic gravity about the return of the new formalism. His prowess as a sonneteer is well known, deserved, and undiminished; but he also understands the poetic sequence, a twentieth-century fascination, and in a poem such as "Wherein the Lawyer from George County Recounts Events Soon and Some Time after He Crossed the Bar," Whitehead counters the fluency of his syntactic transitions with the more abrupt divisions of the seven parts of the poem. His sense of design is tested here, and Whitehead scores high marks in an area often ignored by narrative poets of his accomplishment.

"I couldn't / wait to see the empty basket, / light, structurally transcendent," writes A. R. Ammons in "The Ridge Farm," the opening poem of *Sumerian Vistas* (Norton), and the phrase "structurally transcendent" accurately describes not only the objects of his vision—like Frost, these objects are many—but also the implicit ideal that governs his lines—unlike Frost, his lines are volatile, given to a purposeful instability. Ammons is an epistemological poet, and "nature," as he calls it, has always provided him with his tropes and schemes. But in this collection, particularly in "The Ridge Farm," he juxtaposes a kind of teacherly instruction ("I go to nature not because / its flowers and sunsets speak / to me (though they do) . . . but / because I have filled it with unintentionality") and the high Romanticism on which his best poems depend ("I wouldn't

give up a hair of / the beautiful / high suasions of language, / celestial swales, hungering the / earth up into heaven, no.") Although the book is uneven in its accomplishment, its best lines are possessed by Ammons's uncanny sense of temporality, of the evanescent moment, and in this respect, his verse retains its unabashed individuality. Although Reynolds Price would seem an unlikely companion for Ammons, *The Laws of Ice* (Atheneum) depends upon a similarly Heraclitan perspective. The first two stanzas of the title poem are svelte, to-the-point, inspired: "Ice has laws / (Oxygen, fire, / Lord Gravity / Have laws") but loose— / "A mother's call. / Human life / (Yours, mine) / Will glide down decades / Free as oil." The central section of the volume gathers together 35 poems entered into a notebook, a work which spans the period of time during which Price discovered that he had developed cancer. The tone of the work, as he explains, is meant to be "sufficiently Horatian to permit both the minutiae of a diary and more sizable concerns," and having cited his illustrious model, Price proceeds with aplomb to record those minutiae. And his treatment of his contraction of cancer is exemplary—Price continually balances his own tragedy with the "more sizable concerns," and the solid, yet lyrical wisdoms of the work scrupulously avoid the morbidities that often mar the records of personal tragedy. Price's decorum is Sapphic—not Horatian—in its passion and sensitivity, and "Days and Nights" is a finely conceived, well executed work.

Although Sydney Lea's work has often been discussed in terms of its regional affiliations—he is, the argument runs, yet another poet of country affairs—his third book, *No Sign* (Geor-

Dust jacket of Ridge Music: Poems, *by Harry Humes. The University of Arkansas Press, 1987. Jacket design by Chiquita Babb. Courtesy of the publisher.*

gia), renders the designation less helpful. Conversational rhythms and the record of daily events are often attempts to transcend, through exhaustive enumeration, the earthbound particularity of the events that they record; insisting on the primacy of the phenomenal world, Lea's poems ironically imply that only an inspired perception imparts value to that world. They represent vigorous reclamations both of moral value and the luminous landscape, and he has managed the task with grace and insight. Harry Humes, in *Ridge Music* (Arkansas), might easily fall prey to the regional label were it not for his remarkable fluencies as a miniaturist. The etched perfections of a vignette momentarily lift his poems from their immediate context, as in "Winter Storm Watch," which ends, "Everywhere now, by rose-hip berries / and frozen stream, silence gathers. / By morning it will be whiter, / deeper, called a single name." The poem is one of fundamental energies; the transition from metereology to seminology occurs effortlessly here, and it is a transition that must be made all accomplished poets of the natural world. RECOMMENDED: Denise Levertov, *Breathing the Water* (Norton); Julia Randall, *Moving in Memory,* Julia Randall (Louisiana); Robert Pack, *Clayfield Rejoices, Clayfield Laments* (Godine); Gerald Stern, *Lovesick* (Harper and Row); William Stafford, *An Oregon Message* (Harper and Row); William Matthews, *Forseeable Futures* (Houghton Mifflin); Edward Field, *New and Selected Poems* (Sheep Meadow); Dabney Stuart, *Don't Look Back* (Louisiana State University); Robley Wilson, *Kingdoms of the Ordinary* (Pittsburgh); Ruth Stone, *Second-Hand Coat: Poems New and Selected* (Godine); Patiann Rogers, *Legendary Performance* (Ion/Raccoon); John Morris, *A Schedule of Events* (Atheneum); Wendell Berry, *Sabbaths* (North Point); Carolyn Kizer, *The Nearness of You* (Copper Canyon); John Engels, *Cardinals in the Ice Age* (Graywolf); Alan Shapiro, *Happy Hour* (Chicago); Robert Duncan, *Ground Work II* (New Directions); Hyam Plutzik, *The Collected Poems* (Boa Editions); Charles Edward Eaton, *New and Selected Poems, 1942-1987;* Jane Shore, *The Minute Hand* (University of Massachusetts); Donald Finkel, *The Wake of the Electron* (Atheneum); Lincoln Kirstein, *The Poems of Lincoln Kirstein* (Atheneum); A. Poulin, Jr., *A Momentary Order* (Graywolf); Harry Matthews, *Armenian Papers: Poems, 1954-1984* (Princeton).

International Poets

New Directions has published in a bilingual format Octavio Paz's *Collected Poems* and Jose Emilio Pacheco's *Selected Poems,* two volumes that provide an authoritative introduction to twentieth-century Mexican poetry. Paz, born in 1914 and now the elder statesman of Mexican letters, and Pacheco, born in 1939, and perhaps Paz's heir apparent, represent at once the most seriously experimental and the most lovingly formal poets of our century. Paz's collection begins with *Sunstone,* first published in 1957 and newly translated here by the editor, Eliot Weinberger, and the compelling fluencies of its ordered narrative voice and its freer imagistic progressions constitute what became for Paz a poetic method. It is a method largely unfamiliar to the reader of English and American verse—although it has influenced a branch of American poetry, often mislabeled surrealistic—and its distinctive features are highlighted by the work of Pacheco, particularly, as Paz argued in an introduction to the *New Poetry of Mexico,* by Pacheco's pursuit of perfection. For Pacheco, this perfection consists of a visionary iconoclasm combined with a traditional formalism, and his various accomplishments have accurately been compared to those of Hart Crane's *The Bridge.* Read together, the work of Paz and Pacheco can undeniably claim authority in twentieth-century Mexican writing, but as these volumes admirably illustrate,

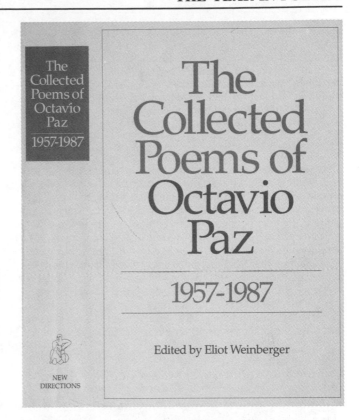

Dust Jacket of The Collected Poems of Octavio Paz, 1957-1987, *edited by Eliot Weinberger. New Directions, 1987. Jacket design by Herman Strohbach. Reprinted by permission of New Directions Publishing Corp.*

they can also command the international audience who values the experience of following any literary tradition as it is capably and vigorously developed. Vincente Aleixandre's *The Shadow of Paradise* (California) has been translated by Hugh A. Harter. Aleixandre, a Spaniard who was awarded the Nobel Prize for Literature in 1977, survived the Civil War and began this long poem in 1939, four months after the fighting ceased. Completed near the end of the World War II, the poem, as its title indicates, bears eloquent witness to the renovative powers of the pastoral imagination, buffeted by the hardships of political upheaval. It is a poem of imaginative resistance, and its publication in English, with the original text opposing, culminates an extraordinary year for Spanish poetry.

Both Seamus Heaney and Paul Muldoon published substantial collections during the year, and Muldoon's book, *Selected Poems, 1968-1986* (Ecco), should finally remove him from Heaney's long shadow. Although Muldoon studied with Heaney—which has given many readers and critics the unreasonable license to speak of influence and favor—Muldoon's verse values the irreverent manipulation of traditional literary techniques and immediately parts company with Heaney's more conserving technical vision. "Wind and Tree," the first poem of Mudoon's selection, constructs an analogy between individual perception and the wind that "happens where there are trees": Coleridge's Eolian harp, providing the tonal response to the wind that moves over its boxed strings, comes to mind. And when Muldoon pauses to remark that in a grove of trees, "one tree will take / another in her arms and hold," he eschews the communal strength, confessing that "I think I should be like / the single tree," a posture that accurately predicts his impassioned avoidance of the political labels often foisted upon writers from Northern Ireland, his homeland. Muldoon's narrative gifts, exemplified in the long poems "Immram," "The More a Man Has the More a Man Wants," and "7, Middagh Street," are considerable, and his tales share much with the picaresque tradition. Urbane in technique, provincial in tone, and unbounded in their toleration of wayward subject matters, Muldoon's poems are brisk and unpredictable, and this shrewd selection will introduce American readers to one of Ireland's finest young poets.

The Haw Lantern (Farrar, Straus, and Giroux), Heaney's seventh volume of poetry and the third since his own collected edition was published in 1980, comprises a diverse assemblage of voices, influences, and intentions: in "The song of the Bullets," which begins "I watched a long time in the yard," we *hear* Auden's "As I walked out one evening"; in "The Mud Vision," we *feel* the presence of the "flirtatious male" of Auden's "In Praise of Limestone" when Heaney writes in a kind of neo-camp diction that "punks with aerosol sprays held their own / with the best of them"; and in such poems as "From the Frontier of Writing" and "From the Republic of Conscience," Heaney *intends* to bring the one frontier in concert with the other by using an elaborate analogical scheme.

The volume, in fact, is filled with situations and dilemmas that seem imaginative analogies for the actual life, the daily life of Northern Ireland that often debases poetic language, substituting an ideology for a tensioned representation. That Heaney has avoided such deflations in this volume testifies to his unusual development, one that seems genetically incapable of repetition and sameness. *The Haw Lantern* requires the reader to develop several sensibilities unexercised by the previous poetry, and that is one of its signal strengths because, once developed, these sensibilities assume a strategic importance in the American reader's comprehension of Northern Ireland's complex array of literature, morality and ethics.

Born in Lincolnshire in 1926, Elizabeth Jennings published her first book of poems in 1953. Her new *Collected Poems* (Carcanet) is based on sixteen previous volumes, and although the obvious development of the verse distinguishes her as a poet of restless energy, the obsessive dedication to musical precision assures her reputation as one of England's staunchest lyricists. "Fragile," begins her short poem "Autumn," which then continues, "notice that / As autumn starts, a light / Frost crisps up at night." The carefully modulated associations of "crisps up," in the contexts both of heat and cold, reflect the extreme variations of temperature often characteristic of autumn days and nights, and such a scrimshawed excellence is not in Jennings's work indicative of a narrow discipline, but of a pervasive poetic attention. The subjects that fall under her scrutiny receive meticulous examination, but her unflagging combination of severity and originality insure that her work offers fresh perspectives. Of an equally rigorous regimen, Evan Boland's work relies on Celtic sonorities tempered by the invigorating restraints of understatement, and her fourth volume *The Journey* (Carcanet) finds her voice secure and confident in its treatment, for example, of growing up Irish in England:

> The bickering of vowels on the buses,
> the clicking thumbs and the big hips of
> the navy-skirted ticket collectors with
> their crooked seams brought it home to me:
> Exile. Ration-book pudding.

The colloquial tones of the phrasing and the dire austerity of the subject matter give Boland her special sound, and in this poem, as in many others in this collection, she continues to cultivate the voice of political awareness and lyrical grace, an accomplishment that has occasionally evaded a few of her more ballyhooed compatriots.

RECOMMENDED: Tomas Transtromer, ed. Robert Hass, *Selected Poems, 1954-1986* (Ecco); Jaan Kaplinski, *The Wandering Border* (Copper Canyon Press); Margaret Atwood, *Selected Poems II: Poems Selected and New, 1976-1986* (Houghton Mifflin); John Ormond, *Selected Poems* (Poetry Wales Press); John Silkin, *The Ship's Pasture* (Routledge and Kegan Paul); C. H. Sisson, *God Bless Karl Marx!* (Carcanet); Frank Kuppner, *The Intelligent Observation of Naked Women* (Caranet); Michael Hartnett, *Collected Poems* (Carcanet); Christopher Middleton, Two Horse Wagon Going By (Carcanet); John Ash, *Disbelief* (Carcanet); Kofi Awoonor, *Until the Morning After: Collected Poems, 1963-1985;* Yehuda Amichai, *Amen* (Milkweed); Dezso Tandori, *Birds and Other Relations* (Princeton).

The Year in Drama

by Robert Cohen

New York Theater

August Wilson's *Fences* won the 1987 Pulitzer Prize for Drama, the Pulitzer board overriding its own nominating committee which had selected Neil Simon's *Broadway Bound; Fences* took every other dramatic award in sight this year, (Tony, Drama Critics Circle, Outer Critics Circle, Drama Desk, American Theater Critics Association, etc.), but its accolades greatly exaggerate its importance. *Fences* is one of the better plays of the past few years, but neither its ambition nor its achievement are particularly momentous.

Last year in this space I mused as how *Broadway Bound* was Neil Simon's *Death of a Salesman;* here, believe it or not, I must report that *Fences* continues to follow this apparently indestructible (and perhaps unimprovable) Arthur Miller model. *Fences,* like the other two plays, is staged in and in front of a two story house in a rundown district of some postwar Northern American city—which might as well be Brooklyn, as it is in the other plays (although director Lloyd Richards, in the published edition, tells us it's Pittsburg.) Like its counterparts, the play shows us an American family on the low edge of middle class: a loyal Mom who holds the clan together; a faithless but (we are given to understand) ultimately noble Dad; two grown sons about to move out of the shabby house; and an unseen mistress, apparently as victimized as victimizing. There are also the model's obligatory scenes: Son confronting Dad, seeking recognition for his Real Self as opposed to Dad's Fantasy Ideal; Betrayed Wife defending Straying Dad to Confused and Outraged Son, and Final Requiem at play's end where it is revealed that Dad Never Really Knew Who He Was. That this family is black rather than Jewish is the novelty here, but it's hardly a cutting edge; the play is a classic American family drama, and, while powerful at times, it's a classic we're getting tired of.

The Dad to whom, in *Fences,* attention must be paid, is Troy Maxson, a Negro league baseball player who never made it to the majors. Troy argues racial discrimination—but the fact is that he was simply in jail for his playing days—while Larry Doby was knocking them out of the park in Cleveland, and Jackie Robinson was stealing second in Brooklyn. Clean up your act, black man, Wilson is telling Troy, and this satisfying racial positivism largely accounts for the huge crossover crowd that nightly filled the 46th Street Theater.

There are deeper levels of discrimination beneath ballpark segregation, however, and this leads to Wilson's underlying theme. Being in jail turns out to be the least of Troy's problems, for mere talent won't buy him out of the ghetto of his own mind. The wonderful set (James D. Sandefur) prominently features a baseball hung from a tree in the front yard; when hit, the ball flies off, only to swing right back again—as do the various Maxsons. There is no quarreling with Wilson's social observation here, nor with the effectiveness of his and Sandefur's

Playbill for Fences. Playbill® *is a registered trademark of Playbill Incorporated, N.Y.C. Used by permission.*

terrific stage metaphor; it's in the development that things get a bit sandlotty.

Troy, like Willy Loman, lives on the edge of the postwar economy; he's a garbage collector, and although, in these his grandparenting years, he has advanced from lifter to driver, his hard-won promotion doesn't give him satisfaction or security. His wife, Rose, and their son, Cory, try to offer him both, but he isn't taking from those quarters: Troy's greatest affection goes instead to his buddy Bono; his deepest love is to his demented brother Gabe; and his profoundest loyalty is to his bar and his bottle. What plots exist concern Troy's sporadic efforts to block son Cory's emerging manhood, and Troy's equally futile travails with unseen mistress with whom

15

he fathers a child during the course of the play; these seem environmental happenings, however, rather than meaningful or consequential indices of a larger picture. There are some brutal confrontations, but much of the play consists of a sort of Amos and Andy drinking blather between Troy and Bono, and the play's dramatic climaxes are both forced and stunted; they're loud, but they don't convey anything, and they end without impact. At the end of the first act, Cory swings a bat at his father, and Troy wrestles him to the ground, triumphantly crying "Strike one!" Has he proven his son an impotent weakling? Has he set Cory onto a trial of manhood? Has he embarked on a tragic course of Oedipal dimensions? What is the strike three of this sequence? A second strike is called (what are second acts for?), but to little point; Wilson has set up an inconclusive pattern which is ultimately irrelevant, and the play's points, by the end, have dissolved in bathos and confusion. The analogy drawn by the title image—is Troy fencing his family in or the world out?—is trite, even silly; it's there just to give the events some sort of dignified dramatic focus, and nobody really believes in it, including Wilson.

James Earl Jones starred as Troy, and Frank Rich, of the *New York Times,* said that this was the performance of Jones's career; I rather think that Jack Johnson in *The Great White Hope* has that honor, and that Jones is basically repeating that role here with less effect. He is full of bombast and authority, and tremendously amusing in his Kingfishly gleefulness, but it is not a very sensitive performance, and seems calculated more to impress than to articulate human qualities; we don't have much feeling for Troy, and we have no idea why he treats his children as cruelly as he does. Mary Alice, however, is magnificent as the suffering but enchanting Rose; she is the very embodiment of grace and courage in the family wars, and the audience all but brings her home with them. Courtney Vance, as Cory, is an inexperienced actor and this shows; in his baseball bat confrontation he simply didn't know what to play, and at crucial moments wallowed in incoherent hysteria; he was attractively articulate, however, in his military garb at Troy's funeral; Mr. Vance has a considerable future, which his honors for this role should not hinder unless he takes them too seriously.

Fences is a fine play if we don't try to pretend that it's a great one; it has had a distinguished regional performance history for three years, and has already done more to desegregate the Broadway audience than any nonmusical play since *A Raisin in the Sun.* Wilson will probably write better plays; it's likely he will become one of our greatest dramatic writers, and his *Joe Turner's Come and Gone,* which I saw in La Jolla in 1988 (and which will be reviewed here next year, after its New York opening), already shows masterpiece potential. Wilson can tell a story, build dialogue, and work the emotions, and he can capture the attention of the American theatergoing public without resorting to cant or claptrap. In Lloyd Richards, the director of his plays, he has a talented and sympathetic patron and guide. No one in the theater will be blithe to his subsequent offerings.

The most becalming New York play of the year was also a crossover hit, as gently persuasive as *Fences* was aggressively dense. *Driving Miss Daisy* is a startlingly little play, with three characters and minimal staging in a tiny house, and there's neither a dramaturgic innovation nor a raised voice in the whole evening, but at the final fade there's a silence as deep as I have experienced in the theater in recent years. Daisy, when we meet her, is a 72-year-old retired fifth-grade teacher, and

Hoke is her chauffeur; she's Jewish, he's black, the setting is Atlanta, and the two hours traffic of the stage covers the next twenty-five years of their mutual lives. Not too much happens; there is some grumpy bickering and southern whimsy, and prejudice is never too far below the surface: Daisy's synagogue is bombed, and Hoke doesn't quite get invited to the United Jewish Appeal's Martin Luther King banquet (it's a beautifully delicate scene), but author Alfred Uhry, in his first straight play (he is the author of several musical books and librettos), has exquisitely and unsentimentally delineated a love relationship, and it is quite quietly thrilling. "This is not a Christmas present," says Daisy, handing Hoke a Christmas present. That present is a fifth-grade reader, left over from Daisy's teaching career; it is an apt gift to the illiterate Hoke, but Hoke bestows on her his own pedagogical gifts as well. This is, naturally, a hopeful drama, but it does not attempt to be or do anything beyond its perfectly simple means. "How do you know the way I see unless you look out of my eyes?" asks Hoke. It's not a profound line—but when you know these people as well as we do by play's end, it breeds an intense cognition. Morgan Freeman won several awards for his portrayal of Hoke, but I cannot imagine he could have been better than the splendid Arthur French, whom I saw in the part, with the equally wonderful Dana Ivey in the title role. Ron Lagomarsino directed with great skill.

Of course, the giant Broadway hit of the year was the musical adaptation of Victor Hugo's 1861 novel, *Les Misérables;* there's probably not been such a hot ticket in New York since *My Fair Lady,* and the thought of thousand-seat houses selling out six months in advance made not only some theater owners happy, it made a lot of theater lovers happy too. A huge hit galvanizes not just Broadway and its lucrative subsidiaries, it heightens the excitement for the entire theater world, even the extremist avant-garde and anti-commercial.

But *Les Misérables* is not just commercial; in fact it may ultimately prove to be the second greatest play of the Romantic movement, though it followed the movement's end by about a hundred years. (Not to worry: the first greatest play of the movement, *Cyrano de Bergerac,* followed the Romantic Age by about twenty years—Romanticism is the only dramatic period whose masterpieces came after the period had come to a close.) Romanticism, sadly, is one of those great dramatic movements respected more for its credos and theories than for any actual works; it is almost impossible to take seriously in today's more wizened climate (just try reading Schiller's *Fiesco* sometime), and has only survived on stage as transmorgrified into grand opera: Verdi, Wagner, and Puccini created the only lasting Romantic theatrical triumphs. Nonetheless, Hugo retains our respect as France's chief idea man of this movement: his preface to *Cromwell* was Romanticism's manifesto, his *Ruy Blas* and *Hernani* were Romanticism's key dramas; and his great novels are often considered Romanticism's only true prose masterpieces. None of Hugo's plays, however, have stood the test of time—and none remotely have the authority of this new and semi-operatic *Les Misérables,* which is or will be playing to rapturous 1988-89 crowds in New York, London, Paris, Moscow, Helsinki, Budapest, Sofia, Tokyo, Tel Aviv, Sydney, Barcelona, Oslo, Munich, Stockholm, Toronto, Athens, Rio, Reykjavik, Warsaw, and Copenhagen. *Les Misérables* is far and away Hugo's best play, even if he didn't write it; it's the play he *should* have written.

The current stage version began as a French recording in 1980, then became an English musical through the collaboration of

Playbill for Les Misérables. *Playbill® is a registered trademark of Playbill Incorporated, N.Y.C. Used by permission.*

Royal Shakespeare Company directors Trevor Nunn and John Caird. The original authors, Alain Boublil (text) and Claude-Michel Schonberg (music), have also seen their work supplemented by many other collaborators and translators; the program credits on this show run on for pages. But Hugo's spirit seems intact, and the towering moral force of *Les Misérables* is the production's dominant quality, as it is in the novel. Not to say this is not just a little silly, of course; the morality of Romanticism is an unearthly goodness, which transcends sentimentality (if it does) only by being so adamant, so overwhelming, so outrageously extreme. *Les Misérables* is not just sentimental, it's hypersentimental; it is a sentimentality so extreme that it bursts through on the other side, into absolute irreality: the feelings the play engenders have virtually nothing whatever to do with life. Homeless-mother panhandlers work the audience right under the marquee of the Broadway Theater; the theater patrons studiously avoid them, so as to shed unfettered tears for homeless-mother Fantine safely inside, on the other side of the proscenium, a hundred years dead. *Les Misérables* reaches our hypothetical sentiments: our sentiments about our sentiments. It is, to say the least, the most un-Brechtian production I have ever seen.

The story, for latecomers to Hugo, is of the splendid Jean Valjean, nineteen years on the chain gang for stealing a loaf of bread (to feed his starving niece), finally paroled and thrust into the vagaries of nineteenth-century urban Europe (echoes of *Nicholas Nickleby, Sweeney Todd,* and *Threepenny Opera* abound). Caught stealing the bishop's silver, he is released when the bishop refuses to accuse him, and he repays that kindness by some kindnesses of his own: first to the shopgirl turned prostitute Fantine, and then to Fantine's daughter Cosette, who becomes his surrogate daughter. But destiny charges after him in the person of the implacable officer Javert: pure nemesis in a French flic. The play's sprawling action occurs in Valjean's jail, in the city slums, on the fiery barricades of the abortive 1832 revolution, and in the palaces and sewers of Paris; it is picaresque adventure but without much swashbuckle—moral fervor allows little relish. Virtually everyone dies singing in mid-note.

Schonberg's music is intensely Gallic, with driving recitatives and nasal sustentions in the manner popularized on these shores by Edith Piaf; the production drives too: it has no spoken text to break the score, and no more than half a dozen breaks for audience applause in its three and a half hours; the sustained build to the first act close is monumental, and the audience explodes in a beautifully prepared-for ovation—one which almost dwarfs the standing ovation that all-but-automatically follows each performance. *Les Misérables* is an experience more than a drama, and you have to give yourself over to it or you'll break out in giggles. If you do give yourself to it, you'll be standing with the other folks by play's end.

The star of Lanford Wilson's new play, **Burn This,** was John Malkovich's wig; an enormous flaxen heap of black silky strands. It tossed, it tumbled, it shook, it swirled, and it simply HUNG there in all its inky malevolence and twisted glory until you feared Medusa was surely come again. Joan Allen, as Anna, a sophisticated Manhattan dancer-choreographer, has the misfortune to fall in love with this hank, or at least with the semi-human being (his name is "Pale") who from time to time appears behind it, and I felt nothing but trepidation for her. This is Lanford Wilson trying to write a Sam Shepard play, and I don't think it works. Wilson, who is probably our greatest dramatic craftsman (I don't think there's a more brilliantly structured American play than *The Rimers of Eldritch*) has abrogated his dramaturgical gifts to write a contempo crowd pleaser here; Pale, a man who, we are told, likes avalanches, is a Shepardian male animal in such ineffable pain that some woman simply has to come along—for mythic reasons, apparently—to lead him over his troubled waters (which include rampant insolence, violence, arrogance, rudeness, crudeness, faithlessness, and the enthusiastic abuse of various controlled substances.) Wilson tries to control the agenda by making Pale's rivals look pale by comparison (Anna's top-of-the-play lover is an ineffective, selling-out screenwriter, and her Soho-loft roommate is a gay advertising director); this makes her collapse into Pale's welcoming arms at the final fade comparatively explicable, but horrible, too—we know she will have her face bashed in (or worse) within the month. Wilson writes with felicity: the moments are engaging, the (frequent) mordant comedy is entertaining, the characters are compelling, and there are moments of stunning theatricality; this is a Broadway hit, and will doubtless garner some big awards. At the same time, the treatment of idiosyncratic, masochistic obsession, while undeniably effective in a perfume magazine ad, endows **Burn This** with a kind of heterosexual meanness I find unbecoming, or at least too counterintellectual and unattractive to praise.

I didn't like Tina Howe's **Coastal Disturbances** very much at all, and found its wide acclaim overly generous; to me it was a ho-hum summer romance, sort of a *Gidget* with F-words. If there was ever a play that was "made" by its leading actor, this is the one: we simply fall in love with Annette Bening as a spacy young woman ("Miranda Bigelow") who leaves an affair and lands on the beach; we enjoy watching the airhead lifeguard, Timothy Daly ("Leo Hart") fall in love with her too. But we wouldn't want to spend a lot of time with either of them; she's just too ditsy, he's just too awkward, and so for the most part is the play. The individual scenes are amusing enough; Bening is a fetchingly neurotic waif, Daly looks great in swim trunks, and there are some bubbly moments of laughing and scrambling in the sand. But this is about it: Howe's play is a mildly diverting pseudo-slice of life, the language is early actorish, and the characters' preoccupations are numbingly trivial. Aside from the leading couple, whose appeal is mainly giggly and physical, the grownups aren't worth spending any time with at all; when the elder couple invites Leo into their tent for a champagne celebration at play's end, we fully understand why he declines: nothing that they (or he) could say would be of interest. There are also some awful children who, unfortunately, are not any less awful on stage than they would be in life. Indeed, the only really interesting character in Howe's play is the heavy: a witty and sophisticated art dealer who comes onto the beach to bring Miranda back to the urban jungle. Granted, he looks a bit like Richard Nixon wearing his natty city wear on the sand, and he has a few sharp (57th Street) edges, but only the Lady Chatterly tradition (or is it sentimental fantasy?) keeps Miranda on the sand with her hunk. This is a girl (and a play) that needs some sharp edges; neither has them.

I was also relatively unimpressed with *A Shayna Maidel,* a shallow and sentimental treatment of a subject that deserves better. *Shayna* (the title means "pretty girl" in Yiddish) is about two Polish sisters: one who, as a child, escaped the Nazi death camps and moved with her father to America, and one who, sick with scarlet fever at the time, remained in Poland through the Holocaust, and somehow survived. The sisters reunite in post-war Manhattan, barely knowing each other, as Luisa (the survivor) finds Raisa, now Rose, ensconced in her 1950s model American apartment—as sweetly naive as Luisa is drearily war-weary and terrified. With its repeated flashbacks to Better Times in the Old Country, full of prayer shawls, schoolgirl giggles and ethnic dancing, the play tries hard to be Yiddishly affecting, but it tries too hard; it's trite, preachy, and sentimental, and you're a step ahead of every word of it—or you are if you've seen this sort of thing before, and who hasn't? Many tears are wrung by the last scene—fully a third of the audience was wearing yarmulkes the night I saw it—but they are the tears of the Holocaust watch; the play is simply a clumsy reminder of our century's horror, and it doesn't inform or accuse or enlighten. There is one powerful confrontation in the play: Luisa accuses the father of running out on the family and not sending money back for their rescue—and she's proven right: the father, it turns out, had too-cleverly saved his shekels against the improbabilities of the unthinkable. But the issue—and all hopes of dramatic interest—is dropped flat on the floor, where it is tramped upon by flashbacks of the family dancing the hora in Better Times, and father is let off as one of those gruff-but-really-lovable Jewish character types. Perhaps the author, Barbara Lebow (who, according to the program, is devoted to writing plays about "disenfranchised segments of the population—including homeless and addicted individuals, prisoners and the elderly—to help raise public awareness") simply didn't want to raise public awareness too high, and so scare off the yarmulkes. A less indulgent playwright would have wrestled with papa's calculated greed as well—which in fact

seems to have made him a wealthy New Yorker, like most of *Shayna's* audience proved to be.

Two English plays, both wonderfully intelligent, dazzled New York this year. Christopher Hampton's *Les Liaisons Dangereuses* was the real stunner, and will be seen everywhere over the coming years; it will possibly even return to New York with an American cast, replacing the Royal Shakespeare Company version that played out its limited Broadway run by season's end. What a wonderful play this is! And what a delicious production! *Les Liaisons Dangereuses* is, quite simply, about sex; and the retention of the French title (from the Cholderlos de Laclos novel of 1781) is simply part of Hampton's plan to abstract the true wickedness of seduction into a juicy diversion; erotic and intellectual by turns, wittily aphoristic, even moral and political by play's end. It is the Don Juan/Casanova story, played out in the shadow of the French Revolution, and it touches—deftly and occasionally firmly—on just about all of our private preoccupations.

Liaisons is anything but conventional drama. It's boy meets girl, boy gets girl, girl gets boy, boy gets got; it's the story of seducers seduced, and of the psychological ramifications of sex without love: and it's mortally penetrating—at least to its principal characters. Although loosely regarded as an amoral play, even an immoral one in some quarters, *Liaisons* makes a most shocking point: that the deepest human instinct is for love, not sex, and that love-deprivation is far more pathogenic than enforced celibacy. All this comes through without the slightest preaching; Hampton has fashioned his drama as a latter day Wildean grotesquerie:

La Marquise de Merteuil [advising a friend's daughter to marry a man she's not in love with]: When it comes to marriage one man is as good as the next; and even the least accommodating is less trouble than a mother.

Cecile: [in love with Danceny] But what about Danceny?

Merteuil: He seems patient enough; and once you're married, you should be able to see him without undue difficulty.

Cecile: I thought you once said to me, I'm sure you did, one evening at the Opera, that once I was married I would have to be faithful to my husband.

Merteuil: Your mind must have been wandering, you must have been listening to the opera.

Cecile: So, are you saying I'm going to have to do that [have sexual relations] with three different men?

Merteuil: I'm saying, you stupid little girl, that provided you take a few elementary precautions, you can do it, or not, with as many men as you like, as often as you like, in as many different ways as you like. Our sex has few enough advantages, you may as well make the most of those you have.

This is biting; it's acidulous wit in the classic English fashion; and it's unrelenting without being cloying: Hampton's diction is magnificently precise throughout, and with the stunning performances of the RSC cast that brought the play to Broadway, *Les Liaisons* was the most whole and perfect piece of work in New York this year. One could (and many did) argue with its totality; one could hardly question its parts. A concluding word about the set: the play takes place in a variety of salons and bedrooms in and around Paris and Vincennes, yet the setting is a single and unchanging unit whose identity is established simply by shifts in the lighting—and by the actors' skills at creating their environment. The play was initially conceived for a more conventional multiple set staging at the RSC's Barbican Theater in London, but was "bumped" over to the much smaller Other Place at Stratford to make room for *Les Miserables;* Bob Crowley's resulting "comprised" setting, lushly dressed with overstuffed highboys, chaise lounges, and dressers outrageously spilling over with fabric, provided a brilliant intensification of the play's action and a consolidation of its theme. Chris Parry's lighting proved a perfect flow between scenes, and Ilona Sckacz's wonderful harpsichord bridges, in literal harmony with Otts Munderloh's sound design (there is a surprise masterstroke at the beginning of the final scene) contributed mightily to the triumph.

Breaking the Code was Broadway's other London hit; this brilliant if occasionally lazy play by Hugh Whitemore was one of two in New York (the other was the short lived *A Most Secret War* by Kevin Patterson) dealing with the homosexual British mathematician, Alan Turing. Turing broke the German "enigma" code during the Second World War; he could not, however, break the social code of postwar England, and his suicide in 1954 is a testament, Whitemore suggests, to our institutional incapacity to integrate justice with genius. The play is about integration on a deeper level, however: Turing devotes himself after the war to exploring the mathematical foundations of an emerging computer science (the set resembles nothing so much as the insides of an early pre-solid-state computer, a computer that Thomas A. Edison could have invented), and he is consequently preoccupied with the generation of aritificial intelligence—and its implications of free will and the final integration of thinking with feeling, the *Entshiedungsproblem*, as he calls it. Tolstoy and Wittgenstein become principal players in Turing's mental drama, as do Lytton Strachey and Maynard Keynes, for artificial intelligence is placed squarely in the path of natural (though homosexual) concupiscence, and the upshot is that Alan Turing, Order of the British Empire, lands in jail.

What makes *Breaking the Code* a minor masterpiece is, above all, the performance of Derek Jacobi in the principal (and only real) role; Jacobi assumes an affecting stammer, a ganglion of fidgets, tics, and disgusting habits, and a wonderfully pathetic pleasantness: this is a creature impossible to forget. Turing's wrestling with the *Entshiedungsproblem* becomes Jacobi's tormented effort to match his character's passions to his defects, and to create—in himself and in us, the audience—the natural intelligence that can produce and control an artificial one. The structure of Whitemore's play is largely indifferent, and the jumps back and forth in time seem hastily arranged; this is more illustrated lecture than play, and it's occasionally lame dramatically—Whitemore lets us off easy much of the time. But the argument is compelling, overall, and Jacobi's performance galvanizing; *Breaking the Code,* in this production, is one of the most entertaining intellectual experiences you can have in the theater.

The New York Shakespeare Festival, which has been responsible for so much fine new theater in the city, added to its laurels with Eric Begosian's *Talkradio,* and Caryl Churchill's *Serious Money,* both of which played at the Festival's downtown Public Theater at Astor Place.

Last year, Begosian's one-man monologue, *Drinking in America* was generally admired at the American Place Theater, although not so much in these pages; but his *Talkradio* is more of a play, although the monologic structure somewhat remains. Barry Champlain (born Paleologus, or "archaic reason," we are told) is the brutally abrasive talkshow host of Cleveland's

radio program, "Nighttalk;" Begosian has him (and plays him—Begosian being both author and leading actor here) as on the eve of going national with his coruscating telephonic interface with America. Barry's nighttalk is all but toxic; his online correspondents are, in his words, a "bunch of yellow-bellied, spineless, bigoted, quivering, drunken, insomniatic, paranoid, disgusting, perverted, voyeuristic little obscene phone callers." And that's just what he tells them when he's *not* angry—which he is for most of the play. For his part, Begosian's Barry is filled with rage, with perverse self-importance, and with a sure sense of unendurable humiliation—from what sources we know not. "Radio is his life," we are told—from one of a number of characters who address the audience directly in the play's least effective moments—and we find out little else of interest about him. Not much actually happens here—one call is revealed as a hoax, another caller is invited into the studio (and arrives), and there are several dozen hangings-up; still, the acidulous recriminations that burn up the phone lines burn traces in our minds: Barry's conversations are livid, passionate, and occasionally unforgettable. You will never hear a radio talk show again without thinking of Eric Begosian, cigarette in hand, railing against the audience that adores him. "You're pathetic. I despise each and every one of you. You've got nothing. Nothing. Absolutely nothing. No brains. No power. No future. No hope. No god. The only thing you believe in is me." This play doesn't have much forward motion, and it is spotted with empty mouthings and clumsy showings-off, but the authorial voice penetrates—particularly in the author's own performance—and it penetrates deep.

Serious Money was an enormous hit at the Royal Court Theater in London, and in its 1987 transfer to Joseph Papp's downtown Public Theatre in New York; it failed, however, to earn a sustained run at its subsequent 1988 Broadway opening with a new American cast. At the Public it was a rousing if special success, and rightfully so. Caryl Churchill is, perhaps, the most innovative playwright on the current scene; her *Cloud 9* successfully rewrote virtually everything we used to think could and couldn't be done on stage, and made us care about the characters too (an astonishing combination of feats), and *Top Girls* required a new orthographic system just to be put into print (the speeches there coincide, break off, and overlap with absolute abandon.) *Serious Money,* which is a farce about British securities trading, arbitrage scandals, insider tipping, and Ivan Boesky, and which amazingly divined the market crash of '87 with near precision, is written, believe it or not, in rhyming prose (some would say verse, but the orthographers will determine that, I suppose, when it's finally published.) There are also two grotesquely obscene songs (the entire, much-repeated refrain of the first act closer is a one-syllable, four-letter word for a strictly female organ), and much of the rest of the time everybody is talking simultaneously and VERY fast. There are about fifty telephones on the set (which is by Peter Hartwell), and most of them are in use most of the time (and that's not in the background, it's the principal dialogue!) There's a helter-skelter feeling about the work even beyond this: all the leading actors double, triple, and quadruple in major roles, and without much in the way of character differentiation; even when you are given the chance to hear what one person is saying, you're not entirely sure who that person is supposed to be. There's a deep level of confusion, then, projected by *Serious Money,* but that's certainly part of its appeal; you're mesmerized by the style; fixated by the whirlwind. One of the most salient aspects of insider trading is that *we* are not the insiders, we are the outsiders, and nothing on stage so far has brought us to this understanding as clearly as Churchill's work.

Since, as they say, Neil Simon turned serious on us, shallow comedy is no longer available on Broadway: well, not true. Larry Shue's *The Nerd* delivers just what the title offers: a full length sitcom with live actors. The play works, albeit meagerly; it has a surprise ending, and it pokes fun at a foible or two. Shue, who died tragically in a plane crash in 1985, was one of our most promising young comedians (his *The Foreigner* is playing somewhere in America every weekend), and this play shows his skill. It was a great hit in London, where it was the highest grossing play in the West End, and it packs them in at the Helen Hayes in New York. The play doesn't seek to be anything but entertaining, and therefore neither, in mentioning it, shall I.

Regional Theater

Outside of New York, Lee Blessing's *A Walk in the Woods,* which opened at the Yale Repertory Theater under Des McAnuff's direction, seems to have been the play of the year: and in fact it was so designated ("Best Play Outside of New York") by a group calling itself the American Theater Critics Association. I say "seems to have been" because no one can see every new play opening in the United States in any year; even the assertively named Association must rely on each voting member's reading the bulk of the manuscripts under consideration. But Blessing's play certainly had my vote as well: it's a thoroughly brilliant play; indeed, it's the best new play I saw in 1987.

A Walk in the Woods is a two character play set on and around a park bench, but that's as close as it comes to *The Zoo Story* or *I'm Not Rappaport,* erstwhile exemplars of this form. The bench here is in the woods outside of Geneva, and the characters are the heads of Russian and American negotiating teams seeking to resolve a longstanding arms control impasse; the play is, of course, based on the famous 1982 "Walk in the Woods" meeting of Paul Nitze and Yuli Kvitsinksy under similar circumstances.

Blessing is not pretending to report actual history, however, and his play, although dealing with some historical elements, is essentially a work of speculative fiction. In his *Walk,* Leningrad-born Botvinnik is the disarmingly lighthearted humorist of the pair; with his exclusively Italian suits, Botvinnik is also the best dresser. Honeyman, from Wausau, Wisconsin, is the straight-laced and hard-driving idealist, trying to steer the negotiations back on track at every opportunity; what his life lacks in fun, Honeyman makes up for by steely (if good-spirited) ambition. But this is not a play about throw-weights and on-site verifications; it is about the nature of friendship—both personal and political, both spontaneous and strategic. "Is it good, do you think, for arms negotiators to become friends?" asks Honeyman. "Someone has to," responds Botvinnik. Honeyman is unimpressed. "Making friends is a fine thing, but not on someone else's time, so to speak," he offers. But his offering becomes a new part of the negotiations, and counter-

Lawrence Pressman and Michael Constantine in Lee Blessing's A Walk in the Woods. *Photograph by Micha Langer for La Jolla Playhouse.*

offers fill the air throughout the play. "Be frivolous with me," orders Botvinnik. "But what about cruise missiles?" asks Honeyman. "Have you ever slept with a black woman?" counters Botvinnik.

Four scenes make up this play; a Summer, Fall, Winter, and Spring that witness despairingly minute shifts in superpower positioning, exquisitely reflected by the nuances of feeling and expression of Blessing's diplomats in the Geneva woods. This is extraordinary dramaturgy: it's a spellbinding two-hour dialogue without overt plot, without hortatory moralizing, even without much in the way of intrigue or suspense; Blessing daringly structures his play around the evolution of a friendship between two middle-age professionals, poised between their idealistic hopes and the dread of ultimate resignation. And Blessing succeeds: the drama holds like a high wire act without a net. In passing, as it were, Blessing provides a brilliant and often original analysis of the human factors in superpower confrontation, with perceptive notions of key historical and psychological factors. I believe that no one could leave this play without a more lucid view of the complexities in contemporary arms politics, and the ramifications of even the slightest movement within those complexities.

Blessing's play is also more than just a feat of the intellect. It is a wry and witty comedy, and a moving human drama. As staged at the La Jolla Playhouse in California (it had opened at the Yale Repertory Theater in Connecticut), it was also a stunning stage treat. Richard Riddell's lighting and Bill Clarke's set gave us achingly beautiful seasons in the Swiss forests ("Who is to blame?" asks Honeyman. "It is not America," replies Botvinnik, "It is not the Soviet Union. . . . The real problem is Switzerland. . . . We should put the table at the bottom of a missile silo.") Clarke's set, a forest floor with 25 tree trunks reaching up and out of sight—tree trunks that could, on occasion, remind one of ballistic missiles—was backed by an interior wall; the forest is not, in this production, wholly divorced from the conference room, but rather a subdivision of it. Des McAnuff's direction, and the performances of Michael Constantine (as the Russian) and Lawrence Pressmen, were subtle, clear, and superior in every respect. A subsequent 1988 Broadway opening, with the same director but different actors, proved somewhat less successful—apparently because the acting was broader and more geared to the shallower gags and easier laughs that some feel are required by Broadway audiences.

"Listen to me. The worlds swarm with an infinity of creatures, those we see, those we never see; Naga snakes who live in the depths of the earth or in vast palaces on the sea's bed; Rakshasas, monsters of the forest's night who live off human flesh; Gandharvas, frail creatures who glide between us and the sky; Apsarasas, Danavas, Yakshas and the long glittering chain of gods who live like all beings in the shadow of death." With these words, and about 60,000 more, Peter Brook brought his celebrated production of *The Mahabharata* to the United States in the Fall of 1987. The play is based on the original Sanskrit epic poem, which, written over a period of seven or eight centuries on both sides of the B.C./A.D. line, is about fifteen times the size of our Bible. Brook and Jean-Claude Carriere spent about ten years shaping it into a nine-hour French drama, which Brook directed with an international cast (his producing company is called the Centre International de Recherches Theatrale); it premiered at the Avignon Festival in the summer of 1985, and, after a successful season in Paris, Brook translated it into English, re-cast and re-rehearsed his actors, and brought the show to Los Angeles.

And it is a show. Brook continues to mine the Artaudian fields he began to work in the late 1960s: with the (seemingly) simplest invention, and the rawest of mechanics, he tells a story that is passionate, spellbinding, and escalating: the war with which the drama culminates is as violently thrilling as anything I've seen on stage—yet utterly devoid of blood, mutilations, or graphic combat. Brook works with the elements—fire, water, air (often smoke-filled for accent) and earth comprise his setting—and humans inhabit these elements as tentatively on Brook's stage as on the Great Stage we all occupy. There's a plainness to this massive tale; destiny is worked out by dice games and chariot wheels stuck in the mud, and for nine hours we live in the plainness too. Brook's play has yet to be performed in an ordinary theater: in Avignon it was presented in a rock quarry, in Paris in the shell of a burned out vaudeville theater (the Bouffes du Nord, Brook's principal staging home), and in Los Angeles in a made-to-order studio; all the staging locales had natural clay floors which could hold the muddy pond, the river, and the kerosene-fueled circles of fire which figure in the script. Plain. And extravagant.

There's a voyeuristic detachment in seeing someone else's epic; we Westerners can, of course, be persuaded that Brook's strange creatures are gods, but for the most part non-Hindus neither fear their divine wrath nor bask in their magnificence, and we thereby miss the (necessarily unstated) background: it is story to us, not allegory. We are dazzled by Brook's extraordinary creations, even mesmerized by them, but we don't root for the home team—in *The Mahabharata,* we don't even get a home team. The division between the warring Pandavas and Kauravas do not kindle any of our allegiances; the "long glittering chain of gods," are, to us, spectacular curiosities, but they are not enchantresses nor monsters. There were long standing ovations following the *Mahabharata* performances (in Paris and in America) but little post-mortem discussion; the play stands just enough apart from our lives to leave little to reflect upon, apart from dramaturgical technique and cross-cultural adventure. Those latter, however, could carry a powerful impact: *The Mahabharata* was the lesson of the year, the trip of the decade. Henceforth, I suspect, we'll be watching out for those Rakshasas in the forest's night.

Vladimir Gubaryev is the science editor for *Pravda,* and was the first journalist on the scene at Chernobyl; he is also the author of four plays and several documentary films, so his play based on the Chernobyl experience, *Sarcophagus,* has an extraordinary importance: all the more so since the play appeared in print a mere two months after it was written, and four months after the April/May 1986 explosion—astonishing timetables by Soviet standards—and it appeared on stage both in Russia and abroad quite rapidly after that; I saw it in Los Angeles in September 1987. *Sarcophagus* wins the *glasnost* award for the year, for without the vaunted openness of the Gorbachav regime, we would never have heard of the play here, and it's likely that we would not have heard of it there either; under Brezhnev or Chernyenko it almost certainly would never see the light of a Russian day. (Under Stalin, Gubaryev himself wouldn't see the light of day.)

All this importance does not a good play make, however. Gubaryev's effort is fascinating, and the subject is powerful, but his writing is often clumsy—sometimes laughably so. It's not, strictly speaking, a realistic play: the setting is a mythical Moscow radiation treatment center, where fatally irradiated patients may not be visited or telephoned; rather they are compartmentalized for their final hours in individual cubicles at the rear of the stage. One patient, Bessmertny (his name means "The Immortal") resides more or less permanently in the center; he has survived his sickness for 487 days when the play begins and the Chernobyl victims arrive; all have died by day 488. Bessmertny serves as a bitterly comic chorus to the play's action, which revolves around an investigation of the causes of the explosion, a compassionate account of caring clinicians in a futile task, and a rather sophisticated analysis of Russian rouble-passing in lieu of crisis management. An American doctor (modeled on the real Robert Gale) makes an appearance, and the expected call for both superpowers to exercise due vigilance is resoundingly delivered. The arguments are not decisive, however, for Gubaryev is not interested in (or capable of) fingering a villain; it is said that he is, indeed, a proponent of nuclear energy, and only seeking to alert the public to the dangers thereof. This he does, powerfully and without question; the audience is suitably alarmed and wryly provoked; we leave the theater racked with the magnitude of the horrific suffering these little gamma rays can cause.

But *Sarcophagus*'s textual clumsiness is hard to ignore; this seems like a play written for schoolchildren. One might think that the author had worked for *The Weekly Reader* rather than *Pravda:* "What do you mean, exactly?" the characters dutifully inquire of each other, with all the naive earnestness of characters in the senior play. The spectacle of superb actors (Nan Martin, Alan Mandel, Robert Symonds, Tom Rosqui in Bill Bushnell's Los Angeles Theater Center production) stolidly exchanging these dumbbell lines was distressing, no matter how grave the subject at hand. I suspect this is largely a generic problem in contemporary Soviet writing; for, in fact, *Pravda* turns out not to be so different than *The Weekly Reader* when you think of it. It is pathetic that the country that gave us the psychological subtleties of Chekhov, the mordant ironies of Tolstoy, and the philosophical complexities of Dostoevski should be routinely putting forth such primitive and simplistic writing as that offered by the daily Soviet press, by leading Soviet dramatists (Mikail Shatrov, for example, at least through the mid 80s) and by Vladimir Gubaryev on this occasion. *Glasnost* is immensely welcome, but we should be aware that one of its first achievements will be to show us just how pedestrian the writing in the Soviet theater has become. *Sarcophagus* succeeds at the level of serious investigation of serious issues, but it fails at the level of world class drama dealing with world class (and world future) problems.

It was presumably a lack of *glasnost* that drove Janusz Glowacki out of Poland some years ago; his interesting play, **Hunting Cockroaches,** looks in on a Polish emigré couple who have landed, among the eponymous cockroaches, in the bedroom of a lower east side apartment at four in the morning. That's more than just when the play apparently takes place; where these emigrés live, the author suggest, it's always four in the morning. Jan and Anka are the insomnious couple: he's a writer who doesn't write, she's an actress that doesn't act; both of them are professionally impotent and sexually inert (although perhaps its the other way around) in a country where the geographical boundaries between the states are made with neat straight lines. "That's what you call a neat job," says Jan, "Montana, Wyoming, North Dakota, South Dakota, Missouri . . . this country was laid out by someone who had technical training. Buildings, streets, everything, even people are well made. That's what you'd call a good piece of work." Europe is not a good piece of work; there "the boundary lines between all the countries twist, and turn, and twitch like worms in a can." Trouble is, Jan and Anka are a couple of worms

themselves, trying to fit themselves into America's straight lines; they can't, or won't, or don't adjust. The play is a series of highly amusing nightmares: immigration officers, would-be patrons, agents, homeless bums, and plainclothes Polish cops pop out from under the bed (the apartment's door is never used); and the phone rings its dreadful summons: is it the KGB? The immigration office? Burglars? Jan and Anka don't answer it. "All the Polish emigrés here are going crazy," says Anka. They turn out the light—but don't fall asleep. Glowacki's work is intermittently amusing, and there is a brightly poignant ending where Anka tries out a stand-up comic routine for us: this will be her breakthrough into the land of the straight lines. Under Arthur Penn's direction, *Cockroaches* was a success in New York and Los Angeles (where I saw it, with Swoosie Kurtz and Malcolm McDowell.) It's a static play; there's no plot, no argument, no violence, and no sex, and with the characters lying in bed with the lights out much of the time, the audience is inclined to take things pretty easy; we become almost as pleasantly inert as the characters. Let's score this one a couple of hours well spent in somebody else's life, but without the ingredients that might charge you up about things east and west, or male and female, or, well, anything at all.

August Wilson's *Fences* is discussed at the top of this essay; he has two newer plays now making regional rounds after their Yale Rep openings, *Joe Turner's Come and Gone,* which is headed for Broadway in 1988, and *The Piano Lesson,* which I saw at New Haven at the end of 1987. *The Piano Lesson* is, again, a collection of powerful dramatic scenes that don't yet come together; it's clearly not a finished work at this time, but may become so. The general drift is wonderful: a beautiful old

Starletta DuPois and Lou Myers in August Wilson's The Piano Lesson. © *Gerry Goodstein.*

hand-carved piano holds center stage in the current (1936) household of the venerable Charles family—this is an ex-slave family from Mississippi, now living in Pittsburgh, and the piano was once bartered for "one and one half" of the family ancestors. The "half" was Papa Boy Walter, then aged nine; Papa Boy Walter's father carved the piano's embellishments, and his grandchildren are the principal characters here, Berneice and Boy Willie, who now dispute what should be done with the family heirloom. Boy Willie, up from the country, wants to sell it and buy a plot of land, and Berneice wants to keep and treasure it as the center of family history (and, perhaps, family culture.) There are wonderful characters in this play: Boy Willie is an inspired one-man talkathon, Lymon is his adorably shy Mississippi companion, Avery is a properly charismatic minister and exorcist, and Wining Boy is a charming dissolute; they are all well meshed by director Lloyd Richards, and you feel a member of their family. The play's highlight is a working song, perhaps a slave song, that the men break into around a table; it echoes a harmony beyond Pittsburgh and Mississippi, a harmony with its roots in Africa and centuries of Black history before the slave ships. There's a ghost that haunts the play, which unfortunately doesn't lend either enlightenment or credibility, and which haplessly deconstructs the play's conclusion; other reviewers have pointed this out, and I hope that Wilson and Richards can rethink this and a few other structural weaknesses before the play and its wonderfully-drawn characters make their seemingly incvitable trek to New York.

Maybe they don't write 'em like they usta', but Louis Lippa has written the best Odets play I've ever seen, and his *The Stone House* proved a very worthwhile success at the People's Light and Theater Company's fine premiere production at their wonderfully attractive theater in the countryside outside of Philadelphia. Tom Bianchi is the principal character in Lippa's play, set in 1937 Philly; Tom wants to head off to Spain to fight the Monarchists, his wife Mary wants him to stay home and care for her and their retarded daughter, Flora. The dialectic is classic:

TOM: People should pay attention to what's going on in the world.

MARY: People should pay attention to what's going on in their own house. Straighten that out first. After that you can straighten out the world.

Attention must be paid to something, that's for sure. The strength of Lippa's play is in the intensity of the conflict, and the sure, inescapable escalation of the arguments. The issue is precisely the one argued by Jean Paul Sartre, whose friend asked Sartre for advice: should I stay with my ailing mother or fight with the Republicans in Spain? Sartre replied that he could not advise, that what his friend chose to do would existentially define who he was, and there was no essential (as opposed to existential) answer to his friend's dilemma. Lippa agrees, and the play thereby has a true to life if rather dramaturgically unsatisfying ending. Tom simply makes a choice, and we go along with it, mainly for sentimental reasons. The play's other strength is Lippa's beautiful depiction of the Bianchi family, particularly the lovely and mentally-disabled Flora. On the downside, *The Stone House* lacks a deep psychological analysis of the situation: Tom's idealism is painted as a pure moral force, whereas it could be shown to contain some points of prideful egotism, à la Dr. Stockmann in Ibsen's *Enemy of the People,* or a nihilistic deathwish, as in Eliot's *Murder in the Cathedral* or Bolt's *A Man for All Seasons.* To take a thesis

as simple and direct as Lippa's, and a stage format as established as domestic realism, the author must give us the deepest and subtlest analysis available, and no one here quite rises to this occasion. But the play is powerful theater, and should be seen elsewhere.

The Berkshire Theater Festival was the launching pad for Tom Griffin's *The Boys Next Door* (it originally opened at the McCarter in Princeton); the play (with some members of the Berskshire cast) opened late in the year in New York, and is now headed for a film. This is a play about mentally handicapped adults, living in a home for such persons, and the play is also an appeal for this sort of relatively unencumbered foster care for the semicapable retarded. It is a funny pay; in part ruefully so, as we are laughing at what in normal life would be stupidities, and we are occasionally ashamed of ourselves. At times, *The Boys Next Door* seems like a naturalistic version of the three stooges or the Marx brothers; Griffin treats the retardation of his characters with sensitivity, but still allows himself the opportunity to throw them into farcical adventures. There are deeply affecting moments, particularly at a dance of the retardates (it's a mixer with a corresponding women's home), and there are terrifically funny moments as well; this is a good play with some stunning acting challenges, and it should have a long life

Joe Grifasi and John Amos in Tom Griffin's The Boys Next Door. *Photograph by Walter H. Scott.*

in academic and community theaters, particularly if the film does well.

I enjoyed *Roza,* the musical by Julian More (book and lyrics) and Gilbert Becaud (music), which was directed by Harold Prince at the Center Stage in Baltimore, and again at the Mark Taper Forum in Los Angeles, en route to Broadway where it fizzled very quickly. I say enjoyed because no other word will really do; *Roza* is a curious stage piece: essentially a character study in two rather disconnected acts, with enough oddities to keep the audience engaged if not exactly on the edge of their seats. Madame Roza, played by Georgia Brown, is an aging Jewish ex-madam, living out her last days in one of the ethnic neighborhoods of Paris (*Roza* is adapted from *La Vie Devant Soi* by Roman Gary); in the first act she is earning her keep by maintaining a foster home for the children of prostitutes; in the second act she dies. Her neighbors, her "kids," and her friends constitute the lackadaisical action, and if there was ever an opportunity to use the phrase "raffish charm" without self-consciousness, here it is. The music, typical of Becaud, has a driving momentum, relentlessly channelled into a tiny mid-octave range, and the few numbers that break out of that range virtually explode; "Don't Make Me Laugh," which culminates in hysterics, is a new genre of theater song. Bob Gunton, as

a heavyweight boxer turned transvestite hoooker, is superb, and his song, "Diff'rent," attempts to characterize the entire show. It does, but being different here is not quite enough. *Roza* is enjoyable, and, for the time being, unique, but the momentum of the Becaud songs is not matched by a forward dramturgical movement in the story; frequently we remain indifferent to the bustle on stage, which seems so much excess energy. The actors' raffishness does not become ours; we don't want to share it or to live it, and, in the last analysis, it is not as charming as we, and the authors, had hoped.

Although I can only give my own unqualified enthusiasm to three shows (*Miss Daisy, A Walk in the Woods, Les Liaisons*), three is a lot for one year; there were also plenty of outstanding moments, powerful scenes, wonderful performances, and brilliant innovative leaps of the imagination on American stages this year: it was a winner all the way around. A carelessness in storytelling seems the commonest weakness, particularly when playwrights still try to generate plot payoffs; let's hope that 1988 brings our writers to a firmer skill in guiding us through their dramatic adventures.

University of California, Irvine

The Year in World Literature

by William Riggan

Hispanic, Third World, and Slavic authors stood out most prominently among the ranks of foreign-language literary works published during 1987, both in quantity and in quality. The Germanic literatures also made respectable showings, but it was definitely an off year for most other European writers, particularly the perennially strong French and Italians.

European Literature

From Spain proper came three noteworthy new titles. The octogenarian poet-artist Rafael Alberti continued his lengthy, productive career with a new selection of verse titled *Los hijos del drago* (**Children of the Dragon**); the mood is more somber here than in much of his earlier work, imparting a sense of dark finality, though the visual and technical skills are as sharp as ever. Juan Goytisolo's novel *En los reinos de taifa* (**In the Kingdom of Taifa**), a sequel to the previous year's *Game Preserve*, continues its predecessor's examination of the many contradictions and conflicts in Spain's history involving such "foreign" elements as the Moors of medieval times and the political activists of the 1960s. The novelist Gonzalo Torrente Ballester collected a good many of his best recent essays on literary-cultural topics in *Cotufas en el golfo* (literally "**Delicacies in the Gulf**," but figuratively "**Pie in the Sky**"), a delightful blend of congeniality and erudition.

Leading the parade of significant new German-language works in 1987 was the 1981 Nobel recipient Elias Canetti's *Geheimherz der Uhr* (**The Secret Heart of the Clock**), his notebook and diary writings from the years 1973-85; a loose mix of aphorisms, confessions, observations, and ideas (though curiously devoid of all topical reference to current events in the world at large), the texts offer a challenging, engaging look into Canetti's artistic world and work. The young Austrian Peter Handke brought out new books during the year: the novella *Nachmittag eines Schriftstellers* (**Afternoon of a Writer**) follows its protagonist on his "uneventful" afternoon walk through his modest-size city, viewing its people and places and phenomena through his hyperperceptive eyes and thus conveying by example what and how an artist "sees" what lies perfectly visible for all but goes unnoticed by most; *Die Abwesenheit* (**The Absence**), on the other hand, billed itself as a fairy tale, but more in the manner of Goethe's hermetic model than that of the Grimms, as it carries its four archetypal characters (an old man, a soldier, a woman, an actor) across continents and eras on an endless quest born of vague allusive longings and mystically sensed needs for satisfaction of the soul.

The West German novelist Martin Walser's novelette *Dorle und Wolf* astutely explores the psychological and psychosocial consequences of divided loyalties through the story of the East German double agent Wolf Ziegler and his attempts to quit his dual life and remain with family and friends and government job in the West. Gabriele Wohmann offers lighter and rather more romantic fare in *Der Flötenton* (**The Sound of the Flute**),

Dust jacket of Die Abwesenheit, *by Peter Handke. Suhrkamp Verlag, 1987. Courtesy of the publisher.*

an expansive (480 pages) and populous generational drama featuring chance meetings in locales such as Lisbon, brief affairs with lingering afterglows, and the binding threads of memory, small duplicities, and family loyalties. Peter Härtling constructed his sensitive novel *Waiblingers Augen* (**Waiblinger's Eyes**) around the historical figure of Wilhelm Waiblinger, an early nineteenth-century poet and friend of Hölderlin whose brief life ended by his own hand in Rome after several misfortunes of he heart in Tübingen. The 75-year-old Luise Rinser spins a Kafkaesque dream novel in *Silberschuld* (literally "**Silverguilt**"), whose first-person narrator is led through a mysterious city "beyond the border"—a city enclosed by a silver wall and filled with labyrinths, waterless harbors, creatureless zoos, unborn children, even the shades of her own guilt-ridden ancestors—on a fantastic journey toward knowledge, purgation, and redemption.

Important new works from other European writers were rather sparse in 1987. From France, the octogenarian Julien Green's newest novel deserves special mention: *Le pays lointain* (**The Distant Country**) evokes the pre-Civil War South in the United States in an elegantly told panorama of passion and intrigue among several leading families of Virginia and Georgia. The outstanding poet and critic Yves Bonnefoy produced a book in each genre in 1987: a selection of prose essays and meditations titled *Récits en rêve* (**Dream Narratives**), and the Goncourt Prize-winning verse collection *Ce qui fut sans lumière* (**This Which Passed in Darkness**), a limpid, autumnal volume which is as fine as anything he has ever done, in the estimation of most commentators. The Nobel Peace Prize recipient Elie Wiesel's latest novel, *Le crépuscule, au loin* (**The Twilight Far Away**), weaves together at least a dozen plot threads involving madness, suffering, betrayal, and survival; as critics have noted, all of Wiesel's fiction—this new work included—invokes a dialogue with the divinity amid the depiction of a downtrodden individual's struggle against fate, with greater authorial interest in the struggle itself than in its outcome. The Swedish Academy member Lars Gyllensten produced in *Sju vise mästare om kärlek* (**Seven Wise Masters about Love**) an exquisitely crafted set of love stories that together constitute "a discrete education in the stages of moral education," to cite one critic. Italy's talented Mario Soldati offers in *El Paseo de Gracia* (**Grace Street**) a wonderfully detailed depiction of Italian movie society and the "dualistic"—not to say "duplistic"—behavior that kind of world fosters even in its most admirable characters.

East European Literature

From Eastern Europe came several very interesting new books. The Polish novelist Tadeusz Konwicki mixes novel and diary in intriguing fashion in *Moonrise, Moonset,* a fictionalized memoir of his participation in both the anti-Nazi underground of 1944-45 and the Solidarity movement of 1980-81; not yet published in Poland, the text is perhaps the finest work yet to emerge on the pre-martial-law period, and the best book yet produced by the author of the acclaimed novel *A Minor Apocalypse*. A new novel by Konwicki that *was* permitted to appear in his homeland, *Bohin,* re-creates the world of his paternal grandmother, the joint proprietess of a large estate in Lithuania and a dynamic, sensitive individual closely involved in the sociopolitical entanglements of the mid-1800s. Konwicki's countryman Karol Wojtyla, better known as Pope John Paul II, permitted the publication of his *Collected Plays and Writings on Theater* in 1987, and the volume is perhaps more significant for what it reveals of the future pontiff's nature and mind than for the plays' literary merit as such; though not exactly moral tracts, the dramas do concentrate on human frailty and explore issues related to the human soul, a "theater of the word" which unfortunately proves rather static as theater. *A Cup of Coffee with My Interrogator* by Ludvík Vaculík became the first collection of the banned Czech writer's chronicles and essays to appear anywhere outside Prague's clandestine literary network and contains witty, short commentaries on "everything from Gandhi to *glasnost*.'" Meto Jovanovski's *Cousins,* reportedly the first Macedonian novel to be translated into English, tracks the comically inept country cousins Srbin and Shishman through their bumbling encounters at the front lines of a war involving Serbs, Bulgarians, Greeks, and the French; the result was an open indictment of fanaticism and warmongering and, despite overtly homiletic tendencies, proved entertaining and of more than passing literary interest.

The Romanian playwright Marin Sorescu came to the attention of Western audiences and readers in the bilingual publication of *Vlad Dracula the Impaler,* a stark drama in which the now-venerable figure of Vlad Tepes or Dracula is presented as "an enlightened madman and martyr who inflicts pain and suffering in the belief that he can overcome evil"; such individual actions, the author implies, are useless and ineffectual against the tide of history. Ismail Kadare, Albania's sole true claim to membership in the European literary community, was represented by no fewer than three new publications: *Chronicle in Stone,* only the second of his dozen-plus novels to have appeared in English as yet, actually chronicles the fate of the author's beautiful, fabled, walled native city of Gjirokastër (Greek: Argyrocastron) under its successive occupations during World War II; *L'année noire* (**The Black Year**), published in French translation in 1987, recounts the political and military machinations in and around the court of the German prince Wilhelm von Wied following his ascent to the throne of the new Albanian state in March 1914; and *Koha e shkrimeve* (**Epoch of Writings**), published in Tirana, collects two recent short novels (including the original of *L'année noire*) and eight short stories dealing with several completely different eras of Albania's "haunted history."

Russian Literature

Four émigrés—two poets and two prose writers—led the year's production in Russian literature. Topping the news was of course Joseph Brodsky's selection as the 1987 Nobel laureate in literature almost simultaneously with the publication of his latest verse collection, *Urania,* and its companion English-language volume *Homage to Urania,* which gathers several new and recent compositions, including the masterful, 1,400-line "Gorbunov and Gorchakov" and the celebrated "Roman Elegies" cycle; the two collections themselves, aside from the worldwide acclaim occasioned by the Nobel announcement, reaffirms Brodsky's status as the finest contemporary Russian poet and an international literary figure of the first rank. *Beyond the Limit* fully introduced Irina Ratushinskaya to American readers with a 47-poem cycle written during her incarceration at a "strict regime" camp for women political prisoners; the young poet, who was released in late 1986 and allowed to emigrate, possesses a lyric gift and an intelligence and art which have reminded many readers of her great predecessors Marina Tsvetaeva and Anna Akhmatova. The Borgesian side of prose writer and critic Abram Tertz (pen name of Andrei Sinyavsky) was revealed to Western readers in the collection *Fantastic Stories.* The novelist Vladimir Voinovich's *Moskva 2042* (Eng. *Moscow 2042*) meanwhile attempts a definitive futuristic satire of both the Soviet state and the messianic aims of such prominent exiles as Aleksandr Solzhenitsyn; though good for frequent laughs and often outrageously black humor, the work is on the whole less inspired than such earlier Voinovich masterpieces as *The Adventures of Private Ivan Chonkin.* As always, opinion was rather more divided on the latest Western editions of the USSR's two most prominent resident poets, Yevgeny Yevtushenko and Andrei Voznesensky. Yevtushenko continues to address matters of topical interest and urgency in *Almost at the End,* eulogizing the *Challenger* astronauts, for example, and condemning such exploitative Western figures as Columbus, Bismarck, Napoleon, and Pinochet while lauding a bulldozer worker and Che Guevara. *An Arrow in the Wall* mixes a bit of Voznesensky's experimental prose with his poetry and incorporates several items from earlier Western editions of his work, but its most satisfying inclusion is an entire section of poems written during the 1980s and hitherto unavailable in print. *In Search of Melancholy Baby* (original *V poiskakh grustnogo bebi*) by the émigré author Vassily Aksyonov offers an amusing series of impressions of American life

as encountered by the author during his coast-to-coast travels
and in his daily life in Washington.

Near Eastern Literature

Third World authors offered both great diversity and high quality in their 1987 productions. From the Near East, for example,
came new works by leading writers of Israel, Egypt, and Turkey. The Hebrew novelist Aharon Appelfeld uses enchantingly
dreamlike prose in *To the Land of the Reeds* to evoke the
increasingly ominous world and destiny of Jews in Central and
Eastern Europe during the late 1930s. In *After the Holidays* (a
phrase which in colloquial Hebrew is the equivalent of the
Hispanics' *mañana*) Yehoshua Kenaz employs a deceptively
simple narrative à la Kafka to reveal the frightful subsurface
of a community of European immigrants in Jewish Palestine
prior to World War I; the work has been hailed by Israeli critics
as one of the year's best in Hebrew, and the English translation
offers a faithful reflection of the original. Egypt's finest active
fiction writer, Naguib Mahfouz, has been concerned for the
last two decades of his career with portraying his nation's
failure to achieve the hopes of the 1952 revolution, particularly
social justice and more equal distribution of wealth. The first
English edition of the 1965 novel *The Beggar* adroitly conveys
this theme in its portrait of one man's psychological deterioration and torment, emblematic of the "beggaring" of Egyptian
bourgeois society in general. Mahfouz also saw in 1987 the
first English publication of his sensitive early novel about the
poverty and suffering of an Egyptian family during World War
II, *The Beginning and the End*.

Mahfouz's far less heralded countryman Sherif Hetata presented an equally searing and stylistically innovative, if politically somewhat programmatic, indictment of the Sadat regime
and its often repressive police-state tactics in *The Net,* whose
Arabic original appeared in 1982. The Persea Books (New
York) edition of the late Turkish writer Nazim Hikmet's *Selected Poetry* was the closest thing yet to a "Best of Hikmet"
volume in English (or any other major language), incorporating
numerous new translations with previously published pieces
and very little of the unabashed communist propaganda and
rhapsodic revolutionary verse he also churned out in great quantity during his prolific career. Turkey's perennial Nobel candidate Yashar Kemal continues his recent preoccupation with
myth and fable in *The Birds Have Also Gone,* a transparently
direct and symbolic tale of three peasant youths in Istanbul and
their futile effort to capitalize on an old folk custom by trapping
and selling birds for ritual release to appease heaven; the nostalgia and sentiment are a bit thick for Western tastes, but the
colorful exoticism of Kemal's subject and milieu will likely
compensate in the opinion of many readers. Greece's famed
poet Yannis Ritsos issued the eighth installment of a planned
nine-volume prose cycle, *Lighostévoun i erotíseis* (**The Questions Diminish**), featuring both dramatic monologues and expository tales involving figures both mythical and earth(l)y.

Latin American Literature

From Latin America came some rich offerings. The Mexican
novelist Carlos Fuentes's long-awaited *Cristóbal nonato* (**Christopher Unborn**) presents a satiric, metafictional look at the
Mexico City of the near future (1992, the 500th anniversary
of Columbus's discovery of the New World), a horrifyingly
filthy, overpopulated, rat-infested ruin of a metropolis on the
brink of total economic and political collapse. Fuentes's countryman Octavio Paz, Spanish America's leading poet, brought
out a bilingual edition of his collected verse of the last 30

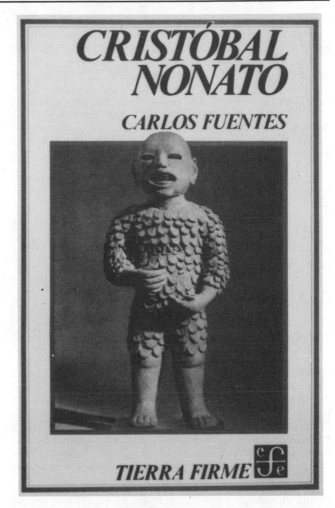

Dust jacket of Cristóbal Nonato, *by Carlos Fuentes. Fondo
de Cultura Económica, 1987.*

years—*Collected Poems, 1957-1987*—nearly 200 pieces in all,
with English renderings by such noted poets as Denise Levertov, Charles Tomlinson, and the late Elizabeth Bishop. The
1982 Nobel laureate Gabriel García Márquez of Colombia returned to the chronicle form of *A Death Foretold* for his account
of *La aventura de Miguel Littín clandestino en Chile* (**The Clandestine Adventure of Miguel Littín in Chile**), an uneven work
on the Chilean filmmaker's secret 1985 visit to his homeland
to film "the reality of his country after twelve years of military
dictatorship"; despite its rather pat political line and the somewhat self-congratulatory attitude of all involved, the story proves
brisk, even thrilling at times, and often infectious in its tweak-
ing of so authoritarian a regime. A far more sober and complex
view of the Chilean situation is found in *La desesperanza* (**Hopelessness**), the exile author José Donoso's first major work in
a decade; alternately hallucinatory and graphically naturalistic,
mirroring the national dilemma in the personal traumas of its
protagonist Mañunga Vera, the book in every way lives up to
its title as a "document on despair." With *Y así sucesivamente*
(**And Thus in Succession**) the octogenarian Argentine author
Silvina Ocampo presented the first in a new series of publications she has promised her readers, in this case twenty-two
short stories and a poem; the stories in particular offer more
of the keen psychological perception so highly praised by Borges
in Ocampo's writing, as well as subtle humor, ironic twists of

plot and incident, and a polished, sophisticated, limpid style. The texts in the late novelist Juan Rulfo's *Obras* (**Works**) were selected by the author prior to his death in January 1986 and thus represent his final literary testament, so to speak; included are his famous 1955 novel *Pedro Páramo,* a complete story collection from 1953, two previously uncollected novellas, a full-length screenplay, and two shorter film scenarios. And from Brazil, the dazzling talents of novelist Marcio Souza were on display for the seventh time in ten years in *O brasileiro voador* (**The Flying Brazilian**), an irreverent fictionalized biography of the nearly sacrosanct figure of pioneer aviator Alberto Santos Dumont.

African/West Indian Literature

New works by several long-established writers from widely dispersed regions highlighted the year in African letters. In *Ces fruits si doux de l'arbre à pain* (**These Sweet Fruits of the Breadfruit Tree**) the Congolese novelist Tchicaya U Tam'si produced one of the most provocative and challenging works in several years from Francophone Africa, a complex study in political intrigue and psychological-ethical questions built around the trial of a putative mass murderer over which the protagonist must preside during the early years of independence. In *La pluie* (**The Rain**) the Algerian Francophone author Rachid Boudjedra probed the dark inner world of a somber and potentially self-destructive young Arab woman driven to tearful despair by her dreary life as medical director of a urogenital clinic and by the vicious rejection she has seemingly suffered from family and society alike. The Moroccan novelist Tahar Ben Jelloun was the surprise winner of the 1987 Goncourt Prize for fiction with his novel *La nuit sacrée* (**The Sacred Night**), the sequel to his acclaimed *Enfant de sable* (Eng. *The Sand Child*); the new book concludes its predecessor's exotic tale of an Arab woman raised as a boy but ultimately freed from her bondage of false identity.

At the other end of the continent the revered South African author and critic Es'kia Mphalele brought out *Afrika My Music,* an autobiography covering the years 1957-83 (his *Down Second Avenue,* on the years up to 1953, is a long-established classic of African literature), a period which included two decades of exile in Europe and the United States before his return home just after the bitter Soweto riots of the early 1980s. Nigeria's Chinua Achebe produced his first full-length novel in nearly twenty years, *Anthills of the Savannah,* a morality tale involving three college friends whose paths lead them to fatal opposition as despotic ruler, government minister, and leading newspaper editor in their West African nation; expectations were perhaps too great for this new work by the famed author of *Things Fall Apart* and *The Arrow of God,* and critical reception has been mixed at best.

From the Caribbean in 1987 came three major new books, one important reissue, and one notable translation. Derek Walcott of Trinidad, one of the finest English-language poets anywhere in the world, published *The Arkansas Testament,* his first large new volume of verse in four years; the new poems are extraordinary in their range and in their mastery of language and lyricism, confirming Walcott's status as "a genuine virtuoso, now and forever a first-rate lyricist, a high-ranking humorist, and a poet of unusually eloquent moral passion" (*New York Times*). Guyana's virtuoso novelist Wilson Harris subsumed much of his earlier fiction in the remarkable new novel *The Infinite Rehearsal;* the work presents itself as the fictional autobiography—by one "W.H."—of a certain Robin Redbreast Glass, born in the year of Hiroshima, author of a new version

Dust jacket of Infinite Rehearsal, *by Wilson Harris. Faber & Faber, 1987. Jacket illustration by Brian Grimwood. Reprinted by permission of Faber & Faber Ltd.*

of *Faust,* and now the haunted resident of a sacred forest redolent of both Eliot and Dante. The whole is richly allusive and densely complex, and the near-unanimous opinion of critics and readers is that Harris has never written better. In *Mahagony* Edouard Glissant delves into the history of his native Martinique, focusing on three very different Maroons from three widely dispersed periods, all cast in an evocative creolized French perfectly suited to the subject matter.

The reissue of *Natives of My Person,* a 1971 novel by George Lamming, brought to the attention of a new generation of readers what is perhaps the Barbadian author's most significant and most ambitious work, an account of a seventeenth-century British colonizing expedition that moves on allegorical as well as historical and realistic levels. *Cathedral of the August Heat* introduces the English-reading public to the Haitian poet-journalist Pierre Clitandre's epic novel of prerevolutionary life among the lowest of the low in Port-au-Prince, replete with the flavor of Caribbean folklore and the force of a visceral, naturalistic style.

Asian/Pacific Literature.

Old masters and new alike were prominent in Asian and Pacific writing in 1987. India's grand old man of letters, R. K. Narayan, created another in his long line of engaging small-town poseurs in the mysterious but compulsively loquacious raconteur Dr. Rann, the protagonist of **Talkative Man.** Japan's venerated fiction writer Masuji Ibuse, now ninety, saw his two finest short novels disseminated to a worldwide audience in faithful English translations bound in a single volume: **Waves,** a fictitious war diary from the twelfth-century conflict between the Heike and Genji clans; and **Isle-on-the-Billows,** a lighter piece set during the later years of the Tokugawa shogunate in the nineteenth century. The novel many consider the finest of Japan's modern period, Shimazaki Toson's **Before the Dawn** (1935), a massive yet thoroughly absorbing drama of the changes wrought in ordinary lives by Perry's opening of Japan in 1853, was finally published in English translation as well this year. Also making its first appearance in English was **The Old Capital** by 1968 Nobel winner Yasunari Kawabata, the ethereal, atmospheric tale of a young Kyoto woman's filial devotion and self-realization. Kenzaburō Ōe, perhaps the most gifted of Japan's middle-generation novelists, brought out an innovative new work titled **Natsuskashii toshi e no tegami** (**Letters to the Time/Space of Fond Memories**), which subsumes many of the characters, episodes, and images from his earlier books, all molded within an "eternal dream time" cosmology derived from Dante yet set in the author's native mountain village of Shikoku; despite such complexity of theme and execution, the work has been received favorably, in good measure because of its more optimistic tone in comparison with several of its predecessors in Ōe's canon. A greater popular success in Japan during 1987 was Haruki Murakami's two-volume novel **Noruwei no mori** (**Norwegian Wood**—intentionally invoking the 1960s Beatles song of the same name), billed as a "100% love story" but featuring a "lover" more in the classically passive Japanese tradition of Prince Genji than in any steamy Western sense of the term. In all else, however—in language, music tastes, eating habits, and life-style in particular—the young protagonist and his circle of friends and lovers are entirely Westernized, and Murakami's novel successfully captures the experience and ethos of one generation of young Japanese for the reading enjoyment of another.

Leaden Wings, an absorbing 1980 novel of daily life in modern China by Zhang Jie, praised at home for its socio-cultural honesty but attacked for its political satire, became one of the first larger recent works of Chinese fiction to appear in translation in the West. Set within a milieu of heavy-industry workers, the book straightforwardly argues that China must grant precedence to democracy and diversity of opinion instead of dogmatism and blind party loyalty; that it manages to do so without falling prey to caricature or oversimplification of issues is an accomplishment of no small degree.

Along the Pacific Rim, the Indonesian writer Ismail Marahimin's haunting World War II novel **And the War Is Over** received the prestigious Pegasus Prize for 1987, an award whose purpose is "to introduce American readers to distinguished works from countries whose literature is rarely translated into English" and which therefore guarantees translation and publication of each year's honored work; set in a small Sumatran village where the Japanese have established a prison camp for captured Dutch soldiers, the novel offers a moving tapestry of interrelations and interactions among the Japanese captors, their Dutch prisoners, and their Javanese workers with each other and with the

Dust jacket of Gabo Djara, *by B. Wongar. Dodd, Mead, 1987. Jacket design by Hal Siegel. Jacket illustration by Linda Crockett. Reproduced by permission of Linda Crockett.*

local populace. **Wings of Stone** continued Linda Ty-Casper's recent series of novels about sociopolitical events in her native Phillipines, tracking the vicissitudes of a returned exile's reintroduction to mid-1980s Manila and the widespread corruption, violence, and physical-spiritual decay that marked the martial-law years. The half-aboriginal (and pseudonymous) B. Wongar published his third novel set in Australia's primitive bush country, **Gabo Djara,** an allegorical tale which mixes science-fiction fantasy and native folklore in its moving tale of a culture facing potential devastation from uranium mining and nuclear testing. And lastly, New Zealand's Keri Hulme followed the enormous worldwide success of her novel **The Bone People** with a collection of short fiction titled **Te Kaihau/The Windeater,** most of whose stories blend the uniqueness of her native Maori culture with the European aspect of modern New Zealand (and her own mixed heritage) by exploring the strong ties that bind families together and the sometimes equally strong, painful clash of traditions that creates disharmony and even disintegration.

World Literature Today

New Authors

Bruce Duffy

19??-

American novelist.

In *The World as I Found It* (1987), Duffy has created a fictionalized portrait of three of the twentieth century's most brilliant men. The novel centers on the life of Ludwig Wittgenstein, the eccentric Austrian who professed contempt for philosophers while greatly influencing philosophy with his theories of language. The rivalries and collaborations among Wittgenstein and his Cambridge colleagues Bertrand Russell and G. E. Moore provide the focus of this first novel, which expands to a general examination of England's intelligentsia.

Some critics fault the novel's scope, finding that excessive biographical detail and wordy, uneven passages occasionally obscure the story. While reviewers note that Duffy's bold ambitions are not always realized, they nevertheless characterize many portions of his first novel as "brilliant," "delightful," "hilarious," "passionate," and "stunning." Duffy's vivid characterizations and witty dialogue are singled out for high praise. Richard Eder, commenting on Duffy's unusual fictional concern, observes, "his purpose . . . is to write about thought as one of the vital signs of life." With few exceptions, critics reflect that *The World as I Found It* admirably achieves this goal.

Photograph by Robert Sherbow

PUBLISHERS WEEKLY

Improbable as it may seem, this long, sometimes complex first novel [*The World as I Found It*], featuring the influential Austrian philosopher Ludwig Wittgenstein and his colleagues/friends/rivals, Cambridge philosophers Bertrand Russell and G. E. Moore, is abundant with life and almost unflaggingly interesting. Deviating only when it must from the record, the lightly fictionalized work progresses chronologically through the convolutions of Wittgenstein's career: his early life in Austria; his arrival in Cambridge; his experiences in the first World War; his unhappy memories of his brilliantly gifted older brothers, both homosexual, both suicides; his relations with a rich, powerful, autocratic father; and his succession of young male friends. All the while Russell is reeling from Lady Ottoline Morrell (of Bloomsbury fame) to a series of wives and other wandering women and the good Moore, already far from young, is marrying happily. The enigmatic Wittgenstein could imagine the unimaginable, but never would we have imagined it possible that he would one day appear as the protagonist of a novel—and a delightful one, at that.

A review of "The World as I Found It," in Publishers Weekly, *Vol. 231, No. 24, June 19, 1987, p. 115.*

KIRKUS REVIEWS

Stunning, bold first novel [*The World as I Found It*] very loosely based on the erratic career of Austrian philosopher Ludwig Wittgenstein.

In a buoyant style, Duffy imagines Wittgenstein's life as a series of collisions, beginning with his turbulent family life and especially with his arrival at Cambridge and his rocky friendships with Bertrand Russell, G. E. Moore, and Lytton Strachey and the Cambridge Apostles. While Russell and Moore vie for Wittgenstein's loyalty, Strachey and the Apostles see a star on the ascendant and move in quickly to enlist him within their ranks. But precisely those qualities that make Wittgenstein a recognizably brilliant student—the exactitude, the elimination of unnecessary detail—render him incapable of a soft berth in academe (a mercy which prevents this work from becoming yet another academic novel). In the meantime, Russell has problems of his own, what with the demands of a mistress, the maintenance of reputation, and the dirty but necessary chore of fending off intellectual and sexual pretenders to the throne. Somewhat off to the side, a perfect foil for the bombastic Russell, stands the ever-tactful Moore, acting as a buffer between Russell and Wittgenstein. Then WW I intrudes, separating Wittgenstein and his friends, who find themselves on opposite sides of the conflict, and we later see Wittgenstein languishing as a schoolteacher in a slovenly Austrian town before going through a spiritual renewal and finally returning to Cambridge to become one of Europe's reigning philosophers. Duffy has concocted letters, rearranged biography, toyed with language and philosophy, and come up with an idiosyncratic tale that, line after line, crackles with sharp wit.

A spectacular first showing.

A review of "The World as I Found It," in Kirkus Reviews, *Vol. LV, No. 12, July 1, 1987, p. 945.*

BARBARA HOFFERT

"This," asserts the author, "is fiction." Though a detailed narrative of the life and times of eminent 20th-century philosopher Ludwig Wittgenstein, "it is not history, philosophy, or biography." Duffy's first novel [*The World as I Found It*] is not for the reader looking to understand contemporary philosophy; indeed, philosophers may object to its use as a gloss on a young man's private anguish. And some readers may wonder whether the many characters borrowed from real life are being fairly represented. But readers who like a broad canvas will find this work appealing, moving as it does from uppercrust Vienna to pre-war Cambridge to the battlefields of World War I and World War II. Alas, there is some infelicitous phrasing here, and the discussions of what's doing in philosophy can read like an encyclopedia. But in scope and ambition this work is finally compelling.

Barbara Hoffert, in a review of "The World as I Found It," in Library Journal, *Vol. 112, No. 13, August, 1987, p. 140.*

RICHARD EDER

Here [in *The World as I Found It*] are nearly 550 pages of a most unusual, even preposterous venture: a novel constructed out of the lives, the thoughts, the appetites, the egos and the very toenails and pocket watches of the philosophers Ludwig Wittgenstein, Bertrand Russell and G. E. Moore.

It is hard to known which is more outsized; the talent of Bruce Duffy, the author, or his nerve. Sometimes they are the same thing, sometimes not. Duffy is a superb writer though not always a prudent one. The successes of *The World as I Found It* are astonishing; its defeats are less astonishing, given its ambition, though perhaps they are not always necessary.

"Passion" may be more accurate than "ambition." This is Duffy's first novel, and he is equipped to be a very fine novelist and perhaps more; but in this case, he is novelizing in the service of a passion that both makes this an extraordinary book and sometimes gets in its way.

Duffy introduces plenty of philosophy, as clearly as possible; particularly in the case of Wittgenstein, the major character, and Russell, his patron and antagonist. But his purpose—and much of the astonishing success—is to write about thought as one of the vital signs of life.

He makes vivid characters out of the three men, and he makes their ideas traits of these characters. With Wittgenstein, ideas are energy, ego and a mystical will to prevail. With the arrogant and insecure Russell, they are the will to maneuver. With the gentle Moore, they are the will to give way to any better argument.

A great deal more than diplomacy is war by other means. Poetry—read Robert Lowell's biography—is war by other means. Cooking and seduction are wars by other means. Philosophy, Duffy tells us, is war (or with Moore, conscientious objection) by other means.

The author asserts in a brief preface that he has used the principal lines of the three lives—diaries and letters are freely quoted—but that he has transposed and invented details. It is a novel by texture, to put it roughly, and a triple biography by plot; real bones with a fictional skin and a large life. It is a fusion that suggests Jacques Maritain's phrase: "The dreamers of what is true."

Duffy's Wittgenstein, son of a rich and overbearing Viennese steel magnate, comes to Cambridge as a young man to study under Russell. He is a most unabashed disciple; before long, he is subjecting Russell's work on mathematical logic to devastating criticism.

The book recounts their collaboration and growing differences; it portrays quite brilliantly Russell's fascination with the younger man whose rigorous logic is voiced with a prophet's certainty. Best of all, it gives a subtle picture of a philosopher's mixture of excitement and agony at being overborne by a deeper mind.

In one of many witty vignettes, the author has Russell telling Ottoline Morrell, his Bloomsbury lover, of how he destroyed the work of the German philosopher Gottlob Frege; and of Frege's cordial acknowledgments. Lady Morrell is mystified by Russell's complacency. "He is in your debt," she says ironically. The real irony, of course, is that it was Frege who sent Wittgenstein to study with Russell.

Philosophic dueling provides some of the book's most exhilarating moments. There is a superbly comical and instructive scene that has Russell, Wittgenstein and Moore—who throughout is a kind of balance-wheel between the others—attending a Cambridge discussion group toward the end of their lives. Wittgenstein stalks out after one speaker accuses him of picking up a poker to threaten him; Russell shrieks with frustration at seeing his rival depart before he can tackle him.

Moore is sketched rightly, but what emerges is a stunningly graceful portrait. He is an innocent with large appetites. Duffy writes several splendid pages that describe Moore making his prodigious way through an enormous and greasy Cambridge meal. His late-life courtship of a student is funny and touching; later, Duffy provides a brilliant account of how their marriage balances her need for intimacy and his for abstraction.

Russell's portrait is less subtle—as Russell himself was less subtle—but it is vastly entertaining. Duffy gets full measure of his restlessness, the need for attention that made much of his philosophizing rather shallow, his egotism and his perpetual philandering. The school that he runs with his feminist wife is a wacky mixture of the earnest and the cock-eyed. Russell interviews the new woman teachers and urges them, in gravely paternal tones, to sleep with him.

Duffy can so pleasure us with a phrase that some of the pleasure rubs off on the character. Describing Russell's snobbish one-upmanship, he calls him "master of the seemingly good-natured slight, fraught with elan and bonhomie, which fizzed up like a fatal heartburn in the person slighted."

Wittgenstein is the book's center both of gravity and energy. He is the figure with whom Duffy risks the most, achieves a lot, and sometimes fails. Where the other two appear and disappear, suiting the author's firework rhythms, with Wittgenstein, a full-scale fictional biography is attempted.

His childhood in the oppressive pre-World War I wealth of Vienna is spelled out. So is the overbearing presence of his enormously successful father. Meals are described, course by rich course; and concerts and family gatherings are presented with a steamy weight that makes *Buddenbrooks* seem like a French farce.

Wittgenstein's burdens are set out: the suicide of his older brothers, his guilt over concealing his Jewishness, his homosexuality. There are long sections on his ordeal in the World War I trenches, and his spells of brooding rustication in Norway, and later as a village schoolteacher in Austria.

It is an impressive, tormented portrait. It succeeds by dint of cumulative detail in suggesting convincing parallels between the strains and ambiguities of Wittgenstein's life, and the extraordinarily severe—and paradoxically liberating—restrictions he put on the meaning and uses of language.

In truth, the biographical detail is excessive; it weighs down and distorts the rich intellectual and emotional play in the lives and strivings of the three philosophers. If much of the writing is quite marvelous, there are whole pages of routinely presented facts and expository intellectual history. Duffy's formidable fictional ability to bring moments and characters to life raises novelistic expectations that are frequently dashed by the "and then . . . and then . . ." plodding of the biographical form.

It is, of course, an easy way out for a reviewer to suggest that more editing would have helped. Clearly, it would have had to be administered by a manic energy equivalent to the author's. No doubt, quite a bit was done, in any case, and perhaps exhaustion set in.

Still, if its mid-section and later sagging is a problem, *The World as I Found It*—a Wittgenstein phrase suggestive of his passionately provisional approach to reality—is a treasure-house, even if unwieldy. It would take a much longer review to suggest the variety of ungroomed pleasures to be found in it, along with the complex and moving portrait of a man whose intellectual energy burned like an acid so pure and corrosive that there was no container it could rest in. (pp. 3, 12)

> *Richard Eder, in a review of "The World as I Found It," in* Los Angeles Times Book Review, *August 30, 1987, pp. 3, 12.*

An Excerpt from *The World as I Found It*

Wittgenstein returned to his kites, but the sick feeling persisted and with it a certain floating anxiety. And so he buried himself in his work, looking *out* into the phenomenological world to keep the worsening weather of his boiling inner world contrite and contained.

These were big, aerodynamically curved kites he was flying, wide wings in need of galloping winds. For such winds, the University of Manchester had established the Upper Atmosphere Kite-Flying Station near Absdell, a cottage standing on a point where the headlands shear off into the Irish Sea.

For two days Wittgenstein had been there. For two days this feeling had been building. The kite, a ten-foot-tall red dihedral of laminated spruce and doped silk, had taken him four weeks to build, and in the twenty-knot wind it took right up, the stretched silk rattling like a jib sheet as it tore line from a winch wound with four thousand feet of 150-pound piano wire.

The sky was wreathed with cirrus. The wind was blowing out to sea. Behind him the brass cups of an anemometer whirled. He had a barometer and stopwatch, inclinometer and notebook, science and its methods—all forgotten now as he watched the kite sweep away.

Air desires. Water encircles and engulfs. The scourging waves recurred and pulled, seamlessly merging like stairs, without human meaning, without ever ending. As he looked down from that bluff, the waves seemed as meaningless and futile as the generations, no sooner surging than they were wiped clean of what they had just brought, falling back into an oceanic blackness, with a slow explosion of all that had passed before. Ocean or air—it was either the engulfment of will or the steady pull of desire that destroyed him. As a boy, and even now, he had suffered periodic bouts of agoraphobia, a fear not of height but of space. This fear came in different guises. At times he felt he would actually dissolve, perishing like an open flask of ether into the world's greater volume. Then at other times he saw it was not space he feared but the queasy feeling of *not knowing what he would do,* imagining that, like an unstable substance, he would somehow explode if ever fully exposed to the concupiscent air.

In the rising wind, spears of sharp sea grass were whirring like scissors. Clouds covered the sea and waves battered the rocks, spurting up in steamy plumes as the last birds beat back to shore. Across the sky, like a cornea filling with blood, came a fearful darkening. The piano wire was humming, and ever so faintly he was trembling, thinking what a thing it was to dread one's own self— to see the self as enemy or other, not as companion, guide, sanctuary.

Why is the will so powerless to stop the thing that life has set in motion? he wondered. Did he suppose that if he were to find value, some gloss of value might rub off on him? In all the sea there is a single pearl. In all the world there is a single, mirroring form that binds and reflects all other things. Desire was his crime, he saw. His father was right: surely, it was vain and sinful to want this thing. Surely, for this presumption punishment awaited. The ocean need not be deep for one to drown, nor need the grapes be high to be just past reach and hence all the sweeter. The dream is incomparably stronger than the dreamer.

His stomach sank with the barometer. Sore from thinking, sore from wanting—to him it seemed that even sex was easier. In his head a hum, a rhythm was hovering. On his lips, a question was forming . . .

Where in the world is value to be found?

It was the question of his life.

CARLIN ROMANO

[Bruce Duffy is not] the first to recognize that Ludwig Wittgenstein—*the* giant of 20th-century philosophy and the central figure in [Duffy's *The World as I Found It*] . . . pursued truth a little too colorfully to be left on the non-fiction shelves.

Iris Murdoch's first novel, *Under the Net* (1954), featured a barely disguised portrait of him in Dave Gellmann, anti-metaphysician. Austrian writer Thomas Bernhard retooled Wittgenstein as a suicidal mathematician in his novel, *Correction*. Randall Collins, in *The Case of the Philosopher's Ring* (1976), dispatched Sherlock Holmes to probe the theft of Wittgenstein's brain.

The man plainly attracts novelists like fleas. And the reason is simple—he was a walking soap opera.

Born in 1889 in Vienna, the son of steel magnate Karl Wittgenstein, Wittgenstein bounced on Brahms' knee as a child. As a young man, his brilliance in logic led him to study with Bertrand Russell in Cambridge, where Russell called him "the most perfect example I have ever known of genius as traditionally conceived."

Wittgenstein's ideas about language's link to the world seemed to jibe with Russell's, and Russell tried to make him a disciple. But Wittgenstein resisted. Haughty, eccentric and obsessive, he clashed with both Russell and G. E. Moore, both of whom believed that philosophical work should end at 5 p.m.

Indeed, Wittgenstein's personal life teemed with unconventionality. Three of his brothers committed suicide, and Wittgenstein often threatened the same. He renounced his fortune and lived in Spartan lodgings. He disparaged philosophy and urged admirers to leave it. According to one controversial biography, W. W. Bartley III's *Wittgenstein*, he was a self-loathing homosexual, given to bouts of promiscuous cruising that revolted him.

During World War I, he fought in the Austrian Army and wrote the only book published in his lifetime, the *Tractatus*. After the war, he decided to teach elementary school in Austrian villages. In 1929, however, he returned to Cambridge. The so-called "later Wittgenstein" rejected the "early" one's theories, writing that all philosophers could do was identify "bumps" that the understanding suffers by "running its head up against the limits of language." He died in 1951, hugely influential.

Duffy's ambitious approach fully exploits the known facts on Wittgenstein, Russell and Moore, imagining anything necessary to fill in the gaps. *The World as I Found It* should be welcomed as manna by many readers starved for intellectual content in their fiction. But a book that strives as hard as Duffy's to be literature also asks to be judged by high standards. Here, alas, it fails.

Because Duffy regularly bloats his story with the beliefs and histories of minor characters, the book lacks "the severe criteria of harmonious balance" that Duffy recognizes in Wittgenstein's own work. *The World as I Found It* pans from Wittgenstein to Russell to Ottoline Morrell (Russell's mistress) to David Pinsent (Wittgenstein's friend) to Pinsent's mother to D. H. Lawrence to Dora Russell to Russell's mistresses and even, most ludicrously, to the dog at Russell's school, Beacon Hill.

Duffy, in short, can't seem to decide where he wants to go with his material. The novelist who chooses a great thinker as his protagonist usually has a tool for a client—we expect an ulterior message. Duffy's is unclear.

An even more damaging misstep is Duffy's wordiness, deeply antithetical to the elegant styles of his three philosophical stars. At one point, Duffy's Moore tells Wittgenstein, apropos of the *Tractatus,* that "it seems as if it was painful for you to say even one word more than was necessary to express your meaning." Duffy, instead, regularly wallows in poetic overkill while straining after epiphanies: "Now the picture of his life cast its shadow across the world. Bitterly, he thought of how fiercely he had fought to save himself. And for what? Flatulent heart. Fraudulent life. The shadow ran through a sieve, spilling lies in the vain hope of distilling even a few grains of truth."

Elsewhere, when not denying his thinkers purple, Duffy encases them in prosaic packages. Typical is this size-up of Wittgenstein: "The irony was that he was at the height of his intellectual powers and he knew it, which should have been liberating but was instead a sorrow, when he saw how little had been achieved for all his efforts." The man who asked what is left when we "subtract the fact that my arm goes up from the fact that I raise my arm," did not think in such clichés. . . .

Duffy tends to Americanize his leading men, presenting each as if he had a 30-second attention span for philosophy and was wholly the product of his libido. Wittgenstein is Bartley's tormented homosexual. Russell is a rake so incorrigible he can't concentrate on logic even during Wittgenstein's doctoral exam. Moore hardly has a thought beyond food and marriage.

As a result, they neither ring true nor entertainingly false. Explaining an intellectual's vision by his personality or childhood is, admittedly, the safe approach after Freud. Yet much evidence about Russell, Wittgenstein and Moore suggests that they constructed their mature personalities *to conform with* their philosophies.

Now there's a challenging novel. Duffy hasn't written it.

> Carlin Romano, "Philosopher's Frolics and Other Follies," in Book World—The Washington Post, September 27, 1987, p. 8.

PERRY MEISEL

When the wealthy and cultivated young Ludwig Wittgenstein burst upon the hermetic world of Bertrand Russell and G. E. Moore at Cambridge in 1912, three lives were changed forever. The Viennese Wittgenstein struck even Russell as perhaps more than his match. The unflappable Moore shared in a fierce but collegial relation that survived two world wars. As a combatant in the Austrian Army late in World War I, Wittgenstein completed the only book he saw fit to publish during his lifetime, *Tractatus Logico-Philosophicus* (1921). Returning to Cambridge in 1929, he began to question his own assumption in the *Tractatus* that the study of language could yield systematic rules, preferring instead to delight in the indeterminacies of linguistic reference, and composing, among other works, *Philosophical Investigations,* published in 1953, two years after his death.

So alluring is Wittgenstein's appeal that it has stirred Bruce Duffy . . . to produce a historical novel [*The World As I Found It*] centered on Wittgenstein and his English friends. Its sweeping arrangement of fact and fancy is vivid, passionate and funny. Mr. Duffy adheres faithfully enough to the outlines of

Wittgenstein's life as we know them (a full-scale biography has yet to be completed), although his book is really an accomplished orchestration of the spheres of Russell's urbanity, Moore's domesticity and Wittgenstein's wanderlust that is organized around three key points in Wittgenstein's experience—his first years at Cambridge, his service in World War I and his return to England.

Mr. Duffy intersperses his absorbing narrative with deft flashbacks that fill in the pasts of all three men (the death of Wittgenstein's father in Vienna is probably the novel's most extraordinary sequence). He writes with great wisdom about love, work and fame, painting raucously humorous and uncommonly moving portraits of his three principals. Russell stews deliciously in his inwardness; Moore gobbles his meal at high table at Trinity with such methodical relish that his philosophical hedonism is explained more convincingly than it is in most academic accounts.

The rendering of Wittgenstein is more dramatic and less naturally inward, testimony to his daunting intractability as both a man and a thinker. Wittgenstein's melancholy narcissism was so profound that it frequently turned into its opposite—the feeling that he hardly existed at all. In reply to a friend's request to take his photograph, Wittgenstein remarks: "You may develop your film & find no image whatsoever."

The novel's title comes from a passage in the *Tractatus* ("If I wrote a book called *The World as I Found It,* I should have to include a report on my body") that concludes with the difficult statement that such a book would be "a method of isolating the subject, or rather of showing that in an important sense there is no subject." Mr. Duffy exemplifies Wittgenstein's point both by apprehending him within a matrix of social contexts, and by dramatizing the elusiveness of subjectivity in the dream of a world he fashions with a prose that aspires to a combination of visionary expansiveness and postmodern terseness.

There are, to be sure, a few hitches. Bertrand Russell did not, *pace* Mr. Duffy, split infinitives. Nor did Lytton Strachey have a booming voice—it squeaked. There are also some lapses into melodrama—a visit to a Yiddish theater in Vienna, a family friend-turned-Nazi and Wittgenstein's painful acknowledgement of his Jewish roots at the onset of World War II. Such moments aside, Mr. Duffy's is an achievement in both fiction and historiography which deepens Wittgenstein's mythology and should attract a wider audience to it.

Perry Meisel, "Young Wittgenstein," in The New York Times Book Review, *October 11, 1987, p. 18.*

Jill Eisenstadt
1963-

American novelist.

Eisenstadt grew up in Rockaway, New York, the working-class beachfront section of Queens that serves as the setting for her first novel. *From Rockaway* (1987) traces the lives of four Rockaway teenagers—Timmy, Alex, Chowderhead, and Peg—for just over a year, beginning with the night of their high school prom. Eisenstadt's narrative then splits to follow Alex's difficult adjustment to her life at the elite Camden College and the aimlessness of her friends back home. Summer brings the group together again on the beach for the final tense scenes of what reviewers describe as a coming-of-age novel.

Dismissed by some as a literary "brat-packer"—one of a group of very young novelists who write minimalist prose filled with references to drugs and sex—Eisenstadt has been commended by others for rising above her peers. Praise has been devoted to her witty and insightful details, her vivid use of the vernacular, and her unpretentious subjects. Detractors call attention to the novel's lack of continuity, undeveloped characters, and numbingly sordid events.

Photograph by Michael Drinkard. Courtesy of Jill Eisenstadt.

PUBLISHERS WEEKLY

If Rockaway, at the Atlantic edge of New York City, were a state of mind, it would be energized despair. Or so it seems for the teenagers in this finely tuned first novel [*From Rockaway*] who have spent their lives in "Rotaway" and are unlikely to get out. They drink a lot, do a little dope, talk about sex more than have it and feel no more in charge of their lives at 18 than they did in Catholic grammar school. After high school, only Alex will go away to college. The rest of her group will stay: Timmy, a dropout and a lifeguard, Alex's ex-boy friend and still in love with her; "Chowderhead," Peg and the cruel Sloane, lifeguards too, the horizons of their lives as narrow as the beaches of their summers are wide. When Alex leaves for school, Timmy misses her with an utter and believeable acuity; meanwhile, he and Chowderhead work at a deli, the movie theater burns down, and Peg takes a "hat walk"—a drink in every bar on the mile-long boardwalk. In Maine, Alex stumbles through her first semester, going to Dress-to-Get-Laid parties, reading anthropology texts and falling in love with Joe—not a Rockaway type. . . . Combining innocence and experience, hope and hopelessness, Eisenstadt's characters seem particularly modern; if her book were a movie, it would suggest both *Saturday Night Fever* and *St. Elmo's Fire*.

A review of "From Rockaway," in Publishers Weekly, *Vol. 232, No. 6, August 7, 1987, p. 434.*

CYNTHIA COTTS

The commercial success of *Bright Lights, Big City* and *Slaves of New York* has inspired a generation of scribblers—the kind who would take the celebrity life and skip writing the book, if they could. Given the prototypes, I didn't expect the derivatives to be flawless. But it's shocking just how bad they are. . . .

From Rockaway follows a gang of teenagers through one year's rite of no passage. Lucky Alex gets a scholarship to a hip college in New Hampshire while her old boyfriend, Timmy, languishes in menial jobs, waiting for her return. . . .

A nice boy, Timmy isn't as reckless or cruel as his lowlife friends. But I wish he'd at least had an obsession, like Alex's father, who keeps 95 clocks running in sync. Mostly, Timmy just runs in place.

Alex doesn't unfold much, either. She is so full of quiet pride at having escaped to college that she stops answering Timmy's letters. In school she enjoys anthropology, repeating tribal anecdotes to her friends, but despairs of turning in a paper on time. Instead, she obsesses about Joe, a skinny, bespectacled kid whose atheist parents delivered him in a room full of tripping people and recorded it on film. Joe works hard at inscrutability, flirting heavily with five girls and running away when they're half undressed. Whether he's a virgin or gay (or just a cokehead) is never resolved. . . .

From Rockaway reads like a catalogue of adolescent behavior. Back home, that means barhopping and getting in fights, fucking outdoors, killing seagulls, and ripping off the place where you work. At college it means comparing lists of everyone you've laid, listening to your roommate get laid, eating breakfast at the cafeteria to figure out who got laid last night, and wishing you had a trust fund.

I'm not sure that even clever writing could save these characters from the awful clichés of their lives. But the opportunity never arises. At the eleventh hour, . . . Timmy is discovering that "God is chickenshit next to the ocean." . . .

[Eisenstadt uses] a third-person limited narration, peering through different characters' eyes without developing any one viewpoint sure to inspire our sympathy and trust. . . . [She tends] to change point-of-view mid-scene—a good strategy when it's intentional, but here no more than a tic.

I'd drop my allegations if the language in [this book] . . . was precise, musical, anywhere near hallucinatory. Metaphors are so sparse that when they appear, I'm tempted to write "nice!" in the margin. . . .

Eisenstadt's narration roves like a camera's eye, registering little emotional response in her subjects. She relies heavily on a stream-of-consciousness technique, which she or her editor seems to consider justification for sentence fragments trailing like beach tar throughout. Especially frustrating is her failure to reprise cameos and elaborate themes. What happened to that blue-haired slut June Blackmore for instance? And what's Alex's take on self-destruction? Any kind of scheme or symmetry would have done for Rockaway what Greek mythology did for Dublin. . . .

Eisenstadt's [chapters] run long and routinely fail to find a bull's-eye, let alone ream it. *From Rockaway* has enough potentially dramatic scenes (theater burning, kids drowning, violent rituals of male bonding) that she could have at least rendered one as a set piece. . . .

Eisenstadt gives too many mundane details and no particular resolution. . . .

> Cynthia Cotts, "Children of the Darned," in VLS, No. 58, September, 1987, p. 31.

SVEN BIRKERTS

[In *From Rockaway,* Eisenstadt] can at least create characters who are differentiated by more than just their names.

Alex, Timothy, Chowder and Peg are first introduced to us on the night of the senior prom. They are riding around in a chauffeured stretch-limo; they are as drunk as can be. But they stand out.

The four meet up with the rest of their gang on the beach at Rockaway. There they greet the sunrise and chaff one another about the future.

Alex will be the only one to get away. The others will move on to wage jobs or the local junior college.

Breaking away and hanging on are what *From Rockaway* is finally all about. Plot complications are minimal. At the core of the novel is the reft relationship between Alex and Timothy. She leaves for college and breaks his heart. He has just enough intelligence and sensitivity to understand that the split is final and enough true passion to refuse the truth. He knows, too, with a bitterness that can erupt into fury, what the rest of his life will be.

From Rockaway is a slight, if engaging novel. Perhaps its true fate is to end up on celluloid. (The book already has been optioned.) I can see it working. Like *Saturday Night Fever*, it pushes the energy of desire against the low ceiling of possibility. Subtle acting might round out some of the flatness in Eisenstadt's fashionably minimal prose. The basic human conflicts are all there.

> Sven Birkerts, " 'Rules,' 'Rockaway' Make a Point of Aimlessness," in Chicago Tribune—Books, September 13, 1987, p. 10.

PAUL RUDNICK

From Rockaway, a first novel by Jill Eisenstadt, is touted, via its press release, as "A stunning group portrait of unshockable youth," as an East Coast *Less than Zero.* The book is nothing of the sort; *From Rockaway* is a sweet, wistful coming-of-age saga, a fragmentary view of teen-agers vibrating between high school flings and adult responsibilities.

Rockaway, also dubbed "Rot-away" and "Rockapulco," is a New York suburb, "just a tiny strip that hangs off Queens as if it isn't sure whether it wants to break away and become an island or hang on tighter, desperate not to be abandoned." *From Rockaway* concerns itself with a gaggle of lifeguards, male and female, who live for the beach. These kids are not a wildly political set; one guy, nicknamed Chowder, "hates Reagan for being in Santa Barbara where it's warm. The guy doesn't even surf, what a waste." The lifeguards lead casual, beer-drenched lives, rife with Prom Night antics and make-out sessions, until fate muscles in, in the form of high school graduation; "It's strange," says one, "to all of a sudden have to be something."

The novel covers the year after graduation, in which Timmy and Chowder, the dudes, continue their lifeguarding and daydream of careers as firemen; they wind up enrolling in the Famous Bartenders School. Timmy and Chowder are homeboys, idlers, big-shouldered louts doomed to be outpaced by their live-wire girlfriends, Peg and Alex. "Good old Timmy," Alex sighs, "exhaustingly loyal to everything." Peg, "beautiful, aggressive, carefree" strides through the book, drinking the guys under the table; Alex packs off for a New England college, the lone escapee from Rockaway's lower-middle-class aimlessness and endless gray winters.

Alex is astounded by New Hampshire, where "trees are not puny, diseased things, they're climbable. Leaves hardly resemble the tannish sawdust balls at home." Alex makes new chums among the undergraduate trust-fund strata; she attends "Dress to Get Laid" parties and plunges into masochistic trysts, all the while receiving passionate post cards from Timmy. Peg crashes the campus; Alex is grateful for Peg's rowdy habits, for reminding her that "Rockaway girls don't need toilet paper."

Alex returns to Queens for her summer break; the novel climaxes when Timmy is unable to save a child from drowning.

Timmy undergoes the Death Keg ceremony, a ritual in which his fellow lifeguards bury Timmy up to his neck in the sand, "a vertical make-believe grave"; a bonfire is lit and a drunken chant welcomes Timmy to "The Murderers Club." The Death Keg is a nightmarish event, intended to purge Timmy and his co-workers of guilt over the dead child. Afterwards, the lifeguards assemble at 2 a.m. on the Gil Hodges Memorial Marine Park Bridge; they taunt each other to dive into the ocean below, to join "The Brass Balls Bridge Jumpers Association."

These final scenes are over-heated rite-of-passage stuff, a tad too symbolic; teen-age dares become true tests of courage and an unknown future is represented by the lethal tides of the Atlantic. The earlier sections of *From Rockaway* are unpretentious, honest and affectionate, as Eisenstadt depicts tiny shifts in post-adolescent friendships and love affairs. None of the characters are particularly vivid, and this feels intentional; the characters become underdefined, mere sketches, rather than full-blooded folk worth reading about.

Eisenstadt shines in the details, in snapshots, in describing a Catholic mother who permits her son to munch Lucky Charms, a breakfast cereal, "because the leprechaun on the label made it vaguely Irish." . . . Eisenstadt is sharp on parental quirks; Alex knows that "It doesn't take all that much to please her mother: neatness and beige."

The minutiae of a lifeguard's amiable days are also well-documented, anchoring the book in fresh experience. The lifeguards inhale pure oxygen from their lifesaving tanks to deflect hangovers; they wrap Alka-Seltzer tablets in bread and feed these nuggets to unwary gulls; "The birds' insides explode." The volcanic ceremonies that close the book remind us that lifeguarding entails an ever-present specter of death; these teenagers, their noses slathered with zinc oxide, are nearly destroyed when a rescue aborts in tragedy.

From Rockaway is less a novel than an album, a series of feisty, compassionate literary Polaroids. The book's range is kept deliberately narrow, limited to a single year in the lives of people who don't do much. Eisenstadt is a thoughtful writer; she never satirizes or patronizes her small-town crowd. While this is commendable, Eisenstadt is clearly capable of larger work, of a more rigorous assignment. *From Rockaway* is small but endearing, flecked with the moments in life when, as the author observes, "there's nothing left to feel except young and a little sad." (pp. 3, 16)

> Paul Rudnick, *"Beach Dorks and Wistful Chicks,"*
> in Los Angeles Times Book Review, *September 13, 1987, pp. 3, 16.*

An Excerpt from *From Rockaway*

Cicadas are drawn to the green stripes on orange lifeguard bathing suits. Fly directly at you in their fat, blind cicada way, while mosquitoes, they circle with a purpose. Hover, then strike. And biting flies are silver black with green eyes. Once moths become moths they have no stomachs or mouths and they die.

Timmy lists insects to stay awake on the tower. To stop thinking of Alex. To test the brain cells his mother is convinced he's destroying. Hundreds of them at a time.

He read that, about the moths, almost a month ago. That proves his moth brain cell's still intact.

He examines the upside-down cicada on his hip. It must not care about being upside down since its legs aren't moving. It's the eighth one on his hip so far today.

"Number eight," he tells his partner, Sloane, and flicks it off.

"I just leave 'em," Sloane says. "I'm sick of flicking. I just leave 'em."

Timmy checks Sloane's suit for cicadas, expecting a whole row. Four or five maybe. None. One measly fly on the chair arm. He wonders if it's true what Alex once said: "Flies throw up every time they land." But there is no visible vomit. In places where Sloane's hairy arm makes shadows, the wood of the chair looks darker.

"You're it!"

"You're it!"

At first they sound like girl voices, so high and hysterical-like, but, turning to look, Timmy sees about five boys scattering on the dry sand.

"How long have my eyes been closed?"

"Coupla hours," says Sloane, laughing. They watch the game. "What's that called again?" Sloane wants to know, "That game, what's that called?"

"Peas and butter." The peas-and-butter brain cell is fine.

"Yeah, that's it."

"You're it."

"You're it."

A new round. The towel is buried. Home base is a wire trash can.

"Hot peas and butter! Come get your supper!" wails "it," in this case a fairly big kid, pinkish limbs and a thumb up his nose. Then the fun begins: who can find the rat-tail weapon.

Yes, it's the same game Timmy and Sloane once played, except they used belts.

"Warmer, you're getting warmer," and, "Coolish . . . freezing." As soon as the wet towel's found, twisted up, clutched in the fist, it's—POWER. No limit to the whippings.

"Those were the days, huh?" Sloane says. "Now ya gotta take it out on your girlfriend."

Timmy doesn't answer. He thinks of the time he came home with a bruised face from some kid's, possibly Sloane's, unfair belt buckle, and how his mother made him pray. She made sure.

Yeah, those were the days. He leaves Sloane to watch the game, turns back around. Checks the water and resumes his list. Tells himself he's safe on his chair, the high chair. Old and safe. But the sounds keep coming at him and he is not that old.

Spiders and walking-sticks and those little white bugs that invade plants and boxes of cereal. There are more species of bugs than of all the other animals put together. There are more bugs in one acre of a field than there are people in the entire world. The tide is getting high.

"Know anything about bugs?" he asks.

"Yeah," Sloane says. "They're real easy to kill."

Timmy licks the sweat off his upper lip and rubs his eyes. Alex said she once fell asleep driving. Woke up five miles later, not swerving or anything.

He tries to picture this and then Alex at college. Her thick, funny hair when she sleeps on it wet. Wood-color hair to match the summer skin, and eyes bluer and lighter than smoke. She's casually rushing, she does that. Only now it's with books toward cafeterias. Or with strangers into libraries. It bothers him that his brain cells cannot do any better. Termites and praying mantises.

ROCHELLE RATNER

Eisenstadt's fast-paced first novel [*From Rockaway*] chronicles the coming-of-age of four working-class Irish youths growing up in Far Rockaway during the early 1980s. The spirit of the time and place is well captured, and the numerous beach scenes (three of the main characters work as summer lifeguards) are extremely evocative. The characters lead emotionally eventful lives: Alex struggles to escape "Rotaway" on a college scholarship; Timmy searches for the father who abandoned him when he was an infant; Chowderhead temporarily adopts a precocious nine-year-old boy. Still, the reader waits for some major, unifying development. Suddenly emerging as accomplished in her craft, Eisenstadt closes with three excellent chapters, tying in the random elements and providing an unexpected yet satisfying finish.

> *Rochelle Ratner, in a review of "From Rockaway,"*
> *in* Library Journal, *Vol. 112, No. 15, September 15,*
> *1987, p. 93.*

MICHIKO KAKUTANI

[*From Rockaway*] is a well-crafted if not terribly profound first novel that . . . uses Camden College as one of its backdrops. . . . Alex, the heroine of the book, who's known as "the most normal person at Camden," has arrived there on scholarship from Rockaway, L. I., and by contrasting these two worlds, Ms. Eisenstadt is able to develop and sustain the book's narrative tension.

We see Alex at home with her lifeguard pals Timmy, Chowderhead and Peg, and will go on to menial jobs after high school—skinny-dipping at the beach, hanging out at the diner, reminiscing about Catholic school. And we see Alex at school coping with a roommate who wears makeup to bed (just in case her boyfriend drops by), and boys who tell her she's too nice.

Oddly enough, Alex herself remains something of a cipher throughout the book: though we're told she's pretty and somewhat insecure, though we see her struggling to reconcile the easy sophistication of her college friends with the more earnest good will of her childhood pals, we're never quite sure who she is or what she feels. It is in her portraits of Alex's friends from Rockaway—her ex-boyfriend Timmy as well as Chowderhead and Peg—that Ms. Eisenstadt shows promise of being able to create genuine people and define a distinctive world.

> *Michiko Kakutani, "Today's Students," in* The New
> York Times, *September 19, 1987, p. 17.*

DEBORAH KIRK

The misadventures of a group of going-nowhere teenagers in Jill Eisenstadt's first novel, *From Rockaway,* would seem to confirm every parent's worst nightmares about what his or her children do when left to their own devices. The book's central characters are a handful of college-age (though not necessarily college-bound) kids, for whom the tedium of their small, dreary world is relieved only by self-destructive rebellion and atavistic ritual. Their realm is the beach in Rockaway . . . , where many of them work as lifeguards, blowing up seagulls and faking drownings on slow days. What binds Timmy, Peg, and Chowderhead is the suffocating banality of their days on the beach and nights in bars, their friendships cemented by their shared boredom in fast-food emporiums and pizzerias (one of them aptly titled "The Slice of Life"). They talk about getting out in the way that inmates talk about escaping. Their summer at Rockaway is marked by several hauntingly cruel adolescent rites (not quite rites of passage because nothing is learned or gained). Using shock effects with some skill, *From Rockaway* introduces the reader into a little-known subculture on the fringe of New York City. While Ms. Eisenstadt writes fluently and has a sure grasp of her subjects' streetwise vernacular, the novel's relentless focus on this tiresome brat pack fails to generate psychologically valid insights. Possibly, however, this gang is not worth getting to know.

> *Deborah Kirk, in a review of "From Rockaway,"*
> *in* The New York Times Book Review, *October 4,*
> *1987, p. 29.*

THE NEW YORKER

There are no expensive drugs in this slangy, episodic novel [*From Rockaway*] about a group of teenagers from Rockaway, New York—just a lot of beer and marijuana, and a feeling that the future doesn't hold much promise. Of the four main characters—who are, for a change, not preppy or artsy or punk but regular confused nineteen-year-olds—only Alex has made it to college. Her ex-boyfriend Timmy, who didn't finish high school and wants to be a fireman, spends much of the year back home as a lifeguard, along with Chowderhead and Peg. When a swimmer is "lost," we witness a bizarre tradition of the life guards' occupation: the lifeguard responsible is buried up to his neck in sand while his peers drink his "Death Keg" and dance naked in crude reverse celebration. The narrative's tough, fragmented language can be tiresome, but at times there's a pathos to it, and the sensitivity of the characters persists in the face of their aimlessness. Without meaning to, they come up with apt metaphors for the way they see themselves: Chowderhead describes Rockaway as "just a tiny strip that hangs off Queens as if it isn't sure whether it wants to break away and become an island or hang on tighter, desperate not to be abandoned."

> *A review of "From Rockaway," in* The New Yorker,
> *Vol. LXIII, No. 33, October 5, 1987, p. 126.*

JON SAARI

[In *From Rockaway,* Eisenstadt] cares most about striking the right cynical pose and mood. The story, such as it is, is incidental to the author's cool narrative voice and creation of characters who are bored by the world and contemptuous of anything greater than their egos. First sentences in novels often tell readers much about what to expect, and this one is no exception as it captures the chauffeur hired to cart Timmy, Alex, Peg, and Chowderhead around on prom night: "The limo driver, Russ or Gus, has a bald, tan head and a line of whitish crust on his lip edges." Just so the point is not missed, Eisenstadt adds: "He does not try to hide his disgust—'Kids today.'" (p. 116)

Eisenstadt's characters are from lower-middle-class families and do not indulge themselves with credit cards, cocaine, and cars. They face a future of meaningless, nowhere jobs. Eisenstadt's adults . . . are ineffectual and unable to make any connections with their children. Alex, the only one in her group to go away to college, where students go to Dress to Get Laid parties, returns home only to find that her bedroom has been rented by her parents.

From Rockaway . . . has much in common with the film *River's Edge,* in portraying a group of teenagers who are ill equipped to cope and function as social beings. When Timmy, probably the most sensitive of the group, accidentally lets a child drown, the others, much to the dismay of Alex, plan the ritual of the Death Keg, with Timmy and his friends jumping in the dark from a suspension bridge 60 feet above the water. The act seems empty and senseless, at best perversely narcissistic; it stands as a confused climactic symbol of the novel. The most telling fact about *From Rockaway* is that the author's photograph is in color. I've never seen that before. (pp. 116-17)

Jon Saari, in a review of "From Rockaway," in The Antioch Review, *Vol. 46, No. 1, Winter, 1988, pp. 116-17.*

COMMENTS FROM EISENSTADT TO *CLC YEARBOOK*

Asked about the genesis of her first novel, Eisenstadt explained, "I began writing stories about Rockaway in college and became slightly addicted to it. The same characters kept popping up and growing till I had about fifteen stories and realized the novel potential. But that meant I needed a novelistic structure and had to work backwards, or from the outside in. I took about two more years to complete it."

When asked what motivates her to write, Eisenstadt replied: "I fear forgetting things. Little things that delight, interest, sadden, amaze, or amuse me. I would like to make people look at themselves and laugh and forgive. For me, writing simplifies and organizes (artificially) a very incoherent, dense world."

Commenting on her media image, Eisenstadt complains, "Media is scary. They decide what they want you to be (in my case, hip, young, decadent, trendy) and try to make you it. They don't really care who you are."

Candida Fraze
19??-

American novelist and poet.

Mona Emory, the narrator of *Renifleur's Daughter* (1987), is the daughter of an eccentric research chemist with a proclivity for scents and unusual sexual behavior. In a series of vignettes, Mona recounts the sensual and sexual perversions of her parents, who were killed when she was fourteen, and her search to understand their world and her own. Obsessed with her parents' relationship, Mona grows to adulthood emotionally paralyzed by her ambivalent search for, and rejection of, love and sexuality.

Critics characterize *Renifleur's Daughter* as a strange and sensuous work, commenting on the novel's lyrical prose and arresting subject. Fraze, with a poet's attention to pictorial imagery and symbolism, skillfully evokes the many layers of sensation in her protagonist's acutely aesthetic world. Reviewers praise Fraze's creation of a realistic narrative voice and her accurate depiction of the artistic and emotional maturation of her protagonist.

KIRKUS REVIEWS

[*Renifleur's Daughter* is a] first novel—about a young woman's delayed rebellion against the emotionally oppressive world created by her parents—that starts off with a penetrating brilliance but then loses its way and half-dawdles to an end.

"Renifleur" is a psychiatric term for one who is sexually aroused by scents—as was the case with Mona Emory's father: highly opinionated paterfamilias of the Victorian-disciplinarian stamp, professor of chemistry at Georgetown University, worldwide consultant to international perfume manufacturers—and a man in the strict habit, each day after lunch, of taking his docile wife to an upstairs bedroom for sex. While these erotic interludes took place, the children of the family would bide their time by playing obediently in the flower-filled backyard garden—not entirely certain what was happening upstairs, but painfully conscious that *some*thing was. So strong was the sense of her parents' embarrassing eccentricities that when they died in a plane accident in Europe, Mona, the middle child, "felt relieved"—and yet would spend the rest of her early years struggling to free herself from the constricting emotional knots that were the legacy of their decadence-within-the-hidebound. A failed love affair ensues, a brief descent into a pornography ring, a degree as medical illustrator (Mona is a gifted graphic artist), and finally a return home to work with her grandfather (Chairman of the Anatomy Department, also at Georgetown) on his *magnum opus,* a medical textbook. And

then? The novel winds down in a more genre-touched way, with Mona reexamining her childhood—more redundantly than dramatically—until she is impelled at last to take clippers and spade to the old backyard flower garden, declaring her freedom from the perverse hand of the past. Successful art (her own) and promise of romance follow.

An initially rich but narrow premise here injects breath into the novel more in fits than in the whole, though elements throughout can be alluringly masterful, indeed—the medical lore and Mona's work as an artist of anatomy among them. Less commanding is the novel's more uncertain second half, with the author working hard to fill the pages, and the words.

A review of "Renifleur's Daughter," in Kirkus Reviews, *Vol. LV, No. 7, April 1, 1987, p. 493.*

PUBLISHERS WEEKLY

[In *Renifleur's Daughter*, the] narrator of this unusual first novel, 14-year-old Mona Emory, and her two siblings have grown up as "silent observers" in a sensual Eden carefully contrived by their mysterious and aloof parents. Papa, a research chemist for perfume companies, can sniff out any malodorous reality. Mama is beautiful, vague and in his thrall. When they are killed in a plane crash, Mona begins a search for the truths that underlie the enigmatic surface of her childhood. The next 14 years are compressed into a series of telling vignettes that deal not only with the formation of a particular life but with the creative process itself. The rigors of romantic and sexual love, youth and old age, science and art are subtly woven into a lyrical whole. Told in a voice both true and original, the book will make its strongest appeal to young, sensitive readers.

A review of "Renifleur's Daughter," in Publishers Weekly, *Vol. 231, No. 18, May 1, 1987, p. 53.*

ELIZABETH GUINEY SANDVICK

A *renifleur* is one who is sexually aroused by odors, and sexuality figures largely in this disturbing first-person account [*Renifleur's Daughter*] of a young woman traumatized by family life. As Mona Emory moves from childhood to adulthood, she finds only self-destructive ways to deal with the early loss of her parents and her family's emotionless existence and perverse sexuality. Eventually Mona becomes an anatomical and then a pornographic illustrator, a seemingly satisfactory resolution to her degrading search that, while a relief to the reader, still happens too easily. Throughout, the emphasis on symbolism interferes with the flow of the plot.

Elizabeth Guiney Sandvick, in a review of "Renifleur's Daughter," in Library Journal, *Vol. 112, No. 9, May 15, 1987, p. 96.*

An Excerpt from *Renifleur's Daughter*

It was their attachment I wanted, their strong feelings, their grand romance, all of which felt foreign to me. Bodies by themselves didn't have much meaning for me. From my work in the lab, I knew how bodies looked and were put together. I knew what was supposed to happen—which was why I liked Freud and Margaret Mead; they gave the body emotional weight, gave meaning and feeling to physical acts.

"Who wouldn't be jealous?" said Julie. I had told her about the lace and linen, the silk curtains, the urn of flowers; about Mama's perfumes, the starch in the laundry room, the avenues of clean sheets being hung to dry in the laundry yard—white, unblemished, pristine sheets. Their bed was changed every day.

I had felt excluded, I told Julie. I still did. My family had not been like other families. In other families the children came first, not because they were loved more, but simply because they were dependent creatures, because they were *children*. In our family, my parents' love for each other came first. I could never compete with their calculated hedonism, with the good taste of their voluptuousness, with the aesthetics of their love for one another. And as far as Papa was concerned, there was nothing more unfashionable than a baby. Piero was clearly unplanned. After he arrived, Papa sulked and moped. He said Piero didn't smell like our family. He wouldn't hold him or play with him or show him off proudly like a normal father. Being a father of girls was fine, or at least tolerable. But who had asked for another child, and then—what gall!—a boy-child? A rival. Strangely enough, Matt felt the same way. He was used to being the boy in our house—an adopted son and Grandpa's friend. He stayed away after Piero was born. When Grandpa came over for dinner, as he did at least twice a week, I complained about Matt's disappearance. I was six and Matt was my only friend. Charles wouldn't arrive until the following year. On his way back to his apartment that evening, Grandpa paid a call at Matt's house. The next morning, Matt appeared at the door as if nothing had happened. But he and Piero were never great friends.

Papa forced Mama and Piero to move into the guest room, and he took over the bedroom suite. He couldn't stand the smell of a lactating woman. Poor Mama. She was the one who needed to be resting in the silky quiet of the bedroom, the sun filtering through the white curtains, the cool shadowiness of it, the dreamlike quality. But no. He claimed it. He took it for himself, and demanded dinner on trays and pots of tea. He competed not so much with Piero as with Mama. He complained that he was ill, that something terrible would happen and he would never, ever, see Mama again.

Finally, Papa demanded that Mama stop nursing. Piero was eight weeks old. Soon after that, Charles came to stay with his father, and Mama and Papa left on the first of their many trips—to Greece, to North Africa, to the south of France—all for Papa's researches.

MARCELLE THIEBAUX

In modern psychiatry "renifleur" means a person erotically stirred or gratified by smells. Freud used the word, however, to indicate someone obsessed to the point of neurosis. Candida Fraze draws both definitions into her captivating first novel [*Renifleur's Daughter*]. The loosely gathered chapters explore the way sense impressions—chiefly smells—are transmuted into emotion and art in the experience of Mona Emory, the young narrator. Mona's handsome Papa, a finicky esthete, is a research chemist specializing in odors and pheromones. From him, Mona learns that "smells were the key to control, memories, feelings, old desires." Papa carefully orchestrates the olfactory ambiance of their Georgetown house and garden in Washington, where Mona and her friends stop to listen to the sighs drifting down from the parental bedroom. Before long Mona repeats Mama and Papa's sexual idyll with a playmate, Matt, now grown, as they travel through Europe, though eventually a more apt lover for Mona will be Charles, beneficiary of a fragrant chocolate factory. But Mona's life's work distances her from this riot of the senses. As an anatomical artist, she has been trained to render exquisite drawings of the body; later she applies her artistry to living models when she sketches for a pornographer. But, Mona worries, can the artist bask in pleasure and still remain aloof enough to describe it? To get at the "meaning" of the inert body, with its muscles and organs, "you had to unwrap it like a precious package." Yet the mystery of the self, as Mona determines, lies diffused in surfaces, in fleeting colors, textures, artifices and odors. Ms. Fraze, who is also a poet, likes to explore the craft of fiction in pictorial terms. A limpid stylist, she skillfully evokes the sensory awakenings of adolescence, while leaving unresolved her narrator's ambivalence about eros and art.

> Marcelle Thiebaux, in a review of "Renifleur's Daughter," in The New York Times Book Review, June 21, 1987, p. 22.

ROBERT WILSON

Renifleur's Daughter is a strange and intelligent first novel whose subjects are sensuousness and sensuality. The word *renifleur* combines these subjects; it comes from Freud, and its (unabridged) dictionary definition is "one who is sexually aroused or gratified by odors."

The daughter in the title is Mona Emory, the book's first-person narrator, a medical illustrator who lives in her family's big, comfortable brick house in Georgetown, only a few blocks from the university where her father and grandfather have worked in their science labs.

Her father, the renifleur, was a chemist specializing in smells. On a trip to France, where he consulted for perfume companies, his plane crashed, killing him and Mona's mother. Besides Mona, who feels curiously indifferent about their deaths, they leave behind Mona's brother, sister and grandfather, the household including servants, and a lush, climate-defying garden—"a textured, scented place of refreshment . . . and a laboratory of scented plants." Shades of the garden in Hawthorne's weird tale, "Rappaccini's Daughter"?

One of the reasons for Mona's indifference, which has now developed into a curiosity about them, was her parents' daily habit of lunching in the garden with the family and then retiring to their bedroom for what was euphemistically called a nap.

We knew when and how long; we heard noises; we saw the curtains billowing from their window like some kind of sexual ghost. They were raw silk and most of the year the windows were open and the breezes bellied the curtains like spinnakers, with their lower hems trapped inside. . . . After what seemed an endless time, both curtains would fly free of the window . . . wrapping and twisting around one another.

Her parents' obvious sensuality irritated her as a child just becoming aware of her own sexuality, and made her angry at them—at her father for the control he seemed to exert over her mother, at her mother for her passivity.

The story that follows, of Mona's maturation, her coming to terms with her parents' and her own passions, is rich in psychological complexity without seeming slavishly psychoanalytical. Candida Fraze's prose is simple and sensuous, her novel as refreshing as the renifleur's garden.

> *Robert Wilson, "'Renifleur's Daughter': Blossoming Sexuality," in* USA Today, *August 21, 1987, p. 6D.*

COMMENTS OF CANDIDA FRAZE TO *CLC YEARBOOK*

Asked about her literary influences, Fraze replied, "There is not one single author who has influenced my writing. Instead, there are all authors, living and dead, and concomitantly, the idea of conducting a life by the agency of fiction: the idea of living by reading and writing. This idea is, to me, at once alarming and thrilling; terrifying, challenging, and finally, an enormous relief: to announce, yes, this is how I will conduct my life, this is comfortable, this fits—this reading and writing—this is my stance to the world."

Describing the research she undertook to write *Renifleur's Daughter,* Fraze explained, "I spent some time in the National Library of medicine, researching medical illustration and olefactory processes. My family simulated the cocoa testing portrayed in 'Chapter 31-Chocolate'. In short, life is more interesting when it imitates art."

Kaye Gibbons

1960-

American novelist.

North Carolina native Kaye Gibbons's critically acclaimed first novel, *Ellen Foster* (1987), offers a child's-eye view of the rural Deep South. The title character, a spirited eleven-year-old, is passed from one cruel and uncaring guardian to another until her own wit and determination land her in a safe home. An important subplot in the novel concerns Ellen's friendship with Starletta, a black girl whom she learns to love despite initial feelings of racial prejudice.

The novel is narrated by Ellen in alternating episodes related in the present or the past tense, evoking a sense of both spontaneity and reflection. Critics unanimously praise the narration as being rendered in a wise but realistic child's voice, free of artificial coyness. Although the events of *Ellen Foster* border on the melodramatic, reviewers agree that by focusing on Ellen's resourcefulness rather than her trials, Gibbons avoids sentimentality in her humorous and compassionate portrait.

KIRKUS REVIEWS

[*Ellen Foster* is a] short first novel told in the laconic and telegraph-style voice of an 11-year-old girl down South.

Ellen Foster is a kind of Huck Finn, smarter than her years and with wit and resilience in plentiful measure, whose orphan adventures lead her, at last, to a happy home. The story opens with the death of her kind but dragged-into-poverty-and-despair mother, an event that leaves Ellen alone with her father, who, like Huck's Pap, is a piece of mean, worthless, lecherous, drunken white trash. Ellen hides from him as best she can, but finally has to run away from home to escape his half-crazed sexual advances. Ellen's fate then is to live for a time with her rich but snake-mean grandmother, who takes out on Ellen the hatred she feels for Ellen's ne'er-do-well father—who in turn does the decent thing by dying (and, like Huck's dad, does it offstage). Ellen's grandmother herself is the next to go (of flu), after which Ellen is handed on to a hypocritical and shallow aunt (and her ditto daughter), who so enrage Ellen (and give her so little love) that she once again flees, this time to the home for girls run by her "new mama," where she at last finds the stability and love (and cleanliness and order and honesty) she's never had before. At book's end, her old and best-loved friend Starletta—dirt poor and black—comes for a weekend; and though the occasion gives rise to a fleeting brush of platitudes about race relations, the depth of feeling Ellen has (not only for her friend, but for having a place to invite her to) is lovely, psychologically on target, and affecting. A reader may doubt that at her age, and in her poverty-driven circumstances, the unlettered Ellen could really be as worldly

as she's sometimes portrayed (she names an imaginary boyfriend Nick Adams), but by and large the innocence of her wit and the tough stoicism of her voice avoid an Eloise-like coyness and ring true—and touching: "I am not exactly a vision. But Lord I have good intentions that count."

A child's-eye tale of evil giving way to goodness—and happily far more spunky than sweet.

A review of "Ellen Foster," in Kirkus Reviews, *Vol. LV, No. 6, March 15, 1987, p. 404.*

PUBLISHERS WEEKLY

Its maudlin plot makes this slim first novel [*Ellen Foster*] resemble a Victorian tearjerker, transplanted to the South. The appealing, eponymous 11-year-old heroine is a survivor; despite the cruel vicissitudes life deals her, she is feisty, resourceful and courageous. . . . Through a series of dismal events, we watch Ellen endure suffering, mature and find safe harbor in a foster home with her "new mama." Devoid of self-pity, Ellen narrates her story in a wry, colloquial voice that is generally an accurate rendition of a child's perceptions of the world but sometimes becomes a little too knowing. Especially well developed is the girl's dawning realization, as her empathy blossoms under the weight of her own troubles, that conventional prejudice against black people is unfounded. Some readers will find the recital of Ellen's woes mawkishly sentimental, but for others it may be a perfect summer read.

A review of "Ellen Foster," in Publishers Weekly, *Vol. 231, No. 11, March 20, 1987, p. 70.*

KIMBERLY G. ALLEN

Ellen Foster is the often heart-wrenching tale of an 11-year-old girl who loses her dearly loved mother through suicide and is left to coexist with her alcoholic father. "Old Ellen," as the protagonist refers to herself, is a tough but tender young soul, determined and wise beyond her years. Initially, she is resourceful enough to ferret out money for necessities, but eventually she becomes fearful for her safety and runs away to live with her art teacher. When a court decides she can no longer remain there, Ellen is briefly shuttled between uncaring relatives but eventually triumphs in finding a "new mamma." Gibbons has produced a warm and caring first novel about a backwoods child persevering through hard times to establish a new and satisfying identity. It is written with the freshness of a child but the wisdom of an adult.

Kimberly G. Allen, in a review of "Ellen Foster," in Library Journal, *Vol. 112, No. 7, April 15, 1987, p. 98.*

ALICE HOFFMAN

If one should never trust the person who has had a happy childhood, then Ellen Foster, the 11-year-old heroine of Kaye Gibbons's accomplished first novel, may be the most trustworthy character in recent fiction. *Ellen Foster* is the story of an orphan's harrowing life, told in a direct, engaging first-person narration. Mrs. Gibbons . . . is so adept at drawing her characters that we know Ellen, and, yes, trust her from the start, even though she begins her tale: "When I was little I would think of ways to kill my daddy."

And for good reason. Ellen's daddy is a careless, heartless drinker who is responsible for the death of Ellen's mother in the early pages of the novel. Ellen lives in fear of him, particularly when the men to whom he sells liquor come to her house and drink themselves into a frenzy. Taken away from her father when bruises are noticed on her arm at school, rejected by her aunt, Ellen spends a brief joyful period in the home of a teacher before the courts decide she must live with her grandmother. But her "mama's mama" is a horribly vindictive old woman who mercilessly punishes Ellen, setting her to work in the fields as a warped revenge against Ellen's father. Ellen is subject to a series of misfortunes veging on the Gothic. Her mother and grandmother both die beside her, her father mistreats her before he dies of drink, and then Ellen is sent off, yet again, to live with another aunt and her awful cousin Dora (at Christmas Dora gets every toy on her list, Ellen a packet of white drawing paper).

Throughout her trials Ellen has a constant friend, a silent black girl named Starletta. At first Ellen finds comfort in her conviction that she is superior to Starletta—no matter how awful her fate, Starletta's is worse by virtue of her race—and one of the major elements in the novel is Ellen's recognition of her own racism. Ellen will not eat dinner at Starletta's house, even when she is close to starving ("No matter how good it looks to you it is still a colored biscuit"). Only when desperate will she spend the night: "When I got up in the morning I was surprised because it did not feel like I had slept in a colored house. I cannot say I officially slept in the bed because I stayed in my coat on top of the covers." At the close of the book Ellen has redefined her feelings about Starletta, and yet their friendship is no less important. "And when I thought about you," Ellen tells Starletta, "I always felt glad for myself. And now I don't know why. I really don't."

Throughout *Ellen Foster* there is a dual narrative. In one, Ellen's ordeals are followed consecutively; in the other, she looks back to tell her story. . . .

It is slowly revealed to the reader that Ellen has set out to get herself a new family, and get one she does, after spying a likely candidate—the mother of a foster family—in church.

In many ways this is an old-fashioned novel about traditional values and inherited prejudices, taking place in a South where too little has changed too slowly. Mrs. Gibbons's canvas is a harsh, rural landscape bordered by poverty, brutality and loss. When the modern world surfaces, it is something of a shock, though not an unpleasant one. Ellen herself is amazed, particularly during her stay with her teacher, by a contemporary life outside the confines of her limited experience:

> She said it was good I loosened up. We would run around and she would tell me to let it all hang out. Let your hair down good golly Miss Molly let it all hang out. Go with the flow, she would say. Make up a tune and throw in some words and go with the flow. I had no idea people could live like that.

What might have been grim, melodramatic material in the hands of a less talented author is instead filled with lively humor ("I was too smart to let somebody find me living with a dead lady the second time around," Ellen says after her grandmother dies), compassion and intimacy. This short novel focuses on Ellen's strengths rather than her victimization, presenting a memorable heroine who rescues herself.

Alice Hoffman, "Shopping for a New Family," in The New York Times Book Review, *May 31, 1987, p. 13.*

An Excerpt from *Ellen Foster*

I had to have something to do so mostly I played catalog. I picked out the little family first and then the house things and the clothes. Sleepwear, evening jackets for the man, pantsuits. I outfitted everybody. The mom, the dad, the cute children. Next they got some camping equipment, a waffle iron, bedroom suits, and some toys. When they were set for the winter I shopped ahead for the spring. I had to use an old catalog but they had no way of knowing they were not in style. I also found the best values. The man worked in the factory and she was a receptionist. They liked to dress up after work. I myself liked the toddlers with the fat faces. Some of the children looked too eager.

Do I look like I am a leader of girls? When I got tired of the catalogs I joined the Girl Scouts. They put up membership drive signs at school and it looked OK to me.

There was some extra money in the envelope so I had Starletta's daddy drive me to town to buy my uniform and accessories. She yelled and went limp on the floor when I did not buy something for her. She could not have a uniform because they do not have a colored troop in my county. They might in town.

I suited myself completely. Canteen, socks, bow tie, Rule Book, everything official.

In six months I had all the badges except swimming. I wanted the badges more than I needed to be honest so I signed my daddy's initials saying I had made a handicraft or wrapped a ankle or whatever the badge called for.

I stayed in the Girl Scouts until Christmas. I got tired of going to the meetings.

Christmas came to my house with the people drinking egg nog and decking the halls on the television set. I am glad I did not believe in Santa Claus. As my daddy liked to say—wish in one hand and spit in the other and see which one gets full first.

Although I did not believe in Santa Claus I figured I had a little something coming to me. So on Christmas Eve I went with Starletta to the colored store and bought myself some things I had been dying for and paper to wrap them with.

I knew my mama's mama was having her usual big turkey dinner that night but that was OK because I had turkey sliced up with dressing along with two vegetables and a dab of dessert.

As long as there is a parade on the television.

I got Starletta and her mama and daddy a nice spoon rest. When they were not looking I had the sales lady wrap up the one I saw with the green chicken on it. Then I had the rest of the money for my own self.

It made my heart beat fast to shop. The store was all lit up with Christmas cheer and shoppers with armloads of presents.

I got two variety packs of construction paper, a plastic microscope complete with slides, a diary with a lock and key, an alarm clock, and some shoes.

When I got home I wrapped the presents and wondered if I ought to wrap something laying around the house for my daddy. I did not have enough paper. He did not come home that night anyway.

I wrapped them at the kitchen table and hid them.

When I found them the next day I was very surprised in the spirit of Christmas.

BRAD HOOPER

[*Ellen Foster* is a] commendable first novel narrated by an adolescent girl, Ellen, who relates the day-to-day experiences she endured as a child in a troubled family. . . . Gibbons does not lapse for a single moment in keeping the entire narrative within this spunky character's personal frame of vision and distinctive pattern of expression. It's a humorous and unsentimental novel, never weepy or grim, despite the subject matter.

Gibbons elicits the reader's compassion and admiration for Ellen forcefully yet honestly.

Brad Hooper, in a review of "Ellen Foster," in Booklist, *Vol. 84, No. 1, September 1, 1987, p. 27.*

DEANNA D'ERRICO

By the time (well into the novel) that the origin of her last name is revealed, readers have already come to cherish [the heroine of] *Ellen Foster*. She is an uncommonly strong little girl who has survived insufferable circumstances and abuses: her mother's suicide, attempted sexual abuse by her father and his friends, mental and physical abuses by her grandmother, mental abuse by her aunt, her father's death, and the obtuse probing of a school psychologist.

Through all this, it is a miracle that old Ellen (as she appropriately refers to herself, for she is wise beyond her years) does not lose herself. She is the embodiment of tenacity, surviving with the tools of intelligence, sensitivity, a strong will, and a remarkable sense of humor. She fends off her father's advances by locking herself in her closet; when that no longer works, she runs away. She has the sense to hoard money and to limit her possessions to what will fit in a small box. When the court hands her over to her grandmother, who blames Ellen for her daughter's suicide, she takes up the gauntlet of penance that her grandmother throws down: She is forced to live and work like her grandmother's Black fieldhands. When she must stay with her aunt and cousin, who clearly resent her presence, she thoughtfully stays out of their sight and battles their ill will with a show of kindness. Ellen makes the best of any situation.

Her efforts to find a home fail, and when her aunt turns her out, Ellen takes charge of her destiny. She has observed a woman at church, a single woman who has taken in several unwanted children. (When she asks about them, she is told that they are "the Foster family"—thus Ellen chooses her last name.) She puts on her best dress and presents herself and her box on the woman's doorstep. Ellen endears herself to the kind woman by offering her the $160 she has saved: "But I want to pay you that money so we can keep this all on the up in up. . . . You get the money and I stay here until I graduate from high school. How does that sound?" A few more details and the deal is clinched:

> And then she got teary eyed and I told her there was just a couple of things I needed to know before I unloaded my box and settled in that room she mentioned. What's that? Well I need to know if you are pretty healthy or if you have a disease or bad habits like drinking. Also are you generally friendly or do you have days when you act crazy or extra mean? Why Ellen? I just need to know. OK. I'm healthy as a horse. Nobody here drinks or smokes. And to have a house full of children I think I'm pretty even tempered. How's that? Thanks I said. That's exactly what I needed to know. . . . And while she fixed supper I unpacked my box and laid down to look out the window. I was glad to rest. My arms were sore from toting the box and even when I laid out flat and still my legs felt like they were walking again. But I would not move ever from here.

This passage is indicative of the artful, simple, humorous style with which Ellen tells her tale. Using a technique that is not itself original but that is masterfully employed, Gibbons has Ellen relay her story by interweaving past and present in alternate chapters. The technique works because the reader simultaneously sees where Ellen has been and where she is going—the effect of which is that Ellen *herself* is made the essence of the novel.

Deanna D'Errico, in a review of "Ellen Foster," in Belles Lettres: A Review of Books by Women, *Vol. 3, No. 1, September-October, 1987, p. 9.*

PEARL K. BELL

If much Southern writing today lacks the identifying stamp of locality, there is no mistaking where Kaye Gibbons comes from, even if the word "South" is not to be found in her remarkable first novel, *Ellen Foster.* Gibbons wisely doesn't try to convey the accent of the 11-year-old orphan who tells her own grim story, but it's clear, even to a Northern reader, that we are listening to the voice of a backwoods Southern child. Ellen has a rare capacity for seeing through phonies and figuring things out, but Gibbons never allows us to feel the slightest doubt that she is only 11. Nor does she ever lapse into the condescending cuteness that afflicts so many stories about precocious children. This child does not swagger or perform; she does not invite congratulation. But she does want to tell us exactly what happened, and how she felt about it, and the humor of the telling—not always intentional, and never showy—is another reason that this child is utterly unlike such little monsters as Salinger's Teddy.

Ellen's story is horrifying, but it ends in quiet triumph because she is determined to outwit her predestined fate. . . . Even when she is flung beyond the reach of hope, she refuses to give in. Her mother, a gentle invalid from a well-to-do family, had in youthful folly married a redneck lout. She goes to an early grave, by her own hand, leaving her daughter at the mercy of the drunken brute.

Ellen seems to have known from birth that everything was terribly wrong, that "my family was shaking itself to death." When her father mercifully drinks himself into permanent oblivion, a judge decrees that Ellen must go and live with her crazy maternal grandmother ("mama's mama" to Ellen, never Grandma), who blames the little girl for her favorite daughter's marriage and death. When "mama's mama" dies, Ellen is shuttled between one stone-hearted relative and another, and tries to console herself by making a list "of all that a family should have," because "I thought I would soon bust open if I did not get one of them for my own self soon."

What can a helpless orphan do when, as she puts it, mimicking the judge's pomposity, he "talks about the family [as] society's cornerstone but you know yours was never a Roman pillar but is and always has been crumbly old brick"? But Ellen is one of nature's survivors. She knows what she needs, better than pesky psychiatrists asking dumb questions, and she finds her own way home. Hearing about a foster family in the town (whose name she takes to be Foster), she marches right over, pleads with the "new mama" to let her in, and becomes part of a family after all.

Safe at last, this white Southerner experiences an extraordinary change of mind and heart about her black school-friend Starletta (the name is a master stroke). Gibbons, unlike so many writers of the New South, doesn't evade the racism of Southern life, which she subtly reveals through the tenacious child's mind. Though Ellen is fond of Starletta, she won't drink from a "colored" glass or eat colored food or use the chamberpot that is all Starletta's family has in its tumbledown shack. Yet Ellen is able to figure out "by my own self" why such feelings aren't right, for she clearly sees it is her own white kin, not any blacks, who have made her life a misery. In a chilling passage toward the end of the book, Ellen explains that she's not the same girl who once wouldn't touch Starletta's biscuit even if she was starving:

> But I am old now I know it is not the germs you cannot see . . . that will hurt you or turn you colored. What you had better worry about though is the people you knew and trusted they would be like you because you were all made in the same batch. You need to look over your shoulder at the one who is in charge of holding you up and see if that is a knife he has in his hand. And it might not be a colored hand. But it is a knife.

Ellen is not preening, or exhibiting her wisdom in the way of know-it-all prodigies. She is telling us that she has learned something important from ugly experience, and we believe her.

The voice of this resourceful child is mesmerizing because we are right inside her head. The words are always flawlessly right, helped along by the "old books" Ellen devours even when she has to admit "they're a little fancy for me." Ellen is an original who remains sweet and loving through the worst of times. Thus does Gibbons persuade us, as few writers can, that even a terrible childhood can be a state of grace. (pp. 40-1)

Pearl K. Bell, "Southern Discomfort," in The New Republic, *Vol. 198, No. 9, February 29, 1988, pp. 38-41.*

LINDA TAYLOR

"What a lovely day!" says Ellen Foster's aunt at Ellen's mother's funeral, "And I look at the back of her neck and think to myself my mama is dead in the church, my daddy is a monster, your girl is probably going to pee on me before this ride is over and that is all you can find to say." The narrator is 11-years-old and the tone here, with its combination of subdued anger, simple observation, adult knowingness, direct language and actual truth, is representative of the clarity of the voice to Kaye Gibbons' first novel.

Ellen Foster, set in the Southern States, is one of those novels that you feel compelled to read from cover to cover in one sitting. Gibbons' child narrator comes alive on every page with wit, pragmatism and revenge ("When I was little I would think of ways to kill my daddy") and is wholly credible, because although she has a dark tale to tell, she will not engineer sympathy for her effects. The narrative is balanced between her present ordinary happiness with "my new mama" (a foster mother whom Ellen has shrewdly selected for herself) and an earlier frying-pan-to-fire existence (the bullying behaviour of her drunken father and his attempts sexually to molest her after her mother died). After running away from home, she had been legally forced to live with her "mama's mama" who sent her out to pick cotton with the black workers because she held Ellen responsible for her mother's death. And after her grandma died Ellen was patronised and despised by an aunt and cousin.

The poignancy of the novel shows itself in the way Ellen's vulnerability pokes through the exterior cool: trying to buy herself a new mother with $160 ("I figured it would let her know right away that I mean business"), or painting a picture as a Christmas present for her aunt and cousin, which is dismissed as cheap-looking ("I had to appeal to somebody and look at them making fun of me"). Fresh, instant and enchanting, this is a first novel that does not put a foot wrong in its sureness of style, tone and characterisation. Implicitly, too, it is a novel about sexism, racism, family rancour and child abuse, issues that are dealt with through revelation rather than moral axe-grinding.

Linda Taylor, "A Kind of Primitive Charm," in The Sunday Times, *London, May 8, 1988, p. G6.*

COMMENTS OF KAYE GIBBONS TO *CLC YEARBOOK*

Asked by the *Yearbook* about the inspiration for *Ellen Foster,* Gibbons replied, "I wanted to use the naive narrator to tell a very complex story. I wanted to stretch language, her language, to great distances."

Gibbons cites Flannery O'Connor as her greatest literary influence: "The precision of her language and the boundless depths of her thought have consistently amazed me. Her ability to see joy as well as tragedy in the everyday goings-on of 'good country people' has often redeemed me."

Rod Jones

1953-

Australian novelist.

Hailed as a tour de force by critics, *Julia Paradise* (1987) interweaves the motifs of Freudian analysis with political-historical upheaval in a manner many reviewers find reminiscent of D. M. Thomas's *The White Hotel*. Set in Shanghai during the period of Chiang Kai-shek's Nationalist attack on Communists, *Julia Paradise* offers a disturbing psychological study of a young Australian woman suffering from hallucinations and hysteria, exploring in equal depth the effect her case has on her psychoanalyst. With revolution in the background, the novel develops into an investigation of the relationship between public and private exploitation. Through Jones's subtle and deliberately ambiguous conclusions, *Julia Paradise* offers multiple implications and interpretations.

Critics laud Jones for the intensity and imaginative power of his prose and emphasize the mesmerizing force the novel holds over the reader. Particular praise has been directed at his lush imagery, which lyrically evokes the exotic physical and psychological landscapes of *Julia Paradise*. Most critics are intrigued by the novel's complex interplay of psyche and history, finding several readings necessary to capture all of its rich nuances.

Photograph by Ponch Hawkes

PUBLISHERS WEEKLY

Marked by lush, exotic imagery and a subtle, complex handling of motifs, this slim and powerful first novel [*Julia Paradise*] is a carefully controlled psychological study set in the turbulent times of Chiang Kai-shek's China. Kenneth Ayres is a Scottish physician living in Shanghai in the late 1920s. A fleshy, solitary widower who prefers young, small prostitutes, Ayres spent a year in Vienna studying under Freud and now treats the nervous disorders of English-speaking expatriates in China. Julia Paradise, a missionary with her husband Willy, is a morphine addict and a hysteric. . . . In weekly sessions with Ayres, Julia gradually reveals an intriguing and appalling background. Raised in Australia in the country by her father, a botanist who forced her into a lengthy incestuous relationship, she was mute for many years until she escaped from her father during a flood and literally was netted by Willy. Julia seems to benefit from the talking cure—soon she is talking in bed with Ayres—and the doctor is invited to a celebration at the mission. But the mission school is burned, Willy is seized by Chiang Kai-shek's nationals, and Ayres is told that Julia's history is fabrication. What is fantasy, what is reality are questions that will reshape Ayres's life and which are likely to linger in readers' thoughts.

A review of "Julia Paradise," in Publishers Weekly, *Vol. 232, No. 29, July 24, 1987, p. 174.*

An Excerpt from *Julia Paradise*

Her illness brought about a sudden change in Joachim's attitudes towards rearing the child. Now he became neurotically protective of the little mute, restricting her movements to a cruel and unnatural degree. The child, who had always taken her morning lessons out of doors, was now shut away inside the dark house. Lessons consisted entirely of reading in English. Although she was unable to speak or, apparently, to hear, Julia spent hours with books.

Joachim found that he was able to be at home more, and began to knuckle down at last to the composition of his monograph on the propagation of Pacific coral. Each morning he spent alone in his study, sifting through all the data he had tipped into a scatter of drawers through the years, and writing it all up carefully, in German, with his fountain pen, in a leatherbound ledger-sized journal he had purchased as a youth and had kept all these years for the purpose.

Each afternoon he took his daughter on nature excursions, although the routes he chose for her through the garden were always quite safe.

They made a strange sight in the Queensland sun, the European 'doktor' with his neatly-trimmed goatee, his felt hat and walking stick, in his light cotton suit, and the small girl, her face grown into a mask of pale seriousness, with that quizzical look the deaf mute develops. She had no freckles now, not even a touch of the sun in her features, her long black hair tucked up under the brim of her sun hat, her delicately boned wrist cocked against the thought of any sudden attack from the bushes along the garden paths. Her eyes, flicking from side to side as she walked along the path had, as the summer passed, grown more and more disturbingly dark.

The child had a way of looking through her father which puzzled him. He did not read in it any rebuke for his actions. Behind that cool stare there was something taunting. Or as though she were inviting him to share a glimpse into the place where she continued to live.

During the season when it rained at the same hour every afternoon he often came upon her on the veranda on the southern, cooler side of the house, which he had filled with pots of his exotic plant specimens. One day she had her back to him and was apparently unaware of his approach, although Joachim was never entirely convinced of the genuineness of her affliction. The sound of the torrential rain drumming on the roof and in the trees was very loud.

Unseen by her, he spoke, describing all the wickedness he had in store for her, while the girl continued to stare ahead into the rain. When at last he walked around in front of Julia, for a long moment she seemed not to see him. These bouts of apathy he began to think of as her 'absences', in the mental notation of the scientist.

ELIZABETH WARD

Near the end of this astonishing—and astonishingly compressed—novel [*Julia Paradise*], the principal male character, a Scottish Freudian analyst practicing in Shanghai in the troubled year of 1927, experiences a moment of profound despair: "He felt that he had lived for nearly thirty-five years in this world and he had understood nothing."

A reader who falls under the spell of *Julia Paradise* for a few hours (it can be read in a single evening) or a few weeks (such is its imaginative power) might be forgiven for wondering how it is possible to live so intensely in a particular fictional world and yet emerge, like Kenneth Ayres, having "understood nothing." Australian writer Rod Jones' first novel is a brief tour de force of "glittering disorientation," to borrow a phrase describing the eyes of Julia Paradise herself on her first startling appearance in the foyer of the Shanghai Astor House Hotel. The characters are like "shadows," whose movements we observe through doors or windows of "frosted glass," a recurrent metaphor in the early parts of the novel.

A quotation from Flaubert's *Letters* serves as an ironic epigraph: "Yes, stupidity consists in wanting to reach conclu-

sions. We are a thread and we want to know the whole cloth. . . ." The critic, like the analyst, stands warned against the hubris of interpretation. It is certainly a theological axiom and, for all I know, a psychoanalytical one, too (although this is in part a novel about the limits of psychoanalysis) that we do not begin to understand anything until we are able to acknowledge we have understood nothing.

The novel is divided with deceptive artlessness into three parts. It is Shanghai, 1927. Kenneth Ayres, nicknamed "Honeydew" for the brand of tobacco he uses, is a bored, grossly overweight Scottish doctor who amuses himself treating the minor nervous disorders of British colonial "wives and . . . daughters" passing through the hotel where he lives. . . . "In China, that pestilential dreamscape of suffering, he had no interest at all." He cultivates an opium habit and, less harmlessly, a sexual obsession with very young Chinese girls, or "Wendies." But when William Paradise, an Australian Christian missionary, brings his disturbed wife Julia to Ayres for a consultation, the doctor is seduced from his languor by Julia's apparently textbook case of hysteria compounded by an addiction to morphine and the poetry of Coleridge. Ayres, the diligent student of Freud, is arrogantly sure of his diagnosis.

The second section takes the form of a third-person narrative account of Julia's own memories. "Ayres was convinced that he was finally being allowed to approach the psychic events of her childhood which lay at the root of her hysterical illness." Set in "the Duck River region in Northern Australia," Julia's story evokes a steamy, exotic, overgrown landscape dominated by the figure of her German scientist father—overweight, leprous and monstrously selfish—who exploits her sexually until she is at last delivered by a spectacular flood, fetching up at the very door of her future husband, the Methodist clergyman, Willy Paradise. It seems that the origins of the adult Julia's "malevolent zoöptic universe," all that lurid baggage of fantasy and hallucination, are being here laid bare.

The third section introduces an unexpected switch of perspective, setting off the gradual subversion of Ayres' confidence in his own scientific judgment. As he is drawn more tightly into the web of Julia's illness, the web takes on the appearance of an intellectual trap, a "net cast with such casual accuracy across his path: the hints planted, her silky narrative woven to confound him, an entire childhood left hanging in the air." Puzzling discrepancies emerge. Certain details of Julia's narrative parallel Ayres' own life and habits so closely that he feels at first uncomfortable, then—along with the reader— mocked and confounded.

Surrounding and complicating all of this are the politics of China's long civil war. Kuomintang troops are advancing on Shanghai. The Paradise mission is seized. At every point the European and Australian characters' involvement with politics and with the Chinese themselves acts as a commentary upon their inner moral lives, and vice versa. The well-intentioned but inept Willy Paradise is arrested and later presumed shot. A female German Marxist revolutionary plays a minor but symbolically significant role: once having looked into her face, it always seemed to Ayres afterward "that he had been looking into the face of the future, the face of the twentieth century."

Julia Paradise touches with extraordinary subtlety on the various interrelationships, both real and metaphorical, among the great modern historical movements—Freudianism, Marxism, colonialism, feminism, revolution. On how many levels, for example, does the key phrase, "the despair of repeated rape," reverberate throughout the novel? But there will be no easy resolution. For "Honeydew" Ayres, "as in life, the mysteries remained, became subterranean and mapped out only in his dreams." So it must remain for the reader. The novel does map itself out subliminally, in the recesses of the mind, if allowed to rest there a while after one or two readings, as it may well have grown in Rod Jones' mind in the first place, a dream woven or "mapped out" from a memory of *Kubla Khan*: "Weave a circle round him thrice, / And close [your] eyes with holy dread / For he on honeydew hath fed, / And drunk the milk of Paradise." (pp. 4-5)

Elizabeth Ward, "Rod Jones: A Startling Debut," in Book World—The Washington Post, *September 27, 1987, pp. 4-5.*

WRAY HERBERT

It is difficult to read Rod Jones's haunting first novel, **Julia Paradise,** without being reminded again and again of Joseph Conrad. It is not only the colonial Far East setting—in this case Shanghai—but also the kind of Westerner found there. Like the trader Almayer in Conrad's own first novel, or the skeptic Axel Heyst in his more mature *Victory*, Mr. Jones's Kenneth (Honeydew) Ayres is stuck, spiritually more than actually. He is a British psychoanalyst and expatriate who stopped off in Shanghai on a whim in the early 1920's and stayed. He has no motive for being where he is or doing what he is doing; the people of China don't interest him, except in the most unsavory ways. And his life is guided by a dull and plodding scientism that provides him no fulfillment—a theme that Conrad also found intriguing and one he explored time and time again.

Having drawn these parallels, I should add that **Julia Paradise** is utterly original. Ayres's particular form of scientism is Freudian analysis, and at the core of the book is a psychoanalytic case study: the case of Julia Paradise. . . . She has been suffering hallucinations, seeing animals and fire where none exist, and has been going through cycles of extreme mania and despondency. In addition, as Ayres discovers, she is addicted to narcotics, and as he weans her from the drugs he treats her neurosis with a most unusual variation of Freudian analysis: in his bed, the immense Ayres and the boyish Julia Paradise have sex while she free associates about her childhood in the Duck River region of Australia.

And what a childhood it was, involving years of sexual abuse at the hands of her deeply disturbed father and an early case of hysterical muteness. She describes her early years to Ayres in intimate detail, and indeed the talking cure takes. Her symptoms disappear, and she returns to the mission, but Ayres is obsessed. It seems he has a sexual compulsion of his own, and Julia Paradise's eroticism has kindled a fire in his mind. He begins spending more and more time in his darkened room with his opium pipe.

Outside his room, and outside his nasty, self-centered little world, China is in a state of political upheaval. Chiang Kai-shek has begun what is to be his unsuccessful campaign to drive the Communists from the country. But Ayres is oblivious to politics, and that, Mr. Jones seems to be saying, is his failing. Stuck with his dreary Freudian vision, he doesn't notice a powerful political vision that is transforming the 20th century—the vision of Karl Marx.

Freud and Marx are played off each other in this novel, the latter's ideas embodied by the German intellectual Gertie Platz, missionary, revolutionary and lover of Julia Paradise. It is she who finally transforms Ayres, providing him with a vision of the future and awakening in him a sense of commitment to people that had never informed his healing practice.

Despite the precision of Mr. Jones's prose, there is a lot of ambiguity in this slim volume. Did the childhood events that Julia Paradise narrated really take place, or were they fantasies? Or did she invent them deliberately as part of another agenda entirely? This is a book to be read and reread. So rich are its pages that I found myself backtracking constantly to uncover a detail that, apparently unimportant, later took on significance. In the enigmatic character of Julia Paradise, Mr. Jones . . . has skillfully entwined the personal and political aspects of a committed life, and in Ayres he has offered a model for moral victory over our darker impulses. It is a remarkable accomplishment.

Wray Herbert, "The Fantasy Trade in Shanghai," in The New York Times Book Review, *October 11, 1987, p. 12.*

PETER S. PRESCOTT

Rod Jones's first novel, **Julia Paradise,** is as short and as tightly strung as a crossbow. In Shanghai, in 1927, the distracted young wife of a missionary seeks help from a dissolute British psychiatrist who once studied with Freud. She tells him a detailed story of her Australian childhood—and her father's incestuous demands. Just as we are thinking: Ah, how events shape a woman's psychology, Jones neatly reverses himself. now it appears that an erotic psychology can shape events. Before he's done, Jones puts one more spin on his narrative. There are no flaws in this tour de force, which on a second reading maintains its mesmerizing effect. From the start, Jones's narrative voice assumes complete authority. His story is a cousin to Freud's case histories, to *The White Hotel* and *The Alexandria Quartet*.

Peter S. Prescott, in a review of "Julia Paradise," in Newsweek, *Vol. CX, No. 23, December 7, 1987, p. 94.*

VALENTINE CUNNINGHAM

Rod Jones is an Australian whose sexual farce **Julia Paradise** is not only . . . internationalist . . . but also very [black]. . . . His Honeydew Ayres is an unflappable Scottish medic practising in turbulent late-1920s Shanghai. Hugely fat, opium-smoking, a student of Freud's, he is a fan of J. M. Barrie. He's also hooked on sex with the child-prostitutes whom he labels Wendies.

The case of Julia Paradise, though, does rattle Ayres. She's the neurotic wife of a Methodist missionary, a grown up Wendy, dependent on morphine, a haunter of foul locales, camera at the ready, and a spinner of charged tales about her father's doings in the Australian outback. Consulting-room hypnosis and Tuesday afternoon adultery entice Ayres ever deeper into the labyrinth of Mrs Paradise's narratives of incest, pyromania, bestiality and skin disease.

How much all Ayres hears is true, how much fantasy, Rod Jones's admirably unheated revelations choose never to disclose. And this vagueness is central to the power of the writing, as Scotland, Australia and China are united in a chain of horror, cruelty and exploitation. Here's a glimpse into the twentieth-century heart of darkness, Ayres alleges. And the novel rises magisterially—for all its conscious copycat D. M. Thomas-sisms—to the task of bringing the grim truths of that allegation home.

> *Valentine Cunningham, "Cuckolded in Chiswick," in* The Observer, *March 6, 1988, p. 42.*

ANTHONY DELANO

Rod Jones's **Julia Paradise** is an exceptional achievement, a novel in all but length; brevity is used as a dramatic resource. Australian reviewers saw immediately that he had been travelling the same devious roads as D M Thomas before the British writer settled in to *The White Hotel*. No matter. The stripped-down format and offhand eroticism of this case-fable of a China mission wife in the grip of zoopsiac hallucinations and a doctor whose dissimulations match his patient's induce an icy enthralment.

> *Anthony Delano, "Unrestrained by the Burden of Place," in* The Sunday Times, *London, March 27, 1988, pp. G8-G9.*

David Michael Kaplan

1946-

American short story writer.

The stories in Kaplan's first collection, *Comfort* (1987), are noted for two primary themes: difficult parent-child relationships and elements of the supernatural. Most of the pieces in *Comfort* focus on children emotionally and/or physically estranged from a parent; the stories involve a search for reconciliation, which may or may not be successful. Many of Kaplan's stories show the influence of the magic realist school, invoking fantastical occurrences to illuminate and underscore heightened moments of reality. Reviewers find Kaplan's stories dramatic, believable, and fresh, commending him especially for his seamless interweaving of dreamlike fantasy with everyday experience. Critics also praise Kaplan for the sensitivity and insight he brings to his exploration of troubled human relationships.

KIRKUS REVIEWS

The dozen unexceptional stories that make up this modest debut [*Comfort*] mostly concern parents and children who experience some kind of separation or loss. Despite a few surreal flourishes, Kaplan's slight fictions rely on an all-too-familiar sense of reality for their diminished psychological effects.

The first and finest piece here, **"Doe Season,"** locates a young girl's passage from tomboyhood at the moments she witnesses the gutting of a doe she's shot, the only one bagged by an otherwise all-male hunting party. After this single instance of regionally inflected prose, Kaplan settles into a number of flat tales involving mothers. The absent mother of **"Love, Your Only Mother"** sends untraceable postcards from all over the West to her daughter, whom she left years ago with her father. In **"Magic,"** a young woman meets her lover's unfriendly daughter, who clearly wants no substitute mother, until a bit of genuine magic brings them together. A dead mother hovers over the somber **"In the Realm of the Herons,"** in which a young widower can't cope with his 11-year-old daughter's refusal to mourn her mother's accidental demise. The overly schematic **"Anne Rey"** finds a young art-restorer confronted with an inexplicably deteriorating print at the same time her mother imagines herself developing a brain tumor. Some of this moroseness derives from fathers as well: **"Summer People"** reunites a widower and his divorced and estranged son; in **"Elisabetta, Carlotta, Catherine,"** a young woman, abandoned with her mother long ago, searches, after her father's premature death, for a girl in a picture with him whom she presumes is his illegitimate daughter.

A number of less predictable stories in which equally bland characters seek various forms of comfort fail to relieve the monotonous solemnity here.

A review of "Comfort," in Kirkus Reviews, *Vol. LIV, No. 23, December 1, 1986, p. 1749.*

MARY SOETE

The author of [*Comfort*] depicts with singular success the heart-stopping impact of those heightened moments that illuminate his characters' lives. In **"Doe Season"** (selected as one of the Best American Short Stories of 1985), a tomboy on a deer hunt accepts a terrible invitation to kill. The luminous beauty and horror of her night encounter with the beast typify Kaplan's subtle and convincing way with the supernatural. Levitation, voodoo, witchery, transformation, ghostly visitation—several stories turn on one or another of these phenomena. **"A Mexican Tale"** and **"Elias Schneebaum,"** for instance, sustain the haunting resonance of horror tales. **"Comfort,"** on the other hand, suggests an ironic compromise to a friendship darkened by knowledge of betrayal. This is writing of powerful insight and beauty, a talented first collection. (pp. 107-08)

Mary Soete, in a review of "Comfort," in Library Journal, *Vol. 112, No. 1, January, 1987, pp. 107-08.*

MARY ELLEN QUINN

[*Comfort*] shows a careful, sensitive writer at work. In nearly every story, Kaplan explores parent-child relationships. In **"Doe Season,"** Andy, on a hunting trip with her father, tries to prove herself a worthy companion but ends up confronting her own ambivalence toward being a girl. **"In the Realm of the Heron"** a restorative stay in a summer cabin provides a young girl with the opportunity to deal with her mother's recent death. Similarly, an art restorer faces her aging mother's disintegration in **"Anne Rey."** Sometimes the author's sense of melodrama gets the better of him, and several of his endings seem contrived. But these stories break away from the autobiographical fixations that characterize so many first collections. Kaplan's portrayals of preadolescent girls are especially convincing.

Mary Ellen Quinn, in a review of "Comfort," in Booklist, *Vol. 83, No. 10, January 15, 1987, p. 751.*

SARAH GOLD

Contrary to expectations raised by the title [*Comfort*], there is little comfort to be found in David Michael Kaplan's first collection of stories. The cover, which illustrates [**"Comfort"**], shows two young women sitting and chatting in wicker chairs in front of a bay window—a harmless enough scene. Both title and cover, however, are coolly, cruelly ironic. One of the young women seduces Ted, the lover of the other one's mother, to test his faithfulness. He fails, of course, and the two women agree never to tell. "But at least *we* know," says the seductress. "That's sort of a comfort, isn't it?"

There isn't much more comfort in any of Kaplan's stories. He writes about uneasy family relationships, particularly between father and child. In **"Summer People,"** Frank and his father close up their old summer house for the last time. In the post-summer isolation of the lake, long-standing conflicts and resentments flare up. Kaplan does not offer a resolution; the ending is the more unsettling for failing to deliver the tragedy he sets us up to expect.

"In the Realm of the Herons" is about a father who takes his daughter on a lakeside vacation in the wake of his wife's sudden death. The girl's unexpressed rage at her loss leaves a gaping silence. One day, out rowing alone, the father comes upon an old deserted house, the kind that looks haunted. He animates it with his fantasy of family happiness and insists on bringing his daughter out to see it. Instead of her father's idyllic retreat, she finds a dead heron nailed to the wall, a terrifying vision which looms over the reader long after the father and daughter have rowed away.

In Kaplan's universe, mothers are mostly absent. They have died, fled, or lost their minds. One of the best stories [**"Love, Your Only Mother"**] is about a mother who left years ago; her only contact with her daughter is an occasional bizarre postcard with a message like "The beetles are so much larger this year. I know you must be enjoying them." The cards never reveal where she is, but only where she was some time ago; they arrive like the light of a dead star. These anti-postcards don't say "miss you, wish you were here." They taunt and

tease, saying "I know where you are, but you'll never find me." Such a mother is no comfort at all.

In addition to the human relationships and the unbridgeable distances they seem to encompass, Kaplan infuses his stories with another reality; apparitions and magic, a demon and a witch, mystical events that seem like dreams but may not be. In **"Doe Season,"** . . . little Andy has a mysterious nocturnal encounter with the doe she reluctantly killed hunting with her father. In another tale, a young woman searching for a post-humous reconciliation with her dead father watches a strange Barbados ritual, the raising of a demon who will tell you your heart's desire in return for something you treasure. Elisabetta offers him the photo of her father and a woman and child she has been seeking on the island. The photo is consumed in the demon's flames, but Elisabetta will not get her wish.

The pleasure of these stories is not just in the twists Kaplan gives them, or in their supernatural effects, arresting as they are. These are vivid narratives, full of texture, emotion, and drama. Each moment stands on its own even as it leads toward the climax. The art of storytelling is not only safe but thriving with David Michael Kaplan—and that is sort of a comfort, isn't it?

Sarah Gold, "Cold Comfort," in The Village Voice, *Vol. XXXII, No. 22, June 2, 1987, p. 50.*

An Excerpt from *Comfort*

Later that evening, while Nicanor smoked and I drank a tepid beer, he filled me in on what little had happened in my absence. It was then that I learned Antonio had been executed.

"Did they ever find out who betrayed him?"

Nicanor's eyes brightened in a way I had never before seen. "Ah, there's a strange story about that. It's only a rumor, I tell you. But you will be interested. It's a story a man of learning would appreciate." He leaned closer to me in his straw chair, one hand on his knee, the other gesturing with his cigarette.

"They say that Antonio's family, desperate to find the betrayer, appealed to a local *bruja*—a witch—for help. This *bruja* is known as La Mascarilla. What her real name is no one knows. She lives some miles outside of town where the dry riverbed meets Las Gorgas Canyon. After some days she named Héctor Milla—another cousin of Antonio's—as the betrayer. How she learned this no one knows. Some say she turned herself into a crow and perched outside many windows, watching and listening." Nicanor saw the expression on my face and waved his hand. "This, of course, I don't believe.

"Milla was brought before a village council and inter-rogated. At first he maintained his innocence, but then the *bruja* spoke something in his ear. He became still as stone, and then began confessing his guilt. He could not lie before the witch." Nicanor sat back in his chair, folded his arms, and smiled.

"And what happened?"

Nicanor spread his hands. "Who knows? Some say he was killed, some say no. Some say the witch herself determined his fate. But"—he raised his finger dramatically—"he has never been seen again. Of course, no one admits having been personally present at this trial. Leopoldo made some inquiries, then gave up. Héctor's family is silent.

"You are a man of learning, of reason. You're not ignorant like these people"—he swept his arms wide to include the entire Bolsón—"or like me. In the long run, I think it best not to ask too much. I wait for knowledge to find me: I don't seek it. But you—you are a scholar. A man used to solving mysteries—yes, yes, I know, don't protest. Perhaps you can solve this one, eh?" He smiled in a way that was both ingratiating and mocking. "Perhaps you can find out what happened to Héctor Milla?"

"Why?" I asked.

"Because you are curious." He shrugged. "Because no one else wants to know."

"And if I wanted to," I said, smiling myself now, "where would I begin? You said yourself the Bolsón is endless."

He leaned toward me in the creaking straw chair. "The only point on which all the rumors agree is that both La Mascarilla and Héctor were there that night. Héctor is gone. But the witch isn't."

SUSAN WOOD

The dozen stories in David Michael Kaplan's affecting first collection [*Comfort*] share a common focus on the extraordinary moments of recognition in ordinary lives. He is at his best suggesting how such moments may alter, for better or worse, our relationships with those to whom we are most deeply bound—children, parents, lovers—in love and guilt.

The most successful stories, in fact—and they are in the majority here—concern complicated ties between parents and children. In ["**Comfort**"] a young woman makes a joking pact with her roommate to seduce her mother's lover—with psychologically devastating results. Frank, the protagonist of "**Summer People,**" has spent his adult life trying to get away from his father's excessive judgments of him; they are finally forced into a confrontation while repairing the house where Frank spent his childhood summers. Having watched his father nearly drown, he sits on the dock, "his legs dangling over the edge like a helpless marionette's," choking "as if it were he that had been drowning."

Indeed, parental abandonment, either real or threatened, is a recurring theme. In "**Elisabetta, Carlotta, Catherine (Raising the Demon),**" a beautiful young woman, abandoned by her father as a child, travels to Barbados after his death in search of his illegitimate daughter, whom she has seen in a photograph. She imagines that the child appears to her and asks the question she herself has been wondering about: *"If I was so beautiful,* Carlotta says, *then why did he leave?"* In her imagination she gives the answer she has wanted to believe: "'Carlotta—' Elisabetta murmurs. 'It wasn't your fault, Carlotta.'" The narrator of "**Love, Your Only Mother**" recounts the postcards she continues to get 30 years after her mother suddenly left the family, postcards that are somehow both terrifying and comforting: "Like a buoy in a fog, your voice, dear Mother, seems to come from everywhere."

Mr. Kaplan, like a few other writers of his generation—Ann Beattie and Elizabeth Tallent come to mind—has an uncanny knack for creating wholly believable children. His showpiece is "**Doe Season,**" in which a precocious 9-year-old girl is initiated into the adult world of sexuality and death when she accompanies her father on a deer hunt and kills a doe. Recalling a trip to the ocean in which her mother lost the top of her bathing suit, Andy runs from her father and his friends as he begins to butcher the doe: "Louder than any of them was the wind blowing through the treetops, like the ocean where her mother floated in green water, also calling *Come in, come in,* while all around her roared the mocking of the terrible, now inevitable, sea."

Several of the stories involve elements of the surreal or supernatural, and when these seem to grow naturally out of character and plot, as in "**Doe Season**" and "**Magic,**" they enrich the stories, offering ways we may move beyond ordinary understanding. In the least successful stories in the collection, "**A Mexican Tale**" and "**Elias Schneebaum,**" the supernatural provides the plot itself and seems like so much window-dressing. Among so many fine stories, however, these two are merely aberrations.

Susan Wood, "Children without Parents," in The New York Times Book Review, *June 14, 1987, p. 41.*

JESSICA AMANDA SALMONSON

David Michael Kaplan's first book [*Comfort*], made up of stories from literary magazines and *Atlantic Monthly,* consists largely of tales about children estranged from parents by divorce, misunderstanding, or death. "**Magic**" ideally reflects the author's obsessions. It's about a child given to her father by an apparently disinterested mother, and the resentful child's first meeting with her father's new lover. The woman's ambivalence toward her boyfriend's daughter soon weighs in the girl's favor, culminating in the sharing of an amusingly bizarre piece of genuine magic the father will never know about. This sensitive fantasy is everything many have claimed for Sturgeon.

None of the other child/parent stories have supernatural content, although most incorporate gothic allusions (a voodoo ceremony in "**Elisabetta, Carlotta, Catherine**") or weird dreams (the little girl of "**Doe Season**" dreams she shoves her hand into the open wound of a living-dead deer; the father of "**In the Realm of the Heron**" dreams he tears off his daughter's arms).

That Kaplan is influenced by the magic realists is most evident in "**A Mexican Tale,**" told by a man self-exiled in the frigid North due to a horrific discovery in the tropic South. An entirely successful pastiche of the Latin American fantasists, it is also one of the best horror stories of the year.

Another story to explore issues different from the bulk of the collection is "**Elias Schneebaum.**" Intellectual and eerie throughout, it is just shy of baroque in its discussion of time and reincarnation and its use of ghosts and precognition.

The three overtly supernatural pieces are of the highest conceivable merit, making *Comfort* a treasure to fantasy collectors. The rest of the tales are variations on a theme demanding an interest in the sad relationships between children and parents.

Jessica Amanda Salmonson, "Gothic Allusions," in Fantasy Review, *Vol. 10, No. 6, July-August, 1987, p. 50.*

COMMENTS OF DAVID MICHAEL KAPLAN TO *CLC YEARBOOK*

Discussing his motivation for writing, Kaplan observed: "I think every writer—myself included—writes for two main reasons: one, to create something that was not in the world before he or she wrote it . . . and two, to share that creation with as wide a readership as possible. The first is a meditation, the second a presumption—but a presumption without which no art of any kind would exist."

Kaplan cites John Cheever and Edmund Spenser as the most profound influences on his writing, explaining, "They are centuries and mediums apart, yet linked imaginatively, I believe. . . . In their work, both showed me the ways in which the magical can exist within the ordinary, and—conversely— how the ordinary can be perceived as magical. The boundaries between reality as lived and reality as imagined is permeable, and the writer's job—as they showed—is to pass, through his work, back and forth, from one to the other, ceaselessly."

Antoine Laurent

1952-

French novelist and screenwriter.

In *Cuisine Novella* (1987), Laurent intersperses fantastical plot twists with discourses on the art of fiction. The novel is set largely on a train bound from Paris to Nice, and portrays fashion designer Annabelle's education in the interconnected arts of cuisine and storytelling by a mysterious Marquis.

Most critics find that Laurent's language is frequently overwrought and self-consciously clever and fault the novel's plot and premise. Some observe, however, that the author's inventiveness compensates for weaknesses in structure, noting with favor the novel's originality and wit.

KIRKUS REVIEWS

[In *Cuisine Novella*], first-novelist Laurent stirs up a self-conscious verbal fantasy in which a mysterious master chef lures a chic *couturier* into cooking lessons aboard a Nice-bound train—only to ensnare her in a web of extraordinary fictions.

In a Paris bistro, the black-cloaked Marquis de St.-Lyre spots Annabelle Fleury making faces over a bad dish of champignons á la Provencale. He introduces himself as a master chef and offers to teach her the secrets of creative cooking if she will join him on a two-day train ride to his restaurant in Nice. Aboard the train, the Marquis reveals his secrets—ingredients, methods, and sympathy. To demonstrate that these principles apply to great storytelling as well, he lures her into a series of living fictions—in each of which he exchanges a special object for one of the ingredients needed to create a perfect dish. . . . To get the last ingredient, Annabelle herself concocts a Dorian Gray-like story that shows her the powers of the imagination. It is in Nice, when she tastes all the ingredients of these imaginative journeys combined into a perfect dish, that the dark, charmed addiction sets in.

Laurent shows imagination galore, but too may self-conscious digressions and too much too-smart verbiage make this too-clever soufflé fall flat.

A review of "Cuisine Novella," in Kirkus Reviews, *Vol. LV, No. 12, July 1, 1987, p. 952.*

ROZ KAVENEY

Cuisine Novella [is a first novel] by Antoine Laurent, whose moderately interesting speculations about the procedures of storytelling would have justified a short essay. Laurent is fascinated by narrative clichés, but suffers from the misapprehension that to present them only lightly sautéd by art is to be amusingly camp. His fashion designer Annabelle is accosted

by a stage-managing Marquis, who offers to teach her the simple rules of cooking—ingredients, techniques and sympathy—and gradually reveals himself to believe their culinary application to be but a particular case of their central role in all creation, particularly in storytelling. It is tale-within-a-tale. . . . At various points in the train journey that is the objective correlative of Annabelle's quest, she encounters fictional and filmic co-travellers: those of *Shanghai Express* for example, or those of *Strangers on a Train*. Authors should only indulge in references if their work can stand the comparison. (pp. 30-1)

Roz Kaveney, "Too Little Reality," in New Statesman, *Vol. 114, No. 2936, July 3, 1987, pp. 30-1.*

WENDY BRANDMARK

In Antoine Laurent's *Cuisine Novella,* a master chef in search of the ingredients to champignons à la provençale transforms the compartments of a train into a forest in central Europe, an ancient Egyptian tomb, a Spanish hacienda. The Marquis de St-Lyre meets a young fashion designer in a café in Paris and offers to teach her the art of cooking on a train journey down to his restaurant in Nice. But his pedagogical methods are unusual, his powers magical. The Marquis believes that good cooking, like good story-telling, depends on the right method, the best ingredients and sympathy; if one learns the secret of one art, one can master all the others.

There are echoes in *Cuisine Novella* of the magic theatre in Hermann Hesse's *Steppenwolf*, of Fowles' *The Magus*, but Laurent's tone is lighter, more playful. He wants us to ponder his ideas about the writing of fiction, to admire his artistry, but also to enjoy ourselves. This is a flamboyant novel whose set-pieces would be camp clichés if they were not told with such élan and wit. At times his language becomes over-rich, the events silly, but Laurent succeeds in beguiling us with his audaciously inventive narrative. (p. 23)

Wendy Brandmark, "'Tell Him I Can't See Him'," in The Listener, *Vol. 118, No. 3020, July 16, 1987, pp. 23-4.*

PUBLISHERS WEEKLY

This unusual first novel [*Cuisine Novella*] offers a romp through the pleasures of metafiction by discussing storytelling in terms of the arts of the kitchen. Annabelle, a pretty young dress designer, meets the flamboyant Marquis in a Parisian cafe. Disappointed with a badly wrought dish of *champignons á la provençale*, Annabelle lets the Marquis entice her to his house in Provence, La Fantaisie, to initiate her in the culinary arts. Lessons begin on the railway journey, which occupies nearly the entire novel. The train's "enchanted compartments" open like little theaters or bazaar booths onto fresh stories, as the talk of concocting applies equally to literature and food.

59

Annabelle and the Marquis suffer temporary hallucinations, seeming to turn into the mushrooms, garlic and oil required by the curriculum. Later these ingredients acquire powerful human essences in the culinary process. The novel's envelope structure encloses tales of Egyptian mummies, a Russian tiger lady, a dwarf and Annabelle's own created story of the couture world. Since Annabelle and the Marquis each are gay, romance between them isn't likely, but both become ensnared by their shared infatuation with art. The novel sometimes errs on the side of a baroque longwindedness, but afficionados of the craft of fiction will appreciate its witticism.

A review of "Cuisine Novella," in Publishers Weekly, *Vol. 232, No. 29, July 24, 1987, p. 171.*

An Excerpt from *Cuisine Novella*

As they turn right out of the Marquis' compartment and start to pace through the train, Annabelle muses whether the number 6 possesses special significance. After a few moments, during which the limited gamut of her symbological knowledge—the hexagon, the hexagram, the Seal of Solomon, the six-sided crystalline forms within nature and various other patterns perhaps salient, perhaps farfetched—are all passed in review, she decides that she is wasting her time. Which is surely the wisest conclusion as there is no way to tell whether in this puzzle-proliferating story there is any rune, occult connotation, or, indeed, subtext to be divined from a number generated by nothing more than the tumbling of the dice.

Her steps soon take her past compartments in which she glimpses a collection of long-distance commuters. Some are shielding themselves from human contact with newspapers which they hold up like phylacteries. Others are nibbling away at *Petits Lu* or are sniffing garlic-soused *saucissons.* A number are fretting over objects placed in the folds of the deepest luggage while the rest stare with wide-eyed wonder at the shadow-encloaked features cascading past their line of vision. While the Marquis strides purposefully in front of her, Annabelle tries to fathom what she has let herself in for.

Ambling past one particular compartment's glass front and casually glancing into it, Annabelle can hardly believe her eyes. For instead of the velveteen upholstery and Midi-bound passengers which she expected to see in it, what greets her instead is a group of South American *peones,* their white linen tunics draped with multi-coloured shawls, sitting on a set of wooden slatted seats. Some clutch hens; others have their laps heaped high with vegetable produce, while through the window the viridian heights of the Andes provide a realistic backdrop to the improbable scene. This would be quite sufficiently astounding in itself were she not to encounter in the very next carriage a band of Russian *kulaks* who, fur-swaddled and leather-enwrapped against the asperities of a snow-bound Siberian winter, confront her, rifles at the ready, with the kind of hostile scrutiny which, she suspects, a female intruding on their patriarchal traditions would arouse.

Thoroughly disoriented, Annabelle does not tarry, as the last thing she wants in the middle of this suddenly enchanted carriage is to lose sight of the Marquis. Yet is it conceivable that he has not noticed these scenes ripped out of some exotic travelogue? Or is his attention so fixed on tracking down the right compartment that he has rigorously excluded all extraneous information? Faced by the Marquis' apparent imperviousness, she has to admit that there is nothing for it but to continue.

EMMA DALLY

The witty title of Antoine Laurent's book, *Cuisine Novella,* reflects the humour and energy of this highly imaginative novel.

When Annabelle Fleury, a young fashion designer, is served a disgusting dish of *champignons à la provençale* in a Paris brasserie, the mysterious Marquis de St-Lyne introduces himself to her as a master chef who can teach her the principles of haute cuisine in just two days. He will do this, he tells her, if she first accompanies him on a journey to collect the perfect gastronomic ingredients for the ruined dish before her.

Annabelle rises to the challenge and finds herself making the most extraordinary journey of her life. Taking her on to a magical train where each compartment holds a different drama into which he and Annabelle plunge, the Marquis gradually explains the purpose of his mission. Revealing that it is he who thought up the stories behind the compartment doors, he tries to show her that cooking and storytelling are part of the same process. Both are governed by the same principles, both provide a type of sustenance, and both are ultimately ruled by the imagination. Now they have collected three of the necessary ingredients from the Marquis' own scenarios, he tells Annabelle, and it is time for her to make up her own story in which they can collect the last. After a false start, Annabelle shows that she has learned her lessons well by producing a story at least as powerful as anything the Marquis has done before.

The scope of *Cuisine Novella* is so thoroughly astounding that when we finally learn the Marquis' true reason for luring Annabelle onto his train, there is hardly any more room for surprise.

Emma Dally, in a review of "Cuisine Novella," in Books, *No. 6, September, 1987, p. 20.*

ROBERT PLUNKET

This first novel [*Cuisine Novella*] dealing with the relationship between cooking and storytelling is indeed an original, although it finds honorable antecedents in the fiction of John Fowles and Robertson Davies. . . . Antoine Laurent's concept is an audacious one but he quickly paints—or writes—himself into a corner. In a narrative so obsessed with the techniques of storytelling, his own story must be brilliant, and unfortunately it is not. Poorly paced, at times confusing and full of half-baked theories, *Cuisine Novella* never quite achieves the quality of "sympathy" the author sees as essential to a story's success. Yet in its mellifluous flow of language it is an elegant, literate achievement that marks Mr. Laurent as a writer of unusual gifts.

Robert Plunket, in a review of "Cuisine Novella," in The New York Times Book Review, *September 13, 1987, p. 34.*

HUGH M. CRANE

The Marquis de St. Lyre, master chef, raconteur, and villain of Laurent's first novel [*Cuisine Novella*], promises to reveal the magical connections between cooking and storytelling to unsuspecting (and occasionally obtuse) dressmaker Annabelle Fleury in a quest for the ingredients of a perfect dish of *champignons à la provençale*. Within the confines of a protean train traveling from Nice to Paris, they obtain their mushrooms, garlic, cooking oil, and parsley from an artiste, an Egyptian Mummy, a dwarfish jester from a Spanish court, and the head of a Parisian haute couture house, in return for resolving their tragic stories. Only when Annabelle has learned her arts can the Marquis be released from his own bondage. Laurent regularly refreshes his piquant central metaphor but serves it up in a sometimes overwrought style. His plot remains unsatisfyingly vague, but his story is very, very different.

Hugh M. Crane, in a review of "Cuisine Novella," in Library Journal, *Vol. 112, No. 16, October 1, 1987, p. 108.*

Stephen McCauley

19??-

American novelist.

The Object of My Affection (1987) is set in New York City and explores the relationship of George, a gay kindergarten teacher, and his roommate Nina, a feminist psychologist. Upon learning that she is pregnant, Nina asks George to help her raise her baby; George is torn between his love for Nina and a newfound relationship with a man in Vermont. McCauley, who has been both a kindergarten teacher and a psychology student, tells their story in a breezy and affectionate manner.

Critics have responded warmly to the humor and unabashed cheeriness of McCauley's tale, finding his wry depictions of contemporary New York life to be both insightful and engaging. While some reviewers observe a lack of substance beneath what they consider a soap-opera plot, many cite McCauley's skillful exploration of the lives and loves of his well-conceived characters as a cogent commentary on the need for meaning and human connections in life.

© Sigrid Estrada 1988

RAY OLSON

George and Nina [in *The Object of My Affection*] are a couple of young, idealistic, underpaid New Yorkers who are expecting a baby. The wrinkle in their story is that George isn't the father. In fact, he's gay, and, while committed to Nina and to children, he's not able to promise her he'll be around to be de facto daddy. George is also involved with Paul, a Vermonter who, as it happens, has a five-year-old foster son from El Salvador. To complicate matters further, George loses his job. Although the plot elements carom around like billiard balls, in the end they all find reasonably comfortable, happy repose. McCauley's first novel is a sitcom that recalls nothing so much as a Neil Simon play. It is quick reading, sunny but a little bland.

> Ray Olson, in a review of "The Object of My Affection," in Booklist, Vol. 83, No. 13, March 1, 1987, p. 981.

SUSAN FROMBERG SCHAEFFER

In his very funny, exceptionally vivid first novel [*The Object of My Affection*], Stephen McCauley seems to be asking whether it is possible to come of age at all in what we may eventually term the addled 80's. His narrator, George, a young man from whose point of view we see everything, is a self-described "glutton for unqualified affection" who comes from Boston to New York because he was "convinced everybody ended up there at some point in life anyway, and I figured I should get it out of the way while I still had the energy." George drops

in and out of graduate school, gets a job at a frighteningly upscale kindergarten and moves in with Nina, an almost-psychologist (she has yet to write her dissertation) trying to reconcile her belief in Freud with her belief in feminism. . . .

On the one hand, nothing happens in this novel; on the other hand, everything does. Stephen McCauley's characters are the children of the feminist, Marxist and psychoanalytic movements, and ideas, unbalanced by common sense or happy, anchoring experience, seem to be their undoing. "Do you realize," Nina asks George, "that I've spent my whole life worrying about my weight . . .? I became a feminist thinking I'd stop caring once and for all, and instead I just became guilty on top of everything because it still mattered on me." Howard, the father of Nina's child (he adores Nina, and calls her, variously, the Pudding, the Butterbean, the Puddle, the Brisket and the Munchkin) blames himself when Nina decides to "terminate" him. . . .

George, Nina and Howard all share a determination not to repeat the truly stunning mistakes of their parents, but, confounded as they are by the twin shipwrecks of the past and the present, this seems impossible. Thus they mistrust "relationships,'' ''commitment,'' being in love, and probably love it-self. They flee intimacy, seek intimacy, move to Manhattan, move out of Manhattan, ignore cooking (George produces a memorable tuna and raisin casserole), are obsessed by cooking, attempt to ignore their families or to belong to them. Throughout, they grimly observe the foibles of society around them. . . . In short, they are all, in their own relentless, hopefully cynical way, in search of meaning. . . .

It is one of the great strengths of *The Object of My Affection* that the characters do not find meaning (although they do seem to *glimpse* it), do not reach that safe harbor where, ''relieved to be spared the burdens of youth and nonconformity'' (these burdens ''replaced,'' according to Mr. McCauley, by ''squalling babies''), they stop looking at the world with astonishment, amusement and healthy contempt. We leave Mr. McCauley's characters half hatched from their shells, suspiciously regarding the world, too far out of the egg to go back, too alarmed by the world to step out into it. We last glimpse them flailing about in a world where homosexuality is less of a problem than being a feminist who likes long, painted fingernails. The water that so often threatens to go over their heads begins lapping at our feet, too, and this is Mr. McCauley's triumph: he brings his characters, his *world* astonishingly, captivatingly alive. In a work of fiction, he collapses the barriers between ''fiction'' and ''life.'' *The Object of My Affection* is surely one of the best books about what it is like to be young in these crazy times.

Susan Fromberg Schaeffer, ''George and Nina, Powerless to Be Hatched,'' in The New York Times Book Review, *March 22, 1987, p. 7.*

PATRICIA VIGDERMAN

In the age of television sitcoms, it's easy to forget that domestic comedy once sported elegantly with truths universally acknowledged. As Jane Austen's novels dissect the mismatch between domestic necessity and the heart's desire, her wit lights up the landscape of love. Almost two centuries later, as [*The Object of My Affection* shows] . . . , the domestic dilemma has acquired a male dimension—and humor has lost none of its candlepower over the depths of the soul.

Stephen McCauley's *The Object of My Affection* is narrated by George, a young gay man living with a young woman called Nina who shows up pregnant in the first sentence. In the months between the hot August evening when Nina reveals her condition and the baby's birth the following winter, George lays out the incongruities of his emotional life. The story includes his family (a kind but ineffectual mother, a crude brother, and a father so detached he lives in the basement), his former lover and then a new one, and his job in a kindergarten where almost all the kids have rich but divorced parents. The absurd sophistication of these privileged and damaged children is played as satire—the parents of one child compete to pack his lunchbox with charcuterie patés and salads. Nevertheless, the pain of these young lives underlines how the coming baby will force George and Nina out of the haven they have found with each other. Their play marriage is a comedy of crossword puzzles and second-hand clothes, of ballroom dancing lessons at the Arthur Murray studio down the street—where the rhinestone-shod, Brooklyn-accented teacher pronounces ''dahnse'' like ''Ginger Rodgers in jodhpurs.''

''To be fond of dancing,'' remarks Jane Austen, ''was a certain step towards falling in love'' and, of course, toward getting

married. But the only wedding in George and Nina's future is that of his brother Frank—at which point the family's reaction to Nina's by-this-time obvious pregnancy brings into focus all the loneliness of the novel's enjoyable tapdance.

Perhaps it's a measure of how hard it is to dance the dark side, but George's feelings are not quite well enough lit by the jokes. Too often episodes stray into prime time comedy. There is, for example, the scene in George's childhood bedroom, when Frank comes in to have a fit about what his new in-laws will make of Nina's pregnancy. George responds to the angry opener, ''She's pregnant,'' as if Frank were referring to his own bride. This is diversionary, television humor: it covers for George's sadness rather than illuminating it.

Such shyness about showing the real soul beneath the actions drains energy from the novel and blunts the conclusion. The last scene suggests that relationships, like death, are a function of forces beyond our control, but George's struggle with universal forces has not clearly been at the center of this comedy. McCauley's hero is charming and funny, and the novel's complex story is very skillfully constructed. But some of that skill has gone into putting the reader off the scent. (pp. 24-5)

Patricia Vigderman, in a review of ''The Object of My Affection,'' in Boston Review, *Vol. XII, No. 2, April, 1987, pp. 24-5.*

An Excerpt from *The Object of My Affection: A Novel*

Melissa and I sent up our school day as a series of ten-to fifteen-minute activities and games and lessons, which we shuffled around like a deck of cards to keep the kids' attention as focused as possible. We swapped off the star turn so we'd still be functional by the end of the day. Ordinarily we'd start off with something rousing like a song session; we'd do a kindergarten classic such as ''A-way down south in the yankety yank, a bullfrog jumped from bank to bank . . .'' and then take requests. ''Like a Virgin'' and ''Tired of Being Blonde'' were two favorites. After that we'd go into the alphabet or a science project, then a story, then snack, more lessons, then lunch. Afternoons were mainly devoted to projects that required a lot of physical exertion—hammering and interpretive movement, for example. Most parents liked to pick up an exhausted child at the end of the day, one incapable of making too many demands on their free time.

Midway through the morning, as I sat at the front of the room reading aloud a story about a pig who moves to New York city to become an actress and ends up waiting tables, I broke out in uncontrollable yawns before the end of every sentence. Melissa sat on the floor at the back of the reading area staring off into space with one of the kids settled on her lap inquisitively running his hands over her bright red crew cut. Her eyes were glazed over as if I were boring her, too, into a stupor. By the time I'd read through half the story, the kids were wrestling and rolling around on the floor and bopping each other on the head with the Marimekko pillows scattered around for them to recline on.

''All right, all right,'' I said, putting aside the book. ''You need to be quiet, right now.'' It was standard practice throughout the school to express every disciplinary request as a matter of dire need. Unfortunately, most of the kids saw through the tactic and used it on each other. It wasn't uncommon to hear, "You need to give me that book, Bethanne, or I'll kill you," coming from the back of the room.

"You *need* to be quiet," I repeated, more harshly this time.

A little girl with waist-length blond hair and an elfin smile raced to the front of the room, put her hands on her hips, and said in a mocking and sarcastic tone, "You *need* to be quiet, class."

The kids shrieked with laughter and collapsed on each other in hysterics. Rose, the blonde, spun around in wild circles with her arms outstretched and her hair lashing against my chair.

"You need to sit down, Rose," I told her.

"You need a blood transfusion, George."

Rose's father was a prominent surgeon in Manhattan. She had a large medical vocabulary she used to diagnose the real and imagined ills of her classmates. She was a pretty girl who was probably destined for great beauty and success in life providing she wasn't ravaged by adolescent acne and eating disorders.

"Rose, dear," Melissa said, stirring herself from her coma, "this is kindergarten. This is not the Johns Hopkins Medical School, this is kindergarten. Try to keep that in mind."

"My father went to Johns Hopkins," one child intoned from beneath a pillow. "That's in Maryland."

"My mother went to Smith," another screamed.

"My mother *could* have gone to Smith but she went to Radcliff."

Within seconds the class turned into a shouting match. Parents' academic credentials and professional accomplishments were flying around the room like bullets. I didn't know what to do. For one thing, neither of my parents had gone to college, so I had nothing to contribute. I finally took them outside to the playground, hoping they'd exhaust themselves in the smoggy heat.

JOHN COTTER

Stephen McCauley does his darnedest to make a go of it with *The Object of My Affection.* His bright and brittle work does, in fact, have a lot going for it: wry-and-witty, thrust-and-parry writings; some entertaining characters; even-handed, humorous representation of gay life; telling shots at compulsive liberals; even the premise itself.

But he never quite succeeds because we never come to understand the relationship between George, a PhD dropout and now a hand-holding kindergarten teacher at a yuppie Manhattan school, and Nina Borowski, a striking blond psychologist who shares his penchant for strange foods, odd hours and minimal housekeeping.

McCauley draws a warm portrait of their easygoing affection— pigging out together on late-night desserts; calling out crossword-puzzle answers between bedrooms; dressing up and step-

ping on each other's toes at Arthur Murray dance classes; escaping to Coney Island. But he never reaches to the source of that affection.

And so George's struggle to reconcile his needs and life style with his loving affection for Nina doesn't so much end as subside, leaving the story wry and dry.

John Cotter, "A Good Soldier and Other Tales," in Book World—The Washington Post, *April 5, 1987, p. 10.*

ALICE H. G. PHILLIPS

The courtship in Stephen McCauley's first novel, *The Object of My Affection,* might have danced for ever around its crisis— never fulfilled but never a disappointment, either—since George is gay with no doubts about it, and his beautiful room-mate and best friend, Nina, prefers her men straight. Their mutual attraction and accommodation, as they continue to pursue less satisfactory relationships with other men, is, as narrated by George, utterly believable—eating pizza and watching figure-skating on television in bed together seems a warm way to spend a Saturday night. But the question behind their story is: knowing whom you care about and whom you like to sleep with, what kind of semi-permanent structures can you build?

Nina shakes the foundations of their cosy housekeeping arrangement among the rundown brownstones and overgrown back gardens of unfashionable Brooklyn when she gets pregnant by her boyfriend Howard (whom she thinks she loves but doesn't want to take care of or be taken care of by). Realizing, however, that the thought of a baby excites her more than anything has for years, she decides to become an unwed mother, and asks George if he will help. As she says, they don't have to get stuck playing conventional roles, the way she and Howard inevitably would (although Howard, a legal-aid lawyer, is as committed to equal sharing of child-care as he is to defending juvenile delinquents).

George, as it happens, likes children: in fact, he teaches infants at a smart Manhattan school, from whose rooms issue many of the book's funniest scenes and endearing insights. Despite some reservations, he agrees to play family with Nina. But as the months go by and he becomes involved with a man who has an adopted Salvadoran son, he comes to feel that the arrangement is neither entirely natural nor fair. It is a chaste, romantic dream, or, depending on how you look at it, a stilted version of the ideal American family that his own family failed to be. George consummates the relationship with Nina for a single night, stays until the baby is born, and then joins his lover Paul and Paul's child in Vermont. Paul's politically active mother, who has adopted Nina as her protégé, moves into George's old room and takes up the role of grandmother; Howard is a frequent caller.

This is a generous and gentle first novel, held together by its narrator's self-deprecating and yet confidently comic voice. Although it embraces failed lives, self-abasements and the disillusionments of gay love, it remains optimistic and funny (George on a rare visit to a bathhouse: "In three hours I'd taken two saunas, four showers and watched an educational film on sexual risk reduction in a TV lounge where they'd formerly shown porno tapes"). McCauley has not quite mastered the art of narrative tension, but his feeling for character is exact; except for George's former boyfriend, who vacuums walls, one would have liked to live longer with all of them.

Alice H. G. Phillips, "Unnatural Arrangements," in The Times Literary Supplement, No. 4406, September 11-17, 1987, p. 978.

JAY MICHAEL DICKSON

Stephen McCauley's recent book *The Object of My Affection* seems almost revolutionary for a novel about modern urban life from a new younger writer. Simon and Schuster is even billing the book (in almost a self-mockery of its publicity for Bret Easton Ellis' *Less than Zero* three years ago) as "a first novel that does *not* intend to be this generation's *Catcher in the Rye,* and a tale of New Yorkers that has not one scene in a club or boardroom." Although McCauley's storyline is every bit as contemporary and clever as that of many of his over-publicized literary peers (those whom *Vanity Fair* has dubbed "the young and the wasted"), his tone is decidedly different from that of the Jay McInerney/Tama Janowitz/Bret Easton Ellis/Jill Eisenstadt/*ad nauseum* set in that he eschews their jaded nihilism for a style both breezy and charming.

From the book's very first scene we have the sense of something refreshing in the book's tone that flouts our expectations for contemporary fiction. George Mullen and Nina Borowski, the story's protagonists, are getting dressed to go dancing at a New York nightclub—but, unlike what we might expect from characters in, say, a Jay McInerney story, George and Nina do not go out and snort Bolivian Marching Powder. Instead, they become "overheated and exhausted" from dressing, and stay in their Brooklyn apartment that night to snack on popcorn and beer and read trashy fifties-era mystery novels ("Four Gorgeous Gals," promises the cover of Nina's mystery "And Each of Them Spelled TROUBLE!").

This touch seems both delightfully human and realistic in its mundaneness. "I liked the idea," says McCauley, "of writing about ordinary lives—people living in ordinary circumstances." Yet McCauley's characters live in what can hardly be called "ordinary circumstances." Nina, who is finishing her psychology dissertation, finds herself pregnant by her insufferable boyfriend Howard, a legal-aid attorney who distressingly refers to her as "the Munchkin" or "the Butterbean." Finding Howard altogether impossible, Nina instead opts to have her baby with her gay roommate George—who is becoming involved with another man living in Vermont with his adopted son from Central America. (p. 14)

For McCauley, the real essence of his characters' lives seems to be their desire to construct new familial bonds in their lives. George's real need for love and a family is evident from his job teaching kindergarten in an upscale and trendy Manhattan school (replete with all-cotton futons covered with Marimekko sheets for naptime). George's explanation for why he took the job—"I'm a glutton for unqualified affection"—is of course key to the entire book. Despite McCauley's characterization of his book as a "silly, chatty, humorous novel," *The Object of My Affection* emerges as a thoughtful and complex study of the need for constructing a family in the eighties. As McCauley notes, none of the characters in the novel has a satisfying family life, "but that's what they all want. That's what we *all* want. I myself am spending my whole life trying to find that." George and Nina's quest for real affection and for setting down roots allows them to bend their individual politics to consider a life together, however impractical and unfruitful such a marriage may prove to be. But this desperate need for affection is dealt with gently, almost unobtrusively. Only when George goes

back with Nina to his home in Boston for his brother's wedding is he forced to consciously articulate the problems of relating to a family: his conservative brother, embarassed by Nina's obvious pregnancy and George's homosexuality, insists that the two pose as husband and wife for the wedding.

Suddenly, the issue of George's sexuality becomes an articulated problem in the novel. Before this, the issue has been treated almost tangentially, despite the obstacles it poses for George and Nina's relationship. George himself admits,

> I'd never considered my sexuality a problem. I'd never really considered it much at all. I'd always felt on the outside of everything in life, so I just took it as part of the package when I realized I couldn't care less about going all the way or any of the way with the girls I occasionally took to the movies.

George's coming out is treated with almost comic airiness, in contrast to the plethora of contemporary novels that deal with this issue in extensive detail (when confronted with his sexual identity by his mother, George blithely replies, "Well, as usual, Ma, you're right"). "I think there have been too many novels that deal with that theme," says McCauley, "and deal with it as if . . . the only way you can have gay characters is to deal extensively with their sexuality as an issue . . . somehow that's interpreted as politicizing the novel." (pp. 14-15)

McCauley's concerns seem to lie less with the politics of his characters and more with what he terms "the real humanity, the real essence of people's lives." Significantly, there are no truly unsympathetic characters in *The Object of My Affection;* even George's heel of an ex-boyfriend, Joley, is treated with compassion and levity. As George explains,

> Still, I loved him—or was childishly infatuated with his good looks and his false air of sophistication and his condescending attitude toward me, and later for all the unglamorous traits that lay beneath the thin fashion-plate veneer. Often, what's most attractive about a person is that part they're trying hardest to conceal, the part they think is least likable. You find out about it and it becomes a secret bond between you, something you never talk about but hold close to your heart and are continually touched by. . . .

Stephen McCauley's own ability to look past his characters' superficialities, despite his light and unpretentious style, and thus get at their "essences" makes him a rare writer indeed among his generation. He has written a first novel "contemporary" in its sociological details but singular in its concern with matters of the family and the heart. (p. 15)

Jay Michael Dickson, "A New Writer: Stephen McCauley," in The Harvard Advocate, Vol. CXXII, No. 1, November, 1987, pp. 14-15.

COMMENTS OF STEPHEN McCAULEY TO *CLC YEARBOOK*

Asked whether *The Object of My Affection* is autobiographical, McCauley responded: "The novel is autobiographical mainly in the sense that the narrator's view of people and the world is close to my own. . . . Any of my own experiences I used are set in a completely different context. I think the truth is that I became more like George, the narrator, as I wrote the book, rather than the reverse. I became very fond of him and wanted to emulate him.''

Discussing the inspiration for his writing, McCauley explained: "I want to write a novel about two people who love each other deeply, but are not exactly 'in love.' A love story in which the two main characters can never have a completely satisfying relationship no matter how important they are to each other. It seems to me most people I know are trying to make some sense of the new options available in life and love while feeling the pull of family and tradition and the past. I think I was inspired to write this novel by living in the middle of what feels like great emotional turmoil.''

Terry McMillan
1951-

American novelist.

Mama (1987) charts the turbulent course of a black American family through the 1960s and 1970s. Opening in a small industrial town in Michigan, the novel centers on Mildred Peacock, a poverty-stricken mother of five, as she struggles through adversity to provide the best for herself and her children.

Reviewers praise McMillan's realistic detail and the powerful characterization of her heroine, finding Mildred engaging in her energy and zest for life. Some critics found *Mama* flawed, citing uneven prose quality, lack of narrative focus, and heavy-handed sociological overtones; nevertheless, most consider McMillan a writer of promise.

© Jerry Bauer

PUBLISHERS WEEKLY

[In *Mama*] Mildred Peacock is broke and has no future prospects. She lives in a dilapidated house in a poverty-stricken Detroit suburb. She has a violently abusive, alcoholic husband who can't hold a job but keeps a mistress. She has five children, though she's only 27. She's black. One would think that a book about this woman's life would be dreary. The surprise of this accomplished first novel, however, is its zest and its extraordinarily positive portrayal of an impoverished family's struggle to overcome its problems. The book will be compared with Alice Walker's *The Color Purple*, partly because of the quality of its prose and partly because some of the thematic material—what it's like to be a poor, black woman in America—is similar. But where Walker's novel describes how things used to be, McMillan's narrative is firmly contemporary. *Mama* is a solid performance.

A review of "Mama," in Publishers Weekly, *Vol. 230, No. 22, November 28, 1986, p. 65.*

JANET BOYARIN BLUNDELL

Mama, a first novel, tells of a proud black woman, Mildred Peacock, and her five children. . . . Mildred's closest bond is to her oldest daughter, Freda, and their lives parallel each other's progress from despair to hope. The book's main weakness is that the author apparently could not decide what to leave out. She also has not decided who her audience is: at times she seems to be writing to blacks, at other times to be explaining things to naïve white readers. Although the story has power, it lacks focus and a clear point of view.

Janet Boyarin Blundell, in a review of "Mama," in Library Journal, *Vol. 112, No. 1, January, 1987, p. 108.*

DEBORAH G. ROBERTSON

Uneven pacing and obtrusive sociological commentary put considerable strain on first novelist Terry McMillan's [*Mama*]. On the other hand, we ultimately care about her characters—poor black residents of a small Michigan town. "Mama" Mildred raises her family of five very different children through several husbands and too many ups and downs to count. Her children grow up, marry, have their own children, and move across the country and back again. Mildred can't seem to settle down either. She's always looking for a better man, a better time, a little more money. She loves her kids, but she's so worn out she can hardly show it. Eventually all the kids and Mildred each show their best and worst sides, which makes them realistic and memorable. McMillan's got her finger on the way people act, even if the news isn't all good.

Deborah G. Robertson, in a review of "Mama," in Booklist, *Vol. 83, No. 9, January 1, 1987, p. 684.*

THE NEW YORKER

[*Mama* is a] tough novel about a tough family—one boy, four girls, and their mother—in a black suburb of Detroit. In 1964, few there have heard of Martin Luther King, and still fewer of Malcolm X. "What you know good?" is a demand for local news. Twenty-one years later, the children, scattered from coast to coast, "know bad," from rape to drug addiction; but they also know kindness, and some of them know college. . . . Terry McMillan has composed this, her first, novel in a sort of dialect—"thang" for "thing"—that is easy to read and rings true. There is a nicely ironic clash, near the end, between the mother's "What you dranking?" and one daughter's "I stopped drinking;" it says everything about how far the daughter has come, and why the mother must let her go.

A review of "Mama," in The New Yorker, *Vol. LXIII, No. 4, March 16, 1987, p. 104.*

An Excerpt from *Mama*

The kids were already on the sun porch watching Saturday morning cartoons when Mildred emerged from the bedroom. She had a diaper tied around her head and a new layer of pancake makeup on to camouflage the swelling. The kids didn't say anything about the purple patch of skin beneath her eye or her swollen lip. They just stared at her like she was a stranger they were trying to identify.

"What y'all looking at?" she said. "Y'all some of the nosiest kids I've ever seen in my life. Look at this house!" she snapped, trying to divert their attention. "It's a mess. Your daddy was drunk last night. Now I want y'all to brush your teeth and wash those dingy faces 'cause I ain't raising no heathens around here. Freda, make these kids some oatmeal. And I want this house spotless before you sit back down to watch a "Bugs Bunny" or a "Roadrunner," and don't ask me no questions about them dishes. Just pick 'em up and throw that mess away. Cheap dishes anyway. Weren't worth a pot to piss in. Next time I'm buying plastic."

The kids were used to Mildred giving them orders, didn't know any other way of being told what to do, thought everybody's mama talked like theirs. And although they huffed and puffed under their breath and stomped their feet in defiance and made faces at her when her back was turned, they were careful not to get caught. "And I want y'all to get out of this house today. Go on outside somewhere and play. My nerves ain't this"—she snapped her fingers—"long today. And Freda, before you do anything, fix your mama a cup of coffee, girl. Two sugars instead of one, and lots of Pet milk."

ELIZABETH ALEXANDER

Only a truly bodacious heroine could merit a book named *Mama*. Mildred Peacock, the sharp-tongued star of Terry McMillan's first novel, is up against financial straits and a brutal first husband, aptly named "Crook," the father of her five children. . . .

Mildred and her children—Freda, Angel, Bootsey, Doll, and Money—live in the depressed town of Point Haven, Michigan, where black folks work at the Diamond Crystal Salt Factory, or manufacture spark plugs at Prest-o-Lite, or clean white folks' homes, or don't work at all. Mildred's neighborhood is so ingrown that she has known Crook's mistress, Ernestine, since childhood. . . .

Mama opens when "most folks had never heard of Malcolm X," and finishes close to the present. During those years, Mildred struggles through single-motherhood, low cash, dependence on drink and "nerve pills," and a host of other problems. She sends Crook packing to Ernestine early on in the book, and the pages that follow describe her subsequent marriages, jobs (among them gambling-party hostess), attempts to outwit bill collectors, and efforts to raise her children right. Her successes are matched by disappointment; her son becomes addicted to heroin, and Mildred's own habits nearly kill her. McMillan romanticizes nothing, presenting Mildred not as a black "Mama" monolith but as a complex woman.

When the eldest girl, Freda, leaves home for work and school in California, the book's focus widens, comparing her life with her mother's. The narrative point of view, so far primarily Mildred's, moves more frequently to her now-grown children. Since Mildred is very much a mama, some of this shifting makes sense, but while the children are interesting, none is nearly so compelling as the mother. . . .

This book has Zora Neale Hurston's vernacular humor and John Irving's absurdity. McMillan is a master of black humor in both senses of the phrase. Her details and names are exact and telling, from Mildred's fake-fur house shoes to her stepmother, Miss Acquilla, sitting in front of her TV soaking her feet in a roasting pan and watching *The Price Is Right*. . . .

McMillan loves a simile, and those that work are dazzling, such as Mildred's description of her pregnant belly "swelled up like a small brown moon"—but not all of them work. McMillan also overdoes it with signposts for the changes of the 1960s through which her characters move. First there is pressed hair and platinum wigs, and then there are Afros; first there is liquor, then reefer, then heroin, and then cocaine. But these are minor distractions from McMillan's Mildred, who knows how and when to lie, loves her children fiercely, and would rather go to the Ebony Fashion Fair than on a tropical vacation.

Elizabeth Alexander, "Hot 'Mama'," in The Village Voice, *Vol. XXXII, No. 12, March 24, 1987, p. 46.*

MAUREEN FREELY

Mildred, in *Mama,* is black and seriously poor. . . .

Another heartwarming martyr story? Not quite. Mildred might be strict about household chores, but she also believes in having a good time. She drinks whisky out of a jam jar, mistrusts God, and she always makes sure she gets her man, one way or another. There is plenty of violence, too, much of it perpetrated by Mildred, who is also shameless about lying to debt-collectors and fiddling the taxman. Althoug her children benefit from the civil rights movement, they also inherit her fondness for the bottle and the wrong men. But like their mother, they are ferocious survivors of America's worst nightmare, and Terry McMillan tells their story with an unforgettable combination of compassion and sass.

Maureen Freely, "Croaking with Hideous Voices," in The Observer, *May 10, 1987, p. 20.*

KAMILI ANDERSON

Mildred Peacock, an undereducated, Black, single mother (divorced), is struggling to raise her five children in a harsh, northern urban environment. She suffers the stereotypical slings and arrows of poverty, anguish, and despair. Yet no one suffers more than the reader, for Terry McMillan's writing is as dismal and erratic as the lives of the characters she creates in her first novel, *Mama.*

The novel has no "hook," no outstanding or magical literary quality that might elevate it to the level of entertainment or rapture. The inauthentic, stilted dialogue and amateurish prose mar this story of lives on the brink, lives that elicit neither insight nor sympathy due to the author's lack of stylistic control. The characters come across as pitiable nobodies going nowhere fast, presented as they are without any of the embellishment that is required of even mediocre fiction. We are left to view them as vicious victims of the vicious cycles of poverty, ignorance, and poor judgment.

With irresponsible and often reckless abandon (for which McMillan, I presume, desires that we blame "the system"), Mildred neglects her children, save for an inconsistent concern for their material well-being. She repeatedly mispends her meager funds, then evades, with no particular style or flair, her creditors across the country. She is also addicted to any number of substances, as is her oldest daughter (who is allowed second voice in the story), and her hapless only son. Unsuccessful in her attempt to portray Mildred as the tough, stoic, resourceful, Black woman—doing what she gotta do—McMillan instead creates a character for whom a reader—even one not in search of his or her "mother's garden"—would be hard pressed to feel compassion for. *Mama* makes you want to cry "Uncle."

Kamili Anderson, in a review of "Mama," in Belles Lettres: A Review of Books by Women, *Vol. 3, No. 1, September-October, 1987, p. 9.*

CHRIS GORDON OWEN

Mama, the title character of Terry McMillan's novel, is an uneducated, glass-slinging, pill-popping, drink-guzzling woman with a chain of ex-husbands, former homes in Michigan and California, tribulations and frustrations galore, and five children whom she adores and screams at, throws out of the nest and welcomes back. We stay with the family until the oldest daughter, a writer and graduate student, has reached a new acceptance of Mama, excesses and all. The novel's loose structure may reveal an autobiographical thread woven into the material, but McMillan's affection for her characters holds the novel together despite its sloppiness. Or does it hold together because of the sloppiness, the downright vigor of life?

Chris Gordon Owen, "First Novels Play with Classic Themes," in New Directions for Women, *Vol. 16, No. 5, September-October, 1987, p. 17.*

Lawrence Osborne

1958-

English novelist.

Set in Europe during and after World War II, *Ania Malina* (1987) relates the story of a hospitalised British soldier who becomes obsessed with a fellow patient, a young French-Polish girl. Brought back together after the war, the two wander across southern Europe, enmeshed in their strange and mutually debilitating relationship.

Critics cite *Ania Malina*'s richly textured, complex prose as the novel's most striking feature, praising Osborne's evocative imagery and technical skill. Also noteworthy are the novel's slow-paced sensuality and air of pervasive gloom, which, according to critic Allen Joseph, make "this hauntingly elliptical novel . . . a strikingly mature and self-contained metaphor for modern alienation."

KIRKUS REVIEWS

Ambitious and densely textured first novel [*Ania Malina*] about the doomed love of an Englishman for a young Polish girl after WW II.

Jamie Lovecraft, at 28, is wounded in France in the closing days of the war; and in a hospital in Laon he meets the 16-year-old Ania, herself badly injured during a bombing, and falls in love with her beauty and precocious innocence. Ania's father is dead (he was French), and her Polish mother temporarily disappears in the end-of-war chaos; in result . . . Lovecraft becomes Ania's lover-guardian as he embarks upon his aimless and disillusioned life as a postwar expatriate. Intellectual but world-weary, and touched—symbolically?—by disease (there are hints of thyroid, hints of heart), Lovecraft suffers with the pain of the doting older man as Ania entertains younger suitors, though she stays with Lovecraft as he finds rooms in cheaper and cheaper Paris hotels. . . .

The wounded, doomed world here is rendered in prose sometimes slow but more often brocade-rich; the prevailing mood of decadence and loss are caught often in cinematically-perfected moments that please the eye as much as the ear—and that linger. However derivative in texture or plot—or in the character of the worldly but despairing Lovecraft—the execution here is unsurpassable.

A review of "Ania Malina," in Kirkus Reviews, *Vol. LV, No. 7, April 1, 1987, p. 506.*

PUBLISHERS WEEKLY

Set in battle-scarred Europe during and immediately after World War II, this intriguing first novel [*Ania Malina*] deals with a man's obsession with a younger woman. While convalescing in a French hospital, British soldier Jamie Lovecraft meets Ania Malina, a hospitalized Polish girl. Letters to his sister mention Ania only briefly at first, but later dwell obsessively on the girl and her physician, Dr. Kessler. As the story shifts seamlessly into first-person narrative—first by Jamie, later by Ania—Jamie is discharged and moves to Paris. Re-introduced to Ania by Kessler, he finds that the young woman's existence now centers on dancing and drinking. The more shabbily she treats Jamie, the stronger his preoccupation grows. The sensual imagery (which occasionally verges on the grotesque), pervasive sense of doom and lacings of French may limit the novel's appeal somewhat, but its polished prose and fine characterizations merit attention.

A review of "Ania Malina," in Publishers Weekly, *Vol. 231, No. 19, May 15, 1987, p. 267.*

SHELLEY COX

The horrors of war and the complexities of obsessive love color this short but ornate first novel [*Ania Malina*]. James Lovecraft, a wounded British soldier, meets Ania, a teenaged, Polish-French refugee, while both are recuperating in a French hospital in 1945. Entranced, and believing her an orphan; Jamie seduces her, and the two begin a tour of the Mediterranean that is increasingly threatened by Ania's bizarre behavior. By switching his narrators, Osborne eventually reveals the tormented soul within the enigmatic Ania, seen by others as a Lolita-like temptress. Though flawed by overwriting and too-precious imagery, the work shows a promising subtlety and talent.

Shelley Cox, in a review of "Ania Malina," in Library Journal, *Vol. 112, No. 11, June 15, 1987, p. 86.*

MERLE RUBIN

[In *Ania Malina*, Lawrence Osborne] is intent on understanding the relationship between the past and the present and on finding ways to express the contradictory, but equally "real" realities of war and peace, love and hate, dislocation and restoration. . . . [The] novel focuses on a woman with a mysterious past who seems to symbolize or embody the unknown. . . .

[In *Ania Malina*,] as feminist critics may note, we find the standard "male" practice of writing about women as objects—not just sex objects, but objects of knowledge, to be investigated, explored, and understood. Yet much can be learned from such explorations, even if what is finally learned is the impossibility of truly "mastering" any body of knowledge.

Ania Malina is a hypnotic, beautifully written, painterly book that broods on themes from Nabokov (obsession with a "nymphet") and Thomas Mann (the links between eros and thanatos;

the aesthetic appeal of illness). The story begins in a French field hospital in 1944, when Jamie Lovecraft, a sensitive young British soldier recovering from an injury, becomes fascinated by a fellow patient, a blond girl who reminds him of his younger sister. When the mysterious Dr. Kessler considers them well enough to be discharged, Jamie and Ania begin the nomadic odyssey that takes them from ever-cheaper Paris hotels to the Italian lakes and finally to a Polish sanatorium.

For most of the book, we see Ania through Jamie's eyes: She seems passive, unfathomable, like a painting or puzzle that he tries to unravel. She is first seen as the victim of an air raid, then as the victim of a lingering malady—and, in some sense, a victim of Jamie and the doctor, who ''define'' her as an invalid—later as the all but immobilized, bandaged victim of the doctor's medical/erotic interest, and finally, as the victim of something she knows. And yet, her knowledge of a horrifying wartime experience proves she is not merely the passive creature she appears to be. Ania is not merely a pretty girl, poring over the glossy magazines Jamie brings her, trying to emulate models and movie stars. Beneath the surface are depths that Jamie suspects but never really sees, depths of memory and imagination that doom this frail girl, whose nickname ''Ania Malina'' means pineapple raspberry, to a knowledge that is more than she can bear. All is revealed at the novel's conclusion, a *tour de force* in which horror is transformed into art, and art enables us to better comprehend horror. . . .

[*Ania Malina*] is a novel about universals—war and peace, love and death.

> Merle Rubin, *"Europe, Mystery and Women in Flight from War,"* in Los Angeles Times Book Review, *September 20, 1987, p. 8.*

An Excerpt from *Ania Malina*

By the time she had risen it would sometimes be nine o'clock. Already three hours would have been wasted. I would commence my breakfast again and take care to relish—it was the normal compensation—the resistant cluster of curls like bunches of grapes that swung down to the level of her collar-bone. I would watch, with routine pleasure, her fingers curl around the Chinese jug to lift it over the coffee, the weary partition of her section of the loaf, the timid sips, the methodical collection of fragments of crust that had fallen on to her dressing-gown. But even this nervous domesticity took months to achieve. It was not easy. At first I was tender with her. In our first room I brought smouldering almond croissants to her bed every morning enfolded in transparent tissues. I would tear off the wings and immerse them in coffee (she liked them damp and semi-bitter), feeding her as they feed baby whales. Or else it was *madelaines, coeurs de pamiers, chaussons aux pommes* and miniature *tartes tatins* which crumbled over her chin and broke into a buttery dust that stuck to the grease on her lips. Later in the day I would encounter these flakes at the back of her mouth and the taste of butter on her fingers. They made her lips sweet and rancid and even at night her mouth made me think of a baker's oven. I laid winter irises by her coffee. Even at the hospital I had found blue anemones, chicory and cornflowers. I was a serious romantic with blue flowers, absolving a centaur's guilt.

This peaceful and humble breakfast ritual began in our first room in the rue Cécile. The room itself was an abomination, combining the profane and the divine by its proximity to the shabby Gothic church of Ste Cécile, adorned with living gargoyles of tramps slumbering on its ledges, and the fruit-like cupola of the Comptoir National d'Escompte de Paris, which cast a beam of shining pride—in the form of a golden pineapple—into the depth of our darkness. Here there was a balcony where Ania could display her elbows to the street and where she could lean from our haughty tower and shake out her hair as if she had risen from bed behind Japanese screens, in the perfume of laziness, in a private order of faithful cats and whispering maids. Behind her would lie newspapers filled with crumbs, and a purple lampshade over the bed would make visible, with a dry light, the detritus of a full moon's pleasure. The walls were lime-coloured lawns of imitation velvet and the cheap metal of the fixtures—door handles, light switches, towel rails—was cold under the fingers. The plastic tiles, like a vast photographic jigsaw of a parquet floor, were cracked and curled up savagely at the corners. The first night we slept there, I saw her mouth quiver at the sight of the flames of mould flowing downward from the painfully visible complex of pipes. Her eyes sought out the source of each river of corruption. He gaze dilated with disbelief: my promises had been a lie.

Yet it is impossible to overcome with disdain the importance of these temporary habitations. I had no nostalgia for my father's English house, dull-red as the blood on a butcher's counter, spreading endless banal roots into his soil as if afraid of the speed of the earth's rotation, heavy as a bull's flanks and still with chill nobility. The hotel room has no history, it is destructible, assembled from scraps and pieces of string. It has no reality in terms of memory and custom, which is why I embraced it. From our balcony I looked down with detached contempt at the yellow crockets and spire-lights of Ste Cécile, clustered together to preserve a vagrant power. And from the Brésil I felt myself raised above the fundamental alimentary commerce and the congestion of voices. In every room it has been the same . . . in the rue Thimonnier, in the rue Greneta, in the rue Marie-Stuart, the rue Riboutté, the rue de la Tour d'Auvergne, in the avenue Trudaine . . . shifting stage-prop bedrooms. The greased pipes and shabby photographic illusions of the Hôtel du Brésil summarized a domain of which we were the children. I saw my chains holding me to this world, spun out of warm sheets, crumbs of sweet pastry and the loaves laid with exquisite solemnity cross-wise like swords upon the tables. . . .

ALLEN JOSEPHS

On the surface [*Ania Malina*] is the story of an English soldier's fascination with a young Polish refugee. In late 1944, Jamie Lovecraft (age 28) discovers Ania Januszewska (age 15) in a French hospital near the small town of Laon where he is recuperating from an eye wound, she from a bombing that broke her leg. Their bizarre relationship is no ordinary love story, however; nor is this an ordinary first novel.

Lovecraft, who narrates the events, tells us the Polish girl keeps a diary about her prewar past entitled "Ania Malina," "her real and baby name put together to create a writer different from herself, a woman still merged with, drowned in, her childhood." Ania is the constant center of his attention and the obsessive focal point of the novel. Yet we learn very little about this mysterious girl since she remains an engima to the narrator, and the brilliance of his observations about her reflects from her opaqueness the way bright light bounces from a mirror. By the end of Lovecraft's narrative neither he nor the reader has entered Ania's hermetic world. Instead we are left to ponder the nature of Lovecraft's peculiar fascination with her.

His narrative is divided into four sections, the first of which, "Unsent Letters," is a series of esoteric, detached epistles to Lovecraft's sister, relating his acquaintance with Kessler, the Swiss doctor at Laon, who seems to have an ambiguous relationship to Ania, and his own enchantment with the young girl. Like many things in this novel, the reason these baroque letters are unsent (and if unsent why written) is never explained.

In "L'Hôtel du Brésil," the second section, Lovecraft abruptly abandons the epistolary mode and switches into standard first person, recounting his reunion with the wayward Ania in Paris after the war, and explaining how he eventually persuades her (by bribing her with gifts and alcohol) to live with him. He comes to think of her as his "adopted child," and tells us, "I could not resist keeping her once the bond was formed."

Since Lovecraft had been cut off financially by his father, he and Ania live in the sordid Hôtel du Brésil. Although he once calls her "the woman I loved," we see little affection between them. She insults him, dances with younger men in cheap bars, escapes from him and runs away all night with a sailor. Finally Dr. Kessler gives Lovecraft money to take her away.

Lovecraft takes Ania to Italy. Awkward and out of place, they descend gradually by train into the ever more violent south. In Naples Ania vomits blood. In Volterra she develops a dry cough and begins rewriting her diary, "the part of her life that had vanished." She admits to him that she has a mysterious sickness (which seems rather unmysteriously like tuberculosis); informs him she is "lunatique"; and coughs up "flowers of blood on her pillow . . . a dark, rich lung-blood".

In "The Eye of the Sea," Ania has come to a sanatorium in the Polish mountains. Lovecraft visits frequently, believing he "was still a saviour," even though her illness has gotten worse. She also has violent outbursts and lapses of memory, and at times must be forcibly restrained. It is unclear whether she is insane, unstable or merely rebellious. At any event, Lovecraft continues adoringly to observe her and futilely to paint her portrait in words time and again. In the end, his efforts come to naught: Ania swallows pieces of a broken plate and dies. No trace of her is left, in his closing words, to betray "the passing of an ephemeral inhabitant."

The closing section is called "Part Two: Ania Malina," but in fact these entries from her diary seem more like an appendix. Written in the sanatorium, they recount her treatment after the bombing, including daily sexual manipulation by Dr. Kessler, and her days in Paris with Lovecraft, in whose company she "felt lonely." The last entry relates the horrible sufferings of her cousin Piotr, who was burned, then shot and left for dead by the Germans in Warsaw. He survives and is told to lie still and wait, something she is finally unable to do.

Ania Malina is an unusual first novel on two levels. Lawrence Osborne is not afraid to make Lovecraft, whose name is clearly ironic, at times intentionally pedantic and tedious. The richness and self-conscious virtuosity of Lovecraft's prose expose a character whose sterile intellectual brilliance has no emotional counterpart. On a deeper level this hauntingly elliptical novel becomes a strikingly mature (Mr. Osborne was born in 1958) and self-contained metaphor for modern alienation. Often what is missing tells us more than what is said.

Allen Josephs, "In Love with a 'Lunatique'," in The New York Times Book Review, *October 18, 1987, p. 52.*

H(arry) F. Saint

1941-

American novelist and short story writer.

Saint, a New York businessman turned writer, set his first novel, *Memoirs of an Invisible Man* (1987), in the world of Wall Street. Saint's protagonist Nick Halloway, a small-time securities analyst, has been made invisible by a nuclear blast and is fleeing from Federal agents who want to exploit his condition. *Memoirs* details the comical and frightening reeducation of Nick as he manages his daily existence and finds his invisibility useful in getting stock market tips.

Critics praise Saint's imaginative exploration of the state of invisibility, although some note that he treats the subject in excessive detail. The author's cynical insider's view of high finance has received particular praise. With few reservations, reviewers find the novel's plot entertaining and suspenseful, the characterizations and dialogue realistic, and the situations humorous.

PUBLISHERS WEEKLY

In Saint's heralded first novel [*Memoirs of an Invisible Man*], the tired plot of the film *The Invisible Man* undergoes a sparkling update. A clash between a scientist and an antinuclear demonsrator at a nuclear energy plant catalyzes an explosion that renders Nick Halloway, a securities analyst, invisible. Realizing that he will become a caged, scrutinized guinea pig if he surrenders to federal intelligence agents, Nick makes a run for his freedom. Saint has hit on a wonderful narrative device: insert one fantastic premise into the life of a Yuppie, but keep the rest of his world functional and, therefore, challenging. Nick displays the distinct sensibilities of a fugitive and a Wall Street smart guy as he invisibly fends for himself in the jungles he knows best—the East Side of Manhattan and the trader's desk. Unerringly incorporating both humor and poignancy, with dialogue that rings absolutely true and suspense sustained at high pitch throughout, this supple fantasy attends so cleverly to plausible elements that it entertains from beginning to end.

A review of "Memoirs of an Invisible Man," in Publishers Weekly, Vol. 231, No. 8, March 6, 1987, p. 102.

CHRISTOPHER LEHMANN-HAUPT

Is there anyone alive who hasn't dreamed of being invisible? Many writers have, too, from Plato to H. G. Wells to J.R.R. Tolkien. But to judge from [*Memoirs of an Invisible Man*] . . . , there's still plenty of life in the fantasy that one fine day a certain character wakes up to find he has disappeared. . . .

© Jerry Bauer

[H. F. Saint] explores the state . . . conscientiously—the problems of walking down stairs, clearing one's throat in public, watching one's food get digested or being, as in the case of Nick Halloway, the memoirist of Mr. Saint's novel, the only human specimen available for government study.

The result is any number of impressive effects, most spectacularly the zone of invisibility produced by the accident. This area includes a two-story house that special government agents must delineate with colored wire to explore its disappeared interior—a visual effect that alone should justify the forthcoming film version of the book.

Naturally, these agents don't want to lose poor Nick, and just as naturally, Nick doesn't want to end up their guinea pig. So they chase and he runs, and for two-thirds of the novel we chew our nails as Nick is driven from his Manhattan brownstone to various men's clubs and then to a succession of temporarily vacant East Side apartments. Actually, this goes on a little too long as halfway through the book we begin to wonder why Nick doesn't take the offensive and do what he inevitably ends up doing a hundred pages later.

But the details are by and large so plausible, especially the psychology of Nick's isolation and his observations of others when they think they are alone. And the prose is so elegantly knowing, particularly the sport it makes of the Wall Street types who inadvertently help Nick out of his pickle. Despite a couple of clumsy plotting maneuvers, *Memoirs of an Invisible Man* sustains our interest to the end. . . .

Mr. Saint elicits the sometimes brutish contingency of social life in New York City. Once Nick Halloway disappears, the very least of his problems is cutting himself off from friends and business colleagues. The crushing loneliness he feels as he goes unseen from one cocktail party to another cannot be so different from that of many people who are plain to the eye.

Mr. Saint even suggests a psychological rationale for cheating the stock market by trading on inside information, as Nick ends up doing to save himself. All such people may want is simply not to be invisible.

Christopher Lehmann-Haupt, in a review of "Memoirs of an Invisible Man," in The New York Times, *April 2, 1987, p. C24.*

STANLEY TRACHTENBERG

Invisibility . . . proves more of a disability than an advantage to Nick Halloway, a securities analyst intent on both sex and stock market opportunities in H. F. Saint's carefully plotted first novel, *Memoirs of an Invisible Man.* Hoping to find both at a small company involved in nuclear fusion, he is changed to an altered state in the time-honored manner; he is the victim of a laboratory explosion.

Almost at once, Nick finds himself pursued by a team of government intelligence agents, headed by a ruthless colonel almost as faceless as his quarry. With a limited supply of invisible objects salvaged from the accident, Nick heads for New York, where he lives precariously in men's clubs and vacant apartments while he attempts to invent a new identity literally out of thin air.

Resourceful in eluding an adversary with seemingly limitless resources of its own, Nick turns to the stock market, where he manages to amass a fortune as the ultimate inside trader. His manipulations provide a wry picture of the manic pressures which, he becomes aware, lead investment banking to mean anything that can be done in a suit.

Only when the focus on logistics shifts to a conspiracy thriller, however, does the novel pick up suspense. Nick discovers a rogue operation protected by highly placed government figures who care little about cost and less about success or failure. Their only concern is avoiding public scrutiny.

Despite his occasional wisecracks and the unequal odds which make Nick more sympathetic than the agents chasing him, there is not much moral difference between them. As a result, it is hard to care what happens to him until he meets and falls in love with Alice Barlow. More vulnerable, Nick becomes more human.

Necessarily overheard more than visualized, Nick's encounters present a problem in narration as well as survival. Like the shoppers who stumble across him on a Bloomingdale's escalator, we keep bumping into things we can't see. More reassuring than scary, our screams, like the ending of this cheerful entertainment, are not less satisfying for being predictable.

Stanley Trachtenberg, "Invisible Men: Although They Are out of Sight, They Possess Uncanny Insight," in Chicago Tribune—Books, *April 12, 1987, p. 7.*

GARRETT EPPS

Nick Halloway, protagonist of *Memoirs of an Invisible Man,* tells us that he could have titled his autobiography "Memoirs of a Securities Analyst." To judge by the hoopla surrounding the book—on the book flap, we learn that *Memoirs* "has already been acquired for translation into ten foreign languages and will be made into a major motion picture by Warner Brothers"—the Wall Street angle has made this first novel a success. Being invisible, you see, lets Nick slip into corporate suites and learn about pending mergers and takeover bids; he then calls his broker (needless to say, he has never seen him) and buys the stock.

But in fact, there's disappointingly little about arbitrage in *Memoirs.* This book is an action thriller, written by someone who's thought a good deal about what it would mean to be invisible and who has a reasonable imagination for action and, equally important, for unusual sex scenes.

Nick Halloway is 35, an analyst with a New York brokerage firm. He is unmarried, with a bachelor apartment on East 88th Street in New York, and is enamored of Anne Epstein, a *New York Times* reporter whose sex appeal is exceeded only by her humorless ambition. Nick lures Anne into the New Jersey countryside, ostensibly to witness a demonstration of the latest in nuclear fusion containment techniques. He's planning a tryst at a country inn; she has in mind an exposé of the nuclear power industry.

Student radicals (apparently, in H. F. Saint's imagination, these still exist) disrupt the lab's electric power supply, and in the ensuing explosion, a small chunk of Jersey real estate, and Nick, are rendered completely invisible.

Government agents are soon pursuing Nick to use him for espionage. He survives at first by sneaking into Manhattan men's clubs after hours (the book's most memorable image is of the empty place in the dark waters that marks Nick's passage during a late-night swim); then by living in apartments left by vacationing New Yorkers. To fund his escape, Nick opens a brokerage account and begins his career in insider trading. . . .

But the agents, led by a relentless spook in his way as invisible as Nick, are still after him. Nick seeks refuge with Alice Barlow, a beautiful artist who believes she is having an affair with a ghost. (In the book's most memorable sex scene, the two grapple in a cab; the driver watches astonished as his female fare appears to make love to the empty air.) When the bad guys capture Alice, Nick must find a way to free her and begin a new life outside Manhattan.

All in all, it's an exciting story, cinematic and suspenseful, and I am looking forward to that "major motion picture." But Saint has transformed this entertaining plot into a remarkably boring book.

To begin with, Nick himself is a distinctly dull dog. Saint revels in letting us know what a cipher he has chosen for a hero: "probably most people found me a bit boring," Nick says early in the book. This is confirmed later when Nick eavesdrops on friends who believe he's left the Street to join the Hare Krishnas. "I defy anyone to name an interesting fact about Nick," says one. "That's pretty much the whole point of Nick."

Nick, being invisible, is suddenly a figure of great interest to those who know he's alive. But an invisible bore is still a bore. Nick's major interest (far more absorbing, so to speak, than Wall Street) seems to be his own digestive processes, about which he tells us far too much. But then, Nick tells us far too much about everything, which brings up the second major flaw in *Memoirs*. It seems not to have been edited at all. The suspenseful plot is all but buried in flabby, repetitious verbiage.

The pervasive sogginess is more glaring because Saint has explicitly invited comparison to H. G. Wells. Remember Griffin, the eponym of Wells' *Invisible Man*? . . . By comparison, Nick Halloway is a nebbish, and the only pity I felt was for the wretches who must translate this soggy pudding of a book into 10 foreign tongues.

> Garrett Epps, *"Disappearing Act on Wall Street,"* in Book World—The Washington Post, *May 3, 1987, p. 7.*

An Excerpt from *Memoirs of an Invisible Man*

I learned from a telephone call to the Social Security Administration that I would have to "come in in person" for an interview, bringing "an original birth certificate and two means of identification." The nearest office was on East Fifty-eighth Street. I went in—"in person"—although I had nothing to bring and knew I would do badly in an interview. It turned out to be on the twelfth floor, which for me meant trudging up eleven flights of stairs. The office itself was a single large room, one end of which had been more or less fenced off with a metal desk and several racks of pamphlets to serve as a waiting room. There were two rows of decrepit metal chairs, on which half a dozen people sat staring aimlessly into space. Waiting, probably, for their names to be called.

I went around behind the racks into the main office area, where there were fifteen or twenty drab grey metal desks, positioned at random on the linoleum floor. There were very few people applying for social security cards, and most of them were aliens or minors, so that it took me several hours to figure out the whole procedure for processing applications. The applicant would hand in his completed application together with his birth certificate and "evidence of identity" and wait to be called for an interview. After the interview, which seemed to serve no function at all in the process, the interviewer, having noted the documentation provided, would sign and stamp the application. The application form then made its very gradual way to one of two women seated in front of computer terminals, and the information was keyed in and transmitted directly to a central computer somewhere in Maryland. The application form itself was then placed in a folder where it was held for several weeks before being forwarded for permanent filing at yet another office in Pennsylvania. I spent most of the morning watching the women at the terminals, paying particular attention when they signed off for lunch and then signed on again afterward.

At five minutes after five, when the room was entirely empty, I switched on one of the terminals and logged on, typing in the same password and information I had seen one of the women use in the afternoon. I called up the format for entering a new name into the system and typed in "Jonathan B. Crosby." That would be different enough from "John R. Crosby" that I would be able to pick out my mail, but not so different as to invite comment from the postman or building staff. I entered the Fifth Avenue address and gave myself a birth date that made me exactly twenty-one that day—old enough to allow me to establish accounts but young enough to make plausible my lack of a credit record.

Jonathan B. Crosby's newly assigned social security number appeared on the screen, and I committed it to memory. Happy Birthday, Jonathan.

DAVID FINKLE

Updating H. G. Wells's *Invisible Man* to the 1980's, so that the protagonist is the victim of an accident at a particle physics experimental laboratory, is a clever idea. Making the invisible hero a securities analyst pursued by a relentless Government agent in a book published during the year of Dennis Levine, Ivan Boesky and the musical blockbuster *Les Misérables* is positively prescient.

Who, a reader wonders, is this H. F. Saint, and how does he come, in *Memoirs of an Invisible Man,* his first novel, to tap so directly into the *Zeitgeist*?

A partial answer is that he is a man with a droll sense of humor. The newly vanished hero, Nick Halloway, supposing momentarily that he has become a ghost, reflects, "To haunt New Jersey through the ages seemed an odd doom." Mr. Saint is also observant about the Manhattan setting; Nick notes, "I have experimentally determined that in every refrigerator between Eighth Street and Ninety-sixty Street there is at all times a bottle of champagne." And the author, a businessman, knows about investing and is handy with timely cynicism on the subject; Nick thinks, "The investment banks perform all sorts of interesting services and acts—in fact, any service that can be performed in a suit, this being the limitation imposed by their professional ethics."

In addition, Mr. Saint has read not only Wells but also Kafka's *Metamorphosis* and a substantial number of existential novels. Furthermore, he has seen the science fiction classic *The Incredible Shrinking Man* and probably, some time back, listened regularly to *The Shadow*—"Who knows what evil lurks in the hearts of men?" Nick asks at one point. It is this mismatched bibliography that keeps *Memoirs of an Invisible Man* from being the knockout adventure the setup leads the reader to expect. Mr. Saint never seems to have decided exactly which of Nick Halloway's literally and figuratively invisible antecedents is the right role model—or maybe he did, choosing for too much of the novel the wrong ones for the wrong reasons. The tip-off comes early when Nick, becoming accustomed to invisibility, concludes, "Rather than a magical state of extraordinary freedom, it would be a series of tedious practical problems."

Invisibility as a symbol can be a metaphor for liberation or limitation, and in choosing to make the dehumanizing limits society imposes on the population the point he emphasizes, Mr. Saint picks the shallower and drearier thesis. Nick, at times with the aid of two of the dumbest women to have shown up in literature in a couple of decades, repeatedly takes refuge in those lairs of the faceless upper class, luxury apartments and men's clubs. . . .

Only when the novel is rounding to a close does Nick think, "My mistake was that I was always running, always retreating passively out of their way." It is also Mr. Saint's mistake. If only, as the invisible author behind Nick Halloway, he had given his charaacter the occasional surreptitious goose.

David Finkle, *"Escape from a Men's Club," in* The New York Times Book Review, *May 10, 1987, p. 15.*

WENDY BRANDMARK

Until an accident at a nuclear fusion lab in New Jersey turned him into a living ghost, Nick Halloway [in H. F. Saint's ***Memoirs of an Invisible Man***] led an ordinary life as a securities analyst in New York. He was a rather shallow man whose relationships were short-lived, whose goals were material, whose one risk was the attempted seduction of a young journalist on an empty commuter train. After the accident, his body still exists; he can be touched, heard but not seen. . . .

Nick's difficulties as an invisible fugitive force him to re-evaluate his old life. Moving unseen among his old friends, he learns what they think of him and sees, as an outsider, the sordidness of the world of stockbrokers and security analysts, the world he once accepted as his own. His freedom, even his intimacy with women, everything he once took for granted, are threatened by the power of the state. Nick never completely defeats his pursuers, but he wins our respect. He discovers his humanity when he loses sight of his body.

Part thriller, part comedy, part science fiction, this is a compelling, often frightening novel. H. F. Saint makes the bizarre condition of his hero believeable through skilful use of detail and a dry, matter-of-fact style which translates the fantastic to the everyday: Nick must plan his meals carefully, for the digestion of his food can actually be seen; he develops a strategy for getting into revolving doors; he learns to cope with invisible eyelids. Through Nick's invisible eyes, the commonplace becomes fascinating, and we gain a fresh vision of a familiar world. (p. 23)

Wendy Brandmark, *"'Tell Him I Can't See Him'," in* The Listener, *Vol. 118, No. 3020, July 16, 1987, pp. 23-4.*

Glenn Savan
19??-

American novelist.

White Palace (1987) is a contemporary love story with a Pygmalian theme, in which issues of social class and class mobility define and shape a love affair. Max, a recently widowed young advertising copywriter, develops an inexplicable passion for Nora, a middle-aged, uneducated waitress who personifies every characteristic he dislikes. As their relationship progresses, Max and Nora struggle with his contemptuous superiority and her insecurity in their attempt to find a common ground.

Some reviewers have expressed unease with the characterization of Nora, finding Savan's broad class and sex stereotypes condescending; others observe that Max's growing understanding and affecetion for Nora presents her in increasingly sympathetic and realistic terms. Critics praise Savan for his narrative skills, noting that the novel's engaging plot and energetic delivery make for an absorbing and enjoyable read.

© Jerry Bauer

JOHN MUTTER

[In *White Palace*] Max Baron, a 27-year-old advertising copywriter in St. Louis, meticulously mourns his wife, Janey, a Jewish-American Princess who died two years earlier in a car accident. Prissy, educated and insular, Max is astounded when he falls in love with Nora, a "middle-aged woman who worked at a White Palace (read White Castle) and lived in a house as filthy as his mother's, who pronounced insurance with the accent on the first syllable, who harbored lost bags of pork rinds under the cushions of her sofa, and who, as far as he could tell, he didn't even like." But Nora is great in bed (unlike Janey) and has a knack for getting to the nub of issues. At first, there is an uncomfortable sense that Max is slumming, but then his obsession with Nora takes a human turn and his life is altered drastically. There is a strangely '50s feel to this book (Max and his friends drink Scotch, say "for chrissakes" and watch home slides), and Savan leaves few thoughts and feelings to the imagination. But the fast-paced narrative and the satisfying ending make for a fun read.

John Mutter, in a review of "White Palace," in Publishers Weekly, *Vol. 231, No. 18, May 8, 1987, p. 66.*

MICHIKO KAKUTANI

An isolated man or woman who is offered the possibility of renewed communion with the world through the redemptive powers of love—variations on this theme have played leading roles in works by writers as disparate as Shakespeare, Hawthorne and the creators of the screwball romances of the 1930's

and 40's. In each case, arrogance, intellectual pride or simple hardheartedness must be unlearned if tragedy is to be averted; wisdom and spiritual insight are gained only in the wake of much confusion and self-doubt.

Max Baron, an up-and-coming advertising man in *White Palace,* Glenn Savan's absorbing first novel. . . , is just such a hero. On first meeting, he's an overly fastidious young man, aggressively rational and more than a little uptight—in one friend's words, "Mr. Moderation-in-Everything." As a child, growing up poor in northern St. Louis, Max used to chide his slovenly mother on her messy housekeeping—"it had been Max who ran the vacuum cleaner, Max who scrubbed the floors"—and he has since blossomed into a first-class yuppie fussbudget. He has a watering schedule for his plants; lines up his Oriental rug flush with the cracks in the hardwood floor, and adheres to a rigorous reading regime of Shakespeare, Tolstoy and Twain.

Though it has been two years since his beautiful wife, Janey, died in a car accident, Max remains obsessively devoted—constantly rerunning memories of their marriage in his mind and declaring that he has "made a conscious decision to be celibate for a while."

"You're turning into that crazy old woman in Dickens," one of his friends tells him, "the one who just sits there in her rotten wedding dress staring at her rotten wedding cake." Indeed, at the age of 27, Max has become "a prematurely aged little old man."

Then, of course, something happens: Max meets a new woman—a waitress in the local White Palace hamburger joint. At 41, Nora seems an unlikely mate for someone of Max's tastes and background: unlike Janey, she's uneducated, poorly dressed and ill-mannered. She lives in a filthy shack littered with garbage and soiled clothes, and spends her free time reading *Cosmopolitan* and books on Marilyn Monroe.

Given our egalitarian aspirations, it's unusual, in contemporary American literature, to meet someone so blatantly typecast as a girl from the wrong side of the tracks, and at first, Nora tends to strike us as an especially unpleasant package of slatternly stereotypes. She drinks and swears too much; she's lusty without being beautiful, manipulative without being charming. She lives on junk food, spends too much time watching television, and pays little attention to politics—habits that Max finds irresponsible and hateful.

White Palace is narrated from Max's point of view, however, and as he slowly comes to terms with his class prejudices—as his condescension gives way to understanding—Nora begins to appear as an increasingly complex and sympathetic figure. Like Max, we come to appreciate her self-sufficiency (even when she's unable to pay her heating bills, she refuses to ask Max for money), her hardheaded sense of reality, her refusal to put up with his social slights.

As for Max, he, too, grows as an individual—through his exposure to Nora. What has begun for him as a drunken seduction quickly becomes a sexual obsession, and as his infatuation starts to turn into genuine affection, he's forced to reassess his feelings and intentions. Nora, he realizes, has destroyed the illusion of self-control he once so cherished, and at times he sees their affair as "so remarkable, so peculiar, so intense, so unconnected to anything he had known before or since" that it seems like a holiday from his real life.

Is a friend correct when she suggests that his obsession with Nora is just another reaction to Janey's death—that an affair with such an unlikely woman is simply a defensive tactic, a means of avoiding commitment to someone who might become a permanent part of his world? Does the fact that his friends disapprove of Nora mean that he should reassess their relationship? And what about his ongoing efforts to play professor to her Eliza Doolittle? Does his desire to remake Nora in Janey's image indicate that something is wrong?

There are moments when Mr. Savan needlessly annotates Max's actions, interpreting what is already obvious to the reader. And there are also moments when his efforts to convey Max's increasingly tormented state of mind push his prose into corny, melodramatic convolutions: "In the outer world, where Nora held sway, all was madness, chaos, and unshackled instinct—a regular thirteenth-century plague-ridden Europe, steeped in darkness and coming apart at the seams."

Still, we hardly notice such passages, so unerring are Mr. Savan's storytelling instincts. He has a brisk, almost cinematic style that enables him to cut effortlessly back and forth between the various worlds inhabited by Max; we see him at work in a downtown advertising agency, at home with his mother and his former in-laws, and alone with Nora in her suffocating little house. In doing so, he not only creates an immensely readable narrative, but he also manages to give us nearly complete access to his hero's emotional as well as day-to-day life. Indeed, by the end of *White Palace,* Max Baron has emerged as that happy thing—a thoroughly recognizable hero, at once sympathetic and detestable, vulnerable and proud.

> *Michiko Kakutani, in a review of "White Palace,"
> in* The New York Times, *June 10, 1987, p. C25.*

JOHN BLADES

[*White Palace* is] set in St. Louis, a city that's been unjustly neglected in American fiction. As an old St. Louis expatriate (the whole truth comes out), I can testify to and appreciate the authenticity of the author's simulated city, from such mainline establishments as the Cheshire Inn to more disreputable haunts like Cousin Hugo's. But the book's authority and its impact don't depend on Savan's physical recreation of the city. He populates his fictional St. Louis with a couple of seriocomically mismatched lovers and tosses them into a plot that can best be described as surefire, since it is basically the one that Somerset Maugham used in *Of Human Bondage.*

In Savan's modern variation, Max, a prissy, 28-year-old yuppie ad man, falls obsessively in love with Nora, a slatternly waitress at White Palace restaurant (in actuality, the White Castle). At 41, Nora is not only much older than Max, she's from another planet. An inhabitant of "dogtown," a hillbilly quarter of St. Louis, she's physically and mentally unattractive: pear-shaped, foul-mouthed, barely literate and unwashed, smelling of "booze, cigarettes . . . the meat and stink of White Palaces."

Why Max finds Nora (or Mildred, as he occasionally calls her, acknowledging the literary origins of the character and his plot in Maugham's *Of Human Bondage*) so "perversely intoxicating" is never made exactly clear, or even very plausible. But Savan is such a brashly assured writer and *White Palace* such a model of energetic, fast-forward storytelling that this first novel is compulsive reading, all the way to the bittersweet, if disappointingly evasive, end.

> *John Blades, "First Novelists Deliver on the Paperback Route," in* Chicago Tribune—Books, *June 28, 1987, p. 3.*

An Excerpt from *White Palace*

"Am I ever going to see you again?" she asked him.

He dropped his eyes and watched her veiny hands pumping the muscles of her forearms through the red material of her robe, the knuckles going from yellow to pink to yellow again. She had, of course, every right to ask this question, but the bluntness of it, and the bitter tone in which she asked it, unstrung him.

"It's a simple enough question," Nora said. "Am I ever going to see you again?"

He waffled. "Why does this have to be all my decision?" he asked her.

"Because I'm the one doing the asking. And that gives you all the power. Or didn't you know that?"

He put his back to the wall and his hands into the pockets of his tuxedo pants. Around his feet lay curved, like a sleeping snake, a pair of her fallen panty hose. He felt unfairly cornered. The only thing he could possibly do was to thank her for a memorable afternoon, kiss her good-bye, and get the hell out. What else could he do? Ask her for a date? But he raised his eyes again to that unpretty, destroyable face and lost his courage.

"How old are you?" he asked her.

Nora lifted her chin. "Take a guess."

"Please, Nora—no guessing games. Just tell me."

"I'm older than I look—or so I've been told."

"And how old is that?"

"I'm forty-one," she said. "I'll be forty-two come this December. And you're how old? Twenty-seven? Lord, there's one hell of a spread there, isn't there? I'll bet you've never been with anyone near as old as me, have you?"

"No," he said. "I haven't."

"So what-all else would you like to know about me? Hell, you've just taken me for a test drive—now it's only natural you'd want a look under the hood. So just ask away."

She waited.

"Why don't you just interview me like you did last night? You already know what I'm like in the sack—or is that all you're interested in knowing?"

"Now, wait a minute, Nora. Let's not forget that you were the one who seduced me. I didn't ask for this."

"You didn't put up much of a fight, either."

"I was outmatched."

She leaned against the wall beside her shrine to Marilyn Monroe and let her arms hang down at her sides, as if she were daring him, through this defenseless stance, to do his best to hurt her. "You think I'm just a dumb ignorant hoosier, don't you?"

"Nora—"

"Don't bullshit me. That's what you think, and that's what I am. I never got past the ninth grade, and I've been working at that White Palace for going on six years now because I'm not qualified for any other kind of work. And I'll tell you something else about me. I'm not in the habit of picking up men in bars. Oh, I used to be. I used to be in the habit of doing a lot of things, which I'm sure you'd rather not hear about. But I just got so sick and tired of all the fucked-up rednecked bastards I kept falling in with that I just gave up on men entirely. Do you know you're the first man I've been with in over a year? Not that I haven't had my share of offers—I've had plenty, let me tell you. But lately I've just gotten this funny idea about myself. I've started thinking that maybe I deserve better than the only kind of man who's likely to be interested in me—which is a laugh, I guess. And then I met you." She crossed her arms again now and kicked away a lone red shoe that was lying at her feet. "I'm sure I'd have to be an even bigger fool than I already am to think you'd want to have anything to do

with me. After all, I'm not exactly your type, am I? But there's just something about you. I'll be damned if I know what it is—but there's just something about you." She stared at Max, blinked at him once, and sighed roughly through her nostrils. "So when you kept on sitting there and drinking with me last night at Cousin Hugo's, I thought to myself, well hell, Nora, stranger things have happened. That's what I thought. Stranger things have happened." She shrugged. "So there you are. I'm too goddamned old for you, I'm poor, I'm ignorant, I'm not pretty, and I'm sure you'd be ashamed to introduce me to any of your friends. So what are you going to do, Max?"

The impossible, diabolical thing was, he wanted her. He wanted her right now, just as she was, with her exposed face and her plucked eyebrows and her lingering stale smell of sex; he wanted to take her right here on this floor, down among the litter of shoes, panties, crumpled Kleenex, fluffballs of dust—he wanted to damn all common sense and circumspection and descend once again into that oblivion.

But he also knew what he had to tell her.

"Nora—I'm sorry."

She showed him a half-smile of contempt.

"Do you know," she said, "for a minute there I really did think you were going to up and surprise me?"

TOM JENKS

Savan's *White Palace* is an unusually good, fast read, and Savan does write wrought-up, explicit sex, which can't be quoted in a newspaper. . . .

Shrewd, hard-bitten, aging Nora works the register at a White Palace hamburger joint. Max is a very handsome, widower yuppie. Nora has every reason to want him, and no reason to believe he could want her, even for sex. They are together accidentally, and what happens is so unlikely they can't believe it themselves. Max falls in love with her.

They seem set for tragedy, but Savan works comic, romantic and satiric edges. Through Nora, Max has an opportunity that few of us have, to step outside his life and see it plain. His best friends—wealthy, fat Horowitz and mordant Klugman— are revealed in their easy greed and petty depravities (sexual kinks, cocaine, the fetish of possessions). They try to diagnose, discourage his attachment, or are simply indifferent, caught up in themselves. From Nora's self-abnegating "How come you're so good to me?" we are carried on a rich tide of social and sexual reversals (she's bolder, direct, more of a man than he) to Max's "I'm the one who's not good enough for you."

Max overcomes his priggishness, abandons the shrine he's made of his wife's death. His heart swells, his head shrinks, his feet touch the earth. He lends Nora books to read. He's an English teacher turned ad man. One night when he wants to make love, she's absorbed in *Huck Finn*. "What I'm in the mood for," she tells him, "is finding out what happens next." Savan's joke: Literature kills sex (and unintentionally, I think, the idea that Max is no match for Huck). Later, Nora will begin to put herself through school but says, "The last thing

I want to know is how I'm going to end up.'' More than fear, it's faith.

Savan offers life as mystery, suggests that you can only know "who really belongs to you, and then act accordingly. The rest is out of your hands.'' That's as profound a thought, and as well expressed, as you'll find in *White Palace.* Savan's no stylist. The coarseness of his tale, his familiarity with his characters, his love for their love, the curiosity of a situation that tweaks downward mobility as much as upward are what recommend and sustain the book.

Savan is not our next McInerney. Instead, through Max, he sets up his own comparisons—Twain, Blake, Dostoevsky, Shakespeare, George Bernard Shaw—and though the book would have been stronger without the self-conscious, English major references, without many of the convenient coincidences and repetitions in plot (Max's wife dies in an auto wreck, his mother is run over by a bus), and would have been funnier without the jokes that feel set up, without the parade of brand names and pop icons to key the satire, from beginning to end Savan's ambition remains good-natured. You hardly mind that the women in *White Palace* smoke and the men don't, that the women are either mother or authority figures, that Max's advertising bosses are an attractive, sharp-witted lesbian and a cold bitch with body odor. The portrayals are brighter, keener than stereotype and caricature but often paler, more mechanical than characters. Accurately measured, not against McInerney or even an older generation, Salinger, Roth, but against the ordinary, sometimes remarkable business of living in the full awareness of our own mortality, measured, that is, against absolute reality, *White Palace* is a surprising, mid-American love song, which is just what it should be.... (p. 12)

Tom Jenks, ''Literature as Life Style,'' in Los Angeles Times Book Review, *August 2, 1987, pp. 1, 12.*

MEG WOLITZER

A postfeminist *Pygmalion, White Palace* is a fable of love and transformation set in present-day St. Louis. Glenn Savan's Henry Higgins takes the form of 27-year-old Max Baron, a handsome, literate, upwardly mobile advertising man, while 42-year-old Nora Cromwell—a loud redneck waitress at a hamburger joint called White Palace—is his Eliza.

The relationship between these two, built on a foundation of pure lust, feels inauspicious from the start. Max, recently widowed and melancholic, is repelled by Nora, and yet finds himself drawn to her. In his first novel, Mr. Savan writes skillfully about sex, as he does about most subjects. When Max first spends the night at Nora's house, he is dazed by the chaos he finds there. Hers is a house so messy it feels lifted right out of a George Booth cartoon: ''Nora flicked on the hallway light and Max stopped in his tracks.... The place might have been trashed by a goon squad.... The scene unnerved him; he felt like a fireman gazing at a blaze that he wasn't licensed to put out.''

The author is convincing in creating the opposing worlds of Max and Nora—one ordered and sane, the other frenzied and anarchic. While Max is someone we are meant to like and relate to, from his collection of record albums (Bach, Haydn, Vivaldi, Mozart) to his library (Tolstoy, Dickens, Twain), Nora is a slovenly woman with Tammy Wynette and the Oak Ridge Boys near her stereo, and *This Shining Promise,* and

The Joy of Sex on her shelf. In *White Palace,* brand names are meant to tell us a lot about the characters, which is not surprising, since the protagonist works in advertising.... But Mr. Savan relies too much on our knowledge of popular culture, and one wishes he had allowed a few more of his own insights about the world to come through.

Although the novel's considerable strength lies chiefly in its succinct and highly engaging prose, *White Palace* becomes problematic when Mr. Savan turns his keen eye toward Nora. She is described with as much close observation as any of the ''trash'' items in her house, and finally one tires of the many references to her physical self, including her ''bottom-heaviness.'' Toward the end of the novel, when one of Max's otherwise likable buddies confides to his friend that he ''just can't seem to get very sexually interested in a woman I don't despise a little bit,'' the reader can't help but feel that this man is also speaking for Max. It's as if Mr. Savan is telling us that somehow, in this age of postfeminist enlightenment, it's O.K. to have such feelings, as long as you can admit them.

These lapses make Max less appealing, which is too bad, since the story is so convincing that we *want* to root for him. Finally, despite the weaknesses, we do. As Nora comes into her own, and Max's life simultaneously begins to plummet, there is a real tension to the narrative, and a darkness the writer handles well. Mr. Savan gives us a wonderful moment in which Max turns the lens on himself, and notes that ''their relationship was beginning to look like *Pygmalion,* with a twist: as the play progresses, Professor Higgins discovers that he has taken on a cockney accent, and by the end of the last act, he's on a street corner in Soho, selling flowers.''

Meg Wolitzer, ''Eliza Doolittle is a Redneck,'' in The New York Times Book Review, *September 13, 1987, p. 18.*

JOYCE MAYNARD

White Palace seems to take its inspiration less from any literary masterpieces past than from the most recent issue of *Variety.* (p. 116)

White Palace tells the story of a young professional named Max, and I have to admit that warning bells went off for me when I read his name. As the daughter of a man named Max, who was not remotely cute, hip or trendy, I have watched with some interest and amusement the way that name (almost unheard of in the years of my growing up) has come close to being the ultimate cute/hip/trendy name for dogs and babies.... So—to get back to *White Palace*—when I learned my hero was to have the moniker of the balsamic-vinegar-and-mesquite-barbecue set, I had to ask myself what I was in for.

A cute/hip/trendy love story, is what. Our hero, Max Baron, is a teacher turned advertising copywriter. From the first, Savan takes pains to convey to us just how bright, witty and attractive Max is (picture Tom Hanks, or maybe Kevin Kline, on the big screen). Max married his pretty, rich and generally perfect high-school sweetheart, Janey, and once seemed destined to spend the rest of his life happily sipping wine and eating Brie, playing racquetball and making tender (if less than earth-shattering) love to his wife. But the game plan has been shaken up due to the fact that Janey heading out one night on a minor errand, crashed the car and died, leaving Max an eminently available bachelor once more.

When we meet him, he has been living an orderly but basically miserable widower's life for nearly a year, to the despair of friends and all the women who would like to date him. Then he meets Nora, a cheap, tawdry-looking, wide-hipped and pockmarked waitress at the White Palace diner, and after getting drunk with her, takes her to bed pretty much by mistake. Savan makes plain all the things that are wrong about Nora. She's ignorant. Ungrammatical. Slovenly. Coarse. Nora has never heard of spaghetti carbonara, listens to the Oak Ridge Boys and favors Wonder Bread and American cheese. But the fact is, Nora is also one incredible lover, and the sex between the two is close to apocalyptic.

That's the situation for you: Up-and-coming young man, down-and-out older woman—Mr. Right meets Ms. Wrong, and discovers depths of passion and pleasure he never dreamed possible. Only problem is, he can't introduce her to his friends. And she knows it.

I don't buy it. For starters, I don't find Max as witty and lovable as I'm meant to, overwrought descriptions of his physical charms notwithstanding ("It just seems that a man as good-looking as you would have women falling all over him all the time," Max hears more than once). Furthermore, I can't get all stirred up about his ad-agency angst, and most of all, I don't buy his passion for Nora. At the bottom of it, that's because Nora, as written by Glenn Savan, doesn't exist.

There's something almost insufferably insulting about the way Savan portrays this woman. He gives us the brand names of the products she keeps on her kitchen shelf, and piles on the lower-class speech patterns the way, 40 years ago, B-movie scriptwriters used to write dialogue for black butlers and no-good Indians. In the end, he never takes her seriously enough to show her experiencing any believable sensations besides orgasms. She's a fantasy figure—a low-down, dirty tramp with a heart of gold whose existence seems only to matter as it relates to our hero, Max. (She had a son who died a few years back. But nothing that's ever happened in her life, clearly, has been as big and awe-inspiring as the fact that someone like Max Baron would fall for her.) In the end, this love affair reads like a condescending anthropological exploration into the curious and comical habits of the pink collar set. (pp. 116, 118)

Max's waitress lover has a heart of gold, of course. But the greatest demonstration of humanity, the book suggests, comes from Max—a man noble enough to consort with one as humble as Nora. A man big enough to slum it with the little people. Coming soon to a theater near you.

[**White Palace**] belongs to the long, ignoble tradition of *Love Story* and its ilk. . . . (p. 118)

Joyce Maynard, "Soon to Be a Major Motion Picture," in Mademoiselle, *Vol. 93, No. 11, November, 1987, pp. 116, 118-19.*

Valerie Sayers

19??-

American novelist.

Sayers was born and raised in South Carolina, the setting of her warmly received first novel, *Due East* (1987). Mary Faith Rapple, the heroine of *Due East*, is fifteen, unmarried, and pregnant. She's also an unusually bright and feisty young woman who, with her pregnancy, becomes a defiant loner in her sleepy little town. The novel explores the tentative relationship between Mary Faith and her father, Jesse, in the trying months of her pregnancy—a relationship suffused with a shared but unspoken grief for Mary Faith's mother, who died of cancer three years earlier.

Alternate chapters of *Due East* are narrated by Mary Faith in the first person, with the others told in the third person from the point of view of Jesse. Critics note that this device captures the father-daughter conflict in delicate counterpoint and illustrates the gap in communications between them. Reviewer Carl Mitcham sees in the final chapter, which is composed of the two narrative voices interwoven, a structural parallel to the tentative emotional rapprochement between Mary Faith and Jesse.

Critics praise Sayers for her realistic and sympathetic portrayals of father and daughter, her compact, resonant prose, and her scrupulous attention to detail. Although a few critics suggest that the novel's plot is perilously close to soap opera, they note that Sayers is ultimately convincing. Commenting on the ease with which *Due East* envelops the reader in its world, Jack Butler commends Sayers for her "rare knack of appearing to simply open up a reality, as if it were so close before her eyes that she doesn't have to create it so much as invite us in."

Photograph by Alex Gotfryd

much more than merely promising: it marks the arrival of a true writer.

A review of "Due East," in Publishers Weekly, *Vol. 231, No. 4, January 30, 1987, p. 368.*

PUBLISHERS WEEKLY

[*Due East,* a] very accomplished first novel, . . . is about a father and daughter both growing up in a small South Carolina town. Mary Faith Rapple, who is 15 and pregnant by a suicidal fellow high school student, narrates her story in the first person: she is determined to have her baby, whatever her widower father Jesse and her other relatives think. Jesse, whose story is told in the third person (and the seamless way this is done is only one of the mature skills of the book) wants to find out who the baby's father is—and in the process falls into an unlikely and untidy romance of his own. Not, then, a novel of violent incident; but the narrative tone the author has given Mary Faith is so wry and unerring a combination of innocence and sophistication, foolish Jesse is observed with such sympathy, and the world of a sleepy seaside town is so beautifully caught that by the tender conclusion the reader has been transported into an unfamiliar but truthfully rendered world. It's a novel that's

CATHERINE PETROSKI

Valerie Sayers' *Due East* is one of those beautifully realized novels that takes over the reader's life. It is the story of 15-year-old Mary Faith Rapple and her father Jesse, and some characters who are not exactly present: Mary Faith's dead mother and her unborn, illegitimate child. It is the story of a way of life in Due East, a South Carolina tidewater town, and of how a daughter and husband, devastated by the same woman's death, find an unlikely way to mend that loss.

Due East is also about substitutes and the diversionary tactics through which we fool ourselves about ourselves: Mary Faith tries substituting an affair with one of her teachers just as Jesse takes up with Nell, the teacher's mother. This sounds like a highly schematic arrangement, but in Sayers' accomplished hands many unlikely events become plausible. As its chapters alternate point of view between Mary Faith and Jesse, Sayers' novel captures and resolves their conflict: youth's passionate errors in judgment and age's attempts to cope with those passions in a loving, positive way. To represent this conflict without condescension is a major order for a novel, but on this and many other scores, *Due East* succeeds. In our society, the Rapples would not be viewed as successful people, but as characters, they succeed in enlisting our sympathies in their struggle, and the creation that is Mary Faith remains a point of reference long after the last page is read.

> Catherine Petroski, *"Three Debuts Prove the Vitality of the Novel,"* in Chicago Tribune—The Arts, *March 8, 1987, p. 7.*

JACK BUTLER

One thing I like about *Due East,* Valerie Sayers' first novel, is that the author names her chapters (and her prelude). It seems a quaint practice, in very much the right sort of way, as if Ms. Sayers has thought over each of her chapters especially hard. You sit down to open 23 little presents instead of just one great big one.

Mary Faith Rapple is a 15-year-old girl in the town of Due East, S.C. (she turns 16 during the story), who has got herself pregnant. She is desperately lonely, her mother, Faith Rapple, having died three years before and her father, Jesse Rapple, who has never been demonstrative anyway, having withdrawn into his grief. She and her father live in gritty poverty—he's a fairly gentle ne'er-do-well who runs a service station when he isn't drinking or brooding. At school she inhabits the twilight zone between the successful and popular cheerleader types and the angst-ridden, anarchistic, superintelligent underachievers—the sort of students who used to be granted at least the bizarre dignity of weirdohood, but who have lately been reduced to mere impotent nerddom.

One of them is the fellow she eventually seduces, Michael (Mick) Jagger—if you think the name lays the comic irony on thick, wait till you find out what his name was *going* to be. After the seduction, Michael, more in love with his sense of guilt than with Mary Faith, commits suicide. She puts him out of her mind, decides to have the baby anyway and at first insists that it will be a virgin birth, not so much to protect Michael as out of defiance—out of refusal to owe anything to his memory or to anyone else's guardianship.

It is not immediately obvious just how desperate Mary Faith is, since most of the story is told in her voice and since she is a much brighter than average, tough-talking, self-sufficient young woman who finds most of her neighbors lacking in either decency or common sense. She is so bright that she has won the Latin Award, has a shot at a Radcliffe scholarship and helps tutor a course in mathematics for the young wives of the marines on a nearby base. The novel perhaps suffers a bit in the middle chapters from just this delineation of extremes: Mary Faith is so shrewdly perceptive and the people who frustrate her are so unrelievedly small-minded and mean that the story nearly degenerates into the familiar tale of the good and sensitive teenager against the cruel and insensitive world.

This sermonizing against narrow-minded piety reaches its apex, ironically, during a sermon delivered by the squinchily named Baptist preacher, Dr. Beady. He holds Mary Faith up to scorn, and even her father fails to defend her. Dr. Beady is a slimy

character, right enough, and there are plenty like him (just turn on your television)—but the opposition is almost too pure, so that the scene comes off like a set piece.

Mostly, though, the book just wraps itself around you. Ms. Sayers has that rare knack of appearing simply to open up a reality, as if it were so clear before her eyes that she doesn't have to create it so much as invite us in. Not that she isn't good with details. She is. Another thing I like about *Due East* is the texture, the density of its observation. Michael Jagger, for example, at one point spray-painted nipples on the statue of the Virgin Mary. This just won't do, of course, so the Roman Catholics clean the statue up—only now, "Mary's breasts are round white points on a browning body." Early on, having felt the eyes of the town busybodies follow her down the street, Mary Faith says: "I didn't mind. It was like having a dog trailing afer me, or a guardian angel." That's a very fine "or." . . .

In *Due East* things convincingly go askew. The characters formulate plans and follow them into total confusion. Jesse Rapple stumbles into a seduction when he tries to find and accuse the father of the unborn child; Mary Faith plots yet another affair that twists away from her, out of desire into the man's sense of guilt. Constantly misunderstanding one another, held together by contradictory fantasies that they do not communicate or forced apart by disappointment when, in truth, they want the same things—these are people in deep trouble, lost souls.

Some misfiring of intention might seem the stuff of comedy, and in fact the book begins like a domestic comedy of errors—the dumbly frustrated Jesse insisting on knowing who got Mary Faith pregnant, she retreating to her claim of virginity. But this is no comedy. This is a bitter wafer, an antistory parallel to that other virgin birth, that old, old story. It is a hard-eyed if not hardhearted tale, and gives nothing up to sentimentality. The true miracle in this story, if there is one—there is just one moment at the very end that suggests it—is that its characters are able to conceive warmth, peace and affection in the midst of unrelenting woe.

> Jack Butler, *"Mary Faith Pleads Virginity,"* in The New York Times Book Review, *March 8, 1987, p. 9.*

SAM STAGGS

[In *Due East*] Mary Faith Rapple, fifteen, is pregnant. The father of her child, who was a classmate of Mary Faith's at Due East High School, has committed suicide by taking an overdose of Quaaludes. Such a predicament would test the mettle of a teenager in a liberal, affluent milieu, but for a spouseless, impecunious mother-to-be in a small South Carolina town, where the Baptist preacher thunders at her from the pulpit, the situation could prove harrowing. Mary Faith, however, has strength and maturity enough for a dozen—she's something of an unwed Earth Mother.

More woes befall her as the novel unfolds. Her father and her late mother's twin sister try to make her have an abortion, even though Mary Faith yearns for a child. Her forty-year-old father, involved in a squalid love affair with a fifty-year-old crone who also gets pregnant, suffers a near-fatal coronary. And Mary Faith is kicked out of school.

Due East, which is Sayers's first novel, might easily have collapsed under such an infelicitous load of problems. But

Sayers writes with a steady hand. She interjects the right amount of comedy to avoid soap opera, while keeping the novel completely realistic in its own quirky way. Observing her characters dispassionately, Sayers reveals the faults and virtues of them all. In such a charged situation, a less skillful writer might have portrayed them as unequivocal heroes or villains.

Sayers wisely resisted using Mary Faith as narrator throughout the novel. Instead, Mary Faith narrates alternate chapters in the first person, with the other chapters told in the third person from her father's point of view. This narrative device expands the novel, like mirrors added to a small room.

Ultimately, *Due East* is an undersized novel. It's like a low-budget movie directed by a superb craftsman who, given the right breaks, might make a blockbuster in a few years. And it is not without serious flaws. The greatest one is Sayers's failure to explain why the father of Mary Faith's baby killed himself. He was sensitive, rebellious, and adopted; he was also given to reading Dostoyevsky. Sayers apparently thinks his being a slight misfit justifies his convenient self-destruction. The novel is weakest when Mary Faith sees herself as a heroine, practically slapping herself on the back for her liberalism. Still, it is a novel with resonance; the characters won't turn you loose after you've finished the book. When Mary Faith stands up in church and says to the preacher who rebukes her, "I do *not* beg your forgiveness," you want to know just how indomitable she will be when she grows up. You also leave the book convinced that Sayers will become a prominent voice in southern fiction.

Sam Staggs, in a review of "Due East," in Wilson Library Bulletin, Vol. 61, No. 9, May, 1987, p. 70.

An Excerpt from *Due East*

"Where have you been every night, out drinking? Momma would've died."

"Mary Faith, leave your mother out of it. Keep a civil tongue in your head."

"Well, I want to know where you've been."

Jesse stared hard at his daughter, at the light, intense eyes. "I've been out trying to arrange things for you," he said, and filled his mouth with bacon sandwich.

She picked at her food for a minute and then said, fiercely, "It's been *lonely* here."

He swallowed his sandwich.

"It's been lonely," she said again, and threw the wad of paper napkin across the table. "When I lie in my bed I can hear Momma in the sewing room. I shouldn't have to listen to that."

"Mary Faith!"

She started to cry again. "Well, I can," she said, wiping her eyes. "I can hear her making me a maternity dress."

"Mary Faith," he said quickly, "I'm going to take care of things for you. You're not going to have to worry about a maternity dress." About a year after Faith was gone, she'd said she could hear her mother in the kitchen, cleaning out under the sink, or that she could hear her in the garage, straightening. That was when he'd taken her to Dr. Black, who had said to take her to a psy-

chologist. "Mary Faith, you didn't mean you could really *hear* your momma, did you?"

"Oh, Daddy," she cried. "Do you have to be so literal?"

"I just want to make sure—"

"You leave me all alone in the house and sure I hear things. I can hear things in her room and in your bedroom and in the kitchen. And I start imagining that for the rest of my life I'll be lying alone in bed or cooking for myself. Only I won't. I'm not going to be alone anymore, don't you see, because I'm going to have a baby. And I'll tell you something else, when I have this baby I'm not ever going to leave her alone at night, not ever, not to go out drinking at some stinking bar. And don't you ever ask to have breakfast with me again, because me and my baby have been doing fine at breakfast all alone without you." She ran to the counter for her books.

"Mary Faith! You get back here to this table." He thought she hesitated at the counter.

"I mean it, Mary Faith."

She picked up her books and looked back at him, her face smoothed into composure, the same face that had met him these past weeks. "Daddy," she said, "I have to tell you one more thing. I'm sorry to have you worrying about money. Don't worry about money, because I'm going to address envelopes at home, or something like that, and we'll get by. But if you don't want my baby in the house, then I guess you don't want me. So please don't say it one more time, because you *know* Momma wouldn't have wanted me to have an abortion." She walked out the back door.

BRET HARVEY

My mother used to say about certain kinds of food or drink: "It puts its little hand in yours." [*Due East*] does that; it slips in step beside you, puts its hand in yours and leads you, without fuss, into Mary Faith Rapple's kitchen in Due East, South Carolina, and into Mary Faith Rapple's immediately interesting 15-year-old mind. Mary Faith lives alone with her father, Jesse, a gentle man who runs a gas station in town and always has curls of oil around his fingernails and oily curls in his hair. Her mother has been dead for three years, and Mary Faith's doing a pretty good job of taking her place. She vacuums the house before school, sees to it that her father has breakfast, and fries up crab claws for his supper. When she tells him she's five months pregnant, Jesse doesn't shout or hit the ceiling; he just says, "No," in a way that reminds Mary Faith of the "no" he said when her mother told them at the same supper table that she had cancer. When Jesse asks her who the father is, Mary Faith refuses to say. In fact, she says she doesn't know how it happened. "Maybe it's kind of like a virgin birth?" she whispers hopefully. . . .

Jesse gets it into his head that his daughter's seducer is Stephen Dugan, the local intellectual, who runs the tutoring program Mary Faith volunteers for twice a week. In the course of tracking him down, he stumbles into a relationship with Stephen's mother, Nell. . . . Meanwhile Mary Faith turns to Stephen Dugan for help in her dilemma and ends up trying to seduce him.

Sex is part of everything in this novel the way it is in life. It's just *there*, making people do things but not always identifying itself. Mary Faith and Jesse always have sex on their minds. The difference between them is that Mary Faith knows it. She's just discovering sex, and she treasures the knowledge. . . .

Jesse, on the other hand, is buffeted by all his impulses. He's surprised and pained to catch himself having sexual thoughts about his daughter, and bewildered by his passion for leathery Nell Dugan. . . .

Father and daughter are both haunted by Mary Faith's mother's terrible death from cancer, though they can't talk about it to each other. Jesse fears that he might have made his wife sick by getting so big when they made love. . . . Mary Faith remembers standing over her unconscious mother in the hospital, reporting to her which stains came out in the wash.

The heart of this book is the relationship between father and daughter, which is clogged with unspoken tenderness and disappointment. Sayers knows just to let their relationship play itself out in her characters' actions. When Mary Faith is humiliated in church by the preacher, her father unexpectedly puts his arm around her shoulder "lightly—not leaning me toward him or squeezing me, but just resting it there, something he'd never done before. . . . I had never felt that sensation before, the sensation of being borne up by him." Buoyed by his support, Mary Faith defiantly rises, sasses the minister, and walks out of the church, confident that her father is right behind her. Only he isn't. He hasn't quite had the courage for that. Sayers's technique of moving back and forth between Mary Faith's point of view and Jesse's feels so right and organic that you almost don't notice that Mary Faith speaks in the first person while Jesse's thoughts are described by an omniscient observer.

In the end, Jesse, Mary Faith, and her baby are together in their little house. Things have gotten pretty bad, with the baby keeping Mary Faith up nights and Jesse on his feet at the gas station all day long and coming home worn out, hoping Mary Faith will have supper ready and knowing he should help her and not knowing how to offer. The last scene of the novel freezes father, daughter, and infant at the supper table in that nightmarish, new-baby aftermath of frayed nerves and exhaustion. After hours of fretting, the baby suddenly quiets on Jesse's shoulder, and in the peace that settles over the kitchen, something finally settles between Mary Faith and Jesse and the dead woman who troubles them. They rest and eat and you can practically hear the gentle clink of fork against plate.

> Bret Harvey, *"Faith, Hope, and Clarity," in* The Village Voice, *Vol. XXXII, No. 20, May 19, 1987, p. 52.*

CARL MITCHAM

After the fall, and an angel with flaming sword stood "at the east of the garden of Eden" to bar Adam and Eve's return, imagine that "the mother of all living" had been unable to bear children. Following a series of miscarriages, however, she finally gives birth to a daughter, and then when her daughter is but twelve-years-old, Eve dies. What would life have been like for a forty-year-old Adam and his teenage daughter?

Valerie Sayers's novel [*Due East*]—at once richly realistic and a bricolage of religious allusions after the manner of many other Southern writers—is one response to such a question. . . .

The story of the nine months from fall 1980 to summer 1981 of Mary Faith's pregnancy—a pregnancy that is, on many levels, a response to the death of her mother, Faith—is told in alternating chapters of Mary Faith's first-person narrative and a third-person description of what is happening with her father. Each reaches out for the other and reacts to what are perceived as failures of love. The disjunction in narrative voices mirrors a deeper failure to bridge the gap between them. Jesse is upset that Mary Faith has gotten pregnant and wants her to have an abortion. Mary Faith is disappointed her father wants to kill the baby when her own mother had such trouble in carrying a child to term and never gave her husband the son he desired. (p. 329)

Pain of separation and distance and lack of communication is the fundamental reality of this novel, but it is a reality that is largely understated and often only indirectly expressed. Indeed, this too is part of its character. There is a good deal of coming and going in the story, almost soap-opera twists and turns of plot and subplot (Jesse is having an affair with a fifty-year-old widow who gets pregnant, the teacher of the local GED program is breaking up with his wife, etc.) and some moderately florid sexual scenes, but the real action of the novel takes place not in heated discussions or emotional outbursts; it happens at a deeper level, below the surface.

Indeed, despite its southern gothic façade, this work of fiction is subtly enough told told that the most minor remarks often have a depth of significance belied by the superficial lucidity of the text. At one point Mary Faith is remembering how "Michael Jagger's voice sounded like a foreigner's to me, and I didn't get it. He'd been in Due East all his life, probably." The force of that "probably" is only fully revealed when his mother eventually tries to befriend Mary Faith. The reader must be careful not to understand this novel too quickly.

In a certain sense, in fact, this is not a novel in the popular sense. Although plot and tension keep one reading at a rapid pace, the point of view as indicated by the opening prelude is actually one of cool retrospection, and character development is minimal—precisely because what is really happening is doing so on a deeper level. The voice of Mary Faith is not (and is not meant to be) the real voice of a fifteen-year-old, but a kind of restrained third-person first person, if you will. The voice that speaks for her father, Jesse, is equally laconic.

The key role played by silence or the inability to speak is emphasized by the occasion when Michael Jagger's parents try to convince Mary Faith to come to live with them.

> "I don't know what to say," Jesse said. The trouble was, he did know what to say—he knew to say: Get out of here. This is my daughter. Your son is dead. I am taking care of things.

But he doesn't say it. He looks to his daughter who, he thinks, "should be jumping up to his side, this minute, telling these Jaggers that she meant to stay with her father." Yet Mary Faith "kept her eyes lowered, her head bowed. 'I haven't made up my mind,' she said quietly." In their needs father and daughter once again silently betray each other.

The deepest silence, however, is not between Mary Faith and her father, but between Mary Faith and her mother—and between Mary Faith and God. Mary Faith hates her mother for her saccharine piety, and for dying and leaving her alone at age twelve; she further hates herself for having such feelings, and God for not answering her prayers first to let her mother live and then, as she was suffering, to let her die. (pp. 330-31)

The last chapter, entitled "Firstborn Son"—born on August 15, the feast of the Assumption—is an achievement that can be adequately appreciated only by one who has read the book. The narrative voices shift and intertwine. For the first time, there is not just third-person Jesse Rapple or first-person Mary Faith, one or the other, but both. In a spare twelve pages, with not a merger but a shift back and forth between narrative voices, a rapprochement is realized between father and daughter, one that is both real and yet devoid of any easy solutions to the life ahead. It is the simple touching between a forty-year-old man and his rebellious teenage daughter for the first time since his wife and her mother died, in the birth not just of a son named Jesse after his grandfather but of a tentative new life.

This novel is not only a good story and good literature; it is also good spiritual reading. It is a fictive study of our rejection of God, the motherhood of faith, and how both depend on and transcend our relationships with others. It can help us ask questions about our own lives and come to know better both ourselves and God. (p. 331)

> *Carl Mitcham, "Footsteps That Did Not Follow,"*
> *in* Commonweal, *Vol. CXIV, No. 10, May 22, 1987,*
> *pp. 329-31.*

DEANNA D'ERRICO

I have only praise for Valerie Sayers' first novel, *Due East.* The plot moves at a brisk clip, revealing in one surprise after another the inner lives of its cast of interesting characters, mostly through the alternating point of view of Mary Faith Rapple and her father Jesse. Sayers' command of language and dialogue and her powers of description are awe-inspiring. She compresses much into a few words, in the way that accomplished short story writers do. She has an uncanny knack for choosing the perfect word to evoke a mood or idea. Consider, for example, the effect of the word *pranced* in the following sentence:

> But he did feel guilty, so he did take the list, and found himself in the Piggly Wiggly on Saturday morning, surrounded by the working women of Due East, who had all come from the beauty parlor and who seemed to know exactly where everything was and pranced around behind their shopping carts delighted with their own efficiency. . . .

Mary Faith is several months pregnant and waiting for her father to notice. She is beginning to think he will never notice, that she will get through 9 months and a delivery, and that one night he will say, "How did that baby get to the supper table?" . . .

Mary Faith tells us that the father was a sensitive boy who read Dostoyevski and drew political cartoons. After she seduces him, he is wracked by guilt and commits suicide. His identity is ultimately revealed to Jesse, but by that time Jesse has taken a tumultuous journey through his own heart and mind. Most notably, he has an affair with Nell Dugan, who is the antithesis of the deceased wife that he and Mary Faith unconsciously still mourn. The affair, the details of which are poignantly drawn, leads him to an awareness of his loneliness, which in turn, paves the way for a reconciliation between him and his daughter.

Characteristically, the reconciliation is not smooth, nor do Mary Faith and Jesse acknowledge it in words to one another. In the maddening way of characters in a Victorian novel, Mary Faith and Jesse do not communicate the things that would unite them. They test one another. Each longs to be understood by the other; each strives to heal the wound of loss they both still feel. But each waits for the other to fulfill these longings— Mary Faith waits for tangible signs of acceptance and support from Jesse; Jesse thinks he has given signs and awaits acknowledgment from Mary Faith.

In the closing scene, Mary Faith and Jesse are still at odds over their expectations of one another, but Sayers subtly implies that the baby, who has by its very arrival made them a whole family again, will be the force that dissolves their loneliness and alienation.

> *Deanne D'Errico, in a review of "Due East," in*
> Belles Lettres: A Review of Books by Women, *Vol. 3, No. 1, September-October, 1987, p. 9.*

EMMA DALLY

The heroine of Valerie Sayers' *Due East* is a motherless, pregnant teenager in the American South called Mary Faith Rapple. Mary Faith would rather let the whole town believe she is having a virgin birth than reveal the name of the baby's father. And in spite of her poverty and her academic ambitions, she resists all pressure to have an abortion.

Mary Faith is a delightful character and so is Jesse, her endearing father. He has struggled hard to provide a good home for Mary Faith since her mother died three years before, and his valiant efforts to confront his daughter's condition cause him an assortment of difficulties.

Due East is a novel to savour. Its characters are real and attractive, its portrait of small-town southern life vivid and involving. Valerie Sayers is a writer of considerable talent, and in *Due East* she has made a promising debut.

> *Emma Dally, in a review of "Due East," in* Books, *No. 8, November, 1987, p. 24.*

DAVID BENEDICTUS

I enjoy conspiracy theories. They are so convenient. You can get shot of all your ancient paranoias and never have to prove *anything*. . . .

There are a great many clever novel-writers amongst American women; far fewer women politicians in positions of power. It could be argued that American women, lacking the aggressiveness of the men and being closer to the heart of things, could actually damage the course of multi-national arms deals and presidential committees and interfere with aid to Nicaragua and warships to the Gulf, and wreck that ingenious Meccano Set construction which enables rotund and balding politicians, bursting out of their Brooks Brothers suits, to Make A Lot Of Money. What if these literary women got organised?

So, whoever it is thinks: Let them write novels. Encourage them. Pay them advances. Subsidise their publishers out of one of those convenient slush funds. And, since nobody much will read their books, it doesn't even matter if they are a tiny bit critical of the system, does it? Keep them writing. Keep them off the streets while the *herrenvolk* get on with the business of high finance and rocketry and all that jazz.

Well, it's a neat theory. And to judge from the books these American women write one gets the impression that there's something pretty wretched going on which Washington ought to know about. Valerie Sayers, for instance. In *Due East* we are concerned with a South Carolina ménage. Mary Faith Rapple, a pretty 15-year-old, lives alone with, and housekeeps for, her father Jesse, grieving for his dead wife, Faith. (The names are heavily symbolic, but then so are the names of the political fellows, Nixon and Poindexter, Hart and Goldwater, and Jim Wright, for example.) Mary Faith is pregnant by sad and inadequate Michael Amos Jagger who took thirty pills and tranquilised himself into the hereafter. But Jesse, who runs an unprofitable gas station, prefers to believe that the father is Stephen Dugan, because Stephen employs Mary Faith to help out at the adult education classes. Mary herself claims to be immaculate.

When Jesse starts seeking consolation in the scrawny arms of Stephen's beer-swilling mother, Nell, one begins to see a pattern emerging which can only end in tears. Stephen's impotence, Nell's abortion, Jesse's coronary and Mary Faith's birthpangs ensure that the tears flow freely in Due East, South Carolina, and that Valerie Sayers' righteous indignation has been safely channelled into domestic waters. She does not even hint—as she surely would if she were British—that the tribulations of a poor family may be laid at the doorstep of the Nigel Lawsons of this world. But she does well to be angry, and tells a good tale.

David Benedictus, "Barbecued Spare Ribs," in Punch, *Vol. 292, No. 7666, December 2, 1987, p. 90.*

ALICE H.G. PHILLIPS

There are many twists in **Due East** to the old Southern themes of innocence, transgression and redemption, but the biggest is the character of Mary Faith. Housekeeper for her widowed father, who was left emotionally numbed by his wife's death, she has grown up alone and different. She lost her religious faith watching her mother call on Jesus to end her pain—"My mother died of cancer. I believe in cancer cells"—and now relies strictly on native wit and silence. She had hardly talked to a boy before her brief, odd affair with the class misfit, Michael Jagger, but for years had secretly dreamed of seducing a shy classmate and having a baby that would make up for the five her mother miscarried. Mary Faith is bound and determined to bear this baby and support it.

Mary Faith chronicles her long pregnancy through the heat of a Southern summer in alternate chapters of clear, astringent prose. (When dreaminess and longing are allowed to creep in, they ravish.) Mary Faith's relations with the tormented Michael Jagger, forever urging students to protest about this and resist that, to think for themselves and reject "respectability", are delicately portrayed through his series of letters to her. She rereads them, thoughtfully, after his suicide, realizing that she has used him, and loved him without knowing it. The novel's other chapters, written in the third person, open out the fictional world, following Mr Rapple on his distraught wanderings round the tackily developed town and spying on his comical affair with a lascivious widow. Minor characters are vividly sketched, from the school principal who reluctantly lets Mary Faith stay on because he's afraid of a court action by the American Civil Liberties Union, to Aunt Lizann, whom Mr Rapple says should work for the FBI "and report on people's innermost feelings from a block away".

Alice H.G. Phillips, "Body Heat," in The Times Literary Supplement, *No. 4432, March 11-17, 1988, p. 276.*

Joanna Scott
1960-

American novelist.

Scott won nearly unanimous praise for the startling inventiveness of her first novel, *Fading, My Parmacheene Belle* (1987). Narrated in the first person by an unnamed, aged fisherman, who thinks of life in terms of piscatorial metaphors, the novel is a rich mixture of fable and allegory. Confronted with loss and change by the death of his wife, Scott's narrator seeks to discover the meaning of his life. Accompanied by a teenage runaway, he embarks on a picaresque journey of discovery to his wife's birthplace, the sea.

Critics cite Scott's strikingly original language as the novel's most praiseworthy feature, commending the eloquence and emotional intensity of her narrator's highly personal dialect. Although a few reviewers observe that the difficulty of Scott's language can be alienating, most agree that *Fading, My Parmacheene Belle* is a notable achievement. Scott's second novel, *The Closest Possible Union*, was published in the spring of 1988.

© Jerry Bauer

PUBLISHERS WEEKLY

A Parmacheene Belle is a trout lure, "the most taking fly" says the narrator of this strikingly original and powerful first novel [*Fading, My Parmacheene Belle*]. A Parmacheene Belle is what he calls his wife of 53 years who has just died of cancer, though while she was alive he called her Wife. Walking out on the funeral before its end, he throws a chair—Wife's chair—at their severely retarded grown son and, fearing he's killed the son, takes off for the woods. There he falls into a wary alliance with a runaway teenage girl whose modern habits appall him. They live for a while in the city, then head to the ocean, Wife's original home, meeting with kindness and abuse along the way. Getting farther from the familiar, growing more attracted to the girl, the narrator uncovers the extent of his attachment to his spouse and, facing the depth of his loss, turns back toward home. In deeply rhythmic language rich in metaphor, Scott explores the pain of loss and limitation, of sorrow and isolation, and brings her narrator—aged, scathed and not necessarily comforted—out the other side. He called her Wife, she called him Man, but during their life together she worked her way inside of him in a way readers will not doubt or easily forget.

A review of "Fading, My Parmacheene Belle," in Publishers Weekly, *Vol. 231, No. 4, January 30, 1987, p. 369.*

CATHERINE PETROSKI

Can anyone think of a more intriguing title than *Fading, My Parmacheene Belle?* What? the reader thinks—what's a parmacheene belle, what's fading, what's this book about?. . . Told by a crusty first-person narrator, this is the story of a man whose wife has just died after 53 years of marriage. He has a lifetime of sorrows and barely allowed joys to sort out by himself, now that Wife's presence no longer distracts him from coming to terms with the meaning of things. In a rage of mourning, the old man strikes out at their only surviving child, whose mental retardation he interprets as a cosmic comment on his marriage. Believing he's killed the young man, the father takes off on a quest of resolution—he's going to deal with all the unanswered issues, all the unfinished business of his life. He meets a 15-year-old girl, also on the run, and the two form an unlikely, amazing bond.

What sets Joanna Scott's novel apart . . . is its particularity, its emotional intensity and its extraordinary language. It is a work that grows out of a situation one wouldn't expect a novel to be about, about characters who would not be deemed good character material by many writers. Because of its remarkable voice, it is also a novel that is covered with its own—and this can't be stressed too much—its *very* own dialect. Reading *Parmacheene* is like encountering a new strain of English, one that has its own grammar and logic and lexicon, and as we absorb the rules of the old man's language, we are drawn into his world. Scott's novel is something of a shock in this respect, and while many readers may not survive it, those who do will witness a virtuoso performance.

> Catherine Petroski, "Three Debuts Prove the Vitality of the Novel," in Chicago Tribune—Books, March 8, 1987, pp. 6-7.

NANCY RAMSEY

Elusive title aside, [*Fading, My Parmacheene Belle*] is a remarkably inventive first novel, narrated in the first-person voice of a curmudgeonly old angler whose wife . . . has just died. Their idiot son and the wife's cousin are now the extent of his family; dizzy with anger and disbelief at his loss, the widower hurls a kitchen chair at the two. Terrified at the possible consequences of his action, he runs off into the forest, where he serendipitously meets up with a 15-year-old cosmetic-toting, pot-smoking amateur prostitute runaway. Together this "expert pair of renegades" embark on an adventure of mythic proportions as they make their way from the mountains, which the wife (she is not referred to by name) saw as "nought but impediments," toward the ocean, which she lived by as a girl. Along the way, the reader is introduced to the underground world of a nameless Eastern city, and is invited to share the old angler's process of self-discovery. "I tell you after fifty-three years you do gain an intimacy with the woman. She shares your name and you grow used to her presence on the mattress. But if the wife wants to proceed to the grave, if she wants to leave you to fend for yourself, then you must call an end to the union, you must prepare yourself for a long separation." Rage alternates with the reflective stance of a man entering the final stage of his life in this moving, wise novel.

> Nancy Ramsey, in a review of "Fading, My Parmacheene Belle," in The New York Times Book Review, March 22, 1987, p. 28.

CHRISTOPHER LEHMANN-HAUPT

[In *Fading, My Parmacheene Belle*,] the protagonist of Joanna Scott's unusual first novel has his highly personal way of seeing the world. . . .

[If] one were to strip this story of its language, there would not be much original about it. It lacks the humor and invention of, say, Charles Portis's *True Grit*. At times, it is even forced and a little clichéd, at least so far as the plot is concerned.

But the mad eloquence of the old narrator redeems *Fading, My Parmacheene Belle*. A blend of the bucolic and the biblical, it achieves its own peculiar tragicomic poetic vision. "I tell you the world is poisoned and the young people do not understand," the old man despairs, upon catching the "mermaiden," as he calls his companion, trying to give her body to a young man for money. "One day they will be covered with malignant sores, their spines will curve, the fish will die, and the rivers will turn to blood. . . . Such loveless activity will speed the catastrophe forward and if I have any influence remaining I must drive these children apart, I must take hold of the girl and make off with her." . . .

[Joanna Scott's] unusual imagination promises a rich future of writing.

> Christopher Lehmann-Haupt, in a review of "Fading, My Parmacheene Belle," in The New York Times, March 26, 1987, p. 21.

An Excerpt from *Fading, My Parmacheene Belle*

Now I cannot help but wonder what the wife must think as she watches me stroll across the cemetery in company with this young tart, the wife surely mistakes my intention, so to give her clearer indication of my relation to the girl, I take hold of her wrist and drag her across the slushy lawn past tombstones all with familiar family names, we ascend the rise and soon I see the new mound indicating the wife's plot. The girl has quieted now, surely she senses my loss, she falls silent, finally respectful of the dead. I would take her to observe the memorial, I would point out the costly weeping angels marking Pappy's site, but there is a stooped figure beside the grave, a man in a brown cap and a mackintosh, leaning heavily on a silver cane.

At first I mistake him for a monument, but I see him exude a long breath, a loving sigh, as he shifts his cane to secure himself on firmer ground. It is a stranger conversing with the spirit of my wife, a stranger gazing endearingly upon her place, joining the angels in their sorrow. Who is this man and how did he serve her? I want to know, but instead I lead the girl away, I stagger backward and veer off so I am heading for the parking lot, furious at this additional betrayal.

"Why did you leave your car here, old man? Has someone died?"

Has someone died? she asks, naïve child, *Has someone died.* As if she needed to be told that there is an end to every beginning.

"No one has died," I say.

From a safe distance I turn to observe the man, even from here I can see how he grovels in adoration, he is solitary in the cemetery and has come to speak privately with the wife, and I tell you I despise this stranger, my eyes blur as I consider how there was adequate time spent apart from the wife, time available for her to convene with adulterers. I convict the nameless figure, I blame him for my fifty-three years, I detest him until I see he is not so much a stranger as I had thought.

With concentrated effort I bring the bowed legs, the mackintosh, the stooped shoulders into focus: it is the cap that provides sure identification, for the cap is the brown worsted that belongs to me, the same I left at home. *The man is me.* I am here, in my fishing cap with my Parmacheene fly pinned to the brim, and there, in my brown worsted, both with the girl and at the gravesite of the wife. I tell you I want to go to the man who is me, I want to reach out to him, for he is no longer an adulterer, he is a dedicated mourner, he wears my own gray mackintosh among the rows of tombstones. I want to take my place beside him, for I left early from the funeral ceremony and had no opportunity to say farewell. I would go to him, but I expect he would not acknowledge me, his stance suggests a relentless worship that will not be disturbed, he will remain beside the wife while I have upon my arm a young thing of bones, sinew, and flesh, and I do not have time to waste accompanying the man in his grief. I will leave him to watch over the wife while I attend to the girl and we continue. After all, it is the fault of the wife that I am forced onward, so I feel no compunction for my haste, let the other man who is me suffice. I have a responsibility to life while he has come to dwell on death. I grip the wrist tightly, I will not release her and approach the wife, no, I will not travel across the sod to mourn.

ELAINE R. OGNIBENE

"To be mad and shamed. To have a home and give it up. To be an aged man, to be alone in the dark wood." Reading these words, one might imagine the protagonist of Joanna Scott's *Fading, My Parmacheene Belle* to be a contemporary Lear, suffering and searching for the wisdom to match his years. Unfortunately, Scott's nameless narrator, a man in his 70s whose wife of 53 years died leaving him bereft, fails to discover the truth about his family or himself. In his fisherman's fable, he presents himself as an outcast and embarks on a cyclical quest to "discover the source" of his wife and himself by traveling to her oceanside home. Unlike Lear, however, he lacks the ability to grow in wisdom, human sympathy, or love.

In a fit of anger after his wife's funeral, the old man flings a chair, striking and perhaps killing his retarded son whom he calls the "Idiot." Fleeing into the woods, he unexpectedly meets a 15-year-old runaway who shares her candy bar and her wild stories. The "mermaiden" triggers an ambiguous mixture of sexual desire and protective parental instinct in "Old Tom Trouble." Taking off in his Buick Skylark, the two wind their way through rough country escapades, small-town scams, and the blighted urban underground whose inhabitants provide a rare moment of solace. In the seaside section with its carnival-like characters, the girl commits suicide, and the old man returns home still suffering, still searching, still alone.

Scott's first novel, though highly inventive as well as intelligent and clever in its sustained use of fishing metaphors, disappoints because her main character is unsympathetic, and her message is finally unclear. Setting aside syntactical aberrations that suggest ramblings of an old man in distress, the reader finds Scott's narrative disruptive in other ways. The dominant tone of bitterness, blame, and self-pity coupled with the selfish and contradictory nature of the narrator undercuts his assertions that he is a suffering "spirit," a "seasoned angler," a compassionate "observer" of life, or a remorseful man. Like Hawthorne's faithless Goodman Brown, this character sees treachery everywhere, including in his wife, whom he blames for fading too fast; in his former best friend, whom he constantly accuses of conspiracy; and in his institutionalized son, whom he rejects for not being able to fish and, therefore, for not being a man.

While one can appreciate Hawthornian ambiguity—the shadow ground between fact and fancy—in this novel the author's failure to name the two main characters, the wife, or the wife's illness mystifies. In addition, the sequences of dream versus reality blur important distinctions; questions rise and remain unresolved. Is the old man's relationship to the girl that of seducer or surrogate parent? Which metaphor fits which character? Where do thematic undercurrents of environmental pollution or industrial waste lead?

Much else about fishing is unclear in this novel besides the fishing metaphors. An experienced angler and writer friend of mine agreed and commented upon the remoteness of some references, for example, knowing that leaders are hollow for flotation or that gravel spills occur in stream beds used for trout fishing. He also observed how strange it was that, in a time of crisis, the obsessed fisherman "never really goes fishing to deal with death or to sort things out."

At the end of the novel, therefore, when lonely and locked out from his home, his son, and his single friend, the old man moans, "Believe me when I say I have learned almost nothing," the reader nods assent but sadly does not care. (pp. 9, 15)

> *Elaine R. Ognibene, in a review of "Fading, My Parmacheene Belle," in* Belles Lettres: A Review of Books by Women, *Vol. 3, No. 1, September-October, 1987, pp. 9, 15.*

CHRIS GORDON OWEN

Joanna Scott's narrator in *Fading, My Parmacheene Belle* is a man in his 70s who is dealing with his wife's recent death. Joined by a fifteen-year-old girl, he sets out on a phantasmagoric journey to the ocean near which his wife used to live. What did the old man and his wife mean to each other? Was he only a helpless fish caught by a seductive fly? Only when he has found some answers can he return home.

In this symbol-laden novel, the man and girl are not just traveling along actual highways and through real towns. Youth is seeking a kind of atonement; age is winding back through 53 years of marital memories and doubts. Contributing to the mythic atmosphere is the absence of names for the main characters (except for labels like the Mermaiden, the Angler, the Idiot One). But this device and the sometimes obscure, often turgid language keep us at an emotional distance from a narrator who might otherwise endear himself to us with his loyalty, sensitivity and remarkable willingness to venture down new roads.

> *Chris Gordon Owen, "First Novels Play with Classic Themes," in* New Directions for Women, *Vol. 16, No. 5, September-October, 1987, p. 17.*

DAVID PROFUMO

While the sport itself is traditionally riddled with fictions, angling has seldom proved a successful theme for the novel. Its metaphorical overtones are better suited to poetry, or the philosophical reflections of which 17th-century readers were fond; extended fictional treatment tends to produce whimsy and tedium. . . .

But this first novel [*Fading, My Parmacheene Belle*] from Joanne Scott, an American, is an honourable exception, combining as it does astute psychology with a vein of dark humour which maintains a constant and intriguing tension. The nameless narrator is an old backwoodsman who has lost his wife after 53 years of grinding marriage. Restless and solitary after her funeral, he comes to realise that his life has been manipulated by his former crony Gibble, whose cousin he was lured into marrying. . . .

Believing that in his rage he has murdered their idiot son, whom he despises, the ancient angler takes to the woods, where he experiences the terrors of the night, spectres of guilt and loss haunting him until he is convinced that the diabolical Gibble (the historical figure of devil-as-angler) is casting a fantastic spell over him. Uncertain of what is phantasm and what is real, he falls in with a hash-smoking teenage prostitute who is also on the run, and this unlikely duo head together towards the sea.

She is the antitype of every woman he has ever met, and to her he is an anachronism, but they reach a tenuous understanding. She dubs him Old Tom Trouble, and steers him through the nightmarish modern world of which he has had no knowledge. Vague, erotic desires are rekindled in him by the girl he calls the streetwalker or the strumpet, but his otherworldly background prevents him from seeing the irony that she is a hooker—for in every other respect he sees the world as an analogue of angling, a place of deceit and devouring, confinement and flight.

Through a series of surrogate parental relationships along the way, Joanna Scott sustains the story and at the same time hints at its mythic aspects without ever quite insisting on the *pèlerinage de l'âme*. While nobody actually goes fishing, the piscatorial metaphors strengthen the book without seeming farfetched: Old Tom, with his scaly skin, thinks of himself at times as a landlocked salmon with an urgent migratory instinct, and in one especially well-found image he considers the male catfish, who hatches the eggs in his mouth, and then turns to cannibalism.

The old man's mental history is tortured and extravagant, and the novel fashions it in an unrelenting prose that is by turns precise and visionary. The world it conjures up is grimy and infected, but the author stops short of impassioned polemic, and focuses on the pathetic and the human, a story of a man struggling to rediscover his past, 'the boy whose imagination worked upon the world until there was no world to be known separate from his dreams'.

David Profumo, *"Fishing for Complements," in* The Spectator, *Vol. 260, No. 8335, April 9, 1988, p. 34.*

COMMENTS OF JOANNA SCOTT TO *CLC YEARBOOK*

Discussing the origins of her first novel, Scott states, "I have a series of inspirations to thank for this book: In the fall of 1984 a friend told me about an elderly woman who, two weeks before she died of cancer, set out her husband's best suit so he would be sure to wear it to the funeral, and then she drove herself to the hospital. I decided to invent my own version of this woman, to write her story using the voice of the man who owned that suit. But before I created a voice for the husband I wanted to give him a hobby, and I chose—arbitrarily, ig-

norantly—fishing. Since I knew little about the sport I went to the library and poked around in 19th century anecdotal anthologies on gamefishing. When I came across a long, loving description of a particular fishing fly, a 'parmacheene belle,' I was struck by its immense metaphorical possibilities. But my main inspiration, from first page to last, was the thrill of the narrator's first words: 'I will tell you.' I was astonished by his inflexible determination to tell, to be heard. With the parmacheene belle as the axle of the fiction, those declarative words became the driving force, pushing the narrative on as the old man tries to give his life significance and rid himself of guilt.

"A few reviewers have commented on the differences between this narrator and the writer (as they have in my second novel, narrated by a fourteen-year-old boy), but to me that is like pointing out differences between a mathematician and a theory. In my fiction I am more interested in creating complex, idiosyncratic sensibilities with a logic of their own than in recording experiences, and the drama in both my first and second novels arises when a character's faith in his logic is shaken. In *Fading, My Parmacheene Belle,* a woman dies and an old man realizes that he cannot trust the world. On board an illegal slaveship in *The Closest Possible Union,* a boy learns that he cannot trust the confidences of those around him.

"If someone writes, 'The World is a Dancer,' we might well be intrigued by the equation, but we probably respond with skepticism as well. Skepticism—or, more precisely, the struggle between skepticism and belief—is one of the basic forces influencing the style of my fictional voices. People reveal themselves through both their confessions and their lies, and they hone their skills of skepticism as they mature. Yet I find that even while I probe for the secrets embedded in language, while I listen with raised eyebrows to speeches, sermons, commercials, or read newspapers, cookbooks, memoirs, roadsigns, I still want to be persuaded by what I hear or read. . . . I want to trust language. And I write with the assumption that I share this with readers: a need to believe and a relentless skepticism. Parables and riddles are made possible (and perhaps necessary) when belief and skepticism vie for control. Fables are made possible. Fiction is made possible. And so, with my first novel, I introduce my narrator to the public with the words, 'I will tell you exactly how it was . . .'—an obvious lie born out of his desire to confess, a lie that I wanted—even as I wrote—to believe.

I began this novel in my last year in the graduate writing program at Brown University where I studied with John Hawkes and Robert Coover. The transformation of my words, from the first illegible draft to the finished book, still seems an alchemist's trick, and yet sometimes I recoil from the exposure and wish that I had published anonymously or even posthumously. But I enjoy dialogues with readers, too. Intimacy is my object. I want to make my skeptical readers forget themselves; I want to make them believe—for a moment—that the dream is their own."

David Foster Wallace

1962-

American novelist and short story writer.

The Broom of the System (1987) is a pastiche of stories within stories, journal entries, unattributed conversations, transcripts of psychotherapy conversations, stream-of-consciousness reflections, and third-person narrative. Set in and around Cleveland in 1990, Wallace's novel chronicles the confusing existence of Lenore Stonecipher Beadsman, switchboard operator for the publishing firm of Frequent and Vigorous. When Lenore's great-grandmother and self-appointed intellectual mentor disappears from her nursing home, Lenore's search to recover her becomes the catalyst for a process of self-discovery.

Lenore's great-grandmother was a student of Wittgenstein—a narrative element which signals Wallace's preoccupation with language. His skillful use of contemporary idiom has been noted with favor by many reviewers, as has his practice of inventing new words. Several critics observe that the novel's plot serves only as a platform for the author's verbal and philosophical extravagances; some find his theories too weak to support such experimentation. Nevertheless, critics applaud the lively imagination and exuberant energy of Wallace's creation, comparing him frequently with Thomas Pynchon.

Photograph by Dianne Nilsen. Courtesy of David Foster Wallace.

A review of "The Broom of the System," in Publishers Weekly, *Vol. 230, No. 24, December 12, 1986, pp. 48-9.*

PUBLISHERS WEEKLY

This sprawling, energetic novel [*The Broom of the System*] has its moments of humor and creativity, but the neo-'60s territory has been mapped before, and more effectively, by others, particularly Thomas Pynchon. The meager plot centers on the search for a 92-year-old woman, a former student of Wittgenstein who is working on new developments in his philosophy of language, and who is believed to be hiding in the Great Ohio Desert, or G.O.D. Main characters include the woman's great granddaughter, Lenore Beadsman, a bland woman who works as a switchboard-operator for the Cleveland publishing firm of Frequent & Vigorous. ("I think it's just that my family tends to be kind of weird, and very . . . *verbal.*") Lenore's lover is her boss, Rick Vigorous, a tediously angst-ridden, middle-aged man in therapy who fears his penis is too small and recites in excruciating detail the dreary fiction submitted to his house. In addition to its unfocused intellectual underpinnings, this novel is hampered by poor writing, which is passed off as experimental: run-on sentences; phrases like "untalkaboutable" and "non-woundish"; childish word plays, including characters named Judith Prietht and Peter Abbott; and complete paragraphs that read ". . . ." (pp. 48-9)

MICHIKO KAKUTANI

[*The Broom of the System* is] an unwieldy, uneven work—by turns, hilarious and stultifying, daring and derivative—but at the same time, it's a novel that attests to . . . its young author's rich reserves of ambition and imagination.

From its opening pages onward through its enigmatic ending, *The Broom of the System* will remind readers of *The Crying of Lot 49* by Thomas Pynchon. Like *Lot,* it attempts to give us a portrait, through a combination of Joycean word games, literary parody and zany picaresque adventure, of a contemporary American run amok. Like *Lot,* it features comic and willfully symbolic characters with odd, cutesy names—a publisher named Rick Vigorous; a roommate named Candy Mandible, an Amherst student named Stonecipher Beadsman (also known as the Antichrist), and a talking cockateel named Vlad the Impaler. Like *Lot,* it uses stories within stories to examine the relationship between real life and fiction, language and perception. And like *Lot,* it focuses on a woman's quest for knowledge and identity.

As her name might indicate, Lenore Stonecipher Beadsman is engaged in an effort to decipher the mysteries of the world about her, and she's also trying to figure out exactly who she is. At the same time, she's trying to find her namesake and great-grandmother, who's mysteriously disappeared from a nursing home. This first Lenore Beadsman was a student of Wittgenstein (a circumstance that gives Mr. Wallace plenty of opportunities to hold forth on the nature of reality and language), and she'd set herself up—in a somewhat sinister way—as her great-granddaughter's spiritual and intellectual mentor. . . .

Although much of the world in *Broom* seems familiar—its backdrop is more or less Cleveland, the language employed by its characters more or less contemporary American slang—Mr. Wallace has set his story in the very near future (1990 to be exact) and in doing so, has allowed himself certain imaginative liberties. The result is a wonderfully odd, new world—recognizable but funny and perplexing at the same time. It's a world where state officials commission the construction of a desert (the Great Ohio Desert, otherwise known as G.O.D.) to give residents a vacationland with all the symbolic value of a wilderness-frontier; a world where television has become the dominant cultural touchstone. College students play a game called "Hi Bob," inspired by "The Bob Newhart Show," and neighbors hang out at a bar called Gilligan's Isle that takes its entire motif from the old television show.

Many of Mr. Wallace's conceits are amusing, and some are genuinely daring—the reader intermittently feels that the author wants to use Lenore's story as a Nabokovian armature on which to drape serious philosophical and literary discussions. The problem is that pretension often substitutes for real intelligence, wordiness for eloquence. Indeed *The Broom of the System* is pockmarked with superfluous verbal riffs (on things like geriatric acne), repetitive digressions, and nonsensical babbling that reads like out-takes from a stoned, late-night dormitory exchange. What are we to make, for instance, of the following: "No matter," says one character. "Meaning as fundamentalness. Fundamentalness as use. Meaning as use. Meaning as use. Excuse me?"

Clearly Mr. Wallace possesses a wealth of talents—a finely-tuned ear for contemporary idioms; an old-fashioned story-telling gift (as evidenced, in particular, by the stories within stories contained in this novel); a seemingly endless capacity for invention and an energetic refusal to compromise. For all its problems, *Broom* is no mean achievement—and yet only a shadow of what the author might accomplish given the application of some narrative discipline and the exchange of other writers's voices for a more original vision.

> *Michiko Kakutani, in a review of "The Broom of the System," in* The New York Times, *December 27, 1986, p. 13.*

RUDY RUCKER

This is a hot book; this is a terrific novel. The publishers are talking Pynchon, and there are definite similarities. The names for one thing: Biff Diggerence, Mindy Metalman, Sigurd Foamwhistle, Judith Prietht. The ramshackle, exfoliating, synchronistic plot reminds one of Pynchon, too, as does the book's

fractal tales-within-tales formal structure, as does the author's passionate concern with his characters' lives. But *The Broom of the System* is assuredly not by Thomas Pynchon; it is by 24-year-old David Foster Wallace. . . .

As a good novelist must, Wallace has an eidetic memory for dialogue. When his characters rap on in their flat-tire Valspeak, we realize that we've heard talk like this for a few years now, even though we've never seen it written down this well. "'No, I mean I could not believe it. When he said it to me, I just totally freaked out. I totally freaked. I was like:' the girl gestured." How great! Girls are always saying, "I was like:" and then gesturing or making a noise, and Wallace has found a way to write it down. I was like:

" . . ."

" . . ." is another of Wallace's linguistic creations. It's something his characters say instead of mumbling. " . . ." They say it a lot. It's good and it works, though often—and here we touch on a weak point—it feels like too much trouble for the reader to trace back through a half-page of unattributed phrases and " . . ."s to figure out who's supposed to be talking. Padding is padding, even when it demonstrates a point. Even so, most of Wallace's book is a fast, pleasant read. By the way, one more nice trope he coins is "Fnoof." That's what his characters say when they're sleeping. "Fnoof fnoof."

The book's main character is Lenore Beadsman. In the first chapter we see her as a teenager in 1981, witnessing an Animal House-style courting scene between two Amherst boys and her Mt. Holyoke sister's roomies. The rest of the book is set in 1990. Lenore is embroiled in a relationship with an older man named Rick Vigorous, who has a really really tiny penis and who has unbelievably foul dreams. "Kind of hard to take a man seriously who wants a spanking for Christmas," as Lenore's friend Candy Mandible says about Rick. He wears a beret to cover his bald spot. Rick represents, I would hazard, the aspect of Wallace's personality that got him to start this book. We often hear Rick talking, and get to read or hear, verbatim, a number of stories that Rick has made up. They're good stories, in a sick way, but by the end of the book we're as tired of Rick Vigorous as Lenore is: "I think new heights of spasmodic weirdness are being reached."

Early in the book, Lenore's great-grandmother disappears from her rest home. As Lenore searches for her, she bounces into and off of most of the people who have mattered in her life. The book's first Animal House scene takes on deeper and deeper resonances. At the climax, Lenore seems to attain what she's been blindly struggling towards for some nine years: self-determination and adult love. Lenore and her eventual true love might be thought of as representing the aspect of Wallace's personality that got him to finish this book, or rather, the aspect of Wallace's personality which finishing this book has helped him express.

It's a cathartic experience, with a lot of laughs, and a lot of deeper meanings. The missing great-grandmother (who may have absented herself precisely to force Lenore's maturation) was a student of Wittgenstein at Cambridge, which fact ties into a really heavy-duty network of images about language and communication. (p. 1)

The book's title comes out of the communications network as well. It's from a Wittgensteinian example that asks which part of a broom is more fundamental. Two equally good answers are: the bristles if you use it to sweep; or, the handle if you use it to break windows. "Meaning as fundamentalness. Fundamentalness as use. Meaning as use." Like a real object, *The Broom of the System* is rich enough to suggest many uses: avantgarde lit, vulgar comedy, *Bildungsroman,* romance.

One of the loveliest romantic passages of all occurs within a substory about a man who was in love with his neighbor's son. The man watched the boy for years but he only touched him once, as the boy's mother recalls.

> What happened was that in the middle of talking, for no reason, he just reached out a finger, very slowly, and touched Steve. With just one finger. . . . It was like, sometimes when you're standing in front of a clean window, a very clean window, looking out, and the window is so clean it looks like it's not there. You know? And to make sure it's there, even though you know it's there, really, you'll reach out and just . . . touch the window, ever so slightly. Just barely touch it. That's what it was like.

This is a wonderful book. (p. 13)

Rudy Rucker, "From the Mixed-Up Future of Lenore Beadsman," in Book World—The Washington Post, *January 11, 1987, pp. 1, 13.*

An Excerpt from *The Broom of the System*

"We made a deal that we wouldn't talk about Jay-appointments, remember?"

"You're so pale you're practically transparent."

"Well, you can touch my chest if you want, like in that stupid story."

"Pardon me?"

"That one story, the first one you had me read? Where the old man touches the little boy to make sure he's not a window?"

"You didn't care for that story? What was it called. . .?"

" 'Love.' "

"Yes, that's the one."

"I liked that other one, though. That 'Metamorphosis for the Eighties.' I thought it was a killer. The part when the people threw coins at the rock star on stage and they stuck in him and he died was maybe a little hokey, but overall it was deadly. I put a big asterisk on it for you."

" . . . ."

"You don't want your stew anymore? I didn't mean it about the mouths. Eat up."

"But you didn't much care for the other one, then."

"Maybe I'm wrong, but I thought it sucked canal-water, big time."

" . . . ."

"Oh no, did you really like it? Am I ignorantly stomping on a good thing, that you liked?"

"My tastes are for the moment on the back burner. I'd simply be interested to hear why you dislike it."

"I'm really not sure. It just seemed . . . it was like you said about all the other troubled collegiate stuff. It just

seemed artificial. Like the kid who wrote it was trying too hard."

"I see."

"All that stuff about, 'And then context came in, and Fieldbaum looked bland.' "

"Fieldbinder."

"What?"

"Wasn't the protagonist's name Fieldbinder? In the story?"

"Right, Fieldbinder. But that stuff about context, though. Shouldn't a story *make* the context that makes people do certain things and have the things be appropriate or not appropriate? A story shouldn't just *mention* the exact context it's supposed to try really to create, right?"

" . . . ."

"And the writing was just so . . . This one line I remember: 'He grinned wryly.' Grinned wryly? Who grins wryly? Nobody grins wryly, at all, except in stories. It wasn't real at all. It was like a story about a story. I put it on Mavis's desk with the ones about the proctologist and the snowblower."

" . . . ."

"But I'll take it right back off if you liked it. You did like it, didn't you? This means my tastes aren't keened to the right pitch, doesn't it?"

"Not . . . not necessarily. I'm trying to remember where I got the thing. Must have been some kid, somewhere. Troubled. Trying to remember his cover letter . . ."

"Although it was well typed, I noticed."

" . . . ."

"Let me just try one little smidgeon of your stew, here."

"Think he said it *was* almost like a story about a story. The narrative center being the wife's description of the occasion on which Costigan touched the son. . . . Almost a story about the way a story waits and waits but never dies, can always come back, even after ostensible characters have long since departed the real scene."

"Really not all that bad."

"What?"

"The broth is pretty good. Creamy. I guess it's just the oysters I don't like."

"I seem to remember he said he conceived it as a story of neighborhood obsession. About how sometimes neighbors can become obsessed with other neighbors, even children, and perhaps even peer into their bedrooms across the fence from their dens . . . but how it's usually impossible for the respective neighbors to know about such things, because each neighbor is shut away inside his own property, his house, surrounded by a fence. Locked away. Everything meaningful, both good-meaningful and bad-meaningful, kept private."

" . . . ."

"Except that ocasionally the Private leaked out, every once in a while, and became Incident. And that perceived

Incident became Story. And that Story endured, in Mind, even behind and within the isolating membrane of house and property and fence that surrounded and isolated each individual suburb-resident.''

ROBERT ASAHINA

"A story, please."

"I did read a rather interesting one recently."

"So let's hear it."

"OK, here goes. A man named David Foster Wallace writes a novel called **The Broom of the System.** . . . The man certainly can write, but he seems to have a serious problem with the style of fiction now in vogue. Instead of writing one of those minimalist novels that take place somewhere between the K-Mart and the trailer camp, where everyone speaks in monotones and everything is described in short sentences written in the present tense and all the women have Ann in their names somewhere, the man decides to write an incredibly complicated *metafiction*, if you'll excuse my French, of the kind not seen since the heyday of John Barth and Donald, not Frederick, Barthelme and William Gass and William Gaddis and, oh yes, Thomas Pynchon."

"Gee."

"Wait, there's more. The novel is set in 1990 in Cleveland, Ohio, though it's not like the Cleveland I know, and I should know, since I'm from Ohio myself. For one thing, most of the state has been turned into the Great Ohio Desert, whose initials, if you're paying attention, as you must in this kind of metafiction, should suggest the sort of word games the author is playing. For another, the heroine, whose name is Lenore Stonecipher Beadsman, works at a publishing house called Frequent and Vigorous, and, as one of the characters asks, 'Who ever heard of a publishing house in Cleveland?' Not me, and I should know, since I work in publishing myself."

"Still, I'm hooked, I admit it."

"Anyway, the author sometimes writes incredibly long sentences filled with blind references, and sometimes dialogues like this one, where you don't know who's speaking to whom, and sometimes first-person journal entries, and sometimes short pieces of fiction within the larger novel, and he even uses the good old-fashioned omniscient third person."

"That's a relief."

"Well, yes and no, because even then it's hard to know what's going on, although it's something about Lenore's search for her great-grandmother, who's also named Lenore, which can be confusing, who's disappeared from the nursing home owned by the conglomerate run by Lenore's father, which manufactures baby food and is in a market-share struggle with Gerber. Lenore herself is struggling between Rick Vigorous, late of Hunt and Peck and now head of Frequent and Vigorous, though he really isn't as far as Lenore is concerned, and Andy Wang-Dang Lang, soon-to-be ex-husband of Mindy Metalman, who used to live next door to Rick in Scarsdale and was a roommate of Lenore's father, as well as his rival, Robert Gerber."

"Whew!"

"And that's just the beginning. There's also a talking cockateel named Vlad the Impaler, which winds up as the star of the Christian Broadcasting Network, a gymnast who's been trained by her father with a cattle prod and plenty of snide remarks about suburbia, where a planned community had the shape of Jayne Mansfield, and people don't connect with one another because they're locked inside their tract houses. Indeed, *connections* are a big theme in the novel, seeing as how Lenore is a telephone operator at Frequent and Vigorous, and the switchboard's always on the blink."

"Hmmm. But what is the novel really *about*?"

"Actually, that's not the kind of question you're supposed to ask about metafiction, or any kind of fiction these days, because even the minimalist variety isn't supposed to *mean*, it's just supposed to *be*, while the art is in the interpretation, since writers have abdicated responsibility for *meaning* to readers, and isn't it funny how current academic critical theory and contemporary fiction go pen in hand? Anyway, if I may be so bold, I think the author wants to say something profound about Self and Other, and Inside and Outside, and all those other Philosophy 101 dichotomies, and I should know, since I studied philosophy in graduate school. Or at least he's always having his characters refer to them, and he's even made Lenore's great-grandmother a disciple of Wittgenstein's, although Russellian and Heideggerian concepts also freely float throughout the *texte*, if you'll excuse my French. Of course, with this kind of writing, you never know what to take seriously and what not to, since the tone is so laden with irony, and that's something else that metafiction and minimalism have in common."

"Big help. Let me ask something easier: What does the *title* mean?"

"Oh, you'll have to read the novel, but here's a clue: Meaning is use. Look *that* up in your Philosophical Investigations."

"Is it my imagination, or are we nearing the end of this review?"

"At last you're entering into the self-referential spirit of the book and the review. Except that the review is ultimately about the book, whereas the book essentially seems to be about itself, 'a game consisting of involved attempts to find out the game's own rules,' and not about Lenore, whose life is 'told, not lived,' or any other character. Now you might find all this wordplay 'hideously self-conscious. . . . Or, at any rate, consistently, off-puttingly pretentious,' to quote Lenore against the author, in self-referential retribution, and why can't a character speak against her own creator? But if by *coincidence*, which is another persistent motif and an all-too-convenient plot device in **The Broom of the System,** you're as 'weird about words' as the author is, then maybe you'll regard the novel as a brilliant debut. Which is to say, it's quasi-Thomas Pynchon for those with a taste for the genre, quasi-Tom Robbins for those without. Obviously, for those who remember Philosophy 101, it can't be both. But, then again, it could be neither." (pp. 1, 9)

Robert Asahina, in a review of "The Broom of the System," in Los Angeles Times Book Review, *February 1, 1987, pp. 1, 9.*

CARYN JAMES

Stanley Elkin, an author never accused of being a minimalist, once recalled his defense when an editor advised, "Stanley, less is more." "I had to fight him tooth and nail in the better restaurants to maintain excess," Mr. Elkin said, "because I don't believe less is more. I believe that *more* is more. I believe that less is less, fat fat, thin thin, and enough is enough.'' Today, nearly a dozen years later, the very mention of a first novel by a 24-year-old barely out of college might make a reader say, ''enough is enough''—enough pared down, world-weary creative writing projects. So *The Broom of the System* is an enormous surprise, emerging straight from the excessive tradition of Stanley Elkin's *Franchiser,* Thomas Pynchon's *V,* John Irving's *World according to Garp.* As in those novels, the charm and flaws of David Foster Wallace's book are due to its exuberance—cartoonish characters, stories within stories, impossible coincidences, a hip but true fondness for pop culture and above all the spirit of playfulness that has slipped away from so much recent fiction.

Cleveland in 1990—the setting for most of the story—borders the Great Ohio Desert (or G.O.D.), a manmade area filled with black sand, meant to restore a sense of the sinister to Midwestern life. The confused heroine is 24-year-old Lenore Stonecipher Beadsman who, despite her proximity to the sinister G.O.D., has a ridiculous life. Her friends hang out at Gilligans Isle, a theme bar; her grandfather designed a Cleveland suburb in the precise outline of Jayne Mansfield's body; her brother Stonecipher Beadsman IV is nicknamed the Antichrist; and her boyfriend, Rick Vigorous, half of the publishing firm of Frequent and Vigorous, is insane about Lenore but impotent when he's with her, so he tells her stories as a substitute for sex.

Poor Lenore is also under the influence of the great-grandmother for whom she was named, a woman who had been Wittgenstein's student and who has taught her great-granddaughter that words create reality. Gramma has convinced Lenore: ''All that really exists of my life is what can be said about it.'' Circumscribed by what others say, Lenore feels not quite in control of her own existence.

When Gramma Lenore disappears from her room at the old folks' home, the search for her provides the book's flimsy plot. Her precious notebook from Wittgenstein's class has vanished as well, but Gramma has left other clues behind, such as the ominous drawing scrawled on a label from a Stonecipheco Baby Food jar. (The family business is Gerber's top rival.) It depicts, Lenore guesses, ''the barber who shaves all and only those who do not shave themselves... The big killer question ... is supposed to be whether the barber shaves himself. I think that's why his head's exploded, here.'' She also suspects a connection between Gramma's disappearance and the way Lenore's pet cockateel, Vlad the Impaler, has a new, enlarged vocabulary. (''Women need space, too,'' squawks the bird.)

The heart of the novel, though, is its verbal extravagance and formal variations, reflecting Lenore's belief that language creates and imprisons her. Beyond the comic narration of her life, there are excerpts from Rick's journal, transcripts of Lenore and Rick's individual sessions with their mutual psychiatrist, the stories Rick tells Lenore. To her, those stories are the means by which Rick tries to control her; given Gramma's theories, Lenore might as well be a character in Rick's thinly veiled autobiographical tales. What's the difference, Mr. Wallace seems to ask, between the real Lenore and the masked version in Rick's stories? And, by extension, what's the difference between the real-life reader and Lenore in *The Broom of the System*?

Though such Chinese boxes are mere staples of metafiction, Rick's stories have a more interesting pattern, one Lenore can't see. These weird tales—of a woman who has a tree toad living in a small hollow in her neck, or of children who can die from uncontrollable crying jags—depict families in distress. No family is as stressed out as the inscrutable line of Stonecipher Beadsmans, of course. With remarkable authorial control, Mr. Wallace makes Rick's stories suitably awkward and clichéd, yet affecting within the fictional world of the Beadsmans.

Mr. Wallace's collection of fragmented set pieces owes a lot to Wittgenstein's theory of language games—at least as Gramma demonstrates it. ''Which part of the broom was more elemental . . . the bristles or the handle?'' she asks her grandson. When he answers the bristles, she yells, ''*Aha,* that's because you want to *sweep* with the broom. . . . If what we wanted a broom for was to break windows, then the *handle* was clearly the fundamental essence of the broom, and she illustrated with the kitchen window.''

Similarly, Mr. Wallace aims to create his own language game, a fictional system in which ''something's meaning is nothing more or less than its function.'' The philosophical underpinnings of his novel are too weak to support this, though. There is too much flat-footed satire of Self and Other, too much reliance on Philosophy 101. (The Antichrist refers to his phone as a lymph node, so he can honestly tell his father he doesn't have a phone.) And the novel falls off drastically at the end, when a tortured running joke turns into a contrived explanation and characters we expect to appear never show up.

But the author's narrative command carries him over the low spots. This is not, after all, a minimalist tightrope-walk where a few wrong choices can produce empty posturing instead of precisely understated fiction. A saving grace of excessive novels is that a few missteps hardly matter; *The Broom of the System* succeeds as a manic, human, flawed extravaganza.

Caryn James, ''*Wittgenstein Is Dead and Living in Ohio,*'' in The New York Times Book Review, *March 1, 1987, p. 22.*

ORSON SCOTT CARD

Wallace's first novel, *The Broom of the System,* falls into that area where literary fiction and science fiction seamlessly meet. Call it absurdism, existential comedy, or alternate reality, it contains some of the best and liveliest storytelling in the English language. R. A. Lafferty and Samuel Beckett, Rudy Rucker and, now, David Foster Wallace; the audience for these brilliant writers must discard all expectations from the start.

Broom is set in 1990 in Cleveland, perched on the edge of the Great Ohio Desert—the G.O.D., as it is called. Lenore Beadsman, scion of the founding family of a giant baby-food corporation, works as a $4-per-hour switchboard operator for the publishing company Frequent & Vigorous; Rick Vigorous, her boss, is also her insanely jealous lover, getting information about her from the unethical psychiatrist they both visit.

Lenore's great-grandmother, who must live in a room heated to 98.6 in order to maintain her body temperature, has disappeared from her old-folks' home, taking a score of residents and staff with her. Beyond that the plot gets complicated.

It also gets funny. The humor is sophomoric sometimes—for instance, an operator named Judith Prieht and a repairman named Peter Abbott. Sometimes it is satirical, as with the plastic adult-size highway-legal cars made by Mattel, and the town in the shape of Jayne Mansfield's nude profile, with zoning laws requiring realistic colors, making it a favorite landing approach route with airline pilots.

The humor often achieves true brilliance, however, the kind of incisive wit that is too funny to be summed up, as with the unforgettable scene in a restaurant as the spectacularly obese Bombardini orders dinner, or the scene in Lenore's apartment where her parrot echoes *all* the words her roommate said in preparing to dump a boyfriend.

Wallace's incipient MFA gives him license to bore, but he rarely uses it.

What he *does* is shake loose all expectations of form. The story is written in dialogue, in monologue, as a diary entry, in present tense, in past tense, as a clipping from a paper—every imaginable voice and form seems to be in this book. Yet Wallace makes it all come together as a unified vision of inspired madness. This is Wallace's first novel. God help us all when he gets some practice. (pp. 41-2)

> *Orson Scott Card, in a review of "The Broom of the System," in* The Magazine of Fantasy and Science Fiction, *Vol. 73, No. 2, August, 1987, pp. 41-2.*

Prizewinners

Literary Prizes and Honors

Announced in 1987

ACADEMY OF AMERICAN POETS AWARDS

FELLOWSHIP OF THE ACADEMY OF
AMERICAN POETS
  Josephine Jacobsen
THE LAMONT POETRY SELECTION
  Garrett Kaoru Hongo, *The River of Heaven*
IVAN YOUNGER POETS AWARDS
  Jon Davis, Debora Greger, Norman Williams
WALT WHITMAN AWARD
  Judith Baumel, *The Weight of Numbers*

**AMERICAN ACADEMY AND INSTITUTE OF
ARTS AND LETTERS AWARD**

GOLD MEDAL FOR BELLES LETTRES AND
CRITICISM
  Jacques Barzun
AWARD OF MERIT MEDAL FOR DRAMA
  A. R. Gurney, Jr.
AWARDS IN LITERATURE
  Evan S. Connell, Ernest J. Gaines, Ralph Manheim,
  Sandra McPherson, Steven Millhauser, Robert
  Phillips, Roger Shattuck
MILDRED AND HAROLD STRAUSS LIVINGS
  Diane Johnson, Robert Stone
HAROLD D. VURSELL MEMORIAL AWARD
  Stephen Jay Gould
JEAN STEIN AWARD FOR POETRY
  Wendell Berry
MORTON DAUWEN ZABEL AWARD
  Paul Metcalf
RICHARD AND HINDA ROSENTHAL
FOUNDATION AWARD FOR FICTION
  Norman Rush, *Whites*
ROME FELLOWSHIP IN LITERATURE
  Padgett Powell
SUE KAUFMAN PRIZE FOR FIRST FICTION
  Jeannette Haien, *The All of It*
WITTER BYNNER PRIZE FOR POETRY
  Antler

BOLLINGEN PRIZE IN POETRY

  Stanley Kunitz

BOOKER-McCONNELL PRIZE FOR FICTION

  Penelope Lively, *Moon Tiger*

COMMONWEALTH POETRY PRIZE

  John Ashbery

**DELMORE SCHWARTZ MEMORIAL POETRY
AWARD**

  Lee Young

DRUE HEINZ LITERATURE PRIZE

  Ellen Hunnicut, *In the Music Library*

EDGAR ALLAN POE AWARDS

BEST NOVEL
  Barbara Vine, *A Dark-Adapted Eye*
FIRST NOVEL
  Larry Beinhart, *No One Rides for Free*
SHORT STORY
  Robert Sampson, "Rain in Pinton County," in *New
  Black Mask*
CRITICAL/BIOGRAPHY
  Eric Ambler, *Here Lies: An Autobiography*
GRAND MASTER AWARD
  Michael Gilbert

PRIX GONCOURT

Tahar Ben Jelloun, *The Sacred Night*

GOVERNOR GENERAL'S LITERARY AWARDS

FICTION
  Alice Munro, *The Progress of Love*
DRAMA
  Sharon Pollock, *Doc*
POETRY
  Al Purdy, *The Collected Poems of Al Purdy*

HUGO AWARDS
NOVEL
Orson Scott Card, *Speaker for the Dead*
NONFICTION
Brian Aldiss and Dave Wingrove, *Trillion Year Spree*
NOVELLA
Robert Silverberg, *Gilgamesh in the Outback,* in *Isaac Asimov's Science Fiction Magazine*
NOVELLETTE
Roger Zelazny, "Permafrost," in *Omni*
SHORT STORY
Greg Bear, "Tangents," in *Omni*

JAMES TAIT BLACK MEMORIAL PRIZES
FICTION
Jenny Joseph, *Persephone*
BIOGRAPHY
Sr. Felicitas Corrigan, OSB, *Helen Waddell*

LENORE MARSHALL/NATION POETRY PRIZE
Donald Hall, *The Happy Man*

LOS ANGELES TIMES BOOK AWARDS
FICTION
James Welch, *Fools Crow*
POETRY
William Meredith, *Partial Accounts: New and Selected Poems*
BIOGRAPHY
Kenneth S. Lynn, *Hemingway*
HISTORY
Robert J. Lifton, *The Nazi Doctors: Medical Killing and the Psychology of Genocide*

THE NATIONAL BOOK AWARDS
FICTION
Larry Heinemann, *Paco's Story*
NONFICTION
Richard Rhodes, *The Making of the Atomic Bomb*

THE NATIONAL BOOK CRITICS CIRCLE
AWARDS
FICTION
Reynolds Price, *Kate Vaiden*
POETRY
Edward Hirsch, *Wild Gratitude*
CRITICISM
Joseph Brodsky, *Less Than One: Selected Essays*
BIOGRAPHY
Theodore Rosengarten, *Tombee: Portrait of a Cotton Planter*
NONFICTION
John W. Dower, *War Without Mercy: Race and Power in the Pacific War*

NEBULA AWARDS
NOVEL
Orson Scott Card, *Speaker for the Dead*
NOVELLA
Lucius Shepard, *R & R,* in *Isaac Asimov's Science Fiction Magazine*
NOVELETTE
Kate Wilhelm, "The Girl Who Fell into the Sky," in *Isaac Asimov's Science Fiction Magazine*
SHORT STORY
Greg Bear, "Tangents," in *Omni*
GRAND MASTER AWARD
Isaac Asimov

NEW YORK DRAMA CRITICS CIRCLE AWARD
August Wilson, *Fences*

NOBEL PRIZE IN LITERATURE
JosephBrodsky

OBIE AWARD
Richard Foreman, *The Cure* and *Film Is Evil: Radio is Good*

O. HENRY AWARDS
Louise Erdrich, "Fleur," in *Esquire*
Joyce Johnson, "The Children's Wing," in *Harper's*

PEN AWARDS
PEN/FAULKNER AWARD FOR FICTION
Richard Wiley, *Soldiers in Hiding*
ERNEST HEMINGWAY FOUNDATION AWARD FOR FIRST FICTION
Mary Ward Brown, *Tongues of Flame*
PEN/BOOK-OF-THE-MONTH CLUB TRANSLATION PRIZE
John E. Woods, for *Perfume: The Story of a Murderer* by Patrick Süskind
PEN/JERARD FUND AWARD
Nancy Dougherty, *The Hangman's Wife*
SHEAFFER-PEN NEW ENGLAND AWARD FOR LITERARY DISTINCTION
Andrew Dubus

PULITZER PRIZES
FICTION
Peter Taylor, *A Summons to Memphis*
POETRY
Rita Dove, *Thomas and Beulah*
BIOGRAPHY
David J. Garrow, *Bearing the Cross: Martin Luther King, Jr. and the Southern Christian Leadership Conference*

HISTORY

Bernard Beilyn, *Voyagers to the West: A Passage in the Peopling of America on the Eve of the Revolution*

NONFICTION

David K. Shipler, *Arab and Jew: Wounded Spirits in a Promised Land*

TONY AWARDS

BEST PLAY

August Wilson, *Fences*

WORLD FANTASY AWARDS

NOVEL

Patrick Süskind, *Perfume: The Story of a Murderer*

NOVELLA

Orson Scott Card, *Hatrack River,* in *Isaac Asimov's Science Fiction Magazine*

SHORT STORY

David Schow, "Red Light," in *Twilight Zone*

LIFETIME ACHIEVEMENT

Jack Finney

YALE SERIES OF YOUNGER POETS AWARD

Brigit Pegeen Kelly, *To the Place of Trumpets*

Prizewinners

Featured in 1987 Yearbook

Joseph Brodsky
Nobel Prize in Literature

Orson Scott Card
Speaker for the Dead
Hugo Award
Nebula Award

Rita Dove
Thomas and Beulah
Pulitzer Prize: Poetry

Richard Foreman
The Cure and *Film Is Evil: Radio Is Good*
Obie Award

A. R. Gurney, Jr.
American Academy and Institute of Arts and Letters: Award of Merit for Drama

Larry C. Heinemann
Paco's Story
The National Book Awards: Fiction

Edward Hirsch
Wild Gratitude
The National Book Critics Circle Award: Poetry

Penelope Lively
Moon Tiger
Booker-McConnell Prize for Fiction

Alice Munro
The Progress of Love
Governor General's Literary Award: Fiction

Sharon Pollock
Doc
Governor General's Literary Award: Drama

Reynolds Price
Kate Vaiden
The National Book Critics Circle Award: Fiction

Al Purdy
The Collected Poems of Al Purdy
Governor General's Literary Award: Poetry

Peter Taylor
A Summons to Memphis
Pulitzer Prize: Fiction

Barbara Vine
A Dark-Adapted Eye
Edgar Allan Poe Award: Best Novel

August Wilson
Fences
New York Drama Critics Circle Award: Best Play
Pulitzer Prize: Drama
Tony Award

Prize Commentary

American Academy and Institute of Arts and Letters: Award of Merit

The Award of Merit, established in 1942, is one of the most prestigious prizes bestowed by the American Academy and Institute of Arts and Letters. Awarded annually, the prize consists of a medal and one thousand dollars and recognizes outstanding achievement in painting, sculpture, fiction, poetry, or drama. The award is given to individuals who are not members of the award-giving body and recognizes their entire work.

Booker-McConnell Prize for Fiction

Britain's most important prize for fiction, the Booker-McConnell Prize is awarded to the writer of the year's most distinguished full-length novel written in English by a citizen of the British Commonwealth and published in the United Kingdom. Publishers submit the books for consideration and a five-member committee selects the winner of the award, which includes a monetary prize of ten thousand pounds. The prize was established in 1968 by the international food company Booker-McConnell Limited and is administered by the National Book League.

Edgar Allan Poe Awards

Informally known as the "Edgars," the Edgar Allan Poe Awards were establihed in 1945 by the Mystery Writers of America and are given annually for the year's outstanding works in the mystery genre. The winners are selected by the General Awards Committee from works submitted by publishers. Scrolls are awarded to all nominees, and the winner in each category receives a ceramic bust of Edgar Allan Poe.

Governor General's Literary Awards

Established in 1936 by the Canadian Authors Association, the Governor General's Literary Awards are now administered through the Canada Council. The prize is given for superior works of fiction, poetry, drama, and nonfiction published during the year by Canadian authors. Awards are given both for works in English and works in French, bringing the total annual number of awards to eight. The winners, who are chosen by an eighteen-member committee, receive a specially bound copy of the award-winning work in addition to a cash prize of five thousand dollars.

Hugo Awards

The Hugo Awards, established in 1953, are sponsored by the World Science Fiction Society and are chosen through the vote of the people who attend the Annual Science Fiction Convention. The Hugo is awarded for notable science fiction works in several categories. Each winner receives a trophy of a chrome-plated rocket ship. Informally named after Hugo Gernsback, an early publisher of science fiction, the award's official title is the Science Fiction Achievement Award.

The National Book Awards

The National Book Awards were established in 1950 by the National Book Committee. Administered by the Association of American Publishers, the National Book Awards, which were known as the American Book Awards from 1981 to 1986, are given annually "to honor and promote books of distinction and literary merit." Books written by American citizens and published in the United States are submitted by publishers and reviewed by the nominating committees. The winners in the categories of fiction and nonfiction are chosen by the Academy of the National Book Awards. Nominees receive one thousand dollars, and winners receive ten thousand dollars.

The National Book Critics Circle Awards

Awarded for books published in the previous year, the National Book Critics Circle Awards honor superior works by American authors. The purpose of the National Books Critics Circle, which was founded in 1974, is "to raise the standards of the profession of book criticism and to enhance public appreciation of literature"; awards are bestowed for the best fiction, poetry, biography, criticism, and nonfiction. The winners are judged by the twenty-four members of the National Book Critics Circle Board of Directors; each winner receives an honorary scroll.

Nebula Awards

Established in 1965 and bestowed by the Science Fiction Writers of America, the Nebula Awards are presented to significant works (in several categories of the science fiction genre) that were published in the United States during the previous year. Winners are nominated and chosen by the organization's membership. The trophy awarded is a lucite sculpture embedded with a nebula formation.

New York Drama Critics Circle Awards

The purpose of the New York Drama Critics Circle Awards is to encourage continued excellence in playwriting by recognizing the year's best play (American or foreign), best foreign play (when the "best play" is American), and the best musical. Eligible dramatists are those who have had a new play produced during the year on or off Broadway in New York City; winners are chosen by the vote of members of the Circle. The award has been given by the New York Drama Critics Circle since 1935 and includes a scroll and one thousand dollars for the best play and a scroll for the other playwrights.

Nobel Prize in Literature

One of six Nobel Prizes given annually since 1901, the Nobel Prize in Literature is generally considered to be the highest recognition a writer can receive. Established under the terms of the will of the Swedish-born Alfred Bernhard Nobel, the Nobel Prizes are given to those "who, during the preceding year, shall have conferred the greatest benefit on mankind." Nobel willed the literary portion of the award to go to "the person who shall have produced in the field of literature the most outstanding work of an idealistic tendency." The award recognizes the author's entire body of work and is open to writers of any nationality. The Nobel Committee of the Swedish Academy nominates candidates and selects the winner. The Nobel laureate receives a gold medal, a certificate, and a honorarium that varies each year but always exceeds one hundred thousand dollars. The awards are presented in Stockholm, Sweden.

Obie Awards

Established in 1956 by the Plumsock Fund and *The Village Voice,* the Obie Awards recognize excellence in off Broadway and off-off Broadway theater productions. The awards are given in various categories and a panel of jurors, experts in the field, select the winners from the year's productions. The prize consists of a certificate and five hundred dollars.

Pulitzer Prizes

The Pulitzer Prizes were established in 1904 by Joseph Pulitzer, founder of the *St. Louis Post Dispatch,* and have continued through his willed endowment since 1917. Administered by the Graduate School of Journalism at Columbia University, the prizes recognize outstanding American works that address some aspect of American life; they are awarded in various categories within journalism, music, and literature. The fifteen-member Pulitzer board receives nominations from the separate juries of each category. The winner in each category is awarded one thousand dollars.

Tony Awards

Formally titled the Antoinette Perry Awards, the Tony Awards were founded in 1947 by the American Theatre Wing "to award the achievement of excellence in the theater" and are administered by the League of New York Theatres and Producers. The awards recognize the year's best play produced at one of the eligible Broadway theaters and also honor many other categories related to dramatic production. From a list of nominees, winners are selected by some 560 people involved in various aspects of the theater. The award itself bears images of the masks of comedy and tragedy on one side and the profile of actress Antoinette Perry on the other.

Joseph (Alexandrovich) Brodsky

Nobel Prize in Literature

(Also transliterated as Iosif, Josif, Yosif, or Josip; also Alexander or Aleksandrovich; also Brodski, Brodskii, or Brodskij) Russian-born American poet, essayist, and translator.

Many commentators consider Brodsky the finest contemporary poet to emerge from the Soviet Union. At the age of forty-seven, he became the second youngest person to receive the Nobel Prize in literature; he is the fifth Russian-born author to be so honored, preceded by Ivan Bunin (1933), Boris Pasternak (1958), Mikhail Sholokhov (1965), and Aleksandr Solzhenitsyn (1970). In bestowing the award, the Nobel Academy praised Brodsky for his "all-embracing authorship imbued with clarity of thought and poetic intensity."

Despite opposition from the Soviet government, which condemned his writings as subversive and degenerate, Brodsky established a distinguished reputation as a poet, both in his own country and in the West. He became as well known for the punishments he suffered under the Soviet system—numerous interrogations and arrests, confinement in mental hospitals and a labor camp, and eventually exile—as for his literary work. For most of his career Brodsky's poetry has been suppressed in his native country. After Brodsky's laureateship was announced, the Soviet literary magazine *Novy mir* published six of his poems. Declared the magazine's poetry editor, Oleg Chukhontsev: "It is impossible to imagine modern poetry without Joseph Brodsky."

Brodsky was born in Leningrad in 1940 to Jewish parents. Disenchanted with formal education, he left school at the age of fifteen to pursue his own studies, and he worked at a series of menial jobs. At about the age of eighteen, Brodsky began to write poetry; he also taught himself English and Polish in order to translate the works of foreign poets he admired, such as John Donne and Czeslaw Milosz. Although he was unable to join an official writers' union, his works were widely circulated in *samizdat* (underground publications); he added to his notoriety with compelling recitations of his work at poetry readings. By his early twenties he had attracted many admirers, including poet Anna Akhmatova, who regarded him as a writer of exceptional promise.

At this time Soviet authorities started to investigate Brodsky as a possible subversive. This was partly because he had belonged to a dissident political group as a teenager; however, some commentators allege that anti-Semitism played a part in the state-ordered persecution of Brodsky. In February of 1964, he was arrested on charges of "social parasitism" under a controversial law meant to punish vagrants, speculators, and others who refused gainful employment. Although Brodsky argued that his activities as a poet and translator constituted legitimate work, the judge at the trial reacted scornfully to this defense. "Who has recognized you as a poet? Who has given you a place among the poets?" she demanded of Brodsky, to which he retorted, "No one. And who included me among the ranks of the human race?" Author and educator Frida Vigdorova, out-

© Jerry Bauer

raged by what she perceived as a miscarriage of justice, took notes during the trial and had them smuggled out of the USSR. Vigdorova's transcript was printed in several journals in the West.

Brodsky's trial became a *cause célèbre,* symbolizing to many Western observers the Soviet Union's repressive treatment of its citizens. Many prominent persons in the Soviet Union, Europe, and North America, including Akhmatova, composer Dmitri Shostakovich, and the Hungarian-American scientist Dr. Edward Teller, protested the verdict that condemned Brodsky to five years of labor in a farm near the Arctic Circle. As a result, his sentence was reduced to eighteen months, and after his release he was allowed to work as a translator. However, Brodsky was still regarded as an undesirable element in Soviet society. In 1972 officials forced him to leave the country, despite his protests. "I do not cease to be a Russian poet," he stated in a letter to Soviet leader Leonid Brezhnev shortly before his exile. "I believe that I will return; poets always return, in flesh or on paper." After leaving the Soviet Union, Brodsky settled in the United States, where he has worked as an instructor of literature and creative writing at several universities. He became an American citizen in 1977.

At the time of his emigration, Brodsky feared that living in an English-speaking country would erode his command of Russian. Nevertheless, he adapted well to bilingualism. Although he continues to write most of his poems in Russian, he has translated some into English, and has written others, such as his tributes to Robert Lowell and W. H. Auden, in the language of his adopted country. Critics have compared him to Vladimir Nabokov for his rare ability to produce excellent literary writing in both Russian and English. American publishers have released several collections of his poetry in their original Russian, as well as translations of his work. *Stikhotvoreniia i poemy* (1965), the first published collection of Brodsky's verses, was assembled by an American publisher while Brodsky was still serving time in labor camp. Other collections followed, including *Ostanovka v pustyne* (1970), *Elegy for John Donne and Other Poems* (1967), *Selected Poems* (1973), *Chast rechi* (1977; *A Part of Speech*), and *Uraniia* (1984; *Homage to Urania*).

As a poet, Brodsky approaches his craft with reverence. He believes in poetry's importance as a constructive moral, social, and intellectual force, especially as an expression of individualism versus authoritarian repression. Although his government prosecuted him as a pornographer and a political subversive, Western critics contend that his poems contain nothing pornographic and very little mention of politics. His themes are for the most part metaphysical and aesthetic: meditations on death, the inexorable process of time, and the transcendent nature of art. The philosophy reflected in his writings is soberly realistic, yet informed by a profound aesthetic idealism. He imparts his thorough knowledge of the rich and varied history of his craft and draws inspiration from an eclectic variety of predecessors. Reflected in his style are the classical allusions of Western poets such as Dante Aligheri and John Donne; the traditional rhyme and meter of eighteenth and nineteenth century Russian poets as well as the influence of the more contemporary Russian writers Marina Tsvetaeva, Osip Mandelstam, Pasternak, and Akhmatova; and the innovative freshness of modernists such as Auden and T. S. Eliot.

Brodsky's poems written prior to 1961 are mostly brief, simple lyrics written in free verse. In his twenties, however, Brodsky worked in longer, increasingly complex forms. Critics note that Brodsky's early poems are his most personal, while later works treat more universal subject matter. However, there are recurrent themes that characterize all of his writings. These include a preoccupation with death and decay, evident in his "Bolshaia elegiia Dzhone Donnu" ("Elegy for John Donne") and "Ostanovka v pustyne" ("A Stop in the Desert"). Repeatedly, he makes allusion to classical Western mythology, as in "K Likomedu, na Skiros" ("To Lycomedes on Scyros") and "Enei i Didona" ("Aeneas and Dido"), as well as Judeo-Christian theology, reflected in "Isaak i Avraam" ("Isaac and Abraham") and "Gorbunov i Gorchakov" ("Gorbunov and Gorchakov").

The long poem "Gorbunov and Gorchakov," one of Brodsky's most well-known works, demonstrates his characteristic method of presenting traditional matter with contemporary immediacy. It concerns two inmates of a Soviet mental hospital. While their predicament is portrayed realistically—Brodsky himself was twice placed under observation in asylums in the USSR, for political reasons—the cycle of suffering, betrayal, and redemption they enact parallels the story of Jesus Christ and Judas Iscariot. The poem also contains an element of the absurd; this strain is intensified in the poems written after

Brodsky's exile, such as "Babochka" ("The Butterfly") and "Kolybelnaia Treskovogo Mysa" ("A Cape Cod Lullaby"). However, perhaps the most typical characteristic of his writings, exemplified in the "Elegy for John Donne," is his devotion to art and his belief in language as a vital, liberating force.

In *Less Than One* (1986), a collection of occasional essays for which he won the National Book Critics Circle Award, Brodsky demonstrated that his literary skills extend to prose as well as poetry. These essays, all originally composed in English, include critical studies of poets whom Brodsky admires, such as Akhmatova, Auden, Mandelstam, and Derek Walcott; reminiscences of his life in the USSR, as in "A Room and a Half"; and general commentaries on literature, notably "Catastrophes in the Air." Repeatedly, these essays examine the conflicts between intellectuals and the Soviet state.

Throughout his career, Brodsky has earned recognition from both critics and his peers as an extraordinarily gifted writer. A few commentators demur from the common opinion that he is the best Russian poet of his generation; they protest that sympathy for the oppression Brodsky has suffered has led others to overrate his talents. As from his beginnings in Leningrad, however, Brodsky continues to win admiration and respect for his poetic skills, his intellectual prowess, and his absolute devotion to his vocation as a poet, educator, and man of letters.

(See also *CLC*, Vols. 4, 6, 13, 36 and *Contemporary Authors*, Vols. 41-44, rev. ed.)

TRANSCRIPTION OF THE TRIAL OF JOSEPH BRODSKY

[*Brodsky was twenty-four years old when he was brought to trial on charges of social parasitism. The trial was held on February 18 and March 13, 1964, in the Dzerzhinsky District Court of the city of Leningrad. The judge in the case, Mme. Saveleva, found Brodsky guilty and sentenced him to five years in a labor camp. Frida Vigdorova, a Russian author and educator, took detailed notes during the trial; these later appeared in several publications in the West, making the Brodsky affair an international cause célèbre. In the following excerpt from Vigdorova's transcript of the court's proceedings, translated from the Russian by Collyer Bowen, Brodsky and his supporters contend with the prosecution's attacks on his character and professional integrity as a writer.*]

The First Hearing of
the Iosif Brodsky Case

JUDGE: What do you do?
BRODSKY: I write poetry. I translate. I suppose . . .
JUDGE: None of this "I suppose" business. Stand up straight! Don't lean against the wall! Look at the court! Answer the court properly! (*To me*): Cease taking notes immediately, or I will have you thrown out of the courtroom! (*To Brodsky*): Do you have a permanent job?
BRODSKY: I thought this was a permanent job.
JUDGE: Answer precisely!
BRODSKY: I wrote poetry. I thought they would be printed. I suppose . . .
JUDGE: We're not interested in what you "suppose." Answer why you were not working.
BRODSKY: I was working. I was writing poetry.

JUDGE: We are not interested in that. We are interested in knowing what institution you were connected with.

BRODSKY: I had some agreements with a publishing house.

JUDGE: Did you have enough agreements to live on? Enumerate them as to what they were, the date, and for how much money.

BRODSKY: I don't remember exactly. All the agreements are in the hands of my lawyer.

JUDGE: I am asking you.

BRODSKY: Two books containing my translations were published in Moscow . . . (*He enumerates them*).

JUDGE: How long have you worked?

BRODSKY: Approximately . . .

JUDGE: We are not interested in "approximately!"

BRODSKY: Five years.

JUDGE: Where did you work?

BRODSKY: In a factory. With geological groups . . .

JUDGE: How long did you work in the factory?

BRODSKY: A year.

JUDGE: Doing what?

BRODSKY: I was a milling machine operator.

JUDGE: But in general what is your specialty?

BRODSKY: I'm a poet, a poet-translator.

JUDGE: And who said that you were a poet? Who included you among the ranks of the poets?

BRODSKY: No one. (*Unsolicited*) And who included me among the ranks of the human race?

JUDGE: Did you study this?

BRODSKY: What?

JUDGE: To be a poet? You did not try to finish high school where they prepare . . . where they teach . . .

BRODSKY: I didn't think you could get this from school.

JUDGE: How then?

BRODSKY: I think that it . . . (*confused*) . . . comes from God . . .

JUDGE: Do you have any petitions to the court?

BRODSKY: I would like to know why I was arrested.

JUDGE: That's a question, not a petition.

BRODSKY: Then I have no petition.

JUDGE: Does the counsel for the defense have any questions?

DEFENSE: I do. Citizen Brodsky, does the money you earn go to the support of your family?

BRODSKY: Yes.

DEFENSE: Do your parents also work for a living?

BRODSKY: They live on a pension.

DEFENSE: Do you all live together as one family?

BRODSKY: Yes.

DEFENSE: Therefore, your earnings became part of the family budget?

JUDGE: You are summarizing rather than asking questions. You are helping him answer. Don't summarize, just ask questions.

DEFENSE: Are you registered at the psychiatric clinic?

BRODSKY: Yes.

DEFENSE: Have you undergone hospital treatment?

BRODSKY: Yes, from the end of December 1963 to the fifth of January of this year (*1964*) in the Kashchenko hospital in Moscow.

DEFENSE: Do you not feel that your illness prevented you from working in the same place for a long period of time?

BRODSKY: Perhaps. Probably. However, I don't know. No, I do not know.

DEFENSE: Did you translate poems for an anthology of Cuban poets?

BRODSKY: Yes.

DEFENSE: Did you translate Spanish *romanceros*?

BRODSKY: Yes.

DEFENSE: Were you connected with the translators' division of the Union of Writers?

BRODSKY: Yes.

DEFENSE: I ask the court to add to the case a testimonial of character from the office of the division of translators . . . A list of published poems . . . Copies of the agreements . . . A telegram: "We entreat you to sign the agreement as soon as possible." (*Defense enumerates.*) And I ask that citizen Brodsky be sent up for a medical examination to determine the state of his health and to see whether or not it has kept him from regular work. In addition I ask that citizen Brodsky be released immediately. It is my opinion that he has not committed any crimes and that he is being unlawfully held in custody. He has a permanent address and he can be called to appear before the court at any time whatsoever.

The court withdraws for consultation. Then it returns and the judge reads the decision.

JUDGE: To send [Brodsky] for an official psychiatric examination during which it will be determined whether Brodsky is suffering from some sort of psychological illness or not and whether this illness will prevent Brodsky from being sent to a distant locality for forced labor. Taking into consideration that from the history of his illness it is apparent that Brodsky has evaded hospitalization, it is hereby ordered that division No. 18 of the militia be in charge of bringing him to the official psychiatric examination.

JUDGE: Do you have any question?

BRODSKY: I have a request, that I might have paper and pen in my cell.

JUDGE: You will have to ask the chief of the militia for that.

BRODSKY: I asked him and he refused. I want to have paper and pen.

JUDGE: (*Softening*) Very well, I will tell him.

BRODSKY: Thank you.

When everyone was gone from the courtroom there was a huge number of people, especially young people, to be seen in the corridors and on the stairs.

JUDGE: What a crowd! I didn't think there would be such a crowd!

FROM THE CROWD: They don't try a poet every day.

JUDGE: But we don't care whether he's a poet or not!

According to the opinion of defense counsel Mme. Z. N. Toporova, Judge Saveleva should have released Brodsky from custody so that he himself could have gone the following day to the designated psychiatric hospital for the examination, but Saveleva kept him under arrest so that he was sent off to the hospital under guard.

• • • • •

The Second Hearing of
the Iosif Brodsky Case

The conclusion of the examination reads: Psychopathic traits do exist in his character, but he is capable of working. Therefore administrative measures can be taken.

Those arriving at the trial are greeted with the following sign:

THE HEARING OF THE PARASITE BRODSKY

The large hall of the Builders' Club is full of people.

ATTENDANT: Stand up! The court is coming!

Judge Saveleva asks Brodsky what petitions he has to the court. It turns out that neither before the first hearing nor before the second was he informed about his case. The judge announces a recess. Brodsky is led out so that he can become familiar with his case. After a while they bring him back and he says that the poems on pages 141, 143, 155, 200, 234 (he enumerates) do not belong to him [editor notes: Page numbers presumably refer to unpublished manuscripts of Brodsky's poems believed seized by Soviet police at the time of his arrest]. *In addition he asks that the diary, which he wrote in 1956, that is when he was 16 years old, not be included in the case. Counsel for the defense joins in this request.*

JUDGE: As far as [Brodsky's] so-called poems are concerned we will take this into consideration, but as far as his personal notebook is concerned there is no need to exclude it. Citizen Brodsky, since 1956 you have changed jobs 13 times. You worked in a factory for a year, and then for half a year you did not work. During the summer you were with a geological expedition and then for four months you did not work . . . *(She lists the places where he worked and the intervals which occurred between jobs).* Explain to the court why you did not work during the intervals and why you pursued a parasitic way of life.

BRODSKY: I did work during the intervals. I did just what I am doing now. I wrote poetry.

JUDGE: That is, you wrote your so-called poems? But what was the use of your changing jobs so often?

BRODSKY: I began to work at the age of 15. I found everything interesting. I changed jobs because I wanted to find out as much as possible about life and people.

JUDGE: And what good have you done for your country?

BRODSKY: I wrote poems. That's my work. I am convinced . . . I believe, that what I have written will be of advantage to people not only now but to future generations as well.

VOICE FROM THE CROWD: Listen to that! What an imagination!

ANOTHER VOICE: He's a poet. He should think that way.

JUDGE: So, you think that your so-called poems are of use to the people?

BRODSKY: Why do you refer to them as my "so-called" poems?

JUDGE: We refer to them as your "so-called" poems because we do not have any other conception of them.

PUBLIC PROSECUTOR SOROKIN: You speak about future generations. What are you? Do you feel that people don't understand you now?

BRODSKY: I didn't say that. It's simply that my poems have not been published yet and people don't know them.

SOROKIN: Do you feel that if they were known they would be given recognition?

BRODSKY: Yes.

SOROKIN: You say that you have a widely developed curiosity. Why did you not want to serve in the Soviet Army?

BRODSKY: I will not answer such questions.

JUDGE: Answer!

BRODSKY: I was deferred from military service. It was not a case of "not wanting" to serve; I was deferred. That's a different thing. I was deferred twice. The first time it was because my father was ill and the second time it was because of my own illness.

SOROKIN: Is it possible to live on the money you earn?

BRODSKY: Yes. Every day in jail I signed a paper to the effect that 40 kopecks [approximately 40 cents] had been spent on my welfare that day, and I used to earn more than 40 kopecks a day.

SOROKIN: But one has to buy shoes and clothes.

BRODSKY: I have one suit—an old one, but it is a suit, and I don't need another.

DEFENSE: Have your poems been evaluated by specialists?

BRODSKY: Yes. Chukovsky and Marshak spoke highly about my translations, better than I deserve.

DEFENSE: Did you have any connections with the translators' division of the Union of Writers?

BRODSKY: Yes. I appeared in an anthology entitled *For the First Time in Russian* and I read translations from Polish.

JUDGE: *(To the counsel for the defense)* You are supposed to ask him about his useful work, and instead you are asking him about his public appearances.

DEFENSE: His translations constitute his useful work.

JUDGE: It would be better, Brodsky, if you would explain to the court why you did not work during the intervals between jobs.

BRODSKY: I did work. I wrote poetry.

JUDGE: But this did not prevent you from actually working.

BRODSKY: But I was working. I was writing poetry.

JUDGE: But there are people who work in factories and write poetry, too. What prevented you from doing this?

BRODSKY: But all people are not the same. Even the color of their hair, the expression of their faces.

JUDGE: That is not your discovery. Everyone knows that. But explain to us, rather, how we are to evaluate your participation in our great progressive movement toward Communism.

BRODSKY: The building of Communism is not only just standing at a workbench or plowing a field. It's also intellectual labor which . . .

JUDGE: Leave off these high-flown phrases! Tell us, rather, how you plan to organize your labor activity for the future.

BRODSKY: I wanted to write poetry and to translate. But if this is contradictory to any generally accepted norms, then I will take on a permanent job and still write poetry.

ASSESSOR TYAGLY: In this country every person works. How is it that you have been doing nothing for such a long time?

BRODSKY: You don't consider what I do to be work. I wrote poetry and I consider this work.

JUDGE: Have you drawn any conclusions for yourself from what has been written in the press?

BRODSKY: Lerner's article was untrue. That's the only conclusion I have made.

JUDGE: So you have not drawn any other conclusions?

BRODSKY: No, I have not. I do not consider myself a person leading a parasitic way of life.

DEFENSE: You said that the article entitled "The Near-literary Drone" published in the *Evening Leningrad* newspaper is not true. In what way?

BRODSKY: The only thing that is correct in it is my name. Even my age is not right. Even the poems are not mine. In this article people whom I scarcely know or don't know at all are called my friends. How can I consider this article true and draw conclusions from it?

DEFENSE: You consider your work useful. Will the witnesses whom I have summoned be able to confirm this?

JUDGE: *(Ironically to Defense)* Is that the only reason you summoned witnesses?

PUBLIC PROSECUTOR SOROKIN: *(To Brodsky)* How could you make a translation from Serbian all by yourself without making any use of someone else's work?

BRODSKY: You are asking an ignorant question. Now and then an agreement with a publishing house comes with an interlinear translation. I know Polish and I know Serbian, but not as well. However, they are related languages, and with the help of an interlinear translation I was able to do my translation.

JUDGE: Witness Grudnina!

GRUDNINA: I have been supervising the work of young (beginning) poets for more than 11 years. For seven years I was a member of the committee on work with young authors. Right now I am guiding the poets in the upper classes in the Palace of the Pioneers, and I am also directing the circle of young literary enthusiasts from the Svetlana factory. At the request of the publishing houses I compiled and edited four collective anthologies of young poets in which more than 200 new names appeared. Therefore I have first-hand knowledge of the work of almost all the young poets in the city.

I know Brodsky's poems from 1959 and 1960 as the work of a budding poet. These poems were still in the rough, but they showed a brilliant originality of figures and images. I did not include them in the anthologies; however, I considered the author capable. I did not meet Brodsky personally until the fall of 1963. After the publication of the article entitled "The Near-literary Drone" in the *Evening Leningrad* I sent for Brodsky to come for a talk with me, since the young people were besieging me with requests to intervene in the affair of the slandered man. To my question—What was he doing now?—Brodsky answered that he had been studying languages and working on literary translations for about a year and a half. I took some manuscripts of his translations so as to become familiar with them.

As a professional poet and a literary scholar I affirm that Brodsky's translations have been done on a high professional level. Brodsky has a specific talent for translating poetry that one does not find very often. He showed me work that he had done encompassing 368 lines of poetry, and in addition to this I read 120 lines of poetry which he had translated and published in Moscow editions.

From my personal experience in literary translation I know that such a volume of work would take an author not less than half a year of solid work not counting time spent in getting the poems published and consultations with specialists. The time necessary for such business is impossible to calculate. If we evaluate the translations which I have seen with my own eyes even at the lowest prices paid by the publishing houses, then Brodsky has already earned 350 new rubles [approximately $400] and the only question that remains is when will everything that he has done be published in full.

In addition to agreements for translations Brodsky showed me agreements for radio and television for which the work had already been completed, but likewise had not yet been paid for in full.

From conversations with Brodsky and with people who know him I know that Brodsky lives very modestly, denies himself clothing and entertainment, and spends the major part of the day at his desk working. The money which he receives for his work he gives to his family.

DEFENSE: Is it necessary to have a general knowledge of the works of an author in order to be able to make literary translations of his poetry?

GRUDNINA: Yes, for good translations like those done by Brodsky one has to know the author's works and get a feeling of his style.

DEFENSE: Is the pay for translations less if one makes use of interlinear translations of the poems?

GRUDNINA: Yes, it is less. In rendering the poems of Hungarian poets into verse from interlinear translations I received one old-ruble less per line.

DEFENSE: Is it general practice among translators to work from interlinear translations?

GRUDNINA: Yes, everywhere. One of the most prominent Leningrad translators, A. Gitovich, translates from Old Chinese by using interlinear translations.

ASSESSOR LEBEDEVA: Can one learn a foreign language on one's own?

GRUDNINA: I learned by myself two languages in addition to those which I learned at the university.

DEFENSE: If Brodsky does not know Serbian, can he, despite this, make a first-rate literary translation?

GRUDNINA: Yes, of course.

DEFENSE: But do you not consider the use of an interlinear translation a reprehensible utilization of someone else's work?

GRUDNINA: God forbid!

ASSESSOR LEBEDEVA: Here is a book I have been looking at. There are only two short little poems of Brodsky's in it.

GRUDNINA: I would like to offer certain clarifications concerning particular aspects of literary work . . .

JUDGE: No, that won't be necessary. However, what is your opinion of Brodsky's poetry?

GRUDNINA: My opinion is that as a poet he is very talented and that he is head and shoulders above many who are considered professional translators.

JUDGE: But why does he work by himself and not frequent any literary organizations?

GRUDNINA: In 1958 he asked to belong to my literary group, but I heard that he was an hysterical young man and so I rejected him myself. This was a mistake and I regret it very much. Now I will gladly receive him into my group and will work with him if he wants to do it.

ASSESSOR TYAGLY: Have you yourself ever seen him actually at work on his poems, or has he been profiting by someone else's work?

GRUDNINA: I have not seen him sitting and writing, but I have not seen Sholokhov sitting and writing at his desk either. However, that doesn't mean that. . . .

JUDGE: It is awkward to compare Sholokhov and Brodsky. Is it possible that you have never explained to the young people that the State demands that they study? After all, Brodsky has gone through only seven grades of school.

GRUDNINA: His field of knowledge is very great. I became convinced of this from reading his translations.

SOROKIN: Have you read his bad pornographic poems?

GRUDNINA: No, never.

DEFENSE: Here is something I want to ask you, witness Grudnina. The following constitutes Brodsky's production for 1963: poems in the book entitled *Dawn over Cuba*, translations of poems by Galchinsky (to be sure, not yet published), poems in the book entitled *Yugoslav Poets, Songs of the Gaucho* and publications in *Kostër* [The Bonfire]. Can this be considered serious work?

GRUDNINA: Yes, beyond a doubt. That is a full year's work. And payment for this work will not necessarily come immediately, but several years hence. It is incorrect to evaluate the efforts of a young author by the amount of money he has received in payment at the given moment. A young author may meet with failure which may necessitate a long reworking of what he wrote. There is a joke to the effect that the difference between a parasite and a young poet is that a parasite eats and does not work whereas a young poet works and does not always eat.

JUDGE: We are not pleased with this statement of yours. In our country every person receives according to his effort, and therefore it cannot be that he has worked a great deal and received little for it. In our country, where such a great share of the wealth is allotted to the young poets, you say that they go hungry. Why did you say that young poets do not eat?

GRUDNINA: I did not say that. I said that it was a joke in which there is a grain of truth. Young poets have very uneven earnings.

JUDGE: Well, but this depends upon them. We do not have to explain that. Alright, you have explained that your words were a joke. We will accept this explanation.

A new witness is called: Efim Grigorevich Etkind, Member of the Union of Writers and a teacher at the Herzen Institute.

JUDGE: Let me have your passport inasmuch as your last name is pronounced somewhat unclearly. (*She takes the passport.*) Etkind . . . Efim Gershevich [sic!] . . . You may speak now.

ETKIND: As part of my public literary work, which is connected with the education of beginning translators, I often have the opportunity of reading and listening to the translations of young writers. About a year ago I became familiar with the works of I. Brodsky. These were his translations of poems of the marvelous Polish poet Galchinsky whose poetry has not yet been widely translated here. The clarity of the poetical phrasing, the musicality, the passion and the energy of his verse produced a strong impression on me. I was also struck by the fact that Brodsky learned Polish by himself without any outside help whatsoever. He read Galchinsky's poetry in Polish with just as much enthusiasm as he read his own Russian translations. I understood that I had to do with a rarely gifted man and—not less important—a man with perseverance and a capacity for work. The translations which I had the opportunity of reading later served to reinforce my conviction. There were, for example, the translations he did of the Cuban poet Fernandes, which were published in the book entitled *Dawn over Cuba,* and those of the contemporary Yugoslav poets which are being printed in an anthology by the Goslitizdat [State Publishing House of Literary Fiction]. I talked a great deal with Brodsky and was amazed at how much he knew about American, English, and Polish literature.

The translation of poetry is the most difficult sort of work, demanding diligence, knowledge and talent. A translator can expect countless failures in this business and the material recompense is a thing of the distant future. A person can translate poetry for several years and not earn a single ruble for it. Such work demands unselfish love for poetry and for the labor involved in it. The study of languages, history, the culture of another people—all of this is, by far, not acquired immediately. Everything that I know about Brodsky's work convinces me of the fact that a great future awaits him as a poet-translator. This is not only my own opinion. The office of the division of translators, when it found out that the publishing house had broken the agreements made with Brodsky, came to a unanimous decision to intercede with the director of the publishing house to have Brodsky given some work and to have the agreements with him reinstated.

I know for a fact that the same opinion is shared by the great authorities in the field of translation—Marshak and Chukovsky, who . . .

JUDGE: Speak just for yourself!

ETKIND: Brodsky must be presented with the opportunity of working as a poet-translator. Far away from a large city where there are neither the necessary books nor a literary milieu, it is difficult, almost impossible. I repeat, I am deeply convinced that in this field a great future awaits him. I must say that I was greatly amazed to see the announcement: "The Hearing of the Parasite Brodsky."

JUDGE: However, you knew this combination of names.

ETKIND: Yes, I did, but I never thought that such a combination would be accepted by the court. With his poetical technique nothing would prevent him from just turning out hack work, and he would have translated hundreds of lines if he had worked lightly and easily. The fact that he has earned little money does not mean that he simply does not like to work.

JUDGE: But why is he not a member of any collective?

ETKIND: He has attended our translating seminars . . .

JUDGE: Well, seminars . . .

ETKIND: He belongs to the seminar in the sense . . .

JUDGE: And what if without any sense?" (*Laughter in the courtroom*) That is, I want to ask, why didn't he belong to any unified group?

ETKIND: We don't have any membership and therefore I can't say that he "belonged." But he attended our meetings and read his translations.

JUDGE: (*to Etkind*) Have you had any misunderstandings in your work or in your private life?

ETKIND: (*Surprised*) No. However, I haven't been to the institute for two days now. Perhaps something has actually happened there. (*The question remained incomprehensible to the public and, apparently, to the witness also.*)

JUDGE: In speaking about Brodsky's knowledge, why did you stress foreign literature? And why did you not say anything about our own national literature?

ETKIND: I spoke with him as with a translator, and therefore I was interested in what he knew about American, English and Polish literature. His knowledge is great, varied and not superficial.

SMIRNOV: (*Witness for the prosecution, head of the Department of Defense*): I don't know Brodsky personally, but I want to say that if all the citizens of this country reacted toward the production of material wealth as Brodsky does, then it would take us a long time to build Communism. The mind is a dangerous weapon for its owner. Everyone has said that he is a smart fellow and practically a genius. But no one has said what sort of a person he is. He has grown up in an intelligent family, but he has only seven years of formal education. Let those present say whether they would like to have a son with only seven years of schooling. He did not join the army because he was the sole supporter of his family. But what sort of a breadwinner is he? Here they say that he is a talented translator, but why doesn't anyone say that he's all muddled up in his head? And what about anti-Soviet verses?

BRODSKY: That's not true!

SMIRNOV: He needs to change a lot of his thoughts. I am suspicious about the certificate that Brodsky was given in the "nerve" clinic concerning his nervous illness. This is nothing but his fancy friends ringing all the bells and demanding: "Save the young man!" But he should be treated with forced labor, and no one will help him, no fancy friends. I do not know him personally. I know about him from the newspapers. And I am acquainted with the certificates. I'm suspicious about the certificate which deferred him from service in the army. I'm not a doctor, but I'm suspicious about it.

BRODSKY: When I was deferred as the sole breadwinner of our family, my father was sick. He was in bed suffering from a form of necrosis, and I worked and earned our living. And after that I was sick. Where did you learn about me so as to speak that way about me?

SMIRNOV: I became acquainted with your personal diary.

BRODSKY: On what grounds?

JUDGE: I withdraw the question.

SMIRNOV: I read his poems.

DEFENSE: During the hearing it has turned out that certain poems do not belong to Brodsky. How do you know that the poems you read actually are his? After all, you are talking about unpublished poems.

SMIRNOV: I know and that's that.

JUDGE: Witness Logunov?

LOGUNOV (*Assistant to the executive director of the Hermitage Museum*): I do not know Brodsky personally. I met him for the first time here in the courtroom. To live as Brodsky has been living is no longer permissible. I would not envy the parents of such a son. I have worked with writers and I have circulated among them. I compare Brodsky with Oleg Shestinsky. Oleg has traveled with a propaganda team; he finished the State University of Leningrad and the University of Sophia. And Oleg has also worked in a mine. I wanted to appear here to emphasize the fact that one must work hard and give up all one's cultural habits. Then the poems which Brodsky puts together would be real poems. Brodsky must begin his life anew.

DEFENSE: The witnesses should, however, be made to stick to facts. But they . . .

JUDGE: You may give an evaluation of the witnesses' testimony later. Witness Denisov!

DENISOV (*Pipe setter of the UNR-20*): I do not know Brodsky personally. I am familiar with him from the press releases. I appear here as a citizen and a representative of our community. After the newspaper release I became indignant over Brodsky's work. I wanted to become familiar with his books. I went to the libraries. They didn't have his books. I asked acquaintances if they knew such a person. No, they didn't know him. I'm a worker. During my life I have changed jobs only twice. But Brodsky? I am not satisfied with Brodsky's testimony that he knew many specialties. You can't learn a single specialty in such a short time. They say that Brodsky passes himself off as some sort of poet. Why wasn't he a member of a single organization? Doesn't he agree with Dialectical Materialism? You know Engels considers that labor created man. But Brodsky is not satisfied with this idea. He figures it otherwise. Perhaps he is very talented, but why doesn't he make a name for himself in our literature? Why doesn't he work? I wish to suggest the opinion that I, as a worker, am not satisfied with his labor activity.

JUDGE: Witness Nikolaev!

NIKOLAEV (*Pensioner*): I do not know Brodsky personally. I want to say that I have known about him for three years from the pernicious influence which he has been exerting on his age group. I am a father. I know from experience how hard it is to have such a son who doesn't work. More than once have I seen Brodsky's poems in the hands of my son. A *poèma* in 42 chapters [sic!] and other odd poems. I know Brodsky from the Umansky affair. There is a proverb: Tell me who your friends are. I knew Umansky personally. He was out and out anti-Soviet. Listening to Brodsky I recognized my own son. My son also told me that he considers himself a genius. Like Brodsky he doesn't want to work either. People like Brodsky and Umansky exert an evil influence on their age group. I am amazed at Brodsky's parents. They apparently have encouraged him. They've gone along with him in unison. From the form of his poems it is apparent that Brodsky is able to compose poems. But no, these poems have brought nothing but harm. Brodsky is not simply a parasite. He is a militant parasite! With people like Brodsky we must deal without mercy. (*Applause*).

ASSESSOR TYAGLY: Do you feel that Brodsky's poetry has influenced your son?

NIKOLAEV: Yes.

JUDGE: Influenced negatively?

NIKOLAEV: Yes.

DEFENSE: How do you know that they were Brodsky's poems?

NIKOLAEV: There was a folder, and on the folder was written: "Iosif Brodsky."

DEFENSE: Did your son know Umansky?

NIKOLAEV: Yes.

DEFENSE: Why do you think that it was Brodsky and not Umansky who exerted an evil influence on your son?

NIKOLAEV: Brodsky together with him. Brodsky's poems are disgraceful and anti-Soviet.

BRODSKY: Name my anti-Soviet poems. Quote even a line of them.

JUDGE: I will not allow any quoting!

BRODSKY: But I want to know what poems he's talking about! Perhaps they are not mine.

NIKOLAEV: If I had known that I was going to appear in court I would have photographed them and brought them with me.

JUDGE: Witness Romashova!

ROMASHOVA (*Teacher of Marxism and Leninism in the Mukhina school*): I do not know Brodsky personally. But I am familiar with his so-called activity. Pushkin said that talent is first of all work [editor notes: A careful check of Pushkin's complete works reveals no such statement by the Russian writer]. But Brodsky? Does he work? Does he work on his poems so that the people will be able to understand them? I am amazed that my colleagues have created such a halo about him. It can only happen in the Soviet Union that a court of law would speak so benevolently to a poet and would advise him in such a comradely fashion to go and study. As secretary to the Party organization at the Mukhina school I can say that he is exerting a bad influence on the youth.

DEFENSE: Have you ever seen Brodsky?

ROMASHOVA: Never. But his so-called activity gives me the right to judge him.

JUDGE: But can you bring any facts to bear on the case?

ROMASHOVA: As a teacher of young people I know what they have to say about Brodsky's poetry.

DEFENSE: But do you yourself know his poetry?

ROMASHOVA: I do. It's horr-ible! I don't feel that it's possible to repeat them! They are hor-ri-ble!

JUDGE: Witness Admoni! Please give me your passport, since your last name is unusual.

ADMONI (*Professor at the Herzen Institute, linguist, literary scholar, translator*): When I found out that Iosif Brodsky was being brought to trial for parasitism I considered it my duty to present my opinion also before the court. I feel that I have a right to do this on the strength that I have been working with young people for 30 years as a teacher in university courses and on the strength that I have been dealing with translations for a long time.

I know I. Brodsky hardly at all. We say "hello" to each other, but I believe we have never exchanged as much as two sentences with each other. However, during the course of, approximately, this past year or somewhat longer I have been following his translation work intently, both in his appearances at the translators' evenings (where the translators get up and read their translations) and also in his publications. Because these translations are talented and brilliant, and on the basis of these translations of Galchinsky, Fernandes and others, I can with complete responsibility say that they demanded a tremendously great amount of work on the part of their author. They testify to the great mastery and cultural level of the translator. And wonders do not exist. Neither mastery nor culture comes by itself, but demands steady and persistent work for its attainment. Even if a translator works from an interlinear translation, he must, in order that the translation be worthwhile, form for himself an idea of the language he is translating from. He must acquire a feeling for the structure of the language, and he has to know the life and the culture of the people, and so forth. And Iosif Brodsky, in addition to this, even learned the languages themselves. Therefore it is clear to me that he is working, that he works intensively and persistently. And when today I learned—just today—that he had finished only seven grades of school, then it became clear to me that he must really have made a gigantic effort in order to acquire such mastery and such a cultural level as he possesses. What Mayakovsky said about the work of a poet is applicable to the work of a poet-translator: "You can go through thousands of tons of verbal ore for the sake of a single word."

The ukase by which Brodsky has been brought to account is directed toward those who do too little work and not against those who do not earn enough. Parasites are people who do not do enough work. Therefore the accusation against I. Brodsky as a parasite is nonsense. It is impossible to accuse of parasitism a person who works as I. Brodsky does, who persistently works a great deal, with no thought as to large earnings, who is prepared to limit himself to the bare essentials so as to be able to perfect himself in his art and to create worthwhile artistic works.

JUDGE: What was it you said about not judging those who do not earn enough?

ADMONI: I said that the essence of the ukase consists in the necessity of judging those who do not work enough and not those who do not earn enough.

JUDGE: What do you mean by this? Have you read The Ukase of May Fourth? Communism is built only by the effort of millions.

ADMONI: Every effort that is useful to society should be respected.

ASSESSOR TYAGLY: Where did Brodsky read his translations and what languages did he read in?

ADMONI: (*Smiling*) He read in Russian. He translates from foreign languages into Russian.

JUDGE: If a simple person asks you a question you should explain to him and not smile.

ADMONI: I am explaining that he translates from Polish and Serbian into Russian.

JUDGE: Speak to the court, and not to the public.

ADMONI: Please forgive me. It's a professional habit—to speak addressing the listeners.

JUDGE: Witness Voevodin! Do you know Brodsky personally?

VOEVODIN: (*Member of the Union of Writers*): No. I have been working in the Union for only half a year. I was not personally acquainted with him. He does not come very often to the Union, just to the translation evenings. He apparently understood how his poems would be received and therefore he didn't go to any of the other organizations. I read his epigrams. You would blush, comrade judges, if you read them. They have been here speaking about Brodsky's talent. Talent is measured only by public acclaim. And this acclaim does not exist and cannot exist.

A folder of Brodsky's poems was handed over to the Union of Writers. There are three themes in the poems. The first is the theme of estrangement from the world; the second is a pornographic theme; and the third is the theme of non-love for one's country and its people in which Brodsky speaks about another homeland. Wait, I think I can remember it . . . "Monotonous is the Russian crowd." May these disgraceful poems remain on his conscience! Brodsky as a poet does not exist. Translator—perhaps, but poet—no! I completely support the statement of our comrade who spoke about his son whom Brodsky influenced perniciously. Brodsky tears the youth away from work, from the world and life. This is Brodsky's great antisocial role.

JUDGE: Have you discussed Brodsky's talent with the committee?

VOEVODIN: There was one short meeting in which Brodsky was mentioned, but it did not turn into a broad discussion. I repeat: Brodsky confined himself to semi-obscene epigrams and he rarely came to the Union of Writers. My friend, the poet Kulkin loudly announced once from the stage his indignation at Brodsky's poetry.

DEFENSE: Does the entire committee share the opinion of the report that you wrote about Brodsky?

VOEVODIN: We did not coordinate the report with Etkind, who maintains a different opinion.

DEFENSE: And is the content of your report known to the rest of the members of the committee?

VOEVODIN: No, it is not known to all the members.

BRODSKY: How did you get hold of my poems and my diary?

JUDGE: I withdraw the question. Citizen Brodsky, you worked only as the opportunity arose. Why?

BRODSKY: I already said that I worked all the time. I worked at a regular job and then I wrote poetry. (*In desperation*) That's work—writing poetry!

JUDGE: But your earnings are not very large at all. You say that you receive 250 rubles a year, but according to information gathered by the militia it is only 100 rubles.

DEFENSE: At the preceding hearing it was decided that the militia was to verify the information it had about his earnings, but this was not done.

JUDGE: We have here an agreement that was sent to you from a publishing house. But this is simply a piece of paper not signed by anyone.

A note is sent to the judge from someone in the audience, informing her that agreements are first signed by the author and then by those in charge of the publishing house.

JUDGE: I ask that no more notes be sent to me.

PUBLIC PROSECUTOR SOROKIN: Our great nation is building Communism. An amazing faculty is developed in a Soviet person—the enjoyment of socially worthwhile work. Only that society blooms where there is no idleness. Brodsky is far removed from patriotism. He has forgotten the main principle: He who does not work does not eat. And Brodsky has been leading the life of a parasite for many years. In 1956 he quit school and went to work at a factory. He was 15 years old. During that same year he was dismissed. (*He repeats the list of places where Brodsky worked and the intervals between regular jobs and he again calls this idleness. It seems as if all the explanations of the defense witnesses of the fact that literary pursuits also constitute work had not even been uttered.*) We ascertained that Brodsky received only 37 rubles for one piece of work, whereas he said that it was 150 rubles!

BRODSKY: That's only an advance! A part of what I will receive afterwards!

JUDGE: Brodsky, be silent!

SOROKIN: Wherever Brodsky worked he made everyone indignant with his lack of discipline and unwillingness to work. The article in the *Evening Leningrad* excited a great response. An especially large number of letters was received from young people. They sharply condemned Brodsky's behavior. (*He reads some letters.*) Our young people feel that Leningrad is not the place for him, that he should be severely punished. He completely lacks any concept of conscience and duty. Every man considers it a pleasure to serve in the army, but he evaded it. Brodsky's father sent his son to the dispensary for consultation and he brought back a certificate that was accepted by the gullible military commissariat. Before he was called up before the military commissariat Brodsky wrote to his friend Shakhmatov, who is now sentenced: "I have a meeting with the Defense Committee coming up. Your desk will become a reliable sanctuary for my iambs." He belonged to a group which reacted to the word "work" with satanic laughter and listened to its *Führer* Umansky with respect. Brodsky is united with him in his hatred for work and for Soviet literature. The selection of pornographic words and conceptions enjoys especial success here. Brodsky used to address Shakhmatov as "sir," and not otherwise! Shakhmatov was sentenced. That's the type of foul-smelling hole from which Brodsky appeared. They speak about Brodsky's talents. But who says it? People just like Brodsky and Shakhmatov.

A SHOUT FROM THE COURTROOM: Who? Are Chukovsky and Marshak like Shakhmatov? (*Guards lead the person out.*)

SOROKIN: Brodsky is defended by rogues [*proshchelygi*], parasites [*tuneyadtsy*], lice [*mokritsy*] and insects [*zhuchki*]. Brodsky is not a poet, but a person attempting to write his little rhymes [*stishki,* a derogatory diminutive]. He forgot that in our country a person is supposed to work, to create material wealth: workbenches, bread or poetry. Brodsky must be made to work by force. He should be sent out of this hero-town. He is a parasite, a cad [*kham*], a rogue, a morally filthy person. Brodsky's admirers spatter saliva. But Nekrasov said:

"A poet—that you may not be,
But a citizen you're obliged to be."

Today we are judging not a poet, but a parasite. Why has a man been defended here who despises our homeland? The moral character of those who defended him here should be investigated. He wrote in one of his poems: "I love another homeland" [*Lyublyú ja ródinu chuzhúyu*]. In his diary there is a notation: "I have long thought about going beyond the red line. Constructive thoughts are ripening in my red-haired head." He also wrote the following: "The town hall of Stockholm inspires in me more respect than the Kremlin at Prague." Marx he calls an "old belly-lubber (glutton), framed with a garland of pine cones." In one letter he writes: "I wanted to spit upon Moscow!" That's what Brodsky and those who defend him are worth! (*After this a letter is read from a girl who writes with disrespect about Lenin. What connection her letter has with Brodsky is absolutely unclear. It was neither written by him nor addressed to him.*) At this moment the judge turns to address me.

JUDGE: Stop taking notes!

I: Comrade judge, I ask for permission to take notes.

JUDGE: No.

I: I am a journalist, a member of the Union of Writers. I am writing about the education of youth. I ask for permission to take notes.

JUDGE: I do not know what you are writing. Stop!

FROM THE PUBLIC: Take the notes away from her!

Sorokin continues his speech. Then the defense counsel speaks, but I can give only his main points for I was forbidden to take any more notes.

MAIN POINTS OF THE DEFENSE COUNSEL'S SPEECH:

The Public Prosecutor used information which is not at the trial, which came up during the trial for the first time and which Brodsky was not asked about and about which he gave no explanations.

The authenticity of the information taken from the special hearing of 1961 has not been verified by us and we cannot verify the quotes made by the Public Prosecutor. With respect to Brodsky's diary, it refers to the year 1956. It is the diary of a teenager. The Public Prosecutor introduced as evidence of public opinion letters of readers written to the editors of the *Evening Leningrad* newspaper. The authors of the letters do not know Brodsky, they have not read his poetry, and they have judged him from a newspaper article which is tendentious and in many places factually not true. The Public Prosecutor insulted not only Brodsky by calling him a "cad," "parasite," and an "anti-Soviet element," but also the personages who intervened on his behalf—Marshak, Chukovsky, and the honorable witnesses. Conclusion: Since he did not have any objective proofs at his disposal the Public Prosecutor made use of unpermissible methods.

What does the prosecution have at its disposal?

(a) A list of the places where Brodsky worked from 1956 to 1962. In 1956 Brodsky was 16 years old. He actually could have studied and continued legally to live at his parents' expense until he was 18. His frequent changing of jobs is a result of certain psychological traits in his character and an inability immediately to find his place in life. The intermissions, in particular, are explained by seasonal work with expeditions. There is no reason to speak of his evading work up to 1962.

(*The defense lawyer speaks about her respect for the assessors, but regrets that among the assessors there is no one who is competent in questions of literary work. When a teenager is tried there is definitely an assessor present who is a pedagogue; if the accused is a doctor then a doctor is necessary among the assessors. Why is this fair and sensible custom ignored when it becomes a question of literature?*)

(b) Brodsky has not had a regular job since 1962. However, the publishing agreements which were presented from November 1962 and October 1963, a statement from the television studio, a statement from the magazine *Kostër,* and the book of translation of Yugoslav poets testify as to his creative work. The *quality* of his work. There is a statement signed by E. Voevodin which is sharply unfavorable with inadmissible accusations even of anti-Soviet activities, a statement reminiscent of the documents of the worst period of the cult of personality. It turned out that this statement was not discussed by the Committee, is not familiar to the members of the Committee, and is the personal opinion of the prosaist Voevodin. There is the testimony of such people as Marshak and Chukovsky, the best authorities and masters of translation—witness V. Admoni, prominent literary historian, linguist and translator; E. Etkind, authority on translated literature, member of the office of the division of translators and member of the committee on work with young authors; and the writer and philologist Grudnina, who has spent much time working with young poets. All of them evaluate Brodsky's work highly and speak about the great amount of time required in order to publish what he wrote during 1963. Conclusion: Voevodin's testimony cannot refute the opinion of these personages.

(c) Not one of the witnesses for the prosecution either knows Brodsky, received his poetry from him, or has heard him speak. The witnesses for the prosecution give testimony on the basis of certain unverified documents which they have somehow received, and express their opinions in giving condemning speeches.

This is all the material which the case for the prosecution has. The court must exclude the following from its deliberation:

1. Materials from the special hearing held in 1961 according to which it was resolved that with regard to Brodsky the case be dropped.

If Brodsky had committed an anti-Soviet crime then or later, or had written anti-Soviet poems, this would be a situation for investigation by the agencies of the department of national security.

Brodsky was actually acquainted with Shakhmatov and Umansky and was under their influence. But fortunately he got free of this influence a long time ago. In the meantime, the Public Prosecutor read us notes from those years, thus lifting them out of time and context, which naturally inspired the wrath of the public against Brodsky. The Public Prosecutor created the impression that Brodsky even now holds his views of long ago, which is completely untrue. Many young people, who entered the company of Umansky, thanks to the interference of sensible and mature people, were returned to normal life. The same thing was taking place with Brodsky during the last two years. He had begun to work a lot and to produce. But then he was arrested.

2. The question of the quality of the poetry of Brodsky himself.

We still do not know which of the poems entered here at this hearing actually belong to Brodsky, since from his own testimony it is apparent that there are a number of poems which do not belong to him. In order to judge whether these poems are decadent, pessimistic or lyrical we must have an authoritative literary examination of them, and this question cannot be solved by the court or by either side.

Our task is to establish whether Brodsky is a parasite living off unearned income and leading a parasitic way of life.

Brodsky is a poet-translator who contributes his work toward the struggle for peace by translating poets of the brotherly republics, countries of people's democracy. He is not a drunkard, not an immoral person, not a money-grabber. He is rebuked for receiving too little compensation, consequently for not having worked.

(The lawyer gives information concerning the specific nature of literary work and the way it is paid for. She speaks about the huge amount of time that is expended in preparing translations, about the necessity of learning foreign languages and studying the works of the poets one translates. She explains about the fact that not all the work is accepted and paid for that is presented.)

The systems of advances. The sums of money that figure in the case are not exact. According to Brodsky's testimony they are greater. This should have been verified. The sums are insignificant. What did Brodsky live on? Brodsky lived with his parents who supported him while he was becoming a poet.

He had no sources of unearned income. He lived frugally so as to be able to spend his time working at his favorite task.

Conclusions:

Brodsky's guilt has not been established. Brodsky is not a parasite, and measures of administrative action may not be taken against him.

The significance of the Ukase of February 4, 1961 is very great. It is a weapon for delivering the city of any actual parasites and idlers. An unfounded application of the ukase will discredit the idea of it.

The decision of the Plenum of the Supreme Court of the USSR of March 10, 1963 makes it incumbent on the court to treat critically the materials presented, that it not permit the condemnation of those who work, and that it observe the rights of those who are brought before it to become familiar with their cases and present proofs of their innocence.

Brodsky was detained without grounds from February 13, 1964 and was *deprived* of an opportunity to present proofs of his innocence.

However, even the proofs presented of what has been said at the hearing are sufficient to form the conclusion that Brodsky is not a parasite.

The court withdraws for consultation. A recess is announced.

(pp. 6-17)

THE COURT RETURNS AND JUDGE READS SENTENCE:

Brodsky systematically does not fulfill the duties of a Soviet citizen with regard to his personal well-being and the production of material wealth, which is apparent from his frequent change of jobs. He was warned by the agencies of the MGB (Ministry of National Security) in 1961 and by the militia in 1962. He promised to take on a permanent job, but he made no decisions, he continued not to work, he wrote and read his decadent poems at evening gatherings. From the report of the committee on work with young writers it is apparent that Brodsky is not a poet. He was condemned by the readers of the *Evening Leningrad* newspaper. Therefore the court will apply the Ukase of February 4, 1961: to send Brodsky to a distant locality for a period of five years of enforced labor. (p. 17)

Joseph Brodsky, in an excerpt from "The Trial of Iosif Brodsky," translated by Collyer Bowen in The New Leader, *Vol. XLVII, No. 18, August 31, 1964, pp. 6-17.*

SIMON KARLINSKY

[Karlinsky is a Manchurian-born American critic and professor of Slavic languages and literature. His publications include Marina Cvetaev: Her Life and Art *(1965),* The Bitter Air of Exile: Russian Literature in the West, 1922-1972 *(1977), and* Russian Drama from Its Beginnings to the Age of Pushkin *(1985); he also edited* The Nabokov-Wilson Letters *(1979). In the following excerpt Karlinsky offers a brief description of Brodsky's early work.]*

The most notable poet to have so far emerged from these clandestine publications [privately circulated mimeographed journals in Soviet Union] is Iosif Brodsky, who became famous after the Soviet authorities put him on trial for being a "parasite'' and a ''sponger.'' The transcript of his trial, published in the West, left no doubt that what was really indicted in Brodsky's person was the whole notion of writing socially useless poetry. After being sentenced to five years at hard labor, and spending almost two years carting manure in a remote northern area, Brodsky was quietly released this year. A piece of poetry he has written since his release has just reached the West; it is a cycle of poems dedicated to the memory of T. S. Eliot. A selection of Brodsky's poems, most of which appeared in Soviet underground journals, was published in 1965 by the Inter-Language Literary Associates, Washington, D.C. Brodsky's poetry is uneven, often murky and verbose, but at its best it has a seriousness and a profundity no other Soviet poet can match. He uses surrealistic imagery freely, his acknowledged foreign influences—John Donne and Eliot—are not on any Soviet approved list; and if Okudzhava's jaunty songs admit only a possibility of a tragic view of life, Brodsky's brooding elegies are at times permeated with an oppressive sense of doom which only the eternal values of art and nature are allowed to overcome. (p. 551)

> Simon Karlinsky, ''Yevtushenko and the Underground Poets,'' in The Nation, New York, Vol. 203, No. 17, November 21, 1966, pp. 549-53.

ERNST PAWEL

[*Pawel is a Polish-born American novelist, critic, biographer, and short story writer. His works include the novels* The Island in Time *(1951) and* In the Absence of Magic *(1961) as well as the biography* The Nightmare of Reason: A Life of Franz Kafka *(1984). He has frequently written about the USSR and Eastern Europe. In the following excerpt Pawel comments on Brodsky's trial and assesses the political and literary characteristics of Brodsky's first translated work,* Elegy for John Donne and Other Poems.]

Given some verve and imagination, the annals of jurisprudence can be read as an underground history of the absurd; and what must have been one of its more exotic happenings took place on February 18, 1964 in the Dzherzhinsky District Court of Leningrad, where the then 24-year-old poet Joseph Brodsky was being tried on a charge of vagrancy. (*Parasitism,* in Soviet legal terminology, and a considerably more serious offense.) (p. 17)

As a trial, this exercise in lunacy violated all standards of fairness and procedure, apparently including certain elementary safeguards provided by the Soviet constitution. But tempted though one may be to dismiss it as a witches' cabal or an institutionalized castration rite—judge, defense attorney and one prosecutor were women—the final verdict would seem proof of sound judicial reasoning, if nothing else. For Judge Saveleva, upon hearing an impressive array of more or less prominent literati describe Brodsky as a poet of great talent and promise, sentenced him to five years at hard labor. Which demonstrates an uncommon degree of insight into the relationship between poetry and the state generally, and between Brodsky's poetry and the Soviet state in particular.

The tension between true poet and any given social order is axiomatic and, moreover, basic to their respective functions; but the specific forms and areas of conflict reflect a broad range of extraneous factors. And though the outcome is seldom in doubt—the ancient bromide about pen and sword being a dubious half-truth tossed off by some scribbler about to have his head cut off—the circumstances, issues and degree of violence attending the struggle provide valuable clues both to the poet's

world and to his place in it. Thus, at least in the technical sense, there exist certain affinities between Mandelshtam and Brodsky; the difference in their respective destinies illustrates changes in Soviet society—Mandelshtam never had his day in *any* kind of court—that in turn are bound to shape the poet's work.

The nature of dissent, in other words, is fatally linked to the nature of the establishment; and if Yevtushenko, Voznesensky *et al* represent the radical reaction to initial liberalizing trends under Khrushchev, Brodsky has taken the inevitable next step and become totally apolitical.

And Mme. Saveleva, I suspect, showed shrewd judgment in regarding such an attitude as dangerously subversive. (pp. 17-18)

In the relative silence of Russia sounds still carry a long way; there are people who listen, and a poet's *No* is liable to lead him into a confrontation with those who don't like what he has to say.

Brodsky's scornful and contemptuous *No* covers a very broad range that includes the entire gothic edifice of politics. Unlike a Yevtushenko, whose very challenge to dogma and tradition is still formulated in the language of orthodox faith, Brodsky is a thoroughgoing agnostic utterly, provocatively indifferent to the issues, ramifications and ideology of power in both its practical and doctrinal manifestations. Yevtushenko, though a mere six years older, belongs to a different generation, hence to a different breed; for in the nuclear age the generation gap seems to have been superseded by a series of radical mutations. Brodsky, child of his time, shares the vision of those who keep their eyes not on the last war but on the next one. His stand in court was certainly of a piece with the spirit of his work, and the stance of determined non-involvement—as Judge Saveleva proved astute enough to realize—is the moral equivalent of draft card burning. (p. 18)

Until recently [Brodsky's] stature had to be taken largely on faith, especially abroad. Locating a poet in the landscape of politics or anti-politics may offer clues to the thrust of his work but certainly not to its quality; second and even tenth-rate talent has suffered in the cause of freedom. Brodsky's work was, and still is, proscribed in the Soviet Union, circulating only in typescripts or underground publications. In 1965, however, a selection of it was published in New York by Inter-Language Associates—necessarily incomplete, possibly a by-product of the cold war, and yet of major importance in that it afforded readers familiar with Russian their first direct contact with a poet acclaimed not only by the Soviet anti-establishment but also by such venerable and knowledgeable judges as Anna Akhmatova, Korney Chukovsky and Dmitri Shostakovich.

Thirty-one of the poems from that book . . . have just come out in England under the title of *Elegy to John Donne,* and I fear that as a result the English-speaking reader with no Russian will now need more faith than ever to believe in Brodsky's genius. For the translations range in quality between failure and disaster, and few convey even a pale gleam of the original. (p. 19)

[The poems in *Elegy for John Donne and Other Poems*] are the poems of a very young man—a description not intended here in the pejorative sense but, on the contrary, meant to convey one ingredient of their magic. The unexpected freshness of Brodsky's vision startles and delights; he has the courage of his naiveté, and talent to spare. But along with courage and talent go a control and mastery of his craft rare at any age.

Emphatically not the sort of thing one picks up in school; and in fact Brodsky is emphatically a drop-out, lucky or gutsy enough to have steered clear of the Literary Institute, a sort of sausage factory for stuffing state-approved littérateurs. This lack of formal training may have cost him some points in court, but it enabled him to absorb poetry in the only way in which it can be absorbed—at the source. Though he quit school at fifteen, Brodsky seems to have done outstanding work as translator of English, Polish, Spanish, and Serbo-Croat literature—of itself a rugged and efficient proving ground. However, his initial choice of this particular specialty, far more highly regarded in the Soviet Union than in the United States, also tells something about the cast of his particular genius, for most of his contemporaries, programmatically or otherwise, hew to an exclusively native tradition best exemplified by Yesenin, who refused to learn so much as one word of a foreign language lest it pollute the purity of his Russian. . . . Significantly enough, the last great poet—and regarded as such by Brodsky—thoroughly familiar with cultures beyond Russia was Pasternak.

For the truth of the matter is that Brodsky has no obvious affinities with any of the contemporary Soviet poets; he seems about as remote from the Yevtushenko school of didactic provocation as he is from Voznesensky's daring and radical experiments in form. Moreover, he also will not quite fit any larger tradition, though Blok, Pasternak, Mandelstam and Akhmatova are discernible influences and have obviously contributed to at least a definition of his goals. He is basically his own man, going his own way. No mean achievement in itself, at twenty-three. (pp. 20-1)

But even the work contained in this volume—I am now referring to the Russian-language edition—shows evidence of considerable growth. The circumstances surrounding its publication make it difficult, if not impossible, to establish a definitive chronology, yet the general pattern of development emerges clearly, regardless of the precise order in which the poems were originally written. Basic to it—and to the difference between Brodsky and almost all of his contemporaries—is his enormous, his almost Biblical regard for the word and, beyond it, for the role of language in its most elemental sense as the instrument of poetry. The startling and evocative power of the shorter and presumably early pieces derives chiefly from this devotion to the sound and color of words, shared by Blok and Pasternak but long since gone out of fashion. Unfashionable positions tend to be dangerous as well as lonely, but such considerations are unlikely to sway Brodsky, who from the evidence is not afraid to go it alone. (p. 21)

From the internal evidence of the work it seems safe to assume that the shorter lyrics, sonnets and poems represent the earlier part of Brodsky's creative output, yet even this incomplete selection covers a wide range of topics and techniques. Their most striking common attribute again is an inevitability of language that seems as effortless and natural as only true art can ever be; but what it articulates is no mere poetic temper but also a tough and contemplative intelligence.

An example is the poem **"Eternal Fight"** conceived as a response to Alexander Blok's famous patriotic song cycle *On the Fields of Kulikovo,* exalting the 1380 victory of the Muscovite princes over the Tartars. . . . Brodsky replies from the perspective of some 50-odd years later, in a mood and idiom existential rather than political. . . .

Any comparison between Brodsky and Blok would be fatuous at this stage; yet voice and temper recall the lyricism of Blok's early verse, and the longer dramatic poems concluding the Brodsky volume would seem to foreshadow a development not unlike that of Blok's own later career. Whether or not Brodsky will ever come to write his version of *The Twelve* remains to be seen and may not, unfortunately, depend merely on his creative genius.

So far, all we have to go on is that by the time he was twenty-three, Brodsky had written a fair amount of strikingly original verse, including at least three long poems, one of which—**"The Procession,"**—not included in the translations, not only marks a new maturity and vastly greater scope but already represents an extraordinary achievement in its own right. At which point he was denounced, hounded, hauled into court, and shipped off to a labor camp.

Prominent Soviet writers and intellectuals interceded on his behalf, and he has since been released after some rather gruesome experiences. He is now reported to be living in Moscow, presumably still writing. Thus far, however, none of what he completed since his release has been published anywhere, and there exists the very real and ominous possibility that his silence will prove to be the ultimate comment by a great poet on the state of the world, his own as well as ours. (p. 22)

Ernst Pawel, *"The Poetry of Joseph Brodsky,"* in *Midstream, Vol. XIV, No. 5, May, 1968, pp. 17-22.*

ARTHUR C. JACOBS

[A] selection of Brodsky's poems which has since been published in English translation [*Elegy for John Donne and Other Poems*] shows him to be a highly serious poet with considerable potential.

His poetry, as far as someone with no real knowledge of Russian can tell, is quite apart from what one thinks of as the main current of Russian verse. His translator, Nicholas Bethell, refers to the influence of Alexander Blok and Anna Akhmatova, but though they may help to shape individual poems, he reads in general very much like a man on his own. Certainly, he seems completely unlike the two best known of the younger Russian poets, Voznesensky and Yevtushenko.

How far Brodsky's isolation as a poet springs from his Jewishness is an extremely interesting question, and will undoubtedly be developed in critical discussion of his work. At least one poem draws specifically on his awareness of Jewish experience, called **"A Jewish Cemetery by Leningrad."** This seems to me the best constructed, most tightly written poem in the book, a moving evocation of the Diaspora seen as the expression of a worthy idealism under intolerable conditions. Brodsky is able to write of Judaism with dignity, and without quaintness, and the feeling of his poem will be easily recognised by Jews, particularly young Jews of his generation, elsewhere.

With the rest of his poems Brodsky shows considerable ambition, but it is measured ambition, as though he has a cool insight into the nature of his talents. Some of his longer poems tend to sprawl a bit, but one is seeing them through translation and must allow for that. Other, shorter poems suffer from a young man's too easily romantic attitudes, and there is a tendency to build up repetitive phrases, which I find distracting, but which may be more effective than a translation can convey. What translation does convey is a dry, sardonic self-awareness, a gift for expressing creative loneliness without self-pity. . . .

What we have are . . . the poems of a very young man, produced and circulated under conditions of considerable hardship. I agree with those critics who feel that Brodsky's work shows promise of a high order.

Arthur C. Jacobs, "A Russian-Jewish Poet," in The Jewish Quarterly, *Vol. 16, No. 4, Winter, 1968-69, p. 33.*

OLGA CARLISLE

[*Carlisle is a Russian-born American nonfiction writer, critic, editor, and autobiographer. Among her works are* Voices in the Snow *(1963), which features interviews with such distinguished Soviet authors as Boris Pasternak, Yevgeny Yevtushenko, and Anna Akhmatova;* Poets on Street Corners: Portraits of Fifteen Russian Poets *(1968); and* Solzhenitsyn and the Secret Circle *(1980), an account of her involvement with the first publication of Aleksandr Solzhenitsyn's novels in the West. In the following excerpt from* Poets on Street Corners, *Carlisle characterizes Brodsky as one of the finest young poets of his generation.*]

One cannot tell yet if Brodsky will become a major poet, as Akhmatova predicted. In his work . . . there is sometimes a tendency towards wordiness; a hollowness may be felt occasionally underneath the rhetoric. Perhaps what is absent is the nineteenth-century humanism, which had its last representatives in Pasternak and Akhmatova. Compared with them, many young Soviet writers have a certain simple-mindedness common to youths of many countries today. Like the hippies of America, they attempt to answer the world's problems through a return to immediate perceptions. But in the case of Brodsky, one feels that his interest in traditional literary and religious concepts has enriched his work and will continue to help him grow. (p. 399)

Brodsky's poems are intensely personal. Most of them are about death—a private death. When they deal with life, his vision is somber. They echo Mandelstam's late poems, but on the whole Brodsky's literary ancestors are not easy to trace. Edward Arlington Robinson and Robert Frost are favorites of his, and at present he is engaged in translating John Donne into Russian. More than any other young Soviet poet today, he is under the influence of English classics and of contemporary American writers. But his perceptions are purely Russian. . . . (pp. 399-400)

Not long ago while in Moscow I heard Brodsky's voice on tape, reading his **"The Great Elegy for John Donne."** The voice was extremely youthful and frenzied with anguish. The poet was reciting the elegy's detailed catalogue of household objects in a breathless, rhetorical manner, in the tradition of the poets of the Revolutionary generation. His passion gave life to each thing enumerated, and this somehow made the very long poem seem short. There was a touch of Surrealism to this work—a new, Soviet kind of Surrealism—in the intrusion of everyday detail into the poem. However, Brodsky's Surrealism takes on a more metaphysical dimension in some of his short poems. These are as good as anything written in the sixties in Russia. (pp. 400-01)

Olga Carlisle, "Joseph Brodsky," in her Poets on Street Corners: Portraits of Fifteen Russian Poets, *Random House, 1969, pp. 397-421.*

KEES VERHEUL

[*Verheul, a Dutch critic, nonfiction writer, and autobiographer, is the author of* Kontakt met de vijand *(1975), a travel book about* Russia; The Theme of Time in the Poetry of Anna Akhmatova *(1971); and the autobiographical* Een jongen met vier Denen *(1982). In the following excerpt Verheul discusses Brodsky's use of poetic forms and his allusions to classical mythology.*]

Perhaps one of the first qualities [of Brodsky's poem **"Aeneas and Dido"**] which strikes the reader who is somewhat familiar with the poet's work is the absence of some of the surface features which would generally seem to characterize the "Brodsky style." Its rhymelessness contrasts with the ingenious virtuosity of rhyme effects which is displayed in most of his other, both shorter and longer, poems. Its syntax is, comparatively speaking, extremely straightforward: the sentences are relatively simple and the even syntactical flow is never interrupted by the lengthy interpolations which belong to the idiosyncracies of his style. The vocabulary of **"Aeneas and Dido"** moreover belongs in its entirety to the classically unobtrusive literary "middle style" and completely lacks the baroque contrastiveness of solemn Church Slavonic expressions, tough city slang, barbarisms etc., which in other Brodsky poems determines the flamboyant vividness of the speaker's mode of expression.

These various "negative" features are not, however, restricted in the work of Brodsky to the one instance of the poem under discussion. There is a whole group of lyrics which stands as it were in a stylistic opposition to the more superficially characteristic Brodsky manner. From an examination of his oeuvre as collected in *A Stop in the Desert* it appears that his stylistic individuality cannot be sufficiently defined in terms of only one form of expression, but should be interpreted rather in terms of a marked polarity between technical virtuosity and rhetorical complexity on the one hand, and restraint and concentrated simplicity on the other. The majority of the poems which are written in the relatively sober key are prosodically based on a rhymeless iambic pentameter, the traditional "blank verse." This technical form is used by Brodsky in a large number of poems, short lyrical pieces, as well as extensive reflective or narrative works. Not only from the point of view of prosody but also, and more importantly, because of their "tone," their syntax and choice of vocabulary, these poems are to be seen, I think, as taking their stylistical starting point, within the framework of the Russian literary tradition, from the great blank-verse monologues of the later Akhmatova and the heritage of the classical elegists of the early nineteenth century, especially Pushkin and Baratynsky. It is significant that one of Brodsky's lyrical blank-verse poems should have in fact as its title the name of the genre **"Elegy,"** while another poem, which has rhyme but no stanza division and is in many ways stylistically similar to his shorter blank-verse works, is called **"Pochti elegiia"** (**"Almost an Elegy"**).

The relationship with the classical Russian elegy and Akhmatova's elegiac monologues of the 1940s and 1950s is perhaps most clearly felt in the earliest of Brodsky's longer experiments with the blank-verse form, the title poem of *A Stop in the Desert*. The situation which this poem presents, a speaker reflecting about the passing of historical time as he looks at the ruins of a building, belongs to the stereotypes of the genre as it was developed in the sentimentalist school of Batyushkov and Zhukovsky. Such lines as

> I kak-to v pozdnii chas
> Sidel ia na razvalinakh absidy.

> Once at a late hour
> I was sitting on the ruins of the apse.

unmistakably betray the poem's ancestry. The Akhmatovian element comes to the foreground in the casual, quasi-improvisatory tone of the speaker's voice, constantly specifying and restricting his observations with such adjuncts as *vprochem, tol'ko, tochnee* (however, only, rather), and in the urbane and poignant irony which often colors his speech. These influences, which in **"A Stop in the Desert"** do not yet seem to be fully absorbed into the poet's personal idiom, almost completely disappear from the surface of Brodsky's subsequent long poems in blank verse. His long preoccupation with this poetical form has become the basis for a remarkable artistic development which has allowed him to use it, with growing originality and control, as an adequate vehicle for themes which seem to be still expanding in richness and significance.

It is characteristic for Brodsky as a conscious literary craftsman that in the case of his blank-verse poems the rhymelessness is not the outward sign of a general looseness of poetic structure, but rather seems to function as a positive quality which activates the possibilities of a meaningful artistic organization on other levels of the text. The very absence of a regular sound repetition as it were forces the reader's attention towards a perception of other, purely syntactical or semantic patterns in the poem, and the author seems concentrated upon a maximal intensification of such patterns to "make up for" the relative lack of a more superficial formal quality. Seen in this light Brodsky's experiments with the "rhymeless sonnet" are to be considered as part of his attempts to achieve a strongly integrated poetical diction depending as little as possible on merely prosodical factors. As I have observed in the beginning of this essay, this tendency is balanced elsewhere in the poet's work by a contrastive experimentation with intricate stanzaic forms and subtle rhyme effects.

As an example of the way in which Brodsky constructs a blank-verse work upon the development of such "interior" patterns the poem **"Aeneas and Dido"** deserves, I think, some special attention. There are only a few poems of his in this metrical form in which the theme is expressed with such a high degree of artistic concentration and at the same time such perfectly maintained naturalness. Judged by the classical standards of literary taste, it doubtlessly deserves a place in any future anthology of Russian verse. (pp. 490-94)

Among Brodsky's shorter poems **"Aeneas and Dido"** is the most clearly narrative in conception. His oeuvre as a whole presents a wide variety of themes: from the lyrical (situations connected with the intimate life of the "I") and the reflective (statement and exploration of general truths and values, often stylistically associated with his "baroque" and "ornamental" mode of expression) to the narrative and the dramatic. All of them seem to have been present from the beginning of his career. But if there is an evolution in this respect, this seems to lead him ever more in the direction of the narrative and dramatic pole. This appears, I think, not only from such important larger works among his recent output as **"Gorbunov and Gorchakov"** and **"Post aetatem nostram,"** but also from the growing significance of the narrative element in his shorter works. The latter point can be conveniently illustrated by a comparison of three blank-verse poems: **"A Stop in the Desert"** (written in 1966), **"K Likomedu, na Skiros ("On the Way to Lycomedes of Scyrus,"** 1967) and **"Aeneas and Dido"** (1969). The first work is predominantly reflective; the thoughts which the speaker develops in his monologue take their starting point from a specific circumstance (the destruction of the Greek church in Leningrad), but they remain on the whole abstract,

turning upon the moral aspects of the time process inherent in history and upon the role of Christianity in the development of Russian culture. The speaker himself is not individualized as a figure; the only personal information we receive about him is contained in the fact that he knows a "Tartar family" in the neighborhood of the Church. For the rest he functions in the poem as no more than the subject of his reflective monologue. In the poem from 1967, **"On the Way to Lycomedes of Scyrus,"** the situation is radically different. We also have to do here with a generalizing reflection, this time on the subject of a paradoxical moral law which causes heroic deeds to be followed by a humiliation of the "hero" instead of a reward, but it is presented in a semi-narrative and dramatic form. The myth of Theseus who after having slain the Minotaur loses his beloved Ariadne to the god Dionysus serves as a narrative "mask" for the present situation of the "I". The monologue is dramatic in a complex way: in the first lines the speaker introduces himself as someone whose fate resembles that of Theseus:

> I leave the town, as Theseus left
> His labyrinth

But in the rest of the poem the comparison as such is never stressed and the speaker presents his own situation so consistently in terms of the classical myth that the reader is apt to forget his separate existence. After a short appearance in the opening sentence he almost completely withdraws behind his "mask." This play of identity, making the speaker an almost anonymous figure, seems to work as a device pointing towards another level of interpretation: that of the author behind the poem and the circumstances of his private life.

Abstract reflection, lyrical or dramatized, is completely absent from the surface of **"Aeneas and Dido."** Insofar as the poem has an abstract theme this is true only by implication. The main difference with the preceding two poems lies in the fact that here there is no speaker-figure to present in the course of his monologue a certain set of thoughts and considerations. . . . [The] narrative structure of **"Aeneas and Dido"** is based, even insistently, on the use of the third person "he" and "she." The first person never occurs and instead of a monologizing speaker there is an implicit narrator. Only in one place (lines 17-19) do we find what seems to be a generalizing observation:

> But, as is known, precisely at the moment
> Of despair a fair wind
> Starts to blow.

As already appears, however, from its hackneyed triviality, the intention of this remark is purely ironical. The irony arises primarily from a play with the psychological perspective. After the poignant tragedy of the preceding lines the "despair" would naturally seem to be Dido's, but the "fair wind" which is supposed to relieve it is, of course, only "fair" for Aeneas. The breezy pseudo-comfort of the statement thus only serves to stress the utter hopelessness of her position.

Just as the Theseus poem, **"Aeneas and Dido"** is set in a decor from classical antiquity. Within the framework of the present essay it is impossible to provide an extensive analysis of the varying significance of the "classical" motifs which form such a predominant feature of the poetry of Brodsky; some general observations must suffice. In some cases the classical paraphernalia have a merely "decorative" function, helping to establish a particular neo-classical stylistic quality. But when it really belongs to the essential aspects of the poetic structure, the classical background has a direct bearing on the presentation of the theme; it may be used either to give it a certain universality or to put it in a special historical perspective. "Universality" seems to be the principal effect of the mythological frame in which the theme is presented in **"On the Way to Lycomedes of Scyrus"** and **"Aeneas and Dido."** The "perspectivism" which arises from a simultaneous projection of distant historical planes may be observed, for instance, in the poem **"Anno domini"**—where the present situation of the speaker and his surroundings is hidden under the ironical "mask" of a narrative scene which is set in late antiquity—and on a larger scale in the recent cycle **"Post aetatem nostram,"** where the description of the everyday life of a town in the pre-Christian world functions as a symbol of our post-Christian future.

The classical motifs in Brodsky's work are organically related to one of the main recurring themes of his poetry—the catastrophic decay of our culture and its traditional moral and spiritual roots. On the lyrical level this is paralleled by the equally persistent theme of the tragic instability and distintegration of personal relationships, resulting in separation, betrayal, departures. In the narrative structure of **"Aeneas and Dido"** these two themes are succinctly combined: historically Aeneas' "betrayal" of Dido is connected with his mission as founder of the Roman empire and thus he ultimately causes not only the destruction of her personal life, but also that of her empire. Dido's death prefigures the ruin of her city. At the end of Brodsky's poem this motif is developed in a kind of thematic (as well as temporal) rhyme:

> And (she) saw how in the haze of the pyre,
> Which trembled between flame and smoke,
> Carthage silently crumbled down
>
> Long before the prophecy of Cato.

It is unnecessary to decide which of the two is the primary element of the comparison: the ruin of Dido's personal life, or the future downfall of the Carthaginian empire. What makes **"Aeneas and Dido,"** I think, at the same time one of the most typical and most successful works of the author is the classical simplicity and coherence with which it unites in an "objectified" vision the depth of an intense personal drama with a sense of historical disaster. (pp. 497-500)

> *Kees Verheul, "Iosif Brodsky's 'Aeneas and Dido',"*
> *in* Russian Literature Triquarterly, *No. 7, Fall, 1973,*
> *pp. 490-501.*

STEPHEN SPENDER

[Spender, an English poet and essayist, belonged to the influential literary-political "Oxford Group" of the early 1930s, along with W. H. Auden and C. Day Lewis. His works of poetry, including Ruins and Visions *(1942),* The Generous Days *(1969), and his* Collected Poems, 1928-1985 *(1985), reflect a nostalgic, prewar style of lyrical romanticism. In later decades, his critical writings, such as* The Making of a Poem *(1955), have overshadowed his accomplishments as a poet. Spender has edited a number of anthologies and translated works by such writers as Rainer Maria Rilke and Georg Büchner. In the following excerpt from a review of* Selected Poems, *Spender comments on the elements that characterize Brodsky's poetry, particularly the recurrent theme of suffering.]*

Some years ago in New York I heard a famous American poet tell a famous Soviet poet that he could find it in his heart to envy his Russian colleagues because poetry was taken so seriously in the Soviet Union by the government that poets were imprisoned or sent into psychiatric wards or into exile. At the time the remark struck me as frivolous. But reading the poems of Joseph Brodsky (who has of course left the Soviet Union) I can see that Russian poets are nearer the centres of anguish which American poets want to write about than are the Americans, and that this may indeed provide reason for a wry envy. If a Russian poet laments his situation as a poet in Soviet society, we all know what that situation is: the society oppresses him for the independence of his views and for not singing its praises. But if a rather successful American poet writes in extreme terms about the sickness of his country, he may well appear to others to be the spoiled child of the system he is complaining about, and even at times to himself to be communicating nothing but his own sickness.

When the Russian poet, in other words, takes as his theme suffering, victimisation and misunderstanding, we know that all these are likely to be objective facts rather than subjective symptoms. When Brodsky writes about solitude, the result is not just another poem about the 'poet's failure to communicate within the conditions of our materialistic society'; it is the communicated suffering and courage of someone who has been sent into exile, labour camps, prisons. . . .

Brodsky is someone who has tasted extremely bitter bread and his poetry has the air of being ground out between his teeth. He sees things from a point of view which is ultimately that of Christians who have devoured bread and gall as the sacraments of the Mass: it should not be supposed that he is a liberal, or even a socialist. He deals in unpleasing, hostile truths and is a realist of the least comforting and comfortable kind. Everything nice that you would like him to think, he does not think. But he is utterly truthful, deeply religious, fearless and pure. Loving, as well as hating.

The ground-bass of these poems [in *Selected Poems*] is, then, that they are *dans le vrai*. Above this, there is a great deal else. Firstly, a respect for tradition: his poetry is continuous with the line of Pasternak and Anna Akhmatova, who befriended him (when she was in London some years ago she told me that she thought he was the most interesting of the young Soviet poets), and full of reverence for the traditional wherever he finds it—in Greek mythology, in Russian classics, and especially in English poetry ranging from Donne to Byron, T. S. Eliot and W. H. Auden. His poems can be intensely personal, and are sometimes private and cryptic, reminding me then more than anyone of Montale. What most move him, it seems, are the snatched moments of happiness with various women whose names or initials recur in his work, or separations which are seen to belong to the iron world of eternities determined:

> Separations in this world
> hint at partings beyond.
> It's not just in this lifetime
> that we must sleep apart.

Like Lorca with the word 'green', or the refrain 'it was five in the afternoon', Brodsky can build up a musical pattern of rhetoric on a repeated phrase: in the **"Elegy for John Donne"**, for instance, on the word 'sleep', or in another, untitled poem, on the word 'black' and the idea of blackness, with its implicit opposites of the white and the shining:

> Why did he blaze black light from those great eyes?
>
> (p. 915)

The conflict between the modern and the Biblical world is sardonically and characteristically conveyed in **"A Halt in the Desert"**, where he describes the destruction of a Greek Orthodox Church in Moscow, in preparation for its replacement by the glass-and-steel October Concert Hall:

> A huge power shovel clanked up to the church,
> an iron ball dangling from its boom, and soon
> the walls began to give way peaceably.
> Not to give way would be ridiculous
> for a mere wall in face of such a foe.

Unfortunately . . . one is never quite allowed to forget that one is reading a second-hand version rather than original poetry. (p. 916)

Stephen Spender, "Bread of Affliction," in New Statesman, *Vol. 86, No. 2230, December 14, 1973, pp. 915-16.*

MICHAEL SCHMIDT

[*Schmidt, a poet, editor, novelist, and critic, is managing director of Carcanet Press and coeditor of the poetry journal* PN Review. *His works include poetry collections, such as* Black Buildings *(1969),* A Change of Affairs *(1978), and* Choosing a Guest: New and Selected Poems *(1983), as well as the novels* The Colonist *(1980) and* The Dresden Gate *(1987). In the following excerpt Schmidt reviews Brodsky's* A Part of Speech, *evaluating the poet's stature and comparing him to other Russian poets of his generation.*]

In *A Part of Speech* Brodsky has chosen those of his earlier poems which illuminate his more recent work—as it were, the antecedents to the poems of his exile, those composed during and since 1972. One misses here some crucial pieces, especially the poem to Donne. Brodsky owes to Donne and the Metaphysicals (whom he has translated into Russian) certain debts of metaphor, organisation and tone. He is a wit of a high order: he plays in and through language. He is passionately alive to his tradition, much as Tsvetaeva and Akhmatova (both guides in his work) were. But it is odd: he is more philosophical, less physical, less particular, than the poets of their generation. When he echoes Mandelstam's 'Do preserve what I've said for its taste of misfortune and smoke', that evocative combination of abstract and acrid concrete is replaced by 'a time of cold, / a day of fear'. It is less real, a gesture rather than an experience. The tendency of Brodsky's generation has been to move away from the vivid celebratory and elegiac particularism of the great generation into a language more public in tenor. Brodsky's language generally stays closer to particulars of perception and experience, even in its witty elaborations, than that of his contemporaries does. Exile has not destroyed his art because it has destroyed neither his memory nor his eye.

I would risk a generalisation here. Poets such as Yevtushenko, Voznesensky and others for whom 'plot' (in the narrative sense) has come to replace subtler notions of form, belong to contemporary history. They will continue to be read—even poems such as 'Babi Yar'—for what they tell of general attitudes and sentiments. Brodsky, by contrast, is part of a broad Western tradition. His work, of less value to the historian or journalist, extends its tradition. It is by nature and by design part of the Judaeo-Christian and classical stream (which one cannot, at present, confidently call the 'main stream'). His refusal to play dissident roles is part of his vocation as a poet. He is reluctant to be used.

In his poetry there are continual daybreaks and sunsets, a Russian sense of immense distances, and some force or energy from the distance (wind, history or metaphysical power) break-

ing on the present where it is apprehended and which it will inevitably include. The subtlest treatment of this theme is the superb "**Nunc Dimittis**" of 1972. More recent (and secular) treatments seem less assured. . . .

What can be said of Brodsky, now he is 40? Of the recent poems, "**Lullaby to Cape Cod**" seems to be a masterpiece; "**The Butterfly**" proves his lyric and philosophical gifts are intact. He has been as unable as Seamus Heaney to resist the spell of Robet Lowell. Exile and middle age have made him no less allusive and oblique. And yet, with a substantial achievement behind him, Brodsky paradoxically remains a poet of promise.

Michael Schmidt, "Time of Cold," in New Statesman, *Vol. 100, No. 2587, October 17, 1980, p. 25.*

PETER FRANCE

[*France is the author of* Poets of Modern Russia *(1982). In the following excerpt from that work, France discusses Brodsky's themes and aspects of his prosody.*]

From the beginning Brodsky's poetry looks into the dark. He is like Eliot's Webster who was 'much possessed by death and saw the skull beneath the skin'. His characteristic themes in the early poems are death and time, youth and age, paradise lost. Brodsky is a Jew, but his poems relate to both the Jewish and the Christian traditions and constantly reveal a feeling for the importance of religion and the gap left by its decline in our century, particularly in Soviet Russia. This is perhaps best seen in his well-known poem "**A Halt in the Desert**" ("**Ostanovka v pustyne**"), which centres on the destruction of a Greek Orthodox church in Leningrad and the idea of faithfulness to the past.

The darkness of the horse is 'terrifying'; it is also magnetic. Set against the ordinary darkness of the night sky, and even more so against the cheerful brightness of a fire, this absolute blackness seems like the essential reality. Early in the nineteenth century Tyutchev wrote a number of poems around the vision of a fundamental darkness over which day is cast like a bright curtain. Brodsky says the same thing when he writes—both literally and figuratively—that 'inside our bodies we are black'. It is because of the absolute nature of the blackness that, like Hughes, he is driven to search out more and more points of comparison, attempting vainly to find words for something beyond words. As La Rochefoucauld said, but using the opposite comparison, 'Neither the sun nor death can be contemplated steadily.'

Given this preoccupation with time, death and nothingness, it is not surprising that Brodsky should have been drawn to T. S. Eliot (for whom he wrote a funeral poem in imitation of Auden's poem on the death of Yeats) and to the English metaphysicals, particularly Donne. The attraction is due not only to a similarity of vision, but to a similar approach to poetry; Brodsky's writing is often witty, thought-provoking and full of interesting metaphors and what would once have been called conceits. Indeed in many poems he seems to abandon himself to an absurd logic, startling his reader with unexpected images and figures of speech. But like Eliot, he combines this verbal inventiveness with a strong feeling for tradition. Quite apart from the overt allusions he makes to specific poems and poets of Europe, he is always aware, as Mandelstam had been, that his poetry is a further development of an ancient line. As he writes, he is answering the poets of former times and other countries. It thus comes naturally to him to choose classical subjects or subjects from the Bible in order to speak of our own times. We are the descendants of the ancients; their culture is our culture. At the same time, again as for Mandelstam or Eliot, this relationship is problematic. The biblical names Isaac and Abraham are no longer what they were; in Brodsky's words, 'Isaac loses a sound in Russian' and . . .

> Isac in fact is only a butt-end now
> of the candle that once all men called Isaac.

When he writes sonnets, they have fourteen lines, but in other respects they depart from the time-honoured sonnet form, and although they may speak of Hector, Ajax and Vesuvius, they really concern a present which is quite unlike the heroic past. (pp. 201-02)

Parting is one of his principal themes. This is of course one of the time-honoured subjects of the lyric poet, but in Brodsky's case it has been given new poignancy by his forced absence from his native country. During his banishment to the far north in 1964-5 he wrote an impressive long poem of absence called (after Byron) **"New Stanzas to Augusta"** (**"Novye stansy k Avguste"**). Since 1972 the exile has been more total, exile from Russia, its people and its language. This naturally finds expression in many of the poems he has written since then, though it should not be thought that these are simply responses to a particular personal situation—exile is a necessary feature of human life, at any rate for poets, and we may recall Tsvetaeva's words: 'Every poet is essentially an émigré.'

Unlike the early poems, many of Brodsky's poems of the late 1960s and the 1970s are political or moral in their concerns. Through all his wit, he appears as a writer seriously committed to the values by which people can live, nostalgic for a lost state of faith and stability and often very black in his perception of the modern world, whether in Russia or the West. As he puts it in a traditional way in a poem with the nostalgic title **"To Eugene"** . . . , 'Living is tedious, my Eugene. Wherever you travel, everywhere cruelty and dullness are there to exclaim: Good day, here we are too.' At the same time, in exile, his poetry inevitably dwells on his own solitary situation and on those same metaphysical issues which were present in his writing from the beginning. (pp. 205-06)

> *Peter France, "Poets of Today," in his* Poets of Modern Russia, *Cambridge University Press, 1982, pp. 188-219.*

EDWARD J. BROWN

[*Brown, an American critic and educator, is the author of* The Proletarian Episode in Russian Literature, 1928-1932 *(1953);* Russian Literature since the Revolution *(1963);* Stankevich and His Moscow Circle *(1966); and* Mayakovsky: A Poet in the Revolution *(1973). In the following excerpt from* Russian Literature since the Revolution, *Brown commends Brodsky's poetic gifts and examines his characteristic style and themes.*]

Brodsky's poetry deals with the persistent unsolved questions of existence: time, origins, space, life and death, along with the psychological puzzles of dislocation, depression, and insanity. While it conveys a sense of ultimate bafflement with such problems, the total effect of his work is a kind of happy transcendence achieved by sheer exuberant virtuosity of imagery and language. Brodsky's poetry, even when it deals with melancholy and death, should have a positive therapeutic value: just as the reading of Mandelshtam's poetry was said to be

"good for the lungs and a cure for tuberculosis," so Brodsky's lines might be useful in psychiatric practice. Even when he speaks of death Brodsky's poetry makes death its own, appropriates it totally, triumphantly realizes its utter blackness and emptiness. One of his best poems, on the blackness of a black horse, forces the language to yield up every image of blackness it has, to reveal all possible inflections of the words for black and dark. As the black horse approaches the lonely campfire,

> He was black, he felt no shadow.
> So black he couldn't be any blacker.
> As black he was as midnight pitch.
> As black as the forest before us.
> As black as the inside of a needle.
> As that place in the chest between the ribs.
> As the hole in the ground where a seed is planted.
> I think it must be black inside us.

And in the poem **"Elegy for John Donne"** we experience not loss but riches in the long, illimitable list of all the things that "sleep" now that the poet, John Donne, is dead:

> John Donne has gone to sleep, and everything is sleeping.
> The walls are asleep, the floor, the bed, the pictures,
> the table is asleep, the rugs, the locks, the hook,
> the whole wardrobe, the buffet, the candle, the curtains . . .

The long poem **"Gorbunov and Gorchakov"** is a dialogue in an insane asylum between two committed madmen, who discuss with a certain mad logic all the anguish of their lives in the hospital, their dreams, their hangups, their preferences, their philosophical and political beliefs, their opinions of one another. The dark passages and strange whorls of a madman's mind we explore with sympathy, stunned recognition, and, it would seem, enhanced understanding.

For Brodsky, God does exist, in some sense, but his attributes are a matter of poetic conjecture:

> God looks down. And men look up:
> But each has a peculiar interest of his own.

The Artificer may be too subtle for us, but his work we can know. The lyric **"The Butterfly"** is an intellectually and strophically intricate meditation on the short, literally fleeting life of a complex little miracle of pattern and color, the butterfly. (pp. 354-55)

It is fascinating to read Brodsky's poems because, filled as they are with the inventory of light and life, they present the negative of those things, darkness and death, as matters for contemplation not totally immune to the power of human thought. As Milosz put it, "His larger enterprise is to fortify the place of man in a threatening world."

Brodsky is quintessentially the poet of exile, one who was prolific after leaving the homeland and who writes beautifully about the lands and the experiences of his exile, Florence, London, Ann Arbor, and Cape Cod. His work is still another example of the Sorrento photograph effect. A number of poems might be used to illustrate his subjective apprehension of those places: **"Mexican Divertissement," "December in Florence," "Lithuanian Divertissement,"** but the best of these and one of his most characteristic and strongest poems is **"Lullaby of Cape Cod,"** which masterfully develops the themes of exile and wandering, inexplicable survival, and space and time as mysteries in a lonely human life. Translation can only weakly reflect the original, and paraphrase must violate the structure of meter and rhyme, but a judicious mixture of the two can perhaps convey something of the poem's profundity and power. The setting is a seaside resort on Cape Cod on a stiflingly hot summer evening at the hour "between the dog and the wolf," when that part of the globe is immersing itself in night, when a steeple crowned by a cross "apathetically darkens and disappears, like a bottle forgotten on the table." Stifling heat and the disappearance of objects in the advancing dark are the chief sensual images of the poem. The opening line, "The eastern end of the empire sinks into night," locates the poet in one of the two empires where his life has been spent, and contains a reminder of the *other* empire where he was born. (p. 356)

[Images] of isolation and immobility at a single point in space—paradise—provide a counterpoint to the leitmotif of free exile, the exploration of time and space, that is the accepted lot of the poet, whose work is the summit and realization of life. The poem began with the free fish, the poet's figure, coming up onto land, caught in the net of houses, surviving somehow on the land, and journeying deep into the continent. It ends with another free fish, the cod, an exile from the sea, knocking at his door.

Iosif Brodsky along with Solzhenitsyn, Sinyavsky, Aksyonov, and in the earlier period Nabokov, Khodasevich, Tsvetaeva, and many others forms the exile stream of modern Russian literature, a gift lavished upon the world by a state that, like Shakespeare's base Indian, "threw a pearl away, richer than all his tribe." At the time it expelled Brodsky, and the others, that state clearly could not distinguish pearls from worthless baubles. And how could it? As Shklovsky puts it, "When Christ was alive the state could not understand his Aramaic, and it has never understood simple human speech." The Soviet state could hardly be expected to understand Brodsky's strong and simple language. (p. 358)

> Edward J. Brown, "Exiles, Early and Late," in his Russian Literature since the Revolution, *revised edition, Cambridge, Mass.: Harvard University Press, 1982, pp. 345-87.*

JOSEPH BRODSKY (INTERVIEW WITH DAVID MONTENEGRO)

[*In the following excerpt from an interview with David Montenegro on April 8, 1986, Brodsky discusses his own poetry, as well as his general theories of poetics.*]

DM: You've just published **Less Than One,** your first collection of essays. Do you find prose gives you a new latitude? What problems and pleasures do you find in writing prose that you don't find in writing poetry?

JB: Well, to begin with, I simply happened to write those pieces over the years. On several occasions, I've been commissioned for one thing or another, and I just wanted to do whatever was asked of me in each particular instance. What pleases me really about the book is that it's something that was never meant to be. Perhaps a collection or two of poems was in the cards, but a book of prose—especially in English—wasn't. It strikes me as something highly illegitimate.

As for the difficulties or differences, essentially the operations of prose and poetry are not so different. In prose, you have a more leisurely pace, but in principle prose is simply spilling some beans, which poetry sort of contains in a tight pod.

DM: You once wrote that prose is hateful to you because it doesn't have poetry's discipline.

JB: How shall I put it? To use an almost paradoxical term, that's one of prose's shortcomings. That's specifically what makes prose lengthy. What I value about poetry, if I can simply estrange myself to look with a kind of cold, separate eye at these things, is that in verse your mind—reader's or writer's—moves much faster, for verse is overtly final and terribly concise, it's a condensed thing. In prose there is nothing that prevents you from going sideways, from digressing. In poetry, a rhyme keeps you in check.

Basically, my attitude towards prose—apart from its being the vehicle of making a living because, in fact, prose is paid for, if not more handsomely, at least more readily than poetry—the thing that I can say in praise of prose is that it's perhaps more therapeutic than poetry. For poetry's risk, its uncertainty, its anticipation of failure is terribly high. And after a while one gets rather edgy or bilious.

In prose, I think, it's harder to fail. You simply sit and write, and as the day passes you've written several pages. Then the next day, and so forth. That in part perhaps explains why there are so many novels around. Prose gives a writer confidence whereas poetry does exactly the opposite.

DM: Efim Etkind, in his book *Notes of a Non-Conspirator,* called you a very modern poet. He said even when you were quite young you were presenting problems to yourself and dealing with problems presented to you by your times. What new problems does the modern poet face unlike those faced by the nineteenth-century poet, or even the poet prior to World War Two?

JB: That's a big question indeed. Now one of the main problems that a poet today faces—modern or not modern—is that the body of poetry prior to him—the heritage, that is—is larger, which makes you simply wonder whether you have anything to add to that body, whether you're simply going to modify some of your predecessors or whether you're gong to be yourself.

But basically it's not so much the question asked at the threshold, whether you're going to modify somebody or not. You ask this subsequently, with the benefit of hindsight. It's a question you ask yourself because of the critics around. But it's precisely because you have such great people before yesterday who breathe on your neck, that you have to go a bit further, where theoretically nobody has been before. It simply makes it more difficult to write, because you are quite conscious of not wanting to be a parrot. And the people before you were quite great. To think that you can say something qualitatively new after people like Tsvetaeva, Akhmatova, Auden, Pasternak, Mandelstam, Frost, Eliot, and others after Eliot—and let's not leave out Thomas Hardy—reveals either a very enterprising fellow or a very ignorant one. And I would bill myself as the latter.

When you start writing, you know less about what took place before you. It's only in the middle of your life that you come to amass this knowledge, and it can dwarf you or mesmerize you.

That's one thing, one problem for the modern poet. The other is obviously that the modern poet lives in a world where what had been regarded as values, as virtues and vices, say twenty or thirty years ago, have, if not necessarily swapped places, at least been questioned or compromised entirely. A modern poet presumably doesn't live in a world which is ethically, let alone politically, as polarized as was the situation before the war. But I think the polarization is still quite clear. I don't really know what Etkind had in mind. Presumably, what he had in mind was a difference between the modern poet and a poet, let's say, of the turn of the century. Our predecessors perhaps had more to believe in. Their pantheon, or their shrines, were a bit more populated than ours. We are one way or another, in a sense, awful agnostics.

But there are agnostics and agnostics. I would say that the poet worships perhaps only one thing in the final analysis, and that has no embodiment except in words, that is . . . language. His attitude towards the Supreme Deity who is absent is more of a reproach for His absence than a pure jeering or else hosannas. Perhaps I am modern in that I am living in my own time and to some extent I reflect—what I write reflects—the sensibility of the people who speak my language towards their reality. In that respect, of course, I am modern. What else could I be? Old-fashioned? Conservative? Well, I'm conservative in terms of form, perhaps. In terms of content, in terms of the attitude towards reality, and the sensibility, I am fairly—well, I hope—*au courant.* (pp. 527-29)

DM: As a poet, you're conspicuous in that you often use religious imagery. Do you think it's still effective? Is it a common language?

JB: In my view, yes it is. At least it's common vis-à-vis my Russian audience. And I'm either generous or cynical enough to think that my Russian audience is not that qualitatively different in the final analysis from my English audience. But maybe that's wishful thinking on my part. I think it's still a language comprehensible to a certain percentage of people, and that's enough. For no percentage of the people is merely a small one. How small are, let's say, ten people, or six?

DM: Marek Oramus, while interviewing Zbigniew Herbert, said that Herbert *corrects* mythology. How do you approach it?

JB: You animate it, you try to make sense out of all of this, out of all that you've inherited. That's what you do. You're not really correcting it, you're making sense out of it. It's simply interpreted. It's the function of the species to interpret the Bible, mythology, the Upanishads, anything we have inherited, including our own dreams.

Basically, each era, each century, not to mention each culture has its own Greece, its own Christianity, its own Orient, its own mythology. Each century simply offers its own interpretation, like a magnifying glass, in a sense. We're just yet another lens. And it simply indicates the distance that grows between us and myths, and I think the attempt to interpret is essentially proportionate to the distance.

DM: You mentioned in one essay—and I'll just quote you— "At certain periods of history it is only poetry that is capable of dealing with reality by condensing it into something graspable, something that otherwise couldn't be retained by the mind." What are some other functions of poetry? What is the power of language through poetry?

JB: Poetry sells perhaps better as the record of human sensibility. To give you an example, the age of the Augustan poets. I think if we have a notion of Roman and of the human sensibility of the time it's based on Horace, for instance, the way he sees the world, or Ovid or Propertius. And we don't have any other record, frankly.

DM: This might not be pertinent at all since the poet's fascination with language isn't with its utility, but what does poetry now provide that prose doesn't, that religion doesn't, that philosophy doesn't? How strong is language in fending off a sense of chaos, in defending people or their sensibility from brutality?

JB: Well, I don't really know how to answer this, except by pointing out the very simple fact that speech is a reaction to the world, some kind of grimacing in the darkness or making faces behind the bastards' backs, or else controlling your fright or vomit. It's a reaction to the world, and in that sense it's functional. Protective? Does it protect you? No, more than likely not. It really *exposes* you. But it's quite possible that the exposure leads to the real test of your quality, of your durability. To say the least, producing something of harmony today is tantamount to saying in the face of chaos: "Look, you can't break me, not yet." And "me" in the language stands for everybody.

I don't really know what the function of poetry is. It's simply the way, so to speak, the light or dark refracts for you. That is, you open the mouth. You open the mouth to scream, you open the mouth to pray, you open the mouth to talk. Or you open the mouth to confess. Well, each time presumably you are forced by something to do so.

DM: When you first arrived in the United States in 1972, you said one fear you had was that your work would suffer a kind of paralysis because you would be living outside the environment of your native language. But, in fact, you've been prolific. What effect *has* living here had on your poetry?

JB: I don't know. I guess what I was saying then simply reflected my fears. Prolific I was. I would imagine that I would have been as, if not more, prolific, with no less interesting consequences for myself and for my readers, had I stayed at home. I think that fear expressed in 1972 reflected more the apprehension of losing my identity and that self-respect as a writer. I think what I was really unsure of—and I'm not so sure today, as a matter of fact—was that I wouldn't become a simpleton, because the life here would require much less of me, not as subtle an operation on a daily basis as in Russia. And indeed, in the final analysis, some of my instincts have dulled, I think. But, on the other hand, by being apprehensive about that sort of thing, you're trying to make up your own mind. And, after all, you perhaps break even. You end up as neurotic as you would have been otherwise. Only faster, though you can't be sure of that either.

DM: You used the word stereoscopic before. Do you think being in another country gives you a sort of double vision?

JB: But, of course, if only because here a great world of information is available to you. I was talking not long ago with a friend of mine, and we were discussing the shortcomings of being away from our country. And we came to the conclusion that perhaps the usual apprehension of the individual as well as of his public or of his critics is that, once outside of danger, out of harm's way, one's instincts, one's pencil get duller. One's notion of evil becomes less sharp.

But, I think, on the contrary, in fact you find yourself really in a rather remarkable predicament vis-à-vis, let's say, the evil . . . well, vis-à-vis the dragon. That is, you can observe him, you can ascertain and assess him in a better fashion. You can see with greater clarity—precisely because of all the data available to you here which wasn't there—all his scales, all his spikes, all his teeth. On top of that, you are not mesmerized. Your attention is not clouded by the fear of being grabbed by that dragon at any time. So basically, if you are to take him on, you can find yourself as well armed as the dragon is. In fact, you establish a certain parity at this safe distance. And on top of that, you have always suspected that you are, perhaps, as bad as the dragon yourself, and given the chance you would be just as nasty and monstrous as he is. That is, you have always suspected there is more of a monster in you than of Saint George. It's not customary for a certain type of writer to regard himself as a fallen angel. One would rather regard oneself as a devil, as one of the devils.

And maybe the fact that I stayed, as you say, prolific reflects simply the availability of data. Maybe it reflects simply the realization that monstrosity is everywhere, while in Russia I thought of it as being our local specialty.

DM: It sounds as if you're implying an identification of the victim with the assailant.

JB: But of course. No, I would say simply your notion of the dragon becomes far more subtle. That is, you realize you may play Saint George *ad infinitum,* because the animal is everywhere. And in a sense, you become, your armor becomes, in the final analysis, your own scales. And clarifying these things on paper conspires to bring the subsequent charge of being prolific. Prose is a more natural medium for that sort of job, for pondering. And to answer your very first question, the thing that many fail to realize is that there is a great bond between a poem and essay writing. Both employ the technique invented, of course, in poetry by poetry, of montage. It's not Eisenstein, it's poetry. It's stanzas with those frame-like shapes.

DM: It's the parts trying to become the whole.

JB: Yes, exactly.

DM: In comparing two of your poems, **"Elegy for John Donne,"** an early poem, and the more recent **"Lullaby of Cape Cod,"** I was struck by how similar they are in many ways, but also how drastically different. Both are set at night, both are very solitary poems. The earlier poem seems to show a spiritual struggle. There's a definite battle going on. I think in the John Donne poem, you had the categories clearer: spirit, flesh, and so forth. And therefore the struggle was much more intense. But in the later poem, there's less certainty. There's a sense of exhaustion—maybe even a spiritual exhaustion. Instead of snow, there's the heat. You repeat the word "stifling." And also, there's the sheer weight of the material world. Despite the list of objects, in the earlier poem there's a sort of resurrection. In the later poem, everything seems to be drugged, heavy, as if it can't wake up. What do you think of this reading?

JB: There is some similarity, come to think of it. I never thought about it. I don't really know. Perhaps this is a valid comparison and a valid observation, and perhaps there is some sort of a genealogy of the kind that you're talking about. But I don't think so. I think the only thing it testifies to is, at best, not so much the evolution of the views as the consistency of the device.

I sort of like **"Lullaby of Cape Cod."** You should be aware of the fact that it's ninety-three lines longer in the translation than it is in the original. In the original, it's a bit more concise. And I think it's a far more lyrical work than **"Big Elegy."** In **"Big Elegy"** there is indeed a certain clarity of the spirit. It is a vertical job from the threshold. But **"Cape Cod Lullaby"** I was writing not as a poem with a beginning and end, but more as a lyrical sequence. It was more like playing piano than singing an aria. Actually I'd written that poem because it was the Bicentennial, you see, and I thought—well, why don't I

do something? There is one image there, I think, where I use the Stars and Stripes.

DM: As you did with the word "stifling," you often use repetition and anaphora. It seems to me, your poetry is centrifugal. You start from a center and move outward, turning and separating different aspects of the subject. Whereas Akhmatova would be more centripetal.

JB: True, there is obviously a difference of temperaments. She seldom operates in big forms. She is a poet of great economy, and she's a more classical poet. Well, I wouldn't like to be compared to her.

DM: What gives you the least confidence now in poetry? Is there any particular problem that you're trying to solve?

JB: The poems are always particular when you are writing this or that one. I'm not trying to bill myself in any spectacular fashion, but I think as somebody who has always written in meter and rhyme, I do increase the purely technical stakes. Those two aspects, especially rhyme, simply are synonymous with compounding your own problems from the threshold, from the first impulse to write, which is fairly frequently a blissful one, in my case, or the sense of guilt. But I know what I'm going to do more or less from the moment I set out. That is, I more or less have the sense of form at the moment I'm starting with some sort of content, and the form gives you a great deal of headache.

DM: Like Auden, you have a fascination with form. Do you think structure itself sometimes leads you into new content?

JB: Presumably, because by and large it's very seldom that one knows at the outset where one is heading. Simply by virtue of being a citizen of a different era, you're *bound* to invest the ancient form, old form, compromised—if you will—form with a qualitatively new meaning. That creates contrast, it creates a tension, and the result is always new. It's bound to be new. And it's terribly interesting. Apart from anything else, sometimes you write about certain things precisely for the form's sake, in many ways. That's not to say that you're trying to write a *villanelle* and la-di-da to check whether your facility is still there. No, it's simply because, otherwise, to write about certain things wouldn't be as appetizing a prospect. After all, you can say only so many things, you can express only so many attitudes towards the reality of this world. In fact, all the attitudes in the final analysis are computable. And forms are not. Or at least the interplay of an attitude and the form in which it is expressed in writing increases the options.

DM: Some poets now don't use rhyme and meter, they claim, because they feel such form is no longer relevant to experience or experience doesn't have the continuity or structure that such form implies.

JB: They're entitled to their views, but I think it's pure garbage. Art basically is an operation within a certain contract, and you have to abide by all the clauses of the contract. You write poetry, to begin with, in order to influence minds, to influence hearts, to *move* hearts, to move people. In order to do so, you have to produce something which has an appearance of inevitability and which is memorable, so that it will stick in the mind of the reader. You have to wrap it in such a fashion that the reader won't be able to avoid it, so that what you have said will have a chance of entering his subconscious and of being remembered. Meter and rhyme are basically mnemonic devices. Not to mention the fact to which Ezra Pound alerted us, I think way back in 1911 or 1915, by saying there's too much free verse around. And that was in the teens of the century.

DM: Or as Robert Frost said, free verse is like playing tennis without a net.

JB: Well, it's not tennis. And not cricket either. (pp. 531-35)

DM: If you object to the next questions, please tell me.

JB: Go ahead.

DM: I want to ask you about the trial.

JB: That was many moons ago. Nothing interesting about it.

DM: We can read the shorthand account of it, but what was it like from your point of view? It was a mock trial. It must have seemed absurd, though it was no joke. It must have made you angry.

JB: It didn't make me angry. In fact, it did not. Never. No, a joke it wasn't. It was dead serious. I can talk about that at length, but in short . . . how shall I put it? It simply was an enactment of what I knew all along. But it's nice when things are *enacted,* you know. I knew who the masters were, and I knew that I had no other choice, that one day sooner or later it was going to happen that I would be in that position. I didn't expect a worse position; I didn't expect a better position. It didn't surprise me in the least that it happened, and the only thing I was interested in was what kind of sentence I was going to get. It looked rather dreadful, because there were lots of people. It looked like what I've seen of a Nuremberg trial, in terms of the number of police in the room. It was absolutely studded with police and state security people.

It's funny how—looking back now with the benefit of hindsight—I didn't really pay very much attention to what was going on, because attention was exactly what the state would have liked you to display. Or feel, indeed. The state wants you to get . . . well, you don't allow yourself to get scared, and you just think about something else. You pretend it isn't happening. You simply sit there and, as much as you can, you try to ignore it. In fact, the only time I was moved during the whole thing was when two people stood up and defended me—two witnesses—and said something nice about me. I was so unprepared to hear something positive that I was a little bit moved. But other than that, no. So, I got my five years, and I walked out of the room and was taken to the prison, and that was it.

DM: You had already spent three weeks of interrogation in a hospital?

JB: It was more than that. It was the mental institution. But that wasn't for the first time. It wasn't the first arrest either. It was the third, I think. I'd been twice to mental institutions, three times to prisons. All that sort of thing. And since it wasn't terribly new or terribly fresh, I wasn't shocked then.

DM: Why did you feel that this would eventually happen?

JB: Because one way or another I knew that I was running my own show, that I was doing something which amounts essentially to private enterprise in what is otherwise a state-owned economy, so to speak. And I knew that one day I would be grabbed.

It's simply the different tonality, the different use of the language. In a society where everything belongs to the state, to try to speak with your own voice, etcetera, is obviously fraught with consequences. It's not so interesting. It's simply an idiotic

situation, and you find yourself in the position of a victim, as a sort of martyr. Well, you find you're sort of ashamed of it. It's *embarrassing.*

DM: You said once that your months of forced labor near Archangel in 1964-65 were perhaps the most normal time in your life.

JB: True, almost two years of it.

DM: In fact, the people there, you said, treated you well, like a son.

JB: Well, a son . . . that was a bit too much. As one of their own, yes. (pp. 535-37)

DM: In 1965 you were released and you remained in Russia until 1972. You did a lot of writing during that period also. Were you interfered with by the authorities?

JB: Not very much. They would interfere with publication, but with life as such, no. Several times there would be subpoenas for interrogations and this and that. . . . (p. 537)

DM: A last question. Absolutes are something you deal with a lot in your prose. What absolutes would you say we have to live by if our sense of good and evil is somewhat oversophisticated perhaps, or sophisticated to the point of paralyzing us? What other types of absolutes are there, if any, or do we need them?

JB: Well, there is one. It's kind of a funny thing to be asked. And it puts me immediately in a position where I am tempted to proselytize, to a certain extent. But, first of all, one shouldn't really allow oneself into that situation where one's sense of good and evil gets so, as you say, sophisticated. Basically there is one criterion which nobody with sophistication would refuse: that you should treat your own kind the way you would like to be treated yourself. It's a tremendous idea offered to us by Christianity, in a sense. It's a terribly selfish idea, and it finally established the bond.

DM: It turned the urge toward self-preservation into a social value.

JB: But of course. Frost said once, to be social is to be forgiving. And that's basically the requirement, to forgive because you would like to be forgiven yourself, not only by the Almighty, but by your fellow beings. And I thought the other day—well, I looked—now it's going to be a little bit maudlin, but then in effect I prove my profession—out of the window and I saw a star. Then I thought, that star over there, presumably, with some help, is the domain of the Almighty, all the stars, etcetera. Then it occurred to me that this thought about loving your neighbor as yourself travelled here from quite afar. I thought, how appropriate is the origin. That is, the stars being the origin of this idea. For a star to like its neighbor, it takes something, yes? It's kind of interesting to think about, to think it through. I don't really know. . . . (pp. 539-40)

Joseph Brodsky, in an interview with David Montenegro, in Partisan Review, *Vol. LIV, No. 4, Fall, 1987, pp. 527-40.*

EDWARD MENDELSON

[An American critic and editor, Mendelson is often identified with his work on W. H. Auden, for whom he has served as critic, bibliographer, editor, and literary executor. He is a contributor to such magazines as the Times Literary Supplement, London Review of Books, *and* New Republic. *His* Early Auden *(1981)*

was nominated for the National Book Critics Circle Award. In the following excerpt on Less Than One *Mendelson praises Brodsky as a powerful critic and describes the moral stance that unites his poetic philosophy with his resistance to the Soviet state.*]

Joseph Brodsky, like Joseph Conrad, writes flawlessly in a language he learned in exile. Only an occasional oddity in Conrad's syntax hinted that he sometimes thought in some other language while writing in English; only Brodsky's pleasure in puns and verbal echoes hints that he still sees the English language as an exotic garden of delights. His prose has the energy and precision of a master, and, at times, the moral authority of a prophet.

Most of the essays in *Less Than One* concern 20th-century poetry in Russian and English, but the book is framed by two memoirs of his childhood in Leningrad. The political passions of these memoirs inform everything else in the book. (As Conrad's homeland was ruled by the czar, so Brodsky's homeland is ruled by the czar's successors.) The school where every morning Brodsky "prepared himself to hear drivel" and the factory where he worked afterwards seem to be two versions of the same institution, each justified by the same lies. Later, when Brodsky was convicted of "social parasitism," prison seemed the same institution in yet another form. In a world in which no one could learn responsibilities, he developed the fear that he might be unequal to any task at hand, that he could not act as a unique person—in short, that "one is perhaps less than 'one.'" Now, he implies, he continues to feel that he can write as a unique and individual "one" only by constant acts of resistance and assertion.

Brodsky uses the same language to describe the act of writing a poem and to describe the act of resisting the state. Like Goethe's Faust he regards freedom not as a state of calm but as the product of unending struggle—more precisely, as the struggle itself. For Brodsky, formal verse is the only kind worth writing, precisely because rhymes and stanzas are as limiting and intransigent as a police state. A poet wins success only by resisting the featureless anonymity that regular forms would otherwise impose. In an age of avant-garde experiments, Anna Akhmatova (the subject of one of Brodsky's most eloquent essays) chose to work within the conventions of classical forms, but she "sounds so independent because from the outset she knew how to exploit the enemy."

Exploiting the enemy is Brodsky's preferred technique in politics as in literature. In a commencement address—one of the rare examples of that genre worth reading—he recalls a labor-camp inmate who performed so extravagant a display of overwork that the guards were too embarrassed to demand more. As Brodsky points out, the gospel verse that urges you to turn the other cheek is more than an instruction to return good for evil. The verse goes on to urge you to give your cloak to the thief who takes your coat, and to go two miles when you are compelled to go one. "The meaning of these lines," Brodsky writes, "is anything but passive, for it suggests that evil can be made absurd through excess."

In the same way, the density and complexity of great poetry make absurd the arbitrary limits of form and meter. Brodsky's poetry, like his politics, is built on "the hope that the victim will always be more inventive, more original in his thinking, more enterprising than the villain. Hence the chance that the victim may triumph." Hence the triumph of the poets he admires.

Brodsky's vision of oppression and resistance is the source of both the major strengths and the minor weaknesses of this book. He has devoted a lifetime to the search for ever more ingenious means of revolt, ever more creative ways of using power against itself, and no critic has a wider and more active understanding of the ethical implications of poetic language. His essays on Russian writers—Dostoevsky, Akhmatova, Nadezhda Mandelstam, Marina Tsvetaeva, Andrei Platonov—convey even to a reader who knows no Russian the moral force of the choices reflected in their vocabulary and their grammar. His essays on Western writers—Eugenio Montale, Derek Walcott, W. H. Auden—are equally committed and convincing. Brodsky makes an equation between the sharpness of a poet's ethical instincts and the keenness of the poet's ear. He proves the equation in a pair of breathtaking essays that analyze, syllable by syllable, a single poem by Tsvetaeva and a single poem by Auden.

Both these essays are extraordinary in their combination of detailed literary understanding with concerned ethical intelligence, but the essay on Auden's "September 1, 1939" is a special triumph. Brodsky can hear precise gradations of tone in his adopted language, and he can draw moral parables from patterns of rhyme. He reports that when he began writing English prose, his "sole purpose then, as it is now, was to find myself in closer proximity to the greatest mind of the twentieth century: Wystan Hugh Auden." Few critics have achieved such proximity to the mind and art of any author.

Yet Brodsky is so powerful a critic that he can transform his subjects into versions of himself. Without recognizing that he is doing so, he praises Auden's poem for the same reasons that Auden eventually renounced it. Auden saw the poem as "infected by an incurable dishonesty," in part because he saw it as a poem in which he manipulated language for his personal ends rather than as a poem in which language had a chance to speak for itself. For Auden, a successful poem was a hymn of praise to the language in which it was written. For Brodsky, a successful poem is a cunning act of resistance against a language that tries to exploit the poet as its own instrument. He finds the "millennarian" fantasy of Communism "embedded" in the Russian language, and he honors the novelist Andrei Platonov for attacking "the very carrier of millennarian sensibility in Russian society: the language itself."

Throughout this book Brodsky is on the attack. . . . But Brodsky is not entirely happy with his own stance. He rebukes dissident Russian writers for attacking only those forces that are outside themselves—very much as he seems to do in his own work. "No matter how poisonously sarcastic one gets, the target of such sarcasm is always external: the system and the powers-that-be." He notes that Auden, in contrast, never applied a pejorative term to others without also applying it secretly to himself. Brodsky has in fact adopted Auden's method as his own, and the ethical drama played out within his essays—a drama in which he argues as eloquently with himself as with his enemies—has all the intricacy and depth of an enduring work of art.

Edward Mendelson, "Against the Limits of Language," in Book World—The Washington Post, *May 25, 1986, p. 7.*

ALEXANDER ZHOLKOVSKY

[*Zholkovsky, a Russian critic and educator, is the author of* Themes and Texts: Essays in a Poetics of Expressiveness *(1984) and coauthor of* Poetics of Expressiveness: A Theory and Application *(1986).*

In his essay, excerpted below, Zholkovsky offers a brief overview of Brodsky's career as a poet and presents a detailed analysis of his style and characteristic themes.]

Iosif Brodskij (Joseph Brodsky) is almost unanimously considered the best living Russian poet and heir to the grand poetic tradition. In the erudite spirit of the Silver Age, he is also a translator of poetry into Russian, professor of Russian literature, editor of critical anthologies, bilingual essayist, and, like many of his predecessors, practitioner of the Russian art of poetic performance. His human rights profile places him in the pantheon of Russia's poets *qua* cultural heroes opposed to/victimized by the powers that be. Brodskij is a poet in exile, but unlike other Russian émigré writers, he has become a member of the Western intellectual establishment and, in the manner of a Turgenev or a Herzen, he is "spreading the Russian word" in the West. A versatile intertextualist with a rare command of English, he brings together elements of traditional and contemporary Russian culture and Anglo-American heritage in a poetic synthesis that transcends national boundaries. (p. 404)

Brodskij's work spans almost three decades and two continents, or rather, "empires," as he will have it. He has written in several genres, with a clear predilection for larger forms: longer poems, or *poèmy* (e.g., **"Isaak i Avraam," "Posvjaščaetsja Jalte," "Post aetatem nostram"**); cycles of poems (e.g., **"Litovskij divertisment," "Pis' ma rimskomu drugu," "Meksikanskij romansero"**) and numerous mini-cycles of two or three related poems; long lyrical poems, often concatenations of numbered strophes (e.g., various **"Strofy," "Stixi na smert' T. S. Èliota," "Pamjati T. B.," "Pis' mo generalu Z."**); and, finally, individual lyrics, which he likes to collect into "books" (e.g., **"Anno Domini," "Čast' reči"**). His favorite genres are elegy, sonnet, epistle (mostly "in memoriam"), travelogue, as well as variations on classical (Greek, Roman, Biblical) or local (Lithuanian, Mexican) themes. In two-odd decades Brodskij has gone through several changes of style and assimilated a variety of influences. Critics more or less agree on a list of "mentors," which includes Kantemir, Deržavin, Puškin, Baratynskij, Axmatova, Mandel'štam . . . , Majakovskij, and Cvetaeva; Norwid and Gałczyński; John Donne, Andrew Marvell, and George Herbert; T. S. Eliot, W. H. Auden, and Dylan Thomas; Cavafy; and perhaps a few others. . . .

Yet, Brodskij's poetic physiognomy has remained rather stable. He is an intellectual poet . . . , fusing high seriousness, sophisticated argumentation, irony, uninhibited play with tradition, and colloquial—to the point of profane—street wisdom and lexicon into an original poetic idiom of his own. He relies on complex, deliberately puzzling metaphors. His sentences tend to be long, convoluted, with frequent enjambments, making the period or stanza, rather than the line, his typical unit of discourse. . . . In this and other respects he tests the limits of traditional Russian verse in a new round of the "prosaization" of Russian poetry. But like many previous reformers, he does not go far beyond the pale. His is the mainstream high tradition. He experiments with rhyme (compound punning rhyme is his staple fare, though he occasionally resorts to blank verse), meter (he uses *dol'nik* and accentual verse, as well as lines of unequal length, sometimes forming *calligrammes*, as in **"Babočka"**), and elaborate stanzaic patterns . . . , but on the whole it can be said that he sticks to "regular" rhymes, meters, and stanzas to provide a strong backbone for his whimsically sprawling banter.

Thematically, he is an archetypal poet of exile and the void, whose actual emigration seems to have materialized from his poetry (indeed, his first book was entitled *Ostanovka v pustyne*). [According to critic Edward J. Brown,] Brodskij "deals with the persistent unsolved questions of existence: time, origins, space, life and death, along with the psychological puzzles of dislocation, depression, and insanity. While (his poetry) conveys a sense of ultimate bafflement with such problems, the total effect . . . is a kind of happy transcendence achieved by sheer exuberant virtuosity of imagery and language. . . . As (Czesław) Miłosz put it, 'His larger enterprise is to fortify the place of man in a threatening world'." . . .

Such is the core of Brodskij's vision and style, of his epistles from elsewhere, his long-windedness, his linguistic, poetic, and intellectual showmanship (inherited from eighteenth-century Russians and assorted Europeans). It is all an incantation, an ongoing effort to fill, or at least ward off, the surrounding void with words, words, words. (pp. 405-06)

Alexander Zholkovsky, "Writing in the Wilderness: On Brodskij and a Sonnet," in Slavic and East-European Journal, *Vol. 30, No. 3, Fall, 1986, pp. 404-19.*

FERNANDA EBERSTADT

[*Eberstadt, an American novelist and critic, is the author of the novel* Low Tide *(1985). In the following excerpt Eberstadt praises the brilliance and energy of the essays in* Less Than One.]

A Part of Speech, the collection of [Brodsky's] poems issued here in 1980 (almost all of them translated from the Russian), reveals a poet stunningly precise in his imagery, technically playful, and, with exceptions, chilly in temperature. Now his first volume of prose [*Less Than One*]—a collection of essays on poetry, history, geography, politics, and metaphysics—has just been published to considerable acclaim.

For a poet, estrangement from so satisfying and so intricately inflected a mother tongue as Russian might be thought a sorrow more silencing than imprisonment or censorship. Brodsky, however, is a man fortified by an unflagging sense of mission. Unlike the majority of Russian and Eastern European writers living in the West, Brodsky has adopted the English language as his own, and brought to it an independence of thought, a thickness and subtlety of texture, and an omnivorous appetite for idiom that are uniquely his.

Less Than One contains eighteen essays, written over the last ten years of Brodsky's sojourn in America; all but three of them were composed in English. The author's photograph on the back jacket of this volume delivers some clues as to the particular qualities of mind which his readers may expect to find within: the poet, freckled, seasoned, and disdainful, scowls at us with narrowed eyes and gimlet mouth, looking less like one's idea of an aesthete than like a Boer farmer defending his land from the mob. (p. 74)

A reader coming fresh to Brodsky's work will be struck initially by the wide and hard-hitting inventiveness of his diction. Brodsky uses language shore to shore, covering vast amounts of verbal territory in short order. His prose is tough, resourceful, and, though sometimes quite difficult or obstructed in its efforts to express everything as precisely and truthfully as possible, nonetheless glaringly alive. His prose style is notable for its abrupt shifts of gear, from a high elegiac strain, to deflating slang, to technical jargon. The deflating impulse, in particular, yields some felicitous phrases, as (for instance) when Brodsky tersely dismisses as "bald and uptight" the image of the young Lenin that adorns almost every surface of public Soviet space.

Joined with Brodsky's tendency to drive English usage beyond its borders is a sometimes ornery independence of mind. By his own account, Brodsky is a writer who from earliest youth fought with his fists, walked out of classrooms, and disbelieved what he was told. His habit of thinking hard about time, space, and the meaning of history, his insistence on figuring out everything for himself, proved a healthy antidote to the loss of will which Soviet life induces in its subjects. Brodsky is (in consequence?) an immensely opinionated writer—such epithets as "witless," "scum," and "drivel" come frequently to his pen—whose own vision of the world is imprinted on every page of this collection like lines on the palm of a hand. Indeed, **Less Than One** may be most memorable for its heady onslaught of idiosyncratic aphorisms, observations, and verdicts, some of which are merely contrary—such as Brodsky's contention that to "an unprejudiced man," monotheism is synonymous with autocracy and polytheism with democracy—some overly elliptical, some even repellent in their crabbed and arrogant misanthropy, but many of which possess a startling justice that makes one sit up and think twice.

Although the majority of the essays that make up **Less Than One** are high in quality, a few have more feathers than flesh to them. Among the latter, **"On Tyranny"** is a shopworn jeremiad against the banality of evil and the blights of high technology, mass production, and overpopulation. (Brodsky, who hails from a tyrant state which houses barely thirty people per square mile, might be expected to know that evil and degradation in this world do not come from allowing parents to have as many children as their hearts desire.) **"A Commencement Address,"** taking its text from the Sermon on the Mount, enjoins an audience of well-to-do American youngsters to imitate Christ by turning the other cheek when hounded and overwhelmed by an invincible enemy—under the circumstances, an invitation not so much to civil disobedience as to massive self-pity.

At their best, however—which is most of the time—Brodsky's essays combine passion, common sense, and nerve with an intellectual seriousness that has few parallels in present-day criticism. In this category belongs especially the gritty and elegiac title piece about the poet's youth in Leningrad as a Jew, a high-school dropout, a factory worker with a library card, and, later on, a jailbird. In this memoir Brodsky describes with great precision the peculiar character of his postwar generation with its badly made clothing, its love of culture and of intellectual complexity, its rejection of Soviet reality, and its utter isolation. In **"A Flight from Byzantium,"** the East is held to embody the essentially spatial principle that all things are merely intertwining patterns on a carpet, whereas the West represents dynamism, autonomy, and time; the essay, written in the form of a diary, is riveting, both in its intellectual brilliance and, in quite a different way, in the intensity of its loathing for things Oriental, especially Japanese tourists. Arresting, too, is Brodsky's portrayal of his parents in **"In a Room and a Half."** Here he writes of what it is like for Soviet émigrés like himself "not to be allowed to see their mothers or fathers on their deathbed; the silence that follows their request for an emergency visa to attend a relative's funeral." . . . (pp. 74-5)

The temperament which pervades this collection of essays is one of old-fashioned conservatism running to reaction, with all that implies by way of an insistence on man's inherent wickedness, resistance to notions of progress, enmity to Rousseauian utopianism, and, not least, disdain for the modern world. Indeed, although Brodsky today is a free man who writes much about the meaning of freedom as against the many forms of slavery which evil inspires, the freedom he has in mind is personal, inner, freedom. His belief that a poet must defend an ideal of "civilization" against modern "social reality" has seemingly dissuaded him from endorsing the political freedoms he now enjoys. In his own ostentatiously neutral phrase, Brodsky in coming to the West has merely "switched Empires" (as he writes in the poem, **"Lullaby of Cape Cod"**), and is as committed to criticizing the irresoluteness and materialism of the democracies as he is to berating Soviet totalitarianism for its dullness and brutality.

If this is one respect in which Brodsky may be seen to part company with many conservatives, another would surely have to do with the central conviction which animates all his work, and to which he adheres as to a religious truth: namely, that language is a supreme and lawmaking deity, and that poets are that deity's anointed priesthood. Why? As he explains in **"To Please a Shadow,"** his tribute to Auden, whereas all other things in the world are subject to the depredations of time, poetry, the verbal articulation of perception, represents a restructuring of time—i.e., of nature—itself. From this stipulation of the preeminence of language over the natural world follows Brodsky's belief that poetry, not religion, is the unique source both of metaphysical truth and of moral value: "It is this law," he writes, "that teaches a poet a greater rectitude than any creed is capable of." Or, as he put it in a response to Milan Kundera published in the New York *Times Book Review*, "an individual's . . . aesthetics give rise to his ethics and his sense of history—not the other way around."

Making a religion of art is, of course, not an impulse peculiar to this poet—although Brodsky may indeed be alone in restricting the realm of art to poetry. But neither, unfortunately, does Brodsky escape the intellectual and spiritual consequences of his position, most conspicuous among such consequences being the arid and cockeyed solipsism that comes of exalting man's creation above God's. The worship of art over all things leads him, moreover, to enter claims on its behalf which neither art nor artists can fulfill. For an example we need go no farther than Brodsky's astonishing contention that W. H. Auden was "the greatest mind of the 20th century," and that "reading him is one of the very few ways (if not the only one) available for feeling decent." Finally, one cannot help noticing that although Brodsky treats admirably with the forms that poets use, he skimps on what it is that poets actually say in their poems (dismissing almost parenthetically, for instance, Auden's Freudian, Marxist, and religious "terminology"). Yet if "A rhyme turns an idea into law," as Brodsky maintains it does, is not a law-abiding reader obliged to pay serious attention to the ideas that poets legislate, some of which have been very awful ideas indeed?

Nonetheless, so subtle and so invigorating are Brodsky's love and understanding of poetry and its makers, so searching and adroit his readings, that **Less Than One** might *almost* serve to vindicate its author's energetic canonization of his own profession. (pp. 75-6)

Fernanda Eberstadt, "For Art's Sake," in Commentary, *Vol. 82, No. 5, November, 1986, pp. 74-6.*

JEFFREY WAINWRIGHT

[*Wainwright is an English poet and critic. The poems in his collections* The Important Man *(1970),* Heart's Desire *(1978),* and his Selected Poems (1985), often deal with political and historical subjects. In the following excerpt Wainwright examines the political and philosophical views expressed by Brodsky in Less Than One.]

Towards the end of **'In a Room and a Half'**, the final essay in *Less Than One*, Joseph Brodsky describes the weekly phone calls which were the only contact with his parents he was able to have since his exile from the Soviet Union in 1972.

> We couldn't say much during those exchanges, we had to be either reticent or oblique and euphemistic. It was mostly about the weather or health, no names, a great deal of dietetic advice. The main thing was hearing each other's voice, assuring ourselves in this animal way of our respective existences. It was mostly non-semantic, and small wonder that I remember no particulars except Father's reply on the third day of my mother's being in the hospital. "How is Masya?" I asked, "Well, Masya is no more, you know," he said. The "you know" was there because on this occasion, too, he tried to be euphemistic.

Euphemism, as here, can possess great tenderness and delicacy through its obliqueness. It is its own kind of exposure. But these essays all work to dissolve euphemism for modes more exactly descriptive of what he intends to say. Brodsky is as forthright and unqualified about the importance of the writers, mainly poets, whom he chooses to write about, as about the significance of poetry itself, as about the exercise of Soviet state power. He writes this memorial essay for his parents in English, deliberately, 'because I want to grant them a margin of freedom', since it was in Russian, in their own language, that, 'shuffling through numerous state chancelleries and ministries', they were refused a visa to visit their son before they died; 'the state considers such a visit "unpurposeful",' Brodsky makes this very clear. However, as the passage about the phone calls implies, the forthright is not the only utterance of value. The physical voice, its non-semantic being, is the real communication here. This, I think, is part of a second principal preoccupation in these essays, which is to pursue the sense that what is essential to poetry has little to do with what is superficially clear, and everything to do with the body of its sound. It is the aesthetic sense, of which this is part, that for Brodsky takes the leading role. Recalling, again in **'A Room and a Half'**, his childhood visits to the Russian Naval Museum where his father once worked, he writes:

> A child is always first of all an aesthete: he responds to appearances, to surfaces, to shapes and forms. There is hardly anything that I've liked in my life more than those clean-shaven admirals, *en face* and in profile, in their gilded frames looming through a forest of masts on ship models that aspired to be life-size.

The development of this aesthetic intuition is what Brodsky follows in his reading and view of poetry as revealed in the twelve essays on Russian and other literature in this collection. A third major obsession in the book—evident in these quotations—is with memory. Two major meditative memoirs stand at either end of the volume: **'A Room and a Half'**, and at the beginning, **'Less Than One'**. That essay opens: 'As failures go, attempting to recall the past is like trying to grasp the meaning of existence. Both make one feel like a baby clutching at a basketball: one's palms keep sliding off.' In the midst of his own and others' unavoidably and urgently political lives (to put it euphemistically), Brodsky, by his recall of the past, and by his striving to define what makes poetry, is, in fact, 'trying to grasp the meaning of existence.' His image of the

baby and the basketball smiles at the possible pretentiousness of the opening sentence, but this belies Brodsky's customary style. This *is* what he is about. No euphemism will really do. His procedure is not analytic, except that in the literary essays he concentrates on his subject with a fierce closeness. Rather he moves to his concerns in accordance with the fluctuations of his mind as, he says, the 'tail' of memory 'coils, recoils, digresses to all sides'.

The 'tail' is straightest when in the toils of politics. Brodsky sees the mark of the Stalinist terror which wrought such havoc on the generation that included his mentors the Mandelstams, Akhmatova, Tsvetaeva, as upon the Soviet state yet. His alienation from it is unequivocal and total. He is not however in these essays a political commentator or philosopher. The reader would have to work hard to tease out a critique which could form an alternative politics, and there is nothing here on the politics of the society to which Brodsky has come, or of those within it as alienated as he himself was at home. But this is because he expects nothing of politics, perhaps little of human beings' efforts at social organisation at all. The cast of his thought is fundamentally existentialist, more particularly Kierkegaardian. On the first page of this book he claims to have refuted in his own mind, at ten or eleven years of age, Marx's dictum that being determines consciousness when he saw that this was true 'only for so long as it takes consciousness to acquire the art of estrangement'. Estrangement has thenceforth been his condition: more interested in the individual human being than in theories about him; with the meaning or purpose of human lives rather than with scientific or metaphysical truths about the universe; and with the *freedom* of individuals. This summary of existentialist attitudes (derived from Leslie Stevenson's *Seven Theories of Human Nature*) seems appropriate to indicate those which emerge through Brodsky's essays. History has no bosom to offer, and about its own travails he is gently understanding: 'History is bound to repeat itself: after all, like men, history doesn't have many choices.' The free consciousness of individuals is however constrained by the existence of Evil, and Brodsky is scornful of the Russian intellectual and literary tradition of consolation and life-affirmation. Solzhenitsyn he chides for 'resistance to the notion of man being radically bad.' By contrast,

> Tsvetaeva's voice had the sound of something unfamiliar and frightening to the Russian ear: the unacceptability of the world.
>
> It was not the reaction of a revolutionary or a progressive demanding changes for the better or the snobbery of an aristocrat who remembers better days. On the level of content, it was the tragedy of existence in general, par excellence, outside the temporal context.

The stare from these sentences is discomfiting. In his adopted political hemisphere, Brodsky's characterization of the Soviet Union will find many who claim recognition. And 'individualism' is a good thing—to the baby with the basketball: 'Go for it!'. But, 'the unacceptability of the world', 'the tragedy of existence in general'? Does he mean us? Did the graduates of Williams College really take to heart his Commencement address which began by telling them that they would 'come into direct physical contact with what is known as Evil', and some of them as 'potential villains'? 'Villains', 'what is known as', a little euphemism, but does he really have to put it like this? As one long habituated to 'demanding changes for the better', I certainly step back from his vision disconcerted. But the cumulative effect of these essays is to demonstrate its authenticity for Brodsky. There is nothing merely acidulous about it. An autodidact through school, factory, military service, and prison camp, it is evidently the product of fierce meditation. But if the history and experience which possesses Brodsky, and for which he brims with disgust, scorn, and anger, is but 'the tragedy of existence in general', then why the disgust, why the anger? Is not this only what is to be expected? Sonorities about the 'human predicament' usually disguise comfort and complacency, and rage is inelegant. But Brodsky continues to rage. For him the history of twentieth-century Russia constitutes an

> anthropological tragedy, a genetic backslide whose net result is a drastic reduction of human potential. To quibble about it, to use political-science mumbo-jumbo here is misleading and unnecessary. Tragedy is history's chosen genre. Had it not been for literature's own resilience, we wouldn't have known any other.

'Political-science mumbo-jumbo' can indeed be nothing better than euphemism, and something like Brodsky's sense of 'the tragedy of existence' will work against those deceptions. The possibility that that sense is right commands respect, but so too does the quibble that there is possibly something called 'human potential', or even some point to 'demanding changes for the better'. 'The affirming flame' (Brodsky has a long piece on Auden's 'September 1st, 1939') does not quite gutter yet.

As that last long quotation indicates, for Brodsky resistance to the tragedy of history forms more around literature than politics. Not that literature relates directly to life, for it is not topical, not a news-report. The work of an authentic writer like Dostoevsky is not mimetic:

> He simply felt that art is not about life, if only because life is not about life. For Dostoevsky, art like life, is about what man exists for. Like Biblical parallels, his novels are vehicles to obtain the answer and not goals unto themselves.

Brodsky's ideas about literature are developed in essays mainly devoted to particular writers whose works draw him, and in some cases, he confesses, to whom he was drawn by their images—obedience to that childhood aesthetic sense, and respect for his father's profession of newspaper photographer. He writes with great textual concentration about the Russians already mentioned, and also about Cavafy, Montale, Walcott, and Auden. His pieces on Cavafy and Montale are especially illuminating, and show how he identifies his very detailed concerns with the techniques of metre, rhyme, and diction, with ethics. The aesthetic and the ethical are linked for him in that, as for Flaubert, strong enough concentration upon the aesthetic intuition and detail leads ethical content. (See Flaubert's 1875 correspondence with George Sand. When she accuses, 'You no longer look for anything but the well-turned sentence,' he replies, 'When I come upon a bad assonance or a repetition in one of my sentences, I'm sure I'm floundering in the False.') Brodsky admires Cavafy's 'poor' language stripped of all 'poetic paraphernalia—rich imagery, similes, metrical flamboyance', and similarly Montale's reaction against both the 'inflated harmony' of D'Annunzio and its exaggerated opposite in Marinetti and the Futurists. Here he is discussing Montale's use of rhyme.

> Apart from its function as a kind of linguistic echo, a sort of homage to the language, a rhyme lends a sense of inevitability to the poet's statement. Advantageous as it is, the repetitive nature of a rhyme scheme (or for that matter, of any scheme) creates

the danger of overstatement, not to mention the distancing of the past from the reader. To prevent this, Montale often shifts from rhymed to unrhymed verse within the same poem. His objection to stylistic excess is clearly an ethical as well as an aesthetic one—proving that a poem is a form of the closest possible interplay between ethics and aesthetics.

Euphemism may in some circumstances at least possess tact and sensitivity. Overstatement may have boldness, or at least bravura. As with all poetry, the task is to find the true line between. But finding that line is not an analytic, linear process. 'Poetic thinking always has a synthesising quality', what Montale calls 'a kind of bat-radar technique'. Brodsky finds the same characteristic in Mandelstam, and, in the essay **'The Child of Civilisation',** he writes of poetry as 'an art of references, allusions, linguistic and figurative parallels.' 'What dictates a poem is the language, and this is the voice of the language which we know under the nicknames of Muse or Inspiration.' So strongly concerned with the qualities and rights of the individual in so much of his thought, Brodsky's poetics are positively not individualistic. The 'classically "great line"', he writes in the Montale essay, 'flatters the audience and by and large is self-serving'. Individualistic flamboyance is part of a worldliness that poetry eschews. He is discussing an elegy of Montale's here which recognizes other kinds of reality, that 'psychological acquisitions become more real than real estate', and so we can understand that Montale is 'speaking into silence' when he addresses his dead wife:

> With my arm in yours I have descended at least a million
>   stairs,
> and now that you aren't here, a void opens at each step.
> Even so our long journey has been brief.

Art does not, Brodsky asserts, imitate life.

> If art does anything of this kind, it undertakes to reflect those few elements of existence which transcend "life", extend it beyond its terminal point—an undertaking which is frequently mistaken for art's or the artist's own groping for immortality. In others words, art "imitates" death rather than life; i.e., it imitates that realm of which life supplies no notion: realizing its own brevity, art tries to domesticate the longest possible version of time. After all, what distinguishes art from life is the ability of the former to produce a higher degree of lyricism than is possible within any human interplay. Hence poetry's affinity with—if not the very invention of—the notion of afterlife.

As with Tsvetaeva faced with 'the unacceptability of the world', 'on the plane of sound, it was a matter of the voice striving in the only direction possible for it: upwards.' I cannot enter in any full or literal way into Brodsky's (Kierkegaardian) metaphysics here, and yet I think it is still possible to comprehend his meaning. Art does not return the world simply to us; it does not console or uplift, make life bearable; it does not by strokes deflect the triumphs of history. So when the chariotwheels of that triumph bear down, what does verse do, what is it for? Of Anna Akhmatova, writing her poems in such dire extremes, Brodsky writes:

> She simply tried to manage the meaninglessness of existence, which suddenly gaped before her because of the destruction of the sources of its meaning, to domesticate the reprehensible infinity by inhabiting it with familiar shadows. Besides, addressing the dead was the only way of preventing speech from slipping into a howl.

The poem becomes something with which to try to manage, something with which to make a meaning even if that sound is to be uttered into a void.

For someone whose ultimate meanings and allegiances are not confined to the here-and-now, Brodsky's physical world, in the three meditative memoirs in this book, has an extraordinary palpability. His **'Guide to a Renamed City'** is luminous, and the portraits of his parents in **'A Room and a Half'** have great presence. Memory, in these essays, is such a presence, and loss—'elements of existence' extended 'beyond its terminal point'. The remembrances are efforts, perhaps failures, of meaning. That some moments from his childhood come into his mind with 'mesmerizing clarity' convinces him of the importance of memory, 'what moments *are*': existence, one atom of what constitutes an entire, perishable life, and as such, as vast and as complex as the interior of Pascal's mite. But we are not so faithful to memory. As children we rush always towards the future, craving adulthood, so that memory is laid waste behind us, until, so far from being that individual whose consciousness is free of existence, we realize that we have become an effect whose cause is detached and lost. Yet perhaps this is as it should be, 'presumably the whole point is that there should be no continuum: of anything.' That is one of the laws of nature. Autonomous, not linked, 'outbound for the future', the failures of memory are fortuitous and pragmatic, a prudent economy of brain cells. Working ironically here, drawing his reader through such reasonable propositions, Brodsky exposes these 'natural laws' as a euphemism for callous forgetfulness, and as something that serves the interest of the state. The state, any state, in the course of controlling the present, will seek to control the past. But of his parents:

> They loved me more than themselves, and most likely wouldn't understand my guilt feelings toward them at all. The main issues were bread on the table, clean clothes, and staying healthy. Those were their synonyms for love, and they were better than mine.

His father's naval cap, his mother 'in her yellow-pink, crêpe de chine dress', bread on the table, clean clothes, dietetic advice, a phone number, Nadezdha Mandelstam memorizing Osip's poems, these are the 'mere details, fragments' that constitute resistance against what is called 'real life'. They do not make up a whole picture of a continuum to be followed. Each moment is itself, not mere brushwork for the future, as each person is an end and not a means. (pp. 36-8)

Jeffrey Wainwright, ''The Art of Estrangement','' in PN Review, *Vol. 14, No. 2, 1987, pp. 36-8.*

RICHARD KOSTELANETZ

[*Kostelanetz, an American poet, novelist, artist, short story and novella writer, critic, and editor, uses innovative techniques, such as multi-media collages, in his experimental fiction and poetry. These works include* Visual Language *(1970),* Come Here *(1975),* Illuminations *(1977), and* Epiphanies *(1983). Among his nonfiction writings are* The Theatre of Mixed-Means: An Introduction to Happenings, Kinetic Environments, and Other Mixed-Means Performances *(1968),* Autobiographies *(1981), and* Conversing with Cage *(1987). In the following excerpt Kostelanetz offers his opinion that Brodsky, while a fine poet, has been overrated by critics.*]

Two decades ago, the general managers of professional football teams discovered that the highly specialized job of place-kicking could be done by sometime soccer players, most of them born and raised abroad. . . . It was Alex Karras, then a star tackle, now a television star, who charged that with such place-kickers a great American game has disintegrated to the level that guys who never did anything else with a football, guys who can hardly speak English, now scream, ''I vin it, I keek it.''

This bit of ancient history comes to mind with Joseph Brodsky's new book of essays [*Less Than One*]. Within the fifteen years he has been in this country, Brodsky has become the most successful poet of his generation (which is also mine). . . . Brodsky is a good poet, accomplished in undistinguished ways, somewhat obvious and bombastic. He is by no account better than a hundred others his age—a generation that, at least in America, has an abundance of good poets, though none commonly recognized as great; but since a lot more worldly success has come his way, some examination is in order.

The truth is that Brodsky is admired by people who understand biography better than poetry, and the former is easier to merchandise, especially in America. The immigrant, especially from an Iron Curtain country, has an instant autobiography unavailable to the native born; and it would seem that the major purpose of this new book is to contribute to the myth of the young Russian who learned literary English, translated some of it, [and] was imprisoned for independent literary activities until he was kicked out of Russia. . . .

If Brodsky has actually written any classic poems, I cannot find them in the English translations I have read. (Much reportedly remains untranslated.) I notice that his admirers here are no more sure. While reviewers quote passages from individual poems as illustrative of something or other, they are reluctant to identify any one of them as great. Brodsky's poems do not appear in anthologies of American poetry, not even Helen Vendler's *Harvard Book of Contemporary American Poetry*, which strives to be a compendium of received opinion. I know of only one American poet colleague who reads Brodsky's work with pleasure, and have thus concluded that it ultimately is no more written for poets than for the common reader. Émigré literati I know tell me that Brodsky's reputation here is based upon tokenism, our publicity machinery rewarding one and only one member of every identifiable minority (black, midwestern, etc.); if Solzhenitzyn is America's sole famous émigré novelist, so Brodsky is our token Russian poet.

The occasional essays collected in this new book are not substantial. They range from perfunctory back-slapping appreciations of older poets (Derek Walcott, Eugenio Montale) to extended analyses of two poems (one in Russian by Tsvetaeva, the other by W. H. Auden). There is one memoir of his native city, Leningrad, and another of an awful trip to Constantinople. There are brushes at political commentary, but nothing as classic as the political prose of another émigré poet—Czeslaw Milosz's *The Captive Mind*. If Brodsky has read any American poets younger than Robert Lowell, he does not say. In the end, *Less Than One* has no cohesive subject, other than Brodsky's celebrity. (p. 29)

The principal distinguishing mark of Brodsky's prose is a grandiosity that comes largely from exaggeration and from taking poetry, and language, too seriously. It is the kind of so-called ''grand manner'' I associate first with poets of an older generation, especially in Europe, and then with the illusion that from a grand style necessarily follow great ideas. Consider the book's opening paragraph:

As failures go, attempting to recall the past is like trying to grasp the meaning of existence. Both make one feel like a baby clutching at a basketball: one's palms keep sliding off.

This last metaphor is a confection inconceivable to me, who have never seen (and cannot imagine) infants ever having the opportunity to clutch an inflated basketball. In English, such inflated phrasing is indicative of the limited specialist, of those who can say ''I keek it; I vin it.'' And within the world of American poetry, Brodsky has never been more than a place-kicker, a sideshow import whose praise-winning boots appeal to those inclined to appreciate flashiness more than substance. (pp. 29-30)

> *Richard Kostelanetz, in a review of ''Less than One: Selected Essays,'' in* Boston Review, *Vol. XII, No. 4, August, 1987, pp. 29-30.*

SEAMUS HEANEY

[*Heaney is an Irish poet, critic, editor, and educator. His poetry, written in a lush, concentrated style, is informed by the language and culture of his native rural Northern Ireland. Among his collections are* Eleven Poems *(1965),* Death of a Naturalist *(1966),* Wintering Out *(1972),* Selected Poems *(1980),* Station Island *(1984), and* The Haw Lantern *(1987). In the following excerpt Heaney, who first met Brodsky in 1972, offers an appreciative description of his literary aesthetics.*]

There was applause in Stockholm when Joseph Brodsky was named the winner of [the 1987] Nobel Prize in Literature. There probably always is at these occasions, since applause is what they are all about, but this particular outbreak of handclaps was reported to have been more animated and partisan than usual. Not partisan in any political, East-West, superpower sense, but in the singularly personal, converted, *parti pris* manner some poets inspire—for with poets the reader is constantly invited to cross a line that usually allows for some distinction between being a reader and being a supporter.

A dissident? He would resent the vulgarity of the word, the way it erodes individual destiny and emulsifies unique choices and distresses into a unit of complacent diction. ''The only things which poetry and politics have in common are the letters *P* and *O*.'' Joseph declared when we did an interview in Dublin a couple of years ago. (p. 1)

If anyone ever deserved to be called by James Joyce's steely and honorific kenning, it is Joseph Brodsky: he is absolutely the penman. Yet, if we are to read the full implications of his stunning **"Commencement Address"** in the prose collection *Less Than One,* we see that his esthetic finally inheres in the wielding of an ax: devoted as he is to the artfulness of art, he is the last man you would expect to find parading a lily. Nevertheless there is something Wildean in the typical Brodsky flourish, a cultivation of the unforeseen in order to disclose the undeniable, an embrace of positions that would have life live up to the demands of art and not vice versa. He has defined the usual reason why a writer writes as being ''to give or to get a boost from the language,'' reminding us thereby that the corollary is also true: the reader reads for a similar boost. What distinguishes one writer from another resides in the exact nature of the boosts they afford, but it seems to me that the Anglo-Irish playwright and the Russian-Jewish poet share some fundamentally writerly characteristics—in their combination of stylistic panache and intellectual pugnaciousness, their allergy to boredom, their subversion of cliché and their creation of a

''plane of regard,'' as Mr. Brodsky calls it, by the attainment of a certain pitch of expression.

Oddly enough, some crucial details of their biographies also correspond. Both courted the role of outcast to the point where they were imprisoned, and both were therefore driven into subsequent exile. It would drastically misrepresent the nature of Mr. Brodsky's residence in the United States, however, to suggest that since his expulsion from the Soviet Union in 1972 it has involved anything as demeaned and posthumous as that suffered by Oscar Wilde in Paris.

Indeed, he has been treated here more as prophet than pariah, although he has contrived to keep himself personally well in the background. He runs for conversational cover the minute anyone brings up his tribulations as a veteran of the forced labor camps, and in general he scrupulously resists the glamour of his refusenik past. Always fighting-fit in print, he has been careful to distinguish between the *less-than-one-ness* of his generic human ordinariness and the arrogance of the persona his ''one'' attains in a sentence. One overbears somewhat, after all, by the mere employment of the pronoun ''one'' in any locution. ''One'' is born out of writing rather than out of the given biological or domestic conditions. ''One'' refuses the historical circumstance in order to flaunt the possibility of freedom and singularity. Mr. Brodsky's original way of reasserting this old Romantic faith is to insist on the otherness of poetic invention and to indulge in its sublime effrontery by affirming that poets' biographies are almost identical—''their real data are in the way they sound,'' their vowels and sibilants, meters, rhymes and metaphors. . . .

Poetry constitutes a rule, a habit, a *disciplina* for every practitioner, but there are degrees of intensity in the observance of the rule. Of Joseph Brodsky, however, it could be said—as Osip Mandelstam said of his old schoolmaster, the Symbolist V. V. Grippius—that he has established personal relations not only with Russian poetry but with the whole pantheon of the classical and vernacular literatures of Europe and the Americas, ''splenetic and loving liaisons filled with noble enviousness, jocular disrespect, grievous unfairness—as is common between members of one family.'' Naturally, this intimate, face-to-face relationship with the masters keeps ''the plane of regard'' very high. It is not just that Joseph received the laying on of hands from Anna Akhmatova, Nadezhda Mandelstam and W. H. Auden, and was thereby placed in filial succession within two great poetic traditions. He is also a writer who, by the memorization of what he loves in the literature of the past, has incorporated the demands of that literature into his mentality. The stylistic consequences of great poetry are to be felt in the pitch, strenuousness and concentrated vigilance with which he reads not just books, but the world. (p. 63)

I have been paraphrasing to some extent things this poet has written about Nadezhda Mandelstam, for it is in those jubilant, exacting essays praising his heroines and heroes that we find an idiom applicable to himself. Obviously, he was braced by his encounters with survivors of the great Russian generation, and it is the happy fate of those who are plunged into Joseph's own hawk-keen, gossipy conversations about poetry to experience a similar refreshment. The action is swift and genially merciless, like a game of Space Invaders played with reputations. But it can also be rhapsodic, as he goes into a kind of mesmeric vocal overdrive and sets quatrains by Hardy or Auden or Akhmatova sailing upon air and ear. I assume that his students learn thereby how unmechanical an exercise rote-learning can ultimately be; certainly his poet friends learn again to love those possessions of the language they might otherwise take too much for granted, and are vividly reminded that they stand in the space of reality marked "poetry," where the dimensions of the art, its survival and continuing worthiness, have passed into their keeping.

But to proceed only in these high terms is to give too solemn an otherworldly impression of the man and the poet, for Joseph Brodsky thoroughly exemplifies the meaning of the term "this world-ness," which the Russian Acmeists coined to rebuke the cloudy aspirations of the Symbolists. His metaphors may wish to travel farther faster and his aphorisms, in their compulsion to delight and astound, do keep jumping ahead of themselves, but the display element in the writing is always governed by a helplessly laconic feel for things as they are. Many of those things are to be cherished because they will be robbed from us by death; others are evil and should be unrelentingly assailed. Poetry is on the whole the fitter instrument for the celebration, prose for the assault, although the very idea of such demarcation is nonsense when one is dealing with a sensibility as igneous and impetuous as Mr. Brodsky's. Who else would have hit upon the notion that prose is usually threatened by its own "esthetic inertia"? And who else could have combined generalizing power with autobiographical heartbreak as irresistibly as he does in the prose threnody for his parents called **"In a Room and a Half."**

This was written in English. The spirits of those two loved ones were confined in life not only by their living quarters: "If there is an infinite aspect to space, it is not its expansion but its reduction." They were also confined by a Russian language that was itself incarcerated in bureaucratese. But now, commemorated in English by their son, they are released into a new linguistic afterlife and are themselves translated. The process in this case is complete; the language passes through us, and us through it, as if it were air, knowledge, palpable intuition.

But in the case of Mr. Brodsky's poetry, which is written in Russian and which revealed him to great Russian readers as their great contemporary poet, the process of translation is more problematic and resistant. Here the event—the Russian poem—has to be reinvented or else it becomes, to reapply a phrase of Robert Lowell's, the record of an event. In the past the reinvention has been achieved with recognizable success by English-speaking poets who worked—for once the verb is the proper one—in collaboration with the author, although in a note to his *A Part of Speech* (1980) he tells us that he sometimes took the liberty of reworking those workings "at the expense of their smoothness."

In other words, like other strong poets, Mr. Brodsky sets the reader's comfort below the poem's necessities, and in order further to impose upon English the strangeness and density of his imagining, he is now the official translator of his own lines. So, in spite of his manifest love for English verse, which amounts almost to a possessiveness, the dynamo of Russian supplies the energy, the metrics of the original will not be gainsaid and the English ear comes up against a phonetic element that is both animated and skewed. Sometimes it instinctively rebels at having its expectations denied in terms of both syntax and the velleities of stress. Or it panics and wonders if it is being taken for a ride when it had expected a rhythm. At other times, however, it yields with that unbounded assent that only the most triumphant art can conjure and allow:

Freedom
Is when you forget the spelling of the tyrant's name
And your mouth's saliva is sweeter than Persian pie,

And though your brain is wrung tight as the horn of a ram
Nothing drops from your pale-blue eye.

This is what the applause in Stockholm was all about. (pp. 63, 65)

Seamus Heaney, "Brodsky's Nobel: What the Applause Was About," in The New York Times Book Review, *November 8, 1987, pp. 1, 63, 65.*

JOSEPH BRODSKY

[*The following excerpt is Brodsky's Nobel lecture, translated by Barry Rubin.*]

For someone rather private, for someone who all his life has preferred his private condition to any role of social significance, and who went in this preference rather far—far from his motherland to say the least, for it is better to be a total failure in a democracy than a martyr, or the crème de la crème, in a tyranny—for such a person to find himself all of a sudden on this rostrum is a somewhat uncomfortable and trying experience.

This sensation is aggravated not so much by the thought of those who stood here before me as by the memory of those who have been bypassed by this honor, who were not given this chance to address *urbi et orbi,* as they say, from this rostrum, and whose cumulative silence is sort of searching, to no avail, for release through this speaker here.

The only thing that can reconcile one to this sort of situation is the simple realization that—for stylistic reasons, in the first place—one writer cannot speak for another writer, one poet for another poet especially; that had Osip Mandelstam, or Marina Tsvetaeva, or Robert Frost, or Anna Akhmatova, or Wystan Auden stood here, they couldn't have helped but speak precisely for themselves; and they, too, might have felt somewhat uncomfortable.

These shades disturb me constantly; they are disturbing me today as well. In any case, they do not spur one to eloquence. In my better moments, I deem myself their sum total, though invariably inferior to any one of them individually. For it is not possible to better them on the page; nor is it possible to better them in actual life. And it is precisely their lives, no matter how tragic or bitter they were, that often move me—more often, perhaps, than the case should be—to regret the passage of time. If the next life exists—and I can no more deny them the possibility of eternal life than I can forget their existence in this one—if the next world does exist, they will, I hope, forgive me, and the quality of what I am about to utter: after all, it is not one's conduct on a podium which dignity in our profession is measured by.

I have mentioned only five of them, those whose deeds and whose lot matter so much to me, if only because if it were not for them, I, both as a man and writer, would amount to much less; in any case I wouldn't be standing here today. There were more of them, those shades—better still, sources of light: lamps? stars?—more, of course, than just five. And each one of them is capable of rendering me absolutely mute. The number of those is substantial in the life of any conscious man of letters; in my case, it doubles, thanks to the two cultures to which fate has willed me to belong. Matters are not made easier by thoughts about contemporaries and fellow writers in both these cultures, poets and fiction writers whose gifts I rank above my own, and who, had they found themselves on this rostrum, would have come to the point long ago, for surely they have more to tell the world than I do.

I will allow myself, therefore, to make a number of remarks here—disjointed, perhaps, stumbling, perhaps even perplexing in their randomness. However, the amount of time allotted to me to collect my thoughts, as well as my very occupation, will, or may, I hope, shield me, at least partially, against charges of being chaotic. A man of my occupation seldom claims a systematic mode of thinking; at worst, he claims to have a system—but even that, in his case, is a borrowing from a milieu, from a social order, or from the pursuit of philosophy at a tender age. Nothing convinces an artist more of the arbitrariness of the means to which he resorts to attain a goal—however permanent it may be—than the creative process itself, the process of composition. Verse really does, in Akhmatova's words, grow from rubbish; the roots of prose are no more honorable.

If art teaches anything (to the artist, in the first place), it is the privateness of the human condition. Being the most ancient as well as the most literal form of private enterprise, it fosters in a man, knowingly or unwittingly, a sense of his uniqueness, of individuality, of separateness—thus turning him from a social animal into an autonomous "I." Lots of things can be shared: a bed, a piece of bread, convictions, a mistress, but not a poem by, say, Rainer Maria Rilke. A work of art, of literature especially, and a poem in particular, addresses a man tête-à-tête, entering with him into direct—free of any go-betweens—relations.

It is for this reason that art in general, literature especially, and poetry in particular, is not exactly favored by champions of the common good, masters of the masses, heralds of historical necessity. For there, where art has stepped, where a poem has been read, they discover, in place of the anticipated consent and unanimity, indifference and polyphony; in place of the resolve to act, inattention and fastidiousness. In other words, into the little zeros with which the champions of the common good and the rulers of the masses tend to operate, art introduces a "period, period, comma, and a minus," transforming each zero into a tiny human, albeit not always a pretty, face.

The great Baratynsky, speaking of his Muse, characterized her as possessing an "uncommon visage." It's in acquiring this "uncommon visage" that the meaning of human existence seems to lie, since for this uncommonness we are, as it were, prepared genetically. Regardless of whether one is a writer or a reader, one's task consists first of all in mastering a life that is one's own, not imposed or prescribed from without, no matter how noble its appearance may be. For each of us is issued but one life, and we know full well how it all ends. It would be regrettable to squander this one chance on someone else's appearance, someone else's experience, on a tautology—regrettable all the more because the heralds of historical necessity, at whose urging a man may be prepared to agree to this tautology, will not go to the grave with him, or give him so much as a thank-you.

Language and, presumably, literature are things that are more ancient and inevitable, more durable than any form of social organization. The revulsion, irony, or indifference often expressed by literature toward the state is essentially the reaction of the permanent—better yet, the infinite—against the temporary, against the finite. To say the least, as long as the state permits itself to interfere with the affairs of literature, literature has the right to interfere with the affairs of the state. A political system, a form of social organization, like any system in general, is by definition a form of the past tense that aspires to impose itself upon the present (and often on the future as well); and a man whose profession is language is the last one who can afford to forget this. The real danger for a writer is not so much the possibility (and often the certainty) of persecution on the part of the state, as it is the possibility of finding oneself mesmerized by the state's features, which, whether monstrous or undergoing changes for the better, are always temporary.

The philosophy of the state, its ethics—not to mention its aesthetics—are always "yesterday." Language and literature are always "today," and often—particularly in the case where a political system is orthodox—they may even constitute "tomorrow." One of literature's merits is precisely that it helps a person to make the time of his existence more specific, to distinguish himself from the crowd of his predecessors as well as his like numbers, to avoid tautology—that is, the fate otherwise known by the honorific term "victim of history." What makes art in general, and literature in particular, remarkable, what distinguishes them from life, is precisely that they abhor repetition. In everyday life you can tell the same joke thrice and, thrice getting a laugh, become the life of the party. In art this sort of conduct is called "cliché."

Art is a recoilless weapon, and its development is determined not by the individuality of the artist, but by the dynamics and the logic of the material itself, by the previous fate of the means that each time demand (or suggest) a qualitatively new aesthetic solution. Possessing its own genealogy, dynamics, logic, and future, art is not synonymous with, but at best parallel to, history; and the manner by which it exists is by continually creating a new aesthetic reality. That is why it is often found "ahead of progress," ahead of history, whose main instrument is—should we not, once more, improve upon Marx—precisely the cliché.

Nowadays there exists a rather widely held view, postulating that in his work a writer, in particular a poet, should make use of the language of the street, the language of the crowd. For all its democratic appearance, and its palpable advantages for a writer, this assertion is quite absurd, and represents an attempt to subordinate art, in this case literature, to history. It is only if we have resolved that it is time for Homo sapiens to come to a halt in his development that literature should speak the language of the people. Otherwise it is the people who should speak the language of literature.

On the whole, every new aesthetic reality makes man's ethical reality more precise. For aesthetics is the mother of ethics. The categories of "good" and "bad" are, first and foremost, aesthetic ones, at least etymologically preceding the categories of "good" and "evil." If in ethics not "all is permitted," it is precisely because not "all is permitted" in aesthetics, because the number of colors in the spectrum is limited. The tender babe who cries and rejects the stranger who, on the contrary, reaches out to him, does so instinctively, makes an aesthetic choice, not a moral one.

Aesthetic choice is a highly individual matter, and aesthetic experience is always a private one. Every new aesthetic reality makes one's experience even more private; and this kind of privacy, assuming at times the guise of literary (or some other) taste, can in itself turn out to be, if not a guarantee, then a form of defense, against enslavement. For a man with taste, particularly with literary taste, is less susceptible to the refrains and the rhythmical incantations peculiar to any version of political demagogy. The point is not so much that virtue does not constitute a guarantee for producing a masterpiece, as that evil, especially political evil, is always a bad stylist. The more substantial an individual's aesthetic experience is, the sounder his taste, the sharper his moral focus, the freer—though not necessarily the happier—he is.

It is precisely in this applied, rather than Platonic, sense that we should understand Dostoyevsky's remark that beauty will save the world, or Matthew Arnold's belief that we shall be saved by poetry. It is probably too late for the world, but for the individual man there always remains a chance. An aesthetic instinct develops in man rather rapidly, for even without fully realizing who he is and what he actually requires, a person instinctively knows what he doesn't like and what doesn't suit him. In an anthropological respect, let me reiterate, a human being is an aesthetic creature before he is an ethical one. Therefore, it is not that art, particularly literature, is a byproduct of our species' development, but just the reverse. If what distinguishes us from other members of the animal kingdom is speech, then literature—and poetry in particular, being the highest form of locution—is, to put it bluntly, the goal of our species.

I am far from suggesting the idea of compulsory training in verse composition; nevertheless the subdivision of society into intelligentsia and "all the rest" seems to me unacceptable. In moral terms, this situation is comparable to the subdivision of society into the poor and the rich; but if it is still possible to find some purely physical or material grounds for the existence of social inequality, for intellectual inequality these are inconceivable. Equality in this respect, unlike in anything else, has been guaranteed to us by nature. I am speaking not of education, but of the education in speech, the slightest imprecision in which may trigger the intrusion of false choice into one's life. The existence of literature prefigures existence on literature's plane of regard—and not only in the moral sense, but lexically as well. If a piece of music still allows a person the possibility of choosing between the passive role of listener and the active one of performer, a work of literature—of the art which is, to use Montale's phrase, hopelessly semantic—dooms him to the role of performer only.

In this role, it would seem to me, a person should appear more often than in any other. Moreover, it seems to me that, as a result of the population explosion and the attendant, ever-increasing atomization of society (i.e., the ever-increasing isolation of the individual), this role becomes more and more inevitable for a person. I don't suppose that I know more about life than anyone of my age, but it seems to me that, in the capacity of an interlocutor, a book is more reliable than a friend or a beloved. A novel or a poem is not a monologue, but a conversation of a writer with a reader, a conversation, I repeat, that is very private, excluding all others—if you will, mutually misanthropic. And in the moment of this conversation a writer is equal to a reader, as well as the other way around, regardless of whether the writer is a great one or not. This equality is the equality of consciousness. It remains with a person for the rest of his life in the form of memory, foggy or distinct; and, sooner or later, appropriately or not, it conditions a person's conduct. It's precisely this that I have in mind in speaking of the role of the performer, all the more natural for one because a novel or a poem is the product of mutual loneliness—of a writer or a reader.

In the history of our species, in the history of Homo sapiens, the book is an anthropological development, similar essentially to the invention of the wheel. Having emerged in order to give us some idea not so much of our origins as of what that sapiens is capable of, a book constitutes a means of transportation through the space of experience, at the speed of a turning page. This movement, like every movement, becomes flight from the common denominator, from an attempt to elevate this denominator's line, previously never reaching higher than the groin, to our heart, to our consciousness, to our imagination. This flight is the flight in the direction of "uncommon visage," in the direction of the numerator, in the direction of autonomy, in the direction of privacy. Regardless of whose image we are created in, there are already five billion of us, and for a human being there is no other future save that outlined by art. Otherwise, what lies ahead is the past—the political one, first of all, with all its mass police entertainment.

In any event, the condition of society in which art in general, and literature in particular, are the property or prerogative of a minority appears to me unhealthy and dangerous. I am not appealing for the replacement of the state with a library, although this thought has visited me frequently; but there is no doubt in my mind that, had we been choosing our leaders on the basis of their reading experience and not their political programs, there would be much less grief on earth. It seems to me that a potential master of our fates should be asked, first of all, not about how he imagines the course of his foreign policy, but about his attitude toward Stendahl, Dickens, Dostoyevsky. If only because the lock and stock of literature is indeed human diversity and perversity, it turns out to be a reliable antidote for any attempt—whether familiar or yet to be invented—toward a total mass solution to the problems of human existence. As a form of moral insurance, at least, literature is much more dependable than a system of beliefs or a philosophical doctrine.

Since there are no laws that can protect us from ourselves, no criminal code is capable of preventing a true crime against literature; though we can condemn the material suppression of literature—the persecution of writers, acts of censorship, the burning of books—we are powerless when it comes to its worst violation: the neglect of books, the non-reading of them. For that crime, a person pays with his whole life; if the offender is a nation, it pays with its history. Living in the country I live in, I would be the first prepared to believe that there is a set dependency between a person's material well-being and his literary ignorance. What keeps me from doing so is the history of that country in which I was born and grew up. For, reduced to a cause-and-effect minimum, to a crude formula, the Russian tragedy is precisely the tragedy of a society in which literature turned out to be the prerogative of the minority: the celebrated Russian intelligentsia.

I have no wish to enlarge upon the subject, no wish to darken this evening with thoughts of the tens of millions of human lives destroyed by other millions, since what occurred in Russia in the first half of the 20th century occurred before the introduction of automatic weapons—in the name of the triumph of a political doctrine whose unsoundness is already manifested in the fact that it requires human sacrifice for its realization. I'll just say that I believe—not empirically, alas, but only theoretically—that, for someone who has read a lot of Dickens, to shoot his like in the name of some idea is somewhat more problematic than for someone who has read no Dickens. And I am speaking precisely about reading Dickens, Sterne, Stendahl, Dostoyevsky, Flaubert, Balzac, Melville, Proust, Musil, and so forth; that is, about literature, not about literacy or education. A literate, educated person, to be sure, is fully capable, after reading some political treatise or tract, of killing his like, and even of experiencing, in so doing, a rapture of conviction. Lenin was literate, Stalin was literate, so was Hitler; as for Mao Zedong, he even wrote verse. What all these men had in common, though, was that their hit list was longer than their reading list.

However, before I move on to poetry, I would like to add that it would make sense to regard the Russian experience as a warning, if for no other reason than that the social structure of the West up to now is, on the whole, analogous to what existed in Russia prior to 1917. (This, by the way, is what explains the popularity in the West of the 19th-century Russian psychological novel, and the relative lack of success of contemporary Russian prose. The social relations that emerged in Russia in the 20th century presumably seem no less exotic to the reader than do the names of the characters, which prevent him from identifying with them.) For example, the number of political parties, on the eve of the October coup in 1917, was no fewer than what we find today in the United States or Britain. In other words, a dispassionate observer might remark that in a certain sense the 19th century is still going on in the West, while in Russia it came to an end; and if I say that it ended in tragedy, this is, in the first place, because of the size of the human toll taken in the course of that social—or chronological—change. For in a real tragedy, it is not the hero who perishes; it is the chorus.

Although for a man whose mother tongue is Russian, to speak about political evil is as natural as digestion, I would here like to change the subject. What's wrong with discourses about the obvious is that they corrupt consciousness with their easiness, with the quickness with which they provide one with moral comfort, with the sensation of being right. Herein lies their temptation, similar in its nature to the temptation of a social reformer who begets this evil. The realization, or rather the comprehension, of this temptation, and the rejection of it, are perhaps responsible to a certain extent for the destinies of many of my contemporaries, responsible for the literature that emerged from under their pens. It, that literature, was neither a flight from history nor a muffling of memory, as it may seem from the outside. "How can one write poetry after Auschwitz?" inquired Adorno; and one familiar with Russian history can repeat the same question by merely changing the name of the camp—and repeat it perhaps with even greater justification, since the number of people who perished in Stalin's camps far surpasses the number of German prison-camp victims. "And how can one eat lunch?" the American poet Mark Strand once retorted. In any case, the generation to which I belong has proven capable of writing that poetry.

That generation—the generation born precisely at the time when the Auschwitz crematoria were working full blast, when Stalin was at the zenith of his God-like, absolute power, which seemed sponsored by Mother Nature herself—that generation came into the world, it appears, in order to continue what, theoretically, was supposed to be interrupted in those crematoria and in the anonymous common graves of Stalin's archipelago. The fact that not everything got interrupted, at least not in Russia, can be credited in no small degree to my generation, and I am no less proud of belonging to it than I am of standing here today. And the fact that I am standing here today is a recognition of the services that generation has rendered to culture; recalling a phrase from Mandelstam, I would add, to world culture. Looking back, I can say now that we were beginning in an

empty—indeed, a terrifyingly wasted—place, and that, intuitively rather than consciously, we aspired precisely to the re-creation of the effect of culture's continuity, to the reconstruction of its forms and tropes, toward filling its few surviving, and often totally compromised, forms with our own new, or appearing to us as new, contemporary content.

There existed, presumably, another path: the path of further deformation, the poetics of ruins and debris, of minimalism, of choked breath. If we rejected it, it was not at all because we thought that it was the path of self-dramatization, or because we were extremely animated by the idea of preserving the hereditary nobility of the forms of culture we knew, the forms that were equivalent, in our consciousness, to forms of human dignity. We rejected it because in reality the choice wasn't ours, but, in fact, culture's own—and this choice, again, was aesthetic rather than moral.

To be sure, it is natural for a person to perceive himself not as an instrument of culture, but, on the contrary, as its creator and custodian. But if today I assert the opposite, it's not because toward the close of the 20th century there is a certain charm in paraphrasing Plotinus, Lord Shaftesbury, Schelling, or Novalis, but because, unlike anyone else, a poet always knows that what in the vernacular is called the voice of the Muse is, in reality, the dictate of the language; that it's not the language that happens to be his instrument, but that he is language's means toward the continuation of its existence. Language, however, even if one imagines it as a certain animate creature (which would only be just), is not capable of ethical choice.

A person sets out to write a poem for a variety of reasons: to win the heart of his beloved; to express his attitude toward the reality surrounding him, be it a landscape or a state; to capture his state of mind at a given instant; to leave—as he thinks at that moment—a trace on the earth. He resorts to this form—the poem—most likely for unconsciously mimetic reasons: the black vertical clot of words on the white sheet of paper presumably reminds him of his own situation in the world, of the balance between space and his body. But regardless of the reasons for which he takes up the pen, and regardless of the effect produced by what emerges from under that pen on his audience—however great or small it may be—the immediate consequence of this enterprise is the sensation of coming into direct contact with language, or more precisely, the sensation of immediately falling into dependence on it, on everything that has already been uttered, written, and accomplished in it.

This dependence is absolute, despotic; but it unshackles as well. For, while always older than the writer, language still possesses the colossal centrifugal energy imparted to it by its temporal potential—that is, by all time lying ahead. And this potential is determined not so much by the quantitative body of the nation that speaks it (though it is determined by that, too), as by the quality of the poem written in it. It will suffice to recall the authors of Greek or Roman antiquity; it will suffice to recall Dante. And that which is being created today in Russian or English, for example, guarantees the existence of these languages over the course of the next millennium also. The poet, I wish to repeat, is language's means for existence—or, as my beloved Auden said, he is the one by whom it lives. I who write these lines will cease to be; so will you who read them. But the language in which they are written and in which you read them will remain, not merely because language is a more lasting thing than man, but because it is more capable of mutation.

One who writes a poem, however, writes it not because he courts fame with posterity, although often he hopes that a poem will outlive him, at least briefly. One who writes a poem writes it because the language prompts, or simply dictates, the next line. Beginning a poem, the poet as a rule doesn't know the way it is going to come out; and at times he is very surprised by the way it turns out, since often it turns out better than he expected, often his thought carries further than he reckoned. And that is the moment when the future of language invades its present.

There are, as we know, three modes of cognition: analytical, intuitive, and the mode that was known to the biblical prophets, revelation. What distinguishes poetry from other forms of literature is that it uses all three of them at once (gravitating primarily toward the second and the third). For all three of them are given in the language; and there are times when, by means of a single word, a single rhyme, the writer of a poem manages to find himself where no one has ever been before him, further, perhaps, than he himself would have wished for. The one who writes a poem writes it above all because verse writing is an extraordinary accelerator of consciousness, of thinking, of comprehending the universe. Having experienced this acceleration once, one is no longer capable of abandoning the chance to repeat this experience; one falls into dependency on this process, the way others fall into dependency on drugs or alcohol. One who finds himself in this sort of dependency on language is, I guess, what they call a poet. (pp. 27-30, 32)

Joseph Brodsky, "Uncommon Visage," in The New Republic, *Vol. 198, Nos. 1 & 2, January 4 & 11, 1988, pp. 27-32.*

Orson Scott Card

Speaker for the Dead

Hugo Award
Nebula Award

(Also writes under the pseudonym Brian Green) American novelist, short story writer, dramatist, and critic.

Speaker for the Dead (1986) is the second installment in the planned Ender trilogy, Card's saga about humanity's struggle to coexist with alien beings. The first book in the series, *Ender's Game* (1985), also won Hugo and Nebula Awards for best novel. A devout Mormon, Card frequently weaves religious and philosophical ideas into his science fiction adventure stories. These spiritual concerns intensify in *Speaker for the Dead,* as elements of theology as well as debate on the morality of war are integrally related with the novel's action.

Speaker for the Dead is set three thousand years after the protagonist of the series, Andrew "Ender" Wiggin, destroys a race of extraterrestrial beings in a senseless battle. Reviled as a genocidal monster, Ender atones for his crime by serving as a historical apologist, or "speaker for the dead." Using the lessons of tolerance and nonviolence he has learned in his time travels, Ender helps a group of human space colonists deal with a threatening species of intelligent aliens. Several critics consider *Speaker for the Dead* a stronger novel than *Ender's Game* and a demonstration of Card's growing maturity as a writer, especially in his development of more well-rounded and compelling characterizations. While many of Card's earlier novels are faulted for excessive violence, *Speaker for the Dead* is praised for its thoughtful and compassionate treatment of all characters, aliens and humans alike.

Praise is not unanimous, however. Alarmed by Card's presentation of a heroic white male race murderer, critic Elaine Radford condemns the Ender series as a thinly veiled defense of Adolf Hitler. Card indignantly refutes this view. "There is no justification whatever in the text of *Ender's Game* or *Speaker for the Dead* for calling me a fascist, a racist, a genocide, or a sexist," he responds; "on the contrary, in both books I spoke as eloquently and powerfully as I could in favor of compassion and empathy, and against all four tendencies that she accuses me of." Indeed, the majority of reviewers accept Card's contention. Asserts critic Michael R. Collings: "*Ender's Game* and *Speaker for the Dead* succeed equally as straightforward SF adventure and as allegorical, analogical disquisitions on humanity, morality, salvation, and redemption."

(See also *CLC*, Vols. 44, 47 and *Contemporary Authors,* Vol. 102.)

Photograph by Jay Kay Klein

the Buggers. In his new identity, Wiggin plays a vital role in preventing war when a second nonhuman intelligent race—even more incomprehensible than the Buggers—is discovered. This book lacks the sheer dramatic power of Ender's transformation from child into warlord as portrayed in its predecessor. However, it benefits from increased dramatic unity, a well-developed background and supporting cast on the colony planet Lusitania, and the author's customarily stylish writing. Not quite as good as *Ender's Game,* this work is still a fine novel in its own right and will be much in demand among Card's growing audience.

> *R. G., in a review of "Speaker for the Dead," in Booklist, Vol. 82, No. 8, December 15, 1985, p. 594.*

BOOKLIST

Card's sequel to *Ender's Game* takes up where the first novel left off, with Ender Wiggin becoming Speaker for the Dead out of remorse over his role in the unnecessary destruction of

PUBLISHERS WEEKLY

Card's novel *Ender's Game* introduced Ender Wiggin, a young genius who used his military prowess to all but exterminate the "buggers," the first alien race mankind had ever encountered. Wiggin then transformed himself into the "Speaker for the Dead,'' who claimed it had been a mistake to destroy the alien civilization. Many years later, when a new breed of intelligent life forms called the ''piggies'' is discovered, Wiggin takes the opportunity to atone for his earlier actions. This long, rich and ambitious novel [*Speaker for the Dead*] views the interplay between the races from the differing perspectives of the colonists, ethnologists, biologists, clergy, politicians, a computer artificial intelligence, the lone surviving bugger and the piggies themselves. Card is very good at portraying his characters in these larger, social, religious and cultural contexts. It's unfortunate, then, that many of the book's mysteries and dilemmas seem created just to display Ender's supposedly godlike understanding. A fine, if overlong, novel nonetheless.

> *A review of "Speaker for the Dead," in* Publishers Weekly, *Vol. 229, No. 4, January 24, 1986, p. 64.*

RICHARD E. GEIS

[*Ender's Game*] is far-future sf, in which mankind has spread to many, many worlds—and initially suffered a traumatic almost-loss to the Buggers (insectoid aliens who attacked and almost wiped out humankind). The high-command recruited the best of the child geniuses of Mankind and trained them for war in a special academy.

Andrew Wiggin was one such genius, and became THE best military strategist and tactician of all.

Ender's Game is the story of how he was trained—mercilessly—to be the commander of all mankind's space fleets in the final war against the Buggers.

And it is the story of how he was tricked into becoming the greatest criminal in the history of mankind.

The novel is direct, real, bedded in military ruthlessness and military values. It's the best sf ''military academy'' novel I've ever read.

Speaker for the Dead follows Andrew ''Ender'' Wiggin 3000 years later after he has spent years traveling in ftl from star system to star system atoning in his way for what he was tricked into doing as a child.

Speaker is a multi-viewpoint novel, with many real people, with another alien species at risk—the ''Piggies''—and with complicated moral values involved.

Scott has woven a constantly escalating storyline which deals with religion, alien/human viewpoints and perspectives on instinctual and cultural levels, the fate of three alien species (including a singular computer/ansible intelligence named Jane, a remote colony/research/study base on a planet called Lusitania, horrible deaths, tragic secrets, and quite possibly the fate of mankind itself. . . .

Scott Card is a fine writer, with great insight, great idealism and love. *Speaker for the Dead* is an affirmation of those values and traits.

He thinks that yes, mankind can learn to recognize intelligence and self-consciousness in any form and accept it as human, as equal. He has created in Ender Wiggin a giant of compassion and intelligence and perspective.

These novels, especially *Speaker for the Dead,* will probably leave you feeling good about humanity and the future.

But I think it is an exercise in wishful thinking, a Liberal-Wimp delusion, and that in the real world the lone genius, his

cohorts, the Piggies, the Buggers and the people of Lusitania are going to be wiped out, because the xenophobia and fear of a potential plague from Lusitania which could imperil mankind, would rule over any empathy or compassion or intellectual argument.

Clearly the final resolution of this saga is one novel away: the fleet is forty years from reaching Lusitania, and Ender Wiggin is still the greatest military genius who ever lived.

I may be presuming too much about Scott and Ender, may be condemning too soon.

Whenever the next Ender novel appears, I'll read it with great interest, and great enjoyment: I'm sure of that. (p. 15)

> *Richard E. Geis, in a review of "Ender's Game" and "Speaker for the Dead," in* Science Fiction Review, *Vol. 15, No. 1, February, 1986, pp. 14-15.*

MICHAEL R. COLLINGS

Speaker for the Dead is a sequel to Card's *Ender's Game* (1985), and the most powerful work Card has produced. *Speaker* not only completes *Ender's Game* but transcends it; the novel shares the compassionate lyricism of *Songmaster,* the excitement of alien landscapes of *A Planet Called Treason,* the mysteries of time and its effects on civilization of *Capitol* and *The Worthing Chronicle,* and the sense of a fantastic tapestry woven around wholly believable characters of *Hart's Hope.*

Read in conjunction with *Ender's Game, Speaker* demonstrates Card's mastery of character, plot, style, theme, and development. Many of the elements that drew harsh criticism for earlier novels—overt violence, destructive sexuality—have been refined. Still present, they draw less attention to themselves because they are inherent in the structure and development of the novels; the Xenocide Ender must kill again—not only to save an alien race and his own humanity, but to complete the cycle of awareness, guilt, and redemption. Like so many of Card's characters, he has an extraordinary talent that has divorced him from much of humanity; in the final chapters of *Ender's Game* and throughout *Speaker,* Andrew Wiggin makes his painful way back into the community of ramen (sentient beings).

Throughout, Card balances action with thought, science fiction with archetypal themes and images, science with faith. The novel incorporates religion as subject and religious individuals as characters, yet avoids becoming polemical or stereotyped. Indeed, most frequently such characters are inverted; the Christ-figure finds himself at the foot of an alien Cross, crucifying another savior. The inversions are carefully paced—with the result that *Ender's Game* and *Speaker for the Dead* succeed equally as straightforward SF adventure and as allegorical, analogical disquisitions on humanity, morality, salvation, and redemption.

Lest that last sentence seem too strong, I must add that both novels are compelling simply as psychological studies of strong characters. Both are highly recommended for readers interested in the cultural complexities and ambiguity the best science fiction novels explore.

> *Michael R. Collings, "Adventure and Allegory," in* Fantasy Review, *Vol. 9, No. 4, April, 1986, p. 20.*

An Excerpt from *Speaker for the Dead*

"Look in yourselves at this moment," said Andrew. "You will find that underneath your hatred of Ender the Xenocide and your grief for the death of the buggers, you also feel something much uglier: You're afraid of the stranger, whether he's utlanning or framling. When you think of him killing a man that you know of and value, then it doesn't matter what his shape is. He's varelse then, or worse—djur, the dire beast, that comes in the night with slavering jaws. If you had the only gun in your village, and the beasts that had torn apart one of your people were coming again, would you stop to ask if they also had a right to live, or would you act to save your village, the people that you knew, the people who depended on you?"

"By your argument we should kill the piggies now, primitive and helpless as they are!" shouted Styrka.

"My argument? I asked a question. A question isn't an argument, unless you think you know my answer, and I assure you, Styrka, that you do not. Think about this. Class is dismissed."

"Will we talk about this tomorrow?" they demanded.

"If you want," said Andrew. But he knew that if they discussed it, it would be without him. For them, the issue of Ender the Xenocide was merely philosophical. After all, the Bugger Wars were more than three thousand years ago; it was now the year 1948 SC, counting from the year the Starways Code was established, and Ender had destroyed the buggers in the year 1180 BSC. But to Andrew, the events were not so remote. He had done far more interstellar travel than any of his students would dare to guess; since he was twenty-five he had, until Trondheim, never stayed more than six months on any planet. Lightspeed travel between worlds had let him skip like a stone over the surface of time. His students had no idea that their Speaker for the Dead, who was surely no older than thirty-five, had very clear memories of events 3000 years before, that in fact those events seemed scarcely twenty years ago to him, only half his lifetime. They had no idea how deeply the question of Ender's ancient guilt burned within him, and how he had answered it in a thousand different unsatisfactory ways. They knew their teacher only as Speaker for the Dead; they did not know that when he was a mere infant, his older sister, Valentine, could not pronounce the name Andrew, and so called him Ender, the name that he made infamous before he was fifteen years old. So let unforgiving Styrka and analytical Plikt ponder the great question of Ender's guilt; for Andrew Wiggin, Speaker for the Dead, the question was not academic.

TOM EASTON

Last July, I heartily recommended Orson Scott Card's ***Ender's Game***. Now that book too has a sequel, ***Speaker for the Dead***. *Game* left child military genius Ender Wiggin full of remorse after having destroyed the alien buggers, and gifted with a chance for redemption. He had come across a last surviving bugger queen (the aliens are hive creatures) and accepted the duty to find it a place to reestablish its species. He had also

written a great and influential work, *The Hive Queen and the Hegemon,* using the pseudonym of "Speaker for the Dead."

Speaker takes place some three thousand years later. Ender still lives, for his civilization is one of slower-than-light travel and instantaneous communication via ansible (a bugger invention). His pseudonym has become his—and others'—profession, for there is a need for people who can be summoned by ansible to travel to a world where someone's life needs explanation to his or her survivors and heirs. It is the time dilation of frequent relativistic travel that has kept Ender and his sister, Valentine, around for thirty centuries.

Like ***Game***, ***Speaker*** deals with issues of evil and empathy, though not in so polarized a way. Soon after Lusitania's colonization, the planet turned out to have a native sentient species, the piggies. The authorities immediately curtailed the colony's activities, surrounding it with a fence that only the colony's two xenologists could cross. The xenologists in turn were barred from revealing human technology or culture, while the biologists could study only what was within the fence. A plague strikes, the biologists find a cure but they die, leaving their daughter, Novinha, alone. In time, she allies with the xenologists, Pipo and his son Libo, and finds joy. But then Novinha links the plague with the peculiarities of piggy biology, Pipo goes to the piggies to check her discovery out, and the piggies kill him in a remarkably gruesome way. Riddled with guilt, Novinha buries her discovery for fear that it will kill Libo too, refusing to marry him because marriage would give him access to her files. But the piggies kill him anyway.

Speaker is a tale of guilt and tragedy driven by fear of the alien, by lack of empathy. When news of the "murders" reaches the rest of human civilization, the fear that the piggies may be another variety of buggers enters the equation. And then Ender arrives, drawn to be Speaker for the Dead, to explain the deaths of Pipo, Libo, and Novinha's maddened husband, Marcão. His clear vision, his depth of insight into the human soul, drawn from his own hell of guilt, soon resolve all problems. The colony rebels, an interspecies accord takes shape with grand promise for the future, and Ender achieves his own joy.

Less brash than ***Ender's Game***, ***Speaker for the Dead*** may be a much better book. Don't miss it, and be prepared for another sequel. Card does leave room for one. (pp. 183-84)

Tom Easton, in a review of "Speaker for the Dead,"
in Analog Science Fiction/Science Fact, *Vol. CVI,*
No. 6, June, 1986, pp. 183-84.

ELAINE RADFORD

[In the following excerpt, Radford claims that Card deliberately modeled his fictional hero Ender after Adolf Hitler and that Ender's Game *and* Speaker for the Dead *are allegorical defenses of race hatred, misogyny, and genocide. For Card's response, see the excerpt below.]*

Let me tell you about a book I just read. It's the story of a young boy who was dreadfully abused by the grown-ups who wanted to mold him into an exemplary citizen. Forced to suppress his own emotions in order to avoid being paralyzed by trauma, he directed his energy into duty rather than sex or love. In time, he came to believe that his primary duty was to wipe out a species of gifted but incomprehensible aliens who had devastated his kind in a previous war. He found the idea of exterminating an entire race distasteful, of course. But since he believed it was required to save the people he defined as human, he put the entire weight of his formidable energy behind the effort to wipe out the aliens.

You've read it, you say? It's *Ender's Game* by Orson Scott Card, right?

Wrong. The aliens I'm talking about were the European Jews, blamed by many Germans for gearing up World War I for their own profit. The book is Robert G. L. Waite's *The Psychopathic God: Adolf Hitler.*

I don't know of any pair of novels that have been as consistently misinterpreted as Card's *Ender's Game* and *Speaker for the Dead.* Even a reader with a rudimentary knowledge of twentieth century history might be expected to guess that the character of Ender Wiggin, the near messianic superhero, is based on that of Adolf Hitler. Card himself is the "Speaker for the Dead" who seeks to understand and forgive the genocidal dictator's behavior by demonstrating that his intentions were good. Because Hitler/Ender committed genocide to preserve the existence and dignity of what he defined as human, he is not a monster but a true Superman who willingly shouldered the heavy responsibility thrust upon him.

For those who missed the point of what he was doing in *Ender's Game,* Card sums up the Speaker philosophy near the beginning of *Speaker for the Dead.* "Speakers for the Dead held as their only doctrine that good or evil exist entirely in human motive, and not at all in the act. . . ." Toward the end, he has a child voice the inevitable corollary, "When you really know somebody, you can't hate them." To which I can only say, "Bullshit." You can easily hate someone you know very well—ask a few people who have had to learn a great deal about their abusers in an effort to head off some of their attacks—and, in any case, adults remain responsible for their actions no matter how good their intentions. Certainly, it isn't OK to kill somebody because you think he *might* try at some time in the future to kill you. Why then is it OK to wipe out whole races for the same reason? What in the world made responsible science fiction readers and writers embrace Ender Wiggin, a.k.a. Adolf Hitler, as a hero?

It isn't because the books are skillfully written. *Ender's Game* is plotted around the weariest cliche going, the game that becomes real. *Speaker for the Dead* is a preachy, tedious text that substitutes coincidence and the Superman's omniscience for plot drivers. The characters in both books, to quote a friend, are constructed of the highest grade cardboard. But since Norman Spinrad has already detailed Card's amazing lack of originality in plot and character construction, I won't indulge in a literary hatchet job here. I'll only say that I suspect that we take Ender/Hitler to our hearts because fascist ideals remain frighteningly alive in all of us. We would all like to believe that our suffering has made us special—especially if it gives us a righteous reason to destroy our enemies.

Perhaps you feel that I exaggerate. I can hear you thinking: How could anybody equate that abused little boy with the Great Dictator? What kind of dirty mind does this Radford person have, anyway? In reply, I will now demonstrate that the Ender/Hitler connection is clearcut and central to the structure of both novels. I'll leave it to you to decide what it means that so many people found it so easy to identify with Ender Wiggin.

The Formative Years

To see what Card's up to, let's first look at Ender's formative years. Because eugenics works in his universe, Card grants the government the ability to predict the Wiggin children's genius from their parents' genes. Since the first two children are dis-

qualified from Battle School on personality grounds, the parents are asked to try again—producing Ender, whose early years are a nightmare of persecution because he's a Third child in an overpopulated world. His only friend is his sister Valentine, with whom he'll eventually wander about the galaxy in a quasi-incestuous relationship.

The reader is left with several questions that aren't easy to answer without comparing Ender's background to Hitler's. Why invoke eugenics, at best a pseudo-science and at worst an excuse for controlling one's "inferiors"? Why is it so important that Ender be a Third, to the point that Card gives the word a capital T? And why, oh why, the unnecessary and offensive hints at incest with his sister, the only member of the family that Ender is close to?

Alan Bullock writes in *Hitler: A Study in Tyranny,* the following synopsis of Hitler's early years: "Adolf was the third child of Alois Hitler's third marriage. Gustav and Ida, both born before him, died in infancy. . . . There were also, however, the two children of the second marriage with Franziska, Adolf Hitler's half-brother Alois, and his half-sister Angela. Angela was the only one of his relations with whom Hitler maintained any sort of friendship. She kept house for him at Berchtesgaden for a time, and it was her daughter, Geli Raubal, with whom Hitler fell in love."

It's all here, isn't it? Hitler was three times a third—the third child of a third marriage, and, because his older siblings died in infancy, the third child actually present in the home. Since his mother didn't conceive again until Hitler was six, Hitler, like Ender, spent his formative years as the third of three children. Like Ender, he eventually grew away from all of his family except his older sister. The main difference is that it was her daughter, and not Angela herself, with whom he engaged in a chaste but emotionally compelling love affair. (After Geli killed herself to escape her uncle's attentions, the doctor confirmed that she died a virgin. Likewise, Card makes us wait until well into the second novel before he tells us that Ender hasn't consummated his love for Valentine.)

Similarly, both children's lives were deformed by physical and emotional abuse. Ender escapes the abuse of his peers to join the Battle School—where he is, of course, abused by adults. Hitler was literally treated like the family dog by his father, who expected him to answer to his whistle and accept vicious beatings—beatings which were all the more terrible to the boy because he had an undescended testicle and deeply feared losing the other. Both cases represent awful violations of a child's body and spirit in the attempt to mold the kind of character that adults have decided the child should have.

The Logic of Misogyny

As an adult, it's in his relationships with women that Ender displays some of his most obvious parallels with Hitler. Indeed, as with the incest theme, some elements of *Speaker for the Dead* are inexplicable unless you're aware of Hitler's dyed-in-the-bone misogyny. In a world where the Wiggin genes are "crying out for continuation," Ender's chastity until his marriage at the age of 37 is puzzling. But, again, when we look at the Hitler connection, all becomes clear. Probably because of his childhood trauma, Hitler remained chaste for an unusually long time. He isn't known to have felt love for any woman until—are you ahead of me here?—age 37.

Another bizarre element is the fact that Ender chooses a bitter, self-destructive woman for his mate. Why? I presume it's to remind us that Hitler too chose self-destructive women. Of the seven close to him, six killed themselves or made serious attempts to do so.

In his eagerness to help us understand Ender/Hitler, Card comes close to justifying misogyny. At the Speaking of Marcão, Ender says that Novinha solicited beatings from her deceased husband in order to atone for her adultery. Marcão wasn't really a violent person, you understand, since he never hit anyone but his wife. How false and ugly that seems to those of us aware of the truth about abusive behavior, which is that abusive people will take out their frustrations on anyone—woman, child, dog, or elderly parent—that doesn't have the power to fight back. In this central chapter, meant to help us understand how speaking the truth heals a community, we see only a new lie traded for the old: Marcão may not have been the great guy we pretended he was, but hey, it was all his wife's fault.

Women have heard this tired story too many times before. It's called Blaming the Victim.

The author's contempt for women shows most clearly in his creation of Jane, a sentient supercomputer. Now there is no reason on God's green earth for Jane to present herself as female or even human. But Card knows that the reader would die laughing at the image of a neutered computer focusing on Ender like this: "And with all that vast activity, her unimaginable speed, the breadth and depth of her experience, fully half of the top ten levels of her attention were always, *always* (Card's emphasis) devoted to what came in through the jewel in Ender Wiggin's ear." Hard to swallow, isn't it? But Card expects us to understand when he depicts Jane as a woman in love. Surely the reader will recognize that a woman, no matter how intelligent, has nothing better to focus on than a man!

The Necessity of Genocide

The most explicit parallel between Hitler and Ender is that they're both genocides. Hitler, of course, ordered the death of millions of Jews, Slavs, homosexuals, physically and mentally handicapped persons, and so on. Ender exterminated an entire intelligent species. Most people, I hope, agree that mass murder, much less genocide, is quite indefensible. Yet, as we follow Ender's life after he wipes out the Buggers, we're invited to understand and forgive [his] actions.

Why? How? Here are two answers: "I would prefer not to see anyone suffer, not to do harm to anyone. But then I realize that the species in in danger. . . ." "I thought I was playing games. I didn't know it was the real thing. But . . . if I had known the battle was real, I would have done the same thing. We thought they wanted to kill us." The first words are Hitler's, the second Ender's. But the idea is the same, an appeal to good intentions: To save our people, we had to eliminate the threat presented by the existence of the stranger.

And that's a valid argument, if you're still a child and no one has ever told you what the road to Hell is paved with. It's a matter of historical record that Hitler honestly believed that the people he defined as human were in terrible danger from "inferior races." He did not merely use the threat to Nordic racial purity to become Fuhrer. Rather, he became Fuhrer because there was simply no other way to institute the sweeping racial programs his beliefs required. As Waite writes in *The Psychopathic God:* "The horror of Hitler was this: he meant what he said, he lived by his ideals, he practiced what he preached." And this, precisely, is the horror of Ender the Xenocide.

That's why Card lays such great stress on Valentine's silly "orders of foreignness," which give the people in *Speaker* such a convenient vocabulary for their racism. Says a "brilliant" student in *Speaker*, "Through these nordic (!) layers of foreignness we can see that Ender was not a true Xenocide, for when he destroyed the buggers, we knew them only as varelse (the truly alien)." To Hitler, of course, Jews, Blacks, and Slavs were equally alien, so by the same argument he is also innocent of genocide!

Forgiving Hitler

The most offensive thing about Ender is that he goes Hitler one better. Where the Fuhrer would have been content to kill everybody he thought might possibly one day represent a threat to his people, Ender does kill everybody—and then proceeds to steal their heritage. Ender the Xenocide becomes the first Speaker for the Dead, writing the book that will define what the Buggers are for three thousand years. It is as if Hitler not only exterminated the Jews, he then went on to write his own story of what the state of Israel might have been.

If there is anything uglier than silencing the voice of the alien because she is alien, it is then filling in the silence with your own version of what she was. Yet Card represents this act as Ender's redemption.

For the reader who isn't convinced that writing a book (no matter how highly acclaimed) makes up for exterminating a race, Card offers an alternative, albeit rather contradictory, excuse for his genocide's actions—genetic determinism. Although this "science" has been shown to represent such an oversimplification that it's a downright distortion, Card makes it the foundation of the biology of his universe. From the very beginning, authorities can breed geniuses more easily than you or I could establish a strain of purebred blue budgies, and never mind that breeding for color and size involves at most a few genes, while breeding for intelligence would require a total understanding of the complicated interactions between whole chromosomes. In Card's strange world, children can inherit advanced qualities like a talent for xenobiology—a bizarre combination of genetic determinism and Lysenkoism since these characteristics were presumably artificially acquired at some point in the past. (Or does Card imagine that there is literally a gene for xenobiological talent that we can breed for? How could such a thing evolve? Surely our genes would have to be macroscopic to carry all the information he assumes they do.) In any case, his pseudo-science serves primarily as an excuse for ugly actions running the gamut from genocide to vivisection.

At the very beginning of *Speaker*, Card has the thirteen-year-old Novinha exclaim, "But you can't understand the piggies just by watching the way they *behave*! (Card's emphasis) They came out of a different evolution! You have to understand their genes, what's going on inside their cells." The reader may chuckle at the idea of understanding a race's psychology from its genes—but Card plots later events so that Novinha's odd statement is entirely borne out. Environment (except for childhood traumas aimed at garnering reader sympathy) is nothing. Inheritance is all.

So what does this have to do with Ender/Hitler? Everything. Hitler, of course, believed in precisely this kind of oversimplified pseudo-scientific mishmash, and that's why he thought that applying the methods of the budgie breeder to human beings would work. Since there are no pet stores to accept your culls when you're breeding people, he built the death camps. And if the world really worked that way, I suppose you could say he was justified. If intelligence and moral character were actually reducible to a couple of recessive genes just waiting to be cultivated, then you *could* breed a race of Supermen using Hitler's methods. Indeed, short of genetic manipulation on a level we haven't mastered yet, his methods would probably be the *only* way to breed said Supermen.

(Perhaps Hitler should have asked some budgie breeders first. They could have told him that the culls often turn out to be the smartest, most personable birds—because they're taken into people's homes and given personal attention. Beautiful show budgies who do nothing but preen and sire young don't say, "Look at the pretty bird." But Hitler—and Card—already know that intelligence is mainly inherited and easily correlated with other desirable traits, so why bother to see what actual breeders say?)

Ender, of course, *is* a Superman—the greatest one. Breeding, not training, made him what he is. Remember, he brutally murdered a schoolboy for strategic reasons *before* he was accepted into Battle School. Although his training helped refine his talents as a killer genius, all the pre-arranged trauma and intensive schooling in the galaxy would have gone for naught had it not been for his superior genes. Card therefore Speaks for Ender by saying that the boy killed for the noblest reasons and couldn't have done otherwise anyway. So why should we attach moral meaning to his actions?

This interpretation also explains the clunky ending to *Ender's Game.* Having saved the world just by being what he is, Ender proceeds to demonstrate his innate nobility by wallowing in his own guilt. Sure, he isn't to blame and he knows it—but why not be a real Superman and prove how sensitive you are while you're saving the world?

Speaker's ending is even more ludicrous. Having spent most of two novels telling us why we can never understand the alien, Card has Ender pull a quick turnaround at the last minute so that Bugger, human, and piggie can live together in harmony. (This in a universe where tolerance is so rare that premarital sex is unthinkable and whole planets are chartered on the basis of narrow religious, racial, and national affiliations!) Just a little understanding and a quickie resurrection by our local Superman are enough to unravel the twisted knot of racially predetermined hatreds. Hitler's made it to Brazil to put what he's learned to use in the interest of racial harmony between European, Indian, and African. He's even brought a few Jews with him to lend the Brazilians a hand!

I'm sorry, Card, but it doesn't wash. It's just too cheap. In the real world, the murdered don't rise from the dead when the Great Leader decides that the times are right for tolerance. Shakespeare, speaking of another figure oft-cited as the model Superman, said it better: "The evil that men do lives after them; / the good is oft interred with their bones. . . ." So it was with Caesar, so it is with Hitler. All the understanding in the world doesn't change the fact that this man deformed the face of the twentieth century and that we are all of us living with his destructive legacy. Perhaps you meant to focus on the good men do rather than their evil when you wrote: "*Destroyed everything he touched*—that's a lie, that can't truthfully be said of any human being who ever lived." Perhaps you meant to help us enlarge the sphere of our capacity for forgiveness. No doubt, in any case, that you meant well.

But it doesn't really matter, does it? As long as people are struggling against anti-Semitism, misogyny, and all the other ways of oppressing the different, it seems inappropriate to focus overmuch on the delicate feelings of the oppressor. Look at the fact that the Fuhrer was sincere and re-define his life as dedicated rather than evil? Forgive Hitler? Card, from your privileged position as a white male American Christian, you have no right to ask us that. (pp. 11-12, 48-9)

> Elaine Radford, "Ender and Hitler: Sympathy for the Superman," in *Fantasy Review, Vol. 10, No. 5, June, 1987, pp. 11-12, 48-9.*

ORSON SCOTT CARD

[*In the following excerpt, Card defends* Ender's Game *and* Speaker for the Dead *against Elaine Radford's charges (see excerpt above) that these novels are apologies for Nazism and genocide.*]

I have made it a policy never to respond to negative reviews of my work, particularly when they are so obviously wrong as to be self-defeating. In Radford's case, however, she purports to have textual proof that I actually intended some of the nonsense she pretends to find in my two most recent novels, and to avoid letting her article stand as an unrefuted basis for future critical commentary, I have no choice but to respond. (p. 13)

The best response, however, is this: Read ***Ender's Game*** and ***Speaker for the Dead.*** I am confident that if you do this, you will see that Radford's review reveals nothing about the books and a great deal about herself. You will then have no reason to bother reading the rest of my response, since most of the points I make will already be obvious to you.

But if her review leaves you thinking that you have no desire to read such awful fascist, sexist, racist, genocidal novels, if from her review you think you now know something about me and my fiction, then it is to you that the rest of my response is addressed; I hope you will be fair-minded enough to read my account of what my stories are about before you decide whether Radford's version of their "meaning" is correct.

I'm always sorry when a reader misunderstands a story of mine. It's bound to happen, of course, since every reader brings his or her own set of prejudices and expectations to the tale; storytelling is a collaborative art, and what ends up in the reader's memory depends in large part on who the reader was in the first place.

On the broadest level, it should be obvious to every reader of ***Ender's Game*** and ***Speaker for the Dead*** that I do draw one key parallel between historical monstrosities like Hitler, Stalin, and Amin, and my character Ender: they are thought of in the public mind as loathsome mass murderers. Despite their similar public image, however, every other element of Ender's story is designed to show that in his case the image is not reality—he is *not* like Hitler or Stalin, exactly the opposite of what Radford claims. Far from using Ender to try to make people approve of Hitler, I use the *contrast* with Hitler, Stalin, and other genocides to illuminate the character of Ender Wiggin.

Ender vs. Hitler

Except for a couple of trivial coincidences, there are no biographical similarities between Hitler and Ender. So let me point out some of the obvious, clear, and intentional moral differences between Ender and Hitler.

Ender Wiggin had no notion he was killing real aliens—he thought he was still playing games. Hitler knew perfectly well he was killing flesh and blood people.

Ender wasn't even a teenager yet; he was a child who saw only the world that adults had allowed him to see. Hitler committed his crimes as an adult, with full understanding of his actions.

Valentine's hierarchy of foreignness—Utlanning, Framling, Raman, Varelse—was consistently used by her and Ender in an effort to bind aliens and strangers together, to make co-operation or at least coexistence possible. The category of Raman was meant to eliminate the automatic assumption that aliens are non-human, irrevocably "not like us," and rather to discover key points of similarity on which good relations and understanding could be built. Hitler's classification of Ar-yan versus non-Aryan was used for exactly the opposite pur-pose: to dehumanize the groups he hated, to provide a moral foundation for destroying them. In short, the hierarchy of for-eignness in *Speaker* is exactly the opposite of racial theory.

Hitler killed himself while proclaiming that the German people were unworthy of him; Ender Wiggin retreated from the rest of humanity in part because he believed himself unworthy of them; but instead of self-destruction he spent the rest of his life promoting empathy and understanding among human beings.

Hitler's avowed goal was the complete obliteration of another race. The humans in *Ender's Game* never imagined that they were obliterating another species; rather they thought they were destroying an invading species' ability to make war. Genocide was the result of not understanding the effect on the buggers of the death of the hive queens. Does Radford really believe that I was claiming Hitler's near-obliteration of European Jews was an *accident*? That he and his underlings didn't know their death camps might kill *all* the Jews? Yet if I made Ender's crime so obviously different in intent from Hitler's deliberate genocide, how can she imagine I meant Ender's story to be an apologia for Hitler?

Ender, as soon as he discovered that true nature of what he had done, took upon himself the full responsibility for it, pro-claimed himself a criminal to the very people who wanted to make him a hero, and did his best to keep such a thing from ever happening again. Hitler and his fellow mass-murderers denied and concealed their actions as long as possible, and when it was undeniable, refused to accept responsibility even for what they knowingly did.

(On this point Radford insists on having it both ways. She at once ridicules the statement that "Speakers for the Dead held as their only doctrine that good and evil exist entirely in human motive, and not at all in the act" (she alludes to the old, and false, adage that the road to hell is paved with good intentions) which seems to imply that she thinks that people are morally responsible for all the consequences of their actions, regardless of their intent; yet when I have Ender take that same attitude, holding himself responsible for the deaths of the hive queen and all her people, she ridicules this: "Why not be a real Superman and prove how sensitive you are while you're saving the world?"

(Our legal system today holds, in principle, that while good intentions often lead to error, they do mitigate against guilt. Drunken drivers who kill people are convicted of manslaughter, not murder; the insanity defense implicitly depends on the idea that it matters whether someone understood the consequences of his acts. It is certainly Radford's right to deplore this kind of moral relativism, but I fail to see what it has to do with Hitler, who fully intended and understood all the evil things he did, and Ender, who did not.)

When Ender pseudonymously tells the story of the hive queen, Radford calls this "stealing their heritage," and says, "It is as if Hitler not only exterminated the Jews, he then went on to write his own story of what the state of Israel might have been." Ender has had perfect telepathic contact with a living member of the species; in telling her story he glorifies his vanquished enemy and depicts his own act as a terrible crime. Does Radford think this makes him *like* Hitler? Did Hitler ever tell stories sympathetic to the Jews?

And Radford's notion that when someone who is not of a community writes a story about that community he is "stealing their heritage" is racist in the extreme—it denies the possibility that people who are from different backgrounds can ever em-pathize well enough to tell the truth about each other. She probably thinks men can never write accurately or honestly about women, or whites about blacks, or Americans about foreigners. Talk about bigotry.

There *is* a science fiction novel that attempts to deal with a Hitlerian monster, not sympathetically, but in such a way as to help us understand how a human being can justify to him-self—and to others—such monstrous behavior: M. J. Engh's brilliant novel *Arslan*. It is a difficult fictional task, which Engh carries out to perfection, in my opinion, making it a challenging, disturbing book. But *Ender's Game* is not that book, if for no other reason than that Ender Wiggin is a child, unaware of the connection between game and reality, when his only "Hitlerian" act is performed—which, in my belief, makes him morally innocent, though causally responsible.

Psychobabble

Radford knows that her reading of *Ender's Game* and *Speaker for the Dead* is eccentric: "I don't know of any pair of novels that have been as consistently misinterpreted as Card's," she says. That's right, everybody is stupid except her. Such self-confidence! This universal "misinterpretation" does not cause her for one moment to doubt the validity of her eccentric read-ing, even to the point of declaring it to be obvious: "Even a reader with a rudimentary knowledge of twentieth-century his-tory might be expected to guess that the character of Ender Wiggin . . . is based on that of Adolf Hitler."

Oddly, I have a much better than rudimentary knowledge of twentieth-century history, and I never guessed it. My problem, I suppose, is that I never read the psychobiography of Hitler that she read and believed. I had my fill of psychobiography with Fawn Brodie's nonsense about Thomas Jefferson, Joseph Stalin, and Richard Nixon; Radford seems to have Brodie's gift for making much of the psychological implications of very small details, while completely ignoring the obvious major patterns of the story.

I have listed some obvious, undeniable moral differences be-tween Ender and Hitler. I was amused by the infinitesimal biographical parallels she finds between them, and on which she bases her entire case. Out of such nonsense are doctoral dissertations made; but the problem with her parallels is that they can't have any causal connection with the books. I had no idea what age Hitler was when he married, or that Hitler was a third child—off-the-top-of-the-head knowledge of those details is not part of a "rudimentary knowledge of twentieth-century history," but rather a sign of an obsessive fascination with Hitler, which seems to be Radford's problem, not mine. If I had been attempting to parallel Ender and Hitler I might indeed have looked up such facts; but since I was not, it never occurred to me to research the details of Hitler's life in order to avoid them. After all, every character is going to have some detail of his life in common with some actual historical figure. It hardly proves a connection.

Ender is a third child in *Ender's Game* in large part because *I* was a third child. (Every family with at least three children has a third child—I do hope Radford does not hold all those parents responsible for making a parallel with Hitler.) Ender's childhood is based, albeit loosely, on my own; his relationship with Peter and Valentine is based, not on my actual relationships with my older brother and sister, but rather on the way I conceived those relationships to be when I was Ender's age. Ender's revised understanding of Peter late in Peter's life parallels in emotion the same revision I went through in my teens as I discovered that my childish view of my older brother was hopelessly wrong.

In other words, my source, as with most writers, is my own experience of human behavior. My source is certainly not petty and irrelevant details of Hitler's life, like his age at marriage and his birth order. If I wanted to draw a close parallel with Hitler, I would hardly use biographical details so obscure that only Radford, of all my readers, would detect them. When I have something to communicate with my audience, I communicate it.

And as for the "incest theme," it does not exist except in the fervid imagination of critics who already decided to hate the book for unrelated reasons. I can't help but feel sorry for Radford and other critics who apparently can't conceive of a close relationship among siblings without assuming that incest is involved. This is the same sort of thinking that persuades some people that close friendships between people of the same sex must always imply homosexuality. God help them if their own children actually love each other.

But the most obvious mistake that Radford makes, the one that discredits her entire argument that Ender "stands for" Hitler is this: If I were trying to make Hitler seem good through Ender Wiggin, wouldn't I attempt to justify his genocide? It would have been so easy just to make the buggers exactly as evil as everybody thought they were—to say it was *true* that they had to be killed to save the human race. Yet at the end of *Ender's Game* and throughout *Speaker for the Dead* I make exactly the opposite point—that the destruction of the buggers was unnecessary for human survival, that it was a terrible thing to happen, and that it is entirely appropriate for Ender to devote the rest of his life to trying to restore to the hive queen the life he took from her and her people. Even if there were a parallel between Hitler and Ender, this hardly counts as an attempt to "forgive Hitler."

Eugenics?

Radford's claim that *Ender's Game* includes a eugenics theme is astonishing. There was no program of eugenics in the book—only a program of testing young children to find early signs of the talents needed for making war. It is a science fictional premise of the book that in this future human beings have discovered more accurate ways of testing young children than we have now. And the book makes it clear that even those carrying out this testing regard it as an appalling necessity, not something they approve of, and that it has no guarantee of success.

Eugenics? Ender's parents were not brought together as part of a breeding program. They merely happened to get married. No notice was taken of them until their first child, Peter, tested

remarkably high. The officials who asked the Wiggins to have a girl next were not using tried and true scientific facts of their time; they were rolling the dice, hoping that sex might make some difference in the direction they wanted. It didn't work out, but the fact that both children were consistently bright suggested to them that the fortuitous combination of genes that Ender's parents provided might well lead to good results in a third child; so a third child was authorized.

Again, it was a gamble. Not eugenics at all, but crossed fingers on the part of those charged with, as they believed, saving the world. For all we know, they tried the same thing dozens of other times, with no good results. But at this point, knowing that their invasion fleet was soon to arrive, they had no choice but to try anything. And this time, by chance, the third child was the commander they wanted. I wrote about this particular event, where the gamble paid off, because my story was about this particular child; the story about a third child who didn't work out would be another book entirely. Ender's superiority in one particular area of human endeavor was not the result of eugenics, it was the result of normal genetic variation in the different members of a species.

This is hardly Hitler's "racial theory" model in action. Indeed, the fact that the battle school has children of every race, nation, and religion is designed to show that genius of this sort was possible everywhere; in the case of the child-commander nicknamed, for racial reasons, "Rose the Nose," the racial assumptions that people have about him, based on the notion that Israelis are somehow "natural" military leaders, are clearly shown to be false.

And far from denying the power of environment, as Radford claims, I do the opposite with the character of Bonzo Madrid, whose upbringing clearly creates the moral system that at once makes him Ender's enemy and gives Ender the ability to destroy him. It is not his Spanish heredity that does this, but rather his Spanish view of manliness, obviously a learned rather than inborn trait.

In fact, the whole battle school process is *educational,* and everything they do to Ender in it is designed to manipulate him into becoming the finely honed command machine that they want. They obviously believe that nature and nurture (or malnurture, in this case) must be combined to create the leader they are looking for.

I can't even guess where Radford gets the idea that "talent" as a xenobiologist or whatever is passed from parent to child in *Speaker*. Rather, this is a society where children are encouraged but not required to follow their parents' occupations—like most societies in human history. Pipo's and Novinha's families tend to get involved in xenobiology because the piggies and other alien lifeforms are their family obsession—they grow up focused on these subjects, which are entirely ignored by the rest of the community. This is not heredity, it's environment. Radford's claim that it is genetic is the product of her own imagination. I find absurd the idea of *interests* being inherited, though I do believe some general abilities may be inherited.

Radford discredits herself entirely when she ridicules Novinha's statement, "But you can't understand the piggies just by watching the way they *behave*! They came out of a different evolution! You have to understand their genes, what's going on inside their cells!" Obviously, Radford has decided the undecidable—that genetics is irrelevant in determining species behavior patterns. While I certainly agree that the specific decisions of human beings are probably not rooted solely in their genes, only someone deliberately ignorant or disdainful of genetics would hold it to be categorically impossible for larger behavior patterns of a species to have some genetic ingredient, or to be driven by a genetic imperative.

At no point in *Speaker* does anyone claim that understanding genes is *all* that is required to understand behavior; merely that in studying an alien species, complete understanding is impossible without also understanding evolution. That is already true of human behavior, as anyone but B. F. Skinner would affirm. And since, in the 3,000-years-from-now future of *Speaker for the Dead,* the science of genetics is far, far advanced in method from our elementary understanding today, one would think Radford would grant me the basic premise of all science fiction: that future science may discover things that are not known today; that, in fact, are believed false today. It was Radford, not I, who actually wrote a story in which radiation from a TV set caused a viable dinosaur-like mutant to be born. I was willing to grant her that ridiculous premise in order to receive the overall story she wanted to tell; she of all people should know that science fiction would get nowhere without reliance on ideas not now believed to be true, or technology not now possible.

Feminism

It is toward the end of her article that Radford reveals what I suspect is the real foundation for her loathing of both books. She is a radical feminist, who has swallowed the phony idea that all behavioral differences between males and females of the human species are learned; that there is no female predisposition toward behaviors different from that of males.

This idea enjoyed great political currency in the seventies, and there are many people who believe it today. There are people who believe all sorts of silly things. But it would truly be astonishing if the human species were the only advanced organism in which evolutionary rather than environmental pressure did not make at least some behavioral differentiation between males and females.

The idea of general differences between males and females is presented early in *Ender's Game,* and may well have made her angry enough to lead to her blind misreading of the rest of the book. No book can survive a hostile reading; the very confusion and baselessness of her other attacks on my books suggests that this, the only one of her attacks that has some basis in the text, may well be the root of her hostility.

The ironic thing about this is that if it came down to voting on public policy concerning differences between the sexes, Radford and I would probably vote almost identically. In no way do I believe that just because biology pushes us toward certain behaviors, we should enthrone such differences in law. After all, biology gives us a predisposition toward violence against rivals, a behavior pattern we devote much of our legal efforts toward punishing or preventing; biology also gives us a predisposition toward acquiring as large a "territory" as possible, yet I regret our legal system's obsession with protecting private property, often at the expense of the public good. Likewise, laws that made women chattel and second-class citizens (if citizens at all!) were and are reprehensible, and I have spoken and voted for equal opportunity and treatment under the law regardless of sex. I also believe that at least some androgyny is required in a whole, healthy human being, and that any society that oppresses one group to benefit another is sick.

Yet only the most thickheaded political feminist could deny the *possibility* of the sociobiological hypothesis that human females are genetically predisposed (but not rigidly forced) toward a monogamous strategy of reproduction, high on nurture and low on adventure, while human males are genetically predisposed toward a polygamous strategy of reproduction, broadcasting seed with all possible vigor while eliminating competing males. This doesn't mean I approve of this difference—I'm a committed monogamist myself—but it does mean I have some justification in having future scientist in my fiction take such general tendencies in human behavior into account. Unfortunately, some feminists resist any ideas contrary to their claim that there is no genetic difference between men and women with exactly the same vigor and degree of rationality as fundamentalists who resist any deviation from the book of Genesis or Marxists who decry any need for correction or revision of Marx's theories. It has nothing to do with evidence, and everything to do with faith.

Even so, beyond that assertion of moderate genetic difference, one can hardly claim that either book has anti-female views unless one is determined to find them even where they do not exist. For instance, while there are fewer females than males in the battle school in *Ender's Game,* the one commander Ender relies on most and drives hardest, and one of his most loyal friends, is the girl Petra. The society in which she moves (the battleschool) is not egalitarian, but the author's point of view here—and Ender's—is certainly *not* sexist.

Ender may conceive of his sister Valentine as a perfect on-a-pedestal female icon, but the passages from Valentine's point of view should make it plain that the author has no such image of Valentine or any other woman, and in fact the author obviously has great sympathy with Valentine's successful effort to escape the domination of her older brother Peter.

Contrary to Radford's assertion, Jane's obsession with Ender is not because she is a "female" and he is a "male," but because her particular genesis was in Ender's fantasy game; she was born seeing the world through his eyes and with moral vision. She conceived herself to be female because of Ender's powerful reliance on his memory of Valentine as an Artemis-figure (the Huntress, Mary, the Virgin Queen—not Aphrodite). Jane herself was not a generalization of females, she was a particular new life-form that Ender, in part, created, and which reflects back to him the person that he most needs this new life-form to be.

Radford's misreading is most pernicious when it comes to Novinha. At no point does Ender or anyone else say or imply or think that she *invited* or *deserved* Marcão's ill-treatment of her. But the fact remains that, like many abused wives, she remained in her poisonous marriage even though escape from it would have been relatively easy. Many psychologists who work with abused wives have commented at length on the fact that some women repeatedly return to their abusing husbands, even when safe avenues of escape are available. I didn't invent this—it's an observable fact of life—and Novinha's reason (a secret sense of shame and guilt) is one of the most-cited reasons for such behavior. Far from saying something awful about women, Novinha simply reflects observed reality in the 1980's—hardly one of the most daring or controversial ideas in the book. For Radford to find it so is almost willfully silly.

The strong marriage laws that require full access of both partners to each others' files are not anti-female—Novinha would have just as full access to Libo's, if they married. Radford may not like such lack of privacy in marriage, but then the book never implies that I approve of it, either, merely that it is the way of life and law in this particular future.

In this future society I describe, women have equal access to all positions of public authority—the mayor of the colony is a woman, as are many other influential office-holders, and no big deal is made about that fact. The Catholic Church is shown retaining its current male-only hierarchy, which Radford must certainly admit is the most likely future, if the Catholic Church survives at all; yet the strange new monastic order I created, the Children of the Mind of Christ, is absolutely egalitarian in its treatment of the sexes, even if its treatment of sex itself is, in my view at least, perverse.

In short, you have to ignore most of the male-female relationships in these books in order to detect an authorial anti-female bias. Radford, like many others devoted to political causes, is so obsessed that she finds male chauvinism where McCarthy found Communists—under every bed, behind every bush, and in every work of art she doesn't understand.

Winding Up

Most of Radford's other comments fall into the category of assuming the future I depict is the future I approve of, and then getting mad at me for it. The fact that some (not all) colonies are granted under specific religious licenses seems to bother her; but throughout history one of the impulses that drives people to leave familiar surroundings to settle new lands is a desire to band together in a community that has similar beliefs—the American Puritans and Quakers, for instance. There are other impulses, of course—desire for wealth or new identity; pressure from another migrating group; a conquest-oriented system of ethics; utopian vision, to name just a few. But given the great expense and danger involved in interstellar colonization in the future, I thought it plausible to look toward the past to find the motivations that would impel people outward, crossing space the way our forebears crossed oceans. Even so, I made it plain that there were laws enforcing religious toleration.

Radford is entitled to her misreading of my book. She is even entitled to believe that she has discovered my "hidden agenda." She can even believe that I'm not even aware of my own unconscious motivations—after all, psychoanalysis of the author, being itself a creative art, is a prime tool of the incompetent critic. I only wish that she would answer what she hates about my books the way Joe Haldeman answered, or seemed to answer, attitudes he disliked in *Starship Troopers*—by writing his own book, *The Forever War*, a masterpiece in its own right, which stands as a permanent alternative-cum-refutation to *Starship Troopers*. Let Radford answer novel with novel, story with story.

But her kind of malicious review, with its veiled and open attacks on my character and her unjustified assumptions about my motives, has no place in serious critical discussion. What she has done is the most transparent kind of guilt-by-association, trying to link me with ideas and systems that I (and most other people) abhor, even though the book clearly and specifically takes exactly the moral position she pretends to uphold. There is no justification whatever in the text of *Ender's Game* or *Speaker for the Dead* for calling me a fascist, a racist, a genocide, or a sexist; on the contrary, in both books I spoke as eloquently and powerfully as I could in favor of compassion and empathy, and against all four tendencies that she accuses me of. To attack fascism, racism, genocide, and sexism is the duty of all good people—but it is also the duty of good people to correctly identify the fascists, racists, genocides, and sexists before vilifying them. There may well be valid grounds for critics to declare my work to be inferior art; but there is no justification at all for Radford's attack on me as a human being.

The most frustrating thing about this whole painful process is that by allowing her to set the agenda for this dialogue, I have used up all these pages without barely touching on the *main* ideas and moral values put forth in these two stories of mine. What a profound waste of everybody's time.

Her sneering final remark about my "privileged position as a white male American Christian" makes her precisely what she falsely claims I am—someone who assumes that because someone seems to be a member of a group of people who are "different" from her, he is identical with all the other members of the group, and can be discussed or attacked on the basis of that membership.

How can Radford know that I have never been part of a persecuted minority, that I have never been a victim of the cruelty of a privileged elite?

How dare she assume that I have not had some source of suffering in my life that might well entitle me to ask forgiveness for someone whom the world despises?

How dare she assume that those who liked *Ender's Game* and *Speaker for the Dead* liked it because of their love of a fascism that only she has ever detected in the book?

Couldn't their liking for the book as easily be because they have at some time in their lives felt the isolation, the helplessness, the terrible guilt that Ender felt in *Ender's Game;* felt a need for the compassionate understanding that Ender brings to people in *Speaker for the Dead?*

I hope that is what most readers have found in these novels, because that is what I tried to put in them. And if someone finds hate or persecution or the glorification of evil in these stories, I can only answer, in the end, that I don't believe I put those things there, and if you found them, it is because the desire to find them was in your heart before you ever read my book. (pp. 13-14, 49-52)

Orson Scott Card, "Response," in Fantasy Review, *Vol. 10, No. 5, June, 1987, pp. 13-14, 49-52.*

Rita Dove
Thomas and Beulah

Pulitzer Prize: Poetry

American poet and short story writer.

Thomas and Beulah (1986) has strengthened Dove's reputation as a leading lyric poet of her generation. Dove's previous collections, *The Yellow House on the Corner* (1980) and *Museum* (1983), won praise from reviewers for their technical excellence and unusual breadth of subject matter. Critics observe that unlike many poets of the 1980s, who tend to concentrate on their own perceptions and emotions, Dove adopts an objective viewpoint, and that, while she often writes about herself and her family, she also imbues her work with an awareness of history and social issues. In *Thomas and Beulah*, Dove once again demonstrates her ability to combine the personal and historical. This interconnected set of poems commemorates the lives of Dove's grandparents and offers a general chronicle of the collective experience of black Americans during the twentieth century.

Dove explained how this work came about: "*Thomas and Beulah* is based very loosely on my grandparents' lives. My grandmother had told me a story that had happened to my grandfather when he was young, coming up on a riverboat to Akron, Ohio, my hometown. But that was all I had, basically. And the story so fascinated me that I tried to write about it. I started off writing stories about my grandfather, and soon, because I ran out of real facts, in order to keep going, I made up facts for this character, Thomas. Then this poem 'Dusting' appeared, really out of nowhere. I didn't realize that this was Thomas' wife saying, 'I want to talk. And you can't do his side without doing my side.'. . . . So *Thomas and Beulah* became actually two sides of the same story."

The resulting work is a series of short lyric poems, divided into two sections. "Mandolin," the opening sequence of poems, is written from the viewpoint of Thomas, a former musician haunted since his youth by the death of a friend. "Canary in Bloom," the other sequence, portrays the placid domestic existence of Thomas' wife Beulah from childhood to marriage and widowhood. Through allusions to events outside the lives of Thomas and Beulah, including the Great Depression, the black migration from the rural South to the industrial North, the civil rights marches of the 1960s, and the assassination of President John F. Kennedy, and by concluding with a chronology of major events in the lives of the characters, Dove emphasizes the couple's interconnectedness with history. Dove remarked: "I'm always fascinated with seeing a story from different angles, but also, in the two sequences, I'm not interested in the big moments. . . . I was interested in the thoughts, the things which were concerning these small people, these nobodies in the course of history."

In their reviews of *Thomas and Beulah*, critics observe that although the poem sequence has no conventional plot, Dove succeeds admirably in telling her story through imagery and character development. They praise the dramatic quality of the understated yet revealing vignettes that portray the life stories

Photograph by Fred Viebahn. Courtesy of Rita Dove.

of Thomas and Beulah. Finally, they extol Dove's use of language, calling it richly lyrical, colloquial yet musical.

(See also *Contemporary Authors*, Vol. 109.)

ROBERT McDOWELL

[McDowell, an American poet, essayist, and editor, is coeditor of The Reaper, *newsletter of the American Baptist Theological Seminary. In the following excerpt, he hails Dove as a revitalizing force in contemporary poetry.]*

Rita Dove has always possessed a storyteller's instinct. In *The Yellow House on the Corner* (1980), *Museum* (1983), and the forthcoming *Thomas and Beulah,* this instinct has found expression in a synthesis of striking imagery, myth, magic, fable, wit, humor, political comment, and a sure knowledge of history. Many contemporaries share Dove's mastery of some of these, but few succeed in bringing them together to create a point of view that, by its breadth and force, stands apart. She has not worked her way into this enviable position among poets without fierce commitment.

Passing through a graduate writing program (Iowa) in the mid-seventies, Dove and her peers were schooled in the importance of sensation and its representation through manipulation of The Image. The standard lesson plan, devised to reflect the ascendancy of Wallace Stevens and a corrupt revision of T. S. Eliot's objective correlative, instructed young writers to renounce realistic depiction and offer it up to the province of prose; it promoted subjectivity and imagination-as-image; it has strangled a generation of poems.

How and why this came to pass is less important, really, than admitting that it is so. Literary magazines are gorged with poems devoid of shapeliness and scope. Imagistic, cramped and confessional, they exist for the predictably surprising, climactic phrase. An historically conscious reader, aware of literary tradition, might understandably perceive an enormous cultural amnesia as the dubiously distinguishing feature of such poems. Such a reader will rue the fact that the writing and interpretation of poetry has diminished to a trivial pursuit, a pronouncement of personal instinct. If this is the dominant direction of a discouraging Moment, then Rita Dove distinguishes herself by resolutely heading the other way.

Unlike the dissembling spirit indicted above, Dove is an assembler who gathers the various facts of this life and presents them in ways that jar our lazy assumptions. She gives voice to many positions and many characters. Like the speaker/writer of classic argumentation, she shows again and again that she understands the opposing sides of conflicts she deals with. She tells all sides of the story. Consider the titles of her books, their symbolic weight. The personal turning point *House on the Corner* evolves, becoming the public Museum (symbol of preserved chronology); that, in turn, gives way to the names of two characters whose lives combine and illustrate the implicit meanings of the personal House and the public Museum. . . . (p. 61)

"These poems tell two sides of a story and are meant to be read in sequence." So begins *Thomas and Beulah*. Their story is told twice: from Thomas's point of view in the twenty-three poems of "**Mandolin**," and from Beulah's point of view in the twenty-one poems of "**Canary in Bloom**." The time, according to an extensive Chronology at book's end, covers the years 1919-1968. Most of the story takes place in Akron, Ohio, a city, which the Chronology also tells us, had a Negro population of 11,000 (out of a total population of 243,000) in 1940.

The chief narrative method employed, the story twice-told, does not rely so much on action; it relies on reactions of characters to events and circumstances that affect them even though they are wholly beyond them. The questions generated by this approach are chilling and clear: if two characters, deeply involved with one another, interpret events (inner and outer, private and public) so differently, what does this suggest about our manipulation of history; what does it say about our reliability as witnesses, as teachers of successive generations; what is true?

Truth in *Thomas and Beulah* is found in the characters themselves. In "**The Event**," the first poem in the section entitled "**Mandolin**," Thomas leaves Tennessee for the riverboat life. He travels with a good friend, Lem, and a magical symbol, a talisman which gathers pain and wards it off—his mandolin.

In a turn that explodes the deliberate echo of Mark Twain's *Huck Finn*, Lem dives overboard to collect chestnuts on a passing island and drowns. This tragedy, at the outset of his journey, will haunt Thomas for the rest of his life. We observe his arrival in Akron in 1921, deftly and desperately playing his mandolin for pay. He is a driven figure, confronting his guilt and his second-class citizenship in a racially divided country. His half-hearted attempts to sell himself in such a country will drive the more sheltered Beulah to find fault in him. It is a key element of his tragedy that he faults himself for it, too. . . . (p. 67)

After their marriage, the promise of equality and upward mobility is profoundly betrayed. The world is threatening, malicious after all. In "**Nothing Down**," they buy a new car for a trip to Tennessee, but the symbol and the dream it represents are destroyed when they're passed by a carload of jeering whites; in "**The Zeppelin Factory**," Thomas lands construction work, laboring on the largest building in the world without interior supports (another appropriate, unforgettable symbol for the world we make) and hates it; Thomas ponders the impending birth of a third daughter against the backdrop of union violence ("**Under the Viaduct**"); Thomas walks out of a movie house to witness a splendid natural phenomenon ("**Aurora Borealis**"), but even this double barreled symbolic magic is overpowered by the grim facts of the world around him. Finally, he finds even his oldest companion, his mandolin, estranged. . . . (p. 68)

Only in his own good heart is Thomas vindicated, and the physical manifestation of his goodness is his family. In "**Roast Opossum**," he spins two tales for his grandchildren: hunting opposum for Malcolm, a tale of horses for the girls. This tender poem makes a case for salvation implicit in one generation's nurturing another by gathering and making palpable history and myth, fact and fiction. In such ritual we discover our one defense against the inhuman things we do to one another.

The section concludes with three elegiac poems covering the events of Thomas's declining health and eventual death. "**The Stroke**" contains a lovely memory of Beulah during pregnancy and his certainty that the pain he feels is Lem knocking on his chest. In the end, Thomas appropriately suffers his final heart attack behind the wheel of his car ("**Thomas at the Wheel**").

Whereas Thomas's life is a perpetual scramble toward definition, Beulah's, as presented in "**Canary in Bloom**," is preordained. She will marry; she will bear children. These restrictions force her to develop an inward, private life. For example, her fear and distrust of male figures is established early in "**Taking in Wash**." Her father comes home drunk:

> Tonight
>
> every light hums, the kitchen arctic
> with sheets, Papa is making the hankies
> sail. Her foot upon a silk
> stitched rose, she waits
> until he turns, his smile sliding all over.

This is the seed of her reaction to her suitor and future husband. She would prefer a pianola to his mandolin; she hates his yellow scarf. When they marry, "rice drumming / the both of them blind," she sees Thomas as "a hulk, awkward in blue serge." Her father places her fingertips in Thomas's hand, and men in collusion have delivered her up to her fate.

From this point on, Beulah's story seeks the form, the shape, of meditation. In "**Dusting**" she fondly remembers a boy at a fair, comparing that magical location and meeting with the hard news of her life. In **"Weathering Out"** she daydreams through her seventh month of pregnancy, glad to be rid of Thomas as he daily hunts for work. In the sad **"Daystar"** she reclines in the backyard while the children nap and dreams of a place where she is nothing. In **"The Great Palace of Versailles"** she works in a dress shop, frequents the library, and temporarily loses the facts of her own life in the magic of lords and ladies.

Beulah's development of a rich inner life is the result of meditation with an outward eye. Throughout her long battle with the prescribed role she was born to play, she continues to cope admirably and compassionately with the world outside. She manages her family; she feeds transients during the Depression; she shows kindness to the daughter of a prejudiced neighbor. As the poems progress her wisdom deepens. Her attitude toward Thomas softens, too. . . . If she does not change her life, Beulah through wisdom comes to understand it. She also comprehends the lives of her daughters. At their husbands' company picnic—a segregated picnic—Beulah remembers the march on Washington and its effects on the lives of her children. Her meditative impulse blossoms. Her preferred inner life squares off against the world of iniquity, and the succeeding generation is better off for it.

When I consider the discouraging Moment I mentioned at the beginning of this article, when I despair of it, I turn to only a few poets of my generation and am revitalized. Rita Dove's development through three volumes reminds us of the necessity for scope in poetry. A wide range of talent in service to an assembling vision is the tonic we need for discouragement. (pp. 68-70)

Robert McDowell, "The Assembling Vision of Rita Dove," in Callaloo, Vol. 9, No. 1, Winter, 1986, pp. 61-70.

PETER STITT

The locus of *Thomas and Beulah,* Rita Dove's third book of poems, is . . . the author's own sense of family. The characters named in the title were Dove's maternal grandparents: Beulah was born in Georgia in 1904 and emigrated with her parents to Akron, Ohio, in 1906, and Thomas was born in Tennessee in 1900 and made his own way to Akron in 1921. The two were married in 1924 and eventually raised four daughters. The first part of Dove's book is devoted to the story of Thomas and the second to that of Beulah. The very absence of high drama may be what makes the poems so touching—these are ordinary people with ordinary struggles, successes, and failures.

The poems are occasional; in the absence of a definite plot, Dove gives them continuity by reference to a recurring motif throughout each section—to someone or some thing that was important in the early life of that character. In the case of Beulah, this role is played by the powerful personality of her father, who was part Cherokee. For Thomas, the recurrent motif is the death of his friend Lem, with whom he left Tennessee to embark upon the riverboat life. . . . The materials of these poems are essentially factual—family history. Dove manages to assert herself and achieve control through, among other things, narrative understatement; as Hemingway once said, what you don't say is even more important than what you do say. (pp. 1031-32)

Because of the brooding presence of Lem's death, the poems in Thomas' section have more emotional resonance than those in Beulah's. One also has the feeling that Rita Dove knew Thomas better, despite the greater kinship one might expect between the two women. The reason for this emerges in a poem called **"Roast Possum,"** where we see Thomas telling stories, "A granddaughter / propped on each knee." In interviews, Robert Penn Warren has attributed his narrative ability to the fact that he spent his summers as a child listening to his Grandfather Penn tell stories. Apparently, a similar situation prevailed in the early life of Rita Dove. In any case, there is a powerful sense of community, residing both in a family and in a place, lying at the heart of this book, and it is this that provides a locus to the poems. Rita Dove has taken a significant step forward in each of her three books of poems; she must be recognized as among the best young poets in the country today. (p. 1033)

Peter Stitt, "Coherence through Place in Contemporary American Poetry," in The Georgia Review, Vol. XL, No. 4, Winter, 1986, pp. 1021-33.

HELEN VENDLER

[Vendler is an American critic specializing in modern poets. Her works include On Extended Wings: Wallace Stevens' Longer Poems *(1969),* Part of Nature, Part of Us: Modern American Poets *(1981), and* Wallace Stevens *(1986). In the following excerpt, Vendler commends* Thomas and Beulah *for its dramatic power.]*

Thomas (born in 1900 in Wartrace, Tennessee) and Beulah (born in 1904 in Rockmart, Georgia) are husband and wife; they are modeled, one guesses, on Rita Dove's grandparents (the cover photo [of *Thomas and Beulah*], a snapshot of a middle-aged black couple standing in front of their car, is credited to Ray A. Dove and dated 1952, the year of Rita Dove's birth). Though the photograph, and the chronology of the lives of Thomas and Beulah appended to the sequence, might lead one to suspect that Dove is a poet of simple realism, this is far from the case. Dove has learned (perhaps from Charles Wright's "Tattoos") how to make a biographical fact the buried base of an imagined edifice. But unlike Wright, who writes meditations almost Chinese in their stillness, Dove is principally a poet of dramatic force—a quality found relatively rarely in lyric, a genre by its nature reflective, circling, and static.

Before I come to Dove's management of dramatic power, I should sketch the story behind the sequence. When Thomas and Beulah marry, he is twenty-four, she twenty. Thomas has already lost his best friend, who, after a drunken dare from Thomas, drowned in the Mississippi leaving only his mandolin behind. Thomas carries the mandolin north with him to Akron, plays it halfheartedly, and eventually hangs it from a nail on the parlor wall. Thomas works in Akron for Goodyear, at the Zeppelin factory; after the Depression puts him out of work, he sweeps offices part time. Over the years, he and Beulah have four daughters. Thomas becomes domesticated enough to sing in the church choir. When the war comes, he works again for Goodyear; Beulah works in a dress shop, then makes hats. At sixty-three, Thomas dies of his second heart attack; Beulah dies six years later, at sixty-five. Their lives span the first sixty-nine years of this century; they represent, among other things, the migration of rural southern blacks to the industrial cities of the north. This great social movement—one of the most important for American history in the twentieth century—

finds here its first extended poem. But the sequence of poems is also the history of a marriage.

Dove's epigraph reads, "These poems tell two sides of a story and are meant to be read in sequence." We have Thomas's side ("**Mandolin**," twenty-three poems) and Beulah's side ("**Canary in Bloom**," twenty-one poems): together they make up Thomas and Beulah's story. The poems comprise a true sequence: that is, most are richer for, and in fact only intelligible in, the context of the rest. The first poem of "**Mandolin**" is called, simply, "**The Event**": in it we see Thomas and Lem, Lem's drowning, and the mute mandolin left behind. I came across this poem a few years ago in *The Ontario Review;* it was the first poem I had ever read by Dove, and it sent me out looking for her first two books, *The Yellow House on the Corner* and *Museum;* I was not disappointed. . . . When I first read ["**The Event**"] and some of its companions from "**Mandolin**," I experienced the best of all poetic delights—feeling that something was very beautiful and not knowing why. New forms of beauty declare themselves only gradually. It seems to me now that a rapid succession of dramatic "takes" is Dove's perfected form; she almost always refuses editorializing, musing, and "leading" the reader. Her brilliance lies in her arrangement of content; as the elements of meaning find their one inevitable form, juxtaposition alone takes on the work of explanation. (p. 50)

For the Depression year of 1934, when Thomas is unemployed, Dove finds a poetry of what could be called the disarticulated. When the work that holds a day together is gone, the day falls apart into its separate scraps. Dove updates 1934 unemployment with images from contemporary unemployment. Thomas doesn't even have a coal furnace to occupy himself with; the house has a gas heater. It is hard to stay indoors idle. He won't drink (because drink caused the death of his friend), but drink is the temptation of the unemployed. So is infidelity. Dove doesn't say any of this outright, but it is all deducible from her elegant shorthand. . . .

Detail has drama in Dove. The Beulah poems have their own details—a dustcloth, stained wallpaper, hats. The domestic confinement offers less to Dove's imagination than the more varied life in the Thomas poems, but the closing picture of Beulah's deathbed as the sun enters the room is one that haunts the mind. Stevens said in his elegy for Santayana that it is poverty's speech that seeks us out the most, and "the afflatus of ruin," as Stevens called it, is present in Dove's elegy for Beulah. The poem is called "**The Oriental Ballerina**," after the small figurine of a Chinese ballerina that dances on Beulah's jewel box. Dove's principle of composition here is a cinematic crosscutting between the exotic claim on Beulah of the beautiful (expressed in clothes, hats, jewel boxes, idealized female grace in the paltry ballerina) and the poverty of her death. (p. 51)

Thomas and Beulah manages to keep intact the intensity of the drama and inexplicability of life and marriage. The mutual criticism of Dove's Akron couple, their enterprise and defeat, while specified to a degree that is satisfying as fiction, will remind readers of analogous episodes in the years 1900-1969 undergone by their own parents or grandparents. Dove does not suggest that black experience is identical with white experience, but neither does she suggest that it is always different. Beulah's experience of motherhood—her terror of doing it wrong, the exhaustion of having no privacy, her irritation at the grown girls—is universal. But Beulah's anger when her daughters take her to the Goodyear company picnic after Thomas's death will be personally familiar only to black readers:

> Now this *act of mercy:* four daughters
> dragging her to their husbands' company picnic,
> white families on one side and them
> on the other, unpacking the same
> squeeze bottles of Heinz, the same
> waxy beef patties and Salem potato chip bags.

Over the segregated picnickers floats the Goodyear company symbol—"a white foot / sprouting two small wings." Beulah's interior monologue, here as elsewhere, has the naturalness and accuracy of art concealing art. Dove has planed away unnecessary matter: pure shapes, her poems exhibit the thrift that Yeats called the sign of a perfected manner. (pp. 51-2)

> Helen Vendler, *"In the Zoo of the New," in* The New York Review of Books, *Vol. XXXIII, No. 16, October 23, 1986, pp. 47-52.*

EMILY GROSHOLZ

[Grosholz, an American poet, is the author of The River Painter *(1984). In the following excerpt, she praises Dove's striking poetic language and character portrayal in* Thomas and Beulah.*]*

[Rita Dove] understands the long-term intricacies of marriage, as the protagonists of her wonderful chronicle *Thomas and Beulah* testify. In her wise and affectionate portrait of two people whose lives interweave because of marriage, Dove emphasizes their separateness by arranging the book in two halves, Thomas' story (vignettes from about 1920 to his death in 1963) followed by Beulah's in similar sequence. The ordering reveals how differently each perceived their union and the lifelines leading up to and away from it, and doesn't gloss over hostilities and disaffection. For all that, the couple's devotion is clear and each is in the other's final thoughts.

But *Thomas and Beulah* is arresting not only as a study of character, but for the brilliance of Dove's style, which has the same pitch and inventiveness as that of Gjertrud Schnackenberg and Alice Fulton. (Of course, for that very reason their work is otherwise quite dissimilar.) Dove can turn her poetic sights on just about anything and make the language shimmer. (pp. 160-61)

History in *Thomas and Beulah* is subordinated to the demands of biography and lyric, but it is present by innuendo in many of the poems, and explicitly in the chronology supplied at the end of the book. Northward migrations of black workers between the wars, breadlines and hobos during the Depression, strikes and union organizers, the civil rights movement, the March on Washington, "a crow's wing mov(ing) slowly through / the white streets of government," form the background of her story. The history of black politics and the church in this country cannot be disentangled; the poem "**Gospel**" begins: "*Swing low so I / can step inside—* / a humming ship of voices / big with all / the wrongs done / done them. / No sound this generous / could fail: / ride joy until / it cracks like an egg, / make sorrow / seethe and whisper." The drift of these lives is celebratory; despite plenty of hard times, nothing is ruined and most of the loss is redeemed, expunged and sweetened. "Yet how healthy / the single contralto / settling deeper / into her watery furs! / *Carry me home,* / she cajoles, bearing / down. Candalabras brim . . ." ("**Gospel**"). Dove's optical, tactile music makes a present harmony out of the future and the past. (pp. 161-62)

> Emily Grosholz, *"Marriages and Partings," in* The Hudson Review, *Vol. XL, No. 1, Spring, 1987, pp. 157-64.*

An Excerpt from *Thomas and Beulah*

Weathering Out

She liked mornings the best—Thomas gone
to look for work, her coffee flushed with milk,

outside autumn trees blowsy and dripping.
Past the seventh month she couldn't see her feet

so she floated from room to room, houseshoes flapping,
navigating corners in wonder. When she leaned

against a door jamb to yawn, she disappeared entirely.

Last week they had taken a bus at dawn
to the new airdock. The hangar slid open in segments

and the zeppelin nosed forward in its silver envelope.
The man walked it out gingerly, like a poodle,

then tied it to a mast and went back inside.
Beulah felt just that large and placid, a lake;

she glistened from cocoa butter smoothed in
when Thomas returned every evening nearly

in tears. He'd lean an ear on her belly
and say: *Little fellow's really talking,*

though to her it was more the *pok-pok-pok*
of a fingernail tapping a thick cream lampshade.

Sometimes during the night she woke and found him
asleep there and the child sleeping, too.

The coffee was good but too little. Outside
everything shivered in tinfoil—only the clover

between the cobblestones hung stubbornly on,
green as an afterthought. . . .

LISA M. STEINMAN

[*Steinman, an American poet and scholar specializing in modern
American and British poetry, is the author of the collection* Lost
Poems *(1976). In the following excerpt, Steinman comments on
Dove's ability to achieve deep resonance in her work through the
repetition of key images and phrases.*]

[*Thomas and Beulah*] engages history, in this case, personal
history. . . . *Thomas and Beulah* refers obliquely to twentieth-
century American history, but from the family album snapshot
on the cover through the appended "Chronology" (first item:
"1900: Thomas born in Wartrace, Tennessee"), we read this
book as a family chronicle. However, the poems themselves
are not about an individual's *relationship* to her history, nor
about the weight of history. They are, more, history allowed
to speak for itself. The title page tells us that the "poems tell
two sides of a story and are meant to be read in sequence."
The history contained in *Thomas and Beulah*, indeed, is found
in the unfolding story—or juxtaposed stories—told of the youth,
marriage, lives and deaths of two people. We even forget that
the poems are historical, in part because they mix past and
present tense, in part because of the frequent use of the past
and present progressive, and in part because of the vividness
of the characters revealed. (p. 433)

[There] is no editorializing, and no morals are drawn; the lives
stand only for themselves, although through image and sound—
one could say through the poetry—the reported lives are enriched and given meanings articulated more fully than they
could be by the people described. For example, "Straw Hat"
describes Thomas, who at age twenty-one arrives in Akron
from Tennessee after a few years on riverboats where he sang
to his friend Lem's mandolin playing. "Straw Hat" reads:
"He used to sleep like a glass of water / held up in the hand
of a very young girl." The language is simple, but the image
and alliteration capture the sense of a now-gone childhood and,
by contrast, the water in which Lem drowned. The image of
the girl also leads the reader into Thomas's courtship of Beulah
in the next poem, "Courtship," where:

> King of the Crawfish
> in his yellow scarf
> mandolin belly pressed tight
> to his hounds-tooth vest—
>
>   . . . .
>
> [Thomas] wraps the yellow
> silk
> still warm from his throat
> around her shoulders. (He
> made
> good money; he could buy
> another.)
> A gnat flies
> in his eye and she thinks
> he's crying.

Given such apparently sparse language, a surprising amount is
said. Thomas's youthful cockiness is captured (in the phrase,
"King of the Crawfish," as much as in the description of his
clothes). We are also given Thomas's point of view; the par-
enthetical aside seems almost his stage whisper, telling us that
the scarf is more a sign of his well-being than of love; the same
is suggested when we see he is willing to use a chance encounter
with a gnat to his advantage. At the same time, though, the
fact that the scarf is "still warm from his throat" comments
on more than Thomas's ability to talk a good line; it suggests
he *is* sharing something of himself, as well.

"Courtship" gains in meaning from the gathering sense of
Thomas's character in the first half of the book, and it also
resonates with the poem, "Courtship, Diligence," in the last
(Beulah's) half of their volume. "Courtship, Diligence," opens:
"A yellow scarf runs through his fingers / as if it were melt-
ing." We think of the phrase, "butter wouldn't melt in his
mouth," and also of how, from Beulah's perspective, Thomas's feeling he has money (and scarfs) to throw away seems
more like mismanagement, or emotional miscalculation, than
financial success. . . . Helen Vendler has suggested that Dove
offers us a poetry of "the disarticulated," of those whose lives,
and therefore histories, are fragmented [see excerpt above]. . . .
It is worth adding that most of the language in *Thomas and
Beulah* could have been spoken by the people whose story is
told, which is to say that the poems do not seem to impose on
their subjects. Rather, they slowly build a context for the objects, images, and scraps of reported speech and song that
appear and keep reappearing. This is an impressive achievement, although it also means that the poems have more power
taken together than individually. To give one more example:
when Thomas watches the "shy angle of his daughter's head,"
sees his son-in-law swallow, and feels for the first time "like /
calling him *Son*" ("Variations on Gaining a Son"), attentive
readers confronted only with this poem will recognize the oblique

reference to fishing and to the commonplace, "hooking a man." But it is only in the context of the other poems about Thomas, about his own marriage, about his more literal fishing trips (in **"Lightnin' Blues"** and **"One Volume Missing"**), and about his desire for a son that these lines have their full impact. This is, of course, an appropriate way to reimagine and re-present the lives traced in the book, since they are lives not fully examined by those who live them. The marriage of Thomas and Beulah, in particular, is clearly one where communication is tacit, contained precisely in repeated phrases and motions that have gained meaning over the years. The poems re-enact both the accretion of meaning and the taciturnity, perfectly right for this subject, although, given other subjects, one might want more. (pp. 433-35)

Lisa M. Steinman, "Dialogues between History and Dream," in Michigan Quarterly Review, Vol. XXVI, No. 2, Spring, 1987, pp. 428-38.

JOHN SHOPTAW

[In the following excerpt, Shoptaw commends Thomas and Beulah for its tragic, elliptical chronicle of two ordinary lives.]

At the beginning of Rita Dove's arresting new volume of poetry [**Thomas and Beulah**], we are given directions for reading which turn out to be true but impossible to follow: "These poems tell two sides of a story and are meant to be read in sequence." The impossibility is not physical, as in the instructions prefacing John Ashbery's long, double-columned poem Litany, which tell us that the columns "are meant to be read as simultaneous but independent monologues"; rather, the impossibility in reading the two sides of Rita Dove's book—Thomas's side (I. **"Mandolin,"** 23 poems), followed by Beulah's side (II. **"Canary in Bloom,"** 21 poems)—is biographical and historical. The lives of Thomas and Beulah, whether considered together or individually, lack what would integrate them into a single story. The events in **Thomas and Beulah** are narrated in a strict chronological order which is detailed in the appended chronology. The subjection of story time to historical time, unusual in modern narratives, gives Dove's sequence a tragic linearity, a growing sense that what is done cannot be undone and that what is not done but only regretted or deferred cannot be redeemed in the telling. . . .

As a narrative, **Thomas and Beulah** resembles fiction more than a poetic sequence—Faulkner's family chronicles in particular. Dove's modernist narrator stands back, paring fingernails like an unobtrusive master or God. (p. 335)

Any choice of genre involves an economy of gains and losses. Objective, dramatic narration—showing rather than telling— has the advantage of letting the events speak for themselves and the disadvantage of dispensing with the problematics of narrative distortion and a camera-eye or God's-eye view. **Thomas and Beulah** tells it like it is and assumes it is like it tells us.

The most surprising thing about **Thomas and Beulah** is the severance not between narrator and story but between story and story. In **"Wingfoot Lake"** Beulah's in-laws attend a segregated Goodyear picnic: "white families on one side and them / on the other, unpacking the same / squeeze bottles of Heinz, the same / waxy beef patties and Salem potato chip bags." The "two sides of a story" are similarly segregated in Dove's volume, cordoned off by the roman numerals I and II. **Thomas and Beulah** tells no joyous love story, as we might expect, nor a tragedy of love lost. The lives of Thomas and Beulah rarely

intersect: There are few common events in their stories and no Faulknerian climax in which their worlds collide. They rarely think about each other (Beulah's name does not even appear in Thomas's side); and when they do, it is with an absent-minded fondness. Their lives' desires lie elsewhere. The love of Thomas's life is Lem, who dies in the volume's brilliant inaugural poem **"The Event."** The easy-going cadences of the opening stanzas obscure the irony that this is not the honey-mooning couple we expected:

> Ever since they'd left the Tennessee ridge
> with nothing to boast of
> but good looks and a mandolin,
>
> the two Negroes leaning
> on the rail of a riverboat
> were inseparable: Lem plucked
>
> to Thomas' silver falsetto.

On Thomas's drunken dare, Lem dives into the water toward an island mirage, which sinks into the river like Atlantis along with Lem. All Lem leaves Thomas is "a stinking circle of rags, / the half-shell of a mandolin." The commonest images, circles and lines, are the most capable of variation. One of the signs of Dove's poetic power is the changes she rings on that Orphic half-shell, the surviving Aristophanic hemisphere of their round of love. The other half rises to heaven, becoming the blue vault of the sky. A Zeppelin disaster in 1931 merely replays Thomas's own tragedy. In a wonderfully interlaced poem, **"Nothing Down,"** Thomas and Beulah pick out a "sky blue Chandler," while in the alternating italicized stanzas, Thomas combines the memories of a blue flower overhead and a young Lem in a tree into a prophetic, ghostly gesture of forgiveness. But the car, as we learn from the chronology (which adds its own silent ironies to the volume), is repossessed during the Depression. The sense of guilt and loss stemming from Lem's drowning in 1919 drives Thomas for the next half a century to his death. Thomas spends his wedding night playing Lem's mandolin; his disappointment over not having any sons stems from his not making another Lem; the parable of the possum playing dead recalls Lem; even his stroke is Lem's doing:

> he knows it was Lem all along:
> Lem's knuckles tapping his chest in passing,
> Lem's heart, for safekeeping,
> he shores up in his arms.

The closest relative of Thomas's elegiac side of the story turns out to be Tennyson's In Memoriam, in which the poet deals with the death of his friend Arthur Hallem.

The bifurcations and divisions in **Thomas and Beulah** extend to the very grammar of its sentences, which are marked by the frequent appearance of free modifiers and absolute phrases. These constructions, uncommon in modern poetry and fiction (Faulkner, again, uses them more than any other American writer, though less often than Dove), consist of a participial phrase (free modifier) or of a noun and a participial phrase (absolute) which are syntactically separated from the main clause or noun they modify. Both Thomas's sequence ("as the keys swung, ticking") and Beulah's ("the walls exploding with shabby tutus") end on these constructions. A stanza may employ several in a disjunctive series, as in **"Courtship,"** when Thomas asks Beulah's father for her hand:

> Then the parlor festooned
> like a ship and Thomas
> twirling his hat in his hands
> wondering how did I get here.
> China pugs guarding a fringed settee
> where a father, half-Cherokee,

smokes and frowns.
I'll give her a good life—
what was he doing,
selling all for a song?
His heart fluttering shut
then slowly opening.

This pronounced style can tell us much about *Thomas and Beulah*. Since their verbs are subordinated and nominalized, such constructions tend to fragment action into a series of still shots. Although there is persistent imagery of a bomb ticking and finally exploding ("the walls exploding in shabby tutus"), *Thomas and Beulah* is in fact a drama devoid of suspense in which nothing ever happens, or in which **"The Event,"** Lem's drowning, sets the narrative aftermath in motion. There is no Faulknerian passion or war or rape or murder or incest. Like most of us, Thomas and Beulah meet and marry and work and have kids and die without much intention or commotion. The book is realist not in the obvious sense of treating the sordid and grim elements of experience but in the essential sense of privileging ordinary experience over the strange. If the strange was the dark continent of the South, the ordinary is the undiscovered country of the Midwest. (pp. 336-38)

There is no loss in Beulah's side of the story equivalent to the loss of Lem; her side consequently lacks the haunting pathos of Thomas's. Because it is not a relic, Beulah's canary makes insignificant music when compared to Thomas's mandolin. The gap in Beulah's side is not an unrecovered loss but a promise unfulfilled. Beulah misses what she never knew; her never-never mirage island keeps its distance. An absence, however, is inevitably understood or felt as a loss. What we miss we must have had, and all empty names are markers. Dove dramatizes the positing of a loss in place of a fundamental absence in **"Dusting,"** the best poem in the second half of *Thomas and Beulah*. . . . (pp. 338-39)

[There is a] name appearing for the first time in **"Dusting,"** whose face or landscape cannot be remembered because it has not yet been discovered: Beulah. Coined first in *Isaiah* and most famously in *The Pilgrim's Progress*, Beulah names the Promised Land. In Hebrew *Beulah* means "married." As Thomas is separated from Lem, Beulah is divorced from Beulah. Beulah's heart is set on Beulah-Land, which goes by several names. In **"Magic,"** a giant Eiffel Tower appears in the sky as "a sign / she would make it to Paris one day." In **"Pomade,"** a friend's fragrance "always put her / in mind of Turkish minarets against / a sky wrenched blue". . . .

It appears last, and for what it is, in **"The Oriental Ballerina,"** as daylight comes to Beulah's deathbed. Beulah's last moments are accompanied by a mechanical ballerina, a paltry Angel of Death, pirouetting on her jewelbox to "the wheeze of the old / rugged cross" on her radio. Ironic juxtapositions of the exotic and the homely, the beautiful and the vulgar organize the poem. What finally dawns on Beulah is not a Beulah-Land but an unbridgeable nothing which the name has hidden. . . . In **"One Volume Missing"** Thomas buys a used encyclopedia "for five bucks / no zebras, no Virginia, / no wars." And no Zion, as in the "A.M.E. Zion Church" which sold it. *Thomas and Beulah*—with its gaps, divisions, and deletions—comes also as an incomplete set. But that is Dove's bargain. For us to read any of her fragmentary alphabet, the never-never volume which would integrate the Goodyear picnic, Thomas and Lem, Thomas and Beulah, the main clauses and their absolutes, Beulah and Beulah, and the narrator and her stories must remain missing. (pp. 340-41)

*John Shoptaw, in a review of "Thomas and Beulah,"
in* Black American Literature Forum, *Vol. 21, No.
3, Fall, 1987, pp. 335-41.*

Richard Foreman

The Cure
Film Is Evil: Radio Is Good

Obie Award

American dramatist and director.

Richard Foreman is widely regarded as one of America's most important and original avant-garde playwrights. In 1968 he founded his own production company, the Ontological-Hysteric Theater, with the goal of revolutionizing contemporary theater. In the twenty years since, Foreman has seen thirty-one of his plays produced, has directed the work of numerous other playwrights, and has been recognized by five *Village Voice* Obie Awards for his writing, directing, and artistic directorship of his theater company.

Foreman's work is distinctive even in the world of avant-garde theater for the extreme disparity between his written text and the actual experience of a performance. A one-man theater-creator, the writer usually also directs, produces, and designs each of his plays, combining language, music, and intricate stage props to create a unique and elaborate brand of performance art. Eschewing the traditional supports of drama—character, plot, psychological development—Foreman's plays are instead a living expression of his own sub-conscious activity. In place of a linear narrative, his work relies upon the incorporation of symbols from a personal iconography he has created over the years. His scripts are the product of random notebook jottings, consolidated after a period of months into an unorthodox free-for-all of words and images. The resulting work evokes meanings that are hauntingly elusive, layering fragments of dialogue into a fluid whole that suggests many ideas but seldom achieves solidity. Foreman describes his art thus: "I have always conceived of my theater as being a kind of mental and intellectual sensory gym, where I could work out the kinks of my perceptual analysis. I'm interested in trying to find ways to make physical the various abstractions that one's imagination spins and projects."

As a stage designer, Foreman transforms space by the use of sliding panels, dramatic lighting shifts, and spiderwebs of string which frame the performance area. His sets are not stable, but move throughout the performance to challenge notions of constancy and perception. Incongruous architectural elements and pop-culture props jar with one another and vie for space on a crowded stage. Foreman's productions are a multi-media experience, involving bright lights which flash at the audience, and a soundtrack of interspersed music, buzzers, and electronic noise. Rather than form a backdrop for his words, his designs expand and reinforce his texts by becoming a part of the conceptual framework of a performance.

Foreman's work has been noted for its extreme egocentricity: as an enactment of the author's thought processes, it is necessarily highly personal and self-referential. Reflecting this, his directorial style is unusually autocratic: until the production of *Film is Evil: Radio is Good,* he did not change lines in rehearsal, or allow actors input into the creative process. In fact, in a number of his plays, all or most of the dialogue has

Photograph by Lois Greenfield. Courtesy of Richard Foreman.

been either projected on screens or played back on tape, while the actors present the visual patterns he has staged for them. Foreman developed this technique to get rid of the personality of the individual performers: "I'm basically interested in staging what is going on in my head while I'm writing the play, and I find that when actors start talking normally it just doesn't sound like that."

Foreman first became interested in the theater at age nine after watching the D'Oyly Carte company's productions of Gilbert & Sullivan operettas. He began working in drama while an undergraduate at Brown University and received an M.F.A. in playwrighting from the Yale School of Drama. Early in his writing career, he counted Gertrude Stein and Bertolt Brecht as his principal influences, and indeed has directed productions of their works. In 1968, Foreman began to write pieces "for the theatre which I wanted to see, which was radically different from any style of theatre which I had seen." Foreman located the failure of contemporary theater in its conscious attempt to manipulate audience reponse. In contrast to the prevalent style of experimental theatre in the 1960's, which concentrated on

159

breaking the barriers between the audience and the stage, Foreman's early works were deliberately aloof and alienating. Not only could they have existed without an audience present, but they often did, as baffled viewers frequently left before the evening was over.

The Cure represents a departure from Foreman's plays of recent years, which were composed on a large scale with numerous actors. Instead, it is a chamber piece, employing only three leads and no secondary characters. The stage set has been called "a Victorian fun-house of horrors": painted in sombre colors, and bedecked with string, whirling pinwheels, and steering wheels dangling from the ceiling. A soundtrack of Foreman's creation cues the performers into alternate periods of serenity and frenetic activity by means of his usual collection of bells and buzzers. The actors' voices are projected over body-mikes, giving an impersonal distance to their pronouncements on identity, dreams, and communication as they haphazardly seek "the cure." The play's imagery is eccentric: the automobile is employed as a symbol of sexuality, and, in a scene frequently cited by critics, cornflakes invade the creative process, as one character attempts to write *War and Peace* using breakfast cereal rather than words. In premonition of *Film is Evil: Radio is Good,* which follows *The Cure* in Foreman's chronology, the radio is a frequent motif.

Film is Evil: Radio is Good has been hailed by critics as a ground-breaking and significant work in Foreman's ouevre, in which for the first time he decisively moves beyond incoherence to assert a definitive artistic viewpoint. The theme of the play is encapsulated in its title and repeated by its players throughout: that radio, by stimulating only one sense, allows creativity to emerge, while film suppresses the imagination by supplying the image our mind would otherwise be required to create. Film is merely physical, while radio is spiritual. The play is set in a laboratory-like radio station presided over by a defiant broadcaster, steadfastly proclaiming these truths against a backdrop of the encroachment of film. The play is bisected by a 15-minute film entitled "Radio Rick in Heaven and Radio Richard in Hell," also directed by and starring Richard Foreman.

Critics have judged *Film is Evil: Radio is Good* to be more complex and provocative than Foreman's earlier works, finding it suggests the ambivalent relationship of humanity with technology. Foreman has built his stylistic career around the notion that art is purest when presented in its unaltered, pre-conscious state; in his latest play, his characters struggle with the inevitable corruption of consciousness by the machines of expression. *Film is Evil: Radio is Good* is less aggressive toward the audience than previous plays, but retains the intensity and energy that characterize Foreman's best work. Reviewers have found the play exhausting, but stimulating.

The film short that forms the centerpiece of Foreman's play has been praised, both for the direction and for Foreman's acting ability. Several reviewers have expressed disappointment at the dramatist's apparent anti-film bias, as his tight and expressive sample shows an obvious talent in the area of cinema direction. Interestingly, Foreman credits his exposure to underground films in the sixties with a revelation that launched his theatrical career. "These people made their own movies, and let the rough edges show," he said. "Most of my work up to that point had been writing and rewriting to get rid of things in the language that sounded rough or corny or unsophisticated to me. What these movies did for me, primarily, was to make me realize that you could accept all that and show it for what it is."

At the time, he even considered working in cinema rather than live theater. He attributes his decision to use film in his most recent play to a desire to move into filmmaking.

Foreman agrees with the majority of critics who feel that his work has become less aggressively personal in recent years and attributes this change both to a maturing personal style and to the influence of Kate Manheim, the actress with whom he lives and who has played the female protagonist in most of his plays. In *Film is Evil: Radio is Good* in particular, Manheim's suggestions in rehearsal resulted in the rewriting of at least a third of the script. Still, despite the increasing accessibility of his work, Foreman stated in his Obie acceptance speech that "next year I hope to write a play people will really hate."

(See also *Contemporary Authors,* Vols. 65-68.)

MEL GUSSOW

For 18 years, Richard Foreman has been exploring and annotating his dreams, creating scores of plays that have led him from small SoHo lofts to major theaters and festivals. Once again he is in SoHo, at the Performing Garage with a new dream play called *The Cure*—and the evening is filled with the playwright-director's fanciful esoterica.

In previous pieces he has been in search, usually in company with his prototypical heroine, Rhoda (played by Kate Manheim), of nothing as elusive as the meaning of life. More often, Rhoda has been looking for a devious way out of a maze or a daze or a locked-room labyrinth. Here, Miss Manheim (her character is unidentified, but she acts like the ubiquitous Rhoda) is after "The Cure." One could have told her at the beginning of the quest that "the cure is in the pain." Diagnosis is all.

So come with him now as Mr. Foreman—one wants to say Dr. Foreman—diabolically invites the patient into his laboratory-living room. As designed by the director, the place is a Victorian fun house of horrors. Because Mr. Foreman is the architect as well the landlord, the environment is strung with string, tripped with pulleys and festooned with pinwheels and pedestals. Each of the mechanical objects eventually become part of the grand design, offering a kind of emotional as well as physical entrapment to the play's three characters. . . .

In the background, we hear the sinister sounds of a score by Mr. Foreman. . . . The music may be a simulation of the beating hearts of the characters, as they are waylaid by the events of the play. Periodically they respond with a danse macabre.

Exegesis is nonexistent, but there are clues to this particular *Cure*. As motifs, Mr. Foreman offers the car as sexual object, corn flakes as creative stimulant, and fruit for all purposes as he tries and fails to get the core of the argument. According to the program, his next New York venture will be a play entitled, *Film Is Evil, Radio Is Good,* and, perhaps foreshadowing that work, *The Cure* favors the radio far above all other instruments of communication.

Though a sign informs us that "no secrets" will be held, mystery is endemic. Non sequiturs float through the play, each of them intended—to use a Foreman line—as "an internal gesture of the mind." It should be said that *The Cure* is not oppressively obtuse. As an animated curio cabinet, it is fascinating for most of its 70-minute duration.

Keep your eye on the corn flakes, as they substitute for the write stuff. Miss Manheim uses the cereal to transcribe *War and Peace,* which she pretends to do by sticking flakes on a screen. At another point, Mr. Kelly sheepishly steps forward carrying a small, nondescript rock. He holds it as if it were a prize sculpture, and says, "There will be no more graven images." If that strikes you as amusing, you should enjoy **The Cure.** Otherwise you may just be disoriented, but, as always with Mr. Foreman, the search is itself the solution.

Mel Gussow, "'The Cure', by Richard Foreman,"
in The New York Times, *May 28, 1986, p. C17.*

GORDON ROGOFF

Hovering like a warning or an admonition over the tiny space in which Richard Foreman's **The Cure** moves through its subdued meditations is a sign saying NO SECRETS. As usual with Foreman, the words don't slip easily into a category or conclusion: Most of the time, he has set up oppositions and unanswerable questions which act as a dialogue with the self. This time, however, with NO SECRETS hanging over the proceedings, he does something new and ironic—a confrontation of the most private theater artist we have with the impulse to tell everything he knows and feels.

It isn't probable that Foreman's privacy can be breached even by Foreman himself. That he's theatrical is, I suspect, his personal salvation: using a voice and iconography all his own, he releases himself to open struggle, a continual play of words and energies that probably make his bad dreams bearable. In **The Cure,** what is seen and heard most certainly must be all we need to know. While there may be a temptation to cast interpretative veils over his signals and images, it is sufficient to take the journey as given—no more, no less than what it looks like or seems to be at any passing moment.

Designed by Foreman, the set looks like a fun-house funeral parlor. . . . Foreman gives his actors a space that is deliberately unsettling and only pseudocomic. Yet one thing is clear: unlike most imagistic theater, **The Cure** is not trying to paint pretty pictures.

The pictures here are almost accidental deferences to the theatrical mode. Foreman's biggest open secret is his passion for words. Placing the three actors—Kate Manheim, David Patrick Kelly, and Jack Coulter—in a hermetically sealed parlor, Foreman gives them nothing to do but enact or present the story of a writer possessed by language and argument. At one moment, as if summoned by a sudden glimpse into ecstatic realms, the men dash and shake their bodies into staccato riffs; at another, they suddenly clap their hands repeatedly on their knees. Kelly is imperturbably cool; Coulter leers and lurches, trapped in his own strenuously induced steam heat. Meanwhile, Foreman spreads a glistening pattern of questions, observations, and half-answers over almost every move and tic. "Can the truth be conveyed in a story?" He has an actor ask, and we know implicitly from the work itself that Foreman finds stories a lie.

Wearing body-mikes so that their voices are heard over speakers, the actors are further distanced by the continual accompaniment of alternately ominous and whimsical music, that too scored by Foreman. Can it be an accident that the tunes and rhythms have an effect not unlike the scores for Chaplin's silent

films, a kind of tinny, filtered music-hall quality suggesting paranoid games? Consider, too, that **The Cure** is also the title of one of those films. (With Foreman, some of the fun lies in playing the games.) With one of those old-fashioned radio signals denoting the hour or the announcement of the station, each section is halted and a new one begins. Foreman's theater is a conspiracy on behalf of words: these orderly, marked divisions are designed to convey us into a listening mood; the text may be densely packed, but Foreman makes it unavoidable.

With po-faced intensity, the actors move from one object to another while speaking their litanies. "Here is an important dream," says Manheim, telling us that she "woke up one morning and found the world was all I desired of it." She doesn't, however, tell us what those desires were. Another section begins with the demand to find out something—"how to punish a man approximately five feet eight-and-a-half inches tall." And again, nobody finds out how to do any of it. In still another section, the actors declare that nobody knows much about them, but repeatedly they conclude that they don't care. Further on, they are implored not to guess or analyze. Warned later that "it's not wise to talk about things that scare you, make you cry, make other people mad at you, or jeopardize your economic security," Manheim replies that she "never does—such things are private." Yet she can't avoid her own subversion: "Sometimes I talk about them without knowing."

Toward the end of this one-hour ceremony of the half-alive, Foreman flirts dangerously with what looks like a conclusive statement: "The cure," we learn, "is in the pain." This is turned quickly, however, into its opposite—"There is no cure." And then again, it becomes another question: "The pain of the cure is the cure?" The danger has passed just as swiftly as it emerged. Foreman is no more likely to provide homilies than any other inquiring artist. If a man thinks he's eating normal cornflakes, someone is bound to tell him that he's wrong. "You'll never solve it," says Manheim.

If he can't solve it, at least he can share some of the pain. Manheim's brittle presence—limping wrists and high heels conveying her over territory that never quite explodes under her focused assaults—is the walking-talking emblem of Foreman's quizzical distress. In one of those lines that keeps escaping into his own prepared oblivion, he has her say that she heard the "glacial cracking of her own emotions." Quoting Alfred North Whitehead's "Nothing in excess" as "the motto of the philistine," Foreman provides an excess of vigorous speculation that is as glacially cracked as Manheim's elusive emotions. **The Cure** may remain private at the end, but if you can bear its solemn fun, it offers the gift of what theater does better than the other arts these days—what Foreman calls here "an internal gesture of the mind." Glacial, yes, but uninsistent and deeply felt.

Gordon Rogoff, "Internal Gestures," in The Village
Voice, *Vol. XXXI, No. 22, June 3, 1986, p. 81.*

LISA MERRILL

The Cure, Richard Foreman's latest work with the Ontological-Hysteric Theater, presents audiences with another opportunity to foray into Foreman's fascinating and idiosyncratic dream world. Whether or not you have ever seen his work before, you know the feeling: you wake from a dream or a hallucination and remember images, sensations, a charged line whose significance seemed indisputable at the moment of utterance; now sounding trite or obscure in the retelling. "Truth is veiled, or it would blind you,'' one of Foreman's characters explains. Later, upon reflection, when you try to decipher the specialized symbol system, just as when we analyze our own dreams, a strictly literal narrative eludes us, but the potency of the individual images is indisputable.

In *The Cure* Foreman's "veiled truths" are set in an interior room draped in red and grey fabric, trimmed with black lace. Except for small circles that whir and turn periodically all around the stage "picture," and such strange furnishings as two black-curtained voting booths at opposite sides of the stage, a large throne-like chair and a plush red car seat-sofa on a table top, we could be witnessing an old horror story. The room is both ominous and garish. . . .

The three performers might be in a drawing room comedy or a murder mystery, an association which Foreman heightens through his imaginatively scored background music.

At different times, each performer drops a scarf, another picks it up like a veil, and speaks from their interchangeable positions on the "throne." Each addresses the other as a "beautiful childhood person," and mentions issues that "nobody knows about."

But the text is not a literal exchange between characters. Certain icons predominate. Manheim, perched seductively on the table-top car seat, speaks about her manipulation of her car as the two men, hands crossed over their crotches, jump frenetically towards her. Later the car image reappears as each performer hangs onto a steering wheel suspended from the ceiling.

Other symbols of modern day life take on mythic and comedic significance as well. Manheim's pedantic talk about the attempt to describe one's experience is made ridiculous as she tries to rewrite *War and Peace* using individual cornflakes instead of a typewriter. Even the self-consciousness of contemporary art is spoofed in lines like, "I've had more visionary experiences than you could shake a stick at." . . .

Foreman's work demands audience involvement. Lights flash at the audience, musical notes jar and punctuate the action. At one point, even our perceptions are questioned directly (albeit rhetorically) when Kelly asks us, "Are you staring at the fruit or listening to the radio?"

With our senses engaged simultaneously, but in ways which contradict rather than reinforce each other, we are forced to respond in a visceral rather than intellectual manner. The music is loud. Can "therapeutic radios cure you?" We intuit organic connections when characters ask, "Do radios" like fruit "grow radios?"

The Cure in this disoriented, post-modern, but strangely "retro" world ends almost where it began. Although the performers state that the "cure" for a trivialized, neurotic dream state is in "the cry of pain" which is the radio, at the end Manheim is back "making a total career" out of the "manipulation of her car." But there is a larger consciousness at work here, nonetheless. As the piece closes, the performers acknowledge that, "Alternately, I could have touched people in ways which were not trivial." Certainly that is what Foreman attempts to do here. To a large measure, he succeeds.

> *Lisa Merrill, " 'Cure' Displays Power of Foreman's Dream World," in* The Villager, *June 5, 1986.*

KEVIN GRUBB

Since the late 1960s, Richard Foreman's 30-odd (and odd they are) plays have swung from intensely personal statements to more accessible collaborative efforts and back again. . . . Traipsing through . . . varied [performance] spaces with plays that deal with issues no less contemplative than the meaning of life, Foreman uses words, music, props, and highly stylized sets (frequently resembling alchemists' laboratories) to set forth ideas generated as much from external stimuli as from profound self-reflection.

In his latest piece, *The Cure,* Foreman returns to the type of theater for which he is best known. Three characters (Kate Manheim, David Patrick Kelly, Jack Coulter) engage in a vigorous display of confession through nonlinear fragments of dialogue punctuated by spasmodic gestures and ominous music. As one man, identified as Paul in the final minutes of the play, announces early on, "The time has come to tell the truth. This art tells the truth"—though, as evident here, the truth is indeed stranger than fiction.

To penetrate any Foreman play (barring his collaborative works and restagings), one first contemplates his external world. *The Cure*'s set employs signature Foreman stagecraft: strings stretched tautly across the ceiling (these suspending the words "No Secrets"—a reference to the popular Carly Simon album? I think not), objects puzzling in appearance and comic in function—pinwheels, a black, red, and gold oar, silver rods that look like spirals of DNA—and lights that shine in the audience's eyes. The visual assault is coupled with a typically raucous Foreman "soundtrack" of bells, beeps, and blips, audible cues that set the actors in, or out of, motion. This frantic animation, which sometimes makes the stage spin out of control, belies the harmonious orchestration and choreography of the overall production. More than in previous Foreman works, *The Cure* strives to articulate the playwright's esoteric themes. Words, phrases, and ideas are repeated as if to underscore key points. "Knowing is no good unless you feel the urgency of the theory," says one man, who later walks around the stage carrying a pedestal of potted flowers on his back.

Although Foreman's final pronouncement is that "the pain of the cure is pain," broad comic flourishes save the production from becoming merely disparaging. When Paul stammers, unable to explain the opposite idea of the idea he's trying to express, he is presented with a box of corn flakes—the "cure" for his confusion. With the flakes he attempts to rewrite Tolstoy's *War and Peace,* an endeavor that must be seen to be appreciated.

For most of its 70 minutes, *The Cure* hypnotizes the audience with sustained wit and energy, though theatergoers unfamiliar with Foreman may find even this distilled "internal gesture of the mind" difficult to apprehend.

> *Kevin Grubb, in a review of "The Cure," in* New York Native, *June 16, 1986.*

An Excerpt from *The Cure*

KATE: There's nobody here yet but you can take off
　　　　your shoes and sox and relax
　　　　There's nobody here yet but you can drink as
　　　　much as you like

There's nobody here yet
    but you can gorge yourself on fresh fruits
        and take the pits from those fruits and
            place those pits in a circle enclosing
    your physical body.

DAVID: Follow this carefully—

KATE: I heard what you said.

DAVID: Therefore, look—

KATE: (don't look, listen)

DAVID: A bowl of conceptual, theraputic fruit

KATE: A bowl or radios
Thought radios?
I mean THERAPEUTIC radios? They cure
  me?

DAVID: Therefore, a collection of dried pits.

KATE: They cure me?

JACK: Plant them in dried earth

KATE: Do radios grow radios?
No. They grow plants

DAVID: (in the ear?)

JACK: they grow plants which grow fruits which
hide

KATE: HERE IT COMES, THE 29TH STREET
    TROLLEY
AND THERE ARE ALOTTA DWARFS
    INSIDE
SHAKING THEIR THUMBS
AND SPITTING THROUGH THEIR RAT
    TEETH

JACK: The cure is in the pain.

KATE: HERE IT COMES, THE A BUS,
FILLED WITH LADIES WHO PUT THEIR
    POCKET BOOKS
INSIDE THEIR POCKET BOOKS
AND SKIP BIG LUNCH

JACK: The cure is in the pain.

KATE: HERE IT COMES, THE UNIVERSITY
    LOCAL
STUFFED WITH TUB THUMPERS
WHO PIT THEIR BRIGHT IDEAS
VERSUS THE OLD MAN OF THE
    MOUNTAIN
IN HIS COAT OF MANY, MANY, MANY,
MANY . . .
  radios
    But
      what ARE those plants, really?
        And what are those fruits?
        (when you bite, do you engage the
        ear, more than the eye?)
        When you bite, does it hurt?
        Does it hurt a fruit? And does
        the hurt fruit cry out

    There is no cure
   The cure is the cry of pain
    The cry of pain is the radio
      The pain of the radio in the ear
      is the cure
   The pain of the cure, is the cure

DAVID KAUFMAN

The excitement that used to occur over a new work of Richard Foreman's had everything to do with the now exhausted notion of *breakthrough*. Though not alone in his mission, he was among the most successful at redefining the limitations of his chosen medium—theater. With a persistence and a consistency that can best be apprehended as obsessive, Foreman stretched conventional boundaries and demonstrated that the periphery could prove more substantial than what used to obtain as the center. Rather than detract from his achievement, his insistence on the prerogative of the artist to be megalomaniacal became an integral part of his *oeuvre*, possibly even the most resilient part. ''The scripts themselves read like notations of my own process of imagining a theatre piece,'' claimed Foreman some years ago in a brief, manifesto-type statement. . . .

The key to Foreman . . . has been his inexhaustible ambition to ''comment upon'' his own works, which exist primarily as testimonies or commentaries on his own thought processes.

Thus begins and ends the tautological process of Foreman's Ontological Hysteric Theater, a fiercely idiosyncratic style of performance art featuring an imprint that is always indentifiable as Foreman's, whether it surfaces as one of his own conceptions (in recent years, **Penguin Touget, Egyptology, Africanus Instructus,** and currently **The Cure**) or as it's applied to others' scripts. . . .

In addition to citing Gertrude Stein and Brecht as primary influences, Foreman has often alluded to Jung while discussing his own creative process. So it should come as no surprise that no symbol better describes Foreman than Jung's uroboros, the archetypal snake consuming itself by eating its tail, creating the image of a circle and representing the chain of death in life. The head is perpetually lost in a tautological tailspin, finding replenishment only in the act of erasing itself. . . .

If, as Foreman the theorist reveals, the great dilemma or imperative for the artist in this century [who] finds that art is engulfed by an overwhelming self-consciousness, by a cerebral process that undermines or even obliterates the more creative impulses, then Foreman himself emerges as perhaps the greatest practitioner of such an offense. How can we avoid recognizing that this particular artist doth protest too much, even as he registers his complaints to justify his own practices. Foreman, the performance artist, evinces a pathological tautology no less pronounced than the self-cancelling properties proclaimed by Foreman the thinker.

The inclination to ascribe Foreman's minimalist and abrasive tactics to faddishness is a seductive one, but ultimately it proves misleading. His Ontological-Hysteric Theater pieces are typically busy, hectic, and eclectic in both appearance and feeling. But beneath the superficial chaos, there resides an abiding simplicity and—dare I say it—serenity. The performers' periodic bouts with frenetic, epileptic-like seizures are preceded and followed by more customary, zombiesque behavior.

Over the years, the cumulative effect of his pieces has been to construct an immaculate representation of his personal iconography: the use of strings which *frame* the works even as they extend them geometrically, implying intersections with our own lives at points that Foreman cannot control. . . . the idiosyncratic use of performers as objects as opposed to subjects or characters—objects that Bonnie Marranca so aptly described as ''demonstrators'' since, she explains, they ''serve as the media of Foreman's ideas;'' the rarefied use of language which is seemingly elevated only to make Foreman's contempt for words that much harsher (language and words are implicitly inadequate, according to Foreman, but they remain necessary—evils); the use of Victoriana items, automatically evoking a sense of disguise and repression, which, in turn, convey Foreman's fundamental conviction, that the truth can be approached but it cannot be perceived (Foreman's grim view of the human condition suggests that few are called, but *none* are chosen); the use of incoherence as a game to remind us that sequence is essentially artificial, at best a convention, but finally one of an infinite variety of possibilities. (The ultimate failure of Foreman is that this alternative arrangement of sequence, his freely acknowledged "incoherence," is finally not viable or workable—more a style than an artistic statement or an imparted perception.)

All of these elements are present in Foreman's latest work, *The Cure*. In his response to *The Cure* for *The Village Voice*, Gordon Rogoff cautions, "While there may be a temptation to cast interpretive veils over his signals and images, it is sufficient to take the journey as given—no more, no less than what it looks like or seems to be at any passing moment [see excerpt above]. This admonition strikes me as a gross oversimplification of Foreman's motives.

In a noticeable departure from the dozen or so Foreman works I've seen during the past six years, Foreman confines himself to three performers in *The Cure*, each of whom is overly familiar at this point and can be viewed as a part of his iconography: Kate Manheim, David Patrick Kelly, and Jack Coulter. He positions them in a setting which Mel Gussow in *The Times* [see excerpt above] summarizes as a "Victorian fun house of horrors" and Rogoff refers to as "a fun house funeral parlor." These descriptions are as accurate as their independent derivation implies.

It should also be said that at this point, the eccentricity of a Foreman set resembles nothing so much as the interior of Foreman's mind. Next to Fellini, Foreman is the one contemporary artist who has released a consistent image of his dream-scape. The Persian rugs and dangling antennae are offset by rich brocades, gothic candles, black lace, massive thrones, and classical busts (in this case, three replicas of Michelangelo's David, initially shrouded in white chiffon). Only the box of corn-flakes up on a ledge seems anachronistic, and it later becomes perhaps the most significant prop. Hovering over the stage on a pair of strings, the phrase "No Secrets" seems particularly pregnant, informing all of the proceedings. The title of the work itself suggests a sense of resolution, and indeed Coulter's first line reinforces such a notion:

"The time has come, to tell the truth." "Art," he continues, "this art, tells the truth." But moments later we're told that "it's hidden. . .because you'd be blinded by it." Manheim allows that "You'd protect yourself," and Kelly proffers that it "Can't be conveyed in a story."

Foreman's basic mistrust of stories (which is synonymous with his disdain for our feeble and outmoded reliance on plot) shows up later as a series of self-mocking puns. Kelly announces, "Nobody knows my name, but I don't care, I don't care, I don't care." Manheim joins in, "Nobody knows what books I like, but I don't care, I don't care, I don't care."

We don't know the answers to these ostensibly mundane questions; but whether or not *we* care, there is the gnawing sense that they *do*, despite their protestations to the contrary. The one irrefutable fact here is that Foreman will not permit his "characters" to care about such matters. It's precisely these quotidian concerns that prevent us from focusing on the deeper issues, Foreman seems to be saying.

As far as character-information goes, we must content ourselves with, for example, Manheim's telling us that "I've had more visionary experiences than you can shake a stick at," or her subsequently teasing Kelly and Coulter with, "What's your name? I bet it's a very good name. What's your profession? I bet it's a very good profession. What's your taste in clothes? I bet you have very good taste in clothes." But as soon as she asks, "What's your phone number?" she recoils in fear that she might get too close; and Foreman's theme of alienation is swiftly manifested.

Though Foreman would have us believe that "paranoia" is dismissable, as he has Coulter say, "Such concerns are neurotic, therefore finally trivial," *The Cure* becomes little more than another exercise in paranoia, reminiscent of all Foreman's Ontological-Hysteric Theater works in just that fashion. Near the end, Coulter pontificates, "The cure is in the pain," and Manheim further qualifies, "There is no cure—the cry of the pain is the cure."

Although far from obvious, and although he would probably be the first to deny it, Foreman is an extraordinary purist, a supreme perfectionist. In his essay on Truth—**"How Truth— Leaps (Stumbles) Across Stage"**—the best his reductive rationale or his Cartesian mode can allow is that, "I have to assume that in my dreams I'm not lying to myself." He can only approach the truth negatively or inversely, by deriving the one frame-of-reference when he isn't "lying" to himself. Every other impulse is suspect. Truth is, to this purist, strictly unobtainable, even if it implicitly remains the one goal worthy of pursuit.

The most concrete insights to this stance are revealed in an interview Foreman had with Roger W. Oliver. . . .I quote at length since it strikes me as the most definitive, political position Foreman had ever divulged:

> . . .in America, the conservative/reactionary forces are generally the result of a particular kind of character structure, a character structure which gets very nervous if things don't seem to be black or white. You have to decide if this is good or this is bad, so you know where you stand, know what to fight against, know what to embrace. The reactionary/conservative structure wants to divide the world up in that fashion. And if there are certain gray things in the environment, they want to use their intellect to try to clarify whether those things are really black or really white. They end up neatly dividing the world into good and bad. Now I think that my plays are exercises in learning how to live—with lucidity and happiness—in a totally ambiguous environment, in a world where *everything* is gray, which is of course how the world is!

Or is it? If only it were that simple.

In the meantime, *The Cure* remains a quintessential example of Foreman's once ground-breaking Ontological-Hysteric Theater company. Though for different reasons, it offers aficionados and newcomers alike much to ponder. Catch it quickly, before it evaporates into the ontological oblivion of historically important theater works.

David Kaufman, "Cogitat Ergo Dramatis Sunt (Or Are They?)," in Soho Arts Weekly, *June 18, 1986, p. 12-A.*

MEL GUSSOW

The title of Richard Foreman's quizzical new comedy, *Film Is Evil: Radio Is Good*, almost says it all. This is a cryptographic mystery about the encroachment of visual imagery into the world of sound. The heroic forces of broadcasting are represented by the proprietors of a small, unidentified radio station that suddenly finds itself besieged and undermined by a chorus of threatening cinéastes.

Because Mr. Foreman is the author, director and designer, one can expect unpredictable displays of creative energy. In this eerie environment, film is evil, radio is good—and "theater" is enlivening, although elliptical. . . .

Mr. Foreman has transformed the [stage] . . . into a cavernous radio studio of the imagination—the Foreman equivalent of a Louise Nevelson environment lined with Joseph Cornell boxes. The stage is gewgawed with gargoyles and curios, including clocks and flashing signs indicating that the author's ego is active (the word "ego" lights up when the show is "on the air").

Coming after last season's show *The Cure,* the new play offers additional evidence that Mr. Foreman has recaptured the playfulness and spontaneity of his chamber pieces of the 1970's, after a more recent career staging operas and plays on a grand scale. . . .

[A] new Foreman character, Estelle Merriweather, . . . merrily weathers the storm of broadcasting inclemency. . . . [She] acts as interlocutor and advance warning system, cuing her colleagues . . . when trouble is lurking on the silver screen. She is undeterred by the aggressive forces of cinemalice.

Movies, we are told, steal one's image and warp one's brain. Radio, on the other hand, is pure. It stimulates rather than suppresses the imagination. The baleful chorus . . . attacks—and radio reacts. But before the battle can become too polemical or semiotic, Mr. Foreman interjects sight and sound gags. Cartoonlike creatures appear—a snowman and a duck that looks suspiciously like Howard, the grossest canard of the movie industry.

Though the play runs on a bit too long, it never loses its fervor. . . .

Midway through the exercise, a screen appears onstage and the play is interrupted by a short film, **"Radio Rick in Heaven and Radio Richard in Hell,"** written and directed by Mr. Foreman, who also—a first—stars. . . . Belying the title of the play itself, the film is good, wasting no words or pictures and serving as an acute annotation of themes raised by the live performance. As an actor on screen, Mr. Foreman has presence and a mobile, though dour, face and, as we already knew, a deeply sepulchral voice. Were Mr. Foreman not so pro-radio and anti-cinema, he might have a filmic future as actor and auteur.

> *Mel Gussow, in a review of "Film Is Evil: Radio Is Good," in* The New York Times, *May 5, 1987, p. C15.*

MARILYN STASIO

Avant garde theater director Richard Foreman has never been at a loss for cleverness. His amusingly titled new work, *Film Is Evil: Radio Is Good,* represents yet another wrinkle on that clever brow.

In keeping with the esthetic conundrum explored here—ear-art versus eye-art—Foreman has set his piece in a bizarre radio station where everybody runs around in lab coats looking very serious.

The studio is jammed with desks, files and other office paraphernalia, along with the microphones, buzzers, bright lights and rope-lines that have become the director's signature pieces.

But despite the frenzied antics of the cast—which includes . . . a snowman—Foreman avoids his usual bag of tricks and seems more involved in the debate.

Kate ("I tempt; therefore I am") Manheim has never been more fascinating than as the artist's alter ego. There's something downright lustful about her hunger to understand the issues: is it true that eye-art appeals to the brain, while ear-art reaches the heart? Or, is radio, like other displaced art forms, really just "a voice from the grave?"

The actress bounces these points off the other two principals, David Patrick Kelly and Lola Pashalinski; and Foreman himself appears, in a 15-minute film, to ponder the dilemma of the artist's ego.

But nothing, naturally, is resolved; Manheim has the last word when she brushes aside all the bedlam and demands that the studio be "very, very quiet."

> *Marilyn Stasio, "Medium Is Message," in* New York Post, *May 6, 1987.*

DAVID KAUFMAN

Along with Robert Wilson, with whom he has both more and less in common than might at first be apparent, Richard Foreman is probably our most steady, prolific, and important *avant-garde* theater practitioner. His extensive career will be celebrating its Twentieth Anniversary next year.

During the past decade, not only has Foreman continued to create new pieces for his Ontological-Hysteric Theatre Company, but he has also grafted his eccentric vision of theater onto the words of other writers. . . .

As for his productions of his own scripts, Foreman's last two, *Africanus Instructus* and *The Cure,* were not nearly as effective as his 1983 opus, *Egyptology,* where the images felt organic and appeared to amount to the sum of the diffused parts of what had been written.

Now Foreman is offering his newest original work, *Film is Evil: Radio is Good,* and, happily, it suggests that some artistic growth is taking place for the first time in years. Evidence of such evolution is always a cause for celebration, but doubly so in Richard Foreman's case, since he has, over the years, contributed an inestimable amount to the ways we now can look at theater—or indeed *must* look at theater.

While many Foreman followers would probably agree that his Ontological-Hysteric pieces have for the most part been redundant, it would be considerably harder to derive a consensus on what his work is about. Personally, I am inclined to agree with an ambivalent Stanley Kauffmann when he wrote 10 years ago that Foreman's "gifts are more pictorial than theatrical" and that works "read" more like "enacted notebooks" than completed thoughts. Or, as Kauffmann wrote even a bit earlier, Foreman's work "is much more stimulus than accomplishment."

Be that as it may, Foreman's works have always been distinctive and have inadvertently reminded us that Style, with a capital "S," involves a look and a feel (i.e. an idiosyncrasy) that belongs to the given artist. A long, hard look at the oeuvre reveals a consistency that allows us to identify the artist by a single piece, or even only a segment of the piece. Along these lines, think of Fellini's films for example, or even Bob Fosse's choreography.

Still, regarding Foreman, Stanley Kauffmann's notion of "notebooks" should be pursued since it becomes a key for getting a handle on Foreman. Even Foreman's own essays in his most recent anthology (*Reverberation Machines*) consist more of fragmentary entries and discontinuous musings than of extended discoveries or fulfilled ideas. Here, as in his own plays, Foreman invests an extraordinary faith in what is arbitrary and spontaneous.

Both his work and his commentary on his work suggest that he became obsessed with, or fixated on, the conviction—so popular in the '60s when his idiosyncratic aesthetic began to ferment and take root—that art is most pure when it is kept under wraps in its interior well, its spring, which is often considered the unconscious or at least preconscious state. To tame it for the sake of displaying it is tantamount to corrupting it, proceeds the logic of this refrain.

"Sense *can't* [Foreman's own emphasis] be avoided," he writes in the beginning of one of these essays. "If it first seems to be non-sense, wait: roots will reveal themselves." These "roots" that Foreman alludes to are his *sine qua non*. They come as close as anything can to describing his understanding of what must remain inarticulate in all of his work. With obvious limitations, they make accessible his apprehension of what he insists is only pure as long as it continues to be unavailable. According to Foreman, the mind sullies whatever it seizes or processes. His work, at the same time that it is steeped in itself and seems overly intellectual or megalomaniacal, basically praises that which eludes him.

With an obstinacy that justifies itself (and indeed suggests to us, his audience of bystanders, that Foreman is an artist of the purest sort), his belief that these "roots" will "reveal themselves" deems that they do just that. They become palpable and most manageable to him and to us on levels that fiercely guard against definition and that perpetrate what is mysterious.

Confirming this trust in what is mysterious above all else, and certainly above what can be understood primarily by the mind, each subsequent work incorporates reference points or signposts from what has come before. . . .

Since these icons or tokens sprang from the mysterious resource of Foreman's subconscious mind to begin with, they acquire additional meaning whenever they get repeated, as they are lifted into the context of the more current opus from that which has come before. An extreme example of this is his use and re-use of the character named Rhoda, or his consistent employment of the actress Kate Manheim. With Foreman, association and reference become ends in themselves.

If *Film is Evil: Radio is Good* is a departure for Foreman and an event in his career, then it's because for the first time he seems willing to make a statement beyond demonstrating that incoherence is the best we can hope for. The statement is the equivalent of the moral that is encapsulated in the title. Indeed this is Foreman's first title which is not willfully arcane or only self-reflective, but a statement-of-intent unto itself. The piece becomes, in effect, an indictment against all those factors which have led to this deplorable point in time when film and

image-worship have usurped humanity of its ability to be part of, or even to appreciate, what is natural. By implication, this piece also explains why Foreman has devoted his life to theater, which is as much alive as film is dead.

Time and again, this theme is made explicit throughout the piece: early when one of the characters proclaims, "When something comes to the ear it goes straight to the heart;" later, when the obverse is represented by another figure who nonchalantly reports, "Some of us guys from the radio station decided that what comes in from the eye, goes out like mental shit."

The central character, Estelle Merriweather . . . defines her mission as the need to "dehypnotize the brain," or in other words to remedy the brainwashing effect that film has had on all of us. The 20 minute film in the middle of this piece . . . reinforces the message concerning the evils of film, even while it extends the major impulse behind all of Foreman's work. When Foreman says near the end of this film, "I'm waiting for someone else to explain it, while I vanish," he is summarizing his effect, if not his motives, for the past 20 years.

In her well-considered response to Foreman's 1975 work, *Pandering,* Bonnie Marranca captured the essential impact of Foreman when she wrote, "The audience is left to fill in the blank." What she failed to recognize is that it has been no different for Foreman, and he has himself been "left" to occupy the void he cannot evade. In *Film is Evil: Radio is Good,* he is more willing to take a stand than he ever has before.

David Kaufman, "Finding Incoherence, He Goes Beyond It," in Downtown, *May 20, 1987, p. 20-A.*

An Excerpt from *Film Is Evil: Radio Is Good*

KATE: *(Enters.)* After an evening at the movies . . . I came back alone to the radio studio.
I laid down my pocketbook, and gloves. Then . . . I went to a secret cabinet . . . and took out the forbidden silver book
. . . of my spiritual potential. I began reading, word by word, when a voice inside my head told me to look up and when I raised my head from the book, there was someone on the other side of the room.
Far away from the microphones
There was someone. There was someone on the red wallpaper. My flesh fell to the ground! I was stripped by lightning!
Oh! That imperishable moment: Truth!
The body of God is on the wall of my poor studio. Why? He is in a landscape, one I drew years ago. What beauty. What gentleness and elegance in him! Look at his shoulders and the way he holds himself. He's wearing a dress of yellow silk with blue ornaments. He turns around and I see his calm, radiant face. Then six women carry a corpse into the room. A woman with snakes around her arms and in her hair is near me.
LOLA: Estelle, dear: You've seen God. And the demon has gone. But he will come back.
KATE: The demon!
LOLA: Intelligence.
KATE: You don't know the good you do me, Helen.
LOLA: Estelle, we love you. Look into your heart!
KATE: I understand, everything.
LOLA: Can you see me, Estelle?

KATE: Yes—

LOLA: Do you have any questions to ask me?

KATE: No.

LOLA: Certainly you must have some questions to ask me. For instance, you may want to ask whether the image in whatever form is evil. Whether is does good or bad to the human soul.

KATE: Here's an idea of my own invention: De-hypnotize the brain.

(Enter DAVID.)

DAVID: That's the subject I've started THINKING about—

LOLA: Shhh! *(To KATE).* Go on, Estelle.

KATE: How do you de-hypnotize the brain? Here's my method. Take that beautiful music you've been listening to—

DAVID: What music?

KATE: And by an adjustment of consciousness—render it: nonbeautiful.

DAVID: Fool, fool, foool.

KATE: Oh—you'd discover something interesting.

LOLA: Those experiments are secrets that are never to be spoken of. Estelle, human beings who say such things in words must be punished.

KATE: *(Pause).* How do you know such things?

LOLA: Don't speak. Don't ask.

GOD: Hello there, everyone. I'm sure glad to make your acquaintance. The first thing I'd like you to do is wake up. Wake up, Paul, to your spiritual ambitions.

KATE: That sounds like a great idea—I've been broadcasting that to the whole world on semiprivate megahertz, but who's listening?

LOLA: Somebody MUST have listened, dear.

KATE: I don't think anybody's been listening

DAVID: I was listening. *(Pause.)* I think—

KATE: OK, then tell me, what was the message?

DAVID: Let me think about this. *(Pause.)* Film is evil. Radio is—

KATE: That wasn't the message.

DAVID: I heard it. Lots.

KATE: It wasn't MY message.

DAVID: Who else?

KATE: Radio Rick. That's what he's into.

DAVID: Who?

KATE: Radio Rick.

DAVID: The big Boss?

KATE: The brains—you know—
>   Radio Rick is on the air.
>   Radio Richard just don't care.
>   Radio Rick comes loud and clear.
>   While Radio Richard flaps his ears.

DAVID: I'd like to talk to him direct.

KATE: You can't.

DAVID: I'd like to meet him, to ask some questions—

KATE: You can't meet him face-to-face.

DAVID: Why not?

KATE: You'd burn up. *(She exits.)*

DAVID STERRITT

As a moviegoer, I'm not sure I like the title of Richard Foreman's latest theater piece, which has just won the 1987 Obie award as best new Off Broadway play of the season. It's called *Film Is Evil: Radio Is Good.*

It would be hard to say whether Mr. Foreman means that slogan or not, since this is a typical Foreman show—making few direct statements but containing many layers of meaning all fractured into tiny slivers of theatrical language and gesture.

Foreman does take pains, though, to spell out a plausible reason for believing such a thing. Radio awakens our imaginations, his play didactically tells us, by appealing to only one of our senses. Film, which fills our eyes and ears at the same time, deadens the heart and dictates to the mind.

This isn't a new argument, and Foreman doesn't dwell on it long. It's just a starting point for his latest intellectual journey into the heart of contemporary culture, which he sees as the breeding ground for all that's most stimulating and most treacherous in human experience. . . .

As usual for a Foreman play, the action is a free-for-all of ideas and feelings, all engaged in rollicking battle on the most slippery terrain the author can provide.

It's so slippery, in fact, that the centerpiece of *Film Is Evil* turns out to be a film. Shot in black-and-white and called **"Radio Rick in Heaven and Radio Richard in Hell,"** it's a 15-minute-long beauty, as tight and sardonic as anything Foreman has done in some time.

The main characters of *Film Is Evil: Radio Is Good* are two women and a man whose lives revolve around a mysterious radio station. It would take many words to unravel their strange, often inscrutable relationship and the story (more of a jigsaw puzzle than a conventional plot) that binds them together.

Suffice to say that at least two symbolic struggles—one between art and technology, the other between image and actuality—seem to be raging away in their hearts and minds, with the radio station becoming a kind of focal point for their mental energies.

Foreman has little interest in the narrative and psychological developments that are the mainstays of ordinary theater. He's less a playwright than a modernist poet of the stage—making fluid theatrical sculptures out of bits and pieces of meaning that reflect, in their very fragmentation, the fractured sensibilities of humanity in the media-bombarded 20th century.

Film Is Evil: Radio Is Good shows him at his most complex and provocative, and also at his most obsessive—one feels exhausted by the intensity of the brief but verbally and visually relentless proceedings. . . .

The film segment . . . shows Foreman to be a surprisingly strong actor—as well as a better movie director than his earlier film (and video) work has suggested. I hope he decides film isn't *so* evil after all and continues to develop his obvious talent in that area.

> David Sterritt, *"Foreman's Latest Play Is His Most Complex and Provocative,"* in The Christian Science Monitor, *June 1, 1987, p. 26.*

RICHARD FOREMAN

SCHECHNER: In **"How I Write My (Plays: Self)"** you write: "At a certain point I pick up one of my notebooks, look casually through it and decide 'Hum . . . go from here to here and I have a play,' which means that the text of any given work is a series of 'change of subjects'." In other words, you try to do as little editing as possible. But *Film Is Evil: Radio Is Good* seems so much more organized thematically than your other work that I can't believe you just harvested it from one of your notebooks.

FOREMAN: That habit of composition has been gradually changing; I don't do it that way anymore. I still make scratches in my notebooks and every couple of months I say, "Gee, I better type up all this material." And it goes into the pile. I tend to have a more active pile—stuff I've written in the last 9 to 16 months—and an older pile. Generally, I start out with the active pile, with a batch of material that needs amplification. Then I look through the two piles to find other pages that might be added and fit, and I combine things without too much rewriting—that's the way *Miss Universal Happiness* (1985) and *The Cure* (1986) were written.

Film Is Evil was totally different. When it started out I thought it was going to be like the others. But then, in rehearsal, a good 30 percent of the play was added, mostly because Kate (Manheim, the leading performer in Foreman's plays) . . . would say, "it needs a scene about this" or "why isn't there a scene where Radio Rick calls up on the telephone?" Many speeches were rewritten, amplified. In rehearsal I cut a lot—at least half of what I started with—and rewrote the rest. I'd estimate that 30 to 50 percent of the words were created in rehearsal. And that is the first time I've done that.

SCHECHNER: It shows in the way that the themes of the play seem to be external to you rather than private.

FOREMAN: Yeah, yeah.

SCHECHNER: How did that come about?

FOREMAN: I think that began to be the case around *Egyptology* (1983) and in *Miss Universal Happiness*. Less in *The Cure*, obviously. (p. 125)

SCHECHNER: What about the themes of *Film Is Evil: Radio Is Good*?

FOREMAN: . . . For many years a background theme that has surfaced slightly in my plays has been the Jewish tradition's prohibition of images. And from the early days, I'd always been lumped in the "theatre of images" even though I always told people it wasn't really the image I was interested in. It was the dialectic between the image and how the word qualified it. I also felt that even though I was called theatre of images a lot of more normally oriented people—Bob Wilson, for instance, who liked my work—I've no idea what he thinks nowadays—used to say, "Your work is so good but oh, it's so ugly all the time." And I thought so too. The imagery that I was dealing with was not making pretty pictures, it was a dialectical examination of the problematics of seeing.

But since I was at the same time an image-oriented person, and since I knew as a good Jew that you weren't supposed to make images of God, you were not supposed to be fixated on the image, it's really been a serious concern in my life. I've never liked totally image-oriented performance or film or art.

SCHECHNER: So the word and the ear are privileged? Isn't the reason for the Biblical prohibition that the image is fixed in space, local, coming from a single spot, entering a focused eye, while the word is diffuse, filling all available space, entering from any/everywhere—therefore a metaphor of omnipresence?

FOREMAN: Yeah, sure, everybody knows that. There are layers and layers of ramifications. I hope I don't have to sit here imagining all the ways in which the word has a specific kind

of psychological and metaphysical significance different from the image.

SCHECHNER: The film part of *Film Is Evil: Radio Is Good* was unclear. It should have been the evilest thing in the play, but it wasn't.

FOREMAN: It wasn't, because the reason I wanted to make this play was because I wanted to make a film again. Hopefully to get something I could show to people so that I could get money to make a real film. That's why I did it.

SCHECHNER: Did that film preexist the play?

FOREMAN: No, but up to the last minute I thought I was going to make another film. I have a lot of fragments of old film scripts. And this film was ten pages out of a longer film I wrote after I made my film *Strong Medicine* (1978), called *Unconscious Motives of the Motion Picture Industry*. It was about a corrupt world in which everybody was only interested in being filmed. The film in *Radio* was a short scene rewritten from it about an Eastern guru who disappears in front of the cameras.

Now, I wanted the irony to be present that film is being glorified—by me, too! I'm very ambivalent about all this, obviously. I do think film as it exists is pretty evil. I suppose people—myself included—still imagine film can be redeemed through a different style of filmmaking.

SCHECHNER: Or is it evil because it's so seductive?

FOREMAN: I've spoken a lot over the years about the danger of seductive art. I'm sure there are many people who think I've become more seductive—many of my early supporters think I've sold out, that I'm not as rigorous as I used to be.

SCHECHNER: In *Film Is Evil*, as distinct from your early work, film is the sensuous object instead of the bodies of women.

FOREMAN: Ah. Perhaps—yeah.

SCHECHNER: If you look back at your early work there were always naked women. Here the sensuous object is an image of yourself made by you. And isn't *Radio* the first time that Richard or Rick—your name—has been used in a piece?

FOREMAN: Except for *Rhoda in Potatoland* (1976), briefly.

SCHECHNER: But in this one you're really central, your name at least.

FOREMAN: Yeah.

SCHECHNER: And you go to heaven or hell, depending.

FOREMAN: Well, I think I am in heaven and hell at the same time. That's why Radio Rick is in heaven and Radio Richard is in hell.

SCHECHNER: But the film in your piece is what you're being damned for—being in love with yourself in your own film. Does it also mean that an image is permanent while words vanish?

FOREMAN: Well, that's a very ambiguous and disturbing issue in my life. The reason I made *Strong Medicine* was because I wanted something that would live on. I'm feeling that urge again and I'm not sure it's a healthy urge. I haven't resolved that.

SCHECHNER: I want to get back to what we started with—methods of composition. (pp. 126-28)

FOREMAN: One other thing I should say. There's one other method of composition that has come in the last three years maybe. Large sections of *Radio* are in these almost song forms, almost free poetic forms. And these are written specifically to tape loops. I put tape loops on and wait to see what comes.

SCHECHNER: What do you mean exactly?

FOREMAN: In the shows I use all this music all the time. And generally the music is two, three, or even four tape loops playing at the same time. I have these all on cassettes so they run for half-an-hour.

SCHECHNER: Right.

FOREMAN: So I'll put two loops into my machines and I'll play these two musics that are repetitive loops and as they play I'll wait for words to come in response to those loops.

SCHECHNER: You'll be writing the lyrics to your own music, which is determining the rhythm of what you write?

FOREMAN: Who knows? And then when I stage the play, I often don't use the same loops. (p. 129)

SCHECHNER: As you're writing do you ever edit the loops too, or are those given?

FOREMAN: Given. I find they really turn me on. . . .

SCHECHNER: Let's talk about directing. Again it seems—with Kate having so much input—that this isn't the way you directed ten years ago.

FOREMAN: Oh, no, no. This is a different situation and, obviously, my relation to Kate is different than to other actors. I never allowed any performer to suggest as much, to alter as much, as she did in this show. Actually, one of the motives I had in this show was to serve her more. (p. 130)

Most actors will still say that I'm not exactly Mr. Freedom, but I am more than I used to be. I still tend to choreograph most of what's happening on stage. However, I am not interested in directing big plays by other people anymore. I doubt I will do them. I know how to manipulate 20 or 100 people across the stage in big swirls of action and I'm sort of tired of being a traffic cop. I think I do it very well, but I am interested in seeing how I can work with three or four or five people. *The Cure* for me was very important for that reason. I sort of wondered if I could conceivably do a play with three people.

SCHECHNER: Right, right. But in relationship to *Radio,* you gave Kate freedom and she suggested things, but what about Lola Pashalinski, David Kelly, and the NYU students?

FOREMAN: No, no. It was really only Kate.

SCHECHNER: You have the actors, you have the text, you have the scenography, and you have the choreography within the scenography. The text comes first and you revise it. When does the scenography come? And how is it related? *Radio* felt more like your early works with their tunnel vision, their compulsive repetition of scenic items. . .I'm trying to delve into your creative process.

FOREMAN: I looked at the room, picked the text, and designed the set last summer [1986, more than six months before rehearsals began]. I made a model of the room. I can't tell you how many versions of every set I go through. Thousands of sketches. I'm exaggerating, but a lot of sketches. Then I make physical models and sit with one for a day, and wake up the next morning thinking, "Oh, that's awful." I'd say I generally go through 12, 15 different models. (pp. 130-31)

The next thing I do is go through my stack of tapes and select different loops. Generally I'll record some new loops. Then I go through the script page by page making choices of what music would go where. It's very casual, it happens very fast. In rehearsals most of that music is changed, but I have a basis for beginning.

Then generally what I do is look at every page of the text very quickly—about as fast as I'm talking to you now. "Page one, oh, look at that. OK, maybe we could use a pie in somebody's face there. So we'll try six pie plates there and then after the pie plate in the face the person can be on snowshoes. OK, page two. . ." I go through it that fast, just making notes, things that occur to me about what I could do for staging.

These days I don't think too much more about the staging until we begin rehearsing. Then I look at my notes and I say, "OK, we've got pie plates and snowshoes in this scene. OK, 20 of you over there. Now, let's see, Kate, why don't you take the pie plate and throw it in Louis's face?" So it's really just giving the building blocks, the toys—like kids playing in a playpen, combining all these toys in different ways. (p. 131)

SCHECHNER: More about scenography. There were Hebrew letters around the room [in *Film Is Evil: Radio Is Good*]—where's that from? It's not like an ordinary set because there's no discernible logic for what's there or not there.

FOREMAN: I knew from the beginning I wanted it to be a radio station. I had this idea of piling in a lot of furniture. I've always liked to have my sets suggest several superimposed layers of where they are. The Hebrew letters? I don't think they were part of the original scheme of things. As we were rehearsing, I realized how much I was talking about the Jewish prohibition of images.

SCHECHNER: Are they in any order? Are they kabbalistic?

FOREMAN: No, no, I don't know Hebrew. I used Hebrew letters before, in the Paris version of *The Book of Splendors* (1976). You see these plays are my life, my autobiography.

SCHECHNER: Did it occur to you to put yourself in this play, at least to put the sound booth where the audience could really see it?

FOREMAN: Very quickly it passed through my mind, but—

SCHECHNER: Too corny?

FOREMAN: No, I just didn't—

SCHECHNER: Right. What about some of the anomalous images—what's a snowman doing in a radio station?

FOREMAN: Well, he was in some of the pages I selected which were from a play called *Dead Snowmen*. Some of the content of those pages seemed appropriate to the thematics of *Radio*. There's all that talk about "men of ice." Of course I've always been accused in my private life as well as my theatrical life of being a slightly aloof, cold figure—so that was something I played with. This particular play talked about that, the snowman occurred, I chose those pages, I thought the snowman would work well in a radio studio—I don't know what else to say.

You know, I do work pretty intuitively, for better or for worse.

SCHECHNER: The snowman was funny but kind of scary, too. He's white, everybody else is in black. He just appears, this gigantic playful polar bear, something wild, out of place: entering this very rectangular space is this round, white, carrot-nosed Snowman.

FOREMAN: Yes, he's scary. If I really want to make the effort I can sit down and do the same kind of analysis, both psychological and symbolic, that you could. I don't enjoy doing that anymore.

The struggle in my life has been to try to come to terms with impulsive things on all levels. I've really always wanted to get free of the obsessive intellectualization that was manifest in all my manifestoes. For many years I was shy about telling people how I wrote these plays because I thought they'd say, ''Oh, look it's just free association, it's just whatever comes up in his head.'' And I felt, oh boy, I'll be punished for that. So the task for me is to admit to all that, to say, ''Look, it works.'' Today I'm less interested than I once was in theoretical analysis after the fact—even though what *Film Is Evil: Radio Is Good* is about is blatantly obvious. (pp. 132-33)

SCHECHNER: What's the future of this production of *Film Is Evil: Radio Is Good*?

FOREMAN: None.

SCHECHNER: That's one of the shameful things about our theatre. I'm not for keeping things forever. But here's a significant work and after a few weeks, it's gone. (pp. 134-35)

FOREMAN: I've always made new work, it's the only thing that interests me. It has something to do with the fact that I want to give up the theatre. I don't think people take me seriously. But I really do because of the problematics of trying to put on stage something that relates to a place where I can get my head when I'm a little more relaxed, where I know my head is open to something that's a little better than where it's at when I'm living my normal, daily life. I know I don't really succeed. I've always told people I was ambivalent about art, I don't know if they took me seriously about that either. But as I get older I'm increasingly ambivalent. I see I've spent my life, just as 20 years ago I casually said all artists did, making little paintings about the way I think life should be. I said that, but for a long time when I made my plays I was able to really pretend to myself psychically that the world I was making in my plays, which made me relatively happy, was really the world I existed in. It isn't the case, it satisfies me less and less, because I know it's not real. And that tension, that problematic, has always been the real content of my work, what's kept me making more work, and I can only make more work because I know the plays essentially on a certain level, are lies, are garbage, and are junk—so I try again.

Getting out of the theatre means trying to figure out how to do something which won't have the weight of a play. Film is evil, radio is good obviously. Where's theatre being talked about in this? Well, it is being talked about, somewhere. The idea of going into a darkened room and just turning on something and hearing a hum has always been my ideal theatre. What I'd like to do is to make a theatre that is no more than a La Monte Young tone sustained for the rest of my life. I must say that I'm going to performances of *Radio*—and I like this play, I think it's very good—I see the people coming, I see them sitting there watching, it, I don't really care. I really don't. (p. 135)

Richard Foreman, in an interview with Richard Schechner, in The Drama Review, *Vol. 31, No. 4, Winter, 1987, pp. 125-35.*

KATE MANHEIM (INTERVIEW WITH RICHARD SCHECHNER)

SCHECHNER: Richard [Foreman] told me you were very instrumental in shaping the mise-en-scene for *Film Is Evil: Radio Is Good*. That's different than the myth that Foreman does everything.

MANHEIN: It's a tricky subject, let's see what we can dig up because it's not easy. When I started working for him I was in a position where I did everything I was told. I did not question that—at the time. Now I'm in a position where I systematically refuse to do anything I'm told. Of course, Richard's still the director. Then we have a further step which is the constructive part of this whole thing. But I can't see that. I can only see this play at the end of the road that we'll be doing for another two weeks and then, as far as I'm concerned, it's finished. And it's that way with each play. My contribution vanishes. Richard still has a written text that can be published. I have nothing. (p. 136)

SCHECHNER: What changes did you make in the mise-en-scene, the writing, or the scenography?

MANHEIM: I work a lot from intuition so it's hard for me to explain very rationally how it happened. I detected right away that Richard was giving many too many things to the students and that I didn't have a big enough part and David Patrick Kelly didn't have a big enough part. So then all of a sudden Richard switched things around and I found myself in a play with a lot of students saying things and this character Paul Antonelli doing everything else, everything was about him. If I am in these plays I want to have a big part, I want it to be centered around me, otherwise forget it, it has no meaning for me.

I used to say that these plays were soap operas of the life of Richard Foreman and Kate Manheim. They are very autobiographical, even though a lot of it we don't think of, it's just there in the texture of it, in the words. So I just kept at Richard to make it mold to my unconscious of the moment. It's hard to explain these things.

SCHECHNER: How does your intuition get translated into the mise-en-scene?

MANHEIM: One day at home I said to Richard, ''You know, I think it would be good if I could be broadcasting about the weather a lot. We should have these big speeches about the weather.'' Ten days after that Richard found the Estelle Merriweather name, it was not in the play before, but I never got a speech about the weather. (p. 137)

SCHECHNER: How do you feel enacting a male consciousness? In the earlier plays you were often naked, an object, and Richard says he wrote those plays by lifting his unconscious right out of his notebooks. You were a big part of that conscious manifestation of Richard Foreman's unconscious. You were both yourself, Kate Manheim, and a figment of this man's unconscious.

MANHEIM: Yeah.

SCHECHNER: How does it feel to enact for 17 years the female of a male?

MANHEIM: I didn't think of it that way. I thought of it as a way to get over certain shynesses, particularly about being naked and about speaking out loud. It was sort of my way of getting over certain difficulties. I knew it was sort of the story of our life but I didn't question it in terms of woman and man. Now I'm questioning it a lot but I'm not quite sure I'd put it in terms of sexes.

SCHECHNER: How would you put it?

MANHEIM: I've become so sexless over the years, it's another thing I'll have to work on.

SCHECHNER: Not so much in **Radio** but in the other plays I've seen you in, sexless is the last word I'd use to describe if not you then your persona. But again, it's a male vision of sexy—the black silk stockings, the garter belt, the merry widow bra.

MANHEIM: But just a minute, this male gaze, it must not have only to do with Richard because all these costumes were my idea. Richard never said put on a black garter belt. That's not his cup of tea at all. Or maybe it is, but he would never say so. (p. 138)

SCHECHNER: So this image of Rhoda or Sophia is really Kate Manheim's, not Richard Foreman's? But Richard says that he puts on stage as much as possible what's in his head. If garter belts are not his cup of tea . . .—then you are controlling the stage image. The words may be Foreman's, but these plays are so strongly pictorial—what is seen of the female is from you, is your construction.

MANHEIM: Well, yeah, These plays are my way of living my life.

SCHECHNER: What's going on is a struggle between two consciousnesses. You speak Foreman's words but show yourself in your own way. Does that make you the more unconscious to the two—words being the domain of the conscious mind and images of the dreaming mind?

MANHEIM: I suppose we could say that. There has certainly been a struggle. (p. 139)

SCHECHNER: I think **Radio** is different from other Foreman plays. The actors are more visible as characters, there's a story, it's thematically more organized, closer to a play Richard might direct rather than one he wrote and directed.

MANHEIM: I was very instrumental in that. The play he had at the beginning—he went into his drawers and he took pages randomly from various scripts and shuffled them all together. He's done that for a lot of his plays but it doesn't show as much as this one did. And I just kept telling him it made no sense, it had nothing to do with "film is evil, radio is good." I kept trying to piece it together so that it would make some sense.

SCHECHNER: Now people are saying this is the best Foreman play as a playscript. It's your input then that people are appreciating?

MANHEIM: It's become increasingly unbearable to me to be in something that doesn't make sense like **Miss Universal Happiness**. I liked very much **Africanus Instructus,** which I wasn't in. (pp. 141-42)

SCHECHNER: Your experience in **Radio** is different than in the other plays because of your input.

MANHEIM: Yeah, it's a little less painful to do. There're still some things, left to me, I'd get rid of. The vision of God on the wallpaper—I hate that.

SCHECHNER: And the hood?

MANHEIM: Ah, the hood. The hood is left over from **Georges Bataille's Bathrobe** (1983) that we did in Paris. I hated so much being in **Radio** that I kept trying to be off stage or covered up. I said, "Can't I be off stage until after the movie?" And that's when he thought of putting me up in the booth. And then I said, "My entrance at the beginning is not so spectacular. I think I should wear a ski mask or dark glasses." I forget whether it was Richard or me who thought of adding the hood. I wanted to have on lots of different layers at the beginning that later I would unpeel. (p. 142)

> *Kate Manheim, in an interview with Richard Schechner, in* The Drama Review, *Vol. 31, No. 4, Winter, 1987, pp. 136-42.*

ERIKA MUNK

> [*Erika Munk is the theater editor of* The Village Voice *where she writes on theater, books, and cultural politics. In the following excerpt Munk finds* Film Is Evil: Radio Is Good *to be a potent and emotional exploration of the fate of humanity in a world dominated by technological media.*]

At one point in Richard Foreman's New York University production of **Film Is Evil: Radio Is Good** (1987), a row of signs lit up along the side of the stage. In small letters they announced we were "on the air," in large ones they simply said "EGO." They were reminiscent of the exit signs in a movie theatre, too. A nice image, leading the spectator in many directions at once. Ego was indeed on the air, and—this being theatre—in the air, but ego certainly offered no way out of the many dilemmas which are the play's subject.

On the contrary, Ego as vanity, ego as the desire to hear one's own voice and see one's own image, ego as the will to control others by manipulating voices and images, has thrown our part of the human race—the "developed" world—into a self-reflecting pit where autonomy is lost, and art-making, in its attempt to recover that autonomy, has to do battle with the self-reflective and manipulative techniques which it is at the same time using. This means, among other things, that no matter how "advanced" or "elite" a particular form of theatrecraft is, it has to take mass culture into serious account.

Film Is Evil: Radio Is Good takes place on a sound stage hung with Hebrew lettering and a multitude of clocks whose hands are close to midnight, or perhaps noon: we may be at the end of an era, or the beginning of one. Throughout, the invisible delights of radio (made, of course, quite visible on stage) are pitted against the tyrannical images of film—Echo against Narcissus. Film is coercive, radio is freeing. Film is aggrandizing, radio is faceless. Film is devouring, radio is soothing. Film makes you sit, radio lets you walk. Film is physical, radio is spiritual. However mysterious or hilarious any moment on stage may be, however many layers of meaning can be drawn from it, this argument is the play's constant text. Foreman's characters are struggling with the various ways in which human consciousness has been displaced by the machines of expression; they are dealing with the results of our unending violation of the first two commandments, with the consequences of turning our all-too-human selves into god and worshipping our own images.

These are hardly new subjects. Over the last 15 years or so, serious thinking about "the media" has changed Western ideas of oppression, expression, and reality: oppression can be intangible, expression impersonal, reality incorporeal. That art is now more often about artforms—especially the forms of mass culture—than about anything else has become a cliché. The very existence of an unmediated (forgive the pun) anything-else has become an open question. In American theatre this question has been dealt with extensively but indirectly: commercial productions embrace the tone, shape, and subject matter of commercial television, pandering to their audiences while conditioning them to expect exactly the same thing from live theatre as from the tube, though at a vastly different price. Most experimental performance either satirizes the mass media in the gingerly and gentle fashion we satirize something we can't imagine living without, or fools around with inserting rebellious content into standard sitcom or MTV forms. (pp. 143-44)

So for Foreman not only to make live theatre out of thinking about media, but to present the process of this thinking framed and distanced, is a splendid, paradoxical, touching project. We may have reached, as one character says, "the end of in-itselfness," but Foreman tells us about it in the most in-itself, fleshy, fallible medium of all, and with this paradox illuminates the grief and pratfalls of people who've lost themselves as a result of their own inventions and are looking desperately for a way out.

The play as seen is more extremely different from the text as read than is usual even for experimental work. And yet there's a possibility—not a large probability, but the glimmer of a chance—that this script, unlike other Foreman texts, could be directed by someone else, in some totally different way, and still keep the integrity of its ideas and its feelings about the world. It's not easily pleasing in the manner of Foreman's work with Stanley Silverman, but it's not hermetic like the earliest plays nor eccentrically referential like the larger and (to my mind) slicker productions at the Public Theater. The word "accessible" is demeaning to both artist and spectator, but certainly the subject(s) of this piece are important and comprehensible to anyone likely to be in an experimental theatre audience. I say this merely to indicate that in describing the play as seen at NYU I do not mean to fix Foreman's staging as an absolute and immutable approach.

Kate Manheim played a radio broadcaster named Estelle Merriweather, so far the most complex and least victimized version of the ever-questioning character she has performed in Foreman's work for almost 20 years. She appears first as an ominous dark figure crossing the stage, and announces her independence with her opening line to her admirer, himself a fragment of a Foreman alter ego: "I have an announcement to make. You are not my Prince Charming." Most of the time she wears white, like a lab assistant, as she praises radio, fights the camera, and rejects the hero. Periodically she dons a high, black, hoodlike cap, something for a sorcerer or an inquisitor. She veers, that is, between technology and mysticism, and her mystical being could be godlike or simply alien: "Did you ever hear me late at night, broadcasting to whoever may be out there in the darkness?" She drifts between bossy coolness and a wry yearning that would be lyrical if she didn't catch it at the last minute, while lines like "Man has failed and must be elevated to ritual" come out of her mouth.... (p. 144)

The man she speaks of is not generic "Man." Her non-Prince Charming, Paul Antonelli, was performed . . . as a sweetly serious, confused soul, another radio (rather than film) person, prone to passivity and diffidence—though in one scene he burst into lust with two women in a pew. He seems to be named for Saints Paul and Anthony. Foreman doesn't leave Man, or men, at that, however. There is also didactic man—"Don't run away until I can find out how to explain everything"—and controlling man, the man behind the camera. All of this is Foreman's joke on Foreman, a form of extraordinarily self-involved modesty: poking fun at himself as the creative artist who attempts to use and document the performing artist, as the intellectual taming the creature of instinct or emotion or spirituality, as stereotypical man vis-à-vis stereotypical woman, Foreman deflates the stereotypes while slyly clinging to his belief in them.

In *Rhoda in Potatoland* (1976), after more than a decade of playing the visible puppeteer—who sat at his sound-and-light board somewhat to the side of the performance space, cued the action, pressed intolerably loud buzzers, shone lights in the audience's eyes—Foreman stood up at a crucial moment, left the controls, and came on stage to argue with Rhoda. Now an ordinary technician works the controls, high up and almost out of sight. Foreman seems nowhere to be seen. This is, however, an illusion. There is a film within the play, which Foreman directed and in which he stars—so he is not only the playmaker, a character within the play, and one ideological pole of the play's argument, but filmmaker and actor, too.

This egocentricity would be oppressive if Foreman hadn't taken it so far, apparently in order to point it out. "Look how trapped in my head I am!" he seems to be saying. "Isn't that silly? Aren't you in the same boat? Are you noticing that the more elaborately we evolve our art-and-information technology, the more we're thrown on the self? And have you noticed how the more we're thrown on ourselves the feebler our grip becomes on what that self is?" In the film, a third of the way through the play, there are two moments which embody the paradoxes of freezing our own images and throw a shadow on the rest of the play.

The first moment is political. The camera fixes on Foreman's intelligent, friendly, unassuming spaniel-eyed face, and stays there. The longer it stays, the more authoritative, and then authoritarian, and then threatening, the face becomes—without really changing very much at all. The simple fact of an image filling a scene turns that image into something larger than, and different from, both the originary and its first few seconds as an image. This is how dictators, and celebrities, are made.

The second moment has to do with the nature of human identity, and comes at the end of the film. Foreman humbles himself before the camera, that is, before our eyes, putting the audience in the position of looking through the lens. He kneels down in a Moslem attitude of prayer, an obsequiousness almost comical, almost satiric—and vanishes. Poof! Into the air, like a miracle, or maybe the ultimate disaster: such loss of self in the process of making art out of the self can be read many ways.

Those two moments, not necessarily central points of the film, crystallize an interesting shift from using Manheim as the camera's subject and object to showing that the director himself is the true focus of his own voyeurism—a twist on the by now often overworked analysis of "the gaze" and its "masculine" function.

The essence of this particular maleness is self-involvement, and the female is so far objectified that she becomes a prop, not a person. Manheim, who has been the focal point on stage for so many Ontological-Hysteric productions. . .is completely secondary in **"Radio Rick in Heaven and Radio Richard in Hell."**

In the play itself, Kate/Estelle is still central: Foreman makes it clear that who she is and how she is seen depends on the medium employed. (Whether she agrees that her being is merely contingent is another matter, and Foreman lets us know in many ways that his artistic choices aren't necessarily her true reflection.) As she's seen through, or associated with, different media, Estelle takes on different kinds of reality. When the film is finished, Estelle, on stage, lapses into a comically hyperlyrical speech; bookish and old-fashioned, it's a startling contrast both to the cold, disjunctive style of Foreman's filming of the same actions, and to the way she usually speaks in the play.

Of course theatre, for all its three-dimensional mortality, is just another medium competing for artistic turf, though the script barely mentions this omnipresent fact. (It doesn't have to, considering not only that this *is* theatre, but extremely theatrical theatre—Foreman's staging providing a constant gloss on the film/radio debate.) The third major character, Helena Sovianavitch, though she owns the radio station, embodies the spirit of the histrionic—all flesh and mannerisms—and [she] managed, with every grand gesture and rounded elocution, to show the audience that live performance is less threatening but more engaging than dead electronic art precisely because it doesn't try to replicate or replace reality. . . .Acting out a tradition long antedating the antimimetic and antisentimental performance style of Foreman's own staging, [Sovianavitch] undidactically urged us to consider how theatre over the centuries had been an opening wedge for media domination by engendering confusion between histrionics and life and tempting people to perform themselves. Perhaps the moment when religious ritual became theatre—if indeed there ever was such a moment—was the moment of the Fall.

Certainly, as the play unfolds, Estelle's search for an alternative to film is more and more clearly religious, and the playing space is deluged with Jewish and Christian artifacts. This is "a fallen world that worships a multitude of graven images." A smug little golden calf is wheeled in, followed not long after by Paul, carrying a side of veal (referred to as "carcass" in the text). Female student actors are constrained by heavy contraptions strapped to their waists, supporting arches over their heads that spell Charity, Purity, Love, and Virtue. Later, the students, girls and boys, hold placards with Christ-like faces painted in pure East Village expressionism. Helena walks around with a collection plate on an enormously long handle. A devil-mannequin perched on the back wall provides a constant, tiny reminder of Faust's compact. That film (and perhaps all technology) represents a fall from grace is clear; that the corrupted, diminished, venal, or silly religiosity threading through almost every scene can be of any help at this late date isn't clear at all.

Estelle also searches for hope in books, but they are as irreducibly from the past as are the relics of old faiths. A table is strewn with medium-sized, silver-colored volumes, decorated with tiny, glittering red hearts. No one seems able to read them, though now and then Estelle will give a speech in a prose so rhetorically at odds with Foreman's usual laconic, affectless dialog that it must have come from their pages. They are basically dead texts, hearts and all. Or hearts above all: the Manhattan audience laughed very hard at the line, "In today's world some people experience a certain deficiency of emotion."

Yet *Film Is Evil: Radio Is Good* suffers no deficiency of emotion. The piece was produced with Foreman's usual energy— or hysteria—and all my interpretations are not only provisional, or possibly wrong, but much too tidy in light of the way the event moved. The space filled abruptly every now and then with people dancing in sudden frenzy, freezing mid-motion, dancing again. The deep stage was crammed with constantly changing props; lights and music hurled the spectators from one emotional tone to another. No matter how much intellectual fantasizing the production prompted, every thought was enmeshed in sensuous action. This action was not aggressive toward the audience, as it so often was in Foreman's earlier work.

There was also a deeper level of emotionality, beyond all this complex and busy vividness: no one laughed at the words, "The microphones in this beautiful modern studio have turned to ice." Foreman has not suddenly sunk into any sentimental-realist "feeling," but this piece has a new and powerful sense of balked connections, of loss and desire, of a terror in the face of our new world which neither man's explanations nor woman's searches can alleviate. This terror goes far beyond the film-is-evil-radio-is-good arguments among the characters, and exists most powerfully as a subject which the play doesn't even mention, but which I assume—perhaps rashly—that Foreman has set as an unspoken frame around his action.

The play seems to be taking place some unspecified number of years ago, so the audience knows something the protagonists don't: the film/radio argument has come too late and is already irrelevant. The play's oppositions are misleading, almost a game. Television is the subtext; the real poles are mechanical media and the living, spiritual self. Both radio and film started what most advanced technology is completing: consider Hitler's radio speeches, or the bizarrely similar iconography of Nazi, Stalinist, and New Deal propaganda films. Television has taken off from these ill-omened starts, and there's no turning back. Every moment of joy in the production was alive, while all the discussion was about the nonimmediate, about media fixed in time or removed from flesh. For the audience, this inbuilt tension creates the work's meaning. But for the characters, the situation is hopeless. Estelle says, "Here's an idea of my own invention. De-hypnotize the brain"; she pulls the plug so she can listen to things as they really are—and then listens through earphones.

A friend argued that the play is not about technology or social control or a deep change in the sense of self that's come upon us, but simply about artforms. Yet I can't imagine a work called *Painting Is Evil: Music Is Good* that would be imbued through and through, as this play is, with the feeling that our lives are at stake. (pp. 145-48)

Erika Munk, " 'Film Is Ego: Radio Is God,' Richard Foreman and the Arts of Control," in The Drama Review, *Vol. 31, No. 4, Winter, 1987, pp. 143-48.*

A(lbert) R(amsdell) Gurney, Jr.

American Academy and Institute of Arts and Letters: Award of Merit for Drama

(Also writes as Pete Gurney) American dramatist, novelist, and scriptwriter.

Gurney is known for his witty, mildly satirical portraits of life among the upper-middle-class of America's Northeastern seaboard. Through finely-crafted comic vignettes, he portrays the manners and foibles of his bourgeois characters. Gurney's works are often compared to those of short story writer and novelist John Cheever and playwrights Philip Barry and S. N. Behrman. While Gurney shares Cheever's insider's view and his open identification with the white Anglo-Saxon Protestant (WASP) community in New England, his plays differ from those of Barry and Behrman—who wrote from the perspective of outsiders and view the community as a permanent institution. Gurney presents WASP society as a culture gradually losing its once formidable power and privilege and blends affectionate descriptions of their customs with poignant social criticism. Gurney observed: "What seems to obsess me is the contrast between the world and the values I was immersed in when I was young and the nature of the contemporary world. The kind of protected, genteel, in many ways warm, civilized, and fundamentally innocent world in which I was nurtured didn't seem in any way to prepare me for the late twentieth century. I tend to write about people who are operating under these old assumptions, but are confronting an entirely different system of values."

Gurney began writing plays and musical revues while he was an undergraduate at Williams College. During his post-graduate study of drama at Yale University, two of Gurney's one-act plays were included in Best Short Plays collections. Gurney's early work includes musicals and such one-act plays as *The Bridal Dinner* (1962), *The Rape of Bunny Stuntz* (1964), *The David Show* (1966), and *The Golden Fleece* (1968). *The David Show* was his first major off-Broadway production. After writing *Scenes from American Life* (1971), his first two-act play, Gurney concentrated primarily on full-length works. During the 1970s and 1980s he wrote an average of a play a year, and his works were produced in regional, off-Broadway, and London theaters. Nevertheless, he gained relatively little critical or popular recognition until the success of *The Middle Ages* (1977) and *The Dining Room* (1982).

Like his earlier play *Scenes from American Life, The Dining Room* is a series of interconnected episodes dramatizing the traditions of upper-middle-class Northeasterners and their responses, over several decades, to the changing manners and morals of American society. The play is set in a dining room, where an assortment of some sixty characters—played by five or six actors in multiple roles—enact humorous or poignant scenes of WASP life. This use of an unusual staging device or dramatic idea is typical of Gurney's work. *The David Show,* for instance, transplants figures from the Biblical story of King David to an American television studio of the 1960s, while each character in *Sweet Sue* (1986) is portrayed simultaneously

© Gerry Goodstein 1988

by two actors. In The *Perfect Party* (1986), Gurney employs a deliberately artificial farcical style similar to that of Oscar Wilde's *The Importance of Being Earnest.* In similarly mannered fashion, he imparts a dimension of allegory to his story. Gurney tacitly compares the protagonist of this play, an arrogant university professor who attempts to create "the perfect party," to a dramatist longing to stage the perfect theatrical event.

Although Gurney is best known as a comic playwright, critics praise his ability to create moving dramatic situations. In plays such as *Children* (1974), his adaptation of the John Cheever story "Goodbye, My Brother," he portrays the tensions underlying family relationships as well as the powerful emotions beneath the reserved exterior of social manners. Gurney's most well-received plays, including *The Dining Room, The Middle Ages,* and *The Perfect Party,* combine engaging humor with poignant moments of social criticism. Despite the fact that many of his plays have received mixed reviews, Gurney has earned a solid reputation as a gifted playwright. In particular, critics praise his elegantly humorous chronicling of the social milieu that has become so closely identified with his work.

(See also *CLC*, Vol. 32 and *Contemporary Authors*, Vols. 77-80.)

CLIVE BARNES

When a play is about David and Goliath and you find yourself rooting for Goliath, you might well conjecture on what the author did wrong. *The David Show* . . . is monstrous, pretentious and, perhaps most of all, vain.

Written by A. R. Gurney Jr., it takes sophomoric humor to new depths in its efforts to place the story of David—as told in the first two Books of Samuel—in the context of a television show. Oh, come, Mr. Gurney, I'm no TV lover, but TV was never so bad. Not even the Ed Sullivan Show.

David is the sharp organization man, smiling empty, media-style smiles, and battling to acquire Saul's throne with all the pointless expertise of a Madison Avenue ad man in search of an account. Saul is like a retired football coach, and Jonathan a depressed hippie, drinking cheap beer and courting rejection. Bathsheba is a man-eating Wasp, stinging her good Jewish boy into fame and fortune. Samuel—poor old Samuel—is reduced into some kind of TV linkman, telling the story, and the arranging the action of David, the new style TV-king.

Perhaps some concept of a Biblical epic as a TV minispectacular—mind you in this instance they missed out on the commercials, which, as anyone who watches TV will tell you, are the only endurable aspect of it—is valid. But Mr. Gurney's vanity was to imagine that he could write it. His jokes fell as flat as Holland in the monsoon season, and his insights were as probing as a blind caterpillar with gloves on. . . .

And so we leave the smooth nothingness of Mr. Gurney's play with its empty intellectual beaches and gently lapping waters of inconsequentiality. And as we leave we idly ask why? Why should a producer, presumably an intelligent man, with all the world to choose from, have imagined that this was worth his money and—to be personal—my time.

Clive Barnes, "'The David Show' Arrives," in The New York Times, *November 1, 1968, p. 34.*

EDITH OLIVER

[*The David Show*] takes place in a television studio. Against the back wall of the set are two crossed flags—the Stars and Stripes and a white flag bearing a gold Star of David. There is a small monitor screen in one corner, and various lights and technical appliances are scattered around the stage. Samuel, the High Priest, enters in clerical robes. He will shortly be crowning David King of the Jews, and although he would rather have performed the ceremony in the temple, David—who soon joins him, dressed in a navy-blue business suit—wanted it done over television, the temple being too "ethnically oriented" for a coronation as important as this one. They are in the studio for a runthrough of the broadcast. So far in the play, most of the lines are television inside jokes, and the idea seems just a droll one for a night-club skit. Then, suddenly, . . . the show turned into the first bright comedy of this Off Broadway season, and the first true satire—with the wit and underlying seriousness that satire demands—in Heaven knows how long. This metamorphosis took place, perhaps a bit more slowly than I've

indicated, as we were introduced to the rest of the characters. David's old friend Jonathan, with whom he used to sing psalms, with guitar accompaniment, at various bars around town, is a pot-smoking, scruffy, vaguely bisexual, wise, ethically sound, and . . . delightfully disreputable hippie. Ham, David's black slave and currently his production assistant, is a subtle, ironic fellow. . . . King Saul, whom David is about to replace on the throne, is an old Southern general (without, by the way, the slightest hint of Texas about him) and a total square. . . . The funniest character is that of Bathsheba, wife of Uriah the Hittite, mistress of David, and a Philistine if ever there was one in that crowd. . . . Bathsheba, a girl with a non-stop spate of glittery, italicized chatter, was given throwaway lines like "when I was a girl at Farmington," and her aplomb enabled her to rise above any social disaster—which, come to think of it, is not a bad description of Jonathan, David's old buddy and her greatest trial. Her iron hand almost but not quite slipped out of its velvety concealment whenever she was in danger of not getting her own way. ("David, get rid of Samuel. I've got a good God-is-dead Episcopalian. Now don't *argue*. I've seen a whole dinner party *ruined* by one argumentative Jew.") Her acceptance of hurt, poise intact, when David jilts her after she has told him that her husband is dead and she is free to marry him was impressive and surprisingly touching. (p. 115)

David, of course, is the most complex character of the bunch— a fast-talking young man on the rise who uses everyone and then sloughs off everyone, until he finally gets his comeuppance. Samuel, calm and unshakable, refuses to crown him until he has fought Goliath. Near the end, David stands alone, spotlighted on a semi-darkened stage with slingshot in hand, and it dawns upon him that his Goliath is his own enormous shadow on the wall—his own black, crooked soul. It was an effective scene that was somehow in keeping with all the sharp, funny scenes that had gone before. . . . As for Mr. Gurney, there is little to add except that he is a gifted playwright—a sparse breed at the moment—with an accurate ear for the kinds of things that are being said right now, and an understanding of the kinds of people who are saying them.

The David Show was not a flawless play—the comedy went overboard every once in a while and got a bit too broad for its own good—but it was unconventional and up-to-date, and each scene made its point. (pp. 115-16)

Edith Oliver, in a review of "The David Show," in The New Yorker, *Vol. XLIV, No. 38, November 9, 1968, pp. 115-16.*

CLIVE BARNES

Pages from American history—past, present and future—are the sociological subject matter of A. R. Gurney Jr's *Scenes from American Life*. . . .

Mr. Gurney is presenting vignettes of American life-styles from the Depression years, through World War II, Korea, Vietnam, and onward to some ghastly police state of the nineteen-eighties, where the military and their computers have taken control, and the whole country is behind barbed wire and under surveillance. The lucky ones are emigrating to Canada.

The scenes are set in Buffalo, where Mr. Gurney was born and raised. He has now left, which, in the light of his play, is nothing but understandable.

To an extent these free-ranging sketches wandering through time are exercises of style, the kind of thing a young playwright might very well attempt. Yet some of the writing—indeed, most of the writing, is excellent, and Mr. Gurney's splintered view of a splintered society is effective and chilling.

The play has no coherent story. There might be a hero. Certainly there is a young man called Snoozer, who is christened in the very first scene—cheerfully and tearfully splashed with his first bootlegged martini—and is mentioned vaguely throughout the play. In the final scene Snoozer himself actually makes an appearance, and seems to be a perfectly ordinary young man. Of course, this is Mr. Gurney's intention: To show us perfectly ordinary people in perfectly ordinary Buffalo.

They get married, they go to dancing schools, they flirt, they quarrel, they learn about life. The events of the world impinge on them—a Roosevelt, a Hitler, dim stirrings of civil rights, social unrest, then finally militancy, insurrection and the authoritarianism—seen first in tiny hints of curfews and state ordinances demanding that car doors be kept locked, until it engulfs the nation.

Some of Mr. Gurney's pictures are naive and obvious; others have a brisk honesty. A sensitivity group trying to grope its way to freedom from embarrassment and understanding of its children is very funny. Less funny, but also curt and telling, is a scene where a mother has lunch with her daughter, just before a matinee of *Kiss Me Kate,* and discusses whether she should have a coming-out party or a college education.

This is not only a picture of a town, but also a picture of a class—upper middle-class WASP. Immediately after the war there can be no Jews in the country club, and colored folks are never black, and they can be patronized but not seen. The picture is tribal as much as geographical. These people go to the right schools and the right parties. They go boating and swimming in Lake Erie—until pollution takes over. And even when they have to put electric fences around their communities they show proper concern for their dogs.

Unfortunately, Mr. Gurney sees better than he interprets. The actual mosaic structure of the play does tell against it. This is a society in a spiraling dance of death, but Mr. Gurney never explains why. The people are more foolish than craven, and while they are conservative, mean and often petty, it is never clear what they do or don't do to deserve the terrible fate Mr. Gurney has in store for them. Perhaps they were just unlucky.

Possibly the play would have been more pointed if some of the characters had remained consistent through the play. It is the nature of sketches never to know personal conclusions, and I felt that a few continuing life-histories winding through this Decline and Fall of the American Empire would have given the play more continuity and force.

Clive Barnes, " 'Scenes from American Life' at Forum," in The New York Times, *March 26, 1971, p. 33.*

IRVING WARDLE

[*Wardle is an English editor, nonfiction writer, dramatist, and drama critic of the London* Times. *He is the author of the drama* The Houseboy *(1973), as well as the biography* The Theatres of George Devine *(1978). In the following excerpt, he lauds* Children *as an important drama about family relationships.*]

[*Children*] is a quietly conservative story of middle-class family life, and it strikes me as the best mainstream play to come out of America since the debut of Arthur Miller.

As its author, A. R. Gurney Jnr, is known to British audiences only from a few one-acters, it might help if I labelled him roughly as America's answer to Peter Nichols. Besides his similar range of subject matter, he shares Nichols's capacity to say important things through trivial events, his dispassionate sympathy towards all his characters, and, above all, his power to discover arresting dramatic patterns in commonplace experience without telling any lies.

Given Mr Gurney's nationality, and this subject of this play, these are precious gifts. Families have always dominated the American stage; and in my lifetime they have been viewed through a thick fog of authorian hang-ups and Broadway protocol. No trace of the fog lingers over Mr Gurney's family portrait: no sense of revenge writing, no hysterical confrontations, rattling skeletons, or Oedipal mechanics, and absolutely no suggestion that love solves everything. In this play, at least, the form has grown up; permitting one to look back to the output of William Inge, Robert Anderson and Co as the work of children.

Such, in fact, is the point of the play, which introduces a mother and her family of married children and shows that none of them has grown up. We see them at a Fourth of July reunion at their summer home, and follow their lives for a single day. The place is idyllic . . . , but already by 7 am the humans are messing things up.

Barbara, recently divorced, sneaks in guiltily and informs brother Randy that she has spent the night with a girl friend. For a while the picture builds up in the standard American style: bright sunlight and wholesome people all due for their comeuppance when night falls.

The first shadow is the unexpected return of Pokey—the most difficult child of the family, and the mother's favourite. This releases the news that mother is about to remarry, and the house to pass into the possession of the three children. With their own children firmly excluded from the terrace, Barbara and Randy themselves start reverting to childhood, squabbling over their rival plans for the house, and exposing each others' weak spots in the fight. . . .

Barbara comes over as censoriously disappointed, masking her sense of failure with glib theorizing: . . . Randy (a schoolteacher) as an athletics fanatic driven into a rage by losing any kind of game. Meanwhile, unseen inside the house, Pokey continues to stir up trouble with demands that would mean the sale of the house, and with his implacable disapproval of his mother's second marriage.

The plot drops in several lurid suspicions without actually involving the characters in anything improbable. Technically it is a wonderfully accomplished piece of story-telling. . . .

Pokey, simply an awkward brother to his two siblings, becomes an ominous symbolic presence to the audience: at once the most childish of all the characters, and the means by which the others are exposed. All the marriages are brought into danger. Layer after layer is peeled off the characters. (Barbara, we find, has WASP values thrust upon her, and has spent her married years pining for the family's despised yardman.) Even the mother finally drops her mask of responsibility and prepares to storm out and enjoy her last 10 good years.

I called the play conservative because it is about preserving things of value. The house is a vanishing bit of America. The family have had it for 80 years and it is worth keeping, no matter who lives in it. Other people, just as selfish and destructive, managed to preserve it. It gives some small ground for human optimism to see it preserved once again.

Irving Wardle, "Family Life without Broadway Fog,"
in The Times, *London, April 9, 1974, p. 13.*

EDITH OLIVER

[*Children*] is set on the front porch, facing the sea, of a summer house on a resort island off the New England coast. The members of the well-to-do family in residence are a middle-aged, still attractive widow; her divorced daughter, Barbara; her tantrummy son, Randy.... *Children* is based, in a loose sort of way, on John Cheever's short story "Goodbye, My Brother." . . . It lacks the reverberations and the mystery of the original—but then Mr. Gurney is not trying for them; he is off on a different tack. The play is experimental in that the protagonists—or, at least, the characters who control the plot and precipitate its climax—do not appear, though they are just as well and fully drawn as the others. They are another son, called Pokey (whose outline is dimly visible through a screen door at the end), and his Jewish wife, Miriam. These two have not visited the island in years, during which time Pokey has held a succession of unsatisfying jobs. The mother has invited the entire family (voices of many children in the background) for the weekend of the Fourth to tell them that she is giving up the house to her sons and daughter (by the terms of their late father's will) and will shortly be married to a friend so close that they all call him "Uncle Bill." Pokey immediately makes it clear that he wishes to sell out to his brother and sister; they, in turn, realize that they will have to sell the entire property in order to raise the cash for his equity. Much that has been repressed in all of them rises to the surface. Randy's hatred of Pokey explodes into violence (Cheever); Jewish, bra-less Miriam, who allows her children the freedom to use dirty language, to drink Cokes with their meals, and to watch television, and who has strong ideas about being useful in life (Gurney), proves to be as much a catalyst as her husband, and she has a profound effect on Randy's wife, Jane. Another unseen character who should be mentioned is a rich local builder, formerly the family's yard boy; the difference between the general attitude toward him (utter contempt) and toward Miriam (curiosity and slight distaste) is interesting, for the play is, among other matters, about Us and Them.

Us are, of course, the old Protestant gentry, as they comport themselves in various situations—some crucial, some trivial—when face to face with the social upheavals of the present. This was also true to a certain extent of Mr. Gurney's delightful *Scenes from American Life,* which a colleague of mine admiringly and accurately compared to the novels of Booth Tarkington. Here, too, the tone is rueful and ironic and "civilized," but the undertone is much darker and the dramatic elements much more overt. The experiment of making the offstage characters do the work—drama by indirection, so to speak—is successful; one is held from beginning to end.

Edith Oliver, in a review of "Children," in The New
Yorker, *Vol. LII, No. 38, November 8, 1976, p. 167.*

FRANK RICH

In one of the many vignettes that make up A. R. Gurney Jr.'s new play, *The Dining Room,* an aunt proudly poses with her collection of Waterford crystal for a photo-snapping nephew. The aunt is all smiles and coos. She's most pleased that the nephew has left his studies at Amherst to come down and take her picture.

But eventually she makes the mistake of asking the boy just why it is that he's taken such a sudden interest in both her and her stemware. And, to her horror, she discovers that he is doing an anthropology class project on "the eating habits of vanishing cultures." The nephew has chosen "the WASP's of the Northeastern United States" as his subject. His aunt's crystal fingerbowls, he explains, demonstrate "a neurotic obsession with cleanliness associated with the guilt of the last stages of capitalism."

Mr. Gurney's play . . . is a similar anthropological study, though not nearly so stern or dry. *The Dining Room* is set in an archetypal WASP dining room—austere dark wood table and sideboard, parquet floor, sterile white walls, Oriental rug—and it offers a series of snapshots of a vanishing culture. In each scene we meet the members and servants of a different WASP family, as they gather together for holidays, birthdays or dinner parties, or fall apart by dint of arguments, infidelities, deaths or changing mores. While the characters belong to various generations and various 20th-century decades, they are all exemplars of an insular upper-middle-class way of life that social history has outrun.

The Dining Room isn't flawless, but it's often funny and rueful and, by the end, very moving. Mr. Gurney, a novelist as well as a playwright, was the author of one of the Public Broadcasting Service's John Cheever dramatizations (*O Youth and Beauty*), and he learned some lessons well. If he doesn't share Mr. Cheever's gift for subtlety, he does share his compassion and ability to create individual characters within a milieu that might otherwise seem as homogenous as white bread. Though dozens of people whirl in and out of Mr. Gurney's metaphorical dining room, they all come through as clearly and quickly as the voices we hear in a Cheever story like "The Enormous Radio." . . .

[One] wishes this play had fewer forced, *Preppie Handbook* style jokes and fewer theme-italicizing scenes, in which contemporary characters want to remodel or do away with the dining room and all the ghostly tradition it represents. . .

The Dining Room is most resonant when the action speaks for itself. Nowhere is this truer than in a beautiful Act II encounter between . . . a proper, Wall Street father, and . . . his married daughter. [The daughter] has come home because she wants "to start all over again." Her marriage is over, and neither her children, nor a new lover nor a brief lesbian fling has arrested her fear that "I don't know where I am." But her father, while polite, doesn't want her back. [He] mixes a drink, offers a few useless words of distant, lawyerly advice, then turns away as if his anguished child had left the room. As in all of Mr. Gurney's most powerful scenes, we're reminded that even in the most privileged of homes, there's not always freedom from want.

Frank Rich, "Vignettes by A. R. Gurney Jr.," in
The New York Times, *February 15, 1982, p.15.*

JACK KROLL

As we all know, Wasps are an endangered species. A. R. Gurney Jr.'s new play, *The Dining Room,* is a wry and tender elegy for these disappearing creatures of tweed and tea. In fact, in one of the many interlocking episodes that make up the play, a young man gets his aunt to pose with her precious china, place mats, pistol-grip cutlery and finger bowls for his anthropology-class project on disappearing cultures. All the scenes take place in that ancient Wasp habitat, the dining room, the antiseptic yet somehow warm arena of good manners, polite conversation and generational indoctrination. The dining room is going the way of most of the amenities of the old American ruling class, and Gurney sets his amusing, sharp-eyed charades of genteel deliquescence right there among the stiff-backed chairs, long mirror-polished table and swinging doors that once led to faithful servants puttering in the kitchen. . . .

The play hopscotches about in time, from the zenith to the nadir of Waspdom. Zenith: a father, hearing that a homosexual relative has been insulted at his club, leaves his family to do battle with the offenders like Sir Gawain trotting off after the Grail. Nadir: a daughter returns home after a broken marriage, a busted love affair and a lesbian liaison, but there's no longer room for her in her father's house or heart. Gurney scatters other telling vignettes: a grandmother, wide-eyed in smiling senility, keeps leaving a family dinner because she doesn't recognize her family; an aged father instructs his son with gruff poignance in the arrangements for his funeral; a son arrives home to find his mother dallying with a friend of the family.

Gurney, who has carved out a place for himself as something of a theatrical John Cheever, does not cut to the deepest Cheeverian depths. But his play is intelligent, warm and affecting.

> *Jack Kroll, "Family Hold Back," in* Newsweek, *Vol. XCIX, No. 11, March 15, 1982, p. 64.*

FRANK RICH

To be privileged, we're often told, is to be free: those born to wealth and social status have a head start in finding the happiest and most productive path through life. But the writer A. R. Gurney Jr. good-naturedly insists on reminding us that it isn't necessarily so. In plays like *The Dining Room, What I Did Last Summer,* and now *The Middle Ages,* he says that even that most privileged of Americans, the upper-middle-class WASP, can be as trapped as anyone else. For Mr. Gurney's characters, living well is *not* the best revenge—it's the last and weakest defense.

Not surprisingly, there's often been a pleasing echo of John Cheever in Mr. Gurney's fine work in *The Middle Ages,* . . . one hears the lilting strains of Philip Barry. Set over a 30-year period, beginning in the mid-1940's, this romantic comedy tells of Barney and Eleanor—two likable, would-be lovers who waste most of their adulthoods by failing to fall into each other's arms.

The Middle Ages is both slighter and less transporting than *The Dining Room*—it was written earlier, in 1977—but it is often sweet and funny. At its best, it is less a gloss on the extended mating dance of C. K. Dexter Haven and Tracy Lord in Barry's *The Philadelphia Story* than a sharply observed, elegiac portrait of a troubled and fast-vanishing world. With unsentimental compassion and without caricature, Mr. Gurney actually makes us mourn for people who, at their worst, use expressions like "perfectly ghastly" and raise their eyebrows over any proper name that sounds Jewish (whole cities like Harrisburg not excepted).

The play unfolds in the wood-paneled trophy room of an urban men's club founded by Barney's great-grandfather. "Here's where we really live," says Barney, and so Mr. Gurney's characters do when they're not dining. Through Barney is a

lifelong rebel against his patrician heritage—he graduates from adolescent locker-room rowdiness to radical politics and bisexuality at Berkeley—he is irresistibly drawn back to his ancestral club for state family occasions. So is the more conventional Eleanor, who spurns Barney's affections to marry his unseen "straight little brother," a lawyer with whom she raises three children in the suburbs.

As Barney and Eleanor circle around each other over the years, Mr. Gurney makes the sad case that his characters have little choice over their fates at all. No matter how hard Barney tries to rebel, he still finds that he is "doomed to a lifetime membership" in both the club and his class. Though Eleanor finds Barney's adventures titillating—she likens him to "one of those fabulous uncles in children's books, like Uncle Wiggly or Doctor Doolittle"—it isn't until she's passed into middle age, via the women's movement and divorce, that she can consider reaching out to her quixotic brother-in-law.

As set forth by Mr. Gurney, this couple's confining world indeed suggests the middle ages of history, as defined by Barney in his doctoral thesis: it's "a quiet, dull life punctuated by ceremony." If Cole Porter is the background music, the foreground is defined by sublimated emotions, strict manners and an orthodox faith in such institutions as Princeton University and Cerebral Palsy charity balls. In the play's best scene, at once antic and poignant, the young Barney tries to seduce Eleanor with tollhouse cookies and smoked oysters—the hottest aphrodisiacs that his upbringing allows him to imagine.

The playwright falters when he states his themes explicitly or over-uses his setting as a metaphor for the declining 20th-century fortunes of WASP America (a failing of *The Dining Room* as well). We hear the plot gears shift noisily when he piles up the offstage events that keep reuniting his putative lovers or sketches in the parallel romance of Barney's widower father and Eleanor's divorced mother. The final resolution of all four characters' futures is abrupt and mechanical.

> *Frank Rich, "Gurney's 'Middle Ages' Opens," in* The New York Times, *March 24, 1983, p. C17.*

WILLIAM A. HENRY, III

Three decades pass. Somewhere just offstage, things are happening: the personal pageantry of weddings, christenings, funerals; social upheavals ranging from suburbanization to the sexual revolution. But only the echoes of change are heard in the trophy room of a venerable men's club, the sole setting of *The Middle Ages.* In a time of ethnicity, the club remains a haven for an embattled Wasp old guard. For the younger generation that departs on a picaresque journey through the chaotic world outside, the club is a beacon, a symbol of the formative power of tradition even on those who would escape its sway.

The Middle Ages, like A. R. Gurney Jr.'s other plays about the declining Protestant elite (*Scenes from American Life,* the current off-Broadway hit *The Dining Room*), is a wistful, elegiac comedy that preserves a tight-lipped emotional reserve: confrontations that could be tragic are played for rueful laughter. Unlike most of Gurney's other plays, however, *The Middle Ages* has a well-knit, symmetrical plot. It offers two love stories, a star-crossed one between a clownish boy and the girl who occasionally impels him to grow up, and another, almost accidental, between the boy's father ("My mother got so bored she died") and the girl's divorced, social-climbing mother. The play is also a moving struggle for control and forgiveness between the autocratic father and his farcically self-destructive son. . . .

Like the historical Middle Ages, the present era strikes Gurney as a time to conserve a dwindling heritage. His central character admires the medieval period as "a quiet, dull life punctuated by ceremony." That describes precisely the ordered, ancestor-worshiping existence of the families in *The Middles Ages* and, more broadly, of virtually all families. By the play's end, Gurney's rebel reconciles himself—and the audience—to the serene rewards of dull domesticity.

> *William A. Henry, III, "Elegy for the Declining Wasp," in* Time, *New York, Vol. 121, No. 14, April 4, 1983, p. 79.*

PERRY PONTAC

[*The Dining Room*] is a series of little vignettes of considerable importance, all dealing with the white Anglo-Saxon Protestant world as observed in various North-East American dining rooms over the past 50 years or so. Its numerous scenes, alas, are too brief to be touching, too corny to be amusing, and too superficial to be performed with any depth.

The play, however, is, in structure at least, highly original and even successful. There are 60 characters played [by six actors], . . . and even the set is called upon to play multiple rôles serving as a variety of middle-class dining rooms. The scenes are played without a break between them, a new group of characters often entering just before the end of the old scene. Sometimes the table is shared by characters from different scenes at the same time, their respective episodes being alternatively but never confusingly highlighted. (pp. 32-3)

[The] play, however original its structure, seems to derive its style of dialogue, characterization and situation from American television series. All that is lacking is the incessant background music for the serious scenes and the incessant laughter for the ones that are intended to be funny. A scene between a father and his married daughter who wants to leave her broken marriage and return home ends with the exchange: 'I can't go back, Dad.' 'Neither can I, sweetheart, neither can I.' That final 'neither can I' confirms the dialogue's undistinguished patrimony. Furthermore, Mr Gurney's stage-craft is not always sure. One scene begins with the line, 'My husband who was—what?—your great uncle', a rather unlikely exchange between relations, however illuminating to the audience.

Why, one might wonder, has the play been so successful in the US? Perhaps present-day America, deeply stuck in a golden age of reactionary nostalgia, relishes such glorification of good, old-fashioned predictability. Perhaps in New York the play seems (as it does not in SE 10) relatively honest and unmanipulative, lacking some (if not all) of the calculated sentimentality of the local Broadway product. At Greenwich, however, there seems to be little profundity in Mr Gurney's examination of the Eastern Seaboard, no dangerous or surprising depths at all, only a vast ocean of shallows, without pearls of wit or gems of wisdom. (p. 33)

> *Perry Pontac, in a review of "The Dining Room," in* Plays & Players, *No. 359, August, 1983, pp. 32-3.*

JOHN LEONARD

[*The Dining Room*] is all Wasp. Northeastern White Anglo-Saxon Protestants are looked at by A. R. Gurney Jr. as if they belonged to one of "various vanishing cultures," with interesting eating habits and confused sexual mores. They are not adorable. This is anthropology. It is not a particularly good play. . . . But it lets the actors whip up a hurricane. . . .

We have a dining-room table. It is a long table, pointing toward many windows that look at cultivated gardens. At this table, many well-bred riffraff—a cast of six plays 50 parts—after martinis and scotch, consume celery soup and leg of lamb and Earl Grey tea and brandy. Their three-pronged forks are silver; their knives have pistol handles; their butter plates are Staffordshire; and their wineglasses are by way of Steuben. Between courses, they talk about Episcopal boarding schools, anorexia, Amherst, sailfish, lesbianism, the Boston Symphony, and the Boston Red Sox. After dinner, maybe, they will play bridge. They have last names like Thatcher and first names like Standish and Binky, and they will buy Toyotas and correct one's grammar.

We are in sub-Cheever country, and Gurney hasn't yet figured out whether he hates or loves the people whom John Cheever, with reservations, managed simply to forgive and pray for. Gurney sentimentalizes even as he excoriates. He is fond of impossibly earthy Irish maids, and seems to believe with the chilly Wasps that "every generation has to make the *effort*," and wants to think that it's a good idea for fathers to raise their sons as attentively as "the purple finch feeds its young." But he tells us, simultaneously, that these Cheever people are "just ghosts," preposterous in their self-regard and self-denial. At Thanksgiving, they carve one another up, and there is nothing left.

Gurney is ambivalent, which I admire. Less admirable here is his inability to find a line between satire and smothering, or sociology and reviling, or affectionate disdain and let's-nail-the-condescending-bastards-to-their-own-family-crest. He is buffaloed, country-clubbed. Still, he has watched. He gets the little things right. (pp. 154, 156)

> *John Leonard, "Leave It to Cosby," in* New York Magazine, *Vol. 17, No. 42, October 22, 1984, pp. 154, 156.*

A. R. GURNEY, JR.

> [*In the following excerpt, Gurney comments on the new direction his writing has taken with such works as* The Snow Ball, The Perfect Party, Another Antigone, *and* Sweet Sue.]

It's no secret to say that drama is a restrictive medium, and that those of us who try to write plays are hedged in on all sides by tough laws of dramaturgy which we break only at our peril. To compound the problem, American playwrights, dependent as we are on the uneasy generosity of private enterprise, would seem to be even further encumbered by economic inhibitions that require us to be downright miserly about the number of characters we use or the settings in which our plays take place.

Of course, all playwrights everywhere have long been used to dancing in various chains. Aeschylus was bound by the ritual rule that only two characters on stage at one time were allowed to exchange dialogue. Molière had to be scrupulously tactful about church and court under the shadow of Louis XIV. Samuel Beckett embraces and makes a virtue of the very spareness which good contemporary drama is asked to impose upon itself.

When I was teaching drama courses at the Massachusetts Institute of Technology, I used to tell my students that it is the very pressure of these esthetic restrictions that gives drama so much of its particular power. I would point to the thrilling resonances of offstage events in Greek drama, or the special sense of enclosed space that emerges in Ibsen or Chekhov. "What's left out lends importance to what's put in," I'd say, and we'd explore the glories of artistic structure, as in the sonnet, or the sonata form, or a good play.

What's more, as a playwright, I seemed to find the restrictions of drama particularly suitable for the people I like to write about—the American East Coast bourgeoisie, the much maligned so-called WASP's. These people themselves carry with them a large stock of inherited obligations and inhibitions, and so they seemed to be naturally at home in a form so carefully strictured. Perhaps I was simply a writer who felt comfortable with rules, writing about people who tried to live by them. In any case, there has been for some time some creative confluence between myself and my characters as we struggled within the confines of inherited form.

Four years ago, however, my wife and I sold our house in Boston and moved to New York, and certain things began to happen to my writing. I became more interested in probing and pushing the walls of dramatic form, and obviously the characters in my plays began to do the same. I'm sure the contagious energy and excitement of the city affected me, as well as its turbulent ethnic diversity. I also felt liberated for the first time in 25 years from the oppressive obligations of academic life. And I have to say, too, that the critical atmosphere in this city became, at least for me, suddenly more hospitable. In any case, I found myself stretching and breathing more freely.

Indeed, in the last three years, I've found myself on some sort of a creative high. My mountainous labors may well have produced a series of mice, but no one can deny that I've been writing up a storm and having a good time doing it.

First I wrote a novel called *The Snow Ball*, which in effect said goodbye to the old WASP world of Buffalo, N.Y., which I had been concerned about for so long. Working in fiction, too, was like jogging down an open road far beyond the limitations of the stage. I think it was very helpful in limbering up.

Then I came in, and sat down, and wrote three plays in disgustingly quick succession. All are somewhat interconnected, and all demonstrate some kind of impatience with conventional dramatic form. Let me quickly add that I don't think for one minute I've achieved any breakthroughs in the history of Western drama. But for a 55-year-old father of four, newly arrived in the big city, shaking off the chalk dust of 25 years in the classroom, I've had a good time kicking up my heels.

Frisky as I may feel I'm not foolish enough to evaluate my own work, but I will try to describe what I was up to in each play as it pertains to this sense of pushing against the traditional restrictions of drama.

The Perfect Party came first. It is still very much bound by the classical units of time and place. It all takes place in one room, and stage time pretty much parallels actual time. The play also gives due respect to the producer's checkbook by asking him to pay for only five actors, whose Herculean task is to evoke, describe, participate in and comment on a rather large party taking place just off stage.

Where the play may take a step forward, at least for me, is in its attempt to expand the possibilities of language and plot. The people in this play are impossibly articulate, reveling in the sheer pleasure of being able to say exactly what they feel or mean, and occasionally to be outrageously vulgar. The plot of the play as well also presses against the borders of plausibility and certainly of good taste. I suppose you could say that in this one, I'm still writing about WASP's, although one reviewer pointed out that its cast of characters is 40 percent Jewish. Certainly the host of *The Perfect Party* is WASPy, but by the end of the play I think both he and I would be impatient with such reductive stereotyping. (pp. 1, 6)

I wrote my next play, *Another Antigone*, as a kind of companion piece to *The Perfect Party*. *Party* deals with a professor at home; *Antigone* shows one at work. *Party* pokes fun at ethnic stereotyping; *Antigone* explores the serious damage such stereotyping can do, on both sides. Furthermore, it works with the archetypal conflict between a man who insists on rigid rules and a woman who insists on breaking them. I try to break a few myself in this one, moving away from the strict confines of a single stage space or chronological time. Finally, I tried to explode what Aristotle calls unity of action. I hope there are seriously tragic elements in this play, grounded in the Antigone story, but the frame here is comic. One thing sure; the play doesn't seem to be about WASP's at all. . . .

The last play to emerge from this strange playwriting binge I've been on recently is called *Sweet Sue*. . . . Possibly prompted by Antigone, it began as a treatment of the Phaedra story, but ended simply as a contemporary love story between an older woman and a younger man.

The strange thing that happened here, however, was that I found myself writing it so that two actors would play each role. There's nothing terribly new about this device: O'Neill tried it and so did Peter Nichols. But as I wrote *Sweet Sue*, I discovered the two versions of the character didn't want to shake down into any particular psychological or esthetic category. No one "stands for" the id or the alter ego or the unconscious, for example. I just wanted to paint the same picture with additional colors, and so two actors needed to be there. I found the result enabled me to tell the story much more easily, and at the same time to add a complexity to the texture of the play which I couldn't achieve by staying within the bounds of a traditional two-hander.

Now, none of this experimentation has broken any major sound barriers. It's no big deal. There have been times in the long history of drama when momentous steps have been taken—when Aeschylus asks that a third actor actually speak, for example, or when Shakespeare bursts on the scene in an explosion of poetic pyrotechnics. But I have recently discovered that drama, for all its traditional rigors, is always being pushed and pressed and tested as much as possible. And I'm beginning to relish its resilience. (p. 6)

A. R. Gurney, Jr., *"Pushing the Walls of Dramatic Form,"* in The New York Times, *July 27, 1986, pp. 1, 6.*

RICHARD HORNBY

[*American critic, dramatist, and educator, Hornby is the author of the play* The Kidnappers (1986). *In the following excerpt, he discusses Gurney's farcical use of theatrical conventions in* The Perfect Party.]

A. R. Gurney's new play, *The Perfect Party,* . . . is another of his comedies about "the Wasp culture of the Northeastern United States," as a character in one of his earlier plays says. It has become common to compare Gurney with Updike and Cheever, who have dealt with the same culture in fiction, but where their writing tends to be understated and psychologically suggestive, Gurney's plays are broadly satirical and verbally adroit, more in the tradition of Shaw and Wilde, as well as recent British writers like Alan Ayckbourn or Christopher Hampton. Everything is above board; the resonances are literary and sociological rather than psychological.

The Perfect Party concerns a college professor named Tony, whose obsession is to create just that, a "perfect" party, with an ideal mixture of guests, superb conversation, perfect dress, perfect timing, and so on. It is hard to imagine such an obsession occurring in real life, particularly with a college professor (I'm one, and I certainly don't share it), but then, odd obsessions are the stuff of comedy. No motivation is given for Tony's *idée fixe;* like Gwendolyn's desire to marry a man named Ernest in *The Importance of Being Earnest,* it is simply a given circumstance, even though here it is so all-consuming as to cause Tony to resign his job, and dream of becoming a famous professional party consultant—as if there were such a thing! All this points up the self-referential nature of Gurney's drama, his technique of constantly reminding the audience that they are not seeing real life, but rather a *play,* with literary antecedents and obvious dramatic techniques.

Thus, Gurney brings in a character who is going to "review" Tony's party for a major New York newspaper, an obvious artificiality that is not justified but instead presented as a theatrical joke, since there are critics in the audience (including me) who are reviewing Gurney's play. There are repeated references to literary writers (Tony is, after all, a professor of literature and history), including Updike and Cheever (another joke on the critics) and Wilde. Tony compares the party to a play, referring to the guests before the party begins as being "off-stage"—where the actors playing the guests literally are. When the would-be party reviewer, an aggressive and self-centered woman whose obsession to become famous equals Tony's, complains that the party is set up too safely, lacking "danger," Gurney trots out the traditional device of having Tony play his own wicked twin brother, a turn of events that is not so much a dramatic development in the Aristotelian sense as it is a meta-dramatic satirizing of the device itself.

Naturally, all of Tony's attempts at perfection go wrong, as they always do in farce, and naturally there is a tacked-on happy ending, as artificial and self-referential as Macheath's escape from the gallows at the end of *Threepenny Opera.* Gurney's theme is the decline of social ritual in our lives. He points this up not only by what is depicted, but by calling attention to his own play as a theatrical ritual with obvious artificialities.

Gurney is thus very much a playwright of our time. The fact that his plays succeed is evidence of a significant change in the American theatre, which has been dominated for decades by psychological realism. (pp. 474-75)

> Richard Hornby, *"Role Playing, Self Reference, and Openness,"* in The Hudson Review, *Vol. XXXIX, No. 3, Autumn, 1986, pp. 472-76.*

GARY SEIBERT

[*In the following excerpt, Seibert praises Gurney's exuberant use of language in* The Perfect Party.]

Eric Bentley, in his *The Life of the Drama,* claims that when his son was beginning to get the hang of talking, he accidentally revealed to him the function of language—in life and in the theater. As Mr. Bentley was speaking to his more-or-less infant son, the latter stated firmly and with no stuttering: "Daddy don't talk. ME TALK!" And he has been talking ever since.

According to the wise Mr. Bentley, his son and all his human brothers and sisters have been talking ever since for many reasons—sometimes for profit, but most of the time for fun. . . .

The Perfect Party by A. R. Gurney Jr. provides a champagne toast to the English spoken by a small American tribe on the Eastern seaboard. Admittedly, Gurney's way is not the only way language can soar for the sheer glory of it. It is surely one way, and an elegant one to boot.

This language is spoken crisply and provocatively by an ex-university professor ("ex" because he chucked his tenured teaching position to dedicate his every breath to throwing the "perfect party"), his wife, their friends and a critic from a "major New York newspaper." This talkative cast illustrates another facet of Mr. Bentley's theory of language gleaned from the mouth of his babe. He maintains that his son and all people who are not autistic, not only want to talk now, but want to talk forever and grandly and profoundly and funnily and elegantly! Each of us tries to do just that in our lives, but are prevented by all the others who want to do the same thing. But in the theater—ah, that's something different.

Happily for us, A. R. Gurney has created characters in *The Perfect Party* who spout elegant Cheeveresque American English that is grand and funny. We would not mind if they talked forever. Even more happily, they seem to be pounding out a message that is worthwhile. Through them Gurney asks questions about the nature of language, its relationship to society, to intimacy, to the quest for meaning in a world of computers and personal double talk. He asks about the relationship of language to the fragile construction of social realities, and what it reveals and what it hides from both speakers and listeners. He investigates how the language of our lives relates to the underlying and ever-present drama of our lives. He has his characters think out loud about the human race's natural drive to turn apparently random lives into meaningful scripts.

He implies that if we Americans keep our eyes and ears glued to television soap operas, day and night, if we keep dousing our eyes in MTV videos, if we insist on casting ourselves as heroes and heroines who make guest- and starring-appearances in the everyday sitcoms of our neighborhoods, casually creating ourselves in the image and likeness of trivialized (and, therefore, perpetually young and sexy) versions of a made-for-T.V.-miniseries, we will become what we watch and say and hear in the same way we may become what we eat—junk. And this transformation or trivialization will occur much to our own and the world's peril.

Gurney seems to be growing as a playwright in the happy direction of the British Alan Ayckbourn who has been seriously plumbing the depths of the simultaneously hilarious and despairing British middle classes. But, because he writes so much and so complicatedly and about the middle class (much like the beautiful blonde who, because she is beautiful and blonde, is judged dumb), many critics have mistakenly consigned him to the Neil Simon School of Shallow Playwriting. I happily report that Gurney, for at least-two-thirds of the play's trajectory, keeps his ideas and laughs humming along in delightful synchronicity. Further, beneath the laughter and WASPish chutzpah, he manages to reveal an idea.

Nor is he afraid to make allusions, an activity most American playwrights prefer to avoid as they desperately hope not to offend, intimidate, patronize or lose their audience. He joyfully assumes his audience reads. (If he is not careful, he may give academe a good name.) With the missionary zeal of a born-again linguist, he investigates the natural relationship between life on the stage and life in the living room as it is reflected in our language. He investigates how we speak about our "performance" at parties and other events in life. He claims it is natural for us to seek structure, not only in our plays and our entertainments, but in our lives. This structure-seeking, in the course of the evening's party, reveals theater's radical (i.e., rootedness in life and vice versa) connection to the way we live, think about living and, most importantly, talk about how we live and think.

Unfortunately, he allows some of his playwrighting seams to show as the play's action and idea frazzle out in the last half of the second act. On the way, however, he amply shows that he has been doing a lot more than correcting papers and attending faculty meetings during his years as a university teacher. He has been observing the life of the drama and the drama of life in America; and he has been watching it with his ears.

> Gary Seibert, "*Talking for Fun*," in America, *Vol. 155, No. 12, November 1, 1986, p. 264.*

MEL GUSSOW

As an articulate theatrical chronicler of WASP manners and mating habits, A. R. Gurney Jr. specializes in richly populated and furnished interior landscapes. The playwright is at his most artful when he invents an apparatus as premise—the dining room as an unchangeable environment for multi-generational maneuverings; a "party critic" who reviews a social gathering as emblematic of a way of life. However, in Mr. Gurney's new play, *Sweet Sue,* . . . the idea is simply an exercise in artifice. . . .

[Two] actresses play a single character, as do [two] actors. They do not play two faces of the same character. . . . *Sweet Sue* is not a comedy like Peter Nichols's superior *Passion* in which actors played alter egos, an outward and inward self, with one urging the other to lose his inhibitions.

In the Gurney play, [the actresses] simply inhabit the stage at the same time; they talk to one another, sharing scenes and even sentences. What [one] starts, [the other] finishes, and vice versa, a pattern of dialogue that is confusing until we realize that the lines are interchangeable and that, in this instance, one plus one equals one.

The storyline concerns a middle-aged divorcée who becomes infatuated with her son's college roommate, a guest in her house for a long summer. The question raised is, will she or won't he? Stripped of its clone-like pretensions, *Sweet Sue* courts comparison with a problem play of another era, Robert Anderson's *Tea and Sympathy*. In that drama, a schoolmaster's ladylike wife sleeps with a young student. *Sweet Sue* is something of a reversal; it is the older woman who is in search of a romantic experience. At the end of this twinned rite of passage, one almost expects the young man to whisper, Anderson-style, "Years from now . . . when you talk about this . . . and you will . . . be kind."

With *Sweet Sue,* it is the playwright who is less than kind to his characters. Susan and her shadow, Susan Too, are duplicate halves of a single dull woman; this is a very limited partnership. As a designer of greeting cards, she is supposedly the creator of the smiling face that wishes one, "Have a Good Day"—and that is about the depth of her character. Once a would-be artist, she is now reduced to spending solitary suburban summers, dreaming and re-reading her favorite novel, *Anna Karenina*.

There is no Count Vronsky in her future until the son's roommate shows up, unannounced, on her doorstep. If anything, Jake and his shadow, Jake Too, are even less interesting than the ladies of the house. Except for his handsome appearance and his "have a good day" smile, there is not much to be said for him.

Of course, Susan—still the Sweet Sue of her youth—tumbles. But the play is not really serious about investigating the reasons for and the results of the liberation of the heroine, or the psychological implications of the September-May romance. Instead, Mr. Gurney is content with having Susan reiterate the fact that Freud must have had something to say on the subject.

At the same time, there is a surprising lack of sophistication on the part of the leading character. Even as she eyes the boarder—more than anything, it seems, she wants to sketch him in the nude—she maintains her rigid double standard. She does not want her unseen son sleeping with his unseen girl-friend . . . , and, when Jake has a date, she stays awake until he comes home. Susan's house is a bastion of hypocrisy. In a real two-character play—instead of this mock "four-hand-er"—there would be something at stake, a dramatic conflict that would move the characters from one crisis to another. Here there is circumlocution.

Because of the playwright's expertise, there are a few funny lines and several moments that hint at the situation's comic possibilities. In one such scene, [Susan] tells [Jake] that she is planning to design seven holiday greeting cards that will depict the Seven Deadly Sins. Naturally they disagree as to which sin fits which holiday. . . .

Two or four actors would make scant difference. Nor would the introduction on stage of all the people who are frequently mentioned—the heroine's son and his girlfriend, Jake's new girl who makes mix-ins at the local ice cream shop, or Susan's longtime suitor, Harvey Satterfield. On second thought, Harvey might make a small difference. As a professor of moral philosophy, he might have a provocative perspective on the dilemma of Sweet Sue: the protagonist of a play in which a talented playwright gets less mileage by doubling his cast of characters.

> Mel Gussow, "'*Sweet Sue*', with Moore and Red-grave," in The New York Times, *January 9, 1987, p. C5.*

GERALD WEALES

[*Weales, an American critic, nonfiction writer, juvenile fiction writer, and novelist, is drama critic for the Catholic journal* Commonweal. *His works include* American Drama since World War II *(1962),* Clifford Odets, Playwright *(1971), and* Canned Goods as Caviar: American Film Comedies of the 1930s *(1985). In the following excerpt, Weales describes* Sweet Sue *as shallow and disappointing.*]

Ever since the success of *The Dining Room* in 1982, A. R. Gurney, Jr. has been circling Broadway, coming closer and closer to the showcase that once was the goal of every aspiring dramatist. Gurney, has been at it for thirty years and has built a solid reputation as a playwright without the Broadway imprimatur. Those of us who have long admired his work (I first came across Gurney when I read *The Golden Fleece* in 1972) wished him well as he moved out to a wider audience. However, now that he has finally come to Broadway with *Sweet Sue* . . . the result is disappointing. Gurney's milieu is the comfortable WASP middle class, and his perception is of a society in decline, perhaps happily so. Although he can be overtly preachy, as he was in last season's *The Perfect Party*, he generally allows the social theme to emerge from his comedy. Perhaps to forestall the possibility that his work may be taken as cousin to that of a joking moralist like Jean Kerr, Gurney has used a variety of devices to subvert the straightforward development of conventional comedy. *The Middle Ages* takes place in the trophy room of a men's club over a period of thirty years, and the more ambitious *The Dining Room* lets a group of actors move from one family of characters to another as the titular room chronicles the changes in society. The device in *Sweet Sue* is to allow four actors to play two characters. The two Susans talk to one another, sometimes amiably, sometimes peevishly. In the scenes with Jake, one Susan picks up the other's words, often in mid-sentence, and goes on with the scene only to step aside in her turn. So it is with the two Jakes. For the most part, the gimmick aside, the scenes are to be taken as actual encounters, but Susan is also given to fantasy so that occasionally the Susans and the Jakes act out a might-have-been scene, usually one involving Jake's posing in the nude. As a further complication, one or the other of the Susans speaks to herself in a monologue or to the audience in direct address.

There are moments in *Sweet Sue* in which one of the Susans appears more maternal, the other more seductive; one more professional, the other more personal. Similarly, one of the Jakes sometimes seems more sensitive and romantic, the other more direct and carnal. Yet, there is no consistency in the presentation, no serious attempt to suggest that the doubling represents separate and conflicting aspects of the characters. Perhaps Gurney simply wants to avoid the kind of good angel-bad angel division that Bil Keane now and then uses in his cartoon, "Family Circus," and to suggest that human beings are more complex than neat definitions imply. Beyond that, there is doubt about what course of behavior is good or bad, correct or incorrect within the context of the play itself.

Sweet Sue is about a summer when a woman of uncertain age (late forties, early fifties) does or does not sleep with her son's college roommate, who has come to spend the vacation as a guest in her house and a partner to her son in a house-painting venture. The son conveniently stays offstage—as gratuitous a device as Gurney has ever contrived—so that the woman and the son's friend can interact, as undergraduates like to say these days. Susan, whose husband understandably deserted her (even she says that), has brushed off her art-school skills and made a living as an illustrator of button-cute Hallmark cards; she has raised three children, the last of whom, the son, is about to go out on his own. At this moment, she would like to do something serious as an artist, paint a believable tree (or a nude), and as a woman, find a love more intense than the tepid companionship of the two nice boring men we never see. Jake, a victim of the new sexual freedom, wants a relationship with a woman that is not simply physical, but intellectual and spir-

itual as well. This is a set-up for a replenishing summer romance from which both characters return, their confidence restored, their sense of self strengthened. I confess I do not know whether or not they ever get together. As Jake leaves at the end, Susan follows him, offering him a beer and an invitation to stay and talk. Susan Two then tells the audience how they fell into one another's arms, how they met here, there, elsewhere—including one chilly walk during which Jake bought her a plum-colored sweater—and finally how they agreed to part. Susan comes back on stage, wearing the plum-colored sweater but saying that Jake refused to stay for the beer, thus leaving the audience with an ambiguous explanation for the wryly upbeat final scene between the two Susans.

I further confess that I do not care whether or not Susan and Jake ever get together. They are two of the dullest people ever to come down the pike. Gurney, who has been teaching literature for twenty-five years, has to know that references to *Anna Karenina*, opera, and the Talking Heads do not indicate that the speakers are interesting or witty. Jake is a whiner of sorts, and Susan is given to mean-spirited one-liners which presumably mask her distress, but actually underline her shallowness. Nor are they particularly charming. The coldness in the characters is partly a product of the device that splits them in two. . . . I cannot believe that Gurney intended the characters as I perceive them, but if he did, I presume he is suggesting that both the 1950s, which formed Susan, and the 1980s, which formed Jake, are forcing ground for hollow men. A sensible social point, just the kind that Gurney might well make, but *Sweet Sue* finally comes across like one of Susan's greeting cards, more cute than acute. (pp. 83-4)

Gerald Weales, "Double Jeopardy: Gurney's 'Sweet Sue'," in Commonweal, Vol. CXIV, No. 3, February 13, 1987, pp. 83-4.

JIM HILEY

Actors bother about props, 'business' and projection. Writers worry about the logistics of a scene, and designers about budgets. Directors fret over the actors, writers and designers. By opening night, at least, only the critics are preoccupied with themes. Theatre, and comic theatre above all, is a practical game, with essentially physical rules.

So-called 'high' comedy is no exception, a fact dramatists ignore at their peril. When Lady Bracknell gasps, 'A handbag?', laughter comes from the physical image and Worthing's discomfort, which Wilde positions so acutely that we can *feel* it. And for all the elegant postures, his play is funny because of what people do when prone—who bonked who so many years ago, and who will be bonking who soon.

Oscar's name is invoked in A. R. Gurney Jr's *The Perfect Party* with reckless frequency. His works even occupy a shelf in the dull study of the even duller principal character, Tony, who has ditched an academic career in favour of professional party-throwing. But each mention only reinforces the hopelessness of Gurney's aspirations to 'high' style. This American author's humour derives from attitude, not skill. His dialogue spumes on in a self-perpetuating quest for laughter, unrelated to credible human affairs. The fun—Tony's party, indeed—remains behind the scenes. And unlike the bonking in *The Importance*, it never impinges on what's put before your eyes. Tony's guests represent, we're carefully told, a microcosm of modern American life. A successful party will mean that American society can be made to work, and Tony dreams of triumphant celebrity after realising this optimistic idea. To his fearsomely schematic ends, he invites Lois, a journalist who drones: 'I happen to represent a very major New York newspaper.' The play is full of such inflated talk, but it takes a while to fathom its satirical intent.

Not unreasonably, Tony's wife and friends fear that the lust for perfection will prevent the party swinging. So it turns out, until the microcosm gives up striving and lets its hair down. What this demonstrates, apparently, is that Tony (and America) should be less 'idealistic', settling for muddle and mess both at home and abroad. But the message has to be spelt out. It's certainly not conveyed through character or circumstance. Even when Tony invents a monstrous twin brother—another awkward shade of Wilde—his impersonation disappoints after a scabrously promising build-up. (pp. 36-7)

> *Jim Hiley, "Party Lines," in* The Listener, *Vol. 118, No. 3019, July 9, 1987, pp. 36-7.*

EDITH OLIVER

A. R. Gurney, Jr., who breathes wit and humor, has written, in *Another Antigone,* a play that deals directly and seriously, though never solemnly, with anti-Semitism, a subject he has touched on in many of his plays through the years—in his very funny, satiric *The David Show,* to start with, and in *The Middle Ages,* among others. The antagonists of *Another Antigone* . . . are a professor of Greek drama named Henry Harper and a rebellious student of his, a senior named Judy Miller. The place is a college in Boston, during the latter half of the spring term. Miss Miller astonishes and infuriates Harper by trying to substitute an original play on anti-nuclear protest for her required paper on *Antigone*, thereby making a comparison that reveals, says Harper, a complete misunderstanding of Greek tragedy. "Juvenile polemics," he says, and when, fighting for a high grade, she tells him that she is going to put the play on he replies that he has no time for "show and tell," and that she has no conception of tragedy at all. . . . Enter the dean of the department, a woman who is a close friend of Harper's, and who tries to persuade him to soften his stand: to give Judy a B for effort, anyway—to be fair. But he replies that tragedy is unfair, that "tragedy keeps us real in this happy-ending nation." Then the dean discloses the real purpose of her visit, which is to tell him that he has been accused by someone of anti-Semitism. Judy Miller, it seems, is Jewish, though she is not his accuser. True, he has often compared Greek and Hebraic philosophy, but without prejudice of any kind; it has never entered his mind that Judy is Jewish, nor does it matter to him. As the action proceeds, she becomes more insistent and he firmer; the analogy grows stronger—he feels himself becoming Creon. Then he relents and offers her a passing grade, but that doesn't suit her, and when he hears about an interfering Jewish professor he is nettled and enraged and makes a truly anti-Semitic crack, thus sealing his doom. Exile, he has said, is the fate of the Greek tragic hero. By the end, Judy, too, has grown in stature.

A synopsis can only hint at the dramatic strength and richness of this splendid play, which is as humorous, by the way, as its predecessors. Mr. Gurney . . . appears totally at home in academe and totally at home with every kind of human being. He is an extraordinary writer.

> *Edith Oliver, "The Professor's Dilemma," in* The New Yorker, *Vol. LXIII, No. 49, January 25, 1988, p. 85.*

ERIKA MUNK

[*Munk, an American critic and editor, is a senior editor and drama critic for the* Village Voice. *In the following excerpt Munk deplores the banality of* Another Antigone.]

Chutzpah and *hubris* are very different indeed. *Another Antigone* unfortunately has neither—though it recasts Sophocles by making the conflict between Antigone and Creon a stew of teacher against student, old against young, conservative against liberal, and populist versus classicist, not to mention man against woman and gentile against Jew. The idea of using *Antigone* as the framework for a version of the debate between Allen Bloom and his critics is, God knows, *chutzpadik*, but A. R. Gurney's script tends to be mousy and self-deprecating, not brash and nervy. And the antagonists—a rigid, anti-Semitic professor whose life centers on Reverence for Classic Wisdom; a spoiled, naïvely leftish Jewish student who wants an A for turning Sophocles's play into an iambic pentameter antinuclear tract—could be considered as suffering from their own versions of *hubris*, however small-scale, if they weren't presented with so much thin, smooth, even-handed sympathy. Let Creon be a fascist, let Antigone be a neurotic show-off, just don't let them be so damned banal and nice.

Banal and nice prevail, however. And in the interests of preserving the niceness, the question of anti-Semitism, of which so much was made in the Larger Paper's preopening puffery, is muffled. Professor Harper's job is in jeopardy because he has been accused of making anti-Semitic remarks, which he says are historical observations on the cultural roles of "Jerusalem" and "Athens" over the last 2500 years. Yet when the accusation is first reported, we haven't heard him say anything at all about Jews. Instead, he has been pontificating so neoconnishly he could be Jewish himself. He is portrayed sympathetically, though in the sexist-old-codger mode; when he makes, quite late in the play, one really repellent crack about "the Chosen People," it's startlingly out of character. As he promptly turns again into the sympathetic old codger, the sense of disruption is overwhelming. Perhaps Gurney wrote another, stronger, play from which only this line remains?

Judy Miller, the student, headed for Wall Street while spouting eco-left clichés, is also felled by the banal and the nice, though she seems on the face of it a perfect satirical target. She's supposed to be an academic whiz, though both ignorant and dumb. Her discovery of her Jewish roots and her histrionic final rejection of money and success are thin and mechanical—which might be taken as a reflection on her character, if the entire action of this play weren't thin and mechanical. It's typical of Gurney's Judy that, though she's surely somewhat feminist, her version of *Antigone* changes Antigone's sister Ismene into a male character called Lysander. Or perhaps it's just typical of Gurney's mechanistic writing that he makes her do this so he'll have two couples on stage (the fourth character is the dean of the department, a two-dimensional woman who prods both Harper's conscience and his sense of bureaucratic-academic reality). This is not the Gurney of *The Dining Room*, light and deft, but a heavy-handed creature, lumbering around the subject he avoids.

Despite *The Dining Room* and other Gurney plays I've enjoyed, anti-Semitism is what got me out on a cold night, and Gurney's timidity about that subject is what makes me angry at a piece otherwise too lightweight to deserve more than irritation at its politics, disappointment at its art. No complexity is engaged, no passion expressed, no argument sustained. Israel barely exists, the Palestinians not at all. Who would know that the Jews' place in both radical and conservative thought has changed in the last 40 years, that there are historians who deny the Nazi genocide ever occurred, that the question of whether the leading candidate for the Democratic nomination is an anti-Semite is crucial, that there's murder and racism in Gaza and Jews in New York who defend or protest this? What kind of stupid, uncaring audience is being assumed here? (pp. 88, 97)

Where there could have been *chutzpah* or *hubris,* comedy or tragedy, we get a sitcom iced with self-pity, an insult. (p. 97)

Erika Munk, "The Whining Room," in The Village Voice, *Vol. XXXIII, No. 4, January 26, 1988, pp. 88, 97.*

Larry Heinemann
Paco's Story

The National Book Awards: Fiction

American novelist and short story writer.

Like Heinemann's previous novel, *Close Quarters* (1977), *Paco's Story* (1987) deals with the horrors of the Vietnam War and the resulting trauma of America's veterans. Heinemann, who was an infantry soldier in Vietnam, describes the conditions of war with a personal immediacy that has garnered substantial critical attention. *Paco's Story* traces the odyssey of Paco Sullivan, a severely disfigured Vietnam veteran with the distinction of having been the only man in his company to survive an apocalyptic firefight. The opening section of the novel recounts this battle and the miraculous survival of Paco, who is found three days later in the wreckage by a startled medic. The second section follows Paco's post-war experience in America. A drifter whose mind is numbed by painkillers, Paco ends up in the small midwestern town of Boone after running out of busfare. In Boone he becomes a dishwasher in a roadside diner, where he struggles with his haunting memories and attempts to connect with the people around him.

Reviewers observe that the most distinctive aspect of *Paco's Story* is the novel's unique narrative voice, which is that of a ghost or ghosts of Paco's slaughtered company. Composed in G.I. slang and a colloquial American idiom, the narrative has been called garrulous, cheerful, hip, cynical, brutal, and obscene. Critics agree that this tone is a striking achievement, carrying the story forward fluidly and giving a haunting force to Heinemann's portrayal of the horrors of war and its aftermath. Critics also praise Heinemann's powerful descriptions, mentioning both his painstaking depictions of activity in the diner and the graphic passages set in Vietnam.

Paco is viewed by many as an epic Everyvet who represents the effects of Vietnam's desensitizing brutality on the soldier both in combat and in post-war life. Heinemann, who is writing a non-fiction work on Post-Traumatic Stress Disorder, has created in *Paco's Story* a fictional case study of PTSD. Most critics find *Paco's Story* a moving exploration of the tragedies of modern warfare.

KIRKUS REVIEWS

[The] real achievement of this hip, bitter and ultimately unpleasant novel about a wounded Vietnam vet is in the narrative voice: a nasty, rivetingly specific voice belonging to a dead "grunt" who's describing (for the benefit of an unidentified listener, "James") Paco Sullivan's miraculous lone survival of a bloody jungle firefight and subsequent aimless drifting through a (familiarly) unfeeling, crass America. (pp. 1467-68)

© Jerry Bauer

Paco's Story begins brilliantly, in Vietnam: Paco is lying wounded in the jungle heat, surrounded by the bodies of his fallen friends. On the third day, a medic (whose life is altered fatefully because of it) finds Paco; and Paco is patched together and sent home. The medic suffers a heart attack; he later becomes an alcoholic who recounts the story of Paco's rescue in bars. This is the last attempt the novel makes at meaning. Henceforth, Paco (about whom we know only that he has no home or family) simply drifts, a collection of scars and badly mended bones, while small-town Americans stare blankly, jeer or lecture at him. For a while he washes dishes at a beautifully described greasy spoon called the Texas Lunch; but nothing much happens to him there, and after a while he moves on.

Early chapters here have the urgency and cohesion of formal tragedy. But late chapters let urgency and accumulated tension lapse into a long snarl of bitterness about the legacy of Vietnam—nothing but speeches and affectless, gory memories intended to shock. It's ugly—and too bad. (p. 1468)

A review of "Paco's Story," in Kirkus Reviews, *Vol. LIV, No. 19, October 1, 1986, pp. 1467-68.*

PUBLISHERS WEEKLY

When incoming fire lights up the sky over the good old boys at Fire Base Harriette in Vietnam, the tough soldiers just look at each other and settle in, certain that the nearly 100 of them will die. And all but one are visited by the descending brightness that tears their bodies apart. [In *Paco's Story* the] ghost of one of these soldiers narrates the story of survivor Paco Sullivan, who lies covered with flies and dirt for two days before being rescued. Badly scarred and limping, he returns to the States and becomes an introspective dishwasher in a small Texas town. This is a well-written, ruminative work in an easy-going, down-home dialect that makes the awful memories of the war—thankfully—a little bit distant. Heinemann has a promising talent, but his novel needs a sense of propulsion, not just excellent tales and fine dialogue; and his women should also be more than lusty objects of men's desires. As is, his work is just short of important.

> *A review of "Paco's Story," in* Publishers Weekly, *Vol. 230, No. 16, October 17, 1986, p. 59.*

MARTIN A. BRADY

Larry Heinemann made his initial literary mark with *Close Quarters,* which featured vivid descriptions of the horrors of Vietnam. Billed as a sequel to that tale, *Paco's Story* charts the final, near-fatal battlefield experience of one Paco Sullivan, his eventual recovery in a field hospital, and his return to civilian life, in which he encounters the insensitivities of his fellow citizens back in the States ("Them Vietnam boys sure do think you owe them something, don't they?"). With his "1,000-meter stare," Paco takes a job as a dishwasher in a roadside hash house, haunted by his memories of Southeast Asia and the brutality of war. Heinemann's coarse, sometimes poetic imagery—"the moonlit, starlit image of weeds and reeds and bamboo saplings and bubbling marsh slime burns itself into the back of your head in the manner of Daguerre's first go with a camera obscura"—raises his tale above the level of a starkly depressing Vietnam memoir. . . .

> *Martin A. Brady, in a review of "Paco's Story," in* Booklist, *Vol. 83, No. 6, November 15, 1986, p. 472.*

GERALD NICOSIA

At the very start of *Paco's Story,* Larry Heinemann insists that he is not writing a war story. But Heinemann, author of the finely wrought naturalistic Vietnam narrative *Close Quarters,* has pulled off the feat of having his cake and eating it too. While *Paco's Story* contains vivid descriptions of some of the most brutal and gory incidents of the Vietnam war . . . it is also the tale of one man's quest to be understood as a human being, and "to discover a livable peace."

Paco Sullivan comes home from Vietnam with a unique case of survivor's guilt—he is the only man of his company left alive after an enormous artillery barrage demolishes Fire Base Harriette, a place previously known as "a piece of cake." The instantaneous death of these 92 men, mysterious in itself, is nothing compared to the mystery of how Paco managed to survive for almost two days before he was discovered among the debris, just barely breathing, and finally airlifted back to a field hospital.

The medic who discovers Paco has a heart attack and thereafter refuses to tend any of the wounded; a casualty himself of the carnage of Alpha Company, he succumbs to despair and spends the rest of his life "eating his liver out" in a hometown bar and recounting how his life was ruined by "this *geek,* the guy not dead, but should have been."

Paco, his shattered legs pinned and screwed back together and his blood-stream filled with painkillers and antidepressants, rides a bus as far as his last GI check will take him, and ends up in a little Midwestern town called Boone. There, he takes a job washing dishes in the Texas Lunch ("I wash and God dries," he says) and sets about discovering, like so many perplexed Vietnam vets, what on earth actually happened to him.

One of the reasons *Paco's Story* is so striking is that it is told neither by Paco (whose brain is in a drug- and trauma-induced stupor most of the book) nor by a detached third-person observer, but rather by the ghosts of Alpha Company, the friends and fellow soldiers who left Paco behind as their sole voice. It is the mission of these ghosts, who pursue Paco day and night and reach him most effectively in his dreams, to teach Paco the very thing that most live people don't want to see or hear of: the universality of loss and pain. "Why *you*?" the ghosts respond to his unasked question. "Don't you know? It's your turn, Jack!"

A freewheeling mélange of GI slang and downhome American idiom, the language of the novel, of the ghostly grunts, is as fluid and musically rhythmical as the best of Mark Twain or Nelson Algren. The story gains even more intimacy from the fact that it is addressed to another ghost named James—who could be anyone from James Jones to the James of the New Testament, who exhorted humanity to rejoice in "trials" because they help us to develop "the ability to endure."

Endurance is certainly one of the messages of *Paco's Story,* as is the need to practice kindness and compassion in this world of misfortune. The wounded Paco is a touchstone of human character; he draws the best and worst out of everyone he meets. Whereas the medic found in Paco only a justification for his own self-pity, the owner of the Texas Lunch, Ernest, himself a wounded World War II marine, opens his own hurt heart to Paco, making both of them feel less alienated; and for Mr. Elliot, the dry goods merchant, Paco's neediness unseals the declining era of Czarist Russia from which he emigrated 50 years before.

Heinemann takes pains to let us feel the quality and texture of this man's life and even of his dreams. The novel also contains several mock-epic descriptions—including a blow-by-blow account of Paco's heroic dishwashing technique and a scene of a Chicago bus driver's nightly disrobing that reads like Achilles taking off his armor—that are surely prizewinning material.

Paco's Story is a novel to be read on many levels. Within Paco's dreams and the voyeuristic fantasies of his neighbor Cathy, who watches him from her window day and night, there are manifold powerful images of our modern world—a locked room that keeps refilling with victims, where the painless executioners "never run out of fresh needles or . . . bottles of that pearlescent, metallic-tasting poison"; and, even more poignant, human history as a kind of integument woven of screams, which, were it to be unraveled layer by layer, would release more anguish and horror than the unpeeling of the thousand scars from Paco's skin.

Above all, Heinemann exposes the primary fallacy of war, which comes from the notion that one can inflict pain without having pain inflicted upon one in return; and he shows this interconnectedness to be the primary truth of life itself, the same as John Donne did three centuries ago when he wrote: "No man is an island, entire of itself; each man is a piece of the continent, a part of the main." And so within disfigured, crippled Paco [a nickname that means something like "little brother"] there is a goodly part of each of us.

Gerald Nicosia, "A War Story That Tells the Truth," in Chicago Tribune——Books, *November 23, 1986, p. 6.*

RICHARD EDER

The most profound social distinction is the one between the living and the dead. Ghosts have fallen into the lower classes. . . .

Like others who have written fiction about the Vietnam War in recent years, Larry Heinemann is haunted by its present invisibility only a dozen years after it ended. Hundreds of thousands of veterans, tens of thousands of them dead, fall under that dark American shadow: to be out of fashion, not hot, off of prime time.

Paco's Story, brief and with a remarkable intensity, presses the social claims of those who died literally, and those who survived but whose history, for all the place it has today, might as well be dead. Using the simplest of stories—a grievously wounded veteran gets off a bus in a small Texas town, finds work, stays a while and moves on—Heinemann writes of the two universes that coexist in our country: the large one that can't remember, the small one that can't forget.

Heinemann foreshortens the remembering and forgetting. Paco Sullivan's brief passage through Boone, Tex., takes place not now but while the fighting was still going on, or perhaps recently over.

Even then, the line between those who are at peace and those who are at war is brutally drawn.

Paco's Spanish name and Irish surname make no special point except to declare him a kind of unprivileged Everyman. He is the sole survivor of Alpha Company. It was destroyed, in a single moment, by a barrage of "supporting" fire while defending its outpost against a Viet Cong attack.

And Paco himself was so badly hurt that the word *survivor* scarcely applies. That is the book's theme. It is also the inspired device that makes Paco's encounters such a glowing metaphor for this theme.

Heinemann puts the narration of Paco's sojourn in Boone in the mouths of his dead companions. *Paco's Story* seems to be told by ghosts. I don't think the author means these ghosts literally, although this is purposely ambiguous.

More likely, Paco feels himself to be one of the dead as well, and tells his story on their behalf. He speaks of himself in the third person, as if the living Paco were an accidental surviving limb of his own essentially dead self. It is the way you might speak of an amputated appendix. Not "I was removed," but "My appendix was removed."

The horror that Heinemann wants to rescue from oblivion is expressed in the notion that it is not death that amputates the victim from the survivor, but life that has amputated the survivor from the company of the dead.

The ghostly voice, which by turns is colloquial, brutal, obscene and remarkably cheerful . . . begins by assuming that most

people won't want to hear its story. It is aware of its own low social standing.

Then it goes on to relate tersely and vividly the ordinary hell of Alpha Company's existence, and the special hell of its destruction. It tells of the discovery of Paco's shattered body among the minute fragments of his companions' corpses; and of his slow and painful mending in a hospital. It is a recovery as precarious and unlikely as Lazarus'.

The narration moves forward to tell of Paco arriving in Boone—simply a matter of giving all his money to the bus driver to go as far as it was good for—and of his time there. Continually, it reverts to the war days. It is as if only the terrible past were believable, and as if the everyday life in Boone were an invention too fantastic to sustain.

Paco, crisscrossed with scars, limping and in continual pain, goes from door to door looking for a job. It is a stunning chain of vignettes. He visits an antique shop whose owner, a refugee from the concentration camps, hallucinates that he is his dead son; and to a barbershop where the townspeople look at him as if he were from another planet. Finally, the owner of the local diner, a World War II veteran, hires him as a dishwasher and, without listening to Paco's story, tells him his own story about the bloody days in the Pacific.

Paco tries to hold on to this life, as strange to him as a grafted organ. (Heinemann conveys the effort with a minute description, lasting an audacious and oddly gripping six pages, of just how Paco gathers up, washes and replaces the diner's dishes and pans.) But the graft doesn't take.

Paco, and the larger phenomenon he represents, is not real to the townspeople; they are not real to him. They are two entirely different aquatic species, swimming side by side in the same aquarium.

He is attracted to a young woman who lives next door in his broken-down hotel; and she is aroused by him and his scars. But on her side, it is peripheral fantasy she indulges in while making noisy love with her boyfriend. Paco listens sleeplessly to the lovemaking and is seized by desire. But desire leads him away, and back to the real world of memory. It is a memory, told in dreadful detail, of the rape-killing by Alpha Company of a Viet Cong woman prisoner.

Paco's young neighbor comes close to him only in a dream. She dreams of making love, in the course of which she peels off his hundreds of scars and lays them gently upon her. The image could be grotesque; but it is delicate and heartbreaking.

Dreams are the closest we come, Heinemann is saying in his deeply original and affecting book, to bridging the gulf between our lives and our snubbed, dead history.

Richard Eder, in a review of "Paco's Story," in Los Angeles Times Book Review, *December 7, 1986, p. 3.*

DUNCAN SPENCER

Larry Heinemann is slowly gaining a reputation as the grunt's novelist of the Vietnam War. His is the storytelling of life and death between the laager and the tree line, a life of dirt, fear, dope, alcohol, brutality, curses and evil. He tells, from his own experience as a soldier, the results of fighting a war without will and without authority.

In [*Paco's Story*], his second war novel, the scene has shifted to postwar America, to which his severely wounded hero, Paco Sullivan, has returned. But Sullivan is no hero, nor has he really returned. The war has erased something important in his psyche—though perhaps it would be more accurate to say the war has *replaced* something important in his psyche, so that he instinctively knows that he is dangerous and alone, a man without restraints.

There are thousands of such men in this country, the broken men of the Vietnam war, said to be suffering from Post Traumatic Stress Disorder.... Heinemann's story is to tell us how one gets PTSD, and the answer is by being systematically brutalized by terror, disorganization, pain, lack of leadership—in short the conditions prevalent for much of the time in the field in Vietnam.

He also makes clear that far worse than the horrors of bombardment, booby traps, ambushes and the rest is the complete illegality of modern warfare, whether it is guerilla warfare waged by children with grenades or terrorists with airplane bombs; it is this moral issue which corrodes the human mind and leaves it adrift.

Heinemann's novel is like a nightmare in prose, perhaps the sliding kind, in which the sleeper feels himself slipping farther and farther into the pit in spite of every kind of struggle, a nightmare in which there is no rest, no safety, only the sure approach of an unknown doom. This, too, was Vietnam, so that in the horrific scenes where the hero partakes in the torture, rape and killing of a female Viet Cong, we are drawn through a kind of spiritual death: "We looked at her and at ourselves, drawing breath again and again, and knew that this was a moment of evil, that we would never live the same."

But the truly awful thing was not the rape and the killing, but the gradual way that Heinemann's unhero Paco Sullivan slips down towards it; he breaks during the night, one night of many, when he is forced to kill an enemy with a knife. In what must be one of the most horrific scenes of literary Vietnam, he takes that life and begins to lose his own.

Heinemann is a writer who is always out for the big punch. He cannot hold back. He pours on such a relentless flood of pictures and details that it would have been good for him to receive the kindly admonition of the unknown city editor who scrawled across a writer's copy, "No vivid writing—please!"

He has also chosen an annoying stylistic device, declaiming key points as if he were addressing an unintroduced character, James, though the name is used only in a colloquial way to punctuate sentences. Thus he will pronounce ingratiatingly, "Let's begin with the first clean fact, James: This ain't no war story." Never mind that it *is*. And it is important and true; in the jungle recollections which drift through the book like evil-smelling smoke, Heinemann's experience of Vietnam as a grunt pours out onto the page like wasted agony, pitiful and resonant.

But when Paco Sullivan returns to America, Heinemann retains the same half-stoned pace. The effect is less correct. The tortured compression of the war through soldiers' eyes gets lost in the vastness of this calm country. (p. 6)

[Paco] moves on with his nightmares, and we know that he will never be whole again. For in the night he is heard to cry over and over, "Oh no! Don't kill him!"—which was what the dying Vietnamese had told him, almost tenderly, under his own knife. (pp. 6, 10)

Heinemann is an undisciplined writer with a fine eye and ear.... (p. 10)

> *Duncan Spencer, "When the War Was Over," in* Book World—The Washington Post, *January 18, 1987, pp. 6, 10.*

An Excerpt from *Paco's Story*

[People] think that folks do not want to hear about the night at Fire Base Harriette—down the way from LZ Skator-Gator, and within earshot of a ragtag bunch of mud-and-thatch hooches everyone called Gookville—when the whole company, except for one guy, got killed. Fucked-up dead, James; scarfed up. Everybody but Paco got nominated and voted into the Hall of Fame in one fell swoop. The company was night-laagered in a tight-assed perimeter up past our eyeballs in a no-shit firefight with a battalion of headhunter NVA—corpses and cartridge brass and oily magazines and dud frags scattered around, and everyone running low on ammo. Lieutenant Stennett crouched over his radio hoarsely screaming map coordinates to every piece of artillery, every air strike and gunship within radio range, like it was going out of style, when all of a sudden—*zoom*—the air came alive and crawled and yammered and whizzed and hummed with the roar and buzz of a thousand incoming rounds. It was hard to see for all the gunpowder smoke and dust kicked up by all the muzzle flashes, but everyone looked up—GIs *and* zips—and knew it was every incoming round left in Creation, a wild and bloody shitstorm, a ball-busting cataclysm. We knew that the dirt under our bellies (and the woods and villes and us with it) was going to be pulverized to ash (and we do mean *pulverized*, James), so you could draw a thatch rake through it and not find the chunks; knew by the overwhelming, ear-piercing whine we swore was splitting our heads wide open that those rounds were the size of houses. We don't know what the rest of the company did, or the zips for that matter, but the 2nd squad of the 2nd platoon swapped that peculiar look around that travels from victim to victim in any disaster. We ciphered it out right then and there that we couldn't dig a hole deep enough, fast enough; couldn't crawl under something thick enough; couldn't drop our rifles, and whatnot, and turn tail and beat feet far enough but that this incoming wouldn't catch us by the scruff of the shirt, so to speak, and lay us lengthwise. We look around at one another as much as to say, "*Oh fuck*! My man, this ain't your average, ordinary, every-day, garden-variety sort of incoming. This one's going to blow everybody down." Swear to God, James, there are those days—no matter how hard you hump and scrap and scratch—when there is simply nothing left to do but pucker and submit. Paco slipped off his bandanna and sprinkled the last of his canteen water on it, wiped his face and hands, then twirled it up again and tied it around his neck—the knot to one side. Jonesy laid himself out, with his head on his rucksack, getting ready to take another one of his famous naps. Most of the rest of us simply sat back and ran our fingers through our hair to make ourselves as presentable as possible. And Gallagher, who had a red-and-black tattoo of a dragon on his forearm from his wrist to his elbow, buttoned his shirt sleeves and brushed himself off, and sat cross-legged, with his hands folded meditatively in his lap. In another instant everyone within earshot was quiet, and a hush of anticipation rippled through the crowd, like a big wind that strikes many trees all at once. Then we heard the air rushing ahead of those rounds the same as a breeze through a cave—so sharp and cool on the face, refreshing and foul all at once—as though those rounds were floating down to us as limp and leisurely as cottonwood leaves. We looked one another up and down one more time, as much as to say, "Been nice. See you around. *Fucking shit!* Here it comes."

CHRISTOPHER BENFEY

Paco Sullivan, the dishwasher at the Texas Lunch, is a mystery to the people of Boone. One day he walks into town, leaning on his black hickory cane, looking for a job and a place to sleep. The scars on his arms are a lure for women and a challenge to men. Everyone wants to know Paco's story, and they often end up telling him theirs: Ernest Monroe, owner and operator of the Texas Lunch, wounded at Iwo Jima; Jesse the drifter, back from the war, with his own ideas for a Vietnam memorial. But Paco keeps washing coffee mugs by hand, glancing from time to time across the street to the Geronimo Hotel. In a room next to his, Cathy, the owner's tease of a niece, spys on him from behind the blinds.

Larry Heinemann's second novel . . . has a plot as spare as that of a movie western. (When Paco leaves town he rides into the sunset.) But the odd way the author narrates *Paco's Story* gives this fine novel its eerie and unsettling force. The story is told from beyond the grave, in the garrulous, seen-it-all voice of one of Paco's former buddies, a voice we often seem to be hearing from inside Paco's head. "Let's begin," he says, "with the first clean fact, James: This ain't no war story." It is never quite clear who James is—a fellow ghost? the reader?—but already, in this first sentence, we know two things this book will tackle: how, if not in a "war story," you can write about war; and how you can become "clean" if you've been to war and returned.

Paco Sullivan, we learn, is the sole survivor of a massacre at a Vietnam base camp called Harriette. Paco's legs are held together by pins and screws and his mind is held together by pain killers and whisky. The repeated ritual of washing dishes steadies him and keeps at bay the ghosts that haunt him at night. Mr. Heinemann describes the act of washing dishes as though it's a baptism, a way of cleansing himself of the past. . . .

Mr. Heinemann has a good eye for satire, and he lets his ghostly narrator ruminate on the mysteries of American fast food. "You can always tell the clientele by the look of what's parked in the lot," he remarks, and a brief essay on customers follows. When a cousin of that sentence turns up 40 pages later, "you can always tell the class of a place by the look of the menu they give you," we know what to expect: sly observations on waitresses dressed like "a cross between meter maids and registered nurses," or on menus with "a short snappy narrative [that] describes every little thing as succulent, piping hot, tangy, or chewy; the coffee is famous, the refills endless."

Indeed, the scenes in the Texas Lunch are so vividly and generously imagined that when the inevitable nightmares and memories of Vietnam intrude . . . they seem almost obligatory, concessions to the demands of the genre. Mr. Heinemann is highly conscious of the conventions of war novels; readers may notice allusions, for example, to Norman Mailer's *Naked and the Dead*. He knows he's giving his audience what it expects: "Any carny worth his cashbox . . . will tell you that most folks will shell out hard-earned, greenback cash, every time, to see artfully performed, urgently fascinating, grisly and gruesome carnage." But in *Paco's Story* he's after something more subtle than the carny's art.

Paco isn't just a mystery to the townspeople; he remains a mystery to the reader as well. Toward the end of the novel we learn that Paco's special talent in his company was setting ingenious booby traps. It comes as a surprise, for he has shown no particular inventiveness in his relations with the people of Boone. Maybe he doesn't think they're worth it. Maybe he's run out of improvisation. Even the rascal Cathy has a hard time getting Paco to perk up. But beneath Mr. Heinemann's simple plot one sometimes senses the presence of a suppressed picaresque novel—in a different time, in a different world. Paco might have adventures in Boone as wild as Huck Finn's. (Even the unlikely and unexplained name, Paco Sullivan, suggests a trickster.) Instead Paco the booby-trapper, the man of cunning, has found a momentary and ambiguous peace washing dishes.

When Walt Whitman said that "the real war will never get in the books," he was stating a simple fact. War is unwriteable. The Vietnam War continues to elude our attempts to represent it, just as the sublimity of storms and volcanos challenged artists of earlier generations. Mr. Heinemann's carefully crafted, oblique narrative suggests that the right words are not going to be found in ever-more-graphic, frontal approaches to "gruesome carnage." Its horrors may be as forcefully conveyed by a haunting scene in a greasy spoon as by the tearing of human flesh.

> *Christopher Benfey, "Finding Peace at the Sink,"*
> in The New York Times Book Review, *November 8, 1987, p. 19.*

MICHIKO KAKUTANI

Paco's Story is narrated by the hero's comrades in arms, who died during a devastating firefight. . . .

[These] narrative strategies provide Mr. Heinemann with ways of getting around some of the problems posed by this anomalous war. By juxtaposing time present and time past, he's able to avoid the grim parade of violent events that leave readers of so many Vietnam novels emotionally numb (much the way they felt, watching the war, night after night, on the television news)—seeing the nightmare images of the war juxtaposed with Paco's attempts to wash dishes or get a bus ride actually heightens their horror. By using the collective voice of Paco's dead buddies as his narrator, he's able to avoid having to delineate a whole cast of supporting characters—something that's often a weakness of Vietnam novels, given the military's short rotating tours of duty there, which tended to preclude the old-fashioned novel of male camaraderie. And by making that voice a hip, cynical one, he's able to avoid dealing with many of the troubling political and moral ambiguities raised by the war.

In this reader's opinion, however, the use of Paco's dead buddies never becomes more than a shrewd narrative device. Though it's a well-crafted, often admirable novel, it never succeeds . . . in enveloping the reader in the hallucinatory atmosphere of the war, or in forcing us to examine the complicated ways in which the war relates to everyday human frailties and needs. Instead, *Paco's Story* settles for bluntly telegraphing the sort of messages that have become familiar to us from dozens of newspaper and television reports—that Vietnam vets were often met with scorn, rather than honors, upon their return home; that Paco, like many others, has been so scarred by his experiences that he now simply seeks to survive or cope; that he wonders why he, rather than someone else, managed to survive.

In these respects, Paco is not so different from the heroes of many other novels about Vietnam—all of which invert the classic scenario of a boy going off to war and returning home a man. In such novels as Rob Rigan's *Free Fire Zone,* Ward Just's *Stringer,* and Stephen Wright's *Meditations in Green,* the hero also returns emotionally damaged—alienated from his contemporaries and unable to adjust to the routines of daily life. In fact, one of the larger flaws of this novel is that Paco never emerges as a distinct individual: he comes across as much a vague representative soldier as the generic voice that tells us his story. At the same time, Mr. Heinemann's writing is insufficiently powerful, his vision too myopic, to effectively turn him into the sort of mythic Lazarus-like figure that might otherwise engage our passions.

> Michiko Kakutani, "Did 'Paco's Story' Deserve Its Award?" *in* The New York Times, *November 16, 1987, p. C15.*

REGINALD GIBBONS

[*An American poet, editor, translator, and educator, Gibbons is the editor of* TriQuarterly *magazine. He has received several awards for his collections of poetry, which include* The Ruined Motel *(1981) and* Saints *(1986). Among his editing credits are* TQ20: Twenty Years of the Best Contemporary Writing and Art from TriQuarterly Magazine *(with Susan Hahn) (1985) and* The Writer in Our World *(1986). In the following excerpt, Gibbons takes issue with the disparaging treatment* Paco's Story *received in* The New York Times, *which, according to Gibbons, reflects a strong East coast/literary establishment bias. Gibbons considers Heinemann's novel a beautifully controlled, emotionally searing, and politically relevant work, well-deserving of the National Book Award.*]

By now, Larry Heinemann's second novel [*Paco's Story*], on which he worked for a decade, has won several well-merited prizes and has even brought renewed attention back to his first novel, **Close Quarters.** [Both books] deserve all the readers they can get. Some of those who pick up *Paco's Story* . . . may come to it out of curiosity after noting the blaring haughtiness and disdain that filled several articles in the *New York Times* when Heinemann won the National Book Award for fiction. According to experts out here in Chicago, where of course only a few decades ago everyone wore deerskins . . . , Heinemann is only the third local writer—after Algren and Bellow—ever to win a National Book Award for fiction.

Evidently that seemed at least one too many to the literary denizens of Gotham—where the *New York Times Book Review* had rushed a perfunctory review into print only a week or so before the announcement of the prizewinners, apparently so as not to look scooped if Heinemann won, and where, after the prize was awarded, the daily *Times* ran several columns devoted to doubting the wisdom, or perhaps it was the authority, of the fiction judges. They had committed the error of awarding the prize to someone besides the officially approved authors (estimable in their own right, of course; but in this instance made to look like the mere mascots of the Capital of American

Culture and Art—hereafter referred to as C.A.C.A.). . . . One of the C.A.C.A. columnists later offered personal conjectures on how the judges must have arrived at their mistaken conclusions (and the judges sent an angry, if weary, letter of refutation to the *Times*), and this literary columnist offered its own opinion that Heinemann's book was not very good, anyway. Every mention of this affair (there were four or five separate pieces in the *Times,* by local Chicago count), made it clearer that the merits of Heinemann's book had never been the issue for the literary columnists of C.A.C.A.—they were concerned mostly that the prize go to a writer whom they themselves considered appropriate. (pp. 219-20)

Since what was lost in all this was any fair consideration of the winning book itself, this note is for the purpose of saying that *Paco's Story* is a wonderful piece of work, even if it did win the National Book Award.

It's also the more audacious and courageous of Heinemann's two impressive works. It has a kind of tragic structure which redeems, which makes immensely valuable, the unavoidable presentation of violence and brutality in a book about war. A chorus of ghost voices speaks, from the beginning, to the main character, and says to him what many living veterans would say to us. The unnamed narrator is, in fact, very preoccupied with his own *saying* of Paco's story, and in the new paperback edition Heinemann adds a preface in which he makes clear that the "James" whom the narrator is continually addressing is not another dead soldier, but that colloquial fiction to whom one turns when, with bitter, too-great knowledge, one wants to say something that should have been obvious already, but just isn't. "Let's begin with the first clean fact, James: This ain't no war story." That's how the book opens.

The ghosts are of the dead from one mortal battle of which Paco is the lone survivor, carrying in his head the consciousnesses of all the rest. *Conscience* is not quite the issue; and its not being quite the issue is partly what the book is about: by the time Heinemann comes to the inevitable horror—he outdoes Conrad in honesty, partly by facing racism squarely instead of masking it with false ideals—the wretchedness and waste of the deaths of Paco's battlemates have cut through our moral certainties, leaving us almost too wobbly to focus our consciences on the horror those soldiers themselves created when they were alive. But not quite—and that's the novel's most stunning effort, perhaps.

It is a brief book, very intense and controlled. The individual chapters are as beautifully constructed as fugues, the sentences precise and fastidious; and, to greater purpose, the sentences go far toward suggesting how intensely Paco's survival may depend on the careful, ritual repetitions of humble movement and procedure in an act like washing dishes. The novel has the feeling of having been written small piece by piece; it is filled with grief, fierceness and a dignity wrestled continuously out of the grip of the despair and hopelessness that won't ever let go entirely, after those days of violent death, but which books like this oppose and transform into life again. (pp. 220-21)

> Reginald Gibbons, in a review of "Paco's Story," in TriQuarterly 71, *No. 71, Winter, 1988, pp. 219-21.*

ROBERT TOWERS

The judges of literary prizes probably feel the need for originality almost as strongly as the writers whom they assess. . . . [In 1987,] the judges of the National Book Award for Fiction went well out of their way to avoid the obvious and instead bestowed their wreath upon a novel that received some attention when it appeared but had not, so far as I know, attracted much of a following in the subsequent months. The discovery of an almost unknown work of great merit would indeed be a glorious thing—and a deserved rebuke to those editors and reviewers who had failed to do it timely justice. Is such the case with *Paco's Story,* a second novel by Larry Heinemann which has as its subject the Vietnam War and its consequences for one of the "grunts" who served in it?

The novel begins by proclaiming somewhat defensively that "This ain't no war story."

> War stories are out—one, two, three, and a heave-ho, into the lake you go with all the other alewife scuz and foamy harbor scum. But isn't it a pity. All those crinkly, soggy sorts of laid-by tellings crowded together as thick and pitiful as street cobbles, floating mushy bellies up, like so much moldy shag rugs (dead as rusty-ass doornails and smelling so peculiar and un-Christian). Just isn't it a pity, because here and there and yonder among the corpses are some prize-winning, leg-pulling daisies—some real pop-in-the-oven muffins, so to speak, some real softly lobbed, easy-out line drives.

> But that's the way of the world, or so the fairy tales go. The people with the purse strings and apron springs gripped in their hot and soft little hands denounce war stories—with perfect diction and practiced gestures—a geek-monster species of evil-ugly rumor.

The above passage is worth quoting to illustrate not only the novel's haranguing tone but the metaphoric oddities to which its narrative voice is prone. The voice, we gradually learn, is a collective one, assigned to the dead men of Alpha Company, which, except for one survivor, was wiped out by a nighttime Vietcong assault on Fire Base Harriette.

This ghostly guide constantly exhorts and chides the reader on behalf of that survivor, Paco Sullivan, who for two days lies hideously wounded in the muck and the hot sun, covered with flies, maggots, and gnats, before being discovered by a medic from Bravo Company. . . . Transported by helicopter to a base hospital, Paco, despite his lacerated, splintered, and shattered state and despite the stitches in his penis, is able, a few nights later, to enjoy the sexual ministrations of a compassionate nurse.

Back in the States, Paco, who is apparently without family and (unaccountably) without a veteran's pension, arrives penniless in the small, mid-American town of Boone. There, after encountering rejection and ridicule on the part of local rednecks, he eventually gets a job as a dishwasher in a diner called the Texas Lunch and settles into a room in a shabby hotel across the street. The remainder of the novel is devoted to an account of Paco's isolated and pain-ridden existence in Boone, interrupted by long and nightmarish flashbacks to the Vietnam War and to detailed scenes of horror and carnage in the Russian Revolution and on Guadacanal and Iwo Jima; the latter are supplied—somewhat gratuitously—by other residents of the town. . . .

The most successful parts of the novel are those that instruct us how to do things: how to set booby traps of great variety and ingenuity in the jungle surrounding a fire base—or how to soak, hand wash, rinse, and dry the continuing avalanche of dishes, mugs, glasses, cutlery, pots, and pans in a diner that stays open from six AM to eleven PM six days a week

and is too small for a dishwashing machine. Heinemann obviously relishes the processes involved, and he describes them vigorously and convincingly. Less convincing (though they may well be factually accurate) are the war scenes. In his determination to spare us no detail of broken bone or gushing blood or flesh reduced to pulp, Heinemann becomes monotonous; the impact of a bullet fired at close range into a human skull is much the same, after all, whether the victim be a "zip" (Vietcong soldier), a grunt, or a Jap, and its description gains nothing by repetition. The routine obscenities of military speech continually reproduced, the routine "macho" reduction of all young women to poontang, pussy, or bitches, the constantly repeated imagery of stench, mud, shit, scum, grease, and garbage, the straining after bizarre comparisons ("that rainbow, as solid and superb as a Corinthian column"), and above all the hectoring, coercive voice (as if the ghost were saying, "And now, reader, I'm going to make you *feel* exactly what it's like to participate in the gang rape and throat-cutting of a Vietcong woman")—these produce, in combination with the stereotyped characters and the largely undifferentiated dialogue, a fatigue like that resulting from a prolonged exposure to pornography. In the midst of all this, the character of Paco himself is so rudimentarily conceived that he hardly exists apart from his wretched situation.

In that it tries, in somewhat blatant fashion, to exploit the reader's most accessible and predictable responses of revulsion, pity, and guilt, *Paco's Story* is, I think, essentially a sentimental novel. That it should have been chosen as the best novel of the year suggests that the judges, for whatever reasons, made a sentimental decision of their own. (p. 26)

> *Robert Towers, "All-American Novels," in* The New York Review of Books, *Vol. XXXIV, Nos. 21 & 22, January 21, 1988, pp. 26-7.*

JOHN MELMOTH

Perhaps more than any other since 1914, the Vietnam war was a secret one, the soldiers' sense of isolation more acute, the remoteness of their sufferings from the civilian perspective more extreme. . . . Infantrymen conducted their obscure operations—no ground was taken or lost, the enemy was rarely engaged directly. . . .

And then, after a year, it was all over. Those who survived were brought back into the world, with which they were not always able to cope. Wigged-out, affronted, brutalized grunts were unlikely to make model citizens, husbands and fathers. Far from a home fit for heroes, America had created heroes who could not fit in at home, who were baffled by the requirements of domesticity, scarcely house-trained. "Survivor syndrome" continues to mar the lives of thousands of middle-ageing American men; not just the crazies who shoot up supermarkets and Sunday football crowds, but those who are just depressed, worn out by nightmares and can no longer "hack it". The secret war is still being fought. . . .

From the first, a distinction is made between Heinemann's new novel, *Paco's Story,* and the genre to which it ostensibly belongs: "This ain't no war story." The claim is, however, disingenuous. Although Paco remains close-mouthed on the subject, those around him—a Second World War marine, the medic who dressed Paco's wounds, the Russian émigré shopkeeper—all take a shot at it. The novel manages to deplore the fact that "most folks will shell out hard-earned, greenback cash, every time, to see artfully performed, urgently fascinating, grisly and gruesome carnage'' at the same time as giving them a little of what they fancy. The only survivor of a massive attack on Fire Base Harriette, Paco is terribly wounded and there is no chance that we will be spared the details. It is two days before he can be rescued (''dusted off''), two days in which the sun and the maggots get to work on what the Vietcong have left.

Back in the States, constantly medicated and sedated, Paco settles for washing up in a small-town diner where he can drink, hide out, remember and try to get by. His is a ghost story, told by the dead who did not survive the attack in which he was wounded, who whisper in his ear when he is at his most vulnerable. He himself is a kind of ghost, walking wounded, avoiding involvement, causing hardly a stir, leaving no impression.

Paco's Story lacks . . . impact . . . because, back in the world, Heinemann is no longer content to tell it as it is but casts around for explanations. The fat necks and small minds of his small-town mid-American grotesques, who will not make room for a man maimed on their behalf, are sitting targets which he could hit blindfolded. He writes best when telling the worst; and Hicksville is significantly less demanding in every sense than the Mekong Delta.

John Melmoth, ''Men at Arms, Women in Love,'' in The Times Literary Supplement, *No. 4430, February 26-March 3, 1988, p. 214.*

Edward (Mark) Hirsch

Wild Gratitude

The National Book Critics Circle Award: Poetry

American poet, critic, and folklorist.

In its award citation for *Wild Gratitude* (1986), the National Book Critics Circle commended Hirsch as "one of the more eloquent and thoughtful voices of his generation " and as a poet who "writes movingly about both the beauties and the sorrows of his sharply observed world." Written in a narrative style, the poems in *Wild Gratitude* display both unsentimental personal reflections in such poems as "The Skokie Theatre" and "In a Polish Home for the Aged" and elegaic tributes to artists and writers of the past, as in the poems "Paul Celan" and "Wild Gratitude," in which Hirsch meditates on the life and work of Christopher Smart.

Several of the autobiographical poems in *Wild Gratitude* are set in Chicago and Detroit, Midwestern cities where Hirsch has spent much of his life. He commented: "One of the problems for me as a poet has been to find a style that's lyrical but could still relate to the world I come from, which is urban." The poems "Commuters" and "Three Journeys" capture epiphanal moments and exemplify Hirsch's success, according to critics, in combining urbane observations with a more meditative and literary sensibility. Another aspect of Hirsch's personal background that repeatedly enters his poems is his chronic insomnia. Hirsch stated: "Almost everything in my poetry begins because I'm an insomniac, so I can't imagine writing poetry without it. I've discovered that late at night is not only a good time for writing and thinking but also for setting poems. I feel as if I'm the only one awake, and it gives me the sense of isolation that I want to capture in my work." Both the first and last poems in *Wild Gratitude*, "I Need Help" and "Dawn Walk," feature sleepless narrators. However, while the speaker in the first poem is anguished, the second one marvels at "the simple astonishing news / That we are here." Explained Hirsch: "I begin the book with a plea for help, and end with a statement of gratitude, that we've survived our isolation and found community."

Although reviewers describe Hirsch as an optimistic, life-affirming poet, they also identify a recurring darker aspect in *Wild Gratitude*. The poems "Fast Break" and "Omen," for instance, concern fatally ill persons, while "Leningrad (1941-1943)" depicts the suffering caused by the siege of Leningrad during World War II. Other poems pay tribute to tragic figures in art and literature, including the English poets Christopher Smart and John Clare, both of whom spent portions of their lives in insane asylums. Hirsch demonstrates his concern with suffering in the present as well as the past when he compares Clare to homeless, mentally ill people found in contemporary American cities. The NBCC citation identified in these and other poems in *Wild Gratitude* "a euphoric humanism reminiscent of Whitman and Stevens."

Some reviewers fault Hirsch for an excessive lyricism in *Wild Gratitude*, especially a tendency towards overuse of adjectives. For the most part, however, they praise Hirsch's prosodic skill,

effective use of metaphor, and particularly his ability to portray affirmative qualities in human suffering. "Edward Hirsch is a poet of genuine talent and feeling," asserts critic Peter Stitt; "as he learns to administer with lighter touch his considerable linguistic fertility, he will surely grow into one of the important writers of our age."

(See also *CLC*, Vol. 31; *Contemporary Authors*, Vol. 104; and *Contemporary Authors New Revision Series*, Vol. 20.)

PETER STITT

[*Stitt, an American critic who frequently contributes to* Georgia Review, *is the author of* The World's Hieroglyphic Beauty: Five American Poets *(1985). In the following excerpt, Stitt examines Hirsch's syntax as well as his emotionally charged presentation of subjects.*]

The work of Edward Hirsch has deepened since his impressive first book, *For the Sleepwalkers*. Imagination is dominant in that volume: the world is seen through the eyes of a magic realist and rendered in the words of a master rhetorician. *Wild Gratitude,* Hirsch's second volume, is more full of feeling than bewitchment; as the epigraph (from Auden) promises, it reaches for joy while recognizing deep pain: "May I, composed like them / Of Eros and of dust, / Beleaguered by the same / Negation and despair, / Show an affirming flame."

The attitude of praise and celebration that permeates this volume is established in the title poem ["**Wild Gratitude,**"] which opens with its speaker fondling his cat Zooey and ". . . thinking about the poet, Christopher Smart, / Who wanted to kneel down and pray without ceasing / In every one of the splintered London streets, / / And was locked away in the madhouse at St. Luke's / With his sad religious mania, and his wild gratitude, / And his grave prayers for the other lunatics, / And his great love for his speckled cat, Jeoffry." The lines are remarkable for their speed—the syntax, which favors parallel phrasal structures, and the rhythm, which relies on strings of unstressed syllables, both rush the reader forward from word to word, line to line. The overall effect is one of celebration, and it is only on a later reading that the reader can really hear words that work contrary to this spirit: "splintered," "madhouse," "sad," "grave."

Three of those four words are adjectives; it is striking how often in this book Hirsch relies on modifiers to convey nuance in his poems. Here the technique is used to advantage and does not cause a problem, though other poems seem weak in direct proportion to the number of modifiers that they contain. Sometimes, in fact, Hirsch will couple a noun with what seems its most familiar adjective, as in the poem "**Omen,**" which contains such phrases as: "fitful half-sleep," "hushed sound," "small, airless ward," "stormy clouds," and "cruel dream." The poem, about a case of cancer, also uses the too easy epithet "my closest friend" twice.

One reason for the problems in "**Omen**" is the powerful nature of the subject matter; the poet's feelings seem stronger than his ability to control them through art. Another reason is that Hirsch's style is so highly rhetorical that even the slightest misstep will cause a poem to cross the borderline between effectiveness and excess. It is interesting that one of the best poems in the book should treat the same subject as "**Omen**" with an almost minimalist sense of restraint. "**Fast Break**" uses an extended metaphor drawn from basketball to express the fatal, perhaps as yet undetected, disease beginning to work on an excellent player.

The description, remarkably fluid, begins as "A hook shot kisses the rim . . . / but doesn't drop"; the defensive center takes the rebound and initiates the break with a perfect outlet pass. After several more passes, the last guard who could stop the play

> lunges out
> and commits to the wrong man
>
> while the power-forward explodes past them
> in a fury, taking the ball into the air
>
> by himself now and laying it gently
> against the glass for a lay-up,
>
> but losing his balance in the process,
> inexplicably falling, hitting the floor

> with a wild, headlong motion
> for the game he loved like a country
>
> and swiveling back to see an orange blur
> floating perfectly through the net.

Perhaps the best detail in this poem is that the shot is made; only the player's surprising fall indicates something wrong, some portending interruption to graceful process. Thus the poem, like this entire volume, expresses both joy and sorrow, triumph and pain. Edward Hirsch is a poet of genuine talent and feeling; as he learns to administer with lighter touch his considerable linguistic fertility, he will surely grow into one of the important writers of our age. (p. 105-06)

> *Peter Stitt, in a review of "Wild Gratitude," in* Poetry, *Vol. CXLVIII, No. 2, May, 1986, pp. 105-06.*

THE VIRGINIA QUARTERLY REVIEW

Hirsch is an excellent poet who has mastered his forms, so much so that they are transparent. Unlike much recent verse that is only differentiated from ordinary statement by self-consciously formal devices, Hirsch's poems bring the reader into contact with something besides themselves. They are avenues for the reader into his or her own imagination—of one's own past autumns or private griefs. There is much that is conventional in *Wild Gratitude*—the tributes to various cultural heroes (Sartre, Ives, Hopper), the confessional poems—but even the conventional poems are usually distinguished in some way, and the title poem on Christopher Smart ["**Wild Gratitude**"] is deeply moving. In a wonderful poem like "**I Need Help,**" Hirsch is doing something of critical importance for poetry if it is to continue to be an important medium: he is calling on his community of potential listeners and readers and imagining them as part of a single effort, focused on the poet but more important than the poet. "I need help" writes Hirsch "to fly out of myself." (pp. 100-01)

> *A review of "Wild Gratitude," in* The Virginia Quarterly Review, *Vol. 62, No. 3, Summer, 1986, pp. 100-01.*

DAVID WOJAHN

[*Wojahn, an American poet and critic, is the author of the poetry collections* Icehouse Lights *(1982) and* Glassworks *(1987). In the following excerpt, he commends Hirsch's technical skill and ability to evoke an emotional response.*]

[Edward Hirsch is] fond of dramatic monologues, but even though his poems usually begin as troubled meditations on human suffering they end in celebration. We may not always be convinced that his speakers have earned the celebration they strive for, but we are always convinced of the poet's technical prowess. Like Mr. Hirsch's earlier collection, *For the Sleepwalkers, Wild Gratitude* specializes in two kinds of poems— homages to artists and poets and gritty autobiographical vignettes of urban life. The literary and artistic figures he chooses to write about are often those touched by tragedy. There are poems about suicides, such as the German poet Paul Celan and the Hungarian poet Attila József, as well as poems paying homage to the mad Englishmen John Clare and Christopher Smart. But Mr. Hirsch also offers elegies for his grandparents, recollections of childhood and descriptions of sojourns in Detroit. What makes his new book successful is Mr. Hirsch's ability to merge his concern for the literary with his observations of daily life. In **"Three Journeys,"** he draws an elaborate parallel between a bag lady's plight and that of John Clare:

> Whoever
> has stood alone in the night's deep shadows
> listening to laughter coming from a well-lit house
> will know that John Clare's loneliness was unbending.
> And whoever has felt that same unbending loneliness
> will also know what an old woman felt today
> as she followed an obedient path between the huge
> green garbage cans behind Kroger's Super-Market
> and the small silver ones behind Clarence's grocery.

Of course, Mr. Hirsch runs the risk of sentimentality, but he can usually avoid bathos because of his prosodic skill and his gift for engaging metaphor. And, although his poems are usually long narratives, he punctuates them with bravura imagery:

> Slowly the bridges open their arms
>
>   over the river and the cars
>   fan out in the midst like a peacock's
>   feathers, or a deck of luminous cards
>   dealt into shadows.

But Mr. Hirsch's tenderness sometimes threatens to become merely ingratiating, and even his most surprising effects at times seem rather calculated. These problems would be less apparent if *Wild Gratitude* were a shorter collection. Although none of the poems is a throwaway, Mr. Hirsch's strategies can grow redundant. Such shortcomings, however, are quite minor, the price Mr. Hirsch pays for his wildly abundant talent. In the chilling conclusion of **"Omen,"** a poem about a friend who is dying of cancer, we are given a sense of how moving this poet's writing can sometimes be:

> My friend says the pain is like a mule
> Kicking him in the chest, again and again,
> Until nothing else but the pain seems real.
>
> Tonight the wind whispers a secret to the trees,
> Something stark and unsettling, something terrible
> Since the yard begins to tremble, shedding leaves.
>
> I know that my closest friend is going to die
> And I can feel the dark sky tilting on one wing,
> Shuddering with rain, coming down around me.

> David Wojahn, *"Monologues in Three Tones," in* The New York Times Book Review, *June 8, 1986, p. 38.*

An Excerpt from *WILD GRATITUDE*

In Spite of Everything, the Stars

> Like a stunned piano, like a bucket
> of fresh milk flung into the air
> or a dozen fists of confetti
> thrown hard at a bride
> stepping down from the altar,
> the stars surprise the sky.
> Think of dazed stones
> floating overhead, or an ocean
> of starfish hung up to dry. Yes,
> like a conductor's expectant arm
> about to lift toward the chorus,
> or a juggler's plates defying gravity,
> or a hundred fastballs fired at once
> and freezing in midair, the stars
> startle the sky over the city.

> And that's why drunks leaning up
> against abandoned buildings, women
> hurrying home on deserted side streets,
> policemen turning blind corners,and
> even thieves stepping from alleys
> all stare up at once. Why else do
> sleepwalkers more toward the windows,
> or old men drag flimsy lawn chairs
> onto fire escapes, or hardened criminals
> press sad foreheads to steel bars?
> Because the night is alive with lamps!
> That's why in dark houses all over the city
> dreams stir in the pillows, a million
> plumes of breath rise into the sky.

LIAM RECTOR

[Rector, an American poet and critic, is the author of The Sorrow of Architecture *(1984). In the following excerpt, he praises Hirsch's compassionate approach to his subject matter.]*

Despite the wonderfully strong sentiment and intelligence of [Edward Hirsch's first book, *For the Sleepwalkers,*] I often detected a reliance on adjectives to act as poetic buzz-words, deflating the surge of the voice and rendering a kind of predictable straining after affability. There is little of that in *Wild Gratitude.* Here the sentence and its rushing forth, its proceeding, is still the same basic unit of Hirsch's poetic, but he is much more in command of the material and of the urgencies within each adjective. (pp. 507-08)

Hirsch's sense of innocence often turns to this "When I was a boy" to take measure of the senseless waning of continuity which adult experience imposes. In *Wild Gratitude,* Hirsch returns to that noosphere which in these poems is the transition, often seen as the impossible impasse, between these two worlds—the vigil of dusk, that other shore of insomnia.

> At this hour the soul is like a yellow wing
> slipping through the treetops, a little ecstatic
> cloud hovering over the sidewalks, calling out
> to the approaching night, "Amaze me, amaze me,"
>
> while the body sits glumly by the window
> listening to the clear summons of the dead
> transparent as glass, clairvoyant as crystal . . .
> Some nights it is almost ready to join them.

Hirsch's poetry is a poetry of great empathy and sympathy. . . . Where characters and scenes are cleaved to for their realism and passion, specific to their details, Hirsch's is a poetry which speaks heartbreakingly for what's common, what's binding (even with the isolation of the insomniac) within the tribe. When his work occasionally veers off into the sputtering engine of a soft visionary stance, the adjectives working like amiable pistons, it can fall short. Hirsch must sense this, for *Wild Gratitude* is a remarkable maturing and has a cohesive sense of restraint in its baroque effusiveness. There are many remarkable individual poems, including **"The Night Parade"** ("whores adjusting their uniforms"), **"Curriculum Vitae"** (perhaps the form of our decade?), **"Wild Gratitude,"** and many others. When Hirsch speaks of the poor, or of the lost and losing, his connections is never sentimental but rather harks back to Frank O'Hara's saying "The poor have me always with them." (pp. 508-09)

Liam Rector, in a review of "Wild Gratitude," in
The Hudson Review, *Vol. XXXIX, No. 3, Autumn,
1986, pp. 507-09.*

HANK DE LEO

[*De Leo is an American painter, printmaker, and critic. In the
following excerpt, he commends the compassionate quality of the
poems in* Wild Gratitude.]

Joseph Brodsky has written that "Love is essentially an attitude
maintained by the infinite toward the finite. The reversal constitutes either faith or poetry." The poems in Edward Hirsch's
second book, *Wild Gratitude,* convey a convincing faith of the
finite toward the infinite.

Hirsch has become extremely adept in using otherwise depressing subjects to affirmative effect. As the title implies,
Wild Gratitude is essentially positive in feeling, and it clearly
establishes Hirsch as one of our most engagingly compassionate
poets. (p. 779)

Insomnia figures prominently in this book, as it did in Hirsch's
first book, *For the Sleepwalkers.* He uses insomnia to masterful
effect as a metaphor for the human resistance to and eventual
acceptance of death.... The primitive unease humans feel
toward sleep, the most vulnerable and needed state, is amplified
throughout this book.... The trope of insomnia is not without
its difficulties. There is a regrettable over-reliance on moon,
stars, and night sky symbolism. When Hirsch reaches for an
image of surreal novelty the result can be as unbelievable as
"the moon slowly turning into a swastika" or "Under stars
scattered / Like red kerchiefs through the trees."

The objects of empathy in these poems are not only human.
Through deft use of the richly connotative word "wild" in the
title poem, the poet's cat, Zooey, and Christopher Smart's cat,
Jeoffry ("and every creature like him"), are shown to be wreathed
in the "living fire" that links humans and animals. (p. 780)

The subjects of Hirsch's most powerful and moving poems,
"Indian Summer," "Dawn Walk," "Fever," "Ancient Signs,"
and **"In a Polish Home for the Aged,"** are people who have
been close to the poet, some still living, most now dead. There
is a directness of communication, a clarity of language throughout this book, which reaches the height of passionate feeling
in these poems drawn from his memories. Hirsch takes the
particulars of his own life and expands them, to good effect,
into general reflections on the human condition.

Similar results are sometimes achieved in the poems on historial
figures. Both in the direct homages (such as the finely crafted
and musically evocative **"The Night Parade"** for Charles Ives)
and in the tangentially suggestive homages, Hirsch writes with
precision and strength. (p. 781)

While Hirsch commemorates men and women he's known in
his own life, it's significant that his tributes to writers, artists,
and composers are reserved for men (Kung K'ai, Edward Hopper, Christopher Smart, Charles Ives, Atilla József, Dino Cam-
pana, Paul Celan, John Clare, Sartre). Marianne Moore is the
solitary woman in a similar list of homages in *For the Sleepwalkers.* It's not that Hirsch is simply after bluechip names
from historical canons, he is genuinely engaged in an attempt
to direct attention to the little-read European poets József, Cam-
pana, and Celan.... I have no argument with tributes to great
achievement; who could? But Hirsch's approach presents two
problems. Such a skewed interest in great men unfortunately

implies that women have not made similarly great achievements. Also, there is a timidity among contemporary American
artists (painters and composers are no less guilty than poets)
that keeps them from paying homage to their as-yet-unproved
and still-living contemporaries. Where is the interest in inter-
artistic comparisons of our own generation?

If one can set aside such polemical issues, Hirsch is a strong
poet worthy of a wide audience. He is continually struggling
to come to terms with and find meaning in human experiences.... (pp. 781-82)

Hirsch's striking narrative voice consistently reveals a strong
novelistic strain, something like the story-telling quality in
József. But unlike József, whom Hirsch has "shaking an anarchical fist / at the world in a small magazine" (a reference
to József's famous poem of 1925 "With a Pure Heart" in
Szeged), Hirsch seems to be looking inward to locate his own
quieter and pure heart. (p. 782)

Hank De Leo, "Edward Hirsch: A Second Book,"
in Michigan Quarterly Review, *Vol. XXV, No. 4,
Fall, 1986, pp. 779-82.*

R. S. GWYNN

[*Gwynn, an American poet and critic, is the author of* The Drive-
In *(1986). In the following excerpt, he discusses the subjects of
Hirsch's poems in* Wild Gratitude.]

Edward Hirsch is on terms of easy familiarity with the world
of poets and painters. The title poem of *Wild Gratitude* speaks
of Christopher Smart and his cat Jeoffrey, "and every creature
like him— / Who can teach us how to praise—purring / In
their own language, / Wreathing themselves in the living fire."
In the face of all the contrary evidence that daily life affords
us, Hirsch shows a determination to "let what rises live with
what descends," to find affirmation in "the simple astonishing
news / That we are here, / Yes, we are still here."

Hirsch's first book of poems, *For the Sleepwalkers,* was buoyed
by an enthusiasm for poetic technique (How many books contain *two* sestinas?) and a generosity of feeling that gave one
the impression of a young man so earnest he was apt to lose
sleep over not being able to talk things over personally with
Vallejo, Rimbaud, Lorca, Matisse, and Monet. Even though
European writers and scenes figure prominently in the present
volume, Hirsch is, for the most part, content to stay close to
home, seeing his own country's landscape through Edward
Hopper's eyes:

> This man will paint other abandoned mansions,
> And faded cafeteria windows, and poorly lettered
> Storefronts on the edges of small towns.
> Always they will have this same expression,
>
> The utterly naked look of someone
> Being stared at, someone American and gawky,
> Someone who is about to be left alone
> Again, and can no longer stand it.

It's appropriate that another poem is subtitled "Homage to
Charles Ives," a dedication to one of our typical home-grown
geniuses. Hirsch's free-ranging associations bring to mind Ives's
conceit of simultaneously diminishing and rising musical themes,
merging and supplanting each other like marches from a parade
passing by. (pp. 113-14)

While many of Hirsch's poems portray a version of the American reality that takes place only in the world of *noire vérité,*

others inhabit more familiar settings. Two elegiac poems, **"Omen"** and **"Fast Break,"** confront the deaths of friends. The second of these, as the title indicates, takes its metaphor from basketball. In a single 34-line sentence, Hirsch captures the movement of a perfectly executed play that becomes a friend's memorial: "hitting the floor / / with a wild, headlong motion / for the game he loved like a country / / and swiveling back to see an orange blur / floating perfectly through the net." In **"The Skokie Theatre,"** he recreates the amusing urgency of adolescent love: "Our mouths / were glued together like flypaper, our lips / were grinding in a hysterical grimace / while the most handsome man in the world / twitched his hips on the flickering screen." **"Three Journeys"** provides a typical display of Hirsch's ability to blend the near with the remote. As he watches a bag lady "on her terrible journey past Food Lane's Super-Market, / and Maze's Records, and The Little Flowering Barbershop," he remembers John Clare's poignant account of his escape from the insane asylum and attempt to walk, starving and foot-sore, the eighty miles home. The third journey in the poem is Hirsch's own, or any poet's for that matter, carrying away with him the leftover scraps of experience, memory, and learning that are the stuff of art. These are the sources for which Hirsch expresses his gratitude in poems for which the rest of us should express a like degree of thanks. (pp. 114-15)

R. S. Gwynn, "Second Gear," in New England Review and Bread Loaf Quarterly, *Vol. IX, No. 1, Autumn, 1986, pp. 111-21.*

ROSETTA MARANTZ COHEN

[*Cohen, an American poet and critic, is the author of* Domestic Scenes *(1982). In the following excerpt, she discusses the bleak yet uplifting quality of the poems in* Wild Gratitude.]

Hirsch's writing is characterized by a simplicity and clarity that make one feel one knows him well after reading only a few poems. While many of Hirsch's poems [in *Wild Gratitude*] . . . rely on exotic places and assumed personae, . . . the lyrical voice comes through so vividly that even grim evocations of the Nazi siege of Leningrad or of Paul Celan and John Clare are suffused with a poignant sense of the poet's personal history.

The title of the book is ironic, for while several of these poems manage to achieve a mildly optimistic perspective, the prevailing vision of *Wild Gratitude* is anything but celebratory. Hirsch's world is a place of struggle and fear where even the most familiar things—clouds, paintings, carriage horses—are commuted through memory or association into unhappy omens. . . .

Often the poems speak in voices either dislocated or bewildered. There is, for example, **"The Village Idiot,"** a character from the poet's past whom he sees now "from the wet mirror" of his own bathroom. There is the fevered vision of an old woman who believes "the full moon is German"; that "the empty white face of the moon is saying it wants to arrest her." And then there is the poet himself, who, in a poem called **"Commuters,"** speaks of his own disquieting self-detachment:

It's that vague feeling of panic
That sweeps over you
Stepping out of the #7 train
At dusk, thinking, *This isn't me*
Crossing a platform with the other
Commuters in the worried half-light
Of evening . . .

Every so often these dark visions are answered by revelations, but these are always muted and resigned. Hirsch chooses his heroes from among the downtrodden and oppressed, and his poems generally pivot on an acceptance of the human condition—a condition that is more or less miserable depending on the subject at hand. In **"Three Journeys,"** for instance, which celebrates the life of the poet John Clare, Hirsch comes to understand Clare's nobility only after equating his escape from High Beech Asylum with the pathetic journey of a bag lady whom Hirsch follows over the course of a day. By the end of the poem, Clare has become a kind of Christian martyr,

. . . so desperately hungry
after three days and nights without food
that he finally knelt down, as if in prayer,
and ate the soft grass of the earth,
and thought it tasted like fresh bread,
and judged no one, not even himself,
and slept peacefully again, like a child.

In [**"Wild Gratitude"**], Hirsch's hero is Christopher Smart, a man whose response to the world's abuse was to transform the humblest pleasures of life into the wildest joys. By contemplating Smart's great affection for his cat Jeoffry, Hirsch comes to realize that

It is Jeoffry—and every creature like him—
Who can teach us how to praise—purring
In their own language,
Wreathing themselves in the living fire.

And in a long poem about war-torn Russia, in which all kinds of physical suffering are catalogued, there is again the determination, if not to praise, at least to survive: "Slowly we touched a sharp razor to our necks / And scraped away the useless blue skin / And the dead flesh. Somehow we lived." These resolutions are small consolations in a world so persistently bleak, yet they manage to convince. *Wild Gratitude* is not a depressing book. In fact, it leaves the reader feeling optimistic, as if the power of the language had redeemed the vision. (p. 286)

Rosetta Marantz Cohen, "Empire of Words," in The Nation, *New York, Vol. 243, No. 9, September 27, 1986, pp. 285-86.*

GREG KUZMA

[*Kuzma, an American poet, critic, and educator, is the author of such poetry collections as* Something At Last Visible *(1969),* Good News *(1973),* A Day in the World *(1976),* Everyday Life *(1982), and* A Turning: A Sequence *(1987). In the following excerpt Kuzma characterizes the poems in* Wild Gratitude *as weak and overwritten.*]

Edward Hirsh's *Wild Gratitude* is [a] very much "written" book. . . . Writing here, is overwriting, writing that takes its toll while taking its time, overly structured, repetitive, cautious, unexceptional in diction, formal, concerned more with *how* it looks than what it says, the stanzas shapely, filled, filled up, the poems dangerously long or thick or fat, polite-looking, conventional, competent, calm, and reliable. Hirsh . . . rarely gets excited. Emotions run from mild confession—though rarely personal—to bemused distraction. . . . Hirsh's poems are wordy—a few apt phrases surrounded by a lot of paste. Were they soup, they would be mostly starch. The first poem, **"I Need Help,"** is wiser than it knows; it affects a playful desperation but is not half so urgent as it should be. "I want to build a new kind of machine,'' it announces, then chokes the reader on dozens of slightly surreal, improbable propositions:

> I want someone to lower a huge pulley
> And hoist it back over the mountain. . . .
>
> I want to hold a rummage sale for the clouds
> And send up flashlights, matchbooks, kerosene,
> And old lanterns. . . .

What stands out though, instead of the slightly-bizarre images, is the framing rhetoric: I want to, I know it, I need, I admit, I want, And I need, I have no, I want to, But I can't, And because I can't, and so on. Along the way one forgets, if one ever knew, the reason for the poem or what it's about. **"Fall,"** the second poem in the book, is similar:

> Fall, falling, fallen. That's the way the season
> Changes its tense in the long-haired maples
> That dot the road; the veiny hand-shaped leaves
> Redden on their branches (in a fiery competition
> With the final remaining cardinals) and then
> Begin to sidle and float through the air, at last
> Settling into colorful layers carpeting the ground. . . .

The first two lines are very nice, graceful, intelligent, witty, metaphoric, rhythmically strong. But line 3 with its "dot" gets off wrong, I think, and what follows through the next four lines is a crazy assortment of the commonplace and the obvious offered as if fresh, stirring, or newfound. One cannot tell here if Hirsh intends to be rehearsing the season, in all its redundancies, upon the usual stage, or if he believes he is making discoveries. The ending doesn't help. Is he serious? Are we meant to nod in deep agreement, or laugh at ourselves for how we remain, forever, dazed and dazzled by the slightest things?

> And every year there is a brief, startling moment
> When we pause in the middle of a long walk home and
> Suddenly feel something invisible and weightless
> Touching our shoulders, sweeping down from the air:
> It is autumn wind pressing against our bodies;
> It is the changing light of fall falling on us.

Whatever we might make of **"I Need Help"** or **"Fall,"** the third poem, **"Omen,"** shows how insensitive the method can be. Hirsh's friend is dying, but the poem looks away, will not confront that, does not try. Only six of the poem's thirty lines are given over to the friend, who, they say, is "suffering from cancer" and "fingered by illness" and other clichés. The rest of the poem deals with weather, landscape, the poet's memory of childhood, and is extremely self-involved, seemingly unaware of the cruel irony of juxtaposing the mild discomfort of rain on the roof or childhood's bad dreams with the friend's

excruciating pain. . . . The friend's pain "is like a mule / kicking him in the chest. . . . '' Were the poem to make plain how the poet's prior experience has been clearly inadequate to prepare him for the enormity of his friend's dying, the poem could be read sympathetically. Instead the poet seeks consolation and reassurance in linking weather with tragedy—the gathering clouds and whispering winds and shedding leaves forecast the death of the friend. It is a clumsy maneuver, unfeeling, literary, designed more to dramatize the self and make a poem than to explore that other reality.

Where Hirsh confines himself to subjects more borrowed than forced upon him, sometimes his poems express a sufficiency. . . . Hirsh is good with landscape, especially things twice seen, or first seen and captured by someone else. In a poem about a Chinese painting, Hirsh writes gracefully: "one village / winking through the distant clouds, / another puckering in the gray mist / like a paper orchid wrinkling in water.'' The poem ends well, as does the poem about Edward Hopper's "House by the Railroad,'' which concludes with an effective interpretation of Hopper's tone and style:

> Always they will have this same expression,
>
> The utterly naked look of someone
> Being stared at, someone American and gawky,
> Someone who is about to be left alone
> Again, and can no longer stand it.

But then **"Wild Gratitude,"** the title poem, shows how extremely mechanical Hirsh can be. In a poem heaped up with details so that it reminds us of **"I Need Help,"** the diction is all paired-up nouns and adjectives. Besides the "wild gratitude" of the title there is "swollen belly," "solemn little squeals," religious mania, "grave prayers," "great love," "calm bravery," "warm humanity," "private benevolence," "universal human kindness," and not one of them in quotation marks or italics!—soft clink, rickety stairs, small pleasure, and so on. Elementary as all this is, the poem is just as awkward as it forces significance upon its scant, concluding vision:

> And only then did I understand
> It is Jeoffry—and every creature like him—
> Who can teach us how to praise—purring
> In their own language,
> Wreathing themselves in the living fire. . . .

Hirsh's poems need lots of editing. (pp. 350-53)

Greg Kuzma, "Two from Knopf," in The Literary Review, *Fairleigh Dickinson University, Vol. 31, No. 3, Spring, 1988, pp. 347-53.*

Penelope Lively
Moon Tiger

Booker-McConnell Prize for Fiction

Egyptian-born English novelist, short story writer, and author of books for children.

Lively first earned her reputation as an author of literature for young people and is widely recognized as one of England's best living children's writers. Since her first novel for adults, *The Road to Lichfield* (1977), Lively has attracted a critical and popular audience for her adult fiction as well. Both her juvenile and adult works share a preoccupation with time, exploring the relationships between collective memory, or history, and personal recollection. Lively explains: "the one thing we all share is the capacity to remember; the novelist tries to convey the significance and the power of that capacity in fictional terms, to make universal stories out of the particular story that we each carry in our own head. At its grandest, this theme is the most compelling in all literature."

Like most of Lively's work, *Moon Tiger* (1987) revolves around the nature of time and memory. The novel is structured as the deathbed recollections of Claudia, a popular historian. From her hospital bed, Claudia attempts to write a history of her era by recalling her own life against the backdrop of historical events, particularly World War II, during which she was a war correspondent in Cairo, Egypt. Claudia's memory travels back and forth through time, as she relives her lovingly intense lifelong competition with her brother, her strained relationship with her illegitimate daughter, and her wartime love affair in Egypt with an English tank commander, who was killed in the Western Desert campaign in 1942. Recognizing that this relationship was the pivotal event of her life, Claudia tries to align her memories of her dead lover with her own experiences following his death.

Moon Tiger is told in a series of alternating viewpoints, overlaying Claudia's voice with those of other narrators, including her brother, her daughter, and the author. Critics praise the craftsmanship and technical virtuosity Lively shows in the construction of her impressionistic narrative, in which the remnants of memory gradually coalesce into a whole. Her vivid evocations of the wartime desert campaign and the milieu of occupied Cairo, where Lively spent her early childhood, were particularly admired. While the tone of most of the novel maintains the detached style of historical narrative, the love story which forms the heart of *Moon Tiger* is considered poignant and emotionally revealing. In the words of P. D. James, chair of the Booker-McConnell Prize, *Moon Tiger* is " a complex and beautifully controlled novel."

(See also *CLC*, Vol. 32; *Children's Literature Review*, Vol. 7; *Contemporary Authors*, Vols. 41-44, rev. ed.; *Something About the Author*, Vol. 7; and *Dictionary of Literary Biography*, Vol. 14.)

© Jerry Bauer

SARA MAITLAND

[*Maitland is an English novelist, short story writer, and essayist, who blends Christian ideals and feminist principles in her writings. She won the Somerset Maugham Award for her first novel,* Daughter of Jerusalem *(1978; published in the United States as* Languages of Love, *1981). Her more recent fiction includes a collection of short stories,* Telling Tales *(1983), and a novel,* Virgin Territory *(1984); she has also been a frequent contributor to feminist anthologies. In the following excerpt Maitland praises the technical virtuosity of Lively's narrative and expresses admiration for the intellectual focus of* Moon Tiger, *but notes that the novelist's conservative view of history weakens the impact of her story.*]

Half a century ago there was a World War. I was born after it and there is something very important about the Europeans born before it that I simply do not understand. It seems imaginatively to have severed the century. Penelope Lively, who was born before it, but not as much before it as the central character of her novel [*Moon Tiger*], endeavours to rejoin those severed halves by connecting the history of *everything*, from amoebae onwards, with those individuals who 'do not grow old as we who are left grow old' and the experiences of those who were left and have indeed grown old.

It is a bold attempt, if rather over-neatly packaged. Claudia Hampton is old and dying; she contemplates her whole life from her childhood to her present. Once, long ago, she was a war correspondent on the Western Desert Campaign: there she fell in love with a young tank regiment officer, who was killed in action. She miscarried their child. His life stopped; hers did not.

Claudia Hampton, moreover, is a popular historian who has always treated history in terms of decisive individuals; now she tries to treat her own life as she has treated others, as a fragment of world history. As an honest historian she 'allows' other voices to have their own autonomous commentary: her brother's, her sister-in-law's and, particularly, her daughter's.

Technically, Lively does a really beautifully crafted thing with these interjected viewpoints, picking up a passage from one consciousness, repeating some of it through different eyes and then moving the narrative forward in the second voice: stunningly economical and revealing. But I had a real problem with the book—or, rather, two interconnected problems.

One is formal and I shall return to it; the other is Lively's view of history itself. The novel is based on the unarguable premise that the past creates the present, but it does not apparently interact with it at all. The subjectivity of the historian—although the central emotional context of the book is the subjectivity of this particular historian—does not affect the past. History is presented as a straight line and the present is simply the still point on that line. In this sense nothing can *happen* in the present and this, for me, is the crucial formal weakness of the book: it lacks a dynamic. Claudia learns nothing in the process of her dying; even her dead lover's diary changes nothing in the way she understands her own, or a larger, history. Her dying is simply a narrative vantage point for telling the story of her past. For example, in her daughter's view her mother is wrong about her; but Claudia remains untouched, unaffected by her ignorance, by her failure to acquire important historical data. The reader has 'one over her', as though we were rival academics, but in personal terms her own history teaches her nothing—nor do her reflections restructure that history.

The conservatism of Lively's form thus fits tidily with her conservative view of history: that there is a position from which truth may be observed, even though we frail human beings usually fail to observe it fully or perfectly. The subjectivity of the historian affects what is chosen for observation, but does not affect the thing observed: a point made in the slightly superficial running debate between Claudia and her brother, an economist, about the relative merits of their own chosen fields of study—though their complementarity is stressed by the rather odd insertion of an adolescent incestuous affair and offered, though discreetly, in terms of some rather drear natural gender difference.

Having said that I don't agree with Lively's apparent ideology, and that I think her form overused and static, it may sound a bit silly to say that I liked reading *Moon Tiger:* Lively is both knowledgeable and fluent but, more importantly, she really is trying to write a novel about something important intellectually: how we are to understand our own past.

Too few 'character centred' novelists really bother to bring intellectual debate into the centre of their books and it is enjoyable to see the engagement. (pp. 23-4)

Sara Maitland, "The History Woman," in New Statesman, *Vol. 113, No. 2928, May 8, 1987, pp. 23-4.*

J. K. L. WALKER

Moon Tiger marks a new departure in Penelope Lively's fiction. She has taken a pair of scissors to conventional chronological narrative to present the life and times of her principal character, Claudia Hampton, in an impressionistic sequence of scenes linked by commentary and reflection on the processes of history. The method allows the cool analytic tone and the sense of the past which characterize Mrs Lively's earlier work to be brought overtly to the fore, and the modish disjunction and distancing are lent plausibility by making Claudia a historian, who, as she lies dying in a hospital room, contemplates her life within the context of the age. But this, she reflects, will not be linear history: "There is no chronology inside my head. I am composed of a myriad Claudias . . . everything happens at once"; yet, "the signals of my own past come from the received past".

From this subtle, if at times confusing presentation, characters and events central to the story gradually emerge. Three relationships stand out: those of Claudia with her brother Gordon, a successful academic economist, with whom she has been locked in intimate rivalry since childhood; with her lover Jasper, a glamorous, half-Russian high-flyer; and with their dowdy, disappointing daughter Lisa. Gordon, first seen squabbling with his sister over ammonites on Charmouth beach in 1920, is to be throughout Claudia's life "my sense of identity, my mirror, my critic, judge and ally". Both share a powerful maverick intelligence which links them in a shameless alliance against Gordon's pretty, Surrey-bred, "profoundly stupid" wife Sylvia.

Her intelligence, too, overlays Claudia's role as mother; observing Lisa become ordinary, she becomes bored with her and senses her disapproval but consoles herself by noting that "Intelligence is always a disadvantage. . . . It was an immense relief to observe that Lisa's was merely average." Lisa, too, is allowed her say throughout the novel, but the reflections centre on Claudia's lack of understanding, rather than on her selfishness and intellectual snobbery. We are left wondering whether Lively sees these aspects of her character; for all the multiple viewpoints in the novel, surprisingly little criticism of Claudia the protagonist is filtered through by Claudia the controller.

The public events, too, against which Claudia claims to assess the significance of her life, are fewer than might be expected from the pervasive historical musing: nothing from the 1920s and 30s, the period of Claudia's youth; perfunctory references to Suez, Vietnam and the Bomb during the post-war era. . . . An exception is the central third of the novel, a vivid re-creation of Cairo and the Western Desert campaign in the early months of 1942. This period Claudia sees, in retrospect, as the core of her life. . . . Structurally, this wartime section is distinct from the rest of the novel; its events are not chronologically anticipated and in the telling acquire a momentum lacking elsewhere. The author acknowledges her debt to the memoirs of the desert campaign, such as those of Keith Douglas and Cyril Joly, together with her own childhood recollections of Cairo, and her descriptions of the city and of the dangers of the desert war have colour and authenticity. . . .

A mundane reconstructionist, crassly reassembling the cunningly patterned fragments of *Moon Tiger* into a chronological sequence, might conclude that Claudia Hampton's life is not all that remarkable; that in fact it verges on the sentimental in its central emphasis, the enduring effects of a tragic wartime romance—for the novel ends with excerpts from Tom's campaign diary and Claudia's peaceful death. But even if the material of the novel is thus open to criticism, Penelope Lively's ingenious, historically informed handling of it is a considerable achievement and Claudia Hampton herself a formidably reflective and articulate protagonist.

> *J. K. L. Walker, "In Time of War," in* The Times Literary Supplement, *No. 4389, May 15, 1987, p. 515.*

JONATHAN MANTLE

The landscape of Penelope Lively's *Moon Tiger* is the mind of the distinguished, dying historian, Claudia Hampton; and in particular Claudia's memory of the death of her lover in the Western desert, in 1941. The memory is dim and soon to be extinguished by her own death. Claudia, however, has too strong a heart and too rigorous an intellect to let go of what there is or make do with fantasies of what might have been. Instead, she sets out to make some sense of her life, using more than just the wisdom of hindsight. 'A history of the world' is her declared aim, 'And in the process, my own.'

This grandiose manifesto is in part a device to deter the well-meaning attentions of nurses, family and friends. The history of her life—as a difficult child, bereaved lover, unmarried mother, maverick historian and war correspondent—is indivisible from the history of the century in which she has lived. She subjects both to close scrutiny and finds them wanting.

But the sense which she ultimately makes of her life is also determined by a coming to terms with the need for love. This is triumphantly evident in the passages which describe her reawakening memory of the man she loved. The process by which she gradually narrows down the 40-year 'gap' in their ages, until they are reunited, is beautifully described. This novel is an achievement of a high order.

> *Jonathan Mantle, "Terrains of Thought," in* The Observer, *May 17, 1987, p. 27.*

FRANCIS KING

[*King is a Swiss-born English novelist, short story writer, critic, and poet whose many books include* The Dividing Stream *(1951),* The Last of the Pleasure Gardens *(1965), and* The Action *(1978). In the following excerpt King commends Lively for her masterful blending of fragmented memories into a cohesive and compelling narrative pattern, noting that her descriptions of Claudia's life in Egypt are especially praiseworthy.*]

For those who may be misled by the title of Penelope Lively's new novel [*Moon Tiger*] into thinking that a night-time safari provides its central incident, a 'Moon Tiger' is a mosquito-repellent with a green coil that slowly burns all night, to fall away into a caterpillar-like column of grey ash. Its red eye glows beside the hotel bed in wartime Luxor in which the heroine, Claudia, lies contented beside her army officer lover, so soon to be killed in the desert. But, at a deeper level, its gradual, inevitable disintegration symbolises the transitoriness of all human happiness and indeed of all human life, which is here the author's main preoccupation, as it is Claudia's.

Claudia is a popular historian whom academic historians condemn with phrases like 'technicolor history' or 'the Elinor Glyn of historical biography'. At the start of the novel she is dying in hospital, her head full—when it is full of anything other than drugs—of memories of her past. Her ambition, never to be fulfilled, is to write a history of the world. But what she pieces together is the history merely of a small world that is her own existence, from childhood closeness to the brother whom sibling rivalry drove almost to cause her death, to septuagenarian remoteness from the illegitimate daughter whom she has always shamefully neglected.

One of Claudia's favourite Victorians is William Smith, 'the civil engineer whose labours as a canal constructor enabled him to examine the rocks through which his cuttings were driven and their fossil contents, and draw seminal conclusions.' But as, drifting in and out of consciousness, scarcely aware of the passing of hours or even of days, she herself drives her cuttings into the past, seminal conclusions about all that has puzzled her in life are precisely what she is unable to reach. The fossils—of past loves, past sorrows, past failings, past disappointments—may all be unearthed; but what they have to say remains an enigma.

Technically this is an extraordinarily adroit piece of writing. Its method of excavating fragmentary shards of the past, which are then slowly assembled to recreate an artefact perfect in it wholeness and symmetry, is reminiscent of Fred Maddox Ford at his best. The tense is sometimes present, sometimes past. Claudia is now 'I' and now 'she', and from time to time we see things not through her eyes but through those of other characters—her scholarly brother, her inept sister-in-law, her dim daughter, her conventional mother. As we view Claudia, we see simultaneously the young, ardent, impetuous girl; the tough, abrasive middle-aged woman; and the elderly emaciated patient who, when she tells one of her nurses 'I'm writing a history of the world', receives the jolly answer 'That's quite a thing to be doing, isn't it?', followed by 'Upsy a bit, dear, that's a good girl—then we'll get you a cup of tea.' As Claudia herself puts it, 'A lifetime is not linear but instant.'

Claudia, like most self-sufficient people, is unlovable except to those who fall in love with her. But everyone is obliged to admire her for her intelligence, efficiency and guts. One of the strengths of the novel is that Lively never for one moment indulges Claudia—any more than Claudia herself ever indulges people frailer than she is. Because she seems so impervious, her grief first at the death of her lover and then at the miscarriage of his child becomes all the more poignant, resulting in the finest passages in a generally fine book. In these passages, paragraphs about Claudia's emotions, as she lies sleepless, hour after hour, staring up at the ceiling of her Cairo bedroom, or as she attempts to combat a growing nausea while going through the tasks of the day, alternate with paragraphs about the trivialities around her—her Levantine landlady's complaints about food shortages, her flat-mate's accounts of the 'heavenly new materials' that have arrived at the fashionable store Cicurel or of her social or amatory doings with officers on leave.

The book contains certain miscalculations. When, years later, Claudia returns to Egypt, she strikes up an incongruous friendship with a Texan, the biggest worldwide distributor of lavatory cisterns, who says things like 'Believe me that's quite sumpin', 'Jesus, that's one hell of a massacre', and 'You're one sharp lady, aren't you, Claudia?' Later in the book Claudia becomes surrogate mother to an acne-spotted, homosexual Hungarian youth, forced into exile by the 1956 uprising, who, though admittedly more credible, is so skimped a character that he might almost be an afterthought. But the merits of the book far outweigh such minor defects. (pp. 48-9)

[One] can only be amazed that a woman should have so vividly evoked the to-and-fro of war in the desert. In the case of Lively this is even more remarkable, since . . . she was only a child in Cairo during those years. But even better than these descriptions are those that conjure up the contrasting worlds of race-meetings, performances of *The Mikado* and drinks at Groppi's or the Gezira Club, and of the ordinary Egyptians waging, indifferent to the approaching Germans, their own separate age-old war against poverty, disease and premature death.

At the close of the book and at the close of her life, Claudia rereads the last pages of the diary kept by her lover. Words, and the history that words create, have given him a kind of immortality, perhaps the only immortality for which any mortal may hope. He, part of the past, is still young; the Claudia of the present is old. But there is another Claudia, the Claudia of a shared past. In that past, the two intermingle, become part of each other.

The sun sinks, the sickroom darkens. The 'Moon Tiger' of life and therefore of memory burns itself out. But like Claudia herself, the reader experiences, at this moment of farewell, 'a surge of joy, of well-being, of wonder.' (p. 49)

Francis King, "Death on the Wartime Nile," in The Spectator, *Vol. 258, No. 8289, May 23, 1987, pp. 48-9.*

An Excerpt from *Moon Tiger*

We got to Luxor and fought our way out of the station through the dragomen and the sellers of scarabs and black basilisk heads of Rameses the Second and flywhisks and each other's sisters and got a room at the Winter Palace. We went to bed and stayed there till the late afternoon. We lay naked on the bed with the midday sun slicing in stripes through the shutters; we made love more times than I would have thought possible. He had five days' leave. The first I had known of it was his voice on the phone asking if I could get away for a long weekend. He had been up at the front and he'd be going back there next week. Or to wherever the front by then was—that indeterminate confusion of minefields and dispositions of vehicles in the empty neutral sand. He once described it to me as more like a war fought at sea than on land, a sequence of advances and retreats in which the participants related only to each other and barely at all to the landscape across which they moved. A war in which there was nothing to get in the way—no towns, no villages, no people—and nothing tangible to gain or lose. In which you fought for possession of a barely detectable rocky ridge, or a map position. In which there were suddenly hundreds of thousands of men where there had been nothing, but still the place remained empty. He spoke of the desert as being like the board in some game in which opposing sides manoeuvred from square to square; I used the image in a despatch and got a pat on the back from London office and told him I should have given him a credit. He said he'd wait for that till after the war.

Eventually, at dusk, we got up and dressed and went down for a drink on the terrace overlooking the Nile. Maybe that was the point when I spoke to Gordon's acquaintance. If so, he is gone now; all that remains is the long low fawn shoulder of the hill above the Valley of the Kings with the sun going down behind it in a smoulder of gold and pink and turquoise. And the bland Egyptian evening sounds of ice chinking in glasses, the slap of the suffragis' slippers on the stone of the hotel terrace, the buzz of voices, laughter—the sound of a hundred other evenings, at Gezira Sporting Club, the Turf Club, Shepheard's. But that evening—or the next or the next—is isolated in my head. I know that I sat on a cane chair, the pattern of the cane printing my flesh through my cotton dress, looking at the river, the white swooping sails of feluccas, the sunset sky in which presently glittered the brilliant enhanced stars of the desert. I know how I felt—richer, happier, more alive than ever before or ever since. It is feeling that survives; feeling and the place. There is no sequence now for those days, no chronology—I couldn't say at which point we went to Karnak, to the Colossus, to the tombs—they are simultaneous. It is a time that is both instant and frozen, like a village scene in a Breughel painting, like the walls of the tombs on which fly, swim and walk the same geese, ducks, fish, cattle that live in, on and beside the Nile today.

ROSALIND WADE

[In *Moon Tiger* Penelope Lively] concentrates on one main character, Claudia Hampton, first encountered near to death in a geriatric nursing home. The scene is familiar, yet it is soon apparent that the sick woman is no ordinary nonentity babbling about her past to patient nurses, but was 'someone', as the doctor astutely concludes after a quick glance through the medical records, '. . . written books . . . articles . . . been in the Middle East . . . typhoid, malaria . . . unmarried . . .' thus do such cryptic phrases become landmarks in a purposeful professional career.

This could be lack-lustre but is far from being so; for as the memories flood in during lucid interludes, the curtain is drawn back to reveal the secrets of an eventful life. Claudia was an 'historian' as well as a political journalist, acutely aware of the pitfalls and deceptions inherent in that hotly debated corner of the literary field. How fact reconciles with recollection is one of the numerous sub-themes developed in *Moon Tiger*. Like many war-correspondents posted to Egypt, Cairo became for a time the centre of Claudia's world; for it was there she encountered Tom Southern, perhaps the real love of her life apart from her brother Gordon, whose raffish, earthy child-relationship was so strongly to affect her world.

By Tom she was to be given a child to care for—only the foetus failed to survive—and it was left to another man to provide the daughter, Lisa, with whom she maintained an uneasy, though affectionate relationship. There are many other facets to the mosaic, as for instance the refugee boy, Lazlo, who is permitted to live in Claudia's flat for a while and share her life generally. All fit together as the moment of death approaches, like the pieces of a brain-teasing jig-saw puzzle, taking longer in years and hard-won experience than the comparatively short novel might suggest. Its final strength lies in the pages of italicised diary jottings written by Tom shortly before his death in action. These authentic-seeming extracts put the final touches of conviction to the story, with their timely reminder that the dangers and brutishness of the battlefront are at least as formidable as the emotions occasioned by personal frustration and loss. (pp. 45-6)

Rosalind Wade, in a review of "Moon Tiger," in Contemporary Review, Vol. 251, No. 1458, July, 1987, pp. 45-6.

TONY DUNN

Will Bloomsbury never die? Penelope Lively has won this year's Booker Prize with a novel, *Moon Tiger,* that recycles all the old themes.

Here are Claudia and Gordon, whose brother-and-sister love is deeper than any other attachment. Here are exotic adventures (war-reporting in Cairo) which only confirm the superior civilisation of southern England. Here is a narrator (Claudia) who talks throughout of her beauty and daring, and is incapable of handling children; a dim widowed mother in Dorset; a gay Hungarian refugee; and a father, brother and lover all killed off before the end of the novel. Here, above all, is the best marriage Bloomsbury ever made, between aristocratic sentiment and populist art.

Claudia is a journalist who writes popular biographies but forms "an aristocracy of two" with her brother. When they are reunited after the war he smells, beneath her scent, "a whiff— a rich emotive whiff—of unreachable moments". Stream of consciousness modulates into advertising. Claudia's husband Jasper (*sic*), a half-Russian with a casual double First from Cambridge, graciously applies his talents to television. Claudia's lover Tom Southern (of course), an ex-journalist and now a tank-commander, gives her vertiginous moments of ecstasy in Cairo and, on his death, leaves her a diary of bluffman sentiment.

The descriptions of Cairo and the desert, which occupy the centre of the novel, descend directly from the school of Virginia Woolf. They are obviously meant to be impressive and a lot of care has gone into selecting significant detail and striking metaphors, but the result is utterly unmemorable. The eye slides unchecked down the page through a banal narrative of dust, heat, sand and corpses. Tom's diary must be the dullest posthumous document in fiction.

This kind of writing is a branch of the "artistic travelogue", also practised by Jonathan Raban and Paul Theroux, where self-important solitaries cast a quizzical glance on humble citizens. But the common reader is as much audience for this writing as it is for the hackwork of the popular press. Evelyn Waugh exposed its pretensions in *Scoop* and a solid dose of vulgarity would have done Claudia (and Virginia) the world of good.

Tony Dunn, "Old Themes Recycled," in Tribune, Vol. 51, No. 49, December 4, 1987, p. 8.

ANNE TYLER

[*Tyler, an American novelist, short story writer, and critic, is known for her humorous and moving portraits of eccentric families. Her novels, usually set in her native city of Baltimore,* include If Morning Ever Comes (1964), Dinner at the Homesick Restaurant (1982), and The Accidental Tourist (1985), *which won the National Book Critics' Circle Award. In the following excerpt, Tyler praises Lively's rich and memorable imagery and observes that although* Moon Tiger's *heroine is somewhat alienating, her story is intelligent and emotionally engaging.*]

The heroine of *Moon Tiger,* which won England's Booker Prize in 1987, is a popular historian named Claudia Hampton. The novel's true center, though, is no less than history itself—the abiding backdrop across which mere human beings flutter.

Lying in what is clearly her deathbed, Claudia reflects upon her long and unconventional life. She sees it in terms of assorted scenes, arranged in no particular order. Her childhood, her desultory affair with the man who fathered her daughter, her years as a newspaper correspondent during World War II and, most important, her brief period of happiness with a young officer on the Egyptian front—all this is related not only by Claudia but sometimes by others as well, with the same conversation presented first from one character's slant and then immediately afterward from another's. It's a device that opens windows in Claudia's narrative, and rightly so; for she sees these recollections as part of a much larger story. "I'm writing a history of the world," she tells a nurse, and to herself she adds, "The whole triumphant murderous unstoppable chute— from the mud to the stars, universal and particular, your story and mine."

The random chronology is deliberate, premeditated. She has always thought, she tells us, that a kaleidoscopic approach might make for an interesting history. ("Shake the tube and see what comes out.") Certainly kaleidoscopic is an apt term, with all that it implies of both jumble and dazzle, but the image that lingers longer in the reader's mind is not a rosette of colored glass but a photograph. . . .

Claudia is a bit too brittle, a bit too smugly shocking to be likable to her readers, but the story she tells is another matter entirely. It pulls us in; it engages us and saddens us. It is also unexpectedly funny—just watch her treat the actors in a Williamsburg-style theme park as if they were literal travelers in time. ("Take my advice," she tells one man, "don't start importing labour, you'll avoid a whole lot of trouble later on that way.")

The deft, light-handed style and the thoughtful tone of voice will come as no surprise to longtime admirers of Penelope Lively's books for adults and children. But her earlier books employed a smaller canvas. (*Perfect Happiness,* her most recent adult novel, was an incrementally detailed account of a middle-aged woman's adjustment to widowhood.) *Moon Tiger* takes broader leaps, larger risks. It's a fine, intelligent piece of work, the kind that leaves its traces in the air long after you've put it away.

Anne Tyler, "Life Moves Too Fast for the Picture," in The New York Times Book Review, April 17, 1988, p. 9.

BRIGITTE WEEKS

Moon Tiger is such a profoundly modest novel that it lends itself neither to superlatives nor to snappy summaries. Lively is the exact opposite of a literary showman. She builds her story without pyrotechnics but gives it a deceptively strong hold on life. She is, as one critic remarked, "the kind of writer that Barbara Pym might have been if she had married and had children.'' . . .

The skill with which Lively cuts back and forth from Claudia in her hospital bed, to Claudia in wartime Egypt to Claudia over the years since 1941 is breathtaking in its smoothness. Just when we feel as if the narrative might slip into confusion, it is deftly twitched back on track and a little more of the picture emerges—like a Polaroid exposed to the light.

Layered on top of the flashbacks, flashes forwards and sideways are viewpoint changes: more than one character describes a scene in the first person, each adding new insights. . . .

Lively leads the reader on a kind of paper chase through Claudia's life. The effect is to create a heroine of great complexity. Claudia is combative and thoughtful. She is an unlikely mother and a demanding lover, but there is an energy and an absence of self pity as she lies dying, drifting in and out of consciousness, that compel admiration. Claudia has lived joyously for herself, making her own rules. She's easy to like, warts and all.

Moon Tiger is a quiet yet deeply accomplished novel, just the kind of achievement that could be overlooked by prize-givers and critics. How encouraging that it was not.

> Brigitte Weeks, *"Thanks for the Memories,"* in Book World—The Washington Post, *April 24, 1988, p. 3.*

RICHARD EDER

A lizard on a rock is an image of watchful stillness in a world that moves. The protagonist of *Moon Tiger* is a lizard of sorts— a dry, brilliant, self-willed old woman—but the image is incomplete.

Penelope Lively's novel, told entirely through the old woman's dying memories, filters out the moving world. It is a lizard's story recounted by the lizard; it digests us and brings us down to its own immobility and low blood temperature.

The dying woman is Claudia Hampton, an English journalist and the author of a number of vivid, unorthodox and highly popular histories. In her imperiousness, her talent, her active and unconventional love life, and her passion to formulate the meaning of the modern world for her time, she suggests a variation upon the late Rebecca West.

All her life, love affairs apart, she has put all of her emotion into tackling society's and history's great issues. Now, in her hospital bed, she proposes one final history of the world. And the history of this world she has burnt herself out upon turns out to be a long-postponed search for herself.

She does not write it, of course. She ruminates it; sometimes as a first-person recollection; sometimes in the third person, as if she were trying to give us formal shape. Occasionally, a passage will be repeated, almost unchanged except for the change of person.

Moon Tiger, in effect, turns out to be not so much an account of Claudia's life as of her telling it. The life has its surprises, vicissitudes and passions, but the real passion and conflict is that between a narrator's conflicting impulses to understand and to control. Most of the time, it is the controller, the motionless lizard, that prevails.

Claudia was a rebellious, questioning child, sufficiently praised and successful to develop a high opinion of her own mind; and

a low opinion of practically everyone else's. Gordon, her brother, she considers her only real peer. He is a brilliant economist, dividing his time between Oxford, Harvard and assorted Third World countries that require his advice.

During World War II, she becomes a war correspondent, covering the desert fighting against Rommel. Afterwards, she continues her career as a journalist of the higher sort, writes a celebrated biography of Tito, and another about Cortez. She has a long-term affair with Jasper, a sophisticated and vastly successful producer of televison films; the result is Lisa, whom she brings up with whatever warmth she can spare from her other passions.

Her hospital recollections are a series of vignettes that add up to a brittle and chilly portrait. She recalls Lisa as an aloof child; the recollection is counterpointed by the bedside visits of the adult Lisa who has become a suburban matron and of whom Claudia disapproves for her lack of intellect.

And we learn that Lisa's ''normality'' is a lifetime revenge upon her distant mother and that, besides, she has a lover. Lisa keeps this lover a secret from Claudia ''not because you would disapprove but because you would not.'' Dissembling allows her to survive Claudia's lifelong ascendancy.

We get glimpses of Claudia's civilized and post-passionate sparring with Jasper, of the intellectual electricity in her periodic argumentative encounters with Gordon, of her contempt for Gordon's tremulous wife, of her life as a wartime journalist in Cairo and her grim trips to the front.

It is a highly controlled form of narration; it skips back and forth. ''Most lives have their core, their kernel,'' she tells us. ''I will get to mine when I'm ready. At the moment, I'm dealing with strata.'' Call me when you're ready, the reader may wish to murmur.

The core seems to be reached when Claudia tells of her affair with Tom, a tank commander whom she meets at the front. They see each other on his brief three-day leaves, they make love and visit the Pyramids. After the war, he wants to marry her, buy a farm and have a child.

It touches her in a way nothing else has. Tom tells her she makes him happy, and she reflects: ''I have never made anyone happy before. I have made people angry, restless, jealous, lecherous. . . . Never I think, happy.'' Tom is killed, and her image for their love is the moon tiger—a spiral coil of punk that burns slowly through the night beside their bed to keep away mosquitos and that leaves only an ash in the morning.

Even this, perhaps, is not the core. Claudia reveals her adolescent incest with her brother. Incest, she muses, is narcissism at its extreme. Claudia knows herself, but self-knowledge, by itself, does not furnish a novel.

Claudia, struggling to find meaning in a life that has been hemmed in by pride and a will to power, is aware of her own barren voice. But she has only this barren voice to tell it with.

Except for Lisa, whose mute rebellion gives her a certain autonomy, none of the other characters are much more than projections of Claudia's urgencies. The doomed affair with Tom comes perilously close to the melodramatic tone of a World War II film romance. Tom himself is an amiable shadow.

Narrators can become Frankenstein monsters. Lively has given her chilly solipsist a chilly solipsistic vision. Her way of telling her story defines her perfectly. The trouble is that it constricts everything else. We are left with the lizard alone.

The writing is sharp and witty; and it can be powerful, particularly in the descriptioins of death and disorder just behind the desert war front. A final passage signaling Claudia's death is breathtaking. She watches a tree branch through her hospital window, lit by a late-afternoon sun that has come out after the rain.

"The sun sinks and the glittering tree is extinguished. The room darkens again. Presently it is quite dim; the window is violet now, showing the black tracery of branches and a line of houses packed with squares of light. And within the room, a change has taken place. It is empty. Void. It has the stillness of a place in which there are only inanimate objects; metal, wood, glass, plastic. No life."

But there never was life in Claudia's room. (pp. 3, 9)

Richard Eder, "Lived and Lost and Never Lived at All," in Los Angeles Times Book Review, *May 8, 1988, pp. 3, 9.*

Alice (Laidlaw) Munro

The Progress of Love

Governor General's Literary Award: Fiction

Canadian short story writer, novelist, and scriptwriter.

The Progress of Love (1986) is Munro's third volume of short stories to receive a Governor General's Literary Award. *Dance of the Happy Shades* (1968), her first collection, and *Who Do You Think You Are?* (1978), her fourth, also won the prize. Considered a major Canadian author, Munro writes almost exclusively in the short story form. Although many critics identify her *Lives of Girls and Women* (1971) as a novel, the author herself considers it a set of interrelated stories rather than a single work. She claims to have experimented with novel-writing, but finds the short story form more suited to the narrative shape and pacing her style demands. "I no longer feel attracted to the well-made novel," she explained. "I want to write the story that will zero in and give you intense, but not connected, moments of experience. I guess that's the way I see life. People remake themselves bit by bit and do things they don't understand. The novel has to have a coherence which I don't see anymore in the lives around me." Most of her stories take place in the small towns and rural areas of southwestern Ontario, where Munro has spent most of her life. "As with Faulkner's Mississippi or Hardy's Wessex," commented journalist David Macfarlane, "there are people now—readers of the *New Yorker*, to which Alice Munro contributes regularly, and lovers of the contemporary short story in England, the United States, and Canada—who call the farms and little towns to the east of Lake Huron 'Alice Munro country.'"

Munro's particular talent, according to reviewers, is to create fascinating drama out of the crises and spiritual discoveries of ordinary poor and lower-middle-class Canadians. Munro develops peculiar and universal concerns in the insular, socially restrictive communities inhabited by her characters. Munro stated: "Everybody in the community is a stage for all the other people. There's a constant awareness of people watching and listening. And—this may be particularly Canadian—the less you reveal, the more highly thought of you are." Munro focuses on how family relationships affect individuals from generation to generation. In order to chart the progress of the events she portrays, she makes frequent use of flashbacks and other devices that allow her narratives to move back and forth in time. "I'm very interested in the present, in the culture as it is right now, but I always want to tie it in to what I remember," she explained. "Anyone my age has seen a lot of change in social attitudes, in the fabric of the culture that surrounds people's lives. I'm interested in how that affects people. I want to skip around in time."

Munro evidences a sympathetic approach to her characters, creating individuals who behave in unpredictable ways. By declining to guide readers' attitudes about the people and events she depicts, critics observe, Munro portrays life as a morally neutral, perpetually unresolved process. At the same time, her stories permit readers to draw their own moral conclusions. Many of her pieces relate an incident from several points of

© *Jerry Bauer*

view, as in "White Dump" and "The Progress of Love," allowing readers to judge for themselves which is the most accurate version. For example, in "The Progress of Love" Munro demonstrates how memory distorts reality by allowing her protagonist's recollection of a significant incident in her childhood to be contradicted and challenged by others.

Not all critics agree that Munro's objective authorial viewpoint is satisfactory; some protest that her refusal to make moral statements leaves many of her stories unresolved, diminishing their effect. Most critics, however, praise her narrative method as both lyrical and compelling. Claire Tomalin calls her work "an exploration of those weathers and distances, those landscapes that shift from the known to the almost unimaginable," and Brina Caplan adds: "Rather than an interpretation of lives, *The Progress of Love* offers a rich involvement in their particulars."

(See also *CLC*, Vols. 6, 10, 19; *Contemporary Authors*, Vols. 33-36, rev. ed.; *Something about the Author*, Vol. 29; and *Dictionary of Literary Biography*, Vol. 53.)

PATRICIA BRADBURY

One morning Marietta finds her mother in the barn, standing squarely on a chair with a rope around her neck. "Get your father," the mother yells, and the child obeys, running frantically through the town, dressed only in a nightie, feeling mocked by groups of men when her father cannot be found. Feeling wretched about leaving her mother, whom she fears is dead, she races back but is blocked by a passing train. In the faces of its passengers, she breaks out wailing. Her mother is not dead. She is in the kitchen of a friend drinking coffee. But Marietta carries a hatred, like "a clot of poison", for her father the rest of her life. Such is the seed of **"The Progress of Love,"** the title-story of Alice Munro's exquisite new collection [*The Progress of Love*], for which the word magnificent seems dreadfully pale.

Near the middle of her life, Marietta commits patricide, if only symbolically. In her impoverished home, she burns, bill by bill, the large inheritance her father has left her. When asked what the point of this action was, her daughter, Fame, later replies, "My father letting her do it is the point," referring to a man who had no money all his life. "If anybody had tried to stop her, he would have protected her. I consider that love."

We are comforted by this until pages later, when it's made clear that the father was not there. Fame's story is a composite of what she felt her parents were, but like the barn incident (retold, with a twist, by Fame's aunt), nothing is as it seems.

To borrow a term applied to painting, Alice Munro is a hyperrealist who, like Colville, is compulsively exact in her depictions, but who suddenly throws in an odd angle. So speedily can she crack open one of her characters that we shudder with the recognition that what we know about people is basically what we've imagined.

More than ever before, Munro is a social historian, thinking nothing of placing three generations in a tale and removing, like tissued layers, the deep strata in people's lives. Old houses, like relationships, are sky-lighted or ruined, and underlying every story is a bedrock of stubbornness, a dark lump in the gut, which Munro circles calmly, giving us all we might know while saying it's never enough.

Sex and death are the primary concerns in this volume. Sexuality is everything from unabashed to mute. An ageing woman who loves reading Old Norse in her cottage emerges nude from a lake after being harrassed by delinquents, and to her shocked son and his family she simply says, "I've had a very minor catastrophe. Happy birthday, Laurence!" In another story, a silent trucker keeps travelling farther away from his wife until he ends up in the Arctic driving to oil rigs across the frozen Beaufort Sea.

Death, like sex, is off-camera, for the most part, then reapproached to make the details bearable. In Miles City, Montana, we are taken step by step through a child's drowning, then saved at the last minute because the child lives, only to be pushed through the details of a child's death by means of a mother's imagination. In **"Fits,"** we skirt deftly around a brutal murder, the enactment of which becomes icily potent because so much, including the motivation of the perpetrator, has been left for us to fill in. It is this extraordinary Munro gap, this precise and calculated omission, that is unerringly evocative and profound.

Patricia Bradbury, "The Realism of Munro and the Romance of Turner Hospital," in Quill and Quire, *Vol. 52, No. 8, August, 1986, p. 42.*

MICHIKO KAKUTANI

For the people in *The Progress of Love,* storytelling is a way of seeing and remembering, a mundane but necessary art. In ["The Progress of Love"], the narrator recounts how her father watched her mother burn her unwanted inheritance in the kitchen stove; though probably untrue, the story serves as a testament to what she believes about them and the nature of love. Another woman tells a story about how she met her first husband while singing madrigals at college, a neat story of destiny between "a skinny innocent bit of a lad with a pure sweet tenor" and "a stocky little brute of a girl with a big deep alto." And a third speaks of how she and her husband "invented characters" for their children, casting each daughter in a specific role.

In **"Monsieur les Deux Chapeaux,"** the telling and retelling of familiar stories serves a ritual purpose of alternately soothing and discomfitting various family members, and in **"Jesse and Meribeth"** a teen-age girl tries to impress her best friend by inventing an outrageous story about an affair with a married man—a story that ironically fulfills itself even as it's exposed as a lie.

As this volume and several earlier collections (most notably *The Moons of Jupiter* and *The Beggar Maid*) attest, Alice Munro is herself a remarkable storyteller who, having slowly acquired a faithful audience outside her native Canada, now richly deserves recognition as one of the foremost contemporary practitioners of the short story. Though her tales occasionally display an overcrafted sense of irony (**"Monsieur les Deux Chapeaux,"** which involves two possible attempts at murder, is one such example), the best possess a wonderfully organic coherence. They create complete fictional worlds for the reader, but their wholeness has the pleasing irregularity of something found in nature. Instead of squeezing the ambiguities of relationships and feelings into a neatly molded form, the stories accommodate them, taking on in the process the complicated texture of real life.

Families, the overlapping and intersecting lines of emotions connecting parents and children, husbands and wives, the "dangerous mix-ups" of domestic life—these are the subjects Ms. Munro returns to in these stories and she delineates them with an old-fashioned amplitude of emotion and language. She is concerned not only with the different configurations of love that occur in the wake of divorces, separations and deaths, but also with the "progress" of love, the ways in which it endures or changes through time: how the weight of intimacy can suffocate a marriage, as easily as loft it into new passion; how disappointments, an apprehension of loss, can be handed down generation to generation, mother to daughter, as easily as the capacity for caring; how history repeats itself, when the man who spurns one fiancée for another decides, years later, to leave the wife for another woman.

But while so many of the characters in these stories leave their lovers or their families, few ever exit completely. Instead, they seem to hover about the corners of their former lives, like ghosts who are reluctant to depart—new girlfriends are introduced, quite cruelly, to former wives; anniversaries are celebrated years after a spouse's defection.

Indeed, the characters in Ms. Munro's stories seem perpetually torn between freedom and domesticity, the need for independence and the need to belong. One man seems to trade in wives and girlfriends, regularly, as soon as their failure to live up to a designated role—of "hippie," "trollop," etc.—threatens him with real intimacy; another determines to leave town when his girlfriend hints she might be pregnant.

In **"White Dump,"** a woman relishes the idea of staying behind as her family goes off for an airplane ride, cherishing the prospect of "emptiness, a lapse of attention," that will permit her to momentarily misplace her customary enthusiasm and watchfulness. And in **"Miles City, Montana,"** the narrator also yearns for "a place to hide" from the demands of running a household. She wants to "get busy at my real work, which was a sort of wooing of distant parts of myself," only to realize in the wake of a swimming pool accident that her self-preoccuption has nearly resulted in her daughter's death.

But while death and overt violence occasionally do make their appearance in these stories, the characters tend to be haunted by a more abstract premonition that life is precarious and fragile, that things can shift, fade or disappear with the suddenness of a mood change. A man abruptly leaves his wife and daughter for a woman whose camper has broken down; a woman meets the man who will become her new lover during a celebration of her husband's 40th birthday. Even when everything seems smooth and scheduled and fine, "the skin of the moment can break open." "With all their happiness and hugging and kissing and stars and picnics," a woman can find her husband's side of the bed empty and leap to the conclusion that he's "done away with himself."

In the end, Ms. Munro suggests, one of the reasons for this sense of aloneness and peril is the utter subjectivity of truth, our inability to see things through others' eyes. In ["**The Progress of Love**"], for instance, a woman contends that her late mother tried to hang herself out of a sense of despair; her sister maintains that she did it as a joke, in order to provoke their father. Which version is correct? Can the truth ever be ascertained?

Drawing upon her seemingly infinite reserves of sympathy, Ms. Munro writes, in these stories, from a multitude of perspectives—shifting points of view, from one character to another, as well as back and forth in time. The results are pictures of life, of relationships, of love, glimpsed from a succession of mirrors and frames—pictures that possess both the pain and immediacy of life and the clear, hard radiance of art.

Michiko Kakutani, in a review of "The Progress of Love," in The New York Times, *September 3, 1986, p. C22.*

LYNNE SHARON SCHWARTZ

[*Schwartz is an American novelist, short story writer, and critic. Her works include* Rough Strife *(1980),* Disturbances in the Field *(1983), and* We Are Talking about Homes *(1985). In the following excerpt, Schwartz admires Munro's subtle and unsentimental approach to love and family relationships in* The Progress of Love.]

Because they are an endangered species, we should bless and rally round those writers who have a lot to say. Alice Munro is one of them, a born teller of tales who can transform the anecdotal or apparently digressive into a rich parable of life in our fickle times. After the shallow ponds of much current fiction, Munro's fifth collection of stories has the tang of salt ocean air.

The Progress of Love gives texture and breadth and voice to Canada: the stories range from coast to coast and over decades in the lives of families—isolated farm people, the small-town

poor scrabbling for a living and the urbane well-to-do in their summer houses. Few writers render deprivation so precisely— witness the boarding-house life of underfed adolescent boys stuffing themselves with Fig Newtons in **"The Moon in the Orange Street Skating Rink"** or in **"Jesse and Meribeth,"** working girls endlessly washing their underwear and their hair. "You couldn't turn around in the bathroom without having something flap in your face."

The book is aptly named. In every story, love takes its circuitous, enigmatic route—not only passionate love, but the faintly absurd, faintly perilous self-love that animates adolescent longings, the ambiguous, self-denying love of family, and the corrosive obligatory love that makes Colin, in the disturbing **"Monsieur les Deux Chapeaux,"** his weird, quasi-retarded brother's keeper: ever since a childhood accident when a gun went off in his hands, Colin has dreaded, yet half-consciously wished his brother's disappearance; the brother has become "his job in life."

The outstanding love story, though, is **"Lichen,"** which manages superbly to embody the most tragic aspects of sexual love in one crude and startling image. Middle-aged David is a man who goes through women—younger ones each time—adoring, seducing, working them over emotionally, aging them, then abandoning them. His ex-wife, Stella, whom he still visits, bringing along his successive loves, is settling into the cheerful, useful busyness of certain plucky aging women: her pain at being cast off is invisible. David shows Stella a murky photograph—the kind known as a crotch shot—of his next, 22-year-old conquest. But Stella cannot quite make it out. "'It looks like lichen . . . Except it's rather dark. It looks to me like moss on a rock.' 'Don't be dumb, Stella, Don't be cute. You can see her. See her legs?'" He leaves the photo on a windowsill, where Stella discovers it a week later, faded by the sun.

> And now look, her words have come true. The outline of the breast has disappeared. You would never know that the legs were legs. The black has turned to gray, to the soft, dry color of a plant mysteriously nourished on the rocks.
>
> This is David's doing. He left it there, in the sun.
>
> Stella's words have come true. This thought will keep coming back to her—a pause, a lost heartbeat, a harsh little break in the flow of the days and nights as she keeps them going.

The graphic and specific have been transmuted into the symbolic and universal; the story leaves permanent echoes of shock and pained comprehension.

Stella's feeling of prescience, of possessing supernatural insight, even power, is repeated in other stories: in **"Miles City, Montana,"** where a young mother senses preternaturally her child's danger, and in **"Jesse and Meribeth,"** where an adolescent's self-serving fantasy about being seduced—in romantic, courtly fashion—by an older man, almost comes true— but how sordidly different the reality is. Her employer's husband leads her into a summer house where he strokes her legs, telling her,

> "You shouldn't go inside places like this with men just because they ask you."
>
> And this is how things continue—the stroking and the lecturing, coming at me together. He is telling me I'm to blame, while his fingers start up these

flutters under my skin, rousing a tender, distant ache. . . . I don't understand that this isn't fair.

In "Eskimo" a young woman whose life is trickling away in a dead-end affair with her older, married employer, a cardiologist, encounters on an airplane a 16-year-old Eskimo in an exaggerated, mirror-image situation: she dreams of rescuing the girl by wise words, but in the end loses the thread of her dream, the insight, and lapses back in her own imprisonment.

Of course none of the characters has supernatural powers; Munro's fiction resides in a sternly realistic world, replete with all of reality's mysteries and unaccountabilities. Her recurring, antiphonal subjects are young people yearning to strike out on their own, for money, love, adventure, freedom; and those same people middle-aged or old, either mired in ruts or striking out anew. Their lives hinge on turning points, moments when the critical choices seem illogical, erupting from nowhere, but in retrospect—and Munro is an artist of retrospect—become rooted in inevitability.

Her method is never straightforward or simplistic: each story shows the complexities and convolutions of life in its labyrinthine course. In fact the only flaw is an occasional excess of convolution: with much to present, much time to cover, and many strands to interweave, Munro bisects or lops off scenes to interpolate others, breaking into the narrative to achieve a simultaneity of past and present. When this is overdone, as in the title story or in "White Dump," about an adultery that alters half a dozen lives, the result can be disruptive and distracting.

But this is a flaw of abundance, not vacuity. And the most complex, novelistic story, "A Queer Streak," chronicling the vicissitudes of an eccentric farm family and its strongest daughter, is wry, riveting, and told with impeccable skill. From early childhood Violet has been the mainstay of her scatterbrained parents and doltish younger sisters, Dawn Rose and Bonnie Hope. Amid a nasty family crisis precipitated by Dawn Rose, Violet makes a tactical error and loses her chance at marriage and upward mobility. Defeated, she gives up her future to tend to her family: "That was the way Violet saw to leave her pain behind." But years later, again by a stroke of circumstance, she gets another chance—while in a ludicrous twist, Dawn Rose's early troublemaking is seen by faddish young militants as incipient feminism. This tough-minded optimism, unromantic, thoroughly documented, yet infused with the unfathomable mystery of character and destiny, makes for Alice Munro's best story, and it is her best gift. (pp. 3-4)

> *Lynne Sharon Schwartz, "Alice Munro's Fictions for Our Fickle Times," in* Book World—The Washington Post, *September 14, 1986, pp. 3-4.*

JOYCE CAROL OATES

[*Oates is a prolific American novelist, short story and nonfiction writer, critic, scriptwriter, and poet. Her fiction is noted for its realistic detail as well as its imaginative power in depicting violence and abnormal psychological states. Her works include such novels as* them *(1969),* Childwold *(1976), and* Marya: A Life *(1986); short story collections, including* By the North Gate *(1963) and* Raven's Wing *(1987); and such nonfiction writings as* The Edge of Impossibility: Tragic Forms in Literature *(1971) and* On Boxing *(1987). In the following excerpt, Oates commends the rich texture of Munro's style.*]

Like her similarly gifted contemporaries Peter Taylor, William Trevor, Edna O'Brien and some few others, the Canadian short-story writer Alice Munro writes stories that have the density—moral, emotional, sometimes historical—of other writers' novels. As remote from the techniques and ambitions of what is currently known as "minimalist" fiction as it is possible to get and still inhabit the same genre, these writers give us fictitious worlds that are mimetic paradigms of utterly real worlds yet *are* fictions, composed with so assured an art that it might be mistaken for artlessness. They give voice to the voices of their regions, filtering the natural rhythms of speech through a more refined (but not obtrusively refined) writerly speech. They are faithful to the contours of local legend, tall tales, anecdotes, family reminiscences; their material is nearly always realistic—"Realism" being that convention among competing others that swept all before it in the mid and late 19th century—and their characters behave, generally, like real people. That is, they surprise us at every turn, without violating probability. They so resemble ourselves that reading about them, at times, is emotionally risky. Esthetically experimental literature, while evoking our admiration, rarely moves us the way this sort of literature moves us.

From the start of her career in 1968 with the Canadian publication of the short-story collection *Dance of the Happy Shades* (published in the United States in 1973) through *Lives of Girls and Women, Something I've Been Meaning to Tell You, The Beggar Maid, The Moons of Jupiter* and this new collection, *The Progress of Love,* Alice Munro has concentrated on short fiction that explores the lives of fairly undistinguished men and women—but particularly women—who live in southwestern rural Ontario. When her characters move elsewhere to live, to British Columbia, for instance, like the couple whose precarious marriage is explored in "Miles City, Montana," it is still Ontario that is home. (But: "When we said 'home' and meant Ontario, we had very different places in mind.") Though Ms. Munro's tonal palette has darkened considerably over the last 20 years, her fictional technique has not changed greatly, nor has the range of her characters. By degrees, of course, they have grown older. Their living fulfills the prophetic conclusion of a beautiful early story, "Walker Brothers Cowboy" (from *Dance of the Happy Shades*):

> I feel my father's life flowing back from our car in the last of the afternoon, darkening and turning strange, like a landscape that has an enchantment on it, making it kindly, ordinary and familiar while you are looking at it, but changing it, once your back is turned, into something you will never know, with all kinds of weathers, and distances you cannot imagine.

The most powerful of the 11 stories collected in *The Progress of Love* take on bluntly and without sentiment the themes of mortality, self-delusion, puzzlement over the inexplicable ways of fate. In "Fits" it is observed that "people can take a fit like the earth takes a fit" after an unaccountable murder-suicide has been discovered in a small rural town. (Indeed, "Fits" would have made an excellent title for this collection.) The story yields its secrets slowly, with admirable craft and suspense: the surprise for the reader is that the "fit" at its core is less the sensational act of violence than a woman's mysteriously untroubled response to it.

"A Queer Streak" is a tragically comic (or comically tragic) tale of an ambitious young woman named Violet, a "holy terror" in her youth, whose life is permanently altered by the bizarre behavior of an emotionally unbalanced younger sister. It is a familiar temptation to which Violet succumbs: she decides, against the very grain of her personality, that the loss of her fiancé is a "golden opportunity" and not a disaster. Henceforth she will give up her own life, live for others:

> That was the way Violet saw to leave her pain behind. A weight gone off her. If she would bow down and leave her old self behind as well, and all her ideas of what her life should be, the weight, the pain, the humiliation would all go magically. And she could still be chosen. . . . If she prayed enough and tried enough, that would be possible.

But this moment of revelation is the high point of Violet's life, as we see it.

Violet, who takes on, by degrees, the "queer streak" of her family, is one of Ms. Munro's unromantic, independent heroines—country bred, proud, resilient, courageous even in her old age. Her story might have been even more moving if it did not unaccountably accelerate in its second half (where the point of view shifts to Violet's cousin Dan about whom we know virtually nothing and who is merely used as an instrument to observe Violet). Also, Ms. Munro is curiously perfunctory in summarizing Violet's love affair with a married man—the most intense emotional experience of Violet's life, presumably. Like the adulterous love affair at the heart of **"White Dump,"** it is alluded to rather than dramatized: the reader knows very little about it, and consequently feels very little.

Recurring in Alice Munro's fiction is a certain female protagonist, clearly kin to Violet, but generally more capable of establishing a life for herself. She is intelligent, though not intellectual; "superior," though often self-doubting. She has the capacity to extract from frequently sordid experiences moral insights of a very nearly Jamesian subtlety and precision. She tells us what she thinks; tells us, often, what *we* would think. Not conventionally beautiful, she is nonetheless attractive to men: which leads her sometimes, as an adolescent, into dangerous situations—as in the new story **"Jesse and Meribeth"** in which the adolescent Jesse is scolded by a near-seducer, an older man, for what he correctly perceives as her overwrought romantic imagination: "You shouldn't go inside places like this with men just because they ask you. . . . You're hot-blooded. You've got some lessons to learn." In the more complex, multigenerational **"White Dump"** a kindred girl is drawn into marriage with a man who "depended on her to make him a man," and who will prove inadequate to her passionate nature. In **"Lichen,"** one of the bleakest of the new stories, the heroine, middle-aged, cheerful, at last adjusted to a solitary life, achieves a moral triumph over her fatuous ex-husband simply by maturing beyond him. She is fully accepting of the terms of her freedom:

> This white-haired woman walking beside him . . . dragged so much weight with her—a weight not just of his sexual secrets but of his middle-of-the-night speculations about God, his psychosomatic chest pains, his digestive sensitivity, his escape plans, which once included her. . . . All his ordinary and extraordinary life—even some things it was unlikely she knew about—seemed stored up in her. He could never feel any lightness, any secret and victorious expansion, with a woman who knew so much. She was bloated with all she knew.

She has become, ironically, a kind of mother to him; but she looks so much older than he that he is shamed and frightened at the very sight of her.

In one of the collection's finest stories, **"The Progress of Love,"** the daughter of a woman who sacrificed both herself and her children to presumably Christian ideals of integrity chooses deliberately *not* to believe in those ideals, or to marry conventionally as her mother had done; she becomes, in fact, a real estate agent, selling off the old houses and farms that made up the world of her youth. Long divorced, alone but not really lonely, Euphemia—who calls herself Fame—seeks moments of "kindness and reconciliation" rather than serious love; she wonders "if those moments aren't more valued, and deliberately gone after, in the setups some people like myself have now, than they were in those old marriages, where love and grudges could be growing underground, so confused and stubborn, it must have seemed they had forever." But without the old marriages and all that they yielded of sorrow, repression, loss, romance—what remains? Fame's love affairs are affairs merely, matters of convenience. To celebrate birthdays "or other big events" she goes with friends from work to a place called the Hideaway where male strippers perform.

(While Ms. Munro's Ontario countryside has come to bear a disconcerting resemblance to Andrew Wyeth's stark, bleached-out, clinically detailed landscapes, her small towns have been tawdrily transformed—dignified old country inns recycled as strip joints, convenience stores stocked with video games: "jittery electronic noise and flashing light and menacing, modern-day, oddly shaved and painted children.")

More than *The Beggar Maid* and *The Moons of Jupiter,* the two story collections preceding this one, *The Progress of Love* does contain less fully realized stories. So thinly executed is **"Eskimo"** that it reads like an early draft of a typically rich, layered, provocative Munro story: its male protagonist is off-stage, its female protagonist senses, or imagines, a psychic kinship with a young Eskimo girl she tries to befriend on an airplane flight, but their encounter comes to nothing and the story dissolves in a self-consciously symbolic dream. **"Miles City, Montana"** recounts a child's near-drowning but fails to integrate the episode with what precedes and follows it, and ends with a rather forced epiphany: "So we went on, with the two in the back seat trusting us, because of no choice, and we ourselves trusting to be forgiven, in time, for everything that had first to be seen and condemned by those children: whatever was flippant, arbitrary, careless, callous—all our natural, and particular, mistakes." **"Monsieur les Deux Chapeaux"** and **"Circle of Prayer"** are each rather sketchily imagined, though brimming with life; and **"White Dump,"** potentially one of the strongest stories in the collection, suffers from a self-conscious structure in which time is fashionably broken and point of view shifts with disconcerting casualness from character to character. We catch only a glimpse of Isabel and her lover and must take Isabel's word for it, that she feels "rescued, lifted, beheld, and safe"; we are not even certain whether the author means her conviction to be serious, or self-deluded. And the image of the "white dump"—the biscuit factory sugar dump—is rather arbitrarily spliced onto the story, poetically vivid as it is.

Even the weaker stories, however, contain passages of genuinely inspired prose and yield the solid pleasures of a three-dimensional world that has been respectfully, if not always lovingly, recorded. And Ms. Munro's minor characters, though fleetingly glimpsed, are frequently the vehicles for others' gestures of compassion and pity. (As in **"The Moon in the Orange Street Skating Rink,"** where decades are compressed within the space of a few pages, and Edgar, whom we have seen as a bright, attractive boy of 17, emerges as an elderly stroke victim, seated in front of a television screen, indifferent to the visit of his cousin and to his cousin's offer to take him for a walk. His wife says of him, simply: "No. He's happy.")

The Progress of Love is a volume of unflinching audacious honesty, uncompromisingly downright in its dissection of the ways in which we deceive ourselves in the name of love; the bleakness of its vision is enriched by the author's exquisite eye and ear for detail. Life is heartbreak, but it is also uncharted moments of kindness and reconciliation. (pp. 7, 9)

Joyce Carol Oates, "Characters Dangerously Like Us," in The New York Times Book Review, *September 14, 1986, pp. 7, 9.*

ANNE TYLER

[*Tyler, an American novelist, short story writer, and critic, is known for her humorous and moving portraits of eccentric families. Her novels, usually set in her native city of Baltimore, include* If Morning Ever Comes *(1964),* Dinner at the Homesick Restaurant *(1982), and* The Accidental Tourist *(1985), which won the National Book Critics Circle Award. In the following excerpt, Tyler praises the vivid, unpredictable narrative technique Munro uses in* The Progress of Love.]

The short story is a mere shadow of its former self these days—slim and stripped, positively anorexic. Only a few writers continue to create those full-bodied miniature universes of the old school. In this country, there's Peter Taylor, for one; in Ireland, William Trevor. And in Canada, there's Alice Munro. Some of her stories are so ample and fulfilling that they feel like novels. They present whole landscapes and cultures, whole families of characters.

The landscape is most often rural Canada. The culture is stern and uncushioned, and the characters are uncushioned as well. They are accustomed to doing without; they pride themselves on their fortitude and seriousness. In **The Beggar Maid** they endured abject, ugly poverty. In **The Moons of Jupiter** they tended to live a little more comfortably, but still they were far from frivolous.

The characters in the earlier collections were traveling along the distinct, deeply grooved tracks of their life stories, and it was the tracks themselves that provided the focus—the path, for instance, of the young heroine of the tales in **The Beggar Maid,** proceeding from her pinched childhood toward an urbane, affluent adulthood. In **The Progress of Love,** the focus has changed. The characters in these 11 stories are concerned not so much with the journey as with the journey's hidden meaning—how to view the journey, how to make sense of it. And frequently, they find the answer by juxtaposing certain events from their lives and studying the theme that emerges. It's as if they're solving a child's wooden puzzle, matching a shape to the cutout hollow that will receive it. In the most successful of the stories, the end result is a satisfying click as everything settles precisely into place.

A woman in **"Miles City, Montana"** carries with her the memory of a young boy's drowning that occurred in her childhood. During the funeral, she recalls, she experienced a wave of disgust and anger toward her parents. Now, while taking a vacation trip with her family, she nearly loses her own child to a drowning accident. But the little girl is rescued and the trip continues, while the woman reflects that her anger during that funeral was caused by her realization that parents cannot totally protect their offspring, that the death of a child seems,

to parents, "anything but impossible or unnatural." So, she tells us, she and her husband travel on,

> with the two in the back seat trusting us, because of no choice, and we ourselves trusting to be forgiven, in time, for everything that had first to be seen and condemned by those children: whatever was flippant, arbitrary, careless, callous—all our natural, and particular, mistakes.

What's interesting here is the way the juxtaposed event—the boy's drowning—is dealt out to the reader so artfully. It begins the whole story, whereas most writers would have introduced it only after the mishap with the woman's daughter. Most would have used the near-drowning as a hook to reel in the memory of the actual drowning—a perfectly acceptable device, but it lacks the suddenness and mystery of Alice Munro's method. And then not all of the juxtaposed event is revealed at once. We're told about the woman's long-ago anger, but we're not told the cause. Only at the end does she state the cause, even though she's always known it. This narrative restraint sets up a tension beyond anything the plot alone could evoke. We're pulled along not just by What happened? but also by Why did she feel that way? and What is the significance?

In ["**The Progress of Love**"], which may be the richest in the collection, the juxtapositions are not physical occurrences but moments when a particular viewpoint comes into question. The narrator is the kind of woman often found in Alice Munro's stories: divorced, sophisticated, self-supporting, the unlikely product of a sturdy Canadian farm family with simple tastes and rigid moral values. In apparently random order, this woman displays assorted family memories. She offers her mother's description of the terrifying moment when her own mother attempted suicide; then she tells us how a visiting aunt later described the same event, presenting the suicide attempt as benign and offhand, almost a joke. She tells us how her father, allowing his wife the right to do what she felt was just, stood by and watched her burn a much-needed inheritance in the kitchen stove; then she tells us she learned later that her father had known nothing about the incident. She must have invented his presence, she says; and yet she cannot bear to give up this heroic vision of him. Here we have juxtapositions within juxtapositions, for even if her father had been there, you could view his forbearance two different ways. "I consider that love," she says, but a man who is listening says, "Some people would consider it lunacy." The story is a whole kaleidoscope of varying perceptions. Everything has its other side—like the glamorous aunt who, after scrubbing her face, turns out to be so pale and wrinkled that her young niece almost expects to see "makeup lying in strips in the washbowl, like the old wallpaper we had soaked and peeled."

In **"White Dump,"** it is different points in time that are juxtaposed, resulting in a striking portrait of the exact moment when a supposedly happy family begins to dissolve. In **"Lichen,"** it is the ideal versus the actual: a man over and over abandons women as soon as discrepancies develop in his seamless images of them. And in **"Monsieur les Deux Chapeaux,"** three episodes involving a grown brother combine to inform the hero of the course the rest of his life is going to take.

Not all of the stories are easily entered. Who the narrator is, how old, what sex, what relation to the other characters—sometimes it takes some minutes to find all that out. This kind of problem is, I suspect, exactly what turns most readers to novels, where as soon as you've learned who's who you're set for the next few hundred pages. It's unfortunate that one of the most stubborn champions of the short story form should be contributing to the difficulty.

Still, the struggle's worth it. Once in these stories, you really are inside them; you have a vivid sense of the world that's being described. You can see the farmhouse guest room with its blue-and-white wallpaper and its view of blooming meadows beyond the meshy window screen. You can see the parlor with its decorative plate depicting Niagara Falls, and the summer cottage with its mismatched dishes and its "boring card game that taught you the names of Canadian wildflowers."

You can hear, too. There is some wonderfully precise wording here. A man tells his visiting fiancée that "he had thought she might show up," and the phrase "show up" tells it all: he's no longer happy to see her. An elderly man, learning of another man's plan to move in with a male lover, amiably remarks that "that's him's and your business," and only the uncharacteristic lapse in grammar gives away his shock. A doctor's wife, calling his office, asks if she might speak to "the Great Healer," thereby revealing much, both positive and negative, about their marriage.

Visiting a family on a plain, shabby farm in Ontario, a stranger is given the best bed in the house. "Well," his host says in the morning, "I hope you got some kind of a sleep on that old bed in there?" "This was Mr. Florence's cue to say that he had never slept better," we're told, but instead he dismays the whole family by answering, "I slept on worse." It's a failure not of manners but of language style—two cultures baffled by each other. That we can understand this so quickly, that we can enjoy both men's remarks and sympathize with them, proves how comfortably we ourselves have settled into Alice Munro's guest room. (pp. 54-5)

Anne Tyler, "Canadian Club," in The New Republic," Vol. 195, Nos. 11 & 12, September 15 & 22, 1986, pp. 54-5.

An Excerpt from *The Progress of Love*

In the summer of 1947, when I was twelve, I helped my mother paper the downstairs bedroom, the spare room. My mother's sister, Beryl, was coming to visit us. These two sisters hadn't seen each other for years. Very soon after their mother died, their father married again. He went to live in Minneapolis, then in Seattle, with his new wife and his younger daughter, Beryl. My mother wouldn't go with them. She stayed on in the town of Ramsay, where they had been living. She was boarded with a childless couple who had been neighbors. She and Beryl had met only once or twice since they were grown up. Beryl lived in California.

The paper had a design of cornflowers on a white ground. My mother had got it at a reduced price, because it was the end of a lot. This meant we had trouble matching the pattern, and behind the door we had to do some tricky fitting with scraps and strips. This was before the days of pre-pasted wallpaper. We had a trestle table set up in the front room, and we mixed the paste and swept it onto the back of the paper with wide brushes, watching for lumps. We worked with the windows up, screens fitted under them, the front door open, the screen door closed. The country we could see through the mesh of screens and the wavery old window glass was all hot

and flowering—milkweed and wild carrot in the pastures, mustard rampaging in the clover, some fields creamy with the buckwheat people grew then. My mother sang. She sang a song she said her own mother used to sing when she and Beryl were little girls.

> I once had a sweetheart, but now I have none.
> He's gone and he's left me to weep and to moan.
> He's gone and he's left me, but contented I'll be,
> For I'll get another one, better than he!

I was excited because Beryl was coming, a visitor, all the way from California. Also, because I had gone to town in late June to write the Entrance Examinations, and was hoping to hear soon that I had passed with honors. Everybody who had finished Grade 8 in the country schools had to go into town to write those examinations. I loved that—the rustling sheets of foolscap, the important silence, the big stone high-school building, all the old initials carved in the desks, darkened with varnish. The first burst of summer outside, the green and yellow light, the townlike chestnut trees, and honeysuckle. And all it was was this same town, where I have lived now more than half my life. I wondered at it. And at myself, drawing maps with ease and solving problems, knowing quantities of answers. I thought I was so clever. But I wasn't clever enough to understand the simplest thing. I didn't even understand that examinations made no difference in my case. I wouldn't be going to high school. How could I? That was before there were school buses; you had to board in town. My parents didn't have the money. They operated on very little cash, as many farmers did then. The payments from the cheese factory were about all that came in regularly. And they didn't think of my life going in that direction, the high-school direction. They thought that I would stay at home and help my mother, maybe hire out to help women in the neighborhood who were sick or having a baby. Until such time as I got married. That was what they were waiting to tell me when I got the results of the examinations.

You would think my mother might have a different idea, since she had been a schoolteacher herself. But she said God didn't care. God isn't interested in what kind of job or what kind of education anybody has, she told me. He doesn't care two hoots about that, and it's what He cares about that matters.

This was the first time I understood how God could become a real opponent, not just some kind of nuisance or large decoration.

JULIE BEDDOES

[Beddoes, a Canadian editor and critic, has served as editor of Flare, a women's fashion and lifestyle magazine, and as a senior editor at General Publishing. In the following excerpt Beddoes explores the mysterious layers of meaning in "Fits" and other stories in The Progress of Love.]

Part of the attractiveness of Munro's work is the beauty of her style: sentences and paragraphs slide past the eyes and through the head like music. In *The Progress of Love,* her most mysterious and wonderful book so far, the musicality is another diversionary screen: the passion, craziness and violence of the lives described are seen through many veils, firstly through the coolness of the language, then through their unglamorous setting in the outwardly quiet lives of farmers or small-town shopkeepers, then through the viewpoint of the puzzled narrator. Glimpses through this veiling are provided by shifts in tone or tense, and by hints that we are reading from a point of view different than that which first seemed apparent. These are detective stories with two sleuths, one inside the story, a minor participant in the puzzling events, the other the reader who asks again and again, Who is telling me all this? The answer probably will be a surprise, the most important clue, as subtle as a change of tense.

> The two people who died were in their early sixties. They were both tall and well built, and carried a few pounds of extra weight. He was gray-haired, with a square, rather flat face. A broad nose kept him from looking perfectly dignified and handsome. Her hair was blond, a silvery blond that does not strike you as artificial anymore—though you know it is not natural—because so many women of that age have acquired it. On Boxing Day, when they dropped over to have a drink with Peg and Robert, she wore. . . .

This is the beginning of **"Fits,"** a story in Munro's new collection. A story that starts with a reference to two dead people might be expected to go on to describe the probably extraordinary events that led to the deaths. Instead, we are told how they looked and what they talked about during a perfectly ordinary visit with their neighbours. The hint of familiarity ("does not strike you"—the narrator knows me) is repeated in the account of the visit (so is the conversational narrator's coolness) when Peg's sons are introduced: "—the older one, Clayton, who was a virgin, and the younger one, Kevin, who was not—watched this breezy-talking silvery-blond woman with stern, bored expressions."

The storyteller's position in time soon gets more complicated: "Robert and Peg have been married for nearly five years." This is narrative strip-tease: five years and already a son who is not a virgin? And if they *have* been, when will we come to the implied present tense? Is the couple still lying dead while we hear about Robert and Peg's marriage? On the next page a clue to the connection, or lack of one: "It was entirely by accident that Peg was the one who found them." But this leads into a story about the egg-woman and then about Peg's night-classes. We are told that Robert finds Peg self-contained. Is that a clue to the title? Is it she who fits, if only into herself? Who is telling us all this, what is her relationship to these scarcely-connected events, and when is *now*?

Then we are told what Robert did the day after the egg-woman came as well as more about his courtship of Peg (the precocious sons are from a previous marriage) and a lot about the state of the snow. Is this a clue too?

We get more and more of the events of Monday as told to Robert by various people, with some interpretations that might be his. We have got from page 106 to page 116 and still the tension of tenses: "Robert *had* finished what he was doing. . . ." Is this a story about death or grammar? On page 122 we go ahead to the funeral on Thursday, then back into Peg and Robert's house on the night of the deaths, all the time in past tense, and then some more about the remoter past. On page 130, the next to last, we get to *now*, but the story continues in the past tense. *Now* might be any time that Robert is thinking it over, trying to make it fit, the deaths, Peg's behaviour, how he and she will fit together now it has all happened. But the

story is in the third person. An unknown voice is telling us about Robert trying to fit the self-contained Peg into a new container; the reader of the book has to fit the half-told story of the deaths into the container of Robert's reading of Peg, and that container into the story outside it which will reveal, perhaps, the identity of that third-person voice. But who will be telling that one? Outside the text is more text.

The story pretends to justify its title in the only passage in which strong emotions are shown. Peg's son Clayton is telling his mother of his terror when she and his departed father used to fight:

> "Clayton. We would never either one of us ever have hurt you."
>
> Robert believed it was time he said something.
>
> "What this is like," he said, "it's like an earthquake or a volcano. It's that kind of happening. It's a kind of fit. People can take a fit like the earth takes a fit. But it only happens once in a long while. It's a freak occurrence."

But the title of **"Fits,"** takes on a new significance each time one rereads the story. it's about people who take a fit, whose lives don't fit, how one fits together the puzzles which are the lives of people one hardly knows, and also those of the people one knows best. Peg's calm seems as much a "freak occurrence" to Robert as the violence she has been witness to. The text that doesn't fit inside the text, perhaps, is asking why it too can stay so cool in the presence of such events.

"A Queer Streak," the book's longest story, is divided into two sections. The first is a third-person, past-tense, chronological history of rural craziness and the eventual escape from it of a young woman called Violet. In the second half we see events through the eyes of Violet's nephew, the son of the one who had seemed the craziest.

At first the farm boy sees his aunt's town life as strange and exotic; as he grows up, travels, is educated, he comes to see her as a fairly ordinary woman, until a visit from a member of a yet younger generation stirs up her memories of the tragic past and indirectly leads to her death. But, of course, there's a mystery: is the queer streak in the nephew's mother, in his aunt or in himself? Do both sections have the same narrator? There's a comment on the oddness of the nephew's name, Dane, but we're not told if he knew anything at all about the much odder events in the first section.

The story compares the dull practicality of town people with the eccentricity of Aunt Violet's parents:

> Violet's mother—Aunt Ivie—had three little boys, three baby boys, and she lost them. Then she had the three girls. Perhaps to console herself for the bad luck she had already suffered, in a back corner of South Sherbrooke Township—or perhaps to make up, ahead of time, for a lack of motherly feelings— she gave the girls the fanciest names she could think of: Opal Violet, Dawn Rose, and Bonnie Hope. She may not have thought of those names as anything but temporary decorations. Violet wondered—did her mother ever picture her daughters having to drag such names around sixty or seventy years later, when they were heavy faded women?

If Dane didn't know about his mother's and aunt's childhood, why does he find Violet's life story worth recalling and writing? The narrator tells us that he is gay. Does this make him feel connected in his sexual marginality to his aunt who had a married lover, and is the title a reference to this? If *he* is telling the story why would he make such a crude joke as to give it that title? Again, in the end the mystery is in the telling of the story, not in the events of Dane's and Violet's lives. Dane's narrative (if it *is* Dane's) is both subtext and metatext to another story not printed here.

The undramatic title of the title story, **"The Progress of Love,"** reminds one of a paperback romance or an old-fashioned, three-act play. Its cool style again teases conventional expectations of tranquillity in a small town in southwestern Ontario. And again, while the lives of its characters are full of passion, the story of these lives competes for our attention with the process of recollection. Memory is an unreliable narrator.

The story—the book—starts with the announcement of a death. The coolness of the language of the announcement—and of the entire text perhaps—is explained right away as, "Country manners. Even if sombody phones up to tell you your house is burning down, they ask first how you are." The death is that of the narrator's mother. Events in her own life and those of her mother and her grandmother are told side-by-side as if to examine them for signs of progress. The mother's ordinariness is shown up against her showy American sister. But the sister lacks the capacity for passion: it is the poor farm woman who is capable of such hatred of her father that she burns the money she inherits from him, it is the farmer husband who is capable of such love that he *might* have allowed her to do it. There are two versions of most of the events in this story. The narrator's emotional life is a lot calmer than those of her mother and grandmother but is this the progress of the title or just one version of the story? Calmness and confusion co-exist in the writing as in the written. (pp. 24-6)

> *Julie Beddoes, "Country Manners," in* Brick: A Journal of Reviews, *No. 29, Winter, 1987, pp. 24-7.*

A. S. BYATT

[*Byatt, an English critic, educator, novelist, short story writer, and editor, is a well known literary figure in England today. Her fiction includes two novels of a planned tetralogy,* The Virgin in the Garden *(1978) and* Still Life *(1985)—both of which have been praised for their intellectual ambition and postmodernist techniques and perspectives—as well as the short story collection* Sugar and Other Stories *(1987). Among her critical works are studies on William Wordsworth and Samuel Taylor Coleridge, Iris Murdoch, and George Eliot. In the following excerpt Byatt discerns a thematic preoccupation with the effects of time in* The Progress of Love.]

At the end of a previous collection of stories, *Lives of Girls and Women,* Alice Munro's heroine, having succumbed to sexual passion, and probably lost her chance of a university scholarship, decides to write a novel. The decision transfigures for her the small Ontario town she inhabits. She invents a central character, a black-shrouded Photographer, who makes everyone look frightening. Her life is pictures, which 'seemed true to me, not real but true, as if that town was lying close behind the one I walked through every day.' She plans 'to turn Jubilee into black fable and tie it up in my novel.'

But Alice Munro's art is no power-game, and her fictional autobiographies are no Portrait of the Artist as a Young Woman. *Lives of Girls and Women* ends, not on art, but on the way in which reality continues to be more surprising than the pictures which illuminate and transfigure it. And Alice Munro's art is

not the over-reaching art of the fabulist, but the deceptively transparent pictures of the realist.

Her new collection of stories, *The Progress of Love,* like its predecessors, concentrates on the surprising, indeed shocking, moments, and the equally shocking whole-shaped lives of people mostly originating in rural Ontario. In earlier books, Munro was concerned with initiations and discoveries. Here her subject is time, biological time, the terrible brevity of the successive phases which make up our very short lives. For this theme, the story (or long tale) seems more appropriate than the novel. It packs more punch. The title story ["**The Progress of Love**"], a narrative masterpiece, achieves its effects by roving, apparently casually, between the present—'a hot enough day in September', when the narrator's father telephones her office to say, 'I think your mother's gone'—and other critical moments: in 1947, or in the mother's own childhood, or in 1965 when a hippie commune bought the old family house. The story is so sharply selective that it is impossible for a review to sum it up.

These stories can be divided into those which scan a whole life in this way, and those whose *raison d'être* is a more conventional narrative jolt or revelation. In the second category might come **"Fits"**, where a husband watches his wife's reaction to her discovery of a horribly dead married couple, or **"The Moon in the Orange Street Skating Rink"** where two young men in provincial Gallagher in the early part of the century skate on the rink, and sexually experiment with the foundling skivvy of their landlady—finally and disastrously running off to Toronto with her dressed as a boy. It may be that the stories which seem more *decisively* shocking are those where the central consciousness is male. Munro is good at men and her range is impressive, from the inarticulate violent father of **"A Queer Streak"**, receiving anonymous death threats from a daft daughter, to the gentle, half-feckless, or anxiously conventional divorced husbands of many of her women.

But it is the female experience of vanished or vanishing time that informs the twisting and questing shapes of the very best of these stories. The women of these stories know quite a lot. They know about the greed of young girls, who jeopardise a whole future for the urgency of love now; they know about the tolerance of the middle-aged, remarried or solitary, for the men they once loved, who have moved on, or return intermittently; they know the stolidity or confusions of old age. In **"Circle of Prayer"** Trudy and Janet watch old reruns of *Dallas:*

> 'That's what's so hilarious, Janet says; it's so unbelievable, it's wonderful. All that happens and they just forget about it and go on. But to Trudy it doesn't seem so unbelievable that the characters would go from one thing to the next thing—forgetful, hopeful, photogenic, forever changing their clothes. That it's not so unbelievable is the thing she really can't stand'.

Alice Munro's stories depict that 'going on' but simultaneously they make sure that the reader knows about the terrible finality of 'happenings' that pass by. In **"White Dump"**, Munro, describing Isabel contemplating her first adultery, comments:

> Not much to her credit to go through her life thinking, Well, good, now that's over, *that's* over. What was she looking forward to, what bonus was she hoping to get, when this, and this, and this, was over?

Alice Munro is as good at presenting the particularities of lifestyles we have lived through, as she is at the universal emotions—hope, resignation, slackening and decay—we all endure. She has a sharp eye for a Fifties' shirt or a hippy skirt, and an equally sharp eye for shifting fashions in parenting or ambition. **"Miles City, Montana"** is about death. It opens with the 1940s drowning of an eight-year-old boy the narrator had not much liked. It tells of the near-drowning in Miles City of the very young daughter of the narrator, driving in 1961 from British Columbia to Ontario. We are told in passing that it is now years since the narrator saw her then husband, but he is exactly alive, then and now: his (not overweening) ambition, his insistence on lettuce in his sandwiches, his urban background, his anxiety. The story contains Jackie Kennedy, Whittaker Chambers, Mr Gromyko and a vivid account of the rescue of a fieldful of drowning turkeys in a flood. It contains marriage, the cessation and persistence of love, and the possibility and the fact of sudden death. It gave me intense pleasure and two terrible nightmares.

These stories seem natural and are hugely artful; they seem life-like and are very precisely constructed. They are, to go back to our original distinction, both real *and* true. (pp. 22-3)

> *A. S. Byatt, "Vanishing Time," in* The Listener, *Vol. 117, No. 2996, January 29, 1987, pp. 22-3.*

ANNE DUCHÊNE

[*The Progress of Love*] is Alice Munro's fifth collection of stories in almost twenty years. . . .

No newcomer, then; yet this accomplished writer—so serious, careful and full of sardonic good humour—remains curiously under-celebrated. the blurb here grows a bit hectic about how she "uncovers the unexpected where it crackles underneath", in the lives of "apparently ordinary folk" who in fact "pulse with idiosyncratic life", etc. The truth is that she has such a respect for fact, such a kind of loving humility before domestic, circumstantial detail, that even if one can't always imagine oneself in a Munro situation, one can easily imagine one's neighbour.

Quite a lot of the writer's temper is carried in the closing lines of the title story here:

> It was just as well to make up right away. Moments of kindness and reconciliation are worth having, even if the parting has to come sooner or later. I wonder if those moments aren't more valued, and deliberately gone after, in the setup some people like myself have now, than they were in those old marriages, where love and grudges could be growing underground, so confused and stubborn, it must have seemed they had forever.

This ends a story that spins through concentric circles of the narrator's, her mother's and her grandmother's experience. It commands "the setup some people have now" and its nervous, evanescent growths; it indulges the author's fascination in digging over the matted roots of "love and grudges" from the past; and over the bleak bedrock of low expectations it steadfastly respects the ordinary humane norm—well, animal norm—which prefers and seeks "moments of kindness and reconciliation".

Typically, too, the inelegant energy of the rhythms matches the narrator—a middle-aged Canadian woman who has worked in a small-town estate agent's since leaving home, has borne two children, and divorced, and now looks lucidly on her modified "setup". This little semi-rural town, close to lakes and plains, is the same as the one the author used to call Jubilee—rather more suburban now, but still able to pick up

allusions to Coldwater Baptists. The characters haven't changed, either: mothers and fathers of prime importance, siblings, cousins, aunts and the "best friends" of youth hard on their heels. Husbands and lovers are less reliable, somehow; sneakier, more evasive and self-indulgent. Not on ideological grounds, just from observation: it seems to be the way they are.

The stories themselves, almost all about the commoner pains or the milder divagations of loving, have a great implosive impact wherever theme and image marry. **"White Dump"**, for instance, brilliantly and bitterly yokes a grandmother, her son, his wives and his two children at the moment of conception, as it were, of a divorce, as well as years later. It has a smooth, baleful glitter, like ice, and anyone who read it last year in the *New Yorker* will find it reverberating in the memory. **"Lichen"**, where an ageing woman recognizes her ex-husband's unredeemable immaturity, plays on the same contrast—warmth in nature, in voices, in hope, stricken by the chill and complexity of disappointment. **"Circle of Prayer"**, where a single mother is reassured by a mental defective, allows the same cold sunshine at the end. More disturbingly, **"Fits"** is about the reactions of a preternaturally reserved wife to the killing of her neighbours.

The funeral sermon over these out-of-towners is pronounced, incidentally, by "the United Church minister, who usually took up the slack in the cases of no known affiliation". Humour is present everywhere, in this writing, as naturally as olives exude oil. When it is, exceptionally, absent—in **"Eskimo"**, a study of sensuality—the deprivation is very acute.

All these are contemporary stories, told in cool tones, the characters chastened by forces, or accidents, we recognize. Sometimes, in what someone who hasn't been around for fifty years or so might call the "historical" stories, the author's passionate attachment to detail, and the need to cover a longer span in the same small space, can lead to elaboration rather than illumination; one longs to see the idea seized on the wing, as it were, with less information about plumage, habitat, nesting habits and the rest. **"A Queer Streak"**, about the barminess in a rural family, has to be broken into two parts. It is fifty pages long; most stories here are twenty or thirty—twice as long, almost invariably, as those of 1968. **"The Moon in the Orange Street Skating Rink"** is a densely packed, baroque story about youth fifty years or so ago, and as the title threatens, it is not free from winsomeness.

Preferring the pared-down, more allusive contemporary stories to those with heavier traditional upholstery is not ungrateful. Simply, one wants to see the author, who is still in her midfifties, go on observing and absorbing, grappling and experimenting with time-shifts, and enjoying her own exuberance, without depending too heavily on her own memories of youth.

> *Anne Duchêne, "Respect for the Facts," in* The Times Literary Supplement, *No. 4374, January 30, 1987, p. 109.*

D.A.N. JONES

Let us be sexist. *The Progress of Love* is a woman's book, particularly interesting to men who want to know what women think of them and know about them. Alice Munro is a 56-year-old Canadian who has been married twice: she is particularly concerned with the knowingness derived from broken relationships. One of the 11 skilful stories in this book (her sixth collection) is called **"Lichen"**—a fungoid growth or eruption used as an image for the progress of love. A civil servant called David, his grey hair dyed, has come to visit his ex-wife, Stella: he brings with him his new partner, Catherine, but he is already sick of her and obsessed with a third woman, the pleasingly trollopy Dina. . . .

There are many sharp observations in the dozen pages of this dispiriting story. Stella's house is in an area of remodelled farmhouses or winterised summer cottages by the shores of Lake Huron, plenty of comfortable, retired folk, a weaver and a gay dentist—its sunny bleakness exposed when Stella says: 'It's nice for us pensioned-off wives . . . I'm writing my memoirs. I'll stop for a cash payment.' David remarks casually: 'You know, there's a smell women get. It's when they know you don't want them any more. Stale.' David feels fresh. He tells Stella about the redundant Catherine, nearing forty and dated—'She's a hippie survivor really. She doesn't know those days are gone.' Like a boy, he sneaks off to telephone young Dina, the doomed successor to Catherine and Stella. His freshness pleases Stella's father, as they discuss motor-cars in the Balm of Gilead Home. 'Daddy was so pleased to see you,' says Stella. 'A man just means more, for Daddy. I suppose if he thought about you and me he'd have to be on my side, but that's all right, he doesn't have to think about it.' The fact is that Stella's tolerant knowingness is a form of complicity with David's wilful selfishness—a complicity not uncommon among women who write skilfully about men.

"Lichen" has been singled out because it is so characteristic of Alice Munro's stories. In "White Dump" we read: 'They had found out so much about each other that everything had got cancelled out by something else. That was why the sex between them could seem so shamefaced, merely and drearily lustful, like sex between siblings.' In "Jesse and Meribeth" a schoolgirl has a crush on a married man, who offers her a sort of paternal advice: at once patronising and sexy, he urges her to appreciate 'the reality of other people'—and the schoolgirl thinks: 'What do I want with anybody who can know so much about me?' This girl is influenced by certain children's books in which 'girls were bound two by two in fast friendship, in exquisite devotion': with her special friend she plans to change their names, herself taking a boy's name, Jesse, to the displeasure of their schoolmistress. Jesse is not altogether different from Callie, in "The Moon in the Orange Street Skating Rink", a stoical little boarding-house 'slavey', who likes to wear boys' clothes: she attaches herself to two athletic lads, skaters and acrobats, who try out their limited sex-knowledge on her. Callie says: 'It would take a lot more than that stupid business to hurt me.'

Other women are more easily frightened, like Marietta in "The Progress of Love". She hated barbers' shops, hated their smell, asked her father not to put any dressing on his hair because the smell reminded her. 'A bunch of men standing out on the street, outside a hotel, seemed to Marietta like a clot of poison. You tried not to hear what they were saying, but you could be sure it was vile.' More confident women have their expectations disappointed—like the liberal-minded old lady who allows hippies to swim in her lake and, as a result, returns from her morning swim naked and disconsolate, after an unfortunate experience. 'Christ, Mother!' says her son, throwing her a tablecloth. Her daughter-in-law 'responds to the story' in strange fashion, embarking on an affair with a handsome airman. These clever, powerful and convincing stories are always satisfying, one at a time, when they appear in *Grand Street* or the *New Yorker:* but to read a collection in a book, one after another,

is rather dispiriting. The gentle tolerance is almost nurse-like: some of these characters, one feels, should be denounced.

> *D.A.N. Jones, "What Women Think about Men,"*
> *in* London Review of Books, *Vol. 9, No. 3, February*
> *5, 1987, p. 23.*

MICHAEL GORRA

Alice Munro has . . . [a distinctive] world—by which I don't simply mean that she sets most of her stories in the flat Ontario countryside, all wheat fields and small towns, around Lake Huron. Some of her stories [in *The Progress of Love*] seem, in fact, as if they could be set anywhere, or in any small town, for all that the specific region seems to matter—they don't seem to be about living in that part of Canada in the way, say, that Cheever's stories are about Westchester. I've rarely read a group of stories that concentrate so exclusively on their characters' private lives, to the exclusion of the society that contains them. Munro's stories seem to lack a public dimension—but perhaps that's just my own parochial ignorance of what life in Ontario is like. Because in standing back from these stories one does see that Munro's tightness of focus, her absorption in her characters' private lives, is itself a comment, like that implicit in Katherine Mansfield's stories about New Zealand, on the isolation of the region about which she writes. And that isolation in turn makes it possible for Munro to concentrate so tightly on her characters themselves, so that they stand out against their background like trees against a wheat field.

But that's not finally what I mean about Munro's possession of a distinctive world. What is most characteristic about her work is not her settings, or even the rather ordinary lives of her rather ordinary characters—farmers, shopkeepers, bright girls from small towns who want to get out—but the way she organizes and presents such materials. Munro's stories are never simple uninflected slices of incomprehensible life. Instead they concentrate on a character's memory of the moment at which something crucial was decided, at which she became the person she was going to be—but a moment whose importance she may not have realized until the story's present. Or perhaps, as in "Jesse and Meribeth," not the person she was going to be, but the one she's always been. That story ends like this:

> I felt such changes then—from fifteen to seventeen, from seventeen to nineteen—that it didn't occur to me how much I had been myself all along. I saw Marybeth shut, with her treats and her typewriter, growing sweeter and fatter, and the Crydermans fixed, far away, in their everlasting negotiations, but myself shedding dreams and lies and vows and errors, unaccountable. I didn't see that I was the same one, embracing, repudiating. I thought I could turn myself inside out, over and over again, and tumble through the world scot free.

That last line has a bold simplicity of the sort that every writer wants to be able to end a story with, but that few are brave enough to try; it's almost as fine as Frank O'Connor's "And anything that happened to me afterwards. I never felt the same about again," at the end of "Guests of the Nation."

My favorite of the collection's eleven pieces, though, is "The Moon in the Orange Street Skating Rink." There a rich widower, a banker named Sam, revisits the small Ontario town where he went to business college and sees, for the first time in half a century, his cousin Edgar, with whom he originally came off the family farm, and Edgar's wife Callie, who'd been the "slavey" at the boarding house where they'd lived. Edgar had seduced Callie—and then married her, even though she didn't get pregnant, without seeming to have been much in love. But why? Sam has wondered about that all his life, a question that's really a way of marvelling at people, at their differences, at his first realization that he and Edgar, who have grown up together, might want different things. And as he marvels at the mystery of other people, so does the reader, in story after story, stories so successful at collapsing a whole life into a few pages as to make me feel that most writers who think they need a novel to explore a few characters' personal relations are simply wasting space. (pp. 140-42)

Michael Gorra, in a review of "The Progress of Love," in The Hudson Review, *Vol. XL, No. 1, Spring, 1987, pp. 140-42.*

MARK LEVENE

[*In the following excerpt Levene, a Canadian critic and educator, describes the "language and wisdom" of* The Progress of Love.]

'One of our favorite writers,' declares one of the new literary stars of New York. 'One of the great short story writers,' intones a Canadian socialite. These designer judgments about Alice Munro do not, of course, mean that *The Progress of Love,* the book that has broadened her international reputation, has anything to do with denim or a prized banquette. Whatever its tone, the praise is fully warranted: this collection of eleven intricately narrated stories is close to a masterpiece, close because a few of the pieces repeat patterns with a loosening grip, a sudden loss of attention. Nevertheless, at least three—**"The Progress of Love," "Miles City, Montana,"** and **"Circle of Prayer"**—belonging among the best in the language.

Munro's is a realm of besieged families and warring feelings far removed from the phantom sorrows of the Holocaust and from 'the green places of the world . . . swarming with strong-arm philosophers and armed prophets.' A world of memories, small towns, and rooms where 'the window blinds were down to the sills' and 'the air had a weight and thickness, as if it were cut into a block that exactly filled the room,' it is equally removed from urban nightmares, the exultations of a free-floating intelligence, and dense subversions of narrative process. But Munro is close to the territory of her more technically lavish contemporaries in her fascination with the complexities of telling, of stories, and with the intimate, often frightening link between invention and love. The seismic shiftings that turn compassion to hatred and heartlessness, that suddenly 'split open'—an insistent phrase throughout the collection—are recorded with extraordinary precision, but perhaps it is Munro's supple language that is the book's finest legacy, her magnificent ability to capture nuances of sensibility and appearance. 'I wanted to hide,' says the mother in **"Miles City, Montana,"** so that I could get busy at my real work, which was a sort of wooing of distant parts of myself.'

The narration of [**"The Progress of Love"**] is restless, unsettled, moving backwards and forwards in time, but circling around opposite versions of two stories. Although the narrator's aunt says that the grandmother's attempt to hang herself was just 'to give Daddy a scare,' the narrator tells the story from her mother's point of view as though she were omniscient and the story a self-contained whole because of its dark impact on their lives. 'There was a cloud, a poison, that had touched my mother's life. And when I grieved my mother, I became part of it.' Unable to break into the hardened shape of this tale, the narrator alters a crucial detail in another story as an antidote to the poison. She places her father protectively beside her mother who burns her paternal inheritance. His presence is demanded in the scene because even through distortion she wants to be assured of their love, because through these 'moments of kindness and reconciliation' 'something could stop now—the stories, and griefs, the old puzzles you can't resist or solve.' In **"The Progress of Love"** invention arises from generosity; in **"Miles City, Montana"** verbal and physical creativity are set in a kind of primal conflict. On a trip home to show off her children, the narrator realizes that the radiant and the macabre imaginings of parents—the subtle creation of her children's characters, the 'trashy' shaping of the grim scene had one of the daughters not been able to swim—are both forms of consolation. And both are set against the stark reality of children being born not for 'a new, superior kind of life,' but for death. Her own parents 'gave consent to the death of children and to my death not by anything they said or thought but by the very fact that they had made children—they had made me.'

In **"Fits"** telling is a more profound need than love itself. It is a form of personal and social cohesiveness, a way of maintaining control over mysteries and secrets through shared knowledge. Names, words, the rituals of repeated assurances, the sense of 'a rambling, agreeable play . . . in progress' are central to life in Gilmour. But in her reluctance to describe the murder-suicide she discovered or to detail her own reactions, Peg refuses mutual proprietorship through language. A friend resents her for not saying 'one word' about what happened, and although Peg provides a story for her husband because he would 'want to know,' his discovery of 'one discrepancy, one detail—one lie—that would never have anything to do with him' means the presumption of a diminished love. Peg has appropriated the story, sealed it into her own silent privacy. In **"Jesse and Meribeth"** the wounds produced by both the withdrawals and offerings of imagination are even more raw. The man Jesse had made into a lover for the benefit of her friend strokes her while lecturing on 'the reality of other people.' Learning that reality and malice are inextricable, she cuts Meribeth off in absolute and unexplained silence. The hidden places of memory have a more benevolent echo in **"A Queer Streak,"** a lengthy piece that spans generations, narrators, and changes in rural and town life. Threatening letters have 'suspended' the lives of Violet's family, and when she sends them along with her own written plea to her fiancé, she stages the end of a domestic play in which she had cast herself as the wife of a minister 'intent on power.' She 'imagines' killing herself, then finds that words had 'settled on her, and were like cool, cool cloths binding her.' The golden shades of the landscape become the abstract 'goldenness' of self-abnegation and purpose. 'To give up. Care for them. Live for others.' But the destructiveness of these words is eventually contained by a memory Violet extends to her nephew just before her death: the secret resonance of a sound that became a gift. Her laugh is much like the effect of this whole, majestic book. Munro's perceptions are not comforting: male and female judgments possess a deadly meticulousness, death is ever-present, and imagination is a complex power of distortion. But in its language and wisdom, in the revelation offered by **"Circle of Prayer"** that one minute we stand outside our 'own happiness in a tide of sadness' and the next outside our 'unhappiness in a tide of what seemed unreasonably like love,' the book yields beauty and graciousness. (pp. 7-9)

Mark Levene, in a review of "The Progress of Love," in University of Toronto Quarterly, *Vol. LVII, No. 1, Fall, 1987, pp. 7-9.*

JEAN MALLINSON

[*In the following excerpt Mallinson, a Canadian critic and educator, discusses Munro's narrative technique in such stories as "The Moon in the Orange Street Skating Rink" and "Circle of Prayer," particularly her use of ellipsis.*]

'Progress' is a lively word which changes with the times, but the meaning which seems most appropriate to the title of Alice Munro's new collection of stories [*The Progress of Love*] is 'a Journey of state; a circuit; a passage from one place to another'. The ceremonial procession of a monarch from one royal seat to another and the transit of the sun from one house of the Zodiac to another are called a progress. The sun isn't going anywhere; it is just keeping its accustomed state at its various stations. In Alice Munro's stories, love, like the sun, shines on the clever as well as the not so clever, the homely as well as the beautiful. Love is no respecter of persons; it is impartial, unprejudiced, it can strike anyone at any time. In this sense the stories are classic in sympathy, free from the contemporary bias that love discovers only the young, the sensitive and the good-looking. The stories are an anatomy of love in its variety, its sometimes brutal and comic surprises. Sometimes we know the moment when love, in its progress, has moved on, but love is fitful; often by the time we are aware that it might leave, it has already gone.

If narrative patterns can be seen as extensions of rhetorical figures, these stories are striking examples of the uses of ellipsis. Like all narratives, they are constructed on the basis of an assumed sequence, the continuity of time, but they select material at certain points on the continuity, with bold gaps in between. Sometimes the gap is bridged through another figure, analogy, and many of the stories work through synecdoche, in that part of a life displayed is understood to stand for the pattern of the whole. The narrative device which gives the stories their reach and characteristic flavour is embedding, the placing of units of story in such a way that their significance accumulates and illuminates the main story line. Embedding gives the stories depth by providing a layering of perspectives on one or two focussed events. The way in which the narratives are sustained by embedding in ellipsis is virtuoso, but the style, except now and then in summary or reflection, tends toward the transparent; it does not draw attention to itself. The samples out of which the whole cloth of the stories is pieced together are judiciously chosen to give a sense of the whole, but they suggest that if you probe a life at any part, you get a significant sample—if you know how to sample. Alice Munro knows how to sample. All of which is to say that she is a master of narrative form, and the pleasure which reading her gives is always in part a pleasure in formal disposition. Her skill as writer frees her to render her subjects with economy, richness, and variety.

Ellipsis is daringly used in **"The Moon in the Orange Street Skating Rink"** and **"A Queer Streak"**. The first of these stories begins in a present moment and then jumps several decades back into a past which provides the generating narrative, the one which shows how the characters took the first steps toward where they were going—not at all what they had in mind when they started out. The freshness and buoyancy of this early adventure, centered in and around Kernaghan's boarding house, give it extraordinary charm. The image of the two country boys, Sam and Edgar, practising their acrobatic stunts in the vacant lot across from the boarding house, exists in the story and lingers after it, as a perfect hieroglyph for the comic, lyrical, confident and always doomed aspirations of the young. The girl Callie, part drudge, part urchin, and as spunky as they

come, is wonderfully imagined, a variation on a familiar type, but strikingly individual. The eagerness for escapade which is so bound up with the high spirits of the young is rendered in this story with a deep feeling for the ignorance of and greediness for experience which is characteristic of youth. The ironies of eventual outcomes are expressed reflectively near the end of the story by one of the carefree trio, Callie, Sam and Edgar: 'When Sam looked across at them on the train, and all three of them laughed with relief, it couldn't have been because they saw an outcome like this. They were laughing. They were happy. They were free.'

"A Queer Streak" begins as a kind of country story about traditional matters—three sisters, one of whom doesn't fit in; a life made slovenly by drastic absence of house-keeping; poison-pen letters—and then it turns into a family chronicle of fairly ordinary lives. Part One doesn't conclude; it just stops, and it is not until the end of Part Two that this hiatus in the narrative is filled. By its bold use of ellipsis, this story vaults from one period to another in the same locale, and tells two different kinds of tale. The narrative centre is shifted in the second part, but it is the life of Violet, the misfit sister, which gives continuity to the two parts of the story. The shift in point of view emphasizes the difference between the two parts; while Violet's life is displayed with lyrical intensity in Part One, her life in Part Two becomes obscure, something to be pieced together, no longer centre-stage. The two modes of rendering her life correspond to the style of the two very different love stories which are at the centre of her story in each part, and the difference is related to one of the themes of this collection of stories, which is voiced by the narrator at the end of the title story:

> Memories of kindness and reconciliation are worth having, even if the parting has to come sooner or later. I wonder if those moments aren't more valued, and deliberately gone after, in the set-ups some people like myself have now, than they were in those old marriages, where love and grudges could be growing underground, so confused and stubborn, it must have seemed they had forever.

Violet's first love story is old-fashioned, romantic, full of glances, vows, longings, renunciations, and eventual betrayal by her fiancé, who could not come down off his cloud. Her second love, though it eventually leads to marriage, involves a 'set-up' with a married man. At the end of Part One, Violet sees herself as the heroine of a failed love, a failed life, 'held fast, hiding because she didn't want to be seen, if her life was tragic'. Part Two is a long coda to this romantic moment, and it is full of surprises. After the hiatus in the narrative at the end of Part One we discover Violet busily leading a life for which her early story has not prepared us. Not until the very end of Part Two do we find out the comic resolution to Part One, which literally extricated her from her tragic predicament. The palimpsest of the two parallel images of thorns in the resolution of the two parts is formally beautiful and humanly believable. The dénouement of Violet's first dilemma was laughter, and it is with the memory of laughter that the second part ends.

The overlaying of these two images of extrication is more than analogy; it is almost substitution. But analogy does form the structural basis for two brilliant stories in the collection: **"Miles City, Montana"** and **"Eskimo"**. The latter story treats familiar material, the stuff of soap opera, in a startlingly original way, through a delicately suggested but devastating analogy. The occasion and setting are banal: the beginning of a holiday to Tahiti, the interior of an airplane, and later, a lady's washroom.

The central character is a nurse-receptionist in the office of a doctor with whom she has been carrying on a love affair for years. A couple whom she briefly and disturbingly encounters on the flight at first cast back to her an image which seems bizarre and alien, but eventually they diagram her own entanglement in the toils of a love which compels her in ways which she cannot explain to herself or anybody else.

Some of these stories, like **"Lichen"**, **"Monsieur les Deux Chapeaux"**, and **"White Dump"** are focused and clarified by the image given in the title. **"Lichen"** dwells on love in the old sense of an affliction, a possession which, while it lasts, allows its willing victim no space to manoeuvre at all. The central character, Stella, is a reluctant witness to the display of her ex-husband's bouts of obsessive love, as he moves from woman to woman in fitful trances of 'desire and dependence and worship and perversity, willed but terrible transformations'. The metaphor implicit in the image of lichen in the story draws on the very old analogy between woman and landscape, and it is to Stella that the glimpse of the metaphor is given; she is not solaced, but something is understood. The title **"Monsieur les Deux Chapeaux"** conveys a double meaning in its double image. The antic quality suggested by the title is at odds with the burden of responsibility which the story honours as an essential component of family love, but it is in keeping with the innocently irresponsible personality of the character, a charming but retarded brother, who wears the hats. The concern in this wonderful story is with the givenness of love as responsibility, the absolute imperative of love of this kind, which life hands us so that we live forever under its constraints, and all the other loves life brings us are enmeshed in it. The stunningly original image of the white dump in the story which bears that name subsumes the craving for love and more love which is at the heart of the narrative. This essentially cheerful account of marital infidelity focuses on a woman who, after years of trying to fit into the pattern of the faithful wife, comes unstuck and discovers her vocation for variety. Sophie, an elderly woman character who studies Old Norse literature, is wonderfully imagined. Although she springs, like Callie in **"Moon"**, from a familiar type, she also is a nonpareil. She plays the role of the one who observes without interfering in the latent story which eventually emerges. She is alive to the possibilities which lurk beneath the surfaces which people present to the world. Her feeling for life embodies a sense of character as fate, in a manner entirely in accord with her study of old Icelandic texts. Her presence in the story as a kind of restrained but palpable choric voice creates a larger perspective on its happenings, without judging them. She conveys implicitly but powerfully the sense which many of these stories give, that human character is complete very early in life, and all that time does is to unravel the narratives coiled inside us, to make the potential actual.

The image in **"Circle of Prayer"**, while less visual, is in a sense also an emblem of various patterns in that story, which is about the ways in which people maintain the links which bind them to the past and the future, the living and the dead. Since this is a contemporary story, these links are often improvised. The central invention in the story is just such an impromptu ritual spontaneously devised by a group of teenagers to respond to the accidental death of a classmate. This fluid, evocative story risks more freedom from a stated or implied narrative line than do the other stories which, even across chasms of ellipsis, arrive at some kind of resolution. In **"Circle of Prayer"** various narrative lines are left unresolved in the

convention of the 'slice of life', but this story is an orchestration of various slices. The spotlight is turned here, then there, and certain scenes are illuminated, from the past, the present. Trudy is in a sense the central character, and her predicaments—a failed marriage, troubles with a teenage daughter—are the vehicles for the feeling for life which the story conveys; but she does not bear the burden of the story as a designated protagonist. The clues in the story do not resolutely point in her direction. There are patterns of repetition in the story which accord with the title. People move in circles: you take one woman's husband, another woman takes yours. At one point you are inside the circle of dancers, of lovers, at another point you are outside. The encircling teenagers paying tribute to their dead friend describe a pattern which is repeated in the circle of prayer. But this story conveys a marvellous feeling for the aleatory, the randomness of life's moments of making sense. It suggests that meaning lies not in the resolution of narrative lines—will he come back? Won't he come back?—but elsewhere, and there are three passages in which a different kind of resolution is offered: not a *finis* to a story but a lyrical moment in and out of time. In one of these Trudy stands 'outside her own happiness in a tide of sadness' and later she stands 'outside her own unhappiness in a tide of what seemed unreasonably like love'. She muses, 'But it was the same thing, really, when you got outside. What are those times that stand out, clear patches in your life—what do they have to do with it? They aren't exactly promises. Breathing spaces. Is that all?' There is another such moment at the very end, a seemingly trifling concord which 'radiates, expands the way some silliness can, when you're tired. In this way, when she was young, and high, a person or a moment could become a lily floating on the cloudy river water, perfect and familiar'. These passages record lyrical rather than narrative resolutions; they shift the burden of the story away from event and toward perception, and the discontinuous form of the story reflects this shift.

"Circle of Prayer" also focuses on a theme which is central to many of these stories: the incursion of the drastic, the uncanny into lives that seem ordinary. This sense of the dangerousness of living is poignantly rendered in **"Miles City, Montana"** and is central to **"Fits"**, the title of which is a metaphor for the suddenness with which an unanticipated dire event can dislocate our sense of reality. The response of the central character in this story to an unexplained murder/suicide is to pull away from life's edges, back toward the norm. Yet the edges are acknowledged in image and embedded narrative. The recognition of the uncanny in this story and others, the tactful refraining from overly full explanation, correspond to our deep sense that life is both ordinary and mysterious at the same time.

Peg, the central character in **"Fits"**, 'pale and silky and assenting, but hard to follow as a watermark in fine paper' is a triumph of characterization through gesture, restrained speech and response, without any rendering of her inner life through interior monologue or reflection. She is clearly an ordinary woman without exceptional talent or beauty but her pervasive presence in the story reveals just how inadequate the notion of the ordinary is. Generally in this collection, Alice Munro seems to be moving away from the lyrical rendering of character through identification of the narrator with one central character. The dispersal of the narrator's interest among a whole range of characters gives these stories their classic feel. There are some extraordinary personalities here, like Callie and Sophie and the Crydermans, but the notion of eccentricity has no place in her sense of character. Her depiction of character is always a gesture of inclusion, and her sense of the possibilities of character is very large. The spiritual snobbery which finds one character more interesting than another is absent from these stories. The fact that she does not pick favourites but gives each character his or her due is a sign of her maturity as an artist.

The daring ellipsis which is the most marked structural feature of these stories accords with the distance measured by the theme of many of them: the chasm between the longings of love and the imperatives of life. Most of the stories take place in the area marked by the space between the illusion of freedom from life's constraints, and the actuality of obligation or, sometimes, entrapment. The high point of the state of illusion in which many of the stories begin is expressed at the end of **"Jesse and Meribeth"**:

> I saw Meribeth shut in,. . . and the Crydermans fixed, far away, in their everlasting negotiations, but myself shedding dreams and lies and vows and errors, unaccountable. I didn't see that I was the same one, embracing, repudiating. I thought I could turn myself inside out, over and over again, and tumble through the world scot free.

The discrepancy between this illusion and the coercions of life's events is viewed in these stories sometimes with irony, occasionally with compassion, but more often simply as a dissonance which life hands us. Love, which usually arrives in the disguise of freedom, often carries with it the heaviest imperatives. The gap between freedom and imperative, between the 'I want' and the 'You must' of love is bridged only by the realization that they are versions of the same thing.

These stories are concerned with the setups or arrangements or improvisations which people contrive as dwelling places for whatever it is that draws them toward one another—call it love in its various guises. But there is another kind of love implicit in them: the love of people in their variety and of the forms of language and literature. An author can progress in this kind of love, in the other sense of progress as a moving forward, an increase in excellence. In this kind of love, Alice Munro has progressed very far, and we as readers reap the rewards of her formal skill, reach and daring, and the wide range of her human sympathy. (pp. 52-8)

> *Jean Mallinson, "Alice Munro's 'The Progress of Love'," in* West Coast Review, *Vol. 21, No. 3, Winter, 1987, pp. 52-8.*

Sharon Pollock

Doc

Governor General's Literary Award: Drama

(Born Mary Sharon Chalmers) Canadian dramatist and script-writer.

Doc (1984) is Pollock's second drama to receive the Governor General's Literary Award; six years previously, her play *Blood Relations* (1980) won the first Governor General's Award ever given for a published dramatic work. Pollock has earned distinction in the Canadian theater for her plays as well as for her work as an actor, director, university lecturer, and artistic director of Theatre Calgary. She began her playwriting career with such politically oriented dramas as *Walsh* (1973), which concerns the Canadian government's handling of North American Indians, and *The Komagata Maru Incident* (1976), which presents a historical example of racism in Canada; both works depict the tragic effects of social oppression and injustice.

In recent years Pollock has narrowed her focus from broad political issues to the concerns of individuals, particularly in family relationships. *Blood Relations* is a feminist reexamination of the legend of Lizzie Borden—the nineteenth-century American accused of murdering her father and mother—that focuses on society's repression of women. In *Doc*, Pollock once again explores what she terms "the politics of the home, the informal politics that permeates human relationships." This time, however, Pollock's story is based on the intimate, often painful facts of her own family history. "It is her most personal play to date, a moving, deeply absorbing and undisguised confrontation of the playwright with her own past," declares critic Richard Paul Knowles, "and it succeeds brilliantly because of an unusual combination of great technical skill with genuine depth of feeling."

Comparisons between *Doc* and the circumstances of Pollock's early life are unavoidable. The central character in the play is a country physician known as "Ev," who neglects his family in order to further his career. According to biographical sources, Pollock's father, Dr. Everett Chalmers, was a general practitioner in Fredericton, New Brunswick. Catherine, Ev's daughter, like Pollock, is a writer, and Ev's alcoholic wife, like Pollock's mother, was a former nurse who committed suicide when her daughter was sixteen. While Pollock admits that major elements of the play are borrowed from her own experience, she distances herself and her family from the characters she created. "I'm glad *Doc* has been appreciated by the audience and the critics, but I think there's been too much emphasis that it's an autobiography," she stated. "It's amazing, the number of people who have come up to me and confided that they have had to deal with alcoholism and ambition in their own families. To them the play echoes something in their own experience, the universal experience about the inability to communicate."

Pollock presents her story in a non-linear format, shifting between past and present through the memories of her main characters. Catherine, for instance, is played by two actors; one represents her as a child, while the other portrays the adult

Photograph by Don Johnson

Catherine, who observes and interacts with her younger self in an attempt to resolve her ambivalent feelings towards her father. Although some perceive *Doc* as a negative commentary on the family it portrays, particularly the father, Pollock insists this was not her intention. Indeed, when the play was originally performed in New Brunswick under the title *Family Trappings*, Dr. Chalmers himself provided program notes for the production. As for her family's reactions to the play, Pollock commented, "I have to hope they see that I've used them to tell a story that's larger than our personal story. I have to trust that the love and affection with which I've used very personal material is apparent, even though some of the things might not be pleasant for them to recall." She added: "If it were really me in the play, I'm not sure I could reveal all that about myself."

Most critics, nevertheless, view *Doc* as an explicitly personal statement, although they debate Pollock's intentions. Some consider the play an indictment of a selfish man who has sacrificed his family to his obsession with his career, while others regard Pollock's presentation to be non-judgmental, noting that each character is portrayed in an ambiguous manner. Pollock herself emphasizes the social rather than the personal nature of the play. "As soon as you start dealing with the politics of the family, it's not so easy to know who the bad guys are," she noted. "It's not a black and white issue, but that doesn't mean the issue isn't there. *Blood Relations* is a play in which the woman is in conflict, not with her father—she loves her father—but with the society around her. In *Doc,* in order for the play to work, you have to give equal balance to everybody in it." For most reviewers, *Doc* succeeds both as autobiographical drama and as a universally significant exploration of family relationships.

MARK CZARNECKI

Many writers start their careers with autobiography before broadening their literary horizons, but Calgary playwright Sharon Pollock has taken the opposite route. Although her early plays focused on social issues including native rights and prison reform, recently a more personal element has entered her work. That shift of emphasis has culminated in *Doc....*

In *Doc,* Pollock reveals the havoc that a social crusader can unwittingly wreak on his family. Ev is a retired New Brunswick doctor who has devoted his life to his patients. Trembling with age and the effects of a heart attack, the widower sits alone in the attic of his deserted house. When his daughter Catherine, a writer, returns home unexpectedly, they conjure up family ghosts together in a futile attempt to strike peace.

As the flashbacks unfold, it becomes clear that Ev brutally ignored his wife, Bob, driving her to drink and into the arms of his best friend, Oscar. Catherine refused to acknowledge the domestic horror around her. Eventually Bob committed suicide, leaving Ev a note which he fingers, unopened, through the play.

Without a suspenseful plot, a memory play like *Doc* can easily flag, and, indeed, the first act is slow. In addition, apart from Ev and Bob, the characters remain sketchy.... *Doc* is more ritual than play, a gripping but oppressive exorcism of the demons in Sharon Pollock's past. Coming in the middle of a distinguished career, it stirs curiosity about where the playwright's inspiration will lead her.

> Mark Czarnecki, *"Ghosts in a Family Attic,"* in Maclean's Magazine, *Vol. 97, No. 17, April 23, 1984, p. 52.*

ALAN STEWART

Everyone has his own theories about what makes some things art and others mere recreation or something to fill the time; my own feeling is that anything that is art must illuminate, pretentious as that may sound. It must shed light on our own lives. Everything else, even though it might instruct, amuse, or move us to tears, is lesser, the work of a tradesman rather than an artist.

Sharon Pollock, the author of *Doc*..., is clearly an artist although this is not to say she does not know her trade as well: *Doc*'s exploration of an unhappy family meets all the criteria of the well-made play while at the same time managing to cast an understanding but unsentimental light on other families as well....

[The] play transcends any medical, sociological, or sexual aspects to become a story about the way children regard their parents, not just when the children are young but when they grow up, when they have become the same age that their parents were when the children first remember them. After all, although we use the word child to describe a boy or girl between infancy and youth, it also means a son or daughter of any age.

Pollock illustrates this by putting the actress playing the heroine on stage at the same time as the actress playing the heroine when she was a girl. The two do not communicate all that much but you can tell that the grown-up regrets some of the things that her younger self says and does, notably the girl's hard-line attitude toward the behavior of her mother and father. Granted, the mother is an alcoholic and the father is insensitive toward the needs of his family, but still, the daughter is judgmental as only the young can be, with little understanding or sympathy about why her parents are the way they are.

The grown-up daughter, having realized that her adult life is not exactly a model of successful living, is a lot more capable of looking at her parents not just as mother and father but as people. But all of us are children in the sense that we will always be sons and daughters, and perhaps this is why it is often convenient for us to withold from our parents the understanding we extend to others and above all, to our own adult selves.

Doc got to me in another way as well. Pollock makes the point that it is difficult for parents and children to find common ground upon which to communicate as equals, even when the children become adults. At least, I think she does this; the trouble with the business of art illuminating your own life is that you might use the play as a kind of theatrical Rorschach test.

Anyway, it seems to me that when you are a child, in the sense of being young, it is almost impossible to talk to your parents as equals but even then, we can understand this—they are old, we are young, and the twain rarely meet. I always accepted this as a fact of nature when I was a child, but I thought that at some point, when I was older, we would get beyond this and be able to communicate as people. I thought my parents would treat me the way they treated other people and I would do the same.

But the play argues that this is difficult, if not impossible. When the heroine returns to see her father, even though she is a grown woman and is quite prepared to tell him where to get off, or that she cares for him, or both, it does not really happen. He is still the parent and she is still the child and the relationship is always going to get in the way....

It is ironic that we, and other families, linked to each other by common blood, history and love, should have such difficulty achieving something as basic as equality.

> Alan Stewart, *"A Look at Family Affairs,"* in The Globe and Mail, *Toronto, October 27, 1984.*

An Excerpt from *Doc*

BOB: I need to do more, I need to ... I need ...

CATHERINE: Why don't you just do what you want?

BOB: Sometimes I want to scream. I just want to stand there and scream, to hit something, to reach out and smash things—and hit and smash and hit and smash and . . . and then . . . I would feel very tired and I could lie down and sleep.

OSCAR: Do you want to sleep now?

BOB: No. I'm not tired now. I want a drink now. Want a drink, and then we'll . . . what will we do?

CATHERINE: Why couldn't you leave.

BOB: Leave?

CATHERINE: Just leave!

BOB: Katie and Robbie.

CATHERINE: Did you care about them?

BOB: And your father?

(*Shift. EV enters, carrying a bag. He is isolated on stage*)

EV: We had the worst goddamn polio epidemic this province has seen, eleven years ago. We had an outbreak this year. You are lookin' at the attendin' physician at the present Polio Clinic—it is a building that has been condemned by the Provincial Fire Marshall, it has been condemned by the Provincial Health Officer, it has been condemned by the Victoria Public Hospital, it's infested by cockroaches, it's overrun by rats, it's the worst goddamn public building in this province! When is the government gonna stop building liquor stores and give the doctors of this province a chance to save a few fuckin' lives!

BOB: Haven't you got enough?

EV: Enough what?

BOB: Enough! Enough everything!

EV: You're drunk.

BOB: You'll never get enough, will you?

RICHARD PAUL KNOWLES

[*Knowles is a Canadian critic and professor of English and drama. In the following excerpt, he praises* Doc *as both excellent drama and moving autobiography.*]

Sharon Pollock is one of only a handful of playwrights in Canada who have put together a solid and developing body of work over a number of active years in the theatre, and of that handful she is one of the best.

Pollock's career is unusual among writers, however, in that her earliest plays deal in an essentially detached, dialectical way with social injustice in Canada's past, after which her settings gradually approach the present and her subject matter becomes increasingly personal. In most of her work, however, from her exposures of Canadian hypocrisy and racism in her early history plays, *Walsh* and *The Komagata Maru Incident,* through her historical family dramas, *Generations* and *Blood Relations,* Sharon Pollock has worked on the assumption, stated in the Preface to *The Komagata Maru Incident,* that "until we recognize our past, we cannot change our future." *Doc* is no exception. It is her most personal play to date, a moving, deeply absorbing and undisguised confrontation of the playwright with her own past, and it succeeds brilliantly because of an unusual combination of great technical skill with genuine depth of feeling. . . .

Metadramatic or self-reflective elements have always been central to the work of Sharon Pollock, and increasingly so in recent years, as the playwright concerns herself with acting and acting out, in life and art, as ways of dealing with the past in the present. In *Doc* the device is integrated with rare naturalness into the dramatic action, as the present tense visit of Catherine, the mature writer, is delicately blended with the life of her younger self, Katie, Pollock reveals herself to be a confident dramatist, wonderfully adept at shifting time frames between past and present, particularly between Catherine and Katie, who are played by different actors and who appear onstage together. This allows, for example, Catherine to talk across the years to her parents, who respond as though it had been Katie speaking; seconds later Catherine is probing causes further back in time, or talking with her father in the present. The trick could be precious or confusing in the hands of a lesser playwright; here it carries conviction, and the circular structure, beginning and ending with Catherine's first return home to visit her father, serves not merely as a framing device, but as a measure of the distance that the characters have come, of the change that the acting out, the re-viewing, has registered and affected. The final burning of an unopened letter from Catherine's grandmother, suspected of committing suicide, conveys a sense of exorcism for the characters that the play itself provides for the audience and, one feels certain, for the playwright as well. The experience of the play becomes a record of its composition.

Richard Paul Knowles, "Sharon Pollock: Personal Frictions," in Atlantic Provinces Book Review, *Vol. 14, No. 1, February-March, 1987, p. 19.*

MARC CÔTÉ

Some playwrights read well, others don't, independent of their production potential. All plays must finally be tested on the stage: it is there that their strengths and weaknesses become most evident. Yet Sharon Pollock's *Doc* . . . reads extraordinarily well as a script, a book, a work of literature. (p. 17)

One of the main concerns of [Pollock's] plays has been the attempt to demonstrate the unveiling of truth, both personal and historical. Nowhere is this more evident than in *Blood Relations* (the nagging refrain from it jumping to mind: "Did you do it, Lizzie? Did you do it?"), where Pollock explored the form of the play, the idea of theatre, as she explored the question of Lizzie Borden's murder of her parents. Pollock sacrifices neither content nor form in an attempt to be "original"; her characters and her writing are always interesting and important.

Tensions and conflicts abound in *Doc*. The eldest daughter of a worshipped small-town doctor, Catherine returns home because her father has had a severe heart attack. Using memory as a guide, Pollock has father and daughter confronting their mutual and separate pasts. The play does not have flashbacks, as flashbacks have come to be used: the action jumps from father's memory to daughter's memory. The time sequences are hard to follow, as the two characters grapple with ghosts from their pasts—the father holding the letter that either blames him or absolves him of his mother's death, the daughter facing the memory of her mother's slow decline into alcoholism and, finally her death. As Catherine's mother (Bob) and her courtesy uncle (Oscar) and her younger self (Katie) arise in her memory or the memory of her father, they appear on stage.

The lack of linear time structure is possibly one of the play's greatest strengths. The time shifts, as Pollock indicates in her directions, from the present of Catherine's necessary visit to the past of her father's hopes of becoming a doctor, to the past of the marital troubles that her father's obsessive dedication to his practice causes, to the past of his mother's death, his wife's breakdowns, and the loss of his daughter who, in the end, confesses to her father that she is just like him: she's got to win. The scenes flow one into the other and clearly comment on what has gone before and what is to come after. Catherine, as a mature and successful writer, is able to see herself as the young and confused Katie; she becomes able to see, if not understand, the conditions that led Katie to become Catherine. She is also forced to relive her mother's death, which, as the play unfolds, reveals itself to have been similar in many ways to the death of her grandmother, for which her father is partially held emotionally responsible.

No one in this play is happy, nor is the subject matter uplifting. But Pollock manages to avoid the general feeling of perpetual malaise that has become a trap of Canadian drama; she also avoids condescending to her characters. The people in *Doc* are neither enviable nor pitiable. They are entirely believable and, because of this, easy to empathize with.

Doc has its dramatic predecessor in Ibsen's *Ghosts*. This is not to say that Pollock is derivative of Ibsen but rather to point out the strengths of her work. As time is manipulated in *Doc* the parallels drawn are sharp and clear: there's no guesswork as to what Pollock might be saying. Artistically as only a playwright can, Pollock is speaking directly to her audience. If Ibsen had been able to manipulate time as well and efficiently as Pollock does, *Ghosts* would not be the difficult play it is. (pp. 17-18)

Marc Côté, *"Remembrance of Things Past,"* in Books in Canada, *Vol. 16, No. 2, March, 1987, pp. 17-18.*

CINDY COWAN

[*Cowan, a Canadian dramatist and critic, is the author of the play* A Woman from the Sea *(1986). In the following excerpt, she praises* Doc *for its insightful exploration of family discord and its experiments with theatrical form.*]

Doc is a powerful observation regarding the nature of the family and its role in determining our personal identities. What makes *Doc* even more effective is Pollock's ability to court danger, both personally with her play's subject (which is autobiographical) and, more importantly, with her continued use of innovative theatricality—specifically the bending of time and space, a technique nascent in another of her plays, ***Blood Relations***.

It could be said that *Doc* is a play about the structure of family relationships whose reality lies in awarenesses and patterns of feelings. Its stylized structure is both accessible and extremely satisfying, confirming the notion that we do not perceive our world in a linear, chronological order. Nor does this "unconscious and intuitive patterning of the past" (to quote Pollock's notes) detract from the simplicity of the story of Catherine, a woman in her mid-30s who returns to her childhood home after an absence of 20 years. Her father, Ev—the Doc—still lives there alone. In the course of their visit, Ev and Catherine confront their painful memories of her mother Bob's hopeless decline into alcoholism, leading to her "accidental" death.

Ev's recent heart attack gives impetus to the reunion and underscores their mutual need to answer the question posed by Catherine: "What about Mummy?"

On her return Catherine finds her father contemplating an unopened letter left by *his* mother the night she was "accidentally" hit by a train. Although it is presumed by most of the family that the letter will reveal why Gramma killed herself, it has remained unopened for nearly 30 years. True of most family life, secrets and little white lies are an important dynamic in *Doc*. Catherine's presence acts as catalyst for the shadows and impressions lingering in the house to take the forms of Ev's best friend Uncle Oscar, Katie (the childhood Catherine), and Bob. The action of *Doc* then proceeds through the sometimes shared, sometimes individual memories of Ev and Catherine's interactions with these figures from the past. Pollock allows Catherine the freedom to speak across time and to interact with her childhood self to create some of the play's most sensitive and sophisticated insights into childhood insecurities and fears.

Pollock uses the stage direction "shift" to indicate the changes in Ev's and Catherine's patterning of the past. The shifts are immediate, sometimes three to a page, more often non-linear and sometimes explosive in nature. At other times Pollock accomplishes the magical and subtle change in perspective that is created by the slight twist of a child's kaleidoscope. The play demands that the actors work with a collective sensibility. By this I mean Pollock creates the impression that the story is being told from a shared collective experience. This group dynamic is highly appropriate to a play which deals with the politics of the family and the inherent conflicts as its members struggle for independence.

Much has been written about women's position in the family. Engels, in his *The Origin of the Family, Private Property and the State* (1984), said that the family "is the cellular form of civilized society in which the nature of opposition and the contradictions fully active in that society can already be studied." *Doc* is a disturbing representation of the "cellular form of civilized society" where women pay the price of their identity, tranquillity, and sanity when forced to fit the 50s mold of what a wife's role should be. We are seeing, in disturbing frequency, feminist ideals pitted against family fundamentalists. *Doc* reminds us that there are women like Bob who feel isolated and shunted to the periphery of society when given no option but to remain at home.

Bob's family has geared her to succeed, encouraging her to be not only the first member of her family to finish high school but also to go on into nursing. That she does so is indicative of her own determination and the willingness of her mother to scrub floors to provide the funds for her education. Naturally, Bob wishes to continue nursing after marriage and childbirth. Ev, however, does not want her working in the hospital, even though she is "fast and good," or even in a more benign role as an office nurse. Pollock presents Ev's reasons bluntly and without any sense of wrong: "You're not Eloise Roberts, you're not Bob anymore." Bob asks "Who am I?" "My wife," Ev replies.

Bob lapses into a life of the IODE, bridge and "leisure activity." Her earlier independence, her fire and spirit inherited from the "red Roberts," is reduced to interviewing prospective maids through an alcoholic haze. Catherine voices our frustration with her mother's impotence and demands of her, "Why couldn't you leave? Why don't you just do what you want?"

Bob has no answer, only a vague recollection of responsibility to Ev and her children. But like Catherine we cannot understand why Bob has allowed her relationship with her children to be secondary to her relationship to her husband. I suggest that this is not because she believes that "love will conquer all" but rather because she is seeking power where power may be had—with men.

Ultimately, Pollock does not provide satisfactory indications of why Bob doesn't rebel. We perceive her as self-centred, and sympathize with Ev's predicament, even though he too has neglected his family, giving his practice priority in terms of time, energy, and even loyalty. And even if Ev is a "son of a bitch," it is hard to ignore the truth of his profound sense of social responsibility: "There's so goddamn much misery—should I have tended my own little plot when I looked around and there was so much to do—so much I could do—I did do! Was I wrong to do that?"

Doc could be read as simply the story of a woman's self-inflicted victimization as a result of her inability to grasp what she wants in life. It might also at times confirm the idea that only the fittest and strongest in society should survive. However Pollock lifts *Doc* above this fairly superficial interpretation, compassionately and skillfully layering in her thematic concerns regarding the nature of guilt and forgiveness within the realm of the family, where we might find guidance for living with dignity and equality.

At the conclusion of *Doc,* Ev tells Catherine to burn the "goddamn" letter from Gramma. In doing so Catherine finds not only personal freedom in the knowledge that although "named after Gramma, I'm not like my Gramma . . . I know when trains are coming . . . and when they're coming, I don't go that way then." She also finds the freedom of forgiveness. The burning of the letter symbolizes Ev and Catherine's forgiveness of themselves and each other for their roles in Bob's death. Both recognize that the family exacts a price. Some pay gladly, others begrudge it all their lives. The price of making peace with our pasts must be made, however, for only the family can make sense of growing old, and only the family can give shape and coherence to the lives once shared by Gramma, Uncle Oscar, Katie, Bob, Ev, and Catherine. (pp. 95-6)

Cindy Cowan, in a review of "Doc," in Canadian Theatre Review, *No. 52, Fall, 1987, pp. 95-6.*

JERRY WASSERMAN

Sharon Pollock's *Doc,* winner of the Governor-General's Award, might be seen as a sequel to nearly all her work in the theatre so far. Perhaps more accurately it's her *ur*-play, the archetypal drama Pollock has played out in many different forms over the course of her stage career. Since the early 1970s she has been writing about the victims of patriarchal systems that institutionalize injustice, with her focus split between those on the receiving end and those who do the system's will, the latter often inadvertent victims themselves. In *Walsh, The Komagata Maru Incident,* and *One Tiger to a Hill* the contexts were historical and the perpetrators merely bureaucratic functionaries, instruments of a sinister, anonymous force vaguely understood to be The Government. With *Blood Relations* Pollock moved outside Canada and inside the family structure, but the basic shape of the play remained the same with a couple of key exceptions: the victim is not destroyed, and the source of patriarchal injustice is not government. It is society itself whose biases the oppressive father, Mr Borden, assumes and enacts.

Lizzie of course saves herself by murdering her father and stepmother. But the play remains profoundly ambivalent towards the father; Lizzie even goes so far as to claim love as her motive in killing him.

With *Doc* Pollock goes straight to the psychobiographical source of these earlier plays. More than loosely based on her own family history, *Doc* explores the relationship between Ev, a crusty, highly respected Fredericton physician, and his estranged daughter Catherine, a writer. Pollock constructs the play as a memory piece and psychodrama. In the present, a middle-aged Catherine has come to visit her elderly father after hearing that he's had a heart attack. As they talk, the play moves back and forth in time, concerning itself mostly with the rapid decline of Bob, Ev's wife and Catherine's mother, who died an alcoholic and probably a suicide. Ev is very much himself in both past and present, unchanged except physically, and completely unregenerate. Catherine, however, is Katie in the memory sequences, played by a much younger actress. Her two selves can speak with each other across time and Catherine can do the same with the others as well. (pp. 67-8)

Ev is in some ways a monster, and one strand of the play involves Catherine's leading her father back through the family's history in order essentially to confront him with the incontrovertible evidence of his guilt. Her revulsion over his behaviour appears at first to be the reason why she left home shortly after her mother's death and has rarely seen Ev since. But another part of Catherine, the Katie in her, has always blamed *herself* for her mother's death and identified with the father, both secretly despising Bob for her weakness. So the play is as much about Catherine's attempts to come to terms with her own guilt and achieve some measure of personal reintegration as it is about the clash and potential reconciliation between father and daughter.

From this perspective *Doc* is reminiscent of Michel Tremblay's *Forever Yours, Marie Lou,* in which two sisters with opposing points of view struggle to free themselves from the stranglehold of their dead parents, and his recently translated *Albertine, in Five Times,* which portrays one woman at five different ages speaking to herself across time. (Is there some significance in the fact that Canada's two finest living playwrights should be writing such similar plays?) But again *Blood Relations* really provides the best gloss on *Doc*. There too Pollock divides her female protagonist into two separate characters sliding back and forth through time to try to understand a family tragedy. Lizzie is the prototype for all three of the women in *Doc*, anticipating Katie's deep-rooted insecurity owing to the death of her natural mother, Bob's suicidal tendency and many of her frustrations at living under the restrictive rule of the patriarch, and Catherine's love/hate relationship with the father. *Doc* is the more mature and compassionate play, though, and not just because the playwright-*cum*-daughter, instead of killing her father, accepts, forgives, and in effect celebrates him.

Ev is one of those men who are difficult to like but impossible not to admire. He is tremendously self-assured, strong, stubborn, and impatient, with tunnel vision and the force of will to ensure that whatever he wants done gets done. Like that other larger-than-life Canadian doctor, Norman Bethune, Ev has a fierce sense of social justice and infinite concern for the suffering of the poor and helpless. And he scorns the proprieties:

> I don't care about this hospital thing . . . I cared about those little kids! I looked into their faces, and I saw my own face when I was a kid . . . So goddamn much

misery—should I have tended my own little plot when I looked round and there was so damn much to do— so much I could do—I did do! Goddamn it, I did it! You tell me, was I wrong to do that ! . . . I had to rely on my self cause there was fuckin' little else to rely on, I made decisions when decisions had to be made, I chose a road, and I took it, and I never looked back.

But the cost of that commitment is enormous, and his family has to bear it all. While Ev is out saving the world, little Katie has to try to save her desperate mother, hiding Bob's bottles away and screaming at her to stop drinking while a horrified Catherine looks on from the future. Even worse than Ev's *laissez-faire* neglect is his active diminishment of his wife's humanity, not only preventing her from working but ordering for her what Oscar insists is an unnecessary hysterectomy that leaves Bob feeling neutered, 'fixed like the goddamn cat or the dog.'

The play proceeds like an extended trial with Bob, the victim, by turns eloquent and pathetic, providing most of the evidence for the prosecution while witnesses Katie and Oscar testify for both prosecution and defense. Catherine must be the judge. Bob's death is indeed a crime, but every time the finger of guilt points at Ev, Catherine finds herself looking into an accusing mirror which reflects her own image back at her. She is too deeply implicated to pass easy judgment on her father.

Doc never shrinks from showing us the crimes people may commit in the name of love, self-preservation or a higher good. Nor does it suggest that such crimes are forgivable. But it argues, as Pollock's plays have always done, that motives are never simple and innocence is always relative. Virtually jettisoning plot for the first time in her career, the better to follow the rhythms of intuition and the unconscious, Pollock takes Catherine on a journey that ends with her able to smile at her father and forgive herself for being human. This is Pollock's most emotionally complex and structurally sure-handed work yet. She is at the very top of her game here, and *Doc* is to my mind clearly the play of the year. (pp. 68-9)

Jerry Wasserman, in a review of ''Doc,'' in University of Toronto Quarterly, *Vol. LVII, No. 1, Fall, 1987, pp. 67-9.*

(Edward) Reynolds Price
Kate Vaiden

The National Book Critics Circle Award: Fiction

American novelist, short story writer, poet, dramatist, and essayist.

Kate Vaiden (1986) is a romantic yet realistic evocation of life in rural North Carolina. Like such earlier works by Price as his highly acclaimed first novel, *A Long and Happy Life* (1962), *Kate Vaiden* won praise for its portrait of life in the modern rural South, replete with expertly rendered dialect and regional atmosphere. Critics observe that while Price consistently chooses a narrow setting for his work, they commend his ability to evoke deep spiritual and mythic subtexts in his tales. Price claims that his native North Carolina, where he continues to reside, is "a fertile environment" for fiction. This region, he explained, "is where ninety-five percent of my emotional intensity has been grounded. My early childhood familial experiences have occurred here. It's the most repeated cliché of writers that you're given your basic questions as a human being, the stuff you're obsessed by in your work, before you're pubescent. I happened to be here. Also," he added, "from my point of view, I'm the world's authority on this place. It's the place about which I have perfect pitch. I can't strike a false note when I'm writing about this part of the world."

Kate Vaiden is set in rural North Carolina during the period between the Great Depression and the mid-1980s. Departing from his usual third-person narration, Price employs the viewpoint of an extraordinary fifty-seven-year-old heroine who relates her experiences as an orphaned child, a teenaged mother who regretfully abandoned her illegitimate son, and a wandering free spirit who avoids permanent relationships. "A large part of the novel came from a curiosity about my own mother's life," commented Price. "I wanted to discover more about her, not through research but through fiction, and relate to her generation. I felt that most of my knowledge about her was buried inside me. That is why she became the central figure in a long narrative." While Kate is not meant to be a faithful biographical portrait of Elizabeth Rodwell Price, the author's mother, there are similarities between the two women. Both were orphaned at an early age, both were vibrant personalities, and each was uniquely independent. "Kate was a gypsy who went on the road," Price explained. "I strongly suspect my mother of spiritually being an outlaw, but she never ran away." By writing the novel from Kate's point of view, Price sought to challenge what he perceives as a feminist bias against male writers who try to depict female experience.

Kate Vaiden represents a personal as well as a professional triumph for Price. In the midst of writing the novel, he learned that he had spinal cancer. "I never dreamt I would finish *Kate Vaiden*," the author remarked. The illness eventually left him confined to a wheelchair, but Price reported that he convinced himself to continue his work. He produced a number of works while undergoing cancer therapy, including poetry, plays, nonfiction, and the rest of *Kate Vaiden*, as well as a seventh novel,

© *Jerry Bauer*

Good Hearts (1988), which is a sequel to his earliest work, *A Long and Happy Life*.

According to critics, Price succeeded in his aim of creating a convincing female protagonist in *Kate Vaiden*. Kate impressed reviewers as an engaging, lively narrator who speaks the authentic dialect of rural North Carolina. Price won further praise for his fluid, lyrical use of language and his picaresque narrative, which in its episodic structure resembles Daniel Defoe's *The Fortunes and Misfortunes of the Famous Moll Flanders*. Price's writings have often been called artificial or too heavily mannered, especially in their use of metaphor. Some reviewers cite certain portions of *Kate Vaiden* as melodramatic, and others contend that some of the secondary characters are not believable. Nevertheless, most agree that Kate's story itself is both entertaining and moving. According to several critics, Price's finest achievement in this novel is demonstrated in the fact that an unconventional protagonist violates conventional norms by rejecting the roles of mother and wife yet she is still capable of winning the sympathy and affection of readers.

(See also *CLC*, Vols. 3, 6, 13, 43; *Contemporary Authors*, Vols. 1-4, rev. ed.; *Contemporary Authors New Revision Series*, Vol. 1; and *Dictionary of Literary Biography*, Vol. 2.)

ROSELLEN BROWN

"I'd caused their deaths." Every writer who has produced a large body of work has themes that play as relentlessly as a ground bass beneath the changing melody of plot and character; every book could yield up a single sentence from the center of the author's obsession. Reynolds Price has shaped many of his novels around the lives of children whose mothers have died giving birth to them, or whose conception is in some other way clouded—children, that is, who feel or are treated as if they are guilty from their first breath.

Kate Vaiden, which teems with orphans and murderous and suicidal generations—all the expected passions of a Price book— is nonetheless different from the North Carolina novelist's other work. It is a forgiving, immensely readable story, set mainly in the early 1940's, almost light in feeling (although its tale of early death and frustrated passions is hardly frivolous). But the voice of Mr. Price's heroine blows like fresh air across the page. *Kate Vaiden* even *looks* different from its eloquent but frequently ponderous predecessors, typographically dense from margin to margin.

Only a few of Mr. Price's stories have been told in the first person, notably the richly textured title story of *The Names and Faces of Heroes*. Therefore the full weight of narrative authority has often borne down heavily on his prose; the ominous burden of his concerns shows in the seemingly endless recurrence of certain favorite words: loss, waste, blame, guilt, choice. Lives are unequivocally "stopped" or "saved," characters "know" in an instant whom to trust or flee, and they follow those intuitions more loyally than reason can guarantee. But this time we hear a brand-new narrative voice trying those words, that of Kate Vaiden herself, and she is a candid but rarely portentous guide through the secrets and imperatives of her life. Kate, like most of Mr. Price's creations, has to struggle under a doom not of her making, but she describes and then contrives a hedged escape from it with wit and resolution. She is feisty and full of self-knowledge, "a real middle-sized white woman that has kept on going with strong eyes and teeth for fifty-seven years. You can touch me; I answer." Already the rhythm of the prose promises an author in uncharacteristically good spirits, more exuberant than solemn.

Kate tells us before the first two pages are finished that she abruptly abandoned a baby 40 years ago "while he was down for a nap," and that when she was a child her father killed her mother and then himself. This puts us instantly in Reynolds Price country, but Kate, unlike the characters whose cursed lives not only haunt future generations but even at times carry over from book to book, has clearly, after all this time, made a kind of peace with these events. Her story, told in patient retrospect, puts us in the midst of death, shock upon shock, but the very fact that she is recollecting in relative tranquillity separates *Kate Vaiden* from the minute-by-minute discoveries, the constructions of Oedipal angst, of *The Surface of Earth, The Source of Light* or *Love and Work*.

Having had an invulnerably happy early childhood, Kate remembers her young parents as attractive, fiercely devoted, her mother depressive, her father jealous of what he takes to be his wife's special relationship to her family; Kate's mother, for her part, had been abandoned by a mother who succumbed to the dangers of childbirth (which endlessly shadow Mr. Price's pages). Kate recalls the mysterious circumstances in which her father, Dan, shot his wife, Frances, and then himself, and her own safekeeping by her aunt and uncle. At the age of 11 she seems less scarred by their deaths than one might expect—less

than might even be realistic—but the lesson that passion is profoundly dangerous and that she herself might be the unwitting carrier of some of that danger is waiting, like a cancer, to assert itself when she is older and ready for commitment.

Thinking of lovers as well as family, Kate too comes round in time to the old ground bass: *"I'd caused their deaths."* Abandoned in a flash of gunfire by father and mother and in an equally inexplicable flash of a different kind of gunfire by her sweet early love, she takes to a life of desperate lurches and disappearances. After the age of 16, the most predictable behavior Kate can manage seems to be unplanned periodic flight and reappearance on the doorstep of anyone who promises comfort, then flight again whenever the threat of permanence begins to suffocate her like a Southern summer day. (She does linger long enough to conceive a child by an enigmatic lover with a parentless background to match her own.) She is "led or carried," as she puts it, apparently active in her choices but actually passive in muddled self-defense against being unvalued, unloved: 40 years later she wonders if she was "carried by anything but my selfish hope and steady fear—*Leave people before they can plan to leave you.*"

Thus the old curse of family recurs, and the understandable suspicion that she is tainted: she is, she fears, "a thing people took up and then put down," and her response is to blow across her own life and the lives of others like a leaf, searching for permanence but fleeing when it threatens. (pp. 1, 40)

Gritty and sure of herself at an early age, still she is deeply, invisibly damaged. She and the orphaned father of her son are similar, for example: "Not good enough magnets to hold even *parents.*" Given her conviction that she spreads contagion, Kate's desire to be needed—"used," she says, as a necessity, not as a mere opportunity for warmth, sexual or otherwise— does not seem to express quite seriously enough, uniquely enough, the real terror at her core that prevents her from settling into satisfaction. This would be a believable quest for most women, to be loved for who they are. But Kate's history, she assures us, and shows us the scars to prove it, has separated her from the ordinary: she does not sound like a woman eager to be recognized, for what she *is* is dangerous.

One of the beguiling things about *Kate Vaiden*, though, is that Mr. Price allows some real ambiguity into Kate's story. Of all the unthinkable actions for a woman whose life has been formed and deformed by her parents' sudden disappearance, Kate walks out on her own child, Lee, presumably because she believes he will have a better chance to grow up healthy in the care of someone less suspect than she. But of course the paradox— and are we to judge her for it?—is that she must perpetuate the curse of abandonment in order to save him. Is that, we are allowed to wonder, her real intention or is she merely self-serving? (p. 40)

There are moments when it feels as if we are seeing the ultimate wages of Kate's neglect, her incapacity to commit herself to anyone, adult or child; and other times when the author's mind seems to have wandered from his central preoccupation and to have let Kate off her own psychological hook rather casually. Mr. Price's characters have always been obsessives, and Kate until that point has been no exception. Her behavior is that of a woman possessed by her own history and capable of making searching comments about it. So it seems alternately a relief from an epic self-absorption and a too easy resolution to have her walk out on her own child and then wonder about him precious little through the next four decades. Her delayed search for him is like an undone duty, undertaken only when the shadow of death has fallen across her. Thus the ending, not so much happy as unburdened by regret, feels borrowed from someone else's book. Mr. Price is more convincing at retribution.

But until those final somewhat facile pages, Kate is superbly in control of her own tale. The informality of her voice, with its Southern storyteller's love of vivid metaphor, takes precedence over the depressing facts she has to relate, and her tendency toward conciseness and irreverence let her render the tragic with the poise of distance. Just before she tells us about her father's awful departure from her life she says: "Why did I think I was part of a thing that weighed enough in his mind and heart to gentle him now? All my life I've run like a shot dog to similar conclusions. I live on hope the way most humans do on air and coffee. He did have the finest neck on earth, and it was the last I saw of him alive till more red dust roared up and took him."

This tone gives Kate one thing that has often been conspicuously absent from Mr. Price's novels: a particularized personality (not to mention a sense of humor). Rosacoke Mustian and Wesley Beavers in his first published novel, *A Long and Happy Life,* have their idiosyncrasies, viewed affectionately through a distancing lens. They are country people and their dignity, a matter of innate but surprising superiority over their surroundings, gives them the charm of the exotic, a carefully observed specificity. The father in *The Names and Faces of Heroes,* apparently modeled closely on Mr. Price's own, also possesses a uniquely inflected personality. But a great many of Mr. Price's other characters, though their creator is hugely articulate on their behalf, often seem to sink under the weight of their blood-soaked histories and passions. The more resonant the prose, the more an abstract quality prevails, in which their generic relation to each other—*son, wife, mother*—keeps them from full individuality.

But *Kate Vaiden*, intense and powerful though it is, is never so absorbed in the elevation of circumstance to myth that it becomes unsympathetic. Kate herself gives us a language in which to feel a recognizable life move forward. Mr. Price's successful creation of a female voice may be a tour de force, but it never feels like a showy ventriloquial act. Instead, Kate is a wholly convincing girl and a not improbable woman, her growing up before and during World War II informed by a mass of unselfconscious detail, and the town of Macon made visible under dust and midday quiet. (The only implausibility enters when the author continues the habit of his other novels and overgenerously makes some of the speech and all the written communications of his characters oddly similar in style and eloquent beyond any English teacher's proudest dreams. He also tends to idealize his black characters, who seem to borrow their wisdom from Faulkner—they are clever, earthy and bold.)

I can think of no novelist whose effect on readers is more polarizing than Reynolds Price; his work seems to some darkly poetic, a welcome alternative to the flat, cool, uncompelling shaggy dog stories of "minimalist" fiction, and to others pompous and inflated, a fierce agon composed of shards of memoir obsessively reordered. *Kate Vaiden* should please readers of both persuasions. Mr. Price has found a narrator of great charm whose sad story, from which she manages to set herself free, sounds (as Kate might say) new as morning. (pp. 40-1)

Rosellen Brown, "Travels with a Dangerous Woman," in The New York Times Book Review, *June 29, 1986, pp. 1, 40-1.*

GEORGE CORE

[*Core, an American editor and professor of literature, has edited the* Sewanee Review, *a literary quarterly, since 1973. He is the author of* The Literalists of the Imagination: Southern New Critics and the Profession of Letters *(1974) and coauthor with Walter Sullivan of* Writing from the Inside *(1983). In the following excerpt, Core applauds* Kate Vaiden *as a stylistically fresh and engrossing novel.*]

Kate Vaiden is Reynolds Price's latest novel in a long line of good books that began with *A Long and Happy Life* (1962). This beautifully written and skillfully narrated work bears many earmarks of Price's fiction at its best—and of American fiction, with or without a southern accent, at its best.

In the simplest and most obvious sense *Kate Vaiden* presents the story of a life that, as the protagonist tells us in her very first sentence, is unbelievable. The novel records Kate's first 57 years, up to 1984, and focuses on her life as it unfolds between 1938 and 1948. The action vividly registers southern manners and mores during the Depression, World War II and the war's aftermath. Its principal events occur in piedmont North Carolina, particularly in Greensboro, Raleigh, and in Price's hometown, Macon.

In certain ways *Kate Vaiden* is a mystery in which the reason for the deaths of Kate's parents—her mother's murder by her father, who then killed himself—is not disclosed until the end. The novel is also a version of picaresque in which our "heroine" reveals herself as a modern-day Moll Flanders, a woman possessed of and by a restlessness of mind and spirit that make her unable to give herself wholly to anyone, or to anything, including her only child. The action entails not only Kate's growing up and her drive for independence but her quest for identity and selfhood, and from this standpoint her story constitutes an old-fashioned novel of initiation.

Some readers may grow exasperated with Kate, for she often behaves whimsically as well as willfully. She deserts her adoptive parents, an aunt and uncle who are devoted to her, to join a cousin (their estranged son), and she then abandons the lover who has impregnated her as they are traveling to Raleigh to marry and make a new start. Indeed Kate's life is replete with desertion and betrayals, all of her making. *"Leave people before they can plan to leave you,"* she thinks to herself.

Kate Vaiden is more nearly a character out of ballad and romance than one who can be explained by psychological realism, even though she is hard-headed and unsentimental. The deeper psychology of the novel reveals the compulsive temperaments of orphans and calls into question some matters involving the women's revolution, as Price has said elsewhere.

More readers will be so carried along by the force of her personality and will so relish the power of her language and the quaintness of her tale as to forget the conventions of realistic fiction.

The language is lively and pointed. Kate uses fresh homely phrases—"cold as scissors," "pretty as baby teeth," "hot as the doorknobs of Hell," "welcome as a dogwood bud"; but her knack for metaphor is even stronger when she indulges it at length: "Catholics were scarce as tigers in the South then—strange as Eskimoes and far more subject to wild suspicions." "I felt like a rattler that had missed her target," "If she'd moulted peacock feathers . . . , it couldn't have shocked me more." Often her metaphors point to theme: during World War

II, she says, romance "came at us stronger than any white drug, and seemed free (or cheap) and endless as water."

Kate Vaiden, a novel for all seasons, will stand as one of this season's best. It is especially memorable for its precise social notation, its exact idiom, its wide range of character, and its flowing narrative. (pp. 1, 14)

> George Core, "*Reynolds Price's Ballad of the South,*"
> in Book World—The Washington Post, *July 6, 1986,*
> *pp. 1, 14.*

An excerpt from *Kate Vaiden*

Maybe it was lonesomeness, the reason I failed. I didn't have anybody my age near me. I'd got used to fun at Walter's and Tim's. Most of all though—and worst of all—I'd started to worry that no man would want me, no decent man with a regular job. A teenaged mother with a needy bastard-baby and no big skills, no big nest egg or moviestar looks. From my room in Macon, it looked like a long one-lane road ahead with a boy to raise, like a cast-iron sidecar hitched to my bike. Holt and Caroline were in their early sixties. They couldn't last forever and anyhow I couldn't ask them to support us once I was on my feet. Walter was nowhere I meant to revisit permanently. I'd walked out on Tim. Also I was hungry, not for food or love.

There's no true way for me to say it—what I felt as that hard winter came down. With Gaston and Douglas I'd used my body more ways than any white girl my age I'd read about or known. And for all the harm I'd caused the world, nothing convinced me my body was wrong and ought to be curbed. It was all I absolutely knew I had; everything else in sight could vanish—parents, kin, love—and in my case already had, more than once. My own strong head and limbs had lasted and kept me happy maybe half the time (a more-than-fair average). I couldn't just maim that much of myself by bolting doors on the wide green world and camping-down forever in a house with no man near me under sixty years old.

So on December 21st I wrote to Douglas Lee. I told him the child was born and strong and was named for him. I said I was sorry I'd left the train with no explanation, that I'd been confused. I said I bore him no grudge whatever and didn't want money; but if he was curious to see me or Lee, I'd meet him anywhere in reason. I'd planned to ask Noony to mail the letter.

But once it was sealed, I had the courage to walk downtown on my own—first time since the baby. I was almost there before I thought "Somebody will say something spiteful to me." But I forged on anyway and nobody did. Miss Lula Harris, when I bought my stamp, said "Noony keeps me posted; that boy sounds *pretty*. Bring him down here to see me." I almost fainted but told her I would, the first warm day.

It stayed cold through the whole next week. And Christmas was calmer than I'd ever known it. Christmas Eve we sat up late to hear the last news on the radio. The Allies had rallied in the Battle of the Bulge, and it looked again like we might beat the Germans (people now forget that was ever in question). Then we dressed the little fat cedar-tree Holt had brought in; and I laid out Lee's first

Santa Claus presents—dresses, caps, and a Dopey-doll from Disney's *Snow White*. Caroline brought in hot spiced tea. Before we drank it, I made a short speech. I begged their pardon for what I'd caused and thanked their patience and their generous hearts.

Caroline smiled. "It has been a year."

Holt said "If soldier boys stand it, so can we."

Then we went to bed. But I lay wide awake for hours longer, thinking of last year's Christmas Eve (my vision in the fire with Walter and Douglas) and hunting the cold black dark of my room for any new sight or sign of guidance. I might as well have been Helen Keller in a barrel. So I told God in that case I couldn't be responsible for my next mistakes—not all of them anyhow, being so hungry. Then I slept till dawn.

ROBERT TOWERS

[*Towers, an American novelist, critic, and professor of English literature, is the author of novels including* The Necklace of Kali *(1960) and* The Monkey Watcher *(1964). In the following excerpt, he comments on Price's treatment of his female narrator-protagonist, whom Towers compares with Daniel Defoe's Moll Flanders.*]

Kate Vaiden is Reynolds Price's sixth novel, and it has already renewed interest in a writer whose career had a strong beginning (*A Long and Happy Life, A Generous Man*) but then seemed to sag under the weight of several honorable, talkative, but less than gripping novels. As Price informs us in a prepublication note from his publisher, he has identified two sources from which his new work arose. One was the need to write a story that would have a direct relationship—"at whatever imaginative distance"—to his own curiosities about the past of his dead mother, who had been orphaned at an early age. The other was a wish to confront the tyrannical dictum of feminists "that members of a gender may not function with any security outside that gender's narrow mental and physical confines—a man cannot 'understand' a woman and vice versa."

The impact of early orphanage is indeed central to Kate Vaiden's story, which otherwise, Price informs us, bears slight resemblance to the events of his mother's life. Moreover, the telling of it in the first person involves for Price (who has always been a special pleader, so to speak, for the women in his fiction) a sustained feat of female impersonation that goes beyond mimicry to a sympathetic identification with every inflection of his heroine's highly distinctive voice and every twist and turn of her erratic course. The effect of this impersonation is engaging in the liveliness of the narration and incident.

The time of the novel is from the late 1920s to the present, when Kate, "a real middle-sized white woman that has kept on going with strong eyes and teeth for fifty-seven years," sets out to write her improbable history; the setting is north-central North Carolina—both town and country—with an extended interlude in Norfolk, Virginia, during the Second World War. (p. 55)

Kate Vaiden is crowded with events, and the narration of them speeds up as the novel progresses. Price in fact telescopes . . . forty years of Kate's life into approximately fifty pages, leading us to the point where she sets out to write her history.

In the background of *Kate Vaiden* there lurks another book—equally packed with events—that preceded it by more than two and a half centuries. At a crucial moment in Kate's story, Price contrives to have a spinster librarian hand the girl a copy of the first major narrative in English written by a man fictionally impersonating a woman:

> I turned to leave and there was Miss Mabel, bearing down on me fast with a big green book.
>
> She held it out in both hands. "You've never had this" (she always spoke of *having* a book). Her eyes were bright as icepicks.
>
> I took it—*Moll Flanders* by Daniel Defoe. . . . I said "No ma'm" and checked it out to please her. It was still by my bed unopened when I left. Not till twenty years later did I find another copy, and by then it was too late to ask Miss Mabel if she'd offered me consolation or a warning that hot clear day.

No other reference is made to *Moll Flanders* and this one is easy to overlook. Once alerted, however, a reader familiar with Defoe's novel can find suggestive parallels between Kate's story and that of the early-orphaned, much-married woman living by her wits in early eighteenth-century England. Like Moll, Kate is resourceful, resilient, and brave. They are both ready at fateful moments to cut loose, to cut losses, to move on. Although both form attachments easily, they seem equally unburdened by grief or guilt when the time comes to abandon them. There are similarities, too, in the episodic structure of the two books and even in the plot: the reader may remember that Defoe's novel, like Price's, ends with the reunion (anticipated in Kate's case) of an errant mother and her long-lost (and now successful) son—and in Tidewater Virginia to boot!

Too much emphasis should not be placed on this literary precedent. *Kate Vaiden* is very much Price's original creation. In one respect, however, his novel is at a disadvantage not shared by Defoe's. In *Moll Flanders* the heroine's lack of inwardness and psychological complexity hardly matters to us, any more than it presumably did to Defoe's contemporary readers. But in our more psychologically aware age, we are bound to perceive the discrepancy between the sharp intelligence and generosity of feeling with which Price has endowed Kate on the one hand and the blindness, even heartlessness, of her behavior on the other. Despite its semipicaresque qualities, *Kate Vaiden* exists essentially within the conventions of psychological realism, and Price has simply not made it credible that Kate—unfit though she may be for motherhood—would allow four decades to pass without even seeking news of her son or concerning herself in the least with the welfare and ultimate death of the good people who had raised her and later raised him. Such a woman might well exist, but Price does not persuade us that that woman is Kate.

It becomes clear eventually that Price is, through Kate, making a point about the psychology of orphans—*"Leave people before they can plan to leave you,"* Kate says to herself at a critical juncture. But her moments of insight, which mostly concern her conviction that she is being "led" by God or by some sure instinct of self-preservation, are insufficiently convincing, and her moments of remorse for the human wreckage in her wake are stillborn. The problem may be that Price's identification with Kate's voice and personality is too close to allow for the greater objectivity in characterization that another approach would encourage. But I doubt that many readers would wish the voice—and point of view—to be other than what they are.

It is a testimony to the energy and charm of Price's style that we do not pause long over the improbabilities of the novel (among them the everlasting saintliness of Aunt Caroline and her son Walter) and a tendency to sentimentalize some of the minor characters. The language that Price has found for his narrator is vivacious, regionally colloquial, and playfully metaphorical without falling into the sourthern trap of excessive cuteness—a pitfall that Price in his other work has not always been able to sidestep. The pace of the novel is exhilarating. In the headlong rush of Kate's story, people (an old-maid schoolteacher, a blind piano tuner and his hill-country aunt, Gaston Stegall's heartbroken father) and short scenes flash by, brought into vivid, momentary existence by Kate's eye for unexpected detail and her ear for the true oddities of speech. Alternately touched, amused, or bemused, one finishes *Kate Vaiden* with a sense of its amplitude—and of having been entertained at a consistently high level. (pp. 55-6)

> Robert Towers, "Ways Down South," in The New York Review of Books, Vol. XXXIII, No. 14, September 25, 1986, pp. 55-7.

ROBERT WILSON

In his first novel, *A Long and Happy Life,* which appeared in 1962, Reynolds Price presented a plucky country girl from North Carolina named Rosacoke Mustian. Her kindness, her innocence, her humor, and, yes, her pluck were noted and even celebrated, and she took her place among those other colorful, naive characters from farther south already familiar in the stories of Faulkner, Eudora Welty, and Flannery O'Connor. Like those masters, Price had chosen a narrow rural setting in which to work out his broad themes, and he had endowed his semiliterate characters with wonderful verbal wit and energy, making them both lovable and faintly ludicrous.

His reputation since his first book has followed that of Southern writing in general, which fell out of fashion in the '70s, sometime after Welty's *Losing Battles* (1970), and began to be fashionable again at about the time of John Kennedy Toole's *A Confederacy of Dunces* (1980). Price's novels *A Generous Man* (1966) (in which a younger Rosacoke figures) and *Love and Work* (1968) were well received, but *The Surface of Earth* (1975) and *The Source of Light* (1981) were not. His new novel, *Kate Vaiden,* appears at a time when almost everything Southern, from the sublime Peter Taylor to the ridiculous T. R. Pearson, finds an audience, and Price has been widely, and justly, praised.

In *Kate Vaiden,* Price has invented another extraordinary female character from North Carolina, a country woman who tells the unhappy story of her youth in a voice that is distinct and mesmeric. Kate's speech, which is almost exhaustingly rich in perfect homely metaphors, is both a tour de force and the high point in Price's evolving literary style. At its low point—in *The Surface of Earth*—his writing could be ponderously individual, tending at times toward the mannerism and tortured syntax of bad verse. In this book, Kate's cool self-knowledge and gentle self-deprecation have disarmed Price of his worst rhetorical flourishes, and his prose is both rich and precise.

The narrative concentrates on Kate's first 18 years, recounted at age 57. The gap of nearly four decades between the time her story ends and the time she tells it allows her to remember the painful events of her youth with equanimity and even with humor. It saves the book from melodrama, although the plot is swollen with illness and illicit love, unwanted pregnancy and unexpected death. . . .

Now, in late middle-age, and recently diagnosed as having cervical cancer, she wants to know her son, who is a grown man. Her story will be her introduction to him. Perhaps by telling him the worst about herself she will earn his absolution.

This most difficult question in Kate's confession—why she abandoned her child—also presents the greatest difficulty for the novelist, who must make understandable behavior the world considers abnormal. As Kate puts it, ''I'd shown most other human instincts till then. Why did mothering fail me?'' The novel is structured to solve that problem of her personality, describing all the other attachments and detachments of her youth. (p. 40)

Gaston is the first person whom she allows herself to love after the death of her parents, and he dies in boot camp at Parris Island toward the end of World War II. (''Don't let any human being ever tell you that a female child, just turned sixteen, can't hurt as hard and deep at a crossroads in eastern Carolina as a one-eyed leper in the dust of Judah. She can; I did.'') She never loves Douglas, but he is the father of her child, and his end is even grimmer than Gaston's. As she suggests, she has been abandoned as often as she has done the abandoning. That's one part of her puzzle. Another is her frank pleasure in her sexuality, which would be enviable in either sex even in these enlightened times; imagine it in a country girl coming of age during World War II. It is plausible here, with the help of Price's discreet and tender renderings of her sexual adventures.

Price's writing has always demonstrated a respect for the strength and mystery of women, and a profound interest in their cares. Both Rosacoke and Kate get pregnant as girls, putting themselves at the mercy of the boys who can make them respectable by marrying them. Rosacoke is the more innocent of the two, and her story ends happily. Kate's problems are much more her own doing, yet it is true for her, too, that her sex, as well as her sexuality, has helped to create her fate. Musing on why she never married in the years after she left her son, Kate thinks, ''Fathers can walk out on whole nests of children every day of the year and never return, never send back a dime— that's considered sad but natural. But an outlaw mother is the black last nightmare any man can face.''

Price evokes the same deep sympathy for both of his young women. But Kate has suffered and overcome more, in the world and in herself, and has had half a lifetime to ponder its meaning. She knows herself as few people do, and that self-knowledge distinguishes her from Rosacoke and the whole clan of inspired Southern primitives. The novel does not record the reaction of Kate's son to her story, but she has achieved something better than the approval of her child, or of anyone else. (p. 42)

Robert Wilson, ''Confessions of a Country Girl,'' in The New Republic, Vol. 195, No. 13, September 29, 1986, pp. 40, 42.

JONATHAN KEATES

[Keates is an English travel writer, short story writer, critic, and biographer. Among his works are several travel books, such as Companion Guide to the Shakespeare Country (1983); a short story collection, Allegro Postillions (1983); and the biography Handel: The Man and His Music (1985). In the following excerpt, Keates praises the unpretentious, memorable quality of Price's novel.]

The evident model in **Kate Vaiden** is Moll Flanders: both women in telling their own stories show the same kind of clumsy capacity for endurance, a talent for muddling through which the reader is invited simultaneously to admire and to question. Reynolds Price, no less than Defoe, perpetually eggs on our compassion and then jerks us back towards confronting and adjudicating between the range of moral ambiguities presented to the heroine.

Within the story the surrounding universe is similarly censorious and indulgent. Kate's is that strikingly dusty, laconic, elemental world of the American South, classically described by Faulkner and Flannery O'Connor. Her sins—forsaking her bastard son and setting off across Carolina on an inglorious progress marked by half truths and broken promises—are substantially excused by the bitterness of a loveless childhood and the smothering of early attachments in death.

Reynolds Price ought to be as well known and admired among us as Updike or Bellow. That he isn't may have something to do with the gentleness and detachment of his authorial voice, all the more remarkable at a time when so much American writing strains after nudging sophistication or strident jocularity. Having always been quietly expert at saying neither more nor less than what he means, he has no difficulty in projecting, through the limited expressive resources at his heroine's disposal, a memorably consistent portrayal of a woman for whom autobiography is the ultimate atonement.

Jonathan Keates, ''Southern Discomfort,'' in The Observer, February 22, 1987, p. 29.

Al(fred Wellington) Purdy
The Collected Poems of Al Purdy

Governor General's Literary Award: Poetry

Canadian poet, editor, dramatist, critic, essayist, short story writer, and scriptwriter.

Purdy has earned a reputation as one of Canada's finest and most popular contemporary poets. *The Collected Poems of Al Purdy* (1986) is his second volume to win a Governor General's Award; his first was *The Cariboo Horses* (1965). Sometimes elegaic, often humorous, his poems reflect the rural Ontario milieu where he has spent most of his life. Conveyed in an unaffected colloquial voice with humor and vigor, Purdy's poems typically begin with descriptions of day-to-day life then move to lyrical themes of transitoriness and transcendence. Purdy is also acknowledged as an important influence on younger Canadian poets both for his own achievements, particularly that of effecting a native idiom, and for his encouragement of others in his role as editor and teacher.

As a poet, Purdy was virtually self-taught. Unlike other prominent Canadian writers such as Margaret Atwood and Irving Layton, Purdy never earned a college degree. He left school at the age of sixteen and held numerous jobs while pursuing his literary interests. Purdy patterned his early poetry after Rudyard Kipling, G. K. Chesterton, Bliss Carman, and other traditional poets. Commentators regard most of the poems from this early period as apprentice work. During the early 1950s, Purdy began reading such modernist poets as W. H. Auden, Dylan Thomas, and Layton and started experimenting with open forms. By the time *The Crafte So Longe to Lerne* (1959) appeared, Purdy had begun to develop a less formal, more personal style. Purdy himself considers *Poems for All the Annettes* (1962) to be his first fully mature work. He was in his mid-forties when his seventh poetry collection, *The Cariboo Horses,* established his reputation as a major author; thereafter, Purdy was able to earn his living as a writer and lecturer.

For his *Collected Poems,* Purdy chose only those works that he felt merited preservation; these include several uncollected poems as well as poems from twenty-one of his previously published volumes, arranged according to the decade in which they were composed. Only one selection in the *Collected Poems,* "Rattlesnake," was written before 1955. More generously represented are his breakthrough works from the 1960s, such as *The Cariboo Horses* and *Wild Grape Wine* (1968), as well as those he produced in the 1970s and 1980s, including *Sex and Death* (1973), *Being Alive* (1978), *The Stone Bird* (1981), and *Piling Blood* (1984).

Purdy's verse is informed by a strong sense of geographical location. Many of his poems are set in the area near Roblin Lake, Ameliasburg, Ontario, where he has lived for many years. This awareness of his physical surroundings also characterizes the poems that recount his extensive travels in other parts of Canada and in foreign countries, such as "Arctic Rhododendrons" and "Remembering Hiroshima." Critics observe that there is a rough, unfinished quality to much of Purdy's work. Although his poems are deliberately structured, Purdy's

Courtesy of the Harbourfront Corporation Reading Series

relaxed colloquial voice is capable of a wide range of expression. In such poems as "When I Sat Down to Play the Piano" and "Home-Made Beer," he demonstrates a self-deprecatory, earthy sense of humor. While "Love at Roblin Lake" evidences a similar comic sensibility, it also expresses a more serious yearning for mystical transcendence. In "Love at Roblin Lake" and "Archeology of Snow," this spiritual longing is related through sexual imagery. Purdy also evokes a form of transcendence by relating events of the past to the present, creating a feeling of historical continuity. In the poems "The Country North of Belleville" and "The Cariboo Horses" he alludes to the geographical, natural, and social history of rural Canada, connecting it to the present day. Mingled with the recurring themes of past and present is that of mortality, which, reviewers note, has become more pronounced in his later poetry. While Purdy's newest poems show less of his exuberant humor, they convey more powerfully the transcendent emotions common in his work.

In reviews of *Collected Poems,* critics reaffirmed Purdy's status as one of Canada's most important poets. Although much of the commentary focuses on earlier, established poems, reviewers also commend Purdy's later work. According to critic George Galt, *The Collected Poems of Al Purdy* "is a rare accomplishment, because Purdy's poetry is unique, but also because few poets approaching old age exhibit his fresh imagination and still expanding insights."

(See also *CLC*, Vols. 3, 6, 14 and *Contemporary Authors*, Vols. 81-84.)

AL PURDY

To all the many thousands of poets who have been who are now (and those who will be), poets bad, good, or indifferent—I'm grateful. The same bug that bit those others also took a chunk out of me, infecting all of us with this habit, craft, art, or whatever it is. As a result, I've experienced tremendous feelings of euphoria when writing what I've thought was a good poem. Even at the worst of times, writing poems has been joyous and rewarding. (p. xv)

Inner recesses of the mind are not at your beck and call. Perhaps there are small elves in the head, privileged guests living there and continually busy with their own affairs. The only connection the conscious mind has with them is when they permit a collaboration, which perhaps neither the conscious nor the unconscious was capable of alone. (p. xvi)

You watch them, those little elves who are your guests. You try to familiarize yourself with their habits, and how your own actions will affect them, how your own thoughts might meld with theirs. You say of them: they prefer strange things, they like high drama and soul-stirring events—then find that something quite trivial means more to them than wars and headlines. You try to predict their thoughts during the sun by day and the moon by night, then discover they have their own internal moons and suns.

Their appearance I can only imagine, but I believe they love to dress in odd costumes; I think they look at themselves in a mirror sometimes and admire what they see. Of course, they are very old. I think it's probable that they have been around since human time began and even before that. I'm sure they were hiding somewhere in the heads of those small shrew-like mammals who preceded humans.

For all my efforts, midnight searchings and dawn questions, I know little more about them than when I first decided they actually existed. And it's only when I forget about them entirely that they gently intrude into my thoughts. Gently, but with something sardonic about their attitude to this human with the ludicrous pretensions in whose head they reside.

A "collected poems" is either a gravestone or a testimonial to survival. When you remember all the early deaths among writers, survival can be considered a little out of the ordinary. And, if considered only as a metaphor for gravestone and the end of a writer's life, a "collected poems" will be seen to have just enough validity to make it meaningless.

[*The Collected Poems of Al Purdy*] does not contain every poem I've ever written. However, it does contain the ones I like best. Some of my stuff is simply too awful to include and there seemed no great urgency about other omitted poems.

As a writer, I've always felt like an eternal amateur. Even after writing poems all my life, I'm never entirely confident that the next poem will find its way into being. And then I find myself writing one, without knowing exactly how I got there.

In my lifetime, there have been many other writers whose work I've admired and absorbed. They are constantly nudging me somewhere in my unconscious mind. If I had to name two of the most important influences, D. H. Lawrence and Irving Layton would qualify. As examples, not tutors. And perhaps Milton Acorn gets in there somewhere as well; I learned from him both how to write and how not to write. (Very few people can teach you opposite things at the same time.) I think I've learned from everyone I've read, on some level, though I've digested their writing in ways that make it impossible for me to recognize it in my own work. All of us who write are indebted to everyone else who writes for our enthusiasms and craft (or sullen art).

I have enjoyed being alive and writing a great deal, being ashamed and prideful, making mistakes and stumbling on answers before I knew the questions existed. In a world so abundant with both good and bad things, in which my own unique lighted space of human consciousness burns and flickers, at this moment when the past and future converge to pinpoint now, at an age when the body says, "Slow down, you silly bugger," there are still important things in my life, and still poems I want to write. (pp. xvii-xviii)

> *Al Purdy, "To See the Shore: A Preface," in his* The Collected Poems of Al Purdy, *edited by Russell Brown, McClelland and Stewart, 1986, pp. xv-xviii.*

DENNIS LEE

[*Lee is a Canadian poet, editor, critic, author of children's books, and lyricist. He was a cofounder of the House of Anansi Press and a founding member of Rochdale College, an experimental institute in Toronto. His poetry collections include* Kingdom of Absence *(1967),* Civil Elegies *(1968), which won a Governor General's Award, and* The Gods *(1979). Among his critical works are* Savage Fields: An Essay in Cosmology and Literature *(1977) and* The New Canadian Poets, 1970-1985 *(1985). In the following excerpt from his afterword to* The Collected Poems of Al Purdy, *Lee traces Purdy's development as a poet, expounding on the polyphonic, transcendent qualities of his mature style and affirming his contribution to Canada's national literary identity.*]

In 1944, at a cost of $200, Al Purdy engaged a Vancouver printer to bring out five hundred copies of **The Enchanted Echo**, his first book of verse. The twenty-six-year-old author was less of an ethereal sprite than the title might imply, being lanky and raw-boned in appearance, shambling and somewhat ornery in manner. He hailed from Loyalist country in southeastern Ontario, the region of small towns and rolling farmland north of Lake Ontario (where his forebears had settled in the 1780s). He'd been born there in 1918; his father, a farmer, died two years later. The son grew up in the town of Trenton, in the care of his rigidly religious mother, and left school without completing Grade 10. After drifting through occasional jobs in the area he had joined the air force in 1940, and was now stationed in British Columbia for the duration of the war.

A less likely bard-in-the-making would be hard to imagine. And the fact is, Purdy would turn out to be among the slowest developers in the history of poetry. To trace the process by which he became one of the fine poets in the language is an intriguing experience; for decades his progress consisted of false starts and apparently unproductive slogging. Only in retrospect can we discern the sureness of instinct and the tenacity of purpose which were propelling him.

Purdy had been writing verse since the age of thirteen—but in complete isolation from other poets, and from the central developments of twentieth-century poetry. The writers he knew were Kipling and Chesterton and Turner, Carman and Roberts and Pratt. And the poetry he wrote till he was past thirty is exemplified by the title piece from his book:

> I saw the milkweed float away,
> To curtsy, climb and hover,
> And seek among the crowded hills
> Another warmer lover.
>
> Across the autumn flushing streams,
> Adown the misty valleys,
> Atop the skyline's sharp redoubts
> Aswarm with colored alleys—
>
> I caught an echo in my hands,
> With pollen mixed for leaven—
>
> I gave it half my song to hold,
> And sent it back to heaven.
>
> Now oft, anon, as in a dream,
> O'er sculptured heights ascending,
> I hear a song—my song, but now,
> It has another ending.

With no other models to learn from, this is where Purdy began: in a minor, dated, and artificial tradition. Why he didn't heed the advice he must have had in abundance—to find a job with a future, and stick to writing as a hobby—is beyond ordinary comprehension.

After the war Purdy found himself in Vancouver once more, where he worked in a mattress factory from 1950 to 1955. Then it was back east to Montreal for two years, to the fertile and combative milieu that included Irving Layton, Louis Dudek, and Milton Acorn—Purdy by now having resolved to make himself into a great poet. In 1957 he and his wife built a small house on Roblin Lake, in Prince Edward County (the peninsula jutting into Lake Ontario south of Trenton and Belleville). And there, with no cash, they settled in: Eurithe to earn their keep, he to write—albeit with an acute sense that he had made nothing of his life so far, that perhaps he was a permanent failure.

In 1960, to pause here at Roblin Lake, Purdy was forty-two. He was reading omnivorously, and since 1955 he had published three chapbooks. He'd outgrown *The Enchanted Echo.* But he still had not produced more than a handful of poems worth preserving.

Some of the reason for his slowness must lie in the inscrutable private rhythms of any writer's development. But from the vantage of twenty-five years later, it is hard to resist the conclusion that he was trying, however obscurely, to reinvent modern poetry on his own terms.

About 1952, he had been goaded by a friend into reading the literary classics, particularly the moderns. The effect was drastic. Consciously or not, he had to accept the fact that the whole formal tradition was bankrupt, at least as far as his own imagination was concerned. Rhyme, metrical rhythm, fixed stanza-forms, and the stock Poetical attitudes that Purdy had been parading—these were drawn from a poetic universe in which the rough-hewn autodidact from Trenton could never be at

home, would never be more than a cramped and nervous outsider. If he wanted to be his own large clumsy aching generous eloquent awe-stricken self in words, he would have to throw over the whole of traditional poetry, start somehow back at square one. In his mid-thirties, he would have to begin his apprenticeship.

And at this point, a stubborn independence had taken hold. He would not simply become a disciple of one of the "modernist" masters—of Pound, Eliot, the later Yeats, Williams; nor would he settle for keeps into one of the newer schools, represented by poets like Auden or Thomas. For better or worse, he would negotiate an independent passage—from the weird time-warp of (say) 1910, which he'd been inhabiting, to his own here and now. But doing that on his own terms was to be a painfully slow process.

He might gain momentum from other poets, of course. In the mid-fifties, he wrote like Dylan Thomas for a spell. And around 1958, trying out Layton's verbal flamboyance and self-assertive stance brought a new muscularity to Purdy's work. It could sound like this (in **"Olympic Room [Toronto Hotel]"**):

> They sit on stools like barbaric models
> With Alexandrian pride: young whores
> Requiring observance of male ritual—
> Implicit in the stance of these brown girls. . . .
> I observe their usefulness with joy
> (On the census rolls a puzzling status);
> I peripheral and unemployed,
> Themselves integral with human sadness.

But this was more compacted and stiff-jointed than what he was reaching for; soon he was pressing ahead on his own again. What he needed was a way of writing that fitted him like a skin, that let him enact *his* way of inhabiting the world, in its native inflections. What his hands could touch, what his own nerve-ends knew—these would be the final test of words.

A clear symptom of the transition he was negotiating is the lively but exasperating **"Gilgamesh and Friend,"** from the same 1959 chapbook. By now Purdy has started to loosen up, to flex his muscles for real. And the play of energy in the speaker's consciousness *is* the pent-up something which had been trying, all along, to find its way into his poetry. Letting it invade the very process of composition, so that the poet simultaneously sketches his subject (like a given musical theme) and embroiders it with fancy honks and playful suppositions (like a series of improvised variations)—this was the crucial next step Purdy had to take. . . . Except it wasn't working yet. The set stanza-form just gets in the way, a residue of alien convention. And the ostensible subject, Gilgamesh and friend, disappears under the avalanche of wise-cracks.

By 1960, dug in at Roblin Lake, Purdy was finally in motion. Though it wasn't yet clear that he was going anywhere of poetic interest.

What happened during the next two years was an abrupt quantum-leap, of the sort that defies explanation whenever it occurs. In his collection of 1962, *Poems for All the Annettes,* there are still misfires. But in the best poems, the mature Purdy simply vaults free of three decades of dead-end and marking time, in a riot of exuberant, full-throated energy.

The closed forms of the past are sponged open with a vengeance, releasing a headlong, sometimes dizzying cascade—as in **"Archaeology of Snow."** The line-breaks and phrasing now seem configured by an ongoing play of unpredictable energy, rather than being poured into a pre-existing mould.

(Once having discovered this degree of freedom, Purdy would subsequently settle into a more restrained use of multiple margins and spray-gun layout. But claiming such an extreme plasticity in the way a poem could fall on the page seems to have been a necessary part of the breakthrough to his own voice.)

And the *pace* of a poem is now something Purdy can control. Notice how certain line-breaks occur after a word like "and" or "the" (dragging the reader on to the next line, to complete the unit of thought), while others coincide with a natural pause (recreating the breathers the imagination takes, as it finds its way ahead). A canny modulation between these two kinds of line-break was another sign of his maturation of craft—as in these lines from **"Sons and Lovers"**:

galaxies

We'll lounge dance cavort and leap- frog touch

the cold quaquaversal

commonalty of light

whose source died long before the

first futile egg of the dinosaurs

went bad and

hover enough distance out in space

from the Andromeda Nebula

to wait and watch

in the dark

for violet light to vault from

planet to planet and

keep going

The poem has become an act of discovery, rather than a list of things discovered. It's full of particulars. And it is fluid, constantly in process; often the lid is not quite banged shut at the end. Now, he can catch a wide range of tonalities: from the new, headlong tumble to a delicate equipoise, or the grave, almost liturgical hush to which **"Remains of an Indian Village"** rises.

At forty-four, Purdy had finally come into his own—with all sirens going. The long apprenticeship was over. He had found his way to an open poetry which could be brash, tender, adventurous, self-mocking, sublime; within which he could move in unexpected directions with gusto and abandon.

He had made the same basic journey, from a closed to an open poetic universe, that other major talents have accomplished in this century. But he'd done it in characteristically maverick fashion; he had refused to read Pound and Williams (who would have been natural mentors, on the face of it), and instead made temporary stopovers with Dylan Thomas and Layton (who were not pointing in the directions he would take). He'd found his path, to an unmarked destination, essentially by himself. And by now he had become his own man, a genuine original.

In *The Cariboo Horses,* three years later, Purdy consolidated everything he had learned in the earlier leap, and carried it further. There is now a wonderful sure-footedness in the rangy, loping gait which had become his signature—with its ability to open out into vast perspectives of space and time, then narrow down to focus on a single image or moment. It was with this volume that he reached a wide critical and popular audience, winning the Governor General's Award in 1965. The spate of good and great poems begins, which have taken on normative status in our literature.

One advance Purdy makes here is a new assurance in identifying his subject matter. For years I thought of *Cariboo Horses* as the book in which he claimed his Canadian themes (perhaps because it includes **"The Country North of Belleville,"** one of his first unequivocal masterpieces). And that is accurate enough.

But what's startling, on returning to the book, is to see how high a proportion of Purdy's home-ground it claims. Here are the portraits; the vignettes; the early memories; poems of place; jokey breakneck yarns; on-the-spot reportage; har-de-har asides; delicate evocations of love and the natural world; broad satire; distant times and places; sex and death and poetry, the galaxy and Roblin Lake. It's a kaleidoscope! Even where Purdy would do greater justice to a particular type of poem in later books, *Cariboo Horses* established much of the imaginative landscape, and many of the basic models of what a poem could accomplish, that have informed his work since.

With the appearance of *Cariboo Horses,* in Purdy's forty-seventh year, this story of late-blooming, interminable, and heroic apprenticeship comes to an end. We need a different approach than the chronological to take the measure of the next two decades.

Surveying Purdy's mature poetry as a single body of work, stretching from 1965 to the present, reveals some large, recurring features. We'll pursue two of them here; the first one involves the unique vision of *process* which informs much of the poetry. (It will be useful to flesh out the meaning of "process" as we proceed.)

It's conceivable that growing up in Loyalist country (albeit with no great family stress on tradition) contributed to Purdy's sense of organic continuity in time. Certainly he has written often and well about the persistence of the past in the present, in that milieu. In the two poems entitled **"Roblin's Mills,"** for example, he concentrates so hard on the nineteenth-century inhabitants of his town that he is granted contact with their lives, and communes with their "departures and morning rumours / gestures and almost touchings." And though they must subside again into the past, their continuity can now be gravely affirmed: "they had their being once / and left a place to stand on."

Even when the legacy of the past is indecipherable, that very message of obliterated purpose tells Purdy something about his roots. In **"The Country North of Belleville"** he meditates on inscrutable stone-piles and fences that no longer enclose anything, their farms abandoned. And the choric lament rises in him, "This is the country of our defeat." Both the strength and the failures of the past continue in time.

For Purdy, time is a continuum that permits a commerce of dead with living, of living with dead—rather than being, say, a wasteland or an executioner. That is why his sense of time passing is bittersweet rather than merely bitter.

On the one hand, he must lament what perishes. In **"Elegy for a Grandfather,"** for example, he expands on the old man's death to mourn for everything that dies, in the great passage beginning, "And earth takes him as it takes more beautiful things." Yet on the other hand he can remark (in **"Temporizing in the Eternal City"**) on how "the past turned inside out / protrudes slightly into the present." Looking at the sculpture of Beatrice, he observes "something crouching there / joining the cadences of eternity." Continuity in time may not remove the scandal of transience and death. But it qualifies them in an important, nourishing way.

There are also poems in which the sense of continuity goes beyond the normal processes of time altogether. These are poems of ecstasy; they intuit an eternal *now* in which every moment of past, present, and future participates, in some unfathomable way surviving its own disappearance. This is the moment adumbrated by **"Winter Walking,"** in which "all the heavy people, / clouds and tangible buildings, / enter and pass thru me." (An early wrestle with the meaning of the experience can be found in **"Method for Calling Up Ghosts."**)

This intuition cannot be translated into conventional thought, of course. And Purdy is so suspicious of mystification of any kind that he mostly backs away from pronouncements on the subject, sometimes from doing anything more than pointing to it cryptically. Nonetheless, glimpses of an eternal *now* occur frequently in Purdy, as we shall see. So far, Purdy could simply be seen as having a Burkean sense of the partnership of human beings across time—which indeed he does. But to stop there would be to miss everything weird, wonderful, and distinct in his vision of space/time as a process.

We can glimpse this vision as early as **"Night Song for a Woman"**—perhaps his first fully mature poem, written in 1958. It's a mysterious little piece, truly a "Night Song." Something has happened to Purdy "a few times only, then away"—but what is it? The poem doesn't appear to say, though perhaps "All things enter into me . . ." gestures at an answer. Again, how does Purdy suddenly find himself on this extraordinary jaunt out past Arcturus? And what is it that people would "know about humans" if they listened? Finally, on a very different tack: what enables these disconnected snatches to hang together at all? Palpably they do, in a breathless murmuring which seems suspended in unearthly silence. But what is the source of their coherence?

We won't try to answer those questions yet. But clearly Purdy's universe operates on unfamiliar principles. It is not just that he can suddenly mutate into "a sound / out of hearing past / Arcturus / still moving outward"—but that the phenomenon occurs so abruptly, and is taken so casually for granted. Slipping across the galaxy is apparently as much a matter of course as slipping across the street.

And once we focus on that fact, we realize with a start that the same thing keeps happening—with all sorts of variations—throughout the whole body of Purdy's work. Take a single step in any direction and you're likely to find yourself in the nineteenth century, in long-ago Samarkand, in outer space or the early Cretaceous. The cosmos of Purdy's poetry is one in which familiar laws of movement in both space and time may be suspended without warning, and a different set of principles take over.

In **"Hockey Players,"** a game is suddenly detonated when three players swerve out of quotidian space and into Purdy's alternate cosmos. They end up "skating thru the smoky end boards out / of sight and climbing up the appalachian highlands / and racing breast to breast across laurentian barrens." The experience, of swerving out of the conventional world, and then covering ground so quickly that space collapses into a blur of simultaneity, is pure Purdy.

In **"The Cariboo Horses,"** Purdy watches cowboys riding into 100 Mile House on their "half-tame bronco rebels." He resists the impulse to romanticize the horses; yet even as he does he finds himself carried elsewhere and elsewhen, transfigured in contemplation of "the ghosts of horses battering thru the wind / whose names were the wind's common usage / whose life was the sun's." Only at the end does he return to the dusty scene before him. It's a remarkable affirmation of parallel universes—of a day-to-day world, and of a larger, more luminous one. And in the alternate universe, points far separated in space

and time are virtually simultaneous; we can flash between them in an inkling.

Implicit in the poem is a debate Purdy frequently carries on with himself. Is he merely pasting his fantasies onto a too-too-mundane milieu? Is this just a trick of the mind? Or is there something objective, *given*, in the experience of whirling off to anywhere at all in space/time?

Sometimes Purdy goes all the way over into the alternate cosmos—forgets his misgivings, and affirms flat-out that all time and space *are* simultaneous. Standing **"At the Athenian Market,"** for instance, he moves into a kind of lucid trance in which simultaneity is simply given; now a pile of oranges is "involved with converging lines / of light Phidias the sculptor / laboured over half an / hour ago." And as the sight of "living girls" in the marketplace carries him deeper into trance, he moves to union with "long ago girls"—and then, unexpectedly, further back still, to the first emergence of life from primordial waters, and to the very beginning of evolution, "before these Greek cities / before the sea was named / before us all." Yet in truth Purdy doesn't even seem to be "moving back"; this is a stillness which goes beyond the wild canter of **"The Hockey Players,"** and participates in other points in space/time without stirring an inch.

The poem is characteristic in that it sounds the note of lived, authentic exaltation precisely as it enters the aspect which seems most remote from "real life"—that is, the intuition that all time and space are simultaneous. It's at this juncture that Purdy's poetry regularly takes on the nostril-flare or hush, and the quirky, kindled gait and diction, which make it irreplaceable—and which feel utterly unforced, at home in a mystery they know first-hand and intimately. The intuition feels more real than mundane "reality."

The distant past juts into the immediate present; faraway is near at hand. Space/time is plastic, elastic, fantastic. We don't yet know what that means. But there are examples by the hundred in Purdy's work; start reading with this in mind and they crop up on all sides. The "cosmos of process" is close to being the primary universe of his poetry.

In trying to get perspective on this volatile process, we might examine Purdy's way of focusing the jumps and pans and dissolves which the poems enact.

Sometimes he starts with a local scene, and then whirls away abruptly to a point far removed in space/time. We might call this a technique of "centripetal focus"—of panning or jump-cutting away from here-and-now to there-and-then. And in some of these centripetal poems, he ends on a trajectory that implicitly continues out to infinity—as in **"Night Song for a Woman"** (where the movement is spatial), or **"At the Athenian Market"** (where it's temporal). In other cases, as in **"Cariboo Horses,"** he whirls us out, and out, and then loops us back at the end of the poem to the here-and-now where we began.

On the other hand, there are poems where Purdy works in "centrifugal focus." The initial here-and-now remains the focal point throughout the poem—but it's traversed by energies or temporal perspectives which (commonsense tells us) belong somewhere else in space/time. Thus in **"My '48 Pontiac"** we sit in an automobile graveyard, only to encounter "a doddering chauffeur / who used to play poker with Roman chariot drivers." In **"Spinning,"** the poet turns on his heel quickly enough to meet his grandmother, who died before he was born. In **"Starlings,"** he stands in his yard, contemplating the processes of life and death—and becomes aware of distant space and early evolutionary time impinging; "bacteria glimmer in the stars' experimental / stations." And on and on it goes; if the poet doesn't zoom out to visit the rest of the process, the rest of the process will zoom in to visit him.

I have been speaking of Purdy's alternate cosmos, and referring to it as one of process. So far, the meaning of "process" seems to be mainly that a great deal of high-speed traffic goes on in the space/time continuum.

But there is more to it than that. For it is also characteristic of the process that it is chock-a-block with things which are incommensurable with one another—yet which coexist. Sometimes in discord, at other times flowing into one another. Time and again the poem presents, not a single reality which would enforce a single-keyed response, but that reality and its converse—or (more subtly) two or three further realities which chime off the first, in a discordant but richly complex music of being. That's how the world *is*. Nothing is single; everything skids into the larger process, and by the very act of existing implicates its incommensurable brothers and lovers and foes and a joke and grandparents and death and the dinosaurs, not to mention intergalactic space and a hangover and spring and the first evolving rampant protozoa.

And the world provokes incompatible responses as a matter of daily course—celebration and elegy simultaneously; or a fusion of raucous laughter, grief, and awe of an almost unbearable delicacy. Much of the energy of Purdy's work goes into delivering the Heraclitean flux of this process intact. Our categorizing minds might prefer to keep segments of the world in airtight compartments. But the segments don't cooperate.

A chilling example comes at the end of "**Autumn.**" The piece begins, and for most of its length continues, as a litany of things in their time of decline. But the final stanza erupts in a (centrifugal) vision of three kinds of warring energy. The natural death of the old; crazed new life in the young; and the killers' trade—these are simultaneous.

In poem after poem we get a comparable vision of heterogeneous elements in tension, or harmony, or a funny half-tension/half-harmony. That *is* the mode of coherence of the process. Everything is part of everything else; all meanings are simultaneous, and must be honoured at once.

This brings us to one of the most dazzling aspects of Purdy's writing: his command of *polyphony,* his ability to orchestrate different voices. No reader can get through twenty lines without becoming aware of the constant shifts in levels of diction and pacing and tone, the squawks and blips as Purdy's own consciousness intrudes and recedes, the startling turn-arounds from redneck coarseness to a supple middle style to soaring passages of joy and lamentation. Purdy is one of the living masters of voice.

And at this point, we can discern why "finding his voice" was so difficult, and so crucial. The voice of his poems would have to mime the nature of his subject matter—the process, and himself in it. But the nature of the process is to be protean, chameleonic, constantly swerving and bucking and passing into its own opposite in the blink of an eye. Only when the voice of his poetry became as manifold and self-renewing as the process itself would Purdy be able to write the poems that were beckoning him.

It would be easy enough to present five quotations, or fifty, that speak in different voices. And that would indicate Purdy's

astonishing vocal range. But it would not demonstrate the most important aspect of the matter—which is not simply that he uses many different voices, often in the same poem, but that he's capable of shifting from one to the next in a seamless way, one that mimes a cosmos in which all things flow.

This is not the hard-edge mosaic technique of a Pound, say, where fragment A comes in one voice, fragment B in another, and the two are banged down side by side on the page, with no transition between them. That technique, of juxtaposing voices in a discontinuous mosaic, issues properly from Pound's own vision of things. It has been the main tradition of "polyphony" in this century; it has even been followed by writers who don't share Pound's cosmology, but who lack the stature to find their own distinctive way of writing polyphonically.

Purdy's technique, which lets him modulate seamlessly through a great range of voices, issues from *his* vision of things, from his sense of how the process flows. The polyphonic resources of a poetry like this have not been extensively explored. Yet they are crucial to *hearing* his work, and hence to understanding it.

To observe those resources in operation, we need to examine the vocal trajectory of one poem from start to finish. Let's take a short piece, "**Love at Roblin Lake.**" Exploring it will permit at least a glimpse of the nature of his vocal achievement, and its relation to "process." And it will suggest an approach that helps unlock the riches of other, more major poems.

> My ambition as I remember and
> I always remember was always
> to make love vulgarly and immensely
>   as the vulgar elephant doth
>   & immense reptiles did
> in the open air openly
> sweating and grunting together
> and going
>   "BOING BOING BOING"
>   making
> every lunge a hole in the great dark
> for summer cottagers to fall into at a later date
> and hear inside faintly (like in a football
> stadium when the home team loses)
> ourselves still softly
>   going
>   "*boing boing boing*"
>   as the vulgar elephant doth
>   & immense reptiles did
> in the star-filled places of earth
> that I remember we left behind long ago
> and forgotten everything after
> on our journey into the dark

It may help if we sort out the poem's movement in space/time. Purdy starts by conflating his own lovemaking with that of elephants and "immense reptiles," the latter presumably being the dinosaurs. There is already a fusion of times, though merely because the contemporary lover is wishing himself back to a more primitive past. But starting about line 11, and then much more rapidly in the last four lines, there is an effect like an infinite camera pullback in a movie. Suddenly we see all the traffic of earth—the ambitious lover, the elephants, the long-ago dinosaurs, the planet itself—diminishing to the size of specks, as we unexpectedly pull away from them at accelerating speed. The backwards zoom is taking place in time; we are receding into the evolutionary future, away from the "star-filled places of earth" (a time-layer where humans still coupled with the un-self-conscious instinct of beasts). And the pullback is also taking place in space; we are receding from the little planet earth into the intergalactic dark, where human and pre-human concerns are so far away they seem both infinitely small and infinitely poignant. The sense of bittersweet awe at the end is unnerving, especially since we have swerved such a great distance in so few lines.

This is a poem with centrifugal focus; it whirls away from the initial here-and-now. And it moves out to infinity, rather than looping down again. What's distinctive is that we are looking backwards as we recede from earth, rather than forward to some new point. And the poem makes us simultaneously conscious of the action down on Purdy's little patch of ground, *and* of our vertiginous pullback from it. As much as any poem can be, it's in two places at once.

What gives me the goose-bumps in this little poem has to do, I believe, with the way the process of tonal change enacts the very experience of process which is being described. This is the larger truth about Purdy's poetry that we're after here. He does not simply write *about* the process; he keeps miming it in the very movements of the poem's voice. Let's retrace **"Love at Roblin Lake"** with that in mind. For it is clear that the poem starts in one voice, and ends in another; but Purdy's skill at modulating voices is so great that it's much less clear how we've gotten from the one to the other.

The piece begins with the narrator as a bit of a bumbler, whose voice gets tangled in its own feet right at the outset: "My ambition as I remember and I / always remember was always . . ." The lines take an abrupt little nosedive. The *gros-series* this character is about to deliver about making love "vulgarly and immensely" may give us a yuck or two, may even speak for the sweatily horny strain in us; but given the clumsy, almost coarse tone of his speaking voice, they seem unlikely to rise much above that level. (Few readers will be thinking any of this consciously as they proceed, of course; if the voice works it will simply exert a tactful, pre-conscious pressure *on* our reading, setting the terms in which we experience the poem as a whole.)

The first tonal surprise comes with the archaic "doth," which pops out at the mention of pachyderms and bygone dinosaurs. With that little tonal blip as the giveaway, the speaker now appears as a more sophisticated man: as one who enjoys playing roles, including that of a clod—rather than simply *being* a clod.

The description of rutting, complete with comic-book "BOING BOING BOING," picks up the note of rib-nudging comedy again—only to dissolve into the weird, serpentine, but surprisingly persuasive image of the phallic trench as a hole in the dark which traps summer cottagers who turn out to be ourselves as well, now inside a football stadium and giving muted cheers because the home team is losing. Wherever the poem is going now, it is clearly nowhere we could have predicted at the start (a mere dozen lines ago). But the changing tone of the piece is itself guiding us through this free, uncharted trajectory in poetic space. By now the voice has become plain, yet sinewy and evocative; we have shifted away from the broad, slapdash tonality of the opening, and though it's not at all clear where we're headed, the voice now feels like a trustworthy guide.

Next we discover that we are both inside the stadium, making love and going "*boing,*" and outside it, somewhere in undifferentiated space. And our increasing distance from the stadium action, our accelerating pullback, is mimed as the original "BOING BOING BOING" fades to "*boing boing boing.*" Now the vulgar elephant and the immense reptiles bear a kind

of pathos of distance about them as they echo their earlier appearance. And with the stammer of broken phrases which concludes the poem, we move into an eerie, hedgerow sublime. It may take a few readings before we can analyze where we are, physically or psychically—but at an emotional and imaginative level, the heart-wrenched, awe-struck tone of the ending has already told us:

> going
>   *"boing boing boing"*
>   as the vulgar elephant doth
>   & immense reptiles did
>   in the star-filled places of earth
>   that I remember we left behind long ago
>   and forgotten everything after
>   on our journey into the dark

We are watching the funny, sexy, absurd, and poignant dance of mating performed by one man, by human beings, by all species that have dwelt on earth. We view them both from within the experience and from a remove that is some place like death, or eternity—where laughter, choked-back tears, and a cosmic hush commingle.

And the changing trajectory of voice, together with the sweep of shifting perspectives, helps to define a process in which near and far, present and past, comic and tragic, are somehow simultaneous.

We have a poetry characterized by zoom perspectives on space/time; by the simultanity of things that don't normally jibe; and by constant tonal shifts, which guide us through the process according to Purdy. What do they signal?

Purdy gives us a day-to-day world that is unmistakably the cranky, suffering, shades-of-grey place we inhabit. But at the same time he gives us a recurrent experience, which keeps breaking through in moments of epiphany. It's what theologians call the experience of *mysterium tremendum*—the encounter with holy otherness, to which an appropriate response is awe, joy, terror, gratitude. We have already seen a number of these ecstatic moments, when time seems to lock for the speaker, and the physical world is utterly present and wholly transparent, a window into some ineffable dimension where he is both lost and home. There are many, many more.

For Purdy, *tremendum* is always mediated through things of the world. **"My Grandfather's Country,"** for example, depicts the way it impinges through *place*—through particular landscapes, including this mesmerizing Arctic scene:

> And there are seas in the north so blue
> that a polar bear can climb his own wish and walk the sky
> and wave on wave of that high blue washes over the mind
> and sings to each component part of the hearing blood
> a radiance that burns down the dark buildings of night
> and shines for 24 hours a day of long sea-days

Frequently, as he says in **"The Darkness,"** the experience conveys "some lost kind of coherence / I've never found in people." Thus in **"The Beavers of Renfrew,"** he senses that the beavers still know,

> the secret of staying completely still,
> allowing ourselves to catch up
> with the shadow just ahead of us
> we have lost,
> when the young world was a cloudy room
> drifting thru morning stillness—

And meeting holy otherness in the daily world, he is held by the intuition of an eternal *now*. Everything that has ever meant itself, ever been at all, seems still to live undiminished in that dimension. Hence everything is simultaneous with everything else.

The eternal *now* is not situated by Purdy anywhere specifiable: not in a heaven, nor an afterlife, nor art, nor in his own mind. He has no theories about it; all he can do is recreate its onset on the page, magnificently, as direct experience. Most of the time he scarcely seems to know what to do about its incursions. And the conventional religions which offer a framework for the experience just make him snort. It's a pure, intuited condition which keeps barging into the flux of the quotidian, without altering the mundane terms in which he has to live the rest of his life.

Purdy's poetry recreates the daily world, as it appears in and out of the light of *tremendum*. His life work, in all its variety, makes most sense as a series of responses to that central intuition.

This casts a new light on the distinctive elements of process in Purdy's work. His imagination tugs toward the *tremendum*— where the heterogeneous things of the world exist in coherence. So that is how he records them. It explains the constant zoom perspectives we've noted; to whirl from Roblin Lake to the early life of stone 200 million years ago—that is to mine the eternal *now* to which he's drawn, where all time and space are a dance of simultaneity. And to let the poem's voice ripple through a spectrum of changes—that too is to mime the luminous flow in the *tremendum,* which daily things bespeak in their moments of glory.

That is, the formal jumps and segues in his poems, their insistence on overlaid or clashing realities, their polyphony— these take their deepest origin from the intuition of *mysterium tremendum* in the day-to-day world. Purdy's unique way of moving in a poem, and of orchestrating its elements, derives from his central vision of what the world is like.

Providing the term is kept clear of associations with dogma and churchy attitudes, this vision is properly called "religious." But Purdy still doesn't pretend to know what it *means,* that such an incandescence lurks in the quotidian. The experience is indelible; its meaning is opaque. Questions about God or immortality receive no answer from within the process. The tentative prayer in **"The Darkness"** is about as close as he's let himself come to addressing the "spirit of everyplace / guardian beyond the edge of chaos" as though it could hear him. And it would be the cheapest effrontery on a reader's part to march in and "explain" this impulse in his poetry. Or baptize it. Or even label it possessively. My terms for it, "*tremendum*" and "the intuition of an eternal *now,*" are meant to honour the mystery, not to straitjacket it. And the ecstatic power and incandescent grace which the poetry takes on, as it enters the kinetic stillness, furnish all the validation that I, for one, would ask.

Purdy frets at times that he may be projecting the movements of his own mind onto the world. And it's true; sometimes he does. "Eastbound from Vancouver" strikes me as a willed, slightly frantic exercise of that kind; **"Shoeshine Boys on the Avenida Juarez"** is (among other things) a critique of the tendency. But he also writes from a deeply empathetic imagination, which can tap into some ache and transcendence at the heart of things, and kindle in response. The ecstatic passages of **"My Grandfather's Country," "The Beavers of Renfrew," "Love at Roblin Lake," "Night Song for a Woman"**— these unmistakably touch grace, whatever its name may be.

As do dozens of others. Entering these moments in the poems, we sense a great hush which sustains everything in the world that has moved into them, and renders their all-over-the-map simultaneity and their vocal flow coherent. Such moments don't seem willed by the poet; they seem sponsored by being.

But to end on that lofty note would convey a false impression— not of the vision which animates Purdy's poetry, but of the poems themselves. For one thing, there are some that report anecdotes from a daily world which shows no trace of *tremendum.* (Some of these are vigorous and engaging; others remain pretty prosy and have not been preserved in this volume.) But this is simply to recognize that Purdy spends plenty of time in a humdrum state, like the rest of us.

Of greater interest is the compulsion Purdy feels, to avoid giving even a sublime poem too much polish, too final and finished a surface. There is an offhandedness, even a slapdash quality, which is clearly an intrinsic part of the way he wants a poem to *be* when it is fully achieved. That this is a deliberate policy is evident if we examine his revisions. They can go on for years, decades even, and frequently they polish individual passages to a burnished glow—but often the piece as a whole is left with an in-process, written-while-experienced feel to it; sometimes revision takes it further in that direction. This is an imagination which refuses to be housebroken. And if we approach even a classic Purdy poem too reverently, expecting a rarefied masterpiece, it is likely to light a cigar, tell a bad joke, get up and leave halfway through the conversation. The high style comes and goes as it pleases.

Purdy is not writing out of a lifetime of non-stop illumination. He is a plain man inhabited by towering intuitions, not a beatified mystic. And his loose-jointed, bantery middle style affords a complex artistic leverage. It lets him acknowledge the long, dry stretches between epiphanies—by the very act of including that voice. And it gives him a way of affirming the mundane world without pumping it full of artificial uplift; of honouring his origins, in a way his early verse did not; of keeping his hand in; and of providing a ground-bass, against which the moments of *tremendum* can register more tellingly when they come along. When he does connect with one of the incandescent intuitions, it will enter a poem whose voice can then modulate or erupt—thanks to his immense improvisational talents—into the high style of the epiphany, and thereby re-enact the process it records.

Keeping the poetry loose and informal, till eternity invades and dictates otherwise—this is a form of human and artistic integrity, a way of miming the process without distorting either its mundane or its eternal mode. It accounts for much of the unique temper and form of Purdy's work. The trick for a reader is to find a wave-length that will accommodate, as they occur, both the consciously rough-hewn textures *and* the moments of pure, achieved incandescence. Purdy has in effect redefined "a poem" to mean a piece of writing that plays artfully in the space between those boundaries—never in the same way twice. *That* process is what we're invited to enjoy.

Purdy has entered a "late period" of uncommon stature. And in the poetry of the eighties, there is a greater willingness to speak of first and last things without jokey or belligerent irony, long his defence against sentimentality and pretentiousness. The result has been to further enrich his account of process and *tremendum.*

He's been extending the vistas of the setting in which this one life has been lived. That has meant pushing further back into childhood; further back in the evolutionary history of the planet; further into the being of another species. And he has been returning from those explorations with poems of an extraordinary yet often inscrutable clarity, like music whose harmonics compel us before we can track what they're doing. These communings and quarrels with himself, with the process, and with whatever vouchsafes *tremendum,* are among his finest achievements. And they show no sign of abating.

There would be many other critical approaches that illuminate Purdy's work. We'll take one other here, briefly considering his poetry as a venture in "native speaking."

For half a century, Purdy has been lugging a preoccupation with the spirit of place back and forth across his homeland. The result has been a series of fine poems about locales and events, which assemble into an imaginative map of our place and history—not an exhaustive one, but far more complete than any other Canadian writer's. Without itemizing individual poems, we can say that he has followed the path of first-hand exploration described in **"Transient"**:

> after a while the eyes digest a country and
> the belly perceives a mapmaker's vision
> in dust and dirt on the face and hands . . .
> and the shape of home is under your fingernails
> the borders of yourself grown into certainty

It is a grand gift to the rest of us.

Purdy has "placed" us in subtler ways as well. For one thing, the plethora of imaginative journeys he has taken outward in space/time also coalesce—like the in-Canada trips—into a larger map; this time, an experiential record of what one man has discovered in the universe. (I have in mind his journeys to other times and other species, as much as the literal globe-trotting.) It makes no pretence to being a scholarly world history; the mapmaker's vision is still perceived in the belly and on the nerve-ends. But the vistas of geological time and interstellar space within which Purdy ranges are quite breathtaking. And because everything he encounters can be charged with the *tremendum,* can reveal itself as part of the luminous process of all space/time, his record of "journeys in the universe" stands as a poetic cosmology, an account of meaningful order.

What's notable is that Purdy focuses the whole cosmos from the vantage point of his own home. Sometimes this is explicit; in **"News Report at Ameliasburg,"** he transmits a cacophony of war-reports from global history, then winds down with a report on sunset in his own small village. But with or without the explicit reference point, a Canada-centric relationship of "there" to "here," of "then" to "now," is defined right in the idiom and perspective of the speaker, who is unmistakably a contemporary Canadian by the name of Al Purdy.

And now there is a new thing on earth: a poetic cosmology focused concentrically around Roblin Lake, southeastern Ontario, Canada, North America, planet earth, all space and time. It does not invalidate visions of order centred elsewhere. But here is a muscular, roomy, and persuasive vision of coherence centred in our own here and now. such a thing did not exist before.

To write as a "native speaker" is not just a matter of exploring Canadian places and deeds; nor even just of mapping the world with Canada as imaginative centre. At a still deeper level it is to embody, in words, our historic modes of dwelling here—not by describing them at arm's length, but by enacting them

on the page. And Purdy has articulated our native reflexes and tensions right in the musculature and movement of his poems. To that extent, he has opened imaginative room for us to dwell in.

It would take a whole further essay to explore Purdy's work thoroughly from this perspective. But let me identify some of the native reflexes which inform his work. No one of them is uniquely Canadian, but taken together they have much to do with who we have been here. And never before have we had a body of major poetry which incorporates them so deeply.

The first of these reflexes has to do with the *mysterium tremendum.* Throughout history, various things have served as the vehicle for the encounter with holy otherness: sexual love, battle, religious contemplation, for example. It is central to our history and imagination in this part of the continent that we have approached the *tremendum* through knowing the vast, extreme and eerie land we inhabit. The mystique is strong even among confirmed city-dwellers. And Purdy's poems of the land embody the reflex to a singular degree.

A second native reflex is that of instinctively locating our fragile human settlements, even the big cities, in a surrounding space of almost inconceivable magnitude, and as tenuous moments in a field of time which loops back at once to Stone Age men and out through intergalactic light years. For that *is* the nature of our dwelling here. The land is vast. Much of the literal ground our feet or car-wheels traverse was formed aeons ago. And the time of white settlement is such a thin patina, usually less than 200 years in depth, that once we penetrate even a hair's breadth beneath it we are swept into vast reaches of human and pre-human time. In Purdy, that sense of our dwelling contributes to the deep, frequently joyous reflex of temporal and spatial hop-scotching that we have already observed.

In **"The Runners,"** a speaker declares, "I think the land knows we are here, / I think the land knows we are strangers." That seems to me a paradigm of a third reflex—a deep and positive ambivalence in the Canadian makeup, which resonates across many aspects of our lives. "The land knows we are here." It antedates us, exerts a claim upon us, and somehow makes us welcome if we come to it knowing our place. We are not free simply to master it and remake it according to the dictates of our own wills—as has been a dominant American pattern. We are free to belong to it, gingerly. Yet "the land knows we are strangers." We do not have a history of countless generations here, in which we have domesticated nature and can feel safe in its interpenetration with our civilization—as did our European forbears. Both the speaker's declarations are true to who we are. We exist in a continuing tension, in which we are compelled by both the Old World and the American version of the New—yet neither feels like who we are. It is a destiny of incomplete or multiple answers, of irony, of perpetual lack of full definition. Purdy's poetry, with its grand articulation of being both strange and at home in this place—a sensitive brawler in taverns, a learned rube—embodies that tension in its very fabric.

A fourth reflex has to do with words—and with eloquence, delicacy of feeling, amplitude of spirit. It is central to our social and cultural heritage that these things can be shown, but only if they are masked with defensive irony. And once they *have* been articulated we hear them echoing in a still vaster silence, and subsiding into it very soon again. Purdy's poems enact that reflex, time and again.

In its embodiment of these deep, historical modes of being here, his poetry articulates who we already are—it "places" us in our home space—to an unprecedented degree. We cannot homogenize all Canadians into a single mould, in speaking of this. But whether or not we like all the reflexes which the poems embody, they *are* many of us, and so we can move around in this poetry without having to turn ourselves into denizens of somewhere else, merely to follow its natural lines of movement. At this profound, almost pre-conscious level, Purdy is a supremely accomplished native speaker.

How are we to assess Al Purdy? It seems to me incontrovertible that he is among the finest of living poets, and one of the substantial poets in English of the century. If we have to realign our notions of what great poetry can look like, to accommodate his best work—and it is part of his achievement that we do have to—that is scarcely a novel experience when an original writer of stature comes along.

If we step back several paces, we discover a further perspective from which to situate Purdy, one that sheds a fuller light on his achievement. From the sixteenth century on, the great imperial nations of Europe spread their languages and cultural paradigms around the planet—English, French, Spanish, Portuguese, and to a lesser extent Dutch. And during the twentieth century, after a long colonial period, literature in those languages has become polycentric, as the former colonies have found their own voices—rivalling and in some cases surpassing the old imperial centres. The most impressive contemporary example is that of Spanish and Portuguese writing in Latin America, but the process has been repeated around the globe, in recent decades with gathering potency.

However, it has not simply been a matter of gifted poets and novelists in the ex-colonies picking up their pens and starting to write well in the fashion of their erstwhile mentors. The very language of the metropolitan imagination has had to be unlearned, even as it was being learned from. And a long struggle of independence has been necessary for writers of the hinterlands to imagine their own time and place as what it is, to become articulate as native speakers at all. The titans have been those who first broke through to indigenous articulacy, who subverted and recast the forms of metropolitan imagination so as to utter the truths of the hinterland in native terms. Generally they've done so with a rare fusion of high artistry and folk, even populist imagination. It's clear that Whitman, Melville, Neruda, García Márquez are among the great founders who have claimed a nation's patrimony this way, and in the process recast the whole imaginative vocabulary of their medium. Without pretending to exhaustive knowledge of the subject, I suspect their number also includes Dario, Amado, Guillén, Asturias, Césaire, Miron, Senghor, Rushdie.

In the case of countries colonized by England, the situation is complicated one stage further. American writers made their breakthrough to native speaking very early, in the nineteenth century. In the result American literature went on to such strengths that, by the mid-twentieth century, Anglophone writers elsewhere have had to free themselves from the imaginative hegemony of both Britain and the United States. That said, the challenge of speaking native among English-speaking writers in Africa, India, Canada, Australia, the Caribbean and elsewhere has been fundamentally the same as that faced by a Neruda or a Senghor in *their* situations.

And that situates Al Purdy in a world context. He has been one of the giants of the recurrent process in which, language

by language and country by country over the last sixty years, the hinterlands of empire have broken through to universal resonance by learning to speak local. Purdy has claimed, and in many ways created, an indigenous imaginative patrimony in English Canada. There have been many Canadian writers whose excellence is unmistakable, but in his rootedness, his largeness, and his impulse to forge a native idiom for the imagination, Purdy is one of a distinct breed: the heroic founders, who give their people a voice as they go about their own necessities. . . .

It is a matter of fact that readers abroad have scarcely begun to discover Purdy—or, more accurately, have not yet taken the crucial first step of learning to hear *this* hinterland idiom on its own wave-length, as an instrument capable of genius, at once familiar and foreign. But such tone-deafness in the metropolis is an old story by now; it is the hard luck of London, New York, and elsewhere, which time will rectify.

For those who read Purdy on his own wave-length, meanwhile, his **Collected Poems** is a cornucopia. (pp. 390-91)

> Dennis Lee, "The Poetry of Al Purdy: An Afterword," in The Collected Poems of Al Purdy by Al Purdy, edited by Russell Brown, McClelland and Stewart, 1986, pp. 371-91.

An Excerpt from *The Collected Poems of Al Purdy*

The Horseman of Agawa

(Indian rock-painting under the cliffs of Lake Superior)

It's spring and the steel platforms tourists usually stand on
are not installed yet so we take our chances
but I have to abandon my beer and use both hands for safety
We clamber down rocks unsteady as children
reach slanting stone ledges under the hundred-foot walls
my wife skipping ahead so nimbly I'm jealous of her
and say "Wait for me, dammit" but she won't
then take my shoes off and go barefoot

She sees the painting first and calls "Here!"
her face flattens and dissolves into no expression
I balance myself beside her on the tilted ledge
that slides off into deep water and the rock hurts my feet
but I feel the same way she does as the rock horseman canters
by two feet from my nose forever or nearly
The painted horseman rides over four moons (or suns) on his
   trail
whose meaning must be a four-day journey somewhere
the red iron oxide faded from Lake Superior storms
and maybe two hundred years since the Ojibway artist stood
   there
balanced above water like us
and drew with his fingers on the stone canvas
with fish eggs or bear grease to make the painting permanent
pitting fish eggs and bear grease against eternity
which is kind of ludicrous or kind of beautiful I guess

I have too many thoughts about the horseman
I might select one and say this is a signpost this painting
(in fact I've just done that)
a human-as-having-babies signpost
but also dammit part of the spirit
a thought taken out from inside the head and carefully left here

like saying I love you to stone
I think that after the Ojibway are all dead
and all the bombs in the white world have fizzed into
  harmlessness
the ghost of one inept hunter who always got lost
and separated from his friends because he had a lousy sense of
  direction
that man can come here to get his bearings calling out
to his horse his dog or himself because he's alone
in the fog in the night in the rain in his mind and say
"My friends where are you?"
and the rock walls will seize his voice
and break it into a million amplified pieces of echoes
that will find the ghosts of his friends in the tombs of their
  dust

But I mistrust the mind-quality that tempts me
to embroider and exaggerate things
                    I just watch my wife's face
she is quiet as she generally is because I do most of the talking
it is forty years old and has felt the pain of children
the pettiness of day-to-day living and getting thousands of
  meals
but standing on the rock face of Lake Superior
it is not lessened in any way
with a stillness of depth that reaches where I can't follow
all other thoughts laid aside in her brain
on her face I see the Ojibway horseman painting the rock with
  red fingers
and he speaks to her as I could not
in pictures without handles of words
into feeling into being here by direct transmission
from the stranded Ojibway horseman
And I change it all back into words again for that's the best I
  can do
but they only point the way we came from for who knows
  where we are
under the tall stone cliffs with water dripping down on us
or returned from a long journey and calling out to our friends

But the rock blazes into light when we leave the place
or else the sun shines somewhere else and I didn't notice it
and my secret knowing is knowing what she knows
and can't say and I can only indicate
reclaim my half-empty beer and drink it and tie my shoes
follow her up the tangled rocks past the warning sign for
  strangers
and wait till she turns around. . . .

D. G. JONES

[*Jones, a Canadian poet, editor, and critic, is the founder and editor of the journal* Ellipse: Writers in Translation. *He won a Governor General's Award for his poetry collection* Under the Thunder the Flowers Light Up the Earth *(1977); his other works include* Frost on the Sun *(1957) and* A Throw of Particles: New and Selected Poems *(1983). In the following excerpt, Jones, who has known Purdy since the mid-1960s, explores how the feminine principle informs Purdy's poetry.*]

The afterword [to *The Collected Poems of Al Purdy* (see excerpt above)] presents Al Purdy as one of the foremost English-language poets of the twentieth century. He speaks Canadian; he knows something about country, cadence and silence; and to those of us in the prison house of modern liberal techno-logical discourse, he brings unlikely news of the *mysterium tremendum*. (If I didn't know the man personally, I'd have said that Dennis Lee invented him.) (p. 14)

I would like to suggest that Purdy and his poetry move more freely than most in what Jacques Lacan calls *l'imaginaire*, that,

although he plays with the word of the father, patriarchal dis-course, the power of the Phallus (going "BOING BOING BOING," as Dennis Lee notes), this is comic, a piece of exuberant bravado, that in fact this rather monumental Cana-dian personality has no great faith in the ego or self which is said to emerge at the mirror stage in the child's development and to integrate him/her in the whole (alienating) system of language or the symbolic code—that Purdy slips rather freely into the pre-linguistic imagery which connects him to the body of the mother, an amorphous state that does not so much tran-scend the division of self and other as precede it.

The *mysterium tremendum* in the poetry of Al Purdy is femi-nine, not the phallic Word but the pre-verbal Matrix. The poems speak of the commerce of the big little man with that mysterious body from which he emerges, through which he is sustained, by which he is overwhelmed. The man who goes out to pick wild grapes in **"The Winemaker's Beat-etude"** begins to dissolve ("letting / myself happen") into a herd of lesbian cows until he says:

> I become the whole damn feminine principle so
> happily noticing little tendrils of affection steal
> out from each to each unshy honesty encompassing
> golden calves in Israel and slum babies in Canada and
> a millionaire's brat left squalling on the toilet seat in
> Rockefeller Centre
>
>   Oh my sisters
>   I give purple milk!

                                                    (p.15)

I can begin again more simply and less fashionably by sug-gesting that Al Purdy is a muse poet, that is, more effectively than Robert Graves himself, a true poet, who writes in more or less happy thralldom to the White Goddess: spring maiden, nagging wife, horrific hag.

Take **"Spring Song"**; St. Al is underneath that '48 Pontiac trying to change the oil and is distracted by birds, frogs, rabbits, and the farmer's daughter in short shorts on her way to the mail; he becomes the happy mechanic in the universal body shop. "Here I am," he says, "with both hands high / under the skirts of the world." (p. 16)

I don't think Purdy has ever been accused of being a "myth poet." The reader is disarmed by the fact that each text tends to be so grounded in the occasional, the documentary. And surely his work presents one of the most varied and realistic images of women that we can find. Typically, however, a Purdy poem proceeds to loosen up, to destroy the assumptions of the realistic mode by introducing the mock-heroic, hyper-bole, high and low burlesque, a kind of masculine, mock-epic play, which then allows for the entry of other, more serious or subjective materials, we associate with the modes of ro-mance and myth. So, in these terms, we watch as the white body of the goddess emerges from **"Archeology of Snow,"** warm/cold, present/absent, larger than life. It begins:

> Bawdy tale at first
>   what happened
>   in the snow
>   what happens
>   in bed or anywhere I said
>   Oh Anna

Here the poet is the "hound of faithfulness," sniffing around lost body of love, imprint, as Dennis Lee might say, primal:

I found her

heavy buttocks
in the snow
printed there
like a Cambrian trilobite

What begins as a slightly ludicrous piece of realism, the unorthodox lover staking out and trying to preserve the fossil form of his snow "angel," leads gradually to an epiphany. There is a gradual transformation of the image, from Helen of Illyria to grey lady (dirty snow, "rotten as / an old man's worn out old underpants with ragged crotch") to its dissolution into spring melt water, "brooks / and water and earth are moving / moving." A moving image, says the speaker, admitting she's gone, but then protesting that what the snow surrounds persists, that what it pointed to "is not perishable," that is, in fact, all things co-exist, present or absent, living or dead, and that:

... in the plumed fields of light
and the shapely deeds of our flesh
the lovely omniscience of women
We need to exist but once
in the green shadows
in the sunlit places
and there's no end of humans

The word "omniscience" consorts oddly with Anna's buttocks, "inline interior cross section/outline vivisected," suggesting again that the all-compehending nature of women is not primarily cerebral.

Whatever it is, it is not merely sensual or sexual either. If we read the text in conjunction with **"Poem for One of the Annettes,"** we may be impressed by the fact that, for Purdy, one of the things women comprehend is grief, separation, being pregnant and abandoned. The latter poem gives us a different, though perhaps finally related, view of meltwater, as Annette, as Janine, as Anita "cry the common sickness with ordinary tears," as if:

they would flood the whole quasi-romantic town of
Montreal with the light of (their) darkness and
follow the gutters and sewers glowing down
thru sewage disposal plants by the river and
into the industrial waste of (their) dreams to
the sea
the shapeless mothering one-celled sea—

Oh Anita, they do.

What the speaker in these poems comprehends in and through the figures of women is not simple; it comprehends both a kind of ecstasy and a pathos, both communion and separation. And this duality characterizes the transcendent vision itself. (pp. 16-17)

The "reality" evoked in such poems is that of a single, yet continuously sub-dividing body, not unlike the "shapeless mothering one-celled sea," but with a difference, the consciousness of difference that we associate with sexual differentiation and propagation as opposed to cellular division. The empathy, the sense of pathos extended to women as well as men, to the whole subdividing, if in some sense single body, may perhaps distinguish Purdy's vision from that of Graves', which I gather is rather more ferocious in its portrait of the White Goddess. Purdy does not grieve only for himself, or other men, but for all the Annettes, and that includes not only the bouncing Anna, but the figure in **"The Old Woman and the Mayflowers."** The latter incarnates "almost 80 years of bitchiness"; yet she may have driven into the fields in search of a bouquet of flowers out of some kind of "hag-tenderness," some feeling for beauty.... This is not the voice of a man spellbound by Siren or Gorgon. As in **"Evergreen Cemetery,"** it combines a poignant empathy with a comic distance. For the time being, the speaker reserves the right to be found in the beer parlour and not the cemetery at closing time. Still, it is the ambiguous memory of both identity with and isolation from an essentially feminine white body that grounds the transcendent vision of unity in diversity in many of these texts. (pp. 17-18)

As the recent preface to *The Collected Poems* may testify, Purdy's visit to the Canadian arctic would appear to have been a central event in his adult career. It reactivated, I suggest, in a still more displaced, yet powerful, form the complex of images and mixed feelings associated with the maternal body and informing, it seems to me, the *mysterium tremendum* Lee talks of in his afterword....

Classically, the *mysterium tremendum* has its dysphoric as well as its euphoric face. If here the arctic furnishes a radiantly positive image, elsewhere it provides a more chilling one. Just as Anna may be snow, the arctic may be ice....

The large man from Hastings County at first scorns the dwarf willows in **"Trees at the Arctic Circle,"** until he recognizes how they too clutch at life. They send their roots down, during the brief summer, "down, down, down':

And you know it occurs to me about 2 feet under
these roots must touch permafrost
ice that remains ice forever
and they use it for their nourishment
they use death to remain alive....

Between the present body and the gone body, between the subterranean ice and the polar bear climbing his own wish, walking the sky, washed by wave upon wave of that high blue, we have the brief in-between moment of **"Arctic Rhododendrons,"** the time of lovers, of "small purple surprises / in the river's white racket." "Love is the sound of a colour that lasts two weeks in August / and then dies." The infant's pure ecstasy, the lover's mixed ecstasy, the separate individual's bitter ecstasy of knowing life feeds on a body of death.

It seems to me Purdy's writing moves back and forth across that line between earliest childhood, where there may be no clear discrimination between the child's body, the mother's body, the world's body, and the mirror stage, the oedipal stage, at which one presumably acquires language and a clear-cut image of one's distinct and separate self. And the arctic brought much of that early material into play, though not, perhaps, without some rather extraordinary, even slapstick gestures at displacement. (p. 18)

Not unlike certain Irish writers, Purdy deals with such grave Freudian matters as sex and the family romance, the oedipus complex, civilization and its discontents, by finding them matter for comedy. This may be partly because he does not take the Phallic Father image, his or any one else's, too seriously, not more seriously, at least, than the more amorphous Child-Mother-World image. And when this image dominates we may move away from comedy and slapstick toward a peculiar mixture of lyric and elegy at the heart of many Purdy texts. (p. 19)

I suggest that the experience of the *mysterium tremendum* in St. Al's poetry, of ecstasy and melancholy, turns on the great figure of the maternal or feminine body, waxing and waning in the finally cosmic spaces of the poet's imagination. (p. 20)

D. G. Jones, "St. Al and the Heavenly Bodies," in Brick: A Journal of Reviews, *No. 29, Winter, 1987, pp. 14-20.*

GEORGE GALT

[*Galt, a Canadian nonfiction writer, poet, and critic, is the author of the travel book* Trailing Pythagoras *(1982). His poetry is included in the anthology* Storm Warning II, *edited by Purdy. In the following excerpt, Galt praises* The Collected Poems of Al Purdy *as a work that "will last as long as Canadian writing lasts."*]

[*The Collected Poems of Al Purdy*] is a rare accomplishment, because Purdy's poetry is unique, but also because few poets approaching old age exhibit his fresh imagination and still expanding insights.

Purdy's post-apprentice writing, which began 25 years ago, stands high above what most of his Canadian contemporaries have done (here I place him loosely in the generation born between 1900 and 1930). His distinct style, which has spawned many imitators; his broad sweep across time, the earth, and its universe; a full emotional range, nuanced through despair and boredom to ecstasy, love, and laughter; his ability to give voice to what readers recognize as Canadian experience (without trapping himself as a spokesman for the parochial); and his vast bookish learning, which almost always illuminates a passage where it is deployed, escaping the drag of pedantry—these are the qualities that set him apart from his peers. Of the poets born in the 30 years I have bracketed, only Earle Birney and Irving Layton have achieved the impact on our culture that Purdy can claim. (Draw a smaller circle, around our poetic culture, and you have to include writers like P. K. Page and Margaret Avison).

The publication of Purdy's *Collected Poems* should be a major cultural event, and the book itself lives up to all expectations. . . .

His two books in the 1980s, *The Stone Bird* and *Piling Blood,* along with a dozen new poems in this collection, are a departure from his earlier work—in some ways superior to it and certainly as vigorous.

Ironically, when Purdy was at his most popular, in the first half of the 1970s, he was not writing as well as he had in the previous decade, nor as well as he would later. I think his best books are *The Cariboo Horses* (1965), *North of Summer* (1967), *Wild Grape Wine* (1968), and the two volumes in the 1980s mentioned above. Many fine poems populate the books in between, but there is also a slackness in parts, a suggestion on some pages that the poet can't find his ignition keys and is thumbing a ride in the back seat of his own previous work.

Pieces like **"Place of Fire,"** a poem about writing a poem **"Picture Layout in *Life* Magazine,"** a predictable (though not unmoving) shot at glossy American journalism and **"Ritual,"** a brooding, self-involved list of winter complaints, all strike me this way. They are not clumsy and clichéd, not meritless, but they lack adventure and surprise. Later Purdy seems to have known that his work had staggered through an uneven period. *Being Alive* (1978) included **"On Realizing He Had Written Some Bad Poems."** . . .

Still, during that same period he wrote more excellent poetry than most poets produce in a lifetime. Among the successes are **"Hands,"** about pressing the flesh with Che Guevara; **"The Beavers of Renfrew,"** a meditation on man's place in nature (with the peculiar twist on history that only Purdy can fashion); **"Pre-School,"** a flashback to the clear-eyed awe of first things . . . and **"In the Darkness of Cities,"** an anguished song on behalf of the earth's dispossessed.

Sometime in the late '70s Purdy's writing voice began to modulate from loud solos, which gave full vent to the poet's brash, sprawling ego, into a softer harmony with ambient sounds and sights. . . .

No longer trying to goose the goddesses in heaven, no more a cosmic prankster who "fails magnificently," the poet has now adopted an almost reverential stance, a "hunched figure" pondering the luminous roof of the world. I doubt that any poet could have sustained both the freshness and the manic energy that much of Purdy's earlier work displayed. Something had to give. By turning his high volume down, and using his presence in the poems more as a filter and mixer than as an amplifier, he has moved into softer ballads that explore in new ways his old concerns.

Exactly what the principal concerns of this agile poetry have been since 1962, when *Poems for All the Annettes* first appeared, Dennis Lee elucidates in an afterword. (p. 16)

Out of the rush of everyday incommensurables spring Purdy's unpredictable epiphanies, which are, according to Lee, "what theologians call the experience of *mysterium tremendum*—the encounter with holy otherness, to which an appropriate response is awe, joy, terror, gratitude." Anyone familiar with the poems will recognize the passages Lee means, the near-visionary moments when Purdy leaps over a few million years in a line, or transports the poem halfway around the earth and back again in one breath. It is his ability to traverse time and space, and to make the traversal seem natural and immediate, his giant steps across the back yards of history and prehistory, often climbing inside the skins of creatures who inhabited other times, that give Purdy his huge poetic grasp. . . .

At the end of Purdy's new book appear three poems that reveal an increasing preoccupation with death. In an eloquent introduction [see excerpt above], the poet says a "collected" is "either a gravestone or a testimonial to survival." Nothing feels feeble or terminal in the new poems that close this volume. Purdy's lifespan aside, this book is less a headstone than an iridescent beacon. But inasmuch as such books are inevitably taken as a kind of monument, I'll predict that this one will last as long as Canadian writing lasts. Certainly long after most books from our little slice of the eternal now have been forgotten, the best poems of Al Purdy will continue to give light. (p. 17)

George Galt, "Giant Steps," in Books in Canada, *Vol. 16, No. 1, January-February, 1987, pp. 16-17.*

ANDREW VAISIUS

[*Vaisius, a Canadian poet, editor, and critic, is poetry editor of the literary magazine* Waves. *In the following excerpt, he comments on the various qualities—comic, transcendent, carnal, scientific—of this "wise and humane" poet.*]

[*The Collected Poems of Al Purdy*] offers an omniscient perspective and sombre extension of the poetry of Purdy—twelve new poems are included here. Purdy writes as no one has written before, or few will hence, I am sure. He is easily our finest living poet. *The Collected Poems* reaffirms his stature, strength, reach and vitality. (p. 80)

[*Sex and Death*] contained two of the strongest poems Purdy has ever written: **"The Horseman of Agawa"** and a reprint from the limited edition *Hiroshima Poems,* **"Remembering Hiroshima".** *Sex and Death* fascinated and startled me as something tinged with what the conventional call sinful usually does. I had not read poetry like it before. Some poems didn't make much sense at first but got under my skin enough to prod me to understand them. The volume carried an abundance of metaphors and images. In fact the sheer amount rivalled the proverbial mud thrown against the wall. Certainly some sticks. In Purdy's case great globs stick. "Like new false teeth in orbit with a steak", "It is one of those moments / when a towel in somebody's bathroom / might fall unnoticed", "The idea we are used to / like a far-away train wreck": What sort of man would write things like that? I supposed a genuine, observant, down to earth non-University degreed poet. Purdy sounded effortless, fluent, marvellous and without a doubt Canadian. . . . I realized then it would never pass to label one of his books *Love and Mortality*. No. *Sex and Death,* surely. This is big poetry for a big country.

With the title as a backdrop nightmare, **"Remembering Hiroshima"** doesn't mention names, events or results. It doesn't even posit a nuclear holocaust with concrete detail and gruesome images. It suggests. . . . Purdy exposes a great dollop of vulnerability in that poem, not only personal but social as well. (pp. 80-1)

"The Horseman of Agawa" is written in a similar vein. Purdy traipses back and forth through a few centuries with his wife and encounters the sublime gesture of an Indian rock painter who "drew with his fingers on the stone canvas." Like **"Remembering Hiroshima"** it is a suggestive and vulnerable poem. . . .

> I think that after the Ojibway are all dead
> and all the bombs in the white world have fizzed into
>   harmlessness
> the ghost of one inept hunter . . .
> . . . can come here to get his bearings

It is a love poem about him and his wife edging out over Lake Superior on slanting rocks to view Indian pictographs, and how the paintings reach across time to speak to them. They share the pictographs, but Purdy realizes that the painter "speaks to her as I could not / in pictures without handles of words"— the exact tools of his own craft. "And I change it all back into words again for that's the best I can do / but they only point the way we came from for who knows where / we are." . . . A dignity underpins the poem, also a simple (though not simplistic) acknowledgement that life on earth has a past and a future. Both poems speak of life which transcends the acutely personal and achieves a universality. They represent not only what endures and is memorable in poetry, but also more importantly in life itself. (pp. 81-2)

Of course these two poems do not exhibit all phases of Purdy's talent. His comic poems are legion and well known throughout the decades. Even in the eighties, Purdy who is now in his sixties displays a grumbling kind of humour evident in his forties when he wrote **"Home-Made Beer"** and **"When I Sat Down To Play the Piano"**. **"A Typical Day in Winnipeg"** recounts his misfortune of a dead car battery and the subsequent journey half way through a snow-filled field to find help "thinking: this white stuff is beauty / if you got that kinda mind / which I ain't—beauty is shit." (p. 82)

Purdy is a masterful writer of carnal knowledge. His poems can be bold without being boastful, and tender without being sentimental. They have a white underbelly I can relate to. . . . His love poems might be erotic if you can call a Bull Moose in rut erotic; more likely they are seamy with a gritty likeable nature.

So much for Victorian romance. So much for modern love, too. Purdy is bound to this earth, that is, if he isn't sashaying about the galaxies or prehistoric eras as an ambassador of Here to There. It is that endearing quality which sets him apart from the self-serving and over-indulgent poetry being published these days.

A somewhat rare literary current running throughout Purdy's writing is an interest in the scientific. Few poets bother with scientific thought and theory. Fewer still venture beyond the rudimentary science of the morning newspaper and radio. Purdy displays more than a cursory interest in modern science. His poetic reflections cross paths with geology, biology, anthropology and evolution. In poems like **"Lost in the Badlands"** (an update of **"The Horseman of Agawa"**), **"Gondwanaland"**, **"Moses at Darwin Station"**, **"The Nurselog"** and **"In the Early Cretaceous"**, he employs science as a vehicle for poetry. He doesn't merely observe and record, but layers scientific fact into the poems. Scientific bones marrowed with Purdy grit make for a very palatable soup. Science sprouts a literary dimension it sorely missed, and Purdy's poetics run deeper in a scientific vein. (pp. 82-3)

I enjoyed about half of the new poems included here, but those I enjoyed immensely. Not surprisingly they reinforce Purdy's breadth, reach and ease of language. Al Purdy has always been a wise and humane poet and these new poems affirm those characteristics. Many of them concern death. Certainly it is a little unsettling to read a poem entitled **"Pre-Mortem"** without having an aftertaste of sadness thinking of the poet's own age. . . . My favourite of the new lot is **"Orchestra"**, a crystallised distillation of the sense of awe and wonder and common yapping Purdy has done so splendidly for thirty years. It is part of a body of poetry which I have found necessary to read time and time again for the past twelve years of my own life. He writes poetry that matters; poetry with bone, blood and lungs; at times smart-ass poetry and tangential meandering poetry which gallops or crawls, but always poetry that matters; poetry which pushes that button defining us as humans able to complete with symbols and signs the electrical nerve circuit we know as communication. Purdy has lived a life for all of us, a life rarefied between the pasteboard covers of this book. The life is not one of which I am envious, but one of which I am profoundly thankful. His poems are the closest I'll get to immortality in my lifetime. They are that good. (p. 83)

Andrew Vaisius, "A Life Rarefied," in WAVES, *Vol. 15, No. 4, Spring, 1987, pp. 80-3.*

BRUCE HUNTER

[*Hunter, a Canadian poet and critic, is the author of* Benchmark *(1982) and* The Beekeeper's Daughter *(1986). In the following excerpt, he praises Purdy for his original and all-encompassing voice and extols* The Collected Poems *as a valuable edition.*]

Al Purdy's winning the Governor General's Award for poetry came as no surprise to me. This substantial collection [*The Collected Poems of Al Purdy*] has few contenders. . . . This is a major collection by one of our most important writers.

Purdy has had an enormous influence on Canadian poetry both as a poet and as an editor of the *Storm Warning* anthologies, and he has been instrumental in editing and encouraging the work of younger writers. In these rather chaotic times of pronounced regionalism and the Meech Lake accord, Canadian poetry seems to be the product of splinter groups: the political trendies, stoned-out postmodernists, various feminist caucuses, apologetic male feminists (those wimps!), and the rabid regionalists, whether they be from Queen St. West or the West Coast. All leave the poor reader reaching for an aspirin. Al Purdy, however, seems to have rambled and grumbled his way past all of these self-serving factions and found a voice original enough and with enough substance that he encompasses them all.

Purdy has a distinctive colloquial voice, one that has certainly affected the younger poets, Bronwen Wallace, Erin Mouré, and Andrew Wreggitt, to name a few. However, it is his colloquial treatment of historical themes that sets him apart. Purdy is very well-read and he uses a wide range of material and source in his poems. And this is not the dull stuff of the historians with their onerous lists of official 'stats'. Purdy is one argument for sacking the historians or at least demoting them to what they really are: the file clerks of academe and government. The poet here succeeds in resurrecting history with all its colour and passion. Purdy has used this technique throughout his career. (p. 40)

In this generous selection made by Russell Brown are many of Purdy's best-known poems that range from the Arctic Circle south to the Alberta Badlands and Prince Edward County down to Mexico and South America, from Tofino, to Newfoundland. But Purdy is more than just a poet of time and place, his hapless persona allows him to discuss with wit and humour his own misfitting the scheme of things, in his relationship with his wife, for example. In **"Over the Hill in the Rain, My Dear"**, after trudging four miles to visit a Viking site (his idea no doubt) and getting drenched:

> We squelch miserably into camp
> about half an hour later
> strip down like white shrivelled slugs,
> waving snail horns at each other,
> cold sexless antennae
> assessing the other ridiculous creature—
> And I begin to realize
> one can't use a grin like a bandaid . . .

The succinct verb 'squelch', the downscaling to snail size, the kind of hapless aplomb here, all work towards revealing the humour of the situation. This is the work of a fine poet.

The Al Purdy in his poems is a home-made beer-drinking kind of sensitive guy, a haphazard, philosophical Everyman with a certain delightful and cockeyed whimsy. He also has an astounding ability to see the significant in the apparently insignificant. (pp. 40-1)

This collection is grouped by decades ranging from the forties/fifties, through to the eighties, but Purdy is no over-the-hill poet. The poems from his three recent books *The Stone Bird* (1981), *Bursting Into Song* (1982), and *Piling Blood* (1984), all crackle with energy and insight. How uplifting to see the steady growth of his powers. The last poem in the book, **"The Dead Poet"** from *The Stone Bird*, indicates the poet is anything but diminished.

> I was altered in the placenta
> by the dead brother before me
> who built a place in the womb
> knowing I was coming;
> he wrote words on the wall of flesh

painting a woman inside a woman
whispering a faint lullaby
that sings in my blind heart still.

This collection contains poetry that traverses many continents, but is distinctively Canadian, from a writer who is able to evoke guffaws, tenderness, and awe, often in the same poem. No poet worth his or her words should be without this volume, and any library or school without a copy quite simply has an incomplete literature selection. Al Purdy is a poet whose work encompasses history on both the larger political and social scale, but also on a less grand but no less important scale of the miniature events that form our ordinary lives. To paraphrase something Irving Layton once said, the historians may tell us about the times and their major players, but Al Purdy tells us what really happened and what it all means. (p. 41)

> *Bruce Hunter, in a review of "The Collected Poems of Al Purdy," in* Cross-Canada Writers' Quarterly, *Vol. 9, Nos. 3 & 4, 1987, pp. 40-1.*

RONALD B. HATCH

[In the following excerpt, Hatch examines Purdy's development, his influence on younger poets, and his concern with transcendence.]

Purdy's best poetry [as represented in his *Collected Poems*] combines the purely local with a sense of the transcendent in what seems at first to be a wholly haphazard manner. '**Wilderness Gothic**,' one of his most famous poems, develops as a continual oscillation between a religious and secular universe, capturing modern man's sense of the will to believe with his sceptical, historical orientation to the divine. In Schiller's terms, the poem combines man's elegiac desire to live in a religious dimension with his satiric awareness of the social and mundane determinants of everyday life.

In an overview of Purdy's career, it becomes evident that Purdy's early poetry in the 1940s was largely derivative; he never succeeded in mastering the late Victorian forms to which he first looked as models. Only in the late 1950s, when he and his wife built a house on Roblin Lake in southern Ontario and Purdy began writing about this region in the speech rhythms of everyday life, did he find an expression adequate to his needs. In so doing, he taught younger poets in Canada that the centre need no longer be London or New York, and his famous 'running line' became one of the most important influences on younger poets. This influence has not, however, always been entirely positive, since there has been a tendency to take from Purdy his seemingly simple line and to overlook the way he uses his different 'tenors' to suggest modern man's various allegiances.

In '**Wilf McKenzie**' Purdy describes himself as 'literary plastic man,' an apt description for someone so endlessly inventive, so endlessly moving from one dimension to another. He delights in writing about his travels to exotic places, using travel itself to bring out the sense of 'edge.' He takes the reader to the Galapagos Islands, to Samarkand, to Mexico, and perhaps most tellingly of all, beyond the 'Hyperborean ocean' to Canada's far north. Here as well, one discovers Purdy's delight in evoking the past. Finding a ring of rocks in the bare Arctic, all that remains of a tent village, he steps inside the magic circle to evoke the lost race of the Dorsets, 'what it was like to be alive / before the skin tents blew down.' The past for Purdy is never merely past or something passed over. While his poems begin in the present, what he calls 'my fractional life in this skin tent,' the present moment then expands into duration, with Purdy listening for something else, the fortuitous voice that will place 'a fulcrum under the universe.' Such moments are 'life's gifts / and in the loopholes and catacombs of time / travel,' we are enabled to 'pass thru' and establish connections with the past. Having slipped out of time, Purdy no longer remains a null point in a linear development, but holds within himself the past, summing up in himself all that came before. The future then extends as *his* shadow, releasing him from the seeming deadness of the present.

Although Purdy has often been seen as a colourful regional archivist, this religious sense, what Schiller would have called the 'elegiac,' is clearly at the centre of his best work. Indeed, in his recent poetry, one detects what amounts almost to an obsessive search for the non-temporal dimension, and one suspects that Purdy tries too hard for such moments of illumination, with the poems frequently becoming explanations rather than enactments. (pp. 33-4)

*Ronald B. Hatch, in a review of "Collected Poems,"
in* University of Toronto Quarterly, *Vol. LVII, No. 1, Fall, 1987, pp. 33-4.*

Peter (Hillsman) Taylor
A Summons to Memphis

Pulitzer Prize: Fiction

American short story writer, novelist, and dramatist.

During the mid-1980s, Taylor has earned the widespread recognition many critics have thought his distinguished fiction has long deserved. *The Old Forest and Other Stories* (1985), a retrospective collection of Taylor's stories spanning his career from the late 1930s to the mid 1980s, sparked new interest in the author's work, won the PEN/Faulkner award for fiction, and caused many to hail him as a master of the short story. *A Summons to Memphis* (1986), his first novel, has also received substantial acclaim, including the Pulitzer Prize for fiction. Reviewers frequently offer two reasons for Taylor's relative obscurity in contemporary literature. They note that his quiet, conversational style and focus on respectable white Southern gentry during the pre-Civil Rights era have received less attention than the Faulknerian Gothic manner of many of his contemporaries. Secondly, they observe that Taylor has concentrated almost exclusively on short stories rather than the more prestigious and salable novel form. Before *A Summons to Memphis*, Taylor produced only one long prose work, *A Woman of Means* (1950), which many critics classify as a novella rather than a full-length novel. At the time *A Summons to Memphis* was published, however, Taylor reported that he was at work on a new novel. "I seem to have switched to another form," he mused.

A Summons to Memphis, like all of Taylor's works, is rooted in a specific time and place, the urban Upper South of the 1930s and 1940s. The novel's narrator, Phillip Carver, is shaped by the fateful events of his youth in Tennessee. He recalls how his self-absorbed father moved his family from genteel Nashville to a rougher environment in Memphis, a change so dramatic it traumatized all family members except the father. Phillip becomes emotionally stunted, his mother withdraws from life, and his sisters became embittered spinsters who seek revenge upon the father. Taylor's skill at evoking tragedy from this scenario stems from his experiences in upper-middle-class Tennessee society. His father was a native of Memphis, while his mother was from Nashville; like Phillip, Taylor lived in both cities while growing up. "The difference between the cities has always seemed significant, but I didn't know why," Taylor commented. "One of the nice things about writing is making use of details that seemed important in your life. You discover what they mean to you."

Despite his love of the Southern past, Taylor's observations possess a dark, ironic resonance that convey an equivocal view of this milieu. Although Taylor treats the moral failings of his characters with humor and compassion, he unflinchingly depicts the Carver family's hostile father-child conflicts, and Phillip's resulting emotional alienation. "I'm fascinated by the deterioration of the family," Taylor remarked. Critics extol Taylor's consummate storytelling skill and his exquisitely lucid prose style. Typical of his style, Taylor gradually unfolds his story in an indirect, ruminative fashion, using little action or dialogue. Taylor slowly builds tension by telling his tale through an accumulation of finely-observed details that evoke the manners and morals of the period and disclose the characters' personalities and strained relations. Reviewers are mixed in their interpretations of *A Summons to Memphis*. The father, for example, is either viewed as an autocratic and manipulative man, or as a strong, adaptable figure with weak children. The narrator, according to some, is devoid of real insight at the novel's close, while others claim that Phillip has evolved from his simplistic and self-deceptive view of the past to one more compassionate and aware of complexities. Despite this ambiguity, which a few critics claim is intended, the novel proves for most commentators that Taylor's style can make the transition from short story to novel and still retain its richness and resonance. "That our most distinguished and accomplished writer of short fiction has at last written a novel is cause enough for comment and celebration," declares critic Jonathan Yardley, "but there is much more for which to be grateful. *A Summons to Memphis* is something of a miracle; not merely a novel of immense intelligence, psychological acuity, and emotional power, but a work that manages to summarize and embody its author's entire career."

© Jerry Bauer

(See also *CLC*, Vols. 1, 4, 18, 37, 44; *Contemporary Authors*, Vols. 13-16, rev. ed.; *Contemporary Authors New Revision Series*, Vol. 9; and *Dictionary of Literary Biography Yearbook: 1981*.)

JONATHAN YARDLEY

Seated in his cramped apartment on West 82nd Street in Manhattan, writing in ''these very irregular notebooks,'' Phillip Carver at the age of 49 confronts his aged father and, in so doing, himself. Not long ago he had been summoned to Memphis by his two spinster sisters because his father, two years a widower, had proposed to marry a younger woman; he records in his notebooks that ''I thought I had detected an old-fashioned fury in my sisters' voices which made me fearful for my father's well-being,'' and so he had hastened to Memphis to defend the old man. But the journey turned into much more than an errand of filial mercy; it became a summons into the depths of Carver's own past, a re-encounter with people and events that shaped him, in most cases much against his will, into the man he is now.

Fathers and sons: the theme has recurred over and again in Taylor's mature fiction, most notably in such short stories as ''The Gift of the Prodigal,'' ''The Captain's Son'' and ''Dean of Men.'' In that sense, as in many others, *A Summons to Memphis* is quintessential Taylor. But *A Summons to Memphis* is not a short story, a novella or a play, the forms in which he has previously written; it is Taylor's first true novel, published in his 70th year. That our most distinguished and accomplished writer of short fiction has at last written a novel is cause enough for comment and celebration, but there is much more for which to be grateful. *A Summons to Memphis* is something of a miracle: not merely a novel of immense intelligence, psychological acuity and emotional power, but a work that manages to summarize and embody its author's entire career.

It is also, for Taylor's admirers, a gift. Those of us who love his work have wanted him to write long fiction not in order to conform to bloated American notions about literary success, but for the sheer pleasures and rewards of reading him at greater length. For years these readers have wondered what would happen if the author of such masterpieces of short fiction as ''A Wife of Nashville'' and ''The Old Forest'' simply fell into an expansive mood, and allowed a story to spin itself out to the full dimensions of a book. Now we have the answer, and it seems almost too good to be true: Taylor is as much a master of the novel as of the story.

In tone and method, *A Summons to Memphis* is directly related to Taylor's later short stories. Its narrator is a man of sufficient years to be able to cast a long backward glance, and of sufficient self-awareness to comprehend his own shortcomings as well as those of others—though his self-understanding does have its clear, and revealing, limits. Within the opening pages a number of mysteries and secrets are gradually identified, but we discover their true nature only after a leisurely process in which layer after layer is slowly peeled away. The mood is genial and civilized, but dark matters lie not far beneath the surface; for if *A Summons to Memphis* is a novel about understanding and forgiveness, it is also one about betrayal and retribution.

The first betrayal, and the one to which everything else can be traced, took place in 1931, when George Carver, Phillip's father, was ''deceived and nearly ruined financially by his closest friend and principal legal client back in Nashville, one Mr. Lewis Shackleford.'' Refusing to stay in the same town with this knave, Carver moved with his wife and four children to Memphis, where he established a law practice and soon became a prominent citizen—but where his wife and children, accustomed to Nashville ways, found their lives thrown peculiarly off course. His wife fell into a decline, perhaps more psychosomatic than real, that lasted three decades; his daughters were maneuvered out of prospective marriages and into prosperous, bitter spinsterhood; his elder son was killed in the Second World War; and Phillip renounced both Memphis and the law, moving to New York to become an editor and book-collector.

Now, back in Memphis to see what he can do about his octogenarian father's marital aspirations, Phillip finds all these strains from his family's past intermingling with others from his own in a painful web of memory. He writes at one point that ''my head was full of . . . adult understanding,'' by which he means that the combination of a family crisis and his own arrival at middle age has allowed him to see through veneers of half-truth and self-deception to the truths of his life: to understand how he has misunderstood his father and his sisters, and thus himself. In particular he comes to see that his sisters are ''frozen forever in their roles as injured adolescents'' and that what he had for years thought to be his father's selfishness is something far more complex. . . .

Accepting and remembering are, if anything, the principal business that Phillip Carver conducts in these ''notebooks.'' The ''adult understanding'' he slowly reaches is that one has to live with what one has been given, and that trying to push it out of mind is merely irresponsible and self-deluding. A central reality in Phillip's life is that his father—with, he finally comes to see, the unwitting complicity of his sisters—destroyed his hopes of marriage to the only woman he ever really loved, but he now is mature enough to try to understand why his father did this to him. He is forced to confront the ways in which submission is maintained within families, and the schemes that children and spouses devise in order to cope with it. However ruefully, he learns what his father knows but his sisters never will: there is no such thing as ''a *simple* truth.''

But to describe *A Summons to Memphis* purely in terms of the themes it examines is to overlook the other pleasures it offers: the sly depiction of contrasting folkways in Memphis and Nashville, the nostalgic yet unsentimental excursions into a lost way of life, the rich yet precise and unadorned prose. Above all, perhaps, the prose. . . .

Prose of such subtlety, taste and clarity—prose that so poignantly and exactly evokes a moment, and makes it real—is rare at any time, rarer still today, yet Peter Taylor has been writing it for four decades. Only of late has he begun to receive the attention and admiration he has earned, but with the publication last year of *The Old Forest and Other Stories* he suddenly found a readership. Now, with *A Summons to Memphis,* that readership surely will grow still larger, his reputation still greater. American readers demand novels, and now Peter Taylor has given them one; to say that it is every bit as good as the best of his short stories is the highest compliment it can be paid.

Jonathan Yardley, "Peter Taylor's Novel of Fathers and Sons," in Book World—The Washington Post, September 14, 1986, p. 3.

MICHIKO KAKUTANI

The world delineated in Peter Taylor's highly acclaimed stories—and in *A Summons to Memphis,* his first novel since the brief *A Woman of Means* in 1950—belongs to a nearly vanished past. It's a very definite world, genteel and circumscribed, and set in the Upper South of Memphis or Nashville, where the gentry pass their time fox hunting and attending debutante parties. An accent is enough to establish someone's background here ("I knew at once from his voice," a character says, "not only that he was from Memphis but that he was from somewhere between Cooper and Crosstown and in the Anandale section of town"), and clothes—a choice of shoes or a fedora—instantly betray one's class and social standing.

For many of Mr. Taylor's people, this world has already receded—Hyatt hotels and Holiday Inns have replaced the fine old mansions remembered from their youth, even as the new imperatives of independence and nonconformity have begun to subsume the old duties and traditions. And yet, like all good Southern characters, they remain irrevocably shaped by this past, haunted by memories that resurface when they least expect them.

In the case of the Carver family, the past and present are represented by two cities—"Memphis was today, Nashville was yesterday," as Mr. Taylor tells us very succinctly—and the family's move from one city to another will come to be regarded as an exile of almost biblical proportions. Like most things, it begins simply enough—the result of a falling out between the narrator's father, George Carver, and his former business partner and best friend, one Lewis Shackleford. George apparently regards the move to Memphis as a way to recover from Lewis's betrayal, a way to start over and recoup his financial and emotional losses. His children, however, see it as a decision that "sustained *him* and in some degree destroyed the rest of us."

As the narrator, Phillip, describes it, the move wrested him from all that was familiar and safe, bringing about an adolescent crisis of confidence with lasting repercussions. His sister Betsy would see her engagement to a young man from Nashville fall apart in the wake of the move; his other sister, Josephine, would experience similar disappointments in romance; and their mother, who'd "been born and bred in Nashville," would find the move so disorienting that she would gradually retreat further and further in invalidism, real or imagined.

None of these observations presented by Phillip sound all that compelling—just how different, the reader wonders, could Nashville and Memphis really be?—and it gradually emerges that the bitterness he and his sisters harbor has a good bit less to do with their family's actual move than with their father's willfulness and power: his insistence on unconditional filial obedience and his determination to thwart their independence.

Indeed, it seems that George has single-mindedly tried to undermine his children's attempts at romance and marriage, going so far as to send away the people each of them loved, and in each case, he has succeeded in ensuring their isolation. Once beautiful young women, with retinues of ardent suitors, Betsy and Josephine are now middle-aged spinsters who pass their time with paid escorts and effeminate, younger men. And Phil-

lip, having never quite recovered from an abortive love affair, currently lives in New York with a woman who shares his sense of lowered expectations.

Now, many years after the move to Memphis, many years after their father's orchestration of their lives, these three children—Phillip, Betsy and Josephine—are in a position to turn the tables. In the wake of their mother's death, their octogenarian father—who's been seen squiring lots of younger women about town—has decided to remarry and also to become friends again with his old nemesis, Lewis Shackleford. They're decisions Betsy and Josephine—and perhaps Phillip, as well—are not prepared to tolerate and they set out to squash his plans.

Are their actions meant as some kind of justifiable revenge for the damage George has inflicted on them? Or do they simply want to prevent his remarriage in order to get their hands on his money? Is George as manipulative and selfish as his children contend? Or are they distorting his actions, blaming him for disappointments of their own making?

A masterful and subtle storyteller, Mr. Taylor never answers these questions, but instead allows the reader gradually to see all the ambiguities of the situation. Using his favorite method of narration—a sort of retrospective examination of events that have occurred long ago—he moves his characters back and forth in time, as his narrator, Phillip, circles around events, returning to them as memory and conscience allow. A glimpse of Phillip and his sisters in the present, say, is followed by a glimpse of them as young adults, and then another of them as children. Several central events (Lewis Shackleford's betrayal, the move to Memphis, their abortive romances) are returned to almost obsessively—each time from a slightly different angle. As a result, we get to know the Carver family as we would neighbors or new friends—picking up new bits of information, new interpretations of behavior, as we hear familiar anecdotes repeated over time.

In Mr. Taylor's stories, this narrative approach can work to brilliant effect, creating dense layers of emotional truth, but in the more capacious form of the novel, it makes for a certain passivity. In fact, so much happens offstage in *A Summons to Memphis*—or exists simply in the mind of one or another character—that the reader occasionally yearns for a glimmer of real action, a bit of firsthand dialogue. Such feelings, however, are fleeting, for Mr. Taylor's sympathy for the chiaroscuro of familial emotion, combined with his command of naturalistic detail, remains so assured, so persuasive, that we finish the novel feeling we've not only come to know his characters, but also come to share their inner truth.

Michiko Kakutani, in a review of "A Summons to Memphis," in The New York Times, *September 24, 1986, p. C23.*

ROBERT TOWERS

[Towers, an American novelist, critic, and professor of English literature, is the author of novels including The Necklace of Kali *(1960) and* The Monkey Watcher *(1964). In the following excerpt, he praises* A Summons to Memphis *as a fascinating, if flawed, novel.]*

While a number of Taylor's stories deal with good country people (many of them living in or around the fictional small town of Thornton, Tennessee), his best stories are concerned with what might be called the social establishment of such sizable but provincial cities as Memphis and Nashville—particularly as it existed forty or more years ago. By drawing his characters from this network of "well-born" bankers, lawyers, and cotton brokers, their wives who preside over the social rituals of the community, their debutante daughters, and their sons who have joined the best fraternities, Taylor writes at a distance . . . from most of the other writers that we associate with the South: Faulkner, Flannery O'Connor, Eudora Welty— to say nothing of Harry Crews and Barry Hannah. Taylor's closest blood kin among southern authors is, I think, that now little-read but estimable novelist of a much earlier generation, Ellen Glasgow, who wrote about the Richmond equivalent of such a society in *The Sheltered Life* and *They Stooped to Folly*.

While Peter Taylor has achieved his high reputation as a writer of short stories, not novels, many of his most successful stories—among them **"The Old Forest," "The Scoutmaster," "In the Miro District,"** and **"Porte Cochere"**—are like condensed novels in their impact. Taylor has said that he likes to pack as much material as he can into a short story without losing the intensity characteristic of the form at its best. The family relationships that he explores—particularly those involving the warfare between fathers and sons—tend to be embedded in dense family history and social observation. His approach often seems more ruminative than dramatic as he circles his subject, tentatively drawing closer and closer to the heart of the matter.

Now Peter Taylor has produced a short novel—either his first or his second, depending on how one characterizes the much earlier (and still shorter) *A Woman of Means* (1950). The narrator of *A Summons to Memphis* is a middle-aged Memphis expatriate named Phillip Carver; a rare-book collector and editor, he now leads a life of rather limited expectations in New York with a younger woman, Holly Kaplan. The novel begins with Phillip's reflections on the difficulties faced in the Memphis of his boyhood by old widowers who had middle-aged children and wanted to remarry. Drawing what may seem to be excessively fine distinctions, Phillip says, "At least it is a certainty that remarriage was more difficult for old widowers in Memphis than it was over in Nashville, say, or in Knoxville—or even in Chattanooga, for that matter. One needs to know those other cities only slightly to be absolutely sure of this." The tone is curious: Is Phillip being funny or not? Apparently not, for he goes on to say, with at least limited plausibility, that the difficulty may arise from the fact that in Memphis "everybody . . . who is anybody is still apt to own some land" and "that whenever or wherever land gets involved, any family matter is bound to become more complex, less reasonable, more desperate." The differences between Nashville and Memphis remain a sharp concern of the novel, and the tone with which these differences are dwelt upon remains ambiguous.

On a dreary late Sunday afternoon Phillip, who is alone in his New York apartment (Holly having recently moved out), receives two telephone calls from his unmarried older sisters, Betsy and Josephine, in Memphis: Phillip must come at once to help prevent the marriage of their old father, widowed two years previously, to "a respectable but undistinguished and schoolteacherish woman" named Mrs. Clara Stockwell. For this start, the leisurely, digressive narration moves back and forth in time, from the present in New York and Memphis back to 1931 and even beyond. (p. 56)

Most of *A Summons to Memphis* is devoted to the past. So many aspects of it are explored that two thirds of the novel has passed before Phillip even arrives in Memphis on his current mission. We hear a great deal about Betsy and Josephine's coy, nonsexual "affairs" and the success of their real-estate business in Memphis; about the widowed George Carver's mildly scandalous behavior with "youngish" women in Memphis nightclubs before he meets the more serious threat posed by Mrs. Clara Stockwell; about George's earlier friendship with his betrayer, Lewis Shackleford; about Phillip's boyhood in Nashville and his wartime engagement to a nice Chattanooga girl—the only woman that he has ever truly loved. All of this— and more—is related to us by Phillip with an abundance of documentary detail and a minimum of dramatized action. . . .

Unfortunately, Peter Taylor's way of circling a subject repeatedly before revealing its fictional core—a technique that contributes much to the distinctiveness of the stories—leads in the novel to prolixity and repetition. Taylor has always been inclined to reject the notion that good fiction must show rather than tell, and he has obtained some memorable effects through that lucid, reflective, and informative way of telling employed in his best stories. But without the compression and intensity contributed by the brevity of the short-story form, the telling gets out of hand. The same ground is covered too often without further revelation.

A Summons to Memphis goes to great lengths to avoid emotionally charged scenes of conflict or exchange between characters—those fully dramatized scenes that Henry James (Taylor's mentor in other respects) regarded as integral to the art of fiction; one can in fact read dozens of pages without encountering more than a line or two of dialogue. We never know what George Carver might have said to cause the spirited Chattanooga girl to break off with Phillip without saying goodbye— or what the middle-aged Carver "girls" might have said to Mrs. Clara Stockwell to cause her to bolt at the last possible moment. Everything is filtered through the consciousness of Phillip, and Phillip does not even bother to speculate on these matters. Without ocular proof, so to speak, we simply have to take his word, which does not inspire total trust, about events that sometimes appear inherently improbable. A reader might well speculate, in turn, on Peter Taylor's choice of such a depressive and unforthcoming narrator. Are we meant to regard Phillip sympathetically or ironically? Is he a bit of a fool or one of the walking wounded or both? In any case, he seems an inadequately conceived medium to convey potentially arresting experience.

It remains to be said that admirers of Peter Taylor's fiction will not want to miss *A Summons to Memphis*. It is interesting to see Taylor at work on a more extended scale. While I do not think its aims have been successfully realized, the novel has passages of considerable power, humor, and pathos, and it provides yet another avenue by which we can approach that particular southern province that Taylor has made so distinctly his own. (p. 57)

Robert Towers, "Ways Down South," in The New York Review of Books, *September 25, 1986, pp. 55-7.*

An Excerpt from *A Summons to Memphis*

Nowadays it seems strange to have once lived in a Nashville where phrases like "well bred" and "well born" were always ringing in one's ears and where distinctions between "genteel people" and "plain people" were made and where there was rather constant talk about who was a gentleman and who wasn't a gentleman. When I am back in Nashville now on some publishing business or other, the city seems to me—me, the outsider—just like any other post-World War II city, as much like Columbus, Ohio, as like Richmond, Virginia. I often have to remind myself where I really am. Staying at the downtown Hyatt Regency, I have to remind myself that this is where the old Polk Apartments once stood and where still earlier stood the imposing residence of Mrs. James K. Polk, Nashville's social arbiter for half a century. Or if in very recent years I am staying in Memphis and I happen to put up at the midtown Holiday Inn, I have to make a point of recalling the fine residences that once stood on that site. Yet there is a difference between these two provincial cities even nowadays. Each has its nucleus of high rises at the center and its spreading suburbs for miles around, but still there *is* a difference between them. And it's not just its old money and its country music that makes Nashville different from Memphis. Even with its present-day vulgar, ugly, plastic look and sound there is a little something else left for anyone who was once under Nashville's spell. As one walks or rides down any street in Nashville one can feel now and again that he has just glimpsed some pedestrian on the sidewalk who was not quite real somehow, who with a glance over his shoulder or with a look in his disenchanted eye has warned one not to believe too much in the plastic present and has given warning that the past is still real and present somehow and is demanding something of all men like me who happen to pass that way. I don't know what all this represents precisely. It seems to say something to me not about all that I remember of my Nashville childhood but about all that I have forgotten, all that the Merciful Censor has blotted from my memory. My mother used to tell us that Nashville was fought for against the Indians by the early white settlers and that it was the spirit of the slaughtered Indians hovering over the place that made everybody there so queer. Then she would laugh and say that on the other hand Memphis didn't have any such spirits, Memphis didn't in effect have any soul or any real history. Memphis was a place that had simply been laid out and sold off like any other town. She said she didn't, herself, mind that but that it was a prejudice Father could never quite overcome.

THOMAS D'EVELYN

The art of the short story, like that of the short poem, is the art of knowing what to exclude and when to stop. What's left out counts almost as much as what's finally left in. Recognized as a "master of the short-story form" . . . , Peter Taylor knows how to use the "negative" or "white" spaces between paragraphs and sections—and in the novel, chapters—to register things too deep for words.

So it should come as no surprise when the reader of Taylor's first novel in 35 years reaches what feels like the end only three-quarters of the way through the book. Although not fully resolved in the way a "well-constructed" novel should be by this point, a certain amount has been understood by the main character Phillip Carver, things have changed, appropriate action has been taken. Formally speaking, a story had been told.

Next, there is the white space before a new chapter.

Then we read, "I find that I must write a postscript of a kind that I would earlier have deemed the unlikeliest of possibilities."

The postscript is another 50 pages, roughly the length of a good Taylor short story.

This unlikely postscript does indeed take us beyond what we had any reason to expect, given our familiarity with Taylor's previous work. So far we've witnessed the chronicle of the Carver family, Tennessee gentry. . . . Much has been conveyed, all in Taylor's carefully modulated, storyteller's prose.

As in so many of his stories, Taylor shows us in *A Summons to Memphis* how the Southern family, and by analogy any family, can be seen as the incubi of loneliness and subdued tragedy. Still, new equilibria are established; life goes on. Lucidity and decorum are somehow maintained, if only analogically by Taylor's prose style.

This first part of *A Summons to Memphis* ends with Phillip's return to New York. He has discovered just why his life has not added up, why his youthful romance went awry, and how after the mother's death the Carvers had been working at cross purposes. Considering Phillip's return to New York and his tragic understanding, the novel sounds like a long good-bye to the South and what it represents.

In the last quarter of the book, Phillip moves beyond acceptance to something like expectation of good in his own life, really for the first time. Forgetting has not sufficed. So the novel, this long goodbye, is also a not-at-all tentative hello.

Phillip returns home, again. Going ever deeper in his confrontation with his past and his own responsibility, he recognizes his father and sisters as they really are and have been. He sees his old flame at a resort and is tempted to make a scene. Finally, he makes the connection between his father and sisters and his old romance. In a moving passage, he sees his father in a new light: "There was no self-pity in his face and no regret. He seemed merely a man thinking of what he was going to do with himself this day and perhaps tomorrow."

And Phillip? Can he go home again?

Returning again to New York, Phillip himself confronts not his past but his future. Returning to New York means returning to Holly, a woman from Cleveland with whom he has shared an apartment on 82nd Street. The quality of Phillip's faded concept of himself is most movingly registered in Taylor's handling of this sad relationship. Like Phillip, Holly has lived in the great anonymous city alienated and close to despair, and for similar reasons, as they gradually discover once they begin to talk to each other about the once-forbidden subject of their families. For this novel about family life to end this way, with this aging, almost purely symbolic pair in deep conversation, reflects not only the drift of modern life but also Taylor's ability to salvage meaning from it, meaning of such intensity that these final pages have the power of poetry.

Throughout *Summons to Memphis,* Taylor's style—cool, transparent, and refreshing as water from a mountain spring—serves as well as it ever has to advance his purpose, which is to understand the survival of honesty and integrity in the modern, self-conscious world. With this book there can be no doubt that Taylor belongs artistically in the company of those mostly Southern peers, poets and storytellers, who have always recognized in him something special: the roll-call includes Flannery O'Connor, Robert Fitzgerald, Allen Tate (who makes a delightful cameo appearance in this book), Eudora Welty, Robert Penn Warren. (pp. 21-2)

Thomas D'Evelyn, *"Going Home Again, and Again,"* in The Christian Science Monitor, *October 1, 1986, pp. 21-2.*

RICHARD EDER

The craft in *A Summons to Memphis* is impressive. A middle-aged narrator explores the old web of family relationships, mainly with his father, that he believes has broken him. And he does it through a shattered narrative that struggles for gentlemanly control and is crisscrossed and undermined by myopia, repetition and erratic spurts of attention and wandering off. Narrator and narration, in other words, are identical.

Craft is certainly not all there is to Peter Taylor's first novel in more than 30 years. It is set, like many of his short stories, among the remnants of southern Tennessee's long-gone gentry. There are some shivering moments of recognition in it, the ability to convey a dramatic confrontation in a few artfully told details and an infallible mastery of period, manners and motivation.

But Taylor's old alligators move slowly. The narrator, a bachelor who is effete, though not celibate, has a very long throat to clear before he can really get started. In his self-unveiling, there is more tugging at buckles and buttonholes than is justified by the rather wizened body exposed. The book resembles one of those meals where the waiter expends a lot of time and virtuosity boning a fish so bony that, when the job is done, the results makes a very small presence on the plate and is consumed in about three bites.

Summons explores the reality of a family wound. Phillip Carter, the narrator, begins by assuming that it is a wound; only at the end does he come to question it. It is the wound inflicted by a powerful father upon his wife and children. Or is it, we wonder finally—and Taylor shifts the question with great skill and compassion—the tendency of children to blame their insufficiencies and disappointment on the convenient fact of having a strong father?

Phillip Carver lives a dusty and vaguely unsatisfying life as a rare book dealer in New York. His companion is a woman who provides him with more solace than passion. His sisters, Betsey and Josephine, are energetic and eccentric spinsters living in Memphis and keeping an eye on their father, George, an 80-year-old widower. . . .

Taylor makes a grand set scene out of the family's peregrinations. His portrait of George as a young man is a rich mix of social, regional and personal history. The final battle between the old man and his children—and a final intimacy that dawns between him and Phillip—are witty and touching.

The problem, and it was one I felt with Taylor's last collection of stories, *The Old Forest,* is that his characters are not really up to their complexities. The psychological and social subtleties of these feudal survivors are matched by little grace of spirit. They have thoroughbred twitches but lumpish souls.

Richard Eder, in a review of *"A Summons to Memphis,"* in Los Angeles Times Book Review, *October 5, 1986, p. 3*

MARILYNNE ROBINSON

[*An American novelist and critic, Robinson is primarily known as the author of* Housekeeping *(1981). In the following excerpt, she points out the mythic elements of tragedy in* A Summons to Memphis.]

Peter Taylor is a novelist and short-story writer who for almost half a century has produced fictions about a distinctive world of Southern inland cities, and about a characteristic stratum of society whose members are both provincial and urbane, descended from plantation-owning stock but very comfortably ensconced in the finest neighborhoods of Nashville and Memphis. They marry their own kind and honor the leisurely rituals of their caste, careful stewards of their own good fortune. These are not the tormented souls we are accustomed to finding in literature of the South. The motive force in most of these lives is complacency, the genial expectation that the young will succeed to the quiet privileges that their parents, in enjoying them, have preserved.

Let us call this Peter Taylor's donnée. His work is compared with the fiction of Henry James, and the comparison has value, even though, in terms of style, the two writers are very different indeed. Both are conscious of having as their subject what is called manners, small fields of nuanced and estheticized behavior that, as Flannery O'Connor observed, should never be thought of apart from mystery. Henry James as American in England, Peter Taylor as Southerner in America, write about societies whose bounds and particularities they are intensely aware of, and whose manners they can see as an interplay of stylized gestures, spontaneous or inevitable as they may seem to those who enact them. James, like a Whitman scanning an especially elegant stream of the human throng for glimpses of transcendency, taking esthetics as a holy mystery and a most mannered class as a sort of priestly caste, described a world for whose meaning he imagined no limit, however narrow a world it might be. Thoreau did not bring loftier expectations to his bean patch.

Peter Taylor approaches the mystery of manners another way. He reminds us that people, like spiders, impose geometries on thin air, which are fragile but will be replicated, which are ingenious and also involuntary; that given an angle, we will colonize void and disorder, putting a tiny Euclidean patch on exploding reality. The sense of limit in Mr. Taylor's work alludes to the littleness and frailty and also the resilience and inevitability of the webs we deploy to make experience habitable. While James finds his limited world inexhaustible, Peter Taylor finds the limitedness of his world inexhaustibly suggestive.

Mr. Taylor's gentry behave well at the rate and to the degree that convention is a worthy guide to the conduct of life. They are seldom distinguished for good or evil. Their "manners" are the terms in which their lives are understood, terms that, in Mr. Taylor's world, differ bewilderingly even as between Memphis and Nashville. In his beautifully ironic new novel, *A Summons to Memphis* . . . he describes, with scarcely a smile, how a family is destroyed by a betrayal, rarely mentioned even among themselves, that took place more than 40 years before. (pp. 1, 52)

It is usual to say that a Southern writer is chronicling the passing of a society doomed and overwhelmed. Such statements sidestep the vexed question of the relationship of any fiction to any reality. They seem particularly misleading in the case of Peter Taylor, for on the one hand his stories do not really present themselves as the social anatomy of Tennessee, and on the other hand one recognizes in them an authentic old regime, less regional than provincial, whose decline is neither greatly to be regretted nor likely to happen soon. In describing the disruptions and erosions that beset it, Mr. Taylor is innocent of a common error. He knows it is *because* these social structures are unstable that they will not change. His stories and novels are variations on a theme. He returns again and again to one question: what is stasis? And how is it achieved?

He does not make the odd though familiar assumption that the stability of a society is any proof of its goodness, nor is he interested in reviling people who, despite houseboys and fox hunts, are dead ordinary. It is rather as though he wishes to describe the pressures that toughen structure, as gravity thickens bone. Imagine a sort of adversary, to borrow a word from Job—a pressure, ubiquitous and protean, that has made every creature the fossil of a harrowing history, the porcupine a war machine, the skunk an avenger, the turtle a walking state of siege. In *A Summons to Memphis,* as in all Peter Taylor's fiction, stasis is defended, not voluntarily or even consciously, by means honorable or pernicious as the circumstance requires, not because it is goodness or value or virtue but because it is stasis—as it would not be if it had not found strategies of persistence in this Heraclitean world. Subversion and erosion take dozens of forms, every one of them more or less like fishing moonlight from the sea in a net, or stifling it in a cloud, or drowning it in a flood.

Among the more satisfying ironies in Mr. Taylor's work is a sort of patterning or recurrence of the threat or betrayal that makes of disruption and continuity one thing. In *A Summons to Memphis* the three middle-aged children betray their old father in a way we are told to consider characteristic of Memphis. The novel demonstrates the gradual naturalization of the Nashville family to the norms of a less humane civilization, one, interestingly enough, more dominated by landowning. These wealthy and childless heirs to an old man's fortune, when they learn that he plans to marry, resort almost reflexively to cruelty and coercion to prevent him. The very familiarity of the tale of the mistreatment of an old parent is a great part of the point—none of us would do such a thing, and yet such things get done, and so commonly that when Shakespeare wrote *King Lear* he thought best to begin it in the manner of a folk tale, the story being as plain and ancient as its historical provenance.

Speaking of their father's business partner, the narrator of *A Summons to Memphis* says: "I cannot resist this opportunity to point out how the evil which men like Lewis Shackleford do, men who have come to power either through the use of military force or through preaching the Word of God or through the manipulation of municipal bonds, as was Mr. Shackleford's case, how the evil they do . . . has its effect . . . at last upon myriads of persons in all the millennia to come." This comparing of great things with small is amused, yet the novel proposes a complex reading of the world in which almost impalpable forces work as imperviously as fate, making whole cloth of what is done and what is suffered.

The father, in making his dignified retreat from Nashville, the scene of his betrayal, shocks his family profoundly. . . . So the family is frozen in one moment, the offspring oxymoronically "middle-aged children" far too engrossed with their father. A recoil is built into the situation. The children do as they feel they have been done by. They betray.

In *A Summons to Memphis,* as in tragedy—I take the title to invite such comparisons—what these people do for reasons that are personal and unique to them, and wholly sufficient to account for their actions, coincides neatly with larger patterns that exist outside them. Oedipus went to Thebes imagining himself a stranger. These people have considered themselves strangers in Memphis. Yet, as the narrator makes clear from the beginning, anticipating events as precisely as any oracle, they re-enact a situation he sees as "some kind of symbol . . . of Memphis"—in the typical pattern he observes in that city, "a rich old widower" is "denounced and persecuted by his own middle-aged children" when he decides to remarry. While the energy of malice in the Carver children comes from their being obliged to move to this alien place, its last expression takes a form that makes it clear they are assimilated to Memphis altogether.

The children are not villains or connivers. They are the beneficiaries of the fact that their pettiness has so many precedents as almost to perform itself. Their actions, if they are thought of as freely chosen, are abetted by the recurrence around them of like actions, which make them seem determined. So two apparently contrary models of human motivation are not only affirmed at the same time but shown to be mutually reinforcing. That is a neat piece of work. While the narrator declares people of his sort now to have only an attenuated existence, their past and milieu hold them so powerfully that if attenuation exists at all among them its only effect is to make them, paradoxically, less resistant to such influences—just as, having lost Nashville, the family falls completely under the sway of Memphis. Behavior, like matter, will have one form or another.

A mistral blows through Peter Taylor's world. Although it is manifested often in betrayal of friend by friend, father by son, son by father, most vulnerable of all are the blacks. In many of his stories, they are drawn into near-familial relationships, and then at the same time subject to being scolded or dismissed at any time, at any age, embarrassed for any imagined offense. They have made, as a magnanimous response to intractable necessity, lives for themselves out of interest in the lives of uningratiating people and affection for children not their own, but have enlisted nothing of the duty or loyalty or identification that sometimes shelters the feelings of family. These stories are very painful to read, as they should be. The problems of race in Mr. Taylor's writing are not historical or political so much as they are extreme expression of the strange energy loose in his world, an injuriousness like Poe's gratuitously destructive "perverse."

Black characters are not prominent in *A Summons to Memphis.* All of them servants, they move over the same terrain as the Carver family, standing by the road during the departure from Nashville to gaze wistfully in the direction of the small country town they and the Carvers have come from. To one who has read Mr. Taylor's stories, the presence of the black characters in this novel is a reminder of the potent shocks that can run along the lines of loyalty and family.

Southern writing often seems to me cloyed with the fusty apologetics of 19th-century reaction, to be indebted a little too deeply to Walter Scott and such inventors of the mystique of past and place, the moral opiate inevitably in demand while Scots were being routed from their lands and driven into wretched industrial cities and death from famine and cholera, and while blacks were being carried from their own lands and put to the use of an industrialized agriculture, treated as articles of commerce, with no acknowledgment of their ties to any place or community or family. This subordination of human beings to sheep on one side of the Atlantic and to cotton on the other is smuggled into our consciousness disguised as an old order, and the noble depopulators and the aristocratic slaveholders as the few, fading survivors of a more human world. History holds few examples of such chutzpah.

Even the best Southern writing nevertheless subscribes too willingly to the idea that there is a past that some people have and others lack, and that this past is dignifying and full of a sort of plenary grace upon which the present can still draw. So intimate was the connection between the American South and 19th-century industrialism that during the Civil War cotton workers in Manchester, England, died in the streets. The past is an industrial byproduct.

All this is by way of giving emphasis to my admiration for Peter Taylor's perfect indifference to the blandishments of this tradition, an indifference more remarkable because he sets his stories in wide temporal expanses and gives great play to social and generational influences. The present resonates with the past, but history is not a sort of monosodium glutamate, an instant, all-purpose intensifier of experience.

Peter Taylor's fiction is full of rewards. It is hard for a reviewer to do justice to the pleasures of understatement. Mr. Taylor's tact in preserving narrative surface, allowing fictional "meaning" to remain immersed in its element and preventing the degeneration of question into statement, leaves him open to being seen as another interpreter of an important tradition, when in fact he is as sui generis as middle Tennessee.

A Summons to Memphis is not so much a tale of human weakness as of the power of larger patterns, human also, that engulf individual character, a current subsumed in a tide. The moral earnestness of contemporary thought, the eagerness to praise and condemn, almost forbids the utterance of an important fact, which is that most of the time we really do not know just what we are doing or why, or what appearances our actions would have if we could see them from a little distance. I think the real accomplishment of Peter Taylor may be to have conjured the great slow shapes of epic and tragedy, so they can be glimpsed in the little segment of an ordinary life, restoring to our myths their most unsettling implications. (pp. 52-3)

Marilynne Robinson, "The Family Game Was Revenge," in The New York Times Book Review, *October 19, 1986, pp. 1, 52-3.*

JOHN UPDIKE

[*Considered a perceptive observer of the human condition and an extraordinary stylist, Updike is one of America's most distinguished men of letters. His works include the novel* Rabbit, Run *(1960), its sequels* Rabbit Redux *(1971) and* Rabbit is Rich *(1981), and such short story collections as* Bech: A Book *(1970) and* Trust Me *(1987). In the following excerpt, Updike discusses the characteristics of Taylor's fiction, particularly his prose technique.*]

A Summons to Memphis by Peter Taylor is not quite the distinguished short-story writer's first novel; thirty-six years ago, he published *A Woman of Means,* which, little more than forty thousand words long, might be called a novella. The two books have much in common: a narrator who has been moved from a bucolic Tennessee childhood to a big house in a river city (Memphis, St. Louis), a handsome and strong-willed father recovering from a business setback, a witty but somehow in-

capacitated and mentally fragile mother figure (a mother, a stepmother), two older and wearingly vivacious sisters or stepsisters, a psychological core of ambivalent and ruminative passivity, and a lovingly detailed (architecturally, sociologically) portrait of life in the upper classes of the Upper South between the two world wars. This last is Mr. Taylor's terrain, and he rarely strays from it. The narrator of *A Summons to Memphis,* Phillip Carver, lives in Manhattan, on West Eighty-second Street ("one of the safer neighborhoods on the Upper West Side, but still we have to be very careful"), with a woman fifteen years younger, Holly Kaplan; New York, that bulging plenitude, is felt as a kind of blissfully blank limbo, and the principal charm of his mistress seems to be that she, from a prosperous Jewish family in Cleveland, shares with the forty-nine-year-old Southern refugee a rueful, guilty obsession with the tribal reality left behind. "She felt they had a real life out there in Cleveland that she didn't have, had never had, would never have now." Both Holly and Phillip are in publishing, and their principal activities seem to be reading galley proofs and discussing their families:

> Suddenly, with a sigh, Holly blew out a great billow of smoke and said irritably that I *was really* absolutely obsessed with my family!

> This was an accusation which Holly and I frequently hurled at each other. In the beginning our complaints about our families had been perhaps our deepest bond. We had long since, however, worn out the subject. . . .

In the course of this meandering narrative, it is possible to feel like Holly when she blew out the impatient billow of smoke. After a lifetime of tracing teacup tempests among genteel Tennesseans, Mr. Taylor retains an unslaked appetite for the local nuance. The rather subtle (to Yankees, at least) differences between the styles of Memphis and Nashville are thoroughly and repeatedly gone into, with instructive side-glances at Knoxville and Chattanooga. "Nashville," an old social arbiter of that town explains, "is a city of schools and churches, whereas Memphis is—well, Memphis is something else again. Memphis is a place of steamboats and cotton gins, of card playing and hotel society." The narrator puts it, "Memphis was today. Nashville was yesterday." His own temperamental preference, as we could guess from his leisurely, laggard prose, is for yesterday. . . . (p. 158)

Direct dialogue in *A Summons to Memphis* is sparse, and the plot feels skimped, even snubbed. Though Mr. Taylor tells us a great deal about costumes, furniture, and civic differences, there is a great deal he avoids showing. Indeed, he almost cruelly teases , with his melodious divagations and his practiced skill at foreshadowing and delaying climaxes, the reader of this novel. Its kernel of action—Phillip Carver's trip to Memphis at the summons of his sisters, in 1967—does not occur until well after midpoint. He at last boards the plane on page 132, arrives at the Memphis airport on page 135, and by page 153 is back on a plane, winging his way into more cloudy retrospect and having refused (implausibly, I think) to spend a single night with his father and sisters. And the events while he is briefly there seem oddly betranced; though his vital if elderly father has been frustrated in an attempt at marriage, the old man submits without a peep, and though his son has been summoned a thousand miles for a family conference, he says hardly a word. Concerning an earlier frustration, it is not made clear why or how the father covertly wrecks the romance between Phillip, who is a soldier and all of twenty-three, and Clara Price, who sounds lovely and, even if she does hail from far-off Chattanooga, would appear to be socially acceptable; she and her family live "in a splendid Tudor-style house atop Lookout Mountain"—presumably above bribery and bullying persuasion. Some nuance, no doubt, escaped me, just as, in trying to grasp the scarcely-to-be-forgiven trauma of being moved from Nashville to Memphis, I fastened on the tragic fact that the two girls thereby "came out" in the wrong city and wasted their débutante parties. . . . (p. 161)

In any case, one might argue that the action of the novel is not so much the doings, past and present, of the Tennessee Carvers as the struggle by the self-exiled Phillip, staged in "these very irregular notebooks" of his which we are mysteriously reading, to come to terms with his past—the magnificent, crushing father, the "cluttered-up, bourgeois life," the tenacious, static idyll of the South. . . . From this South, with its omnipresent past, Mr. Taylor, like Faulkner, draws endless inspiration; he stirs and stirs the same waters, watching them darken and deepen, while abstaining from Faulkner's violent modernist gestures. He stirs instead with a Jamesian sort of spoon.

In praise of *A Woman of Means* thirty-six years ago, Robert Penn Warren claimed for it "the excitement of being constantly on the verge of deep perceptions and deep interpretations." We stay on the verge much of the time. *A Woman of Means* did plunge, with the empathy of a James Agee or William Maxwell, into the frightening dark of boyhood, when one is able to observe so much and do so little. Its evocation of a child's helpless, sensitive world seemed to close hastily, but not until our essential loneliness and the precariousness of even the best-appointed home were made painfully clear. In *A Summons to Memphis,* though the canvas is broader and adorned with fine comic splashes, some of the narrative churning brings up only what is already floating on the surface. . . . (pp. 161-62)

James's heavily mirrored halls of mutual regard seem but feebly imitated by reflections like "I knew always that the affair referred to was pure fantasy but I do not know even now whether or not they knew I knew." The diction at times is so fastidious that a smile at the narrator's expense must be intended: "If slit skirts were the fashion, then my sisters' would be vented well above the knees, exposing fleshy thighs which by this time in my sisters' lives were indeed of no inconsiderable size." Some sentences can only be called portly: "But about Alex Mercer himself there was something that made him forever fascinated by and sympathetic to that which he perhaps yearned after in spirit but which practically speaking he did not wish himself to become." Such measured verbal groping among the shadows of morality and good intention has suffered a diminishment since James; he had no commerce with God but had retained the religious sense, and the ground beneath his characters authentically trembles when they—for example, Kate Croy and Merton Densher—commit what they feel is a sin. In Phillip Carver's world, no religion remains, just an old-fashioned code of behavior, and its defense is hard to distinguish from snobbery or, to use a word he uses of himself, "lethargy." He is so imbued with lethargy that he speaks of "debating the question of how many angels could sit on the head of a pin" when in the conventional image, of course, the angels dance. As a young man he registers for the draft as a conscientious objector (in peacetime, early in 1941), but when the draft-board clerk fails to understand and sends in his form with the others, "this was *so* like a certain type of Memphis mentality . . . I could not even bring myself to protest;" he indifferently puts on his uniform and goes off to Fort Ogle-

thorpe. When, six years later, he flees Memphis for New York, "it was as though someone else were dressing me and packing for me or at least as though I had no will of my own"—his sisters are acting through him. And when, in 1967, he discovers himself in the same restaurant as his long-lost love, Clara Price, he doesn't trouble to get up from his chair and present himself; like those angels, he just sits. On his visits home, the dynamism of his ambitious father and animated, vengeful sisters oppresses him; it seems that "the whole family had finally become completely demented and didn't know how consummately and irreversibly life had already passed us by." His narrative can scarcely bring itself to describe present events, and comes to life only when recapturing some moment or fact from the buried past. The prissy, circuitous language (confided to "notebooks" yet elaborately explanatory and in one spot openly concerned about "the reader") is flavored with anachronisms like "for the nonce," "lad," and the word "dependencies" to describe a farm's outbuildings.

And yet this language, with its echo of old usages and once-honored forms, delivers things a less quaint diction could hardly express. . . . The father and sisters are old-fashioned characters, with costumes and settings and histories and psychologies; Phillip, by leaving the hinterland where clothes make a statement and the family "things" are worth inheriting, has become a non-character, a sensate shade dwelling in the low-affect regions of Don DeLillo and Donald Barthelme, a human being who assigns only a limited value, hedged about with irony, to himself. Someday, Phillip Carver fantasizes, he and Holly will simply fade away in their apartment—"when the sun shines in next morning there will be simply no trace of us." The lovers will not have been "alive enough to have the strength to die."

Peter Taylor's apparently cozy Tennessee world is bleaker than Henry James's transatlantic empyrean, for it is a century more drained of the blood of the sacred. The sacred, Mircea Eliade has written, "implies the notions of *being,* of *meaning,* and of *truth.* . . . It is difficult to imagine how the human mind could function without the conviction that there is something irreducibly *real* in the world." For James, the real constituted the human appetites, mostly for love and money, that flickered beneath and secretly shaped the heavily draped society of late-Victorian times. By Mr. Taylor's time, appetite has shrivelled to dread—dread of another's aroma, of being suffocated by one's father's appetites. For all the fussy good manners of his prose, the ugly war between parents and children has been his recurrent topic; one thinks of the short story **"Porte Cochère"** (the house in *A Summons to Memphis* also has a porte cochère), which ends with that old father, in the darkness of his room, while his adult children noisily besiege his door, taking out the walking stick "with his father's face carved on the head" and stumbling about "beating the upholstered chairs with the stick and calling the names of children under his breath." In *A Summons to Memphis,* Phillip Carver wins through to a real, non-trivial insight when he accepts "Holly's doctrine that our old people must be not merely forgiven all their injustices and unconscious cruelties in their roles as parents but that any selfishness on their parts had actually been required of them if they were to remain whole human beings and not become merely guardian robots of the young." The wrongs of the father are inevitably visited upon the son, as part of the jostle of "whole human beings" sharing the earth. Beneath his talky, creaking courtesies, Peter Taylor deals fascinatingly with the primal clauses of the social contract. (pp. 163-65)

John Updike, ''Summonses, Indictments, Extenuating Circumstances,'' in The New Yorker, *Vol. LXII, No. 37*, November 3, 1986, pp. 158, 161-65.

ANN HULBERT

[*Hulbert is a senior editor of* The New Republic. *In the following excerpt, she comments on the dark themes of social disruption and alienation in* A Summons to Memphis.]

Peter Taylor is routinely and rightly praised for the glasslike lucidity of his prose, yet he is interested above all in distortions of perspective. For more than 40 years, he has written about well-born families in the upper South who have lost much of their assurance about what to look up to and whom to look down on. His Tennessee, as Robert Penn Warren wrote in 1948 in his introduction to Taylor's first collection of stories, *A Long Fourth,* ''is a world vastly uncertain of itself and the ground of its values, caught in a tangle of modern commercialism and traditions and conventions gone to seed, confused among pieties and pretensions.'' That world was still a contemporary one then. It no longer is—the old rules of order between the generations, the sexes, and the races are history. Yet they are important history, and Taylor has continued to scrutinize the place and epoch of their passing in fiction that seems old-fashioned—at least on the surface.

Taylor's new novel . . . looks like another contribution to that absorbing enterprise. In a sense it is. *A Summons to Memphis* is largely a gathering of Phillip Carver's memories of growing up happily in Nashville and then unhappily in Memphis in the 1930s and '40s. But Phillip's ''very irregular notebooks,'' which he writes in New York miles and years away from his family past, are also an occasion for Taylor to explore an even more uncertain world than that densely textured South. Scribbling in a gloomy Manhattan apartment in the 1970s, Phillip is suffering from a very contemporary anomie. With his deracinated narrator, Taylor has brought to the surface the psychological theme that has always been at the heart of his social portraiture: how resilient, or else resistant, human character can be in the face of disorder and change.

It is a familiar Southern preoccupation, but Taylor's ''understyle,'' as Warren termed it, and his quiet emphasis on the mysteries of character (he's often compared to Chekhov) set him apart from the gothic regionalism of much Southern writing. He is neither pious about the past nor much impressed by the present, and his ruminations about human motives and actions have always had a deliberately inconclusive quality. Above all, they have never been simple. Certainly they aren't in *A Summons to Memphis,* which might best be described as a dramatic monologue—a virtuosic example of the often disconcerting genre. Taylor lets Phillip do all the talking, but that doesn't mean he trusts Phillip's account of self-discovery or intends us to. Phillip may well rate as Taylor's least reliable narrator, and this book demands—and rewards—vigilance. Phillip's reckoning with his own history, Taylor ironically implies throughout his character's monologue, is hollower than it appears. This dispassionate narrator is strangely bloodless, and in the end he has lost his bearings.

A Summons to Memphis has the outline of a familiar Taylor story: a man is unexpectedly jolted into a confrontation with an oppressive, puzzling past and then has a brief revelation—Taylor's characteristically inconclusive kind of epiphany. (pp. 37-8)

Yet the way Phillip tells the story lends support to an implicit, and considerably darker, version. The prose is as limpid as ever (''like a glass-bottom boat,'' said Randall Jarrell), but Phillip's method is digressive in the extreme: he veers unpredictably between past and present, circles around obviously important memories, repeats himself again and again. His long-winded, hairsplitting manner results in some quite comical passages—to Taylor's obvious delight. But Phillip's own detachment is strangely awkward, not witty. Despite all the minute observations he offers, he is emotionally impassive as he pauses to describe the woman with whom he has lived for years or his best friend from Memphis days, or surveys his family—or assesses himself: ''I think I felt totally indifferent,'' says this man from whom sentiments flee. Each page seems to hold out the promise that Phillip is about to frame a memory in a way that might free him from his aloofness. Yet the happy ending that Taylor stages in the last, frigidly lyrical paragraph of these notebooks is heavily ironic—as his apparently comic conclusions so often are. This narrator is numbly suspended between the past and the future, between the power to will and the power to feel.

Throughout Phillip's monologue, Taylor nudges us toward this deeper reading: here is a man whose ostensible resilience is finally only a sign of abiding passivity. For such an evasive soul, Taylor suggests, a confrontation with his family past can do little to instill, or strengthen, a sense of generous self-possession. Instead it becomes an occasion to avoid responsibility for having become the remote person he is. The convoluted tour Phillip makes of his youthful ordeals reveals a vulnerable man bent on blaming others for his own self-centered vulnerability. (p. 38)

Phillip has sketched a grim caricature of the provincial past that often looms in Taylor's stories. The changing local Tennessee customs that unbalance so many of his characters seem to have disoriented Phillip in a radical—almost surreal—way. For him, the familiar over-bearing power of family traditions and expectations has turned tyrannical. Not that he's presented it so starkly. Shifting constantly among scenes and times, Phillip makes a show of groping for a clearer perspective on a past he's brooded over but never before brought to the surface—yet he's more successful in raising further questions about his own failures to act and react.

Toward the end of his notebooks, Phillip is given what appears to be the reprieve Taylor sometimes offers his protagonists: the chance to put his past, if only provisionally, in more realistic proportion. Yet Taylor implies that Phillip may be as misled about his mature liberation as he was about his youthful enslavement. His supposed act of imaginative sympathy with forceful George Carver serves in the end as another way for Phillip to assuage his uneasiness about his own wan existence—to convince himself that from now on he is choosing it freely. Taylor grants him a few moments of empathy: there is a vivid scene in which Phillip is swept up and out of himself by the old man as the two ride in a car to the wedding his sisters have secretly canceled.

But by the close of the book, Phillip has drifted into dry speculations instead. Sitting in his Manhattan apartment with Holly Kaplan, the woman with whom he's lived peacefully and passionlessly for years, he sips a watery drink and talks endlessly about principles of family reconciliation—about forgiving versus forgetting—rather than about real people. He says he can now see and admire his father as an energetically adaptable man, completely different from himself: ''It was his very oppositeness from me that I could admire without reservation, like a character in a book." Contemplating an unchanged, utterly quiet life ahead, he announces in his last line that he and Holly have emerged "serenely free spirits."

Yet "serenity" and "orderliness" and "reasonableness," the supreme values in Phillip's limited existence, are hardly Taylor's high standards. Conceiving of the past as the realm of determinism, Phillip seizes upon the future as the province of choice—and is left with no true human choices to make. The static, unencumbered fate that Phillip and his companion look forward to with self-satisfaction is sterile—a vision of the weightless contemporary world eerier than any Taylor has presented before. Shut up in his dim apartment with Holly, surrounded by manuscripts rather than children, Phillip may see his notebooks as evidence of the birth of understanding, but in fact they are the testimony of a disoriented soul.

"Peter Taylor has a disenchanted mind," Robert Penn Warren wrote 40 years ago, "but a mind that nevertheless understands and values enchantment"—"the enchantment of veracity," he hastened to say, not of fantasy. The trauma of maturity, Taylor's fiction has always proposed, involves more than seeing through the oppressive pieties and pretensions of the past. But he has rarely so starkly dramatized the real, and more daunting, challenge: to find some humane way of living with precisely the terrifying truth that those family and social customs are meant to camouflage—the chasms between selves. Some of his characters are lucky enough to "see the world through another man's eyes," as the narrator of the story **"Promise of Rain"** puts it, and thus have a chance of truly seeing into their own heads, and above all their own hearts: "It is only then that the world, as you have seen it through your own eyes, will begin to tell you things about yourself." For the less fortunate in Taylor's fiction, the price of myopia is high. Some turn into tyrants at home. Some become victims out in the world. In *A Summons to Memphis* Taylor has suggested an even more alienating possibility in Phillip, who has no real home and rarely ventures into the world: the danger of turning into a "free spirit" trapped within the bounds of the self. (pp. 39-40)

> Ann Hulbert, "Back to the Future," in The New Republic, Vol. 195, No. 21, November 24, 1986, pp. 37-40.

WALTER SULLIVAN

[*Sullivan is an American critic, novelist, and scholar specializing in contemporary British and American literature. His writings include the novels* Sojourn of a Stranger *(1957) and* The Long, Long Love *(1959) and the critical work* Death by Melancholy *(1972); he also coauthored* Writing from the Inside *(1983) with Robert Towers. In the following excerpt, Sullivan discusses Taylor's vision of Southern post-agrarian society as reflected in* A Summons to Memphis.]

Few writers have staked out for themselves more narrowly defined domains than Peter Taylor. His place is middle and west Tennessee, and when a story or play is set in St. Louis or Detroit, the foreign ambience enhances the sense of southern custom. Taylor's southerners in exile remain what they are: second- and third-generation Tennessee agrarians who have made an urban progress in the world. His time is the decade of the thirties, and he is such a master of anachronism that whatever the stated date of a story may be, the attitudes and actions and details recreate the uneasy last decade of the he-

gemony of the southern gentry. His people are the well connected and well-to-do; the middle-class and poor and black characters who appear in his work are defined by their relationships to the wealthy. Think of the unfortunate Miss Bluemeyer in **"The Death of a Kinsman,"** or of Jesse in **"A Friend and Protector,"** or of the girls of the Memphis "demimonde" in **"The Old Forest."** (p. 309)

In most of Peter Taylor's work the characters, their attitudes, and their social intercourse with one another constitute, to a great extent, the story. (p. 310)

As Taylor points out frequently in his work, his aristocrats are the last Agrarians. They left their ruined plantations after the Civil War to engage in business or a profession in the city. They brought with them the old manners and customs, the country sense of family—or "connection" as they would put it; as we are told in **"The Old Forest,"** what they brought from the old order "made them both better and worse than business men elsewhere." Their wives and daughters shared their values and were also better and worse and happier and unhappier than their contemporaries who broke with the past. Taylor's people know who they are; they know how they are supposed to behave; and so at the outset of their lives they have answers to the two questions that most vex the rest of the modern world. They need not search for their identities or enter into endless engagements over what is right or wrong in a given situation. But the past, any mundane past, is imperfect, and freedom is not to be found in its service. Bound by what they believe in, Taylor's character take their stands and await their defeats. (p. 311)

A Summons to Memphis takes Taylor farther from his home base than he usually allows himself to travel. Philip Carver, his narrator, though originally from Nashville and Memphis, now lives in New York. (p. 315)

Philip Carver is not a typical Taylor character. His translation to a job in publishing and a Manhattan flat shared with a Jewish woman from Cleveland seems to have dulled his personality. Making a reluctant passage home, he is uncertain until his plane lands whether he will help his sisters or his father. Since George is at the airport to meet him, he decides he will "stand up" with George; but the intended bride has left Memphis, having been subverted by the sisters. The next family crisis and the next summons to Memphis come when George, having made up his differences with Lewis Shackleford, wants to pay him an extended visit. This time Philip sides with his sisters, but the sudden death of Shackleford renders any loyalty or action supererogatory.

A Summons to Memphis gives the impression of being at once old and unfinished, as if it were written in the early seventies—when the main action takes place—and resurrected now without revision. The book is loosely constructed, often repetitive; and one of the characters, Philip's brother who has died in World War II, is too little a human being, too much a symbol. An editor should have repaired these defects. Of more importance are the uncertainty of George's motives and Philip's fecklessness. Compared to Son in **"A Long Fourth,"** another southern expatriate, Philip seems flat; but Son and Philip exist in different worlds. In 1939 the agrarian South was doomed, but it lived in the manners and affections of Sweetheart and other business and professional men of Memphis and Nashville. It was shared by their wives and children. By the seventies the last survivors of the old dispensation are dead or too old to continue the struggle, the southern custom endures only in such private confrontations as those Taylor delineates here.

Yet the novel embodies a public dimension in an irony that Taylor has not exploited previously. The lives of all the Carvers are distorted by the failure of Lewis Shackleford's business, but it was his success, and the success of others like him, that eradicated the influence of southern agrarianism. Shackleford's character is based on Rogers Caldwell, and Taylor follows his prototype faithfully. In 1917 Caldwell founded the first investment banking firm in the South. When his financial empire collapsed in 1930, he barely escaped prison. But, like Lewis Shackleford, by the end of his life Caldwell was considered a financial genius; and invitations to his Saturday luncheons were prized by Nashville businessmen. His ambition became the common ambition, as the agrarian twilight faded into darkness. What is left by the seventies is remnants—manners privately practiced, standards privately held.

In *A Summons to Memphis* the demise of southern society is seen in the flamboyant dress and suggestive conversation of the aging Carver sisters, in George's dates with young women and his visits to discos, in Philip's alienation from home and tradition. He and his girlfriend from Cleveland see their parents as part of the graying of America, the geriatric crisis that concerns us all. And when Philip's boyhood friend suggests that he give his collection of rare books to a Memphis university, he can only laugh. For him there is no more Memphis, no more family, no more South. Thus the story Peter Taylor has been telling all his writing life reaches its proper end. (pp. 315-17)

> *Walter Sullivan, "The Last Agrarian: Peter Taylor Early and Late," in* The Sewanee Review, *Vol. XCV, No. 2, Spring, 1987, pp. 308-17.*

MAUREEN FREELY

Peter Taylor is one of America's most famous underrated writers. In the four decades since his short stories began to appear in the *New Yorker,* he has been awarded most of the nation's prestigious literary prizes and fellowships, and yet he has never attained the wider recognition of an Updike, a Styron, or a Cheever.

Why? His preferred subject—genteel hometown life in old-world Tennessee—could hardly be called esoteric. Perhaps the problem lies with his deceptively modest prose style, but it is more likely to be his lack of sentimentality. Taylor is more interested in dissecting the American Dream than he is in celebrating it—and that can be unforgivable in a country that still thinks of serious literature as a sophisticated form of cod liver oil.

In *A Summons to Memphis* . . . the narrator, a middle-aged New York publisher, hears from his two spinster sisters that his father is about to remarry. They want to head him off, and they want their brother to help them.

The crisis sparks off a series of philosophical musings about what makes Memphis the kind of city it is, and why middle-aged children are more likely to meddle with their widowed parent's romances in that 'landlocked, backwater' town than they are in Nashville, Knoxville, or even Chattanooga. It is only gradually that the narrator fills in the blanks of his own family history. Despite every effort to be fair, he succeeds in casting his father as an ogre.

It is a shock, therefore, when we finally meet the father. Unlike his children, with their dead weight of malice, he is bursting with hope, plans, forgiveness and goodwill. One longs for him and his son to 'have it out.' But the only reconciliation they manage is long distance, over the phone. At the end of this subtle and disturbing book, one is left with a picture of a man rendered sterile by his own sense of irony—and with nothing but admiration for the author, who is the master of his.

> *Maureen Freely, "Families at War," in* The Observer, *April 19, 1987, p. 22.*

ANITA BROOKNER

A Summons to Memphis has been the success of the season in America, and it is indeed very good, a slow classic rumination on the events of the past which come freighted with just that degree of mystery that makes them unlikely to disappear in the lifetime of the protagonist, Phillip Carver. (p. 34)

The whole Gothic confabulation is masked by a slow meditative style which plunges evermore masterfully into the past. It is in fact the style which raises the status of this novel to the alpha-plus rating, for the emotional premise on which it is built—that the move from Nashville to Memphis ruined four lives—is shaky. Similarly, the truly shocking hatred which the author's perfect and easy manners disguise might have strained the credulity of the reader, were it not for the sad conclusion, in which a diminished Phillip fails to celebrate his freedom, having indeed never had any freedom to celebrate.

A Summons to Memphis is a curiosity. On the one hand its oversize subject-matter takes it out of the normal run of contemporary novels, and has one reaching for adjectives like heroic, or, on the other hand, grotesque. But the deceptively mild clarity with which it is written indicates an unusual capacity to internalise its conflicts and to bring the novel home to its perfect conclusion. A remarkable achievement, different in both matter and style from anything we have read this year, and if not a masterpiece, almost a classic. (p. 35)

> *Anita Brookner, "Revenge of the Weird Sisters," in* The Spectator, *Vol. 258, No. 8288, May 16, 1987, pp. 34-5.*

Barbara Vine
A Dark-Adapted Eye

Edgar Allan Poe Award: Best Novel

(Pseudonym of Ruth Rendell) English novelist and short story writer.

Having established her reputation as one of the finest mystery writers in England, Rendell chose to vary her successful routine by publishing her novel *A Dark-Adapted Eye* (1986) under the pseudonym Barbara Vine. Rendell made no secret of her authorship; she announced that she planned to issue a new series of mysteries under the pen name Vine while continuing to write the kind of detective novels and psychological thrillers that have won her fame. While she is renowned for her taut, perceptive studies of the criminal mind at work, Rendell as Barbara Vine plans to concentrate on "ordinary people under extraordinary pressures." *A Dark-Adapted Eye and A Fatal Inversion* (1987) are the initial books in the Vine series.

While Rendell's most popular works, including *From Doon with Death* (1964) and *Put On by Cunning* (1981), are relatively conventional murder mysteries centering on the adventures of Chief Inspector Reginald Wexford, a small-town police detective, she has experimented with different approaches to the crime genre. In the 1970s, for example, Rendell began to tire of writing straightforward police procedurals and added to her regular output of Wexford novels a series of more offbeat suspense thrillers.

These works, including *A Demon in My View* (1976) and *Live Flesh* (1986), concentrate more on criminals, usually violent psychopaths, and their victims than on the details of plot and crime-solving. Rendell's novels are often praised for their fascinating character studies, as well as their realistic depictions of London and Rendell's native Sussex. "If it weren't for a ridiculous literary snobbery about 'crime writing,'" comments English author John Mortimer, "Ruth Rendell would be acclaimed as one of our most important novelists." Rendell observed: "I don't particularly mind being called a genre novelist because I've found that if I write a book that is good and is literate and critics like it, it gets raised above the genre anyway in reviews and the way it is treated, so it doesn't really matter very much."

In a postscript to *A Dark-Adapted Eye*, Rendell explains the origins of the pen name Barbara Vine. Barbara, she notes, is her middle name; when she was growing up, she was known both as Ruth and as Barbara. To Rendell, each of her given names has come to represent a separate aspect of her personality. "Ruth is tougher, colder, more analytical, possibly more aggresive," she states. "Ruth has written all the novels, created Chief Inspector Wexford. Ruth is the professional writer." Rendell describes Barbara as "more feminine" and adds: "For a long time I have wanted Barbara to have a voice as well as Ruth. It would be a softer voice speaking at a slower pace, more sensitive perhaps, and more intuitive." Reflecting her desire, as Barbara Vine, to study the effects of abnormal circumstances on normal persons, *A Dark-Adapted Eye* focuses on the events that cause Vera, a prim matron living in post-

World War II Britain, to murder her sister. The novel, narrated by Vera's niece Faith, is Rendell's first book written from the point of view of a single character. Rendell remarks: "There would be nothing surprising to a psychologist in Barbara's choosing, as she asserts herself, to address readers in the first person."

Most commentators agree that *A Dark-Adapted Eye* demonstrates Rendell's literary skills, citing her detailed evocation of England during and after World War II and her poignant revelations of the motivations behind her characters' actions. Critics note that *A Dark-Adapted Eye* bears a stronger resemblance to "serious" fiction than Rendell's previous mysteries: the narrative progresses at a more leisurely pace than its predecessors, relying on depictions of psychological tensions and interfamilial intrigues to build suspense; and the author employs such literary devices as shifting time-frames and a circuitous method of storytelling, which evokes the ambiguity of perception. As Gillian Mackay noted: "Rendell has achieved every crime-writer's dream: critical recognition for transcending the form."

(See also *CLC*, Vols. 28, 48 and *Contemporary Authors*, Vol. 109.)

CRESSIDA CONNOLLY

It is perhaps unsurprising that *A Dark Adapted Eye* should contain a murder: its author is Ruth Rendell. . . . In common with some of her earlier work the murderer's identity is revealed early on, enabling her to explore fully the tensions which precede such an event. And Barbara Vine excels at observing the minute undercurrents which can lead to violence.

Faith Longley is forced to re-appraise her family when she agrees to assist a biographer researching a book on her late Aunt Vera. The Longleys are, at first sight, very ordinary middle-class people. Faith's father spent his working life in a bank in outer London, while his two sisters shared a home in Essex where their time was occupied with crochet and baking. They are fastidious and refined people whose only apparent vice is an occasional glass of sherry. How, then, did Vera come to be hanged for the murder of her sister Eden? Faith's recollections are interspersed with extracts from the proposed biography: to form a brilliantly sustained literary paper-chase which gradually peels away the layers of secrecy under which the answer lies.

The novel begins in war-time, when, to escape air-raids, the young Faith is sent to stay with her aunts. Vera's husband is posted abroad and her son away at boarding school. The two sisters live alone and appear devoted to one another, the difference in ages recalling a mother/daughter relationship in which cordiality plays the strong part. When Eden joins the WRNS Vera's only consolation is in the many letters her sister sends. It is only later that Faith remembers Vera's hesitancy as to Eden's whereabouts at that time; she remembers, too, how she saw her younger aunt at a London theatre when she was purportedly stationed on the south coast.

An elaborate subterfuge between the sisters is slowly revealed. Eden leaves the services, secretly, long before VE day and works as companion to an elderly lady of means, which post ultimately secures her a rich husband. Vera, meanwhile, announces that she is expecting a child. This tardy pregnancy causes a few raised eyebrows, as does its supposed duration, for Vera's husband has not visited her for the past ten months. When Eden and her husband settle only a few miles from Vera, it is generally supposed that the former will soon be pushing a pram alongside her nephew's. But Eden is unable to have a baby. The conflict between the sisters becomes rancorous as Eden slowly appropriates Vera's son. It is this 'tug-of-love' which precipitates the murder.

Vera is an austere and punctilious woman whose very features are softened by motherhood and her growing hysteria at the loss of her child is easy to comprehend. Less attractive is the acquisitive and beautiful Eden, frantic to produce an heir for her husband's fortunes. But Barbara Vine's characters are far from straightforward and the sisters' motives are not as clearcut as they seem. *A Dark Adapted Eye* is not a whodunnit but a whydunnit and the reasons are subtle and various.

Barbara Vine is masterly in her portrayal of the moral climate of the Forties and her descriptions of Vera's house conjure up its stifling atmosphere so well that the click of knitting needles is nearly audible. Faith makes regular forays into Eden's dressing table and its changing contents (lipstick, nylons, deodorant) serve as a neat reflection of the passage of time. A whole era is evoked by this novel and with it a kind of family structure in which respect for privacy gets the better of love, with terrible results. (pp. 35-6)

Cressida Connolly, "Extremes of Love," in Books and Bookmen, *No. 366, April, 1986, pp. 35-6.*

KATE CRUISE O'BRIEN

Motherhood in Barbara Vine's *A Dark Adapted Eye* is a tortuous and complex business. Vera Hillyard is a passionate, genteel woman living in rural Essex through the Second World War. Vera has absurd and strongly held convictions about the propriety of eating with her left hand and drinking with the right. 'Not so much *Kinder, Küche, Kirche*,' says her malicious sister-in-law 'as *Kauf, Klatsch, Kettelnadel*'—or shopping, gossip, embroidery needle.

Vera is married to an officer stationed in India, but prefers to remain in England to lavish her fanatical mother-love on her orphaned half-sister Eden, who is blonde and beautiful and never makes a fuss about bedtime. The two sisters lead a narrow rule-bound life, their peace occasionally shattered by visits from Vera's son Francis, who furiously resents his exile at boarding school and who spends his holidays devising 'teases' which mock Vera's proprieties. As war deepens Eden joins the WRNS—'very much the superior of the woman's services' says Vera—and soon there are rumours about Eden and men and rumours about the unexpected baby, Jamie, born to Vera ten months after her husband's last leave. The sisters' cloying love turns to hostility as they fight for possession of Jamie, whom each woman claims as her own.

A Dark Adapted Eye is beautifully told, the enclosed atmosphere of the country in wartime effortlessly conveyed, and Vera—contemptuous, rigid but capable of heroic love—is a notable creation. But Ms Vine is less successful with Eden, whose petulant selfishness seems incompatible with the maternal possessiveness which leads her to risk her brilliant marriage to reclaim her child.

Kate Cruise O'Brien, "Vermicelli Cord," in The Listener, *Vol. 115, No. 2958, May 1, 1986, p. 30.*

PATRICK SWINDEN

[*Swinden is an English critic and scholar specializing in English literature. His works include* Unofficial Selves: Character in the Novel from Dickens to the Present Day *(1973) and* The English Novel of History and Society, 1940-1980 *(1984). In the following excerpt, Swinden compares* A Dark-Adapted Eye *with previous novels by Rendell.*]

Ruth Rendell must be one of the most prolific, as well as the best, crime writers in England today. Within the last year she has published one of her Wexford detective novels, a volume of short stories, and two crime novels. The last of these, *A Dark-Adapted Eye*, comes to us through a *nom de plume*, and follows *Live Flesh* by only a month. They are very different expressions of her genius: the Rendell being a study in claustrophobic paranoia, the Vine a much more expansive treatment of a family secret long buried in the past and resurrected in the present by pressure of varied and complex circumstances. . . .

[The] ramifications of the Longley family in *A Dark-Adapted Eye* are extensive. So much so that a lot of the time spent reading this book will take the form of puzzlement and speculation about who is related to whom, through what devious and sinister channels. And that is how it should be, because the subject of the novel is one of uncertain identity. Ruth

Rendell has always been interested in the strange mix of genetic and enviromental factors that produce criminal behaviour. Now she extends this interest to the offspring of the criminal. She uses a puzzle about a child's identity as a means of opening up what looks like a straightforward case of murder, conviction and execution (the past events of the novel take place in the 1940s) to a re-examination which produces startling conclusions.

Both novels include settings in the Essex countryside. In fact the locations for each of them have been used before in Rendell's collections of short stories. Aspects of the plots of each have also been used before—in *A Demon in my View* and *A New Lease of Death* respectively. . . .

A Dark-Adapted Eye, by contrast [with *Live Flesh*], is full of life and interest. The war and post-war periods are described in meticulous though unemphatic detail, and the way the plot develops through memories of and investigations into a past too shallowly buried and fraught with unresolved mysteries is skillfully controlled. I don't recall, in a crime or any other kind of novel in recent years, such a convincing and deeply understood representation of bonds that tie mothers to sons, and elder to younger sisters. A fatal combination of snobbery and passion produces a uniquely fascinating and intractable family problem, incapable of painless resolution either from within or from without the family concerned. The niece of the two Longley sisters, whose point of view we share, looks on in the past with bafflement, and in the present with increasing horror, as the truth of the matter slowly dawns on her.

The conclusion is darkly provocative, and will disappoint neither crime-buff nor novel reader. If one has to express qualified disappointment with the latest Ruth Rendell, there can be nothing but praise for the first Barbara Vine.

> Patrick Swinden, "Questions of Identity," in The Spectator, Vol. 256, No. 8234, May 3, 1986, p. 30.

An Excerpt from *A Dark-Adapted Eye*

She has come back into my life after an absence that extends over more than a third of a century. Helen and Daniel Stewart have brought her to me and she is here in the house, the awkward guest she always was when she stayed in the homes of other people. I almost fancy that I can see her—not the Vera of the photographs in "the box," young, fair, earnest-eyed, but my thin, nervous, pernickety, often absurd aunt, performing that strange, uniquely characteristic action of hers, as unconscious as a tic, as unconscious as Jamie's flick of the hand, of pressing her palms together and bearing down on her clasped hands as if in some inner anguish. Time and time again these past days she has driven me to our unused littlest bedroom, where "the box" is, and made me lift the lid and turn over the contents, pausing to look at a picture or read a line from a letter, or simply staring in a daydream of nostalgia at the memorabilia of his sisters my father left behind him.

What would poor Vera make of the moral climate of the present day? I can imagine her look of mulish incredulity. A sexual revolution took place and the world was changed. What happened to her and Eden could not have happened today. The motive and the murder were of their time, rooted in their time, not only impossible in these days

but beyond the comprehension of the young unless that moral code is carefully explained to them. Because Vera is with me, is in my house like the sort of ghost that is visible to only one person, the one with the interest, I have tried to tell my daughter something of it, I have tried to elucidate.

"But why didn't she . . .?" is the way her interjections begin. "Why didn't she tell him? Why didn't she just live with him? Why did she want to marry him if he felt like that?" And, "But what could anyone have done to her?"

All I can say, lamely, is, "It was different then."

It was different. Does Stewart, also young, know how different it was? And if he doesn't, will he take my word? Or will I find myself, as I begin to think most likely, giving him the bare facts, correcting his obvious howlers, reminiscing a little, but keeping the real book that is Vera's life recorded on a tape run only in my own consciousness?

PAUL STUEWE

Ruth Rendell's novels have always fallen into two distinct categories: the Inspector Wexford books—police procedurals set in a small country town—and thrillers with psychological disturbance at their core, which often take place in seedy London surroundings where the peeling wallpaper matches the state of the characters' souls. *A Dark-Adapted Eye* is something of a change, as Barbara Vine displays a more literary side of Rendell's authorial personality to stunning advantage. Tricky technical devices such as abrupt shifts in time and deliberately limited points of view have been used to add complex ambiguities to an apparently simple tale of sisterly rivalry; the result is a story that engages us at several different levels. Most of Rendell's fans should be able to keep up with her new persona, although mystery addicts who prefer more traditional clue-by-clue puzzles will probably find the book an unsatisfying, vague read.

> Paul Stuewe, in a review of "A Dark-Adapted Eye," in Quill and Quire, Vol. 52, No. 7, July, 1986, p. 66.

PATRICIA CRAIG

[*Craig, an English critic, was formerly children's books editor of* The Literary Review. *Her works, written with Mary Cadogan, include* You're a Brick, Angela! A New Look at Girls' Fiction, 1839-1975 *(1976) and* The Lady Investigates: Women Detectives and Spies in Fiction *(1981). In the following excerpt, Craig notes that although Rendell has never taken a frivolous approach to crime fiction,* A Dark-Adapted Eye *is her most literary novel to date.*]

[In *A Dark-Adapted Eye* Ruth Rendell], under her new name of Barbara Vine, kicks off in striking style: 'On the morning Vera died I woke up very early.' Vera Hillyard, we learn within a line or two, is scheduled to die by hanging at the usual hour of eight in the morning. It is Vera's niece Faith Longley, Barbara Vine's narrator, who offers this information. What follows is an exhaustive look at the circumstances of the murder committed by Vera, and the life lived by her and her family before this event. We are soon in the past, in the Thirties and

Forties, and engrossed in a story presented with all the expertise the thriller-writer can muster.

The Longley family is a heterogeneous one, accommodating various social classes; class, social behaviour and sexual morality matter in 1939, in ways incomprehensible to those born into a freer society; the murder and the motive, the narrator emphasises, were 'of their time, rooted in their time', and impossible to imagine in a different period. What do we have? Faith Longley, thirty-odd years on, re-creating her wartime sojourns with her father's sisters, Vera and Eden, the second still a schoolgirl in 1939, with her front hair rolled into a sausage shape, at their white-brick cottage in Great Sindon, Essex. Augmenting these recollections are some pieces of research work by an author engaged in examining the Hillyard case.

The Sindon household to which Faith becomes attached is pretty odd, what with querulous, prickly Vera, irresistibly blonde Eden, and provoking Francis, Vera's son, who spends his holidays devising torments for his mother. Within a year or two another child is added to this intractable household, and it's a tussle over the custody of this child, Jamie, that brings about the pivotal outbreak in the drama. But that is some way into the future: in the meantime Faith and her Sindon friend Anne Cambus rifle the life of Mary, Queen of Scots for scenes to play-act in a derelict cottage, while the Battle of Britain rages overhead, and Eden, at her dressing-table, applies cosmetic preparations to her flawless face. All this is set out with the surest feeling for the character of the era.

Ruth Rendell has written many detective novels of a fairly orthodox kind, and, interspersed with these, high-grade thrill-ers in which the course of events is determined by the maladjustment of someone among the leading players. With the second type of novel, it's the author's custom to lumber herself with preposterous or seemingly unmalleable ingredients, and then go on to surprise us by the skill with which she causes everything, in the end, to fall into the place devised for it. It is partly a matter of balance, as she handles two or more converging stories (within each plot), and keeps them from going off the rails. Only a slightly lurid aftertaste gets between these stories and our complete enjoyment of them: there's no element of parody or black comedy in the situations Ruth Rendell envisages, not even when it comes to a man's obsession with a dress-shop dummy, which leads him to act peculiarly in a basement. Why should there be, she might ask, when her theme is criminal derangement and the forms it takes—that, and the openings for depravity afforded by the modern world? Her new novel, under a new name, is equally chary of frivolity, but it also, by and large, cuts out the depiction of paranoia, which is very much a feature of the Rendell thrillers and detective novels alike. Vera Hillyard is not a woman in the grip of some revolting compulsion: it's an intolerable pressure that causes her to act as she does. Ordinary life, in this book, is eroded by a malignant strain, instead of harbouring some such quality. The effect of this shift in approach is to bring the book close to the requirements of serious, rather than 'genre' fiction—a merger which the more accomplished among contemporary detective and thriller writers are always aiming to bring about. (p. 22)

Patricia Craig, "Open That Window, Miss Menzies," in London Review of Books, *Vol. 8, No. 14, August 7, 1986, pp. 22-3.*

August Wilson
Fences

New York Drama Critics Circle Award: Best Play
Pulitzer Prize: Drama and Tony Award: Best Play

American dramatist and poet.

Fences (1985), Wilson's second play to appear on Broadway, received unanimous praise from reviewers and won the most coveted prizes in American theater, including the Tony Award, the Pulitzer Prize, and the New York Drama Critics Circle Award. Wilson's Broadway debut, *Ma Rainey's Black Bottom* (1984), was also awarded the New York Drama Critics Circle Award. Both plays are a part of Wilson's planned play-cycle devoted to the story of black Americans in the twentieth century. *Ma Rainey* takes place during the 1920s, a time of particular achievement by blacks in the arts and the entertainment industry, and examines exploitation of blacks as well as their struggle for upward mobility. *Fences* is set in the urban industrial North during the 1950s and focuses on an outstanding athlete who was denied an opportunity for a major league baseball career.

"I'm taking each decade and looking at one of the most important questions that blacks confronted in that decade and writing a play about it," Wilson explains. "Put them all together and you have a history." It is Wilson's belief that in trying to assimilate into a white culture blacks have lost a sense of connection to their own tradition, which is rooted in Africa and finds modern expression in blues music. Wilson explains: "Blacks in America want to forget about slavery—the stigma, the shame. That's the wrong move. If you can't be who you are, who can you be? How can you know what to do? We have our history. We have our book, which is the blues. And we forget it all."

Wilson's awareness of black heritage dates back to his childhood in the Pittsburgh ghetto called "the Hill." Frustrated by the racism he experienced at school, Wilson dropped out of the ninth grade, thereafter deriving his education from his neighborhood experiences and the local library, where under a section marked "Negro" he found the books of the Harlem Renaissance writers. In these early years, Wilson dreamed of becoming a poet. Influenced by such writers as Amiri Baraka, Dylan Thomas, and John Berryman, he submitted poems to small, mostly black publications associated with The University of Pittsburgh. Though he learned much from practicing this craft, Wilson noted that he had difficulty finding his own voice, having so immersed himself in other poets. In 1968, inspired by the civil rights movement, Wilson cofounded a community theater—Black Horizon on the Hill—to raise black-consciousness in the area; this theater became the forum for his first plays. Wilson purposely avoided the study of other playwrights so as not to hinder the expression of his own voice.

Wilson's first professional breakthrough occurred in 1978 when he was invited by Claude Purdy, a former Pittsburgh director, to write a play for his black theater in St. Paul, Minnesota. It was in this new milieu, removed from his native Pittsburgh, that Wilson began to recognize poetic qualities in the language that had surrounded him in his hometown. His first two plays,

Rollin A. Riggs/NYT Pictures

Jitney and *Fullerton Street*, garnered little notice. Wilson's third play, *Ma Rainey's Black Bottom*, was accepted by the National Playwrights Conference in 1982, where it drew the attention of Lloyd Richards, the artistic director of both the conference and the Yale Repertory Theater. Richards recalls that he immediately recognized in Wilson a significant new voice. Richards directed *Ma Rainey* at the Yale Theater, and later took the play to Broadway. Since then, with Richards in the role of mentor and director, all of Wilson's plays have had their first staged reading at the playwrights conference followed by runs at the Yale Repertory Theater and regional theaters before opening on Broadway.

Set in the late 1950s, on the eve of the civil rights revolution, *Fences* centers on Troy Maxson, a black man who was an outstanding athlete during his younger years but was ignored by major league baseball because of his color. Struggling through middle age as a garbage collector, Maxson's bitterness at his situation results in a family conflict. His son, who aspires to an athletic career, battles against his father's fear and envy of him, and Maxson's wife is humiliated by his adultery. Many critics see in these family divisions and conflicts the influence of such playwrights as Arthur Miller, Tennessee Williams, and Eugene O'Neill. Most agree, however, that Wilson's play, though enriched by the similarities, maintains its originality and addresses universal family concerns.

Wilson has stated, "I come to playwriting out of words, poetry," and, indeed, critics consider his use of language the strongest element of his work, praising both his sharp ear for the rhythms of everyday speech and the musical, often blues-influenced quality of his dialogue. In the words of actor James Earl Jones, who portrayed Troy Maxson onstage, "Few writers can capture dialect as dialogue in a manner as interesting and accurate as August's."

A prolific writer, Wilson has composed two additional plays in his play-cycle since completing *Fences: Joe Turner's Come and Gone* (1987), which is set in 1911, centers on black migration to the North, and *The Piano Lesson* (1988) takes place during the 1930s, portraying a family conflict over a treasured piano.

(See also *CLC*, Vol. 39 and *Contemporary Authors*, Vol. 115.)

JOHN BEAUFORT

[*Fences*] is a work of exceptional depth, eloquence, and power. . . . It is a major addition to the decade-by-decade cycle of plays through which Mr. Wilson is surveying the black American experience in the 20th century. . . . The new segment takes place in the shabby backyard of the Maxson house in a northern American industrial city. . . . Extending from 1957 to 1965, the play's nine scenes thus antedate and implicitly anticipate the civil-rights revolution of the 1960s.

The past confronts an uncertain hope of things to come in the conflict between Troy and his teenage son Cory. A promising high-school athlete, Cory is being scouted for a scholarship at a Southern university. Troy, an ex-baseball star embittered at having been restricted to the Negro Leagues, and suspicious of white men's overtures, refuses to give the needed parental permission. To Troy, who has served time in prison, his promotion to being the first black garbage truck driver in the sanitation department means more than Cory's dreams of glory. The father's obduracy leads to an irreconcilable standoff.

In the meantime, Wilson is filling out the details and dimensions of this black family portrait. Ebullient, hard-working, home-loving Troy supports the household. But it is Rose Maxson, his firm but gentle wife, who sustains their life together. When Troy haltingly confesses a marital infidelity, Rose accepts the innocent child whose mother dies giving birth, but she informs her husband that he is now "womanless." (p. 23)

Like the best of black American drama, *Fences* blends the unique and the universal: the unique because it explores the plight of a minority in a society not yet healed of prejudice; the universal because it is rooted in the human condition. Not surprisingly, some commentators have perceived resemblances between the father-son conflicts of *Death of a Salesman* and those of *Fences*. Such inferred comparisons don't in any way diminish the achievement of Wilson's complex, demanding, and rewarding urban folk play. (p. 24)

> John Beaufort, "'Fences' Probes Life of Blacks in '50s," in The Christian Science Monitor, *March 27, 1987, pp. 23-4.*

CLIVE BARNES

[*An English drama critic, Barnes has written for such periodicals as the London* Times, *the* New York Times, Harpers, Nation, *and* New Republic. *His works include* Inside American Ballet Theatre *(1977) and* Nureyev *(1982). In the following excerpt, Barnes praises* Fences *as an extraordinarily rich and powerful drama.*]

Once in a rare while, you come across a play—or a movie or a novel—that seems to break away from the confines of art into a dense, complex realization of reality. A veil has been torn aside, the artist has disappeared into a transparency. We look with our own eyes, feel with our own hearts.

That was my reaction to August Wilson's pulsing play *Fences*. . . .

I wasn't just moved. I was transfixed—by intimations of a life, impressions of a man, images of a society.

Wilson, who a couple of seasons back gave us the arresting but fascinatingly flawed **Ma Rainey's Black Bottom,** always insists in interviews that he is writing from the wellspring of black experience in America.

This is undoubtedly true. Had Wilson been white, his plays would have been different—they would have had a different fire in a different belly.

But calling Wilson a "black" playwright is irrelevant. What makes **Fences** so engrossing, so embracing, so simply powerful, is his startling ability to tell a story, reveal feeling, paint emotion.

In many respects, **Fences** falls into the classic pattern of the American realistic drama—a family play, with a tragically doomed American father locked in conflict with his son. Greek tragedy with a Yankee accent.

The timing of the play—the late '50s—is carefully pinpointed in the history of black America as that turning point in the Civil Rights movement when a dream unfulfilled became a promise deferred.

The hero is Troy Maxson—and I suggest that he will be remembered as one of the great characters in American drama. . . . (p. 316)

Troy is as complex and as tormented as black America itself. He started life as a refugee from the South, and as a thief and, eventually, a killer.

Life in a penitentiary gave him the iron determination to reshape his life—as did, later, a feverish brush with death.

Prison also taught him baseball; when he came out, he became a temperamental star of the Negro Leagues. And now—in 1957—he can look at the likes of Jackie Robinson and Hank Aaron, making it in the Major Leagues of big-time whiteball, with a mixture of anger, envy and contempt.

A garbage collector, Troy has typically had to fight through his union to become the first black driver of a garbage truck. Equally typically, he hasn't even got a driver's license.

He sees himself as a man fenced in with responsibilities, but he has created some of those fences himself—some intended to keep people out, some to keep people in. . . .

What is particularly pungent about Wilson's play is how the story and the characters are plugged into their particular historic relevance, ranging from the lessons of prison to the metaphors of baseball. It is this that makes the play resonate with all its subtle vibrations of truth and actuality.

This is in no sense a political play—but quite dispassionately it says: This is what it was like to be a black man of pride and ambition from the South, trying to live and work in the industrial North in the years just before and just after World War II.

The writing is perfectly geared to its people and its place. It jumps from the author's mind onto the stage, its language catching fire in the rarefied atmosphere of drama. . . .

Fences gave me one of the richest experiences I have ever had in the theater. (p. 317)

> Clive Barnes, ''Fiery 'Fences','' in New York Post, March 27, 1987. Reprinted in New York Theatre Critics' Reviews, Vol. XXXXVIII, No. 5, Week of March 30, 1987, pp. 316-17.

FRANK RICH

[*American critic Rich has served as a film, drama, and television critic for* Time *and the* New York Times; *he has also contributed articles and reviews to* Ms., Esquire, *and other periodicals. He is coauthor of* The Theatre Art of Boris Aronson (1987). *In the following excerpt, Rich describes* Fences *as an often formulaic but nevertheless masterful dramatic tour de force.*]

To hear his wife tell it, Troy Maxson, the middle-aged Pittsburgh sanitation worker at the center of *Fences,* is ''so big'' that he fills up his tenement house just by walking through it. . . . But the remarkable stature of the character . . . is not a matter of sheer size. If Troy is a mountainous man prone to tyrannical eruptions of rage, he is also a dignified, delicate figure capable of cradling a tiny baby, of pleading gravely to his wife for understanding, of standing still to stare death unflinchingly in the eye. A black man, a free man, a descendant of slaves, a menial laborer, a father, a husband, a lover—Troy embraces all the contradictions of being black and male and American in his time.

That time is 1957—three decades after the period of Mr. Wilson's previous and extraordinary *Ma Rainey's Black Bottom.* For blacks like Troy in the industrial north of *Fences,* social and economic equality is more a legal principle than a reality. . . . Mr. Wilson writes about the pain of an extended family lost in the wilderness of de facto segregation and barren hope.

It speaks of the power of the play . . . that [Troy] doesn't devour the rest of *Fences* so much as become the life force that at once nurtures and stunts the characters who share his blood. The strongest countervailing player is his wife, Rose. . . . [She] is a quiet woman who, as she says, ''planted herself'' in the ''hard and rocky'' soil of her husband. But she never bloomed: marriage brought frustration and betrayal in equal measure with affection. . . .

It's rare to find a marriage of any sort presented on stage with such balance—let alone one in which the husband has fathered children by three different women. Mr. Wilson grants both partners the right to want to escape the responsibilities of their domestic drudgery while affirming their respective claims to forgiveness.

The other primary relationship of *Fences* is that of Troy to his son Cory. . . . [While] Troy wants Cory to settle for a workhorse trade guaranteeing a weekly paycheck, the boy resists. The younger Maxson is somehow convinced that the dreams

of his black generation need not end in the city's mean alleys with the carting of white men's garbage.

The struggle between father and son over conflicting visions of black identity, aspirations and values is the play's narrative fulcrum, and a paradigm of violent divisions that would later tear apart a society. As written, the conflict is also a didactic one, reminiscent of old-fashioned plays, black and white, about disputes between first-generation American parents and their rebellious children.

In *Ma Rainey*—set at a blues recording session—Mr. Wilson's characters were firecrackers exploding in a bottle, pursuing jagged theatrical riffs reflective of their music and of their intimacy with the Afro-American experience that gave birth to that music. The relative tameness of *Fences*—with its laboriously worked-out titular metaphor, its slow-fused Act I exposition—is as much an expression of its period as its predecessor was of the hotter 20's. Intentionally or not—and perhaps to the satisfaction of those who found the more esthetically daring *Ma Rainey* too ''plotless''—Mr. Wilson invokes the clunkier dramaturgy of Odets, Miller and Hansberry on this occasion.

Such formulaic theatrical tidiness, while exasperating at times, proves a minor price for the gripping second act (strengthened since the play's Yale debut in 1985) and for the scattered virtuoso passages throughout. Like *Ma Rainey* and the latest Wilson work seen at Yale (*Joe Turner's Come and Gone,* also promised for New York), *Fences* leaves no doubt that Mr. Wilson is a major writer, combining a poet's ear for vernacular with a robust sense of humor (political and sexual), a sure instinct for crackling dramatic incident and a passionate commitment to a great subject.

Mr. Wilson continues to see history as fully as he sees his characters. In one scene, Troy and his oldest friend weave an autobiographical ''talking blues''—a front-porch storytelling jaunt from the antebellum plantation through the pre-industrial urban South, jail and northward migration. *Fences* is pointedly bracketed by two disparate wars that swallowed up black manhood, and, as always with Mr. Wilson, is as keenly cognizant of its characters' bonds to Africa, however muted here, as their bondage to white America. One hears the cadences of a centuries-old heritage in Mr. Jones's efforts to shout down the devil. It is a frayed scrap of timeless blues singing, unpretty but unquenchable that proves the overpowering cathartic link among the disparate branches of the Maxson family tree.

> Frank Rich, ''Family Ties in Wilson's 'Fences','' in The New York Times, *March 27, 1987, p. C3.*

An Excerpt from *Fences*

ROSE: You gonna drink yourself to death. You don't need to be drinking like that.

TROY: Death ain't nothing. I done seen him. Done wrestled with him. You can't tell me nothing about death. Death ain't nothing but a fastball on the outside corner. And you know what I'll do to that! Look here, Bono . . . am I lying? You get one of them fastballs about waist high over the outside corner of the plate where you can get the meat of the bat on it . . . and good God! You can kiss it goodbye. Now, am I lying?

BONO: Naw, you telling the truth there. I seen you do it.

TROY: If I'm lying . . . that 450 feet worth of lying! (*Pause*) That's all death is to me. A fastball on the outside corner.

ROSE: I don't know why you want to get on talking about death.

TROY: Ain't nothing wrong with talking about death. That's part of life. Everybody gonna die. You gonna die, I'm gonna die. Bono's gonna die. Hell, we all gonna die.

ROSE: But you ain't got to talk about it. I don't like to talk about it.

TROY: You the one brought it up. Me and Bono was talking about baseball . . . you tell me I'm gonna drink myself to death. Ain't that right, Bono? You know I don't drink like this but one night out of the week. That's Friday night. I'm gonna drink just enough to where I can handle it. Then I cuts it loose. I leave it alone. So don't you worry about me drinking myself to death. Cause I ain't worried about Death. I done seen him. I done wrestled with him. Look here, Bono . . . I looked up one day and Death was marching straight at me. Like Soldiers on Parade! The Army of Death marching straight at me. The middle of July, 1941. It got real cold just like it be winter. It seem like Death himself reached out and touched me on the shoulder. He touch me just like I touch you. I got cold as ice and Death standing there grinning at me.

ROSE: Troy, why don't you hush that talk.

TROY: I say . . . What you want, Mr. Death? You be wanting me? You done brought your army to be getting me? I looked him dead in the eye. I wasn't fearing nothing. I was ready to tangle. Just like I'm ready to tangle now. The Bible say be ever vigilant. That's why I don't get but so drunk. I got to keep watch.

ROSE: Troy was right down there in Mercy Hospital. You remember he had pneumonia? Laying there with a fever talking plumb out of his head.

TROY: Death, he ain't said nothing. He just stared at me. He had a thousand men to do his bidding and he wasn't going to get a thousand and one. Not then! Hell, I wasn't but thirty-seven years old. (*Pause*) Death standing there staring at me . . . carrying that sickle in his hand. Finally he said . . . "You want bound over for another year?" See just like that . . . "You want bound over for another year?" I told him . . . Bound over hell! Let's settle this now! It seem like he kinda fell back when I said that, and all the cold went out of me. I reached down and grabbed that sickle and threw it just as far as I could throw it . . . and me and him commenced to wrestling. We wrestled for three days and three nights. I can't say where I found the strength from. Every time it seemed like he was gonna get the best of me, I'd reach way down deep inside myself and find the strength to do him one better.

ROSE: Every time Troy tell that story he find different ways to tell it. Different things to make up about it.

TROY: I ain't making up nothing. I'm telling you the facts of what happened. I wrestled with Death for three days and three nights and I'm standing here to tell you about it. (*Pause*) Alright, at the end of the third night we done weakened each other to where both of us could hardly move. Death stood up, throwed on his robe . . . had him a white robe with a hood on it. He throwed on that robe and went off to look for his sickle. Say, "I'll be back." Just like that. "I'll be back." I told him, say,

"You gonna have to find me!" I wasn't no fool. I wasn't going looking for him. Death ain't nothing to play with. And I know he's gonna get me. I know I got to join his army . . . his camp followers. But as long as I keep my strength and see him coming . . . as long as I keep up my vigilance . . . he's gonna have to fight to get me. I ain't going easy.

LEO SAUVAGE

Of the few legitimate plays that have opened on Broadway this season, August Wilson's Pulitzer Prizewinning *Fences* . . . is far and away the best. . . .

Fences might in fact have been the best play to hit Broadway in many a season, had not the undeniably talented Wilson blurred its impact by mixing up two story lines. Worse, besides being weakly founded, the secondary one is irritatingly misused. . . .

Troy Maxson, at 56, is a bitter man. What gnaws at his pride is not so much that he spends his days collecting white people's garbage; the job at least provides a living for his family and pays for the whiskey he shares with his friend Jim. Rather, he is angry because his considerable baseball talent was never allowed to flourish in the major leagues. (Jackie Robinson would come along 20-odd years too late for him.)

Rose is his second wife, and the mother of Cory, now 17. Troy also has sons from an earlier marriage. . . .

Much emphasis is put on Troy's sex drive. . . . He is quite physical with his wife, and he also keeps a mistress on the side who dies while giving birth to a daughter named Raynell. That's where Rose's patient love for her husband reaches its limit. When he brings the illegitimate daughter home, Rose tells him that the girl will have a mother, but he will no longer have a wife.

My summary cannot begin to convey the dramatic qualities of August Wilson's text, the subtleties of his social and racial observations, the liveliness of the badinage between Troy and Jim, or the strangely significant part played by Troy's mentally retarded brother Gabriel. . . . [All] is flawless—until the author unexpectedly inserts into the narrative his version of the clash-of-generations cliché.

On the surface, the conflict is over a football scholarship offered to Cory by a local college. Troy, recalling his own dashed baseball hopes, will not let his son accept it. Although his motive seems to be protective, he is actually overwhelmed by envy for his son. The painfulness of his past—which, it turns out, also involved a stint in jail—can be detected behind a facade of boisterous exuberance.

As the playwright draws it, the hatred that develops between father and son is all the father's fault: Troy is absolutely stubborn in his conviction that he is always right, and never stops taking his frustrations out on Cory. In the concluding scene, set seven years later, Cory returns after the death of Troy (but avoids the funeral). He is wearing the smart uniform of a Marine corporal, no doubt to signify that enlistment was his way of escaping his father.

Wilson should have saved the inter-generational business for another play—which might just as well have been about white people—and left us with the deeply human story of a black family in the late '50s. Still, that story makes *Fences* a show not to be missed. (pp. 20-1)

Leo Sauvage, "Worlds Apart," in The New Leader, Vol. LXX, No. 5, April 6, 1987, pp. 20-1.

JOHN SIMON

[*Simon is an American critic known primarily for his film and theater reviews. He has written on literature and the arts for such periodicals as* Commonweal, Esquire, The New York Times, The New Republic, *and* New York. *His books include* Singularities: Essays on Theatre, 1964-74 *(1976) and* Something to Declare: Twelve Years of Films from Abroad *(1982). In the following excerpt, Simon finds that despite a loss of spontaneity in the second act,* Fences *brings "life, in all its bittersweetness" to the stage.*]

Fences, by August Wilson, is a dignified, understatedly eloquent, elegant play. "Elegant" may be an odd term to apply to a piece about an underprivileged, oppressed black family precariously surviving in a northern industrial city during the late fifties, with backward glances to a worse past and forward looks at a strenuous uphill path. But "elegant" *is* the word for a work that tries to make sense of a predicament in which race is subsumed by humanity, in which black color is no more defining than the blue collar, and whose ultimate pigmentation is the black and blue of bruises—not so much on the body as on the soul.

Elegant for another reason as well. Because the play is constructed in a way both naturally fluid and artfully controlled, both improvised like the riffs of a jam session and thought-out like the development in sonata form. Paradoxical as it may seem, Wilson has achieved (to change metaphors) the lepidopterological miracle of mounting a butterfly as an exhibit and still keeping the creature alive. How? With a very long, very fine pin that goes not only through the moth but also through us; it may be our sympathetic trembling that makes the creature seem aquiver, our tears that make it shimmer with aliveness.

But alive it certainly becomes. Troy Maxson is an ex-con and ex-baseball pro and present garbage collector; a steady provider for his wife, Rose, and his son Cory; a man of boundless energy and boisterous bitterness. He has been frustrated all along: first by a stern, overbearing father; then by racism in the baseball world and elsewhere; finally, by economic straits that drove him to crime. A semi-solid citizen now, he is still plagued by illiteracy, unfair employment practices, threatening indigence, drink, and a sexual drive his overworked and emotionally unfulfilled wife cannot quite satisfy. A difficult husband, he was once an abused son, which makes him an uncaring father to Lyons, his musician son by a former wife, and an overexacting, seemingly unfeeling father to Cory, his athletically gifted son by Rose, for whom he does care. His attitude toward his brother, Gabriel, a brain-damaged World War II vet, is similarly ambiguous: though he is caring and protective of Gabriel, he also exploits him. Perhaps his purest, least ambivalent feelings are for Bono, a longtime friend and colleague; yet even with him, when the shared alcoholic haze lifts, a bristling wariness sets in.

Out of these relationships, and others with offstage characters, Wilson has fashioned a comedy-drama that, in its first act, is well-nigh flawless. Although its four scenes covering one week in 1957 are of necessity episodic, the episodes flow into one another. Fantasy, mostly in Troy's account of his wrestling

with Death and the Devil, good-humoredly reverts to reality, with Rose as the pungent catalyst. Levity, no less imperceptibly, turns sour or grim, particularly when Cory is accosted right-headedly but wrongheartedly by his canny but confused father. Life, in all its bittersweetness, fills the stage—to be faced with gallant affection or fierce animosity.

In the second act—partly because the temporal gaps are greater, partly because problems are ticked off a bit too hastily and schematically—there is some loss in the spontaneity, dovetailing, and free breathing of the five scenes. But this is always offset by intelligent stating of the dilemmas, assured use of language, unponderous handling of symbols (baseball tropes, fences, Gabriel's horn), and refusal to lapse into either shrillness or sentimentality. Pain and anger are balanced by humor and common sense, and both passion and compassion are played on a muted trumpet that insinuates rather than insists. *Fences* marks a long step forward for Wilson's dramaturgy. (p. 92)

John Simon "Wall in the Family," in New York Magazine, Vol. 20, No. 14, April 6, 1987, pp. 92, 94.

MICHAEL FEINGOLD

[*A contributor to such magazines as* The New Republic *and* Saturday Review *and a theater critic for the* Village Voice *since 1970, American critic and translator Feingold also served as the Yale Repertory Theater's literary manager from 1969 to 1976. Feingold has translated plays by Molière, Henrik Ibsen, and Bertolt Brecht, among others; his own works include librettos to William Shakespeare's* Hamlet *(1984) and* Times and Appetites of Toulouse-Lautrec *(1986). In the following excerpt, he examines the rich and complex implications of Wilson's work.*]

August Wilson's plays are giant rivers of words—superficially slow, turbid, and static, they teem with deep undercurrents which, having once gripped you, bustle you along with unexpected speed till they rise to dizzying whirlpools of action. That this forceful flow may or may not bring you where you thought you were heading—as often as not it will run you aground on a sandbar—doesn't diminish the power of the ride, and to some extent even explains it: Wilson's ambitions extend far beyond simple storytelling, and widen or scatter the focus of his drama as much as they intensify it. A mythmaker who sees his basically naturalistic panorama-plays as stages in an allegorical history of black America, Wilson is also a folk ethnologist, collecting prototypical stories, testimonies, rituals of speech and behavior, which he embeds in his larger compositions. Buried deepest of all, under the dramatist Wilson, the mythmaker-cum-social historian Wilson, and the folklorist-ethnologist Wilson, is a tormented and complex ideologue Wilson, carrying on anguished debates with himself about such politically engrossing matters as black male-female relations, the use of black economic power, and the place of the church in the black community.

This layering of intentions gives the seemingly conversational tone of Wilson's plays a perpetual dark undertow: You never know on which level the next anecdote or sociable remark will turn out to have repercussions that suddenly enmesh the whole story, driving it into wild violence or dashing it on the rocks of cold misery. *Ma Rainey's Black Bottom* was chiefly made up of musicians chatting on the breaks of a recording session; its hero murdered a man (his ideological opponent, as it happened) for stepping on his prized patent-leather shoes. In the surface terms of dramaturgy—"plot line," "character development,'' and so on—the event came out of nowhere and connected to nothing. But audiences experiencing the play instantly saw it as inevitable, the summation of the teasing, the bickering, the hunger, the tension, the competitiveness that had gone on all evening: Levee's fancy shoes, and the fatal consequences of their accidental dirtying, embodied, for a moment, the whole traumatic history of black upward striving in the 1920s.

In *Fences,* the latest of Wilson's plays to reach New York, the time is the 1950s, and the hero is the antithesis of Levee, with his creative musicianship, his youthful wildness, and his desperate craving for the material signs of success. Troy Maxson is a middle-aged garbageman in a northern industrial city, a generation away from the sharecropping rural South of his father. His long-past wild days, which seem to be matters only for reminiscence, have left three visible traces: a spendthrift elder son, born during Troy's loose-living adolescence in Mobile; a life-long friend, met on the prison work gang to which loose living led him; and an obsessive love for baseball, which he played in the hard-scrabbling Negro leagues of the 1930s. Since then he has settled—a steady job, a marriage moving toward its silver anniversary, a teenage son whom, unlike the first, Troy parents carefully if unlovingly, aiming to preserve the boy from the blind frenzy and victimization of his own youth.

What brings Troy's plans crashing down in disaster and bitterness is his failure to face two kinds of change: his own and history's. Not seeing that a home is first of all a center of warm feelings, he shuts love out of his home life, till he's driven to look for it elsewhere—and wrecks his marriage by fathering a child on a younger woman. Not realizing that the the war has paved the way for a change in black Americans' status, he pushes his son out of the football practice that could win him a college scholarship, trying to force him to take up a manual trade. Wilson's patient shifting, from topic to topic and cause to cause, gives us a clear picture of Troy as a tragic case, at once hero, victim, and villain, unconsciously perpetuating a fatal cycle in ways that can be blamed partly on racism, partly on his family history and circumstances, partly on himself. The motives intertwine, leaving no one unindicted or unforgiven.

> *Michael Feingold, ''The Fall of Troy,'' in* The Village Voice, *Vol. XXXII, No. 14, April 7, 1987, p. 85.*

GERALD WEALES

[*Weales, an American critic, nonfiction writer, juvenile fiction writer, and novelist, is drama critic for the Catholic journal* Commonweal. *His works include* American Drama since World War II *(1962),* Clifford Odets, Playwright *(1971), and* Canned Goods as Caviar: American Film Comedies of the 1930s *(1985). In the following excerpt, Weales discusses* Fences *as a traditional family play.*]

At the end of August Wilson's *Fences,* the Maxsons gather for the funeral of Troy, who has dominated the family and the play. His ''mixed-up'' brother Gabe, who had ''half his head blown away'' in World War II and who believes that he has been to heaven, unlimbers the trumpet he always carries ''to tell St. Peter to open the gates.'' There is no mouthpiece, no trumpet blast. After three increasingly desperate tries, Gabe howls in anguish and frustration. Light pours across the scene. ''That's the way that go!'' he says, smiling his satisfaction.

That's not really the way that go, meaning the play as a whole, but the effectiveness of the final scene is a reminder that Wilson stretches the limits of the realistic form his play takes (as he mixed songs and dramatic scenes in *Ma Rainey's Black Bottom*) and that the verisimilitude of his language cannot disguise the lyric qualities in his work. For the most part, *Fences* is a family play in an old American tradition—*Awake and Sing!, Death of a Salesman, A Raisin in the Sun*—in which the conflicts within the family are given definition by the social forces outside. Set in ''a Northern American industrial city'' (i.e., Wilson's Pittsburgh) in 1957, it uses the metaphor of the fence which Troy builds around his backyard as title to a play about the fences between husband and wife, father and son, black and white.

Troy Maxson is a black man in his early fifties, at once an authority figure and a garrulous, playful nice guy. . . . Although he has the strength to buck the system, to get himself promoted from garbageman to driver, he sees the world in terms of his own past. He has become a variation on the tyrant father he ran away to escape. He has come to believe that a black man's only choice is between jail, where he spent some youthful years, and a steady job; he cannot see that there might be other possibilities in the 1950s, roads that were not open thirty years earlier.

A central prop in *Fences* is the baseball that hangs on a rope from the tree in the yard. Troy's device for batting practice, it is a constant reminder for him and for us of his greatest triumph and his greatest disappointment. Having learned to play baseball in prison, he went on to become a star in the Negro League but, despite his talent, the color line kept him out of the majors. Whether out of jealousy or to protect the young man, Troy refuses to sign the papers that would let his son go to college on a football scholarship, a destructive act that leads to a final confrontation between the two and a reenactment of the father-son conflict that sent Troy off on his own. He uses his sense of ownership and control (my house, my yard) not only to stifle his son's ambitions but to misuse his brother, whose disability payments bought the house, and his wife, whom he loves but to whom he brings the child of another woman. . . . Troy fills the last scene even in his absence, and when his son, now a sergeant in the Marines, joins his half-sister in singing Troy's song about Blue that ''good old dog,'' acceptance of and forgiveness for what Troy and his world had made of him prepare the way for Gabe's bringing the light. What remains is Troy's strength, his sense of duty, and his odd vulnerability. ''That's the way that go!'' (pp. 320-21)

> *Gerald Weales, ''Bringing the Light,'' in* Commonweal, *Vol. CXIV, No. 10, May 22, 1987, pp. 320-21.*

Obituaries

Necrology

Jean Anouilh . . . . October 3, 1987

James Baldwin . . . . December 1, 1987

Carlos Drummond de Andrade . . . . August 17, 1987

Erskine Caldwell. . . . . April 11, 1987

Richard Ellmann . . . . May 13,1987

Robert D. FitzGerald . . . . May 25, 1987

Robert Francis. . . . . July 13, 1987

John Oliver Killens. . . . . October 27, 1987

Margaret Laurence . . . . January 5, 1987

Primo Levi. . . . . April 11, 1987

John Logan . . . . November 6, 1987

Charles Ludlam . . . . May 28, 1987

Alistair MacLean . . . . February 2, 1987

Rouben Mamoulian . . . . December 4, 1987

Howard Moss . . . . September 28, 1987

George Ryga . . . . November 18, 1987

James Tiptree, Jr. . . . . May 19, 1987

Glenway Wescott . . . . February 22, 1987

Anthony West . . . . December 27, 1987

Emlyn Williams . . . . September 25, 1987

Marguerite Yourcenar. . . . . December 17, 1987

Jean (Marie Lucien Pierre) Anouilh

June 23, 1910 - October 3, 1987

French dramatist and scriptwriter.

(See also *CLC*, Vols. 1, 3, 8, 13, 40 and *Contemporary Authors*, Vols. 17-20, rev. ed.)

PRINCIPAL WORKS

Humulus le muet [with Jean Aurenche]   (drama)   1929
Mandarine   (drama)   1929
L'hermine   (drama)   1932
   [*The Ermine*, 1955]
La sauvage   (drama)   1934
   [*Restless Heart*, 1957]
Y avait un prisonnier   (drama)   1935
Le rendez-vous de Senlis   (drama)   1936
   [*Dinner with the Family*, 1958]
Le voyageur sans bagage   (drama)   1937
   [*Traveller without Luggage*, 1959]
Le bal des voleurs   (drama)   1938
   [*Thieves' Carnival*, 1952]
Léocadia   (drama)   1940
   [*Time Remembered*, 1954]
Antigone   (drama)   1942
   [*Antigone*, 1946]
Eurydice   (drama)   1942
   [*Point of Departure*, 1951; also published as *Legend of Lovers*, 1952]
Pièces noires   (dramas)   1942
Pièces roses   (dramas)   1942
Médée   (drama)   1946
   [*Medea*, 1957]
Roméo et Jeanette   (drama)   1946
   [*Fading Mansion*, 1949]
L'invitation au château   (drama)   1947
   [*Ring round the Moon: A Charade with Music*, 1950; also published as *Invitation to the Chateau*]
Monsieur Vincent   (screenplay)   1947
Nouvelles pièces noires   (dramas)   1947
Ardèle; ou, La marguerite   (drama)   1948
   [*Cry of the Peacock*, 1951]
Cécile; ou, L'école des pères   (drama)   1950
Colombe   (drama)   1950
   [*Mademoiselle Colombe*, 1951]
La répétition; ou, L'amour puni   (drama)   1950
   [*The Rehearsal*, 1960]
Pièces brillantes   (dramas)   1951
La valse des toréadors   (drama)   1952
   [*The Waltz of the Toreadors*, 1953]
L'alouette   (drama)   1953
   [*The Lark*, 1955]
Ornifle; ou, Le courant d'air   (drama)   1955
   [*Ornifle*, 1970; also published as *It's Later Than You Think*, 1970]

Pauvre Bitos; ou, Le dîner des têtes   (drama)   1956
   [*Poor Bitos*, 1964]
Pièces grinçantes   (dramas)   1956
Becket; ou, L'honneur de Dieu   (drama)   1959
   [*Becket; or, The Honor of God*, 1961]
L'hurluberlu; ou, Le réactionnaire amoureux   (drama)   1959
   [*The Fighting Cock*, 1960]
Pièces costumées   (dramas)   1960
La grotte   (drama)   1961
   [*The Cavern*, 1961]
Théâtre complet. 6 vols.   (dramas)   1961-63
La foire d'empoigne   (drama)   1962
Collected Plays. 2 vols.   (dramas)   1966
Le boulanger, la boulangère, et le petit mitron   (drama)   1968
Cher Antoine: ou, L'amour raté   (drama)   1969
Ne réveillez pas madame   (drama)   1970
Pièces baroques   (dramas)   1974
Pièces secrètes   (dramas)   1977
Pièces farceuses   (dramas)   1984

JANE GROSS

Jean Anouilh, one of France's most prominent and enduring playwrights, died of a heart attack [October 3] at the Vaudois University Hospital Center in Lausanne, Switzerland. He was 77 years old.

Mr. Anouilh's death was announced yesterday by his family. He was mourned by President Mitterand of France and by performers at the Palais Royal Theater in Paris, where one of his plays, *The Fighting Cock,* is being presented.

The actors dedicated their matinee performance yesterday to Mr. Anouilh, while President Mitterand sent a message of condolence to his widow. "A great writer has disappeared," Mr. Mitterand said, "one whose work marked the French theater."

In a writing career that spanned five decades, Mr. Anouilh wrote about 40 plays, many of them marked by gloom and cynicism. Although others might characterize his works as black comedies or tragedies, by turns hilarious and hopeless, Mr. Anouilh preferred a more individual classification system. He referred to a certain works as *Pièces roses,* or "pink plays," and others as *Pièces noires,* black ones.

One of his most popular plays, one of the "pièces roses," was *L'invitation au château,* known in English as *Ring round the Moon.* It was first produced in Paris in 1947 and came to New York in 1950. "The play has a sensuous quality that is wholly enchanting," Brooks Atkinson wrote in *The New York Times* in 1950.

Among Mr. Anouilh's best-known works were *Antigone,* first produced in 1944 and considered a metaphor for the German occupation of France; *The Lark,* a 1953 historical drama about Joan of Arc that, in an adaptation by Lillian Hellman, was the playwright's first Broadway hit, and *The Waltz of the Toreadors,* originally produced in Paris in 1952 and revived in New York as recently as 1985 by the Roundabout Theater Company.

Mr. Anouilh's plays careened from one end of the emotional spectrum to the other. Reviewing *The Waltz of the Toreadors* in *The Times,* Mr. Atkinson described the playwright as a "desolate man" who "knows how to write a remarkably gay comedy." Arthur Gelb wrote in *The Times* that "Mr. Anouilh's balance between grim humor and real pathos is delicate."

Mr. Anouilh once described himself as a comic misanthrope. "I am surrounded by foulness," he said. "The world is foul and it is plain to see. My theater is a fairy tale compared to reality."

Mr. Anouilh drew on such theatrical staples as caricature and plays-within-plays. Often his characters were moral men and women struggling against an immoral world and living at the margins of society. But despite his bleak philosophical preoccupations, Mr. Anouilh stressed that his plays were, first and foremost, entertainment.

"I write plays as a chair maker makes chairs," he said in one of his rare interviews. "Chairs are made to be sat on and plays are made to be played, to provide actors with work and the public with entertainment."

The English poet Stephen Spender once said, "The plays of Anouilh seem to have more poetry of the theater in them than anything a contemporary poet has yet put in metrical lines upon the page."

Although Mr. Anouilh is often described as one of the world's most widely performed playwrights, his work has sometimes seemed more popular with theatergoers than with critics. In a review of *The Lark* in *The Times,* Mr. Atkinson described the play about Joan of Arc as overly "cerebral" and thus inferior to George Bernard Shaw's *St. Joan,* which set the standard 30 years before. Nonetheless, *The Lark* played before enthusiastic Broadway audiences for 229 performances at the Longacre Theater.

Several Anouilh plays were historical dramas that brought new life to old stories. *The Lark,* which featured Julie Harris and Boris Karloff in its Broadway production, was in this category. Another of Mr. Anouilh's important historical dramas was *Becket,* the tale of England's Henry II and the 12th-century Archbishop of Canterbury, which followed the same story line as T. S. Eliot's verse drama *Murder in the Cathedral.* The American production of *Becket,* with Laurence Olivier and Anthony Quinn, won a Tony Award in 1961 as the year's most distinguished play and was later made into a popular and critically acclaimed movie starring Richard Burton and Peter O'Toole.

Other of Mr. Anouilh's plays were contemporary restatements of classical myths, among them *Antigone, Eurydice* and *Medea.* The first of these, a reworking of Sophocles's tragedy, had an inspiring pertinence when it was performed in Paris, with bombs whistling outside, during the German Occupation in 1944. In that context, many Parisians saw Antigone's flouting of Creon's authority as a symbol of the French Resistance.

Mr. Anouilh's beginnings were humble. He was born on June 23, 1910, in Bordeaux, in the southwest of France. His father was a tailor and his mother a violinist who performed at casinos. The young Anouilh went along and watched operettas.

During this teen-age years the family moved to Paris, where Mr. Anouilh later studied law for a year and a half at the Sorbonne. Concerned that his father could not absorb the cost, Mr. Anouilh abandoned law school for a position writing advertising copy for products ranging from noodles to automobiles.

Later, the playwright described advertising copywriting as "a great school" for playwrights because of its "precision, conciseness and agility of expression."

Mr. Anouilh wrote short plays from childhood onward, but his first official connection to the theater came when he worked as secretary to the renowned actor and director Louis Jouvet. Mr. Anouilh wrote his first play at the age of 19, and had his first success at 22 with the production of *The Ermine,* in 1932.

By his middle years, Mr. Anouilh was famous, wealthy and reclusive. He owned several homes in and around Paris and also had a retreat in the Swiss Alps. He reportedly changed his unlisted telephone numbers frequently, disconnected the doorbell at his Left Bank apartment and kept a pair of binoculars at hand in the country to spot unwelcome strangers.

Slightly built, with straw-colored hair, Mr. Anouilh did not carry himself like a celebrity. On opening nights, he hid out in the prompter's box and then crept out of the theater, a slender form in tidy tweeds and round wire-rimmed eyeglasses, retreating silently across the slick cobblestones.

"The public is invited to the premiere," he once said. "My private life is my own affair."

Until age and illness slowed his production, Mr. Anouilh was known as an unusually speedy writer who, for example, was said to have written *Antigone* in three weeks during the Occupation. "It's scandalous," he once said, "that I earn my livelihood by amusing myself as I do."

In addition to his primary writing, Mr. Anouilh occasionally wrote movie-dialogue and translated and adapted the work of such playwrights as Shakespeare and Oscar Wilde.

In recent years, plagued by heart disease, Mr. Anouilh had lived in a suburb of Lausanne, in a home overlooking Lake Geneva.

> *Jane Gross, "Jean Anouilh, the French Playwright, Is Dead at 77," The New York Times, October 5, 1987, p. 18.*

RICHARD PEARSON

During a career that spanned five decades, [Anouilh] wrote about 40 plays and saw his work translated into 27 languages. He also wrote stories for the ballet, dialogue and scripts for movies including *Monsieur Vincent* (1947) and *Deux sous de violettes* (*Two Cents Worth of Violets*) (1951). He directed several movies and in 1959 won the prix Dominique for his direction of *Madame M*.

Although his works did not gain a wide following in the United States, many critics regarded Mr. Anouilh as one of this century's great playwrights. He was hailed for writing that was technically deft and completely human. His plays, especially the ones based on Greek myths, posed seemingly insoluble moral questions.

He wrote of loneliness, old age, the end of innocence, and the breakdown of communication.

The plays featured moral players in an immoral setting with heroes forced to live life on the fringes of a corrupt and bankrupt society. He saw a world largely fueled by cowardice, revenge and hatred. He expressed horror at what man's life was compared to what it could be.

His play *Antigone* was produced in 1944 during the Nazi occupation of France. A modern version of Sophocles' masterpiece, it pitted the innocent, youthful and indomitable idealist, Antigone, against King Creon's voice of power and pragmatism.

French audiences interpreted the work as a "Resistance" play and made Mr. Anouilh a hero for his clever defiance of Nazi power. Mr. Anouilh later said that though he was pleased, he was genuinely surprised. Unlike many of his generation, he did not make a career of beating his breast while boasting of resistance work; he maintained that he had neither the time nor the inclination for politics.

One of his greatest and most popular plays was *Becket,* produced in 1959. It was the tale of Thomas a Becket, a worldly English chancellor who became a sainted archbishop of Canterbury. After defying his king, Henry II, he was murdered on the steps of a cathedral.

The play was a critical triumph and led to a popular film. There were British critics, however, who attacked him on historical grounds, pointing out that the play presented Becket, who was a Norman, as a Saxon. Mr. Anouilh admitted the error, replying that he was a playwright, not a historian.

He had previously been attacked on political grounds for such plays as *Poor Bitos,* a 1956 comedy with a sardonic view of a French liberation politico trying to settle wartime scores against the socially prominent. The play was said to be Mr. Anouilh's favorite, and despite poor reviews, it enjoyed a two-year run in Paris.

Mr. Anouilh had maintained something of a self-imposed exile from his native France since the 1950s. In recent years, he had lived in Pully, a suburb of Lausanne.

He was a lifelong critic of the late French president and wartime leader, Gen. Charles de Gaulle, once calling him "the Jupiter of the theater of human beings." De Gaulle was the man who came to lead France during a period Mr. Anouilh saw increasingly dominated by greed, revenge and a search for lost glory. Many believe that it was Mr. Anouilh's opposition to de Gaulle that prevented him from garnering any of France's great literary honors.

Mr. Anouilh was born in Bordeaux and grew up there and in Paris. He was considered somewhat retarded until his problem was diagnosed as nearsightedness. His father was a tailor who wanted his son to get a good education, his mother a musician who played at casinos and imparted to her son a love of music and operettas.

After studying law at the University of Paris, he worked in advertising. He told a reporter in 1950 that "for three years I wrote copy for products ranging from noodles to automobiles. I consider advertising a great school for playwriting. The precision, conciseness and agility of expression necessary in writing advertisements helped me enormously."

His first published work was *The Ermine* in 1932. His more popular works of the 1930s included *Traveller without Luggage, The Wild One* and *Thieves' Carnival.* During the war, he moved to the front ranks of drama. In addition to *Antigone,* he produced *Eurydice* in 1942 and *Oreste* in 1945.

His postwar work included plays with a psychological bent, including *L'invitation au chateau* (*Invitation to the Castle*) in 1947, *La repetition ou l'amoureux puni* (*The Rehearsal or The Punished Lover*) in 1950, and *Alouette* (*The Lark*), a 1953 work about Joan of Arc.

A 1976 play, *The Script,* was about a group of artists trying to make a movie on the eve of World War II. It ended tragically—with exile for some, suicide for others.

> *Richard Pearson, "French Playwright Jean Anouilh Dies at 77," in The Washington Post, October 5, 1987.*

JULIUS NOVICK

[*Novick, an American critic and educator, is the author of* Beyond Broadway: The Quest for Permanent Theatres *(1968); he is also a drama critic for the* Village Voice. *In the following excerpt, he discusses critical perceptions of Anouilh.*]

Many Americans must have been surprised to hear of Jean Anouilh's death on October 3, at the age of 77. Hadn't he died long ago? Anouilh had a brief vogue among us, after a successful Off-Broadway production of *Thieves' Carnival* in 1955 had proved that he was not *always* too sophisticatedly European for Americans to enjoy; *The Lark, The Waltz of the Toreadors, Time Remembered,* and *Becket* were Broadway successes. His ironic outlook and lapidary style made him one of those playwrights whom American middlebrow critics call ''literate'' and ''civilized,'' while highbrows and lowbrows united in finding him precious and thin. Some of Anouilh's plays are still occasionally revived by college drama groups and by noncommercial theaters—*The Waltz of the Toreadors* was given by the Roundabout only last season—but none of the 13 plays he wrote since *The Cavern* in 1961 has yet been seen in New York.

After his Antigone and Creon had debated the ethics of resistance and collaboration under the noses of the occupying Nazis, Anouilh was embraced by Jean-Paul Sartre as one of ''the young playwrights of France'' (along with de Beauvoir, Camus, and himself) whose aim was ''to forge myths,'' presenting free human beings debating moral choices. But he did not really belong in this company. In spite of his avant-garde past, he was too much in love with the theater—not the theater as he wished to remake it, but the theater as it was. Camus died; Sartre and de Beauvoir went on to other things; Anouilh was overtaken by Beckett, Ionesco, and Genet. Out of fashion among the intellectuals, he remained the king of the boulevards, the favorite of the bourgeoisie he despised, as popular in Paris as Molière had been.

Anouilh was a cynical sentimentalist, combining an ardent love of purity with a deep conviction that purity was doomed in our tawdry, impure world: the purity of political idealism no less than the purity of romantic devotion. Even his pretty, happy-ending comedies, in which his powerful bitterness was laid aside, are so fragile, so delicate, so artificial, that they declare themselves, with subtle poignance, too good to be true. His mooning over lost innocence could sometimes become cloying, but at least he knew that purity is not always sweet: in his work it is often harsh, fierce, even mad. The choice between Antigone and Creon is not an easy one.

A writer's reputation often rebounds shortly after his death. Perhaps it is time for some of those expensively educated dramaturgs who haunt our theaters to investigate Anouilh's unknown plays, and even his familiar ones.

> *Julius Novick, ''Jean Anouilh (1910-87),'' in* The Village Voice, *Vol. XXXII, No. 42, October 20, 1987, p. 112.*

HAROLD HOBSON

[*Hobson, an English nonfiction writer, critic, novelist, and autobiographer, has been a drama critic for the* Christian Science Monitor *and the London* Times *and a television critic for the* Listener. *He has written such nonfiction works as* The First Three Years of the War: A Day-by-Day Record *(1942),* Verdict at Midnight: Sixty Years of Drama Criticism *(1952), and* The French Theatre since 1930 *(1978). In the following excerpt, Hobson examines the philosophy behind Anouilh's dramas as well as their critical and popular reception.*]

Jean Anouilh, who died early in October last, was born in Bordeaux in 1910. He was surely the bravest dramatist of the twentieth century, and though his incomparable theatrical dexterity; his scorpion wit, and his overwhelming passion could not be denied by even the most bitter of his critical enemies, he aroused widespread hatred, and contumely. Many of his plays *L'invitation au château* (*Ring round the Moon*), *L'alouette, Euridyce, Becket, Ardèle, Pauvre Bitos* and others, were produced in London. On an occasion several years back, one of these came up for consideration by the BBC critics. At the luncheon preceding their recording, where the conversation was never broadcast (though often it was more interesting than

the programme subsequently put out) the critics of the week solemnly asked themselves whether any right-wing play, film, or book could possibly have any merit. They decided that such a thing was inconceivable. Even the film critic forgot *The Birth of a Nation*. Their attitude was typical of the temper of the post-war years, which was one of left-wing euphoria. With such a standard of judgement being in the ascendant, it was easy enough for left-wing writers, both creative and critical, to score resounding triumphs. But it was death to a rightwing dramatist like Rattigan. Now Anouilh was the most right-wing dramatist of his time.

He was thus met with almost universal hostility in the theatre. The white wall that surrounded his house in Paris was smeared, in huge, black letters, with the word, unspeakable at the time, 'MERDE'. Anouilh's contempt for the people was such that he did not trouble even to have it removed. But the deep-seated animosity which it displayed, depressed him. He became determined always to emphasize the black side of things. To those who tried to cheer up his often despondent spirits by reminding him that his plays ran for five hundred performances, he would say that he had never had a popular success comparable with Roussin's *The Little Hut,* which ran for a thousand. He preferred to brood over the words of Jean-Jacques Gautier, Paris' most influential critic, who demanded to know how much longer the theatre would continue to endure Anouilh's ferocity of feeling and of language. 'After excess, the excess of excess, then what?' he asked not without sadness, for he was an admirer of Anouilh.

The words which Gautier found so offensive are spoken by Madame la Générale de Saint-Pé to her pitiful husband the General. Both characters appear in *Ardèle* and *La valse des toréadors,* plays which Anouilh himself says were written to set people's teeth on edge. They certainly caused audiences and critics to say that Anouilh was a man who hated life itself. Yet the savagery of both plays is a protest by which young love is, by the passage of the years, brought to degradation and disgust. To Anouilh the highest point of existence is attained only when love remains pure and unsullied. And in *Ardèle* he shows that, whilst the handsome and wealthy characters in the play talk about love and betray it, there are two, both of them hunchbacks, who know how to die for it. In Anouilh love can be, and occasionally is, attained by the most unlikely people.

Plays such as *Ardèle* and *La valse des toréadors* were condemned as a general indictment of humanity and its destiny, without their underlying longing for beauty and faithfulness being perceived, or the skill of their characterisation being recognised. Against the merciless opposition with which his work was met, however, Anouilh battled on undaunted, though the *élan* of his life was almost destroyed.

These works were charged only with a general hatred of life as a whole. But there were two others which actually put him in the greatest physical danger. These were *Antigone* and *Poor Bitos. Antigone* is a case of curious irony. The usual British view is that *Antigone,* produced in Paris during the German Occupation, was a Resistance play. But it was not so seen in Paris in 1943. In the great scene of the debate between Creon and Antigone, all the best arguments are given to the authoritarian, who was identified with the Germans. It received enthusiastic reviews from the collaborationist press, and the rumour ran round Paris that *Antigone* was a Nazi play which no patriotic French theatregoer should go to see. It was not for several months that this view of the play changed, and when it did the Occupation authorities ordered it to be taken off.

But about *Poor Bitos* there could be no change of view. It was unmistakably an attack on the Resistance, whose members it represented, not as heroes, but as jealous cowards trying to pay off old scores. After the end of the war Anouilh was in some danger of being shot for treachery, but luckily was saved by the intervention of Armand Salacrou, and other dramatists who had no desire to see the most brilliant light of the French theatre disgracefully extinguished. It is good that this should have been so, for Jean Anouilh, savage and ferocious at the crucifixion of humanity's highest values, was the greatest dramatist of our time. (pp. 11-12)

> *Harold Hobson, "Jean Anouilh," in* Drama, *London, No. 167, 1st Quarter, 1988, pp. 11-12.*

James (Arthur) Baldwin

August 2, 1924 - December 1, 1987

American novelist, essayist, dramatist, nonfiction and short story writer, juvenile fiction writer, poet, and scriptwriter.

(See also *CLC*, Vols. 1, 2, 3, 4, 5, 8, 13, 15, 17, 42; *Contemporary Authors*, Vols. 1-4, rev. ed; *Contemporary Authors New Revision Series*, Vol. 3; *Contemporary Authors Bibliographical Series*, Vol. 1; *Something about the Author*, Vol. 9; *Dictionary of Literary Biography*, Vols. 2, 7, 33; and *Concise Dictionary of American Literary Biography*, 1941-1968.)

PRINCIPAL WORKS

Go Tell It on the Mountain   (novel)   1953
The Amen Corner   (drama)   1955
Notes of a Native Son   (essays)   1955
Giovanni's Room   (novel)   1956
Nobody Knows My Name: More Notes of a Native Son
   (essays)   1961
Another Country   (novel)   1962
The Fire Next Time   (essays)   1963
Blues for Mister Charlie   (drama)   1964
Going to Meet the Man   (short stories)   1965
Tell Me How Long the Train's Been Gone   (novel)   1968
No Name in the Street   (essay)   1972
One Day, When I Was Lost   (screenplay)   1972
If Beale Street Could Talk   (novel)   1974
The Devil Finds Work   (criticism)   1976
Little Man, Little Man: A Story of Childhood   (juvenile
   fiction)   1976
Just above My Head   (novel)   1979
The Evidence of Things Not Seen   (nonfiction)   1985
Jimmy's Blues: Selected Poems   (poetry)   1985
The Price of the Ticket: Collected Nonfiction, 1948-1985
   (essays)   1985

© Jerry Bauer

LEE A. DANIELS

James Baldwin, whose passionate, intensely personal essays in the 1950's and 60's on racial discrimination in America made him an eloquent voice of the civil-rights movement, died of stomach cancer [December 1] at his home in St. Paul de Vence in southern France. He was 63 years old.

At least in the early years of his career, Mr. Baldwin saw himself primarily as a novelist. But it is his essays that arguably constitute his most substantial contribution to literature.

Mr. Baldwin published his three most important collections of essays—*Notes of a Native Son* (1955), *Nobody Knows My Name* (1961) and *The Fire Next Time* (1963)—during the years when the civil-rights movement was exploding across the American South.

Some critics later said his language was sometimes too elliptical, his indictments sometimes too sweeping. But then, Mr. Baldwin's prose, with its apocalyptic tone—a legacy of his early exposure to religious fundamentalism—and its passionate yet distanced sense of advocacy, seemed perfect for a period in which blacks in the South lived under continual threat of racial violence and in which civil-rights workers faced brutal beatings and even death.

In the preface to his 1964 play, *Blues for Mister Charlie,* noting that the work had been inspired "very distantly" by the 1955 murder of a black youth, Emmett Till, in Mississippi, Mr. Baldwin wrote:

> What is ghastly and really almost hopeless in our racial situation now is that the crimes we have committed are so great and so unspeakable that the acceptance of this knowledge would lead, literally, to madness. The human being, then, in order to protect himself, closes his eyes, compulsively repeats his

crimes, and enters a spiritual darkness which no one can describe.

The novelist Ralph Ellison said [December 1], "America has lost one of its most gifted writers" and praised Mr. Baldwin as "one of the most important American essayists, black or white."

"I would place him very high among writers," Benjamin DeMott, professor of English at Amherst College, said [December 1], "in part because his work showed a powerful commitment to the right values and had a profound impact for good on our culture."

Mr. Baldwin had moved to France in the late 1940's to escape what he felt was the stifling racial bigotry of America.

Nonetheless, although France remained his permanent residence, Mr. Baldwin in later years described himself as a "commuter" rather than an expatriate.

"Only white Americans can consider themselves to be expatriates," he said. "Once I found myself on the other side of the ocean, I could see where I came from very clearly, and I could see that I carried myself, which is my home, with me. You can never escape that. I am the grandson of a slave, and I am a writer. I must deal with both."

Henry Louis Gates, professor of English and Afro-American Literature at Cornell University, said [December 1] that Mr. Baldwin's death was "a great loss not only for black people, but to the country as a whole, for which he served as a conscience."

Mr. Gates said that Mr. Baldwin had "educated an entire generation of Americans about the civil-rights struggle and the sensibility of Afro-Americans as we faced and conquered the final barriers in our long quest for civil rights."

Despite the prominent role he played in the civil-rights movement in the early 1960's—not only in writing about race relations, but in organizing various protest actions—Mr. Baldwin always rejected the label of "leader" or "spokesman."

Instead, he described himself as one whose mission was to "bear witness to the truth."

"A spokesman assumes that he is speaking for others," he told Julius Lester, a faculty colleague at the University of Massachusetts at Amherst, in an interview in *The New York Times Book Review* in 1984. "I never assumed that I could. What I tried to do, or to interpret and make clear, was that no society can smash the social contract and be expect from the consequences, and the consequences are chaos for everybody in the society."

This serene sense of independence was not simply a political stance, but an intrinsic part of Mr. Baldwin's personality.

"I was a maverick, a maverick in the sense that I depended on neither the white world nor the black world," he told Mr. Lester. "That was the only way I could've played it. I would've been broken otherwise. I had to say, 'A curse on both your houses.' The fact that I went to Europe so early is probably what saved me. It gave me another touchstone—myself."

Mr. Baldwin did not limit his 'bearing witness' to racial matters. He opposed American military involvement in Vietnam as early as 1963, and in the early 1960's he began to criticize discrimination against homosexuals.

Mr. Baldwin's literary achievements and his activism made him a world figure and to the end of his life brought him many honors in this country and abroad. The French Government made him a Commander of the Legion of Honor in 1986.

Yet, Mr. Baldiwn was also clearly disappointed that, despite his undeniable powers as an essayist, his novels and plays drew decidedly mixed reviews.

Go Tell It on the Mountain, his first book and first novel, published in 1953, was widely praised. Partly autobiographical, since Mr. Baldwin himself was the son of a minister, the book tells of a poor boy growing up in Harlem in the 1930's under the tyranny of his father, an autocratic preacher who hated his son.

Mr. Baldwin said in 1985 that in many ways the book remained the keystone of his career.

"*Mountain* is the book I had to write if I was ever going to write anything else," he remarked. "I had to deal with what hurt me most. I had to deal, above all, with my father. He was my model. I learned a lot from him. Nobody's ever frightened me since."

But the reception accorded his other works was at best lukewarm, and his frank discussion of homosexuality in *Giovanni's Room* (1956) and *Another Country* (1962) drew criticism from within and outside the civil-rights movement.

In a celebrated polemic in the late 1960's, Eldridge Cleaver, then a member of the Black Panther Party, asserted that the novel illustrated Mr. Baldwin's "agonizing, total hatred of blacks."

Another assessment of Mr. Baldwin was offered by Langston Hughes, the poet, who observed, "Few American writers handle words more effectively in the essay form than James Baldwin. To my way of thinking, he is much better at provoking thought in the essay than he is in arousing emotion in fiction."

Mr. Baldwin's other works included the novel *Tell Me How Long the Train's Been Gone,* the stage plays *Blues for Mister Charlie,* and *The Amen Corner,* and *The Evidence of Things Not Seen,* a long essay on the murder of 28 black children in Atlanta in 1980 and 1981.

Characteristically, Mr. Baldwin did not shrink from acknowledging the lesser view of his works of fiction, nor that his fame had slipped since the early 1970's.

"I'm very vulnerable to all of that," he said in a 1985 interview, referring to what he described in an early essay as the "dangerous, unending and unpredictable battle" of being a writer.

"The rise and fall of one's reputation," he mused. "What can you do about it? I think that comes with the territory. . . . Any real artist will never be judged in the time of his time; whatever judgment is delivered in the time of his time cannot be trusted."

James Baldwin was born in 1924 in Harlem and attended DeWitt Clinton High School in the Bronx. He was a precocious writer, and by his early twenties was publishing reviews and essays in such publications as *The New Leader, The Nation, Commentary* and *Partisan Review,* and socializing with the circle of New York writers and intellectuals that included Randall Jarrell, Dwight Macdonald, Lionel Trilling, Delmore Schwartz, Irving Howe and William Barrett, among others.

Yet, Mr. Baldwin was among the last one would have initially marked for a leadership role in a national movement. Soft-spoken, with a manner of speaking that mirrored his complex writing style, and physically slight, he thought of himself for many years as ugly, and wrote poignantly of his struggle to accept the way he looked. (pp. 1, 21)

Lee A. Daniels, "James Baldwin, Eloquent Essayist in Behalf of Civil Rights, Is Dead," in The New York Times, *December 2, 1987, pp. 1, 21.*

WILLIAM STYRON

[Styron, an American novelist, critic, and nonfiction and short story writer, has won acclaim as a Southern writer in the tradition of William Faulkner and Thomas Wolfe. Among his writings are the novels Lie down in Darkness *(1951),* Set This House on Fire *(1960),* The Confessions of Nat Turner *(1967), and* Sophie's Choice *(1979). His nonfiction works include* As He Lay Dead, a Bitter Grief *(1981), a critical study of Faulkner, and* The Quiet Dust and Other Writings *(1982). Styron and Baldwin became friends in the early 1960s. In the following excerpt, Styron recalls the early years of his relationship with Baldwin, noting the paradox inherent in the camaraderie between a white Southerner and a black civil rights activist.]*

James Baldwin was the grandson of a slave. I was the grandson of a slave owner. We were virtually the same age and we were both bemused by our close links to slavery, since most Americans of our vintage—if connected at all to the Old South—have had to trace that connection back several generations.

But Jimmy had fresh and vivid images of slave times, passed down from his grandfather directly to his father, a Harlem preacher of fanatical bent, who left a terrifying imprint on his son's life. Jimmy told me that he often thought that the degradation of his grandfather's life was the animating force behind his father's apocalyptic, often incoherent rage.

By contrast, my impression of slavery was quaint and rather benign; in the late 1930s, at the bedside of my grandmother who was then close to 90, I heard tales of the two little slave girls she had owned. Not much older than the girls themselves, at the outset of the Civil War she knitted socks for them, tried to take care of them during the privations of the conflict and, at the war's end, was as wrenched with sorrow as they were by the enforced leave-taking.

When I told this story to Jimmy he didn't flinch. We were both writing about the tangled relations of blacks and whites in America and, because he was wise, Jimmy understood the necessity of dealing with the preposterous paradoxes that had dwelt at the heart of the racial tragedy—the unrequited loves as well as the murderous furies.

The dichotomy amounted to an obsession in much of his work; it was certainly a part of my own, and I think our common preoccupation helped make us good friends. Jimmy moved into my guest cottage in Connecticut in the late autumn of 1960 and stayed there more or less continuously until the beginning of the following summer. A mutual friend had asked my wife and me to give Jimmy a place to stay, and since he was having financial problems it seemed a splendid idea.

Baldwin was not very well known then—except perhaps in literary circles where he was much admired for his first novel *Go Tell It on the Mountain*—but his fame was gradually gaining momentum and he divided his time between writing in the cottage and trips out on the nearby lecture circuit, where he

made some money for himself and where, with his ferocious oratory, he began to scare his predominantly radical chic audiences out of their pants.

His charisma, which had no doubt attended him since his days as a boy preacher in Harlem, was quite apparent; he was often trailed to the cottage by Volkswagen-driving, dirndl-clad, guitar-toting girls who, unaware of his sexual orientation, wanted to bed down with him. Somehow he would elude them. I would see him hurrying towards my house. He had a frail, elfin body that moved with the grace of a ballet dancer. Hopping through the snow drifts, his black face frozen in a smile of maniacal glee, he would burst through the door and howl 'Baby, save me from these Northern liberals!'

There was more seriousness in that plea than its jollity revealed. Without being in the slightest comforted as a Southerner, or let off the hook, I understood through him that black people regarded *all* white Americans as irredeemably racist, the most simple of them being not the Georgia rednecks (who were in part the victims of their heritage) but any citizen whatever whose *de jure* equality was a façade for *de facto* enmity and injustice.

Also romantic nitwits like those girls. In the cottage Jimmy was writing his novel **Another Country** and was making notes for the essay **"The Fire Next Time."** I was consolidating material, gathered over more than a decade, for a novel I was planning to write—but for which I had no title as yet—on the slave revolutionary Nat Turner. It was a frightfully cold winter, and a good time to learn something about each other.

I was by far the greater beneficiary. Born and reared in a Virginia community where blacks and whites were firmly walled off from each other as in Pretoria, struggling still to loosen myself from the prejudices that such an upbringing engenders, I possessed a residual scepticism: could a Negro really possess a mind as subtle, as richly informed, as broadly inquiring and embracing as that of a white man? My God, what appalling arrogance and vanity. Night after night Jimmy and I talked and talked, drinking whisky through the hours until the chill dawn, and I understood that I was in the company of as marvellous an intelligence as I am ever likely to encounter.

His voice was lilting and silky, but became husky as he chain-smoked. Disconcertingly homely, with an almost misshaped face dominated by popping eyes and a huge mobile mouth in which when laughing (and he laughed often and explosively) the tongue wagged like a bell-clapper, he was spellbinding, and he told me more about the frustrations and anguish of being a black man in America than I had known until then, or perhaps wanted to know. He told me exactly what it was like to be refused service, to be spat at, to be called 'nigger' and 'boy.'

It was as if he were disgorging in private all the pent-up rage and gorgeous passion that a few years later, in **"The Fire Next Time,"** would shake the conscience of the nation.

Sometimes other people, friends of mine, would come in and join our talk. The conversation might then turn more abstract and political. Certain of these people—well-intentioned, tolerant, and 'liberal': all the things Jimmy so intuitively mistrusted—would listen patiently while he spoke, visibly fretting then growing indignant at some pronouncement of his, some scathing *aperçu*.

'You can't mean that!' 'You mean—*burn*. . .?'. And in the troubled silence, Jimmy's face would become a mask of imperturbable certitude. 'Baby,' he would say softly, and glare back with vast glowering eyes. 'Yes baby, I mean *burn*. We will *burn your cities down*.'

Lest I give the impression that the winter was one of unalleviated solemnity, let me say that this was not so. Jimmy was a social animal of manic gusto and we had loud and festive evenings. He was a master chef of soul food—pork chops and collard greens, corn bread and blackeye peas—and I recollect a house often full of after-dinner dancing, the Twist being in vogue then and Jimmy's wiry and nimble little body gyrating at the focus of the centrifuge.

His waif-like form would have invited pathos had it not been so incredibly stuffed with energy. When summer came and he departed for good, heading for his apotheosis—the flamboyant celebrity that the 1960s brought him—he left a silence that to this day somehow resonates through my house.

After that I never saw him as often as I would have liked but our paths crossed from time to time and we always fell on each other with an uncomplicated sense of joyous reunion. Much has been written about Baldwin's effect on the consciousness of the world. It has been enormous.

I shall speak for myself. Even if I had not valued much of his work—which was flawed, like all writing, but which at its best had a burnished eloquence and devastating impact—I would have deemed his friendship inestimable. At his peak he had the fervour of Camus or Kafka. Like them he revealed to me, both in his art and his life, the core of his soul's savage distress and thus helped me to shape and define my own work, and its moral contours. This would be the most appropriate gift imaginable to the grandson of a slave owner from a slave's grandson.

William Styron, " 'Social Animal of Manic Gusto'," in The Observer, *December 6, 1987, p. 10.*

TONI MORRISON

[*Morrison, an American novelist, nonfiction writer, editor, and educator, has earned acclaim for her poetic novels which combine elements of realism and fantasy in their exposition of black American life. These include* The Bluest Eye *(1970),* Song of Solomon *(1973),* Sula *(1974),* Tar Baby *(1981), and* Beloved *(1987), which won the 1988 Pulitzer Prize in Fiction. In the following excerpt from a eulogy she delivered at Baldwin's funeral on December 8, 1987 at the Cathedral of St. John the Divine in New York, Morrison thanks Baldwin for his three gifts to black American writers: new language to express their thoughts, bravery, and love.*]

Jimmy, there is too much to think about you, and too much to feel. The difficulty is your life refuses summation—it always did—and invites contemplation instead. Like many of us left here I thought I knew you. Now I discover that in your company it is myself I know. That is the astonishing gift of your art and your friendship: You gave us ourselves to think about, to cherish. We are like Hall Montana watching "with new wonder" his brother saints, knowing the song he sang is us, "He is us."

I never heard a single command from you, yet the demands you made on me, the challenges you issued to me, were nevertheless unmistakable, even if unenforced: that I work and think at the top of my form, that I stand on moral ground but know that ground must be shored up by mercy, that "the world is before (me) and (I) need not take it or leave it as it was when (I) came in."

Well, the season was always Christmas with you there and, like one aspect of that scenario, you did not neglect to bring at least three gifts. You gave me a language to dwell in, a gift so perfect is seems my own invention. I have been thinking your spoken and written thoughts for so long I believed they were mine. I have been seeing the world through your eyes for so long, I believed that clear clear view was my own. Even now, even here, I need you to tell me what I am feeling and how to articulate it. So I have pored again through the 6,895 pages of your published work to acknowledge the debt and thank you for the credit. No one possessed or inhabited language for me the way you did. You made American English honest—genuinely international. You exposed its secrets and reshaped it until it was truly modern dialogic, representative, humane. You stripped it of ease and false comfort and fake innocence and evasion and hypocrisy. And in place of deviousness was clarity. In place of soft plump lies was a lean, targeted power. In place of intellectual disingenuousness and what you called "exasperating egocentricity," you gave us undecorated truth. You replaced lumbering platitudes with an upright elegance. You went into that forbidden territory and decolonized it, "robbed it of the jewel of its naïveté," and un-gated it for black people so that in your wake we could enter it, occupy it, restructure it in order to accommodate our complicated passion—not our vanities but our intricate, difficult, demanding beauty, or tragic, insistent knowledge, our lived reality, our sleek classical imagination—all the while refusing "to be defined by a language that has never been able to recognize (us)." In your hands language was handsome again. In your hands we saw how it was meant to be: neither bloodless nor bloody, and yet alive.

It infuriated some people. Those who saw the paucity of their own imagination in the two-way mirror you held up to them attacked the mirror, tried to reduce it to fragments which they could then rank and grade, tried to dismiss the shards where your image and theirs remained—locked but ready to soar. You are an artist after all and an artist is forbidden a career in this place; an artist is permitted only a commercial hit. But for thousands and thousands of those who embraced your text and who gave themselves permission to hear your language, by that very gesture they ennobled themselves, became unshrouded, civilized.

The second gift was your courage, which you let us share: the courage of one who could go as a stranger in the village and transform the distances between people into intimacy with the whole world; courage to understand that experience in ways that made it a personal revelation for each of us. It was you who gave us the courage to appropriate an alien, hostile, all-white geography because you had discovered that "this world (meaning history) is white no longer and it will never be white again." Yours was the courage to live life in and from its belly as well as beyond its edges, to see and say what it was, to recognize and identify evil but never fear or stand in awe of it. It is a courage that came from a ruthless intelligence married to a pity so profound it could convince anyone who cared to know that those who despised us "need the moral authority of their former slaves, who are the only people in the world who know anything about them and who may be, indeed, the only people in the world who really care anything about them." When that unassailable combination of mind and heart, of intellect and passion was on display it guided us through treacherous landscape as it did when you wrote these words—words every rebel, every dissident, revolutionary, every practicing artist from Capetown to Poland from Waycross to Dublin memorized: "A person does not lightly elect to oppose his society. One would much rather be at home among one's compatriots than be mocked and detested by them. And there is a level on which the mockery of the people, even their hatred, is moving, because it is so blind: It is terrible to watch people cling to their captivity and insist on their own destruction."

The third gift was hard to fathom and even harder to accept. It was your tenderness—a tenderness so delicate I thought it could not last, but last it did and envelop me it did. In the midst of anger it tapped me lightly like the child in Tish's womb: "Something almost as hard to catch as a whisper in a crowded place, as light and as definite as a spider's web, strikes below my ribs, stunning and astonishing my heart. . .the baby, turning for the first time in its incredible veil of water, announces its presence and claims me; tells me, in that instant, that what can get worse can get better. . .in the meantime— forever—it is entirely up to me." Yours was a tenderness, of vulnerability, that asked everything, expected everything and, like the world's own Merlin, provided us with the ways and means to deliver. I suppose that is why I was always a bit better behaved around you, smarter, more capable, wanting to be worth the love you lavished, and wanting to be steady enough to witness the pain you had witnessed and were tough enough to bear while it broke your heart, wanting to be generous enough to join your smile with one of my own, and reckless enough to jump on in that laugh you laughed. Because our joy and our laughter were not only all right, they were necessary.

You knew, didn't you, how I needed your language and the mind that formed it? How I relied on your fierce courage to tame wildernesses for me? How strengthened I was by the certainty that came from knowing you would never hurt me? You knew, didn't you, how I loved your love? You knew. This then is no calamity. No. This is jubilee. "Our crown," you said, "has already been bought and paid for. All we have to do," you said, "is wear it."

And we do, Jimmy. You crowned us.

> Toni Morrison, *"Life in His Language," in* The New York Times Book Review, *December 20, 1987, p. 27.*

AMIRI BARAKA

[*Baraka, an American dramatist, poet, essayist, novelist, and critic, rose to prominence as a controversial and influential voice in the black power movement of the 1960s and 1970s. His works include the poetry collections* Preface to a Twenty Volume Suicide Note *(1961),* Afrikan Revolution *(1973), and* Reggae or Not! *(1982), such dramas as* The Toilet *(1962),* Slave Ship: A Historical Pageant *(1967), and* Weimar 2 *(1981), and a memoir,* The Autobiography of LeRoi Jones *(1984). In the following excerpt from a eulogy he delivered at Baldwin's funeral on December 8, 1987 at the Cathedral of St. John the Divine in New York, Baraka praises the author as a gifted man of letters and an inspiring leader.*]

First of all, Jimmy Baldwin was not only a writer, an international literary figure, he was a man, spirit, voice—old and black and terrible as that first ancestor.

As man, he came to us from the family, the human lives, names we can call David, Gloria, Lover, George, Samuel, Barbara, Ruth, Elizabeth, Paula. . .and this extension is one intimate identification as he could so casually, in that way of his, eyes and self smiling, not much larger than that first ances-

tor, fragile as truth always is, big eyes popped out like righteous monitors of the soulful. The Africans say that big ol' eyes like that means someone can make things happen! And didn't he?

Between Jimmy's smile and grace, his insistent elegance even as he damned you, even as he smote what evil was unfortunate, breathing or otherwise, to stumble his way. He was all the way live, all the way conscious, turned all the way up, receiving and broadcasting, sometime so hard, what needed to, would back up from those two television tubes poking out of his head!

As man, he was my friend, my older brother he would joke, not really joking. As man, he was Our friend, Our older or younger brother, we listened to him like we would somebody in our family—whatever you might think of what he might say. We could hear it. He was close, as man, as human relative, we could make it some cold seasons merely warmed by his handshake, smile or eyes. Warmed by his voice, jocular yet instantly cutting. Kind yet perfectly clear. We could make it sometimes, just remembering his arm waved in confirmation or indignation, the rapid-fire speech, pushing out at the world like urgent messages for those who would be real.

This man traveled the earth like its history and its biographer. He reported, criticized, made beautiful, analyzed, cajoled, lyricized, attacked, sang, made us think, made us better, made us consciously human or perhaps more acidly pre-human.

He was spirit because he was living. And even past this tragic hour when we weep he has gone away, and why, and why we keep asking. There's mountains of evil creatures who we would willingly bid farewell to—Jimmy could have given you some of their names on demand—we curse our luck, our oppressors—our age, our weakness. Why and Why again? And why can drive you mad, or said enough times might even make you wise!

Yet this why in us is him as well. Jimmy was wise from asking whys giving us his wise and his whys to go with our own, to make them into a larger why and a deeper Wise.

Jimmy's spirit, which will be with us as long as we remember ourselves, is the only truth which keeps us sane and changes our whys to wiseness. It is his spirit, spirit of the little black first ancestor, which we feel those of us who really felt it, we know this spirit will be with us for "as long as the sun shines and the water flows." For his is the spirit of life thrilling to its own consciousness.

When we saw and heard him, he made us feel good. He made us feel, for one thing, that we could defend ourselves or define ourselves, that we were in the world not merely as animate slaves, but as terrifyingly sensitive measurers of what is good or evil, beautiful or ugly. This is the power of his spirit. This is the bond which created our love for him. This is the fire that terrifies our pitiful enemies. That not only are we alive but shatteringly precise in our songs and our scorn. You could not possibly think yourself righteous, murderers, when you saw or were wrenched by our Jimmy's spirit! He was carrying it as us, as we carry him as us.

Jimmy will be remembered, even as James, for his *word*. Only the completely ignorant can doubt his mastery of it. Jimmy Baldwin was the creator of contemporary American speech even before Americans could dig that. He created it so we could speak to each other at unimaginable intensities of feeling, so we could make sense to each other at yet higher and higher tempos.

But that word, arranged as art, sparkling and gesturing from the page, was also man and spirit. Nothing was more inspiring than hearing that voice, seeing that face, and that whip of a tongue, that signification that was his fingers, reveal and expose, raise and bring down, condemn or extol!

It was evident he loved beauty—art, but when the civil rights movement pitched to its height, no matter his early estheticism and seeming hauteur, he was our truest definer, our educated conscience made irresistible by his high consciousness.

Jimmy was a "civil rights leader" too, *at the same time!*, thinkers of outmoded social outrage. He was in the truest tradition of the great artists of all times. Those who understand it is beauty *and truth* we seek, and that indeed one cannot exist without and as an extension of the other.

At the hot peak of the movement Jimmy was one of its truest voices. His stance, that it is *our* judgement of the world, the majority of us who still struggle to survive the beastiality of so-called civilization (the slaves), that is true and not that of our torturers, was a dangerous profundity and as such fuel for our getaway and liberation!

He was our consummate complete man of letters, not as an unliving artifact, but as a black man we could touch and relate to even there in that space filled with black fire at the base and circumference of our souls. And what was supremely ironic is that for all his estheticism and ultra-sophistication, there he was now demanding that we get in the world completely, that we comprehend the ultimate intelligence of our enforced commitment to finally bring humanity to the world!

Jimmy's voice, as much as Dr. King's or Malcolm X's, helped shepherd and guide us toward black liberation.

Let us hold him in our hearts and minds. Let us make him part of our invincible black souls, the intelligence of our transcendence. Let our black hearts grow big world-absorbing eyes like his, never closed. Let us one day be able to celebrate him like he must be celebrated if we are ever to be truly self-determining. For Jimmy was God's black revolutionary mouth. If there is a God, and revolution His righteous natural expression. And elegant song the deepest and most fundamental commonplace of being alive. (pp. 27, 29)

> *Amiri Baraka, "We Carry Him as Us," in* The New York Times Book Review, *December 20, 1987, pp. 27, 29.*

MAYA ANGELOU

[*Angelou, an American poet, autobiographer, dramatist, editor, scriptwriter, and nonfiction and short story writer, has earned acclaim for her series of autobiographies, including* I Know Why the Caged Bird Sings *(1970),* The Heart of a Woman *(1981), and* All God's Children Need Traveling Shoes *(1986). Her other works include the poetry collections* Just Give Me a Cool Drink of Water 'fore I Diiie *(1971) and* Now Sheba Sings the Song *(1987). Angelou met Baldwin in Paris during the late 1950s; he encouraged her to start her writing career. In the following excerpt from a eulogy she delivered at Baldwin's funeral on December 8, 1987 at the Cathedral of St. John the Divine in New York, Angelou recalls her close friendship with Baldwin.*]

Speeches will be given, essays written and hefty books will be published on the various lives of James Baldwin. Some fantasies will be broadcast and even some truths will be told. Someone will speak of the essayist James Baldwin in his role as the biblical prophet Isaiah admonishing his country to repent from wickedness and create within itself a clean spirit and a clean heart. Others will examine Baldwin the playwright and novelist who burned with a righteous indignation over the paucity of kindness, the absence of love and the crippling hypocrisy he saw in the streets of the United States and sensed in the hearts of his fellow citizens.

I will speak of James Baldwin, my friend and brother.

> A short brown man came to the door and looked at me. He had the most extraordinary eyes I'd ever seen. When he completed his instant X-ray of my brain, lungs, liver, heart, bowels and spinal column, he smiled and said, "Come in," and opened the door. He opened the door all right. Lord! I was to hear Beauford sing later for many years "Open the Unusual Door."

Thus James Baldwin describes meeting and being met by Beauford Delaney, the provocative black American painter who was to enlarge and enrich Baldwin's life. Baldwin's description of Delaney fitted Baldwin as well, for he, too, was small and brown and had the most extraordinary eyes.

I first met Jim fleetingly in the *boîtes* of Paris when he and I and the world were young enough to believe ourselves independently salvageable. But we became friends in the late 50's, just as the United States was poised to make its quantum leap into the future, as Martin Luther King, Rosa Parks and other Southerners were girding themselves for the second Civil War in 100 years and while Malcolm X was giving voice to the anger in the streets and in the minds of Northern black city folks.

In that riotous pulse of political fervor, James Baldwin and I met again and liked each other. We discussed courage, human rights, God and justice. We talked about black folks and love, about white folks and fear.

Although Jimmy was known as an accomplished playwright, few people knew that he was a frustrated actor as well. I had a role in Jean Genet's play *The Blacks*, and since Jimmy knew Genet personally and the play in the original French, nothing could keep him from advising me on my performance. He furnished me with my first limousine ride, set the stage for me to write *I Know Why the Caged Bird Sings*, encouraged me to take a course in cinematography in Sweden and told me that I was intelligent and very brave. I knew Jim loved me when he gave me to Gloria and Paula, Wilmer and David Baldwin and all the rest of his siblings and when he took me to Mother Baldwin and said: "Just what you don't need, another daughter, but here she is." I knew that he knew black women may find lovers on street corners or even in church pews, but brothers are hard to come by and are as necessary as air and as precious as love. James Baldwin knew that black women in this desolate world, black women in this cruel time which has no soundness in it, have a crying need for brothers. He knew that brother's love redeems a sister's pain. His love opened the unusual door for me and I am blessed that James Baldwin was my brother. (pp. 29-30)

> *Maya Angelou, "A Brother's Love," in* The New York Times Book Review, *December 20, 1987, pp. 29-30.*

[ELIZABETH MACKLIN AND MARY HAWTHORNE]

[*The following excerpt describes Baldwin's funeral on December 8, 1987 at the Cathedral of St. John the Divine in New York.*]

The Cathedral Church of St. John the Divine, on the border of Harlem, is so reverberant that the sound of drums—or even of a single drum—fills it. One drum and then, suddenly, eight drums began the funeral service for James Baldwin [December 8] at noon. For the opening procession—a crucifer flanked by two candle-bearers and followed by priests, pastors, acolytes, the cathedral choirs, the Baldwin family, and the pallbearers, all slowly making a half circuit of the aisles—the Babatunde Olatunji Ensemble played "A Drum Salute." For some two hours after that, though, there was stillness, except for occasional clicking cameras or a fussing baby, and the congregation listened as Psalms were chanted, prayers were offered, and Scripture was read, and as friends of Baldwin's spoke about him, or to him. "You made American English honest," Toni Morrison said [see excerpt above]. "You stripped it of ease and false comfort. . . . You went into that forbidden territory and decolonized it. . . . In your hands, language was *handsome* again." Toward the end came Baldwin's own gentle baritone voice, in a recording, singing the gospel hymn "Precious Lord, take my hand, lead me on." It was so quiet that you could hear, a long way off, the muffled ringing of a telephone.

In some ways, it was as if the service ("A Celebration of the Life of James Arthur Baldwin" was the title on a printed program) were a pageant, meant to be seen as a play is seen. The men and women presiding and serving wore their plain dark cassocks and white surplices; the choir wore red robes. Some of the women in the procession were in regal-looking fur coats, and several wore tall, squared African head wraps, one with a parade of zebra stripes around it. And when two jazz musicians played a horn salute the trumpet and flugelhorn shone under the lights.

At the end, a recessional called "Continuum Drums" (also played by Babatunde Olatunji) went on until the church was empty and hollow-sounding. The congregation slowly filed out through the main doors, but didn't leave. Instead, people stood on the wide steps leading down to Amsterdam Avenue—in small groups, mostly, though there was one classroom-sized crew of third graders—and greeted each other, posed with programs for each other's snapshots, called out to those still leaving the church, chatted ("But you *never* wear a tie!") or spoke privately for a long time. They seemed less like isolated mourners than like friends who hadn't seen one another in an age—who had come not as strangers but as a family.

[*Elizabeth Macklin and Mary Hawthorne*], "Notes and Comment," in The New Yorker, *Vol. LXIII, No. 44, December 21, 1987, p. 31.*

MICHAEL THELWELL

[*Thelwell is a Jamaican short story writer, novelist, and educator whose writings reflect his concern with social issues pertaining to black Americans and Jamaicans. Among his works are the novel* The Harder They Come *(1980) and the collection* Duties, Pleasures, and Conflicts: Essays in Struggle *(1987). Thelwell first met Baldwin when the author came to speak at Howard University in the early 1960s. In the following excerpt from a eulogy he delivered at a memorial service for Baldwin at the University of Massachussetts at Amherst on December 16, 1987, Thelwell expresses his admiration for Baldwin's dedication to his ideals.*]

One does not encompass in a few words—or a great many for that matter—the extraordinary, many-faceted complexity of the man, the presence, indeed the phenomenon known to the world as James Baldwin.

"He had in him the elements so mixed . . ."

On the one hand, so infinite a sweetness and gentleness of spirit; an openness to and a capacity for love so deep as to appear almost as vulnerability. On the other, a boldness: a quality of moral courage; a fearless, passionate, militant, unrepentant commitment to struggle and to justice that was heroic.

On the one hand, the penetrating insight of an intelligence so brilliant, sharp and incisive as sometimes to be painful. On the other, the warm personal generosity and profound decency of the man. The slight, almost fragile, physical presence out of which shone a greatness of soul, a radiant moral dignity that was clearly—in the best sense of that term—regal. An aristocracy not of birth, but of spirit.

". . . that nature might stand up and say to all the world, this was a man."

So, where to begin, friends? From which source do we take a text this morning? In the sanctified church out of which he came one must—on such an occasion—take a text. Clearly we must look to one of the many streams that flowed into his art, nourished his vision and informed his genius. A line, then, maybe from: a hymn, a battle hymn? *"We have seen his righteous witness . . ."* or, Shakespeare, a writer whose language equalled his? *"Let us sit upon the ground and tell sad stories of the death of kings . . ."* The King James version? *"Let us now praise famous men . . ."* The affirmation of the spiritual? *"Ain't no grave can hold my body down . . ."* The Blues? *"Yo' was a ramblin' man, Daddy, But yo' spirit never done lef home."* Or, we could go to the streets. A line overheard in a Harlem bar after he had appeared on television in confrontation with a former Attorney General of the United States: *"Whooiee, that little dude be kicking ass, Baby! The brother sho' don't take no shit, do he?"*

Any or all of those would serve.

But, I think, and not merely in deference to Chinua, to our respected senior brother . . . , I shall recourse to the proverbial wisdom of the Ibo elders, as it were, to the source. Our African ancestor said: *"If you want to see a mask dancing, you cannot stand in one place."* And so it was with Jimmy. He indeed was one of the numinous presences, one of the great masked, ancestral spirits of our time, covering so much ground in his prophetic dance that one had to constantly keep moving in order to see it truly.

But those same ancestors also said, *"Truth is like a goatskin bag, each man carries his own."* Truth and Jimmy were friends. Indeed truth was his constant companion, they were one and inseparable. And all of us in this room, we who have spoken and you who have listened, each carry our own version of this truth. Each different, each personal, each in its own way true. So what I will do in the time left me is to share with you a portion of mine. . . .

In the Spring of 1960 I was a freshman at Howard University and a member of a group of young blacks who had begun, in the nation's capital, demonstrations against the racist social practice of the society. It was an exciting time. We sensed that something profound had definitely begun, but had no idea where it would end, or what price would ultimately be exacted. We knew that there would be a price and that someone would have to pay it, but we were determined to "see what the end would be."

This ''militance'' was not well received by the administration, or if the truth be told, a goodly number of our peers. Among many adults there was the feeling that our defiance would only make things worse, embarrass the race and ultimately and inevitably provoke the angry retribution of white America. It was far wiser that you young Negroes, as they called us, looked to your education; stay neat, clean, polite and respectful; suppress them Southern accents, master ''proper'' speech and don't wear your hair in that wild ''African'' bush. In this way white folk might—if we rendered ourselves thoroughly inoffensive— gradually come to ''accept'' us. This we heard daily, though some faculty offered quiet encouragement and a few ''radicals'' like Sterling Brown did so boldly and publicly.

One day we received an unusual invitation. It was in terms so intriguing—and as it proved, prophetic—that I have never forgotten the conversation.

''Mike, does the name James Baldwin mean anything to you?''

''Yeah vaguely . . . isn't he some kind of writer . . . remind me?'' As you can see, at that time I didn't really know his name.

''Well, my friend, he's an extraordinary writer and a very curious and interesting man. He's a small black man from Harlem with this remarkable face—some would say almost ugly—but very mobile and expressive with these big, intense pop eyes. But once he opens his mouth, I guarantee, you will never have heard such intelligence, such brilliance . . . And his personal life is always so complicated, always chaotic, skirting the edge of crisis. He's giving a talk in Georgetown and particularly asked that some of the movement kids be there.'' With an invitation like that how could we not?

Baldwin was returning from twelve years of French exile drawn back as much by the pictures of Little Rock as by two manuscripts packed in his luggage. Within a year these manuscripts would become the best-selling **Another Country** and **Nobody Knows My Name,** an ironic title which would soon be rendered utterly false.

So . . . we, a group of us, make the trek across the city into Georgetown, then as now the preserve of Washington's affluent and powerful, or of pretenders and aspirants to that status, which at that time meant exclusively white folk.

When we entered, the meeting had started. The neighborhood was unfamiliar and we had some difficulty finding the rather imposing house of an affluent former socialist. James Baldwin stood in the center of the packed living room. Completely, as it were, surrounded by white America. We were late, somewhat tense or at least not at all at ease and trying hard not to show it. It was, I think for most of us, our first incursion into the alien territory known as social contact with white folk. All eyes turned to the door, and we had another first: the radiance of that legendary Baldwin smile.

He turned and, seeing the young blacks (no: we weren't blacks yet, still Negroes), the mobile, expressive face erupted into a smile of such immediate and spontaneous charisma and protectiveness that we were immediately at peace. ''Hi,'' he said, ''I'm James Baldwin, and I'm so very glad you came.''

The rest of the evening is not so easy to describe. Baldwin was about thirty-five, in the flowering of his power. Even his gestures and expressions were eloquent and he displayed a precision and poetry of language, an elegance of mind such as I had never seen before. He was never strident or abrasive,

but gracious, indeed almost gentle with even the most obtuse and ill-informed questions, of which there were many. But totally clear, uncompromising, evading no question, side-stepping no issue and never, never, never defensive or apologetic for the race. He made believers of us.

As we watched, marvelled and cheered we could feel movement, the very ground shifting beneath us. The fundamental terms of racial discourse were permanently being transformed and elevated before our eyes. We were receiving confirmation of all—which in inchoate and unformed ways—we had been feeling in our hearts, now given form and utterance in the sparkling, lambent clarity of Baldwinian language.

''No, no my friends you are mistaken. The question is not one of acceptance but of forgiveness. Not whether America will accept us, but whether we can find it in our hearts to forgive you.'' Our hosts who had felt themselves to be enlightened and sympathetic to the Negro problem felt these tremors too. Their questions became more and more uncertain, befuddled and therefore belligerent, as their most comforting clichés and complacent assumptions were one by one rendered unavailable and permanently unserviceable. Of course all of us, indeed the nation, have many times since heard those cadences and felt the weight of those arguments. But to encounter them, at the opening of that fateful decade, for the first time and in the context I have tried to describe . . .

Leaving that meeting we strode through the dark city as though in twelve-League boots. We had *heard* his righteous witness. It was not merely that white racism held no further terror for us, it was that we couldn't *wait* for that sucker to raise its ugly head. We were ready. I think the word of choice now is ''empowered.'' That evening, I see now, was for us the beginning of a unique relationship, involving not only the few fortunate enough to be present, but between James Baldwin and our whole generation of black Americans.

About a year later, when the student challenge had gathered force and Baldwin's fame had grown, that relationship was formalized. We invited Baldwin, John O. Killens and Ossie Davis onto our campus to discuss the black writer's responsibility. Again it was a highly charged evening for the writers and for the students.

In the small hours of morning, as the sun was rising over the capitol, in a small student apartment to which we had adjourned the discussion which had raged all night, there came a moment when Baldwin summarized the meaning of the encounter. Speaking slowly and thoughtfully he said, as I remember, ''As a black writer, I must in some way, some very real way, represent you, my young brothers and sisters. You didn't bestow this responsibility . . . I didn't choose it . . . But there it is. All I can say, is that I will never betray that, . . . never betray you. If you—all of you—will promise me that you never will accept the reductive definitions of your existence that this republic has ready for you . . . I promise you I shall never betray you.'' He never did, betray us or himself.

And he could have so easily, because then those two imposters, fame and celebrity, came pounding and kicking on his door. When James Baldwin burst across the cultural firmament and national consciousness like a new-born comet—the establishment's literati and media came-a-courting, seeking to immobilize him in a fulsome embrace.

''Come on, Jimmy. You still can't be angry. You've made it, you're big time now.''

Jimmy, they never knew who you was.

Because while their journals, magazines and airwaves prated about his "bitter fire," "angry genius," "astounding gifts" and "terrible eloquence" they were incapable, really, of understanding their source or meaning, or that these were not commodities, and that Jimmy would and could not permit them to be packaged into merchandise. What they did not understand was that the source of Baldwin's power came from a style and a vision both of which were firmly and irrevocably anchored in the soul of black folk. The remorseless clarity of his vision lay in a perspective on American reality forged in the fiery crucible of the black experience. And the wisdom and insight of that bitter and ennobling history was simply not negotiable. And further, that magnificent prose, at its finest, was a near perfect instrument for its expression. Because the nuances and poetry of that style were informed by centuries of the rich cultural expression of black America. The best of black American cultural idiom: the blues' earthy ironies; the spirituals' haunting power; the saucy riffs and defiant rhythms of jazz; the awful moral cadences of King James; the gospel's ecstatic shout and the preacher's god-intoxicated growl, were all synthesized into an instrument of remarkable beauty and compelling power.

For the first time, and a brief moment, in the history of this sad republic *the distilled voice of 300 years of African American experience spoke directly to the nation and compelled its grudging attention.* That was his power, his gift and his burden. This is why the little romance with the literati could not last. It was also why Baldwin's vision, loyalties and commitments were not and could not have been for sale, rent or lease. Why his gifts—and the responsibility which attended them—could not be subsumed or assimilated into some smug, complacent consensus of the white literary mainstream.

Had they been, Jimmy would have died an obscenely wealthy man, and spiritually, long before now. Praised in all the wrong places for all the wrong reasons. He would have, indeed, betrayed himself and us. He never did. So the *apparatchiks* of the literary establishment, seeing that his witness could not be suborned, turned overnight from fulsome admiration and importunings to venom.

I will always remember a most instructive lunch in 1964. I, then a senior in college and the author of a grand total of three published short stories, was being courted by an agent, an editor and a critic. "Mr. Thelwell, you really should write a novel," they urged. Then at the end the agent gave a great smile of accomplishment. "Good. Then that's settled. I think the time is ripe! This country *is ready for a new Negro writer. That James Baldwin is finished.* Did you *see Blues for Mr. Charlie?* Really!"

What an unholy marriage of arrogance and ignorance! But it was profoundly eye-opening to a young Negro who might otherwise have had his head turned. Something else I owe to Jimmy. Of course, like Mark Twain, pronouncements of his demise were greatly exaggerated and quite premature.

In recent years it was my honor to travel on occasion with Jimmy to various events. Wherever we went people of my generation—white or black—would approach him, almost with reverence. The blacks would hug him, the whites shake his hand. Always it was with an almost fervent sincerity, Mr. Baldwin:

"Your work changed my life . . . when I was in college . . . ."

"When we were in jail in South Africa we smuggled your book. . . ."

"When I was growing up in Selma, Alabama. . . ."

"I cried and trembled the day I read. . . ."

One night in 1984 in Washington—the tale had come full circle—a group of younger blacks, clearly a new generation, gave a reception for him. I witnessed there an outpouring, spontaneous, heart-felt and joyous, of love and appreciation. I asked him, "Jimmy, how does this make you feel?"

"I feel . . . ," he said simply, "I feel *blest.*"

So he is dead. He died with his integrity intact, his legacy unsullied and with his honorable example as a beacon for our guidance and inspiration. I am in no way ashamed to admit publicly that I have tried to model my work and conduct as a writer and a black man on that example. For our generation of black writers—to the extent we see further than might otherwise have been the case—it is only because we stand huddled on the fragile but formidable shoulders of James Arthur Baldwin. It was an honor and a privilege to have been his friend. (pp. 556-59)

> *Michael Thelwell, "We Have Seen His Righteous Witness . . . ," in* The Massachusetts Review, *Vol. XXVIII, No. 4, Winter, 1987, pp. 556-59.*

JOHN WIDEMAN

[*Wideman, an American novelist, short story writer, poet, critic, memoirist, and educator, writes about lower-class black American life. His poetic, highly impressionistic style has been compared to the work of William Faulkner and James Joyce. His novels include* A Glance Away (1967), The Lynchers (1973), Sent for You Yesterday (1984), *which won the PEN/Faulkner Award for Fiction, and* Reuben (1987). *The following excerpt is a eulogy in verse delivered by Wideman at a memorial service for Baldwin at the University of Massachusetts at Amherst on December 16, 1987.*]

> For James Baldwin
> (1924-87)
>
> What can we say to this
> this knife-edged air
> this ice blocking streams
> this bluesteel sky
>
> How do we speak to you
> who is our voice and
> still now. Too patient to
> laugh at us but smiling
> yes yes
> and the glass in your hand
> your steepled knee
> that elegant rag of many colors
> swirling round your throat
>
> Surely we knew
> it would come to this
> it always does.
> Against fiery last ditch light
> trees are x-rays of themselves
> prisoners stripped, flayed to the bone
>
> One black boy so scared
> pee-pee bout to run down his pantleg
> but he ain't turning round

not today. No woman no
cry. Not today, Mama. Gon tear that
old building down. With love
with fire and bare hands
and words like ten thousand
trumpets shaking hills
to their foundations

Poor boy long way from home
Poor boy long way from home
Poor boy long way from home
Been here—and now he's gone
Been here—and now he's gone

Think of little David
and his sling shot,
monkey shine signifier
blowing the Emperor away

We wait for the earth
to turn and tilt again
the shadow to lift

Rainbow wisdom of the elders
grandfathers, priests, kings
mother shuffle and warrior
woman strut and tons and tons of
babies still to come
our people our breath
your words
tell us the circle is strong
will not be broken
though the clay, the clay
my brother is weak, weak
as a slave ship ought to be
Steal away.
Steal away.

We gather
in this frozen land
beside a river of mourning.
Saints chant: *Be not dismayed*
what ere betides
and you march in your billowing
black robes down the aisle
mount the pulpit and
shout us sing us bound
to a glory man wherever that
might be wherever you are
now catching your breath and
testing it and amen how sweet
it must be free free
at last the cup to your lips
and emptied and full and
go on with your fine self,
child. Home.

  John Wideman, "For James Baldwin (1924-87)," in
  The Massachusetts Review, *Vol. XXVIII, No. 4, Win-*
  ter, 1987, p. 560.

STANLEY CROUCH

[*Crouch, an American critic, musician, and educator, is a music*
critic for the Village Voice. *In the following excerpt, he attacks*
Baldwin's views on racial issues, which Crouch finds extremist.]

By 1963, when he published **The Fire Next Time,** James Baldwin's writing had become almost exclusively polemical, foreshadowing the narrowing of black commentary into strident
prosecution or spiteful apology. Considered the intellectual
component of the Civil Rights movement, Baldwin was a seminal influence on the subsequent era of regression in which
Stokely Carmichael, Rap Brown, Leroi Jones, and Eldridge
Cleaver transformed white America into Big Daddy and the
Negro movement into an obnoxious, pouting adolescent demanding the car keys.

The increasing bile and cynicism of Baldwin's generalized
charges and his willingness to remove free will from the black
lower-class through what he called the "doom" of color, helped
foster a disposition that put the Negro movement into the hands
of those who had failed at taking it over before: the trickle-
down Marxist revolutionaries and cultural nationalists whose
flops and follies of imagination Harold Cruse documented so
well in *Crisis of the Negro Intellectual.* Those people led many
up paths that resulted in imprisonment, spiritual collapse, and
death for goals far less logical than acquiring political power
through inclusion into the social contract. The alienation of
abstract facelessness that Martin Luther King and the civil
rights workers had won so many battles against was given
greater strength when black political talk became progressively
antiwhite, anticapitalist, and made threats of overthrowing the
system itself.

Before he was swept into the position of a media spokesman,
Baldwin had been much more ambitious and much more willing
to address the subtleties of being a serious writer. His first
book of essays, **Notes of a Native Son,** contains **"Everybody's**
Protest Novel," which was written in 1949 and observes that
". . . the avowed aim of the American protest novel is to bring
greater freedom to the oppressed. They are forgiven, on the
strength of these good intentions, whatever violence they do
to language, whatever excessive demands they make of credibility. It is, indeed, considered the sign of frivolity so intense
as to approach decadence to suggest that these books are both
badly written and wildly improbable. One is told to put first
things first, the good of society coming before the niceties of
style or characterization. Even if this were incontestable . . . it
argues an insuperable confusion, since literature and sociology
are not one and the same; it is impossible to discuss them as
if they were."

The turmoil that would so twist Baldwin's intelligence and
abuse the possibilities of his talent is also evident in that first
book of essays, much of the trouble circulating around his
sense of himself as "an interloper," "a bastard of the West."
"Stranger in the Village" finds him reeling toward the emblematic as he writes of some Swiss hicks in an Alpine town,
"These people cannot be, from the point of view of power,
strangers anywhere in the world; they have made the modern
world, in effect, even if they do not know it. The most illiterate
among them is related, in a way that I am not, to Dante,
Shakespeare, Michelangelo, Aeschylus, Da Vinci, Rembrandt,
and Racine; the cathedral at Chartres says something to them
which it cannot say to me, as indeed would New York's Empire
State Building, should anyone here ever see it. Out of their
hymns and dances come Beethoven and Bach. Go back a few
centuries and they are in their full glory—but I am in Africa,
watching the conquerors arrive."

Such thinking led to the problem we still face in which too
many so-called nonwhite people look upon "the West" as some
catchall in which every European or person of European descent
is somehow part of a structure bent solely on excluding or
intimidating the Baldwins of the world. Were Roland Hayes,
Marian Anderson, Leontyne Price, Jessye Norman, or Kiri Te
Kanawa to have taken such a position, they would have locked
themselves out of a world of music that originated neither

among Afro-Americans nor Maoris. Further, his ahistorical ignorance is remarkable, and perhaps willful.

But breaking through the mask of collective whiteness—and collective *guilt*—that Baldwin imposes would demand recognition of the fact that, as history and national chauvinism prove, Europe is not a one-called organism. Such simplifications are akin to the kind of reasoning that manipulated illiterate rednecks into violent attempts at keeping "their" universities clean of Negro interlopers. Or convinced black nationalist automatons that they were the descendants of "kings and queens" brought to America in slave ships and should, therefore, uncritically identify with Africa. Rather than address the possibilities that come both of ethnic cultural identity and of accepting the international wonder of human heritage per se, people are expected to relate to the world only through race and the most stifling conceptions of group history. The root of that vision is perhaps what Shaw spoke of in *Major Barbara,* hatred as the coward's revenge for ever having been intimidated. Baldwin would call it rage, and write, "Rage can only with difficulty, and never entirely, be brought under the domination of the intelligence and is therefore not susceptible to any arguments whatever."

Though his second book of essays, *Nobody Knows My Name,* is the work of a gritty and subtle intelligence, there are more than a few indications of the talent that would soon be lost to polemics. Perhaps the most illuminating is **"Princes and Powers,"** where he takes a remarkably sober look at the Conference of Negro-African Writers and Artists, held in Paris in 1956. Baldwin was faced with an international gathering of black people who were rejecting the justifications used to maintain the colonial structures they groaned under. Here Baldwin introduced themes he would later adapt to the American context: the denial by Europeans of non-Western cultural complexity— or parity; the social function of the inferiority complex colonialism threw over the native like a net; the alignment of Christianity and cruelty under colonialism, and the idea that world views were at odds, European versus the "spirit of Bandung," or the West in the ring with the Third World.

At the time, Baldwin understood quite well the difference between colonized and Afro-American people, whom he rightfully referred to as "the most real and certainly the most shocking contributions to Western cultural life." Though Afro-Americans also suffered under institutionalized prejudice, the nature of their experience was the manifestation of a very specific context. "This results in a psychology very different— at its best and at its worst—from the psychology that is produced by a sense of having been invaded and overrun, the sense of having no recourse whatever against oppression other than overthrowing the machinery of the oppressor. We had been dealing with, had been made and mangled by, another machinery altogether. It had never been in our interest to overthrow it. It had been necessary to make the machinery work for our benefit and the possibility of doing so had been, so to speak, built in."

In assessing the performance of Richard Wright, Baldwin understood the danger of apologizing for brutal, Third World politics that the older writer was condoning. Baldwin didn't miss the implications of Wright's address: ". . . that the West, having created an African and Asian elite, should now 'give them their heads' and 'refuse to be shocked' at the 'methods they will be compelled to use' in unifying their countries. . . . Presumably, this left us in no position to throw stones at Nehru, Nasser, Sukarno, etc., should they decide as they almost surely would, to use dictatorial methods in order to hasten the 'social evolution.' In any case, Wright said, these men, the leaders of their countries, once the new social order was established, would voluntarily surrender the 'personal power.' He did not say what would happen then, but I supposed it would be the second coming."

Listening then to Aimee Cesaire, Baldwin wrote, "I felt stirred in a very strange and disagreeable way. For Cesaire's case against Europe, which was watertight, was also a very easy case to make. . . . Cesaire's speech left out of account one of the great effects of the colonial experience: its creation, precisely, of men like himself." Baldwin could see that Cesaire was a modern man, a writer whose bearing and confidence were proof that, "He had penetrated into the heart of the great wilderness which was Europe and stolen the sacred fire. And this, which was the promise of their freedom, was also the assurance of his power."

Such good sense wouldn't last long in Baldwin's writing. Once he settled into astonishingly lyrical rants such as *The Fire Next Time,* Negro neighborhoods were described as relentlessly grim and so inevitably deforming that only the most naïve could accept Baldwin's having come from such a "ghetto." Ignoring the epic intricacy of Afro-American life, Baldwin began to espouse the kinds of simplistic conceptions Malcolm X became famous for: "It is a fact that every American Negro bears a name that originally belonged to the white man whose chattel he was. I am called Baldwin because I was either sold by my African tribe or kidnapped out of it into the hands of a white Christian named Baldwin, who forced me to kneel at the foot of the cross."

Actually, a good number of Negroes named *themselves* after freedom came and the issue of converting slaves to Christianity was a subject of major debate because it broached the idea of slaves having souls. But such facts were of no interest to Baldwin. Rather, he chose to combine the Nation of Islam's venom toward Christianity and toward whites with an overview so committed to determinism that it paralleled the explanatory recipes of the left. When mature thinking was most desperately needed, Baldwin was losing the ability to look at things the way they actually were.

In effect, Baldwin sold out to rage, despair, self-righteousness, and a will to scandalize. The mood he submitted to was one he had pinned down in **"Princes and Powers."** Alioune Diop, editor of *Presence Africaine,* had delivered a talk and Baldwin perceptively noticed this: "His speech won a great deal of applause. Yet, I felt that among the dark people in the hall there was, perhaps, some disappointment that he had not been more specific, more bitter, in a word, more demagogical." In America, there was a very similar attitude among those fat-mouthing Negroes who chose to sneer at the heroic optimism of the Civil Rights Movement; they developed their own radical chic and spoke of Malcolm X as being beyond compromise, of his unwillingness to cooperate with the white man, and of his ideas being too radical for assimilation. Baldwin was sucked into this world of intellectual airlessness. By *The Fire Next Time,* Baldwin is so happy to see white policemen made uncomfortable by Muslim rallies, and so willing to embrace almost anything that disturbs whites in general, that he starts competing with the apocalyptic tone of the Nation of Islam.

Perhaps it is understandable that Baldwin could not resist the contemptuous pose of militance that gave focus to all of his anger for being the homely duckling who never became a swan, the writer who would perhaps never have been read by so many black people otherwise, and the homosexual who lived abroad most of his adult life in order to enjoy his preferences. Baldwin's increasing virulence had perhaps more than a bit to do with his homosexuality. As a small, even frail, man who wrote of being physically abused by his father, the police, and racists in the Greenwich Village, Baldwin was prone to admire and despise those who handled the world in a two-fisted manner (which comes out clearly in his essay on Norman Mailer, **"The Black Boy Looks at the White Boy"**). He was also given to the outsider's joy when intimidation was possible: "black has *become* a beautiful color—not because it is loved but because it is feared." This same attraction to fear permeated his ambivalent attitude toward Christianity. Condemned to hell as an erotic pariah by Christian doctrine, he was understandably relentless in his counterattacks; at the same time, his alienation did not prevent him from being awed by the particular power and majesty Negroes had brought to the religion. Boldly, though unconvincingly, in ***Another Country*** and ***Tell Me How Long the Train's Been Gone,*** he presented an alternative order in which homosexuals served as priests in a religion based on love.

Baldwin's prose was sometimes coated with the effete sheen of the homosexual straining to present himself as part of an elite, or it could be pickled with the self-defensive snits and bitchiness Lionel Mitchell called "our macho." Beware ye who would condescend: Baldwin's attitude wasn't substantially different from the aggressive defensiveness of any outsiders, be they black nationalists who celebrate Africa at Europe's expense, those feminists who elevate women over men, or any other group at odds with or at a loss for social and political power.

It is also true that Baldwin was the first of his kind, and perhaps the last we shall see for some time; the Negro writer made a celebrity and thrust into the national political dialogue. He had no models to learn from and settled for sassing the white folks when ideas of substance would have been much more valuable. His considerable gift for making something of his own from the language of Henry James and the rhetoric of the black church was largely squandered on surface charges and protest fiction. The talent for writing fiction that Baldwin showed in his first novel, ***Go Tell It on the Mountain,*** never achieved maturity. Though the rest of the novels are uniformly bad, almost every one contains brilliant passages in which Baldwin's long, long sentences were indicative of his intricate sense of consciousness, boasting finely orchestrated details, declarations, and nuances of feeling. But they are, with the exception of the all-white homosexual melodrama ***Giovanni's Room,*** ruined by the writer's contrived and sentimental conception of race. The purple trumpet in his soul played the same tune over and over, one which depicted Negro life as insufferable, saintly, and infinitely superior to that of whites.

Though homosexuality loomed ever larger in his fiction as the years passed, by the last long essay, ***The Evidence of Things Not Seen,*** Baldwin streaks away from the issues surrounding the Atlanta child murders, ignoring particularly the exploitation of so many improverished Negro boys by the homosexual subculture of that city. His eloquence gone, Baldwin reads as though his mind had so eroded that he no longer knew how to build an argument. Very little connects and any subject is an occasion for a forced harangue against the West, the profit motive, Christianity, and so on. It is a disturbingly dishonest book.

One cannot deny James Baldwin his powers, but it is tragic that he was never strong enough to defend and nurture his substantial talent and become the writer even such imposing gifts do not make inevitable. Finally, Baldwin's description of his success as a boy preacher in ***The Fire Next Time*** says much about the decay of a writer who once seemed poised on greatness: "That was the most frightening time of my life, and quite the most dishonest, and the resulting hysteria lent great passion to my sermons—for a while. I relished the attention and the relative immunity from punishment that my new status gave me. . . ." (pp. 35, 38-9)

> *Stanley Crouch, "The Rage of Race," in* The Village Voice," *Vol. XXXIII, No. 2, January 12, 1988, pp. 35, 38-9.*

JAMES BALDWIN AND QUINCY TROUPE

[*Troupe, an American poet, editor, educator, and nonfiction writer, is founding editor of* Confrontation: A Journal of Third World Literature. *Among his works are* Embryo *(1972),* Ash Doors and Juju Gates *(1975),* Snake-Back Solos: Selected Poems, 1969-1977 *(1978), and* Skulls along the River *(1984). In the following excerpt from an interview Baldwin gave Troupe on November 13 and 14, 1987, the author discusses such issues as fame and his thoughts about other prominent black American writers.*]

JAMES BALDWIN: It's difficult to be a legend. It's hard for me to recognize *me.* You spend a lot of time trying to avoid it. It's really something, to be a legend, unbearable. The way the world treats you is unbearable, and especially if you're black. It's unbearable because time is passing and you are not your legend, but you're trapped in it. Nobody will let you out of it. Except other people who know what it is. But very few people have experienced it, know about it, and I think that can drive you mad; I know it can. I know it can.

You have to be lucky. You have to have friends. I think at bottom you have to be serious. No one can point it out to you; you have to see it yourself. That's the only way you can act on it. And when it arrives it's a great shock.

QUINCY TROUPE: To find out?

It's a great shock to realize that you've been so divorced. So divorced from who you think you are—from who you really are. Who you think you are, you're not at all. . . . I don't know who I thought I was. I was a witness, I thought. I was a very despairing witness though, too. What I was actually doing was trying to avoid a certain estrangement perhaps, an estrangement between myself and my generation. It was virtually complete, the estrangement was, in terms of what I might have thought and expected—my theories. About what I might have hoped— I'm talking now in terms of one's function as an artist. And the country itself, being black and trying to deal with that.

Why do you think it occurred. That estrangement between your generation and the country?

Well, because I was right. That's a strange way to put it. I *was* right. I was right about what was happening in the country. What was about to happen to all of us really, one way or the other. And the choices people would have to make. And watching people make them and denying them at the same time. I began to feel more and more homeless in terms of the whole relationship between France and me, and America and *me* has always been a little painful, you know. Because my family's in America I will always go back. It couldn't have been a question in my mind. But in the meantime you keep the door open and the price of keeping the door open was to actually be, in a sense, victimized by my own legend.

You know, I was trying to tell the truth and it takes a long time to realize that you can't—that there's no point in going to the mat, so to speak, no point in going to Texas again. There's no point in saying this again. It's been said, and it's been said, and it's been said. It's been heard and not heard. You are a broken motor.

A broken motor?

Yes. You're a running motor and you're repeating, you're repeating, you're repeating and it causes a breakdown, lessening of will power. And sooner or later your will gives out—it has to. You're lucky if it is a physical matter—most times it's spiritual. See, all this involves hiding from something else—not dealing with how lonely you are. And of course, at the very bottom it involves the terror of every artist confronted with what he or she has to do, you know, the next work. And everybody, in one way or another, and to some extent, tries to avoid it. And you avoid it more when you get older than you do when you're younger; still there's something terrifying about it, about doing the work.

O.K. Let's change the subject and talk about some writers. Amiri Baraka?

I remember the first time I met Amiri Baraka, who was then Leroi Jones. I was doing **The Amen Corner** and he was a student at Howard University. I liked him right away. He was a pop-eyed little boy poet. He showed me a couple of his poems. I liked them very much. And then he came to New York a couple of years later. He came to New York when I came back to New York from Paris. And by this time I knew the business. I'd been through the fucking business by that time. I was a survivor.

And I remember telling him that his agent wanted him to become the young James Baldwin. But I told him you're not the young James Baldwin. There's only one James Baldwin and you are Leroi Jones and there's only one Leroi Jones. Don't let them run this game on us, you know? You're Leroi Jones, I'm James Baldwin. And we're going to need each other. That's all I said. He didn't believe it then but time took care of that.

He believes it now?

Yes he knows it now.

What person has hurt you the most recently?

Ishmael Reed.

Why?

Because he is a great poet and it seemed to be beneath him. His anger and his contempt for me, which was both real, and not real. He ignored me for so long and then he called me a cock sucker, you know what I mean? It's boring. But I always did say he was a great poet, a great writer. But that does not mean I can put up with being insulted by him everytime I see him, which I won't.

What do you think about Toni Morrison?

Toni's my ally and it's really probably too complex to get into. She's a black woman writer, which in the public domain makes it more difficult to talk about.

What do you think are her gifts?

Her gift is in allegory. *Tar Baby* is an allegory. In fact all her novels are. But they're hard to talk about in public. That's where you get in trouble because her books and allegory are not always what they seem to be about. I was too occupied with my recent illness to deal with *Beloved*. But, in general, she's taken a myth, or she takes what seems to be a myth, and turns it into something else. I don't know how to put this—*Beloved* could be about the story of truth. She's taken a whole lot of things and turned them upside down. Some of them—you recognize the truth in it. I think that Toni's very painful to read.

Why?

Because it's always, or most times, a horrifying allegory; but you recognize that it works. But you don't really want to march through it. Sometimes people have a lot against Toni, but she's got the most believing story of everybody, this rather elegant matron, whose intentions really are serious, and according to some people, lethal. . .

We were talking once about the claustrophobia among writers. You said you prefer actors and painters to writers.

Yes. Well, first of all, when I was coming up there weren't any writers that I knew. Langston Hughes was far away. The first writer I met was Richard Wright and he was much older than me. And the people I knew were people like Beauford Delaney and the women who hung out with him; it was a whole world that was not literary. That came later; then it wasn't literary. It came later in Paris, with Sartre and others. But there was something else. And in Paris it had nothing whatsoever to do with race for one thing. It was another kind of freedom there altogether. It had nothing to do with literature. But when I looked back on it years and years later, looked back at myself on the American literary scene, I could see what almost happened to me was an attempt to make myself fit in, so to speak, to wash myself clean for the American literary academy.

You mean they wanted you scrubbed and squeaky clean?

Exactly. You have to be scrubbed and squeaky clean and then there's nothing left of you. Let me tell you a story.

When Ralph Ellison won the National Award in '52 for *Invisible Man*, I was up for it the next year, in 1953, for **Go Tell It on the Mountain.** But at the same time, I was far from scrubbed. I didn't win. Then, years later, someone who was on the jury told me that since Ralph won it the year before they couldn't give it to a Negro two years in a row. Now, isn't that something?. . .

Once, after I published **Go Tell It on the Mountain** and **Giovanni's Room,** my publisher, Knopf, told me I was "a Negro writer" and that I reached "a certain audience." "So," they told me, "you cannot afford to alienate that audience. This new book will ruin your career because you're not writing about the same things and in the same manner as you were before and we won't publish this book as a favor to you."

As a favor to you?

So I told them, "Fuck you." My editor, whose name I won't mention here, is dead now, poor man. I told them that I needed a boat ticket. So I took a boat to England with my book and I sold it in England before I sold it in America. You see, whites want black writers to mostly deliver something as if it were an official version of the black experience. But the vocabulary won't hold it, simply. No true account really of black life can be held, can be contained, in the American vocabulary. As it is, the only way that you can deal with it is by doing great violence to the assumptions on which the vocabulary is based. But they won't let you do that.

And when you go along, you find yourself very quickly painted into a corner; you've written yourself into a corner—because you can't compromise as a writer. By the time I left America in 1948 I had written myself into a corner as I perceived it. The book reviews and the short essays had led me to a place where I was on a collision course with the truth; it was the way I was operating. It was only a matter of time before I'd simply be destroyed by it. And no amount of manipulation of vocabulary or art would have spared me. It's like I think that Al Murray and Ralph Ellison are totally trapped. It's sad, because they're both trapped in the same way, and they're both very gifted writers.

But you can't do anything with America unless you are willing to dissect it. You certainly cannot hope to fit yourself into it; nothing fits into it, not your past, not your present. *The Invisible Man* is fine as far as it goes until you ask yourself who's invisible to whom? You know, what is this dichotomy supposed to do? Are we invisible before each other? And invisible why, and by what system can one hope to be invisible? I don't know how anything in American life is worthy of this sacrifice. And further, I don't see anything in American life—for myself—to aspire to. Nothing at all. It's all so very false, so shallow, so plastic, so morally and ethically corrupt.

> James Baldwin and Quincy Troupe, "Last Testament: An Interview with James Baldwin," in The Village Voice, *Vol. XXXIII, No. 2, January 12, 1988, p. 36.*

BOBBY COOLEY

[*In the following excerpt, Cooley, who is acting director of the African-American Center at Tufts University, responds to Stanley Crouch's negative comments on Baldwin (see excerpt above).*]

Stanley Crouch's article on James Baldwin [see excerpt above] was remarkable for the depth and breath of its truculence. While reading it, I kept thinking that it was the work of an angry man who was settling an old score. How else to explain the host of crimes of which Baldwin is accused: writings of "bile and cynicism"; a 'willingness to remove free will from the black lowerclass through what he called the 'doom' of color"; of helping to "foster a disposition that put the Negro movement into the hands of . . . trickle-down Marxist revolutionaries and cultural nationalists." This is simply amazing.

It is meaningless and dishonest to suggest that Baldwin's writings led to any such "disposition." After all, some of these same Marxists and cultural nationalists attacked Baldwin (sometimes rather savagely, as in the case of Eldridge Cleaver) for being too white and too willing to be "included in the social contract." Crouch does not mention this, and so descends, in his diatribe, into the very ahistoricism and disregard for fact for which he takes Baldwin to task.

Crouch's anger seems to be based on what he construes as Baldwin's anti-Americanism and his distaste for Baldwin's homosexuality. The article fairly drips with America-the-beautiful sentiment, and Crouch even trots out Leontyne Price and Jessye Norman as proof positive that American society is not racist. That these ladies have succeeded in their field in no way disproves the larger case that James Baldwin made against America. And it is very easy to sneer at Baldwin's homosex-

uality; after all, it proves pages of psychohistory: tormented homosexual as angry radical writer. This is all rather a lot of nonsense and goes little way toward helping us to usefully assess the life of James Baldwin the man, writer, the intellectual engagé. It merely expresses one man's dislikes and tribal instincts. The writer from Harlem deserves better.

> Bobby Cooley, in a letter to the editor, in The Village Voice, *Vol. XXXIII, No. 4, January 19, 1988, p. 4.*

DARRYL PINCKNEY

[*In the following excerpt, Pinckney recalls the impact of Baldwin's work on his own ideas about race and literature and reflects on the author's career.*]

Go Tell It on the Mountain, its pages heavy with sinners brought low and prayers groaning on the wind, scared me when I read it as a teen-ager. I was afraid that around any corner in the story of how Johnny Grimes, "frog eyes," came to be saved I ran the risk of exposure. It spoiled my wistful identification with *The Catcher in the Rye,* which all my friends were soaking up at the time. None of them had read *Go Tell It on the Mountain,* though, as did everyone else in the late 1960s, they knew what the name James Baldwin stood for. I was left alone with the book, as if it had been the little box at the bottom of the exam form that only I, as a black, was asked to pencil in. I thought I was better than Johnny, sweeping dust from a worn-out rug on his birthday, but I wasn't sure that the trap of Harlem, 1935, was as long ago and far away as I wanted to believe.

The name James Baldwin had been around the house for as long as I could remember, and meant almost as much as that of Martin Luther King. *The Fire Next Time,* my parents tell me, had an explosive effect unlike anything else since *Native Son* or *Invisible Man,* and in part led to a settling of accounts and an opening of new ones. Some old-timers thought he was too far out, others were jealous of this storefront preacher's Jamesian overlay—"slimy" was my grandfather's word—but Baldwin's prophetic voice was irresistible. It brought an intense moment of unity among Freedom Riders, professionals spawned by the GI Bill, the Blue Vein Circle that considered itself slandered by E. Franklin Frazier's exposé, *Black Bourgeoisie,* and the many who did not think Frazier had gone far enough. In retrospect, Baldwin's cry that blacks were of two minds about integration into a burning house seems hopeless since the power of a minority to threaten a majority with moral collapse depends on how much the majority cares. The climate of the times—perilous sit-ins and voter registration drives, murders and marches, songs of toil and deliverance—had everything to do with the sensation created by *The Fire Next Time.* Of course in those pre-Selma days no one believed that we'd ever have to walk alone.

Baldwin gave expression to the longings of blacks in exalted prose. He was embraced, in the tradition of Negro Firsterism, even by those who never sat down with a book, as *our* preeminent literary spokesman, whether he liked it or not. Neither athlete nor entertainer, but nevertheless a star. I do not know why it became fashionable among militants to dismiss him as absent without leave from the struggle, or as too moderate, conciliatory, a honky lover. He was, it seemed, always there, and he arrived on the stage in the apocalyptic mood. He filled my mind as the single enduring image of the black writer, an example to dwell upon beyond admiration or envy.

It helped that he had a genius for titles, for the phrase at once biblical and bluesy. I was drawn without hesitation to *Tell Me How Long the Train's Been Gone,* and at a time, I must admit, when I was ashamed to request a book from the library that had the word *Negro* or *Black* on the spine, as if there were something Baptist and loud about the connection between me and such a text. I didn't have to be embarrassed to say his name because James Baldwin was more than all right. One day I spotted **"An Open Letter to my Sister, Miss Angela Davis,"** in this paper. I read it over and over, as if it were a poem—"For, if they take you in the morning, they will be coming for us that night"—and was very moved to find joined the two living souls who, because I looked up to them, relieved my fear that I was an Uncle Tom.

For a long time I thought of my being black as an extracurricular activity. Baldwin's novels represented time off from the reading list: I took to them as romances, in the privacy of my room. *Another Country* was the steamiest book I'd ever sneaked off the shelf. There was something illicit in the vulnerability of his black male characters, given the smoky deviations by which his prodigals acted out their torment, and I vaguely expected to uncover in his interracial plots some clue to my own social inhibitions. When no black character appeared in the Paris of *Giovanni's Room,* I knew that he had broken the rules. (p. 8)

He had a way of sometimes signing off at the end of a work—"Istanbul, December 10, 1961"—and that, not the labor of composition, said, to me, that there was indeed a door somewhere to the outside. Wherefore wilt thou run, my son, seeing that thou hast no tidings?

James Baldwin was born into the black church and he came into the world with his subject matter. He was a boy evangelist, a dreamer in school—"I read books like they were some kind of weird food"—a malcontent in the defense plants of New Jersey, then, with the teeth marks still on his throat, an escapee to France, and from these unlikely beginnings he projected a career. "I wanted to prevent myself from becoming *merely* a Negro, or even, merely a Negro writer." He held fast to the steady view, to a premise profound in its simplicity: the conditions under which black Americans lived were unnatural. Out of the fundamental distortions of black life he spun the essays in *Notes of a Native Son,* a work triumphant in the clarity of its paradoxes.

Harlem was central to his journey. He described in celebrated essays and in the stories of *Going to Meet the Man* not a slum, but a ghetto, an unfathomable valley where wasted sharpies, toil-blasted women, idle old men, and sanctified girls stood corralled. "Only the Lord saw the midnight tears." He knew about street corners, teen-age pregnancy, and drug addiction, the urban equivalents of the chain gang. Baldwin's Harlem was a desolate landscape, completely severed from the cultural glories of its past. Though in *Nobody Knows My Name* he was haunted by the South as the source of his "inescapable identity," the Old Country remained opaque, erotic in his polemics, almost fable-like in his fiction, and fathers like Deacon Grimes revealed themselves as kinsmen to Bigger Thomas only when restored to the suffocation of the tenements. He wrote out of the black urban experience of his generation. Harlem was not a capital, not even a metaphor for claustrophobia. It was the real thing.

The journey out of Egypt was his great theme—that, and the search for identity, the necessary shedding of spiritual burdens along the road, the white world as the wilderness. The early

essays are an unequalled meditation on what it means to be black in America. Baldwin came of age as a writer during the cold war. He spent his youth, unlike Wright or Ellison, not in radical politics, but in religion. The pulpit was always present in his work, and this legacy guided a vivid literary imagination that made for his high style, for his arresting lyricism of despair. The refinement of gut feeling and the bravery of his ambivalence were entirely original. I do not think I am alone when I say that for young blacks Baldwin's candor about self-hatred was both shocking and liberating. A message slid under the cell door.

He conceived of race relations as a drama of confession and absolution. He asked questions of the future and dared to believe that to hate and fear white people, to despise black people and the black ghetto, gave to the butch and criminal elite an easy victory. If there were no acceptable version of himself as a black man he would have to invent one, and demystify whites in the process. "No one in the world—in the entire world—knows more—knows Americans better or, odd as this may sound, loves them more than the American Negro. This is because he has had to watch you, outwit you, deal with you, and bear you, and sometimes even bleed and die with you, ever since we got here, that is, since both of us, black and white, got here—and this is a wedding." People, he argued, do not wish to become worse, they want to become better, but don't know how. Eventually he was made to pay the price for his gamble that they, the motley millions, worried as much about us as we, the new day a-coming, did about them; for his insistence on loaded values like love in an age of dubious cool.

Baldwin once warned us that the second generation has no time to listen to the first, but we were caught up in the long, hot summer and then yonder came the blues in the form of the southern strategy or the Nixon campaign, the beginning of the end. The right made quick business of the revolution, as we liked to call it, because those doomed creatures, white liberals, already had been intimidated, purged, told where to go. On our side of the cameras, ideological patricide became the order of the day, and extra dustbins were conjured up to accommodate the gentlemen who failed the how-black-and-bad-are-you test. Someday someone will assess what damage, if any, was done to Baldwin—and to us—by the attacks on him as an apologist for the Jews.

The denunciation of Baldwin in Eldridge Cleaver's *Soul on Ice* precipitated a crisis of inspiration. Where are those Sentas of Black Power who ran around the school lockers with this manifesto of extreme violence and vulgarity? Cleaver equated intellectuality with homosexuality and declared them crimes against the people, worse than "baby-rape." Perhaps, given the bitterness and frustration of those days, the venality of benign neglect, Baldwin would have come to distrust the worth of the intellectual life, the uses of the reflective voice, but I can't help wondering if he didn't take Cleaver's indictment seriously because of the "merciless tribunal" he convened in his own head. The evasive response in *No Name in the Street,* the capitulation in his saying that Cleaver did what he felt he had to do, caused me to think of him as defenseless, adrift, lacking the blustering, self-protecting ego of the important American writer. In any case, today we know where the dude Cleaver is at. As for Baldwin, the baroque sense of grievance was replaced by sermon, and maybe I'm wrong but I think the change in tone came about because he was forced by his volatile constituents to keep up with events as they saw them. His need to be political, in the popular sense, undermined his literary gift.

"Some escaped the trap, most didn't. Those who got out always left something of themselves behind." He often said that he was a commuter, not an expatriate, and maybe the gestures of the engaged writer were part of a larger compulsion to get back home, to honor where he came from, to prove that he had not forgotten. The later novels, *If Beale Street Could Talk* and *Just Above My Head,* place emphasis on the black family as refuge, on reconciliation and belonging, but they are as immobile as urns, as if in them he hoped to lay down his burden of being different, the smart black youth who feared his father and wrote his way out of poverty into the bohemian life. "Nothing is ever escaped," he said early on. But he was not a home boy; he was an elevated extension of ourselves.

It is impossible to read his memoir of Richard Wright without suffering a chill. Baldwin was young and very aware of his own promise, a reminder that before St. Paul de Vence he had his share of crummy rooms. Wright, in exile, sat alone, isolated from other blacks, mocked. "I could not help feeling: *Be careful. Time is passing for you, too, and this may be happening to you one day.*" Then Wright was gone and Baldwin noted the will in the lesson: "Well, he worked up until the end, died, as I hope to do, in the middle of a sentence, and his work is now an irreducible part of the history of our swift and terrible time." I thought of this passage after I read *The Evidence of Things Not Seen,* his report on the Wayne Williams trial in Atlanta, which made it a hard book to face in the first place.

The flow of startling insights and connections had dried up. "The auction block is the platform on which I entered the Civilized World. Nothing that has happened since, from South Africa to El Salvador, indicates that the Western world has any real quarrel with slavery." It was a performance *sopra le righe.*

One heard exhaustion when he, still a striking apparition, murmured rhymes at audiences during his last appearances around town, and everyone remembered that back in the kingdom of the first person his work had the grace and melancholy of obselete beauty, like a Palladian dance hall uptown improbably at rest between empty lots.

> There's not a breathing of the common wind
> That will forget thee.

Among writers, black or white, he had few peers, among those who bore witness none. He was buried from St. John the Divine as a hero of the folk. The drums sounded and one missed him immediately. Against great odds he lived out the life of a brilliant innocent, and went the luckless distance for us all. The first time I met him I had with me a book that was meant to serve the sad function of showing Manhattan how interesting I thought I was. It was a volume from Leslie Marchand's edition of Byron's journals that Mr. Baldwin found himself asked to sign, and sometimes I think his smile as he wrote across the title page said: number got. (pp. 8, 10)

Darryl Pinckney, "On James Baldwin (1924-1987)," in The New York Review of Books, *Vol. XXXXIV, nos. 21 & 22, January 21, 1988, pp. 8, 10.*

Erskine (Preston) Caldwell
December 17, 1903 - April 11, 1987

American novelist, short story writer, nonfiction writer, journalist, juvenile fiction writer, autobiographer, and scriptwriter.

(See also *CLC*, Vols. 1, 8, 14; *Contemporary Authors*, Vols. 1-4, rev. ed., Vol. 121 [obituary]; *Contemporary Authors New Revision Series*, Vol. 2; *Contemporary Authors Autobiography Series*, Vol. 1; and *Dictionary of Literary Biography*, Vol. 9.)

PRINCIPAL WORKS

The Bastard (novel) 1930
Poor Fool (novel) 1930
American Earth (short stories) 1931; also published as *A Swell-Looking Girl*, 1951
Tobacco Road (novel) 1932
God's Little Acre (novel) 1933
We Are the Living (short stories) 1933
Journeyman (novel) 1935
Kneel to the Rising Sun and Other Stories (short stories) 1935
You Have Seen Their Faces (nonfiction) 1937
Jackpot: The Short Stories of Erskine Caldwell (short stories) 1940; also published as *Midsummer Passion* [abridged edition], 1948
Georgia Boy (short stories) 1943
Tragic Ground (novel) 1944
Call It Experience: The Years of Learning How to Write (autobiography) 1951
The Humorous Side of Erskine Caldwell (short stories) 1951; also published as *Where the Girls Are Different and Other Stories*, 1962
A Lamp for Nightfall (novel) 1952
Complete Stories (short stories) 1953
Molly Cottontail (juvenile fiction) 1959
Men and Women (short stories) 1961
In Search of Bisco (nonfiction) 1965
The Deer at Our House (juvenile fiction) 1966
Afternoons Mid-America: Observations and Impressions (nonfiction) 1976
Stories of Life, North and South: Selections from the Best Short Stories of Erskine Caldwell (short stories) 1983
With All My Might (autobiography) 1987

JACK JONES

Erskine Caldwell, the writer who shocked readers and outraged many of his fellow Southerners with unvarnished novels and short stories about squalid life in the cotton country backwoods,

Courtesy of Virginia M. Caldwell

died [April 11] in Paradise Valley, Ariz., after years of battling lung cancer. He was 83.

The author of *Tobacco Road* and *God's Little Acre* as well as nearly 50 volumes of short stories, Caldwell underwent treatment for lung cancer in September, 1986, at Scottsdale Memorial Hospital in Arizona. He had been operated on twice 11 years earlier.

His fourth wife, Virginia, with whom he had been living in Scottsdale for the latter part of his life, said he died shortly before 8 p.m.

Caldwell was one of the most successful writers in history. His books have sold more than 80 million copies worldwide and have been translated into more than 40 languages. *God's Little Acre,* banned in Boston and reviled by many after it was published in 1933, was at one time the champion best-seller with more than 10 million copies. Last year it was still 10th on the all-time fiction list.

Tobacco Road, his 1932 novel, was turned into a stage play and ran for nearly eight years on Broadway, a record at the time.

Caldwell, a Presbyterian minister's son who as a boy saw poverty govern the lives of both blacks and whites throughout rural Georgia and other parts of the South, never seemed perturbed by the criticism he received for putting the seamy images in print.

"I must have had an impact for good rather than bad," he said in 1985, when he returned to Georgia for a state-sponsored writers' program. "And I'm glad I did what I did. . . . There's been a great deal of change in rural Georgia . . . the rural South. If one of my short stories opened someone's eyes, then I have been successful."

In his autobiography, *With All My Might,* released in March by Peachtree Publishers, Caldwell clearly sensed that his career was over. "From the first bright rays of dawn to the shade of evening," he wrote, "the day is done."

He said in that book: "My goal from the beginning has been to be a writer of fiction that revealed with all my might the inner spirit of men and women as they responded to the joys of life and reacted to the sorrows of existence."

He said he had resisted "glorifying the sensational and knowingly falsifying the anguish or the jubilation" of his characters because "the human spirit should not be ravished and outraged in print by ghouls at large."

Although reviled in his early years by many critics, Caldwell once told the *Saturday Review,* "If you are going to take criticism very seriously, then you will stop writing anything."

He recalled for that interviewer that it was his father, the Rev. Ira S. Caldwell, who took him from place to place in the South during his boyhood and showed him the misery of dirt-poor people.

Caldwell was born *Dec. 17, 1903,* in Moreland, Ga., and moved with his parents from one place to another in the Carolinas, Virginia, Florida, Tennessee and back to Georgia. During his high school years in Wrens, Ga., he got a night job shoveling cottonseed into a conveyor belt at the local mill, but his parents made him quit when he fell asleep at the breakfast table.

He then took a summer job turning the hand press at the *Jefferson (County) Reporter* and was soon allowed to set type by hand as well as write short items about local doings. Before long he was also folding the papers and delivering them.

When after seven weeks he asked for a salary of some sort, Caldwell wrote in his 1951 book, *Call It Experience,* the editor said, "You didn't expect me to pay you money for learning the business, did you?"

He quit after being "given to understand that I was not proving to be a loyal worker." But he had discovered that daily newspapers around the state used local stringers to supply news of the small communities, so he began to mail items to papers in Atlanta, Macon and Augusta.

Caldwell also knocked about picking cotton, working as a chauffeur and doing numerous other jobs in order to go to college. He spent a year at a small Presbyterian college in Due West, S.C., but stayed only a year before leaving to work at other jobs and then to enter the University of Virginia, where he worked nights in a pool hall to support himself.

He had begun trying to write, and in 1925—two years short of graduation—quit the university to take a job as a cub reporter on the *Atlanta Journal.* Before long he was on the move again,

settling in Maine with his first wife, Helen Lannigan, to write short stories.

Success came slowly—first with an occasional story published in one of the small magazines that paid little or nothing. Then he sold a novelette, *The Bastard.* Maxwell Perkins, the famed Charles Scribner's Sons editor, spotted his stories and published a collection of them under the title *American Earth.*

With the little money he made from that, Caldwell took off by himself around the country with his portable typewriter and his cigarette-rolling machine, living in a cheap Hollywood hotel room for a while, returning to Wrens, Ga., and finally going to New York, where he turned out *Tobacco Road.*

His fame and his financial security were assured. The royalties from the stage play alone were enough to keep him comfortable for many years. Then came *God's Little Acre,* the runaway best-seller. Its profanity and sexually explicit passages brought not only a ban in Massachusetts but a recommendation by the Georgia Literary Commission that anyone caught reading it should be sent to jail.

A New York magistrate ruled, however, that the novel was literature.

In 1933, Caldwell won the *Yale Review* fiction award.

Three years later, he published *Journeyman,* a novel about a traveling preacher who arrives at a remote Georgia community to drink, seduce the women and arouse the town to a revival meeting orgy. That also was turned into a play—though not successfully—and was also denounced by reviewers as filthy, lewd and immoral.

Caldwell worked for a time as a screenwriter for Metro-Goldwyn-Mayer; his two big assignments were to write short features in a series called "Crime Does Not Pay" and to co-author a logging camp script for Clark Gable. It was never produced.

In 1936, he did a book about the Deep South with Margaret Bourke-White, the *Life* magazine photographer whom he married in 1939 after divorcing his first wife. The success of that effort, *Have You Seen Their Faces* prompted Caldwell and Bourke-White to do a similar book in Europe, *North of the Danube.*

During World War II, he was a correspondent for *Life,* the newspaper *PM* and for CBS in China, Mongolia and the Soviet Union.

He was divorced from Bourke-White and married June Johnson in 1942. He married Virginia Moffett Fletcher in 1957.

Caldwell had three children—Erskine Preston, Dabney Withers and Janet—by his first wife and one—Jay Erskine—by his third.

Until he finally settled in Scottsdale, he was always on the move, living in San Francisco, Tucson, Florida and elsewhere.

He quit smoking in 1972 at the urging of a Mayo Clinic physician and three years later underwent surgery for lung cancer. A few months later, cancer was found in the other lung, and he was operated on again.

He considered recent fiction nothing but "polyester," with authors trying to outdo each other for sheer sensationalism. As for his own *God's Little Acre,* he said: "I did not consider it obscene in that day, so I would not consider it obscene at any time. I am a very conservative writer."

Jack Jones, "Erskine Caldwell, Author of 'God's Little Acre,' 'Tobacco Road,' Dies," in Los Angeles Times, *April 13, 1987, p. 17.*

EDWIN McDOWELL

Mr. Caldwell wrote more than 50 books, including **Tobacco Road** (1932) and **God's Little Acre** (1933), which were two of the biggest sellers of all time but made Mr. Caldwell one of the most controversial writers in the United States.

William Faulkner named Mr. Caldwell one of the five best contemporary American writers, along with himself, Thomas Wolfe, Ernest Hemingway and John Dos Passos.

Mr. Caldwell received generally warm reviews for such novels as **Journeyman** (1933), **Trouble in July** (1940) and **Tragic Ground** (1944), each of which was part of a 10-novel "Southern cyclorama" that included **Tobacco Road** and **God's Little Acre.** Many critics also hailed **Georgia Boy** (1944) and **In Search of Bisco** (1965), the latter an evocative account of the author's unsuccessful search for a boyhood friend.

Yet in recent years, while Mr. Caldwell remained popular in foreign countries, he lapsed into relative obscurity in the United States. It had been years since he wrote a big seller, and for the last 20 years or so he generally shunned interviews and public appearances. Moreover, his spare, direct prose style, which so captivated critics in the 1930's and 40's, eventually fell out of fashion and favor.

Mr. Caldwell enjoyed a brief revival in 1982, the 50th anniversary of the publication of **Tobacco Road.** New American Library marked the occasion by reissuing new paperback editions of **Tobacco Road** and **God's Little Acre,** which together had sold 17 million copies.

The initial success of both those novels owed much to their shock value. Mr. Caldwell's direct style was never more evident than in the unadorned descriptions of Jeeter, Ellie May, Ty Ty, Darling Jill and a galaxy of other poor Southern whites publicly parading their fiery passions, erotic appetites, petty jealousies and frequent fits of anger. Their language would cause little stir today, but 50 years ago it was considered so obscene that the books were banned in a number of cities and removed from the shelves of many libraries.

Mr. Caldwell took the controversy over his "dirty" books in stride, yet he never resigned himself to attempts to force him into a literary or political mold. Because many of his books dealt with the Deep South, some critics tried to link him with the so-called "Southern tradition," despite his insistence that he belonged to no literary school and that many of his books were about other areas of the country and other parts of the world.

Because his early books called attention to the plight of the sharecroppers, he was hailed as America's premier proletarian novelist. That distinction won him a large following in the Soviet Union, where for years he was one of the most popular American authors, but during the cold war it also won him the enmity of some American conservatives, who denounced him as a tool of Moscow.

Through it all, Mr. Caldwell insisted that his purpose had never been to change the world but only to report on it.

"I was not trying to prove anything," he said in 1982. "I was writing about the people I knew, I lived in the same neighborhood as the Tobacco Road fraternity and I went to school in the area. I knew very little about life outside the South. I was only trying to tell a story."

That attitude typified Mr. Caldwell's views generally. Asked in an interview in *The Georgia Review* in 1982 whether he had become involved in the civil-rights movement of the 1960's and 70's, Mr. Caldwell replied that he had not.

"Naturally, I approved of the attempt to desegregate the South because my sympathy has long been that segregation is wrong and should be terminated," he said. "So I watched with interest what went on. But I'm a writer, not a crusader. I leave the crusading to others."

Mr. Caldwell was born Dec. 17, 1903, on what he described as "an isolated farm deep in the piney-woods country on the red clay hills of Coweta County, in middle Georgia." He traveled the region's many tobacco roads with his clergyman father, during which he observed the habits and speech patterns that he would later incorporate into his writing.

He briefly attended the University of Pennsylvania and the University of Virginia, but he left to become a reporter on *The Atlanta Journal,* at a salary of $25 a week.

In 1925 he married Helen Lannigan, with whom he later had three children and from whom he was later divorced, and the following year he settled on a farm in Maine where for the next seven years he tried to succeed as full-time writer.

"I was sort of a caretaker, so I didn't have to pay rent," he recalled. "I raised potatoes so I always had something to eat and I cut wood to keep warm. I had the good fortune to persuade a woman on *The Charlotte Observer* to let me review books. It didn't pay anything, but when I finished the reviews I'd sell the books for 25 cents to secondhand bookstores."

In an autobiography, **Call It Experience** (1951), Mr. Caldwell recounted how he sent one story a day for a week to Maxwell Perkins, the Scribner's book editor who doubled as editor of *Scribner's Magazine.* Mr. Perkins rejected them all, so Mr. Caldwell sent him two stories a week until the editor finally accepted two of them to run in the same issue of the magazine.

When Mr. Perkins said he would pay "two-fifty" for both of them, Mr. Caldwell replied: "Two-fifty? I don't know. I thought maybe I'd receive a little more than that." So Mr. Perkins upped the payment to three-fifty. "I guess that'll be all right," Mr. Caldwell replied. "I'd thought I'd get a little more than three dollars and a half, though, for both of them."

A mystified Mr. Perkins replied: "Three dollars and fifty cents? Oh, no! I must have given you the wrong impression, Caldwell. Not three dollars and a half. No. I meant $350."

By then Mr. Caldwell had already written the novels **The Bastard** (1929) and **Poor Fool** (1930) as well as **American Earth** (1930), a collection of stories.

Soon afterward he sold **Tobacco Road** to Mr. Perkins, and he never again had to worry about succeeding as a full-time writer. Jack Kirkland's stage adaptation of the novel ran for seven and a half consecutive years on Broadway, beginning in 1933, bringing the author $2,000 a week in royalties. Hollywood also bought the book, but Mr. Caldwell described Darryl Zanuck's 1941 movie version as "one of the most conspicuous failures in cinematic history" because of its falsified happy ending.

Mr. Caldwell wrote two dozen novels, 10 short-story collections, an autobiography, a dozen works of nonfiction, plus four books with the photographer Margaret Bourke-White. They married in 1939, two years after collaborating on *You Have Seen Their Faces,* a text-picture book about the South, and subsequently collaborated on books about prewar Czechoslovakia and wartime Russia.

Mr. Caldwell reported from the Soviet Union in 1941 for *Life* magazine, CBS radio and the newspaper PM. He wrote Hollywood scripts for about five years, and he also wrote articles from Mexico and Czechoslovakia for the North American Newspaper Alliance.

In 1942, after a divorce, Mr. Caldwell married June Johnson, with whom he had a son, Jay. In 1957, after they divorced, he married Virginia Fletcher, who drew the illustrations for several of his more recent books. They lived for many years in San Francisco, until moving to Scottsdale, Ariz., in 1977.

In 1984, he was elected to the American Academy of Arts and Letters. In 1985, as part of a program organized by the Georgia Endowment for the Humanities, Mr. Caldwell was invited back to Georgia, which he fled in the 1920's, and there were teas and lectures and even a Sunday picnic in his honor.

Mr. Caldwell said that even then, so many years after the publication of the two novels that brought him fame, there was a woman at the county library who wanted nothing to do with him. "She wouldn't talk to me—she avoided me whenever I came by," Mr. Caldwell said during his visit. "Whenever I walked through the library, I could feel her cold stare."

"There's been great economic and social change in Georgia, as elsewhere in the South," Mr. Caldwell said in an interview in *The New York Times* in 1982. "With all the Federal and state money, there is not the dire poverty that I saw. The remnants of Tobacco Road are still there, back in the ravines and hollows of the mountains, but the sharecropper existence has disappeared and people can apply for food stamps."

As to whether his books had helped accelerate that change, Mr. Caldwell replied: "It's been said that they allowed people to see with their own eyes what they couldn't see from calculated ignorance or blindness. But remember, I didn't try to change or reform the world, I only wanted to report on it." (pp. A1, D13)

> Edwin McDowell, "Erskine Caldwell, 83, Is Dead: Wrote Stark Novels of South," *in* The New York Times, *April 13, 1987, pp. A1, D13.*

DAVE WAGNER

Erskine Caldwell who died in Paradise Valley [April 11], may have been treated unkindly by literary critics, but his fellow writers, including some of the country's best, single him out as one of the most influential writers of 20th-century America.

James Dickey, a native of Georgia, which Caldwell depicted with such withering effect in a dozen or more novels, told *The Gazette* [April 12]: "I defer to no man in my admiration for the best of him. He had the true folk touch.

"I think the best of Erskine Caldwell is wonderfully good. His work is out of the folk tradition, the teller of tales. His short stories are among the best anywhere."

In fact, Dickey once said Caldwell "wrote the best story in the language, **'Crownfire.'**"

Caldwell, 83, died of lung cancer. He had requested cremation and no public ceremony.

Dickey, a leading poet of the generation that followed Caldwell's, shares his opinion with many of his most famous contemporaries.

Saul Bellow, Norman Mailer, Ralph Ellison, William Styron, John Updike and Kurt Vonnegut among others, wrote to express their views on Caldwell's work. The letters were collected into two large volumes that his wife of 30 years, Virginia Moffett Fletcher, presented to Caldwell on his 80th birthday, Dec. 17, 1983. The letters have never been published.

Bellow wrote to Mrs. Caldwell, "I thought your husband should have had the Nobel Prize. A great many readers would have rejoiced at such an award. I became a Caldwell fan in college with *God's Little Acre* and have remained a loyal rooter to this day."

Bellow was awarded the Nobel Prize for Literature in 1976.

Ronald Reagan, fellow Georgian Jimmy Carter and a host of newspaper writers also wrote to Caldwell on his 80th birthday. But it was his fellow novelists who appeared eager to make the point that Caldwell's work was undervalued by critics, if perhaps not by readers. (Caldwell's were among the best-selling novels in U.S. literary history).

Many of the novelists also discussed his influence on them or their work.

William Styron, who won the Pulitzer Prize for fiction in 1965: "Ever since I first read your work in the 1940s your words and spirit have been in my bloodstream as a writer. You are a great creative presence whose wise, funny, sad, revealing books have been an inspiration to the writers who followed you."

Norman Mailer: Caldwell was "one of my first literary heroes, and always one of the best."

John Updike: "I first read you when I was fifteen or so . . . and I haven't been the same since. You popped my eyes open, and have lent courage to all of us who would like to describe life in America as it is."

Kurt Vonnegut: "It seems to me that your predecessors were almost all too polite to write about ordinary Americans as they really look and sound and suffer and celebrate and hanker and calculate . . . In the 1930's, you and a handful of contemporaries pulled off a revolution in American literature as liberating and radical as what the cubists did for painters at the turn of the century."

Fellow Southerner William Faulkner once remarked that Caldwell was among the best five writers in the world who were then working.

Ralph Ellison, author of *Invisible Man* and probably the most influential black novelist of the generation that followed World War II, wrote at length to thank Caldwell for the instruction he had received while attending the stage production of *Tobacco Road* just a few weeks after he had arrived in New York:

> Beyond the borders of Harlem I tended to view New Yorkers through the overlay of my Alabama experience, contrasting the whites I encountered with those I'd observed down South; weighing class against class and southern regional styles against their opposites. Then suddenly, there in a darkened theater, I was snatched back to rural Alabama, and when Jeeter

Lester and the horsing-around couple went into their act I was reduced to such helpless laughter that I distracted the entire balcony and embarrassed both my host (Langston Hughes) and myself.

It was a terrible moment, for before I could get myself under control more attention was being directed at me than at the Lester family. I apologize, but there was nothing I could do . . .

I had seen Jester's type in Macon County but there their capacity for racial violence would have been far more overwhelming than their comical wrong-headedness. Indeed, they kept crowding me and I had been tempted to armor myself against their threat by denying them their humanity as they sought to deny me mine.

Tobacco Road, Ellison concluded, saved him from the temptation and helped him become a writer with a vision broad enough to include all of humanity.

Although the novelists and the critics may appear split on the issue of Caldwell's literary importance, there is no unanimity on either side.

Dickey said Caldwell's work lost some of its force after the initial successes, which were huge by any standards. His 55 novels were published in 43 languages in 80 million copies and the stage production of *Tobacco Road* went through more than 1600 performances.

The problem, Dickey said, was the context of sexual curiosity that surrounded much of the early work. Passages that would not lift the most sensitive eyebrow today were eagerly sought out by "the kind of people who today would be reading comic books."

As a result, Dickey said, "He made an awful lot of money. And he wrote an awful lot of other novels that did the same thing." It was then that the critics turned against him.

Not all of the critics lined up against Caldwell, however. Malcolm Cowley has eloquently championed the novelist for years. "Sometimes he wrote as if he were one of the hungry farmers; as if he had dropped the plow lines that very morning, stabled the mule, and rushed to the typewriter," Cowley wrote in 1979.

Cowley cited two sentences to illustrate Caldwell's gift:

A man walked into a restaurant through the front door and ate all he wanted to eat.

Once the sun was so hot a bird came down and walked beside me in my shadows.

That is writing, Cowley said, "Of utter simplicity and rightness."

At least one contemporary scholar takes Caldwell's stature in stride, at least on the question of the major work. Dr. Marvin Fisher, a professor of English at Arizona State University, stated simply of Caldwell, "He is one of the living legends from the 1930s. In his best work he raised regional themes to national significance.

"In any anthology of the 1930s that includes the work of Faulkner, Hemingway and Fitzgerald, Caldwell will have his place."

A heavy smoker from 1918 to 1972 who twice underwent surgery to remove portions of his lungs, Caldwell said he was glad to serve as a warning to smokers. However, he said, "I don't care anything about fame or recognition."

Caldwell worked as a seaman, cotton-picker, semi-professional football player, bodyguard and real estate salesman before settling down to write. He produced some 53 books and 150 short stories.

Caldwell's first three marriages ended in divorce. His second marriage, to famed photographer Margaret Bourke-White, led to their collaborating on *You Have Seen Their Faces,* a text-and-picture book on the sharecroppers' plight.

Dave Wagner, *"Fellow Literary Greats Remember Erskine Caldwell,"* in Phoenix Gazette, April 13, 1987.

KYLE LAWSON

Erskine Caldwell, who died [April 11] at his Paradise Valley home, will be remembered forever as the novelist who wrote *Tobacco Road* and *God's Little Acre,* steamy tales of life in the Deep South that scandalized America in the 1940s and '50s.

That in spite of a writing career that spanned almost 60 years and produced more than 50 works, such as *Lamp for Nightfall,* *Georgia Boy* (his personal favorite) and *Round About America,* as well as children's books like *Molly Cottontail* and *The Deer at Our House.*

None of these, though many were praised at the time, achieved the notoriety of his two masterpieces.

Sometimes that confused the writer.

"I never thought those two books were all that sexy," Caldwell said some years ago, during an interview in his Paradise Valley home.

"I just wrote about the things people do naturally. Is it sexy to report that cows mate or that humans fall in love and have children?

"I never could consider those works pornographic. But then, I'm a stubborn fellow. I write to please myself. Once I'm satisfied, no one can make me change my mind."

Bluenoses of the day thought him very pornographic indeed. In 1941, hundreds of theater owners refused to show the film version of *Tobacco Road*—even though it was produced personally by Darryl Zanuck and directed by John Ford, the team that had won Oscars the previous year for John Steinbeck's *The Grapes of Wrath.*

(That may have been just as well with Caldwell, who later said, "I didn't think much of that film. Zanuck was afraid of censorship . . . he got panicky, so he changed the ending. He had all the people walking down the road together, singing on the way to the poorhouse. You can imagine how I felt about that.")

Zanuck had some justification for panic. Even Caldwell himself lost count of the number of obscenity trials in which *Tobacco Road* figured. And he was back in court nearly a decade later with *God's Little Acre.*

In 1957, Boston banned that book. A year later, Phoenix censors tried, but failed, to do the same thing.

The unkindest cut of all came when the Georgia Literature Commission declared *God's Little Acre* obscene and removed it from bookshelves in Caldwell's native state. The mayor of Augusta, Ga., put the kibosh on plans to film the novel in his community, saying, "This book is the most libelous depiction of Georgia I have read. It is smut."

Caldwell refused to take offense, "I reflect life as I see it," he said, "and if the mayor of Augusta chooses to lower the Peanut Curtain on the truth, that is his privilege, even as it is my privilege to write it."

Caldwell came by his knowledge of Southern life firsthand. The son of a Presbyterian preacher, he traveled the "circuit" with his father to many of the small towns surrounding Moreland, the Cowetta County community in which he was born in 1903.

He also drove the area doctor on his rounds.

"The doctor tended to the needs of a great many black people, as well as whites of the sort some people call 'rednecks' or 'poor white trash,'" Caldwell said.

"Some of them were real characters. I never forgot them. When you read *Tobacco Road* and the other books, they're the ones you meet."

Caldwell always wanted to be a writer, although the novels came later in his career. He began as a sportswriter for the newspaper in Wren, Ga. That probably was inevitable for a young man who had played pro football for a short time and who remained an avid gridiron fan for life. (Other "pre-writing" jobs included woodcutting, farming, selling and cab driving—"You could say I have more firsthand knowledge of poverty than of scandalous doings," the four times married Caldwell once joked.)

The newspaper "was valuable training, not just because they printed my stories," he said. "It was one of those papers where there never was enough help. I did a little bit of everything, including inking the press. Newspaper work is the best training you can get. From my two years as a reporter, I learned more than in all the years of school and university."

As to why he became a writer, he said: "I didn't like to read. I remember assignments in school books and poetry. I'd do anything to get out of them. I liked short stories . . . but I was not impressed by anyone's fiction. I was not happy with what was being written. That's why I wanted to do it myself—and do it better."

During World War II, he was the Moscow correspondent for *Life* and CBS—and covered later crises in Mexico, Spain, Czechoslovakia and Mongolia.

Among his more unusual assignments was a stint at MGM, working on a screenplay for Clark Gable. Caldwell, true to form, cut the screen idol down to size, putting him on Skid Row. MGM was horrified. Caldwell was fired.

Even as he entered his 80s, Caldwell never stopped having "some project on the front burner, and a half dozen on the back."

"Writing comes pretty easy to me" he told a reporter in 1970. "I don't think much about it. I just sit down and write. I'm not a philosopher, just a storyteller."

And he had no plans for retirement.

"A writer doesn't retire," he said. "He just drops dead."

Nevertheless, in an interview with The Associated Press in 1973, the 70-year-old Caldwell said:

When you're young, you think everything you do is great. But as time goes on, you gain experience. You see your mistakes. Writing is becoming more difficult these days. I find myself taking longer, revising more. You learn the world is going to be harsh on your work. You become your own critic.

In spite of the controversy engendered by his books, they enjoyed great popularity. More than 100 million copies were sold in 43 languages. At one time, only the Bible surpassed *Tobacco Road* and *God's Little Acre* as best sellers.

Caldwell, who lived in Phoenix and Tuscon in the 1950s and was a frequent visitor to Arizona in the years before and after, settled permanently in Paradise Valley seven years ago. He lived a quiet life except for the occasional celebratory event.

But, as ever, his home state remained unimpressed. When the 82-year-old writer returned in 1985 to spend two weeks as writer-in-residence at Fitzgerald-Ben Hill County Library, 160 miles south of Atlanta, his reception was less than tumultous.

"I guess some things will never be forgotten—or forgiven," he told UPS's Joe Parham. "I think that's human nature and I don't think it's anything personal."

But Georgia was behind the times, for it was during the 1980s that the arts community began to polish Caldwell's image.

In 1982, Arizona officials declared November as Erskine Caldwell Month and sponsored a week-long celebration of his work, including a stage production of *Tobacco Road* at Phoenix Little Theatre.

In 1983, France and Poland honored Caldwell, making him a Commander of the Order of Arts and Letters and presenting him with the Order of Cultural Merit, respectively.

In 1984, his own country got around to paying tribute: Caldwell was elected to the American Academy of Arts and Letters.

His reaction was typically Caldwell: "Some people might say it's a little late. I'm just glad they remembered."

> Kyle Lawson, "*Caldwell: Home Town Called Work 'Smut'*," in Phoenix Gazette, *April 15, 1987.*

NATIONAL REVIEW, NEW YORK

Literary reputation is a difficult compound to analyze. In the year 1940, for example, James T. Farrell, John Steinbeck, Thomas Wolfe, Ernest Hemingway, John Dos Passos, and Erskine Caldwell (but not William Faulkner) were thought to be American novelists of the first rank. Faulkner at one point ranked Caldwell among the five best contemporary novelists, along with Wolfe, Hemingway, Dos Passos, and himself. Wolfe's posthumous *You Can't Go Home Again* was reviewed on the front page of the *New York Times Book Review* in terms that would have been hyperbolic if applied to Tolstoi. However, of the writers mentioned above, Caldwell, Farrell, and Steinbeck have entirely disappeared, while Dos Passos and Wolfe are read only here and there. Faulkner and Hemingway have not only lasted but prevailed.

Yet *Tobacco Road* (1932) and *God's Little Acre* (1933) not only sold 17 million copies but received high critical acclaim. During the 1930s and early 1940s Caldwell was regarded as a publishing phenomenon; indeed, his 55 books sold a total of eighty million copies. But his reputation took a nosedive after World War II and never recovered. In 1985 he could not find a publisher for a collection of his stories.

Samuel Johnson held that it takes a hundred years for a work of literature to establish itself as permanent. Many minds, acting over a period of several generations, establish a consensus about it that is not a product of transitory fashion.

It seems likely that Caldwell's earlier celebrity was indeed a product of fashion. During the 1930s, everyone seems to have been eager to read about poor people—sharecroppers, Okies, slum dwellers, proletarians. They constituted a delicious indictment of capitalism; more than that, they were somehow more *real* than the bourgeois or the wealthy. Then taste changed. Caldwell characters, along with Steinbeck and Farrell characters, it had to be said, were pretty limited and dull. Poverty itself is not very interesting, however important.

Caldwell also served up a great deal of raw sex, scandalous and titillating at the time he wrote; but he was certainly been surpassed in that department since. Finally, as a prose writer he lacks the interest of Hemingway, Fitzgerald, and Faulkner, not to mention Henry James.

Sic transit.

"Erskine Caldwell, RIP," in National Review, *New York, Vol. XXXIX, No. 8, May 8, 1987, p. 21.*

Richard (David) Ellmann
March 15, 1918 - May 13, 1987

American critic, biographer, literary historian, editor, and educator.

(See also *Contemporary Authors,* Vols. 1-4, rev. ed., 122 [obituary] and *Contemporary Authors New Revision Series,* Vol. 2.)

PRINCIPAL WORKS

Yeats: The Man and the Masks (biography) 1948
The Identity of Yeats (criticism) 1954
James Joyce (biography) 1959, rev. ed. 1982
Eminent Domain: Yeats among Wilde, Joyce, Pound, Eliot, and Auden (literary history) 1967
Ulysses on the Liffey (criticism) 1972
Golden Codgers: Biographical Speculations (essays) 1973
The Consciousness of Joyce (criticism) 1977
Four Dubliners: Wilde, Yeats, Joyce, and Beckett (criticism) 1987
Oscar Wilde (biography) 1987

WALTER GOODMAN

Richard Ellmann, whose 1959 biography of James Joyce became the definitive work on the Irish novelist, died [May 13] in Oxford, England. He was 69 years old.

Mr. Ellmann, who was Goldsmiths' Professor emeritus of English Literature at Oxford University, was admitted to an Oxford infirmary [May 12], suffering from pneumonia. He was stricken in February 1986 with amyotrophic lateral sclerosis, commonly known as Lou Gehrig's disease, a degenerative disease of the nerve cells for which there is no known treatment.

Despite the debilitating ailment, which had severely affected his speech, he continued to work. During the last weeks of his life, with the help of small machines on which he typed out messages that were then printed on a screen or on paper, he made final revisions on his long-awaited biography of Oscar Wilde. It is scheduled to be published in the United States in January by Alfred A. Knopf.

Mr. Ellmann was born in Highland Park, Mich. He studied at Yale University and served in the O.S.S. in World War II. After the war, he did graduate work at Trinity College in Dublin, becoming engaged in what would be a lifelong love affair with Irish literary figures of the 19th and 20th centuries.

His first two books dealt with William Butler Yeats. He traced the origins of *James Joyce,* his 1959 biography that is considered the definitive work on the Irish novelist, to a 1947 meeting

© Jerry Bauer

in Dublin with Yeats's widow, who showed him an unpublished memoir by the poet in which he recalled his first meeting with the younger writer.

In a front-page review in *The New York Times Book Review,* Stephen Spender called *James Joyce* an "immensely detailed, massive, detached and objective, yet loving biography." The work, which won the National Book Award, stands as the authoritative study of the man whom Mr. Ellmann called "the first writer to show us in English what modern literature really is." Other critics were influenced by his assessment of Leopold Bloom, the central figure of Joyce's controversial masterpiece, *Ulysses.* Mr. Ellmann found nobility in this "nobody—an advertising canvasser who, apart from his family, has virtually no effect upon the life around him." He wrote: "The divine part of Bloom is simply his humanity—his assumption of a bond between himself and other created beings."

Mr. Ellmann's scholarly pursuit of Joyce did not end with the publication of the biography. In addition to serving as editor of Joyce's letters, he kept tracking down new sources and following up on new leads, and in 1982, in time for the Joyce centenary, a revised edition of *James Joyce* containing 100 pages of additional material was published to renewed acclaim. A former colleague calls Mr. Ellmann "a private detective of genius." The fascination with Joyce remained strong. "I have been moved and amused," he wrote "by fresh instances of Joyce's originality and bizarreness."

Visitors to the small old house in Oxford that the Ellmanns moved into in 1970, when he took up his post at New College, might be taken upstairs to the cluttered workroom, where, with evident pleasure and quiet pride, Mr. Ellmann would extract from one of the cardboard boxes on the floor a piece of Joyceana, a scribbled note, perhaps, or a library card from the writer's youth.

Mr. Ellmann had a notable sense of humor and a donnishly droll way with a punchline; he took a puckish delight in gossiping about the peccadillos of literary personages. His high forehead, heavy-rimmed eyeglasses and soft-spoken manner suited his own scholarly persona. His wit remained intact throughout his illness; with speech difficult, he typed out jokes and repartee with visitors.

In the course of a distinguished academic career, Mr. Ellmann taught at Harvard, Yale, Northwestern, Emory, the University of Chicago and Indiana University and lectured widely until his illness made public speaking impossible. Next fall, Emory will begin a lecture series named in his honor. He contributed frequently to such publications as *The New York Times, The New York Review of Books* and England's *Times Literary Supplement*.

In addition to his many critical essays on such writers as Samuel Beckett, T. S. Eliot, W. H. Auden and Ezra Pound, Mr. Ellmann edited *The New Oxford Book of American Verse* and was co-editor, with Robert O'Clair, of two anthologies of modern poetry. Mr. O'Clair, who worked closely with him on the anthologies for almost a decade, remains awed by "Dick's taste, his knowledge, his love of the word." In 1971, Mr. Ellmann was elected to the National Institute of Arts and Letters.

> Walter Goodman, *"Richard Ellmann Dies at 69; Eminent James Joyce Scholar,"* in The New York Times, *May 14, 1987, p. 26.*

ANTHONY BURGESS

[*Burgess, an English novelist and critic, is well known for his darkly humorous satires of contemporary society; the most famous of these is his novel* A Clockwork Orange *(1962). Burgess' experimentation with language is widely acclaimed, and his interest in linguistics is reflected in his critical studies of James Joyce, notably* Here Comes Everybody: An Introduction to James Joyce for the Ordinary Reader *(1965). His recent works include* Flame into Being: The Life and Work of D. H. Lawrence *(1985) and* Little Wilson and Big God: The Autobiography *(1987). Burgess, who admires Ellmann's work as a fellow Joyce scholar, first met him in Nashville, Tennessee in 1966. In the following excerpt, Burgess offers a personal tribute to Ellmann as a friend and colleague.*]

I first met Dick Ellmann in Nashville, Tennessee, in 1966, when he and I were participants in a literary festival. From then on we met frequently—usually at places where James Joyce was being celebrated. It is good to be able to tell a man to his face what his books have meant to one, and I could never tell him often enough of the importance of his *James Joyce* in my life—the most brilliant, witty, scholarly literary biography of the century.

We must be thankful that the crippling disease which killed him, with perhaps merciful speed, held off sufficiently to enable him to finish his *Oscar Wilde*: its appearance this autumn will be one of the great literary events of the year and the best posthumous celebration of a life devoted unremittingly to scholarship. He wrote nothing that was dull, inelegant, or lacking in profound humanity. The term 'humane letters' takes on its full meaning in his connection.

Dick was thoroughly American in his acceptance of what is known as the American lifestyle—I remember his dashing to his room at the Holiday Inn in Nashville to catch the latest instalment of some TV soap—but his genius was focused on Anglo-Irish literature: Yeats and Joyce in particular, though his knowledge of modern literature in general was profound and his assessment of writers from Proust to Virginia Woolf always highly original.

At Oxford he brought American commonsense and a European sensibility to his teaching, and, in his public lectures everywhere, a clarity of exposition and an unfailing humour when expounding his literary insights. He had the courage to shock, as when at Trieste in 1972 he pointed out the structural significance of Buck Mulligan's mock-eucharist at the beginning of *Ulysses* and the real menstrual blood of Molly Bloom at the end. He was always full of surprises.

Where narrower, and bloodless, experts were content to see *Ulysses* as a kind of codex of arid ingenuity, Dick pointed out that its theme was love. He never tired of stressing the importance of the family constellation in Joyce's work. He was himself a family man of intense loyalty, a quality which enabled him to see the fundamental humanity of Joyce.

There is no man who will be more greatly missed. It gives me a small consolation to know that I received one of his last letters, kind and witty as always, saying that he had gained some pleasure from my most recent book. There remain his own books, which will never cease to enlighten and confirm a joy in being a literary man, however imperfect. Yeats's epitaph—'Cast a cold eye / On life, on death'—will not do for him.

> Anthony Burgess, *"Richard Ellmann: A Great Joycean,"* in The Observer, *May 17, 1987, p. 23.*

SAMUEL HYNES

[*Hynes, an American critic, educator, and editor, is the author of such critical works as* The Pattern of Hardy's Poetry *(1961),* The Edwardian Turn of Mind *(1968), and* The Auden Generation: Literature and Politics in England in the 1930s *(1976). In the following excerpt from a review of* Four Dubliners, *Hynes commends Ellmann's outstanding scholarship and literary skills.*]

Richard Ellmann died as this review was being written. It is sad to think that that career is at an end; but what a career it was. More than any other scholar of this century, Ellmann taught us all how to think about Irish writers and their difficult island; he wrote better books on Yeats than any Irishman has ever done, and his [*James Joyce*] is the finest literary biography of this century, and likely to remain so—unless the biography of Oscar Wilde that he finished in his last days is even better. A career of memorable, permanent accomplishment.

Four Dubliners is in a sense a resume of those forty years spent brooding over Irishmen. The four are Wilde, Yeats, Joyce, and Beckett, and to each writer Ellmann addresses an essay.

They are essays of celebration and affection, first of all; Ellmann was fortunate in spending his critical life among writers whom he could like (think of all the sad scholars who have condemned themselves to the company of creeps and bores). But each is also a model of biographical criticism, moving from details of the lives to the work, not to impose explanations, but to reveal the questions and the problems that link them, and so to define the nature of the artist's mind. Ellmann is dealing here not with certainties but with uncertainties, and it is a testimony to his powers of re-creation that his four Dubliners emerge from his pages as complex, contradictory, quirky men, with all their kinks and edges sharp.

Each essay turns on a biographical crux, some point in the life that lights up the work. The occasion in Wilde's life comes early: he is a student at Oxford, feeling a conflict in himself between his spiritual aspirations and the temptations of the sensual world, and choosing *both,* and so committing himself both in his life and in his art to duplicity and concealment. The occasion that Ellmann takes to illuminate Yeats is a late one: his decision, in his sixty-ninth year, to undergo a Steinach operation in order to improve his lagging sexual potency. The operation seems to have done his sex life no good at all, but it nevertheless gave Yeats a potency of another kind, enabling him to write the wild old wicked poems of his last years.

The Joyce instance is really two: two incidents in 1917-18, when Joyce, writing at the time the Nausicaä episode of *Ulysses,* romanced two young ladies, in his peculiar Joycean way, in search not of sexual favors but of literary materials. Beckett's moment is the one at the end of the second war, when he returned to Ireland to visit his mother, and there, at the end of a Dun Laoghaire jetty in a howling wind, experienced his vision—that the dark that he had struggled to suppress was in fact his subject.

The essays in *Four Dubliners* have all been published before—each one twice, in fact, as a Library of Congress pamphlet, and in the *New York Review of Books.* Nevertheless it is good to have them between one set of covers, for they constitute one critical whole. They are united in the common theme of the creative power of duality and uncertainty—the potency/impotence of the old Yeats, the spirit/sensation of the young Wilde, the art/actuality of Joyce, the being/nothing of Beckett. And they also share the Irishness of their subjects—a subject that Ellmann knew so much about that a more accurate title for his book might be *Five Dubliners.* He knew, for example, that talented Irishmen leave Ireland early (all four of his subjects departed in their early twenties); and that having done so, they endlessly look back. And that they go on speaking a language that is touched by their rejected Irishness.

There is another linking principle that is important for literary history. Considering the connection of Beckett to the earlier three figures, Ellmann writes: "Once he fills the scene we cannot help but consider or reconsider the writers who preceded him. And when we do, a strange thing happens. However unlike him they were, at least some of their interests appear to be proleptic of his. Qualities in his predecessors which had previously been less conspicuous he pushes to the fore." The latest term in a sequence rearranges and reinterprets the preceding ones: it's a point that T. S. Eliot made long ago (though he wasn't talking about Irishmen). It makes the subject of this book not four Irish writers but one Irish tradition.

In the end the quality that most unifies the book is the voice and intelligence of the fifth Dubliner. Ellmann has always

written with a grace and wit so genial and so unemphatic as to pass unnoticed (it's the knotted, graceless styles that we pay attention to). You hear that voice, and that intelligence, in quiet stylistic turns like this one, from the Beckett essay. Beckett has returned in 1930 to Dublin, to teach there: "His friends suspected that he was a genius, yet no one knew as yet how his abilities would be deployed. His teaching post at Trinity he quit abruptly because he discovered, and would later remark, that he could not teach others what he did not himself understand, a handicap that most of us endure without bridling."

That mild ironic voice, remarking the eccentricities and follies of humankind—both the artists and their critics—seems to have been natural to Ellmann: it expresses the nature of that genial, intelligent, ironic man. It was not his only style, though, for he also had a high style that can be very moving, a style apt for admiring and celebrating the ways in which artists confront the uncertainties of life and death. Ellmann ends the Beckett essay, and his book, with these sentences: "To explain is to attenuate. As his writings have become shorter, he has seemed to imply that faithful images of life have to be squeezed out. Yet his musical cadences, his wrought and precise sentences, cannot help but stave off the void. Even here, as he says in *Ill Seen Ill Said,* 'Imagination at wit's end spreads its sad wings.' If he means to depress us merely, he may be said to outwit himself. Those sad wings are not only panache, they are also poise. Like salamanders we survive in his fire."

I don't have that style at my command (and just as well, I can imagine Ellmann saying). But if I had it, I would try to use it to suggest the sense of indebtedness that generations of critics feel and will go on feeling for the achievements of Richard Ellmann; we survive in his fire. (pp. xlviii-l)

      Samuel Hynes, in a review of "Four Dubliners—Wilde, Yeats, Joyce, and Beckett," in The Sewanee Review, *Vol. XCV, No. 3, Summer, 1987, pp. xlviii-l.*

JOSEPH RONSLEY

[*Ronsley, an American critic, editor, and educator, is the author of* Yeats' Autobiography: Life as Symbolic Pattern *(1968). A professor of literature at McGill University, he first met Ellmann after bringing him to lecture there on Irish literature. In the following excerpt, Ronsley praises Ellmann's warm personality as well as his contributions to Irish literary scholarship.*]

Readers of the *Irish Literary Supplement* are likely to have been students of Richard Ellmann, whether or not they were formally so at Harvard, Northwestern, Yale, Oxford or Emory. They have been so mainly because of the importance of the subjects on which he has written, the dimension of his work and the originality of his insights, and also because he wrote with striking liveliness and clarity, and genuinely illuminated the literature with which he dealt. Many have been his friends or at least acquaintances, and many have written moving, deeply-felt obituaries for him. So what I have to say is not so much intended to be informative as to be recognizable and to stir memories that we would prefer not to lose.

Despite the universal deference for his scholarly stature and authority, which was taken for granted during his lifetime, the impact on the literary world of his death last May 13 was profound. Each of us apparently discovered that Richard Ellmann was as special a man, or nearly so, to everyone else as he was to oneself. A mystique had grown around him as a literary figure that was unique among scholars and critics, and was akin to that of some of the great creative artists with which he was concerned.

His earliest important professional scholarly work was on William Butler Yeats. His books are still the most useful and readable on the subject, and, when it appeared in 1948, *Yeats: The Man and the Masks* was likely responsible for altering the general perception of hierarchy among poets writing in English during this century. Since then he has written further on Yeats, Joyce, Wilde, and in fact while his focus has been on Irish writers, he has written on subjects covering the entire range of 20th-century literature. This despite his telling me once that he "writes very slowly"! In his concern with Irish writers he never slipped into that quicksand so dangerous to scholars, a general Celtophilia. Rather he has explored the work and lives of some of the greatest literary figures of our day who happen to be Irish, and while giving full credit to the importance of Irishness to their work, he has primarily illuminated the universality on which their greatness lies.

Of course his most overwhelming impact came in his biography of Joyce. Frank Kermode has said that it "fixes Joyce's image for a generation." Anthony Burgess unequivocally called it "the greatest literary biography of the century." David Norris "would go even further and rank it with Boswell's life of Johnson as one of those rare works that transcends mere biography and stands in its own right as a work of art." On the other hand David Clark complained that every time he consulted the book for factual material he found himself distracted from his purpose, caught up fascinated and reading on. On two occasions I have witnessed the kind of probing interview which must have contributed to his biographical work. One of his visits to McGill University coincided with that of a candidate for a position in comparative literature. Ellmann met the candidate in the company of the English department chairman over a drink before dinner, and casually asked some questions. While Dick was not unkind the candidate spent a rather strenuous fifteen minutes answering questions. (He has since become chairman of the program.) The other time was when his visit overlapped that of Irish playwright Denis Johnston, and both spent a night in our home at the same time. Under the guise of casual dinner conversation I learned about Johnston than I had during several previous meetings.

Probably one of the mot compelling aspects of the Joyce biography is the sympathy with which it is imbued, or as Roger Lewis has said, going further, the author's "awe of his subject." Those of us who were formally his students quickly learned that as scholars and critics it is dangerous to underestimate the objects of our study, to be patronizing toward them, to trivialize their thinking or be deluded into thinking we were wiser than they. The cogent wisdom of human truths that lay behind Yeats's symbolic and apparently fanciful mythology, for instance, should be constantly before us in the study of the poet and his work. Without setting aside our critical capacity, the stature of Yeats and Joyce, both as men and as artists, must be kept in mind. And the inseparability of their lives from their art is crucial. This is not to say that the author's life and work are the same. Rather, Ellmann has said, "the way in which you respond to experience must somehow connect to the way in which you write your books." Ellmann is speaking of Joyce here, but his words apply equally to himself. Moreover, Joyce's human frailty along with his strength appealed to Ellmann. It is this combination, after all, that is characteristic of all the great figures of our literary heritage, fictional and living, defining as they do the human condition

and providing a celebration of life, while bringing humility to the sensitive scholar.

Richard Ellmann exemplified in his own life and work this humility and this celebration of life; the common theme running through the many obituaries written for him is that he was endowed with a brilliant mind along with a generous and gracious spirit, an overwhelming humanity, and an almost naive appreciation for the little, seemingly inconsequential things that make up daily life. Declan Kiberd recalls his insouciance toward his own achievements and his profession, Anthony Burgess [see excerpt above] his concern during a conference to catch an episode of a television soap opera, Roger Lewis his delight in an extravagant gourmet dinner at the expense of a magazine's "dining out" column. I recall that on a visit to Montreal he was preoccupied with getting to Woolworth's to buy something he could not get in Oxford. He was not above writing for popular magazines or designing the Oscar Wilde Playing Cards. After he received seven honorary degrees in four different countries we expected him to be a little jaded when he received his eighth (and last) at McGill, but there could be no doubt that he was genuinely pleased and excited with the event—he enjoyed the costume, ritual and all. Roger Lewis speaks of his collecting hoods in a top drawer, and liking them particularly because they were such useless garments. When I first brought Dick Ellmann to McGill to lecture, our department chairman, Donald Theall, was astonished upon meeting him to discover that the great man was also such a "nice man."

Ellmann was seriously and humanely cornered about social and political issues. David Norris describes as "characteristic" the fact that when "I took legal action against the Irish Government to force a reform of the laws criminalising homosexual behaviour, almost the first letter I received was from Richard Ellmann saying that as the biographer-to-be of the most notorious victim of those very laws, Oscar Wilde, it was only appropriate that he should support my efforts. Also enclosed was a substantial cheque." He was directly involved when the issues touched upon literature, but a Joycean light touch can be found here as elsewhere: when in the 1960s during a court hearing in Chicago over obscenity charges against Henry Miller's *The Tropic of Cancer* he was asked as an expert witness if the fornication of elephants could be considered pornographic, he replied simply that elephants do not fornicate. His lighthearted, mischievous, amused and congenial spirit pervades all life's common experiences; he absorbed into his own life the best qualities he found in Yeats, Joyce and Wilde. A close friend, Sylvan Schendler, has pointed out that in dying he appeared to manifest the spirit Yeats found in Mabel Beardsley as expressed in "Upon a Dying Lady." He also embodied the spirit of Leopold Bloom, "a good man," in both his Dublin and Homeric avatars.

There never was any question for Ellmann that love, not death, was at the heart of *Ulysses*. Were it the other way, it could not have been the "holy" book it was. His caring, loyalty and love for his family were obvious to anyone who knew him, and so was his warmth toward his friends and colleagues, and especially the gentle care he gave his students. He was meticulous in his supervision of their work, for a readable style as well as for substance. His students were encouraged to think and work things out independently, but they learned by themselves to be cautious, to pause and reflect before disagreeing with their mentor. Not that he objected to their disagreement. It was simply that after sitting with the issue for a while they usually decided on their own that he was right. In the same way they learned that it was worthwhile to allow him time for leisurely reflection. I seldom came away from a meeting without being just a little wiser than before, without having learned something, and not just about literature but about living my life, Declan Kiberd has spoken of "his stealthy acts of kindness on behalf of his students." Surely as a teacher he is what we all aspire to be, with only varying amounts of success. The universal sense of loss and grief among his former students and his colleagues at his death speaks for an ongoing admiration and affection that places him beyond scholars and teachers who are merely highly distinguished.

> Joseph Ronsley, "Richard Ellmann, 1918-1987," in Irish Literary Supplement, Vol. 6, No. 2, Fall, 1987, p. 5.

ROGER LEWIS

[In the following excerpt, Lewis, a former student of Ellmann's, offers background information on the scholar's final work, Oscar Wilde.]

[Oscar] Wilde was born in 1854 and died in 1900 and it has taken 87 years and Richard Ellmann's new biography [**Oscar Wilde**] to show that the Wilde we thought we knew intimately is, in fact, a stranger, a false idol and travesty of the truth. The real Oscar Wilde, it transpires, was a complex intellect, whose shallowness ran deep. He was the wisest man of his age, and of the next. Ellmann traces Wilde's recreation of himself—his renaissance, the opposite of decadence—in words: he celebrates the playfulness of his plays, the theatricality of his theatre. Wilde belongs, we are told, "to our world more than to Victoria's. Now, beyond the reach of scandal . . . he comes before us still, a towering figure, laughing and weeping, with parables and paradoxes, so generous, so amusing, and so right."

These are Ellmann's last lines, and Wilde achieves apotheosis as *the* existential hero. It is a magnificent achievement, to convert the filigree comedy of *The Importance of Being Earnest* or the sinister sensuality of *Dorian Gray* by the alchemy of biographical investigation into something far more deeply interfused, and almost holy.

But then, that's the Ellmann touch: he rendered the recondite James Joyce familiar; he made the fantastic Yeats domestic. Ellmann, Professor of English at Yale then Oxford, was the greatest biographer of the century for this reason: he knew there was nothing simple-minded about simplicity. "The object of life is not to simplify it," he wrote—and in his eyes we are each of us an incipient artist. "As our conflicting impulses coincide, as our repressed feelings vie with our expressed ones, as our solid views disclose dramatists." Ellmann talked of the secret life underneath the one we appear to live, and averred that one of the pleasures of writing novels or poems is that "this subsurface life can be drawn upon and transformed without incurring the responsibilities of autobiography or history". Novels, poems, plays—they are nonetheless autobiographies in disguise.

To literary critical analysis, Ellmann would marry facts and figures; wed real-life counterparts with fictional characters. The writer Aidan Higgins found him searching an Irish cliff for the exact spot Joyce's Bloom dreams of falling over; for his Yeats he visited the aged Maud Gonne herself. He spent months ascertaining what Wilde's pleasure was, and having ascertained

from pseudonymous articles and stories in turn-of-the-century British and French magazines that it was fellatio, told Norton Smith, professor at Dundee. "Giving or receiving?" asked Norton Smith. "Damn", said Ellmann. "That'll be another six months work." And it probably was.

For in the late Forties and early Fifties there were the Yeats studies, in the late Fifties the Joyce masterpiece, revised in 1982; *pari passu* there were collections of essays and printed lectures—but the big book, promised and toiled over for decades, has been on Oscar Wilde. A legendary manuscript, refined and re-refined, its deadlines have come and gone. Joan Wyatt, secretary at the English Faculty, said: "I know sections by heart. I typed and retyped. Nothing substantial in the changes. He'd add sentences and words—but the whole chapter would have to be done again. That went on for the 15 years I was in Oxford."

Ellmann wanted his book to have no single uninteresting sentence. The biography was started and abandoned "He kept being displeased with it," said Maud Ellmann, the professor's 33-year-old daughter, "and he would give it up. He only got down to it without interruption, when?" "Just in the last two years," said Mary, the widow, without looking up from her card game. "When he retired."

Ellmann circled Wilde, limbering up by writing about him centrifugally—essays, lectures, reviews, prefaces—defining the activity of the magnet by the jitters of the iron filings. Wilde by way of Ruskin, Pater, Arnold, Whistler, Yeats. Meanwhile, draft upon draft of the biography was mailed between Oxford and Emory, the university in Georgia where Ellmann wintered. Why, the question arises, if the James Joyce opus, some thousand pages, appeared within a few years of *The Identity of Yeats* and *Yeats: The Man and the Masks*—why was it taking nearly 30 years from James Joyce to Oscar Wilde?

With Yeats there was Mrs. Yeats and Miss Gonne to meet and borrow a trove of unsorted treasures from; with Joyce there was the brother Stanislaus. Ellmann won the confidence of living relics of dead literary saints. With Wilde there was no testimony other than the absolutely archaeological—though this was serendipitous. Dr. Keith Schuchard, from Emory University, recalled sitting down for breakfast in an Edinburgh hotel next to a man who owned, it transpired, the Lodge Book from Wilde's Masonic days. It was easy to see where Wilde took part in ceremonies: his name had been cut from the page after his disgrace.

There were no eyewitnesses, no firsthand accounts to track down and benignly grill—with the exception of Sir Isaiah Berlin, who recounted conversations with Bernard Berenson about conversations Berenson had had with Wilde at the last century's end. So what Ellmann did was to spend years turning over, page by page, the Wilde archives at the University of California and the Library of Congress. He visited the cellars of Harvard, Yale and Trinity College, Dublin. He explored that vault in Texas where all English authors languish for eternity. Home Office files revealed details about Reading Gaol and the dozens of recondite books its most famous inmate requested. At Magdalen, Ellmann discovered the dusty records and reports about the college's most recalcitrant son: at Brasenose a correspondence with Walter Pater was produced. In the National Library of Ireland, Ellmann located Robbie Ross's calling-card, on the verso of which was a scribbled request for a priest to come and save the soul of a dying man: Wilde.

He found yellowing files of newspapers containing sketches of Wilde about town; from ancient and defunct journals he followed Wilde's lecture tour of America, he collected photographs and daguerreotypes: he was in touch with autograph hunters and dealers; he investigated the history of the Queensberrys and found them to be something other than simple brutes. (They were complex ones.)

Ellmann was in a populous wasteland of unregarded evidence thrown in corners; plus all those other biographies; plus Wilde's letters, which had been systematically edited by Sir Rupert Hart-Davies. All this material is synthesised, showing many new alignments and configurations. He brought fresh interpretation from fresh juxtaposition of fact—all of this accomplished within a magisterial reconstruction and understanding of the historical period and the spirit of the age.

No: the reason for delay, the reason why Ellmann grew into his project as his project grew, is linked with the notion of each of us being a secret dramatist, each yearning to find a shape for our interior life—that Freudian forest of memory and desire. If poems, novels and plays are autobiographies in disguise then so, perhaps above all, is biography a secret route to the self. "Every portrait that is painted with feeling," says Basil Hallward in *The Picture of Dorian Gray*, "is a portrait of the artist, not of the sitter."

The subject of Wilde is Ellmann's *Parsifal*, his *Magic Flute*—the swansong sounded at the beginning. The identification with the writer has nothing to do with the erotic—Ellmann was, as he says of Frank Harris, as heterosexual as a man can be—but a lot to do with writing, its art and craft.

"My father said he was interested in writing a book on Wilde from childhood," Maud disclosed, "from when he was seven or 11. He compiled a commonplace book of all the best epigrams, and loved the absolute precision and adroitness of the language. He wanted the biography to be more than a homage, though I don't quite know what he had in mind. I know he had difficulty with the sexual aspect. The homosexuality thwarted a full identification, or understanding."

"He was fascinated," Lucy, his 31-year-old daughter, said when I later returned to this issue, talking to her in London, "by his own inability to bridge that sexual gap; he was interested in his own embarrassment."

"Did he explore himself in his books?"

"By default, I suppose."

Born into a family of Rumanian Jews, who'd been successful attorneys in America for several generations, Ellmann was made to feel a tinge of betrayal when he chose literature as a career above the law; he'd elected an idiosyncratic destiny, maybe an effete one. He was a member of the Yale Class of 1939, instead of the local Michigan University.

"The sense of exclusion, alienation, tied in with Jewishness—my father's experience of a disdained sect—that's what he identified with in Wilde," said Lucy. "The loneliness. He had a difficult upbringing—turning away from doing law, which was the expected thing. Law wasn't what he wanted."

To impute colourful ostracism would be wrong—but Ellmann had busily to justify himself and his lesser subject without the law. He won prizes and impressive academic credentials at Harvard and Yale. In his college study at Oxford are many works on Jewry. Ellmann was proud and touchy about his religion—touchy about real or imagined slights. It contributed to his sense of being an outsider. A genial twinkling man, there was always sorrow in his eyes.

With Maud, leafing through old albums, I saw a group photo from 1941. There was a long-faced cross-legged pixie in the front row. "My father. He was much thinner then. I only found this picture last week. Quite handsome."

"He took up jogging to lose weight," I said.

"Jogging!" said Mary—a Lady Bracknell intervention. "His entire decline began when he took up jogging. I blame everything on jogging."

The sense of division between aesthetics and family pride, between skinny Stephen and corpulent Bloom, between youth and age, art and responsibility, came to rest in Wilde, literature's lordliest sufferer and most tragic success-story.

There is an additional preoccupation of Ellmann's to be found in his biographies—and it concerns disease and the black comedy of the body. Yeats's vasectomy and the fool's paradise of increased virility informed several essays; Joyce's duodenal ulcers, sarcomas and interest in female micturition were incorporated in the 1982 edition, Wilde's syphilis is big in the present work—the spirochaete's journey up the spine being the covert decay of Dorian Gray.

Fascination with physiology and fleshly caprice had a macabre conclusion. Last autumn Ellmann, at 68, was diagnosed as suffering from motor neurone disease, for which there is no known cure. The Wilde biography was completed as death approached, like the beating of the great wings that so madden Herod in *Salome;* and it was impending death which galvanised the book's final draft. To read the last chapter, about the dying Wilde, knowing about the dying Ellmann, is unbearable. Ellmann, who'd chronicled the last rites of others so often, succumbed to illness himself, his book his testament. Days after his funeral, Catherine Carver, his editor, found by his bed a set of proofs. They'd been minutely gone through and corrected.

"Illness gave him a crazy kind of energy," said Lucy, "at least when it was somebody else who was ill. But he felt it. When my mother was first ill—a sort of stroke—he clattered his typewriter more than ever. He drew on illness."

Motor neurone disease affects the transmission of messages from the central nervous system to the musculature. There is a gradual, painless weakening as body and brain stop communicating. Ellmann grew thinner as he couldn't swallow, and he grew so frail he couldn't dress or speak. It happened with alarming speed. The provinces of his body revolted: "this tomb for those who are not yet dead," as Wilde said of prison. Motor neurone disease was Ellmann's Reading Gaol; trapped in the den of himself.

He died on May 13 this year. (pp. 32-3, 35, 37)

Roger Lewis, *"Declaring His Genius,"* in The Sunday Times, *London, September 13, 1987, pp. 32-3, 35, 37.*

(Jean) Margaret (Wemyss) Laurence

July 18, 1926 - January 5, 1987

Canadian novelist, short story writer, critic, nonfiction writer, and juvenile fiction writer.

(See also *CLC*, Vols. 3, 6, 13; *Contemporary Authors*, Vols. 5-8, rev. ed.; and *Dictionary of Literary Biography*, Vol. 53.)

PRINCIPAL WORKS

A Tree for Poverty: Somali Poetry and Prose [translator]
    (folktales and poetry) 1954
This Side Jordan (novel) 1960
The Prophet's Camel Bell (memoir) 1963; also published
    as *New Wind in a Dry Land*, 1964
The Tomorrow-Tamer and Other Stories (short stories)
    1963
The Stone Angel (novel) 1964
A Jest of God (novel) 1966; also published as *Rachel,*
    Rachel, 1968; and *Now I Lay Me Down*, 1968
Long Drums and Cannons: Nigerian Dramatists and
    Novelists, 1952-1966 (criticism) 1968
The Fire-Dwellers (novel) 1969
A Bird in the House (short stories) 1970
Jason's Quest (juvenile fiction) 1970
The Diviners (novel) 1974
Heart of a Stranger (essays) 1976
Dance on the Earth (autobiography) 1987

Photograph by Paul Orenstein

DON BAILEY

[*Bailey is a Canadian novelist, short story writer, and poet. His writings include* My Bareness Is Not Just My Body *(1971), The* Sorry Papers *(1979), and* Swim for Your Life *(1984). Laurence's novel* A Jest of God *inspired Bailey to write his first short story; later, Laurence became Bailey's close friend and literary mentor. In the following excerpt, Bailey recreates some significant moments from his friendship with Laurence.*]

I first met Margaret in a book. I was serving a long prison sentence for bank robbery. I had time on my hands. Time to read and write myself. My cell was littered with stories and poems I had written but the events and characters remained cold and lifeless. I could record life but not create it.

I had read Balzac, Maupassant and even Chekhov. I hadn't completed grade 8 but I could read. The big dictionary on my desk got a lot of use because I was trying to develop language to express myself and to facilitate my reading so I could understand how other writers did it. But still, in J. D. Salinger's writing, the qualities that floored me also eluded me.

And then one day a copy of **A Jest of God** arrived in the prison library. I took it out and read it in one night. Even after lights

out I kept on under the feeble glow of the fifteen-watt surveillance light we each had so the guards could catch us if we tried to hang ourselves. I persevered because in the character of Rachel Cameron I at last heard the voice I'd been looking for all my life.

"Come along, grade twos. Line up quietly now."

Am I beginning to talk in that simpler tone, the one so many grade-school teachers pick up without realizing? At first they only talk to the children like that, but it takes root and soon they can't speak any other way to anyone. Sapphire Travis does it all the time. "Rachel, dear, would you be a very very good girl and pour me a weeny cup of tea?" Poor grade ones. How did they endure it? Children have built-in radar to detect falseness.

"Come along now. We haven't got all day. James, for goodness sake, stop dawdling."

Now I've spoken far more sharply than necessary. I have to watch this too. It's hard to strike a balance. It's so often James I speak to like this, fearing to be too much the other way with him.

I knew that voice. Like a tennis ball being banged back and forth across a court where one player was logic and the other feeling. A voice that worried about what was right and wrong. One concerned with the vulnerability of others. A knowing voice, intuitively aware that this vale of tears was fraught with risk, and that our every move hurt somebody.

It was a voice my ear had forever longed to hear, both tender and critical, soothing and harsh. The voice of my mother! The woman who when I was two years old walked out of my life. The war had taken my father. Her life was shattered. Now she had returned, not in flesh. But in tone.

In those days a field mouse sometimes found its way into my cell, an intruder on my limited privacy. But in the early morning hours, when I finished reading Margaret Laurence's book, I yearned for the arrival of that rodent, a living creature with whom I could share the joy I felt and the excitement of arriving at a place I'd never been. Home.

I almost rang for the guard. But I was afraid the night man would laugh at my babblings. So instead I began to write in my notebook. Frantically I worked in pencil as the dawn slowly penetrated the gloomy light of my cell. By breakfast I had produced a story called "Ring around the Rosie." Different in content from Margaret's work. Different also in voice. But the story had a voice that echoed credibly in my own mind. It marked my birth as a writer.

During the daylight hours of the next day I typed out what I now referred to as my Margaret Laurence story, stuck it in an envelope and mailed it off to a literary contest that the penitentiary service was sponsoring. Before the results were announced I was granted a parole. I went home to the wife and family I had left many years before. A stranger. Within a week I knew I had a responsibility to leave them again. (pp. 6-7)

The day I was making my awkward goodbyes the mailman brought me two letters. One contained a cheque for fifty dollars and congratulations for winning the prison literary contest. The other letter was from Jane Rule, a writer in Vancouver who had been one of the judges. She was generous in her praise of my work and offered to help me.

And then one day I received a letter from Jane saying that Margaret Laurence had contacted her in an attempt to track me down. Margaret had read one of my stories and wanted to meet me.

I called the number Jane had sent. Margaret answered and invited me to dinner the next night. I was afraid of making a fool of myself. Of saying too much. I imagined my mind going blank in her presence. . . .

Margaret did not answer the door. A beautiful young woman who was sharing the house whisked me inside and ushered me upstairs to the study. Margaret stood to greet me and I knew in that instant she was as shy as I was. She took my hand.

"God, I liked that story," she said.

And then she reached into the bottom drawer of her desk and removed two bottles of liquor. She dug out two glasses and motioned for me to sit down.

"I hope you're a rye drinker," she said, "because the scotch is for me."

That night Margaret became my mentor. Through the next eighteen years we never spoke of it but she helped me get writing grants when I was desperate. She remained loyal and supportive to the voice I tried to articulate. She pointed me towards love and witnessed my faltering steps to make a new life. All she demanded from me was the will to go on.

"A person's got to do what needs to be done," she once said. (p. 7)

Don Bailey, "The Diviner," in Brick: A Journal of Reviews, *No. 29, Winter, 1987, pp. 6-9.*

THE TIMES LONDON

Margaret Laurence, a dominant influence on Canadian literature, and the first of a group of contemporary Canadian women novelists to win international reputation, died [January 5]. She was 60.

She wrote before her time, while Canada was still culturally provincial. Her heroines are early feminists, and her novels explore such matters as freedom and responsibility, and the female predicament, which have since become fashionable as well as important. At the time they caused alarm in parts of Canada.

Her last novel, **The Diviners,** was banned by some school boards because of its explicit depictions of an abortion and a sexual escapade (although it was, together with the rest of her novels, retained on the reading list). She never wrote another.

In an interview in 1984 she said: "I was desperately hurt. I thought I'd get back at them in a novel. But after two years of mulling it over, I realized you don't write fiction to get back at somebody. It was a lousy idea."

She will be remembered for the imaginary but authentic prairie world of Manawaka that she created, in what became almost a single epic work.

Jean Margaret Wemyss was born on July 19, 1926, in the prairie town of Neepawa, Manitoba. Her parents, of Highland Scottish ancestry, died when she was young.

As a child she contributed to her school magazine. She went to United College, Winnipeg, where she graduated with a degree in English. She then got a job as a reporter on the *Winnipeg Citizen.*

In 1947 she married Jack Laurence, a civil engineer, and two years later they moved to England. His work took them to Somaliland and Ghana, and Margaret Laurence started to write: a travel book, short stories, and a novel, all set in Africa. She also began to explore relations between the races as well as the sexes and the classes.

Her first work, **A Tree for Poverty,** published in Somaliland in 1954, contains translations of Somali folktales and poetry. International reviewers started to recognize a new talent.

Three years later, now with two children, they returned to Vancouver. She and her husband separated in 1962 (they were divorced seven years later) and she came to England where she wrote the first three Manawaka novels.

The first, **The Stone Angel** (1964), is told by a proud 90-year-old woman living in the harsh prairies, and gets beneath the skin of senility as well as Canada. Then came **A Jest of God** (1966)—which was made into the film *Rachel, Rachel*—and **The Fire Dwellers** (1969).

The Diviners was published in 1974, five years after her final return to Canada, where she made her home in the hamlet of Lakefield.

The books are provincial, in that the very local setting is integral to her meaning and her characters. But they are universal and fascinating, as her heroines, struggling to understand their own pasts, reflect the great country that has for so long been in search of a national identity. It is not surprising that provincial Canadians found her disturbing.

Margaret Laurence was a big woman, with strong features, and straight black hair. You might have guessed the Highland genes. She had a disconcerting honesty about herself and her country, which made her uncomfortable as well as a true writer.

> *"Margaret Laurence," in* The Times, *London, January 7, 1987.*

TIMOTHY FINDLEY

[*A Canadian novelist, scriptwriter, and dramatist, Findley was a stage actor before establishing his literary career with such novels as* The Last of the Crazy People *(1967),* The Wars *(1977), which won a Governor General's Literary Award, and* Not Wanted on the Voyage *(1984). Findley and Laurence were friends for two decades before her death. In the following excerpt, Findley commends Laurence for her skill and courage as a writer.*]

In what has become one of the best-known passages in Canadian writing, Margaret Laurence brought her masterpiece— *The Diviners*—toward its rolling conclusion: "Morag walked out across the grass and looked at the river. The sun, now low, was catching the waves, sending out once more the flotilla of little lights skimming along the green-bronze surface. The waters flowed from north to south, and the current was visible, but now a south wind was blowing, ruffling the water in the opposite direction, so that the river, as so often here, seemed to be flowing both ways. *Look ahead into the past, and back into the future until the silence."*

Last week that silence came for Margaret Laurence—though only she would have been aware of its presence. For the rest of us, the silence is filled with the sound of her voice.

"A strange place it was," she wrote of the place where she was born; "that place where the world began. A place of incredible happenings, splendors and revelations. . . ." Jean Margaret Wemyss (pronounced *Weems*) was born in Neepawa, Man., on July 18, 1926. Her family always called her Peggy and, even now, if you go to Neepawa and make inquiries, those who knew her as a child still speak more freely of Peggy Wemyss than they do of Margaret Laurence.

When Peggy Wemyss was four years old, her mother, Verna Jean Simpson, died. Her father, Robert, a lawyer, remarried with Margaret's aunt, Margaret Campbell Simpson, but died a short time later—before his daughter and her stepbrother had left their childhood behind. In a memoir, which she completed with her daughter, Jocelyn, just before her death, Laurence pays particular tribute to the women who shared in her Prairie upbringing—her natural mother and her aunt-turned-stepmother whom Margaret always called "Mom."

All those adults had a lasting and creative influence on Margaret Laurence's sense of the world—its demands on human beings and their right to make demands of it. The world you were a child in, she maintained, stayed with you all the days of your life. Its light was the light you always saw by and its dark the dark that colored all your days.

Certainly, everything that Laurence wrote was colored by the devils of her childhood: death, the Depression and what Prairie folk always refer to as "the everlasting drought." the images wrung from her battles and victories over these devils infused her writings with the kind of immediate veracity unique to the greatest works of art. Laurence would have resisted such as assessment of what she did, but what she did had greatness it it, regardless of what she believed. The greatness lay in the way she set her people before us: whole and articulate, hungry for the life she gave them.

Peggy Wemyss—married in 1947 to civil engineer John Laurence and divorced in 1969, the mother of two loving children, Jocelyn and David—ultimately lived alone. But *alone* is perhaps not quite the right word. She lived—as any writer must— in tandem with the artist inside her. Each one drew on the other's strengths and weaknesses in order to come to terms with what Laurence perceived neither as a duty nor as a need to become a writer, but as her right to become whole—as complete as any of the women whose lives she created with such consummate skill.

"It is my feeling," she said, "that as we grow older we should become not *less* radical but *more so.*" Long before she died last week in Lakefield, Ont., her home for the past 12 years, both Laurence the writer and Laurence the woman had achieved through her books and in her everyday life a kind of radicalism the rest of us can only envy. Envy, yes; but not in a spirit of jealousy: only in the spirit of respect. Her writings—most notably *The Diviners* (1974), *A Jest of God* (1966) and *The Stone Angel* (1964)—had incurred, because of their unsparing integrity, the wrath of all wrong-thinking people. And her life—as a dedicated feminist, a Canadian nationalist, a human rights activist and advocate of nuclear disarmament—had become an inextinguishable beacon for others.

Brave, but modest, she was sometimes nervous in the extreme: virtually unable to stand when she made a speech or gave a reading. The questions she faced from the floor of public forums were inevitably tense with the drama inherent in a person who can barely stand up because of her fear, but who knows that she must rise to the occasion. Her body often betrayed her, forcing her to hold fast to the back of the chair in front of her. Whenever it was known beforehand that Margaret was going to make an appearance, a chair and table were provided. Even from a distance, any witness could see her shaking.

Robin Phillips, the noted stage director, once choreographed an entire evening of readings given by writers in opposition to censorship, around the fact of "Margaret Laurence's table." It sat just where it should, left of centre from the audience's point of view. That every writer, that night, making exits and entrances, had to contend with this table—the one they all have to face every day of their working lives—was a marvellous symbolic gesture. That it was Margaret Laurence's table made it doubly symbolic of what that evening was about.

No other writer in Canadian history suffered more at the hands of those professional naysayers, book-banners and censors than Laurence. And that suffering—make no mistake of it—took its toll, both professionally and personally. So be it: she was prepared for that. And, in the long run, she triumphed, knowing that her books had been written, as she said herself, "in order to clarify, proclaim and enhance life—not to obscure and demean and destroy it."

"My lifetime here is a short span," she wrote once, "but I am not here as a visitor. Earth is my home." And we are the better for it. (pp. 52-3)

Timothy Findley, "A Life of Eloquence and Radicalism," in Maclean's Magazine, Vol. 100, No. 3, January 19, 1987, pp. 52-3.

JACK McCLELLAND

[McClelland has been an administrator and former president of the Canadian publishing firm McClelland and Stewart, as well as cofounder of Seal Books. McClelland's professional relationship with Laurence began when he published her first novel, This Side Jordan; since then McClelland-Stewart has released several of her works. In the following excerpt, McClelland expresses his admiration for Laurence's bravery, in her life as well as her writings.]

Margaret Laurence was a deeply private person, yet her readers felt they knew her intimately through her work. When she died of cancer in early January at the age of 60, many people who had not met her felt they had lost a beloved friend.

Although she wrote stories from the age of seven onward, her first book was published in 1954: A Tree for Poverty, a collection of her translations of Somali folk-tales and poetry. Her years in Africa, 1950-1957, also resulted in a collection of stories, The Tomorrow-Tamer (1963); a travel memoir, The Prophet's Camel Bell (1963); and Long Drums and Cannons (1968), a study of Nigerian writing. Her first novel, This Side Jordan, was set and drafted in Ghana and published in 1960.

It was followed by the Manawaka quartet of novels—The Stone Angel (1964), A Jest of God (1966), The Fire-Dwellers (1969), and The Diviners (1974). . . . These novels and her autobiographical story collection A Bird in the House (1970) made Manawaka—inspired by Laurence's prairie birthplace, Neepawa, Manitoba—a permanent part of Canada's fictional landscape. Her strong female protagonists—Morag Gunn, Stacey MacAindra, Rachel Cameron, Hagar Shipley—seem to live beyond fiction, their strengths and weaknesses a reflection of our own. Laurence also wrote books for children, including Six Darn Cows (1979), The Olden Days Coat (1979), and A Christmas Birthday Story (1980).

In the 70s and 80s, Laurence saw repeated attempts to ban her work—particularly The Diviners—from school reading lists. Ironically, one of the challenges to The Diviners came in her hometown, Lakefield, Ontario, where the book was temporarily removed from the high-school reading list in 1978. "Those who most vehemently oppose my books," said Laurence in 1981, "are the ones most proud of never reading them."

Laurence, a founding member of The Writers Union of Canada, was a great friend to young writers. "When you arrive on her doorstep, formality dissolves quickly," writer Alan Twigg recalled in a letter to us after her death. "It's like visiting your mother after a long separation. She is full of warmth and strength. There's a bottle of Blue Nun waiting in the fridge. And Mum already has your lunch ready. Afterwards, you help with the dishes."

"I put a lot of faith in the young," she told Twigg on that visit in 1979. "I put a lot of faith in the ability of people my age to change. I am still prepared to do battle and save the planet."

On the death of one of her writer friends, Hubert Evans, in 1986, she wrote in these pages, "It meant such a lot . . . to talk with this elder member of the writers' tribe, this man of great and valiant spirit." There are several generations of Canadian writers who feel the same way about Laurence herself, a writer who gave of her time and her thoughts generously.

Jack McClelland, Margaret Laurence's long-time publisher and friend, prepared the following tribute for [Quill and Quire].

Margaret Laurence was probably the greatest gift to the literary community that Canada has ever known, not only through her writing, but through her sheer presence—her caring and compassion, her support of other writers, her deep love of all the things that we value most. She was a friend. I loved her. She was one of a small group of distinguished writers who made life in Canadian book publishing so fulfilling for me.

I have been asked if I discovered Margaret Laurence. Of course I did not. She first discovered herself, as all great writers must do. That is the hard part, and the first lesson in courage. She is quoted as having said, "Unless you have to be a writer, in Canada, don't be." No one could be in more certain agreement with that thought than I am. But she had to be a writer, and it was a rare gift that made her one of the great ones.

Her work was first brought to my attention by a mutual friend on the University of British Columbia campus, Gordon Elliott. On his recommendation, I wrote and asked to see a manuscript. This Side Jordan, her first novel, was the eventual result, and the records indicate that it sold almost 1,400 copies in Canada in its first year, 1960.

I wish I could say that I recognized the full potential of this great talent and offered a publishing contract at once but, alas, this is not the case—as I am reminded by a recollection in her memoir, Dance on the Earth, completed just before her death and scheduled for publication in the fall of this year.

I had said, yes, we would like to publish This Side Jordan, but first a British or American co-publisher must be found—a typically Canadian response, and one that remains all too common even today.

A British publisher, however, was soon found: the Macmillan Company of London, in the person of Alan MacLean, who became a life-long friend and associate. (MacLean went on to become one of the greatest British publishers of our time.) Later, Alfred Knopf, probably the single most distinguished publisher in any country in the last half-century, took the unprecedented step of publishing three of her books in New York in one day.

One thing we may not yet understand fully is the deep courage of Margaret Laurence. She had to begin with the instinct and faith of all great writers. I refer here to the courage that is required for the simple act of submitting a manuscript to our publishing system. As a relatively young publisher, I learned something important from Margaret about writers: the anguish, the anxiety, that an author experiences while waiting for a judgement from the publisher—the kind of uncertainty that remained with Margaret long after she had become an established star. Beyond this, of course, is the courage she demonstrated in her writing—in her themes and in the honesty and depth of her characterizations.

On another level of courage, I am reminded of the agony and disquiet that this deeply caring, deeply moral, and dedicated woman suffered as a result of concerted attacks by mindless, self-appointed censors in Lakefield and Peterborough County, Ontario, who attempted to have her works removed from school and library shelves. It was an outrage, an experience that hurt her deeply, but one that she fought eloquently, with grace and conviction. . . .

The final call for courage was one Margaret was well prepared for because she had thought about it and written about it extensively. She wrote with humour, with faith, and with certainty. When she faced death herself, she maintained a strength, an openness, and a degree of cheerfulness that I found almost beyond understanding.

To my regret, I visited her only once during these dread final months. I simply lacked the courage. I did talk with her regularly—and, in fact, I spoke to her the day before she died. I had no notion that she would be gone so soon, nor did her close family. I suspect that she herself knew.

The country has lost a great citizen, whose spirit will endure through the books she has left us. I feel privileged to have touched her life.

Jack McClelland, "Margaret Laurence," in Quill and Quire, *Vol. 53, No. 2, February, 1987, p. 9.*

W. H. NEW

[*A Canadian critic and editor, New is the author of works such as* Articulating West: Essays on Purpose and Form in Modern Canadian Literature *(1972), and* Among Worlds: An Introduction to Modern Commonwealth and South African Fiction *(1975). He is editor of* Canadian Literature *and a former associate editor of* World Literature Written in English. *New counted Laurence as a valued friend and colleague. In the following excerpt, New lauds the qualities of "honour, caring, commitment, compassion" that won Laurence a devoted following.*]

Margaret Laurence was my friend. She died on January 5, 1987, and I miss her. It's not that we knew each other well. We met, I think, only twice—once in Vancouver, and once at a conference in Ontario, where we spent a swift afternoon in amiable anecdote—and we corresponded only occasionally. But she was *there:* there in imagination, there to reach, there as encouragement. She always wrote encouraging letters. It was one of her ways of reaching out to others, which is why she became friend to so many. Even strangers came to know her personally. She responded to requests with kindness and courtesy, read others' work with sympathy and appreciation, *shared* in her community. Dave Godfrey said once, when he was asked whom he wrote for, that he wrote for Margaret Laurence. Though at the time he had never met her, she was already an image, a conduit to understanding. "She is unforgettable," wrote Marian Engle, "because she is *us.*" Through her, as her African journal says of foreign travel, we came to know something more about that strangest of countries, ourselves.

It was by no means a passive, pallid knowledge that connected her with others. Margaret Laurence lived with a fierce desire for the future, a desire *for* the future, a desire that the future not just inherit the past but actively live to fulfil its own potential. Mistakes were something she recognized as human, and sometimes even enjoyed—but stupidity and bias were anathema. Impediments to understanding, they were the real

enemies of the future; they prevented people from making informed choices, prevented people from recognizing what moral behaviour really was, prevented them from valuing the consequences that their own actions would have on others. The stupid and the biased, whatever their declared allegiance to community, always live alone, and Margaret Laurence fought their brand of isolation passionately. She opposed racism, and championed the rights of women; she opposed bigotry, and sympathized with those whom social establishments had disenfranchised. Her essays and stories are full of insights into the selfishness that motivates intolerance, and the hope and desperation that alike sometimes mask as idiosyncrasy. Learning the edges of one's own limitations is not as easy task, but it's what Margaret Laurence asked of all her readers. Hers was a moral desire for the world, fed by a glimpse of an unselfish, true community in which persons, not positions, might thrive.

The broad outline of her life is familiar to readers of her books. Born Jean Margaret Wemyss in Neepawa, Manitoba, in 1926, she was early orphaned (throughout her life she was concerned with tales of roots and origins and home). She was deeply influenced by her Scots-Canadian heritage, her maternal grandfather's sense of order, and the electrifying narratives of the Old Testament: all of which she absorbed and resisted in equal measure, making them her own. Brought up by Margaret Simpson Wemyss (her aunt and stepmother, who figures prominently in the personal manuscript she was completing in the last months of her life), she went on to Winnipeg's United College in 1944. Married to an engineer, Jack Laurence (from 1947 until their separation in 1962), she lived for differing periods of time in Somaliland, the Gold Coast, Vancouver, and England, raising two children, and from 1953 on, publishing regularly. In 1974 she returned permanently to Canada, to live in Lakefield, Ontario; for a term, she was Chancellor of nearby Trent University in Peterborough. Her works were translated into several languages. She won an enthusiastic readership in France, Norway, Germany, and Italy as well as at home, and she was the recipient of many honours, both civil and academic.

The settings of her stories reflect her travels: from the Somali folktales with which she began her public career to the Vancouver of Stacey MacAindra's *The Fire-Dwellers*; from the Ghana of *The Tomorrow-Tamer* to the "Manawaka" Manitoba locale of Hagar's *The Stone Angel*, Vanessa's *A Bird in the House*, and Rachel's *A Jest of God*; from the Nigeria of her friend Chinua Achebe (whom she praised in *Long Drums and Cannons*, and who in turn honoured her understanding of Africa) to the England and Ontario of Morag Gunn's *The Diviners*, she wrote of what she knew. But these works are not in that strictest of senses autobiographical. What she knew extended beyond personal experience. Africa taught her to value ancestors as a way of reaching past them to the future. That's what the Manawaka Cycle then set out to do. In one direction it stretches from Hagar Shipley's childhood to Piquette Tonnerre's youth; in another it reaches from the town dump and the railway tracks and the burned-out Métis settlement to the offices of academe, the salons of propriety, and the many-storied castles-in-the-air—from all of which are dreams and disasters born.

An adept at the craft of words, Margaret Laurence never separated literature from the empirical world of class, gender, place, and age. The Manawaka Cycle focuses on people; it records how separate characters turn into *a* people; it flows, as *The Diviners* has it, both backwards and forwards at once, shaping words out of silence into rhythms of recognition. The way she wrote altered how Canadian writers responded to words. Through her, Canadian cadences became a language of art, rooted in place, yet shared. She proffered alternatives both to received formulas of historical value and to received equations between substance and speech. Canadian readers recognized themselves in her works; others have found there an intricate record of human relationships and the artistry of formal design. These are not exclusive reactions; they are complementary testaments to the continuing power of an ethical art.

That, as a community, we share a moral responsibility for the future was Margaret Laurence's constant theme. She dramatized it in a variety of ways, probing the lives of women, articulating the voices of tale-tellers and diviners. It is a theme she addressed directly in a speech called **"My Final Hour,"** which she gave at Trent University and later published in *Canadian Literature* 100. There is no secret of life, she said, "or any wisdom except the passionate plea of caring." "Cultivate the art of patience," she said. But learn. Learn actively. Avoid the deadly sin of despair. Learn compassion. Remember you are unique, and in so remembering, learn to honour others. "Know that your commitment is above all to life itself." These words—honour, caring, commitment, compassion—spell out what she held to be of value. They are qualities she would never have claimed to possess—only to be seeking to possess, in order to share—but she did possess them. They are part of the reason we collectively called her friend, and why we remember her. (pp. 221-23)

> W. H. New, "Margaret Laurence, 1926-1987," in Canadian Literature, No. 112, Spring, 1987, pp. 221-23.

BARRY CALLAGHAN

[*A Canadian poet, editor, critic, journalist, and short story writer, Callaghan is also founder and publisher of the influential literary magazine* Exile *and* Exile Editions, *a literary press. His works include* The Hogg Poems and Drawings *(1978),* The Road to Compostela *(1981), and* As Close As We Come *(1982). In the following excerpt, Callaghan recounts a conversation he had with Laurence in 1965, when the novelist lived in London. He relates Laurence's views on current literature, including her own writings, and her thoughts on being a Canadian author.*]

Letter home: London, November, 1965.

Went today to Margaret Laurence, who lives in a grey stucco cottage, Elm Cottage, in Penn, just outside of London. . . .

Mrs. Laurence is frenetic. She bolted into the room (the sitting-room is at most 10-by-10 with a tiny alcove to the side) shaking hands quickly, eagerly. She dropped two packages of Cadets onto a side table (Cadets, she said, because they are cheapest), then picked a package up, fumbled for matches, said, "Let's have no formality—call me Margaret and I'll call you Barry," and when I jokingly replied, "I'll go further . . . a hello kiss on the cheek," she said, "No, no, not that friendly," and lit up, throwing the matches onto the table. . . .

"The town where I was born," she said. "I don't think it ever occurred to me that I could spend the rest of my life being a writer. No one there ever had done this sort of thing, but I was very lucky, my mother had been a schoolteacher and was a great reader, so I grew up in a house that was full of books. Still, as a writer, I was probably a slow starter."

"Why did you have to go to Africa," I asked, drawing my chair close to hers, sitting in front of her, "before your imagination really stirred?" (p. 9)

"Well, probably because that whole countryside seems somehow less real than your own country, and therefore terribly exotic. This was tremendously exciting in a way I couldn't believe the Canadian Prairies could be exciting. I realize now that this is nonsense, of course."

"In Somaliland, what seems to have quickened your imagination was the Somali struggle to stay alive with a little dignity in a barren land. . . . Your novels and stories, they're essentially concerned with that primitive struggle, staying alive with just a little dignity?"

"I think this is absolutely true," she said, leaning forward in her chair, "and I think that you find—sort of unknown to yourself—that the same themes tend to emerge all the time in your writing. But when I was writing about Africa, the struggle to survive was strictly a physical struggle, whereas in *The Stone Angel* Hagar's struggle is not only to survive physically, but also to survive in an inner sense. The book I've just finished, *A Jest of God,* I can see the same theme, survival with some dignity, but it's more a question of survival of the personality in a world filled with enormous strains and tensions; survival becomes spiritual."

"Did the political strife in Africa stimulate this interest in survival?"

"The political situation," she said, spilling ashes in her lap, "stimulated an interest in human freedom which, back on the Prairies, I didn't know I had. With my first novel, the whole thing is the question of independence . . . political independence, but even at that time it was also an inner independence. I mean, Nkrumah said: 'Seek ye the political kingdom and all else will follow.' Well, I don't believe that. Freedom for me has become increasingly what is inside rather than what is outside."

"Would you say that's what's wrong with your first novel?"

"Yes, I certainly would. Yes, it's far too external."

"What about politics and the novel? You've written about the struggle between blacks and whites, and a number of short stories in the same context. Can the artist really deal with politics, get involved in actual political situations, without seeming to deliver messages?"

"Personally, I think not. I think very few writers, maybe none, can be novelists and political propagandists at the same time. I think they find themselves writing propaganda. It becomes propaganda rather than a novel because when a writer becomes highly political, he thinks he knows the answers and wants to make you hold the same political point of view, whereas a novel is almost always a kind of discovery. I don't think the writer herself knows entirely what's going to happen, or what's going to emerge, and she has to be prepared for the unexpected. In fact, you partly write to discover something you didn't know before." She laughed and lit another cigarette. "I think there's a very strong sort of evangelical strain in most political writers."

"What do you think of Doris Lessing in this respect? She's written about Rhodesia, you've written about Ghana. . . ."

"Well, I think that when Doris Lessing writes about relationships between people, whether they're Africans or Europeans, she's fine, she's at her best. But her political writing, I find quite quite dull, really. Where she is absolutely super is in this terrific ability for self-analysis; she is tremendously honest.''

"And the English writers in this country who've come out of the lower classes: Alan Sillitoe, or Arnold Wesker . . . is the laying on of a political point of view—in someone like Wesker—is that an attempt to cover up for a fundamental weakness?''

"I think with a great many writers whose obsession is a social or political theme, this is a kind of evasion, an attempt to look away from inner things. In other words, you focus entirely on the outside world." She shifted her black-rimmed harlequin glasses. "The outside world is terrifying, but not quite so terrifying as the inside world.''

"Well, American writers today seem preoccupied with the inner world, even the neurotic, what with characters coming apart at the seams, their conditions explored through elaborate symbols, or fantasy, or even the fancier forms of soft porn . . . but all your stories are technically quite straightforward, even quite old-fashioned. How do you see your work in relation to someone like Norman Mailer . . . or William Burroughs?''

"Well," and she rested her chin in her hand, smiling a little, "sometimes I see my work in terms of deep Celtic gloom, to tell you the truth. I think maybe some of those writers are too far out, and I say to myself, 'Margaret, you're too far in'—but I can't help it. The fact is, I know that my prose style is essentially a traditional one, but for me to try to change simply for the sake of changing, or for the sake of trying to be more 'with it' . . . this would be so phony, nothing would happen—except disaster. So all I can really do is to try and put down things according to my own way of seeing, and if the style changes naturally, by itself, and develops, well . . . well and good, and if it doesn't, I'm stuck with the idiom of myself. Whereas, probably at this point, I think people like Mailer can say a very great deal to people, particularly in the North American culture, which I know I can't.''

"Why can't you?''

"Well, I don't feel I can. The only thing, really, that concerns me is to try to put down things as I see them, because it is all you've got. You've just got your own pair of eyes, that's all, and the thing I would like to be able to do,'' she said taking a quick drag on her cigarette, "more than anything else is to create characters that step off the printed page, 'cause this is what really obsesses me, I suppose, more than anything else. This is still what I look for in a novel. What I'm interested in more than anything else is character. As for Mailer himself, I think that his last book was most unfairly panned.''

"Really? *An American Dream!*''

"Yes. I think it's a terrible book in many ways. . . .''

"I think it's an atrocious book. . . .''

"Well, I don't think it's atrocious," she insisted. "It shows a tremendous interest and understanding of basically the same thing that Hawthorne was writing about centuries ago. I mean, Mailer is obsessed with the problem of good and evil, particularly evil, and I think that in some parts of the book you get a marvelous picture of a man who is quite literally teetering on the brink of madness, but what happens, of course, is that the thing falls down again and again, because the writing starts off very strongly, in a particular chapter, and then it sort of falls to pieces.''

"Sure, he's concerned with evil, but he's got no conception of good. Isn't that where the whole book falls apart?''

"Yes, I think it probably does, just on exactly that, although I don't feel he has no concept of good—but that his concept of good seems pretty unsatisfactory, sort of saccharine . . . this terribly sweet girl who's just too good to be true . . . I didn't find her believable for one minute.''

"I'd say, thinking about right now . . . Mailer's *An American Dream,* Saul Bellow, Philip Roth . . . that their work is riddled with a hatred of women. . . .''

"I would've said *An American Dream* is far more a sort of self-hatred. I mean, the thing that bothers me most about Mailer is this terrifically strong sense of self-destruction. . . .''

" . . . And I think something of the reverse is true here in England, among women writers, a kind of hatred of men. . . .''

"Flamboyant women novelists who. . . .''

"Yes, Doris Lessing I think has a real hatred. . . .''

"Yes, so do I,'' she said. "But I don't think that this is necessarily true for some of the women novelists about whom this has been said, like Edna O'Brien, but as for Lessing. . . .''

"Who are the other American writers you're reading, on this side of the waters. . . .''

"Well, instantly my mind goes blank, I can't think of anything I've read within. . . .''

"Well. . . .''

"The last 15 years, but I liked Bellow's *Herzog,* it was a fantastically good novel, simply because the character of Moses Herzog came across to me so very strongly. . . .''

"What about Canadian writing?''

"I've just got Al Purdy's book of poems, *The Cariboo Horses,* which I like very much, too.''

"Were there any Canadian writers who touched you?''

"When I was quite young I read far more American and English writing, and then I lived away from Canada for quite a while.'' (pp. 9-10)

"You know,'' she said, "I think that I came to the point, writing about Africa, where I felt that if I continued to write about Africa I would be writing strictly as a tourist, and in fact might be spending the rest of my life as a tourist. I didn't want that. I started writing about Canada, it was very much a coming home, mentally, for the first time an attempt not to evade my own past and childhood. Essentially, the same thing very many writers do, come to terms with where you've come from, come to terms with what you are. This came out in **The Stone Angel.** There are many things, many discoveries I didn't like, in fact I deplore, but these things are also in myself, and this is where I came from, this is what I am. You don't get very far unless you come to some kind of terms with it. I don't really want to write anything any more except about people that I can know a bit from the inside.''

"And you've just finished a novel!''

"Yes, I'm very happy, deliriously happy about this, *A Jest of God.* What it's about is an unmarried schoolteacher, a woman in a small Prairie town, Manawaka again, a person who doesn't really make very much contact with the rest of the world, who is very withdrawn and shut in, and it really is the story of her attempt to break out of this kind of shell and also to break away from the influences of the past. . . .''

"Is this the same survival. . . .''

"It is really survival, yes. . . .''

"Getting a little dignity by breaking out. . . .''

"That's right, and also finding even in the most personally appalling circumstances that sometimes you discover dignity at the very depths of the pit, as it were," she said, her gaiety gone, turned inward. "You know. . . .''

"Well, you've gone back to Manawaka in your imagination, and now your Manawaka woman's trying to break out, but you're still here living in England. Why is that?''

"It's just sort of chance, really. At the moment I like it here. I like living close to London. I've gained quite a bit through having met a number of English writers and publishers and so on but I don't intend to stay here for the rest of my life. I'll go back to Canada.''

"What do you make of the whole business of Canadianism? I remember one of the reviewers of *The Stone Angel* said that the real merit of this fine new book was its Canadianism.''

"Really, I feel so," and she closed her eyes, as if in pain, "I feel so strongly against that point of view. I think the thing that matters least about a novel is whether it's Canadian or American or English or African, or what it is. I think the only thing that matters is whether it's a good novel and I hate really to have my writing talked about as Canadian writing. I mean, it is Canadian writing because I'm Canadian, but this is not the central thing. This is not important. It isn't important for me to try to be a Canadian writer—I wouldn't dream of trying—but the only thing that one wants is to be a reasonably good writer. And I think, if only Canadians could quit talking about Canadian writing. We're far more sort of self-conscious about this than other people are. . . .''

"Don't you fear, when you come back to Canada, getting caught up in the whole business of being a Canadian writer, promoting Canadian culture?''

"I don't know whether this is a tactless thing to say or not, but I really am very much afraid of this. In one sense, this is a reason why I'd rather stay here for the moment, because I do think that with the best will in the world, in Canada, the writer gets too much recognition for too small a body of work. This sounds so terribly ungrateful, but I'm not ungrateful you know. I'm terribly pleased that my books have sold well in Canada and so on . . . but I don't think it's a very good idea for a young writer—not that I'm all that young—but a beginning writer to have a great deal of attention given over one or two books. The whole thing is, can you continue, can you go on to where you've written maybe three, four, five novels and then we can see whether you're a good novelist or not. This is really all I want to do.'' (pp. 11-12)

She went on talking with animation about Canada, and how the idea of the "land" has been overplayed and what interests her is people, not poplar trees. She remembers her little town not as picturesque or landscape, but as the home of her domineering grandfather, a man hated by his children and his children's children. That experience, she insisted, was far more interesting, overpowering, than any mound of rock, clump of trees or CPR train-track across the tundra.

She said she would like to live in Toronto, where she could have a coterie of friends, people she could talk with: she yearns for Canada, though Vancouver was apparently a hell, trapped in a world of engineers (the only reference to her husband). Especially, she wants her children to be in Canadian universities, again for social reasons.

When I left she seemed a little sad to see me go, though she was hearty and abrupt in her farewells. . . .

I drove away under a grey sky. It was drizzling. I looked back, the cottage almost hidden by half-dead autumn foliage, a frail wisp of smoke from the stove. I felt she was very alone and vulnerable there, that she must come home and settle. (p. 12)

> Barry Callaghan, "Margaret Laurence in England," in Books in Canada, *Vol. 16, No. 2, March, 1987, pp. 9-12.*

ROBERT FULFORD

[*Fulford, a Canadian journalist and critic, is the editor of* Saturday Night. *His books include* This Was Expo *(1968)*, An Introduction to the Arts in Canada *(1977)*, *and* Canada: A Celebration *(1983)*. Fulford, a friend of Laurence's, interviewed her for CBC Radio in 1974. In the following excerpt, he provides an overview of Laurence's career.]

In one of her rare public appearances, at Trent University in 1983, Margaret Laurence told a little joke about a brain surgeon meeting a novelist. The surgeon says, "Oh, you're a novelist, eh? When I retire, I plan to take up novel writing." The novelist replies, "How interesting. When I retire, I plan to take up brain surgery." That story asserted Laurence's proud knowledge that writing well is as complex as any enterprise on earth and satirized all those fools who smugly imagine that only a lack of time keeps them from being authors. But it also illustrated the paradox of fiction, which is that it appears to be something anyone can do. Brain surgery, after all, requires an expensive education, a place in a hospital, and a platoon of helpers, prerequisites that clearly set the brain surgeon far above most of us. A writer needs only a pad and pencil. This is what gives novelists their special potency as public figures and makes them, when they succeed, more admired and cherished than other intellectuals and artists: we understand intuitively that they are like us, only much more so. Of literate humans, only a minority can write with any verve, a smaller minority can tell absorbing stories, and a still smaller nucleus can write books that embody the shared concerns of society. In this elite group, this aristocracy of scribblers, Laurence—who died in January, at the age of sixty—was a commanding figure for more than two decades. Her life and her writing, which were so entwined that they overlapped and blurred in the public imagination, summarized the ideals of a whole Canadian generation.

The drama of her career took a classic shape: the lonely bookish provincial reacts against small-town life and leaves it, finds that she can't escape her background, and finally redeems it by exhibiting its emotional riches to the world. Literary history tells that story again and again, in every conceivable setting—in the United States, in the first half of this century, it was acted out most famously by Thomas Wolfe, whose autobiographical novels brought Asheville, North Carolina, and a thousand towns like it, into American culture. Like Wolfe, Peggy Wemyss regarded the place where she was born—Neepawa, Manitoba, a farming centre about 125 miles northwest of Winnipeg—as narrow and stultifying. "When I was eighteen," she wrote when she was forty-five, ''I couldn't wait to get out of that town, away from the prairies. I did not know then that I would carry the land and town all my life within my skull, that they would form the mainspring and source of the writing I was to do. . . .'' Like Wolfe, she discovered as she grew older that she had absorbed every nuance of her town's social life and moral imagination; when finally she recast Neepawa as Manawaka, it served as background or jumping-off place for her most admired work—*The Stone Angel, A Jest of God, The Fire-Dwellers, A Bird in the House,* and *The Diviners.* Through her, Neepawa, or its fictional shadow, became familiar territory to hundreds of thousands of readers, and just before her death—as if completing some magic circle—the Margaret Laurence Home Committee Inc. was raising $160,000 to restore 312 First Avenue, the house she lived in from age nine to age eighteen.

She was writing even before she arrived at First Avenue and by the time she was twelve she had filled two school notebooks with a novel; neatly anticipating her own role in the making of our national literature, she called it *Pillars of the Nation.* ''I have been writing most of my life,'' she once said, ''and always knew that I wanted to be a writer, but did not believe for many years that this was something one could do as a profession.'' Books were made by people far away; she could move towards the exalted status of author only by slow, hesitant steps.

Alongside this standard pattern, of fiction seeded obscurely in an isolated young mind, her own story accommodated another familiar romance: the orphan who spends much of her life seeking human connection. Peggy's mother died when she was four, her father when she was ten; the rest of her upbringing was in the hands of her stepmother and grandfather. Perhaps as a result, readers of her fiction were persistently invited to contemplate the meaning of intricate human relationships. Families, clans, tribes were never far from her concern, whether she was writing about tribal culture in her African stories, or studying her own ancestors in Scotland, or consciously forming a link with the Métis in *The Diviners.* These themes brought her characters, and her novels, into the mainstream of the Canadian life of her time and helped make her an emblematic figure. Where an American writer of this century goes forth into the world as a raging individualist—again, Wolfe is the prototype—Laurence expressed, in her books and elsewhere, the more Canadian yearning for community. In her last ten years or so, as a guiding spirit among Canadian writers, she liked to call her profession a ''tribe,'' not only in recognition of the comfort she took from her peers but as a statement of her abiding philosophy.

That philosophy, or set of impulses, became clear in the late 1960s, as the child of Neepawa turned into the mother-figure of Canadian fiction. It was the product, above all, of the West, and in particular of the western history that shaped Canadian social democracy through radical politics and a network of public institutions. One of those institutions was United College in Winnipeg, where Peggy Wemyss enrolled in 1944 and imbibed the United Church tradition—Methodism mixed with the Scots-Presbyterianism of her own background—that was turning into the secularized Christianity we long ago learned to call ''the social gospel.'' Ever after, the aroma of that peculiarly Canadian brew rose from the pages of her books. Whatever was kindly and compassionate in her stories, and whatever was sentimental and uncritical in her essays, echoed that tradition. And because so many other people shaped by the same tradition were helping to set the tone of Canadian

life, Laurence in her maturity became their exemplar, a figure not only in literary history but in the larger history of the Canadian imagination.

More than anyone else of her generation in English-speaking Canada, she lived the vocation of the public writer, conscientiously turning the chaos of life and the feelings of the moment into books that became monuments to her society and its dreams. For this role she seemed, on the surface, altogether unsuited. She was never at ease in controversy. When mean-minded Christian fundamentalists tried to have her work banned from the schools, she reacted not with the contempt the fundamentalists deserved but with mortification and dismay. Other serious writers learn to laugh off such assaults; Laurence's friends reported that she was profoundly hurt, and perhaps her pain was a measure of how close she felt to the community around her. But when speaking in public, even to people who loved her, she was visibly terrified. Her friend Timothy Findley wrote: ''Margaret Laurence had to contend with a body whose nervous system tended to betray her just when she needed it most to be strong. She shook. Her knees gave way. Her hands could be seen . . . reaching for the backs of chairs and the tops of tables—anything to hold her up and stop her from shaking.''

What is most surprising about her, in retrospect, is that her career as a serious writer was—in comparison with most literary careers—so short. Just fourteen years elapsed between the appearance of her first novel, *This Side Jordan,* in 1960, and her last, *The Diviners,* in 1974. Yet in that period she altered our literary geography. In Africa, where she went in her twenties as wife to a civil engineer, John Laurence, she made contact with an alien culture in a way that few Canadian writers have ever done—*The Tomorrow-Tamer* contains superb stories of west African life as it reacted to the violent changes of the 1950s and *The Prophet's Camel Bell* puts Laurence's readers in astonishingly intimate contact with Somaliland. When finally she turned to her own country, she made the Canadian West freshly available as a subject of fiction. Under her influence it became not just the location of a few beautiful but singular books—for instance, *As For Me and My House,* by Sinclair Ross, which helped inspire her—but the source of an endless river of novels carrying the post-pioneer experience of the prairies to the rest of Canada and beyond. Finally, Laurence, more than anyone else, placed heroic and formidable women at the centre of our literature; the heroines she created, above all Hagar Shipley in *The Stone Angel,* made the triumphs of women in modern Canada into a powerful theme. her books often became texts for Canadian feminists, a use she didn't overtly encourage but didn't disdain either. And they became staples of Canadian-literature courses in the high schools and universities, putting her view of Canada, and women, before the generations that followed her.

When those books were appearing—five novels, two books of stories, a book of criticism, a travel book, all in the same fourteen years—her career didn't seem as remarkable as it was. It appeared altogether natural, in fact, and most of her readers assumed, as I did, that it would go on indefinitely. I was astonished when she told me across a CBC radio microphone in 1974, a couple of days before *The Diviners* appeared, that she would probably write no more novels. She had said what she had to say, she felt. Many of us believed that this was a temporary notion, induced by the effort of writing *The Diviners.* But it turned out to be prophetic. From the age of forty-eight until her death she wrote no more adult fiction; just some work for children, a few essays, and the memoir that may appear this autumn, *Dance on the Earth.* It was as if she had been given some messages to deliver, delivered them, and then fell silent. (pp. 5-6)

Robert Fulford, "Orphan from Neepawa," in Saturday Night, Vol. 102, No. 5, May, 1987, pp. 5-6.

ANNE BURKE

[*Burke, a Canadian writer and editor, edits the* Prairie Journal of Canadian Literature. *In the following excerpt, she examines three major themes in Laurence's writings: small town life in the Canadian prairies, the importance of ethnic identity, and women's struggle against patriarchal authority.*]

Laurence was born Jean Margaret Wemyss in 1926 in Neepawa, Manitoba, one-hundred and twenty-five miles northwest of Winnipeg. Neepawa (in Cree meaning abundance) was incorporated by her grandfather. He married Margaret Harrison, the daughter of D. H. Harrison who was the premier of Manitoba. Her stepmother was responsible for founding the town's public library. Laurence's first short story was written for the *Winnipeg Free Press* when she was twelve, at which time she invented the fictional setting of Manawaka. She would later use details like the Whitemud River as the Wachakwa River; Riding Mountain on Clear Lake became Galloping Mountain on Diamond Lake.

Laurence attended Neepawa Collegiate and afterwards, on a Manitoba scholarship, United College in Winnipeg. She worked briefly as a reporter for the *Winnepeg Citizen* and as a registrar for the YWCA in Winnipeg.

In her articles Laurence frequently commented on how she saw herself as a small-town prairie person. In **"A Place to Stand On"**, she explained how all her writing set in Canada, whether the setting is Manitoba or not, contained her memories of the physical appearance of the prairies. (*The Stone Angel* and *The Diviners* are excellent examples.) Her early feelings were ambivalent because she wanted both to leave and to retain the protective environment.

According to Laurence:

I felt the loneliness and the isolation of the land itself, and yet I always considered southern Manitoba to be very beautiful, and I still do. I doubt if I will ever live there again, but those poplar bluffs and the blackness of that soil and the way in which the sky is open from one side of the horizon to the other—these are things I will carry inside my skull for as long as I live with the vividness of recall that only our first home can have for us.

In her introduction to *The Lamp at Noon and Other Stories* by Sinclair Ross, Laurence said he had an enormous impact on her writing since she read the novel *As For Me and My House* at eighteen, "for it seemed the only completely genuine one I had ever read about my people, my one place, my own time." Selections from her work have been anthologized in collections of prairie writing like *Horizon: Writings of the Canadian Prairie* edited by Ken Mitchell, *Writers of the Prairies* compiled by Donald Stephens, and *The Prairie Experience* edited by Terry Angus.

Laurence first read W. L. Morton's *Manitoba: A History* (1957) the summer that she began writing the draft of her most ambitious undertaking to date, *The Diviners.* Although she had read many prairie histories previously, she preferred Morton's. He gave her not only facts which she needed, but also the

sweep of history, a shared overview confirmed in subsequent conversations between them. In correspondence with Clara Thomas, Laurence wrote:

I share, most of all, with Morton, the sense of my place, the prairies, and of my people (meaning all prairie people) within the context of their many and varied histories, and the desire to make all these come alive in the reader's mind.

Laurence was fond of a quotation from the poem "Roblin Mills Circa 1842" by Al Purdy: "they had their being once / and left a place to stand on" which she used as an epigram for *The Diviners.* Her immediate ancestors, both patrilineal and matrilineal, were well-documented in her novels and short stories. Her maternal grandfather John Simpson was an undertaker and cabinet maker, a pioneer in western Canada, who as a boy had walked from Winnipeg to Portage la Prairie after coming to Manitoba by steamer. (He became Grandfather Connor of *A Bird in the House.*) Her father Robert Wemyss and his brother John survived the first World War in France. John, who worked for the United Grain Growers in Wilkie, Saskatchewan, and Robert who (with his wife) died when Laurence was still a child figured prominently in *The Diviners.*

Laurence commented on her own ancestors in an interview for *Journal of Canadian Fiction:*

My family began in Scotland and I was brought up with a great knowledge of my Scots background, but it took me a long time—in fact I was really grown up—before I recognized that, in point of fact, these ancestors were very far away me and that Scotland was just an ancestral memory, almost in a Jungian sense . . . I had to come back and . . . examine my own family, my own roots . . . this is what I have done.

In a note Laurence remarked that she had written many articles about the question of where one belongs and why, and meaning to oneself of ancestors, both the long-ago ones and those in remembered history, before she ever dealt with it fictionally. In **"Road from the Isles"** Laurence stated that she came to a greater understanding of the Scots' clan system through her knowledge of the tribal system in Africa. In **"Men of Our People"** she compared the 1885 uprising of the Metis to the battle of Culloden in 1746 when the clansmen were literally "mowed down" by the British. She viewed both groups as defending a primitive culture against a complex civilization.

She did not read Mannoni's *Prospero and Caliban: A Study of the Psychology of Colonization* (1956) until 1960, but she may have had "dormant" the affinity for the oppressed which this French ethnographer suggested was the problem for human beings. However much people differ from one another, they must possess the will to understand one another.

In Laurence's terms this meant the Biblical injunction from Exodus 23:9 which she chose as an epigram for her collected essays:

Also, thou shalt not oppress a stranger: for ye know the heart of a stranger, seeing ye were strangers in the land of Egypt.

She always based her writing firmly on this foundation, as she explored her affinity with others in ever expanding dimensions throughout her career.

In **"The Loons"** Laurence introduced the Tonnerre family. Here Vanessa's grandmother views the Metis as "neither flesh, fowl, not good salt herring". Their *patois* is full of obscenities.

The men like Old Jules and his son Lazarus do odd jobs or survive on relief. Piquette suffers from tuberculosis. She is vaguely embarrassing for Vanessa, but also generates a new awareness. The false models of Hiawatha and Pauline Johnson do not fit the reality of disease and despair any more than do the mythic proportions of Big Bear, poundmaker, Tecumseh, or the Indian that "ate Father Brebeuf's heart." Piquette is a "dead loss" as an Indian in that respect. Still, she is both a reproach and a mystery, who seeks in marriage to an Englishman what she so bitterly rejected, and dies in a fire. Vanessa observes that Diamond Lake from where the loons have fled was renamed for the tourists with the Indian-sounding name Lake Wapakata. The wild birds like Piquette have gone away, simply died out, or ceased to care.

Stacey has an affair with a writer named Luke Venturi in *The Fire-Dwellers* and it is mentioned on more than one occasion that Luke is wearing an Indian sweater. Stacey wants to begin the world again with him, this time with no lies and no recriminations. We are told that Luke is from a large family and his father works for a building contractor. Luke's unfinished novel *The Greyfolk* is about this continent as desert, the few remaining people being governed by African administrators. The greyfolk can be educated but they are naive, without a knowledge of their past conflagration.

In *A Jest of God* the Ukrainians like the Cree seem to Rachel to be more emotionally free to speak out than the Scots. Yet the town is divided between them, like oil and water. Rachel is the undertaker's daughter who has an affair with Nick Kazlik the milkman's son. Nick is ashamed of his heritage, never making the attempt to learn his family's native language, and he prefers urban values to rural ones. Unlike Nick, Rachel is able to free herself because she faces her past.

There are passing references to the Parthenon Cafe operated by Miklos, the lobby of the Queen Victoria hotel, the Regal Cafe owned by the Chinese Toy who is separated from his wife. These are examples of the varying success ethnics have in attempting to transplant Old World values in the new land.

Laurence referred to *The Diviners* as a very Canadian book. I believe Morag's quest can be seen as the odyssey of a nation, orphaned by its parent countries, who seeks identity among false or inauthentic models. Caught between the old and new pioneers, it has no need of them. (Laurence said, "Scratch a Canadian and you will find a phony pioneer" in **"Where the World Begins".**) One needs to understand the past, the role of tradition and the individual talent in this portrait of the artist as a young woman. School represents a false, if dominant, culture. The sale of the family farm is the lost birthright. Morag is raised in the Logan home and learns from her foster father stories about the Sutherlanders, the Red River settlement, and other Scottish legends of Riel but learns to reconcile them. Morag relinquishes the idea of Scotland for her real home in the prairie town of Manawaka.

In Laurence's novels the women characters are paired with men whose children they attempt to bear. These are Prospero/Caliban combinations (or Apollonian/Dionysian pairs, if you prefer). The women attempt to overcome the old standards of Victorian sexuality and racism, but are in transition, gradually overcoming the loss of parents or parental figures. Nick's sister Julie separates from her truck driver husband before he commits suicide. Piquette dies after leaving or being abandoned by her white husband and her three children die with her in the Tonnerre shack. Morag's daughter Pique (named for Piquette) has

difficulty in a white society. Yet she comes the closest to the Metis metaphor, a vision of the new Canada described by George Melnyk. Unlike the Indian who is the other half of Western history (with the Anglo) the Metis can be a model for those wishing to replace a unitary Anglo society (colonial, anti-west) because it is concerned with extension of the mother country. In "The Metis Metaphor" section of *Radical Regionalism* Melnyk argues that it is a metaphor full of possibilities, one which acknowledges that to be a westerner means a mix of the indigenous and the foreign. The western consciousness is a half-breed consciousness, and he points out the irony that the most dispossessed group in society should provide a model and an identity for all Westerners.

Laurence explained in an interview for *Journal of Canadian Fiction:*

> It took me many years to see that in point of fact what we were doing—not just myself, but almost all Canadian writers—was to try in some way to come to terms with our ancestral past, to deal with these themes of survival, of freedom and growth, and to record our mythology . . . our history . . . perhaps not consciously, but after a while consciously. . . .

Ethnicity forces the characters to face their homelands or the past which is elsewhere than the new land. They encounter the problems of assimilation and experience a split or separation (the duality which Melnyk mentions). If they fear change, they may become like the moles of Laurence's juvenile novella *Jason's Quest* and be dying of boredom. Her major characters seek authentic values in kinship, the Manitoba prairie, family, ancestors, the land, legends, oral culture, whether the poetry tree to shelter the African poor or folk songs in the contemporary world. Her summary of Nigerian dramatists and novelists in *Long Drums and Cannons* may be applied to herself when she spoke of writers being a tribe, and the value of the past.

What is a feminist to make of father?

Laurence saw herself as an iconoclast when it came to her female characters. In **"Ten Years' Sentences"** she said:

> I was fed up with the current fictional portraits of women of my generation—middle-aged mums, either being presented as glossy magazine types, perfect, everloving and incontestably contented, or else as sinister and spiritually cannibalistic monsters determined only to destroy their men and kids by hypnotic means. I guess there are women like the latter, but I don't happen to know any of them. There are no women like the former; they don't exist.

Laurence chose not to adopt the mantle of the feminist movement, perhaps because so much of her work predated the contemporary feminist movement. In "Face to Face" she declared herself "90% in agreement with Women's Lib",

> I don't think enough attention has been paid to the problems men have . . . These are our husbands, our sons, our lovers . . . we can't live without them, and we can't go to war against them.

However, in *Quarry* she did review *Surfacing* by Margaret Atwood as a "Rites of Passage" which corresponded with her own novel *The Diviners*. The narrator is on a quest, a descent into dark regions. She returns with knowledge of her own power (which had frightened her and which she had therefore denied) and a knowledge of her previous unwillingness to be a victim who had victimized others. It is a quest for archetypal parents, or our gods in the face of death. Interestingly enough, a blue heron figures prominently in both novels.

Atwood reviewed *The Diviners* in "Face to Face" by defending it against sexist reviewers. She praised the divorced woman on her own, the reversal of Morag as rejected parent and Christie as saint. According to Marian Engel ("It's the Grit. Laurence is unforgettable because she is us,") Morag is an outsider, a woman without a man, from the wrong side of the tracks, a writer seeking family ties.

I believe the insights offered by feminist psychologist Julia Kristeva, combined with a working knowledge of O. Mannoni will make clear how Laurence perceived the role of woman. Mannoni compared colonial society to the individual personality in Freudian terms. Europeans represent the father figure. As paternal administrators they require ego assurance from their dependents in order to suppress their own feelings of inferiority. The native, removed from tribal life, feels abandoned by his master. His oedipal instincts erupt in hostility, even violence. (Laurence acknowledged that she had little sympathy for the Europeans, despite rewriting these passages in *This Side Jordan*.) For Kristeva, who rejects Freud and rewrites Lacan, the uniquely feminine is at once within the symbolic order of modern class society dominated by the Law which the father embodies and is relegated to society's margins because she is judged inferior to masculine power.

Some basic parallels must be drawn between women and other oppressed groups. In her works Laurence was concerned with the African native, the Metis, the prairie, the Canadian nation. Each was struggling for freedom, an inner liberation, against great odds, the paternal oppressors or archetypal parents being European administrators, the assimilation policy, eastern Canada, European parent countries, respectively. In *The Diviners* Morag learns to reject imprisonment in a tower, whether the prince is Christie over "Prin" her Stepmother or Brooke Skelton her professor and husband. At various stages in Morag's limited understanding she rejects the false fathers/lovers and establishes an identity on her own. In very personal respects Laurence came to terms with her authoritarian grandfather whom she hated for his domination of women, a process she dramatized in *A Bird in the House*.

In her writing Laurence reassessed tribal leaders, whether African (Ibo, Hausa), Metis or Scots. She attacked authoritarianism as a betrayal. It was "like knowing, really knowing, that one's father intended, if he could, to murder you," she said in **"Road from the Isles"**. She attacked imperialism, while acknowledging we are all imperialists. She praised the anarchical society of the Metis, men like Riel and Dumont in **"Men of Our People"**. She attacked cultural primitivism as marginality, and revered an oral culture which is androgynous.

In conclusion, for Laurence, women, like Africans, children, the Canadian nation, must resist the colonizers, the class structure we have inherited, the patriarchal society of the father, husband, would-be lover—imperialism in all of its manifestations.

Anne Burke, "Margaret Laurence: Prairie, Ancestors, Woman," in Cross-Canada Writers' Quarterly, *Vol. 9, No. 2, 1987, pp. 16-17, 29.*

Primo Levi

July 31, 1919 - April 11, 1987

(Also published under the pseudonym of Damiano Malabaila) Italian memoirist, short story writer, novelist, poet, and essayist.

(See also *CLC*, Vol. 37; *Contemporary Authors*, Vols. 13-16, rev. ed.; and *Contemporary Authors New Revision Series*, Vol. 12.)

PRINCIPAL WORKS

Se questo un uomo (memoirs) 1947
[*If This Is a Man*, 1959; also published as *Survival in Auschwitz: The Nazi Assault on Humanity*, 1961]
La tregua (memoirs) 1958
[*The Reawakening*, 1965; also published as *The Truce: A Survivor's Journey Home from Auschwitz*, 1965]
Storie naturali [as Damiano Malabaila] (short stories) 1966
Vizio di forma (essays) 1971
Il sistema periodico (short stories) 1975
[*The Periodic Table*, 1984]
Shema: Collected Poems of Primo Levi (poetry) 1976
La chiave a stella (novel) 1978
[*The Monkey's Wrench*, 1986; also published as *The Wrench*, 1987]
Lilit e altri racconti (short stories) 1981
[*Moments of Reprieve*, 1986]
Se non ora, quando? (novel) 1982
[*If Not Now, When?* 1985]
Ad ora incerta (poetry) 1984
L'altrui mestiere (essays) 1986
I sommersi e i salvati (essays) 1986
[*The Drowned and the Saved*, 1988]

© *Jerry Bauer*

DAVID DENBY

[*Denby, an American critic, writes film reviews for* New York *magazine. In the following excerpt, written in the year before Levi's death, Denby offers commentary on Levi's life and works, calling him "one of the outstandingly beautiful and moving writers of our time."*]

Reading the first few pages of *Survival in Auschwitz*, Primo Levi's recently reissued 1947 memoir, one is at first impressed, then grateful, then astonished. How is it possible that this book, and its equally remarkable sequel, *The Reawakening* (1961), are not famous in America? If one comes to Levi's early books after reading his later works—*The Periodic Table, If Not Now, When?* and *Moments of Reprieve*—one isn't quite prepared for the dramatic nature of his achievement. *The Periodic Table,* a combined memoir and chemico-metaphysical lark, is a kind of eccentric triumph, but Levi's two Holocaust volumes are the fulfillment of a literary ideal long imagined yet widely thought impossible.

Judging the quality of Holocaust literature is, to put it mildly, a delicate business. To misunderstand, or be misunderstood, would be too awful; a literary judgment might be taken as a dismissal of the experience behind the writing (for as experience, certainly, the past of the Holocaust writers is all on the same level, and beyond judgment). Even to praise one writer or another seems odd, discomforting, an assertion of mere opinion when so much more than a literary response is called for.

As everyone knows, the resources of literature are considerably straitened by such a subject. Anyone giving way to moral indignation sounds horribly inadequate in the face of such crimes. And art can offer little refuge. Too many ideas, too much literary brilliance, too much metaphor, symbol, irony—in a word, too much art—may strike us as a vulgarity and an imposition. In weak or grandiose moods, we may be tempted to think that silence is the best of all responses to the unendurable. "The world of Auschwitz lies outside speech as it lies outside

323

reason,'' wrote George Steiner in 1963. ''To speak of the *unspeakable* is to risk the survivance of language as a creator and bearer of humane, rational truth. Words that are saturated with lies or atrocity do not easily resume life.'' In Steiner's influential view, the collapse of German civilization in the Nazi period called into question the value of literature itself.

But Levi, a survivor of Auschwitz, did not suffer the losses to sensibility that many writers about Auschwitz considered almost inevitable. A chemist by trade, shocked into writing by his ordeal, Levi produced books that are precisely a triumph of sensibility. He writes with an even plainness of manner, a refined simplicity and lucidity that encompasses, in the same breath, pain and degradation and the most noble ideals. He is direct and specific, yet never lurid. His suffering and the suffering of others made him an impassioned man, but the emotion finds release in a prose mournful yet tough, grave yet unceremonious, personal yet never self-aggrandizing. The quiet style achieves subtlety, even wit. One might have thought that heavenly angels of gentleness presided at his birth—and then one remembers the experience they condemned him to write about.

In comparison to the high-flown severity of most writing about the Holocaust, Levi's modest effort at description and understanding might seem naive. And perhaps that is why *Survival in Auschwitz* did not cause much of a stir when it first appeared. Here was a survivor, clearly an intellectual, who was innocent of theories about totalitarianism and Nazism, innocent of prophecy and despair. In this book, and in his later work, he was, of all things, a kind of 19th-century humanist—the most ridiculed, the most despised, the most inadequate of all postwar intellectual types. Like some heroically oblivious silent-film actor who maintains his calm amid the whirlings of nature, this old-fashioned and orderly person, this *gentleman,* was absurdly at large not only in the 20th century, but in the worst catastrophe the century had to offer.

A humanist after Auschwitz! There is something almost comical, but immensely satisfying, in the paradox of Levi's identity. He not only violates our sense of what a survivor should be, he violates our sense of what a modern writer should be. He lacks fierceness, anguish, a taste for extremity. He has little drive toward self-examination and none toward self-laceration, no interest in exhuming his soul in all its perversities. He is not a great imaginative genius like Joyce, Kafka, or Céline. And yet he is the great memoirist of the Holocaust—certainly the most extreme of all memories—and one of the outstandingly beautiful and moving writers of our time. As Lionel Trilling said of Orwell, his not being a genius is part of the reason we value him.

Primo Levi was born in Turin in 1919, the child of middle-class Jews with substantial roots in the tolerant soil of northern Italy. Thoroughly assimilated, Levi's family, like most Italian Jews, did not speak Yiddish but an eccentric and seemingly contradictory mixture of the Piedmontese dialect (''rugged, sober, and laconic. . .never written except on a bet'') and bits of Hebrew (''snatched from the language of the fathers, sacred and solemn, geologic''). At the beginning of *The Periodic Table,* published in Italy in 1975, a charming, almost unclassifiable book—part memoir, part scientific treatise, part rumination on such topics as companionship, solitude, and the profession of chemistry as an entry point to the great mysteries of existence—Levi makes an elaborate comparison of his ancestors to argon, a gas that will not interact with any other element:

> Not all of them were materially inert, for that was not granted them. . .But there was no doubt they were inert in their inner spirits, inclined to disinterested speculation, witty discourses, elegant, sophisticated, and gratuitous discussion. It can hardly be by chance that all the deeds attributed to them, though quite various, have in common a touch of the static, an attitude of dignified abstention, of voluntary (or accepted) relegation to the margins of the great river of life.

In describing his family in this ruefully celebratory way, Levi sets the background for his own ironic self-portrait. The character who appears in all three autobiographical volumes is essentially an observer—detached, self-protecting, a young man of moderate temperament without a taste for struggle. Trained in Turin as a chemist, he seems to have found a student's cloistered life, with its regulated competition and achievements, quite congenial. One gets the impression of a quiet, shy, rather defensively haughty young scientist-craftsman, proud of his abilities yet modest in his demands on life.

After school (in the late 1930s) he takes a variety of jobs as a chemist, his career restricted but far from destroyed by the 1938 racial laws. Toward fascism he and his friends cultivate an attitude of contempt, a mood of rejection more aesthetic than political, and entirely inactive. He is drifting, waiting for life to begin:

> We proclaimed ourselves the enemies of Fascism, but actually Fascism had had its effect on us, as on almost all Italians, alienating us and making us superficial, passive and cynical. . .Each of us did his or her work by day, slackly, without believing in it, as happens to someone who knows he is not working for his own future.

Only after the collapse in July 1943 of Mussolini's government, and the beginning of the Nazi occupation of northern Italy, does Levi join the partisans. He is not a communist, a socialist, or a Catholic. He makes the decision without moral or ideological support—as an extension of sensibility, almost—and it is not a success: ''We were cold and hungry, the most disarmed partisans in the Piedmont, and probably also the most unprepared.'' He is immediately betrayed and arrested, and during interrogation, ''partly out of fatigue, but partly out of a sudden surge. . .of haughty pride,'' he admits to being a Jew. The fascists turn him over to the Germans, who deport him to Auschwitz. Years later, in an autobiographical piece written in 1982, Levi dryly summarized the rest:

> The railroad convey that took us to the Lager contained 650 persons; of these, 525 were immediately put to death; 29 women were interned at Birkenau; 96 men, myself among them, were sent to Monowitz-Auschwitz, a *Nebenlager* belonging to I. G. Farbenindustrie. Of these, only about 20 of the men and women returned to their homes. I survived imprisonment by a fortunate chain of circumstances: by never falling ill; by the help of an Italian brick-layer; by being able to work two months as a chemist in an I. G. Farbenindustrie laboratory. I was liberated thanks to the rapid advance of the Red Army in January, 1945. . .During my imprisonment, despite the hunger, the cold, the blows, the fatigue, the gradual death of my companions, the promiscuity of all hours, I experienced an intense need to recount how much I was living. . .

The book produced in answer to that need, in 1947, was called, in its British version, *If This Is a Man* (a literal translation), and in its current American edition, *Survival in Auschwitz.*

Levi, it should be said, was relatively fortunate. His immediate family was not deported; he did not endure before his own eyes, as millions of others did, the death of parents, children, brothers, sisters. He was randomly beaten, as almost all prisoners were, but never tortured. He was not one of the Jews forced to participate in the extermination process itself. He was even able to work, for a while, at his own trade. Surely his pardon from the very worst made it easier for him to write as he did, to compose a record of cruelty and misery almost detached in its clarity. Perhaps literature is possible only in the absence of the final degree of suffering.

In the early pages of *Survival in Auschwitz,* the prisoners, in this case Italian Jews, ride across Europe in freight cars, arrive at the Birkenau siding, and are immediately divided into those to be gassed right away and those to be held in the camp, or moved to related camps, as laborers. There follows an account, superb in its terse eloquence but also familiar, of the steps that reduced Levi and the other Italians to a state of numb abjection by the indoctrination procedures at Monowitz-Buna, the subsidiary camp to which Levi was assigned. The men are then given their work, excruciatingly difficult physical labor. At night, they are forced to sleep in pairs on straw mattresses no more than two feet wide—a space so narrow they have to sleep end to end, each facing the other's feet.

The nights are filled with awful dreams, and also a more immediate problem. Fed nothing but water soup during the day, the men need to relieve themselves every few hours. Yet the block has no latrine, only a bucket next to the night-guard, a bucket that has to be emptied, when it is full, by the last person who uses it. The veteran prisoners know a way out of this: they have "retined their senses to such a degree that, while still in their bunks, they are miraculously able to distinguish if the level is at a dangerous point, purely on the basis of the sound that the sides of the bucket make." Thus the job of removal falls to the inexperienced:

> The night-guard unexpectedly jumps from his corner and seizes us, scribbles down our number, hands us a pair of wooden shoes and the bucket and drives us out into the middle of the snow, shivering and sleepy. It is our task to shuffle to the latrine with the bucket which knocks against our bare calves, disgustingly warm; it is full beyond all reasonable limit, and inevitably with the shaking some of the content overflows on our feet, so that however repugnant this duty may be, it is always preferable that we, and not our neighbor, be assigned to it.

There's a lesson in this more striking than the usual one of man's infinitely adaptable nature under stress. By telling us that it is better to sleep with your feet wet with urine than to sleep facing someone else's feet similarly fouled, Levi is elucidating what for him became the essential activity of survival: the division of every moment of the day into a series of graded sensations of pleasure and pain. Levi moved through physical sensation the way a mountain climber negotiates the varied abutments and hollows of his terrain—now relaxing, now stiffening, now guarding for a fall. And because of his attention to every moment of pain, and his understanding of it as a physical rather than a spiritual fact, Levi may have been able to savor the moments of surcease without being seduced or overwhelmed by them. He was capable of pleasure. This book, which is filled, like all camp memoirs, with degradation and suffering and humiliations beyond all imagining, records moments of bodily comfort so intensely satisfying—an extra bowl of soup, the warmth of the sun during some ghastly forced march—that one almost cries out with joy.

Levi becomes a psychologist of sensation. Greater pains, he says, usually block out lesser ones, a law of mental perspective that effactually prevents the dissolution of consciousness. But he also says, in another context, that small blows may sometimes serve as a restorative precisely because they force one to concentrate on immediate discomforts and therefore to forget the misery of one's general situation. So both large and small pains have their uses. There were many ways to die in the camp, and a few ways to live, but surely those who could not put suffering to use were lost.

In accounting for his own survival, Levi has always stressed how much luck he had, and how much he was helped by those stronger than himself. Yet when he writes of the others, those weaker or less lucky or less adaptable—those incapable of making the calculation of pain from moment to moment—he does so with an unyielding, harsh truthfulness that makes one shudder:

> In history and in life one sometimes seems to glimpse a ferocious law which states: "To he that has, will be given; to he that has not, will be taken away." In the *Lager,* where man is alone, and where the struggle for life is reduced to its primordial mechanism, this unjust law is openly in force, is recognized by all. With the adaptable, the strong and astute individuals, even the leaders willingly keep contact, sometimes even friendly contact, because they hope later to perhaps derive some benefit. But with the *Muselmänner* (camp slang for the doomed), the men in decay, it is not even worth speaking, because one knows already they will complain and will speak about what they used to eat at home. Even less worthwhile is it to make friends with them, because they have no distinguished acquaintances in camp, they do not gain any extra rations, they do not work in profitable Kommandos and they know no secret method of organizing. And in any case, one knows that they are only here on a visit. . .

Levi is not a Jewish saint. In the camps, too much pity, too inclusive a registration of the suffering of others, could lead to a disastrous lapsing out, a loss of concentration and hardihood that would be fatal. As far as we can make out, Levi saved a few drowning people when he could do so without overwhelming risk—and for the rest stuck to his own interests and those of his friends.

Only later, much later, in the stories collected in *Moments of Reprieve,* was Levi able to turn to the *Muselmänner* with anything more than a passing gaze of silent grief. The book is composed of brief sketches, often very bare, in which a single man, separating himself from the crowd and refusing the role of victim, asserts some claim of identity, some version of selfhood. Imposters, scoundrels, religious fanatics, moralists of orthodoxy too gentle to steal even when starving, they all draw on some reserve of ego or craft or idiosyncrasy. They step forward for an instant and recede: the story is their monument, their sole monument. When you read these skeletal stories they seem too thin, but afterward you realize the thinness represents a state of being in which a single impulse briefly survives mortal weakness.

Levi writes of the victims of the camp without "survivor's guilt." But in 1944, when he was actually in the camp, the activity of self-preservation, unheroic in his own eyes, took its toll. In *Survival in Auschwitz,* he frequently asks whether he is still a man, whether his friends are still men. He uses the word "man" in both senses—human and masculine. What he means by masculinity is self-respect, and also an ideal of civility, honor, kindliness. He is not by nature a self-deprecating person, but his ruined state as a prisoner fills him with shame.

In order to live, and also out of simple attraction, he is repeatedly drawn to prisoners shrewder and more resourceful than himself, men who have mastered the art of organizing—of stealing goods from the camp stores or factory and then trading them or fashioning them into something else and trading that. Levi becomes almost vivacious in describing these schemes, the complexity of which, in this setting, can be startling. The intimates of Auschwitz, who had no chance of surviving if they merely obeyed the rules and ate what was given them, appear to have produced a classical model of rational economic behavior out of nothing—out of pieces of wood and stone, scraps of metal, cloth, and bread. For the resourceful, the end result was a bit more food. Levi's own contribution to this agitated and desperate system of barter is relatively minor; in the Buna rubber plant he hacks brooms into pieces, which he then smuggles back into the camp in his clothes, reassembles with steel pegs, and trades off to the block leaders—German prisoners many of them, who pride themselves on the cleanly swept floors of their inhuman quarters.

But the broom trade did not save his life. Levi survived, first, because an Italian civilian worker named Lorenzo gave him some extra soup every day for six months, and second, because his skills as a chemist were of use to the Germans. Before being admitted to the laboratory, however, he has to submit to a bizarre trial—an examination in organic chemistry before a blue-eyed, fair-haired Doktor Pannwitz. For once, the spirit of absurdity nearly overwhelms him. Bald, covered with sores, smelling of turnips and cabbage, wearing torn and filthy clothes, and surely destined in the end for selection to the gas chambers, Levi feels himself unreal. Yet he conquers his dismay and performs. His old student vanity as an exam champion saves him. The remnants of a normal ego remain.

Survival in Auschwitz turns out to be, of all things, a book about the forms of civilization. Levi describes the system of death and survival in the camp, but he also presents a variety of relationships—economics, spiritual, fraternal, and even cultural—that can only be called the contours of a social world. As much as any man of the 19th century, Levi believed in civilization; he believed it possessed a moral and spiritual as well as a juridical value. Naive as it may seem, his stubbornness seems to have carried him through. He was not particularly brave. He did not choose the way of armed revolt, as a few Jewish inmates did, dying in the act of killing some of the S.S. But he was courageous, steadfast, enduring. He means more to us, this mild, cultivated, and defenseless man, more to us than the truculent and motivated types, the saints, the communists, the religious and ideological personalities, all of whom entered the camps armed, so to speak, to resist. Levi went in naked and clothed himself.

A very modest and fragmentary work, *Survival in Auschwitz* has an emotional power entirely disproportionate to its size and ambition. And yet when it came out in Italy in 1947, it sold 2,500 copies and disappeared. Levi had never thought of himself as a writer, so he continued to work in chemistry, supporting himself and his new wife with a variety of jobs. But in the late 1950s, when he was established as a technician in a varnish factory, he spoke at an exhibition in Turin devoted

to the deportations. To his surprise, he discovered that his book had gained, among young people at least, something of a following. *Survival in Auschwitz* was republished in 1958 to great success, and a few years later, emboldened by this acclaim, Levi completed a sequel, known in Britain as *The Truce* (again, a literal translation of the title) and published here as *The Reawakening*. (Both books are beautifully translated by Stuart Woolf.)

The first book ends with a diary-style chapter, "The Story of Ten Days," which tells of the time between the flight of the Germans and the Russian liberation of the camp. For more than a week in January 1945 the sick and starving inmates were left in the camp on their own. To walk out of the camp, in winter, was unthinkable—no one was strong enough—and the corpses piled up on the open ground. The final pages of the book are written in a whisper. At last, on January 27, four Russians on horseback pass through the camp entrance. But Levi is too weak to feel much of anything, even relief. *The Reawakening* picks up from here.

In some ways, it is an even better book than *Survival in Auschwitz*. Though he feels anguish enough, Levi is no longer calling on the bitterest of his memories, and if the writing lacks that last degree of personal sweetness that makes his self-preoccupation in *Survival* a model of integrity, pride, and true consciousness, it is also freer and bolder in describing everything outside himself. The book was written 16 years after the events. By 1961, we can guess, Levi feels no need to hold back, no need to guard against dissolution; even his descriptions of suffering are more fluent and expressive than before. In an early chapter, two Russian nurses with rough hands bathe the surviving prisoners, and Levi writes an account of a man whose limbs have contracted into the fetal position—a man too frightened to take a bath—that is a purer distillation of horror and compassion than anything in *Survival in Auschwitz*. The system of annihilation has receded; the individual case now begins to reassert its claims.

This non-writer has become a master portraitist, both of individual men and women and of postwar cities and landscapes. *The Reawakening* has a peculiar shadowed quality, as Levi now captures scenes attempted less often in the literature of the war, the moment *after*—a time when life has broken down into its constitutive elements:

> In those days, and in those parts, soon after the front had passed by, a high wind was blowing over the face of the earth; the world around us seemed to have returned to primeval Chaos, and was swarming with scalene, defective, abnormal human specimens; each of them bestirred himself, with blind or deliberate movements, in anxious search of his own place, of his own sphere, as the particles of the four elements are described as doing in the verse-cosmogonies of the Ancients.

Europe, as a civilization and a set of social relations, has simply dissolved. The Red Army holds sway, but its grip, in contrast to that of the S.S., is loose, improvisatory, and erratic, an unstable compound of brusque command and benevolence. In this vacuum of power, anomalous groups of people—defeated armies, refugees, survivors—brokenly wander about the countryside or travel in disconsolate convoys here and there.

Levi becomes a traveler himself. He is first evacuated to transit camps in Poland, and then, just when expecting a turn south to the mountains and the sea—Italy—he is sent, along with 1,400 other Italians, to a camp far to the north, in White Russia, near Minsk. There, slowly, and in a misery of homesickness, he recuperates from the camp.

The Reawakening encompasses several types of literature. It is a somber, picaresque tale: an account of strange and resourceful people who met at a time of loose social bonds; a book of adventure, vagabondage, exile, and return; a record of meals cadged, floors slept on, journeys endured. It is also a kind of ironic travel book—a 20th-century travel book, in which the homeless are chased from one disaster to another.

Levi has survived degradation, illness, the near extinction of life. Now, as he restores himself, the sudden pangs of normal appetite break in on his lingering state of debility with an almost terrifying sharpness. Better than any book I know, *The Reawakening* conveys the surge of active convalescence. Every cell strains for health. But in Levi there is also a young man's peculiar, shamed bitterness and nostalgia, a longing for the pleasures that he has not yet enjoyed—sexual love, professional success, the affections of a family.

In his diffident way, he involves us closely in the story of his regained health and spirit, convincing us, without ever saying so, that he is writing about the recovery of Europe. Not economic or material recovery: for him civilization is meaningless without the possibility of pleasure, and this book about the recrudescence of life offers one version of the way consciousness, brought to the brink of nullity, restores itself by slowly increasing its demands for pleasure—the pleasure of companionship, of Italianness as a type of sociability, of landscape and adventure, and then, finally, pleasure in the arts.

Reading these two stirring little books, one begins to see that Levi was protected, and perhaps delivered, by a certain stolidity of temperament, and this very same quality accounts for his special qualities as a writer. We tend to think of the camp survivors as spiritual figures—as marked by a special religious strength or reverence for life. But Levi is such a writer only insofar as he created what Norman Mailer once called "a metaphysic of the belly"—in Levi's case, a metaphysic of spoons, of grease, of shit, of bread. He treated his experience in hell largely as a material phenomenon, not as a metaphor or a dream or a curse. From this we may cynically conclude that when a modern writer confronts the literal abyss rather than the hell he finds in himself, the urge to make metaphors and to undertake spiritual adventures disappears. Yet what I have called Levi's stolidity—his stubborn persistence in a humanistic response to the apocalypse—should be seen not as stupidity or a failure of imagination, but as a personal and cultural achievement of striking value.

Levi adores chemistry. His love for it is the ground base of his identity, more persistent and more pervasive than his Jewishness, or his Italianness, or his history as a camp survivor. *The Periodic Table* can be read in part as a hidden account of how Levi came to write his first two books by studying science. Each of the 21 chapters is named after an element—zinc, iron, gold, argon, and so on—and each element calls forth an area of Levi's experience, or an anecdote or lesson of modern times. In the middle of a chapter devoted to his memories of a university course in chemistry, Levi lists the properties of zinc: "They make tubs out of it for laundry, it is not an element which says much to the imagination, it is gray and its salts are colorless . . . in short, it is a boring metal." Why are we given this unexceptional piece of information? The point falls into place with exhilarating ease:

The course notes contained a detail which at first reading had escaped me, namely that the so tender and delicate zinc, so yielding to acid which gulps it down in a single mouthful, behaves, however, in a very different fashion when it is very pure: then it obstinately resists the attack. One could draw from this two conflicting philosophical conclusions: the praise of purity, which protects from evil like a coat of mail; the praise of impurity, which gives rise to changes, in other words, to life. I discarded the first, disgustingly moralistic, and I lingered to consider the second, which I found more congenial. In order for the wheel to turn, for life to be lived, impurities are needed, and the infertilities of infertilities in the soil, too, as is known, if it is to be fertile. Dissension, diversity, the grain of salt and mustard are needed: Fascism does not want them, forbids them. . . . (As a Jew), I am the impurity that makes the zinc react, I am the grain of salt or mustard.

Mussolini wanted a political life for the nation of pure "spirit," in reaction to which Levi and his friends took refuge in the police-report dryness of quantitative analysis. How many milligrams of iron and lead could be found in a gram of powder? *There* was a truth that couldn't be corrupted by politics. If spirit and matter can be conceived as opposites, the latter became the consoling, revivifying choice. Chemistry, for all its foul acidic odors, smelled clean. Levi was enchanted by the sheer materiality of chemistry and by the neutrality of the elements of life. Recalling an excursion outside the Turin in which he searched for chicken shit (invaluable for making certain lipsticks), he reflects that "matter is matter, neither noble nor vile, infinitely transformable, and its proximate origin is of no value whatsoever." In such effusions—his insistence on the gaiety of the chemist's task—one hears the exhilaration of a young man of sensitive and self-doubting nature who comes to realize that existence can never be an entirely subjective phenomenon. What a relief! The world exists outside "taste," outside "sensibility."

One now understands something that was puzzling in his earlier volumes: the obvious lack of "psychology." No matter how briefly observed, Levi's characters have density of being—he feels the presence of every individual. But they aren't men and women molded by their unconscious. He is fascinated not by the complexity of mental activity but by the interpenetration of desire and matter, and by the sensuous nature of things in all their varying states of degradation, transformation, ennoblement. Even Auschwitz he saw as degraded matter; and therefore he could conceive that it would pass into another state. As a political and philosophical response to the attempted annihilation of an entire people, this can only strike us as inadequate. As one man's response to catastrophe, it is startling and endlessly suggestive.

Chemistry made Levi a powerfully original writer, but then writing brought out his dissatisfaction with chemistry. His old vocation as industrial technician slipped away, and major literary ambitions took over. Fiction beckoned. Our view of him is incomplete (one novel and two books of stories remain untranslated), but after reading his 1982 epic novel, *If Not Now, When?,* we are more impressed than ever, alas, by his modest earlier books.

If Not Now, When? is a strenuous attempt both to embrace the traditions of the Eastern European Jews—the Yiddish-speaking Jews of the shtetl whom Levi had not known before Auschwitz—and to dispel the shibboleth that such Jews never resisted the Nazis. It is a long celebration of *partisanska*, Jewish style—

the wandering life, struggles, acts of sabotage, minor victories and defeats of a group of Russian Jewish irregulars (stragglers from the Red Army, survivors of the *Einsatzkommandos*) who gathered behind German lines during the war. Preparing to write, Levi not only scanned the records of partisan warfare but studied Yiddish. He immersed himself in shtetl literature and the traditions of the rabbis. His generosity and sympathy shows in every scene. A people without military traditions in 1943, his Jewish partisans spend much time debating the ethics and purpose of what they are doing—an exasperating and comical practice that gives this book a gentleness of tone perhaps unknown in the whole of partisan literature.

But something else turns up, too—a willed overexplicitness and rhetoric not seen in Levi's work before. There is too much of this sort of thing:

> They were tired, poor, and dirty, but not defeated: children of merchants, tailors, rabbis, and cantors, they had armed themselves with weapons taken from the Germans, they had earned the right to wear those tattered uniforms, without chevrons, and they had tasted several times the bitter food of killing.

The writing has an incantatory and orotund rhythm—conventional, impersonal, almost crude—that approaches the banality of propaganda, or the narration of a documentary film. Amends are being made here, and reassurance and inspiration offered.

Levi has tried to get all of Eastern Europe into one novel, all of Jewish resistance and martyrdom and ethical striving. And the result is that in *If Not Now, When?* we miss Levi, not only because his gently incandescent presence is so pleasing, but because Levi needs to be a character himself in order to anchor his profoundest impressions of other people. In a century in which the self, as it is defined in our most ambitious literature, makes demands beyond anything ever encountered before, Levi's modesty has a kind of tonic force, even authority. This writer-chemist has opened spaces for the human presence that more omnivorous souls have blocked out of view.

As one reads Levi's dignified and lucid books about the contours of hell, one's awe before the characteristic spiritual striving of modernism—the energies of negation and self-torment, the loathing of rationality, the disgust for culture, the "sympathy for the abyss," as Thomas Mann called it—does not lessen but falls into a different perspective. Literature matters, but it does not matter absolutely. Sanity matters, too. Levi's gravity of tone reveals a temperamental equanimity that can only be called a supreme sense of the fitness of things.

To find its equal you have to go back through the whole of the 20th century—to Chekhov's stories, letters, and his report from a Russian penal colony, *The Island of Sakhalin.* Like Chekhov, Levi was born with the soul of a poet but was drawn to science by both interest and the necessity of making a living. Chekhov wrote newspaper sketches and stories when he was a very young man—he was thrust into literature by personal and historical catastrophe. But the training of the one in medicine and the other in chemistry obviously affected, and perhaps determined, the kind of writer each became. They are not, of course, equals, but they share a marvelously even-keeled sense of life's pleasures and pains, habits of directness and lucidity, and a sense of the dignity and self-sufficiency of the writer as craftsman.

Levi's modesty can be more than just tonic. A wonderful writer, he is also, in his gentle way, and despite what he may think himself, a hero. For he suggests a possibility that modern people, and intellectuals in particular, have regarded with almost punitive irony (as if to kill the hope within themselves): that they might endure some supreme test by holding fast to nothing more than the personal powers they can command. Of course his victory over his circumstances can hardly be appropriated as our own. Still, he has restored knightly luster to qualities we have regarded as inadequate and even pathetic, qualities we have nearly ironized out of existence—dignity, personal cultivation, even lowly patience. (pp. 27-33)

> David Denby, "The Humanist and the Holocaust," in The New Republic, Vol. 195, No. 4, July 28, 1986, pp. 27-33.

PRIMO LEVI [INTERVIEW WITH I. M. THOMSON]

[In the following excerpt, Thomson recounts statements by Levi about his experiences in Auschwitz, his work as a chemist, and his writings.]

Primo Levi endured almost the worst that the twentieth century has had to offer. In February 1944 he was deported, with 650 other Italian partisans, to Auschwitz: 'a name without significance for us at the time, but it at least implied some place on earth'. Levi became *Häftling*—prisoner—174517, and was shortly transferred to Buna, a rubber factory connected to the extermination camp. There he worked as a chemist until 27 January 1945, when the Red Army tanks finally arrived. Only three of the partisans survived. The need to 'tell the story, to bear witness' was afterwards so urgent that, some forty years on, Levi likened himself to Coleridge's ancient Mariner: 'And till my ghastly tale is told / This heart within me burns'.

Levi told his tale in what are now deservedly considered masterpieces: *If This Is a Man* (1947) and *The Truce* (1963)—'the written forms of oral stories which I have told countless times after my escape from Auschwitz'. But is was almost a decade before *If This Is a Man* won recognition in Italy. Levi first sent the typescript to Natalia Ginzburg at Einaudi; she rejected it. But Levi looked back on the incident as fortunate: 'If I'd had an immediate success with *If This Is a Man,* I would have probably given up my career as a chemist, and without chemistry, I would not have written *The Periodic Table.*'

The Periodic Table (1975), a collection of part-autobiographical tales structured around elements of Mendeleev's Table, finally confirmed Levi as, in Italo Calvino's words, 'one of the most important and gifted writers of our time'. Levi devoted himself full-time to writing after 1977, when he returned from his position as manager-technician of a Turin chemical factory. But his connections with the chemical and scientific world remained as strong as ever: some of the most enthusiastic reviews of *The Periodic Table* appeared in *Chemical and Engineering News, Scientific American* and *New Scientist.* And without chemistry, Levi would not have survived Auschwitz: working at the Buna factory meant the SS considered him an 'economically useful Jew'.

Levi draws some fairly eccentric analogies from alchemy and chemistry in *The Periodic Table.* At one point he forges a comparison between the latter and Italian Fascism.

'Too eccentric, you think?', enquired Levi. 'But chemistry deals with Matter, with the clean and the easily quantifiable. Fascism dealt with the Spirit, with the dirty and the "unquantifiable". Under Mussolini, the very air we breathed was polluted with lies and propaganda; the teaching I received at school was contaminated by Fascist ideology. And the stress which the Fascists placed on the Spirit, on the ''life-force'' was bogus: without materials, without Matter, you cannot win a war, something which it took Mussolini a long time to realize: ''Noi non abbiamo le arme, ma abbiamo il coraggio'', he said. Whereas the truth of the matter was that we had neither weapons nor courage.'

After Primo Levi graduated from Turin University in 1941 with a degree in chemistry, he worked as a chemist in a variety of jobs: extracting nickel from a large mine for a Turin metal company; as a laboratory assistant for a Milanese chemical plant. Levi looked back on these days with a certain nostalgia: relatively cheerful times compared to the horrors ahead. I wondered how much he had known then about Nazi atrocities against Jews.

'Nothing', said Levi. 'Well, almost nothing. The Italian newspapers, which at that time merely reproduced Nazi propaganda, gave very vague and partial accounts of how Jews in Poland had been *übertragen*—transferred—to certain ''zones''. From 1942 onwards, vague and sinister reports began to filter through from the Italian soldiers returning from the Russian front. And they nearly all said the same thing: how they had seen the SS force Jews to dig their own graves, or how they had been thrown into rivers, or how Jewish men and women had been made to work on railroads in filthy rags, and how they had been made to lie down on the tracks in front of trains . . .

'There were vague rumours about atrocities committed by Russians against Jews. But they were nowhere near as ruthless as the Germans . . . When the Germans said ''exterminate all'' they meant it: *all* deported, *all* exterminated. The Nazi death camps were operated with the ferocious military rigour which was a Prussian inheritance, the savage discipline dramatized by Büchner in *Woyzeck*.

'It's what is known in Germany as *gründlichkeit:* fundamentalism, going to the very roots of something. Not a very Italian characteristic, to be sure. It's all to do with what I call a ''mancanza di misura'': the inability to know when to stop, to strike a happy medium—something, I believe, which distinguishes you British from the Germans. But *Gründlichkeit* is a very ambiguous quality. Let me illustrate: several years ago a Bavarian girl wrote to me saying how disgraceful it was that Nazi atrocities were carefully glossed over at school. She seemed an intelligent girl, so I wrote back asking certain questions about post-war Germany. The girl sent me a postcard immediately, promising to reply in full as soon as possible. Twenty days later I received a twenty-three-page letter from her, the product of indefatigable research: a thesis, in other words. ''I haven't had enough time'', she wrote at the end of it, ''to write all I wanted.'' Now this is thoroughly *gründlich:* a national characteristic without which there would have been no Auschwitz, just badly-run camps along the Russian lines'.

Levi was captured by the Fascist militia at Val d'Aosta on 13 December 1943. He was then transferred to Fossoli, near Modena, 'where a vast detention camp, originally meant for English and American prisoners-of-war, collected all the numerous categories of people not approved of by the new-born Fascist Republic.' On his way to Fossoli, Levi managed to tear into pieces and swallow his false identification papers, and to bury in the snow a note-book containing the addresses of partisans affiliated to the resistance movement to which he belonged: 'Justice and Liberty'. When the SS arrived at the detention camp, Levi and the 650 other anti-Fascists were herded into deportation trains: 'goods wagons closed from the outside, with men, women and children pressed together without pity, like cheap merchandise, for a journey towards nothingness, a journey down there towards the bottom'. Levi hastily scribbled a postcard to his mother, addressed to her flat in Turin, and threw it out of the train; miraculously it reached its destination.

Turin was where Levi was born, in 1919, and it was where he returned after Auschwitz: 'swollen, bearded and in rags', as he wrote in *The Truce*. He was slight of build, very fair, with greyish-white hair. Horn-rimmed spectacles lent him a slightly professorial air. He had a neatly trimmed grey beard. The study in his Turin flat was almost bare of decoration: just an anglepoise lamp, swivel chair and word-processor. The only concession to ornament, apart from a sketch of a half-destroyed wire fence at Auschwitz, was three bizarre creatures (an owl, penguin and butterfly) modelled out of what looked like wire coat hangers, perched high above a bookcase filled with scientific journals. Our conversation was conducted in Italian, as Primo Levi was rather too modest to admit that he spoke excellent English, as he certainly did.

Levi was in short sleeves, the tattoo reading '174517' visible on his left forearm: 'a typical German talent for classification', he said. Tattooing is forbidden by Mosaic law: Leviticus 19.28 All the more reason, then, for the Nazis to brand the Jews.

And yet Levi admitted to feeling a certain 'nostalgia' (his word) for Auschwitz, and even looked back on his twenty months there as an 'adventure' (also his word).

'An adventure', he said, 'in the sense that my experience of the *Lager* was a sort of rite of passage, and the writing about it an . . . interior liberation. It was only after my humanity had been utterly obliterated, only after I had written *If This Is a Man,* that I felt a true ''man'', a man in the sense of the title of that book. . . . But more a university than an adventure: I would almost say that I ''graduated'' from the *Lager* . . . Auschwitz taught me how to get the measure of somebody in a split second. . . .

''It *is* a little paradoxical to say that I feel a certain nostalgia for Auschwitz, of course. But the *Lager* coincided with my youth, and it is for my youth, and for the few people with whom I made friends at Auschwitz, that I feel nostalgia. Not that I have any desire to go back to the camp as a *Häftling*. Obviously not. But the memory of plays strange tricks on one: it is somehow only the good moments from the past that remain, the happy times at Auschwitz rather than the horrific. . . . I can remember with extreme clarity the time I taught an Italian folk-song to a Hungarian friend, and how he taught me a Hungarian folk-song in return. And I can still recite it, word for word. It's because that particular moment was so *exceptional:* for just a few minutes we were ecstatically happy.'

Was Auschwitz, I wondered, all the worse for Western Jews, who had not already suffered in the ghettos?

'Of course the shock of entering Auschwitz for the first time was less . . . severe for the Russians and Poles. For us Italians it was quite literally a case of having been plucked straight out of our beds at home to a death-camp. One of the first things I noticed at Auschwitz was a strong discrimination at the linguistic level: almost all the Poles, Hungarians and Czechs spoke a little German, whereas the Italians did not. And you were at a considerable disadvantage if you spoke no German. I myself knew a little, but I soon realized that I had to know an awful lot more if I was to have any chance of surviving. I even took private lessons in German, for which I paid with my bread rations. I didn't know, of course, that what I was learning was an extremely vulgar sort of German, full of savage imprecations, insults, blasphemies and imperatives: a *Lagerjargon*, as I now call it. Elsewhere it has been termed a *Lingua Tertii Imperii*, a language of the Third Reich: L.T.I. It was certainly not the German of Goethe or Heine!

'But this didn't matter at the time. Because he who spoke no German was by definition a barbarian. You were not a proper *Mensch*, a human being . . . The Poles were in fact the most numerous at Auschwitz, and the majority of them had already escaped the gas chambers by 1944, when I arrived at Auschwitz, had already learnt the rules of the game. They were incredibly canny people. And robust: robust in both mind and body. Partly this was because Polish anti-Semitism, which has always been very pronounced, gave them a certain . . . identity, made them tough as nails even before they had been deported to Auschwitz. This was never the case with the Italian Jews: most of us felt more Italian than Jewish, so it was hard to come to terms with being persecuted for one's religion. The Italians have never been particularly anti-Semitic anyway. When the Ministry of the Interior introduced the Racial Laws of 1938, most Italians thought them absurd. But there were exceptions, of course: my uncle, for instance, was betrayed as a Jew to the Nazis by a fellow Italian. I myself was arrested by Italian Fascists, not by Nazis. But one's Judaism counted for very little before the last war: my parents had a maid here in this very flat who never realized that she was in the pay of a Jewish family. She was perhaps puzzled by the absence of the Madonna above their bed, but she otherwise presumably took us for a catholic family.'

Levi never practiced the Jewish faith. In fact he professed no religion at all. He admired the importance given to literacy and education by Orthodox Jews, but rarely went to synagogue. In 1982 he publicly condemned the Israeli invasion of Southern Lebanon. I asked him whether he had any desire to settle in Israel after Auschwitz, like the Jewish partisans in his novel *If Not Now, When?* (1982)? He appeared slightly annoyed, and gave a categorical 'no':

'My home has always been in this flat where I was born. There was no need to look for a new home. Only 500 or so Italians settled in Israel after the last war. Hardly any, in other words.'

Levi's most hostile critics have in fact been Jews, particularly American Jews. Levi told me how 'an absolutely crippling' article had recently appeared in the US Jewish magazine, *Commentary*, where a critic accused Levi of having a 'tin ear' for religion, that he was 'an assimilated Jew'. Levi continued: 'I have given some twenty-five interviews in America, and journalists always ask the same old question: "What does it mean to be a Jew in Italy?" Not an awful lot, I reply. The only language I speak at all well is Italian. My best friends are Italian, few are Jewish. There are only 40,000 Jews in Italy today. Not many, really.'

Levi never used his writing to take revenge on his would-be murderers. "It has not been written', he wrote in the Introduction to *If This is a Man*, 'to formulate new accusations; it should be able, rather, to furnish documentation for a quiet study of certain aspects of the human mind.' I asked him about his remarkably forgiving attitude to Dr. Müller, former SS officer at Auschwitz, whom Levi tried to track down in the 1960s.

'Dr Müller, you see, was in charge of the Buna rubber factory, so I was not surprisingly fascinated by him. And by Germany too: for five years I attended the Goethe Institute here in Turin to learn the language which I had learnt so imperfectly at Auschwitz. But this curiosity of mine . . . I'd say that it even kept me alive in the *Lager*—a place where it was extremely easy to die spiritually. I am interested in men like Dr Müller as human beings, as ordinary *Menschen*—which is of course what they are: ordinary men, made of flesh and blood like yourself.'

Levi's honesty in *If This Is a Man* is sometimes quite shocking: there was no point, he says halfway through, in befriending the weak and helpless at Auschwitz, because 'they have no distinguished acquaintances in the camp, they do not gain any extra rations, they do not work in profitable Kommandos and they have no secret method of organising. And in any case, one knows that they are only here on a visit, that in a few weeks nothing will remain of them but a handful of ashes in some near-by field and a crossed-out register.'

'Horribly cynical, you think?' he asked. 'Well, yes: but cynical by your standards, by those of "society at large". Auschwitz was hardly society at large: a microcosmic form of all the evils in the world, to be sure. But it was not "normal" by anyone's standards. I myself occasionally fraternised with the "drowned" at Auschwitz. But not often. Usually one just let them drift by on their way to death. There was no point in lending a helping hand to those beyond help. The Good Samaritan ethic had no place in the *Lager*. Nor does it have much of a place in contemporary Manhattan. But, no: very little of one's moral world could survive behind the barbed-wire fence of Auschwitz; one had to be a martyr not to renounce or . . . compromise it in any way.'

Shocking, too, is the episode in *The Truce* where Levi and a French companion ignore the cries for water coming from the patients in the room next to the Auschwitz scarlet-fever ward, where they had taken refuge after the departure of the Germans.

'Also cynical?' wondered Levi. 'I'm not so sure. You see, it went something like this: we were boiling some soup—a wonderful moment for us because it was the first time we had invented anything for ourselves: how to make the soup, how to construct a stove, how to fetch water—and there was enough soup for eight people. But not for three hundred. And so we shut the door on the patients next door. What else could we do? If we'd shared the soup among 300 people, we would all have perished: as it was, we succeeded in saving a few lives. . . .

'I repeat: one simply cannot apply ordinary moral standards to the *Lager*. . . . When it comes to something like the Auschwitz "Special Squad", the group of prisoners to whom the SS bequeathed the task of managing the crematorium—transporting prisoners to the gas chambers, removing the corpses, extracting any gold teeth, raking out and getting rid of ashes— it is best to suspend moral judgement altogether. The "Special Squad" performed their duties under duress. It was not something for which they volunteered. Anyway, once physical exhaustion and the hunger took their toll, they too were sent to the gas chambers.'

The suspension of moral judgement was the theme of Levi's last book, *I sommersi e i salvati* (1986), a collection of essays on the Nazi concentration camp system. *The Drowned and the Saved* is not simply another addition to what is known in Italy as 'la letteratura concentrazionaria'—quite a lot of which Levi considered 'bad literature'. (And not only the literature: he disliked *Sophie's Choice* with Meryl Streep.) It is a warning, rather, to those who deliver facile judgements of condemnation:

only those who have survived the death-camps can judge. And even they are not properly fit to forgive or condemn, for 'the story has been almost exclusively written by those who have not fathomed the depths of human degradation. Those who did have not come back to tell the tale. Or their powers of observation have been paralysed by suffering and incomprehension.'

But how much of Auschwitz was quite simply beyond comprehension? I mentioned the episode in *If This Is a Man* where a fellow *Häftling* shows Levi the words carved at the bottom of his wooden bowl: 'Ne pas chercher à comprendre.'

'*I tried*', said Levi. 'I tried to understand. Not that it was easy: one's powers of observation were severely limited. None of us even knew where Auschwitz was geographically situated. . . . And it was only months after my escape that I had any idea as to how the *Lager* functioned, how extensive the connections were between slave-labour and German industry. Buna was the product of a contract between the SS and a chemical company, as I later discovered: "We'll help build a death-camp, you supply us with labour for our chemical factory." Buna still exists: it's the largest rubber factory in Poland.

'I've been back to Buna twice, in an effort to "understand" things a little better. Strangely enough, I felt little emotion returning there. Today, Auschwitz has the cold impersonality of a monument: not as I remembered it at all. Birkenau, on the other hand, is much more impressive, surrounded by an enormous wasteland of broken-up barrack-huts, with just dust and mud all around. Not a blade of grass. . . . An odd thing happened to me a year ago, when I was invited by a German pharmaceutical company to visit their plant at Leverküsen. On a strictly professional basis, you understand. "Where did you learn your German?" the management asked. "It's rather rare for an Italian to speak our language." And I said: "My name is Levi. I'm a Jew. And I learnt your language at Auschwitz." Naturally, this caused a little embarrassment . . . But most interesting was the fact that the Leverküsen factory almost exactly resembled the Buna factory at Auschwitz. How little things seem to have changed, I thought.'

Auschwitz remained Levi's great theme; he even admitted that without his experience of the *Lager*—concentration camp—he would never have been a writer: 'Or I would have been a failed writer.' Furthermore, Levi believed the *Lager* was a paradoxical 'godsend', since it gave him his subject 'on a plate': 'But then one could say the same about my great hero Conrad: would he have been a greater writer without the sea?'

When *The Truce* first appeared in English, Philip Toynbee gave voice to what Primo Levi regards as a common misconception: 'Whenever this subject (Auschwitz) is put before us again we find that our vocabulary, and even our normal grammatical structures, have begun to fail us. . . .' (*The Observer*, January 1965). And George Steiner, too: 'the world of Auschwitz lies outside speech as it lies outside reason.'

'It is true that in one or two chapters of *If This Is a Man* I remarked how our language lacks words to express the . . . demolition of man', admitted Levi. 'And it is true that the witnesses at the Eichmann trial said "You cannot understand! Who was not *there* cannot imagine." But both *If This Is a Man* and *The Truce* are written in a language that everyone can understand, in everyday speech. I believe it is the task of every writer to describe what he sees in plain language, and I hope I have achieved this. Not that it is impossible to write about the death-camps in a highly experimental prose with all manner of linguistic pyrotechnics (although I think, *a priori*, this would

be somehow indecent): André Schwartz-Bart described the Holocaust in *The Last of the Just* using a rather unconventional prose; Paul Celan, too, wrote about Auschwitz in some extremely obscure, not to say hermetic poems. . . .

'But I'd say that our everyday language is more inadequate when it comes to describing scientific phenomena: the planets, the galaxy, the world which is invisible to the naked eye. Ours is a language which fails to go beyond what our senses are capable of comprehending. It falls short of the mark. If I say you're tall, I mean you're over six foot, not half a millimetre. And yet half a millimetre is an extremely "tall" measure in the world of atomic science. And the expression "light year" is almost meaningless when describing not only the universe but also the galaxy. . . . Italo Calvino was the only Italian writer to have bridged the gap between our earth-bound language and a science-fiction language adequate to describe the stars. . . .'

Levi, who considered Jules Verne 'a great writer', himself wrote science fiction of a sort: the short stories based on chemistry, astrophysics and molecular biology contained in his *Storie naturali* (1966) and *Vizio di forma* (1971) make up a satire on futuristic technology, or rather on man's indiscriminate and potentially destructive misuse of such technology. Whimsical *novelle*, similar to the sort of thing Calvino wrote in *Cosmicomics* and *Time and the Hunter*, Levi believed the stories to have 'suffered the fate of all science fiction', which is 'to undergo a rapid ageing process'. He was not particularly proud of them.

'But one cannot *not* communicate', said Levi, his Piedmontese accent becoming markedly more pronounced as he returned to the subject of Auschwitz and language. 'Even silence itself means something. If a husband speaks and his wife remains silent, her silence is positively loaded with all sorts of meaning. But silence is a poor way of communicating. . . . I can't stand writers like Samuel Beckett: it is the duty of every human being to communicate. The same goes for the likes of Ezra Pound: writing in Chinese simply showed a disrespect for the reader. Writing should be a public service: so-called "incommunicability" (such an *ugly* word!) went out with the 1960s. . . .'

Levi drew the line at Kafka, however—even though he acknowledged the influence he had on Beckett: 'With *The Trial*', he said, 'Kafka predicted the time when it was a crime simply to be a Jew. I was in fact commissioned by Einaudi to translate the book into Italian. Looking back, I wish I hadn't: the undertaking disturbed me badly. I went into a deep, deep depression. . . . And so I haven't read any Kafka since: he involves me too much. . . .'

Levi remarked that 'precision and concision are the two hallmarks of the chemist', and that these have their counterparts in writing itself:

'When one writes a "weekly report" in a chemical factory, it must be brief and succinct, and it has to be read by everyone, from the men on the shopfloor right up to the directors. Both Goethe and Leopardi said that a book is valid only once it has been accepted by an intellectual élite, followed by a vast public. If it fails on one or the other count, there's something wrong with it. Now, without wishing to sound pompous, I'd like to believe that both *If This is a Man* and *The Truce* conform to this criterion, since they were read by at least a million people in Italy, from high-powered intellectuals to secondary-school children. Naturally the books were read in different ways by different people, but I hope they had something to say for everyone. And I truly believe this is to do with my factory days. . . . *La chiave a stella,* you know, was read by people who would never otherwise touch a book—labourers and factory hands. . . .'

La chiave a stella (1978) just published in Britain as *The Wrench,* concerns the picaresque adventures of one Tino Faussone, a construction worker on bridges, cranes and oil rigs. It has sold well in Italy, although Primo Levi worried about its reception in the English-speaking world: the novel, partly written in Piedmontese dialect, must be something of a translator's nightmare. At any rate, one hopes the almost Rabelaisian humour of *La chiave a stella* will not be lost in translation, since the novel admirably conforms to Levi's belief that 'human beings suffer unjustly; man is great notwithstanding; he is saved by understanding, and by laughter.' (pp. 15-19)

Primo Levi in an interview with I.M. Thomson in
PN Review, *Vol. 14, No. 1, 1987, pp. 15-19.*

JOHN TAGLIABUE

Primo Levi, whose autobiographical writings drew on his experiences as an Auschwitz survivor and his training as a chemist, died [April 11] in Turin. He was 67 years old.

The authorities said they were treating the death as a suicide. Mr. Levi was found by members of his family and neighbors at the foot of a stairwell in the home where he was born, in the Crocetta neighborhood, and he was pronounced dead on arrival at a hospital.

Renzo Levi, the writer's son, said by telephone from Turin that his father had had serious bouts of depression in recent months.

The elder Mr. Levi had undergone minor surgery recently, and friends suggested he was deeply troubled about the condition of his 92-year-old mother, who was partially paralyzed by a stroke last year.

Already well known in Europe, Mr. Levi became prominent among American readers with the appearance in 1984 of the third volume of his autobiographical reflections, *The Periodic Table,* in which he used the chemical elements as a bridge to weave an unusual account of his experiences in the Nazi death camps.

His other books include *Survival in Auschwitz,* the first volume of his autobiographical trilogy; *The Reawakening,* the second volume; *Moments of Reprieve,* a series of sketches of the author's acquaintances from the camps, and, most recently, *The Drowned and the Saved.* He also wrote works of fiction, some of it under the pseudonym Damiano Malabaila.

Primo Levi was born in Turin on July 31, 1919, a descendant of Jews who had settled in the Piedmont, in northern Italy, after the expulsion of Jews from Spain. He studied chemistry at the University of Turin, even after the Mussolini regime barred Jews from institutes of higher learning in 1938, and received a degree in 1941.

In 1943, he quit his job at a Milan pharmaceutical laboratory to join Italian Partisans fighting the Fascist forces of Germany and Italy.

"I was not a very good Partisan," Mr. Levi told Herbert Mitgang in *The New York Times* in 1985. "When my unit was betrayed by an informer, I was interrogated by Italian Fascists and handed over to the Germans. I was put on a train with hundreds of other Jews and sent to Monowitz-Auschwitz, the factory part of the camp that used slave labor."

It was his experiences there, as No. 174517—the number was tattooed on his left arm, a few inches above the wrist—that were to shape his life and work.

His 1947 account, *Survival in Auschwitz*—also published under the title *If This Is a Man*—described daily life in the death camps in rich detail, creating a monument to the triumph of lucid intelligence over Nazi barbarism.

He attributed his survival in the camp to luck, to the Germans' need for chemists—he was given a job in a synthetic-rubber factory—and to an acquaintanceship with a fellow inmate, an Italian bricklayer who was not Jewish, who brought him bread and soup.

In *The Reawakening,* published in 1963, the author described his long and bizarre journey home to Turin after being liberated from the camp by Soviet soldiers.

He also drew on his Partisan days in a novel, *If Not Now, When?* The novel, published in Italy in 1982, chronicled the exploits in the closing months of the war of a band of Eastern European Jewish Partisans who dream of finding freedom in Palestine.

In recent years, Mr. Levi turned increasingly to works of fiction, including novels and short stories, and was a regular contributor of poetry to the Turin newspaper *La Stampa.*

He was the winner of several literary prizes, including the Strega Prize, a prestigious Italian award, in 1979. In 1985 he and Saul Bellow shared the Kenneth B. Smilen fiction award, sponsored by the Jewish Museum in New York.

While devoted to his writing, Mr. Levi continued his career as a chemist, working for a Turin paint factory, SIVA, for almost 30 years. From 1961 to 1974, he was the plant's general manager.

In an interview with *The New York Times* in December 1984, Mr. Levi described himself as "a chemist by conviction," but added, "After Auschwitz, I had an absolute need to write."

"Not only as a moral duty," he said, "but as a psychological need."

That need was reflected in a Yiddish proverb he used as an epigraph for *The Periodic Table:* "Troubles overcome are good to tell."

Mr. Levi wrote in an Italian enriched by snatches of the disappearing jargon of the Piedmontese Jews, which combined Hebrew roots with local endings and inflections.

Mr. Levi, who came from a middle-class family of assimilated Jews, once wrote that "a Jew is someone who at Christmas does not have a tree, who shouldn't eat salami but does, who has learned a little bit of Hebrew at 13 and then forgotten it."

But he remained close to the Italian Jewish community and two years ago he contributed an introduction to the catalogue of a newly opened Jewish museum in Turin.

The novelist Philip Roth, whose account of a conversation with the Italian appeared last October in *The New York Times Book Review,* said of Mr. Levi. . .:

> With the moral stamina and intellectual poise of a 20th-century titan, this slightly built, dutiful, unassuming chemist set out systematically to remember

the German hell on earth, steadfastly to think it through, and then to render it comprehensible in lucid, unpretentious prose. He was profoundly in touch with the minutest workings of the most endearing human events and with the most contemptible.

John Tagliabue, "Primo Levi, Author of Works on Holocaust, Is Dead," in The New York Times, *April 12, 1987, p. 42.*

NICHOLAS SHRIMPTON

'The poet who traversed the Inferno and never lost the tragic scars' was how *La Stampa* commemorated Primo Levi last week. An Italian Jew who survived Auschwitz, and returned to live and work in his native Turin, he was a crucial witness to the horrors of European Fascism: This was a man who suffered and was there. His autobiography, *If This Is a Man,* like much of his later fiction, recounts the terrible experience with unrancorous lucidity.

Though Dante or Lazarus are the parallels suggested by his obituaries, Primo Levi himself, in his latest book of stories to be translated into English, picks a rather different model. *The Wrench* is a series of encounters with a steel-rigger called Tino Faussone. Stuck in hotels or bunk rooms on the far-flung sites of the international oil industry, the chemist Levi and the construction worker Faussone spend their evenings swapping anecdotes.

The garrulous Faussone, of course, talks 10 times as much as the shy writer. But in the fifth story Levi, for once, asserts himself and compares the pleasures and perils of a rigger's life with those of his own. The literary life has its dangers—writers 'live badly, are melancholy, drink, smoke, can't sleep and die young.' Levi, however, is peculiar even among writers, for the simple reason that he is also a scientist. The analogy he draws is with Tiresias.

Tiresias was a prophet, and a human being with a double nature. Born a man, he spent seven years as a woman, and was uniquely equipped to compare the experience of the sexes. The doubleness which Levi claims is not sexual but a cultural one:

> In distant times I, too, had got involved gods with quarrelling among themselves; I, too, had encountered snakes in my path, and that encounter had changed my condition, giving me a strange power of speech. But since then, being a chemist in the world's eyes; and feeling, on the contrary, a writer's blood in my veins, I felt as if I had two souls in my body.

The distinction of the book is that it turns from the horrors of Levi's early experiences to a later world of work, curiosity, and professional satisfaction. As in his masterpiece, *The Periodic Table,* Levi deploys science as an optimistic image of the rational mind, a humane value to set against the darkness of scepticism, indifference and prejudice.

Here, however, the scientific vocation is also used in another way. The dominant voice in *The Wrench* is that of Tino Faussone (a literary device which, incidentally, involves a further Tiresian doubleness, allowing Levi to speak, appropriately, both as Jew and as Italian). Tino's work with his hands is steadily paralleled with the work of his inventor Primo Levi, allowing the tales to accumulate into a remarkable study of *homo faber,* man the creating animal. The stories are uneven, but at their best marvellously moving and suggestive, with a real sense of the poetry of physical matter and the epic quality of the human encounter with it.

Primo Levi began his literary career with an exceptional portrait of man the destroyer. We may perhaps take comfort from the fact that he ended it with so distinctive a vision of man the maker.

Nicholas Shrimpton, "The Art of Being Human," in The Observer, *April 19, 1987, p. 23.*

PHILIP ROTH

[*Roth is a highly acclaimed American novelist, short story writer, and critic known for his satirical portrayals of Jewish-American life. His works include the novels* Portnoy's Complaint (1969), The Ghost Writer (1979), *and* The Counterlife (1987), *which won the 1988 National Book Critics Circle Award, and the short fiction collections* Goodbye, Columbus and Five Short Stories (1959) *and* On the Air (1969). *In the following excerpt, Roth commends Levi for the courage and intellectual grace he demonstrates in his writings about the Holocaust.*]

[Primo Levi] endured the worst evil and then resurrected heroically from that horror one of the century's truly necessary books, *If This Is a Man.* With the moral stamina and intellectual poise of a twentieth-century Titan, this slightly built, dutiful, unassuming chemist set out systematically to remember the German hell on earth, steadfastly to think it through and then to render it comprehensible in lucid, unpretentious prose. He was profoundly in touch with the minutest workings of the most endearing human events and with the most contemptible. What has survived in Levi's writing isn't just his memory of the unbearable, but also, in *The Periodic Table* and *The Wrench,* his delight in what made the world exquisite to him. He was himself a magically endearing man, the most delicately forceful enchanter I've ever known.

Philip Roth, "Primo Levi, 1919-87," in The Observer, *April 19, 1987, p. 23.*

LEON WIESELTIER

The last letter I had from Primo Levi was dark and terse. He wrote of his worry for his ailing mother, and alluded elliptically, but with his characteristic calm, to anxieties he would not describe. He hoped, he said, to pick up his work again soon. A few months later he threw himself down a deep stairwell and smashed himself to death. His suicide is spirit-destroying. For it was Levi who was back from death. It was he who stood for the chance of composure after catastrophe, for the possibility that order and decency awaited the survivors of those camps. When Paul Celan took his own life in 1970, you could not be shocked; the act seemed to have completed the decomposition in his work; to have consummated its logic of leave-taking. But Levi remained attached to the world, despite what it did to him. That was why you cherished him. He hated oblivion. He was intact. Or so it seemed. Now I find myself dusting off an old panic: that the survivors never really survived, but merely lived on; that having died once, they will wish to die again; that they are unrestorable even by love. In his writing and in his person, Primo Levi dispelled such fears. He spoke for the bet that there is no blow from which the soul may not recover. When he smashed his body, he smashed his bet.

Leon Wieseltier, "Disorder and Early Sorrow," in The New Republic, *Vol. 196, No. 19, May 11, 1987, p. 42.*

[ELIZABETH MACKLIN]

The Italian writer and chemist Primo Levi, who died [April 11], at the age of sixty-seven, wrote some years ago about his first experience in a laboratory. The story, called "Hydrogen," was an early chapter in Levi's memoir *The Periodic Table,* in which each chapter is named for the element it recalls: cerium he'd encountered in Auschwitz, iron he'd found in the mountains outside his native Turin, and so on. He told the hydrogen story by way of a joke on himself—his young self mostly, though every so often he seemed to be telling the story on his grown self, too. In 1935, when Levi was sixteen and first chemistry-smitten, he and a more down-to-earth school friend got themselves into an older brother's makeshift but off-limits lab. After fiddling around a while with the dusty Bunsen burner, the two spent a concentrated hour feinting at glassblowing: "Even the slightest puff of breath in excess and the walls took on the iridescence of a soap bubble (until the glass) burst with a sharp little snap and its fragments were scattered over the floor with the tenuous rustle of eggshells." Then they turned to something more satisfyingly chemical, and more certain in its results: the electrolytic proof of the elemental proportions of water. Levi assembled the ingredients—a dry battery, two empty jam jars upside down in a beaker of water, a pinch of salt—and the experiment was set in motion. "I wrote the well-known equation on the blackboard," Levi recalled, "and explained to Enrico that what was written there was actually taking place." The next day, one of the jam jars, half full ("In pliant obsequiousness to theory"), held oxygen; the other, filled up, contained hydrogen—but this Levi's school friend stubbornly disbelieved:

> "Now we shall see," I said: I carefully lifted the cathode jar and, holding it with its open end down, lit a match and brought it close. There was an explosion, small but sharp and angry, the jar burst into splinters (luckily, I was holding it level with my chest and not higher), and there remained in my hand, as a sarcastic symbol, the glass ring of the bottom.

It was this—the sound of glass breaking, the boys' astonishment at the lawfully reacting gas—that came to our mind at the news of Levi's death. "The authorities said they were treating the death as a suicide," the *Times* reported, and the story went on to say that Levi had recently had minor surgery, and that "friends suggested he was deeply troubled about the condition of his 92-year-old mother, who was partially paralyzed by a stroke last year" [see excerpt above].

We also remembered a passage from *Survival in Auschwitz*—Levi's first book, written a year or so after the war—in which he discussed analytically the various inhabitants of the German *Lager,* or prison camp, where he had spent eleven months. In the passage we recalled, he wrote of the distinction made between those prisoners commonly known as Muselmänner ("This word 'Muselmann,' I do not know why, was used by the old ones of the camp to describe the weak, the inept, those doomed to selection," he said in a footnote) and everyone else—the drowned and the saved, he called them. He wrote:

> This division is much less evident in ordinary life; for there it rarely happens that a man loses himself. A man is normally not alone, and in his rise or fall is tied to the destinies of his neighbours; so that it is exceptional for anyone to acquire unlimited power, or to fall by a succession of defeats into utter ruin. Moreover, everyone is normally in possession of such spiritual, physical and even financial resources that the probabilities of a shipwreck, of total inadequacy

in the face of life, are relatively small. And one must take into account a definite cushioning effect exercised both by the law, and by the moral sense which constitutes a self-imposed law; for a country is considered the more civilized the more the wisdom and efficiency of its laws hinder a weak man from becoming too weak or a powerful one too powerful.

But in the Lager things are different.

When we first heard of Primo Levi's death, it seemed to us that there could be no plausible explanation for it, and, of course, no one could say with certainty why, having survived the *Lager* forty-some years ago, he would choose death now. It was Levi, after all, who assembled on paper those cool, light, and passionate words—as orderly and as carefully prepared as glass jars set out to receive acid—for specific use in contemplating large or small disasters and in counteracting despair. Our fear, naturally, was that the efficacy of all his words had somehow been cancelled by his death—that his hope, or faith, was no longer usable by the rest of us. Later, though, when we went and looked, we found that among his words he had left a precise vocabulary—a gift, possibly inadvertent—for the strangely familial pain his death had caused: "a sharp little snap." (pp. 31-2)

[*Elizabeth Macklin*], "*An Obituary for Primo Levi,*" in The New Yorker, *Vol. LXIII, No. 12, May 11, 1987, pp. 31-2.*

RICHARD EDER

[*Eder, an American critic and journalist, has written drama and literary reviews for the* New York Times *and the* Los Angeles Times. *In the following excerpt, he reflects on how Levi's suicide might affect a reader's perception of his work.*]

Years ago, as an apprentice reporter, I saw my first corpse. It was of a deranged pistol-waver who had been shot dead by the police in a New York subway car. Afterward, I remember riding the subway home at 3:30 in the morning, and noticing that what normally seemed scruffy—grimy cars, a drunk or two—suddenly shone. Simply because they were alive, or served life.

That was something of Primo Levi's art. An Italian Jew, a student chemist from a comfortable family and with comfortable prospects; he found himself, after a spell in the Resistance, in the wreckage of Auschwitz.

With death and degradation everywhere, what he noticed was life. The prisoner who hummed Mozart all day through his oversize nose, as if to announce: There is a world elsewhere. The slave laborer who practiced juggling with the building materials he was shifting. A cheerful con man who explained that no matter what happened, he had got the best of Hitler. Looking back, he found more good times than bad.

The theme is in Levi's works of direct testimony: *Survival in Auschwitz, The Reawakening, Moments of Reprieve.* It is in his masterpiece, *The Periodic Table,* where the properties of different chemical elements are metaphors for a series of reflections, anecdotes and fictions about life. It is voiced by the protean construction rigger in *The Monkey's Wrench,* a figure who travels the world building things and showing that "What a Piece of Work Is Man!" can also be read: "What a Man Is a Piece of Work!"

Such a theme could easily have taken the form of sermonizing. With Levi, it never did. Every bit of cheerfulness was paid for by pain; his flowers were not decorations but tiny muscles that broke the heavy soil they grew in. And there were no generalities; everything was as minutely particular as a chemistry experiment. Together, pain and particularity transformed message into art, of such idiosyncratic quality and with such a unique voice, that it was clearly only a matter of time until Levi's work received a Nobel Prize.

Time was not available, of course. Levi died in April, at 67. And the Italian authorities treated it as a suicide.

The death of a great artist is a special kind of loss. Suicide adds an even more special note of shock. With our literary suicides—Hart Crane, John Berryman, Sylvia Plath—we register the shock, look at their work and see, or think we see, the mortal risk-taking.

But this death produced anguish of a far different kind. The man of life who kills himself—far from confirming his work, did this to negate it?

The depths of feeling for Levi in the world of letters has been remarkable these last few years. A great deal has been written about him—I think of Philip Roth, Italo Calvion, Saul Bellow, Irving Howe, to mention a few—and every reader I know seems to regard him as a private discovery. Something about his vision was recalcitrant to fame, to its generalizing. He was just about fame-proof.

And so, the shock and the question: Are we betrayed? Only in the last couple of weeks—as if it took a while to react—there have been editorials in *The New Republic* and *The New Yorker* [see excerpts above]. A writer's suicide is not, to say the least, an easy or customary subject for editorializing. *The New Republic* seemed inclined to think that a shadow had fallen on Levi's work. *The New Yorker* thought differently. . . .

In a way, there is not much to add except a gloss. If Levi's special retort to the Holocaust was on the order of "in the midst of death we are in life," he never suggested that this was more than a corollary to the reverse principle. The chemist achieves, temporarily, a more highly organized state for his elements, but entropy will decay them. *The Monkey's Wrench* will not last forever. If the chemist, the artisan and the artist create orders that will survive them, that is exactly the point. They themselves will not survive.

Levi wrote of life as an immortal principle, not an immortal possession. The stubborn radiance of his notion of what it means to be human is universally accessible but individually transient. It is because the mortal Levi, with whatever depressions and despairs he may have possessed, could write as he did that what he wrote is so valuable.

In **"Story of a Coin,"** Levi wrote of a camp inmate who lived in luxury in return for helping the Nazis keep his fellow Jews in order. Finally, he too went off to the gas chambers; his only reward being to ride in a special coach hooked up to the rest of the death train.

"We too," Levi wrote, "are so dazzled by power and money as to forget our essential fragility, forget that all of us are in the ghetto, that the ghetto is fenced in, that beyond the fence wait the lords of death and not far away the train is waiting."

That would seem to take full account of our April loss. More modest, and more characteristic, is Levi's meditation on the carbon chain that lies behind all life, including his own. He visualizes a single atom in this chain entering his bloodstream and becoming a part of one of his brain cells.

The cell in question, and within it the atom in question, is in charge of my writing, in a gigantic minuscule game that nobody has yet described. It is that which at this instant, issuing out of a labyrinthine tangle of yeses and no's, makes my hand run along a certain path on the paper, mark it with these volutes that are signs: a double snap, up and down, between two levels of energy, guides this hand of mine to impress on the paper this dot, here, this one.

The dot, the period, the carbon atom—giving life to Levi's paragraph and, in due course, ending it.

Two painters I know set up a small shrine in one corner of their crowded studio when they heard of Levi's death. Among the daily and enduring things were a red candle, a bunch of yellow flowers, a clock, half a cup of tea, and a dust-jacket photograph of the writer. One of the painters did a watercolor and gave it to me, and I look at it while writing this. Carbon atom. Carbon atom. Carbon atom. Carbon atom.

Richard Eder, "The Death of Primo Levi," in Los Angeles Times Book Review, *May 31, 1987, p. 11.*

ALEXANDER STILLE

[*In the following excerpt, Stille, who conducted an interview with Levi a year before his death, speculates on how Levi's experience in Auschwitz affected his life and ultimately led to his suicide.*]

When a writer commits suicide it is difficult not to reinterpret his books in light of his final act. The temptation is particularly strong in the case of Primo Levi, much of whose work stemmed from his own experience at Auschwitz. The warmth and humanity of his writing had made Levi a symbol to his readers of the triumph of reason over the barbarism of genocide. For some, his violent death seemed to call that symbol into question. An article in *The New Yorker* [see excerpt above] went so far as to suggest that perhaps the "efficacy of all his words had somehow been canceled by his death—that his hope, or faith, was no longer usable by the rest of us. An author's suicide is seen as the logical conclusion of all he was written or as an ironic contradiction—rather than as the result of a purely personal torment.

Since learning of Levi's suicide I have been trying to reconcile in my mind the writer and the man I had come to know with his violent death.

Levi bore none of the obvious emotional scars common among Holocaust survivors, none of the usual reticence in discussing his past. He was a person of remarkable serenity, openness and good humor, with a striking absence of bitterness. He was able to describe a Nazi prison guard with the same objectivity and understanding he showed in writing or speaking of his fellow prisoners. It seemed a kind of miracle that a person of such gentle temperament and finely tuned intellectual balance could have emerged from the nightmare of Auschwitz. Levi retained the shy sensitivity and inquisitiveness of the chemistry student he was before the war, and yet he had the wisdom and toughness of a survivor who has seen more of life than anyone should.

Levi was free of the vanity and self-importance of many writers perhaps because he had worked for 30 years as a chemist in a paint factory. He was unfailingly generous in response to the many demands on his time and politely answered even the most stupid questions. Slight of build, almost wiry, with a thick shock of white hair and alert eyes, he had a simplicity of manner that belied his considerable intellectual sophistication.

Unlike some survivors who remained rootless after the war, Levi had profound ties to his family and his city. After Auschwitz, he returned to live in the Turin apartment his family has occupied for three generations. He contributed regularly to the Turin newspaper *La Stampa* and stood by the Turinese publishing house Einaudi even after it went into receivership and most of its other prestigious authors had abandoned it.

As a writer Levi grew from being simply an eloquent witness of the Holocaust into a full-blown imaginative novelist. After his first two volumes of memoirs about his wartime experience (*Survival in Auschwitz* and *The Reawakening*), he drew on his life as a chemist to produce *The Periodic Table, The Monkey's Wrench* and two collections of short stories not yet translated into English. Throughout, he remained in the stately old apartment building in Corso Umberto where he and his wife spent much of their time caring for his ailing 92-year-old mother. Their son lived just down the hall. Writing his books in the room in which he was born, working on a computer, Levi seemed both deeply rooted in the past and still intensely curious about the present. But last April 11, just outside his fourth-floor apartment, he hurled himself down the building's central stairwell to his death.

The last months of Levi's life were dominated by personal problems. In November his mother suffered a paralytic stroke, requiring around-the-clock care. Levi himself had been hospitalized for two prostate operations, which, although minor, tired and depressed him. A doctor had placed him on antidepressant drugs, and some have suggested that a reaction to a change in dosage may have led to his seemingly impulsive act. While these circumstances may account for the timing of his death, it is difficult not to search his Holocaust experience for the origin of his underlying despair.

Levi's final nonfiction book, *The Drowned and the Saved,* which has not been translated into English and which I had occasion to discuss with him in Turin a year ago, sheds some light on the last period of his life. While *Survival in Auschwitz, The Reawakening* and *The Periodic Table* are ultimately hopeful books, *The Drowned and the Saved* is a dark mediation on the meaning of the Nazi exterminations after the passing of 40 years. In it he recalls how the Nazis tormented prisoners by telling them that even if through some miracle they managed to survive, no one would believe them when they returned home.

While this was not literally the case, it contains a larger truth. By the end of his life Levi had become increasingly convinced that the lessons of the Holocaust were destined to be lost as it took a place among the routine atrocities of history. Levi was troubled by the sentimental distortions of survivors and sympathetic historians and by the collective amnesia of those responsible for the exterminations. In recent years he had spoken often to students and joined the board of his former high school. He was acutely aware of how remote his experience had come to seem to the youngest generation.

"Holocaust survivors," Levi said in one of our talks, "can be divided into two distinct categories: those who talk and those who don't." Levi, clearly, was in the first category. In our psychoanalytic culture we tend to believe that those who talk are better off and happier than those who don't. But those who prefer silence and forgetfulness may have a successful self-protective strategy. Those who talk are also those who remem-

ber. Levi said he could remember literally everything that happened during his year and a half of imprisonment. Forty years later he could recall entire sentences he had heard in languages he did not even know: Polish, Yiddish, Hungarian and Greek.

Explaining why he kept returning to the subject of Auschwitz, Levi wrote in *Moments of Reprieve,* a collection of autobiographical sketches, that "a host of details continued to surface in my memory and the idea of letting them fade distressed me. A great number of human figures especially stood out against that tragic background: friends, people I'd traveled with, even adversaries—begging me one after another to help them survive and enjoy the ambiguous perennial existence of literary characters."

In *The Drowned and the Saved,* Levi writes about the tremendous difficulty of living with Holocaust memories. Suicide is, in fact, a major preoccupation of the book. He dedicates an entire chapter to the Belgian philosopher Jean Améry, who had been with Levi at Auschwitz and who killed himself in 1978. While any suicide, Levi writes, "is open to a constellation of different interpretations," he believes that in the case of Holocaust survivors the origin is likely to reside in their war experiences. For survivors, he writes, "the period of their imprisonment (however long ago) is the center of their life, the event that, for better or worse, has marked their entire existence." In a passage he quotes from Améry, Levi may have left us an interpretive key to his own death: "He who has been tortured remains tortured. . . .He who has suffered torment can no longer find his place in the world. Faith in humanity—cracked by the first slap across the face, then demolished by torture—can never be recovered."

But while Améry was a man who tried to retaliate against violence, Levi described himself as "personally incapable of responding to a blow with a blow." He responded to the violence of Auschwitz by internalizing it. Acutely sensitive to the suffering of others, he was particularly subject to feelings of guilt for having been unable to do more for those who suffered and died around him.

While many of his readers viewed him as an example of the triumph of good over evil, Levi would probably have rejected that view as an oversimplification. When I spoke with him in Turin, he said that he was especially concerned by a tendency to view the Holocaust in black and white terms, with the Germans as the bad and the Jews the good. "The world of the *Lager* I witnessed was much more complex," he said, "just as the world outside it is much more complex." The architects of the Holocaust created a system that delegated much of the physical punishment of prisoners to other prisoners. By creating an infinite number of subtle divisions and privileges, they pitted the inmates against one another in a brutal struggle for survival.

But to Levi, Darwin's laws were thrown into reverse. "The worst survived: the violent, the callous, the collaborators and the spies," he said. Levi himself did not resort to collaboration—he survived largely through the help of an Italian worker who brought him food and through his job as a chemist in a camp factory—but he was nonetheless tormented by the memory of companions he was unable to help. In his last book he wrote: "Each of us (who survived) supplanted his neighbor and lives in his place. . . . It's deeply hidden like a moth. You can't see it from outside but it gnaws and bites."

During his last months Levi had been talking extensively about his past with the Turinese literary critic Giovanni Tesio, who was gathering material for a biography. A few days before his death, Levi broke off their conversations because the memories of Auschwitz were becoming too painful, Mr. Tesio said recently in an interview. Other friends spoke about a nightmare Levi often had. In the dream, he told them: "I would see myself at the dinner table with my family or at work or in a green countryside. A relaxed atmosphere. And yet I felt a subtle anxiety, the sense of an imminent threat. Then as the dream proceeded, the scene dissolved. The family disappeared. There was no more work. No more countryside. I was still in the camp. And there was nothing real outside of the camp."

Alexander Stille, "Primo Levi: Reconciling the Man and the Writer," in The New York Times Book Review, July 5, 1987, p. 5.

JAMES ATLAS

[Atlas, an American critic, biographer, novelist, and editor, is the author of the biography Delmore Schwartz: The Life of an American Poet (1977) and the novel The Great Pretender (1986). In the following excerpt, he chronicles the various physical and emotional problems that may have contributed to Levi's suicide.]

To claim for himself special powers of intelligence or will would never have occurred to Levi; it wasn't in his nature. Yet reading Survival in Auschwitz, the story of his tenure in hell, I couldn't help feeling that his character must have contributed in some way to the miraculous defiance of statistics. One of the most notable things about this book is its magisterial equanimity. There is no self-pity, none of the lamentation characteristic of Elie Wiesel. "There is no why here," said one of Levi's guards; for Levi, inquiring into the "why of things" was simply what one did. His discourse on the social structure of the camp—the way clothes and rations were distributed, the work details, the insanely complicated rules and regulations—is amazingly precise. Auschwitz was an experiment, the most perverse and barbarous ever devised by man, but it could still yield knowledge, and it was in this scientific spirit that Levi observed "what is essential and what adventitious to the conduct of the human animal in the struggle for life."

For all the suffering it chronicles, Survival in Auschwitz is not a gloomy book. Time and again, Levi manages to find pleasure in the slightest things. On those rare nights when he doesn't have to share his bunk, he considers himself lucky. When the weather is warm, he rejoices because it isn't cold. When the ration of watery gruel is more plentiful than usual, he counts it "a happy day." Hope is the momentary absence of pain. In one memorable scene, struggling to carry a heavy soup pot, he begins to recite a passage from Dante's Commedia to a French comrade:

> Think of your breed; for brutish ignorance
> Your mettle was not made; you were made men,
> To follow after knowledge and excellence.

If Survival in Auschwitz is optimistic, its sequel, The Reawakening, a picaresque chronicle of the months Levi spent wandering the far reaches of Eastern Europe and Russia, is positively buoyant. Liberated from Auschwitz, he found himself shuttled off hundreds of miles in the wrong direction, transferred from camp to camp, an eternal refugee. Yet even as the dream of returning home receded, Levi reveled in his new freedom. The time adrift was "a parenthesis of unlimited availability," he declared, "a providential but unrepeatable gift of fate." Arriving in the ruined city of Katowice, he and his tattered compatriot are "as cheerful as schoolboys." Invigorated by a cup of tea as he's camping out on the floor of a

train station in some distant province, he's "tense and alert, hilarious, lucid and sensitive." He had survived. He was alive.

In his interview with Levi, Philip Roth remarked on the "exuberance" manifest in The Reawakening, its atmosphere of celebration. "Family, home, factory are good things in themselves," Levi replied, "but they deprived me of something that I still miss: adventure." The experience of Auschwitz, catastrophic as it was, enlarged his character. "I remember having lived my Auschwitz year in a condition of exceptional spiritedness," he told Roth, comparing his absorption in camp routine to "the curiosity of the naturalist who finds himself transplanted into an environment that is monstrous, but new, monstrously new." For Levi, Auschwitz was "an education." (p. 80)

For Levi, chemistry was inspirational, both an anchor in the world and a way of interpreting it. When he wrote about his profession in La Stampa, the Turin newspaper to which he contributed an occasional column over the years, it was in a spirit of adventure, and with a lucidity that verged on joy. The behavior of beetles, the challenge of astronomy, the physiology of pain: for Levi, the "two cultures" were one. Science enlivened his writing, made it precise; his job as a chemist got him out of the house. "My factory militanza—my compulsory and honorable service there—kept me in touch with the world of real things."

In 1977, Levi retired in order to devote himself to writing. By now he was a public figure of sorts in Italy, and a celebrity in Turin. When a German television crew showed up to make a documentary and followed him around the streets, people greeted him on the tram. He gave talks in the local schools, answered his ever increasing mail, made himself available to scholars and journalists in his study in the Corso Re Umberto. "He was a person of remarkable serenity, openness and good humor, with a striking absence of bitterness," wrote Alexander Stille, a young journalist who knew about Levi [see excerpt above]. To Roth, he was a vivid presence, voluble, shrewd, preternaturally attentive: "He seemed to me inwardly animated more in the manner of some little quick-silver woodland creature empowered by the forest's most astute intelligence. . . . His alertness is nearly palpable, keenness trembling within him like his pilot light."

His intellectual energy was prodigious. He studied Yiddish in order to write If Not Now, When?, his novel about a band of Jewish partisans fighting for survival at the end of World War II. He translated Heine, Kipling, Lévi-Strauss, and devoted long hours to playing chess with the Macintosh computer he'd installed in his study. Working with his British translator, Stuart Woolf, Levi was indefatigable. He would sit down after dinner, "beginning around nine o'clock, and go on until midnight or one in the morning, and he'd be up again the next day regularly," Woolf recalled in a television program dedicated to Levi. "Auschwitz had conditioned him to living with very little sleep."

Levi seemed happy in his fame; in a memoir called **"Beyond Survival,"** published in 1982, he noted that If Not Now, When? had won "two of the three most coveted Italian literary awards" (the Campiello and Viareggio) and was "meeting with great success in Italy among the public and the critics." On the wall of his study he put up a chart to help him keep track of the translations of his books in many languages. Levi was always dropping in at the Luxemburg, a bookstore near the Piazza Castello that stocked English and American periodicals, to read his reviews. "He was proud of his reputation," recalled Agnese Incisa, formerly of Einaudi. "He didn't have an agent. Everything we did, we had to call up Primo first."

Visitors to the Corso Re Umberto were struck by how close the family seemed. Both of Levi's children were unmarried: his son, Renzo, a physicist, lived next door; his daughter, Lisa, a biology teacher, had an apartment in the neighborhood. Levi's ninety-two-year-old mother, nearly blind and the victim of a paralytic stroke, was confined to her room in the fourth-floor flat. There were two nurses in attendance, and an Arab student, Amir, who helped around the house; but the Levis lived simply, and disapproved of servants. "It was a typical Turinese household," remembered Anna Vitale, of the Comunità Ebraica. "They were well-off, but they didn't live like wealthy people." Levi's book-lined study, furnished with an old flowered sofa and a comfortable easy chair, was his refuge. On the shelves were playful constructions made out of the enameled copper wire manufactured by Levi's factory: a wire butterfly, a wire owl, a bird, and one that Levi described to Roth as "a man playing with his nose." ("'A Jew,' I suggested. 'Yes, yes,' he said, laughing, 'a Jew, of course.'") The only emblem of his trauma was a sketch on the wall of a barbed-wire fence: Auschwitz.

As his mother's condition deteriorated, Levi traveled less and less, but in the spring of 1985 he was given the Kenneth B. Smilen award, sponsored by the Jewish Museum in New York, and his American publishers persuaded him to give a series of informal talks in the United States. *The Periodic Table* had appeared the year before, graced with a blurb from Saul Bellow, and been instantly recognized for the classic that it is. (Twenty publishers turned it down before Schocken Books picked up the rights.) (pp. 81-2)

It was a triumphant journey. "He loved his trip to America," recalled Agnese Incisa. "It gave him a chance to be away." Back in Turin, Levi resumed his tranquil routine. He made weekly visits to his publisher, Einaudi, whose offices were just around the corner. He was collecting material for a book in the form of love letters from a chemist to a young girl—"a sort of epistolary romance," according to Arthur Samuelson, who became Levi's editor when Summit Books acquired the rights to his work. Agnese Incisa remembers going to see him at Christmas 1986 and spending hours with him at his Macintosh computer. "It was the last time I saw him happy."

Suicide among Holocaust survivors is hardly uncommon. Levi addressed the issue himself in *The Drowned and the Saved,* out this month from Summit in a masterly translation by Raymond Rosenthal. He was haunted by the memory of his friend Jean Améry, a philosopher who had survived Auschwitz and committed suicide in 1978. Few suicides occurred in the camps, Levi noted: "The day was dense: one had to think about satisfying hunger, in some way elude fatigue and cold, avoid the blows; precisely because of the constant imminence of death there was no time to concentrate on the idea of death." Suicide, Levi argued, was a reflection of the victim's inward guilt, a punishment for suppressed, unspoken sins; but why punish yourself when you were being punished on a scale beyond what anyone had ever been called upon to endure? At Auschwitz, guilt was superfluous: "One was already expiating it by one's daily suffering."

The subject was clearly on Levi's mind. In one of his *La Stampa* essays, he examined the death of another survivor who eventually committed suicide, the Romanian-born poet Paul Celan.

Celan was a "tragic and noble" figure, Levi conceded, but his inchoate, nearly indecipherable last poems constituted "the rattle of a dying man." They were devoid of hope. "I believe that Celan the poet should be mediated upon and pitied rather than imitated," Levi declared. Three years later, Levi was dead by his own hand.

Perhaps the most devastating aspect of Levi's suicide was its unexpectedness. Even among his closest friends, few were aware of his despair. "He was a happy man, *allegro,*" says the eminent political scientist Norberto Bobbio, who had known Levi for decades. "Three days before his death, he was tranquil and serene." Roth, who visited him in Turin seven months before his death, insisted that "he was as filled with a sense of joy and well-being as a man can be."

But there were those who sensed a darkening in Levi's mood, and not only toward the end. "He was a deeply depressed person," Dr. Roberto Pattono, one of Levi's physicians, told me. "I thought he was suicidal the first time I met him. Years ago, I said to myself: It is only a matter of time." A close friend of the family showed me a poem Levi wrote in the mid-seventies. "It has gotten late, my dears" was the opening line.

"There were brief periods of depression," said Bruno Vasari, the former managing director of Italian public television. It was late at night, and we were sitting in the parlor of his apartment off the busy Via Roma. It was an old-world apartment, full of beautiful things: art books piled up on the coffee table, plush furniture, Impressionist prints up on the walls. Vasari, a large, dignified, soft-spoken man with a mane of white hair, seemed weary. He had been in Mauthausen, he told me—"one of the most brutal camps." He opened one of Levi's books and showed me a poem entitled "The Survivor," dedicated to "B.V." In it Levi had quoted some lines from Coleridge:

> *Dopo di allora, ad ora incerta,*
>
> Since then, at an uncertain hour,
> That agony returns:
> And till my ghastly tale is told,
> This heart within me burns.

"The most important thing for him was to write," Vasari stressed. "One had to live not only to write but to tell one's story, to testify." He left the room and returned with another book: the Bible. He opened it to Exodus 13:8. "And thou shalt shew thy son in that day, saying, This is done because of that which the Lord did unto me when I came forth out of Egypt." "To testify," Vasari said again with quiet emphasis, "in the religious sense." He referred me to the opening passage of *The Drowned and the Saved,* where Levi quotes the boast of an SS man who declares that even if a handful of Jews survive, the world will never believe their story. "Strangely enough," writes Levi, "this same thought ('even if we were to tell it, we would not be believed') arose in the form of nocturnal dreams produced by the prisoners' despair." That was Levi's great fear, said Vasari: that he wouldn't be believed.

Levi had devoted his life to bringing before the world the meticulous evidence of what had happened, what had been done by men to men. He had chaperoned children on trips to Auschwitz, lectured, and given interviews; he had written books. Yet he wondered if he had done enough. "How much of the concentration camp world is dead and will not return, like slavery and the duelling code?" he asked in *The Drowned and the Saved.* "How much . . . is coming back? What can each of us do, so that in this world pregnant with threats, at least this threat will be nullified?'' To those who persisted in asking why the Jews hadn't fled, he replied: What are we doing about nuclear war? ''Why aren't we gone, why aren't we leaving our country, why aren't we fleeing 'before'?''

The Drowned and the Saved, Levi's last testament, is very different from anything he wrote before. What comes through so powerfully in this anguished book is anger—a new emotion for Levi. ''I'm not capable of acting like Jean Améry,'' he once told an interviewer, referring to an episode in which Améry had assaulted a Polish prisoner. Violence was alien to Levi. There's a moving passage in *The Periodic Table* where, confined in a cell at Aosta after his arrest by the Fascists, he shares his crust of bread with a mouse: ''I felt more like a mouse than he; I was thinking of the road in the woods, the snow outside, the indifferent mountains, the hundred splendid things which if I could go free I would be able to do, and a lump rose in my throat.'' That generosity was Levi's essence.

How long could he maintain his equanimity? *The Drowned and the Saved* is a cry of barely stifled rage against the Germans. Why did they do what they did? It was their nature. In the Third Reich, ''the best choice, the choice imposed from above, was the one that entailed the greatest amount of affliction, the greatest amount of waste, of physical and moral suffering. The 'enemy' must not only die, but must die in torment.''

It was this crime against the innocent that obsessed Levi. It was a crime beyond expiation, a wound that festered and would never heal. In his remarkable last chapter, Levi quoted at length from letters Germans had written him, remorselessly showing their evasions and lies, their feeble efforts to justify themselves in the face of what could never be justified. He would not grant the forgiveness they sought. The legacy of the camps was ineradicable. His dead friend Améry had written: ''Anyone who has been tortured remains tortured. . . .Anyone who has suffered torture never again will be able to be at ease in the world.''

For Levi, survival was a gift—perhaps undeserved. He was troubled by the thought that ''this testifying of mine could by itself gain for me the privilege of surviving and living for many years without serious problems.'' Levi considered himself among the lucky few: not only had he lived, he had become a success. ''We are those who by their prevarications or abilities or good luck did not touch bottom.'' The real victims were those who had suffered in silence.

But, in his own way, Levi himself was mute, enduring his life without complaint. Liberated from Auschwitz, he found himself four decades later a virtual prisoner in his own home. From her room down at the end of the hall, his mother, Ester, dominated his existence. She woke up at 6:30, demanded breakfast at 7, called out to Levi day and night. He pushed her around the neighborhood in her wheelchair, kept a vigil beside her bed. When he visited friends, he would rush off after an hour, explaining that he was needed at home. ''He was the most dutiful Jewish son who ever lived,'' says Roth. ''He and Lucia were like slaves to the family situation,'' according to Norberto Bobbio. Levi's mother-in-law, ninety-five, who lived down the block, required equally strenuous ministrations. ''Primo had these two old ladies on his back,'' said of his friends bluntly. ''He was surrounded by sick old women.'' Why didn't he put his mother in a home? ''Out of the question,'' declared Bobbio. ''He was too good a son. He'd seen too much suffering to inflict any of his own.''

Levi was on antidepressants, and briefly saw a psychiatrist, but when she tried to probe his feelings of aggression, he abruptly broke off treatment. In February 1987, he entered the hospital for a prostate operation, and was taken off his antidepressant medicine. ''Don't visit me,'' he told Giovanni Tesio, a scholar who had been interviewing him for months. ''I'm very boring when I feel badly.'' The operation was a success, but it brought on a host of distressing urological problems.

Levi seldom ventured out. ''He wasn't seeing anyone,'' said Agnese Incisa. ''He would come in and sit in the office and stare.'' He refused invitations to speak and failed to attend meetings of his social club, the Famija Piemönteisa, or the weekly dinners with friends at the Cambio, Turin's most exclusive restaurant. ''He was getting worse and worse,'' Ernesto Ferrero, and editor at Einaudi, told Valeria Gandus and Gian Paolo Rossetti, who interviewed many of Levi's friends and associates for the Italian magazine *Panorama* in the weeks after his death. ''We cosseted him, telephoned him, urged him to take his mind off things, busy himself with concrete matters. . . .It was a bad period, but we were sure that it would pass.'' Toward the end of February, Levi broke off his conversations with Giovanni Tesio. ''I don't feel like doing this anymore,'' he said tersely. ''Let's stop.''

One of Levi's most persistent complaints was that he couldn't write. *Non posso scrivere.* He had been a prolific author all his life; his last two novels, *If Not Now, When?* and *The Monkey's Wrench,* the garrulous monologue of an itinerant construction worker, had made his reputation as a novelist. But he was terrified that he had nothing more to say. Largely spared the negative reviews that few writers can avoid, he was perplexed by Fernanda Eberstadt's essay on him in the October 1985 issue of *Commentary,* which claimed that he was insufficiently Jewish, and argued that his later work suffered from ''a certain inhibiting fastidiousness and insubstantiality.'' Levi was a writer who read his reviews.

In April, Levi seemed to improve. ''He was eager to get back to work,'' recalled Dr. Pattono. Stuart Woolf thought Levi ''seemed to be in much better spirits than I'd seen him in on the previous occasion.'' On April 8, Levi wrote a letter to the Venetian writer Ferdinando Camon. ''Primo explained to me how much he would have liked to see his latest book translated and published in France,'' Camon told Gandus and Rossetti, the reporters from *Panorama.* ''The thought that Gallimard, one of the most authoritative publishers on the other side of the Alps, should be interested in his work filled him with enthusiasm.'' The next day, Levi was offered the honorary post of president of Einaudi, then in the midst of a reorganization. He was flattered by the proposal, remembers Norberto Bobbio, and declined it with regret. On April 10, Giovanni Tesio called, and Levi answered in a happy voice. ''*Ciao, Giovanni,*'' he said. ''We should begin again.''

That night, a friend concerned abut Levi's state of mind called to see how he was doing. ''Bad,'' Levi reported.

''At least you can play chess with your computer,'' said the friend.

''Yes, but it beats me.''

The next morning, Levi's wife went out shopping and left him alone with his mother and a nurse. A few minutes later, after he'd gotten the mail, Levi rushed out to the landing and hurled himself over the railing of the wide staircase. Death was instantaneous. (pp. 81-4, 94)

Rita Levi Montalcini, a childhood friend of Levi's and a Nobel laureate in medicine, speculated in a lengthy interview that Levi hadn't committed suicide at all. Perhaps he had plunged over the railing by accident, while calling down to the concierge. More likely, Dr. Montalcini surmised, it had been what psychiatrists refer to as a raptus, a sudden fit of insanity that could have been precipitated by some irregularity in his reaction to the dosage of his anti-depressant drugs. Whatever the cause, it was a frightening way to die, especially for a chemist, who could have found less violent ways to kill himself.

Every suicide, Levi had written, apropos the death of Améry, provokes "a nebula of explanations." Had there been financial problems? The year before, the house of Einaudi had gone into receivership, and Levi stayed on while most of the writers on its list jumped ship. Some people intimated that Levi's loyalty had cost him a lot of money, but Agnese Incisa told me that Einaudi had managed to pay "most of the royalties" from *If Not Now, When?*, despite its own financial difficulties.

Or was it heredity? In *The Periodic Table,* Levi had offered portraits of his eccentric relatives: the doctor uncle who neglected his practice and squandered his days on a cot in a filthy attic on the Borgo Vanchiglia reading old newspapers; his grandmother, who spent the last twenty years of her very long life mysteriously cloistered in her room; a remote ancestor, the uncle of his maternal grandmother, who took to his bed when

his parents refused to let him marry a lowly peasant girl, and stayed there for twenty-two years; his grandfather, rumored to have killed himself over his wife's infidelities, the wife herself half mad. Levi's tone was ironic, but the history is significant.

Inevitably, there was speculation that the Holocaust had reached out to claim another victim. Levi "had built a public image for himself, but inside he was very corroded," testified Ferdinando Camon in *Panorama*. "The operation of memorizing, cataloguing, bearing witness to the Nazi horrors and barbarities took a tremendous psychic toll. This is a suicide that must be dated back to 1945. It did not take place then, because Primo wanted (and had) to write. Having finished his work (*The Drowned and the Saved* ends this cycle) he was free to kill himself. And he did."

Perhaps it did go that far back. As he was wheeled into the operating room last February, Levi rolled up his sleeve and pointed to the number tattooed on his arm: "That is my disease." Reading over *Survival in Auschwitz,* I was struck by the passage where Levi suggested that to come down with diphtheria in a concentration camp would be "more surely fatal than jumping off a fourth floor." That book was written in 1947, in Levi's fourth-floor flat on Corso Re Umberto. (p. 94)

James Atlas, "The Survivor's Suicide," in Vanity Fair, *Vol. 51, No. 1, January, 1988, pp. 78-84, 94.*

Charles Ludlam
April 12, 1943 - May 28, 1987

American dramatist, actor, and director.

(See also *CLC*, Vol. 46 and *Contemporary Authors*, Vols. 85-88, 112 [obituary].)

PRINCIPAL WORKS

Big Hotel   (drama)   1967
Conquest of the Universe   (drama)   1967; also performed
    as *When Queens Collide*, 1967
The Grand Tarot   (drama)   1969
Turds in Hell [with Bill Vehr]   (drama)   1969
Bluebeard   (drama)   1970
Corn   (drama)   1972
Eunuchs of the Forbidden City   (drama)   1972
Camille: A Tear-Jerker   (drama)   1973
Hot Ice   (drama)   1974
Stage Blood   (drama)   1974
Professor Bedlam's Educational Punch and Judy Show
    (puppet drama)   1975
Der Ring Gott Farblonjet   (drama)   1977
The Ventriloquist's Wife   (drama)   1978
The Enchanted Pig   (drama)   1979
Reverse Psychology   (drama)   1980
Le bourgeois avant-garde   (drama)   1983
Galas: A Modern Tragedy   (drama)   1983
The Mystery of Irma Vep: A Penny Dreadful   (drama)
    1984
The Artificial Jungle   (drama)   1986
Salammbô   (drama)   1986
Medea   (drama)   1987

Sara Krulwich/NYT Pictures

JEREMY GERARD

Charles Ludlam, one of the most prolific and flamboyant artists in the theater avant garde, who seemed to be on the verge of breaking into the main stream of American culture, died of pneumonia [May 28]. He was 44 years old and had been suffering from AIDS.

Mr. Ludlam's death stunned a theater community that is struggling daily—mostly, until now, in private, personal ways—with the devastation of AIDS. The announcement of his death and the causes was made by his lawyer, Walter Gidaly.

Only last week, Mr. Ludlam sat in his room at St. Vincent's Hospital in Greenwich Village and discussed a production of Shakespeare's *Titus Andronicus* with Joseph Papp, producer of the New York Shakespeare Festival. A few days before, he had withdrawn as director of the same play at Mr. Papp's Free Shakespeare in the Park and the producer promised to reserve

the play for Mr. Ludlam, perhaps next season, in a space in the Public Theater complex.

Mr. Ludlam had known for just two or three months that he was suffering from AIDS, according to the circle of friends closest to him. For a few days he appeared to have turned the corner, telling a reporter last week that he expected to be released from the hospital shortly. Then his condition quickly worsened, leaving him unable to breathe without a respirator, the victim of a disease that made a formerly healthy man incapable of fighting the pneumonia. AIDS, or acquired immune deficiency syndrome, strips the body of its immunological defenses.

"We lost an extraordinary artist who was just on his way to a tremendous breakthrough in theater and opera," Mr. Papp said yesterday.

With a key role in *The Big Easy*, a feature film scheduled for summer release, and the prospect of completing *A Piece of Pure Escapism*, a major stage project in which he would have played the magician Harry Houdini, Mr. Ludlam seemed ready to move beyond the tiny theaters and faithful audiences that had supported him and into the mainstream.

For two decades, since establishing the Ridiculous Theatrical Company in 1967, Mr. Ludlam recalled the 19th-century theater entrepreneur, producing and directing the plays he wrote and starring in them (often in female as well as male roles) with a company that returned season after season.

He was a master of travesty, creating in a tiny grotto theater on Sheridan Square critically and popularly acclaimed parodies of such familiar genres as the dime novel (*The Mystery of Irma Vep*), film noir (*The Artificial Jungle*) and opera (*Camille, Der Ring Gott Farblonjet*).

Mr. Ludlam also had an eye for the absurdities of modern life, needling art as fashion (*Le Bourgeois Avant-Garde*), psychoanalysis *(Reverse Psychology)*, the cult of superstardom *(Galas)* and his own craft (*How to Write a Play*). During its first decade and a half, the Ridiculous presented its most popular works in repertory, a practice Mr. Ludlam abandoned several years ago in favor of doing only new plays.

Mr. Ludlam, who lived in Greenwich Village, was making forays beyond his own theater, as well. In 1984 he played the title role in the American Ibsen Theater production of *Hedda Gabler* in Pittsburgh, in August 1985 he staged the American premiere of *The English Cat*, by Hans Werner Henze, for the Santa Fe Opera.

"His career was blossoming on so many fronts that he couldn't possibly have accomplished them all," Steven Samuels, general manager of the Ridiculous, said [May 28].

The theater was indisputably Mr. Ludlam's most comfortable domain. Though his plays often were characterized by crossdressing, free use of the double-entendre and comic exaggeration, he resisted attempts to categorize his work as camp.

"One of the problems with accepting a tag like avant garde or gay theater or neo-post-infra-realism," he once said, "is that you're a bit like an Indian on a reservation selling trinkets to the tourists. You have no real interaction with the culture, and whatever impact you may have had on that culture is nullified.

"If people take the time to come here more than once, they see I don't have an ax to grind even though I do have a mission. That mission is to have a theater that can offer possibilities that aren't being explored elsewhere."

With *The Mystery of Irma Vep* and *The Artificial Jungle*, Mr. Ludlam undoubtedly found his widest audience.

The first was a tour de force in which Mr. Ludlam and Everett Quinton, an actor who also was his longtime companion, shared a dozen roles.

Frank Rich, chief drama critic of *The New York Times*, cited it as one of the best plays of 1984, writing

> Charles Ludlam, cavorting in a wild assortment of roles in the Ridiculous Theatrical Company's ingeniously realized parody, *The Mystery of Irma Vep*, wasn't just a brilliant quick-change artist. He was also a valiant theatrical renaissance man (star, director, playwright) who has stubbornly pursued an idiosyncratic artistic vision for nearly 20 years—now to arrive at a new creative peak.

About *The Artificial Jungle*, which combined elements of *Double Indemnity, The Postman Always Rings Twice* and *Little Shop of Horrors*, among others, Mr. Rich wrote that Mr. Lud-

lam "remains our master of the ridiculous, if not yet of suspense."

Mr. Ludlam was born on April 12, 1943, and raised in Northport, [Long Island]. In 1964 he received a degree in dramatic literature from Hofstra University. He joined John Vaccaro's Playhouse of the Ridiculous before founding his own company in 1967. Early productions by the Ridiculous included *Conquest of the Universe*, or *When Queens Collide, Eunuchs of the Forbidden City, The Ventriloquist's Wife* and *The Enchanted Pig*.

Not all of Mr. Ludlam's work met with praise. His most controversial show, a 1985 adaptation of Flaubert's *Salaambo*, was attacked as lurid and grotesque. The playwright defended the play as being faithful to the novel.

Highly regarded as a teacher, Mr. Ludlam taught or staged productions at New York University, Connecticut College for Women, Yale University and Carnegie-Mellon University. He won fellowships from the Guggenheim, Rockefeller and Ford foundations and grants from the National Endowment for the Arts and the New York State Council on the Arts.

Two weeks ago, Mr. Ludlam received a Village Voice Obie award, his fourth, for distinguished achievement. Last year, he won the Rosamund Gilder Award, also for distinguished achievement in the theater. (pp. A1, B6)

> Jeremy Gerard, "Charles Ludlam, 44, Avant-Garde Artist of Theater, Is Dead," in The New York Times, May 29, 1987, pp. A1, B6.

LEON KATZ

[*Katz is an American dramatist, scriptwriter, educator, and critic. Among his dramas are* Three Cuckolds *(1958),* Dracula: Sabbat *(1970),* Son of Arlecchino *(1978), and* Astapovo *(1983). From 1979 to 1981 he was director of Pittsburgh's Floating Theater, which presented Ludlam's* Camille *in 1980. The following excerpt is a eulogy that Katz delivered at Ludlam's funeral on May 30, 1987 in St. Joseph's Catholic Church, New York.*]

To pay tribute to the real Charles's life and work in the midst of all this religious solemnity is no mean feat. His devotion, his absolute commitment to his art, was of the same intensity as religious devotion—but of a very different kind. But in the story of the acrobat of God, the Virgin Mary, you remember, reassures the acrobat: "Your art, too, is prayer." Charles's art, too, was prayer. He celebrated life for all of us with a comic art that amounted to genius, a revelation of comedy at the limit of what is comically conceivable. All of us remember those incredible moments of laughter so convulsive as to be almost unbearable, moments that will stay with us for the rest of our lives.

So many moments, so many epiphanies. The moment in the last act of *Camille* (1973) when Charles as the dying Marguerite greets her lover, and in an ecstasy raises one foot horizontally toward Armand, and then balletically, on toe, trips across the stage to his waiting arms—it was as moving as it was hilarious. And in *The Artificial Jungle* (1987), when Ethyl Eichelberger, as the mother of the murdered husband, learns the truth from the guilty lovers—do you remember her reaction of surprise? From a standing position she does a 360-degree backflip and lands on her feet. Reaction of surprise. We exploded with laughter for five minutes into the next scene. And in the same play, do you remember the lovers about to embrace in bed, and Charles, the dessicated corpse of the husband, in a flash rears up from below and parts those guilty lovers?

Great entrances: Charles as the Egyptian Princess in *Irma Vep* (1984) emerging from the tomb holding the magical talisman with her arms crossed below a pair of shining, plastic, naked breasts. And in *Galas* (1983), the cloth train billowing diagonally across the stage and Charles as Galas, diva, alighting from it—he and Galas both registering absolute conviction that the train is real.

There is talk now of the sad fact that Charles was about to reach the pinnacle of his career, about to enter the mainstream, on the verge of Broadway, of opera, of film, of TV, and the other noble arts. That's absurd. Charles entering the mainstream would not have changed; he would have remained the same artist, the same Charles. If he had entered it, it would have signified only that the mainstream had changed. We have no reason for regret on that score. In his performances, in his thirty-two produced plays, he reached many pinnacles, and left us with their glowing memories. He was fulfilled. He did not have to reach for more.

One of the greatest curtain lines in dramatic literature occurs in *Camille* when Everett, as Nisette, stands over the body of Marguerite and speaks her eulogy: "Much can be forgiven for love, and you have loved much. Toodle-oo, Marguerite."

Our beloved, beloved Charles, toodle-oo. (pp. 8-9)

> Leon Katz, *"In Memory: Charles Ludlam (1943-1987),"* in The Drama Review, *Vol. 31, No. 4, Winter, 1987, pp. 8-9.*

CHRISTOPHER RAWSON

When Charles Ludlam died at 44 [May 28] in New York of pneumonia as a complication of AIDS, we lost a uniquely witty and intelligent man of the theater.

In Pittsburgh, Ludlam had many admirers and some detractors, all earned during his six appearances here as actor, director and playwright—sometimes simultaneously as all three. I found his work both funny and thoughtful, able to combine high-camp wit, pratfall farce and emotional pathos in surprising and disconcerting ways.

The one time I saw him at his own Ridiculous Theatrical Company in Greenwich Village's Sheridan Square was a memorable evening—*The Mystery of Irma Vep,* a crazy comic melodrama in which Ludlam and partner Everett Quinton quick-changed through all the parts. Like most of his more than two dozen productions since 1967, it was his own quirky parody of bits and pieces of high art and low, from Shakespeare, Ibsen and Dickens to horror films and pop kitsch.

Afterward, he and Quinton were happy to meet a drama critic from Pittsburgh, and we went to eat and see a late-night Garry Trudeau *Doonesbury* revue. Ludlam was both charming and thorny, a smart, well-informed, opinionated talker who could be an engaging, often hilarious companion. His humor was deepened by his sensitivity, learning and intense convictions about the autonomy of the artist.

One of his specialties was to act in drag. In Pittsburgh, we saw him play the heroines in both his own version of *Camille,* brought here in 1980 by Leon Katz and the Floating Theater, and, more unusually and controversially, in a non-parodic *Hedda Gabler,* director by Mel Shapiro for the American Ibsen Theater in 1984. Shapiro visited Ludlam in the hospital just before his death.

Earlier, the Floating Theater had sponsored Ludlam's other appearances here in *The Ventriloquist's Wife*—his grisly psychological comedy that anticipated the Anthony Hopkins film, *Magic*—and *Bluebeard,* which contained the funniest sex scene I've ever seen.

His *Stage Blood,* a perversely funny pastiche of *Hamlet,* Chekhov's *Seagull* and heaven knows what else, was staged here by Theater Express in 1979, proving that his authorial wit needed a Ludlam-like skilled comic actor at the center to get it fully airborne.

In 1980 he came here to teach and direct Wycherley's *The Country Wife* at Carnegie Mellon. He told the *Post-Gazette's* Donald Miller that the rebellious students of the '60s, among whom he included himself, had tried to throw away too much of our artistic tradition. "The '70s were a reconstruction period," he said, "and the '80s are *fin de siecle,* a time for masterpieces."

That prideful optimism was characteristic. But the '80s are also a time when that phrase, "as a complication of AIDS," acquired immune deficiency syndrome, will become horribly familiar.

Here's how I choose to remember Charles Ludlam, in his full theatrical panache. I hope it would please him, in spite of the deadly irony.

As the bedridden Camille, cold, deserted and dying, he told his faithful servant to "throw another faggot on the fire." Informed there was no faggot to be found, he painfully propped himself up, looked out over the Stephen Foster Memorial audience with languid incredulity, took a magisterial pause—the audience was howling with glee—and sank back on his pillows, intoning in self-dramatizing resignation, "It doesn't matter. We'll be back in New York tomorrow."

> Christopher Rawson, *"Ludlam Called Witty, Versatile Theatrical Gem,"* in Pittsburgh Post-Gazette, *May 30, 1987.*

MEL GUSSOW

[*Gussow, an American critic and biographer, is a drama critic for the* New York Times. *He is the author of* Don't Say Yes Until I Finish Talking: A Biography of Darryl Zanuck *(1971). In the following excerpt, he praises Ludlam for his original and versatile style of drama.*]

For 20 years, Charles Ludlam made a marvelous career out of being Ridiculous. As the comic genius behind the Ridiculous Theatrical Company, he was a grand recycler of popular culture, an entertainment ecologist, taking old tales and old movies and recharging them with his own extravagant imagination. His art continued unabated, from *Bluebeard* to this past season, *The Artificial Jungle.* Ludlam died on May 28, at the age of 44, ending a career and a brilliant, one-man way of theater.

For all his apparent iconoclasm, he was very much in the classical tradition of the actor-manager. He wrote all of his company's plays—more than 30 of them—directed them and played one or more of the leading roles in every production. He also designed many of his shows. More than anything, he gave his theater its unique character, which was larger and far funnier than life. Inventing himself and his troupe, he created a performance genre.

To be Ridiculous is to be a step beyond the Absurd. Ludlam defined his form of theater as an ensemble synthesis of "wit, parody, vaudeville farce, melodrama and satire," which, in combination, gives "reckless immediacy to classical stage-craft." That recklessness led some people to misinterpret his work as anarchic. It was spontaneous, but it was also highly structured—and always to specific comic effect. Though Mr. Ludlam was a titanic Fool, he was not foolish. He knew exactly what he was doing, whether the object of his satire was Dumas, du Maurier, the Brontës, Molière, Shakespeare, soap opera or grandiose opera—or himself.

I first encountered him in performance 17 years ago when he was playing *Bluebeard* far Off Broadway—with a beard like blue Brillo and diabolical glare in his eye. This was a distillation of every mad-doctor movie ever made. In his role as Bluebeard, he said, "When I am good, I am very good. When I am bad. . .," and he paused to consider his history of turpitude. Then he concluded, "I'm not bad." As hilarious as *Bluebeard* was, it gave no indication of the body of work that was to follow it. Almost every year, sometimes twice a year, there was another Ludlam lunacy on stage. As a critic who reviewed almost all of his plays, I must say that Ludlam was always fun to watch and fun to write about. His flights of fancy could inspire a kind of critical daredevilry, as one tried to capture in words the ephemeral essence of Ridiculous theater.

Looking back on our debt to him, one remembers his rhapsodic, hairy-chested *Camille*; the Grand Guignol vaudeville of *The Ventriloquist's Wife,* in which he spoke both for himself and for his back-talking dummy, Walter Ego; *The Enchanted Pig,* a helium-high hybrid of *King Lear* and *Cinderella*; *Le Bourgeois Avant-Garde,* a Molièresque send-up of minimalism; *Galas,* with Mr. Ludlam as the title diva. The range ran from *Corn,* a hillbilly musical, to *Der Ring Gott Farblonjet,* a three-Ring Wagner circus. There were also sideshows—a Punch and Judy puppet theater in which he played all 22 characters, and *Anti-Galaxie Nebulae,* a science fiction serialette.

The Mystery of Irma Vep (in 1984) was a tour de force, a horror-comedy in which he and his comic partner, Everett Quinton, quick-changed roles in a scintillating send-up of "wuthering" and other Gothic "Heights." For Ludlam, *Irma Vep* became a break-through of a kind. The first of his plays to demonstrate a broader, popular appeal, it has been staged by other companies, in other countries as well as in America's regional theaters. Not all of Ludlam was equal, but his batting average was extraordinarily high—as author, director and actor.

His acting was, of course, his most noticeable talent. As a performer, he unfailingly enriched his own work, as he charted a chameleonesque course, specializing in satyrs, caliphs and fakirs—as well as playing the occasional damsel. He was also an expert teacher of theater, as I discovered some years ago when, over a period of several months, I took an acting workshop with him. In these intensive sessions, we studied and practiced physical, visual and verbal comedy. He was most informative about what he did on stage. For example, he thought of his body as a puppet; through his imagination, he pulled his own strings.

Even with success, he stayed in his own stream, a tiny Off Broadway theater, with his familiar company (a few actors left and a few new ones arrived), making theater on a shoestring. Late in his career, he occasionally directed opera—and plays by others—but, for the most part, he kept doing what he alone did so well. As demonstrated by *Irma Vep* and *The Artificial Jungle,* he never stopped growing. Next in line, while directing *Titus Andronicus* for Joseph Papp, he was scheduled to present his new play about Houdini in his theater at One Sheridan Square. One could easily envision him locked in a box at the bottom of the sea—and breaking out in a phantasmagoric display of theater magic.

Mr. Ludlam was an original theater artist, and, as such, his art will survive—in his plays, in our memories of performances and also in the actors whom he trained and who became his comic co-stars: Black-Eyed Susan, Lola Pashalinski, Everett Quinton, John D. Brockmeyer, Bill Vehr, Georg Osterman and others. Under his inimitable tutelage, they learned how to be Ridiculous in the land of Ludlamania.

At Mr. Ludlam's funeral, a Catholic service at St. Joseph's Church, the playwright Leon Katz delivered the eulogy. Recounting great moments in Ludlam theater, he concluded by describing the climax of *Camille.* Mr. Ludlam's tragicomic heroine had coughed a last cough. Passionately, Armand pledged his eternal love, and then added, "Toodle-oo, Marguerite." As Mr. Katz remembered those last words, the mourners in the church broke into a cascade of laughter. In a wave, they rose and offered Mr. Ludlam his final standing ovation—and a salute of "Toodle-oo, Charles."

> *Mel Gussow, "The Man Who Made Theater Ridiculous," in* The New York Times, *June 7, 1987, p. 6.*

ERIKA MUNK AND CHARLES LUDLAM

[*Munk, an American critic and editor, is a senior editor and drama critic for the* Village Voice. *In the following excerpt, she introduces an article written by Ludlam in 1972 that explains his theory of the seven levels of theater.*]

I first saw a Ludlam play 20 years ago, and what I remember most clearly is a miraculous, unexpected sense of freedom. *Conquest of the Universe*—loosely, even lasciviously, based on Marlowe's *Tamburlaine*—was done in some long-forgotten crummy little midtown space without even bohemian charm. The audience was untouched by affluence. Crazed actors spoke in the tongues of a thousand genres, their genders mutating like drosophila. This was a true poetry of anarchy, and no matter what happened—Tamburlaine speaking Hitler's words, the Loretta Young Show and the Wife of Bath's Tale cheek-by-jowl—Ludlam's affection and compassion, and the wonders he drew out of his then barely-fledged actors, allowed a glimpse of utopia. Other theaters of sexual extremism and deliberate blasphemy existed then, but Ludlam's was distinguished not only by his intellect and artistry, but because it was without posing, malice, or despair. Every moment of wild laughter freed some bind in the spirit and unleashed a kaleidoscope of possibility. In whatever small measure theater can change a life, and whatever large measure it can change feelings about one's life, Ludlam's changed mine.

In 1972, after I'd started a theater magazine called *Performance,* I asked Ludlam to write something, anything. (I'd already published *Turds in Hell* in *The Drama Review;* I remember Charles and Bill Vehr forever rushing in at yet another last moment with new dialogue scribbled on tiny bits of paper they'd pull from their pockets like magicians.) He gave me this.

1. MECHANICAL

The mechanical theater is run by functionaries. The curtain always goes up on time. The most important quality in the artist is dependability. The play is written well in advance by a playwright, preferably dead. The actors count their lines, which they learn with the aid of a tape recorder. And the director knows that any play can be made to "work" with a little "tightening up."

2. SENTIMENTAL

The sentimental theater is a ravishment to the senses. It caters to the audience's likes and dislikes. The most important quality in the artist is beauty. Actors spend a great deal of time in gyms, under sunlamps, and on diets. Food and drinks are served during the performances, which feature music, gorgeous costumes, pleasant fragrances, and comfortable seats. This theater eternally enlists audience sympathy through the theme of love, which depicts two human beings experiencing the same emotion at the same time.

3. INTELLECTUAL

The intellectual theater sets out to prove a theory. Everything is done for a reason. The most important quality in the artist is studiousness. The director adopts the role of a teacher. Performances are living demonstrations of an argument, usually followed by discussion. In fact the audience can hardly wait for the show to be over so they can go home and think about it.

4. SOCIAL

The social theater provides a meeting place for people with something in common. The actors and audience come from the same community. Some of them come to identify themselves with the familiar themes of the plays. Others come to see and be seen. Theatrical companies are composed of families who pass on roles from father to son. Although this theater serves to strengthen a movement by clarifying a group's point of view while affirming its values, it is rarely of any interest to outsiders.

5. ECONOMIC

The economic theater means business: bargaining, buying, and producing a play for sale. Because this theater is primarily involved in a struggle for wealth, the plays it produces stress the importance of money in men's lives. Cooperation is achieved by mutual exchange, and the most important talent is to stay employed. When the money runs out, the theater disappears with it.

6. MORAL

The moral theater is for good and against evil, or for evil and against good. Dissatisfied with the world as it is, producers of moral theater seek to change things with the plays they do. Whether improving human beings for the sake of uplift or corrupting them through some supremely perverse delight in nastiness, they are always sorting out right from wrong. Between the good accomplished by the one and the evil accomplished by the other there is a perfect balance which results in no change whatsoever in the moral condition of Man.

7. SUPREME

The supreme theater is intuitive. The artists of this theater have mastered and internalized the first six levels of judgment. They are spontaneous and lucky. At the supreme level there are no ulterior motives, no striving for one thing to the exclusion of others. If there is anything these artists enjoy as much as

complete success it is a real fiasco. They get better as they get older, giving all they have. Because they have suffered, they accept their applause with gratitude. Their secret is that of the ancient Chinese marksman whose every arrow was found in the dead center of a chalk circle. They shoot their arrows first and draw the circle afterward.

Erika Munk and Charles Ludlam, "The Seven Levels of Theater," in The Village Voice, *Vol. XXXII, No. 23, June 9, 1987, p. 88.*

MICHAEL FEINGOLD

[*Feingold, an American critic and editor, is a drama critic for the* Village Voice *and a founding editor of Yale's drama journal,* Theatre. *In the following excerpt, he lauds the intelligence and inventiveness that Ludlam brought to his theatrical productions.*]

There was so much substance to Charles Ludlam's art, so much intelligence and such a variety of gifts in him as a person, that his loss seems at the moment to have crumbled our theater with one blow, as if the keystone had suddenly been pulled out of an arch.

The descriptions that are starting to fly about, of him as playwright, director, actor, are already a diminution of his stature. They leave out, for instance, his skills as a puppeteer and a ventriloquist, and as a designer for the stage. One of the most enchanted moments of my theater-going was the version of *Bluebeard* in which the good and evil angels were tiny hand puppets, with Charles throwing their voices; the wittiest piece of set design I have ever seen was the sword in the tree in Hunding's house, as rendered by him in *Der Ring Gott Farblonjet.*

The variety of Charles's talents was simply a sign of what made his work so rich and so far-reaching in importance: He was a complete man of the theater, with not only a vision to project, but a tradition to sustain—the classic tradition in which the theater's work is a great continuum, always changing and renewing itself while clinging to everything old that is still of value. Ventriloquism and puppetry, for Charles, were no more alien to this process than the lines of Shakespeare, Molière, and Ibsen he collaged into his scripts, or the traditional burlesque *lazzi* he executed with such hilarious precision. Theater is the art that welds all the arts together, and Charles was a great unifying force, which is why his work could seem at the same time outrageously revolutionary and austerely classical. In treating his stories as objects of fun and lewd sexuality as well as high seriousness, he brought tragedy back to the goat-dance where it was born in ancient Greece, without any pretentiousness or mumbo jumbo.

In this sense, he was not, as has wrongly been assumed by the daily press, an avant-garde artist in the least; he was the reviver and purifier of a thousand traditions that had fallen into corruption, banality, and disrepute. He reinvented the burlesque tradition, the vaudeville and silent-film tradition of physical comedy, the tradition of playwriting as an ongoing conversation with a faithful audience, the tradition of repertory acting. In this last category he evolved, with a company of gifted actors, an entire performance style that, though based on gender-blind casting and conscious artifice, did not scant or neglect the inner life central to Stanislavsky's method—again a matter of being simultaneously classic and modern. The papers described him as having been on the verge of entering the mainstream, but Charles's theater *was* the mainstream; it's the rest of our institutions that lally-gag on the verge, giving us patchy, one-sided versions of this or that aspect of the theater, while Charles Ludlam gave us the whole experience.

He was able to do this because he was so genuinely intelligent, with the true passion for art and the deep joy in the visceral and the sensual that are the marks of real intelligence. In person, I have to confess, he always scared me a little; he was the only American theater artist whom I have ever really thought of as my intellectual superior. Supernally easy to interview, he was not always the easiest man to converse with, as his many-faceted mind could so readily carrying on the conversation by itself. Underneath the mad whirl of ideas challenging each other, though there was a loving, generous, and joyous person, always visible in his devotion to the theater, to its highest possibilities for pleasure and for challenge. Visible, too, in the glee of his performances, because the first thing to be said about Charles as an actor is how captivating his every word and gesture was, in its mixture of intensity and precisely measured exaggeration. As with the matinee idols of old, you instantly wanted to imitate him: As Dr. Bluebeard, rhapsodizing, "The third genital!" as Camille, sitting bolt upright in bed, exclaiming, "No faggots in the house?" As Maria Magdalena Galas, turning her head to ask her maid, in a voice fraught with tension, "How many Normas do I have left?" None, Charles, alas. (pp. 88, 98)

> *Michael Feingold, "The Great Continuum," in* The Village Voice, *Vol. XXXII, No. 23, June 9, 1987, pp. 88, 98.*

ERIKA MUNK

I saw two tributes to Charles Ludlam last week, one—*Tabu Tableaux*—to the man himself, the other—*Donna Giovanni*—to the strength of his theater's ideas. That *Donna Giovanni's* tribute was unintended and a coincidence just made it more meaningful, a sign. Especially as these ideas are neither necessarily so nor quite respectable: crudely, that desiring and being desired are not only humanity's defining states but absurdly funny; that our emotions, which center on desire (debased word, robbed of passion by the past few years of academic theorizing, but what to do? "lust" is too narrow, "love" too sweeping) are as much shaped by their portrayal in all kinds of art as by our experience; that in such a situation, sexual travesty and sending-up both classics and pop genres are *dolce* and *utile;* that truth is best approached by bypassing realism.

Tabu Tableaux was a memorial presented by the Ridiculous Theatrical Company. Scenes from seven of Ludlam's plays alternated with affectionate statements from a wild variety of theater people, among them Eric Bentley, Madeline Kahn, Geraldine Fitzgerald, Judith Malina, Joe Papp. The greatest honor to Ludlam, though, was that he had as his companion and lover a man who could stand in front of a thousand people and speak with heart-wrenching directness of his loss, then step through the mirror, into an unnervingly giggly scene from the unproduced work *Houdini.* There he played Dr. Saint, a medium who is trying to raise Houdini's spirit for his widow (Black-Eyed Susan). Everett Quinton's courage in so clearly holding out to us first one kind of truth and then another was exemplary. The fragment ended with a huge projection—a photo from a *Houdini* rehearsal?—of Ludlam, in chains, behind bars. Though his spirit at that moment seemed flying free.

The scenes from the plays made clear how much the Ridiculous can do on its own with the heritage Ludlam left it; what touched me with the deepest sense of artistic loss were the excerpts from Leandro Katz's film of *The Grand Tarot.* The film didn't look like the performance I saw in a loft in 1969—it's certainly humorless, even arty, while the production was both makeshift and powerfully unsettling—yet it captured what I'd felt then. The images merged and dissolved—glimpses of Ludlam's eyes upturned to heaven under a ludicrous wreath, Black-Eyed Susan, Lola Pashalinski, and Mario Montez all ravishing in huge eyelashes, ropes of pearls, swathes of gauze; a mad Catholicism constantly honored in the breach. A gorgeous sensuality inextricable from the belly laughs of order overturned.

The final slide show, with Ludlam's unendingly mobile face and body in every imaginable persona, had a similar effect. But when stills from *Camille* were projected, I became aware of something disconcerting. A lot of the spectators laughed every time Ludlam was shown in drag, as if so trained by television or the need for denial that they couldn't be moved even by the fact that Camille was dying. Among the many reasons the Ridiculous Theatrical Company should survive is that it might be able to reeducate such people into the recognition of complexity of feeling within style. (pp. 87-8)

> *Erika Munk, "Long Live," in* The Village Voice, *Vol. XXXII, No. 31, August 4, 1987, pp. 87-8.*

Alistair (Stuart) MacLean
April 28, 1922 - February 2, 1987

(Also wrote under pseudonym of Ian Stuart) Scottish novelist, short story writer, scriptwriter, juvenile fiction writer, and poet.

(See also *CLC*, Vols. 3, 13; *Contemporary Authors*, Vols. 57-60, 121 [obituary]; and *Something about the Author*, Vol. 23.)

PRINCIPAL WORKS

H.M.S. Ulysses (novel) 1955
The Guns of Navarone (novel) 1957
South by Java Head (novel) 1958
The Last Frontier (novel) 1959; also published as *The Secret Ways*, 1959
Night without End (novel) 1960
The Dark Crusader [as Ian Stuart] (novel) 1961; also published as *The Black Shrike*, 1961
Fear Is the Key (novel) 1961
All About Lawrence of Arabia (juvenile biography) 1962; also published as *Lawrence of Arabia*, 1962
The Satan Bug [as Ian Stuart] (novel) 1962
Ice Station Zebra (novel) 1963
When Eight Bells Toll (novel) 1966
Where Eagles Dare (novel) 1967; adapted for the screen, 1968
Force Ten from Navarone (novel) 1968
Puppet on a Chain (novel) 1969
Bear Island (novel) 1971
Captain Cook (biography) 1972
The Way to Dusty Death (novel) 1973
Breakheart Pass (novel) 1974
Circus (novel) 1975
The Golden Gate (novel) 1976
Goodbye California (novel) 1977
A Weekend to Kill (novel) 1978
Athabasca (novel) 1980
San Andreas (novel) 1986
The Lonely Sea (novel) 1987
Santorini (novel) 1987

EDWIN McDOWELL

Alistair MacLean, author of *The Guns of Navarone* and one of the biggest-selling adventure writers in the world, died of heart failure yesterday in Munich, West Germany. He was 64 years old and lived near Geneva.

A spokesman for his British publisher, William Collins Sons & Company, said the Scottish-born author had a stroke three weeks ago while visiting a friend in Munich and died in a hospital there.

AP/Wide World Photos

Mr. MacLean wrote more than two dozen books, most of them war adventures or thrillers whose action spanned continents and often took place in airplanes, on ships or in nuclear submarines. They sold millions of copies worldwide, selling especially well in the United States, where he has been published since 1956. A new novel, *Santorini,* a story of espionage in the Aegean, is scheduled for publication next month by Doubleday, his longtime American publisher.

Although many of his books described violent action, Mr. MacLean, according to Charles Poore, a reviewer for *The New York Times,* also wrote "passages of wry comedy in the midst of chaos, death and general destruction." Another reviewer for *The Times* said Mr. MacLean wrote "some of the most stunning suspense to which I've been exposed."

Mr. MacLean's first novel, *H.M.S. Ulysses,* was set aboard a British naval convoy ship during World War II and was based on the author's experiences in the Royal Navy during the war. That book, which he wrote in three months in 1955 while teaching school, became a huge international success. It is also one of the few MacLean books that was not largely the product of his vivid imagination.

His imagination conceived the Mediterrean island of Navarone, the setting for his novel about British saboteurs who undertake to destroy a seemingly impregnable German fortress in the southern Aegean. The book was made into a successful motion picture by Carl Foreman in 1961, starring Gergory Peck, David Niven and Anthony Quinn. Seventeen years later, Mr. Foreman produced a sequel from Mr. MacLean's *Force 10 from Navarone,* published in 1968, but the movie, with Harrison Ford and Robert Shaw, was much less successful than the original.

Other MacLean books include *Night Without End* (1960), *Ice Station Zebra* (1963), *Puppet on a Chain* (1969), *The Way to Dusty Death* (1973), *Goodbye California* (1978), *Athabasca* (1980), *San Andreas* (1985) and *The Lonely Sea* (1986), a collection of stories.

Mr. MacLean also wrote detective stories, two of them, *The Black Shrike* and *The Satan Bug,* published in the 1960's under the pseudonym Ian Stuart. He also wrote children's books.

Many MacLean novels were made into motion pictures, including *The Secret Ways* with Richard Widmark, about an attempt to return to England a British nuclear expert who defected to the Russians; *Fear Is the Key,* a 1973 movie with Barry Newman and Suzy Kendall, and *When Eight Bells Toll,* about the disappearance of ships carrying gold bullion, starring Anthony Hopkins, Robert Morley and Jack Hawkins. While those films often did well abroad, few were box-office hits in the United States.

Mr. MacLean also wrote the screenplay for *When Eight Bells Toll,* and he wrote several original screenplays, including *Breakheart Pass* (1976), a western with Charles Bronson and Richard Crenna. After writing the screenplay for *Where Eagles Dare,* he wrote the novel of the same name. He rarely visited the movie sets, he said, explaining: "I object to the sight of 200 people sitting round seeming to do nothing. I guess it's my Scots soul."

Elliot Kastner, the American film producer who talked Mr. MacLean into writing his first screenplay, said of the author: "MacLean is a natural storyteller. He is a master of adventure. All his books are conceived in cinematic terms. They hardly need to be adapted for the screen; when you read them, the screen is in front of your mind."

Mr. MacLean also conceived an adventure drama for television, *The Hostage Towers,* about a gang of terrorists who seize the Eiffel Tower and demand ransom. That film, starring Douglas Fairbanks Jr. and Billy Dee Williams, was broadcast by CBS. Network executives asked that the author substitute the Statue of Liberty for the Eiffel Tower, but Mr. MacLean refused. He did not write the script, but the characters, the idea and the plot were his. "I don't much care for the television format," the soft-spoken author said. "I write novels—you get someone else to handle the actual script."

An astute businessman, Mr. MacLean, who spoke in a thick Scottish burr, rarely gave interviews. Writing from 5 A.M. until 1 P.M., he would complete a book in a little more than a month.

Edwin McDowell, *"Alistair MacLean Dies; Books Sold in Millions,"* in *The New York Times, February 3, 1987, p. B7.*

ANTHONY LEJEUNE

[*Lejeune is an English novelist, editor, nonfiction writer, and critic specializing in suspense fiction. His works include such novels as* Crowded and Dangerous *(1959),* Glint of Spears *(1963),* The Dark Trade *(1965), and* Strange and Private War *(1987). In the following excerpt, Lejeune, reflecting on MacLean's death, laments the declining quality of contemporary adventure fiction.*]

Any writer's death diminishes us. Extinct volcanoes may explode, brown twigs flower. But, although Alistair MacLean, who died [February 2], was far from extinct in terms of output, there can be no denying that his novels, which began so strongly with *HMS Ulysses,* based on his wartime experiences, had thinned until they were hardly more than outlines for films, which many became.

His later books were, in relation to the rich stream of English adventure stories, much what the James Bond films are to the authentic work of Ian Fleming—but without the jokes. This analogy is informative, since MacLean, sensibly, followed the fashion of the market; the commercial fashion, not an intellectual-trendy one.

Films in general, and thrillers in particular, have been aimed increasingly at a teenage market which is supposed to like nothing but explosions, car chases and a great deal of blood. If these elements are insufficiently present in books bought for adaptation, the stories are filleted and coloured in cochineal to match. MacLean, like a good businessman, simply anticipated the process.

Another present-day tendency, not only in films but in the profitable genre of airport-bookstall fiction, is to boast of stories "ripped from tomorrow's headlines"; their attraction depending less on the perils and triumphs of individual men and women than on the extrapolation and fantastication of current events; on Russian conspiracies, Arab terrorism, CIA machinations, sabotaged oil-rigs, pollution and politics.

This approach, which might seem helpful, really isn't. It actually impedes romance, distracting the writer from his proper purpose. The war stories with which Alistair MacLean began and to which he several times returned, led in this direction too easily.

Critics and literary editors—critics of films no less than books—have contributed to the decline of story-telling. At best they have regarded thrillers, adventure stories and romances as being merely, in Graham Greene's condescending phrase, "entertainment", quite different from and inferior to the gloomy and sensitive novels which, in their minds, constitute literature.

The result has been a gap in what should be a continuous critical spectrum. The normal standard of good writing, craftsmanlike structure, plausibility of character and inherent readability are not fully or consistently applied. So the writers, with nothing but a crass and perhaps misunderstood market to guide them, wander away from the excellence of which they might be capable.

The great adventure story writers, such as Haggard, Buchan, Stevenson, Conan Doyle and P. C. Wren, offered battles and chases in plenty. But the secret of their enduring appeal was more intimate. They had a warmth which the headline-ripping tales quite lack. Even Edgar Wallace and Ian Fleming, whose books translated readily into films, wrote much more than a scenario: their voices were distinct and friendly.

The desire for a story is indeed as basic to mankind as the love of a warm fire and a satisfying meal. By neglecting or despising the art and craft involved, by not applying high standards to the good and bad within all such work, we not only detract from our comfort; we weaken something very close to the heart of the human condition.

Anthony Lejeune, "Alistair MacLean, Craftsman of Story-Telling," in The Times, London, February 3, 1987.

THE TIMES, LONDON

Mr. Alistair MacLean, novelist, died [February 2] in Munich. He was 64.

He was fond of denigrating his own work, insisting that he was a storyteller, not a novelist. He most detested being called a "thriller writer".

His output was prolific if repetitious. He wrote to a formula which appealed to a popular readership. The most enjoyable part of the exercise for MacLean was the research and the development of the plot. "I know the day I start to satisfy readers of The Times, I'm finished."

His name will forever be synonymous with *The Guns of Navarone* and *Where Eagles Dare,* both best-sellers which were made into equally successful films. But his vast wealth lay uncomfortably on his conscience, and he lived, if not frugally, then simply.

Alistair Stuart MacLean was born on April 28, 1922, at Daviot, near Inverness, the third son of a Gaelic-speaking, Calvinist clergyman. He grew up on the family farm and, until the age of eight, spoke only Gaelic at home, at his father's insistence.

As a boy he read Scott, Buchan and Trollope because he was made to. In later life, the Gaelic made him obsessed with the correct usage and structure of the English language.

In 1941 he joined the Navy, and served as a torpedo man below deck on the Murmansk convoys. He was in the Navy for three years altogether, but his disrespect for the service was pronounced from the first.

After the war he got the chance to go to Glasgow University, where he read English literature—"because I could do that without getting my hands dirty". All the same he had to keep himself by working in a post office and sweeping the streets.

He took an honours degree and became an English teacher at Gallowflat Secondary School, near Glasgow. He found little satisfaction in that, either.

He entered a short story competition in the *Glasgow Herald*— for the money, he said. It was a sad and evocative tale about a fishing family in the West Highlands. It won the £100 first prize.

Mr Ian Chapman, then a young editor working in the Bible department at Collins' Scottish office, noticed his wife crying as she read it. Chapman read it himself, liked it, and set off in search of the author, whom he tracked down to a furnished flat on the other side of the city.

All that winter he urged MacLean to tackle a full-length novel, but MacLean was busy on another money-making venture: organizing tourist boats to the Arran Islands.

Chapman's efforts were, however, rewarded with *HMS Ulysses.* It was published in September 1955; by Christmas it had sold 250,000 copies. "I had a go", MacLean later recalled, "and the go went". It remained his favourite book.

It is an autobiographical account of his time in the convoys. It displeased the Admiralty; the critics found it unskilled, unconvincing and slipshod. MacLean never again read the reviews.

Afraid that the book's success had been a flash in the pan, he continued with the teaching. *The Guns of Navarone*—inspired by six months he spent in the Aegean on board *HMS Royalist*— was published two years later. It was as successful as *HMS Ulysses,* and decided MacLean to make writing his livelihood.

He emigrated to Geneva where he found the climate and the tax system more agreeable. There he wrote *South by Java Head* (1958)—an adventurous chronicle of the escape of a mixed group of people from Singapore.

William Collins felt that it was not up to standard, and despatched Chapman to persuade the author to put it aside. When Chapman arrived in Geneva, however, he received a cable from Collins informing him that the film rights had, in the meantime, already been sold on the strength of the proofs. No more was said. . . .

Thereafter, the novels came off the typewriter at the rate of almost one a year, among them *The Last Frontier, Night Without End, Fear Is the Key, Ice Station Zebra, Where Eagles Dare* and *Force 10 from Navarone.*

The plots—adventure mixed according to the modern, fast-moving thriller formula—lent themselves to the big screen. Most were subsequently filmed, among them some notable successes.

The critics consistently found fault; but an obedient public did not, and MacLean's books sold by the million.

In 1961—when he was out of harmony with Collins—he wrote two books under the pseudonym Ian Stuart. Without the name MacLean on the dustcovers, however, *The Dark Crusader* and *The Satan Bug* enjoyed only ordinary sales.

In 1963 a disillusioned MacLean gave up writing and returned to England. He bought Jamaica Inn on Bodmin Moor and three hotels, and set himself up as a businessman. After three years, though, he discovered that running hotels was "a most undemanding pastime". He returned to his typewriter in Geneva.

An American film producer asked him to write a script for *Where Eagles Dare.* His later novels to an increasing extent read like screenplays.

During the 1970s he dabbled for a time as a film producer— "inveigled into it", he said. Satisfaction and genuine happiness were still eluding him, and he found none in the film industry. He quickly became disenchanted with what he saw as time-wasting and actors sitting around all day apparently doing nothing.

His output continued unabated, but many of his later novels are instantly forgettable; thin and unconvincing. In a change of direction he turned to poetry in the uninspiring *From the Wilderness* (1973).

MacLean was a man in search of a "cause". One which he found was cancer, and for the British Cancer Council he wrote (all but the last chapter) *A Layman Looks at Cancer.* To the council's distress, though, he concluded that euthanasia is justified "when people are grey and just vegetables".

Another worthy cause was the preservation of wildlife, on which he wrote at the suggestion of Prince Bernhardt.

His only work of nonfiction is *Captain Cook* (1972), a brief, sober account of the great navigator, explorer and cartographer. Sir Peter Scott also approached him to write an official biography of his father, Captain Scott of the Antarctic.

MacLean kept his own company and encouraged few friendships. He remained shy and modest, and the phenomenal wealth which his books brought did not, at the same time, bring enduring contentment.

It was the Calvinist in him which kept his novels free from sex; besides, "it holds up the action". He admired Chandler, but knew that he was not in that mould.

In later years his favourite reading was scientific journals, particularly those on astronomy and physics. He had originally wanted to be a doctor.

He found it difficult to settle, and travelled extensively in his last years in search of a place to call home. He seldom returned to Scotland, but, when he did, it was always "to carry a coffin". His strong accent, not always easy to follow, never left him.

> *"Mr. Alistair MacLean: Yarn-Spinner for the Millions," in* The Times, *London, February 3, 1987.*

MARTIN SIEFF

When Alistair MacLean died [February 2] at 64 in Munich, West Germany, he had been the most popular adventure and action novelist in the world for more than 30 years. Only Harold Robbins, the master of seamy sex, and French detective novelist Georges Simenon rivaled him for bulk of sales.

But none of his action or espionage rivals, Ian Fleming, Frederick Forsyth, John LeCarre or Len Deighton, could match him for productivity, sales, or the passion and power of his works.

Mr. MacLean's later novels, while not skimping on action or craftsmanship, were straight adventure yarns, turned out with conveyor-belt speed. But the first decade of his output, up to *Ice Station Zebra* in 1963, were like nothing the form had seen.

Their heroes were impelled by moral power to a preordained end, wreaking revenge and establishing justice, no matter what the cost, however ruthless the means. Mr. MacLean's was a Manichaean world of good and evil, of moral choices, and of men redeemed, their true natures stripped bare under suffering and in the crucible of war.

In *Fear Is the Key* the hero uses the villain's love for his son to bring him to destruction, and avenge his murdered wife and child. In *The Dark Crusader,* his darkest work, the hero triumphs at the cost of sending his love to her death.

In contrast to the cynicism, moral equivalence or world weariness of John LeCarre or Len Deighton, all Mr. MacLean's novels are imbued with a powerful, uncompromising moral vision—that there is wickedness in the world and that it must be recognized and fought to the death, come what may.

Unlike many thriller writers, Mr. MacLean was no phony tough fantasist. He served for five years with the Royal Navy during World War II. Significantly, Frederick Forsyth, who comes closest to him in moral power, pace of action and the lean, driving economy of his prose, was also a service veteran who had seen war at first hand.

Mr. MacLean's experience on the hellish arctic convoys to Russia formed the autobiographical basis for his first and greatest work, *HMS Ulysses* in 1955.

It ranks with Nicholas Montsarrat's *The Cruel Sea* as the greatest novel to come out of the maritime war, the story of a ship's crew who redeem their shame in a doomed convoy at the cost of their lives.

He loathed totalitarianism and exposed it mercilessly in his novels. *The Last Frontier* (1959), one of his most moving works, was set in Hungary during the repression that followed the crushing of the 1956 uprising against communist rule and described the repatriation of millions of refugees to Stalin at the point of British bayonets in 1945. This crime was almost entirely overlooked by the literati of his generation.

He loathed Ian Fleming—the creator of James Bond—for the sex, snobbishness and sadism of his novels. Mr. MacLean used no bad language in his books, but their veracity never suffered. In addition to his unmatched narrative drive, his complex plots and his—in the earlier novels—powerfully compelling characters, he was also a master of black, biting wit—a quality for which he was seldom given credit. . . .

Mr. MacLean admired Raymond Chandler, creator of detective Philip Marlowe, above all writers, and said that comparatively his own writing was "merely entertainment." However, it made him a millionaire, owner of the famous Jamaica Inn on the Cornish moors, setting of the Daphne du Maurier novel of that name, and other hotels. . . .

By 1973, Mr. MacLean's works had sold more than 24 million copies, but he retained his simple tastes. Hearing himself described once as a jet-setter, he said, "My idea of a big day out is to go to the local cafe and play table-football with my sons."

He lived in Geneva, Switzerland, many years and regularly visited Dubrovnik, Yugoslavia, scene of the Navarone novels. . . .

Although he was one of Britain's best-selling writers, he once said: "I'm not a novelist, I'm a storyteller. . . . There's no art in what I do, no mystique. It's a job like any other." He allowed, however, "I'm good at my job."

> *Martin Sieff, "The Final Adventure for Author MacLean," in* The Washington Times, *February 3, 1987.*

Howard Moss

January 22, 1922 - September 16, 1987

American poet, critic, editor, dramatist, and juvenile fiction writer.

(See also *CLC*, Vols. 7, 14, 45; *Contemporary Authors*, Vols. 1-4, rev. ed.; *Contemporary Authors New Revision Series*, Vol. 1; and *Dictionary of Literary Biography*, Vol. 5.)

PRINCIPAL WORKS

The Wound and the Weather   (poetry)   1946
The Folding Green   (drama)   1954
The Toy Fair   (poetry)   1954
A Swimmer in the Air   (poetry)   1957
A Winter Come, a Summer Gone: Poems, 1946-1960
    (poetry)   1960
The Magic Lantern of Marcel Proust   (criticism)   1962
Finding Them Lost and Other Poems   (poetry)   1965
The Oedipus Mah-Jongg Scandal   (drama)   1965
Second Nature   (poetry)   1965
Writing against Time   (criticism)   1969
Selected Poems   (poetry)   1971
The Palace at Four A.M.   (drama)   1972
Travel: A Window   (poetry)   1973
Buried City   (poetry)   1975
A Swim off the Rocks   (poetry)   1976
Tigers and Other Lilies   (juvenile poetry)   1977
Notes from the Castle   (poetry)   1979
Whatever Is Moving   (criticism)   1981
Rules of Sleep   (poetry)   1984
New Selected Poems   (poetry)   1985
Minor Monuments   (criticism)   1986

Photograph by Vic Giganti

EDWIN McDOWELL

Howard Moss, a poet who for almost 40 years was the poetry editor of *The New Yorker,* died of cardiac arrest [September 16] at St. Vincent's Hospital and Medical Center of New York. Mr. Moss was 65 years old.

"He was a tremendous force for poetry in this country," said Galway Kinnell, the Pulitzer Prize-winning poet. "He was often accused of publishing 'The New Yorker poem,' but as a matter of fact the variety and quality of poems he published was astonishing. I don't know any pure literary magazine that has had as consistent a quality of poetry as *The New Yorker* under Howard Moss."

With only two published poems to his name, Mr. Kinnell submitted a poem directly to Mr. Moss, whom he did not know,

and the editor telephoned and said he was going to publish it. Many other prominent poets published their early work with Mr. Moss, including James Dickey, James Scully, Anne Sexton, Theodore Roethke, L. E. Sissman, Richard Wilbur, Sylvia Plath and Mark Strand.

Mr. Moss did not hesitate to suggest changes or revisions. "The words in poems are no more sacred than words in anything else," he told *Publishers Weekly* in 1973. "I will often make suggestions on changes, cuts, different punctuation. I would never edit without the approval of the author, but I feel quite free to make suggestions for improvement if we are seriously interested in his work. Think of what Pound did for Eliot, after all."

Not only does *The New Yorker* pay well, in contrast to most other magazines that publish poetry, but it is an important showcase as well. "Most poetry magazines are 90 percent read by poets," Mr. Kinnell said, "but the poems in *The New Yorker* are read by many people who don't buy the magazine for its poetry, including people who just open it and read it in a doctor's or dentist's office."

In part to encourage poets, Mr. Moss invariably bought more poems than the magazine could publish. "If only I could get all the poems I wanted to buy into print promptly," he said, "without being haunted by the thought of all the ones waiting to be published."

When Mr. Moss took a year's leave of absence from the magazine in the fall of 1972, at which time the backlog of poems stood at 130, the magazine stopped considering new poetry submissions for that year.

Mr. Moss was 24 years old when he published *The Wound and the Weather,* the first of 12 volumes of poems. He also published four books of criticism and two plays, and he edited several volumes of poetry, a collection of short stories written by poets and an anthology, *New York: Poems.*

His volume *Selected Poems,* published in 1971, won the National Book Award. His most recent collection, *New Selected Poems,* won the Lenore Marshall-National Prize for Poetry in 1986, the same year in which he received the Academy of American Poets fellowship for "distinguished poetic achievement." In 1971 he was elected to the National Institute of Arts and Letters, the nation's foremost honor society of fine arts.

"He was an extraordinary poet," said Harry Ford, a senior editor at Alfred A. Knopf, who, while at Atheneum Publishers, edited Mr. Moss's last seven volumes. "From the very beginning he had a sense of his own worth as a poet, and it came through." Mr. Moss dedicated *New Selected Poems* to Mr. Ford, who said [September 16] that Mr. Moss had a new volume of poetry "pretty near to completion," and Knopf would probably publish it.

Mr. Moss was born in Manhattan on Jan. 22, 1922, and was graduated from the University of Wisconsin in 1943. He taught English as Vassar College for a year before joining *The New Yorker* in 1948 as a fiction editor. Two years later he asked Harold Ross if he could edit the poetry, and he remained poetry editor until his death.

> Edwin McDowell, "Howard Moss, 65, New Yorker Poetry Editor," in The New York Times, *September 17, 1987, p. 14.*

THE NEW YORKER

[*In the following excerpt, the critic commends Moss, who served on the editorial staff of* The New Yorker *from 1948 until his death in 1987, for his outstanding qualities as an editor, critic, and poet.*]

Howard Moss joined the editorial staff of *The New Yorker* in 1948, and served as its poetry editor from 1950 until he died [September 16]. Not long ago, he said that, according to his rough calculations, he had spent the equivalent of three months of his life in the elevators of this building. Offices being a continuum of a kind, it will be a long while before we lose the happy expectation of meeting him momentarily in the corridors.

Few poets in our time have been able to concentrate their whole lives on poetry. Howard Moss did just that. Poetry implied for him a startling precision of phrase and feeling, a created surprise: qualities that he was always on the lookout for in his scrutinous reading of the poems submitted to this magazine, that he relished in the writers he loved and about whom he

wrote so affectingly, that sparkle in his plays, and that are everywhere manifest in the collections—twelve in all—of his own poems which appeared every few years throughout his writing life.

Inevitably, he met and corresponded with poets, and many became his close friends; in that he counted himself lucky— to be able to talk about poetry at all he considered something of a luxury. He was much prized among his friends for his wit, his insights, and his unflagging humor. As an editor, he was meticulous. One poet said, "So much is compressed into the compass of a poem that one always wondered if the reader would catch it all, take it all in. Howard always did, for he was a superb reader of other people's work—the perfect reader. He took poems in, one at a time. Good poems were for him small miracles. Any observations or suggestions he offered were so perceptive that he made me make my poems better. Few are in such a position. Nobody could have filled it more responsibly." He would teach from time to time, for short spells—a natural extension of his extreme articulateness, his impulse to clarify. In all he did, he made many of us—colleagues, friends, students, readers, other poets—aware of what it meant to be a poet. It was to say things well.

The best of his critical writings were in the mode of appreciation. The writers he loved, like Chekhov and Proust, became to him close friends, and he brought them brilliantly to us. His short study *The Magic Lantern of Marcel Proust* is a masterpiece of jewelled concentration, an appendage to Proust that embellishes the original. It is in his poems, however, that he is most present. He had an exceptional ear for the language, and each of his poems is singularly made, singularly said.

In one of his essays, he wrote, "I would say that the distinction between fiction writers and poets is becoming obsolete, that it might be more useful to think of authors as mirror-writers or window-writers. . . . In America the two schools stem from two major figures, both poets, who may be viewed as their source: Emily Dickinson, the mirror, and Walt Whitman, the window." Howard's reflective glass was both mirror and window, as was Proust's. In all his writing, inner and outer meld. Many of his poems are meditations—on painting, on dance, on landscapes, on gardens—that move from wit to wisdom, in a manner entirely his: quirky, ironic, beautifully cadenced.

In public, he read his poems quietly; and the voice in the poems is a quiet one, though warm with compassion and shared pain:

> Fisherman, though I must remain
> Merely a tourist in this town,
> Consider me for what I am,
> A stranger in a lean time.
> Your landscape feeds our loneliness.
> The sea belongs to both of us.

It was not simply our offices but the office of poet that he graced with his life.

> "Howard Moss," in The New Yorker, *Vol. LXIII, No. 33, October 5, 1987, p. 128.*

BRUCE BAWER

[*Bawer, an American critic, nonfiction writer, and essayist, is the author of* The Middle Generation: The Lives and Poetry of Delmore Schwartz, Randall Jarrell, John Berryman, and Robert Lowell *(1986) and* The Contemporary Stylist *(1987). In the following excerpt, he examines the style and themes of Moss's poetry.*]

If it makes any sense at all, in that impotent and ingrown fraternity known as the American poetry world, to speak of an individual as having "power," then there was arguably no American poet more powerful than Howard Moss, who died on September 16 in New York. As poetry editor of *The New Yorker* since 1950, Moss could single-handedly make a poet's career by printing his work regularly—and indeed he played a major role in establishing the reputations of many important postwar American poets, among them Galway Kinnell, Sylvia Plath, Anne Sexton, and Mark Strand.

Unsurprisingly, the obituary that Edwin McDowell wrote for *The New York Times* [see excerpt above] highlighted Moss the editor. Not until the eighth paragraph (of thirteen) did McDowell mention Moss's own writing, and perfunctorily at that. It was a lamentable lapse—lamentable, for over the years Moss had published more than a dozen volumes of his own work, none of them beneath notice. He was, for one thing, an unusually sensitive literary critic, whose books of prose (the most recent of which was last year's **Minor Monuments**) consisted largely of perceptive and delicately articulated appreciations of such writers as Proust, Chekhov, Mann, and Whitman. But his most distinguished contribution, of course, was as a poet. Moss's poems have been described as mannered, and some of them are, but I prefer to think of them as mannerly—gentle, civilized, quietly thoughtful and clever. Take, for instance, these two stanzas from the early poem "**Burning Love Letters**":

> Fire that cancels all that is
> Devours paper and pen,
> And makes of the heart's histories
> A cold hearth warm again.
> It could as well consume a branch,
> Blank paper or black coal
> That now, in ashy avalanche,
> Scatters the heart whole.
>
> What words led to the end of words?
> Coldly, all separate sighs
> Shiver in flame, flying upwards,
> Merged into burnt lies.
> In somersaults of light, words burn
> To nothingness, then roll
> In dead scrolls, delicate as fern,
> Or hiss like a waterfall.

As these stanzas suggest, Moss did not as a rule go in for radical experiment or spectacular effects. (When he did, on one occasion, write a poem that represented a radical departure from his usual manner, he called it "**Radical Departures.**") He has often been described as a disciple of Auden, but his poems bring other affinities to mind as well; though I don't mean to suggest that they are necessarily of the same stature, they have the urbanity and poise of Merrill, the wistfulness of Jarrell, the cold passion and abstract joy of Yeats, the stylistic extravagance of Stevens, the luminousness—and attentiveness—to nature of Elizabeth Bishop; their music has justly been compared to that of such classic lyric poets as Campion and Herrick. Though full of feeling—romantic love is a favorite topic—most of them are essentially impersonal, free of revealing intimate detail; though rich with intelligence, they are marked less by intellectuality (and certainly show no trace of Auden's interest in ideology) than by wit. They are dense with wordplay, with Petrarchan conceits, with formal and rhythmic invention; in one poem after another a difficult and ingenious rhyme scheme is brilliantly executed. Audenesque generali-

zations—many of them about love and its attendant emotions—proliferate: "Not to be loved is to crave power." "Guilt feeds on the inconsequential." Paradoxes abound: in "**Venice,**" Moss writes that "One cannot tell how really false the real is. / One cannot tell how real the really false is." In "**The Pruned Tree,**" he declares that "my wound has been my healing." (The title of one of his poetry collections is also a paradox: *Finding Them Lost.*) Moss also plays frequently on double meanings: "lie to me, lie next to me." He does this, as Richard Howard has observed, "not because he is frivolous or obsessed, as most men who pun all the time seem to be, but because he relies on the wisdom that is innate in language itself to enforce his moment, on the wit of words as they work together or against each other. . . . Moss has found the homophone to be a figure of order, and in his dependence on the experience immanent in our speech, has reached to the bottom of things."

At the bottom of things, for Moss, is the inexorable passage of time. (**Writing Against Time** is the name of his first volume of essays, published in 1969.) To read through his **New Selected Poems** (1985), which draws on all eleven of his previous poetry collections, from *The Wound and the Weather* (1946) to *Rules of Sleep* (1984), is to recognize that he is, above all else, an elegist. This is to say not merely that he composes conventional elegies, with titles like "**Elegy for My Father**" and "**Elegy for My Sister,**" but that he is always, in his poetry, mourning the passing of something, whether it is a love affair ("**Burning Love Letters,**" "**The Falls of Love**"), a season ("**A Summer Gone,**" "**September Elegy**"), or a day. To borrow a phrase from the end of his poem "**In the X-Ray Room,**" Moss perennially dwells upon "[t]he precious weight of everything that goes." In the accomplished (if somewhat callow) youthful poem that begins *New Selected Poems*, he writes, "Relatives and friends, / A coffin is our end"; and images of ashes, setting suns, and falling leaves recur throughout the hundred-odd poems that follow. Again and again Moss draws punning connections between falling leaves and summer's leave-taking; between the words *mourning* and *morning* (the arrival of the latter often signaling an end to the former); between the two related meanings ("autumn" and "descent") of *fall*. The cycles of nature—the successions of sunsets and seasons, the rise and fall of tides—are omnipresent in Moss's poetry, continually associated with the fact of his own mortality: "The last late leaf / Settles on my upturned, aging hand." His second collection of essays bore the (punning) title **Whatever Is Moving,** and the constancy of change, of movement, is a preoccupation throughout his oeuvre. Movement is, moreover, a prime characteristic of his poetry: "Moss does not write a static poem," Josephine Jacobson observed in a review of *Buried City* (1975) [see *CLC*, Vol. 14]. As Moss puts it in a late poem entitled "**Rome: The Night Before**" (one of many Moss poems that are notable for, among other things, their sense of place),

> Everything permanent is due for a surprise,
> The stopped stunned by the ever-changing.
> What everybody always took for granted
> Astonishes a second before it disappears,
> Like the dinosaur who left a plate of bones
> And was gone for good. In Rome one feels
> Duration threatened day by day,
> Not knowing which of its great works will last,
> Flesh and marble the same mix of mortar.

At times, Moss's poems can seem stiflingly lapidary, overly self-conscious. But this is more true of the early poems than of the later poems, many of which are in free verse and might almost be described as colloquial in tone. In any event, as Dana

Gioia concluded in a recent essay on Moss for the *Antioch Review*, "If a poet has faults, a superabundance of taste, a weakness for description, and a tendency to overpolish seem rather agreeable ones." Certainly the grace, refinement, and deep humanity of Howard Moss's poetry will continue to draw readers to him when many of the more celebrated poets of our day are forgotten. (pp. 35-7)

> *Bruce Bawer, "The Passing of an Elegist," in* The New Criterion, *Vol. VI, No. 3, November, 1987, pp. 35-7.*

James Tiptree, Jr.
August 24, 1915 - May 19, 1987

(Pseudonym of Alice Hastings Bradley Sheldon; also wrote under pseudonym of Raccoona Sheldon) American short story writer, novelist, and essayist.

(See also *CLC*, Vol. 48 and *Contemporary Authors*, Vols. 108, 122 [obituary].)

PRINCIPAL WORKS

Ten Thousand Light-Years from Home   (short stories)
    1973
Warm Worlds and Otherwise   (short stories)   1975
Star Songs of an Old Primate   (short stories)   1978
Up the Walls of the World   (novel)   1978
Out of the Everywhere and Other Extraordinary Visions
    (short stories)   1981
Brightness Falls from the Air   (novel)   1985
Starry Rift   (novellas)   1986
Tales of the Quintana Roo   (novellas)   1986

Photograph by Patti Perret

THE NEW YORK TIMES

A critically acclaimed science fiction author, who wrote under the pen name James Tiptree Jr., killed her husband and herself [May 19] after warning her lawyer to call the police, the authorities said.

Alice Sheldon, 71, and her husband Huntington Sheldon, 84, were found in bed together with single gunshot wounds to their upper bodies, said officials of the Fairfax County police.

Warren Charmichael, a spokesman for the police, said the shooting occurred at about 3:30 A.M. in the couple's home in this fashionable suburb of Washington, D.C.

The police said Mrs. Sheldon had been depressed about the illness of her husband, who had gone blind this year and was bedridden. She called her lawyer to warn him she was planning the killings and warned him to call the police, the spokesman said.

Virginia Kidd, Mrs. Sheldon's agent, said the author telephoned her last week and had seemed "in her usual good spirits."

Ms. Kidd described Mrs. Sheldon as "middling popular" as an author. "She had enormous critical success and was very highly thought of by "intellectuals," Ms. Kidd said. "But she never made the numbers."

Nevertheless, she won the respect of her peers. Isaac Asimov, the noted science fiction writer, said in a 1984 article that she

"has produced works of the first magnitude and has won the wild adulation of innumerable readers."

The *Washington Post* in a March 1986 review called the author one of the finest writers of short fiction in the 1970's.

Mrs. Sheldon's most recent work was *Starry Rift,* a collection of three novellas, published in 1986. The *New York Times* called it "a latter-day space opera, replete with daring interstellar action, life-saving (and life-threatening) technology and a general air of wide-eyed wonder at the vast playground we call the universe."

Other recent books include *Up the Walls of the World,* her first book after two decades of writing short stories, published in 1978, and *Brightness Falls from the Air,* published in 1985.

Mrs. Sheldon served in the Army Air Corps in World War II and later worked in photo intelligence for the Central Intelligence Agency, her agent said.

She started writing science fiction as a way to relax after working on her doctoral dissertation. She taught experimental psychology and statistics at American University and at George

Washington University, both in Washington, D.C., from 1955 to 1968.

"Author Kills Herself and Aged Husband in Suburb of Capital," in The New York Times, *May 20, 1987, p. B11.*

[ANDREW PORTER]

Alice Sheldon, who wrote under the name James Tiptree, Jr., killed her husband and then committed suicide early on the morning of May 19th. The murder-suicide took place at the couple's home in McLean Virginia. Sheldon was 71; her husband was 84. Their bodies were discovered in their bedroom after police received a call from the pair's attorney at 3:34 am. The couple, with two bullet wounds in his head, a single wound in hers, were found in bed, holding hands.

Friends of Sheldon said the pair were devoted to each other, but increasingly suffered from medical problems. Sheldon's husband, who retired from the CIA in the late 1960's, where he was an intelligence analyst, was now bedridden and blind.

In a letter to Robert Silverberg dated December 28, 1976, Sheldon wrote, "I had always meant to take myself off the scene gracefully about now while I am still me. And now I find I can't, because to do it would mean leaving him alone, and I can't bring myself to put a bullet through that sleeping head—to take him too, when he doesn't want to go."

According to Sheldon's agent Virginia Kidd, she had long suffered from clinical depression, and had been threatening to commit suicide for the last twenty years. The depression was compounded when her mother died and the carefully built up identity as James Tiptree crumbled. The revelation that mysterious but extremely talented author James Tiptree Jr. was really Alice Sheldon—a woman, not a man—swept the SF field.

Sheldon was devoted to her mother, Mary Bradley, who sold more than 35 travel books in her lifetime as a travel writer, and whose reports as a World War II correspondent on the German death camps shocked America.

Born in Chicago, Sheldon spent much of her childhood in Africa and India. She served in the Army Air Corps in World War II and worked for the CIA in photo intelligence. She taught experimental psychology and statistics at American University and at George Washington University, both in Washington DC, from 1955 to 1968.

She began writing late in life; her first professional sale was **"Birth of a Salesman"** in 1968. Perhaps her most memorable stories were **"The Screwfly Solution,"** in which aliens set off men's latent hostilities toward women in order to depopulate the Earth before they move in, and **"The Women Men Don't See"** in which a pair of American women, vacationing in the Yucatan, encounter humanoid aliens and leave the Earth with them, reasoning that life with aliens would be better than trying to live with men on Earth.

Jeff Smith . . . is literary executor of Sheldon's estate. All manuscripts, contracts and other material are now in his possession. Sheldon left only one unpublished story, and that has already been turned over to Virginia Kidd, who remains her literary agent. Sheldon left her money to charity. The couple's house was sold several years ago; they were living in it under a lifetime tenancy contract.

Commenting on the Sheldons, two close friends outside their house the morning after the discovery of their bodies. "They lived a beautiful life, very loving", one friend said of the pair. Crying, the other added, "They were very vital, intelligent people. They were finding life very fragile right now".

[Andrew Porter], "Alice Sheldon (James Tiptree, Jr.) Kills Husband, Then Herself in Suicide Pact," in Science Fiction Chronicle, *Vol. 8, No. 10, July, 1987, p. 6.*

JEFF SMITH

James Tiptree, Jr. probably had the largest and closest circle of correspondence friends (I don't think anyone ever said "penpals") in the second half of the 20th century. He was concerned about everyone's physical and psychological well-being, full of praise and appreciation, and incredibly generous with his time and energy. It was hard to explain to others how you could consider someone you had never met—and had no real expectations of ever being able to meet—one of your best friends, but Tip *was* a best friend to many. And when it turned out that he really was Alli Sheldon (several people immediately drew the parallel with L. Frank Baum's *Land of Oz,* in which the boy Tip was revealed as the Princess Ozma), Alli had no trouble keeping the friendship going. And, unlike Tip, *she* could talk to people on the phone, and occasionally receive them in her home. She enriched us even beyond the quality of her fiction.

She and her husband (it was hard at first to think of this quiet but forceful white-bearded man as "Ting," but that soon passed) were extremely devoted. They watched over each other constantly, and while you talked with one the other would lean forward and drink in the scene with pleasure and admiration. Alli told me once that the worst night in her life was the one when Ting's small fishing boat had been swept out to sea by a storm; the emotion in her voice, years later, was overpowering.

My own relationship with Tiptree/Sheldon goes way back. I remember reading Tiptree's first story, **"Birth of a Salesman,"** in the March 1968 *Analog* and thinking it was funny (though I can't claim I predicted great things for its author). I had read a dozen or so Tiptree stories by 1970, when I wrote to him and asked him if he would participate in a postal interview for my fanzine, *Phantasmicom.* (This was based on no great perception on my part that Tiptree was about to blossom into the writer he became, but because in those New Wave vs. Old Wave days Tiptree was being claimed by both camps—and there seemed to be a story in that.)

Much later, Alli said: "When you wrote for that Interview was the first time I was approached personally by anyone, and I told myself, Dammit, say no. But then this business of really loving the SF world and wanting to say so welled up, and I thought I could kind of race over the bio bit without telling lies and start waving Hello." And to *Contemporary Authors,* she wrote: "'Tiptree', realizing that some sort of biographical information would have to be furnished before exasperated blurb-writers hired a detective, decided to take a chance. (Later on, other writers called this act insanely trustful.)"

The letters discussing the editing necessary for the interview led to an on-going correspondence, and a quickly-established friendship. Tip was so warm, so open, that it made absolutely no difference that I never saw his face or heard his voice. We wrote constantly. Elaborate schemes were set up to get mail in and out of Yucatan, where Tip spent every winter. What he sent me might be postmarked Florida, or Texas, or San Francisco, and would have to be sterilized to kill roach eggs. What I sent him would often be dragged ashore through the surf, and have to be dried out before reading. Sometimes these letters resulted in articles for my fanzines, making my efforts more popular than the might otherwise have been.

After the Revelation, the letters turned into phone calls. Better in some ways, but in others it just wasn't the same.

Tiptree the SF writer kept getting better and better. When Alli realized she was actually selling these stories, she started taking them more seriously. The screwball comedies died out early; **"The Last Flight of Doctor Ain,"** which earned Tiptree his first attention, was only his eighth story. By the time **"Love Is the Plan the Plan Is Death"** won the Nebula for Best Short Story of 1973, he was no longer a phenomenon but a well-respected author. That story had been followed in creative succession by **"All the Kinds of Yes," "The Man Who Walked Home," "And I Awoke and Found Me Here on the Cold Hill's Side," "Forever to a Hudson Bay Blanket," "On the Last Afternoon," "The Girl Who Was Plugged In"** and **"The Women Men Don't See."** With several of these, Alli was beginning to feel constrained by her male persona, and for relief she created a new one: Raccoona Sheldon.

Raccoona first surfaced as a fanzine artist, as Tip sent me a page of sketches by an "old friend" for my use. (I told him he should try to get her to illlustrate his magazine stories: "She draws like you write.") The original scheme had been for Raccoona to establish herself as a writer, then for Tip to drown in Mexico and there'd only be one persona left. But Raccoona couldn't live in McLean, so a Wisconsin post office box had to be set up and mail shuttled back and forth. And neither could Raccoona have just picked up Tip's friendships. Raccoona was left out in the cold: since she couldn't be Tiptree she couldn't really be Alli either.

I never had trouble accepting Alli and Tiptree as the same person, but Raccoona has always been *someone else* to me. My favorite story about this "crescendo of confusion" concerns the time Tip wrote to say he was having hand surgery, and was going to feel absolutely helpless for months. Believing Tip to live alone, I was concerned for him—but then the Wisconsin post office, on its own initiative, sent me a temporary change-of-address for Raccoona: she was now in McLean. I was very relieved that Tip's old friend had gone down to help him out. Little did I know they only had one good hand between them.

By this time the Great Tiptree hunt was the game of choice in science fiction circles. Consideration was given to staking out the McLean post office. Even some of Tip's friends were trying to phrase innocuous-sound questions which might elicit revealing answers. I got very depressed at Discon, the 1974 Worldcon in Washington, D.C., by the number of people who were competing to solve the mystery. Since Tiptree was nominated for two Hugos, and since the famous post office box was right outside the city, rumor was strong that Tip was attending incognito. Some people even "knew" this for a fact. (At least one stranger was cheerfully signing Tiptree autographs.) All I knew was that a week earlier he'd been in British Columbia, and he'd said that if he ever *did* attend a convention he would just stand at the edges and observe. Lots of people asked me if he were there; I just said I didn't know.

The Hugo Award ceremony was fraught with more suspense than usual, as people wanted to know not only who would win, but who would accept if Tiptree won. Tiptree didn't win in the novelette category, but did for Best Novella. As MC Andy Offutt implored Tip to come up and receive his trophy, I was providing the anticlimax by walking up on stage myself. This failed to convince people that Tiptree *wasn't* there, but fueled the inexplicable belief some people held that *I* was Tiptree.

In November 1976, just under ten years after the name "Tiptree" had been pulled off a marmalade jar, everything started coming apart. Tip sent me a letter for publication about the death of his mother, and had written similarly to others. I was reluctant to run it because of the number of family details included, and said so. Tip dismissed that fear with a wave of his typewriter: "Nobody could trace anything. I didn't even inform the papers." I wasn't convinced, and decided to check the newspapers myself; if I couldn't find anything I'd publish the letter, but if I could I'd sit on it. This seemed safe; if I found out that Tip's real name was Sylvester Mule or something, so what? I'd never even have to tell him I knew. But instead I found something totally unexpected: that his first name was Alice and that his second name was the by-now-familiar Sheldon. That very day I got a postcard from someone asking, "Is it true that James Tiptree is Alice Sheldon?" This was becoming too complicated to bear, so I wrote a letter describing everything I'd done. It ended: "This is not a demand for information. A postcard saying merely 'Later' will not be the ending of a friendship. But one thing to definitely consider: I am going to be getting questions, and whatever you choose to disclose to or withhold from me, please pass along the Party Line that I'm supposed to tell others."

In reply: "Dear Jeff, How great. At last it's out."

But it wasn't "great." Once Tiptree was exposed (Alli told a select few people, some of whom could keep a secret better than others), he vanished—leaving a number of projects for Alli to complete. And she struggled with them: her first novel, *Up the Walls of the World*; "Slow Music" (in which Tiptree, as a male character, dies and is revealed as a woman); a couple of others. Once, in despair, she took all her notes, all her unfinished drafts, and started feeding them into a fire. Ting physically knocked her over to get at them, and managed to save one notebook, which he gave me for safekeeping. Years later she asked for it back, when she again became productive. (Most of what she burned—*Tales of the Quintana Roo*, **"With Delicate Mad Hands"**—she was able to recreate.)

She was not only productive again, but uncharacteristically satisfied with what she wrote. After hating it through much of its gestation period, she became excited about *Brightness Falls from the Air*. She would call me up and gleefully read me paragraphs from short stories, pleased with her creativity. Of all the time I knew her, she seemed the most satisfied with life—except with her husband's health.

They were learning to deal with Ting's failing eyesight. He got more interested in music. They could continue to travel. When their ten-year lease on the Yucatan ranch expired they went to New Zealand, and last year they planned a fishing trip to Alaska. But eventually Ting's health problems grew too severe. And Alli had long said that neither of them would survive the other.

So, no, what happened was no surprise. And really, that has made it easier to bear. But it doesn't make me miss them any less. (pp. 16, 18)

Jeff Smith, in an obituary of Alice Sheldon, in Science Fiction Chronicle, *Vol. 8, No. 10, July, 1987, pp. 16, 18.*

SOMTOW SUCHARITKUL

A week ago, as I was preparing to travel east to a science fiction convention and the ABA in Washington, three of my Washington area friends telephoned me in quick succession to tell me that Alice Sheldon had killed her husband and herself. I'm sure that all the science fiction community will by now have been made privy to the details of these deaths—it's been on the news and will doubtless have been reported in the papers. But the Sheldons were the most private of people, and I don't think that their last moments should be dissected in public. Others, I am sure are even now dissecting the work of James Tiptree Jr. and Raccoona Sheldon, Alli's alter egos, and surely both among the most important writers our field has ever known. Everyone who loves science fiction is griefstricken at James Tiptree's passing; even those outside our field must needs be appalled at the insensitive inflexibility of a system of justice that, perhaps, forced the Sheldons into this double suicide.

I can't really add anything to those sentiments we all feel, but perhaps I can share a few reminiscences, a few anecdotes. We lived only fifteen minutes away from each other, seldom spoke on the phone, and even more rarely saw each other, but she was, in a very real sense, a constant presence in my life and the lives of others who from time to time inhabited 16 Ancell Street in Alexandria.

I first met the Sheldons when Shawna McCarthy asked me to deliver a Nebula Award (I believe it was for **"The Screwfly Solution"**) to them. It was with some trepidation that I and Walter Miles (who was sharing my house) prepared to meet her. After all, James Tiptree was a legend—I have read and reread her short stories dozens of times. Stories like **"Love Is the Plan, the Plan Is Death,"** with its astonishing evocation of an arachnoid alien sensibility—like **"Houston, Houston, Do You Read?"** and the strikingly original novel, *Up the Walls of the World.*

James Tiptree Jr. turned out to be a whitehaired, distinguished-looking elderly lady who instantly began regaling me with tales of her childhood; the first story she ever told me was of how the first dead people she had ever seen, as a ten-year-old child traveling through Africa, were men crucified on trees. Talking about trees, *there was a monster of a tree growing through the floor* in the middle of their living room—very Wagnerian—and the house was absolutely stacked with bizarre ivory statuettes and strange artifacts, the sort of thing you see painstakingly reproduced in pen and ink on the pages of anthropology textbooks. After treating Walter and me to some kind of exotic fruit juice (she always kept exotic fruit juice on hand) she told more stories, and showed us the typewriters on which she wrote—one for each pseudonym—nontransferable!

In short, it was a splendid afternoon, and a sublimely paradoxical one. This dottily eccentric old woman, who reminded me of nothing more than a favorite grandmother, was also a writer of astounding linguistic precision and originality—and, in the early seventies, the biggest literary enigma in the sf community. But I shall mostly remember her for her kindness. It seemed that every three to six months there'd be a phone call from her—one day I turned on my answering machine to find a ten-minute message praising my novel *Starship and Haiku,* followed by another five minutes of closely argued reasoning as to why I should remove the word "puddle" from the first chapter! Or her postcards (every one of which I've kept) which frequently showed scenes from New Zealand or some other distant locale, with strange commentaries, in spidery script, taped over key parts of the photographs.

The last time I spoke to her was a year ago—before I moved to Los Angeles. She called me and inveighed about how dreadful all the short stories she had just read in one of the "best of the year" anthologies were—we spent a few moments bemoaning the state of the art—and then, abruptly, she was gone. It never occurred to me that I would not see or hear her again. It always seemed as though she would always be there—quirky, cranky, ever-brilliant.

I don't think I've quite absorbed the fact that she's gone yet. It's going to take a long time. It's hard.

Somtow Sucharitkul, "Alice in Tiptree Land," in Fantasy Review, *Vol. 10, No. 6, July-August, 1987, p. 12.*

Anthony (Panther) West

August 4, 1914 - December 27, 1987

English novelist, critic, biographer, nonfiction and juvenile nonfiction writer, and editor.

(See also *Contemporary Authors*, Vols. 45-48; *Contemporary Authors New Revision Series*, Vols. 3, 19; and *Dictionary of Literary Biography*, Vol. 15.)

PRINCIPAL WORKS

Gloucestershire   (guidebook)   1939
On a Dark Night   (novel)   1949; also published as *The Vintage*, 1950
Another Kind   (novel)   1951
D. H. Lawrence   (biography)   1951
The Crusades   (juvenile nonfiction)   1954; also published as *All about the Crusades*, 1967
Heritage   (novel)   1955
Principles and Persuasions   (criticism)   1957
The Trend Is Up   (novel)   1960
Elizabethan England   (nonfiction)   1965
David Rees, among Others   (novel)   1970
Mortal Wounds: The Lives of Three Tormented Women (biographical essays)   1973
John Piper   (biography)   1979
H. G. Wells: Aspects of a Life   (biography)   1984

WOLFGANG SAXON

Anthony West, the critic and novelist, died [December 27] at his home in Stonington, Conn., after suffering a stroke. He was 73 years old and also kept a home on Fisher's Island, N.Y.

Mr. West reviewed books for *The New Yorker* from 1950 into the late 1970's. Many of his essays also appeared in *The New Yorker*, which previously published much of the reportage of his mother—Dame Rebecca West—from around the world.

A collection of his pieces, reflections on subjects ranging from Thomas Jefferson to Winston Churchill, appeared in 1957. An updated version followed in 1970.

Mr. West was the son of Dame Rebecca and H. G. Wells, whom he featured in a biography, *H. G. Wells: Aspects of a Life.* The book appeared in 1984, the year after his mother's death, and was widely regarded as a son's effort to come to terms with famous, difficult—and unwed—parents.

In a like vein, Mr. West's third novel, *Heritage* (1955), was heralded as the story of a son torn between two "high-powered, world-famous and unmarried parents" who grew up to be "a very happy man." Little note was taken at the time that he

had named the fictional narrator, Richard Savage, after an early-18th-century English poet who claimed to be the illegitimate son of the Countess of Macclesfield.

Reviewing the book in *The New York Times*, Orville Prescott wrote: "Although by conventional standards they were wretchedly bad parents, Richard concluded that being their son was a privilege rather than a misfortune," their conduct having been "justified by their genius."

Mr. Prescott called that a "generous verdict," albeit a debatable one, and judged Mr. West's book "an amusing and well-written novel."

The disguise as fiction did not sit well with Dame Rebecca, who threatened to sue any publisher who printed it in Britain. None did until after her death.

Asked to write an introduction for an American paperback version in 1984, Mr. West proved equally unforgiving and merely allowed that he should not have used the name Richard Savage for the "fictional" son.

Christopher Lehmann-Haupt of *The Times,* who reviewed Mr. West's life of his father in 1984, called it "an enthralling yet ultimately troubling biography" and "a memoir-biography" the author had been working at off and on since 1948.

"This is a book whose main purpose seems to be to even the score with anyone who has ever denigrated Mr. West's father," Mr. Lehmann-Haupt wrote. While not really glossing over H. G. Wells's failings, Mr. West keeps coming "back to the subject of Rebecca West, who, when all is written, is the ultimate target of his book."

The reviewer praised the "witty and eloquent" portraits of people who touched Wells's life and acute psychological insights. Yet, Mr. Lehmann-Haupt concludes, "Judging by this brilliantly written book, for Mr. West the agony has never abated."

Anthony Panther West was born Aug. 4, 1914, in Hunstanton, Norfolk, England, his middle name derived from one of the nicknames his parents used with each other. He called himself "a rather unsuccessful student" at school and never went to university.

He spent some years in cattle breeding, dairy farming and traveling before starting to write reviews, in 1937, for the *New Statesman and Nation.* By the time World War II broke out, he was that journal's regular critic of new fiction.

Tuberculosis kept him from military duty, so he spent the war working for the Far Eastern desk of the British Broadcasting Corporation, and then for its Home News division. From 1945 to 1947 he was posted to the Japanese Service.

In 1950, he went to the United States, where he joined the staff of the *New Yorker.*

Mr. West's other books include his first novel, ***The Vintage*** (1950), which was titled ***On a Dark Night*** in Britain. Winner of a Houghton Mifflin Award, it was the story of an English colonel-barrister and a German general, executed as a war criminal, who meet in a contemporary version of hell and explore their lives.

The Trend Is Up (1960) was about the ambitious son of a conservative banking family in Boston. David Dempsey of *The New York Times Book Review,* praised Mr. West—"not a native son"—for his "accurate and sensible" understanding of American life and "valid social observations."

> Wolfgang Saxon, "Anthony West, Critic and Author; Wrote Essays for 'The New Yorker'," in The New York Times, *December 28, 1987, p. D13.*

THE TIMES, LONDON

Anthony West, critic and novelist, but best known for being the son of H. G. Wells and Rebecca West, died in the United States on December 27. He was 73.

The romance between Wells—then a highly successful author and public figure—and the talented and ambitious young Rebecca West, was a fascinating source of gossip among the British intelligentsia for a large part of the twentieth century. Their illegitimate son wrote two versions of the story.

The first, fictionalized version, was the novel ***Heritage,*** which appeared in America in the 1950s but which was withheld from publication here because of threats of legal action by his mother, who was now Dame Rebecca West and a formidable literary figure in her own right. It was finally published in Britain in 1984, after her death.

In the same year West also published ***H. G. Wells: Aspects of a Life***—which made it all too easy to see why Dame Rebecca had been so anxious not to see her son go into print.

There was, to put it mildly, no love lost between mother and son. West hero-worshipped his father, and was convinced that his mother, when Wells refused to marry her, had decided to take her revenge on the child.

Not that Wells emerged from his son's biography as simon-pure. The book, considering the extraordinary emotional background, and the need, as West saw it, to counter aspersions cast on Wells's reputation by his mother, turned out to be a valuable assessment of one of the great writers in the English language.

Anthony Panther West ("Panther" was the pet name by which Wells addressed Rebecca during their affair) was born at Hunstanton, Norfolk, on August 4, 1914 (just as German forces were sweeping into Belgium, and the world that Wells's novels described was in a sense coming to an end).

He was educated at Stowe, and for a time was a dairy farmer and a registered breeder of Guernsey cattle. During and just after the Second World War he worked for the BBC, first with the Far Eastern Desk and then with the Japanese Service.

His potential as a man of letters was acknowledged when he joined the staff of the *New Yorker* in 1950. His literary essays attracted notice on both sides of the Atlantic, as did the first of his half-dozen novels, ***Another Kind.*** His first substantial work of literary criticism was ***D. H. Lawrence*** (1951), which was republished in 1966.

For a time he wrote criticism for the *New Statesman.*

His literary output was considerable in quantity and in merit. Many of those who knew him felt, however, that his place in literature might have been larger had his life not been dominated by so much family bitterness.

> "Anthony West: Chronicler of a Famous Literary Romance," in The Times, *London, December 29, 1987.*

Marguerite Yourcenar

June 8, 1903 - December 17, 1987

(Born Marguerite de Crayencour) Belgian-born French and American novelist, critic, essayist, short story writer, biographer, poet, dramatist, and autobiographer.

(See also *CLC*, Vols. 19, 38 and *Contemporary Authors*, Vols. 69-72.)

PRINCIPAL WORKS

Le jardin des chimères (poetry) 1921
Les dieux ne sont pas morts (poetry) 1922
Alexis; ou, Le traité du vain combat (novel) 1929
  [*Alexis*, 1984]
La nouvelle Eurydice (novel) 1931
Pindare (criticism) 1932
Denier du rêve (novel) 1934
  [*A Coin in Nine Hands*, 1982]
La mort conduit l'attelage (short stories) 1934
  [*Two Lives and a Dream*, 1987]
Feux (poetry and prose) 1938
  [*Fires*, 1981]
Nouvelles orientales (short stories) 1938
  [*Oriental Tales*, 1985]
Les songes et les sorts (essays) 1938
Le coup de grâce (novel) 1939
  [*Coup de grâce*, 1957]
Mémoires d'Hadrien (novel) 1951
  [*Memoirs of Hadrian*, 1954]
Électre; ou, La chute des mosques (drama) 1954
Les charités d'Alcippe et autres poëmes (poetry) 1956
  [*The Alms of Alcippe*, 1982]
Préface à la Gita-Gavinda (nonfiction) 1958
Sous bénéfice d'inventaire (essays) 1962
  [*The Dark Brain of Piranesi and Other Essays*, 1984]
Le mystère d'Alceste, suivi de qui n'a pas son minotaure?
  (drama) 1963
L'oeuvre au noir (novel) 1968
  [*The Abyss*, 1976]
Théâtre (dramas) 1971
Souvenirs pieux (biography) 1974
Archives du nord (biography) 1977
Le labyrinthe du monde (autobiography) 1977
Mishima; ou, La vision du vide (criticism) 1980
  [*Mishima: A Vision of the Void*, 1986]
Le temps, ce grand sculpteur (essays) 1983
  [*That Mighty Sculptor, Time*, 1987]

BURT A FOLKART

Marguerite Yourcenar, who lived in Maine, wrote in French and ended 3½ centuries of misogyny when she became the first

Photograph by Jacques Robert © Gallimard

woman acclaimed an *immortelle* by the prestigious Academie Francaise, is dead.

The internationally esteemed historical novelist was 84 when she died [December 17] after suffering a stroke [in November]. She died in a hospital in Bar Harbor, Me., near her small home of white timber on Mount Desert Island where she was known to neighbors simply as "Madame." She will be cremated and her ashes buried there, a spokesman for her French publisher said.

Little known to the English speaking world until her 1980 admission to the 40-member Academie Francaise—which guards the French language from impurities—Ms. Yourcenar was considered a master of psychological analysis of history through her novels, which were set at disparate points of time and in diverse cultures.

Probably known best for her 1951 novel *The Memoirs of Hadrian*, about the Roman emperor, and *L'Oeuvre au Noir*, (*The Abyss*) about Europe in the 16th Century, Ms. Yourcenar was hailed by critics for her ability to remove herself from her subjects and for her evocations of the past that illuminate the present.

"French letters has just lost an exceptional woman," Premier Jacques Chirac said in Paris. "On the strength of a classical and rigorous style, Marguerite Yourcenar used a very personal tone to find, thanks to history, the occasion for a strong reflection on morality and power."

President Francois Mitterand called her "one of the great writers of this century" and issued a statement saying that "she gave us lessons of nobility, of conscience, and also of the appetite for life."

Jean d'Ormesson, the French writer and editor who nominated the silver-haired, soft-spoken author as a fellow member of the *academie,* said that after Jean-Paul Sartre and poet Louis Aragon, Ms. Yourcenar was the best representative of French literature in the world.

It was his nomination that sparked a furor in France not only because the choice was a woman but also because she was a citizen both of France and the United States.

She also was only the second American, after author Julien Green, who was born of American parents in Paris, to be considered for membership. (He obtained French nationality before his election in 1971.)

Surprisingly Ms. Yourcenar was elected by a 20-12 margin on the first ballot even after warning the *academie* that she would accept membership but would not wear the traditional gold-embroidered uniform nor carry a sword at her inaugural.

And in taking her seat, she paid tribute to the "invisible troop of women that perhaps should have received this honor sooner."

Although she said she was pleased at the distinction, she lent little personal credence to her selection, once describing the *academie* as "a club of elderly gentlemen."

Marguerite Yourcenar was born Marguerite de Crayencour in Brussels, Belgium, to an old, established society family. She was the only child of a French father and a Belgian mother, who died 10 days after her birth.

Ms. Yourcenar was raised by her father, Michel, a nobleman known for his romantic adventures and the first two volumes of her three-volume autobiography dealt with her maternal and paternal lineage.

By age 8 she was fluent in the classics, was accomplished in Latin by the age of 10 and Greek at 12. Her father supervised her education, obtained exclusively at home through a governess and tutors who taught her to read aloud in many languages.

Her father, whom Mrs. Yourcenar once called "the first great friend I ever had and the freest man I ever knew," paid for the publication of a book of poems which she signed Marguerite Yourcenar—a near-anagram of Crayencour. She was 10.

She traveled with her father to England during World War I and then after his death in 1927 throughout Europe and the eastern Mediterranean.

Her first novel, *Alexis,* was published in 1929. Over the years her work ranged from descriptive scenes of her childhood to a novel centered on attempts to assassinate Benito Mussolini.

Robert Nunn, associate professor of romance languages at Bowdoin College in Brunswick, Me. where her manuscripts

and original editions will be kept, said Ms. Yourcenar had a small readership because her works were so difficult.

"They require a great deal of knowledge of history."

Ms. Yourcenar first visited the United States in 1937 to do research at the Yale University library and decided to stay. In 1947, she became an American citizen but failed to notify French officials that she wanted to preserve her French citizenship, which she later lost.

That almost cost her her seat in the Academie Francaise, which agreed to postpone the vote so she could be reinstated as French which she managed only months before her nomination.

Her decision to stay in the United States had been prompted by the outbreak of World War II and her close friendship with American Grace Frick, a teacher who became her prime translator.

During the war she lectured and taught art history at Sarah Lawrence College in New York while translating Virginia Woolf's *The Waves* and Henry James' *What Maisie Knew.* Both volumes were praised for overcoming stylistic difficulties.

The success of *Memoirs of Hadrian* in which she tried to define the character of the Roman emperor, overcame her financial difficulties and permitted her to concentrate on her novels. Although they were warmly received and impactful in France, only three had been translated into English before her nomination to the Academie Francaise.

An eclectic reader and writer, she translated into French many of the Negro spirituals she had heard while traveling the American South while performing a similar service for erudite Greek and Latin poets.

"I try to give an idea, an emotion, as close as I can to what the author wanted to be felt by the reader," the never-married writer once said of her translating talent.

She also studied and wrote on art, mythology, philosophy and genealogy, prompting the noted French literary critic Jacqueline Piatier to call her "an unabashed humanist with old-fashioned values."

And her deeds matched her words as she lent support from her French country cottage in rugged Maine to things ecological, saying that today's primary concern should be what humanity leaves for tomorrow.

Burt A. Folkart, "Marguerite Yourcenar; 1st Woman "Immortelle' in Academie Francaise," in Los Angeles Times, *December 19, 1987.*

ERIC PACE

Miss Yourcenar was a cosmopolitan, versatile woman of letters who wrote in her native French. To English-speaking readers, she was best known for her fiction, especially her 1951 novel *Memoirs of Hadrian.* Her other writings included essays, memoirs and plays. . . .

Roger W. Straus, the president and chief executive officer of Farrar Straus & Giroux, which has published works by Miss Yourcenar, said [December 18] in a statement released at the Manhattan headquarters of the publishing house: "Marguerite Yourcenar was without question or doubt one of the great writers of the 20th century. She is a great loss to the literary community, but her words will be read and remembered forever.''

Born in Brussels of a French father and Belgian mother, Miss Yourcenar grew up in France and traveled widely. On a visit to the United States early in World War II, she decided to stay when, as she once put it, ''the months stretched into years as the war didn't end.'' For the next decade she taught comparative literature at Sarah Lawrence College. She acquired United States citizenship in 1947 but was later reinstated as a citizen of France.

''I am rootless,'' she told an interviewer in 1979. ''To steal from Hadrian, 'I am at home everywhere and nowhere.' ''

Her induction into the Académie Française in 1981 was an accolade that had been denied to Mme. de Staël, Colette and other illustrious French-women in the four-century history of that prestigious society of 40 ''immortals,'' the arbiters of French language and literature.

Commenting on her induction, Miss Yourcenar said: ''This uncertain, floating me, whose existence I myself dispute, here it is, surrounded, accompanied by an invisible troupe of women who perhaps should have received this honor long before, so that I am tempted to stand aside to let their shadows pass.''

She also said the academy was not to blame for not admitting women sooner. ''One cannot say,'' she said, ''that in French society, so impregnated with feminine influences, the academy has been a notable misogynist: it simply conformed to the custom that willingly placed a woman on a pedestal but did not permit itself to officially offer her a chair.''

Miss Yourcenar was respected as a classical scholar as well as a literary stylist. The Oxford University classicist Hugh Lloyd-Jones, writing in *The New York Times Book Review* in February 1985, praised her ''ornamental and mellifluous French prose, studded with the literary allusions which come so easily to such a cultivated writer'' [see *CLC*, Vol. 38].

Miss Yourcenar once said her writing had ''one foot in scholarship, the other in magic arts,'' and her interests were diverse.

Shortly before her death, in an interview with Jean-Pierre Corteggiani for the new quarterly *Normal*, Miss Yourcenar spoke of her views on literature:

> The books I like best are those where there is intelligence, goodness and no injustice. They are very rare indeed. I think that the reason there is so much bad literature, or at least one of the reasons, is that the average person who sets out to be a writer goes around looking for subjects to write about, and editors have the effrontery to ask you: 'Could you not possibly write a novel about . . . or an essay on . . . ,' to which I always reply that I never write anything I have not chosen myself.

Her works ranged from *Memoirs of Hadrian*—an imaginary autobiography of the Roman emperor written as a letter to his grandson Marcus Aurelius—to a volume of stories, *Oriental Tales* (first published in 1938 in French), that drew on the folklore of medieval Japan and other cultures.

She also wrote plays, poems and prose poems and translated into French the lyrics of American spirituals as well as works by such authors as James Baldwin, the modern Greek poet Constantine Cavafy, Henry James, Thomas Mann, Yukio Mishima and Virginia Woolf.

The Hadrian novel was widely considered Miss Yourcenar's magnum opus. The author Stephen Koch wrote in *The New York Times Book Review* in September 1985 that the work ''has riches for anyone interested in history, humanism or the psychology of power'' [see *CLC*, Vol. 38]. When it was first published, he recalled, ''it was immediately incrusted with the mixed and marmoreal honor of being called a classic in its own time.''

Miss Yourcenar's criticism was praised by John Gross in *The New York Times*. Reviewing the English translation of her book *The Dark Brain of Piranesi and Other Essays*, Mr. Gross called her ''an outstanding critic'' [see *CLC*, Vol. 38] and said the essays in the book were notably lucid and ''forceful, deeply pondered, the record of a full imaginative response.''

The rest of her work, which drew on her familiarity with several languages and literatures, remained less widely known until she was named to the Académie Française. In subsequent years, translations of her writing came out more frequently.

In April, *Two Lives and a Dream,* a volume containing three stories by Miss Yourcenar, was published in an English translation by Walter Kaiser in collaboration with the author.

The book had come out in 1982 in France, and the stories it contained were revisions of writing Miss Yourcenar did decades earlier. Farrar Straus & Giroux is to publish a paperback edition in April.

Mishima: a Vision of the Void, a short study by Miss Yourcenar of the Japanese writer Yukio Mishima, was published here in 1986.

Farrar Straus is also scheduled to publish a collection of essays and literary criticism next spring titled *That Mighty Sculptor, Time.* In addition, Farrar Straus is to publish three volumes of autobiography by Ms. Yourcenar, but no publication dates have been set.

The other books by Miss Yourcenar that have appeared in the United States in English translation include, in addition to *Memoirs of Hadrian, Coup de grâce* (1957), *The Abyss* (1976), *Fires* (1981), *A Coin in Nine Hands* (1982), *The Dark Brain of Piranese* (1984), *Alexis* (1984) and *Oriental Tales* (1985).

Miss Yourcenar was born June 8, 1903, the only child of Michel de Crayencour and the former Fernande de Cartier de Marchienne. The name Yourcenar—which she assumed personally and professionally in the 1920's—is an imperfect anagram of the name *Crayencour.*

Her mother died when Marguerite was less than a month old, and she was educated largely by tutors, under the direction of her father. As an 8-year-old, she was already reading the work of the 17th-century French dramatist Racine, and as a teenager she had two small books of verse published.

Then, as an independently wealthy young woman, she traveled widely, wrote essays, poems and fiction, and won praise as a novelist. In 1950, after settling in the United States, Miss Yourcenar and her American friend and companion, Grace Frick, bought the house in Northeast Harbor—on Mount Desert Island off the Maine coast—that became their longtime home. Miss Frick, who translated *Memoirs of Hadrian* and other works by Miss Yourcenar into English, died in 1979.

Miss Yourcenar was known to have prepared a tombstone for her eventual grave, complete up to the final two digits of the date of her death. In the interview with *Normal,* Miss Yourcenar said she had met a Frenchwoman who was horrified that she had even put the first two numbers of her death date on the marker. "So she said 'but why should you not live to the year 2000?' I have absolutely no desire to live till the year 2000," Miss Yourcenar said. "The year 2000 is not for me."

Miss Yourcenar was awarded honorary degrees by Smith, Bowdoin and Colby colleges. She also won numerous European literary prizes, was decorated by the French and Belgian Governments and was a member of the American Academy and Institute of Arts and Letters and the Academy of the French Language and Literature of Belgium.

> Eric Pace, *"Marguerite Yourcenar, Writer and Scholar, Dies,"* in The New York Times, *December 19, 1987, p. 34.*

THE TIMES, LONDON

[Yourcenar's] pen name was a near-anagram of the name with which she was born: Crayencour. She was born in Brussels on June 8, 1903, her mother a Belgian, her father a patrician French man of letters. It was he who brought her up, after her mother died when she was an infant.

He read the French classics to her and taught her Latin and Greek. He privately published her girlhood poems, and provided not only a literary background but specific ideas for her to work on in her own writing. Yourcenar claimed that the characters and stories of her books were all in her head by the time she was twenty.

The theme of the first of her novels to get into print, in 1929, was not historical. But *Alexis; ou le traité du vain combat* was based on a true incident, and created something of a sensation by its treatment of homosexuality at a time when the reading public was only just beginning to get used to Proust. Her sexual themes were in advance of her time. But it was feelings and relationships with which she was concerned, not physical sex.

The originality of her talent showed itself in other novels, such as *Le mort conduit l'attelage,* in 1934; a volume of short stories, *Nouvelles Orientales;* a collection of prose poems, *Feux,* in 1936.

Her shrewd political interest was demonstrated in 1934 when she wrote one of the earliest attacks on the dictators in *A Coin in Nine Hands,* an intricately-structured novel describing an assassination attempt on Mussolini.

With *Mémoires d'Hadrien,* in 1951, which won her several prizes, she became known to the wider reading public. Her talent for historical novels also showed itself in 1968 in *L'oeuvre noir,* a scholarly reconstitution of the life of a sixteenth-century alchemist, and in *The Abyss,* set in the Renaissance.

Yourcenar wrote only in French. But she was translated into more than twenty languages, and latterly her books sold widely. Her move to the United States, in 1947, did not prevent her from continuing to be one of the best-known writers in France, and she also enjoyed considerable success in the theatre with plays on the myths of Electra and of Alcestis.

Just as one of her achievements was to introduce readers of the modern world to classic tales, another was to interpret English and American culture to her fellow-countrymen. She translated Virginia Woolf's *The Waves* and Henry James's *What Maisie Knew.* In *Fleuve profond, sombre rivière* (1964) she adapted Negro spirituals into French.

She was also an essayist. *Le temps, ce grand sculpteur* (1983) revealed not only a characteristically wide-ranging knowledge of topics as varied as the Venerable Bede and the literature of Japan, but also a moving concern for the welfare of animals. Ecology and conservation were among her passions. Feminism, in the fashionable sense, did not attract her.

Her election to the *Académie,* after that élite body had survived three-and-a-half-centuries without any women members, was not achieved without heated debate. Since by that time she had taken American citizenship, there had to be a special dispensation from the President of the Republic.

But in 1981, in a cape designed for her by Yves St. Laurent, and wearing not the traditional sword but a pendant bearing the image of Hadrian, she duly appeared before her fellow "immortals" of the Academy, and in her acceptance speech graciously forgave those who had tried to keep her out. The official grounds for electing her were that her classical erudition, combined with a vibrant contemporary spirit, had made her an exception in the modern age.

Her last work to be translated into English, *Two Lives and a Dream,* was published this year.

> *"Marguerite Yourcenar: France's First Woman Academician,"* in The Times, *London, December 19, 1987.*

LOUIS AUCHINCLOSS

[*Auchincloss is an American novelist, critic, short story writer, essayist, biographer, autobiographer, and dramatist. He is known primarily as an author of novels of manners in the tradition of Edith Wharton and C. P. Snow; these works include* The Indifferent Children *(1947),* Pursuit of the Prodigal *(1960), and* The House of the Prophet *(1980). He has also written major critical studies of Henry James, Ellen Glasgow, Henry Adams, and Wharton. A longtime admirer of Yourcenar's writings, Auchincloss met her in New York in February, 1986, when he spoke at a National Arts Club dinner in her honor. In the following excerpt, Auchincloss recalls Yourcenar, praising the powerful vision of history and humanity in her novels.*]

When I was seated by Marguerite Yourcenar at a dinner given in her honor last February in New York—the occasion of her receiving the medal of the Commander of the French Legion of Honor and the National Arts Club's Medal of Honor for Literature—I placed before her my copy of *Memoirs of Hadrian,* which she had previously agreed to autograph. She had evidently already considered what she would write in it, for she rapidly inscribed her approval of this "good" first edition, the only one not marred by misprints. She then appended in solid capitals the words "LIBERTAS, HUMANITAS, FELICITAS," the motto engraved on Hadrian's coins. Thus moving from the exactly rendered particular to the broader universal, she put me in mind, however irreverently, of the lady with the squint in the Edward Lear limerick who "Could scan the whole sky / With her uppermost eye / While the other was reading small print."

Mme. Yourcenar, who died at 84 on Dec. 17, had a small enough literary output for so long a life, but reading it is apt to produce the extravagant reaction that she knew all there was to know. Somehow the term "historical novel" does not fit her work. She moves so easily and confidently in time and space that a second-century Roman emperor, a 16th-century Flemish philosopher or an anti-Communist combatant in post-World War I Lithuania seems as familiar, or even as "relevant" (to use the sacred word of the 1960's), as Vietnam veterans or anti-nuclear demonstrators. It is as if Yourcenar, orbiting in space, could plummet down into any country in any era and find herself at home. To her it really was one world.

So intent was she on the precise detail that when she lacked the restricting frame of a planned fiction, as she did in writing her autobiography, the facts almost ran away with her. Vivid and fascinating as these volumes are, one is not surprised that her story remained unfinished at her death. A hundred pages were needed for her ancestry alone; hundreds more for her childhood. But in her novels and tales, the strictest order prevailed, and some of the latter she was revising 50 years after their appearance.

I had originally planned to speak that night at the National Arts Club dinner on the subject of power in her fiction, and it was just as well that I decided to change my theme, as I should otherwise have given a touch of anticlimax to the eloquent address on just that subject with which the French Ambassador to the United States, Emmanuel de Margerie, concluded the evening's ceremonies. He pointed out that in any age when writers of fiction dealt largely with the inner self, Yourcenar was one of the few who had treated in depth man's use of power over his fellow men.

I had been an admirer of Mme. Yourcenar's books ever since my college days, when *Alexis* stood out in a literature that still dealt rarely enough with homosexuality. It seemed, however, to me that the story was less concerned with its ostensible subject than with the broader one of love, just as those of her tales that treat historical events are more truly concerned with an ageless humanity. This universal quality in her work, this viewing of men as units of an organized society as well as introspective or neurotic individuals, draws her attention almost inevitably to problems of governance and the effect of rule on those who must impose it. I found myself particularly interested in the three novels that deal most explicitly with this theme: *Coup de grace, The Abyss* and *Memoirs of Hadrian*.

Although I did not meet Mme. Yourcenar until the night of the National Arts Club party, I had corresponded with her the year before to choose a day on which I might call during a visit that I was planning to Northeast Harbor, Me. It always struck me as a bit incongruous that this great Gallic savant should have chosen to reside on the Maine coast, but I imagined that she lived more on the wild and beautiful island that Champlain, discovering it in 1604, had named *I'lle des Monts Déserts* (the Isle of Bare Hills) than she did in the fashionable spa it has since become. At any rate, a meeting could not be arranged, for she had just been elected to the French Academy—the first female "immortal"—and her pretty cottage was being turned inside out as the setting for a television documentary. She protested on the telephone of her inability to receive a single guest; she was enmeshed, a modern Laocoön, in wires. But she was kind of enough to say that what I had written her had taught her something about her work. I was too elated to care whether this were only what Henry James (whose *What Maisie Knew* Yourcenar has brilliantly translated into French) termed "the mere twaddle of graciousness."

The three novels that I see as dealing with power move progressively into the past.

In *Coup de grace*, set in the cold, foggy winter countryside of war-torn Lithuania, the power of life and death is given indiscriminately to individuals and groups fighting savagely and pointlessly in the aftermath of Armageddon. The eerie effect of her prose, praised by survivors of the civil conflict, is the more extraordinary in that she was not present in Lithuania in the years immediately following World War I. Her accomplishment is like that of Stephen Crane in *The Red Badge of Courage* or Stendhal's in the Waterloo chapters of *The Charterhouse of Parma*. And I know of no more shocking passage in modern fiction than the one in which the narrator is obliged to shoot with his own revolver the woman captive who has been his mistress. It is the ultimate madness of power in a world gone mad.

Moving back in time to 16th-century Flanders and Germany in *The Abyss,* Yourcenar transports us to a world that is only half-mad, for her hero philosopher is a priest of the life of reason who makes a gallant struggle to win the minds of his fellows before he perishes, the victim of a bigoted and superstitious church. As *Coup de grace* is set in an atmosphere of misty cold, *The Abyss* is shrouded in a darkness lighted by the golden glints of Flemish palaces and the fire of the Inquisition.

Ironically, it is in her furthest penetration of the past that Yourcenar finds human reason at its strongest and clearest. *Memoirs of Hadrian,* her greatest novel, is cast in the form of a memorial written by the dying Emperor to his ultimate heir, Marcus Aurelius, to guide him in his destiny of ruling the world and to warn him of some of his predecessor's errors. The eloquence and splendor of the style are in keeping with what the imperial philosopher might have written himself, and the supposed monograph is not interrupted by unlikely recollected dialogues or dramatically re-enacted episodes. One can enjoy the illusion of reading a recently unearthed historical document.

To my mind the greatest achievement of what she called her "meditation upon history" lies in the sense conveyed of the essential loneliness of the man who has gained the supreme power and learned to use it humanely. It is a loneliness that his situation thrusts on him, but it is also a condition that he seems to need and almost desire. He cannot bear to be dominated by another human, and he comes to fear that even love will threaten his necessary independence. When love does bind him, toward the end of his reign, it is almost in nonhuman form. Antinoüs, the beautiful, muscular boy, silent, sultry and utterly adoring, seems more like a faithful hound, and when he drowns himself in the belief that his sacrifice will prolong his master's life, it is as if he finally isolated Hadrian from the rest of humanity, condemning him to the solitude of the leader who has had the hubris to emulate a god.

Here is the beautiful passage describing the Emperor's resistance to his passion:

> I was beginning to realize that our observance of that heroic code which Greece had built around the attachment of a mature man for a younger companion is often no more for us than hypocrisy and pretence. More sensitive to Rome's prejudices than I was aware, I recalled that although they grant sensuality a role they see only shameful folly in love. . . . In this passion of a wholly different order I was finally reinstating all that had irritated me in my Roman mistresses. . . . Fears almost without justification had

entered that brooding heart; I have seen the boy anxious at the thought of soon becoming nineteen. Dangerous whims and sudden anger shaking the Medusalike curls above that stubborn brow alternated with a melancholy which was close to stupor, and with a gentleness more and more broken. Once I struck him; I shall remember forever those horrified eyes. But the offended idol remained an idol, and my expiatory sacrifices began.

Louis Auchincloss, "On Power and History: What Marguerite Yourcenar Knew," in The New York Times Book Review, *January 10, 1988, p. 9.*

Literary Biography

Sartre: A Life

by Annie Cohen-Solal

(For Jean-Paul Sartre: see also *CLC*, Vols. 1, 4, 7, 9, 13, 18, 24, 44; *Contemporary Authors*, Vols. 9-12, rev. ed., Vols. 97-100 [obituary]; and *Contemporary Authors New Revision Series*, Vol. 21.)

An Excerpt from *Sartre: A Life*

In her *Petit Catéchism de l'existentialisme pour les profanes* (Little Catechism of Existentialism for Laymen), Christine Cronan offered an accelerated, hypervulgarized course in existentialism, a digest for every occasion: key words, various manifestations, philosophical origins. The book sold like hot cakes. Now everybody could speak of existentialism. "Question: What is existentialism: Answer: Existentialism is the belief that man creates himself through his actions. Question: Who has brought existentialism up to date and made it fashionable? Answer: Jean-Paul Sartre. Question: What is the basic premise of existentialism? Answer: That existence precedes essence." From the most elaborate and sophisticated products to the simplest, thinnest by-products, the fashion of existentialism kept on growing, spreading along a series of concentric circles, and reaching, circle by circle, what Sartre would later call "the total public." Or as Christine Cronan put it, in verse, "In your commitment you will incite / All humanity.... Relentlessly you will create / By your acts alone."

In no time at all, existentialism began to represent, haphazardly, and for no apparent reason, a philosophical current, a way of life, a "religion," and thus become a vast category that could accommodate just about everything French society had rejected as deviant, marginal, dangerous, anarchic. Soon the term "existentialism" grew to encompass all the new ideas circulating at the time. The result was a ridiculous mixture, the pure product of media speculations, the unrecognizable bastard of a collective paternity, all quite extraneous to *Being and Nothingness*, or any other work by Sartre. From German phenomenology, we had thus moved on—much too fast—to an "ism," a meaningless word that everybody seemed to understand, a presumed philosophical movement that everybody seemed to know, a vague and nebulous daily behavior that everybody seemed to adopt.

It is not surprising that Sartre would balk at the uncontrolled skid that this sudden and much too brutal fame wanted to impose on him. Later, he will have to pay for it, but for the moment, he is caught and deformed by this new role. No longer able to control what people say about him or to repudiate the remarks attributed to him, he is stuck in an infernal machine. Soon, he will even have the impression that his own creation is eluding him,

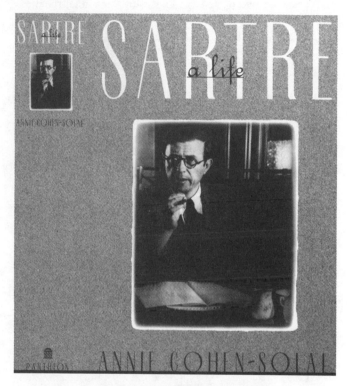

Dust jacket of Sartre: A Life, *by Annie Cohen-Solal. Pantheon Books, 1987. Jacket photograph by Brassaï. Jacket design by Louise Fili. Courtesy of Pantheon Books, a Division of Random House, Inc.*

that he can no longer quite understand it. In three months, and solely because of his own literary production, he has managed to be compared with the most famous men of letters, those very ones who had enjoyed the most intense relationship with the people. The Sartre who is accused of corrupting the nation's youth is compared to Socrates. The Sartre of political commitment speaks, almost despite himself, for Hugo and Zola. If he entered the world of legend as the old lecher luring his virginal prey with a piece of Camembert, he is now quickly evolving, and not without some humor, into the composite offspring of a variety of centuries and a number of forebears, writers, philosophers, men of action. The geographical center of existentialism is perceived as Sartre's neighborhood: Saint-Germain-des-Prés. Gradually, over the past five years Sartre and his group have moved from Le Havre, then Laon, then Montparnasse toward a new center, which, for at least ten years, beginning in 1945 will become, or rather become again, the absolute center of the cultural and literary life of France and even the world. Saint-Germain-des-Prés was often called a village, because of its church, its square, and the narrow streets on both sides of the Boulevard Saint-Germain. And it had layers of cultural tradition—of erudition and adventure, of pleasure and revelry, of science and criticism, of Molière, Diderot, the Benedictine monks and the surrealists. It had sheltered monks, clowns, scholars, actors, revelers, painters, deputies, poets, and writers. Each configuration of this magical place had inscribed itself on the previous one: when, in February 1941, Sartre decided that it would be more comfortable to write near the warm stove of Père Boubal than in his hotel room, he inherited, almost in spite of himself, this tradition.

STEPHEN KOCH

Jean-Paul Sartre—who until 10 years before his death in 1980 was the dominant intellectual voice of post-war Europe—is a fallen hero. Sartre emerged on the Parisian scene during and immediately after the German occupation, stepping from a welter of promising obscurity into a new kind of visibility, from which he rose to an embattled eminence greater than that enjoyed by any other intellectual in this century. Philosopher, novelist, playwright, polemicist, all these activities sustained him in his large role, which was to define the war of ideas for the Europe of his time, and fight among its greatest combatants.

How Sartre reached that pinnacle, and how he fell from it, is the substance of . . . [*Sartre: A Life*]. In addition to his great gifts, Sartre was the stuff from which heroes are made. He had stature: the strength fully to live up to his own seriousness. He had courage: He lived in controversy, and no matter how vicious it became, it could not break him. Finally, he had an unfailing sense of his own fighting place in the crisis of European intellectual culture following World War II.

Yet he was more than all his roles. Twenty years ago, I counted myself among his countless hero-worshipers. I am struck now by a certain strain of romantic irrationality in my admiration. What, exactly, did I admire? To be truthful, while I found his formal philosophy very exciting as a verbal—almost poetic—game, as a description of actual consciousness it seemed first unconvincing and soon merely uninteresting. I never for a moment acceded to his lamentable politics. It was Sartre the writer who moved me, and greatly. His plays engage ideas with unequaled dramatic intensity: I defy anyone to shrug off the infernal machine of *No Exit. Nausea* and his short stories are among the most interesting fiction of his era. His literary and cultural essays—the work in *Situations*—are unforgettably incisive. His memoir of childhood, *The Words,* is among the really flawless pieces of French prose in this century. Despite the slack late work, Sartre was among the most virile and powerful stylists in modern letters. One of many, I took him for a model.

Yet finally I think his glamour derived most powerfully from the musk of some 20th-century romantic magic that Sartre exuded with unchallengeably hypnotic allure. To a degree almost without precedent in this century—the exception is Ernest Hemingway—Sartre was endowed with a talent, a separate autonomous gift, for *fame*. I do not mean empty celebrity. Sartre's fame was part of his heroism, and I invoke the word in its honorable antique sense: fame, the praise and recompense of heroes. He had an uncanny capacity to make himself the most visible part of his relation to any issue. (I'm interested to discover how he was influenced by Hemingway, especially

by Hemingway's knack for making the smallest gesture seem to glow with deliberation and consciousness. ''Me, I'm only a captain.'' Hemingway told him when they met. ''You're a general.'') From all this Sartre conjured up a rough, tough but very cerebral mystique of the isolated ego, a vision of the intellectual as solitary hero, a modernist romanticism of which Sartre made himself the Great Writer and sage. *Nausea* is *The Sorrows of Young Werther* for mid-century. To several generations of the young and bright, it was irresistible.

And it makes a fascinating life, or rather, lives—for there is no Sartre without his lifelong companion, Simone de Beauvoir. The actual outline of their relationship, the subject of so much fantasy and myth about sexual openness, is of enormous interest. Add to their relationship the circles within circles of Parisian intellectuals who formed their apparatus, not to mention the vast network of his love life, and intrigue spreads, to become very grand. (pp. 1, 10)

Though solidly researched and well put together, Cohen-Solal's enterprise is infected with a slack between-us chattiness that's recently been responsible for a great deal of very bad French style. . . .

But [*Sartre: A Life* is] crammed with fascinating information. Who would have imagined, for example, that the title for *Nausea* was suggested at the last minute by Sartre's publisher, that pillar of the bourgeois establishment, Gaston Gallimard? Sartre's original title was a dull, Goethesque *Melancholy*. The change made the book, and identifies precisely the transformation of the romantic heroism over which Sartre presided. I had heard rumored, but never seen confirmed as it is here, that Sartre was a near-alcoholic and an amphetamine addict. I'd hazard that beginning with *Saint Genet* much of his style—an energized, repetitive drive toward some perpetually unattainable lucidity—derives from the effects of that drug. Certainly a number of the awful afflictions of his last years can be traced to it, and in Cohen-Solal's account especially, one senses that through his toxic addictions, Sartre paid a price for his need to stay forever visible, in battle, dominating the scene. We should not omit the painful story of Sartre's years of decline. Simone de Beauvoir wrote about them in a good book, *Adieux,* but certain rather sinister aspects are more fully handled here, especially the way the ailing Sartre used—and was in turn both used and abused by—his last assistant, an opportunistic young fanatic who emerged from the events of '68. It makes riveting reading.

In the larger balance of work, love and reputation, Sartre the artist is now at a low point, Sartre the political sage is close to discredited, and Sartre the man, as the companion of the leading French feminist of her era, in a kind of trouble [his biography] . . . can only deepen. I cannot remember the last time there was an important production in America of a Sartre play. As for the fiction, I'd guess only *Nausea* is still much read—and a recent bump in its career is Denis Hollier's *The Politics of Prose: An Essay in Sartre*, a brilliant, hilarious, and all-but demolishing persiflage of the novel's structure and affectations. (p. 10)

Then there is the almost insurmountable problem of Sartre's politics. In political polemic, heroic stature is not quite enough. It also helps occasionally to be right. A short review makes a full analysis impossible, but it must be said that from the beginning, Sartre's political judgments were systematically and almost ludicrously unsound. He was wrong about Hitler, wrong about the Resistance, wrong about postwar Europe, wrong about the East-West struggle, wrong about totalitarianism, wrong about the future of France. An absolute reversal of the post-humous reputations of Sartre and his youthful companion, and later philosophical and political adversary, Raymond Aron, is only fashion's current testimony to an enduring problem. Exactly where Sartre was likely to be wrong, Aron was likely to be right. It does make a difference.

I find myself gently reproaching [Cohen-Solal] . . . for not summing up the relation to de Beauvoir more fully. Much is explained, but much also remains somewhat mysterious. Theirs was plainly a love match, and a peculiarly stable one at that, even though it floated inside an uncrossable moat of sado-masochism, and the famous "frankness" that defined it served a number of ends other than truth-in-intimacy. Sartre's girl-friends were numberless, part of his great-man apparatus, organized and compartmentalized in a thoroughly hierarchical fashion, with de Beauvoir steady in the center, admirer-in-chief. Except for her, he did not seek out women who were his peers, or even close. (Men either, for that matter.) He seems to have been a charming, generous, gentle, ingratiating lover, far more interested in being admired and loved than he was in "conquest." It was de Beauvoir's job to witness and tolerate—no, love and admire—all this. The balance of this hard intimacy was maintained by elaborate formality; though they could finish each other's sentences, they addressed each other as *"vous."* Her dependency on him (partly denied in her feminism) was obvious and total: his on her was less obvious, and more personally (cruelly) denied. They were essential to each other and their partnership was authentic. Yet one senses that its leading characteristic was its entirely public, and publicized, nature. In fact, much of de Beauvoir's work consisted of writing and talking about it. The fact is that their intimacy was part of a public myth: each others' myth. And yet it was real.

Just as Sartre's stature is finally real. I am no longer much moved by his heroism. But it was authentic. I have come to greatly mistrust his "role"—right and wrong—in politics and culture. Yet he alone could have played it. Finally, he made himself into what the little prodigy and mama's boy dreamed of: one of the greatest French writers of his era. His funeral in April 1980 was one of the impressive events of recent intellectual history. Surrounded by a quite spontaneous crowd of, incredibly, 50,000 people, Sartre's hearse crawled through the Latin Quarter, across Saint Germain, past the cafés he'd habituated, past the bookshops and kiosks and university hang-outs that were his landscape, and then turned south toward Montparnasse. When the black van pulled into sight of the cemetery, the thousands broke into applause. The applause spread; it went on and on. It was the grand recessional of postwar intellectual life of Europe, and one could only lay down one's doubts and grieve. (pp. 10-11)

> *Stephen Koch, "Jean-Paul Sartre: France's Philosopher King," in* Book World—The Washington Post, *June 21, 1987, pp. 1, 10-11.*

SCOTT SULLIVAN

Jean-Paul Sartre spent his life trying to be all things to all men—and to all women. When he died in Paris on April 15, 1980, he left behind a medium-size harem of weeping mistresses, and an intellectual heritage of baffling immensity and ambiguity. By ordinary physical standards, Sartre was a most unimpressive figure. Short and squat, he looked like a frog

and was blind in one eye. To his women, however, he was one of the great seducers of all time. Some Frenchmen, mostly young ones, saw him as the towering moral figure of this century. But most conservatives dismissed him as a flaky, unsophisticated leftist, while the French Communist Party despised him as an ignominious traitor to the Marxist cause. No French author or publisher rushed forward to produce a definitive biography of the controversial philosopher-novelist-playwright.

Now an American publisher has taken the plunge. *Sartre: A Life,* by Annie Cohen-Solal, confronts the wildly contradictory story of Jean-Paul Sartre head-on. It chronicles Sartre's odd, fatherless childhood, his meteoric rise to the front ranks of French intellectual life, his drastic ideological shifts and changes, his consistent failures in practical politics and his equally consistent successes as a lover of women. The Sartre that emerges from Cohen-Solal's big, deeply researched biography is a nexus of phobias and megalomania, both selfish and generous to a fault. It doesn't solve all the mysteries in its subject's complex character, but it illuminates many of them and establishes a solid record for later research. . . .

As an Algerian Jew who spent much of her childhood in Italy and most of her working life teaching in Berlin and Jerusalem, [Cohen-Solal] saw Sartre as a "cross-cultural phenomenon." Impatient with the abstract approach of most French biographers, she spent three years of reportorial digging, interviewing Sartre's relatives, lovers, friends and enemies.

That approach paid off in some solid new insights. Among other things, Cohen-Solal has filled out the portrait of Sartre's father, a brilliant young naval officer who died when his [son was an infant]. . . . Sartre, who lived with his mother till he was 60, always refused to talk about the father he never knew. Now Cohen-Solal argues that the philosopher's rabid anticolonialism derives in part from the fact that his father participated actively in the French conquest of Indochina.

The biographer also managed to turn up the great unknown love of Sartre's life, Dolores Valenti, a French actress living in New York. Cohen-Solal discloses that Sartre proposed marriage to Valenti and even offered to give up his lifelong companionship with Simone de Beauvoir in order to win her over. Valenti turned down the offer, partly because she was married at the time. Later in his life, Sartre worked out quasi-contractual arrangements with half a dozen girlfriends. He set them up in pleasant Paris apartments and looked after their financial needs. In return, the women were expected to get along with one another, and with de Beauvoir.

Cohen-Solal offers a fundamentally enthusiastic view of the author of *The Wall, Nausea* and *The Words.* Her Sartre is "a man for the 1980s," a writer who has "a hot line to young people today." She sees him as having been "the greatest of all Sartreans himself," in the sense that, in his hectic political activism and vast literary projects, he strove unceasingly to "create himself through his own actions." She deals convincingly with Sartre's excesses, his heavy drinking and smoking, his dependence on amphetamines, all of which she interprets as part of a "megalomaniac need to pass beyond his human limits."

The book leaves some important questions unanswered. It does not really explain why the antifascist Sartre had his play *The Flies* produced under German censorship during the Nazi occupation. It fails to account for the sophisticated philosopher's frequent naiveté in embracing questionable leftist causes. It leaves his most famous single act—his refusal to accept the Nobel Prize in Literature—as an incomprehensible instance of reverse snobbery. But Cohen-Solal fills a real need. Her long, careful and loving portrait of Sartre turns a remote and puzzling mandarin into a true existential being, warts and all.

Scott Sullivan, "The Real Jean-Paul Sartre," in
Newsweek, Vol. CIX, No. 25, June 22, 1987, p. 76.

DENIS HOLLIER

[Hollier, a critic and educator, is the author of The Politics of Prose: Essays on Sartre (1986). In the following excerpt, he discusses Sartre's views on the difficulties of biography as a genre and notes that Cohen-Solal has written a remarkably unproblematic, although limited, study.]

Annie Cohen-Solal's book [Sartre: A Life] opens with the story of a suitcase. In 1960 Jean-Paul Sartre, then in the process of writing The Words, the autobiography of his childhood, went on a research trip. He returned to Thiviers, the small town in the southwest of France where his father and his father's family had lived. Perhaps Aunt Hélène, the last surviving relative on that side, would have a key to things. He had not seen her in 30 years. He knocked. Nobody answered. Aunt Hélène had died three months earlier. The following day, back in Paris, Sartre, unperturbed, took up the draft of The Words once again.

This trip to Thiviers, both in its precipitousness and in its curious lack of issue, betrays Sartre's ambivalence about his own responsibility for his personal past. (Roquentin, the protagonist of Sartre's Nausea, sneers at the burghers who save everything. "The past," he says, "is a luxury for landlords." But he conveniently forgets that in his hotel room, he himself has two trunks full of souvenirs.) Walking to the Thiviers station empty-handed, Sartre would never know that in the deserted house there was indeed a suitcase waiting. He had not even tried to have the door opened. A landlord, after all, needs a caretaker. Why should I do it since others will do it for me? Sartre didn't mix his genres. It's up to biographers to carry the suitcases of the autobiographer.

Cohen-Solal found the suitcase, and she opened it. This is not the only thing that she's opened. Each time that is hasn't been too late and she's been able to find the address, she has knocked on the doors of the elderly, to snatch the last memories of childhood from the shades of oblivion. At her bidding these fragile phantoms, their voices quavering, evoke Jean-Paul Sartre the child, turning over to the journalist their stores of school-time memories. They have been waiting for her for 67 years. They knew that one day they would have to meet their obligation: to bear witness before all of humanity that he was just like everyone else, a child who—to play on the famous concluding sentence of The Words—was as good as anyone and whom anyone was as good as.

Sartre made himself dizzy with fantasies about what the life of a Balzac who died before having written a single novel might have been like. But his schoolmates were not worried for him. They knew that this chum who had the discretion not to distinguish himself from them was promised the fame of a biography. Yet their memories are pale, and these desiccated ghosts of Sartre's childhood give to the opening chapters of Cohen-Solal's book the atmosphere of Citizen Kane. The "Rosebud" of Citizen Sartre, however, is not painted on a sled and is not to be found in any of the suitcases through which Cohen-Solal rummages. We find it in The Words, where

Sartre, now a Great Man, complains of having been "poisoned" as a child by a certain book whose aura would inhibit all his future efforts to attain adulthood through commitment and responsible writing: The Childhood of Great Men, a book whose grip on his imagination was probably too secret and too important for him to share with his schoolmates.

The very concept of the interior life always disgusted Sartre. He never referred to it except in sarcastic tones. Once Roquentin begins to work on his diary, this new intimacy with himself makes him nauseous. Consciousness, Sartre repeats, has no interior; to exist means to be outside. He loathed intimate books. The Sartrean memory has nothing about it that is called up by the German word Erinnerung—that is, memory as interiorization. Instead it evokes more of the open house, a public place where so many people have had their word to say that it is difficult, today, to sort out autobiography from biography. Sartre wrote a book of memories not to relive his past, but to liquidate it. Sartre wanted fame to gain a single privilege: to be able to unload his past and his memories onto someone else's shoulders. The only way to redeem his life was to find someone who would take care of it for him.

Philippe Lejeune has shown how the Sartrean autobiography was sired through contact with the media. For Sartre the microphone was what the madeleine and the cup of tea were for Proust. The interview was not only the conduit, it was the atmosphere proper to the blossoming of memory as well. The space of the press conference was necessary for Sartre to be able to remember. This, in any event, is the thesis according to which Cohen-Solal organizes her biography.

"All you have to do," Sartre wrote in 1938, "is to narrate a life in the style of American journalism and the life becomes a social text." The most touching pages of this biography are those in which Sartre, in 1945 and 1946, encounters American journalism and becomes a social text. Sartre himself (whom Camus had sent to New York in the capacity of journalist) is the writer who, in France, elevated journalism to full citizenship in the domain of letters. But here Cohan-Solal reverses the proposition. It is through Sartre, she tells us, that French literature achieved the status of a media event. It is by means of the press that Sartre was introduced to Sartre and made contact with himself. And since journalism is American, it is in New York that Cohen-Solal, as well, makes contact with him.

Cohen-Solal is not an indiscreet biographer. It is clear that she prefers her subject when he isn't writing. She lets him work in peace, without spying on him, without trying to push her way into his study. But she is confident. She knows that sooner or later he will have to leave his desk, leave his books. And if she likes him so much in New York, it's because she can get to see him there. He has stopped writing. During these several weeks he is happy being famous, and in love.

The crowd massed along the shores of the East River to welcome Dickens was the first image of fame that haunted Sartre. The welcome that New York reserved for him suggested a fame both stranger and purer. Since "few of Sartre's works had yet been translated," that welcome crowned a writer whom almost no one had read. At Carnegie Hall, he gave a lecture in French before an audience that hardly understood him. But never mind, "since it was Sartre people had come to discover and appreciate, not his lecture." More: "What the American public noticed was something that no text could have conveyed: his human warmth, his humor, his capacity for contact." By her own warmth, but also by a curious distance from his work, Cohen-Solal's interest in Sartre resembles, in many ways, the interest that New York displayed for him.

Sartre was profoundly alive to the problems inherent in the biographical genre.... In *Nausea,* it is in order to write a biography (not of a "scholar," as Cohen-Solal tells us, but of an 18th-century adventurer, the Marquis de Rollebon) that Roquentin goes to live in Bouville—until the day when, in the library of this provincial town, a sudden revelation makes him see the vanity of the biographical project. He abandons his notecards and leaves Bouville. He has discovered that biography is an impossible genre; it accumulates around its subject eyewitness accounts that, he says, "don't contradict each other, no, but they don't agree with each other either." And he has discovered too that it is not by writing the life of another that a man finds his salvation. "A dead man can never justify the living." For the biographer, biography is not a redeeming genre.

Roquentin's problems, however, did not stop Sartre from writing about the dead. In particular, he wrote a study of Baudelaire that caused a scandal in its day: he dared to pass judgment on a poet without taking the work into account. To show that Baudelaire had the life he deserved, Sartre examined the letters, the diaries, the reports of others. Yes, *Les Fleurs du mal* was consulted, but merely as one document among all the others making up the existential dossier. The study of Baudelaire reversed Roquentin's proposition. Even though for him no dead man would be able to justify a living one, here it is the living (Sartre) who is incapable of redeeming the dead (Baudelaire). The concept of "original choice," which is at the center of Sartre's theory of freedom, implies that all men freely choose what will be their destinies. In his *Baudelaire,* Sartre tracks back to the choice that the poet freely took for his life and for himself, to find how he made for himself the life he deserved.

Cohen-Solal's book is the oddly unproblematic biography of this author who considered biography to be the most problematic of the genres. It escapes both the scruples of Roquentin and the ambitions of Sartre, in its modesty and its directness. She follows the life of her subject without asking whether he has either chosen it or deserved it. And when the eyewitness accounts that she reports aren't in accord with one another, she doesn't try to impose a factitious unity on them. She doesn't explain the work by means of the life. She doesn't even try to explain the life. She tells it. She is neither intrusive nor possessive. Still, if she never exceeds the limits given by her subtitle (*A Life*), this is not through ignorance of the work, but from respect for it: she, after all, knows herself not to be a critic. Sartre's books, their working out, their publication, their reception are referred to when necessary, but always in the background, during intermission. The summaries of his doctrines, his aesthetic arguments, are reduced to a minimum. And when she quotes, it is what has been said (by Sartre himself or someone else, if possible in the course of interviews) rather than what has been written.

It is a law of biography that it attaches itself to the life in preference to the work. But never does Cohen-Solal imply that Sartre, mirroring his biographer, had chosen life over his work. He did everything he could to avoid choice, to prevent his work from detaching him from life. Such is the main purpose of his theory of literary engagement. Sartre's first works on the subject of the imagination already denounced the threat of depersonalization implied in a literature of evasion, in an aestheti-

cism that would turn its back on life. He chose literature, but only in demanding of it that it take its measure from life.

For Sartre, the engaged writer does not dream. He acts. His words, like his silences, produce effects for which he is responsible. No more play. After his wartime internment, in 1941, Sartre solemnly announced to Simone de Beauvoir that he was going *"to act."* His students of the time still remember the lectures in which he analyzed the difference between "gesture" and "action." And in 1943 he has Orestes, the hero of *The Flies,* boast, "I've done my deed, Electra, and that deed was good."

But *The Flies* is a play, and the seriousness of Orestes' "action" and commitment is strangely undermined by the actor's playacting itself. The same ambiguity poisoned Sartre's discovery of "the real," represented to him by the experience of the Second World War. In 1974 he described to de Beauvoir the emotion that made him realize that the war had abruptly stopped being phony, which made him decide that it was time to act. "I remember the strange feeling I had of a film, the feeling that I was acting in a scene in a film and that it was not true." It is correct to say that Sartre, in order to be able to engage himself in the real, spent his life looking for a certain criterion for telling it apart from the imaginary, but it is no less correct that he always confused them.

Cohen-Solal's biography has a leitmotiv. During the Resistance: "He is with them, yet elsewhere."... The more engaged he is, the less he is there. "Already, Sartre had escaped. He had escaped to a place where no one, not even those closest to him, could enter." He who condemned so severely any form of escapism was always escaping. The rioting students of May '68 prompted a scene whose baroque grandiosity recalls the endings of Mel Brooks's films. The world, once again, becomes a stage. And the fundamental choice of Sartre, who based his work (and the difference between it and his life) on the possibility of distinguishing the real from the unreal, was submitted to a hard test.

This test began in the streets, where the Parisian students refused to distinguish the real from the imaginary. They wrote on the walls, "The imaginary is real." And they yelled, "Take your dreams for reality." But Sartre, the engaged writer, did not hear these slogans about giving power to the imagination. He was too far away. These cries were blocked out by another voice, quite close, that he finally consented to hear, one that whispered to him exactly the same thing. He didn't hear them, but he was with them—elsewhere—terminally involved with Flaubert, an author who is strangely classified as a realist when he had chosen the unreal. "Sartre's connection with the student riots of May 1968 is an invention of the press, pure illusion. At that moment, Sartre is elsewhere, back in 1831 ... he is with Flaubert." The war served to frame revolutionary engagement; May '68 was the moment of revolutionary disengagement for Sartre.

No doubt it is a virtue of Cohen-Solal's biography to keep reminding us at all the important historical turning points that Sartre's real place is elsewhere. Its shortcomings, however, derive from this very admission, since Sartre's elsewhere is to be found in what he wrote. And to enter it, opening the suitcases in Thiviers is not enough; we must open the books that after all make up one of the major bodies of literary and philosophical work of our century.

An early entry in Barthes's *Mythologies* concerns the type of "candid" or informal photograph of actors taken when they are off stage, supposedly immersed in routines of daily life. This kind of image apparently exchanges the stage for the real world, but in fact it raises the stakes of irreality. What the professionals of illusion acquire in these new settings is simply an aura of deprofessionalized illusion. Perhaps they had to play roles that demanded them to inhabit faces of ugliness or of age. These photographs restore to them "an ideal face, cleansed (as at the launderers) of the improprieties of their profession. Paradoxical condition: it's the stage that becomes reality, and life is what is myth, dream, fantasy."

The episode of Sartre's New York triumph is dominated by a photograph of this very type. It appeared in *Time* on January 26, 1946, credited to William Leftwich. Ugliness, as is well known, is the major characteristic of Sartre's own iconographic legend. But from this curiously glamorous image, ugliness had vanished. "By what strange miracle," wonders Cohen-Solal, "had the eye of an American photographer been able to find the right angle to draw out of Sartre's face the portrait of a classically sensuous face?" It is a bewilderment not unlike that experienced from time to time by the reader of this biography, from which Sartre emerges, like Barthes's actor, cleansed of the improprieties of his profession, paradoxically all the more unreal for his being depicted exclusively in "real life." (pp. 36-9)

Denis Hollier, "Being and Somethingness," in The New Republic, *Vol. 196, No. 26, June 29, 1987, pp. 36-9.*

H. W. WARDMAN

In four years of intensive effort Annie Cohen-Solal has performed the remarkable feat of writing a comprehensive, well-researched life of Sartre in a lively and challenging style. Intended for the general public, her narrative is clearly-shaped and enlivened by sharply-drawn contrasts. The cover of [*Sartre: A Life*] shows a dapper-looking Sartre in a dark suit, smoking a cigarette and advancing purposefully towards the camera, no longer with Simone de Beauvoir, as in the original photograph. Such, one feels, for this author, is the essential Sartre: self-assured, vigorous, and combative.

One of the problems which confronts Sartre's biographer is how far *Les mots* can be trusted as a source. Annie Cohen-Solal has solved this problem, as she does throughout, by using interviews and consulting family archives. This part of her research results in a much fuller account of Sartre's family background than can be gleaned from *Les mots* or any other literary source. In particular, there is a great deal more than was previously known about the life of Sartre's father, who makes only a brief appearance in *Les mots*. Thus the details of family relationships provide the biography with a firm, traditional foundation.

The author excels in depicting Sartre's early years at the École Normale and later as a highly unorthodox *professeur* at Le Havre, where he succeeded in ruffling the prejudices of the bourgeoisie so maliciously satirized in *La nausée*. Wherever Sartre can be shown to be active and expending his remarkable energies, especially in writing, his biographer does him full justice. She does this also when writing about the so-called 'contingent' love-affairs which were so necessary to his life. She gives an informative account of Sartre's experiences in the army and during the Occupation. On the latter subject, in particular, she has much to say that is new. One of her most successful chapters is entitled, characteristically, 'Un Sulfureux Ambassadeur'. It describes with verve the visits that Sartre

and Simone de Beauvoir paid in the sixties as ambassadors-extraordinary to various capitals all over the world, nearly all of which, except in China, received them with acclaim. The author is understandably critical of some of Sartre's more enthusiastic pronouncements intended for popular consumption at home, especially about the Cuban revolution. But we are not really given much of a chance to see exactly what is wrong with them. After all, Sartre saw himself as an intellectual with a mission. This may have had its pretentious side, but a wider public than the readership of *Les Temps modernes* had to be contacted, or so Sartre evidently thought, even at the expense of some critical rigour.

This biography succeeds equally in its treatment of the tragic years of Sartre's near-blindness and decline in the chapter 'A l'ombre de la tour'. Moved as she is by sympathy as much as by curiosity, the author manages to be impartial in writing about Sartre's relationships, not only with Simone de Beauvoir and his adopted daughter, Arlette-Elkaïm Sartre, who were rivals for his attention, but with the other women who were by now all the more necessary to him both as companions and as nurses. She goes deeply into the complex question of the conflict between Arlette and the Maoist stormy petrel, Benny Lévy, on the one hand, and the editorial board of *Les Temps modernes* on the other. But she does not altogether face up to the charge of complicity levelled by Simone de Beauvoir against Arlette and Lévy. She does not mention the extent of Simone de Beauvoir's grief and devotion to Sartre's body before the burial, as told in *La cérémonie des adieux*. She is fair to Arlette, as Simone de Beauvoir perhaps is not, in so far as, in that work, more prominence is given to Simone than to her rival. But according to Georges Michel, in his book *Mes années Sartre*, while Simone de Beauvoir lay prostrate with grief after Sartre's death, Arlette and Lévy went into his flat and took away what they fancied. Arlette had legal rights whereas Simone de Beauvoir had none. Annie Cohen-Solal does not refer to this episode.

Against her biography's considerable merits must be set a lack of feeling for *nuances*. Sometimes her antitheses are drawn too sharply. It is perfectly apparent from *Le mur* and *La nausée* that Sartre had a social conscience before the war. The impression given here is that his social conscience was born suddenly, as a result of the war. Excessive prominence is given to Sartre's panegyric of life in the Soviet Union published in *Libération* in 1954, after his return to France. Sartre is held up to ridicule for displaying such naivety. . . . It is true, as Sartre later admitted, that this was one of the occasions in his life when he had not been strictly truthful. We are promised an explanation of this lapse, which is not altogether forthcoming. This is the more frustrating because Sartre was making similar observations about life in the Soviet Union several years later.

Sartre's life, as presented here, tends to be punctuated by crises rather too dramatically conceived. Admittedly, the affair of Duclos and the pigeons did provoke a violent reaction on his part. His relations with the P.C.F. are fairly described, although his polemic with such ex-Communists as Claude Lefort is dismissed rather too lightly. Then, with the Soviet invasion of Hungary, came another crisis in Sartre's life. He abandoned his pro-Soviet attitude as suddenly as he had embraced it and devoted himself to the cause of the oppressed in the Third World. There is truth in this account, but it is oversimplified. It was precisely because of his concern for the oppressed that Sartre became a fellow-traveller in the first place. It is only necessary to read '**Les communistes et la paix**' to realize this, but that work, the main literary result of the Duclos affair, is not considered in any depth here. One hears more about Merleau-Ponty's criticism of it. There is reason to think that the author cannot understand why Sartre became a fellow-traveler.

One could also criticize the account given of the first performance of *Les mouches* for relying too heavily on the biographical imagination, not necessarily a faculty to be despised. In an endeavour to evoke atmosphere, snippets are quoted from the play taken from widely-separated contexts. As to *L'etre et le néant,* there would have been at least as much point in referring to Gabriel Marcel's review of it, written in 1943, as to describing the reactions of André Gorz and Michel Tournier. There is a fair discussion of phenomenology before Sartre's departure for Berlin in 1934, but in general the treatment of the works is disappointing.

The style of this biography is undoubtedly vivid; it carries the narrative along at a pace which is sometimes, but not always, appropriate to the subject-matter. The author has an unfortunate habit of 'firing' rhetorical questions at the reader instead of satisfying his curiosity and of using three epithets where one would do. Attempts at explaining certain important changes in Sartre's life are not always enlightening. How far, for example, does the expression 'une boulimie d'écriture', used more than once, take us in an attempt to explain why Sartre gave himself wholly to writing after the failure of his Resistance group, 'Socialisme et Liberte'? In general, the author tends to see Sartre as a sort of human dynamo whose actions she is apt to explain in mechanistic terms. It is not an accident that one of her chapters is entitled 'Dans la salle des machines'. In consequence, her portrait of Sartre lacks the dimension of inwardness.

This book is not free of faults, then, but its merits are considerable; it deserves to establish itself as a scholarly and highly individual account of Sartre, the man, and his life and times which no student of the period can afford to ignore. (pp. 750-52)

*H. W. Wardman, in a review of "Sartre: A Life,"
in* The Modern Language Review, *Vol. 82, Part 3,
July, 1987, pp. 750-52.*

MICHIKO KAKUTANI

In the wake of World War II, Jean-Paul Sartre emerged as France's pre-eminent intellectual: the avatar of existentialism and the model of the engagé writer, worshipped by the angry and the young, a Renaissance man who addressed the major esthetic and social issues of his day in novels, plays, biographies, essays and philosophical tracts. Though his leftist politics were often widely discredited, though his fiction would be criticized as unwieldy and didactic, Sartre remained an enigmatic public figure through his death in 1980. . . .

In [*Sartre: A Life*], the first biography of the philosopher (the book was first published, to considerable acclaim, in France in 1985), Annie Cohen-Solal, a professor of French culture and the author of a study of the writer Paul Nizan, takes on the daunting project of explicating Sartre's life. Told in a fast-paced, almost cinematic style—many scenes are set down in a nervous present tense that perfectly captures Sartre's own hectic mode of existence—the book moves fluently from rigorous examinations of the writer's literary output to chatty examinations of his complicated liaisons with Simone de Beauvoir and a number of younger women. Ms. Cohen-Solal knowledgeably discusses Sartre's vocations as writer, teacher and

activist, and she succinctly traces the evolution of his philosophical vision, sketching in his debts to Husserl, Bergson and Descartes, as well as the process whereby he formulated his ideas in conjunction with Beauvoir and such friends as Raymond Aron and Nizan.

Though it bogs down a bit in discussions of his complicated politics . . . , *Sartre* not only succeeds in situating the writer's work within the context of contemporary intellectual and social currents, but it also gives us an intimate portrait of the man that possesses all the detail and resonance of fiction. We see Sartre as a spoiled, mama's boy: "a 2-year-old child with curly blond hair, beautiful, adored, Poulu the child-king." We see him as an odd, ugly duckling of a teen-ager: a "pompous little monster," whose "stuffy speeches, stale wit, absurd appearance, and Parisian manners" make him the butt of other teenagers' jokes. We see him before the war as "a small, fat, aging provincial teacher" later, as love-sick courtier, all of whose "dreams and certainties collapsed before the dainty, delicate rejections" of an 18-year-old student, and eventually as the famous man of letters presiding over a retinue of disciples and issuing fierce pronouncements to the world on everything from American literature to the viability of Maoism.

The Sartre that emerges from this biography is an enormously difficult man: a natural heretic, egotistical, arrogant, by turns generous and self-serving, sentimental and cruel, a man who more than anything personifies his own belief that man creates himself freely through his own actions. In fact, one of the main effects of this volume is to demonstrate just how grounded Jean-Paul Sartre's work and philosophy were in autobiography, how, like his own heroes, he eschewed all social labels, choosing instead to live his life like a novel, an adventurer intent on inventing himself as he went along.

Having lost his father to tuberculosis as an infant and his mother to remarriage some 10 years later, Sartre embraced the orphan's prerogative of freedom quite early on: in the face of taunting from schoolmates and his own feelings of loneliness and alienation, the short, walleyed boy arrogantly proclaimed his own genius. By the time he'd graduated from the Ecole Normale Supérieure, he'd already succeeded in turning himself into something of a student legend: the class prankster and bon vivant, verbally adept and equally skilled at "displaying his talents as actor, singer, and pianist."

World War II and his experiences as a prisoner of war would effect another dramatic change. "The Sartre of 1945 is no longer the Sartre of 1939," Ms. Cohen-Solal writes, "The war is the great mutation, the great metamorphosis of his life. On his way into the tunnel, he is a high school philosophy teacher with two published books, an isolated person, an individualist hardly involved in the affairs of this world, totally apolitical. On his way out, he is a writer who spreads his talents over different genres, politically active, and intentionally so: a writer who, in the space of a few months, will be an international celebrity."

The third phase, in which he becomes a militant traveler, visiting Castro in Cuba, Khrushchev in Moscow, Tito in Belgrade, would galvanize his commitment to radical social change and complete his rupture with his family's bourgeoise roots. "He will join Socrates, Plato, Rousseau, Voltaire and Marx," Ms. Cohen-Solal writes, "in the tradition of philosophy that tries to rescue society."

By the time he refused the Nobel Prize in 1964, Sartre was both an international celebrity and a kind of has-been, increasingly separated, Ms. Cohen-Solal observes, "from the intellectual currents of his time." He continued to write and agitate, however, relying more and more on amphetamines to sustain his energy. No doubt the drugs contributed to his deteriorating physical condition: by the fall of 1973, he was suffering from hypertension and dizzy spells, and he was nearly completely blind, unable to go on with the one thing that had defined his life. "Everything that has been most essential in my activity up to now has made me above all a man who writes," he declared at the time, "and it is too late for that to change."

> Michiko Kakutani, in a review of "Sartre: A Life,"
> in The New York Times, July 8, 1987, p. C23.

STANLEY HOFFMANN

[*Hoffmann is an Austrian-born American political scientist and educator who specializes in the government of France. Cohen-Solal credits him for his assistance with* Sartre: A Life. *In the following excerpt Hoffmann observes that, while Cohen-Solal focuses on Sartre's life at the expense of his works, she offers a well-researched and nonjudgmental study, illuminating Sartre's complex personality.*]

There are different ways of writing biographies—especially those of writers as monstrously prolific as Sartre. One way is to try to deal both with the events in their private and public lives and with their writings. In the case of Sartre, this would require several volumes and an author who would feel competent to handle philosophy, epistemology, novels, plays, screenplays, politics, literary and art criticism and psychoanalysis.

Another possibility—and temptation—is to try to find in the works the expression, explicit or unconscious, of the writer's personal experiences, traumas and conflicts. In Sartre's case, the links are often obvious. His huge "preface" to the works of Jean Genet, which became a book, and the three enormous volumes on Flaubert are disguised autobiographies, for they deal with writers who represented aspects of his own personality, and whom he wanted (in Genet's case) to celebrate for his defiance of bourgeois conventions and (in Flaubert's case) to vivisect as the very model of the bourgeois writer who, disgusted by his century, deliberately entombed himself in art. Sartre's hatred of his own body, as well as of his adolescence, reappears in his novels. His love for his mother (widowed in 1906 when he was a year old), and his sense of betrayal when she remarried in 1917, can be connected with his fascination with incest and his interest in Baudelaire, who also hated his stepfather. Indeed, his philosophy of being and freedom, his demand that men and women shape their existence in the form of a project—an attempt to master the future—his disdain for and frequent repudiations of his past can be seen as the products of a man whose idyllic early years were abruptly terminated. His adolescence was both stifling and unhappy, his career— after the happy years at the Ecole Normale Supérieure—was slow and filled with rejections, and he therefore lived, for consolation and vindication, in the future.

The emotion that dominated his life, hatred of bourgeois mores, ethics and politics, seems to have been fed by his family background (his father had already rebelled against the bourgeoisie). The famished and ravenous way in which he appeared to want to "possess" the world through the mind and the printed word, the concentrated and almost Stakhanovite way in which he threw himself into writing, especially in periods of intense stress (such as the "phony war" of 1939-40), could all too

easily be psychoanalyzed as revenges and escapes. The problem with this kind of an approach is reductionism: whatever its sources in a writer's nightmares, hang-ups and obsessions, the work has a life of its own. Many of Sartre's plays are about guilt; they cannot be reduced to his own feelings of guilt for being, inescapably, a bourgeois, or for having been indifferent to social and political issues until the war kicked him out of his cozy existence as a teacher, because they examine also some of the most compelling moral dilemmas faced by the Europeans of his generation.

Wisely, [in *Sartre: A Life*] Ms. Cohen-Solal has avoided the pitfall of reductionism. But there are two more possible approaches to biography. One consists in discussing the works at least briefly, and in showing their connection with the author's and the general public's concerns of the moment, without providing an extensive analysis of the content or indulging in psychological reductionism. . . . Ms. Cohen-Solal's choice is different; she leaves the work aside and concentrates on the life. It is, of course, a debatable choice. What is Sartre without his books? In her fascinating and depressing final chapter, she describes the irreparable break between two generations of Sartean companions—the generation of de Beauvoir and of their associates who ran the monthly *Les Temps modernes,* and the younger generation represented by Sartre's adopted daughter (and mistress) and the fanatical Maoist (later to become a rabbi) Benny Lévy, who had become Sartre's guardian and collaborator during his seven years of blindness and illness and drafted several interviews in which Sartre took startling new positions. But it would have been important to know over what intellectual issues the conflict developed.

Ms. Cohen-Solal's choice to concentrate of the life at the expense of the works, however, can be defended. First, there is really no satisfactory way of dealing with Sartre's monumental *oeuvre* except in depth; no one-volume biography could do this. Second, as Sartre's first biographer, she decided not to rely on what had already been published. She investigated family archives and interviewed as many of Sartre's acquaintances as she could find. Her merit is to have been both modest and industrious. Her modesty shows in her decision to let the facts speak for themselves and to editorialize as little as possible. As a result, Sartre's political involvements appear more complex and more futile than in many other more judgmental works about him. Her industry brings us an intensely human writer with all his contradictions, betrayals, miscalculations, blinders and fiascoes. Thanks to the new information she has collected, we have for the first time a clear picture of Sartre's parents and of their families, which seem to belong in the novels of François Mauriac and Roger Martin du Gard. We also learn a great deal that is new about Sartre's thespian antics at the Ecole Normale, about his unconventionally informal and successful methods as a secondary-school teacher of philosophy and about his moral fortitude as well as his pitiful physical weakness in his last years.

That Sartre's account of his childhood in *The Words* was both brilliant and thoroughly unreliable we already suspected. Ms. Cohen-Solal confirms that. His portrait of his maternal grandfather, who he claimed tried to shape him into a bourgeois whiz kid, was deeply unfair. (After reading it, his mother declared that he had understood nothing about his childhood.) Ms. Cohen-Solal also shows that the icon of the perfect, "free" couple painted by Simone de Beauvoir was far from the truth. Craving affection, Sartre was surrounded by a veritable harem. He told de Beauvoir about all these women. But what did he tell them about her? To what extent were his adoption of Arlette Elkaïm and later his cooperation with Benny Lévy acts of revenge aimed at de Beauvoir, who had been his most intimate partner and the longtime critic of his drafts? There is rich material for a bourgeois vaudeville (and drama) here.

What also emerges from Ms. Cohen-Solal's account is his lifelong fascination with youth. He always preferred young disciples to equals. In his enthusiasm for revolutions and revolutionary countries, antibourgeois hatred and the love of new beginnings blended. One of his earliest (unpublished) novels was about a triangle: the master (Wagner), the young disciple (Nietzsche) and the master's wife (Cosima). Later, he wrote about Tintoretto's revolt against his master, Titian. At the end of his life, Lévy played the role of the young disciple, and if Sartre let himself be manipulated by him (as de Beauvoir has stated), was it only out of senility, or because he identified with his tough young aide?

Ms. Cohen-Solal also documents his unhappy relationship with the world of political action. After history had, so to speak, grabbed him in 1940, he wanted to find an all-inclusive meaning in the sweep of human history. It was an ambition that he never carried out—and had he taken seriously the writings of the great Raymond Aron, his classmate at the Ecole Normale, he would have known why it was futile—but one that explains both his long alliance with Marxism and the unresolved tension between this quest for a philosophy of history and his philosophy of freedom. Yet he also wanted to affect events: he needed both dialectic and praxis; however, he was never successful in praxis either. His two attempts at clandestine action in the Resistance were amateurish failures. The revolutionary party he created in 1948 may, as his biographer says, have anticipated the spirit of May 1968 and many of the themes of the 1980's, but it collapsed in internal squabbles very quickly.

The only period in which Sartre became a strident fellow traveler of the French Communist Party and of the Soviet Union was from 1952 to 1956, when many of the older fellow travelers, revolted by Stalinism in Moscow and by Maurice Thorez's party in France, were beginning to desert. The Algerian and Vietnam wars, which Sartre denounced with all his might, were indeed *his* wars. But his hymn to cleansing, anticolonial violence and his blindness to the flaws of the revolutionary forces that were fighting French and American imperialisms marred even his bravest stands.

The fact is that as he went on, especially in the late 1950's and in the 60's, what he wrote came more and more out of his head (he was hyped by drugs that ultimately destroyed his mind, as has already been mercilessly described by de Beauvoir) and less and less out of either his personal experience or his research. The scholar's humble submission to data, so essential in the social sciences Sartre wanted to apprehend, was never his method. Sure of his genius, eager to embrace the whole world and to expand consciousness as far as it could go, he left unfinished most of his major projects—his series of novels, *The Roads to Freedom*, his ethics, his critique of dialectical reason, his biography of Flaubert.

The foe of bourgeois literature and bourgeois humanism, the didactic celebrator of *committed* writing, the lifelong seeker of a new relationship between authors and readers, he ended up being the last great French intellectual guru, in the mold of a Voltaire or a Victor Hugo. He was the intellectual as conscience and prophet, whose authority rested on his aura rather than on his expertise and who was honored as a national asset by the officials and notables (including the Nobel Prize committee) whose very existence this old anarchist despised. The triumphant, omnipresent intellectual hero of 1945-55, whose abundant writings, lectures and stands, whose influential monthly magazine and cultivation by the news media insured his hegemony, finally became the enfeebled, blind recluse.

Today in France, where Marxism has become unfashionable, enthusiasm for the third world unmentionable and selective sympathy for "progressive" regimes intolerable, Sartre is widely seen as a nefarious influence—a man whose prestige perhaps delayed by 20 years the advent of an antitotalitarian, liberal consensus. The prosecution has a strong case. And yet, behind Sartre's political follies, there always was a faith in individual freedom, a desire for human emancipation from all the servitudes of established hierarchies and drudgeries, a nostalgia for those dawns of liberation when Bastilles fall and fraternity fuses people in a project that they define democratically as self-respecting citizens—a residue of France's tradition of anarchic socialism that survived his nasty break with Albert Camus (over Camus's attack on the intellectual's total commitment to revolution) and reasserted itself in his quixotic support for persecuted Maoist newssheets after 1968. There will be other biographies, though there cannot be a "definitive" life of Sartre any more than he was able to write a definitive one of Flaubert. For now, Annie Cohen-Solal's book helps us understand the man's complexity better, and brings him to life in a startlingly touching way. (pp. 3,25)

Stanley Hoffmann, "A Hero Gone Out of Fashion," in The New York Times Book Review, *July 26, 1987, pp. 3, 25.*

JOHN WEIGHTMAN

[*Weightman is an English translator, critic, and educator. He is the author of* The Concept of the Avant-Garde: Explorations in Modernism *(1974) and has translated the works of Jean Guehenno and Claude Levi-Strauss. In the following excerpt, Weightman finds Cohen-Solal's work well-documented, but hampered by its lack of any moral judgment of Sartre.*]

Is Jean-Paul Sartre—philosopher, novelist, playwright, critic, biographer, political theorist and activist—to be revered as the outstanding intellectual and artistic figure of twentieth-century France, or was he, as George Orwell suggested in the early days of Sartre's fame, predominantly a windbag? To rephrase the question in politer terms, was he a great genius or just a colossally gifted word-spinner, strangely—almost frivolously—indifferent to the inconsistencies in his enormous output, and ultimately devoid of any concept of objective truth? Furthermore, was his association with Simone de Beauvoir an archetypal love affair, a pattern for modern heterosexual relationships, or was it largely a fiction that she created and that he never publicly brought into question, once they had both become famous?

On the second issue I have long been disillusioned. On the first, I confess that, over the years, I have oscillated somewhere between the two opposite opinions, always spellbound by Sartre's torrential flow of mind, but constantly perplexed by his shifting dogmatisms. I am still fairly certain that *La nausée* is a masterpiece, an Absurdist classic which will remain along with Camus's *L'etranger* as the expression of a certain cultural moment, but I am now inclined to look upon the vast body of subsequent writing, unique and astounding though it is, as a brilliantly confused mass of words which, moreover, runs counter to some of the essential Absurdist insights contained in *La nausée.* Worse still, I have come to suspect that Sartre was not, as is often supposed, a convinced humanist evolving a philosophy for the godless world, but a very different kind of creature: in his second phase, at least, a thoroughgoing, old-fashioned metaphysician with a wild, Luciferian urge to negate or dominate creation.

It follows that I approach [*Sartre: A Life* by Annie Cohen-Solal and *Sartre: A Life* by Ronald Hayman]...with keen curiosity to see where their authors stand, seven years after Sartre's death. The biographers begin by expressing great admiration for Sartre. Cohen-Solal deplores the fact that his reputation is now in partial eclipse, but declares her confidence in the enduring vitality of his work, without, however, attempting any detailed critical assessment of it. (p. 42)

Both biographers give, for the first time, fully documented accounts of Sartre's complicated life, based not only on the abundant written evidence but also on interviews with a great many of the surviving contemporaries. Cohen-Solal's book, in the original French version, appeared first.... She is the more enjoyable to read, because of her lively, rhetorical style, whereas he remains rather plodding. Both avoid the opposite pitfalls of hagiography and systematic detraction. However, one thing missing in both books is some overall, controlling judgment, not so much in connection with a detailed appraisal of Sartre's work—neither, after all, claims to be writing a "critical biography"—as with the moral tone of his life and mind.

At the height of his fame, it was not unusual to see him as the great modern embodiment of the humanistic tradition of the Enlightenment, the new Voltaire, a liberal philosopher who had stepped down from his ivory tower to do his best, clumsily perhaps but with good will, for the rest of mankind. I myself inclined to this view, and I remember being deeply shocked when another very eminent French writer, with whom I once attempted to discuss Sartre, cut me short with the vicious thrust: *"Ne me parlez pas de ce crapaud, qui est en même temps une crapule"* ("Don't speak to me about that toad, who is also a swine".) At the time, I attributed the outburst to pure jealousy, but I later came to see that there might be a germ of truth in the terrible alliterative formula. In the final analysis, we have to decide whether Sartre's intellectual contradictions, and inconsistencies and indelicacies of behavior, were the inevitable accidents of a great brain struggling valiantly with the complexities of the world, or whether the arose, at least in part, from doubtful philosophical principles and questionable emotional attitudes.

The two biographers do not hesitate to describe Sartre's peculiarities but, having done so, they tend to stand back and accept them as part of the necessary pattern, almost as if Sartre's tremendous lifetime fame somehow smoothed away the necessity for judgment. Cohen-Solal, for instance, demonstrates that the highly colored account of his childhood that Sartre gives in *Les mots* seems often to be at odds with the ascertainable facts, which would explain why his mother, on reading the book, exclaimed in surprise: *"Poulou n'a rien compris à son enfance!"* ("Poulou hasn't understood a thing about his childhood!") His grandfather had not been such a dislikable person, and had in fact helped him a lot; his stepfather was not such an ogre, etc. Also, despite his declared opposition to Freud, Sartre seems to have suddenly decided, without warning, to refashion his childhood as an ultra-Freudian Oedipal fable.

Cohen-Solal calls the book *"une autoanalyse, agencée par un orfèvre qui aurait truqué ses outils, ... un règlement de comptes, ... une ode á sa mère, ... une belle oeuvre d'art"* ("a self-analysis contrived by a practitioner who seems to have falsified his instruments, ... a settling of accounts, ... an ode to his mother, ... a beautiful work of art"). It is certainly one of his most brilliant pieces of writing after *La nausée,* but it breathes a curious heartlessness about people—even, I should say, about his mother, whose remarriage is seen entirely from her son's point of view—as if it were a virtuoso exercise in narcissism, prompted by a fierce self-love/self-hatred, stronger than his interest in any other person. Written some twenty years on, it marks no advance over the limited Existentialist psychology of *L'etre et le néant,* from which any disinterested notion of love of the Other, or forgiveness of the Other, is missing. Cohen-Solal, after stressing how misleading the book is as a guide to anything that might be called "the truth," simply passes on, without drawing any conclusion about Sartre's character.

Both Cohen-Solal and Hayman point out that Sartre, sooner rather than later, broke with all his male friends of comparable intellectual standing—Raymond Aron, Maurice Merleau-Ponty, René Etiemble, Camus, etc.—and lived in a circle of younger male admirers, some of them his former pupils. One wonders what would have happened to his relationship with his best friend, Paul Nizan, had the latter not been killed in the first months of the war. The quarrels all related to differences of opinion, and they show that Sartre was temperamentally incapable of tolerating anyone who disagreed with his dogmatism of the moment, and moreover never apologized, if he later changed his position on the issue that had been the overt cause of the break.

The most striking case was the quarrel with Camus over the review of *L'homme révolté* in *Les temps modernes.* Sartre, who was in a pro-Soviet phase at the time, thought that Camus's theoretical refutation of Marxist ideological certainty was tactically injudicious, because it might indirectly serve the American cause. Instead of doing Camus the honor of criticizing the book personally, he delegated the task to his then sidekick, Francis Jeanson, who produced a rather supercilious article, which Camus resented. There was a public exchange of letters, indignant on Camus's side and unpleasantly consescending on Sartre's, and the two never met again. As far as I can see, Sartre was entirely in the wrong. Whatever the incidental weaknesses of *L'homme révolté,* Camus's basic position on the issue of Marxist ideology was sound, and Sartre had behaved indelicately (just as he had, some years before, on a more trivial level, when Camus, as editor of the left-wing paper *Combat,* had financed him on a reporting trip to America and he had sent all the more interesting pieces to the right-wing daily *Le Figaro*).

Since the quarrel occurred at the peak of Sartre's Parisian reign, most of the intelligentsia slavishly followed his lead, with the result that, even now, Camus's reputation has not fully recovered from the blow. (pp. 42-3)

On the Beauvoir issue, as well, the two biographers are quite frank, but again, perhaps, without drawing all the threads together. Their accounts show that Sartre was the center of Beauvoir's existence, despite the hint of a lesbian element in her makeup. Her books probably represent the most extensive tribute ever paid to a male by a female. Even her description of his decline and death, which some people have interpreted as an act of revenge, can be taken as a last, tender homage to the only man she could set up as the absolute finality, or *terminus ad quem,* that she needed. Had he ever seriously proposed marriage to her—as he did to various other women, but only halfheartedly and for tactical reasons—it seems obvious that she would have accepted him. The other men in her life, including Nelson Algren, were clearly stopgaps, resorted to because, after the first three or four years, Sartre no longer had any vital need of her, except intermittently as a convenient sounding board for his endless monologue.

It was he who, from the beginning, imposed the conditions of their relationship on her. (pp. 43-4)

Beauvoir, the professed feminist, was, in one sense, the consenting victim of Sartre. He went after any woman who took his fancy, whether attached or unattached, and, operating on the . . . convenient principle of "transparency," would give Beauvoir a detailed account of his exploits, if he felt like it. Somewhere in his letters, after recounting a rather sordid episode, he admits *"Je suis un salaud"* ("I am a shit"), but she seems never to have taken him up on this point. At a relatively early stage, she tacitly accepted the role of senior, sexually retired, pseudowife on the fringe of his fluctuating seraglio. Cohen-Solal refers to Sartre's *"harem ouvert et sans limites"* (his "open and limitless harem"). . . . In the end, he adopted the last in line of his mistresses as his legal daughter. . . . There appears to be no evidence that he discussed this step in advance with Beauvoir; it led to friction between the two women, at the same time as Beauvoir, with what seems like pathetic imitativeness, legally adopted her younger companion, Sylvie. Nor is there any indication that, in earlier years, Beauvoir ever found it morally dubious, from the feminist point of view, that four or five mistresses at a time should accept monthly subsidies from Sartre, and live in effect as kept women serving a single male ego. One cannot avoid the surprising thought that Sartre had exactly the same sexual mores as Louis XIV. Each was cock of his particular walk, although—fortunately or unfortunately—the philosopher was not philoprogenitive like the Sun King.

Yet, paradoxically, Sartre was also at the source of Beauvoir's theoretical feminism. The famous opening sentence of *Le deuxième sexe: "On ne naît pas femme, on le devient"* ("One is not born a woman, one becomes a woman") is, rhetorically, an obvious echo of the still more famous opening sentence of Rousseau's *Contrat Social: "L'homme est né libre, et il est partout dans les fers"* ("Man is born free, and he is everywhere in chains"), but it draws essentially on Sartre's belief in the abstract nature of the freedom of the consciousness, or Being-for-Itself, which he arbitrarily assumes to be independent of its physiological siting in the body. His "For-Itself," in fact, is almost as metaphysical an entity as the Christian "soul." . . .

The issue of the freedom of the For-Itself lies at the heart of the immense tangle of Sartrian abstract thought. (p. 44)

I would say that Sartre is an old-fashioned, pre-Enlightenment metaphysician in that, despite his learning and the limits he eventually sets on freedom, he behaves primarily as if he were "pure" spirit, thinking in "pure" language, and divinely master of his thought. He doesn't start concretely from the post-Enlightenment hypothesis that man is an evolved animal, engaged in the ongoing, paradoxical task of trying to understand the whole of which he is only a part, and who is doing so, moreover, by means of language, a historical folk product, the genesis and immediate functioning of which have still not yet been elucidated. Similarly, although he makes much play with the idea of man being "in situation," he constantly seems to forget, at least on the theoretical level, that the "situation" of each individual includes not only his family and his social class, but also the initial, "absurd" datum of his particular genetic makeup, which conditions his reactions to his circumstances. Genes are a primary destiny; freedom, insofar as it can be said to exist, is a variable epiphenomenon of our individual animal nature. The point is, perhaps, easily overlooked by a childless philosopher, without brothers or sisters, who may never have had occasion to notice how strongly marked individual infant temperaments can be, even from the day of birth.

Happily, these strictures do not apply to *La nausée.* In that book, through his narrator, Roquentin, who presumably represents his own temperament, Sartre gives a wonderful description of the awakening of a consciousness to the mystery of life, as if "contingency sickness" were a necessary phase of intellectual puberty, which has to be gone through, even perhaps as late as in adulthood. Roquentin finds his consciousness in a particular body, with which it feels only intermittent solidarity; he is surrounded by the given, incomprehensible rituals of society, is using words that seem to bounce back from the objects to which he applies them, and is obsessed by the flow of time, which can neither be stopped nor recalled. His discussion of the task he is engaged upon—the biography of the eighteenth-century figure, M. de Rollebon—is a perfect critique of the limits of historical writing. His description of the Autodidact, who is reading all the books in the public library in alphabetical order, gently satirizes the human ambition for total knowledge. His delight in the jazz song, "Some of These Days," demonstrates the relief, at once true and illusory, provided by art, and so on. All this represents a subtle development of the more primitive awareness of the Absurd present in the Enlightenment tradition, and would surely have been applauded by Voltaire and Diderot.

For some reason, Sartre's wartime experience caused him to switch from the intellectual delicacy of *La nausée* to the cruder, though always infinitely ingenious, mode of his later thought, connected with the belief in commitment. He himself says, in *Les cahiers de la drôle de guerre,* that his reading of Heidegger, just before and during the war, was instrumental in making him realize his "historicity." . . . At this point, he had still not decided on action and, in any case, it seems odd that a man of thirty-five, who had written so perceptively about history, should have needed both a war and Heidegger to make him see himself in a historical perspective. Besides, there had already been the Spanish Civil War, which had not prompted him to action, although he knew all about the behavior of Malraux and others. If he felt guilty about his parasitical status as an uncommitted intellectual, why did the crisis not occur then? It may be an unworthy thought, but I wonder if his later experience of the prison camp, where he discovered that he could have the same charismatic effect on adults as he had had on schoolboys, did not give him a taste for action—or the rhetorical semblance of action—as an ego-boosting complement to writing. But it still remains puzzling that his "conversion" should have made him think below his previous standard. (pp. 44-5)

Perhaps it was because Sartre had not yet elaborated the abstract system of *L'etre et le néant* that *La nausée* remains, for the most part, so beautifully and concretely phenomenological. The brilliantly satirical presentation of bourgeois "bad faith" in that book is appropriate as the immediate reaction of Roquentin's temporarily alienated consciousness to a social setting in which he is a mere spectator (just as the trial scene in *L'etranger* is a delicate rendering of Meursault's subjective feeling of puzzled half-innocence, although inaccurate and unfair as a description of the general functioning of the law). But Sartre, the would-be political participant, has two major handicaps which occasionally fuse into one.

In the first place, the psychology of human relationships in *L'etre et le néant,* whatever its dazzling ramifications, boils down in the end to a struggle for dominance between conflicting *Pour-Soi* or For-Themselves; hence the slogan in *Huis clos: L'enfer c'est les autres,* which is acceptable as an amusing squib, but misses out the obvious fact that, while other people may be Hell, they are also the only Heaven we know. The battle of the For-Themselves is an undeniable part of reality, and can be translated into other vocabularies—original sin, the *amour-propre* that La Rochefoucauld presented as the mainspring of human action, the selfish gene, etc.—but it cannot, by itself, be a basis for positive democratic activity, which also supposes human solidarity, unselfishness, tolerance, and love, none of which are dealt with adequately by Sartre. While claiming to be democratic, he is saddled with a one-sided negativity which makes democracy impossible. . . .

In the second place, Sartre's political commitment began as opposition to the German occupier, in a black-and-white situation. From the start, incidentally, he showed no aptitude for, or patience with, the practical details of action; Cohen-Solal assembles considerable evidence to this effect. After the war, and during his subsequent career, he kept looking for black-and-white patterns on which to exercise his rhetorical verve, and he could only do this by damning villains and defending victims. The French bourgeoisie was solidified into a permanent villain, essence of villain, one might say, although human essences were supposed not to exist; capitalism was another villain; the Communists were now villains, now victims, according to his mood. . . .

The commitment, which helped so much to make Sartre world-famous can, with hindsight, be looked upon as a resounding and tragic failure. We can either say that he squandered his talents through going in a dramatically wrong direction, or that his failure at least served the cause of literature by demonstrating, with extravagant excess, that literature and politics are fundamentally different activities, whatever links there may be between them. He founded *Les temps modernes* as the engine of war of committed literature, but fell out with all the important original contributors, and the review itself never equaled the achievement of its predecessor, *La Nouvelle Revue française.* The theoretical contradictions in his lively polemical manifesto, *Qu'est-ce que la littérature?* soon became glaringly obvious, as did the discrepancy between his theories and his own literary practice. His novel sequence, *Les chemins de la liberté* did not show the roads to freedom promised in the title, and was left unfinished. No general movement of committed literature came into being. His attempt to launch a political party quickly collapsed. For years, his off-and-on relationship with the Communist party and Soviet Russia was supported by arguments of a byzantine casuistry, if not dishonesty. In the end, he abandoned the Communists to throw in his lot with neo-Maoist groups, whose anarchistic, and sometimes terrorist, activities seemed to him to have a populist quality missing from bureaucratized political parties. He had gone full circle, as it were, from the passive anarchism of his early, precommitment phase to the febrile anarchism of his old age, when he tried to get himself arrested for selling banned newspapers in the streets. (p. 45)

[It] is a fact that Sartre's enormous intelligence sometimes seems to turn itself inside out to become a kind of monumental obtuseness. His exceptional cerebral power is characterized by a sort of inflation, which leads him to erect the most complex verbal structures by means of scholastic variations on relatively simple, and patently limited or dubious, premises. At times, one feels that the whole house of cards is going to collapse into nonsense and, in fact, I think it often does; then again, it can happen that he makes one of his more telling points when he is way out on some verbal limb, like an acrobat saving himself *in extremis.* No writer is more bewilderingly uneven. The reader, about to lose heart after toiling through a desert of doubtful, though fiercely affirmative, jargon, may suddenly find himself in an oasis of delightful perceptiveness, as if a different and altogether more sensitive part of Sartre's mind had suddenly come into play. The superior passage is often an improvisation on some incidental theme, only slightly connected with the main argument. Sartre himself referred to such digressions as *des hernies,* hernias or bulges that he left as they were, because he could neither bring himself to sacrifice them nor incorporate them properly into the text. In some future anthology of his work, they may figure as proofs of the sporadic survival of his talent.

The inflationary style is especially noticeable in his extraordinary biographical-critical studies of Baudelaire, Flaubert, and Genet, in which he displays both a cavalier attitude toward the ordinary rules of evidence and an almost complete insensitivity to the initial physiological identities of the individuals concerned. He presents each as the embodiment of an abstract existential choice, which he imposes on them retrospectively, without paying very scrupulous attention to the recognized facts of their lives, and sometimes by inventing facts or factoids to support his thesis, as he openly admits in the case of Flaubert.

The genre of the *biographie romancée* was given its name in the prewar years by a typically bourgeois man of letters, André Maurois, and one can imagine how scathingly Sartre would have dealt with it in his early phase. Roquentin, in *La nausée,* gives up writing the life of M. de Rollebon because he comes to realize that, however closely he may study the data, he still has to fall back on his imagination to fill the gaps, and this he feels to be a form of dishonesty. He is making the Absurdist discovery that we have no way of knowing the past in any absolute manner. This is just one aspect of the broader Absurdist perception that all knowledge is uncertain. We live in a mystery, in which we make little provisional clearings of human understanding. Such is the inevitable ground bass of all intellectual activity, and it can be experienced as an anguish, or an anguished excitement, as it is, indeed, throughout *La nausée.* But after his "conversion," Sartre, instead of accepting the provisional and relative nature of knowledge as a fact of life with which one has to come to terms, seems to have jumped wantonly to the conclusion that anything goes. Perhaps he was curing his anguish by making subjective dogmatism an act of faith. At any rate, he executes a complete *volte-face*; after showing the limits of knowledge in *La nausée,* he undertook his study of Flaubert with the declared intention of achieving total knowledge, as if the human brain could digest the universe. (pp. 45-6)

[These] so-called biographical studies are, to a large extent, highly idiosyncratic hymns of hate: against the bourgeoisie, against his subjects insofar as he finds them guilty of "bad faith," and against the bourgeois he was trying to exorcise from within himself. . . .

[With] Sartre, biography tends to become a form of displaced autobiography. On the one hand, he is fiercely, although often intelligently, unfair to Baudelaire and Flaubert, because he is hating himself, and all bourgeois, in them. On the other hand, he builds up Genet into a great Angel of Darkness, because Genet's works, which glorify bastardy, sexual inversion, theft, treachery, and murder, can be read, without excessive distortion, as a complete, heroic reversal of all "normal" values, the apotheosis of alienation, on a par with the black universe of the Marquis de Sade. As someone once said, if Genet had not existed, Sartre would have had to invent him to give full rein to his negative impulses.

It is understandable and, in a sense, admirable, that Genet, given his "situation," should have made the existential choice to turn negativity into his positive value. It is less obvious why Sartre, a privileged intellectual, should have believed so strongly in the empty spontaneity of the For-Itself as the necessary negating force of the whole status quo, in the dim, long-term expectation of the socialist millennium, when the need for negation will miraculously disappear, and all will be well. . . .

[Sartre acts with] the impatience of a spoiled, hyperintelligent little boy, who would like to smash the world at once, as if it were an irritating, incomprehensible toy—which is what it may seem to all of us, of course, in certain moods—rather than patiently share the handling of its incomprehensibility with others. Sartre is being unfaithful to his initial awareness of the Absurd by forgetting that, if Absurdism is true, it is valid for everyone, even for the benighted bourgeois, who can never be an essence but is, at worst, an uncertain, provisional, always partly modifiable, crystallization of "bad faith." As Camus, unlike Sartre, came to realize, the only moderately hopeful basis for democracy in the godless world is the principle that we are all brothers and sisters in the Absurd, although a lot of people may not yet have grasped this, and those who have may have difficulty in constantly bearing it in mind.

At other times, I suspect that Sartre never got rid of the idea of God, but remained an atheist, hating father figures of all kinds (with the major exception of Stalin as the mediator of the millennium), and hating the bourgeoisie as an authoritarian father class, a sort of front for the unforgivable God responsible for creation. I used to suppose that he understood the expression "God is dead," as the metaphor it undoubtedly is (a God who never existed cannot have died; only the illusory idea that there is a God can have died), and that Orestes defying Jupiter in *Les mouches*, Goetz parleying with God in *Le diable et le bon Dieu*, and Frantz declaiming to the void in *Les séquestrés d'Altona* were just rather crude theatrical devices, resorted to, with tongue in cheek, because of Sartre's avowed weakness for melodramatic effects. Now, I am not so sure.

Just as he behaves as if God, although dead, kept popping up again in some ghostlike form and had to be constantly challenged and reargued out of existence, so he produces endless variations on the formula "man is the being who projects being God." This again, for humanists, can be no more than an ironical figure of speech; "God" is only a shorthand term for the limits of man's understanding, a hypostatization of the central mystery of the Absurd; how can man—even a man as clever as Sartre—project to be the incomprehensible which baffles him? Yet Sartre often gives the impression that he sees his For-Itself engaged in a sort of duel with the For-Itself of God. If this is actually the case, he is falling prey to the megalomaniacal delusion that he, a man, can somehow, if he tries hard enough, understand the whole of which he is a part, and ensnare it in a web of words. . . .

I am reminded of a famous early article, in which Sartre attacked the Catholic novelist, François Mauriac, and which ended with the memorable sentence: *"Dieu n'est pas un artiste; M. François Mauriac non plus"* ("God is not an artist; nor is M. François Mauriac"). We could perhaps echo it here, in the form: "God is dead; He cannot rise again as M. Jean-Paul Sartre." (p. 46)

John Weightman, "Summing Up Sartre," in The New York Review of Books, *Vol. XXXIV, No. 13, August 13, 1987, pp. 42-6.*

JOHN STURROCK

What dream-life had Jean-Paul Sartre? None that he would want to admit to, for this unbudgeable Cartesian had faith in the operations of the conscious mind alone, and took an unfashionably low view of the unconscious. . . .

But at least once in his life, Annie Cohen-Solal lets it be known [in *Sartre: A Life*], the steely rationalist flirted with depth psychology. Sartre then made morning-after notes on his dreams, thinking to interpret this involuntary pillow-theatre later in the furtherance of his furious intellectual drive towards a total understanding, in this instance of himself. This brief attack of introspection had come upon him at the time he was writing his one slim volume of autobiography, *The Words*, when he felt somewhat short of an inner life.

Ms Cohen-Solal does well to bring in his few recorded dreams, for they complicate her story. She also gives us the diagnosis of a psychoanalyst, once close to Sartre, who declares that they are 'dreams from on high' ('from on top' would have been my translation). Sartre asleep, it turns out, was a very much less egalitarian fellow than Sartre awake. In his dreams he is still the pushy young claimant to glory, the echo of the devastatingly sharp student at the Ecole Normale Supérieure, who had declared 'I want to be the man who knows most about everything.' Ms Cohen-Solal is quite ready to gush over Sartre but she also finds herself having to use words like 'megalomania'; she is admiring but not blindly so.

Sartre: A Life is the second biography of him that we have had in quick succession. Grippingly inquisitive, it stands a lot closer to its subject than did Ronald Hayman's [*Sartre: A Life*] of a year ago. Ms Cohen-Solal has got around, she has talked to a great many people, and because they are far from agreed on what kind of person Sartre was or just what he counted for in France, one gets a vital and muddling picture of him.

The book begins well, by going into the Sartre family background in the Dordogne, which never got a look-in in *The Words*; and it finishes well, with an even-handed account of the pathetic last years of the philosopher's life, once he had lost his sight and with it all sense of his intellectual mission, and was being alternately tended and manipulated by those around him. Ms Cohen-Solal follows him into, and all too often out again from, his many emotional and intellectual associations with others. Some people put up with Sartre, rather more could not; she brings out well enough how his ideas and his passions were ruthlessly fused, and how extremism in his political life derived from the tensions of his merely social one.

This is not a philosophical biography: it does not pursue Sartre's ideas at all deep or far. But it places him meticulously. Sartre the intense but anarchic Paris student is here; Sartre the friendly, bohemian lycée teacher in Le Havre, outraging the parents on speech-day; Sartre the sensual, cafæe-dwelling chieftain of his little Paris clan; Sartre the prime Existentialist, unsuitably jolly prophet of a pessimistic doctrine; and Sartre the vociferous political pundit, travelling the world to give excitable lectures in favour of revolution and of a proletarian entirely of his own imagining. Has there ever been so fluent or venerated a fount of political unwisdom?

Ms Cohen-Solal does not try to reach inside Sartre; she has written a public life of a remarkably public man, who thought the world could be saved if every human being in it became 'transparent' to every other. The case-studies of Sartre are yet to come, but come they must, for this same exponent of an unnerving candour was also the man who after 40 years still addressed Simone de Beauvoir formally as *'vous.'*

The book is badly over-written in places but under-translated throughout: this is a primitive (and anonymous; why?) English translation infuriatingly faithful to the 'historic present' tense in which Ms Cohen-Solal has told much of her story—French readers are used to this, English ones can soon grow to hate it.

> *John Sturrock, "Sartre in Egoland," in* The Observer, *October 25, 1987, p. 27.*

A. J. AYER

[*Ayer is a renowned English philosopher. His many publications include* Language, Truth, and Logic *(1936), which is considered a seminal work in the field of logical positivist philosophy. In the following excerpt, Ayer maintains that Sartre's reputation incorrectly rests on his philosophy, which Ayers considers derivative; instead, Ayer notes that Sartre should be recognized for the brilliance of his dramas, novels, and journalism. Ayer finds Cohen-Solal's biography detailed, but lacking critical assessment.*]

If Jean-Paul Sartre, who lived from 1905 to 1980, is not the foremost French writer of this century, he is the most versatile and the most prolific. For quite a long period he was also the most celebrated. . . .

By most people Sartre is thought of primarily as a philosopher, but I believe that this does him an injustice. The three philosophical books that he published in the 1930s, two on the imagination and one on the emotions, are all slight and derivative from Husserl. The posthumous *Cahiers pour une morale* adds nothing new to ethical theory. *Critique de la raison dialectique,* which was published in 1960, presents an idiosyncratic and obscure version of Marxism. It is on the gigantic *L'etre et le néant,* appearing in 1943, that Sartre's philosophical reputation chiefly rests. An indictment of this book is that it is almost wholly derivative from Heidegger's *Sein und Zeit;* a point in its favour that Heidegger repudiated it.

The social significance of *L'etre et le néant* was that it made Existentialism fashinable in France. I have to confess that it has never been entirely clear to me what Existentialism amounted to. I have tried to show elsewhere that its central doctrine that existence is prior to essence is either trivial or false. For Sartre and his followers its main importance lay in its exaltation of individual liberty and its insistence on social and political commitment.

Sartre's own political commitment was intense but ineffective. It started late. Having been a brilliant student, he vegetated in the 1930s as a teacher of philosophy at a lycée in Le Havre

until the publication of *La nausée,* his first and best novel, in 1938, and *Le mur,* his collection of short stories, in 1939, brought him sudden fame. Having escaped from a prisoner-of-war camp in 1941 he started a writers' resistance movement which soon petered out.

The early numbers of *Les temps modernes* espoused the lost cause of a European third force. He quarrelled with Camus and with his closest collaborator, Maurice Merleau-Ponty, over his favouritism of Russia, remaining a fellow-traveller even after the revelation of Stalin's crimes. His conversion to Maoism after 1968 brought him few followers. What was admirable in this aspect of his life is his energy, his doggedness and his courage.

The best of Sartre's post-war writing, apart from *Les mots* consists, in my view, in his plays, notably *Huis-Clos,* commonly mistranslated into English as *No Exit, Les mains sales* and *Les séquestrés d'Altona.* His journalism was often brilliant but, almost inevitably, ephemeral.

Annie Cohen-Solal's biography [*Sartre: A Life*] first appeared in 1985. It has now been rather badly translated into American by Anna Cancogni. Its virtues are that it gives a very detailed account of Sartre's life. Its main defect is the almost total absence of any critical assessment of Sartre's work.

> *A. J. Ayer, "A Grievance with the Guru," in* The Sunday Times, *London, October 25, 1987, p. 66.*

CARLIN ROMANO

[*In the following excerpt, Romano praises Cohen-Solal for shedding light on the question of why Sartre—with all his intellectual inconsistencies and personal flaws—managed to achieve such influence and renown.*]

What becomes of the broken-Sartred? Seven years after the death of the man who gave *nausea* and *nothingness* a good name, French intellectuals still aren't sure. They live with Sartre's legacy daily. They know he accomplished modern philosophy's greatest PR triumph by fastening a beret to existentialism—a notion previously owned and operated by Kierkegaard and Heidegger—and making it fit. They recognize that when they slip off with nonsignificant others for some *liaisons dangereuses,* the ghosts of Jean-Paul and Simone rebuke them, imploring them to confess, and maybe even brag a bit. Every fresh excavation of recent French history—collaboration, the Resistance, the Algerian war, May 1968—evokes memories of the novelist, playwright, and philosopher who typed his way right up to center stage. Every issue of the Parisian newspaper *Libération,* the leftist daily cofounded by Sartre (now the safe second read of Socialist government bureaucrats), reminds them of his activism. (p. 14)

[The] barrage of recent secondary works on Sartre signals more than the usual desire of reverential professors to fatten the card catalogue of a deceased eminence—they indicate a recognition that Sartre not only belongs to history, but that a certain kind of intellectual life, currently in limbo, belongs to Sartre and can only be reassessed in his company.

The first two major Sartre biographies, Annie Cohen-Solal's hard-digging *Sartre: A Life* and Ronald Hayman's bookish yet more interpretive [*Sartre: A Life*], deliver day-to-day details that partly answer Sartre's 1970s challenge to do to him what he did to Flaubert in his last great biographical project, *The Family Idiot*—absorb and comprehend the writer whole. . . .

These books invite us to ponder how Sartre achieved a Voltairean prominence and influence unmatched by his successors.

Was it the technical superiority of his philosophical work? The brilliance of his literary style? The impact of his personality and ambition? Or does the credit go as much to the play as to the player—a philosophical and social scene waiting for him to happen?

For those who retain some romanticism about intellectual history, the happiest explanation of Sartre's celebrity would be the merit of his philosophical work. Yet, from the beginning, Sartre's existentialism skirted classic philosophical problems, even if it served as a spirited rallying cry. At the start of his first novel, *Nausea* (1938), in which Sartre started to flesh the system out, Roquentin, the independent scholar free of ordinary obligations—job, family, spouse—still doesn't feel free. He senses the viscous, oozing world of material objects imposing itself on him and oppressing him. After an epiphany in the park helps him to appreciate the world's contingency, he realizes the "horrible ecstasy" of his freedom—he is responsible for his own life.

Roquentin's earlier self-deception in regard to his freedom is what Sartre calls "bad faith." But Roquentin's enlightenment does not give him the freedom to make things happen as he wishes—he can't, for instance, regain his former mistress, who has moved to Paris. That was the first hint of the unsatisfactory payoff of Sartre's freedom that continued to plague his philosophy: existential freedom may be freedom *from* a completely predetermined life, but it is not freedom *to* accomplish any particular aim. Roquentin commits himself to writing a novel, which is the young Sartre's end-run around the problem—literature as salvation.

Being and Nothingness (1943) and the famous lecture *Existentialism Is a Humanism* (1946) further complicated the marketability of existential freedom. Sartre asserted that "existence comes before essence," that man does not possess a nature but is simply the sum of his actions—what "he makes of himself." He rejected Freud's unconscious, charging that it encouraged bad faith by inviting people to evade responsibility for their actions. Classically if not consistently Cartesian in his concerns, Sartre declared that two kinds of things exist—consciousness, which is identical with human reality and transparent to itself, and objects of consciousness. The first constitutes being for itself (*l'être-pour-soi*), the second being in itself (*l'être-en-soi*). Between them is nothingness.

Here things got cryptic—that is, the ontology got dark—as Sartre declared in a notable phrase that "Nothingness lies coiled in the heart of being, like a worm." . . . It's fair to say that if Sartre's fame had depended on the clarity of his ontology, he'd now be as celebrated as Alexius Meinong.

Certain aspects of *Being and Nothingness,* however, proved clear enough to raise questions. Sartre considered Freud's neurotics to be conscious deceivers, indulging their bad faith. Like psychoanalysis, however, Sartre's existentialism enjoyed a built-in protection against falsification. Whereas Freud could dismiss objections as resistance, Sartre could dismiss them as bad faith. So philosophers fond of theories that permit falsification—and they flourished in Sartre's heyday—were dubious. Moreover, Sartre set out an elaborate scheme of how relations work between a consciousness and an "Other" (anyone else) that raised further problems.

In Sartre's view, relations necessarily involve conflict and an inability to respect the freedom of the Other. Sartre analyzed, among many relations, shame, desire, indifference, hatred, sadism, masochism, and love. Yet he described them as if they were deterministically locked into place, as when he insisted that real love could never exist because each of us tries to co-opt our loved one. The biographical data we now have on Sartre suggest that he was deeply *engagé* at this point in some fairly obvious extrapolation from personal experience. But even in the 1940s, the inconsistency of the "man is free" side of his philosophy was obvious. If we're all free, why can't we handle our relationships better than Sartre says we can?

The more closely one scrutinized *Being and Nothingness,* the harder it became to credit Sartre with the sedulous philosopher's commitment to impose coherence on his system, or restraint on his exaggerations. (pp. 14-15)

[Sartre] owed his readers an "Ethics" after *Being and Nothingness,* but in a pattern typical of his career, he never redeemed the promise at that book's end to provide one. Nor did he confront another question: Why, if we constitute our worlds, can't we constitute them any way we like? Sartre acknowledged what he called a "coefficient of adversity" (what a layman might call the world's brute facts) as a constraint on how we shape "our" world, but he paid little attention to it and contradicted himself often on the point, even writing that "freedom and creation" were the same.

The sense not just of Sartre's inconsistency, but of his blithe inconsistency, grows when one examines the fiction of the 1940s and the plays such as *The Flies* (1943) and *No Exit* (1944). The *Roads to Freedom* trilogy that Sartre published from 1945 to 1949 (*The Age of Reason, The Reprieve, Troubled Sleep*), which fictionalized parts of his life with Simone de Beauvoir and other literati, seems to mock the intense interest in freedom of its young philosophy teacher, Mathieu, who becomes a soldier. His desperate attempts to get his mistress an abortion, and his stabbing himself in the hand, indicate selfishness and mania rather than freedom. The novels' chief message seems to be that obsession with freedom can itself be a kind of bad faith. *No Exit* also implies its futility.

As Sartre moved into his Marxist stage in the 1950s and '60s, his intellectual life became a never-ending scissors-and-paste job, a mission to preserve the successful elements of Sartre Incorporated's best-selling product—existentialism—while trumpeting Marxism as "the inescapable philosophy of our time." Existentialist commitment—which originally required only a presumptively literary commitment to one's own freely created values—became commitment in words and deeds to the Left. In the *Critique of Dialectical Reason* (1960), Sartre sought to marry existentialism and Marxism after preparing each for the conversion, retooling them like a Reform rabbi finding some "give" in the Torah.

Here the deterioration of Sartre's prose reached new lows—the man who gave us "Hell is other people" now offered the "Hell of the practico-inert." He argued for a Marxism stripped of scientific determinism, a system that took economic causes seriously but left individuals the makers of their own history. Conflict between people resulted from scarcity of resources, not the ontological difficulty of one "Other" casting out another "Other." (pp. 15-16)

By this time, however, Sartre's response to internal contradictions in his work revealed a gradually developed impulse, in the face of criticism, toward unbridled dogmatism and egotism.

One sharp illustration involved Lévi-Strauss's attack, in the last chapter of *The Savage Mind* (1962), on Sartre's *Critique.* Sartre posited a Marxist view of history full of World Views that dominated various periods. With customary modesty, he promised that the second volume would "attempt to establish that there is *one* history of man with *one truth* and *one intelligibility.*" The challenge from Lévi-Strauss turned on complicated issues involving the intellectual sophistication of primitive societies; Sartre maintained the inferiority of the mental lives of primitives, and Lévi-Strauss asserted that Sartre, the self-styled champion of the Third World, betrayed deep-seated ethnocentrism. The philosophical issues at stake were profound and called for serious debate. Sartre fell back on denouncing Lévi-Strauss for the same illness Lukács had diagnosed in existentialism—last gaspism of the embattled bourgeoisie. . . .

Sartre's philosophical writing ultimately leaves the impression that he was more obstinate than philosophical, a magisterial sloganizer and mass marketer of philosophical observations rather than a careful or responsible arguer of them. His corpus perfectly exemplifies the type of French philosophy that Jacques Bouveresse accuses of trying "to compensate for the absence of properly philosophical argumentation by means of literary effects and for the absence of properly literary qualities by means of philosophical pretensions." . . .

Only this year's biographies finally shed light on Sartre's fatal attraction—why he rests predictably on E. D. Hirsch's table of cultural literacy when more original thinkers, such as Hans-Georg Gadamer or Chaim Perelman, remain household names only in their own households. . . .

Cohen-Solal's prose (at least its English version) is more mannered, full of fragmentary, verbless sentences, lengthy quotes that ramble, and subjective asides on French institutions she knows firsthand. Nonetheless, her narrative comes closer to Sartre as human character than Hayman's. Whether the scene is a café, classroom, or prison camp, Cohen-Solal sits down beside Sartre or his intimates, takes out the tape recorder, and turns it on; Hayman gives the impression of observing matters from across the room. For all that, the portraits gibe so well that a consistent picture of Sartre's life emerges, strengthening the conviction that, in his case, character was philosophy as well as fate.

Born in Paris in 1905, Sartre lost his father 15 months later. He spent his first years in the care of a beautiful young mother who spoiled him silly, and a grandfather who filled the house with books and a stern pedagogic temper. When Jean-Paul was 12, his mother remarried, and the family moved to the provincial town of La Rochelle. Sartre made a case for the resentments bred by those circumstances in his own memoir, *The Words.* Both Hayman and Cohen-Solal agree that those years produced much of the narcissism and contentiousness that, by his teens, spawned such self-evaluations as "I've got a golden brain" and "I have never met any man who was my equal."

His college days at the Ecole Normale Supérieure, both biographers report, accentuated his reputation for brilliance and arrogance. Sartre boxed, acted, played practical jokes, performed on the piano, roamed cafés. When Simone de Beauvoir met him in the summer of 1929, he was 24, she 21. In the philosophy exams that year, he would come in first, de Beauvoir second. She began to feel that time without him was wasted: "He was the double in whom I found all my burning

aspirations brought to incandescence." "From now on," he said, "I am going to take you under my wing."

They made their famous pact, initially for two years, ultimately for over 50. Their love would be "necessary" and preeminent, but they would also be free to have "contingent" love affairs on the side. Though short, wall-eyed, and ugly, Sartre attracted women easily, pursued them eagerly, and excelled at seduction. It was not something he wanted to give up, and de Beauvoir never asked him to.

From the beginning, the biographies make clear, Sartre stalked not just achievement but vast fame. At 24, he told de Beauvoir he wanted to become both Stendhal and Spinoza. After graduation, as he taught philosophy at provincial high schools and served his military time, his arrogance remained unchecked: struck by the pomposity of Chateaubriand's tomb, he pissed on it. He could do imitations of Donald Duck, visit brothels, or talk about the links between the novel and philosophy, as the mood struck him.

Both narratives reach a crescendo as they enter the 1940s. One reads of *Nausea* being acclaimed, of Sartre's astounding productivity on several literary fronts, of his careful footwork during the Occupation, and his provocative attacks on established writers such as François Mauriac. The sense of being in the presence of a brilliant PR campaign—not just an intellectual career—takes hold. Here, the first issue of *Les temps modernes* hits the kiosks, there the Baudelaire biography is unpacked from the boxes. The author of *No Exit* could always spot another sidedoor into the world he sought to dominate.

Cohen-Solal is especially good on the breaking atmosphere of postwar existentialism and Sartre's pop stardom—the standing-room-only lectures, the fainting listeners, the angry establishment opponents, the *Time* cover, the publisher who claimed, like a French Col. Parker, "I made Sartre." By the mid-1940s, Sartre's literary armies had converged on the public, the media had pounced, and Sartre conquered Paris, then the world. He was dubbed "the pope of existentialism," and his maxims—life is meaningless, the bourgeois are *salauds* (swine), man is condemned to be free—were seen as marching orders for a generation. By the end of the decade, strangers recognized him on the street.

The downturn came in the 1950s, when Sartre's apotheosis of literature succumbed to an increasingly Marxist tilt. He lost interest in writing fiction and never wrote another novel. Instead, he rallied to socialist and communist causes. For a time, he became a near-complete apologist for Soviet communism, though the Hungarian and Czech invasions eventually pushed him into opposition. Torn between his own work and political action, he increasingly felt that action necessarily took precedence. . . .

All his adult life, Sartre depended on drugs—pep pills, belladenal, orthodine, corydrane—to work and sleep. During the writing of the *Critique,* he sometimes downed 20 corydrane pills at a time, at one point losing the skin on his tongue and going partially deaf. More and more, he wrote off the top of his head, expounding on books or films he had not read or seen, or turning out distorted biographies of other writers. . . .

A compulsive worker who averaged nearly 10 hours of writing per day for some 50 years, Sartre smoked two packs of Boyards daily and wore moccasins "to avoid wasting time on tying shoe laces." He was generous with money, carefree about possessions, careless about manuscripts. He hated to acknowledge any intellectual debt. According to Raymond Aron, he avoided intellectual confrontations or debates with those he considered his equals. He devoted drug-free time to fashioning his literary prose, but tended to dash off his philosophy while stoned.

In the 1960s, his fame grew even larger when he declined the Nobel Prize for Literature, saying a writer should not let himself become "an institution." His politics turned Maoist, and he ignored new philosophical currents in Paris, particularly structuralism, as his dismissal of Lévi-Strauss showed. By the 1970s, Sartre's health charts pointed only one way, and the last 10 years of his life, detailed by both biographers and by de Beauvoir in her memoir *Adieux,* was a stretched-out descent into blindness, bronchitis, incontinence, diabetes, exploitation, and further radicalism.

One of the few issues on which Hayman and Cohen-Solal clash sharply is the Sartre-de Beauvoir relationship. Hayman renders a harsh verdict. De Beauvoir created, he writes, a substitute religion "in which Sartre and socialism were the twin gods." (p. 16)

Cohen-Solal reacts differently: "For several generations, this couple would become a model to emulate, a dream of lasting complicity, an extraordinary success since, apparently, it managed to reconcile the irreconcilable: the two partners remained free, equal, and honest with each other. By accepting Sartre's contract and developing her own autonomy while respecting his, Simone de Beauvoir beat him at his own game."

The clash crystallizes the duck-rabbit choice that Sartre, the walking Gestalt, presents—high-minded *philosophe* or scurrilous *salaud*? Despite her preference for the former view, Cohen-Solal, like Hayman, undermines it through her reportage. Yet because she more or less whistles the philosophy instead of evaluating it—while, at the same time, Hayman limits himself to paraphrasing key points and displaying contradictions in Sartre's work—the biographies might be thought unlikely to exert a direct effect on Sartre's philosophical reputation.

Not so. Sartre's career (not to mention Wittgenstein's) should warn us against underestimating the role of personality in philosophical reputations. Indirectly, the revelations of Sartre's dubious handling of Beauvoir, and the testimony from intimates to how he shirked philosophical combat, confirm the judgment, impolitic during his lifetime but held by many academics, that he was a bit of a poseur where the hard stuff of philosophy was concerned. Similarly, the drug revelations should hurt the recruitment of true believers. Even graduate student exegetes, second to none in their masochism, may balk at unscrambling prose known to have been written under the influence of whole medicine chests.

Indeed, the overview of Sartre offered by both biographers helps explain why he struggled to hard to unite seemingly disparate philosophies in his later years. Sartre remained torn his whole life between hatred of the bourgeoisie and the bourgeois desire to win fame and keep it. The hatred provoked personal rebellion, which required a belief in individual freedom. It also, gradually, spawned a hatred of the capitalist assumptions that supported bourgeois institutions. One intense hatred led to many contradictory intellectual positions. It could be argued that he became intellectual bad faith incarnate, trying to have his free-wheeling existentialism and angry Marxism

both, impudently believing he could spin it all together in his head. . . . But both biographers capture Sartre's colossal pomposity and self-centered deceitfulness, even the intellectual foolishness at times so central to his character (as when he pronounced, on the eve of World War II, that "the war would be modern, with no real fighting in it, just as modern painting had no real subject matter").

Sartre's ambitions and hostilities, anchored to his stylistic panache and enormous capacity for work, in the long run explain his philosophical impact better than the sheer persuasiveness of his philosophy. But one mustn't overlook a factor in his fame to which Sartre himself would have been the first to call attention—its social conditions. He exploited a longstanding truth about public relations and philosophy—that one-track minds exert a disproportionate influence on the "Tradition." . . . Onesidedness goes hand-in-glove with fancy phrasemaking, since qualifying clauses tend to ruin slogans ("I Love New York, At Least Most of the Time"). It also assists teaching, which favors clear spokesmen for alternate positions. Sartre knew the historical script, and he knew how to coin a phrase.

The rigidity of French philosophical culture also provided a greenhouse for the rebellious Sartre's celebrated theses, which hardly arose in a vacuum. (pp. 16-17)

Those factors worked in Sartre's favor, but he also assaulted French culture with an ambition and personality that knew no bounds. . . .

Fortuitously, Sartre's steamrollering, syncretic personality became a kind of three-dimensional argument for his philosophy; its fundamental premise may have been a throwaway line in *The Devil and the Good Lord*: "only human beings really exist." His final obsession with Flaubert attempted to turn that insight into practice—better thinking through biography. Ultimately, though, his life rather than his work proved more successful in presenting his vision of a complete picture of Man, without the inconvenient parts trimmed away. Too many of his French successors chop up Man and put the body parts— the text, the sign, the power structure—under the microscope. Sartre's career demonstrated that the parts explain one another when they're not artificially divided. The egoism, the womanizing, the workload, the talent, the politics, the oratory, the novels, the plays, the philosophy, the café-crawling, the contradictions—they all smacked together like bumper cars.

In the late 1970s, Sartre remarked in an interview that he'd never really believed in existentialism, almost suggesting that it amounted to a kind of sophisticated ruse for attracting women. Even allowing for exaggeration, the comment astonished many longtime students. One senses, however, a core of truth. For at the end of the road mapped by Hayman and Cohen-Solal stands a handy if damning definition of existentialism—Sartre for Sartre's sake. Nonetheless, if today's French *philosophes* lack his impact on France and the world, it's because they toy with mere parts of the human puzzle, enabling the audience to feel safe in turning away. Sartre, by contrast, flung the whole thing before them in living color, and the world couldn't take its eyes off him. (p. 17)

Carlin Romano, "Sartre Imitates Life: The Philosopher as Media Hero," in VLS, *No. 60, November, 1987, pp. 14-17.*

Simone de Beauvoir: A Life . . . a Love Story

by Claude Francis and Fernande Gontier

(For Simone de Beauvoir, see also *CLC*, Vols. 1, 2, 4, 8, 14, 31, 44; *Contemporary Authors,* Vols. 9-12, rev. ed., Vol. 118 [obituary]; and *Dictionary of Literary Biography Yearbook: 1986.*)

An Excerpt from *Simone de Beauvoir: A Life . . . a Love Story*

Volume I of *The Second Sex* rolled off the Gallimard presses in June 1949, and nothing would ever be quite the same again. *Les Temps modernes* had carried the chapter "The Myth of Woman in Five Authors" in February followed by "Woman's Sexual Initiation" in May and "The Lesbian" in June. Cries of indignation rose in the press. Twenty-two thousand copies of Volume I were sold in one week. Volume II appeared in November and sold as many. Similarly, each issue of *Les Temps modernes* had been snatched from the newsstands. The scandal was at its height.

Few books have provoked such an avalanche of bad faith, hypocrisy, rudeness, and indecency. In *Le Figaro littéraire* François Mauriac wrote indignantly, "We have literally reached the limits of the abject. This is the ipecac they made us swallow as children to induce vomiting. Here perhaps is the moment of the final nausea: that which delivers." He appealed to the general public and began an investigation in the name of the readers. He railed against Emmanuel Mounier's collaborator, Domenach, who wrote in the left-wing Christian review *Esprit* that Madame de Beauvoir had given, with her "courageous articles in *Les Temps modernes,* a course in normal sexuality." Domenach had also suggested that such novelists as François Mauriac were furious because de Beauvoir demystified the subterranean reaches of sexuality from which those novelists drew their material.

De Beauvoir chose the provocative slogan "Woman, this unknown" for the eye-catching paper band wrapped around her book. Ever since the advent of men and writing implements there had hardly been a subject more famous, more cursed, more described, more sung, more analyzed, more glorified than woman. De Beauvoir was challenging every novelist, every playwright, every psychologist. Left and right attacked her with the same vehement indignation. Readers felt compelled in the name of truth, goodness, and beauty to send her lewd letters. . . .

Although it *was* placed in the Index, *The Second Sex* was not burned at the executioner's hand, nor was its author condemned to burn for sorcery. Yet an incredible

fanaticism was unleashed against de Beauvoir, and it has not entirely subsided to this day.

To reduce *The Second Sex,* as numerous critics have done, to a dictionary of feminine demands is to miss completely the point of a work based on a philosophical system that poses each individual as its subject. . . .

The originality of *The Second Sex,* like that of Descartes' *Discours de la méthode,* lies in its having proposed that received ideas be systematically questioned. The book's true impact would not be perceived in France until later, when the American feminist movement had attracted attention and brought forth a sudden awareness of feminist consciousness in France. The majority of feminist writers throughout the rest of the world took their inspiration from Simone de Beauvoir. *The Second Sex* was translated into English in 1953, and two million copies were sold in English-speaking countries. It remained on Japan's best-sellers list for a full year. It was translated into German, Arabic, Danish, Spanish, Hebrew, Hungarian, Italian, Dutch, Norwegian, Polish, Portuguese, Serbo-Croatian, Slovak, Swedish, Tamil, and Czech.

Simone de Beauvoir was the most widely read feminist author in the world. The work remains topical, and it has inspired an impressive number of scholarly papers and university theses. This book launched women's studies as a serious academic discipline. Whether a feminist movement is "Beauvoirian" or utterly different—that is, hostile—it can be related beyond any question to this ground-breaking essay.

De Beauvoir did not open the doors to freedom for women alone with her slogan, "One is not born a woman, one becomes one." In demonstrating the effect that culture can have on the human condition, she posed not only the problem of liberation for women but all the problems that are related to cultural oppression. She called into question laws, religions, customs, and traditions, and in her own way she demanded that society and all its structures be reevaluated.

MARIANNE VÉRON

Simone de Beauvoir—now, who could possibly pretend to live completely beyond the ripples of her influence, as if she had never existed? This pioneer in rebellion, fighter for equal rights, advocate of women's sexual freedom and financial autonomy, this theoretician of womanhood—where would we be without her? And if it is true that she was a product of changing times, of the need for women to go out to work while men were getting themselves killed in World War I, it is also true that she was a catalyst, helping to make those changes possible. Simone de Beauvoir was a flesh-and-blood woman, a passionate one, who wanted everything, tasted everything and wrote everything. But she also became a symbol in her lifetime, a myth, a cult.

It would have been fascinating to follow de Beauvoir's intellectual development from the time she studied philosophy and became a teacher against her family wish (for in her time it was unacceptable in the bourgeoisie that a woman earn a living—not to speak of aristocrats like her father who considered it unacceptable for *men* to work for a living) and to follow the progress of her writing, notably of *The Second Sex,* which has since become a bible to so many women in so many nations. But this is where the biographers leave us hanging. For if their subject's family background and early years are recounted in considerable detail—sometimes to the point where de Beauvoir's life seems little more than an excuse for anecdote—her arrival at the Sorbonne brings an end to the intimacy one may have felt with her. We would have liked to know what she studied and felt and said and heard, but all we get is trivia. The reader feels trapped behind a glass window, acting like a small-time voyeur.

In France, the original version of this biography received a prize voted by the readers of *Elle* magazine, and the book remains a must for all those without any serious interests in philosophy, literature or politics. The outside shell of de Beauvoir's life is here, complete with American mink coat and love letters to Famous American Lover Nelson Algren—which preoccupy the authors more than all of World War II. Still, the reader looking for saucy "Existentialist" details will be disappointed, for if we are told a bit of the sex lives of assorted spear carriers, the authors seem to have been dazzled by Saint Simone's halo and don't dare ruffle her robes.

One has to read Sartre's letters to de Beauvoir in order to discover what it was that linked them so strongly all their lives long. After reading at length about each and every café she spent time in, and with whom, and feeling one has sniffed every glass of liquor she ever drank, we begin to wonder whether by any chance we've missed the moment when she may have lost her virginity to Sartre. And later, in 1943, while Sartre was a POW of the Germans, the mother of a female student who was under de Beauvoir's spell accused her of abducting a minor. "Friends intervened and the criminal charge was dropped but, after twelve years of teaching, de Beauvoir was barred from the University, and she was lucky that the matter went no further for the offense carried a jail sentence. She could no longer teach in France; she would have to find a new way of earning a living." Now, wouldn't it have been interesting to know the significance of homosexuality in the life of the author of *The Second Sex,* then and later?

Years later, in 1970, at the age of 62, de Beauvoir signed a manifesto of the MLF, the French Women's Liberation Movement, requesting the right for women to have abortions and claiming to have had an abortion herself. Clearly since Simone de Beauvoir did tackle such sexual and ancillary questions frontally, provoking the establishment loudly and deliberately, the reader would obviously like to know how she faced them personally. But it seems that the presence—and then the shadow—of de Beauvoir paralyzed the authors. It would have been a hard assignment to obtain such private information, and the authors don't give it to us. The result is that we feel very much left outside.

All this changes in the final chapters, covering the last years of her life, when age excused her from having a private life, and she threw herself into militant action on the multiple fronts of feminism, demonstrations against the Vietnam War, the struggle against capitalism and imperialism and allied causes. By this time, the authors had come to know their heroine, and they could interview her on the subjects then of greatest concern to her. But there are three decades of de Beauvoir's life which we can only watch through the glass window, with the feeling of killing time with Saint Simone.

Marianne Véron, "Simone de Beauvoir: Passions of the Mind," in Book World—The Washington Post, *June 21, 1987, p. 11.*

HÉLÈNE VIVIENNE WENZEL

[*Wenzel is the editor of* Simone de Beauvoir: Witness to a Century *(1987), a collection of essays focusing primarily on Beauvoir's contribution to feminist history. In the following excerpt, Wenzel finds Francis and Gontier's analysis of Beauvoir's life and work somewhat undeveloped, but concludes that their work is compelling.*]

Who is Simone de Beauvoir that her life and love story should command our attention for about 400 pages of text [in *Simone de Beauvoir: A Life . . . a Love Story*], including extensive bibliographies, myriad footnotes and a seemingly cosmic index? For starters, fresh on the heels of the May, 1968, student-worker revolution in Paris, in which she took a very active and supportive role at age 60, De Beauvoir emerged as an international figure in the second wave of feminism. Her two-volume work, *The Second Sex,* was universally adopted as the only existing text capable of grounding the old "woman question" and the new politics of feminism in theory. Indeed, since the publication of this far-ranging work in France in 1949, one could hardly speak or hear of "woman" or "woman's condition," let alone "feminism," without "Simone de Beauvoir" and *The Second Sex* tripping over each other as they rolled off the tongue. Most people probably first learned about De Beauvoir through *The Second Sex*—now more widely read and circulated than when it was first published. Wanting to amplify this narrow image of a far more complex and compelling figure [in *Simone de Beauvoir: A Life . . . a Love Story*], Claude Francis and Fernande Gontier limited their treatment of De Beauvoir's years in the women's movement from 1970 to her death in 1986, at age 78, to a very condensed 13 pages. What they present, instead, is the life of a woman, who before, after and during her involvements in women's causes was also novelist, essayist, and autobiographer; who was at one and the same time an intellectual, a socialist, and an existentialist; who was over and above all one of the ultimately indivisible union known as "Sartre and De Beauvoir."

De Beauvoir first encountered Jean-Paul Sartre, France's most illustrious 20th-Century intellectual, philosopher and political renegade, when they were students at the Sorbonne. Together, they studied for their "aggregation," the most advanced and competitive examination for teachers in the French system, and passed it, Sartre in first place, De Beauvoir in close second, a not insignificant order that would be echoed throughout the rest of their lives and their writings. Their love affair, which began in 1929, became a lifelong primary (if shortly thereafter non-sexual) partnership, negotiated with multiple contracts. It endured world events of cataclysmic proportions, intellectual and political commitments of questionable merit, and celebrity and infamy for each. Over the course of 50 years, this "essential" relationship included, by mutual consent, but more at Sartre's bidding than at De Beauvoir's, a sizable cast of "contingent" lovers. . . . For De Beauvoir, Nelson Algren was perhaps the most important contingent relationship in her life. He was also the most unwilling to accommodate the Sartre-De Beauvoir indivisibility.

As the authors proudly tell us in their "Notes and References," "The point of departure for this biography was our tracking down of the handwritten, unpublished letters that Simone de Beauvoir wrote to the American author Nelson Algren, with whom she had fallen in love." Written in English, the letters began when they met in Chicago in 1947 and extended beyond their rupture in 1951, to 1960. The excerpts from these letters reveal a heretofore unpublished, undiscovered De Beauvoir; a sensual, sexually reawakened 39-year-old woman in love, who had to do battle with her conscience and her body over the limitations imposed by the contract she had forged with Sartre two decades earlier, and this new passionate love for Algren. As the biography reveals, De Beauvoir had many, many fewer contingent relationships, and with the exception of the Algren letters, she was always circumspect about them, even in her autobiographies, relegating the stuff of sex and passion to fictional rewrites.

It is at times unsatisfactory that the authors do not further extend their inquiry into the reasons why, and how, De Beauvoir's contingent love relationships were different from Sartre's. Indeed, it is very disturbing to read on the one hand the graphic sexual descriptions that Sartre, the self-avowed womanizer, in the name of "transparency," conscientiously wrote to De Beauvior of his many very young mistresses and passing fancies; and on the other, only repetitions and overextended explanations of the carefully worded thoughts and responses that De Beauvior had already published. Wouldn't it have been preferable had the authors decided to go beyond, or at least outside, the limitations of the autobiographical word, had not stuck so closely to De Beauvior's own texts, and to restatements of her oft-repeated dicta about these relationships? These criticisms notwithstanding, the perspectives cast on Sartre, De Beauvoir and their entourage are provocative: Their love lives emerge as humorous and dramatic, at times unbelievable, and always disconcerting.

This biography of De Beauvoir complements, extends and at times contradicts her own monumental four-volume autobiography. It is the most comprehensive study of her life to have emerged amid the profusion of works which have been written on and about her since the women's movements began, or since her death. . . . The original French version appeared simply as *Simone de Beauvoir* in 1985, before her death. This American translation with the addition of the subtitle "a life . . . a love story" contains an introduction that was not present in the French edition, some different photos, and a new last chapter describing De Beauvoir's brief illness, her hospitalization and her unexpected death on April 14, 1986, one day short of the sixth anniversary of Sartre's death. In addition to saying "farewell" in this final chapter, the authors use the introduction and the footnotes to the chapters to share with the reader some of the responses that De Beauvoir had to their original manuscript.

If Francis and Gontier's point of view is somewhat less incisive or developed than we would have wished it to be, and if there is sometimes an overwhelming amount of detail, it is nevertheless a compelling book about a remarkable woman's life, and her love affair with herself and the world. (pp. 2, 9)

> *Hélène Vivienne Wenzel, in a review of "Simone de Beauvoir: A Life . . . a Love Story," in* Los Angeles Times Book Review, *July 5, 1987, pp. 2, 9.*

CLAIRE TOMALIN

Simone De Beauvoir lived and worked in a formidable tradition of French women of letters—Madame de Staël, George Sand, Colette—all of whom refused to bow their heads to the rules binding their sex, lived as flamboyantly as macaws, and used their abundant, crackling intellectual energy to produce books which both scandalised and sold. Of this powerful tribe, the most didactic was de Beauvoir, not surprisingly, since she trained and worked as a teacher of philosophy (and indeed it was the income from teaching that gave her the independence she needed as a young woman in the 1920s). She set out to change the lives of her own sex, believing that effectiveness in the world was what gave men their superiority over women.

The Second Sex was published 40 years ago, and it's quite a shock to re-read it today, because some of the constraints it describes seem so distant and barbarous: bourgeois families desperate to catch suitable husbands for their daughters, pregnancy in an unmarried woman considered wholly catastrophic, legal abortion unknown, small girls denied the freedom of practical clothes (to name only a few points discussed).

There is no doubt that de Beauvoir set out most of the programme of feminist reform in the second half of this century. She led the attack on the moralising and misogynistic aspects of psychoanalysis. Her chapter on lesbianism is a model of sanity and demystification. She is neither for it nor against it:

homosexuality, she points out, may be either a way of escaping from something, or a way of accepting something about oneself.

She is well aware that existence can be monotonous and unsatisfying for men as well as for women, and her description of the kind of happiness many women with constricted domestic lives enjoy is amazingly true and fair. *The Second Sex* is a rich, bold book, with something original and interesting in every section (and one or two absurdities, like the confident generalisation that Scandinavian women are sexually cold). . . .

De Beauvoir's other outstanding writing is autobiographical. There is the superb sequence of books that begins with *Memoirs of a Dutiful Daughter* and includes the account of her mother's death, perfectly poised between feeling and observation. Autobiography also crops up in parts of her novels; there are memorable pages, for example, in *The Blood of Others*, describing her flight and return to Paris as the German army arrived in 1940.

Claude Francis and Fernande Gontier set themselves a hard task in taking on [in *Simone de Beauvoir: A Life . . . a Love Story*] a writer who has written so well and fully about her own experience. They point out some of her inconsistencies and failures of memory, but their version of her life is nothing like as interesting as her own. They offer no real discussion of her work, no analysis of her character; and they begin with a particularly disastrous bit of falsification, by presenting de Beauvoir in the guise of an Isolde, and insisting that the most interesting aspect of her life was her love for Sartre (an unlikely Tristan).

Worse still, whereas de Beauvoir's prose was impeccable, this narrative is cobbled together out of clichés which the translator has done nothing to improve. Words are on everyone's lips, everyone who matters is there, a thrilling new eroticism takes hold of the young, the foundations of society are rocked: de Beauvoir's pedagogic pencil would have made short work of that kind of writing.

As to the famous pact with Sartre, made at the end of their student days, it was no Wagnerian potion but a promise that they would always be honest towards and come first with one another. This they seem to have stuck to, or at least as well as most couples stick to promises. . . .

Their decision to remain childless seems to have been the least successful aspect of the arrangement. . . . They were always acquiring 'family' in the shape of dependent younger people (often their lovers) and ended by adopting young women whom it is hard not to see as surrogate daughters. Perhaps we shall hear more about this when Deidre Bair's authorised biography appears.

Claire Tomalin, "Out of Bondage," in The Observer, *July 26, 1987, p. 23.*

JANE McLOUGHLIN

Time is going to cheat Simone de Beauvoir: co-star Jean-Paul Sartre will be remembered as the father of existentialism, the philosopher-poet, and she will be sold short, if we are not careful, as universal auntie of the women's movement. And if to call it "being sold short" offends the ghetto feminists, that is undoubtedly how Simone would see it. The great clarion call of her life was "Liberty, Equality, Fraternity", but only in later years did she concentrate her attacks on the liberation

of women as a specific group, and even then they were just a part of more generalised attacks on oppression within society. To believe that her importance as a philosopher or a writer begins and ends with *The Second Sex* is quite wrong.

On the other hand, it is easy enough to do. Hers is a great love story, extraordinary for the intellectual fruits of its joint labours. It is remarkable, too, that a woman of Mme de Beauvoir's calibre should have tolerated a man who, genius or not, appears to have been a male chauvinist pig of a very high order. Even she would drop everything—her own work, her relationship with American writer Nelson Algren, her personal plans—to help J-P Sartre finish a philosophical or political treatise.

Then again, what made Simone de Beauvoir remarkable to her contemporaries is not particularly remarkable now. The outlaw relationship with Sartre, the contingent lovers, the intellectual aspirations, the imperative to work and the idea that identity established through work is more powerful than sex or maternity—it all now seems simply the natural course for a woman following her own choices. Indeed, it seems extraordinary that so many women today live any other way. Her feminism is based simply on the truth that without independent work, a woman has no identity—which would hardly make front-page news in *Spare Rib*.

Women have adopted her as a heroine of their own, though, because she affirms that a great love is compatible with great work. She offers an optimistic exception to the rule that one nearly always precludes the other. This has militated against efforts to place her in a wider context than that provided by a literary version of Morecambe and Wise.

Claude Francis and Fernande Gontier do not attempt such an assessment [in *Simone de Beauvoir: A Life. . .a Love Story*]. They hint that de Beauvoir may sometimes have felt marginalised when she accompanied Sartre on foreign tours, but it is never clear whether her willingness to participate on such terms was a way of resentfully staking her claim to equality in their joint work, or whether she felt she would have been marginalised still further into the women's ghetto if she had refused.

The reader misses the answer to such questions. One of the problems of writing a biography of de Beauvoir is that she did the job so thoroughly and inimitably in her novels. This is compounded by the pervading impression that the authors were constrained by the threat of her disapproval, and their susceptibility to uncritical—even unchallenged—reverence for her achievements. It seems both they and she are apt to take themselves a mite too seriously.

On a subject so full of passion, anger, idealism and intellectual self-flagellation, this is a strangely passionless book. It is detailed, factual, reflecting the authors' access both to previously unpublished letters and to Simone de Beauvoir herself. At very few points can we stand back and see Simone de Beauvoir as other people saw her. We are told how she wore her hair, how blue her eyes were, but there is no testimony of others' emotional reaction to her. The reader is turned into a tourist taking a guided tour round a national monument.

For instance, we are told that in 1970 Simone de Beauvoir signed a pro-abortion manifesto, putting her name to the declaration, "I have had an abortion." Possibly this abortion was symbolic, like Jimmy Carter's adultery in his heart; but whether real or "idealistic", it does not seem to occur to the authors to ask. What remains is an impression that it didn't much matter one way or the other, as long as the rationale was right—thus contributing to the curious academic chill of this book.

> Jane McLoughlin, "Cherchez la femme," in Punch, Vol. 292, No. 7648, July 29, 1987, p. 54.

BETTY ABEL

In *The Prime of Life* and *Force of Circumstance* Simone de Beauvoir told her own story: now there is a biography [*Simone de Beauvoir: A Life. . .a Love Story*] written by two trusted authors who have been allowed access to an unpublished correspondence consisting of 1,682 letters, another sort of autobiography which the writer herself handed over to them before her death. Claude Francis and Fernande de Gontier had been well known to Simone de Beauvoir for more than ten years and so they knew much that has not been revealed elsewhere than in their account of her life. The source book of her novels is contained in the letters, written between 1947 and 1960. (p. 166)

Simone de Beauvoir dominated feminist views throughout the world for fifty years although, retaining her principles where the marriage bond itself is concerned, she never intended to marry Sartre and they both believed in a sexual freedom rarely found in the early twenties and thirties in France or Europe generally. License was not, however, in question, but only a rational belief in occasional separations even when these involved an infidelity which few partnerships could survive. Many of the letters now quoted for the first time reveal how great was the strength of their attachment, based as it was not only on physical passion but also on political and philosophical radicalism.

The literary and political experiences through which Simone de Beauvoir lived, the people who were her friends, the journeys she made (to Africa, the USA, Central America, Russia and China) provide rich and gripping material for the present well-researched biography. Her range as a novelist was wide but home-based, for she showed in her first famous novel, *The Mandarins*, an easy and experienced grasp of French university life. This theme, with excursions into bourgeois domesticity to provide its contrasting *milieu*, is endemic to all her fiction. The justification for a biography of considerable length to have been translated into English is the far-reaching influence and fame of her writing, both autobiographical and fictional. She is established in European literature as much for her stylistic grace as for her political radicalism.

In spite of the difficulty of assembling so much new material and not repeating already well-documented facts, the two authors of the biography have successfully presented a meticulous and precise picture of one whose mark on her times is likely to remain deep and lasting. (p. 167)

> Betty Abel, in a review of "Simone de Beauvoir: A Life. . .a Love Story," in Contemporary Review, Vol. 251, No. 1460, September, 1987, pp. 166-67.

LILLIAN S. ROBINSON

[*In the following excerpt Robinson reflects on the role* The Second Sex *played in the feminist movement and on the relationship between Beauvoir's feminism and her larger political activism. She faults Francis and Gontier for their lack of substantive discussion of these topics. Robinson also examines Beauvoir's relationship with Sartre and concludes that Francis and Gontier* fail to explore or understand the ideological basis for Beauvoir's choices.]

For those of us who have come under Beauvoir's influence, the continuing importance of *The Second Sex* does not reside in the particulars of its observations and conclusions. It is possible to disagree with much of what she says and still see the book as a landmark in the history of feminist thought and method. *Thought* above all, for it is a powerful declaration that the woman question should be approached by applying the powers of the mind. "Phallic feminism," her opponents call it. "Using the brains you were born with," some of us retort, though it is not just raw intelligence that is required, but the rational—the *passionately* rational—pursuit of new understanding of the female condition on the basis of insights drawn from physiology, history, literature, psychology, mythology, sociology, anthropology and personal observation.

The assessment of *The Second Sex* and its role in feminist thought is one of the places where the biography [*Simone de Beauvoir: A Life . . . a Love Story*] by Claude Francis and Fernande Gontier is weakest, for the authors give short shrift to content, paying far more attention to the book's worldwide success, the scandals surrounding its publication, and its (quantitatively expressed) influence. Substantive discussion is preempted by an exaggeration of that influence. It is simply wrong, for instance, to state, as the biographers do in two places, that *The Second Sex* was the basic text for women's studies as an academic field, when its greatest impact has been outside the academy, and when it is such a damnably difficult book to use in the classroom. And it is downright silly to claim that "in 1960 the American women's movement adopted *The Second Sex* as the theoretical basis for its activities." (p. 15)

[In a 1984 interview with Hélène Wenzel,] Beauvoir makes it clear that she never developed an overall politics that either "fit" feminism into a general design or placed it at the forefront. Her views were clear and consistent, but they do not constitute a system. . . . Beauvoir herself tells Wenzel that the stages of her experience were formed less by a specifically female life pattern than by "politics, events . . . the Resistance, Liberation, the war in Algeria . . . those are the things that marked eras . . . for me . . . [I]t's the historical events, the historical involvement one has in these larger events. It's much more important than any other kind of difference."

The Resistance, Algeria, Vietnam—these are not simply labels for phases of Beauvoir's life, but indicators of social movements with which she identified and in which she took an increasingly active role. The war for Algerian independence was pivotal to Beauvoir's political evolution. Her horror at the torture and condoning of torture committed in her name as a Frenchwoman alienated her from her compatriots, and led her to offer material aid to what the state called "terrorism" and support for draft resisters and deserters. Her personal anguish over Algeria and, later, over the US role in Vietnam is the essential and gripping subject of *Force of Circumstance,* the third volume of her autobiography. . . .

[Although] Claude Francis once edited a collection of photographs and quotations entitled *Simone de Beauvoir et le cours du monde,* she and Gontier have little to say in the biography about the public events of Beauvoir's time. They give a scant fifteen pages to the Algerian war, barely two to the International Russell Tribunal on US War Crimes in Vietnam, some scattered remarks to her relation to feminist activism. (p. 16)

What I miss in [this book] . . . is the woman who cried out against oppression and torture, who said that her countrymen's crimes in Algeria were making a horror of her old age, who marched and testified and organized and wrote, courting official arrest and imprisonment and unofficial terrorist retaliation. And the connection between that activist and the distinguished writer, the feminist theorist, the great lover.

"The great lover"—what an odd term to slip off my pen! Usually, it means Casanova, Don Juan, at the very least Jean-Paul Sartre, the heterosexual male ardently pursuing his casual relationships. Yet the English translation of the Francis-Gontier biography—whose French title is an unadorned *Simone de Beauvoir*—is subtitled *A Life . . . a Love Story*. Under a rubric like that, one fully expects a soap opera, and that expectation is fully realized. Beauvoir's autobiography and the two novels that have autobiographical dimensions contain both revelations and reticences about the author's sexual life. Francis and Gontier pursue the revelations, ignore the reticences. This would not be any more disturbing than the biographers' filling in or revising other aspects of the memoirs, were it not for their evident lack of sympathy for the kinds of love affairs Beauvoir had, affairs based on serious, committed, loving feelings for more than one person at a time. Their particular problem has a double source: in scholarship and in language.

The point of departure for their biography, Francis and Gontier tell us, was their discovery of Beauvoir's handwritten letters to the American writer Nelson Algren, all 1442 pages of them (1682 pages, if you believe the French version). Faced with the passionate tone of these letters, the biographers appear to be at a loss to explain what they see as a contradiction between her assurances of deep and undying love for Algren and her perpetual return to Sartre. Although they had the priceless opportunity to talk with Beauvoir herself about non-monogamy in theory and practice, they end up as puzzled as Algren himself, who apparently believed he was entitled to "a woman of his own." If anything, the biographers, overestimating and misinterpreting the value of their archival *trouvaille* of however-many-pages it was, end up on Algren's side. They even imply that it was his anger at Beauvoir that did him in, that she—her non-monogamy and her "indiscretion" in revealing the details of their love—killed him by remote control.

I refuse to debate whether an old man with a bad heart actually can die of frustrated long-ago love or even a fit of pique, much less whether Algren "should" have been feeling the destructive emotions he expressed on his last day of life. I will even admit, as Beauvoir did, that the third parties to her relationship with Sartre frequently got badly hurt in their encounters with the permanence of that couple. But I do expect a biography of a serious feminist thinker to place at least as much value on her original ideology as on some guy's conventional expectations, to respect the sexual innovator over the sexual conservative, the woman over the man.

In his last interview, the one that may have been fatal to him, Algren fulminated about Beauvoir's quoting from his letters in her autobiography: "Hell, love letters should be private. I've been in whorehouses all over the world and the women there always close the door, whether it's in Korea or India. But this woman flung the door open and called in the public and the press." What I'd expect a *feminist* biographer to ask at this point is why it's okay for him to have bought the sexual services of women in impoverished countries and then used the experience rhetorically, but not okay for Beauvoir to write about her deepest feelings. I'd also appreciate some inquiry as

to how the author of *The Second Sex* happened to fall in love, while she was working on that very book, with a man who seems never to have given a moment's critical thought to the existing gender arrangements. Instead, I'm being asked to feel sorry for this man!

Algren once complained in print about the theory of non-monogamy itself, as articulated in Sartrian discourse: "Anybody who can experience love contingently has a mind that has recently snapped. How can love be *contingent*? Contingent upon *what*?" Which strongly suggests that it never occurred to Algren to read his rival's work, in which the notion of *contingence* is laid out. The English word "contingent" has more definitions than apparently dreamed of in Algren's philosophy, but it does not adequately translate what Beauvoir meant when she told Algren that theirs was a contingent love, not a necessary one. . . . The problem is that translator Lisa Nesselson follows Beauvoir's lead and sticks with the related but ill-fitting word throughout, creating the impression that her biographers agree with Algren that Beauvoir's ideas about sex and love were unique, as well as grotesque. (pp. 16-17)

Sartre's letters proved the only source of insight around [on Sartre and Beauvoir's relationship].

In the name of perfect honesty, Sartre and Beauvoir told each other about their other lovers—in some detail. . . .

Sartre manifestly expected Beauvoir's complicity in his confessional and it would seem from his half of the dialogue that he got it. He not only assured her, as any lover might, that she was the best of all women, he made her feel that she was, by sharing with her how essentially absurd every other woman was. The length of the correspondence and of the relationship it reflects would indicate that, at least in those years, she was in fact complicit in this construction of her own superiority. Perhaps what is remarkable about Beauvoir, after all . . . is her ability to say so much that is meaningful about the condition of women, although the relationship that empowered her as a writer survived through placing her "above" that condition. Perhaps, too, the relationship itself has to be judged that way: by the work that it made possible. From this perspective, they were clearly doing *something* right. Which doesn't prevent the letters, which she was the one to make public, from being, to put it mildly, a let-down.

And maybe that is the real point. Beauvoir edited these letters herself, publishing them as part of the struggle over Sartre's memory. *She* saw them as a vindication. In that sense, they reflect her authenticity, and the student of Beauvoir's life and thought cannot afford to flinch from what they reveal. It is this authenticity, the truth to the subject, that I miss in . . . Francis and Gontier's praise. . . . For, in order for someone to be our teacher, she does not need to be perfect, she does not need to be right, but she does need us to be prepared to learn from her—whether or not we like everything that we learn. (p. 17)

Lillian S. Robinson, "Simone, Our Teacher," in The Women's Review of Books, *Vol. V, No. 2, November, 1987, pp. 15-17.*

CAROL ASCHER

[*Ascher, an American critic and anthropologist, is the author of* Simone de Beauvoir: A Life of Freedom *(1981), a biocritical study of Beauvoir's life and work. In the following excerpt, she finds Francis and Gontier's biography weakened by their obvious idolization of Beauvoir. She further objects to the emphasis the authors place on Beauvoir's romances at the expense of intellectual criticism.*]

For those whose thirst to understand Simone de Beauvoir is unquenchable, each new book is a promise and a temptation. Moreover, we are in a great period of Beauvoir research. Simone de Beauvoir died on April 14, 1986, only a little over a year ago, and her death—though ending the personal interviews and writings that continued almost into Beauvoir's last days—is already making available new perspectives and information. . . .

Francis and Gontier have written an adoring biography [*Simone de Beauvoir: A Life . . . A Love Story*], which at times imitates Beauvoir's own energetic and moving memoir style. Their description of Beauvoir's childhood brings into sharper focus the mix of real poverty and elite social standing she grew up in. For readers who have loved her memoirs, this book also reveals satisfying new information about the identity of some of the disguised names in her books. And the authors present new material based on passionate letters Simone de Beauvoir wrote to Nelson Algren during her long affair with him.

But the many failings in this biography show how difficult it still is to write a full and balanced portrait of this woman, who was herself a prolific writer and who "mothered" so many potential biographers over the last decades. Throughout, this account verges on potboiler romance, at the same time it suffers from vagueness and imprecision suggestive of coverup.

Francis and Gontier clearly love Beauvoir; thus they are rather good at conveying why others have fallen head over heels for her, but they tell most stories with more protectiveness than she would have mustered for herself. Nor, in matters of love and sexuality, do they probe behind Beauvoir's version of her life. Thus her life-long relationship with Jean-Paul Sartre is described with girlish adoration. It is, oddly, only an incidental remark by Nelson Algren, which is included without comment, that gave me a new insight. Algren saw them as "a sort of business enterprise, a single entity, Sartre de Beauvoir & Co."

In fact, the biography details the last years of Sartre's life, when major strains seem to have occurred between him and Beauvoir—interestingly, not because of other women, which had been routine, but because of a man who was replacing Beauvoir as his intellectual mate. Yet Francis and Gontier floridly insist:

> Their love story was literature's most disconcerting. It was a revolutionary romance, for it relegated to the fringe all traditional morality codes. All codes of conduct, customs, taboos, the bonds and boundaries, shackles and constraints, all the barriers constructed by popular wisdom to stand in the way of this redoubtable force that had the power to sweep everything else aside.

As serious as the idolatry, which causes the writers to ignore details they themselves have set down, is their lack of interest in Simone de Beauvoir as writer and intellectual. Though pages are devoted to Beauvoir's various love affairs, the authors scarcely touch Beauvoir's ideas—and don't attempt to untangle the delicate and complicated cross-fertilization that went on between her and Sartre. *The Ethics of Ambiguity* gets a single paragraph. *The Second Sex* receives four pages about the reactions of the public, but nothing about the book itself. Though it is clearly difficult to write about thinking and writing, the very texture of Simone de Beauvoir's life is thus distorted.

Carol Ascher, "de Beauvoir Books Promise and Tempt," in New Directions for Women, *Vol. 16, No. 6, November-December, 1987, p. 17.*

Rebecca West: A Life
by Victoria Glendinning

(For Rebecca West: see also *CLC*, Vols. 7, 9, 31; *Contemporary Authors*, Vols. 5-8, rev. ed., 109 [obituary]; *Contemporary Authors New Revision Series*, Vol. 19; *Dictionary of Literary Biography*, Vol. 36; *Dictionary of Literary Biography Yearbook: 1983*. For Victoria Glendinning: see also *Contemporary Authors*, Vol. 120.)

An Excerpt from *Rebecca West: A Life*

The failure of this flawed and gifted man makes a pitiful story, and any daughter might wish to defend such a father from the glib judgement of strangers. Cissie, though she took her mother's side as the girl, could not, as a grown woman, reject him. She created a myth out of the wonderful father she had and did not have.

The impossibility of knowing exactly what had happened between her parents made her ambivalent about the opposite sex. She longed for men to be strong and supportive, while believing that they were generally inadequate and destructive. She was to guard her independence ferociously, while expressing resentment towards the men who encouraged her to do so. Because her father had left the family penniless and *déclassé,* money, clothes, and food became her emotional currency, carrying an inflated symbolic value.

She was frequently to say that human beings did not have enough information about the conditions of their existence, and that as a writer she tried to discover it for herself. The versions, or stories, that she told herself out of her need to handle this first crisis are reflected in all her writing. An artist, she wrote, is goaded into creation "by his need to resolve some important conflict, to find out where the truth lies among divergent opinions on a vital issue." His work is often "a palimpsest on which are superimposed several incompatible views about his subject."

She made such a palimpsest not only in her work but out of the story of her life. The need to make a pattern out of random happenings led her to interpret her experience as if it were a dream, and to restructure her past as if it were, as she said, "a bad book" which had to be improved. Although she drafted and redrafted the raw material of her life until she was on her deathbed, she knew it was a hopeless task. Destiny, she wrote, cared nothing for the orderly presentation of material; "it likes to hold its cornucopia upside down and wave it while its contents drop anywhere they like over time and space.

Dust jacket of Rebecca West: A Life, *by Victoria Glendinning. Alfred A. Knopf, 1987. Jacket design by Gun Larson. Courtesy of Alfred A. Knopf, Inc.*

Brave are our own human attempts to correct this sluttish habit." But it is "only by making such efforts that we survive." . . .

The story of Cicely Fairfield, who became Rebecca West, is not only a narrative but a web of perceptions, constantly modified. Part of the purpose of telling it is to disentangle what really mattered to her from what did not. There are some events which become experience, she wrote, and "many more which do not." There is also often a gap between what she felt, or decided, had happened and how it seemed to somebody else. Human beings felt insecure, she wrote, unless they could find out what was happening around them. "That is why historians publicly pretend that they can give an exact account of events in the past, though they privately know that all the past will let us know about events above a certain degree of importance is a bunch of alternative hypotheses."

FAITH EVANS

[*Evans is the editor of the Virago Press edition of West's* Family Memories. *In the following excerpt, she praises Glendinning for her responsible yet sympathetic portrayal of a complex woman.*]

Three-quarters of a century ago a young journalist on the *Freewoman* made a name for herself by exposing male pretensions. (She was using the same method when she was 90 and a Dame, but by then it was for the *Sunday Telegraph.*) In September 1911 Rebecca West went for H. G. Wells, describing him as 'the Old Maid among novelists.' . . .

To such a challenge the middle-aged masculinity of Wells was bound to rise. Soon he and Rebecca West had begun the relationship which, with its silly sketches and its animal and baby talk, makes awkward reading today but which lasted, on and off, for 10 years.

Those were, after all, the days when writers engaged in private discourse through their public work—Wells particularly, though Lawrence and Bloomsbury did much the same. In a collection of essays published as late as 1928, *The Strange Necessity,* Rebecca West still could not resist adding sexual banter to ·literary criticism. Pondering the legacy of her 'literary uncles'—Wells, Shaw, Galsworthy and Bennett—she mocked the feebleness of Wells's love scenes and told him that his prose tended to 'suddenly lose its firmness and . . . shake like jelly.' She also incensed James Joyce by the way she interrupted her critique of *Ulysses* with an imaginary stroll round Paris buying hats and dresses. She had meant it as a compliment, casting herself as Leopold Bloom and Paris as Dublin; but Joyce failed to appreciate the value she set upon mixing high art (literature) with low (fashion).

Rebecca West's obsession with clothes, which she perceived as both a female weakness and a female strength, is only one of many contradictions in her sense of herself. One of her late reviews began: 'There is of course no reason for the existence of the male sex except that one sometimes need help in moving the piano.' But for all her fighting talk, she suffered deeply from lack of the male presence. Her father, an attractive but feckless Anglo-Irish journalist, was rarely at home, disappearing altogether when she was eight; she had no brothers; and Wells pigeon-holed her as a mistress, an occasional delicious treat (for him). These absentee men in her life took up residence in her imagination and reappeared in her fiction: the perfect young brother in the book about her childhood, *The Fountain Overflows*; Laura's trustworthy father in her Russian novel *The Birds Fall Down.*

The possibility of betrayal was always there, and when, in later life, it became a predominant theme of her work, she began to encounter real, self-confessed difficulties in separating plain fact and paranoid fiction. Rebecca West cannot, then, be approached in any conventional way.

In this first full-length attempt to tell her story [*Rebecca West: A Life*], Victoria Glendinning . . . often has to act as adjudicator, deciding when to present alternative viewpoints (in the many family feuds, for example) and when to put in a good word for someone who has been unfairly pilloried in life or in art or in both (Wells's wife Jane, for example, or Rebecca West's sister Lettie, the conformist Cordelia in *The Fountain Overflows*). She never shirks her biographical responsibilities, yet she never lets her subject down. It is an assured performance that seems to gain impetus as the years and the problems increase.

Rebecca West's sense of rootlessness, combined with her fierce but not always progressive intelligence, meant that as she grew older she felt the feminist dilemma of security versus independence in its acutest form. In 1930 she married, some years after her relationship with Lord Beaverbrook (depicted in her novel *Sunflower*) had come to nothing, making her fear, not for the last time, that she caused impotence. Her husband was a wealthy, anonymous, though not uninteresting banker called Henry Andrews, with an encyclopaedic knowledge of international train timetables.

The marriage surprised her Bohemian friends, who named him 'the Elk.' Mr and Mrs Andrews acquired a country seat in Bucks, travelled the world on journalistic assignments, kept pigs and labradors, and had countless friends, not all of them titled and rich. She wrote continually, but much of the second half of her life was plagued by disputes with her son by Wells, Anthony, which continued until and indeed beyond her death in 1983. . . .

What Rebecca West would have especially appreciated in her biographer, in addition to the mastery of those ideals of grace and tolerance that she herself sometimes failed to achieve, is her wit: 'As Henry grew older, deafer and blinder, he drove faster and faster.' And if Victoria Glendinning too often lets social busy-ness take priority over intellectual context, she does offer a proper analysis of Rebecca West's politics, above all her consistent stand against Soviet Communism, which she herself identified with Fascism.

This major clearing of the biographical undergrowth will lead the way to more extended criticism of the work, much of it now reprinted. Surprisingly little has been written about the oddly unchanging nature of Rebecca West's literary style, and the unusual versatility of her output. All her writing shows an absolute refusal to be constrained by gender, particularly the controversial political journalism, those ambitious declarations of faith in which great public events are judged by observation of individual behaviour—her two-volume epic about Yugoslavia, *Black Lamb and Grey Falcon,* and *The Meaning of Treason,* her investigation into the world of espionage.

For almost a century Rebecca West encouraged women to reject the parochial, always reaching beyond traditional boundaries to the great philosophical debates: the struggle between good and evil, illusion and reality, male and female. To abandon yourself to this brilliant and exasperating writer is to abandon yourself to a great many alternative versions of history—and of womanhood.

> Faith Evans, "Speaking Up for Women," in The Observer, *April 12, 1987, p. 22.*

ALEXANDRA PRINGLE

[*Pringle has written the introduction to the Virago edition of West's* The Harsh Voice. *In the following excerpt, she praises Glendinning for presenting a balanced view of West's unhappy life and indomitable spirit.*]

Even in her 80s, Rebecca West kept up the business of life with remarkable vigour; or so it seemed to those who visited her elegant, no-nonsense Knightsbridge flat. Skilfully deflecting earnest questions about her long career, she talked of the present, of television, of Italian shoes or modern art. Her wit illuminated the conversation to the end, just as it had enlivened all her writing—from early radical journalism in the *Free-*

woman to her final article, on being 90, which appeared in *Vogue* in 1982.

It is therefore disheartening, if not really surprising, to find that Victoria Glendinning's balanced, humane biography [*Rebecca West: A Life*] presents an unhappy woman. There have been many accounts of West as brilliant foe of convention, indomitable crusader, passionate lover and impossible mother. Now we are shown someone—and I think Glendinning is very close to the truth—who was not a bohemian, scarcely even a rebel.

Glendinning portrays a more conventional person. West may have been some young woman *terrible*, but she aspired to respectable matronhood. The traumas of her Edwardian childhood are known through her marvellous *The Fountain Overflows* and from the lovely first half of her flawed novel, *The Judge*. From her wastrel Anglo-Irish father she inherited a liking for political debate and developed a disastrous taste in men: from her brave, talented Scottish mother she learnt about independence. Growing up in bourgeois Edinburgh without the support of respectability, West developed a strong understanding of those who fail to fit in.

From the first, her writing was various and ruthlessly intelligent. She wrote fiction, criticism, journalism, biography and travel books. In all these fields her work radiates competence.

But her emotional life was a disaster. Like many women doomed to fall in love with married men she really wanted to "live decently in a house with children". It was her misfortune, which she shared with other literary women, to succumb to the (to me, mysterious) charms of H G Wells, and doubly or quintuply her misfortune in getting pregnant the second time they made love.

West might have made an excellent matriarch in a home full of children. But she was ill-equipped with one illegitimate son. Small moustachioed Wells was no help: "I *hate* being encumbered with a little boy." It was a tragedy that, instead of blaming the father who had deserted him, Anthony West spent a lifetime in search of revenge against his mother.

She never had a decent time with any man. After her 10-year affair with Wells, she plunged into a brief relationship with Lord Beaverbrook. She became obsessed, but for Beaverbrook, small, not moustachioed, she was only a diversion. Victoria Glendinning now tells the previously concealed story of West's marriage to the banker Henry Maxwell Andrews. He seemed a typical Englishman, restrained, quiet, sensible. But in fact he was a gambler who had lost heavily on the stock market. Early in their marriage he turned physically from Rebecca and sought younger women. Despite appearances, it was his wife who earned the major part of the family income. Together, outsiders pretending otherwise, they feigned respectability in their country house in Buckinghamshire.

West's marriage was, for a brilliant woman, a dull and prolonged sentence. Glendinning has to contrast her vitality of mind with the banal truth of "my sexual life, or rather death". In all West's work there was a fight between the will to live and the ease with which people can die. Her fighting joy in the stuff of life—music, food, clothes, people—was constantly undermined by her feeling that "like Job", she was "persecuted by God (and by man, woman and child)".

Glendinning writes of her task that "Rebecca's unhappiness is easier to document, because it outraged and frightened her, and she recorded it". A virtue of her book is that it does so unflinchingly, yet also celebrates the triumph of West's writing, with its desire to turn from life to art.

> *Alexandra Pringle, "Passionate Lover, Impossible Mother," in* The Sunday Times, *London, April 12, 1987, p. 59.*

MICHELENE WANDOR

[*Wandor, an English dramatist, poet, and short story writer, has written and edited numerous studies of women in the theater. Among her most recent works are* Carry On, Understudies: Theatre and Sexual Politics *(1985) and* Guests in the Body *(1987). In the following excerpt, Wandor commends Glendinning for her ability to explain West's many contradictions and praises her balanced portrait of West.*]

My first introduction to the writings of Rebecca West was through her updated book on spying, *The Meaning of Treason,* and her first novel, *The Return of the Soldier.* The former, with its tumbling, vivid prose, began with the trial of William Joyce (Lord Haw-Haw) in 1945, and ended with Kim Philby in the early 1960s; I emerged from its reading intrigued and infuriated. West dissected the complex anatomy of the spy, discussed the vexed question of national security (whose nation? whose security?) and was violently anti-Communist without ever trying to justify her arguments.

From the novel I emerged not very impressed; here was a story in which women competed with each other for a man and which ended with a silly and unnecessary gesture of female self-sacrifice. Very Mrs Humphry Ward, I thought, and not at all worthy of the reputation of a supposed feminist. Later, with the publication of Anthony West's novel *Heritage* and his biography of his father, H. G. Wells, painful evidence of a tortuous not-quite-ménage à trois emerged: at the age of 19, the young Rebecca met and was wooed by the successful, married H. G. Wells. Out of this semi-clandestine relationship Anthony was born, to adore his father and publicly blame his mother for his own unhappiness.

The extraordinary achievement of Victoria Glendinning's biography [*Rebecca West: A Life*] is to anatomise a tempestuous character and explain her life in a way that begins to make sense of her many contradictory features: a woman who established herself as an outspoken feminist journalist while still in her teens, yet allowed herself to be shunted away from family and friends for the birth of her child. Rebecca West stayed with H. G. Wells for years after she should have broken free; Glendinning pinpoints her dilemma: '. . . she longed for men to be strong and supportive, while believing that they were generally inadequate and destructive.'

Here is the core problem for the bourgeois radical feminist (my analysis, not Glendinning's) who can simultaneously despise men and desperately need to depend on them. Such feminism cannot lead to an independence that exists in its own right and demands an equal relationship with men. When Rebecca West later married, it was to a man who soon stopped having sexual relations with her and, as she found out after his death, was an inveterate philanderer. However, her genuine need to control her own destiny enabled Rebecca West to become the incisive political journalist she undoubtedly was and also, perhaps, this very independence made it difficult for her to carry through her undoubted love for her son.

Glendinning, who knew Rebecca West, takes careful pains to show how much Anthony's public laundering of family relations hurt her, but she is also frank about Rebecca's wild, sharp, wickedly witty and always emotionally direct responses to personal and professional events. She is clearly on her subject's side, although sometimes she goes too far. She states, for example, that Rebecca was 'an honorary Jew' because so many of her friends were Jewish; quite apart from the sheer silliness of such a phrase, it jars with Rebecca's later assumptions that anti-Semitism was somehow a 'natural' response.

Glendinning claims that Rebecca West can be seen as a role model for 'radical, independent women' of the 20th-century. Good God, I hope not. Such a profoundly unsatisfactory personal life is certainly no useful role model for today's women.

And yet there is a sense in which Rebecca West stands as a reminder of the continuing need for the striving spirit of female independence. Glendinning makes the interesting point that Rebecca West reinvented her own life, people she knew and events that pained her. Of course, we all rewrite our lives as we go along to some extent and, while this reinvention may have helped West cope, it is also a salutary reminder that the security of women's place in our culture still needs to be assured by controversial, stroppy, prose-loving and opinionated women writers. Rebecca West certainly had all those qualities.

Michelene Wandor, "Lamb and Falcon," in New Statesman, Vol. 113, No. 2925, April 17, 1987, p. 27.

FRANCES SPALDING

[Spalding, an English biographer and educator, is the author of Roger Fry: Art and Life (1980) and Vanessa Bell: A Bloomsbury Portrait (1983). In the following excerpt Spalding observes that, by focusing on West's entire life, Glendinning places West's affair with H. G. Wells in the proper perspective.]

'Just how important is something that ends when you are thirty?' This remark, dropped en passant by Dame Rebecca West to her future biographer, referred to that which the public would not let her forget: her affair with H. G. Wells. In her eighties she still sometimes dipped into his books, kept on her kitchen shelves, while waiting for the kettle to boil. So Victoria Glendinning recounts in her prologue, all too aware that Rebecca West's question, uttered in protest, still overshadows her entire life.

Regrettable though it is that this affair has detracted from the protean interests informing Rebecca West's career, it cannot be lightly dismissed. Her association with this man more than twice her age coincided with the onset of her career and lasted a decade. If, as Peter Levi recently wrote, one of Wells's attractions was his magical smell, another, in 1913, was his massive reputation. Contact with this polymath, in Rebecca West's case, replaced university education. What she might have got from her father, a journalist who talked to his children as equals on current affairs, was withdrawn when he left home in 1901 when Rebecca was eight. Wells's example, on the other hand, taught the application of history and knowledge to contemporary life. Reading Rebecca West's account of the Nuremberg Trials or her two-volume masterpiece, **Black Lamb and Grey Falcon,** we get the impression that she, like Wells, had a world picture which gave meaning to past and present. Her novels also display a forceful intelligence. But her manipulation of detail, her analytic powers and humane breadth are perhaps better placed in the service of journalism, in those

acerbic critical commentaries which are surely her foremost achievement.

Tragically, in 1984 her reputation was disfigured when her son by Wells, Anthony West, proved that much of the information she had given Wells's historians was 'phoney'. She was, he claims, building a dossier that would win her a good posthumous press. How does Victoria Glendinning deal with this [in **Rebecca West: A Life**]? As a biographer, she neither pretends to omniscience nor allows a too partisan view to undermine detachment. Only gradually do we discern the extent to which she is able to ameliorate the damage. At first she hedges: Rebecca West's stories about Wells, she argues, have the authenticity of myths, poetic but not objective truth. Obliged to admit a gap between what Rebecca West felt or decided had happened and how others saw it, her chief strategy is to attack the attacker: Anthony West's denigration of his mother is fuelled by 'the resentments of a lifetime'; he is also tarred with the same brush, for both mother and son add 'a fabulist's gloss to every detail of every misunderstanding'.

The resentments and misunderstandings are understandable. Denied the right to identify with his parents, Anthony West was brought up to regard his mother as his aunt and Wells as no more than a genial, friendly male who arrived now and then in a car. This is no recipe for happiness and it is surprising that Rebecca West perpetuated the pretence. But one contradiction revealed here is that this iconoclast (she had joined the suffragettes at the age of 16), this radical and independent woman increasingly felt compelled to surround herself with all the accoutrements associated with conventional high society; chic furnishings, good clothes, French paintings. After her marriage in 1930 to Henry Maxwell Andrews these so characterised her life that Virginia Woolf saw her personality in terms of 'a lit-up modern block, flooded by electricity'.

If she demanded a life of appearances it was partly to make up for the penniless, classless state incurred by her family after her father's departure. More equivocal is her fascination with guilt. It attracted her to St Augustine whose life she wrote and whose every phrase, she elsewhere admits, sounded in her ears 'like the sentence of my doom and the doom of my age'. . . . In addition, she felt that there was something in herself that invited tragedy. This biography upholds her opinion, for it describes a deeply flawed and unhappy life. But it also sets the record straight, balancing the positive against the negative aspects of her nature, the life-enhancing characteristics against the devouring and malignant. By broadening the focus of attention Victoria Glendinning puts the affair with Wells into perspective without diminishing it. If Virginia Woolf was correct in her assertion, that all Rebecca West's difficulties came from 'the weals and scars left by the hoofmarks of Wells', this same woman 50 years later avowed that being with Wells was on a par with 'seeing Nureyev dance or hearing Tito Gobbi sing'. (pp. 34-5)

Frances Spalding, "All's Well That Ends Wells," in The Spectator, Vol. 258, No. 8284, April 18, 1987, pp. 34-5.

PETER KEMP

[Kemp, an English critic and educator, is the author of Muriel Spark (1974) and H. G. Wells and the Culminating Ape (1982). In the following excerpt, he finds Glendinning's book an "instructive and fast-moving survey" of a life that was ultimately idiosyncratic and self-centered.]

The problem with writing a life of Rebecca West is that she wrote so many of them herself. Not content with producing autobiographical fiction, she also fabricated fictitious auto-biography—memoirs meant to mislead, doctored reminiscences, self-centred and self-justifying screeds which twist facts into flattering forms. As Victoria Glendinning points out [in *Rebecca West: A Life*], "she drafted and redrafted the raw material of her life until she was on her deathbed". Partly, this was to reassure herself; partly, to solicit the support of posterity. She devoted, her son Anthony acidly observed, "a great deal of time and no inconsiderable part of her creative energy to building a dossier that would win her a good post-humous press".

By a harshly sardonic nemesis, it's her son Anthony—temperamentally resembling his mother, his father H. G. Wells noted—who has done most to sabotage this scheme. Remarking in his *H. G. Wells: Aspects of a Life* that "like George Sand before her, she thought of her life history as something that could easily be improved by editing", he has specialized in caustic commentary on his mother's versions of events: cuttingly annotating her habit of conflating people and incidents from widely differing times and places into some episode gratifying to her self-image, underlining with relish farcical blunders like her claim that her mother (buried in 1921) had chortled with derision at Wells's *The Secret Places of the Heart* (published in 1922). . . .

Featuring with uncomfortable prominence in tales told by writers close to home wasn't a new experience for Rebecca West. The early phase of her affair with Wells, in which they gamily frolicked under the pet-names of Panther and Jaguar, was put on show in his *The Research Magnificent* where, as Amanda—nicknamed Leopard—she is given covert warnings by her mate Cheetah that he doesn't intend to be permanently penned in with her. . . .

These experiences—and her own penchant for populating her fiction with friends and foes . . .—kept Rebecca ever alert, Victoria Glendinning reveals, to spotting herself in other people's pages. *Finnegans Wake*, she believed, brimmed with unkind references to her and her taste for hats. Charmian in Muriel Spark's *Memento Mori*—who resembles Rebecca in having a domineering sister called Lettie, an unfaithful husband and a writer-son who resents her—was, perhaps with cause, seen as another portrait. In addition, it seems, she saw herself distortedly reflected in Wyndham Lewis's *The Roaring Queen*, Hugh Walpole's *The Young Enchanted*, Storm Jameson's *A Cup of Tea for Mr Thorgill* and Iris Murdoch's *The Sacred and Profane Love Machine*.

Given this inflamed streak of bibliomania and her own taste for unrelenting literary vendettas—even in her eighties, Glendinning observes, she was using her position as reviewer for the *Sunday Telegraph* "to settle a few old scores"—it's unsurprising to learn that she devoted anxious thought to who should write her life-story. Characteristic of her suspicion and self-esteem was her decision to designate two biographers: one to produce a full-length study, the other a shorter work. Stanley Olson is assembling the larger tome. Victoria Glendinning was selected for the shorter one. . . .

Choosing her wasn't perhaps Rebecca West's canniest decision. True, Mrs Glendinning's researches into the lives of Elizabeth Bowen, Edith Sitwell and Vita Sackville-West indicate a sympathy with blue-blooded bluestockings and *grandes dames* not always able to differentiate between social prominence and

artistic distinction, which Dame Rebecca must have found reassuring. True, as one who "knew her for the last ten years, and saw her often and with pleasure", she writes as an admiring friend, lauding her subject's books and applauding her wit (regrettably little of which gets into these pages). Certainly, there's nothing here resembling Wells's unsparing insights into Rebecca's character or her son's savage accounts of such scenes as her being carried raving from the Ritz by her husband and a waiter after a contretemps over lunch. But Glendinning's scrupulousness as a biographer constrains her to include material which, even if its implications aren't fully spelled out in her book, can be alienating.

Rebecca's compulsive lying is sometimes rather kindly glossed as "imaginative fluency". The tales where facts are altered to chime in with her feelings have, Glendinning gamely suggests, "poetic truth when they do not have objective truth", while her "later stories about her past were miniature novels, encoded texts". All the same, you're left in no doubt about the daunting drawbacks to a biographer presented by Rebecca's self-dramatizing and self-pitying fables about "my awful childhood, my worse girlhood . . . my life with that insane sadist H. G.".

Negotiating such pitfalls nimbly, Glendinning offers an instructive and fast-moving survey of the life, interspersed with appreciative but rarely very penetrating glances at the literature. While as much of Rebecca West's story as can be extricated from her falsifications is unravelled, her personality and the factors forming it receive scrutiny of a more benevolent kind than she herself generally trained on her fellow-creatures.

What rapidly becomes apparent is that West's character was diagnosed most acutely by two men always very much to the fore in her herd of *bêtes noires*: H. G. Wells and Arnold Bennett. When he first met her, Wells recalls in his autobiography, he found her "a curious mixture of maturity and infantilism". Bennett, in a review headed "My Brilliant but Bewildering 'Niece'", noted that "she must, at all costs, 'perform'. She must be odd"; often this results, he remarked, in "mere irresponsible silliness". Evidence to back this up stands out everywhere in her work—especially in her habit of confusing paradox with perversity or daubing some witless assertion with metaphor in an attempt to smarten it up: Joyce "pushes his pen about noisily and aimlessly as if it were a carpet-sweeper"; "Ibsen cried out for ideas for the same reason that men call out for water, because he had not got any".

The tone of such ersatz epigrams is that of the adolescent show-off: callowly clever and over-confidently contrary. And in a sense, this book discloses, Rebecca West remained fixated in this phase for life. . . . This late-teenage pattern of response—enjoying shocking others from a privileged position—was something she never broke free of. Reflecting the formative importance of her early family life, her autobiographical novel sequence, begun with *The Fountain Overflows* and intended, she said, as a "Saga of the Century", can't stop contemplating it. The lengthy first book covers just a brief span of her girlhood. By the end of *Cousin Rosamond,* the third volume in the series, Rose and Mary Aubrey—versions of Rebecca and her sister Winnie—are, though now mature women, still living like adolescents, obsessed by their youthful years and constantly harking back to them. Similarly, it seems, the as-yet-unpublished memoirs Rebecca wrote in later life endlessly returned to and re-worked her childhood background.

What she was most concerned with camouflaging, Glendinning shows, was the decamping of her feckless father from the family home. During her infancy, Cicely Fairfield, as she then was (she adopted the *nom de plume* Rebecca West in her late-teens arbitrarily and as a concession to her mother's qualms, she insisted—though it's hard to believe that the name of Ibsen's histrionic heroine hadn't a special appeal for her), lived in South London at 21 Streatham Place, just off Brixton Hill. A semi-rural backwater of market gardens, buttercups and stables, this was romanticized in her novels into a paradise of lush trees, graceful villas and gorgeous flowers "growing out of wet earth dark as plum cake". Like her two sisters, Cissie was enchanted by her father, a journalist and speculator. Regarding himself as one who had come down in the world, he dazzled his daughters with tales of grand antecedents: in later life, Rebecca would devise genealogies linking her to noble families; her sister Lettie, of a more religious disposition, traced the Fairfields back to Saint Margaret of Scotland, Saint Louis of France, two Spanish saints and a Russian one. But though Charles Fairfield harped on the family's glorious past, he did little for its floundering present. Chronically philandering and foot-loose, he eventually strayed away and stayed away: after a business trip to West Africa, he returned to England but not to his wife and daughters, taking himself off to Liverpool, where he remained for five years before dying destitute in Toxteth.

Not surprisingly, these paternal vagaries kindled in Cissie a fiery commitment to feminism. This first showed itself when she was fourteen and living with the family in genteel reduced circumstances in Edinburgh, from where she dispatched a letter to the *Scotsman* decrying "the subjection of women" and "sex degradation". After three years at RADA had convinced her that she wasn't suited to an actress's life—as Victoria Glendinning indicates, she was, with her facial twitch and psychosomatic rashes, too physiologically histrionic to be professionally theatrical—she began her journalistic career writing for the *Freewoman,* an organ of the suffragette campaign, and later the *Clarion,* with its socialist rallying calls.

These early articles—vigorously opinionated, courageously outspoken, often fierce and funny in their stinging, whiplash attacks on Establishment pomposity, complacency or hypocrisy—are arguably the most trenchant and stirring pieces Rebecca West ever wrote. This is partly because of the comparative brevity required—leaving no scope for the de luxe verbosity she allowed herself in later years. Another is the very clear-cut nature of the issues involved: blatant social and sexual inequities are bitingly denounced. Startlingly precocious, these short reviews and occasional terse essays sometimes collapse into self-advertising smartness but, at their best, have a cutting edge of real intellectual mettle.

Shortly after this extraordinary début, though, Rebecca's career changed course drastically: within just over a year, she'd moved from *Freewoman* to kept woman. (p. 431)

The New Woman then found herself living through the old, old story. Determined to stay with his wife Jane (an especial hate figure in Rebecca's later mythology), wanting just sporadic recreation and stimulation with his new lover, Wells housed her in obscure lodgings—at the seaside, in the country—visiting her irregularly and infrequently. Partly drawn to Wells because of what she'd seen as his paternal qualities—he was in his mid-forties to her early twenties—Rebecca was, in time, caught in a plight not dissimilar to her mother's. It's no puzzle to see why her first novel, *The Return of the Soldier,* should take male unreliability as its subject, with a shell-shocked husband going absent without leave from his marriage and being discovered doting on another woman.

As Rebecca worked on her next novel, *The Judge,* deep-rooted differences between her and Wells emerged on the literary level as well as in their antagonistic expectations about their affair. Wells disliked the book's saturated and amorphous nature: typically, Rebecca had scuppered the possibility of its following the course she first intended by overloading it with material about the central characters' earlier life. But, though antipathetic attitudes to writing increasingly divided the pair, what most contributed to their split was Rebecca's clamouring for marriage. As an ardent young radical, she had sarcastically denounced wifehood as often no more than prostitution. But as Wells had noticed, she was always "at once a formalist and a rebel"—or, as a friend later put it, "a combination of the most unconventional and conventional person in the world." Craving position and respectability as well as a reputation for daring talk and bold behaviour, she eventually left Wells. (pp. 431-32)

[With her marriage to financier Henry Andrews and] with the acquisition of Ibstone House—an eighteenth-century property in seventy acres, with 3,000 bottles in the wine-cellar, paintings several deep on the celadon green walls, flower bulbs ordered by the ton, and terraces adorned with antique sphinxes whose faces resembled Madame de Pompadour and Madame Du Barry—Rebecca continued that metamorphosis from *enfant terrible* to *grande dame* that was to reach its apotheosis in her final widowed years in Kingston House, Kensington. The imperious figure enthroned there in the gilt Regency chair with the claw feet and armrests carved as lions' heads seems a long way from the mocking, mutinous young suffragette. Yet this book lets you see what they shared: an unflagging determination to seize attention by being startlingly combative and self-assertive.

Though Glendinning begins by claiming that the story of Rebecca West is "the story of twentieth-century women", her biography convinces you that it's the opposite of this: passionately personal and self-centred. West's writings—fiction, polemic, reviews, investigative reporting, political commentary, travelogue—look wide-ranging. Her identities—Cissie Fairfield, "Aunty" Panther, Rebecca West, Mrs Henry Andrews—seem protean. But behind it all lies a stubbornly fixed and surprisingly unbudging idiosyncrasy. Far from being representative, she seeks to stamp her peculiar problems and obsessions on everything she surveys. *The Meaning of Treason*—a topic likely to strike a chord in one who felt she'd been so often betrayed—can be glossed by her in unusually subjective ways. *Black Lamb and Grey Falcon,* hailed by Glendinning as "a great work of romantic art", seems more an artless exercise in self-indulgence. Given Rebecca West's temperament, it was perhaps inevitable that the muddled vehemences of the Balkans should claim her quivering sympathy. But it's still surprising that a book purporting to offer serious historical and political analysis should end up as little more than a technicolour map of its author's personality and predicaments. Though written when she was almost fifty, its pages are hallmarked by her continuingly girlish traits. Mugged-up reelings-out of historical background redolent of the school swot alternate with high-coloured tableaux—lovely doomed empresses, noble monks, handsome peasants, vile tyrants—which remind you that the first author she admired was Alexandre Dumas, and underline the accuracy of Wells's claim, when she was sneering at his *Outline of History,* that she "wanted history full of wonderlands".

Like most of West's ambitious works, the book contrives to be not only overwrought ("It was the body of our death, it was the seed of the sin that is in us, it was the forge where the sword was wrought that shall slay us") and over-long but also over-simplified. The crudely polarized vision of the world she harboured—allies versus enemies, fine art versus coarse vulgarity, radiant virtue versus obscene evil—is weirdly projected on to the murky, problematic arena of the Balkans. A region riven by blood-feud, treachery and slaughter gets praised as the idyllic preserve of natural simplicity. In this "world where men are still men and women still women", homosexuality—another of West's bugbears (she declined to become a Roman Catholic because this would entail "constant and degrading contact with priests who are homosexual")—is happily absent, she feels sure. Beneath this hymning of the Balkans as a haven of healthy, uncomplicated relationships, Rebecca's yearnings for the straightforward partnership she never achieved can be heard. Glendinning's reminder that **Black Lamb and Grey Falcon** was written when the Andrewses' marriage was running into problems casts a sadder light on the paraded connubial cosiness—the ceaseless referrings and deferrings to "my husband"—that can seem so risible a feature to the book.

Fiction should have been a more promising field for an imagination that never lost a childlike power of unexpected, vivid response. Jagged mountain peaks perturbed her, Rebecca West said later in life, because they recalled the graphs of rising and falling copper prices her speculating father scrutinized so anxiously when she was a girl. Images of this kind, fresh from childhood memory, regularly vivify her often antique-sounding prose, so heavily encrusted with words like "clamant", "helleboric", "coign" and "volute". Looking back results in moments of pungent sensuous immediacy—as when harshly lit trees at a sickening party remind Rose Aubrey of "the prodigious green of vegetables I had sometimes eaten in my childhood, which had been boiled with pennies by cooks who knew nothing of metallic poisoning".

Modelling itself on the work of her idol, Proust, Rebecca West's "Saga of the Century" tries to emulate it by being long, nostalgic about childhood, full of musical reference and high society scenes. But personal proclivities intrude calamitously. Though Glendinning calls **The Fountain Overflows** "a generous book", it is frequently spiteful and self-regarding. Alongside a flattering picture of Rebecca as a musical prodigy with psychic gifts is set up a grotesque caricature of her loathed sister Lettie—excoriated, in the person of Cordelia Aubrey, as a soulless bossy prig who bawls out orders in her sleep, tortures the family's musical sensibilities by her mawkish and mechanical sawings of the violin, and attracts the embarrassing dotings of a lesbian frump in garish clothes (an earlier fiction, **The Salt of the Earth,** had a character resembling Lettie poisoned). For Proust's emotional and psychological subtleties, the sequence substitutes West's own naively hierarchized view of life: saints, artists, vulgarians, villains.

Those in the former two categories tend to be impeccably turned out; those in the latter two, hideously dressed. And this sartorial signalling is symptomatic. Near the start of **Black Lamb and Grey Falcon,** West wept over some embroidered frocks that had run in the wash, claiming they had been "important testimony". . . . In **Sunflower** she spoke of "the beauty of tragedy, and the beauty of good clothes, which is one and the same beauty". Rebecca West's career, Victoria Glendinning declares in her introduction, "has turned out to be a sadder story than I expected". One dispiriting feature is the ossifying of

the scathing young suffragette—who scoffed that "women who spend their mornings hovering round drapery shops are hardly dignified"—into the dressy attitudinizer who couldn't distinguish between high culture and *haute couture*. (p. 432)

Peter Kemp, "Literary Lives: The Illusive . . . ," in The Times Literary Supplement, No. 4386, April 24, 1987, pp. 431-32.

A. S. BYATT

[*Byatt, an English critic, educator, novelist, short story writer, and editor, is a well known literary figure. Her fiction includes two novels of a planned tetralogy,* The Virgin in the Garden *(1978) and* Still Life *(1985)—both of which have been praised for their intellectual ambition and post-modernist techniques and perspectives—as well as the short story collection* Sugar and Other Stories *(1987). Among her critical works are studies of William Wordsworth and Samuel Taylor Coleridge, Iris Murdoch, and George Eliot. In the following excerpt, Byatt praises Glendinning as a tactful biographer who offers new insights on West's marriage; Byatt further suggests that Glendinning was dismayed by West's penchant for self-destructiveness.*]

The early pages of Victoria Glendinning's **Rebecca West: A Life** give hints that this always courteous and tactful biographer feels less than perfect ease with her latest subject. The epigraphs are all chosen from Rebecca West. Two warn that what people say about each other, and even more, about themselves, is a form of fiction and untrustworthy. The other says that good biography, like good fiction, 'comes down to a study of original sin, of our own inherent disposition to choose death when we ought to choose life.' I get the impression—faint but persistent—that Ms Glendinning is moved to a pained exasperation with Dame Rebecca's more self-destructive choices, and also with a capriciousness, a tendency to unreason, to embroider and distort facts, which render her untrustworthy.

Rebecca West was various if not Protean—the same trenchant wit spoke through the novelist, the journalist, the political thinker, the feminist, the literary critic. It was a wit which could modulate into sentiment, or become rigid with indignation, darting and precise and a little out of control. Victoria Glendinning sees West's life and work as a product of an unresolved conflict between her sexuality, which included her socially conditioned idea of what a 'real woman' should be, and her intelligence, which she feared made her unacceptable to men. Rebecca West herself wrote 'I have never been able to write with anything more than the left hand of my mind; the right hand has always been engaged in something to do with personal relations.' And on the first page of her unpublished memoirs: 'I was never able to lead the life of a writer because of these two overriding factors, my sexual life, or rather death, and my politics.' (p. 16)

Victoria Glendinning treats [West's sexual] relationships with a kind of appalled and occasionally amused sympathy, like a good clear-minded friend unable to warn another woman about inevitable disaster and disillusion. On Rebecca West's eventual husband, Henry Andrews, about whom I was most curious, she is illuminating. Henry, by this account, was an amateur scholar and gentleman, and gave Rebecca what she partly wanted, a respectable country life in a lovely house, cherishing furniture and local friends, gardening, preserving fruit. West seems to have loved him partly because, like herself, he had acquired, rather than inherited, his position and identity. . . . Discovering his many infidelities after his death, West became bitter. 'I *understand* the male attitude but don't *like* it. I don't think it's pleasant for a husband whose wife is successful to feel an irresistible compulsion to go off with a tart. . . . There is something so desperately unlovable, even unlikeable, about the male sex.' This biography makes clear that the central problem of her life, both privately and in public, as a convinced and eloquent feminist, was the relations between men and women.

There is much else in this brief biography, however, ranging from precisely described sensual pleasure in lobsters and *haute couture* to descriptions of West's tenaciously held and often auto-destructive political attitudes, whether in relation to the Balkans, to the Nuremberg trials and capital punishment, or to McCarthy's Communist witchhunts in the 1950s, where her fear of Russian domination led her to some extravagant statements. There is a persistent paranoia, leading to the writing, rewriting, sending and occasional repression of a series of hysterical (and often hysterically funny), furious letters of condemnation to friends and family. There are epigrams and shrewd literary insights, which were expected. She was a great survivor and a doughty fighter; she loved white satin and Bonnard's colours and lobsters. But she wrote 'A fresh lobster does not give as much pleasure to the consumer as a stale one will give him pain' prefacing this with 'the bad is more easily perceived than the good.' Victoria Glendinning, resolutely even-handed, appears to have been surprised by the preponderance of the bad and the stale and painful in this variegated life. Some of her best pages are on Rebecca West's Manichaeism, which West herself analysed in her marvellous short life of St Augustine and in **Black Lamb and Grey Falcon**. The world, she felt, inclined towards the dark, as H. G. Wells, that tough optimist, had said she herself did, telling her 'It is your nature to darken your world.' . . . Victoria Glendinning contemplates this darkness ruefully, with dignity, and says what can be said for the vivid, the lively, the bright. (pp. 16, 21)

A. S. Byatt, "Towards the Dark," in Books, *No. 3, June, 1987, pp. 16, 21.*

MOLLY TIBBS

Rebecca West knew that there was something in herself that invited tragedy—although she was excellent at surmounting disaster, and could scribble a dinner menu while her heart was breaking—and Victoria Glendinning found that her life was, indeed, a sadder story than she had expected. The two standards upon which the canopy of tragedy was erected consisted of the defection of Rebecca's philandering father when she was only eight years old, and the long and damaging liaison with married, cake-eating H. G. Wells, whom she loved dearly, and who confessed in later life that he ought to have liberated her. The discomposing birth of their son, Anthony West, and his resentment at his uncomfortable status provided a further theme of bitterness, and, we learn, Lord Beaverbrook's failure to satisfy Rebecca's passionate expectations upset her emotionally for a number of years. H. G. Wells once wrote that she had a 'splendid *disturbed* brain' and Victoria Glendinning comments pithily [in *Rebecca West: A Life*] that 'Its splendour owed something to its disturbance. There is always a price to pay.'

Miss Glendinning has a gift for encapsulating insights into her subjects' personalities in striking epigrammatic lines, such as 'Those who found her imperious could not possibly know that she saw herself as an underdog.' It is significant that Rebecca West, who had part consciously and part unconsciously obfuscated and fudged the sensitive areas of her life, ultimately chose a talented biographer who is psychologically skilled, accurate

and fair. . . . The burden of papers was, as might be expected, far from light, Rebecca's 'most passionate concerns were art, morality, history and politics' and her long life in pursuance of those concerns was lived to the full, with an overflowing fountain of letters and autobiographical writings. She kept on re-writing her life.

Certain papers held in the Beinecke Library at Yale were not made available to this official biographer, because of a restriction placed on them by Rebecca West during her lifetime: these include her letters from H. G. Wells and her correspondence with her husband, Henry Andrews. This unfortunate limitation does not, however, appear to detract from a balanced biography. The schooldays could have received a little more attention. There is ample treatment of the political writings and journalistic achievements. Difficult, and, one suspects, comparatively uncongenial aspects, such as the Yugoslavian commitment, are tackled head-on, and with authority. Miss Glendinning's introductory *mot* is that Rebecca West's life is the paradigm of twentieth-century woman, and although at first sight this is a mere, fashionable gambit, she triumphantly pursues her argument that 'she was both an agent for change and a victim of change' to its justification. (pp. 333-34)

Molly Tibbs, "A Balanced Biography of Rebecca West," in Contemporary Review, *Vol. 250, No. 1457, June, 1987, pp. 333-34.*

SARA MAITLAND

[Maitland is an English novelist, short story writer, and essayist. In her works, she blends Christian principles and feminist ideals. She won the Somerset Maugham Award for her first novel, Daughter of Jerusalem *(1978; published in the United States as* Languages of Love, *1981). Her more recent fiction includes a collection of short stories,* Telling Tales *(1983), and a novel,* Virgin Territory *(1984); she has also been a frequent contributor to feminist anthologies. In the following excerpt, Maitland comments that Glendinning's biography offers a careful analysis of West's private conflicts but fails to provide insights on West's public persona, in particular her involvement with feminism.]*

[No] one would question either Rebecca West's significance in literature and ideas, nor Victoria Glendinning's competence as a biographer. I can only conclude that by the time I came to read [**Rebecca West: A Life**] I was weary with the whole idea of literary biography—the exaltation and conflation of the person and her works—because I ended up simply bored, and I do not know why. I wished rather that Glendinning had given us more background: for example, West's early involvement with militant suffragism was crucial to her and to her whole life and development—Glendinning makes this clear, but she gives insufficient information about the wider context of feminism and the suffrage struggle and therefore doesn't make it clear why *that*—rather than something else—should have so engaged West. (In fairness, though, Glendinning is much better at providing background on Yugoslavia and West's later involvement there.)

Primarily, Glendinning is concerned with West's emotional and literary activities, which, of course, is fair enough for a biographer, but for one who existed so much 'in the world' as West the reader needs more history and less hysteria. Given Anthony West's prominent account of his mother's dealings with him, Glendinning probably does have some obligation to set the record straight, or at least straighter, and she manages to be meticulously careful about the ins-and-outs of that poisonous mother-son relationship; but in the last analysis I am more interested in the public figure and her cultural location than in the private neurosis of someone I can never now meet, and this balance is not always sufficiently well maintained. West is so dashing as well as so profound in her public persona, that her emotional life seems particularly insignificant, especially as Glendinning does not adequately explain or explore the gap between the two.

But following my logic no biographies would be written. This one is honest, well informed, thorough and as generous as possible to almost all the parties. But I'd rather read West's own writing.

Sara Maitland, "Remarkable Women," in The Listener, Vol. 117, No. 3016, June 18, 1987, p. 24.

JUSTIN KAPLAN

[Kaplan, an American biographer, editor, and educator, has received the National Book Award and the Pulitzer Prize for his biography of Mark Twain, Mr. Clemens and Mark Twain (1966), and the American Book Award for Walt Whitman: A Life (1981). In the following excerpt, he characterizes Glendinning's account as candid and evenhanded, though at times inadequate and graceless.]

Starting with *The Return of the Soldier* in 1918, Rebecca West published half a dozen significant novels in the United States and her native Britain. But it was chiefly as a fiercely engaged, quite personal critic, journalist and travel writer that she established her reputation. Her most celebrated book, *Black Lamb and Grey Falcon* (1941)—500,000 words about Yugoslavia—was a work of romantic art in the tradition of George Borrow, Charles Doughty and T. E. Lawrence. Victoria Glendinning, the author of [*Rebecca West: A Life*], quotes John Gunther's recognition that *Black Lamb and Grey Falcon,* for all its historical and descriptive substance, was eventually "not so much a book about Yugoslavia as a book about Rebecca West." She approached the geopolitical reality of the Balkans and the wreckage of the Austro-Hungarian Empire as if it were a model for her own psyche, a battlefield for eros and thanatos, "warlike romantics" and "warlike intellectuals," male and female principles.

By 1947, when she was 55 years old, *Time* magazine was calling her "indisputably the world's No. 1 woman writer." She had just published *The Meaning of Treason,* a study of the Judas principle as she saw it unfold during the trials of William Joyce (as Lord Haw-Haw he had broadcast Nazi propaganda to wartime Britain) and others charged with betraying a primary allegiance. Separately and cumulatively, however, *Black Lamb and Grey Falcon,* in which she sided with the Serbian nationalist Draza Mihajlovic against the Communist Marshal Tito, and *The Meaning of Treason,* which she updated in 1964 to include Kim Philby, Guy Burgess and Donald Maclean, hardened her into zealotry. Ms. Glendinning reports that West "compiled a private list of closet Communists mainly in British public life which tended to include anyone who had crossed swords with her and which, were it not for her own high seriousness, would be hilarious."

Although graceless, Ms. Glendinning's description is admirably candid. Throughout the book she shows West to be a formidable, frequently rebarbative public and private person with a taste for histrionics (she had originally planned to be an actress). Virginia Woolf told her sister Vanessa Bell that West was "hard as nails, very distrustful, and no beauty . . . a cross between a charwoman and a gipsy, but as tenacious as

a terrier." H. G. Wells, West's lover for 10 years and the father of her son, Anthony, said that she possessed "a curious mixture of maturity and infantilism" and "a splendid *disturbed* brain." He admired her rough-tongued wit even though he was one of its targets. "All our youth," she said, surveying the post-Victorian literary scene, "the Big Four [Wells, George Bernard Shaw, John Galsworthy, Arnold Bennett] hung about the houses of our minds like Uncles." . . .

Apart from her liaison with Wells, West had an unreciprocated passion for the press magnate Lord Beaverbrook and a 38-year marriage to a businessman-dilettante, Harry Andrews, known to the Bloomsbury circle as Chinese Torture. Like the other two, Andrews was a habitual philanderer. The closest she knew to happiness with him, West said, was "the relief I felt when he died." There were plenty of other men in her life, among them John Gunther, the French diplomat and boudoir athlete Prince Antoine Bibesco and Francis Biddle, the American chief prosecutor at the Nuremberg trials. Nevertheless, she felt that there was "something in me" that put men off and terrified several of them into impotence. It was mainly for this reason, according to Ms. Glendinning, that West, then in her mid-30's, decided to be psychoanalyzed. . . .

[Glendinning] testifies with considerable conviction to West's contradictory personality, her abiding frustrations and resentments, her alternations of vanity and self-hatred. The many names she lived under may be an index of her turbulent identities. Soon after she made her start on *The Freewoman*, a feminist weekly, Cicely Isabel Fairfield, who signed letters to her sisters "Anne" and in married life became Mrs. Henry Andrews, took the pseudonym Rebecca West from a character in Ibsen's *Rosmersholm.* Ibsen's Rebecca West, the mistress of a married man, eventually drowns herself. West "came to regret the Ibsen connection," Ms. Glendinning says, "insisting that she chose the name in a hurry when the paper was going to press." During her affair with Wells, she was "Panther" to his "Jaguar"; they named their son Anthony Panther West; and he in turn was brought up to call his mother "Panther" or "Auntie Panther." In her last years some of these names "clashed in my head," West said. "I could not choose between them."

"It has turned out to be a sadder story than I expected," Ms. Glendinning writes. Lying close to the heart of this sadness are West's long, bitter, mutually recriminatory dealings with her son. . . . In her attempt to rescue West from Gehenna, Ms. Glendinning is an evenhanded advocate for the claims and counterclaims of both Rebecca and Anthony and, additionally, those of Wells, who was married and refused to divorce his wife, Jane, despite Rebecca's periodic ultimatums. By taking Rebecca to bed he had been a willing accessory to her sexual liberation. But once Anthony was born, Wells was unable to recognize that it was far more difficult for Rebecca to be a "free mother" than a "free woman." "For ten years I've shaped my life mainly to repair the carelessness of one moment," Wells wrote to her. "It has been no good and I am tired of it."

The type of swift biographical portrait and conspectus that Ms. Glendinning aimed to write involves literary standards she is often not up to. There are many incoherences, disjunctions, pat psychological formulations and passages of mechanical narration in which time passes as on a clock. She is reluctant to speculate when speculation appears to be most in order, for example about the authorship of a series of vicious but undeniably informed letters Rebecca received after her marriage.

Ms. Glendinning's comment on them is hardly to the point: "By a meaningless coincidence, they read like a vulgar parody of Virginia Woolf's elliptic diary notes." Her contextual explanations—for example, of the nonaggression pact between Prince Paul, the regent of Yugoslavia, and the Axis powers—supply the obvious or omit the essential. Much to her credit, however, she resists the temptation to depersonalize and mythologize West into a simple emblem of struggle against gender stereotypes, although that struggle is a vital part of the story. West comes through as her own woman. Wells said, "I had never met anything like her before, and I doubt if there was anything like her before."

Justin Kaplan, "*Men Had Reason to Fear,*" *in* The New York Times Book Review, *October 18, 1987, p. 3.*

SAMUEL HYNES

[*Hynes, an American critic and educator, has written and edited numerous studies of English literature and literary figures. He is the author of the introduction to* Rebecca West, a Celebration: A Selection of Her Writings Chosen by Her Publisher and Rebecca West *(1977). In the following excerpt Hynes praises Glendinning's economical biography, and offers an overview of West's life and career, characterizing her as a woman whose extraordinary ideas made her a social and intellectual outcast.*]

When in the spring of 1912, a young English writer named Cicely Fairfield decided to call herself Rebecca West, it was assumed that she had taken her new name from the rebellious heroine of Ibsen's *Rosmersholm.* Ibsen had created The New Woman, and it was reasonable that a 20-year-old girl who was just setting out to write about social and sexual matters in a journal called *The Freewoman,* and who intended to be a free woman in her own life, should claim an alliance with him.

But there was another, earlier Rebecca West who was, one might argue, a more significant ancestor. That Rebecca West was one of four English women executed for witchcraft in 1647. Two of the four repented, but West and one other "dyed very Stuburn, and Refractory with out any remors, or seeming Terror of Conscience for their abominable Witchcraft." ... The later Rebecca West didn't die for her beliefs and practices; rather, she made a reputation out of them, and a long, successful career. But her Stubborn and Refractory ways caused her trouble all her life, and made her the problematic figure that she was, both in the world of letters and in English society—a disturbing, threatening, unclassifiable female who said what she thought and did what she wanted.

It doesn't seem too fanciful to call such a woman a witch. For witches are women who live outside society's limits of toleration and would rather die than come in, and West was that sort of woman. And witches have more power than men think they should have, and she was that sort, too. The power that she had was, first of all, intellectual: she was brighter than most men, and that made men nervous. It was also verbal: she had a witty, acerbic style, and she used it like a knife. And as if that weren't enough, she had sexual power: she was a beauty, but more than that, she was clearly a woman of great sexual force—such force, indeed, that she came to believe that she rendered some men impotent simply by her own sexual energy.

With such powers, it is not surprising that she made herself known in London literary circles very quickly. She was not yet 20 when she began writing for *The Freewoman,* 23 when she published her lively, irreverent book on Henry James,

barely 25 when *The Return of the Soldier,* her brilliant first novel, appeared. By the end of the war, she had made her reputation as a journalist in England, and was beginning to be known in the United States. (pp. 46-7)

But she had made another kind of reputation as well. She had had an affair with H. G. Wells and had borne a son; and what was worse from society's point of view, she had kept the child with her (being a Stubborn and Refractory woman). So she became to conventional people a shameless hussy, and to more liberal ones England's principal example of The Liberated Woman. The tinge of notoriety, of the not-quite-acceptable person, stayed with her; even now I would guess that more people know that Rebecca West had Wells's bastard than know the title of any book she wrote.

Rebecca West hated her reputation as a rebel, though it was never in her nature to cease thinking rebelliously. She felt that it had excluded her from her rightful position in the hierarchy of letters, not only in her early, outrageous days, but even at end of her long life. When the *Times Literary Supplement* published a front-page celebration of her work on the occasion of her 81st birthday, she wrote gratefully to the editor, praising him for his courage. "I have forced my way into recognition," she wrote, "but I am treated as a witch, somebody to be shunned. My books . . . have always been treated as if they were maleficent spells."

By the time she wrote that letter, West had written the books on which her literary reputation rests, or would rest if it were stable—teeters is perhaps a better word: six novels, three books of criticism, the monumental, unclassifiable *Black Lamb and Grey Falcon,* the two volumes of postwar trials. And she had gathered her share of praise, one might think. *Time* had called her "the world's No. 1 woman writer," and the *Evening Standard* had billed her as "The Greates Journalist of Our Time." She was rich and famous, and she was a Dame Commander of the Order of the British Empire. Yet she saw herself as a witch in the world's eyes, a woman who had had to force herself into recognition. Whatever the praise, it had been insufficient; there was more to Rebecca West than that.

One obstacle to recognition, in her mind, was clearly gender. She saw herself not simply as an unappreciated writer, but as a shunned woman. Gender was a subject that she had thought and written about all her life, from her first suffragist articles to her late, unpublished memoirs. Though she was a feminist, she was not optimistic about the relation between the sexes. Men, she concluded, do not like women; "or perhaps men do not like, period." She thought it possible that men are deficient in the capacity for love, and she found it difficult to love them. . . . (pp. 47-8)

Yet, bad bargain though they were, men were necessary to women, even to a woman as independent as Rebecca West was. How else is one to explain the most surprising event in her whole life, her marriage? In 1930, when it took place, she was world-famous as a journalist, socially in demand for her wit and beauty, and self-supporting on a fairly grand scale. She spent summers on the Riviera, wore elegant Paris clothes, and sent her son to a Public School. Yet she married Henry Andrews, who was as dull as an English summer, an unsuccessful banker whose strongest trait was his incompetence. . . . West complained endlessly about him to her friends, but the marriage lasted until his death in 1968. Evidently the condition of being married gave her something that she needed. But it also took something—took energy, took time, took self-respect when her husband began to stray—that was drained from her work, and diminished her accomplishment. Or so she thought.

But if it had not been Henry it would have been somebody else, as she sadly recognized, for sexuality was an essential element of her being. . . . [The] first page of her unpublished memoirs contains this sentence: "I was never able to lead the life of a writer because of these two overriding factors, my sexual life, or rather death, and my politics." . . .

Sex and politics appear in that sentence as obstacles to a full literary life, but they were also two preoccupying subjects of West's work. There were others, too: law, history, religion, psychology, literature. We are, I trust, beyond the point of calling such copious minds masculine; but it is nevertheless true that she ranged more widely in her interests, and put more various ideas into her writing, than any other woman writing in English in this century has done. And perhaps that too was a factor in her lack of recognition, for she could not be contained within any category into which woman writers could be assigned. She said as much to Victoria Glendinning, near the end of her life: "I should like to have been a novelist. I should like to have been a historian." Glendinning replied, as all of us would: "But you are a novelist, you are a historian." But the point is that she wasn't: she wasn't, that is, that comfortable type, the woman novelist, nor even a woman historian. She wasn't a woman anything. Her English publisher, Jonathan Cape, called her "a writer of scattered books," and that is accurate; but it isn't a category to make a reputation in.

Still, Cape got the first term right: she was, above all, a writer. Not a journalist, not a woman writer, but simply a writer, an artist who wrote wonderful prose, who took chances with language and cadence, and who wrote poetically even of prosaic subjects. To this one should add that she was, all her life, a speculative writer, moving through and beyond the observed facts to moral meanings. Here, as an example of what I mean, is the end of her account of the trial of John Amery, convicted of high treason in a London court after the war. Before passing judgment, the judge spoke to Amery, reminding him that British internees had warned him of his crime. His remarks seemed to be irrelevant, at that point in the trial. "Yet," West wrote:

> if what the Judge said had little application to Amery, he seemed to say it because his mind had been shocked into flight underground to some place near the sources of our general destiny. The Judge said slowly, with accusation and querulous wonder in his voice, "They called you traitor and you heard them." It was as if he spoke to all men, marveling at their knowledge of good and evil and their preference for evil, and looking at his own heart from far away that he might see the cause.

That is a characteristic passage—so deliberately cadenced and so expansive, moving from one man in a courtroom to our general destiny, and the evil in the hearts of men.

One might argue that the wonderment that she heard in the judge's voice was West's real subject all of her life—that men should know good and evil, and choose evil. She scrutinized that subject from many angles, but she found no orthodox institutional explanation of it. She called herself a Socialist, but she had no party; she professed to believe in the Christian conception of man, but she had no church. In her thinking, as in her living, she was herself.

I have wondered, thinking about her life and work, whether the biography of such a woman is not inevitably a diminishment of her. Here is the life, so troubled and untidy, so full of the failures of love and the small vanities and follies of anybody's existence. And there is the work, so intelligent, so searching, and so individual. Does one explain the other? Only in the most superficial sense, I think. (p. 48)

[One] must admire the thoroughness and economy with which [Glendinning's *Rebecca West: A Life*] gets a long life told— all the affairs, the troubles with her son, the unhappy marriage, the long battle with old age—and with tact and sympathy. Glendinning is a skillful biographer, and she is also clearly a kind and intelligent woman. Yet her book does diminish her subject, because it does not offer a convincing, full-face portrait of the other side of Rebecca West—of the witch, whose powers of thought and imagination were great enough to write those extraordinary books. The books are mentioned here, along the way, but they are not really confronted, and the ideas and the human perplexities that troubled her mind, and drove her into art, are here more like interruptions in the story than like obsessions.

For that other story, the witch's story, we will have to wait. . . . Perhaps it can only be discovered in Rebecca West's own version, in the books that she wrote; perhaps it is only there that her extraordinary power will reveal itself, undiminished by the tribulations and pleasures of a woman's life. (pp. 48-9)

Samuel Hynes, "The Wild West," in The New Republic, *Vol. 197, No. 16, October 19, 1987, pp. 46-9.*

JOHN GROSS

[*Gross, an English biographer and literary critic, is the author of works on Charles Dickens, Rudyard Kipling, and James Joyce. He is also the editor of* The Oxford Book of Aphorisms. *In the following excerpt, Gross finds Glendinning's book compelling, but faults her for failing to analyze in depth West's literary and political life.*]

Rebecca West spend much of her long life amid the fumes of private quarrels and public controversy. Her gifts were formidable but often misdirected, and her contradictions were almost as impressive as her achievements. She was even better than most of us at believing what she wanted to believe.

All this makes her an exceptionally tricky subject for a biographer, and although Victoria Glendinning has already proved her mettle with admirable biographies of Elizabeth Bowen, Vita Sackville-West and Edith Sitwell, in Rebecca West she faced an altogether more daunting challenge. It wasn't made any easier by the fact that she was committed to writing a relatively short book, as Rebecca West requested in her will. . . .

The first thing to say about *Rebecca West: A Life* is that, like Ms. Glendinning's earlier biographies, it is consistently readable. Her wit is unforced, her narrative glides along easily and compellingly. The book's second obvious virtue is that it displays Ms. Glendinning's feeling for character to full advantage.

The early chapters, for example, have many of the qualities of a good novel, of the old-fashioned generation-spanning variety. The account of how the young Cissie Fairfield evolved into Rebecca West . . . lays open rich layers of social history; and while it would have been easy to have drawn up a stern indictment against her father—a philandering, fantasy-spinning journalist who abandoned his family and ultimately came to nothing—Ms. Glendinning is at least as interested in conveying his charm, his pathos and above all the disturbing spell he cast over his daughter.

An even finer balance of sympathies is in evidence when we come to the celebrated, perhaps too celebrated, affair with H. G. Wells, which began when Rebecca West was 20, and its bitter aftermath, her endless feuding with the child neither she nor Wells had originally bargained for, Anthony West. Ms. Glendinning patiently unravels the rights and wrongs, and recognizes that it was the affinities between mother and son no less than their grievances that helped to inflame the conflict: "She could read his psychological processes as fluently as he could read hers, and each added a fabulist's gloss to every detail of every misunderstanding."

The imbroglio with Wells, though one rather flinches from reading any more about it, could hardly fail to lack dramatic interest. What is more surprising is that the most gripping pages of the book should turn out to be the account of Rebecca West's marriage, which lasted for nearly 40 years, to the banker turned freelance financier Henry Andrews.

Andrews was scholarly and well-intentioned; he was also vague and slow-moving . . . , and very far from being the pillar of strength Rebecca West had been looking for when she willed herself into falling in love with him. At one stage, and you suspect she might have said the same thing at many other stages, she confided to a friend that he was "complete hell to live with."

Yet the two of them made the marriage work, and achieved a fair degree of happiness. As Ms. Glendinning says, in one of her penetrating asides, "the ideal Rebecca clung to the ideal Henry, however much the selves that they were in everyday life fell short of those ideals."

Ms. Glendinning writes almost equally well about Rebecca West's lesser affairs, notably her frustrated passion for the press baron Lord Beaverbrook, and she conjures up many other aspects of her private life with shrewdness and sympathy. As long as she sticks to the personal and the domestic, her account could hardly be improved on.

But an adequate appraisal of Rebecca West ought to pay at least as much attention to the literary and the political. What are we to make of her as a writer?

"Her books remain, and are read," says Ms. Glendinning. "This is what matters." But what we think of the books when we have read them also matters, and it seems to me that as a novelist, at least, her lasting importance is far from being as self-evident as Ms. Glendinning seems to imply. The case needs to be argued.

Her own stature as a writer is bound to have some effect on how we take the slashing dismissals of other writers—Tolstoy, Yeats, Thomas Hardy, scores of others—that were part of her stock in trade, and that Ms. Glendinning tends to report neutrally. Is it quite enough to say that "reverential postures did not come naturally to Rebecca West"?

What is beyond dispute, I think, is that she was a superb journalist, and that her greatest achievements are to be found among what might loosely be termed her journalistic writings: *Black Lamb and Grey Falcon,* the travel book about Yugoslavia that is so much more than a travel book, and her two post-World War II studies of treachery, espionage and crime, *The Meaning of Treason* and *A Train of Powder.*

To do justice to those works, however, you have to be prepared to grapple with their politics, and Ms. Glendinning backs away. While I can understand her reluctance to get involved in the ferocious disputes about wartime Yugoslavia reflected in *Black Lamb and Grey Falcon,* I don't think that as a biographer she can afford to be quite so evasive; and as for her gingerly discussion of *The Meaning of Treason,* she fails to set Rebecca West's anticommunism properly in context or bring out its true importance. She comes close, in fact, to treating it as a form of mental disturbance.

Good though all the good things in Ms. Glendinning's books are, they leave a lot unsaid.

            *John Gross, in a review of "Rebecca West: A Life,"
            in* The New York Times, *October 20, 1987, p. C21.*

PENELOPE FITZGERALD

[*In the following excerpt Fitzgerald examines the revelations of personal psychology to be found in West's books, characterizing her as a writer of passionate commitment and genius. Fitzgerald finds Glendinning's biography to be an objective and skillful recounting of a rich life.*]

There were giant-killers in those days. Storm Jameson, rallying English writers in defence of peace and collective security, had to toss up to decide between Rebecca West and Rose Macaulay for the place of honour. Between these three women enough power should have been generated even for an impossible cause. They were tireless collectors of facts . . . and what courage they showed, what endurance, what determination to call the world sharply to order, what unanswerable wit, what impatience for justice. They were all prepared to outface the mighty, but they also judged themselves, on occasion, more strictly than anyone else would have dared. . . . 'As we grow older,' said Rebecca West, 'and like ourselves less and less, we apply our critical experience as a basis for criticising our own consciences.' It isn't surprising that her son grew up with the 'idea that a woman was the thing to be, and that I had somehow done wrong by being a male.'

But Rebecca also wrote in her old age: 'I was never able to lead the life of a writer because of these two overriding factors, my sexual life, or rather death, and my politics.' Here she is both attacking and defending herself, for she felt that the world, on the whole, had treated her basely. From the age of 18 she made her own life, but she was not altogether satisfied with the results. She would have liked to subsume, perhaps, the lives of both her sisters, Lettie, the correct benevolent professional woman, Winnie, the contented housewife, 'living decently in a house with children'. She would have liked to live in Rosmersholm without drowning herself, and in the doll's house without letting it defeat her. Her voice, which she found so early, is that of an elder sister, not the youngest. Samuel Hynes has even called it 'episcopal'—'praising the righteous, condemning heretics, explaining doctrine'. She found it easy to attract, almost as easy to dominate, and 'if people do not have the face of the age set clear before them, they begin to imagine it.' Authority, then, became a duty, and yet 'I could have done it,' she believed at times, 'if anybody had let me, simply by being a human being.'

Some of her first pieces, for the *Freewoman,* the socialist *Clarion* and the *New Statesman,* were reprinted by Virago in 1982. They were written in her teens, or just out of them, when she first arrived in London, a phenomenon, a marvellous girl, reckless, restless, brilliant and indignant. All her life she remained pre-eminently a journalist. To the very end, in illness, in fury, in distress, and when almost spent, she continued to react, as a plant does to the light, to new information or even to gossip. She was always on the alert, as Our Correspondent from the moral strongholds of the 20th century. Her first novel, however, the beautiful *Return of the Soldier* (1918), seemed to class her as what was then called a 'psychopathological writer'—with her older friend May Sinclair, who had organised London's first medico-psychological clinic. *The Return* is the case-history of an officer invalided home from the trenches. He is an amnesiac who cannot react either to his wife or to the memory of his dead child. His only surviving emotion is for a girl he once loved, who by now is a dreary little straw-hatted woman, 'repulsively' faded and poor. This woman courageously shows him the dead son's clothes and toys, which have been locked away. He is cured, but this, of course, means that he will have to return to the Front.

When Rebecca called this novel 'rather Conradesque', she was thinking of the unvoiced struggle between good and evil, woman's attempt to heal, man's invention of war. In 1922, when Freud's *Beyond the Pleasure Principle* appeared in translation, she related his theory to her own view of the life-and-death struggle: it became, for her, part of the fierce self-justification of a natural fighter—she did not hold with Freud's majestic hypothesis that human beings unconsciously recognised the 'sublime necessity' of the return to the inorganic state. Like many passionately committed writers, she created a God and then took Him to task for falling short of her standards. Her case against Him was that He made sacrifice and suffering a condition of redemption: 'pain is the proper price for any good thing.' This was also the basis of her complaint against Tolstoy and against St Augustine, whose life she was commissioned to write in 1933: he 'intellectualised with all the force of his genius' the idea of atonement through suffering. Rebecca set herself to wipe out not guilt but cruelty, by the exercise of reason. *The Harsh Voice* and the much later *The Birds Fall Down*, the monumental *Black Lamb and Grey Falcon* and *The Meaning of Treason* are essentially variations of the same battle. Blake, she believed, was on her side, so was Lawrence—though this disconcertingly meant claiming both of them as champions of the mind. 'The mind must walk proudly and always armed,' she wrote, 'that it shall not be robbed of its power.' What was her mind like, though—'her splendid disturbed brain', as Wells called it—and how far did she ever free it, if that was what she wanted to do, from her emotions? It has been called androgynous, but May Sinclair came closer to it when she said: 'Genius is giving you another sex inside yourself, and a stronger one, to plague you with.'

This plague took the form of an extreme temperament. All her life Rebecca West was betrayed by the physical, collapsing under stress into illness and even hallucination. She was a romantic in the highest sense of demanding universal solutions. 'I believe in the Christian conception of man and the French Revolution's interpretation of his political necessities.' But she was also romantic in a much simpler sense. *The Return of the Soldier* takes place in ancestral Baldry Court, perfect in its 'green pleasantness', except that the post arrives too late to be brought up with the morning tea. *Parthenope* is set in Currivel Lodge with its haunted croquet lawn. The character of Nikolai in *The Birds Fall Down* was based on a Russian tutor—though he has become a Russian count. Isabelle, the heroine of *The Thinking Reed,* is young, exceedingly beautiful, 'nearly exceedingly rich', tragically widowed. She hunts the wild boar,

her underwear is made to measure, her first lover 'was not less beautiful as a man than she was as a woman'. As a novelist, Rebecca West liked to write about people who were rich or good-looking or high-born or all three, and her public liked to read about them. There was a converse: she found it difficult to forgive ugliness or coarseness—the crowds outside the court in the Stephen Ward case were worse because they had 'cheap dentures'. All this was part of the great impatient shake with which she left the narrowness and just-respectability of her early life. As her son was to put it, 'shabby-genteel life in Edinburgh marked those who had to endure it to the bone.' *The Thinking Reed* was said to be about 'the effect of riches on people, and the effect of men on women, both forms of slavery', but, like *The Great Gatsby*, it shows that although money produces corruption, it also produces an enviable and civilised way of living, and there is nothing we can do about it. Good writers are seldom honest enough to admit this, but Rebecca West did admit it. With her limitless energy and enthusiasm, she called for harmony, but not for moderation. All that the reader can do, very often, is to trust the driver as her arguments bowl along in splendid sentences or collect themselves for a pause. 'Men and women see totally different aspects of reality.' 'A great deal of what Kafka wrote is not worth studying.' 'Authentic art never has an explicit religious and moral content.' These are sweeping statements—though sweeping, of course, can be a worthwhile activity.

Victoria Glendinning says in the introduction to [*Rebecca West: A Life*], that it is 'the story of 20th-century woman', but that it is a sadder story than she had expected. She has divided her book into episodes: 'Cissie', the unstoppable young new arrival in London; 'Panther' (this was Wells's name for her), fearlessly launching into questions of history, politics and morality, and into bed with Wells; 'Sunflower', the fiery successful international author and unsuccessful mistress of Beaverbrook; 'Mrs Henry Andrews', the awkwardly married famous writer; 'Dame Rebecca'. The divisions are helpful, though rather like breakwaters trying to hold back a high tide. It is a fine biography, which for several reasons can't have been easy to write. To start with, Stanley Olson, who became a friend of Dame Rebecca's in 1974, was entrusted with the full-length Life. To conform with this, Victoria Glendinning decided to cut down on the later years. Rebecca lived to be 90, and the elision somewhat weakens the sense of endurance and of seeing the century through, also of that indestructibility—surely an active rather than a passive quality—which is dear to the British public. Another difficulty must have been the richness of the literary and political background, or battleground, and the sheer number of subsidiary characters. For all of them there was 'an overwhelming mass' of material. The only evidence missing seems to have been some diaries and papers which are restricted during the lifetime of Anthony West, and the correspondence with Beaverbrook, which Rebecca and Max burned together at her flat in 1930. With great skill Victoria Glendinning concentrates attention on the story she has been asked to tell. Rebecca was to the end, as one of her housekeepers put it, 'black and white and crimson and purple and wild'. Victoria Glendinning treats each episode, black or white, with calming, professional good sense. She makes very few direct judgments, only once or twice risking a sad question—'How could she behave so unwisely or so badly?' Some of the story has been paraded almost too often, some not at all. The book is equally successful with the well-known and the unfamiliar aspects, particularly with Rebecca's marriage to Henry Andrews, who is usually thought of, if he is thought of at all, as a wealthy, totally faithful, slightly deaf, typically English banker with whom she found security and a country life. Slightly deaf he certainly was, but he soon ceased, it turns out, to be a banker, was partly Lithuanian, and was unable to resist a long series of tepid affairs with younger women. In Buckinghamshire, where they bought a house and farm, he was quite at a loss. 'Rebecca wanted to do everything, having a flair for everything.' . . . Henry pottered, and was considered in the village to be a comical old bugger. When he died, in 1968, he left 30 almost identical dark suits from Saville Row, each with money in the waistcoat pocket, ready for giving tips. Yet he lived with Rebecca and travelled with her and drove her about, often losing the way; and he was a man about the house. Victoria Glendinning re-creates him with something like tenderness, and points out that 'it was not so different from many marriages.' It is only strange as the choice of the brilliant and stormy woman who wrote that 'the difference between men and women is the rock on which civilisation will split.'

But perhaps 'strange' is not the right word, because consistency was never Rebecca West's main concern. In *The Meaning of Treason* (revised in 1962 to include studies of Philby, Burgess and Maclean), she sometimes confuses treachery with treason and examination with cross-examination, but this doesn't affect the dazzling intelligence of her case-histories. As to why she wrote, she gave a number of explanations. She began 'without choosing to do so—at home we all wrote and thought nothing of it.' 'My work,' she said, 'expresses an infatuation with human beings. I don't believe that to understand is to pardon, but I feel that to understand makes one forget that one cannot pardon.' She also said that she wrote her novels to find out how she felt. Victoria Glendinning believes that 'she most revealed herself when describing somebody else.' She has, therefore, to look even more attentively than most biographers at the correspondence of what Browning called House and Shop. This is a complex matter when it comes to the later work, in particular *Black Lamb and Grey Falcon*. In 1936 Rebecca was sent to Yugoslavia by the British Council (who might have guessed what would happen) as a lecturer, and she went there again in 1937 and 1938. Her book was a testament to the country with which she had fallen in love on a majestic scale. It was not finished until 1942, when the Yugoslav resistance to the German invasion had given it a new intention. The travel book was still there, with Rebecca as the passionate explorer and interpreter and Henry supplying—not always convincingly—the statistics, but it had deepened into a vast meditation on the history, politics, geography and ethnology of Eastern Europe, following, as she said, 'the dark waters' of the Second World War back to their distant source. To do it justice, Victoria Glendinning has had to summarise the troubled history of the southern Slavs (Rebecca was heart and soul with the Serbs), the shifts of British policy and the devices of the SOE and the Foreign Office. At one extreme, there is the 'emotional, curly-haired Serbian Jew' who acted as Rebecca's official guide and fell in love with her; at the other, is her vision of Europe's history as a crime committed by man against himself. The exposition here could not be clearer. When Rebecca declared that she had never made a continuous revelation of herself, she was admitting that she made a discontinuous one. The novels are probably the best place to look for her. 'Non-fiction,' she said, 'always tends to become fiction; only the dream compels honesty.' So the biographer arrives, with admiration and caution, at her own view of Rebecca West's view of herself. (p. 17)

Penelope Fitzgerald, "Dame Cissie," in London Review of Books, Vol. 9, No. 20, November 12, 1987, pp. 17-18.

MARGHANITA LASKI

[As Victoria Glendinning recounts in *Rebecca West: A Life*], for ten years, from 1913 when she was twenty years old, Rebecca West was H. G. Wells's mistress, an affair that began in rapture and ended in ugly recriminations, made nastier by the running vendetta against Rebecca by the son of the union. The pair had other things in common too, though no more than with many of the rest of us. Both resented the—as it seemed then—unduly inferior social levels to which they were born. Both had less satisfactory sex lives than they dreamed of and felt they were entitled to. Both fantasised their own lives, contemporaneously and retrospectively. And both were writers. (p. 82)

It appears that Glendinning's book, getting on for 300 pages, is to count as the short life Dame Rebecca wanted written. . . . Is this person's life worth writing about, apart from the work? Glendinning suggests that in other times she might have been an abbess or a witch. I see her as a forceful Jewish matriarch, a bully-woman, and not too inaptly since she was often thought of as Jewish, had many close Jewish friends, and envied Jewish family life. But in any such imagined roles, indeed in her own, is she worth a biography, let alone with a "full" biography to follow?

I judge that she is not. What I think she is greatly worth, and Wells too, is assessment as a writer, not only in a detached literary context, but in the relationships established, the influences wielded, by both writers over their readers. This makes it the stranger that Glendinning has nothing to say about the work from this point of view, little of it as cool assessment, and of this, some crassly inept. (p. 88)

Victoria Glendinning's treatment of her author's books is so cursory as to give the impression that she is leaving that ground to a critical study of them now in the making. What little she does is sometimes right and worth saying. She is right to say that the Yugoslav book of 1941-42, *Black Lamb and Grey Falcon,* is a work—she says a *great* work, but I think not—of "romantic art constructed over a framework of research and scholarship. Judged by the strict criteria of this framework, it is excessively unbalanced, sometimes wrong, sometimes silly."

She is right to say (that is, I agree with her) that the long-short stories of 1935, *The Harsh Voice,* are the best Rebecca ever wrote; but simply to say that they "are about love, hate and money" is quite grossly inadequate—and in any case, one of them is far more accurately described as being about insensitivity and murder.

On Rebecca's first book, *The Return of the Soldier* of 1918, Glendinning is unpardonably casual. She gives the publication date wrongly in her text as 1917 (though correctly in the Bibliography), and fails to notice (or to tell us) that it is dedicated to J., her pet name for Wells. . . . This story, Glendinning says at the beginning of a paragraph, is about "the healing significance of parenthood", and at its end, that it is a story about salvation through unselfish love. Neither will do. Remembrance of his dead child is the story's device to restore the shell-shocked soldier to full recollection, but whether this is salvation or damnation is the book's core question, left with the reader. I have always found this a hauntingly important story; surely, in any biography of Rebecca, her first novel, written under conditions of loneliness and ill-health and yet reflecting nothing of this, deserves extended attention.

So far, indeed, as the work is concerned, it is on the novel of 1936, *The Thinking Reed,* that Glendinning falls shortest. She notes that it is dedicated to Rebecca's husband, but not in what terms. The dedication reads:

> Vivamus quod viximus, et teneamus
> Nomina, quae primo sumpsimus in thalamo,

an expression of gratitude for the pleasures of the marriage bed, embarrassing as it stands, and the more so once we have learned from Glendinning's book that, after the mid-1930s, Henry visited Rebecca's bed no more.

But I am convinced that Glendinning (and several other people) have got *The Thinking Reed* all wrong. It is a funny novel, she says—and so, in bits, it is. But she accepts Rebecca's own description of the novel's themes, "the effect of riches on people, and the effect of men on women, both forms of strategy". I have always thought this one of Rebecca's *post-facto* rationalisation fantasies. I am sure that *The Thinking Reed* is a romantic novel, an intelligent woman's popular romance, an up-market version of *The Pursuit of Love*, and I have read and enjoyed enough popular romance to recognise one when I meet it. All through Rebecca's life, I believe we see a Cinderella yearning for her Prince—in this story the life that the cool, beautiful, intelligent American Isobelle can live in France after marriage to the rich motor-car manufacturer, who is not, as Glendinning makes him, a Jew: the distant Jewish strain is something his devoutly Catholic family never refers to.

To see that Rebecca's ambition, or even part of her ambition, was to be firmly established as a rich woman in the right society is to find that many inconsistencies in her life fall into place. To see her writing, or part of her writing, as the work of a romantic novelist too intelligent for that role is to explain much. As the life of an interesting woman, Glendinning's book is good; and if anyone wants to count it as art, nothing against this, though less undeniably for it than in her earlier lives of creative women. But, more than most people, what Rebecca West needs now far more than a Life is a sensitive critical appreciation of her works. (p. 90)

> Marghanita Laski, "Lives or Works? On H. G. Wells & Rebecca West," in Encounter, Vol. LXIX, No. 5, December, 1987, pp. 82-4, 86, 88, 90.

V. S. PRITCHETT

[*Pritchett is an important English man of letters. Along with his short stories, for which he is most highly praised, Pritchett's ouvre includes critical essays, travel writing, and autobiography. In the following excerpt, he details West's life history, paying particular attention to the childhood influences that affected the course of her life.*]

She "lived her life operatically, and tinkered endlessly with the story-line, the score, and the libretto." These frank words come from [*Rebecca West: A Life*], Victoria Glendinning's sympathetic and searching life of Cicely Fairfield, known to us as Rebecca West.... Ms. Glendinning is a well-known, prize-winning biographer.... [With] Rebecca West she is alert to the pathos, the grand drama of sweeping judgment. She understands how the tunes of temperament change.

Why did the young Miss Fairfield choose to be Rebecca West? (She disliked Ibsen's plays.) To re-imagine herself? To catch attention? To stand apart from her sisters, one of whom was already making an impression as a distinguished doctor and would eventually become a barrister, while the other sister was blamelessly conventional? We must look back to Rebecca's Puritan Scottish mother, of crofter stock, and her fantasizing

Anglo-Irish father. The parents met in Australia, where they were poor immigrants. He had become a painter and a clever, restless journalist, inclined to parlous mining speculations and casual love affairs. The marriage was a union of two lonely people. Hating Australia, he brought her back to Scotland. No Puritan he. He came from wild Kerry, and his fancy was filled with talk of rank and with the Anglo-Irish obsession with grand cousinage. The daughters listened in their childhood to his tales of an ancestor who had been a cousin of Sir Walter Raleigh, of a connection with the great Sackvilles which somehow gave them all descent from an aunt of Anne Boleyn....

More interesting was the father's political talk. He was an admirer of Edmund Burke and corresponded with Herbert Spencer. When he brought his family back to Scotland, he worked in Glasgow on the Glasgow *Herald,* and then moved them to London. Eventually, he vanished abroad on some speculative pharmaceutical deal, pursued women, and abandoned the family completely for five years—it is possible that his wife threw him out—and was found dead in lodgings in Liverpool. In the meantime, the mother raised the family in Edinburgh. Her gift was musical, and her taste for Schumann and the influence of music in general were to be strong in Rebecca's writing. In Edinburgh, the Athens of the North, the clever girls soon won scholarships to excellent schools. Rebecca's desire was to become an actress, and when she was seventeen she went to London to the Academy of Dramatic Art. There, for all her gifts and although she did get one or two minor parts, she failed. Why? The beautiful girl was histrionic. The victim of high-strung nervousness, she reacted to strain with involuntary grimaces and was plagued by uncontrollable itchings. In short, she could not unself herself and become other people. She inherited from her father a literary gift, but it would have startled him to see her succeed as an ardent feminist. He had been a strong Tory, and loathed the notion of woman suffrage: suffragettes, he said, were "unsympathetic and repellent." He would have been shocked by the articles she wrote for *The Freewoman,* though he certainly would have admired her mastery of the irreverent metaphor, which caught the attention of Bernard Shaw. We hear her dismissing the British intelligentsia as "the left-wing carriage-trade." ... Such wit in her writing and conversation led the young woman to the famous, but it had its price. One of her lifelong friends, the distinguished journalist Charles Curran, who was of great help to her when she was writing her long, incisive investigative studies of crime and treachery, said of her that she "has several skins fewer than any other human being, it's a kind of psychological haemophilia, which is one reason why she writes so well, and why she is so vulnerable." (p. 132)

The young woman, who had been a "displaced person" as a child, not unnaturally sought the glamour of wealth and respectable certainty. We come at last to her marriage with Henry Andrews, notoriously a pedant, apparently rich, and a bore. He passed as a solid English country gentleman, but he, too, had been a displaced person. He came of Polish or Lithuanian stock, had been educated in Great Britain, and had spent several years in a prison camp in Germany during the First World War. He dabbled in merchant banking, not always happily: he was really by nature a fussing academic. (When he and Rebecca set up in a rather grand country house in Buckinghamshire, the local villagers were mystified by him and lightly called him "a comical old bugger.") For Rebecca, he had one valuable gift: he was a linguist. This was indispensable to her on her visits to Yugoslavia before 1939, when she wrote what is thought by many to be a masterpiece of romantic travel, *Black*

Lamb and Grey Falcon. As her biographer says, Rebecca became "one of nature's Balkans." (p. 133)

Ms. Glendinning has made much of Rebecca West's admiration for Proust and the music of his long-winded and branching sentences, and of his influence on her. This is true up to a point; in her novels (except in *The Fountain Overflows*) we often have the sensation of claustrophobia. Wells complained that in the narrative of her early novel *The Judge* she was dilatory and began too far back. This is also true of her last novel, *The Birds Fall Down*—an ambitious historical story in which an innocent girl is used to carry a message to czarist dissidents. We are soon lost in the décor and the overfurnishing of the intrigue. Too many people appear, too completely. The whole story is too brilliantly labored. It is astonishing that while she was working on this very long book the manic side of her temperament was driving her to write scores of letters to friends, explaining here, attacking there, as she poured out the wrongs of her personal life: the tedium of her marriage; the persisting quarrel with her son, Anthony; her feuds with her critics, who rightfully accused her of political extremism. Her health was bad. After a serious operation, she had hallucinations: she said that the wretched Henry Andrews was trying to poison her with doctored soup sent over from a London restaurant.

In 1968, Henry died. His organized fussiness was revealed. In the waistcoat pockets of thirty Savile Row suits—all the suits the same—a hundred and eighty-seven pounds was found: money the prudent man had reserved for tips! A more disturbing discovery was that he had been in the habit of casually picking up girls. Rebecca was enraged. She had only briefly been unfaithful to him—once with a doctor and once in Nuremberg, with a judge at the trial. In itself rather an odd choice.

Rebecca West lived on until she was ninety. She sold the Buckinghamshire mansion and moved to a terrace in Kensington, a few doors from the Iranian Embassy that later sheltered terrorists. A highly trained anti-terrorist squad attacked the building, and she eagerly watched the affair from her window until she was dramatically rescued in a scene of gunfire. The incident is an ironic and unexpected crown of her career. She could almost have invented it. (pp. 133-34)

> V. S. Pritchett, "One of Nature's Balkans," in The New Yorker, Vol. LXIII, No. 44, December 21, 1987, pp. 132-34.

TERRY TEACHOUT

The surest shibboleth of the committed ideologue is a willingness to praise bad art. This willingness, of course, is frequently the product of necessity. Most of today's feminist writers, for instance, are literary sloganeers whose artistic seriousness is fatally undermined by their enthusiastic adherence to a political agenda. Those women writers who deserve to be taken seriously, on the other hand, are often politically indifferent at best, hopeless heretics at worst. To be sure, some of them have lived private lives which recall the more extravagant pages of a Mary McCarthy novel. But one is hard-pressed to come up with a woman writer of indisputable significance who has devoted anything like a substantial part of her professional energies to the feminist cause.

Enter Rebecca West. Widely praised as the greatest journalist of her time, her involvement in the English feminist movement during the early years of the century was both extensive and significant. Moreover, the details of her personal life can still

bring a flush of righteous fervor to the most ascetic cheek. Here was a woman who actually *suffered* for the cause, who bore a child out of wedlock at a time when such things were not yet the common coin of popular journalism. To top it off, she was impregnated by no less a figure than H. G. Wells, proving that all men, even the most superficially progressive, are ruthless oppressors under the foreskin.

An admiring biography was clearly inevitable, and it has now appeared. Victoria Glendinning, who knew Rebecca West during the last decade of her life, is one of those women writers who specialize in writing books about other women writers. . . . *Rebecca West: A Life* would seem to fit the pattern quite nicely, and Glendinning's heavy-handed introduction accordingly smacks of the will to adore: "The story of Rebecca West, who lived from 1892 to 1983, is the story of twentieth-century women. She was both an agent for change and a victim of change." (p. 13)

Not only is *Rebecca West: A Life* frankly admiring of its subject, it emphasizes straight biography over criticism to an annoying degree. Miss Glendinning's original commission is to some extent responsible for this imbalance. . . . "There is room not only for a detailed biography in the future," she explains in her introduction, "but for studies of aspects of her life and work which this first biography has not been able to cover fully." This sounds reasonable enough. But certain "aspects" which have been omitted from *Rebecca West: A Life* for the ostensible sake of compression are absolutely central to the coherent telling of Rebecca West's story, and one soon begins to suspect that their omission was effected on other than strictly literary grounds. (pp. 13-14)

Fay Weldon, in her monograph on Rebecca West for Penguin's "Lives of Modern Women" series, directs the novice reader to her novels, squirming past *The Meaning of Treason* as quickly as possible: "I suspect she looked too myopically through patriotic glasses, and failed to grasp the hopefulness of what she saw—as concepts of loyalty and morality, for centuries poles apart, at last began to fuse."

This line is echoed throughout the pages of *Rebecca West: A Life,* in which every opportunity is taken to diminish Rebecca West's mature political convictions as a quirk, an idiosyncrasy, even a sign of mental disturbance. ("She was, in New York, appallingly run down in health and spirits, and obsessed with the theories of communist infiltration which had been her subject matter for the preceding months.") The proportions of Miss Glendinning's book, which deliberately stresses "the early and middle years," also serve to obscure the fully formed writer in favor of the impassioned young controversialist of feminist legend.

The problem with this approach, aside from the inevitable distortions which it imposes on the story of Rebecca West's life, is that it emphasizes that part of her work which is least likely to last. The rapidity with which Victoria Glendinning glosses over much of the later work diminishes the interest of the book as a whole. *The Court and the Castle,* for instance, is written off in a one-sentence footnote. Rebecca West remarked in *Black Lamb and Grey Falcon* that her work "could not fuse to make a picture of a writer, since the interstices were too wide." In the absence of an adequate consideration of her literary and political views, this rueful self-description becomes all too accurate.

The feminists, to be sure, lack the perspective necessary to see Rebecca West whole. Nor is Glendinning particularly helpful in this regard, given her apparent ignorance of modern European and American politics. (pp. 14-15)

Fortunately, Victoria Glendinning's political obtuseness has not prevented her from writing a readable book. Not that *Rebecca West: A Life* is a masterpiece of the biographer's art. One feels certain that the "short" biography Miss Glendinning was asked to write was intended to be a brief life, a *tour de force* of penetration and grace similar in approach to Rebecca West's own book on St. Augustine. Instead, Glendinning has given us a book of awkward length, neither short enough to be graceful nor long enough to be inclusive. Important episodes are given short shrift or . . . omitted altogether.

Even more important is Miss Glendinning's failure to provide any kind of sustained discussion of Rebecca West's work. Her reputation has been in eclipse for a number of years, and while her politics are in large part responsible, the fugitive nature of the literary genres in which she regularly worked is equally to blame. Rebecca West herself analyzed this problem shrewdly when she told a graduate student in search of thesis fodder that "I was a writer wholly unsuitable for her purpose" because "the bulk of my writing was scattered through American and English periodicals," adding that she "had never used my writing to make a continuous disclosure of my own personality to others, but to discover for my own edification what I knew about various subjects to me."

Still, there is enough information here to give the reader a fairly solid grasp of the high points of Rebecca West's eventful life. Whatever Victoria Glendinning's political agendas, she strikes exactly the right note for a good popular biography: sympathetic but candid. Though her book is finally inadequate, it does a substantial number of things well enough. One awaits with considerable interest the full-length biography which Stanley Olson is writing, but at least Miss Glendinning has now made it possible to consider in some detail the main themes of Rebecca West's work side by side with the details of her long and troubled private life. (p. 15)

> Terry Teachout, "A Liberated Woman," in The New Criterion, *Vol. VI, No. 5, January, 1988, pp. 13-21.*

DONNA RIFKIND

Rebecca West moved through life with a singular and almost religious urgency. Her need for knowledge was limitless, her love for dramatic displays of knowledge abundant. Although she may be accused of occasional untruthfulness and of frequent excess in both her work and her life, she probably never wrote a dull word or expressed an uninteresting idea. Even at the end, when West was ninety, a housekeeper described her life as "black and white and crimson and purple and wild." Her personality elicited strong feelings in others: she had hundreds of fiercely loyal friends and not a few enemies. Admirers of her writing speak of her with near-cultic devotion, while her own son (who died last December) spent much of his own writing career vilifying her for real or imagined injuries. Soon after her marriage, when she was thirty-eight, her husband wrote to her: "I hope you will recall how when I was lonely your work recalled to me the ideals and enthusiasms of my youth and gave me strength not to compromise. In the same way, many whom you will never know are surrounding you with their blessings." It seems an injustice that the first of two biographies commissioned by this vivid individual before her death in 1982, *Rebecca West: A Life* by Victoria Glendinning, should be as flat and formal as a newscast. . . .

Rebecca West bears signs of having been hastily written—and written more out of a sense of duty than from a patient willingness to evince the spirit of the woman's life and work.

How best to characterize that life and work? In her introduction, Miss Glendinning asserts that her subject's story "is the story of twentieth-century women," but this is not at all true, because Rebecca West was an individualist to such a degree that she often defined her milieu most clearly when she stood in opposition to it; as a feminist, a socialist, and later as an anti-Communist, she maintained a truly independent point of view, never needing to seek refuge in a particular faction in the course of fleeing another. She was a prodigious rather than an emblematic figure: an individual who seemed larger than life not because she was a representative woman but because she had more than the usual amount of resources, and more courage, to respond to the requirements which her world presented to her.

The same is true of her position as a writer. She was not a representative journalist, or novelist, or critic, or travel writer, although she worked in all those genres. Hers was a synthesizing rather than a specializing mind. She worked as if there existed a grand, glittering emporium called Knowledge where she was a preferred customer, and something in her personality drove her to collect knowledge of as many diverse subjects as she had time to pursue. She wrote more, one suspects, out of a need to satisfy that driving restlessness to *know* than out of a wish to address a particular audience or to master a specific genre, and as a result it would be difficult to gauge exactly what kind of people her large audience was composed of. The body of work she left is more or less inimitable, but to explain the nature of her intellect one might perhaps most profitably compare her with an American contemporary of hers, the journalist-turned-man-of-letters Edmund Wilson, himself a writer whose synthesizing mind looms much larger in his public's imagination than do any of his particular books. In the case of both Wilson and Rebecca West we sense at the source of their achievements a desire above all to gather up information which they could shape into artful prose, in an effort to make the most possible sense of their world. (p. 44)

[One] begins to suspect Miss Glendinning is more comfortable with the romantic aspects of her subject's life than with the intellectual and political material.

For example, we get plenty of information about Rebecca's unsatisfied infatuation with the newspaper tycoon Lord Beaverbrook, including some tabloid-style teasers like the following: "Rebecca, who had never been unfaithful to [Wells], was interested in another man—an interest that was to become an obsession." But we sense Miss Glendinning's relief when, in another section, she finishes a long passage about Rebecca's involvement in Yugoslavian affairs just prior to and during World War II—an involvement which led her to write her great book on the subject, *Black Lamb and Grey Falcon*. Having given a rudimentary and rather awkward account of the political situation in the Balkans and of Rebecca West's view of it, the author retreats (gratefully, it seems) into a cozy discussion of her subject's country-house life and her pleasure in canning, gardening, and making butter.

Miss Glendinning also seems less than comfortable with the large fact of Rebecca West's anti-Communism, which she attempts at several points to attribute to mere paranoia or to other kinds of mental illness. But West herself would no doubt have protested that. Far from being a quirk, her anti-Communism was absolutely consistent with the rest of her political beliefs; her hatred of totalitarianism was of primary significance among her democratic-socialist positions, and she detested any political doctrine which threatened the individual's freedom in the way she felt Communism did. Miss Glendinning's misrepresentation not only neglects the importance with which West regarded the malignity of Communism (she called it "Fascism with a glandular and geographic difference"), but it also weakens the biography's already brief discussions of West's works, especially *The New Meaning of Treason*—originally published in 1947 as *The Meaning of Treason* and updated in 1964—which seeks to examine the motivations of the Fascist and Communist traitors of World War II and after.

Another serious fault of the biography is its inattention to the books Rebecca West was writing throughout her long life. Titles and dates are duly provided, but Miss Glendinning devotes a minimum of space to discussing the works. She claims in her introduction that "there is room not only for a detailed biography in the future, but for studies of aspects of her life and work which this first biography has not been able to cover fully." While this seems a munificent invitation to future scholars, in fact the statement betrays a large error of judgment. For while it is not true for many writers, in the case of Rebecca West her life was mixed into her work—and her work into her life—to such a degree that to ignore the work in favor of the life is to miss a great deal. The most interesting thing about Rebecca West was not the course of her life, although that was interesting indeed. It was her intellect, that great synthesizing machine, a sparkling and marvelous engine whose contents she manufactured into books, that was and remains of the most vital importance. To ignore her works in any biography of her, long or short, is to ignore the essence of the woman. (pp. 45-6)

If she does not wholly succeed in persuading her readers that art is our salvation, or that the maintenance of the idea of the nation is essential to society, Rebecca West does succeed in assuring us of her complete conviction as a writer. If nothing else, we believe in her need for belief. It was that conviction that allowed her constantly to push the necessary half-inch below the surface, a half-inch below anything Victoria Glendinning has managed to reach in this biography. Certainly it is unfair to expect that a biographer's talent and dedication match her subject's. But in this case Miss Glendinning's cool, dutiful tone and superficial presentation betray a lack of engagement that dampens the spirit of her subject. *Rebecca West: A Life* convinces us only that there is plenty of material for a future biographer to work with. . . . (p. 46)

Donna Rifkind, in a review of "Rebecca West: A Life," in The American Spectator, *Vol. 21, No. 4, April, 1988, pp. 44-6.*

Hemingway

by Kenneth S. Lynn

(For Ernest Hemingway: see also *CLC*, Vols. 1, 3, 6, 8, 10, 13, 19, 30, 34, 39, 41, 44; *Contemporary Authors*, Vols. 77-80; *Dictionary of Literary Biography*, Vols. 4, 9; *Dictionary of Literary Biography Yearbook: 1981*; *Dictionary of Literary Biography Documentary Series*, Vol. 1. For Kenneth S. Lynn: see also *Contemporary Authors*, Vol. 1, rev. ed. and *Contemporary Authors New Revision Series*, Vol. 3.)

Hans Malmberg/Black Star

An Excerpt from *Hemingway*

To a casual observer, Ernest's adolescent relationship with Grace might have seemed delightfully warm, especially when they got to talking about music, for her interest in the subject had taken firm root in his own sensibility. On a more mundane level, baked goods were another bond between them. Although Grace generally tried to stay out of the kitchen, she did enjoy producing cakes and cookies—much to the delight of the eternally hungry Ernest. Even after he went off to work in Kansas City, she continued to cater to his sweet tooth with packages sent special delivery.

A saccharine sweetness likewise characterized her manner of addressing him; indeed, as it became clear to her that he, not Marcelline, was her most gifted child, her gushing over him became so fulsome that it might have been an embarrassment, had he not learned to turn it aside with a bantering humor and Jewish nicknames. (Mother Hemingstein he called her, Mrs. Stein for short.) The light touch, in sum, became the socially acceptable means through which he was able to bring to the surface of their encounters his covert hatred and contempt for his mother. And when he reached his middle teens, these feelings were furthered darkened by an unconscious sense of betrayal. For in the summer of his fifteenth birthday he was given the astonishing news that his mother was once again pregnant. The baby arrived on April 1, 1915, and—April Fool!—turned out to be a boy. No sooner did his mother name him Leicester Clarence than Ernest started calling him Leicester De Pester, after a character in the comic strips. But the sobriquet was too cumbersome, as well as insufficiently expressive of how he felt about having a male sibling after so many years of being the only cock on the walk, so he reduced it to The Pest.

For her part, Grace never doubted that her handsome boy truly loved her. On February 15, 1916, she grouped together in one of her scrapbooks two recent photographs of him. One showed him looking glum with his mouth turned down; in the other, a shy smile wreathed his face. The first picture, Grace noted, is "the way he looks whenever his fathers speaks to him," and the second is "the way he looks whenever his mother speaks to him."

Undoubtedly, she showed him the comment, but its coquettishness did not avail to halt his progressive withdrawal from her, a withdrawal that was particularly noticeable during the vacation months in Michigan. In the summers of 1915, 1916, and 1917 he slept most nights in a tent behind Windemere, or in another tent across the lake at Longfield Farm, or in a camp he established for himself at Murphy's Point, or in the homes of friends in Horton Bay. "Thinking of his mother's exuberant vitality, the rich curves of her every move, the warmth of her vital personality," Ernest's favorite teacher, Fannie Biggs, would reminiscently remark in 1952, "I wondered if Ern would find a wife with the lush motherhood he knew." This vibrant appreciation of another woman's ripeness may very well say less about Ernest than about Miss Biggs, for rumor had it that she was a lesbian. In assuming that he responded to his mother as she did, she did not reckon with the complexity of his feelings. While there is every reason to believe that he was entranced by the descriptions of *Fortitude* of the passionate embraces between Peter Westcott, the would-be novelist, and his mother, the onetime concert singer, within his own family he fled from the very possibility of restaging them.

With his departure for Kansas City in the fall of 1917, he placed a much greater distance between himself and Grace. She would send letters winging after him, however, one of which was highly critical of his conduct, and his instantaneous response to it would provide the first indication of his fate. Although he had reached the point of wanting to break completely free of her, he would not be able to bring it off, nor would he be able to do so in the future years, not even after he had all but ceased to write to her. All his life, his mother would remain the dark queen of Hemingway's inner world.

BENJAMIN DeMOTT

[*DeMott, an American novelist, critic, and educator, has published several novels and volumes of essays. In the following excerpt, he admires Lynn's coherent discussion of the crucial influence of Hemingway's childhood on his life and work, but reproaches the biographer's frequently derisive tone toward his subject.*]

For close to a quarter of a century the Hemingway legend has been undergoing approximately annual touch-ups. In *Hemingway,* Kenneth Lynn praises nine previous biographical studies; six appeared after 1981. (p. 91)

Lynn's revisions, which concern Hemingway the macho man, are not reverent, and introduce a hitherto neglected villainess—the novelist's mother. Grace Hemingway kept the hero-writer-to-be in dresses and shoulder-length hair (a "loose, tapered coiffure") well past toddlerdom—rather longer than was customary. . . . In addition, Grace Hemingway paired Ernest with his older, often intimidating sister Marcelline, treating them like "twins of the same sex" (sometimes male, sometimes female), pressing Ernest simultaneously to be and not to be "a 'real' boy." "Caught-between his mother's wish to conceal his masculinity and her eagerness to encourage it, was it any wonder that he was anxious and insecure?"

The younger Hemingway children were sent equally confusing sexual signals. Hemingway's sister Ursula wore a Rough Rider costume and was nick-named Teddy. (Like Ernest and their father, Ursula committed suicide; she and Ernest seem at one point to have been lost in fantasies both androgynous and incestuous.) Grace Hemingway's husband appears also to have endured sexual humiliation. While young Ernest was in his observant teens, Dr. Hemingway threw a woman out of the house whom he evidently suspected of being involved in a lesbian affair with Grace.

On the appearance last year of an abbreviated version of *The Garden of Eden,* a novel Hemingway shelved in mid-life, readers commenced asking unaccustomed questions about the writer. The book was awash with transsexual fantasies, and Kenneth Lynn claims that it "compelled reluctant recognition of the possibility that [Hemingway] was not the writer, nor the man, he was thought to be. . . ." But that recognition was, in Lynn's view, clouded and evasive. The world of letters pretended to see the sensibility revealed in *The Garden of Eden* as "new," when in fact it had been "there all along."

Lynn had been engaged for some while in studying the sensibility, probing its roots in life situations and tracking its development from the earliest stories onward. The core of his argument here is that the extraordinary anxieties and insecurities of the writer's youth and adolescence exerted shaping influence not only on his work but on his relationships with siblings, friends, lovers, and competitors.

Lynn's achievement as biographer is that he sets up a field of coherent relationships among previously difficult-to-read phenomena. His book stresses the pervasiveness, through the entire writing career, in texts of utterly different character, of motifs and images—from emasculation to bobbed hair—that betray the novelist's entrapment in the sexual uncertainties of his youth. This material is connected, in turn, with other details of behavior—Hemingway's bullying and braggadocio, his constant testing of himself for bravery, his unwillingness to suffer any rival reputation in any literary, sporting, or sexual endeavor. And before the end of the work the Hemingway style itself—the famous spareness and reticence—is interpreted in light of behavioral patterns. Repeatedly Lynn imagines the operative forces from inside, attempting to spell out their interaction. (pp. 91-2)

No life or style generates its logic solely from within, and, aware of this, Kenneth Lynn seeks to ground his tale firmly in history. He establishes that the remarkably fluid, unisexual dress and hairdo conventions prevailing at the turn of the century tended to encourage Grace Hemingway's indulgence in kinky conceits. The pivotal historical reality of the age—the Great War—served Hemingway's special need, providing him with a heroic explanation for wounds that Lynn believes were embarrassingly unheroic in origin. And a contemporary sexual revolution offered an objective, legitimizing framework for secret personal fixations. . . .

Everywhere in this life story social and psychological history are interfused, and, happily, Lynn isn't the kind of biographer who affects to know precisely where and how to separate them. On the other hand, neither is he a biographer whose tone and manner give unfailing assurance of large-mindedness—the ability to journey deep into a troubled heart without becoming derailed by derision. The first hint of derailment occurs in the prefatory assumption that literary reputation shrivels whenever "transsexual fantasies" surface. Why do such fantasies cause us to conclude that an artist is less than "he was thought to be"? Stoniness also enters into Lynn's mocking dismissals of the generation of Hemingway biographers ("fools") that believed that the sick man in **"Big Two-Hearted River"** had been psychically crippled by the war. Must every new explanation destroy all preceding explanations?

And contempt rules this biographer's discussion of sentimental leftist critics who took seriously the naive, "engaged" Hemingway of *The Spanish Earth* and *To Have and Have Not.* Nobody's evidence that Hemingway's "faults were terrible" is more compelling than Kenneth Lynn's. And, to Lynn's credit, he struggles to balance consciousness of the faults with appreciation of the author as a "conflicted, haunted man who produced from his torment some of the most memorable fiction of the century." The Nobel laureate is saluted on the closing page as a writer whose curiosity, gusto, adventures, and art "affirmed the possibilities of life in this tough world." But the alternating patches of baiting and generosity elsewhere are distracting, as is the book's undervoice, which murmurs almost ceaselessly, *We have found you out.*

How will reputational hierarchies shift as a result of the re-evaluation that is now—perhaps—inevitable? Reading about this writer's torments had the effect, on me, of sharpening affection for a Hemingway contemporary who was rich-souled enough to live into his transsexual fantasies with humane humor as well as passion: James Joyce, of course. As for standing of the best and worst in Hemingway's *oeuvre:* it's been years since the macho worst has commanded respect, and I can report, on the basis of rereading, that the best—the story **"Hills Like White Elephants"**—seems rather more poignant than before. (p. 92)

> Benjamin DeMott, *"Papa's Mama Trouble,"* in The Atlantic Monthly, *Vol. 260, No. 1, July, 1987, pp. 91-2.*

SCOTT DONALDSON

[*Donaldson, an American educator, biographer, and critic, has written numerous studies of American literature and the American experience. His works include* The Suburban Myth *(1969),* Conversations with John Cheever *(1987), and* By Force of Will: The Life and Art of Ernest Hemingway *(1977). In the following excerpt, Donaldson praises Lynn for his well-researched, insightful picture of Hemingway as man and artist.*]

"And all the legends that he started in his life / Live on and prosper / Unhampered now by his existence." The lines come from a 1923 poem Ernest Hemingway wrote about Teddy Roosevelt, a man he idolized as a boy growing up in Oak Park and deprecated as a young foreign correspondent living in Paris. But as Kenneth S. Lynn points out in his new psychologically oriented biography [*Hemingway*], Hemingway's poem might as well be about himself. Like T. R., he was one of the great legend builders. The myth became pervasive: Hemingway the *macho* man, warrior-lover-sportsman-writer-drinker-expert, tough as nails Papa in his beard at the bullfights.

During his day, Hemingway bestrode the world like a colossus, and colossi present nearly irresistible targets to those who come after. Two wives, three siblings, and two sons have so far had their say about him, and so, it lately has come to seem, have about half the literary biographers extant. Any new attempt to depict Hemingway must therefore pass a freshness test, and Lynn's *Hemingway* passes easily. The book is very different from anything else on Hemingway. It is the best full-scale biography since Carlos Baker's groundbreaking *Ernest Hemingway: A Life Story* in 1969, and the most insightful study yet of the inter-connections between the artist's life and his writing.

Lynn's thesis is that Hemingway was crucially wounded, not in World War I but in the house on North Kenilworth Avenue. The damage was done not by an Austrian trench mortar shell, but by his mother Grace Hall Hemingway, a woman of powerful personality who dominated her husband and enveloped her second child Ernest in a miasma of sexual confusion. She immediately drew her baby "into a deliciously intimate dependency." For six months he slept in her bed, where—she recorded in her scrapbook—he "lunches all night." Later, when disputes arose between mother and son, she would remind him of those loving nights at her bosom.

Still more damaging, according to Lynn, was Mrs. Hemingway's decision to treat Ernest and his sister Marcelline, 18 months older, as twins of the same sex. . . . Grace Hemingway often sent conflicting signals, and her son grew up in an atmosphere of sexual confusion.

The Garden of Eden—both the long unfinished novel Hemingway wrote and set aside after World War II and the drastically reduced version of it recently published by Scribner's—manifestly uncovers a curious sexual ambivalence. David and Catherine Bourne cut their hair the same length, dye it the same color, and reverse the male-female role in love-making. Moreover, both of them make love to the bisexual Marita. Forty years after Hemingway abandoned his novel, *The Garden of Eden* came as a shock to many of his admirers. One of the virtues of Lynn's biography is to make it clear that the sexual experimentation of David and Catherine is only the most explicit example of a duality that exists almost everywhere in his fiction.

Hemingway frequently identifies as author with the women-victims of insensitive males. The fetish about wearing hair the same length exists in all his novels, along with a frequently articulated desire of the lovers to immerse themselves in each other. Thus in *A Farewell to Arms,* Lynn maintains, Frederic and Catherine should be regarded as two halves of an androgynous whole.

What *Hemingway* offers is a fresh and convincing interpretation of Hemingway's life, in large part based on his work. Like all biographies with a thesis, Lynn's finds the evidence it is looking for, and sometimes the effect is to diminish a novel or story somewhat by transforming it into one more item on a covert agenda. Yet only rarely do his readings invite objection, almost always he is persuasive.

The reason is that Lynn writes with great authority. He has done his homework, and then some. A practicing historian, he is careful to point out that many little boys were dressed as girls at the turn of the century, but that this practice almost always ceased by the time they were 2. An accomplished biographer, he can bring a cast of characters to life in a few brief paragraphs, particularly Hemingway's fascinating companions of the Paris years: Gertrude Stein, Ezra Pound, Ford Madox Ford, Harold Loeb and Robert McAlmon, for example. A thorough researcher, he makes judicious use of many unpublished letters and a few unpublished stories in bolstering his argument. And he has clearly read and evaluated almost everything written about Hemingway.

To be sure, this biography has its shortcomings. Given his psychological bent, Lynn is constantly speculating. Perhaps Hemingway meant this, perhaps that, or could it be that he meant the other? On occasion, he seems guilty of traces of mean-spiritedness toward Hemingway, his mother, Malcolm Cowley, supporters of the Loyalist cause in Spain, martini drinkers, and anyone on the left. And the book does not so much come to a conclusion as simply end after 600 pages. But there's a lot to learn in those pages about the Midwestern youth who constructed a monumental image of himself to hide behind while he wrote some of the greatest fiction of the century. (pp. 1, 5)

> Scott Donaldson, *"The Hidden Hemingway,"* in Chicago Tribune, *July 12, 1987, pp. 1, 5.*

ALFRED KAZIN

[*Kazin, a highly respected American literary critic, is best known for his essay collections* The Inmost Leaf *(1955),* Contemporaries *(1962), and particularly for* On Native Ground *(1942), which charts the rise of American Modernism. His most recent collection,* An American Procession *(1984), examines the period in American literature from the 1830s to the 1930s. He is also the author of* Bright Book of Life: American Novelists and Storytellers From Hemingway to Mailer *(1980). In the following excerpt, Kazin condemns Lynn's Freudian treatment of Hemingway, finding it condescending, misleading, and devoid of any sense of Hemingway's achievement as an artist.]*

Even before he became a legend and began to play it up, Hemingway's first readers seemed compelled to confuse the writer with the man. He virtually told them to do this: Hemingway's stories clearly reflected early experiences. Then came the image of him as a 20th-century Byron, piled up from literary associations (he was a great reader) that he was not shy in offering. Tough, hard, even brazen in the personal myth he made of war and peace alike, "the Hemingway hero" was cruelly, indifferently erotic. Yet he became the symbol of a doomed romantic tenderness, the epitome of world-weary youth frantic for love and sport in a mad, bad world.

The very tension and terseness of Hemingway's intimidating style provided the shock that a new era needed. The mastery over experience that this style seemed to display turned Hemingway's "objective" and "emotionless" art into a personal triumph. Of all 20th-century American writers, he was the last frontiersman. Yet still his subject was literature. The reader could not escape the force and savvy of him, the fierce addiction to nature, the truculent competitiveness. He was a savage, notoriously dangerous to know, who claimed Cézanne as his teacher.

So "Hem" came with the territory he had created. And how he loved this, the insatiable "champion" over everyone else, the fascinator in every saloon, the international sportsman living it up from Paris to Africa, Cuba to Montana, adored by many women (and many wives) to whom he was ritually unfaithful. When he shot his head off in the last, long-expected Hemingway short story, John F. Kennedy and Fidel Castro were united in mourning. (p. 27)

Of all the many portraits of Hemingway I have encountered, Kenneth Lynn's obsessively Freudian attempt to show Hemingway as an unconscious homosexual is the most relentlessly researched and the most condescending. Lynn's chief concern with Hemingway's writing is to demonstrate that the bedeviled fellow's real subject was his erotic conflicts. There is nothing in [*Hemingway*] to account for Hemingway's addiction to literature, nothing to show what in his own mind led him to become a writer, nothing about the early fascination with landscape that became the safeguard of his artistry. But there is a very great deal, delivered in the armchair Freudian's most clinically superior tone, about the exaggerations, distortions, and lies Hemingway practised in transferring his personal experience to literature. Apparently "transference" is all a writer needs, is as routine behind a typewriter as it is on both sides of the psychoanalytic couch.

So Hemingway's difficulties in facing up to himself . . . become *the* Hemingway story. Even the famously reduced and spare Hemingway style, once the astonishment of the Western world, acknowledged even by Soviet writers as the one style that "catches the tempo of our time," is passed off and explained in this summation of Hemingway's terrible case:

> To be a boy but to be treated as a girl. To feel impelled to prove your masculinity through flat denials of your anxieties (*Fraid a nothing* had been your motto as a child) and bold lies about your exploits. To be forced to practice the most severe economy in your attempts to "render" your life artistically, because your capital of self-understanding was too small to permit you to be expansive and your fear of self-exposure too powerful. To make a virtue of necessity by packing troubled feelings below the surface of your stories like dynamite beneath a bridge. To be tempted by your enormous ambition into writing a novel, despite the risks inherent in amplitude.

At another point Hemingway's style is put down as "severely limited, puritanically repressed." But in truth everything about Hemingway's mediocre apprentice work, and the gassiness that eventually overcame him, show that the prime Hemingway style was entirely *made*, a conscious feat, like the Cézannes whose uncanny placing of rock and tree inspired him.

Lynn writes as if Hemingway's "concealment," his fear, his ignorance of "who he actually was" are the material of his art. It is bad enough to interpret everything about an original artist in terms of a (supposed) psychological case history. Homosexuality seems to have become the last noteworthy itch by which to explain human personality. Lynn nowhere says that Hemingway *was* a homosexual; he was just pointed in that direction by a pretentious overbearing mama who kept the babe in dresses, paired him with his sister, and so dominated her husband that he committed suicide. (Dr. Hemingway believed himself to be mortally ill.)

But it is just obtuse, on the basis of some inflated Freudian assumptions about Hemingway's "trans-sexual fantasies" (most directly given in the unpublished original manuscript of *The Garden of Eden,* written by a battered writer getting more and more unhinged), to assume that Hemingway's babyhood was "bizarre" enough to cripple him for life. Building on maternal habits that were decidedly not bizarre for upper-class families of Hemingway's time and place, Lynn's thesis is that Hemingway wrote straight from his life to the page. The problem was that the poor dope didn't know the "truth" about himself.

Lynn's heavy-handed approach to Hemingway's babyhood, to Hemingway's art, does not show the fascination with Hemingway so marked in the vast literature about him. Armed with Freudian hindsight, Lynn seems less interested in Hemingway than in the case he provides. . . . Despite the relentless coverage of Hemingway's many faults and betrayals, and the replication of what every reviewer said about every Hemingway book as it came out, what is really intrinsic and central to Hemingway—his passion for the word, for the American wilderness and its romantic truth—is missing from this book. How ever did such a madly assertive, ferocious egotist come to such delicacy of tone, feel such pain at the dismantling of nature in America; retain such a special sense of what "in our time" is wrong with history and therefore with ourselves?

In place of such literary and historical considerations, we are told (hardly for the first time) how vulnerable, to the point of violence, Hemingway could be. No other writer, especially no well-selling novelist on the Scribner list, was allowed to live: Hemingway was abominable to the friends he was putting into his books, even as he cavorted with them, flashing his famous charm. All true. But Lynn is also insistent that Hemingway had a thing about women's hair, liked to have girlfriend or wife wear it cropped short "like a boy's." He was fond of lesbians, and wanted to sleep with Gertrude Stein because she was his mother all over again. "When Gertrude savaged him eleven years later in *The Autobiography of Alice B. Toklas,* she showed how well she had figured him out, even though she knew none of the bizarre details of his background. . . . Did she sense on the day she met him that this muscular young man was hiding something?"

This accusation of "hiding something" is the special edge Lynn brings to every view of Hemingway. Nothing could be more misleading in its treatment of the subtle transpositions between experience and imagination. By common consent *The Sun Also Rises* now seems the most enduring, the most compact, of Hemingway's novels. He was, as the saying goes, a writer more "lyric" than "dramatic," more suited to the short story than to the novel. (pp. 27-9)

The Sun Also Rises has survived because, among other reasons, it is a fabulous historical novel, a novel of the greatest joy and treachery in a now never to be recovered period, when all the world was getting over one war and awaiting another. It has survived because it is so distinct in every word, in every line, that a brief brilliant period on the edge of still another European cataclysm is forever with us in all its "fiesta" and meanness. Its very meanness, the other side of its shining eroticism, has kept it alive. Hemingway had a grudge against history. It was one of his old-fashioned traits.

How does Lynn treat this unique, this glitteringly brilliant and ever-alive work of art? Letting no occasion slip that invites a discussion of women's hair, he reminds us that Lady Brett Ashley, the very same who in sweater and skirt looked like she was "built like the sides of a yacht," also had cropped hair "brushed back like a boy's." Impotent Jake Barnes in the novel is hopelessly in love with her. But since the model for Brett, Duff Twysden, was involved with a decidedly not-impotent Ernest Hemingway, it follows that said Hemingway was really attracted to. . .a boy. Lynn so confounds Lady Brett with Duff that we get this: "Furthermore, [Brett] affects a man's felt hat, just as Duff did, and can hold her liquor with equivalent gallantry. Hemingway's lady friend, in short, would make the journey from life to art virtually intact."

Nonsense. No "real" person ever gets into a book intact. The very act of writing someone into a book makes that person different. Take Hemingway in Lynn's book. Can we really believe that the miserable, frightened, horribly conflicted mother's boy who appears in this book as "Hemingway" is the man who in life, while tortured by many things (especially the criminality that prevails as politics "in our time"), wrote what he wrote? Dazzled us and frightened us as no writer has dazzled and frightened us since? (p. 29)

> *Alfred Kazin, "A Farewell to Art," in* The New Republic, *Vol. 197, Nos. 2 & 3, July 13 & 20, 1987, pp. 27-9.*

CHRISTOPHER LEHMANN-HAUPT

[Lehmann-Haupt is a Scottish-born American critic who has been the chief daily book reviewer for The New York Times *since 1969. In the following excerpt, he characterizes Lynn's biography as an essential contribution to Hemingway studies; he notes, however, that Lynn is often overly speculative and disparaging in pursuing his thesis.]*

Kenneth S. Lynn's *Hemingway* is only the third full-scale biography of the writer to appear since his suicide in 1961—after Carlos Baker's *Ernest Hemingway: A Life Story* (1969) and Jeffrey Meyers's *Hemingway: A Biography* (1985). Still, the appearance of Mr. Lynn's study may strike readers as superfluous, especially coming so soon after Mr. Meyers's dramatic narrative. And after all, it's not exactly as if Ernest Hemingway lived his life in secret.

Yet Mr. Lynn's book is essential. By bringing to light certain key events in Hemingway's early childhood, he not only deals with material that his predecessors either overlooked or actively denied, he also puts his subject's life and work into a new perspective. . . .

Born 18 months after his sister Marcelline, Ernest provoked his overbearing mother, Grace, to act out her own childhood resentment at the arrival of her brother, Leicester, when *she* was 2 years old. "How much nicer it would have been for Grace if she and little Leicester had been twins of the same sex," Mr. Lynn observes. "How much nicer, correspondingly, it would be for Marcelline—her mother's surrogate—if she and little Ernest could be turned into twins. Thus, she took early action to assert her authority over even the sexuality of her son," by outfitting him in dresses and keeping his hair long until he was 6.

The consequences for Hemingway's unconscious, Mr. Lynn speculates, were a fear of castration and a longing for sexual role reversal that were evident in both his behavior and his art. His mother's early treatment of him explains his wanderlust, his ambivalence toward women, his death-defying, death-seeking physical abuse of himself and virtually every other aspect of "the sickness unto death that was Hemingway's life."

It also explains what critics hitherto have overlooked in his art, argues Mr. Lynn—why "his pursuit of a purer prose style" was as much an escape from "his mother's operatic language" as it was an attempt "to dissociate himself from a wartime rhetoric of glory and honor." Why despite his image as a hairy-chested writer, he was fully capable of viewing things from the female point of view, as he does in such stories as **"Up in Michigan"** and **"Hills Like White Elephants."**

And it explains why critics have misread such works as **"Big Two-Hearted River"**: it is not the war but bad relations with his mother that lie beneath the surface where, for Nick Adams, "the fishing would be tragic.". . .

Mr. Lynn's reading of Hemingway's life is not without its shortcomings. His habit of elbowing us with his psychoanalytic insights can sometimes be annoying, especially when he fails to offer a source for his speculations. "Their appearance, in short, made them look like twins," he writes of Pauline and Jinny Pfeiffer, Hemingway's second wife and her sister, "and Hemingway seemed to like that." To whom Hemingway "seemed" to feel that way, Mr. Lynn doesn't say.

He seems to take undue pleasure in disparaging the critics with whom he disagrees. It's one thing to challenge misreadings of the biographical facts behind Hemingway's fiction. But does it finally matter all that much to the power of **"Big Two-Hearted River"** whether the source of Nick's psychic wounds is his mother or the war? A wound is a wound is a wound, and it is the rawness of whatever is bothering Nick that lends power to his great fishing story.

Lastly, Mr. Lynn's treatment of his subject's confused sexual identity seems overspecific, as if the problem were unique to Ernest Hemingway. To some degree, all artists who attempt to imagine human behavior must necessarily come to terms with their unconscious sexual polarity. True, it is given of Mr. Lynn's biography that Hemingway produced great art, at least until the 1930's, when he began to lose the battle with himself. But too often, instead of praising his subject for winning a universal struggle, he assumes a disparaging tone about psychic weaknesses, as if they were some moral failure on Hemingway's part. To paraphrase one of Mr. Lynn's favorite observations: this makes us wonder what the author is revealing about himself.

All the same, he makes a powerful case for his interpretation of his subject's psychic struggle. And not only does it seem common-sensical in this day and age to argue that the degree of Hemingway's machismo only reflected the degree to which he was struggling with opposing tendencies, it also makes for a dramatic rendition of Hemingway's life. One read Carlos Baker's life with impatience over the accumulation of miscellaneous details. One read Jeffrey Meyers with gratitude for at least shaping Hemingway's story. One reads Kenneth Lynn with excitement. Whatever the merits of his interpretation, he has shaped Hemingway's life and death into a story that approaches tragedy.

> *Christopher Lehmann-Haupt, in a review of "Hemingway," in* The New York Times, *July 13, 1987, p. C18.*

REYNOLDS PRICE

When Ernest Hemingway chose to die in 1961, he was the most famous writer in the English-speaking world. He may well have been the most admired—and by a wide range of readers. The fame has endured this crowded quarter-century; even today his bucket-sized grinning head is recognizable by more average citizens than any living writer's. The admirers, though, have radically diminished in number.

There are more than enough reasons why. Most readers now see what some saw at once—the late fiction is often self-imitative. His hatreds have aged badly. And he cooperated in the media's dissemination of an image that quickly turned from ludicrous to atrocious—the boozy Great Writer, trailing wives and sons as he consumes the Earth in thunderous strides, hands red with the blood of helpless beasts.

His present critical standing is so bad that many readers—convinced that Hemingway is our greatest American novelist—begin to wonder if he has a public defender left. His biographers can hardly be called advocates.

Recent years have seen numerous attempts; they begin in admiration but generally end in disillusion. The events they tally in compulsive repetition, laid end to end, form so grim a figure that Hemingway's oldest son recently complained—where is the loving and lovable father that he and his brothers knew?

It's past time too for admirers of the fiction to ask the next question—where in all this boring repetition of fear, deceit, lust, hate and noisy pride is the serene center from which Hemingway produced many supreme short stories and four great novels? Or is he the Richard Wagner of the novel—a moral monster secreting great art? Such an anomaly may be possible in music but not in prose fiction, a medium in which the writer's mind is bared by the instant.

Kenneth Lynn seems to have begun his turn in admiration. His preface promises to show us "a conflicted, haunted man" who triumphed heroically in the fiction. He also promises more than the earlier lives—the man *and* the work; the heroic art, not merely the bleak daily record.

But he quickly proceeds to rely, like his predecessors, on a catalog of visible daily events—the acts of Hemingway as revealed in documents or recalled by his more talkative kin, friends and enemies. In his favor, Lynn attempts to suggest

the quality of the books, which are now of course his subject's only enduring acts; but he lacks the skills of a literary critic.

First, he fails to understand the difference between fiction and autobiography (thus his misleading tendency to see the fiction as imperfectly transformed autobiography). Second, he admires only a stingy portion of the work. Third, though a trained historian, Lynn makes few attempts at suggesting the atmospheres in which his characters moved. Last—and most damaging—Lynn's attempts to show the fiction as the redemptive pearl in an otherwise bad oyster are defeated by his inability to evoke the lucid air and water of Hemingway at his best and to illustrate his huge and vital contributions to the ongoing art of fiction. (Hemingway has been a far more fertilizing model than Faulkner, for instance.)

So, when Lynn has detailed his version of the familiar calendar, he deposits us at the same dead-end as earlier biographers—the spattered wall of a life that wasted its own gifts and brutalized the lives it touched. Even Lynn's promise to make something significant of Hemingway's fascinating attraction to androgyny seldom results in more than a list of symptoms.

To show so little of an artist as rich and various as Hemingway, a man who still has more than a few living and loving admirers, is to repeat the current scandal of our literature—the near-total failure of literary biographers to describe an artist truly. Artist or field hand, those of us who escape sanctity can pray to be redeemed in the future by the memory of our works—the things we made and gave, the atmosphere of our minds and acts as it survives in the minds of those who cherished, as well as those who loathed, us.

> *Reynolds Price, "The Life of Hemingway: Where's Papa?," in* USA Today, *July 17, 1987, p. 4D.*

JONATHAN YARDLEY

So much has been written about Ernest Hemingway in the quarter-century since his death that one approaches a new biography with trepidation. Is there anything left to say, any fresh and revealing way to assess this immeasurably influential writer and infinitely complex human being? Yes, there is, for in his quite monumental biography Kenneth S. Lynn has much to tell us that is new, provocative and convincing. His ***Hemingway*** is at once a distillation of all previous scholarship—in itself no mean accomplishment—and an excursion into territory that, though not precisely unexplored, has never before been examined with such care and insight.

This exploration involves a certain amount of Freudian speculation, with which I am generally uncomfortable, especially when it is practiced by an amateur. But Lynn gets away with it for two reasons: he is scrupulous about staying within the bounds presented by his evidence, and from that evidence he makes what seems to me a quite unimpeachable case. To anyone who has read Hemingway's fiction and observed his life with a degree of attentiveness, Lynn's conclusions will not come as a great surprise; but it remains that no one else has drawn these conclusions so boldly or argued them so effectively....

If there is an element of debunking in Lynn's argument—he has no patience with the "Papa" mythology, is quick to point out the many forms that Hemingway's posturing assumed, and documents his treachery towards friends and rivals in unstinting detail—it is secondary to what is in fact an admiring and deeply sympathetic portrait. As one who has long felt Hemingway the writer to be much overrated and Hemingway the man to border on the contemptible, I am persuaded by Lynn that Norman Mailer's judgment, as quoted by Lynn, is correct:

> It is not likely that Hemingway was a brave man who sought danger for the sake of the sensations it provided him. What is more likely the truth of his own odyssey is that he struggled with his cowardice and against a secret lust to suicide all his life, that his inner landscape was a nightmare, and he spent his nights wrestling with the gods. It may even be that the final judgment on his work may come to the notion that what he failed to do was tragic, but what he accomplished was heroic, for it is possible that he carried a weight of anxiety with him which would have suffocated any man smaller than himself.

Lynn's biography—again I risk oversimplification—is constructed around Mailer's hypothesis. . . .

It is in Hemingway's stories that Lynn finds much of the evidence with which to substantiate his interpretation of the writer's "inner world," and he uses that evidence most persuasively. He believes, and certainly he is correct, that only Thomas Wolfe among Hemingway's contemporaries was so autobiographical a novelist; he therefore regards his fiction as legitimate corroboration of, and in some instances surrogate for, the facts. If anything, Lynn convinces me—though he does not advance the argument himself—that it is Hemingway rather than Wolfe who should get both credit and blame for the narcissistic currents that now course through American fiction; more than we have thus far realized, his influence lay not merely in style but in content.

Though it surely is unintentional, Lynn also persuades me that Hemingway's fiction is more interesting as autobiographical evidence than as fiction. His judgments about the work generally seem to me acute—he admires the first two novels and a number of the stories, mostly the early ones, but dismisses most of the later work and is suitably contemptuous toward the "lachrymose sentimentality" of *The Old Man and the Sea*— but he finds more to admire than I do in the celebrated Hemingway style and he is more patient than I am with Hemingway's literary mannerisms.

But that is of no moment. What matters is that Lynn has made the definitive case for Hemingway as a tortured man who sought to resolve his conflicts through literature and who fought a brave, honorable fight before succumbing at last to the same suicidal impulse that claimed both his father and his younger brother. In making this case he of necessity covers much ground that already has been traced to the point of extreme tedium, but to his immense credit he manages to breathe new life into all of it. More than any previous biographer—more, in particular, than the well-intentioned but pedestrian Carlos Baker— he places the events of Hemingway's life in proper perspective; he gives ample consideration to the crucial years with Hadley in Paris, for example, but dispatches the childish swashbuckling during World War II in a few pages.

Lynn is especially interesting on Hemingway's relationships with and attitudes toward women. Among Hemingway's critics it has for some time been assumed that, as I put it some years ago, "he regarded women as instruments of his own pleasure and discarded them when the purpose had been served." But Lynn contends that a legacy of his relationships with his mother and sister was "an ability to look critically at the insensitive ways in which men handled women" and that "the alienation of women from men (as well as vice versa) was one of his

themes." Using in particular the testimony offered by Mary Hemingway's diaries and by the posthumous novel *The Garden of Eden*, Lynn makes as especially strong argument that Hemingway had a "helpless fascination with androgyny and sexual transposition," one that informed both his private life and his fiction.

What becomes clear above all else in Lynn's portrait is that Hemingway was a painfully haunted man: haunted by a mother whom he hated and did not understand, by a father whom he loved but did not respect, by a Midwestern childhood that inspired both nostalgia and loathing, by a sexual insecurity that drove him to outperform all men, by a longing for applause and celebrity, and in the end by the self-destructive image he created for himself—the image of "Papa"—that "would interfere with the free working of his creative imagination" and ruin him as a writer. It is, as Lynn well knows, a sad story and in many respects a peculiarly American one; he tells it with empathy and compassion; and with great admiration for the good heart that beat behind the pitiable facade.

> *Jonathan Yardley, "'Papa' Was a Mama's Boy,"*
> in Book World—The Washington Post, *July 19, 1987,*
> *p. 3.*

DIANE JOHNSON

[*Johnson is an American novelist, critic, and biographer whose novels, including* Fair Game *(1965),* The Shadow Knows *(1974), and* Lying Low *(1978), focus on the personal and social alienation of modern women. In the following excerpt, Johnson finds Hemingway a sympathetic and detailed exploration of Hemingway's sexual identity and its relation to his writing. Although she notes that at times Lynn's interpretations of events are extreme, she commends him for showing the human, vulnerable side of a great writer.*]

Reviewing two biographies of Ernest Hemingway in 1985, Raymond Carver wrote in these pages of the influence Hemingway had had on him and other American young men who wanted to be writers and "managed to work Hemingway's name into just about every conversation we had." What they liked, even if they hadn't read Hemingway, was his daring, for, by the 1950's, his wartime and sporting exploits had given his life exemplary status, and his name iconographic magic having to do with writing and maleness. As John Updike put it in a review of one of Hemingway's novels, "an entire generation of American men learned to speak in the accents of [his] stoicism." He might have added that women, those who wanted to be writers at least, had also learned the cadence of his prose.

The whole question of manhood is, it seems, a matter for the cultural historian; it is connected to wars, the changing status of women and other things outside books. This elusive property seems to preoccupy half the human race because of its difficulty of achievement (for isn't it really a synonym for "conduct"?). Definitions of manhood have changed, but Hemingway's was the received version of his time (for women too), and he tried to exemplify in his life what he wrote about. It is too bad that assessments of his writing have tended to depend on assessments of his conduct, and to equate his failure to live up to his own lights, as inferred from his suicide, to mean somehow that he was a bad or overvalued writer. The modern world of male sensitivity groups and paternity leave has felt uncomfortable with the crudely phallic emblems of masculinity—the gun and the fishing rod—that decorate his plots, with his enjoyment, today so suspect, of killing defenseless wild animals and with his supposed inability to write about women. And so some have derided his books, which is really rather unfair, as if we were to throw out Jane Austen now that women are more independent and need not look to marriage as the sole possible female destiny.

The outlines of Hemingway's life have been told, since his death in 1961, by numerous biographers, in ever-darkening tones. He was born to an upper-middle-class doctor's family in Oak Park, Ill., worked as a reporter in Kansas City, served in World War I with the Red Cross and was wounded (he was 18). He was a reporter in the Spanish Civil War and World War II, was married four times, was the father of sons, a big-game hunter and teller of splendid manly tales. He won a Nobel Prize in 1954, and at the age of 62, in the twilight of his fame, after hospitalization for depression and alcoholism, shot himself to death at home in Idaho. His suicide seemed to call his work into question and prompted people to cast a cold eye on his own accounts of his life. They were found exaggerated or distorted, as if this must also mean that his stories falsified something about life, or men and women, or war. From a hero to a liar and a coward, from a major artist to a character, whose terse, mannered realism became the subject of parody and no longer of imitation, this after a time when his had been the way of writing—true, based on experience, sentimental, lean, outdoorsy—that had most influenced young writers (male and female).

The rapid decline of reputation after the death of a major literary figure is pretty much the usual thing, but Hemingway's has been slower to repair because of his treatment of endangered species, his posing and brawling and, of course, his suicide. With *Hemingway*, one has the feeling that Kenneth S. Lynn, at least, has recovered from disappointment and squarely faces the issue of Hemingway's masculinity, about which, it has been hinted, he protested too much.

Mr. Lynn finds special significance in the fact that Hemingway was raised for his first few years in little dresses (like, though, other boys of the day), as if he were the twin of his older sister, and in the dominant nature of his apparently overbearing mother, about whom Mr. Lynn uncovered lesbian gossip— although he doesn't say where. He thus (to oversimplify) finds in Hemingway's whole life "a larger drama of sexual confusion," with sisters who may or may not have wished to be boys, lots of cross-dressing and an obsession with women's short hair, and a "concerted effort to conceal his continuing psychological involvement" in this drama "by showing the world how manly he was." These preoccupations have been noted by other biographers but given less weight and they were made quite explicit in the recent posthumous compilation *The Garden of Eden*.

Certain questions may well occur to the reader. For one, what exactly is sexual confusion? Evidently it's more what you want to be than whom you want to sleep with—Hemingway gave no evidence of being attracted to men. It does seem undeniable that he recurs to the subject of heroines who are forever cutting their hair and trying to appear like boys and to heroes who like them this way, but Mr. Lynn does not make much of the fact that hair bobbing and gender definition were the preoccupations of Hemingway's and even of his parents' generation. There had been a revolution in women's clothes. Would you bob your hair or not? Bosoms were out. Should women smoke? The feminist issues in Hemingway are those in George Meredith, the reigning British novelist of Hemingway's childhood, or

even earlier, and one does not get a sense from Mr. Lynn of how widespread their importance was. All those entrenched male and American behaviors—hunting and the like—clearly did possess ritualistic importance for many men besides Hemingway, but many men, including Hemingway, must have been fascinated and attracted to the new emerging woman, however anxious she may have made them feel. No doubt the wish to settle, once and for all, the matter of Hemingway's psychosexual state has much to do with our continuing interest in what constitutes manliness.

It is not Mr. Lynn's intention, and not his effect, to make Hemingway seem to be living a sexual lie. After all, good writers are androgynous. The overwhelming impression is a sympathetic and detailed one of a writer trapped by other factors—by his own charm and energy, by literary adulation, by alcoholism—in a more conspicuous life than he could manage. It was too bad for him that he was a more fascinating person than most, and he paid a serious price for that, and so did his work, during and after his death. His childhood, in little dresses and so on, seems rather more ordinary than one would have thought, not really very strange—at least not to anyone who grew up in a small Illinois town, with its Congregational Church, dancing class, prom, school paper (called, inevitably, *The Line-O-Type*), pranks, hunting, sexual experiment, warmly affectionate female friendships and family strains—which in Hemingway's case foreshadowed the eventual tragedy of his father's suicide. So that at the same time that the author gives a rather extreme interpretation of Hemingway's start in life, the concreteness of this biography lends a certain convincing reality others have lacked.

He is also interesting on the subject of biographical evidence and the whole history of Hemingway criticism, rejecting, naturally, many earlier interpretations of the works and particular incidents, but at least bringing the reader up to date on the history of any controversy. (pp. 3, 25)

In discussing the relation of life and work, Mr. Lynn assumes a rather direct connection, a procedure usually acceptable but occasionally strained. For instance, in his account of **"Up in Michigan,"** a story Hemingway wrote just before his first marriage, to Hadley, Mr. Lynn observes, reasonably enough, that it "raises the question of what had been going on in the author's mind in regard to the Dilworths"—family friends whose names he had used, in particular using the name of the wife for that of a young waitress whom the young man forces to have sex with him on a dock. But Mr. Lynn's next question—"Was he by any chance trying to rid himself, on the eve of taking a bride almost eight years his senior, of a sexual attraction to a much older woman?"—may seem to the reader to venture too far into the realm of speculation. Then Mr. Lynn points out, and the reader agrees, that the same story refutes charges that Hemingway can't identify with women in his fiction since, here, he does.

It always seems, when a writer's life has captured people's imagination, that both biographers and readers are upset to hear that the writer has somehow altered the truth, even though that is what writers do. And whatever the artistic or psychological reasons for doing it, alterations seem to shadow the artistic achievement, at least until truth can be separated from its integument of lies. Mr. Lynn has a good go at this. But he is no more charitable than most biographers about the peculiar reality problem many writers actually have—the inability, once they have formulated a fictional version of a real event, to remember what really happened. In a way, the writer, whose imagination works oddly anyway, is the last person to be trusted for the truth embedded in his own fiction, just as, say, most of us have difficulty saying which of our early memories are directly remembered and which supplied us by family accounts.

How the biographer uses literary evidence to infer a life, and life to explain stories, as well as what the reader will accept, is almost a matter of individual taste. At any rate, Mr. Lynn insists that it was Hemingway's experience of "knowing how it felt to look like a girl but feel like a boy that was the fountainhead of his fascination with the ambiguities of feminine identity." Yet the reader cannot help but think that if other boys were dressed in clothes that to us today look like girls' clothes, then that is the way boys dressed then, and it is only we, looking back, who think they must have felt like girls. On the other hand, Mr. Lynn makes some really interesting connections: for instance, he notices that the name of Jacob Barnes, in *The Sun Also Rises,* could allude to two prominent lesbian acquaintances of Hemingway's—Natalie Barney, who lived at 20 rue Jacob, and Djuna Barnes, who lived at the Hôtel Jacob. "From these two associations," Mr. Lynn writes, "Hemingway derived the name of a man who is passionately in love with a sexually aggressive woman with an androgynous first name and a mannish haircut, a man whose dilemma is that, like a lesbian, he cannot penetrate his loved one's body with his own." This seems likely.

In the final analysis, whatever Mr. Lynn means by sexual confusion or sexual duality seems finally not scandalous but, instead, a compliment to Hemingway. And the author modifies an existing impression of a boorish man's man—whose work was "brutal, cynical, and callous," in the words of the Nobel citation (which upset him)—with the assessment that he was, in many instances, his women characters too and that he appreciated and identified with them. Hemingway, in Mr. Lynn's version, actually lived the kind of courageous and painful life he wrote about. There was no hypocritical discrepancy between the life he lived and the one he extolled. He was trying all along to face and write about problems of fate and conduct, especially conduct. In this sense he was moral and valiant, and *Hemingway* helps us recover a view of his life as having been, despite its end, a success. Perhaps its end was in keeping. Of his work, there can never have been any doubt. (p. 25)

Diane Johnson, "Mama and Papa," in The New York Times Book Review, *July 19, 1987, pp. 3, 25.*

RICHARD EDER

There is a rather small thesis in charge of Kenneth S. Lynn's very large biography of Ernest Hemingway. To relate it, skeletally: Hemingway's fleshy, pretentious and overbearing mother would sometimes dress him in girls' clothes when he was 2 and 3, and have him photographed along with his slightly older sister, Marcelline.

My impression of sepia photographs circa 1900 is that it was not altogether uncommon to dress tiny boys in girlish clothes. But Kenneth S. Lynn sees in it the beginning of a lifelong sexual hang-up.

Hemingway's male warrior-hunter self-image was a cover for a partly feminine nature, Lynn holds, and he investigates his writing for evidences of it. For example, in the short story, **"Up in Michigan,"** the writer portrays a quasi-rape not from the man's point of view, but from the woman's.

True enough; well observed, and possibly evidence for arguing that insofar as he was an artist—rather than a self-caricaturing life-styler—Hemingway commanded a range of sensibility that encompassed both sexes. So did Tolstoy, Shakespeare and Sophocles, of course.

The trouble is that Prof. Lynn allows the point to hijack his nicely loaded general-cargo vessel and sail onto some precipitous rocks. He treats it as a drastic and hitherto unsuspected secret; one that must radically upset our notion of the man and the writer.

Accordingly, Lynn conducts a kind of sexual stow-away-chase through Hemingway's novels and short stories. He is looking for women who cut their hair short and are sexually aggressive, and for men who like to make love belly-up.

In *The Garden of Eden,* the point is conspicuous and has been considerably remarked upon. Catherine gets a haircut to resemble David's and their love-making deliberately mixes up their sex roles. But of course, *Garden* was a swollen collection of drafts and false starts, drastically edited after Hemingway's death into a small and shaky book. It is hard to figure what in the way of a general statement can be derived from it about the artist and man, as opposed to the disintegration of the artist and man.

Lynn goes to the major works, but his point shrinks as he does so. With the other Catherine, in *A Farewell to Arms,* he notes her short hair and the fact that she was the nurse and Frederic the patient for the early part of their relationship, and that Frederic was on his back in a hospital bed. . . .

With *For Whom the Bell Tolls,* Lynn goes so far as to assert that critics, who hailed the book as a sign of recovery from the writer's long decline, missed two of the really significant things about it. One of these is what he calls the "obsession with death." Whether "obsession" is the right word, considering the subject—the hopelessly murderous Spanish Civil War—is at least debatable. The second major point, he writes, is "the curiousness of the love affair." Sure enough, this consists of Maria's short hair and the fact that in their love-making, she and Robert Jordan felt that they had become indistinguishable from each other.

To be surprised that the critics didn't pick out short hair and the fusing of two lovers, as a key to the novel, may indicate how far Lynn has let his theme run away with him. After all, he does not claim that Hemingway was a homosexual, still less a lesbian. Short of that, the particular kind of sexual fantasy Hemingway gave to his protagonists seems to me of interest, but not infinite interest. It casts a modest, though real light, but Lynn has overcharged it with outsize batteries.

Thesis apart, Lynn's *Hemingway* is a thorough, detailed and often sensitive job. I don't think it provides any major new insights about this most abundantly written-about writer, but it documents extensively the largely familiar story. . . . (p. 3)

Sometimes the detail seems little more than scholarly pugnacity; an attempt to stake out a tiny plot in an overcrowded field. Pages are spent taking issue with others over the precise nature of the leg wound Hemingway incurred serving in the Red Cross in World War I, and over just how brave he had been. Were there bullets in the wound as well as shrapnel? What precise degree of prowess was indicated by the Italians' award of a silver rather than a gold medal?

Lynn's thoroughness, on the other hand, is useful in making more understandable the mercurial quality of Hemingway's moods; his ability to be generous, winning and brutal without apparent transition; his tendency to turn upon and discard those friends and lovers upon whom he expended such energy and genius in acquiring. He is frequently illuminating in his efforts to show links between facets of Hemingway's life and its reflections in his highly autobiographical work.

The pain, lifelong, is spelled out vividly. Lynn's Hemingway is a man of rankling resentments. He wanted to be godlike as hero, lover and artist, but had serious shortages in each department.

He could be disastrously clumsy as an outdoorsman, he was perpetually getting sick or hurt, his sexual abilities seem to have been erratic, and when he was not a very, very good writer he was often a very, very bad one.

Falling short or running dry was unacceptable agony. He could not allow himself to age. Instead, he engaged in a slow, spectacular suicide that called itself living life to the full, until it stopped calling itself anything. (pp. 3, 12)

Richard Eder, in a review of "Hemingway: The Life and the Work," in Los Angeles Times Book Review, *July 26, 1987, pp. 3, 12.*

FREDERICK CREWS

[*Crews, an American critic, is known as a practitioner of psychoanalytical literary criticism. In addition to his famous parody of literary theory,* The Pooh Perplex: A Freshman Casebook *(1963), he has written* Out of My System: Psychoanalysis, Ideology, and Critical Method *(1975),* Skeptical Engagements *(1986), and several works on American novelists. In the following excerpt, Crews hails Lynn's biography as "brilliant and provocative" and details how this revisionist study offers dramatic new perspectives on Hemingway's life and fiction.*]

Kenneth S. Lynn's **Hemingway** is hardly a book that its subject would have enjoyed reading. If the touchy and pugnacious bruiser were still among us, Lynn would surely want to keep a bodyguard at his side for the next several years. Nevertheless, he has written not only one of the most brilliant and provocative literary biographies in recent memory, but also the study that Hemingway most urgently needs at this point in his critical fortunes.

Though superficial appearances indicate otherwise, Hemingway's literary stature continues to be subject to the downward revision that began on the day in 1961 when, depressed, paranoid, and stupefied by heavy doses of electroshock therapy, he blew out his brains with a shotgun blast. Throughout the Sixties and Seventies, feminists and others took their own shots at the tottering idol, whose cult of macho sporting values and stoic mannerisms began to seem hollow and foolish. So much insistence on correctness of attitude in the face of a melodramatically hostile fate; so much self-flattery in the creation of one autobiographical hero after another, always a god to his adoring woman; so much scorn for the weakling, the pervert, the aesthete, the castrating bitch! Wasn't the whole thing—and Hemingway's famous tight-lipped style along with it—a contemptible sham?

Today, when remoteness in time has begun to confer indulgence toward the writer's personal failings, we hear less of such talk. Instead, we find ourselves in the midst of what looks like a Hemingway boom. (p. 30)

One may wonder, however, whether this flurry signifies a true reversal of the critical deflation or merely a scholarly and commercial feeding frenzy over the newly accessible Hemingwayana in collections at the John F. Kennedy Library, the University of Texas, and elsewhere. In large measure, what has been restored to us is Hemingway the celebrity—the figure that he himself, the supreme self-publicist of modern letters, created in the Thirties and shrewdly marketed through articles and interviews depicting a life of action, courage, and connoisseurship. It says something about our own shallow decade that so many of us are happy to revert to that trivial conception of our most influential novelist. In the long run, however, the resuscitation of the Hemingway legend will be seen to have merely postponed an inevitable reckoning. Quite simply, the legend is false, and its certain demise will leave Hemingway once again exposed to his most adamant detractors.

What Hemingway requires is an ideal reader who can discard everything that is meretricious in our image of him but then do justice to the literary art that remains. Put this way, the task sounds straightforward enough. The trouble is, however, that the reality behind the legend is so unpleasant in several respects that biographical debunkers have had no stomach for the work of critical reconstruction. From the former idolator Carlos Baker's reluctantly revelatory *Ernest Hemingway: A Life Story* to Bernice Kert's *The Hemingway Women* and Jeffrey Meyers's *Hemingway: A Biography*, those who have had the most eye-opening things to say about Hemingway the man have not cared even to attempt critical reformulations.

After Kenneth Lynn's contribution, however, nothing will be the same in any branch of Hemingway studies. Though his ambitious inquiry builds (with acknowledgment) on the work of other biographers, Lynn carries the process of demythification even farther than did Jeffrey Meyers, whose coolly objective and well-researched book has been treated in some quarters as a breach of decorum. We will see that no aspect of Hemingway's conduct, however intimate or embarrassing, escapes Lynn's clinical eye. Yet his intelligence is fully balanced by his humanity. Instead of merely refuting Hemingway's boasts, Lynn offers us our first cogent and sustained explanation of the psychological, familial, and environmental pressures that helped to make the willful yet deeply cautious author what he was. The result is an admirable combination of justice and compassion—but that is not all. In showing that Hemingway secretly entertained broader sympathies than his manly code implied, Lynn is able to return to the fiction with fresh appreciation.

To be sure, the Hemingway who emerges is a troubled and diminished figure in comparison with the mythic presence that once dominated our literary scene. But he is not the exposed fraud we have grown accustomed to meeting in ideological diatribes of recent decades. Rather, he is the Hemingway who once wrote to Scott Fitzgerald, "We are all bitched from the start and you especially have to be hurt like hell before you can write seriously. But when you get the damned hurt use it—don't cheat with it. Be as faithful to it as a scientist."

To arrive at that vulnerable and exacting artist, we must first learn to forgo the Hemingway legend. But the task is not as easy as it looks. The legend, it is important to grasp, comes in two versions—in effect, one for the credulous mass public and one for relatively wary critics. If the simple version is clearly doomed, its more sophisticated counterpart still has plenty of eloquent defenders.

At the primary level, the legend says that Hemingway was a great sportsman, aficionado, and stoic, religiously devoted to maintaining poise in the face of mortal danger. This is the image cultivated by the surviving Hemingway clan for the sake of its business ventures, including Hemingway Ltd., a corporation formed to market the label "Hemingway" for use on tastefully chosen fishing rods, safari clothes, and (surely the ultimate triumph of greed over taste) shotguns. In contrast, the critics' version of the legend is a limited exercise in damage control. It allows that the hero may have been morbid and fear-ridden but asserts that even his debilities were acquired in a noble, portentous manner—namely, in the traumatizing experience of being hit by shrapnel in World War I. Thanks to the wounding, Hemingway is awarded a red badge of tragic historical consciousness.

Although Lynn provides the most decisive refutation of both accounts, his conclusions about Hemingway the alleged sportsman were already implicit in other biographies. Scholars have known for some time that Hemingway—clumsy, weak-eyed, slow-footed, accident-prone, and, in the words of his third wife, Martha Gellhorn, "the biggest liar since Munchausen"—always talked a better game than he played. To hear him tell is, no subtlety of sport or combat had eluded his skills or analytic acumen. True specialists, however, were often unimpressed not only by his prowess but also by his claims to expertise.

More important, Hemingway's sense of fair competition was stunted by irrational needs. As a recreational boxer, he became notorious for administering low blows and knees to the groin, mercilessly pounding smaller and weaker friends, sucker-punching one man who was still lacing his gloves, and doing the same to another—indeed, smashing his newly donned glasses—while the latter was *un*lacing a glove. After his eye-hand coordination had been sacrificed to alcoholism, he disgusted his hunting companions by claiming some of their kills as his own. And in recalling deep-sea fishing trips with the later Hemingway—who was fond of shooting at sharks with a machine gun or pistol, and who once wounded his own legs in the process—Arnold Gingrich characterized his overbearing friend as a "meat fisherman" who "cared more about the quantity than about the quality," disdained the true angler's concern for proper methods, and was all in all "a very poor sport." In his zeal to throw more punches, ski more recklessly, catch more fish, and slaughter more animals than anyone else, Hemingway was not a sportsman but a man possessed.

If the writer's compulsive side is inescapable, however, its origins are still a theme of lively controversy. Under the influence of Malcolm Cowley, Philip Young, and Hemingway himself—who grudgingly came to find a certain utility in this line of argument—most commentators from the Forties until now have traced his psychic problems to the Austrian mortar shell which had allegedly shattered both his equanimity and his belief in public causes. As articulated in the backup legend, the famous incident at Fossalta di Piave at once attests to the hero's preternatural valor, imparts an agreeably leftward spin to his grandest themes (the emptiness of politicians' abstractions, the need for a separate peace), and provides a concrete external basis for the not-so-grand ones (night fears, loss of nerve, castration, impotence, nihilism).

Thanks to careful research by Lynn and, before him, Michael Reynolds, this story now stands exposed as a fiction. Hemingway, it seems, grossly misrepresented the immediate aftermath of his wounding, when, with over 200 shell fragments lodged in his lower body, he allegedly carried a fellow victim 150 yards through machine-gun fire to safety, absorbing several direct hits but somehow picking himself back up and completing the herculean ordeal. The truth appears to be that young Ernest received many flesh wounds from shrapnel, that he showed solicitude for others while waiting to be evacuated, but that during his recovery he embroidered the story to compel maximum awe from parents, friends, and reporters, some of whom were even left with the impression that he had been a member of the Italian equivalent of the Green Berets rather than a Red Cross volunteer dispensing cigarettes and candy from a bicycle.

The most significant distortion, however, was not Hemingway's doing but that of critics enamored of the overworked "postwar disillusionment" or "wasteland" thesis. This banality has served to lend a darker, more mature tinge to the fiction of the Jazz Age, which at its best (*The Great Gatsby*, *The Sun Also Rises*) is thought to constitute a wise commentary on the moral collapse of the West. Since the books in question reflect scant historical analysis and are patently jejune in some respects, the critics' job has been to catch deeper echoes between the lines. (pp. 30-1)

Did Hemingway lose his boyish innocence in 1918, acquiring in short order a fissured psyche and a bitter sense of historical disillusionment? Lynn proposes that we need only consult surviving letters and photographs to see that, on the contrary, the teen-age adventurer was more elated than shattered by his brush with death. (One of the reproduced pictures, taken shortly after the explosion, discloses a buoyant, handsome youth, not quite nineteen, beaming triumphantly at the camera from his hospital bed in Milan.) "It does give you an awfully satisfactory feeling to be wounded," he wrote home. It was, he said in another letter, "the next best thing to getting killed and reading your own obituary"—a line that could have been spoken by Tom Sawyer. Obviously, Hemingway was trying to calm his parents' fears. Even so, the adeptness of his sprightly rhetoric sits poorly with the conventional idea of his thoroughly unnerved, shell-shocked condition.

As Meyers had already perceived, Hemingway's escape without so much as a broken bone "made him feel invincible, . . . made him want to challenge fate." Nothing in his subsequent conduct suggests that he returned from Italy with a subdued temper, much less a revulsion against killing or a grasp of the issues and ironies behind the war. No doubt the wounding did render him more "existential," heightening both his bravado and his morbidity. What it assuredly did not do, however, was to equip him with the insight and compassion that his friendliest commentators have wished to lend him. On the contrary, it appears to have launched him on a career of braggadocio and hedonistic thrill seeking (financed by other people's money) that would put him gravely out of touch with the social and political consciousness of later times.

For Hemingway's most compliant critics, however, thoughts of war and death are wonderfully ennobling. Consider, for example, their response to **"Big Two-Hearted River,"** certainly an admirable work, but not necessarily one that reverberates with world-historical import. Especially since Malcolm Cowley's influential introduction to the *Portable Hemingway* in 1944, this story of a solitary trout-fishing expedition has been thought to depict its hero's struggle against an underlying panic stemming from the shell shock that figures in other Nick Adams stories written some years later. Hemingway himself belatedly claimed to have adopted this poignant way of reading his tale. "In the first war, *I now see,*" he wrote to Cowley in 1948, "I was hurt very badly; in the body, mind and spirit; and also morally. . . . **'Big Two-Hearted River'** is a story about a man who is home from the war. . . . I was still hurt very badly in that story" (italics added).

In 1981, however, Kenneth Lynn had the temerity to point out that the published text of **"Big Two-Hearted River"** neither mentions the Great War nor alludes to it in any definite way, and that in this tale Nick Adams neither moves about nor thinks like a man who has recently undergone a physically and spiritually crippling trauma. His escape, through the satisfactions of expert camping and fishing, from an unstated preoccupation is all but complete. As for Cowley's thesis, Hemingway apparently saw in it an opportunity to put his anxieties into the past tense and assign them a public cause. Which reading requires fewer extraneous assumptions? Surely it makes sense, as Lynn urges, to be guided by the story itself rather than by the retrospective gloss that Cowley successfully urged upon the rarely veracious Hemingway.

Nevertheless, Lynn's challenge to the "wound" reading has been received as a virtual sacrilege. Two years ago, writing in *The New Republic,* R. W. B. Lewis sounded the alarm: "Lynn's critical attitude [toward **"Big Two-Hearted River"**], however absurd, was only incidental to a larger intention: to insist that American literature in general is and has been sun-drenched and happy, and wholly free of the dark Russian morbidity attributed to it by Cowley and his fellows." This gratuitous claim can serve as a gauge of the passions that get involved not just with Hemingway criticism in general but specifically with the Fossalta question. For Lewis, Lynn's failure to be adequately pious about the crushing effects of the war constitutes nothing less than a "nativist" and reactionary program to break the links between the Continent and modern American literature in general.

Hemingway's "postwar disillusionment," such as it was, proved to be a belated and derivative manifestation. *A Farewell to Arms* was published in 1929, long after the acclaimed antiwar novels by Dos Passos and Cummings and in the same year that Remarque's *All Quiet on the Western Front* appeared in English. By then, a bitter view of the slogans of 1914 had become virtually obligatory as a token of tough-mindedness. Moreover, Lynn emphasizes that Lieutenant Frederic Henry's famous embarrassment over "the words sacred, glorious, and sacrifice" is represented not as a wartime revulsion but as a preexisting bias; that is the way he has "always" felt. Lynn's analysis concurs with a brilliant reading by Millicent Bell, which reveals the seeming pacifism of *A Farewell to Arms* to be a curiously private and psychologically regressive affair.

Similarly, Lynn reminds us that some of Hemingway's stories about the prewar Nick Adams already hint at the depressive anxiety with which the wounded Nick will have to contend. Far from maintaining that Hemingway's writings are "wholly free of . . . dark Russian morbidity," Lynn finds them typically saturated in a mood of indefinite resentment, pessimism, and urgency about maintaining control. Indeed, he takes that mood far more seriously than do critics who try to derive it from Hemingway's alleged awareness of failings in modern capitalist civilization. The writer's politics, Lynn repeatedly shows, were suggestible and riddled with inconsistencies. His psychic makeup, on the other hand, was invariable—and deeply strange.

The prime article of faith for Hemingway's cultists is of course his thoroughgoing maleness. Already in his lifetime, however,

that was a topic of considerable speculation. James Joyce saw the brash American as "the sensitive type" trying to pass for tough. A colleague on the Toronto *Star* who knew him at age twenty remarked, "A more weird combination of quivering sensitiveness and preoccupation with violence never walked this earth." "What a book," hissed the novelist's former confidante Gertrude Stein, "would be the real story of Hemingway, not those he writes but the confessions of the real Ernest Hemingway. It would be for another audience than the audience Hemingway now has but it would be very wonderful." (pp. 31-2)

One of Hemingway's most constant traits was his compulsion to demean the sexual credentials of others—usually people who had wounded his literary or erotic vanity. In stories, novels, and poems he skewered friends and enemies alike, taking pains to make them easily recognizable and portraying them as impotent or homosexual. Four years after Max Eastman had publicly drawn the obvious conclusion from such sniping that "Hemingway lacks the serene confidence that he *is* a full-sized man"—the wounded lion cornered Eastman in Maxwell Perkin's office, yelled, "What do you mean accusing me of impotence?" and physically assailed him.

But there is evidence that Hemingway did suffer from recurrent impotence in his four marriages, and his pre- and extramarital amours either quickly fizzled or never progressed beyond hand holding. . . . "I wish to hell it were true," said Mary when asked if her husband had been a magnificent lover. Throughout his adulthood Hemingway's relations with women were characterized not by the libidinal freedom of which he bragged but by a babyish, demanding dependency punctuated by sulks, tantrums, and flights to the next would-be protectress.

To say this much about Hemingway's sexual misery is to bring the story up to Kenneth Lynn's point of departure. As Lynn insists, more needs to be established about Hemingway's sexuality if we are to account for the peculiar tremulousness of his fiction. Ever since news of the *Garden of Eden* manuscripts began spreading a decade ago, it has been widely suspected that his secret theme was androgyny—and this has now become the leading motif of Lynn's *Hemingway.*

Androgyny is named just once in Hemingway's published work, in a startlingly sympathetic discussion of El Greco in *Death in the Afternoon.* The painter, Hemingway wrote, "could go as far into his other world as he wanted and, consciously or unconsciously, paint . . . the androgynous faces and forms that filled his imagination." Now, thanks to Lynn's carefully reasoned analysis, Hemingway's own "other world" has become sufficiently distinct to be beyond conjecture.

Exhibit A, of course, is the posthumous *Garden of Eden,* a work whose dissociated effect can be explained in part, but only in part, by the collage-like job of editing that was required to make it look like a consecutive story. But even this composite text, screened by Hemingway's second son, Patrick, for any hints of the unsavory, is manifestly about androgyny.

What made *The Garden of Eden* printable from the family's standpoint was no doubt the fact that two female characters, not the Hemingwayesque writer-hero, instigate the story's kinky games. All the bisexual impulses that are overtly represented belong to David Bourne's maniacal bride Catherine and their mutual friend Marita, a lesbian whom Catherine praises as "a girl and boy both." Superficially, it is not David's (or Hemingway's) fault that he and Catherine are taken for brother and sister, or that Catherine keeps cutting her hair like a boy's, or that she gets him to dye his own hair—thus turning him into her same-sex twin—or that her ultimate fantasy in bed is to trade roles with him. And of course David is just obeying instructions from Catherine—though with telltale alacrity!—when he has sex with the boy-girl Marita, who has recently come from a lesbian encounter with Catherine.

A gullible reader could overlook the motiveless, masturbatory quality of this transformational daisy chain and imagine that Hemingway was merely venting some of his usual misogyny. But as Lynn makes us aware, the same theme of sex-crossing and even some of the same language can be found in other fictions dating back to the Twenties. In that nominal war novel *A Farewell to Arms,* another and more celebrated Catherine proposes that she and her man get identical haircuts:

> "Then we'd both be alike. Oh darling, I want you
> so much I want to be you too."
>
> "You are. We're the same one."

In *For Whom the Bell Tolls* it is the Hemingway stand-in, Robert Jordan, who takes enough of a recess from preparing to kill fascists to suggest that he and Maria "go together to the coiffeur's" and be rendered indistinguishable. While cuddling they tell each other, "I am thee and thou art me." And in *Islands in the Stream* it is once again the woman (does it really matter?) who leads:

> "Should I be you or you be me?"
>
> "You have first choice."
>
> "I'll be you."
>
> "I can't be you. But I can try."

Such passages make it difficult to doubt that an imagined switching of sex roles constituted the heart of Hemingway's erotic ideal. And, as Lynn goes on to show, the nonfictional record is entirely consistent with the fictional one.

This is not to say that the strident homophobe Hemingway was disposed toward literally bisexual activities. Whatever he wanted from eros, he sought it from women alone. Lynn shows, however, that the sexual inclinations of women themselves were of more than ordinary interest to him. Hemingway found himself libidinally drawn to lesbians—even to the butch and burly Gertrude Stein, who told her rapt apprentice about women's ways with women and taught him how to crop the hair of his first wife, Hadley. His second wife, Pauline, took female lovers (including Elizabeth Bishop) after Hemingway abandoned her, and in happier days he gloried in her boyishness, just as he had done with his sporting chum Hadley. With all four wives he exhibited the same fetishism of hair length and color, seeking twinlike effects with himself. . . . (pp. 33-4)

If Ernest Hemingway felt himself to be in essence "a girl and boy both," how did he get that way? And what prompted him to encase his androgynous core in a suit of hypermasculine armor? Though any answers must be speculative, Lynn shows us some remarkable and touching correlations between what was done to the writer in his earliest years and the volatile and unhappy man that he became.

Lynn has realized more fully than anyone thus far that the place to begin looking for explanatory clues about Hemingway's values and predilections is not Fossalta or Paris or Pamplona but Oak Park, Illinois, where he grew up. We now know that he felt himself continually judged against the local standards of sobriety, chastity, decorum, refined culture, and Protestant altruism—standards that had been impressed upon the dutiful cello student and choirboy by both his puritanical and capri-

ciously punitive father and his ambitious, domineering mother. Like Oak Park's other world-class maverick, Frank Lloyd Wright, the mature Hemingway dramatically flouted those standards. In doing so, however, he remained caught in an anxious, resentful quarrel with them.

If Frederic Henry has "always" gagged on words like *sacrifice* and *glory,* that may be because they were instruments of intimidation in his creator's early years; and they remained so as both parents continued to express dismay over their famous son's freedom of language and theme. ("What is the matter?" wrote Grace Hemingway upon first looking into *The Sun Also Rises.* "Have you ceased to be interested in loyalty, nobility, honor and fineness of life?") Once out of Illinois, Hemingway took pains to reverse every feature of Oak Park respectability, even to the extent of encouraging his son Gregory to get repeatedly drunk on hard liquor at age ten and of renting a Cuban prostitute to relieve his other son Jack of his hypothetical (but long departed) virginity at age nineteen. Yet no parent could have been less forgiving than Hemingway's own conscience in damning him for trading on his charm, wasting his time and talent, surrounding himself with flatterers, and marinating his brain in Scotch. Wherever he fled, Oak Park waited in ambush for him.

When Hemingway wrote about scenes from boyhood, they were set not in that priggish Anglophile suburb but in the woods and remote towns of northern Michigan where he had passed his relatively unconstrained summers. The rural outdoors was his father's masculine territory—the only area where Dr. Clarence ("Ed") Hemingway, in his teenage son's view, had found even a partial refuge from their mutual nemesis, Grace. The author-to-be saw his "Papa" as the cowed and castrated husband par excellence, broken in spirit by a woman who arrogated male authority and who squandered the family's resources on lavish, ego-preening projects. In some of his Nick Adams stories Hemingway alluded to Ed Hemingway's weakness, implicitly put the blame on Grace, and represented his own impressionable self in terms that suggested an already desperate wish to escape a comparable fate.

As Bernice Kert has demonstrated in *The Hemingway Women,* Grace Hemingway possessed several constructive traits that her son chose to overlook. She was more tolerant of boyish mischief than her husband was and, unlike him, she was more concerned to reward achievement than to lash out against impropriety and sin. Ernest's literary precocity was not just a gift but a tribute to her encouragement and tutelage. For these very reasons, however, his lifelong, virulent, well-documented hatred of the mother he always called "that bitch" must be regarded in a symptomatic light. Like his father, and in a pattern that stretched back and ahead through four unlucky generations, Ernest was constitutionally depressive. In laying his nervous melancholy at Grace's door and arming his mind against all Circes everywhere, the writer was attempting to externalize and forestall a doom that may have been imprinted in his genes.

If nature supplies the flawed clay, however, it is nurture that molds the features into a unique image. Here is where Lynn's *Hemingway* stakes its boldest claim to originality: in showing how pervasively the writer's mind was ruled by his sense of what Grace had done to him. The story is bizarre, and some readers will want to put it down to gratuitous Freudianizing on the biographer's part. But Lynn is not in fact rehearsing Oedipal universals or purporting to trace repressed infantile memories; he is merely reconstructing the inferences that Hemingway himself drew as he coped with his mother's conduct, pored over the scrapbook she had compiled about his childhood, and pondered the rumors about her that were common gossip in Oak Park.

Those rumors said that Grace Hemingway enjoyed a lesbian relationship with her young voice pupil and housekeeper Ruth Arnold, who lived with the family for eleven years until Ed, who took the gossip seriously enough to become alarmed, screwed up his courage for once and ordered Ruth out of the house. (The juggernaut Grace was safely off in Michigan at the time.) Ernest Hemingway was twenty years old and in a sullenly rebellious frame of mind when he witnessed the ensuing parental showdown and took his father's side; but throughout his adolescence he must have known what people were whispering. After Ed's suicide the two women stirred further talk, and further resentment from Ernest, by resuming their joint residence in nearby River Forest.

Lesbian or not, Grace had her own obsession with sexual identity. To be sure, the fact that side dressed and coiffed Ernest as a girl for the first two and a half years of his life does not set her apart from many another turn-of-the-century mother. Perhaps that is why previous biographers have attached no importance to such memorabilia as a photograph of two-year-old Ernest in a gown and bonnet, cutely captioned "summer girl." But the biographers should assuredly not have passed lightly by the 1962 memoir written by Hemingway's sister Marcelline, one and a half years his senior. There Marcelline explained that Grace wanted the children not just to look alike but "to feel like twins, by having everything alike." (pp. 34-5)

Continually experimenting with outfits and hair styles, she created twin "brothers" as often as "sisters," and at times she showed pride in the sporting exploits of her little man. In all likelihood what Grace wanted, beyond an enactment of some private cross-gender scheme, was a boy whose sexual identity would remain forever dependent upon her dictates and whims. If so, she gruesomely got her wish. The apparent effect of all that dolling and doting was not so much to lend Ernest a female identity as to implant in his mind a permanently debilitating confusion, anxiety, and anger.

Naturally, Hemingway despised Marcelline as fiercely as he came to hate the mother who had glutted him with caresses until she abruptly turned her attention to the next sibling, Ursula. And the strong attachment he subsequently developed to Ursula carried an incestuous intensity, as if he had to validate his maleness through this other sister's love. But the idea of incest, in Hemingway's bemused imagination, was just another means of swapping identities. Later, as an adult, he could only entrust himself to a woman—and then only provisionally, before feelings of entrapment set in—if he mentally conscripted her into the game in which he himself had been initiated by Grace. *Odi et amo*. It is little wonder that Hemingway's writings abound not only in castrating shrews and shattered men but also in sibling-like lovers whose deepest fantasy is to trade sex roles or merge into androgynous oneness.

The virtue of Lynn's account is that it brings into coherence an array of facts—from Hemingway's obsession with lesbianism and hair length through the combination of browbeating and dependency in his love relations—that have hitherto appeared puzzling, though not exactly anomalous. Many commentators have sensed that someone who was not only mesmerized by the castration-defying bravado of the *corrida* but also compelled to sneer at the squeamishness of the unconvinced had to have been caught up in a quarrel with self-doubts.

And with increasing certainty after the shot-gun blast in 1961, they have known that the writer whose imagination reverted to goring, maiming, crucifixion, exploded body parts, and agonies of childbirth was by no means a simple realist of the out-of-doors. No one before Lynn, however, has established the specific connections between Hemingway's family situation and his fragile personality.

Take, for example, the writer's locker-room, know-it-all side—his claim to definitive expertise on every male topic from boxing and hunting through battle tactics. Lynn shows that such assertiveness would have fit the psychic needs of a boy growing up in the shadow of an older sister with whom he was constantly paired and compared. Likewise, the man who saw betrayal everywhere succeeded the boy who, appealing to one parent for refuge from the other, invariably found the adult ranks closing against him in sanctimonious solidarity. The man who dubbed himself "Papa" while still in his mid-twenties and who sought record-sized kills of fish, beasts, and German soldiers was bent not only on outdoing his woodsman father but on magically repairing the unmanning to which he thought that father (along with himself) had been subjected by Grace Hemingway. And topping everything, the mental hermaphrodite had been systematically deprived of a stable male identity. All in all, we cannot be surprised that even in his final years, family grievances remained uppermost in Hemingway's mind. (pp. 35-6)

The critical lessons of Lynn's *Hemingway* are chiefly two. In the first place, Lynn enables us to realize why the short story and not the novel proved to be Hemingway's suited genre. The amplitude of a realistic novel calls for broad sympathies and a conscious, integrated understanding of characters and conflicts. A writer whose professed values serve as preventatives against self-insight will find it hard to sustain his characters' development over many chapters or to avoid recourse to stereotypes and posturing. Such, on the whole, was Hemingway's predicament as a full-length novelist; he wavered between being "true to the hurt" and propagandistically disowning it. As Lynn reminds us, even the acclaimed novella *The Old Man and the Sea* seems, on rereading, like a strained and padded effort, bolted together with clunky symbols.

In contrast, Hemingway was temperamentally inclined toward the economy of phrase and gesture required by a ten-page tale. . . . Within a short story, Hemingway's characteristic shuttling between mute physical details and irritable, elliptical conversation is hauntingly suggestive. We needn't know, any more than the author himself does, precisely what lurks within the gulf that every sentence barely skirts. . . . Hemingway's tales at their best are unforgettable because their actions have the cruel finality of fate itself, without the possibility of recourse to values and theories—not even Hemingway's own.

The other benefit that discerning readers of Hemingway can draw from Lynn's study is encouragement to trust their instincts, rather than Hemingway's reassurances, when they think they have noticed deviations from the writer's macho norm. In particular, they will find that some of Hemingway's most durable works undercut their own impulse to distinguish simplistically between the he-man and the weakling, the compliant kitten and the castrating bitch.

Consider, as a seemingly intractable test case, **"The Short Happy Life of Francis Macomber."** Like **"Big Two-Hearted River,"** this powerful story has usually been read in the light of Hemingway's own summary of it, delivered a decade and a half after its composition. "Francis' wife hates him because he's a coward," Hemingway said to an interviewer in 1953. "But when he gets his guts back, she fears him so much she has to kill him—shoots him in the back of the head." That is Hemingway the famous misogynist speaking. But once again Lynn demonstrates that the tale refutes its forgetful teller. Mrs. Macomber is no murderer; in stating that she "had shot *at the buffalo* with the 6.5 Mannlicher as it seemed about to gore Macomber" (italics added), the text unambiguously establishes the killing as accidental. As Lynn insists:

> Just as the wife in **"Kilimanjaro"** is finally relieved of blame by her husband for the tragic waste of his talent, so a critically important narrative detail absolves Margot of responsibility for Macomber's tragedy.

This is much more than a crux resolved; it is one sign among many that Hemingway *could* sometimes identify with a woman's point of view and thus mitigate the tendentiousness of his schematizing.

For a final and more complex example, let us consider Hemingway's best novel, *The Sun Also Rises,* whose "official" reading was laid out by Carlos Baker in 1963. "The moral norm of the book," wrote Baker, "is a healthy and almost boyish innocence of spirit, and it is carried by Jake Barnes, Bill Gorton, and Pedro Romero. Against this norm . . . is ranged the sick abnormal 'vanity' of the Ashley-Campbell-Cohn triangle." In all probability, Hemingway would have endorsed this way of regarding his novel. Yet surely it is much too constraining. Do we in fact experience Brett and Cohn as unredeemably bad? And is the casual anti-Semitism voiced by Bill and Jake somehow "healthier" than Mike Campbell's bullying version? Unless we can find a way of approaching the book that transcends Hemingway's vulgar code, many of us will remain immune to its narrative power.

In one sense Baker was right: from its opening page, *The Sun Also Rises* makes Robert Cohn its embodiment of every trait that violates the Hemingway outlook. We know for certain, moreover, that the sneering at Cohn was inspired by Hemingway's petty but permanently injurious vendetta against his friend and benefactor Harold Loeb, whose romance with Duff Twysden, unlike his own, had been sexually consummated. Yet we now also know from Lynn's biography that everything Hemingway wanted to say about Cohn/Loeb's naive romanticism and self-pity applied at least as well to his own.

On closer inspection, as several critics have noticed before Lynn, the resemblances between the two "steers" Jake and Cohn seem more impressive than the differences. Furthermore, Jake doesn't simply take pleasure in watching Cohn get humiliated in a setting that he, Jake, has largely staged; he also shows flashes of self-detestation for that very baseness. In Jake Barnes the author has given us his most revealing, if still oblique and alibi-ridden, self-portrait. It is a picture of someone who has good reason to feel himself less than a man, who therefore waxes by turns snappish and maudlin, yet who longs for escape from his private hell into the matador's reticent and impersonal "purity of line." Precisely because Jake *is* Hemingway (indeed, his name in the earliest surviving manuscript was "Hem"), he captures not only his creator's adolescent manifest values but also his mean streak, his fits of remorse, his secret passivity, and his eventually suffocating need to be right about everything. The characterization is far more nuanced than Hemingway could have first intended when he set out to "get" Harold Loeb and create an autobiographical hero who would be disqualified only by a technicality from being Duff Twysden/Brett Ashley's one true love.

And if Carlos Baker's "healthy" Jake escapes black-and-white categories, so does his "abnormal" Brett. According to the Hemingway code, Brett's habit of undermining men's sexual self-respect ought to be unforgivable. In fact, however, her constant yearning to be a "good chap" and mend her ways makes her one of the more appealing figures in the book—more so, surely, than the wooden Pedro Romero, who is novelistically inert precisely because he embodies Hemingway's ideal and nothing else. As Lynn points out, Brett's penitent side was drawn from life—not Duff Twysden's life or Zelda Fitzgerald's, but Hemingway's own. Thanks to his capacity for unorthodox identifications, he gave us in Brett what most of his fiction would sorely lack: an independent woman who is not automatically an object of scorn.

There is no need to go overboard here and decide that *The Sun Also Rises* is a wise and compassionate book. As Lynn shows, Hemingway couldn't afford to decide what he finally thought of the sportsman-eunuch-bigot-pimp Jake Barnes, and his novel is not just irresolute but seriously muddled. Readers who think they have found consistently humane ironies in the text—indications, for example, that the author is not crudely anti-Semitic or that his vision of excellence transcends the image of Pedro Romero in his tight green pants—are deceiving themselves. And so, I would add, are those who take this cattiest of *romans à clef* as a reliable guide to masculine values.

Yet Lynn has revealed that *The Sun Also Rises* is swept by countercurrents of feeling that neither the idolators nor the iconoclasts among Hemingway critics have been prepared to recognize. If it had been a more thoroughgoing "Hemingway novel" in Baker's sense, the final image of Jake and Brett in the taxi—together but forever apart—would have meant nothing to us. Instead, of course, it is a crystalline moment—the nearest approach Hemingway would ever make to the pathos of authentic tragedy.

In replacing the comforts of myth with acute psychological, social, and literary analysis, Kenneth Lynn has not only laid bare that "real Ernest Hemingway" whom Gertrude Stein once fathomed; he has also provided a model of the way biographically informed criticism can catch the pulse of works about which everything appeared to have been said. In short, he has made Hemingway interesting again. For many readers, of course—the potential clientele of Hemingway Ltd.—that contribution will appear superfluous and offensive. In view of the now exposed hollowness of the official cult, however, no one has done more timely justice to what Alfred Kazin once called Hemingway's "brilliant half-vision of life." (pp. 36-7)

Frederick Crews, "Pressure Under Grace," in The New York Review of Books, *Vol. XXXIV, No. 13, August 13, 1987, pp. 30-8.*

JAMES W. TUTTLETON

[In the following excerpt, Tuttleton praises Lynn's biography for its psychological insight, noting that its exploration of Hemingway's androgynous fantasies prompts a critical reevaluation of his canon based on the important element in the perennial theme of sexual identity and relationships rather than neuroses.]

With the publication now of Kenneth S. Lynn's **Hemingway** readers are at last in a position to begin to understand the psychological and emotional dynamics of Hemingway the man and to grasp how the elements of his inner life are manifest in the forms of his fiction. Lynn brings to his task the tools of a mature critic and biographer who is already well known for a variety of excellent works of literary and cultural criticism including *The Dream of Success, Mark Twain and Southwestern Humor, William Dean Howells: An American Life, Visions of America, A Divided People,* and *The Air-Line to Seattle.* But never before has Lynn or anyone else demonstrated the depth of psychological insight and understanding that is here brought to Hemingway's life and work. Lynn's biography, I hasten to say, is not clinically psychoanalytic; there is no obfuscating technical jargon here—no far-fetched recourse to psychic condensations, obscure displacements, or bizarre dream symbols invoked to explain the latent content of Hemingway's thought and work. (pp. 70-1)

The ultimate value of Lynn's biography is that it returns us to the idea that a writer's overt "political" themes—say, the effect of the "dirty war" on Nick Adams, Jake Barnes, or Frederic Henry—may conceal affective states originating in the very personal wounds received in childhood, wounds of which the author was not fully conscious. Even the elements of a literary style, according to Lynn, may be a manifestation of this kind of ill-understood trauma, rather than a reflection of the brevities of journalism or the corruptions of language in the patriotic rhetoric of wartime. . . . (pp. 72-3)

But if Hemingway's affective disorders had their origin in Grace Hemingway's disorientation of her son's sexual identity, it is worth remembering that androgyny has a literary history and a cultural provenance and may, at a particular time, be merely a theme, like any other. Freud had dignified for Hemingway's generation clinical matters that literature had mythicized and that sexologists like Krafft-Ebing had cloaked in Latin secrecy. Writers of the time were quick to bring to the surface of literature the new "psychological science." Sherwood Anderson, whose influence on Hemingway is demonstrable, wrote about such an imaginative sexual transformation in "The Man Who Became A Woman." Pound likewise invoked the double-sexed Tiresias in *Canto I* and made the Ovidian metamorphosis of men and women (into beasts, into trees, into the forms of one other) a central motif of his epic. And T. S. Eliot in *The Waste Land* (1922) objectified in Tiresias ("Old man with wrinkled female breasts") both the genital wound that fascinated Hemingway and the motif of the two sexes merged into each other. Hemingway was not oblivious to these elements of literary modernism. Is it any wonder, then, that at the heart of *The Garden of Eden* he presents a symbol of androgyny: Rodin's statue of the merging sexes based on the *Metamorphoses* of Ovid? (References to the statue are unfortunately excised in the Scribner's edition.)

All writers, if they are any good, are capable of imagining what it is like to have the body of a member of the opposite sex and to have the feelings of that sex. The cultivation of an androgynous sensibility is a necessity of the artist; certainly it is a feature of what Keats called "the chameleon poet," who, emptied of himself, can be filled with the ideas and feelings of another wholly alien to him. But the imaginative taking over of another person's identity, especially of another person's sex, is especially problematical for the writer who already has a weak ego and an insecure sense of his own sexuality. Lynn has brilliantly shown what it was that caused Hemingway to be so anxious and insecure of his own masculinity and how he masked his confusions by flamboyant posturing as the Man's

Man. It is hard to disagree with his conclusion that while Hemingway's "faults were terrible he was also a more truly heroic figure than even the gaudiest version of his myth would grant him."

The effect of Lynn's biography is to send us back to the novels and stories with a new and heightened sense of how intimately Hemingway longed to experience the sensibilities and sensations of a woman and how he dramatized those feelings. If Barbara Probst Solomon is correct in thinking that *The Garden of Eden* is "a sort of summa of Hemingway's aesthetics," with sexual metamorphosis as its cornerstone, the put-down feminist critics will have to take another look at his work, for things are evidently not as they seem. Stories like **"Up in Michigan"** and **"Cat in the Rain,"** viewed in the light of Lynn's account of Hemingway's inner conflict, take on a new poignance and depth and set at naught the claim that Hemingway's women characters are nonentities. And the great novels in the Hemingway canon now require a full critical reconsideration, not as case studies of a neurosis but as dramatizations of some very old issues in male-female relationships—issues first suggested in Plato's myth about the androgynous soul in search of its twin. (pp. 73-4)

James W. Tuttleton, "The Androgynous Papa Hemingway," in The New Criterion, *Vol. VI, No. 2, October, 1987, pp. 67-74.*

THOMAS P. McDONNELL

[*In the following excerpt, McDonnell attacks Lynn for his commission of "biographical heresy"—the interpretation of fictional works as autobigraphy. McDonnell also finds Lynn's analysis of Hemingway's life and works uninformed, irrelevant, and malicious.*]

When I learned some time ago that the critic Kenneth S. Lynn was bringing out a book on the late Ernest Hemingway, hard on the heels of the large biographical study by Jeffrey Myers, I anticipated a reasonably cogent analysis of the stories, the several novels, and the most important of the nonfiction as well. Instead, what we now have on hand [in *Hemingway*] is more of the same—the gossipers and the neo-Freudian biographers pecking away at a life that was already shattered long before the man, in a moment of agony, became his own executioner. With that one shot, the myth of the public persona of Ernest Hemingway should have been put to rest forever.

But it hasn't been put to rest at all. (p. 36)

I think that we have had overmuch of judging the man instead of the works. There are infinite numbers of characteristics that we can serve up in order to make Hemingway look bad—but why should anyone want to do this, unless there are types among us who had long ago sharpened their claws for just such a job?

The fact is that Hemingway, despite the hairy chest and he-man facade, was what we should now call vulnerable. He was vengeful, a falsifier, a womanizer, a poseur, and accident-prone to a disturbing degree. But he was also a good companion, in many ways heroic and selfless, someone to count on when the going got tough. Though admittedly difficult, he was himself often abandoned by others when he most needed their help. He had that instinctive curiosity which the young writer must have, and he was among the first of the postwar Americans to recognize the relationship of modern art to the formation of a new prose style. In the current biographical assault, Hemingway has not been gauged, he has been gouged.

The gouging has been particularly noticeable when focused on the two Hemingway books that the critics seem most disposed to attack: one at possibly the low-point of his career, in *Across the River and into the Trees* (1950), and the other at a brief but recoverable high-point in *The Old Man and the Sea* (1952), each amazingly enclosed within a two-year period of publication. On the first of these titles, the vultures would descend at once. . . . As for the latest big biographical assessments of the matter, Kenneth Lynn proves to be fairer than Jeffrey Myers, whose discussion distorted the contemporary critical response to the novel. (pp. 36-7)

Professor Lynn is as misleading on *The Old Man and the Sea* as Professor Myers had been on *Across the River and into the Trees*. The 1952 book is a miracle of American writing, a thing of incandescent strength and clarity, but its virtues, no less than its continuing popularity, fail to win over the academic critic. Professor Lynn wonders how a book could be so highly praised "that lapses repeatedly into lachrymose sentimentality and is relentlessly pseudo-Biblical, that mixes cute talk about baseball ('I fear both the Tigers of Detroit and the Indians of Cleveland') with the crucifixion symbolism of the most appalling crudity ('he slept face down on the newspapers with his arms out straight and the palms of his hands up'),'' and so on.

God forbid that any fiction in the age of Joyce Carol Oates should evoke the order of genuine feeling that Lynn calls "lachrymose sentimentality." Here is a long short story which moves on several levels at once, mainly of a resolute old age in relationship to the youth of the boy who loves the old man more than his own parents, and based of course on the wisdom of experience they have shared. The talk about baseball is not cute by any means; it is essential and savors of the great (and by the way continuing) Cuban love of baseball itself, and it deepens the bond between the old man and the boy. And, for God's sake, indeed, the old man slept at the end with palms upward because they were stripped bloody raw from the friction of the fishing lines. Lynn may never have gone fishing or, to judge from his writing, have ever done any work with his hands. *The Old Man* is one of the most remarkable examples we have in the genre of nature-writing on the sea itself. It is a story in which Hemingway gave to manly behavior the very delicacy of a feminine presence.

Lynn shares with Myers an appreciation for one of the finest brief memoirs in the annals of American literature, *A Moveable Feast* (1964), which, though slightly soured by Hemingway's own denigrations of some of his contemporaries, remains a superb piece of writing on the art of writing. It was Edmund Wilson who early recognized that when "Hemingway begins speaking in the first person, he seems to lose his bearings, not merely as a critic of life, but even as a craftsman." This is generally the case, no doubt, but it is also an insight which Wilson had recorded, in his outstanding essay on Hemingway in *The Wound and the Bow* (1941), long before the appearance of *A Moveable Feast*. For those who want to confront the central fact about Hemingway, this almost fictionalized memoir forces us to ask what kind of a writer he happened to be.

Ernest Hemingway happened to be a short story writer. Above or aside from everything else he wrote—the novels, the journalism, and the nonfiction—it is in the short story form that Hemingway excels and still maintains a high place in world literature. This is not simply to acknowledge familiar masterpieces like "Big Two-Hearted River," "The Snows of Kilimanjaro," or "The Short Happy Life of Francis Macomber," etc., for it is also to recognize the short stories that are essentially contained in the several major novels themselves. *The Sun Also Rises* is several short stories, while the posthumous *The Garden of Eden* (1986) is several more. *For Whom the Bell Tolls* may be the only authentic novel that Hemingway wrote, and yet even that is diffuse and ill-constructed. Maxwell Perkins to the contrary, it is too bad that an editor more devoted to art than the marketplace (novels are more marketable than short stories) did not hold Hemingway to the form he was born to write.

The startling conclusion to all this is that with three major biographies of Hemingway already on the shelf . . . we do not have readily at hand a study of the author that is either critically autonomous or biographically satisfying. One can at least accept, I think, the *Hemingway* of Jeffrey Myers as the best of the crop so far; whereas it is most difficult, if not impossible, to accept Kenneth Lynn's *Hemingway* on any level, if only because, in both principle and practice, it so severely offends what C. S. Lewis has called "the personal heresy"—or, as we may call it here, the biographical heresy. The great Christian apologist and literary critic opposed any method of criticism which attempts to interpret imaginative works as autobiography. He disdained biographical criticism, as such, and said that in his opinion "all criticism should be of books, not of authors." Although Lewis applied this dictum chiefly to classical poetry, it may usefully be applied as well to the 20th-century prose of Ernest Hemingway.

Here we have, then, the incredible demand of biographers like Myers—and especially the pusillanimous Lynn—who lay down the law that the fictionist shall be disallowed to recreate his raw materials in anything other than strict biographical terms. Lynn's critical method is *to expose* Hemingway for not conforming to this ridiculous dictum. It was also typical of the *New York Review of Books* (August 13, 1987) to bless Lynn's practice of this curiously illiberal doctrine in its extended commentary, by Frederick Crews, of the Lynn biography [see excerpt above]. One might have guessed, however, that something was amiss when *NYRB* chose to draw attention to the article with the cover-title "Kinky Hemingway." Kinky he may have been, but surely not more so than some of the rest of us. In any case, so much for the scholarly approach.

Hemingway was a writer. In our century, he left us with a new way of storytelling. And yet here is a presumed biographer, Lynn, who seems incapable of dealing with his subject's most important works (*The Old Man,* for one) and who makes no attempt at all to put his subject's failures into perspective or to see in them any redeeming value whatsoever. It is hard to say this, but Kenneth Lynn has joined the faction of pimp-critics whose preferred aim is the depreciation of Hemingway's works through the continuing and undaunted practice of the biographical heresy: Expose the man; demean the works. A great deal has been made of Lynn's critique of "Big Two-Hearted River," which up to now has been regarded as an allegory for the healing of the hero's wounds sustained in war, partly supported by Hemingway himself. But the point is, who cares? Not even the remarks aside of Ernest Hemingway can destroy a good story or harm a superlative piece of American writing. The incredible paradox is that while the biographical critics have discovered that Hemingway was, after all, a terribly complex individual, they continue to treat him as an irreducible buffoon and to pervert the interpretation of literary works that have already earned their place as autonomous works of art. When Lynn or Myers can write a single paragraph as good as the opening sentences of virtually any Hemingway novel, when either can teach us as much of the human heart as the shortest of his short stories, and when they have learned even the rudiments of constructive literary criticism, then and only then we might be interested in anything they have to say on the subject of modern literature. (pp. 37-8)

Thomas P. McDonnell, "Hemingway and the Biographical Heresy," in Chronicles: A Magazine of American Culture, Vol. 11, No. 11, November, 1987, pp. 36-8.

WILFRED M. McCLAY

[*In the following excerpt, McClay hails Lynn's book as a groundbreaking work in the field of Hemingway scholarship, arguing that the biography puts aside the veil of public myth that previously obscured the author's inner struggles. McClay calls for a critical revaluation of Hemingway's oeuvre, viewing his work as a barometer of the fascination with androgyny in the twentieth century.*]

Everyone knows Ernest Hemingway. Or, at least, they think they do. It is hardly possible not to, for Hemingway is one of the inescapable presences of our century. . . .

But the Hemingway the world knows is very different from the man who stares out in poignant vacancy from the dust jacket of Kenneth Lynn's new biography [**Hemingway**]. His puffy-lidded, exhausted, vaguely pleading eyes attest to a longstanding torment, and a sense of looming defeat. The deep creases in his face and the wavy sweeps of his unruly hair and beard converge and swirl, like the whirlpools of angst in a Van Gogh self-portrait. In this extraordinarily evocative photograph, one begins to sense the fathomless, helpless melancholy of the gifted man who, despite his receipt of a Nobel Prize, worldwide acclaim, and a lifetime's worth of honors, finally turned a twelve-gauge, double-barreled shotgun against himself early on a Sunday morning in the summer of 1961, and blasted away his entire cranial vault. This Hemingway is a very different man from the Hemingway of grandiose myth.

So, too, is the Hemingway depicted in the pages of Lynn's biography, one fact which immediately distinguishes it from most of what has been written about Hemingway. Over the years, Hemingway and his work have generally been approached in two quite different ways: in a spirit of uncritical admiration, or in a spirit of unrestrained debunking. (p. 43)

Lynn's biography sweeps the landscape of Hemingway scholarship clean, leaving standing little of what has been said and written in the past. Skeptical readers may well come to the book wondering how anything new could possibly be said about Hemingway after all these years. They will come away from the book wondering how so much was misread, for so long, by so many. . . .

Lynn has in fact done Hemingway an enormous favor—one the novelist could never have done for himself—by lifting from his shoulders an immense, largely self-imposed burden of fancy and falsehood, thus making it possible for us to read his work freshly, as the tale of a ceaseless, and finally tragic, inner struggle.

To be sure, many elements of that struggle have been adumbrated before. We know, for example, that his father's suicide,

about which he spoke frequently in both his life and his work, haunted him for the rest of his life. But no one before Lynn has realized how central a role his mother played in that drama. Contemptuous of suicide as a form of sinful cowardice, Hemingway flushed with shame whenever he thought of his father's weakness. But then he was likely to erupt into a rage at his domineering mother, whom he believed to have driven her husband to such extremes. And indeed, Grace Hall Hemingway was a physically imposing, self-possessed woman, used to having her own way in everything, whatever the cost. Known for her tomboyish ways as a young girl, Grace ruled the Hemingway household with an effective combination of naked assertiveness and well-timed attacks of fatigue. Fancying herself an artist, she disdained the humdrum duties of the *Hausfrau,* to such an extent that Hemingway's father had to take care of the food shopping and much of the cooking, on top of his demanding practice as a physician. . . . Grace's egotism and self-indulgence, in tandem with her husband's strange submissiveness to her will, would leave an indelible mark on the young Ernest. . . . The strange combination of extreme callousness and extreme dependency which marked Hemingway's dealing with women had their beginning with Grace. And the manipulative intent he sensed behind Grace's unctuous recitation of shallow Protestant pieties was the true source of the nausea he felt, long before he went to war, when he heard people speak of high ideals.

One of Grace's whims, which other Hemingway biographers have passed over far too lightly, was her elaborate fantasy that Ernest and his older sister Marcelline were to be raised as if they were twins of the same sex. Undoubtedly this urge was grounded, as Lynn suggests, in the limitations of Grace's own upbringing—but the psychological damage to Ernest and Marcelline was profound and lasting. (pp. 43-4)

Laboring under the double burden of his parents' unhappy relationship and the disorienting pretense of his "twinhood," Hemingway could not escape being chronically uncertain of his masculinity and emotionally crippled in his relations with women. . . . Thus, the residue of his strange childhood became incorporated into the persistent imagery of twinhood in his work; into Hemingway's ability to think himself imaginatively into female characters, as in the story **"Up in Michigan"** or the novel *A Farewell to Arms*; into Hemingway's peculiar erotic preoccupation with short-haired, boyish, or lesbian women; into the Hemingwayesque male-female relationships which so often strain to resemble buddy-buddy male friendships (and view the specter of pregnancy and childbirth as a cruel destroyer); and even into the great Hemingway love scenes which, as Lynn points out, are filled with erotic whisperings and playful pillow talk about the exchanging of sexual roles. . . . [The] recurrence of the same kinds of images and conversations, in story after story, novel after novel—from such early stories as **"Soldier's Home,"** through *The Sun Also Rises,* and most graphically of all, in the recently published fragment of *The Garden of Eden*—makes it clear beyond question that Hemingway's own erotic ideal was bound up in the confusion and commingling of the sexes, and that the seeds of this ideal can be found not in Paris, but in Oak Park.

In the earliest works, which Lynn still regards as his best, Hemingway found a way to give uncanny expression to the things that troubled him most, without ever revealing precisely what they were. These stories are more like cryptic, fragmentary, lyric poems than straightforward works of narrative prose, and it was in such shorter forms that Hemingway excelled. As

Lynn observes, he always said that he wanted "to make people feel more than they understood," and in a vividly compressed, meticulously controlled masterpiece like **"Indian Camp"** or **"Big Two-Hearted River,"** he could pull it off, because the brevity of the form itself spared him the necessity of expounding on matters he dared not touch directly. But from the moment he began to tackle the novel (in *The Sun Also Rises*), he found himself adrift in a more complex literary form, whose demands did not permit him to play hide-and-seek with his anxieties so easily.

Unfortunately, it was in those very years that the Hemingway myth began to take root, and its imprisoning effects on Hemingway's creative imagination were already clearly visible by 1932, with the publication of his pretentious ode to the Spanish bullfight, *Death in the Afternoon.* Max Eastman immediately dubbed it "Bull in the Afternoon," and not without reason, for as Lynn points out, its hero was not a haunted Jake Barnes or Nick Adams, but "an overbearing know-it-all named Ernest Hemingway." With each passing year, Hemingway found the temptations of the myth harder to resist, even though dependence on it increasingly meant living a lie, and what is worse, exiling himself from the emotional wellsprings of his art. A work like *The Garden of Eden,* which put aside the mythic mask, was far too dangerous, too revealing of precisely the things Hemingway wanted to hide, for it ever to be finished, let alone published in his lifetime. Even his remarkable success with *The Old Man and the Sea* in 1952 did not really alter the downward curve of his career, for that was a book bathed in a sort of crowd-pleasing sentimentality and crude symbolism that the younger Hemingway would have disdained. In the end, the power of the myth overwhelmed all, and the mask merged with the face. But, as the shotgun blast on that July morning proved, the mask could never remake the man in its own image.

When the dust begins to settle after the initial impact of Lynn's book, those who genuinely admire Hemingway's art will find that his new biographer has given their man a new lease on life. Virtually every major work in the Hemingway *oeuvre* will now have to be rethought and reinterpreted, in line with this new understanding of their author. And such interpretations will likely have implications extending far beyond the tight coils of his troubled psyche. Indeed, his work may eventually be seen as a progressive fever chart, sensitively registering the early stages of one of this century's most troubling social and psychological transformations: the progressive blurring and erosion of sexual differentiation. Androgyny had just come widely into fashion in the 1920s, especially in such avant-garde continental centers as Paris and Berlin, at the very moment the expatriate Hemingway was beginning his serious literary career. No doubt Hemingway was captivated by the sights of kinky Paris for reasons that were ultimately quite personal: his love-hate obsession with his forceful mother, and the feminine component submerged in his own quivering sensibility. Nevertheless, he was also bearing witness to a disturbing cultural undercurrent that has only gathered strength as our century has progressed. In this respect, his example ought to have a sobering effect upon contemporary sages who regard this development with enthusiasm, and who put forward androgyny as a cultural ideal towards which right-thinking men and women must strive. For as Hemingway's life would suggest, those who tinker with the traditional conceptions of gender may be playing with fire. (pp. 44-5)

Wilfred M. McClay, in a review of "Hemingway,"
in The American Spectator, *Vol. 21, No. 1, January, 1988, pp. 43-5.*

LEM COLEY

Kenneth Lynn's *Hemingway* opens with generosity and balance: "while his faults were terrible he was also a more truly heroic figure than even the gaudiest version of his myth would grant him." But eventually Lynn wanders from this theme.

Hemingway has two strands that diverge in the reader's memory. First it tells the scary tale of Hemingway's Oak Park childhood and the literary consequences. The future toast of *Esquire* was born into a prototypical seedbed of modernist alienation—bourgeois comfort, bloodless liberal Christianity and the lingering tentacles of Victorian sexual repression, trips to the Field Museum and the Art Institute, an artistic mom and an energetic dad. Lurking in the wings, need it be said, disorder and early sorrow. It has long been known that Hemingway hated his mother. Lynn explains why. . . .

Cross-dressing infant males wasn't a big deal then, but in this case it went on far too long. Grace manipulated her son's fundamental identity with the perverse energy of a willful child who dresses, undresses, punishes, and rewards her dolls. Ernest was "confused and demoralized by his mother's changeable treatment of him." And the larger context was that her strong, reproachful, dominating personality broke Hemingway's father and put a hex on Ernest that he never shook off despite fame, wealth, and genuine achievements. In Lynn's words, "All his life, his mother would remain the dark queen of Hemingway's inner world."

Hemingway's anxious struggle to keep that inner world off the clean, well-lighted surface of his fiction is, according to Lynn, the missing key that explains that fiction. For example, **"Big Two-Hearted River"** is not about a young man traumatized by World War I. Lynn would have it that for Nick Adams "the activity of his mind that keeps threatening to overwhelm his contentment could be rage"—in this case, rage directed at Grace Hemingway. Lynn argues that **"Two-Hearted River"** makes no reference to the war and that the fishing trip which supplied background for the story took place in 1919 when Ernest fought with his mother. She threw him out of the Michigan house and told him he was not a man, in a pious, murderous letter closing with scripture and Christian love.

I suppose it can never be settled which dog is not barking in **"Big Two-Hearted River."** . . . Lynn reminds us that **"Now I Lay Me,"** another Nick Adams story, mixes troubled family recollections with war material: "What counts supremely in the story is not the northern Italian frame . . . but the childhood memories within the frame."

Like anybody with a theory, Lynn works it too hard. Certainly anyone who reads the letter Grace handed Ernest in 1919 may agree that rage towards his mother is one item in the swamp Nick Adams doesn't want to fish. Still, it's reductive to dismiss the effect of the war on Hemingway. Any work of art will lead us back to the artist's psyche, but that should not short-circuit wider meanings.

Nor is *Farewell to Arms* a war story. Rather it is a "study in affective disorder." The disorder is Hemingway's as well as Frederic Henry's, and here Lynn's analysis of a writer trying but finally unable to deal with "the remote origins of his personal problems" is quite moving. . . .

Employing his case history as a Geiger counter, Lynn finds new ore in well-mined works. One of his most contentious explications insists that **"The Short Happy Life of Francis Macomber,"** is not the story of ultimate war between the American genders Hemingway and Edmund Wilson said it was. Like anyone who has ever taught **"Macomber,"** Lynn notices that, according to the text, Mrs. Macomber kills her husband accidentally while shooting at the charging buffalo. "It is not wifely malevolence that brings Macomber down, but his own dangerous aspiration to be recognized as intensely masculine." For Lynn, the white hunter and Macomber are two projections of Hemingway. The hunter is the outer image he aspired to be, and Macomber is the wounded boy he was. This is an engaging, plausible idea, but overall Lynn's version doesn't work. He turns Margot Macomber into a caring, sharing ecofeminist who loves her husband, and the red-faced white hunter into a brute. This ignores too much of the story. Margot, very excited before the lion hunt, pulls away from her husband after his debacle and kisses the hunter in the car, then taunts Macomber and makes no secret of her infidelity.

Lacking space to take up all of Lynn's critical labors, I will just say that even those who dislike his conclusions and interpretations will be prodded to rethink and reread. Lynn's findings and opinions may not replace, as he thinks they do, all other views of Hemingway, but he has definitely added a dimension to these famous books, which had begun to seem like marble monuments of a lost age when masterpieces rolled off the press every year like new models from Detroit.

The family history and literary stuff are fascinating and important, but the rest of the biography is not. The sensitivity and freshness that Lynn brings to the works seem to desert him when he takes up the life. Sympathetic to Hemingway the child, Lynn's aversion to Hemingway the man rises off the page like the stench of death Pilar describes in *For Whom the Bell Tolls*. The reader hardly notices at first, so accustomed are we to the idea of Hemingway as a miles gloriosus. The Lillian Ross profile, the boxing anecdotes, the Max Eastman story, the evident cruelty of *A Movable Feast,* the vituperation of the letters, have long since done their work.

But Lynn brings a special relish to his job. In 1918, when Hemingway was in New York preparing to go to Italy, he wrote his newspaper cronies in Kansas City and his family that he was engaged to Mae Marsh, a famous actress of the day. He was obviously kidding, but for Lynn it becomes another example of Hemingway's dishonesty. On several assignments for the Toronto *Star,* Ernest sold dispatches to other news services under an assumed name. Lynn refers huffily to shabby journalistic ethics. When Edmund Wilson considered publishing a brief notice of *Three Stories & Ten Poems,* Hemingway wrote asking him to wait until *In Our Time* was out so Wilson could write a longer review covering both books. Lynn calls this manipulation. . . .

This censorious, belittling tone never lets up. At times the reader gets the bizarre feeling that Lynn has been somehow taken over by Grace Hemingway's attitude towards her son. Hemingway is the sole villain in all four marriages: weak, dependent, also selfish and domineering. He either leaves his wives alone, which is bad, or forces them to go places with him, which is bad. To friends and fellow writers Hemingway is usually the treacherous opportunist—envious and quick to strike.

Now, Lynn isn't making all this up out of thin air. There can be few American writers about whom we know so many discreditable things. But Lynn takes anybody's word against Hemingway's and seems to begrudge him his better moments. Ernest's neighbors, the Cubans of San Francisco de Paula,

remember with great affection the writer who donated $2000 for an aqueduct; outfitted their kids with baseball uniforms and equipment, then drove them to games in his pickup; and roamed the streets with gangs of boys at Christmas throwing strings of firecrackers into the barbershop. But you won't find him in this book.

Books reflect the intellectual climate of their times as rings on a tree record the weather. *Hemingway* is an artifact of the American male intellectual's twenty-year encounter with feminism, an important artifact because it holds so many features of that complex encounter—confrontation, détente, assimilation, and fear.

Lynn judges Hemingway by standards feminism has taught us to apply. He was an inconsiderate husband who saw marriage and children as a trap and resented babies for crying all night. He wanted his wives to be squaws and could not brook the competition of third wife Martha Gelhorn, an ambitious, adventurous journalist with a mind of her own.

The he-man role model for a generation is subjected to the two-pronged attack perfected by feminists: as an avatar of the rogue male, Hemingway was a competitive, aggressive bully, a butcher of fish, fowl, and beast. Then the second prong: insecure in his sexuality, less brave and virile than he pretended to be, the he-man was not one.

On the other hand, Lynn has exposed the silent fears of contemporary males by telling the story of a boy scarred by a powerful woman. He is careful to show not only that Grace was stronger than Dr. Hemingway, but also that both grandmothers were stronger than their husbands. Lynn makes the Hemingway family sound like people we know. Dr. Hemingway did the shopping and much of the cooking. Something of a public figure, Grace had her own career and at times earned more than her husband. An early feminist, according to Lynn, she took vacations away from her family when she felt overworked, often staying at a Nantucket boarding house run by a women's rights activist. Her closest relationship was apparently with a younger woman whom Dr. Ed suspected of taking his place and threw out of the house. Lynn calls it "one of the few enduring victories of his marriage."

With this background we can see why a writer who made masculinity an aesthetic object and its loss an aesthetic subject is such a disturbing figure today—both anachronistic and contemporary, engrossing and repellent. Out of the long rearguard action against his own pursuing furies Hemingway made edifying tales and a cautionary life. Kenneth Lynn, in a book more serious, tendentious, and therefore interesting than the usual literary biography, tells the story of a man and his work so redolent of other times and other manners that we see more clearly who we are right now. (pp. 20, 22-3)

Lem Coley, "Noisy Secrets," in The American Book Review, *Vol. 10, No. 1, March-April, 1988, pp. 20, 22-3.*

WILLIAM H. PRITCHARD

[*Hemingway*] is built on Mr. Lynn's conviction, developed and justified at length in the book's early stages, that Grace Hall Hemingway was (in Lynn's good phrase) "the dark queen of Hemingway's inner world," and that she reigned there for all his life. To simplify what Lynn goes into in extensive detail, it was Grace Hemingway's passion—and that is the word for it—to treat Ernest and his sister Marcelline as if they were twins, dressing them in look-alike outfits. . . . Lynn suggests that it was the arbitrariness and changeability of Grace's sartorial whims that confused the children, and in Hemingway's case hurt him in a major way.

If one is tempted—and I was immediately tempted—to scoff at this line of argument as making too much out of how some mothers dressed their children "back then," a reading of Hemingway's posthumous, editorially stapled-together novel *The Garden of Eden,* gives Lynn's case strength. For the puzzling and insistant fuss made in that book about confusion of sexual identity—especially in much tiresome gushing about the wife having her hair cut short, and dyed, so that she will be "like" the husband—makes sense (if it can be called that) only by seeing how deep the matter ran in Hemingway's psyche. Lynn gives us a way to view this matter and to understand why Hemingway's hatred for Grace—"that bitch," as he loved to refer to her—needed to be worked at full-time, took up enormous psychic energy. Not of course that it was "just" hate. He loved the fact that his mother was proud of him for having been wounded in action (he was in an ambulance unit of the Red Cross) and wrote to her that "When a mother brings a son into the world she must know that some day the son will die, and the mother of a man that has died for his country should be the proudest woman in the world and the happiest." This absolute capitulation to Gold-Star Mom boosterism is merely the other, saccharine side of his nastiness toward her. Like all tough babies, Hemingway was consistently sentimental and cruel by turns, even at once; Lynn's biography misses no opportunity to detail instances of such behavior.

At one point in the book, just before taking up Hemingway's years in Paris, Lynn steps back to give us the following summary of how he imagines his subject's inner life to have been shaped: . . .

> To be forced to practice the most severe economy in your attempts to "render" your life artistically, because your capital of self-understanding was too small to permit you to be expansive and your fear of self-exposure too powerful. To make a virtue of necessity by packing troubled feelings below the surface of your stories like dynamite beneath a bridge.

One could object to this account for the way it turns the writer wholly into the passive agent of his sexual or familial curse, the famous Hemingway style reduced to nothing more than the result of being "forced" to practice economy in the writing of sentences and paragraphs. The brilliant discovery we had thought he made, about how by leaving things *out* of the writing it could be made the more suggestive and troubling, now becomes nothing more than the consequences of minimal self-understanding—this man didn't know himself well enough to let things hang out.

"Freudian" understandings or explanations of how writers got to produce the art they produced—after which the art itself can be dismissed, or at least put in its place—should be treated with impatience or worse. What makes Lynn's dealings with Hemingway something other and better than such non-esthetic procedures, is that he cares about Hemingway's art (especially his early stories and first two novels) but also sees how very odd is that art, how little it invites us to see it as the result of thoughtful, "objective" planning. If all writers could be said to be in the grip of their gift—or their beast—Hemingway was in its grip more than most; he is less likely to be distorted by an approach such as Lynn's, since the distortions, the twists in his art, are so apparent and inescapable.

At the same time, there are at least two American writers whose work yields richer satisfactions and pleasures than Hemingway's and whose biographers, committed to elaborate psychological explanations of their subjects, manage to tell us very little by way of locating and describing the literary value of their work. I am thinking of Leon Edel on Henry James and Lawrance Thompson on Robert Frost. Both biographers relentlessly wielded a theory about how their subjects came to arrive at their respective inner landscapes; both biographers were helpless before the novels or poems which somehow emerged from that landscape. . . . It almost seems that the very intentness with which these biographers fix on a scheme that explains everything, debars them from anything like flexible, critical attention to the poem or novel in question—they are so busy showing how the example confirms their theory that they have no time to listen to what and how it speaks. Kenneth Lynn is a much better critic than either Edel or Thompson; but Hemingway, while not the equal of James or Frost as a writer, was surely—at least in his early stories and novels—a stylist of great delicacy ("a very considerable artist in prose-fiction," wrote Wyndham Lewis, before proceeding to make fun of that artist's fondness for his "Dumb-ox" heroes). Hemingway's style still presents a challenge to criticism and is why one keeps returning to him in the classroom, where passages can be read aloud and pondered. (pp. 218-220)

"No one who looks *at* it, will want to look *behind* it," said Wyndham Lewis about Joyce's *Ulysses.* But from the beginning, those who have looked at Hemingway's sentences felt they needed to look behind them for a significance not found on their surface; it all began with Edmund Wilson finding that Hemingway's "naivete of language" served "actually to convey profound emotion and complex states of mind." But what is the force of "actually," and why should we presume that behind the simple language lies profundity and complexity, or even states of mind? Are we justified in moving from Hemingway's troubled psyche in order to endow his characters and his fiction with a similar set of feelings? Or is it all the magnificent stunt of an illusionist, casting his spell over us for as long as the story takes to tell? Despite his acumen and conviction, I don't think Lynn deals enough with such matters, since—committed to his "strong" interpretation of what lies behind or underneath Hemingway's writing—he neglects to look sufficiently *at* that writing.

In spending so much time discussing (niggling at?) Lynn's reading of some of Hemingway's best work, I have of necessity left most things in the biography untouched. My partial excuse here will be that Frederick Crews his treated the book at great length—and accorded it the highest praise [see excerpt above]. . . . But among its aspects I found particularly illuminating were the pages on *The Sun Also Rises* and *A Farewell to Arms,* especially the earlier novel which Grace Hemingway called "one of the filthiest books of the year" and whose publication, she opined, was "a doubtful honor." (There's nothing like having your mom in your corner!) Lynn gives a brilliant account, by far the best I've read, of Hemingway's relations with the Scott Fitzgeralds. And there are original, sharply-turned, revisionary readings of famous stories like **"The Short Happy Life of Francis Macomber"** and **"The Snows of Kilimanjaro."** Of course any biographer's problems with Hemingway is that after 1930 everything begins to go downhill: the novels get worse, the stories dry up, the behavior becomes more horrendous. Then there is the prodigious drinking to be chronicled, testified to, for example, in Hemingway's "regular Sunday hangover letter" (to his editor, Max Perkins, in 1940) which fills out the scorecard for the previous night's journey from absinthe to red wine to vodka to having "battened it down with whiskys and soda until 3 a.m." Concurrent with the drinking, there were the physical injuries, accidents, and general bodily deterioration. The unpleasant story of it all is told here with thoroughness and some compassion. I think it fair to say that—for all the heavy interpretive artillery directed at Hemingway's psyche, Lynn does not end up, as have some biographers, more or less hating his subject. At one point he quotes Norman Mailer's assertion about Hemingway that "what he accomplished was heroic, for it is possible that he carried a weight of anxiety with him which would have suffocated any man smaller than himself." Lynn's book allows us to follow the accomplishment in detail, indeed see it clearly for the first time. (pp. 223-24)

*William H. Pritchard, "The Trouble with Ernest,"
in* The Hudson Review, *Vol. XLI, No. 1, Spring,
1988, pp. 218-24.*

Ezra Pound: The Solitary Volcano

by John Tytell

(For Ezra Pound: see also *CLC*, Vols. 1, 2, 3, 4, 5, 7, 10, 13, 18, 34, 48; *Contemporary Authors*, Vols. 5-8, rev. ed., 37-40, rev. ed. [obituary]; *Dictionary of Literary Biography*, Vols. 4, 45. For John Tytell: see also *Contemporary Authors*, Vols. 29-32, rev. ed.)

An Excerpt from *Ezra Pound: The Solitary Volcano*

In Genoa, Pound was interviewed by Edd Johnson, an American reporter to whom he stated that if a man valued his beliefs, he would die for them. In a fit of omnipotence, he declared that if he would be allowed to meet President Truman or Stalin he could help resolve the political complications that would surely ensue because of the war. He had a series of other comments: Mussolini was an imperfect man who had lost his head, Churchill a man who stood for the "maximum of injustice enforced with the maximum of brutality," and Hitler was a saint like Joan of Arc, a martyr who failed only because he had not followed Confucius closely enough.

Several weeks later, after a flurry of cables between Genoa and Washington, Pound was handcuffed to a soldier accused of rape and murder and transferred under guard to the Disciplinary Training Center near Pisa. . . . The Disciplinary Training Center was designed to punish and contain the most vicious criminals in the American army, a collection of some thirty-six hundred deserters, brawlers, rapists, murderers, and maniacs. Some of these men were waiting for trials, others were already paying for what they had done with hard labor days that lasted fourteen hours. Most of the men lived in tents which were housed within the barbed wire compounds, but there was also a group of ten wire-and-concrete cages for the most dangerous prisoners or those who had been sentenced to death by court-martial. Pound was placed in one of these isolation cells, a so-called death cell that had been reinforced on the night before his arrival by men working with acetylene torches who welded galvanized mesh and heavy airstrip steel onto the wire grid of the cell. It was a fact that made Pound figure in the speculations of the other prisoners, who must have wondered about the extra precautions and the dangers presented by this new inmate.

Dressed in army fatigues but without a belt or shoelaces to prevent any attempt at suicide, Pound paced his six foot by six foot "gorilla" cage. Protected from dust, sun, and rain only by a tar paper covering, he was tortured by the constant glare of a reflected light set up to shine directly into his cell at night while he tried to sleep on the cold cement floor. No one, not even the guard who delivered his food or who emptied his refuse bucket,

Photograph by Boris De Rachewiltz. Courtesy of New Directions Publishing Corp.

was allowed to speak to him. "They thought I was a dangerous wild man and were scared of me," Pound said later. "I had a guard night and day. Some of them brought food. Old Ez was a prize exhibit." He was mistaken. The precautions were not taken because of the dangers he presented, but because of the possibility that Fascist sympathizers might try to free him. For three weeks the fifty-nine-year-old poet paced his cell, exercised as best he could, sat staring, or read his Confucius and his Chinese dictionary which he had brought with him from Sant'Ambrogio. His eyes were red and inflamed from dust. After a downpour one day, the guards gave him a pup tent and a military cot. But by then the strain had proven intolerable and Pound collapsed, stricken with violent and hysterical terror, nightmares, hallucinations, and cold. He suffered memory loss and lost the ability to identify his surroundings. He stopped eating.

In later years he characterized the experience by saying, "The World fell in on me." Actually, the breakdown was a wordless catharsis, a sudden recognition of the peril of his situation and the price he might have to pay.

Hemingway had once told him that a writer needed to feel terrific pain before releasing his subject. The breakdown was an admission of such pain. Pound, the man of words, was now caught in the most overwhelming moment of his life without the power to summon language. But he might have realized, in some silent corner of his being, that language was merely the artistic fiction of tragedy, the rationalization of pain, and that the flow of words would be invented by the novelist or playwright, or Pound himself in the cantos he would soon begin to write, to stylize and heighten and explain the conjunction of superior forces and the puny human who could dare to defy them.

PAULA M. SEDOR

Ezra Pound is considered a major American poet of this century, but his fame is based as much on the notoriety surrounding his confinement in a psychiatric hospital and his work as a Fascist propagandist as on his achievements as author of *The Cantos* and leading proponent of the imagist movement in poetry. In [*Ezra Pound: The Solitary Volcano*], a biography that is notably unburdened with scholarly baggage, Tytell relates the language to the man and the man to his time, making good use of personal interviews and previously unpublished correspondence between Pound and contemporaries such as Eliot, Joyce, and Yeats. The author neither lionizes his subject nor apologizes for him, but by documenting Pound's intense theatricality and insidious self-pity, he makes it possible for the reader to understand how the man's once-successful role as a mad poet became a reality he could not face.

> *Paula M. Sedor, in a review of "Ezra Pound: The Solitary Volcano," in* Booklist, *Vol. 83, No. 22, August, 1987, p. 1712.*

JOSEPH PARISI

[*Parisi is an American editor, critic, and educator. He is the editor of* Poetry *magazine and* The Poetry Anthology, 1912-1977: Sixty-Five Years of America's Most Distinguished Verse Magazine *(1978). In the following excerpt, Parisi praises Tytell's biography for its vivid portrait of the talented but troubled Pound and for its informative analysis of the poet's works.*]

"Pound is an incredible ass," Robert Frost wrote after meeting him in England in 1913. Like other American writers before and since, feeling unappreciated at home, they had gone abroad to make their mark. In green billiard cloth trousers, pink coat and blue shirt, and with his pointed red beard, single earring and sombrero, Pound had little trouble attracting attention in London and was soon taken up by Ford Madox Ford, who introduced him to the leading literati. But his costume, and theatrics like eating the tulips in dinner-table centerpieces, caused older luminaries to suspect a show-off or charlatan, or worse. He was definitely "not our kind."

Still, if a *poseur*, Pound was also precocious. He quickly absorbed the new aesthetics of Ford and T. E. Hulme, refining them into what would become the tenets of Modernism. Soon even the master, W. B. Yeats, became a disciple, submitting his work to Pound's editorial hand as would so many others. With startling acuity, Pound perceived several as-yet unrecognized talents, and turned literary entrepreneur. He placed T. S. Eliot's "The Love Song of J. Alfred Prufrock" in *Poetry*

(founder Harriet Monroe had named Pound the magazine's foreign editor in 1912), where he also declared the doctrines of Imagism, exemplified by the poems of H. D. (Hilda Doolittle) and James Joyce, whose fiction he promoted tirelessly. Always in action, he founded the short-lived Vorticist movement, issued manifestos, made other "discoveries," translated Provençal and Chinese poetry, wrote his first *Cantos*. Meanwhile, he contributed staggering numbers of articles and reviews to new literary journals. In 1918 alone, he published 117 times and in 1919, 189 times.

Yet, for all this prodigious activity as poet and impresario, Pound never achieved the recognition he felt he deserved in England. Moving to Paris in 1920, he was at first elated and recharged by the stimulating artistic climate of the capital, where he soon met Cocteau, Brancusi, Picabia, Stravinsky, the Dadaists, the Surrealists, e. e. cummings. But again, initial enthusiasm soured, and Pound's ambitions as literary mover and *maître* ended in disappointment. Finally he settled in self-imposed "exile" in Rapallo, on the Italian Riviera.

With lingering resentment, he continued on the *Cantos* that would be his life's chief work, and on translations, critical books, hundreds of articles; he also penned about a thousand letters a year. With growing bitterness, he descended into the quagmire of polemics and hatred—against American politicians, bankers and Jews—which ended in scandal, charges of treason, and his return to the U.S. in ignominy. In grotesque fashion, he had regained center stage.

"As baffling a bundle of contradictions as any man whom I had ever known," recalled the poet John Gould Fletcher in 1937. And 15 years after his death, Pound remains a mystery. His prolific and difficult work has created a major academic industry. With so much scholarly ink already spilled on the problems of his career and character, do we really need another critical biography?

That, John Tytell admits, is the question he posed to New Directions publisher James Laughlin before embarking on this latest survey of "the solitary volcano." Laughlin is reported to have said there was still a need to "explore the myths behind the man rather than merely debunking them."

Instead of "another behemoth biography," Tytell offers in these cleanly written pages [*Ezra Pound: The Solitary Volcano*] a summary of the facts while capturing the exciting flavor of an experimental age, particularly of the '20s and '30s. And, using Pound's own "luminous method" of carefully selected details and quotes (but without his chaos), he does largely succeed in sorting out the historical and psychological factors that created the Pound enigma.

Pound's roles as catalyst and confidant are legendary. Hemingway claimed he taught him more "about how to write and how not to write than anyone else." He later eulogized:

> He defends [his friends] when they are attacked, he gets them into magazines and out of jail. He loans them money. He sells their pictures. He arranges concerts for them. He writes articles about them. . . . He gets publishers to take their books. . . . And in the end a few of them refrain from knifing him at the first opportunity.

Despite his countless efforts—the revision of *The Waste Land* and the indefatigable promotion of *Ulysses* are but the most famous cases—how is it Pound managed eventually to alienate almost everyone, including those he aided most?

Pound's egotism and lack of self-knowledge run as *leitmotifs* through Tytell's book. Like Frost, his old friend William Carlos Williams found Pound an ass, and a patronizing one as well. Many others, friends and critics alike, found him stubborn and condescending, both single-minded and wrong-headed.

H. D., a one-time sweetheart, remarked: "He is adolescent. He seems almost 'arrested' in development." Pound's capacity for delusion and self-pity was indeed great. Yet his feelings of wrongful neglect were justified. As the fame of his protégés grew, so did Pound's jealousy and paranoia. He aspired to power as literary arbiter. But tactful Eliot—impeccably dressed, prim, astutely accommodating—had by the late '20s assumed that role.

When, at their first and only meeting, Mussolini said he found the *Cantos "divertente"* (entertaining!), Pound foolishly believed he could play the part of poet-philosopher to a prince. Profoundly learned in literature, he assumed similar expertise in politics and economics. Simplistic and woefully naive about Realpolitick, he was well-practiced in hatred, his Fascist sympathies and anti-Semitism already of longstanding. His crank letters—Tytell quotes many—were now augmented by vile but disjointed diatribes on Rome Radio. His speeches were often so incoherent the Italians thought he was crazy—or speaking in code.

As in his tracing of the curves of the earlier career, Tytell's account of Pound's descent—the wartime broadcasts, the captivity in Pisa, the insanity hearings, the 13-year incarceration at St. Elizabeths mental hospital—is vividly detailed, lucid, balanced. Like many of Pound's contemporaries, a majority of the examining psychiatrists and many critics, Tytell finds that while the manic poet was an unusual case, he was probably not truly or totally insane. He might have appeared to be, to those unfamiliar with his usual behavior.

Riding from the hospital one day, William Carlos Williams discussed the case with the taxi driver. Perhaps the cabbie was right when he said: "He just talk too much."

Whatever his true mental state, Pound's words were often reprehensible. Whether the egotist played the knave or the fool (or perhaps King Lear) may never be settled. As in his fragmented and frequently obscure work, Pound adopted numerous masks and personas in life. Many of them were not pleasant.

Lawrance Thompson's disclosures of Frost's private life in his exhaustive biography revealed a miserable man; they have not diminished Frost's stature as a poet. Pound's work remains problematic. Tytell's analysis of the evolution of Pound's style and his succinct examination of the complex technique of the *Cantos* provide helpful guides.

With typically outrageous overstatement, in 1922 Pound declared the end of the Christian era. But his literary innovations and midwifery—so well documented here—and his influence upon contemporary writing were to prove that he was *not* a "complete ass" in proclaiming the beginning of "The Pound Era." (pp. 1, 5)

Joseph Parisi, "Demystifying Ezra Pound," in Chicago Tribune, *August 16, 1987, pp. 1, 5.*

BRUCE BAWER

[*Bawer writes regularly about modern literature for* The New Criterion. *In the following excerpt, he discusses Pound's literary genius and his disturbing personal and political behavior. Bawer faults Tytell's biography for clumsy prose and lack of critical discussion of Pound's contradictory behavior; nevertheless, he finds the book absorbing and compassionate.*]

About his contribution as poet, critic and social commentator we may all wrangle endlessly, but one fact about Ezra Pound seems virtually unarguable—namely, that he was one of the most colorful literary figures of this century. To be sure, being colorful was his conscious aim: even in his freshman year at college, as John Tytell observes in his absorbing new biography [*Ezra Pound: The Solitary Volcano*], Pound "accented his sense of difference with a gold-headed cane or a broad-brimmed hat with a swooping feather. He wanted notice." The Idaho-born, Philadelphia-bred poet also wanted to be where the action was—which is why, after a brief stint as an English teacher at a small Indiana college, he relocated to Europe at the age of 23. There he proceeded to carve a sizable niche for himself in the world of high culture—a world whose denizens came either to despise him for his brashness and oddity or to revere him for his brilliance and charisma.

Of course, Pound's attention-getting behavior had a purpose: to advertise modern writing, both his own and that of his peers. For kulchur (as he spelled it, in the labored faux-frontiersman style that he often adopted) was his life. He didn't work at a bank, like T. S. Eliot, or deliver babies, like his old college friend William Carlos Williams; when he wasn't writing his own poetry or criticism, he was reading or editing or publicizing somebody else's. Living in turn (during the years between 1908 and World War II) in London, Paris, and the Italian town of Rapallo, Pound managed not only to write some of the 20th century's most important poetry but to found its most important poetic movement (Imagism), to copy-edit its most important poem (*The Waste Land*), to help its most important poet (Yeats) to modernize his style, and to give its most celebrated serious fiction writer (Hemingway) "the most practical advice" he ever got. What distinguished Pound, above and beyond his literary genius and his ability to recognize literary genius in others, was that he had innate gifts as a critic and impresario—and a paradoxical combination of egomania and selflessness (in cultural matters, anyway)—that made it possible for him to play a dominant role in helping these writers to perfect and promote their work.

How, one may wonder, did a boy from Idaho grow up to be the 20th century's foremost cultural activist? Tytell suggests—quite convincingly—that Pound's activism was a legacy, in large part, of his paternal ancestors, particularly his grandfather Thaddeus Pound, a self-made man who built railroads and served in the Wisconsin assembly; a "model of enterprise and accomplishment" as well as of American-style optimism, Thaddeus was associated in Pound's mind "with the daring and danger of frontier life, the robust vigors that would serve to domesticate a wilderness." That Pound applied his zeal to culture rather than to business or state politics is attributed by Tytell to the influence of the poet's maternal ancestors, the Westons and Wadsworths. These two old New England families—the latter of which claimed as one of its members the poet Longfellow—represented to Pound "history, gentility, and culture." A respect for tradition, a yearning for the new: it is upon this paradoxical combination of elements that the modern sensibility is built.

One can hardly imagine modernism without Pound. More than anyone else, he was responsible for creating a climate in which sophisticated readers came to expect a poem to be not sentimental, metronomic "Victorian mush" but an impersonal and intelligent object—either direct and conversational, as in Williams, or comprehensive and obscurely allusive, as in Eliot. Yet when have readers ever felt more uncomfortable with so prominent a literary figure? To those of us with a high regard for modernism, Pound's centrality to it is unsettling on many accounts. For one thing, his poetry—which ranges from the Imagistic brevity of the two-line **"In a Station of the Metro"** ("The apparition of these faces in the crowd; / Petals on a wet, black bough") to the all-inclusive sprawl of the book-length *Cantos*—represents, on the whole, a smaller achievement than that of Eliot, say, or Wallace Stevens. And the hyperkinetic, hayseed manner of most of his prose is likely to strike a contemporary reader as irritating, even tiresome.

What's more, Pound's judgment on many matters was, to say the least, extremely unreliable. He bought wholesale Ernest Fenellosa's mistaken theory regarding the pictorial function of Chinese ideograms, as well as Rémy de Gourmont's ludicrous notion of a connection between copulation and cerebral development. More disturbing was his fanatical devotion to the crackpot economic theories of the anti-Semitic Major C. H. Douglas (who declared that most of the modern world's troubles were the fault of usury) and to Mussolini (for whom he propagandized during World War II over Rome Radio). Then there is his famous anti-Semitism, which—as Tytell shows at devastating length—was virulent and virtually lifelong. Such phrases as "Jew York" and "Jewnited States" crop up frequently in his early letters; on Rome Radio he declared that "the Jew is a savage" and recommended *The Protocols of the Elders of Zion* to his listeners; after the war—when he was domiciled for 12 years in the psychiatric ward of Saint Elizabeth's Hospital in Washington, D.C.—he spoke up in favor of pogroms and befriended members of various Klan-like and neo-Nazi organizations.

To be sure, many writers of Pound's era, among them Eliot and Hemingway, at times expressed anti-Semitic sentiments; whether Pound's more vocal bigotry was a sign of greater hostility to Jews, or simply a manifestation of his need to outrage—his feeling that "They won't pay attention to me unless I say something sensational"—is open to question. In any event, Irving Howe is probably right in saying that Pound's prejudices were purely abstract and that he never would have wished harm upon any individual; that is, Pound was so preoccupied with Judaism as a concept, as a component of his own grand philosophical system, that he was incapable of recognizing it as an aggregation of human individuals who were actually suffering and dying under his beloved Fascist regime. The sad truth is that for all Pound's sense of responsibility in regard to such abstract entities as culture, the economy, and the state, he was guilty of a reprehensible irresponsibility toward the *hoi polloi*—toward individuals, in other words, who did not happen to be artists, intellectuals or leaders. It was a similar irresponsibility that made it possible for him to maintain two households for many years, one with his wife, Dorothy Shakespear, and one with his mistress, Olga Rudge, and to send his children (whom he couldn't be bothered to have underfoot) to be raised in other homes.

A fascinating figure—and Tytell has written a fascinating book. But it has significant failings. For example, though it is certainly a good deal more readable than many literary biographies, its prose is often deplorable; there are dangling participles and misplaced modifiers in abundance, and numerous instances of imprecise diction (Tytell habitually uses *convince* for *persuade*), pleonasm ("the L'Action Francaise"), and sty-

listic clumsiness. (Tytell writes, for example, such awful sentences as the following: "A bullet-shaped man with shoulders hardly broader than his head, Mencken's grating humor and his explosively opinionated views of American life had organized *The Smart Set* and *The American Mercury*.") And there are odd little lapses here and there: the playwright and screenwriter Ben Hecht is referred to as "an American critic"; the word *blague* is used in one chapter but not defined until the next; the names of Meyer Schapiro and Carl Rakosi and Natty Bumppo are misspelled; and a letter from Delmore Schwartz to Pound—in which Schwartz, incensed at the older poet's anti-Semitism, "resigned" as one of his greatest admirers—is misquoted.

Furthermore, with so much controversial material at hand, it is frustrating that Tytell has so little to offer by way of commentary. Though he . . . is excellent at retailing colorful details and illuminating anecdotes, he provides precious little critical discussion; he reports the comments of others about Pound's work and life but to a considerable extent keeps his own views to himself. At times, consequently, the book seems to be a mere collection of facts and quotations, devoid of a controlling sensibility of its own. (Interestingly, this is the very reaction that one has to many of Pound's poems.) Nor does Tytell satisfactorily explore the crucial questions that Pound's life raises—such as, how could such a symbol of humanistic culture be at the same time such a miserable hatemonger? And if such a dichotomy is possible, what does that tell us about the nature of the connections between art and morality, beauty and truth, the poet and the state? Nor does Tytell offer opinions upon such matters as James Laughlin's disturbing remark, in a 1945 letter to Eliot concerning Pound's postwar arrest on charges of treason, to the effect that "Ezra is 'sane' and the world 'insane'," and that Pound was imprisoned only because "the world . . . habitually hangs or torments men of genius or vision."

To be sure, it is difficult to sort out the Pound we must admire from the Pound we must despise, for his genius seems to have been, in a sense, on a continuum with his madness, the best of him inextricable from the worst. His egomaniacal belief that he could save the world by railing against usury was not completely unrelated to his belief that he could save literature by railing against indirectness, superfluity and gratuitous ornamentation. For what it is worth, moreover, Pound recanted his ugliest statements during his declining years in Rapallo. "Wrong, wrong. I've always been wrong," he told the novelist Richard Stern in the early '60s. In a postscript to the *Cantos* he admitted that he'd been "out of focus" about usury: the real problem was not usury but "AVARICE." And he confessed to Allen Ginsberg (who brought him a Beatles record) that the *Cantos* were "a mess. Stupidity and ignorance all the way through. . . . But the worst mistake I made was that stupid suburban prejudice of anti-Semitism." His final, fragmentary contribution to the *Cantos* is genuinely pathetic: "Let those I love," he wrote, "try to forgive what I have made." For the rest of us, it is not to forgive but to try to understand—and John Tytell, though he hardly makes it possible for us to understand everything, has provided in his book a vivid, sensitive portrait that will go a good way toward clarifying, for all of us, the enigma that was Pound.

Bruce Bawer, "The Emcee of Modern Letters," in Book World—The Washington Post, September 6, 1987, p. 4.

LINDA SIMON

[*Simon, an American critic and educator, is the author of works on Gertrude Stein, Alice B. Toklas, and Thornton Wilder. In the following excerpt, she finds Tytell's biography objective and lucid, but notes that his failure to interpret Pound's enigmatic personality prevents the work from achieving status as the definitive biography.*]

Ezra Pound is a problem. He was romantic hero and monster, troubadour poet and malicious misanthrope, sublime artist and calculating opportunist. Certainly he is not easily explained or, as John Tytell aims [in *Ezra Pound: The Solitary Volcano*], interpreted. There have been many competent biographies, yet always, it seems, room for another view of the contentious, controversial Ezra Pound.

When Tytell approached James Laughlin, Pound's literary executor and, in many ways, his champion, about the possibility of writing a biography, Laughlin was encouraging about "an interpretive biography that could explore the myths behind the man rather than merely debunking them." Tytell decided to present the facts of Pound's life "in a honed and chiseled manner," and the result is a comprehensive, competent, and lucid account of the troubled and troubling poet, although it is only minimally "interpretative." It is a fair and cleareyed look at Pound's poetry and politics by a biographer who is sympathetic but not starry-eyed, respectful but not adoring of his subject.

Pound's youth in Idaho; his aborted career as a teacher; his emigration to London, Paris, and Italy; his relationship with Yeats, Eliot, Ford, Hemingway, Wyndham Lewis, and Hilda Doolittle, among others; his odd marriage to Dorothy Pound and his romantic liaisons; his noisy support of Mussolini; his arrest, incarceration, and decline all are chronicled here. But the motivations behind Pound's often erratic behavior, his abrasiveness, his lack of empathy, his exasperating bravado—these are hardly explored.

Pound emerges no more palpable from Tytell's efforts than he did from the work of Charles Norman, Noel Stock, C. David Heymann, or Hugh Kenner. Tytell has had the benefit of a decade of new research and archival material since Heymann's 1976 biography; but *Ezra Pound: The Solitary Volcano* supplements rather than supplants any previous book, including Stock's more detailed 1970 biography, which was recently updated. . . .

Pound's is a tragic story, full of ironic twists (the editor who pushed for the American publication of *A Draft of XXX Cantos* was none other than Ogden Nash) and dashed hopes. It is a story that will, no doubt, be told again, and the cumulative efforts may serve to enlighten as no single work can.

> Linda Simon, "Revisiting 'Ezuversity' in Two New Biographies of Ezra Pound," in The Christian Science Monitor, *September 30, 1987, p. 20.*

PAUL STUEWE

There's no dearth of good books on Ezra Pound: major biographies by Charles Norman and Noel Stock, Hugh Kenner's magisterial *The Pound Era,* and a host of more specialized critical studies have laid a solid foundation for the understanding of this talented writer and terribly flawed human being. Thus any new biography has to justify itself in terms of fresh evidential and/or interpretive approaches. [In *Ezra Pound: The Solitary Volcano*] Tytell hasn't come close to doing so. The

biographical sections of his book simply rehash material more exhaustively mined by Norman and Stock; his ventures into literary criticism are likewise derivative and often irritatingly superficial. Tytell is also a distressingly slapdash writer, addicted to phrases of the "Pound must have felt" or "Pound may have been influenced by" variety, and he has a less than adequate grasp of the literary milieux in which his subject circulated. This thoroughly uninventive and unnecessary volume reflects no credit on those responsible for its publication.

> Paul Stuewe, in a review of "Ezra Pound: The Solitary Volcano," in Quill and Quire, *Vol. 53, No. 12, December, 1987, p. 30.*

HUMPHREY CARPENTER

[*Carpenter is an English biographer, critic, editor, and writer for children. A specialist on the Oxford Christian group, Carpenter is the author of* Tolkien: A Biography *(1977) and* The Inklings: C. S. Lewis, J. R. R. Tolkien, Charles Williams, and Their Friends *(1978), and is co-editor of* The Letters of J. R. R. Tolkien *(1981). His* W. H. Auden: A Biography *(1981) is considered the definitive portrait of the modernist poet. Carpenter has recently published* Geniuses Together: American Writers in Paris in the 1920's *(1988) and* A Serious Character *(1988), a biography of Ezra Pound. In the following excerpt, he faults Tytell* **for his apparent lack of original research, his cliché-ridden style,** *and his inadequate criticism of Pound's poetry.*]

Hugely written about, Ezra Pound has nowhere come alive in all his contradictory dimensions as a human being. Not, that is, in a full-length life, though writers of article-length personal impressions usually manage to catch something of the enigma. But he has eluded the professional biographer. Charles Norman's 1960 life has vivid patches but is very sketchy on information and does not try to explain the Pound puzzle. Noel Stock's *The Life of Ezra Pound* (1970) is crammed with facts but makes little attempt to show the motivations of its central character. Other less ambitious volumes have been written, usually the work of paid-up Poundians or occasionally of equally committed Pound-haters, both too violently partisan to paint a clear portrait. And so the man whom William Carlos Williams called "one of the most competent poets in our language" and also "the biggest damn fool and faker in the business" remains mysterious. Why did the literary explorer who discovered and published Eliot and Joyce spend the Second World War broadcasting on behalf of the Mussolini régime? Why did the craftsman who wrote *Hugh Selwyn Mauberley* and edited *The Waste Land* churn out the great dreary stretches of un-poetry which make up so much of the *Cantos*? The telling of this strange tale—for all it really requires is good storytelling rather than clever analysis—seems oddly beyond the grasp of biographers.

The latest attempt is by an American writer. . . . John Tytell's title [*Ezra Pound: The Solitary Volcano*] comes from an epithet applied to Ezra Pound by W. B. Yeats in the early days of their friendship. Tytell claims to have drawn on "the reading of thousands of unpublished letters", and there are moments in his narrative when one does recognize a fragment of information culled from the depths of one of the American manuscript collections. Yet most of the quotations printed in his book are the well-worn pieces that turn up in all the other lives, and there is very little evidence of original research.

Worse, his narrative is almost entirely constructed by means of clichés. Paul Jennings once coined the term "actor's bosh" for the particular type of meaninglessness that bad playwrights make their actors spout. *The Solitary Volcano* has some choice examples of biographer's bosh. So we have the young Ezra in Venice in the summer of 1908 "obsessively exploring, observing, recording—the work of the poet", "pensively gazing at the water, sensing the plenitude of the ocean". Tytell is scarcely able to make the simplest statement without indulging in this sort of writerese, and when he turns to the historical background the narrative is equally absurd. So, on Ezra's arrival in London that same year, we are told that men had only recently given up powdering their noses and painting their cheeks, but that the "hard social rules" of Edwardian England were "affected by the new technologies: the wireless telegraph, the telephone, the cinema and the X-ray, the incandescent lamp and electricity, the automobile and the airplane".

Chapter titles ("London: Art for Its Own Sake", "Rapallo: The Politics of Art", and so on) try to suggest a concern with Pound as artist, but the poetry is scarcely touched on—the *Pisan Cantos,* for example, get less than a page and a half—which is perhaps merciful, given that Tytell's attempts at criticism are generally as ludicrous as his narrative. At its better moments *The Solitary Volcano* reads like a compressed entry on Pound in a dictionary of writers: a quality that scarcely seems to justify . . . [the publication] of this curiosity of the biography boom.

> *Humphrey Carpenter, "An Elusive Giant," in* The Times Literary Supplement, *No. 4425, January 22-28, 1988, p. 79.*

Sylvia Plath: A Biography

by Linda Wagner-Martin

(For Sylvia Plath: see also *CLC*, Vols. 1, 2, 3, 5, 9, 11, 14, 17, 51; *Contemporary Authors Permanent Series,* Vol. 2; *Contemporary Authors,* Vols. 19-20; *Dictionary of Literary Biography,* Vols. 5, 6; and *Concise Dictionary of American Literary Biography 1941-1968.*)

BRUCE BAWER

To the general public, the name Sylvia Plath may well be more familiar than that of any other postwar American poet. People may not know Plath's poetry, but—thanks largely to her autobiographical novel, *The Bell Jar*—they know of the morbid anxiety that plagued her during her Massachusetts childhood and her college days at Smith. And they know, of course, of her suicide, which occurred in London in February, 1963, when she was 30, the estranged wife of Ted Hughes (now Britain's poet laureate) and the mother of two small children. Though she was hardly the only major poet of our era to kill herself, Plath, alone among the postwar poet-suicides, was someone that a typical American could understand and identify with—and could even, if so inclined, choose to regard pityingly as a failure, a potential middle-class wife and mother gone astray into poetry and neurosis.

For unlike John Berryman, say, or Hart Crane, Plath longed conspicuously for conventional success and public approval. From her father, Otto—a German-born entomologist who, as Linda Wagner-Martin writes in [*Sylvia Plath: A Biography*], "created the image of father as critic, judge, someone to be pleased"—Plath learned early that "doing things for the fun of doing them was less important than doing them because she could do them better than most people." So driven was she to succeed scholastically that even on the morning after Otto died (Sylvia was 7 at the time) she refused to miss school.

If she felt obliged to be an exceptional student, she also felt obliged to be light and gay—to act, that is, the part of the carefree young lady, and to hide, as fully as possible, the darker thoughts that tormented her. "Like a child," Wagner-Martin explains, "Sylvia seemed to believe that pretending would make any situation improve." Only in her poems and journal, and in a very few letters, was she able to admit her despondency. At Smith, for example, she wrote to a confidante that "Life is loneliness, despite all the opiates, despite the false grinning faces we all wear ... Yes, there is joy, fulfillment and companionship—but the loneliness of the soul in its appalling self-consciousness is horrible and overpowering."

Her life, then, consisted of an ironic combination of extraordinary accomplishment (numerous academic honors, precocious publication, a brilliant marriage) and profound emotional

torment. Her greatest college triumph—a summer editorial internship at *Mademoiselle*—was followed almost immediately by a suicide attempt. Afterwards, Plath characteristically regarded the incident as a demonstration of her failure to be the ideal co-ed. "If I could only be a freshman again," she lamented to her mother. "I so wanted to be a Smith woman." ...

What Wagner-Martin has done is to pare the life down to its bare narrative essentials—at times, indeed, this book reads like a synopsis of a biography—and to cast it in largely feminist terms. She sees Plath as the victim not only of her father's insistence upon academic success but also of the image of the "perfect American girl" propagated by such magazines as *Ladies' Home Journal* and *Seventeen.* These middlebrow magazines, Wagner-Martin argues, taught Plath that *"the only happy woman was the married woman."* Her ambitions warred with her responsiveness to her own culture.

But the important question is, why did pop-culture stereotypes and philistine values matter so much to Plath in the first place? At a time when many other intelligent, creative American women (with less sophisticated parents) managed to look beyond *Ladies' Home Journal* notions of womanhood, why did Plath take

439

these notions so seriously? Wagner-Martin is less interested in addressing this critical question than in repeating simplistic feminist formulas and making sweeping cultural indictments.

Moreover, though she does have some perceptive and interesting things to say about *The Bell Jar*—about, for example, its borrowings from *The Catcher in the Rye*, about Plath's use of symbology based on "the Christ legend," and about the effect of its writing on Plath's poetic voice—Wagner-Martin doesn't devote as much space as one would like to discussions of Plath's verse. This neglect is particularly surprising in view of Wagner-Martin's high regard for Plath's poetry. She seems to take for granted the importance of the poetry and the greatness of the intense, violent poems—the notorious **"Daddy"** and **"Lady Lazarus"** among them—that poured out during Plath's last tragic year. As a reader who rates Plath's poetry a good deal less highly, I had hoped that Wagner-Martin might help me to see these poems through her admiring eyes. (In part, to be sure, Wagner-Martin's failure to discuss the poetry in detail is not her fault; as she explains in her preface, the Hughes family prohibited extensive quotation from Plath's works.)

If there is a villain in Wagner-Martin's book, it is Ted Hughes, who comes off in these pages as irresponsible and uncaring. Basing her conclusions on journals and letters that have only recently been made available, Wagner-Martin strongly implies that what precipitated Plath's suicide was Hughes' sudden distancing of himself from her, perhaps because he was having an extramarital affair. Wagner-Martin even says that, according to Plath's letters of late 1962, "Ted was taunting her with her earlier suicide attempt, saying that if she were to repeat that action, everything would be simpler for him." Hughes denies having said such a thing, and it is certainly conceivable that, given Plath's state of mind, she was lying or hallucinating; but Wagner-Martin buries Hughes' denial in her endnotes. She seems a bit too eager to believe the worst about Hughes; indeed, she seems almost to regard him, as Plath does in her manic late poem **"Daddy,"** as a "vampire," an agent of a fascistic patriarchy.

Yet in her more lucid moments, even Plath appears to have recognized that her own worst enemy was not her father or mother or husband, but herself. In her college journal she criticized herself as "an Over-grown, Over-protected, Scared, Spoiled Baby" who was afraid of independence, afraid "to face the great huge man-eating world." "Stop thinking selfishly," she urged herself, "of razors and self-wounds and going out and ending it all. Your room is not your prison. You are." Alas, Wagner-Martin doesn't offer much in the way of insight into the complex, fascinating psychopathology that informs such journal entries.

> *Bruce Bawer, "Sylvia Plath and the Prison of Her Days," in* Book World—The Washington Post, Oc- *tober 25, 1987, p. 4.*

IAN HAMILTON

[*Hamilton, an English critic and poet, is the founder and editor of* New Review, *a journal of English poetry specializing in the criticism and promotion of new talent. He is the author of* Robert Lowell: A Biography *(1983) and several volumes of poetry, as well as the editor of numerous poetry anthologies. In the following excerpt, Hamilton discusses the difficulties prospective biographers of Plath have had with her literary executors—difficulties which Wagner-Martin also experienced. He observes that the resulting biography adds little to the record of Plath's life.*]

It is now almost a quarter of a century since Sylvia Plath killed herself, at the age of 30. Since her death, there have been several attempts to write her definitive biography, attempts that at some stage or another have run into trouble with those who safeguard the poet's literary estate: her husband, Ted Hughes, and his sister and agent, Olwyn Hughes. Whenever the "truth about Sylvia Plath" is discussed, you can be fairly sure that sooner or later the Hugheses will be mentioned with disfavor, as if the pair of them were somehow in the business of suppressing vital data. Nobody ever seems very clear about what kind of data this might be; the innuendoes persist, though, and it is hard to imagine what will put a stop to them.

On the face of it, the Hugheses can indeed be described as overcautious, not to say obstructive, in their dealings with those who wish to write Plath's life. It is known that there are Sylvia Plath writings under seal in libraries, not to be seen by anyone until the year 2013. It is also known that Ted Hughes destroyed a notebook that records Plath's most private thinking during the last months of her life ("because," he says, "I did not want her children to have to read it"), and that another notebook from 1962 has simply, according to Mr. Hughes, "disappeared." There is also the draft of what might have been Plath's second novel, *Double Exposure*; that too is missing.

These disappearances, coupled with what one hears about the strict way the Hugheses have of granting permissions, can easily be made to sound suspicious, as if Ted Hughes were more interested in protecting himself, or some image of him- self, than in letting his dead wife be heard. And since there are many admirers of Plath who have already cast Mr. Hughes in a villainous role—as the husband who dominated and then wronged her—such suspicions have gained ground over the years. There is a certain glamour in the projected notion of Plath as a woman posthumously victimized, just as (so it is thought by some) she was victimized in life.

It is difficult, with admirers of this sort, to plead for a more balanced view, and [*Sylvia Plath: A Biography*] will not, I fear, make it any simpler. Linda Wagner-Martin is herself in favor of more balance, and she has learned enough about the more intimidating aspects of Sylvia Plath's personality to steer clear of any crudely feminist judgments of Mr. Hughes. Indeed, in her presentation, the marriage ended because Sylvia Plath expected too much from it. Even so, her book is prefaced with complaints about her dealings with the Plath estate. Mr. Hughes, she says, wanted some 15,000 words deleted from her manuscript. Although she made concessions, she did not go along with all of the suggested changes, and she has therefore been denied permission to quote at length from Plath's writings.

What were these changes, and why did they matter so much to Mr. Hughes (his list of objections, we are told, runs to 15 pages)? Were his objections self-interested, or did he straightforwardly believe that this biographer had got things wrong? But surely every biographer gets things wrong in the eyes of those who shared the life under discussion. What did Mr. Hughes see in this book that made him want to alter it so drastically? If the author had chosen to give us the details of her differences with him, some useful demystification might have been achieved. As it is, we go on wondering.

But wondering what? After all, it is not as if the world were starved of information on the life and private thoughts of this ferociously self-centered writer. We know about her glittering Smith College record, her precocious successes as a writer in her early 20's, her breakdowns and her first suicide attempt, her move to Cambridge, England, where she met and married Mr. Hughes—a poet far more self-assured and successful than she was. During the marriage, Plath did her best to be a "good wife" to a husband she adored, and her own literary ambition, which was huge, took—or pretended to take—second place to his. The explosive poems of *Ariel* were written after Mr. Hughes left her for another woman, and it is because of these poems that we have wanted to know about her life. But what more can there be to know? We have in print 500 pages of her journals and 350 pages of *Letters Home*. We have dozens of memoirs and one or two full-length biographies. And, of course, we have the poetry, which in its later stages is scorchingly autobiographical. There are, to be sure, unpublished letters and large sections of Plath's journals that were not included in the edition co-edited by Mr. Hughes. But do these hold secrets that need to be revealed before we can be satisfied that we possess the truth about Sylvia Plath?

Ms. Wagner-Martin has been through all this material and is able to give us some facts we didn't have before. None of these seem wildly controversial, and none reflect all that badly on Mr. Hughes—nor, come to that, on Plath herself. Ms. Wagner-Martin's additions to the record are minor, circumstantial, and to savor them (or, sometimes, even to register that they are indeed additions) we really need to see her book alongside the published journals. One effect of such an exercise is to make the Wagner-Martin text seem thin, impoverished. Even at her most hysterical, Plath has the intelligence and word power to defeat, or outshine, any paraphrase—and Ms. Wagner-Martin is not, in any case, the most subtle of reporters. Another effect is to make us wonder if the journals themselves could not have been less timidly prepared for publication.

For example, in the published edition, there are a number of declared omissions, material plucked from the middle of sentences and paragraphs and replaced by tantalizing dots. These censorings have, needless to say, given rise to uncharitable speculation. But whenever Ms. Wagner-Martin takes it upon herself to fill in these gaps, the result is invariably so tame as to make us wonder why the original omission was ever thought to have been worth the trouble. To take one instance, in the published journal we have this description of Plath's first meeting with Ted Hughes:

> Then he kissed me bang smash on the mouth (omission) . . . And when he kissed my neck I bit him long and hard on the cheek, and when we came out of the room, blood was running down his face. (Omission.) And I screamed in myself, thinking: oh, to give myself crashing, fighting, to you.

Ms. Wagner-Martin has been to the source, and she transcribes as follows:

> Then he kissed me bang smash on the mouth and ripped my hairband, off my red hairband scarf which has weathered the sun and much love, and whose like I shall never find again, and my favorite silver earrings: ha, I shall keep, he barked. And when he kissed my neck I bit him long and hard on the cheek, and when we came out of the room, blood was running down his face.

We note that the second of the two original omissions is allowed to stand, so we must still remain ignorant of how, precisely, Mr. Hughes responded to that bite, but surely the material that *is* filled in need not have been excluded in the first place.

It is this sort of discussion that Ms. Wagner-Martin's book is most likely to provoke. As to Sylvia Plath, the picture we already have of her, and of the marriage, remains essentially unaltered, and Ted Hughes' own brief account of his wife's struggle to determine her "real self" still seems entirely plausible. One of the problems, though, with any biography of this poet is that Mr. Hughes himself has never given his version of the marriage. He has spoken abstractly about Plath's personality, and he has been a loving and scrupulous editor of her poetry, even though the best of it is fueled by an intense anger against him. . . . Plath in her last months was in a vengeful mood most of the time, and one can well imagine that there are unpublished writings that, if released, would seem to invite some sort of line-by-line rebuttal by Mr. Hughes. (p. 12)

And yet does one really want more paraphrase of the prohibited material, more guesswork, more sentences like this one (from Ms. Wagner-Martin): "They spent the night at his second-floor flat on Rugby Street in London, reciting poetry, making love, finding their alter ego in each other—rebellious and isolated, strong and erotic and gifted"? Ms. Wagner-Martin's style veers between colorful empathizing and businesslike terseness ("Summer was slow, relaxed and—for Ted—productive. Everything he wrote was good"), and her book is somewhat unbalanced by her wish to exhibit the fruits of her considerable research. That is to say, if an event is covered by the published journals, she will tend to skimp it, but if it is "new," it gets more emphasis than it necessarily deserves. This again brings us back to the problem of permissions, and to the thought that the next Sylvia Plath biography will surely have to be one that enjoys the full cooperation of Mr. Hughes. In the meantime, there is a question that is too rarely pondered: what would Sylvia Plath have wished to preserve, if she had lived? (p. 13)

Ian Hamilton, "The Tatty Wreckage of Her Life," in The New York Times Book Review, *October 25, 1987, pp. 12-13.*

DIANE MIDDLEBROOK

[*Middlebrook, an American educator and critic, is the author of* Walt Whitman and Wallace Stevens (1974); *she is currently writing a biography of Anne Sexton. In the following excerpt Middlebrook observes that Wagner-Martin's biography succeeds as a sociological exploration of the poet and her era, but is weak in artistic analysis, largely because of Wagner-Martin's inability to quote from Plath's works.*]

Not everyone is still an adolescent at college or during the first childbearing years. The Sylvia Plath of this biography mostly was: all preface, all expectation, preoccupied with her body, an identity still in the crucible. . . .

[In *Sylvia Plath: A Biography*], Linda Wagner-Martin approaches Plath more or less sociologically. In this she has had Plath's own full cooperation. Erik Erikson called adolescence the Age of Ideology; Plath's most popular writing, focused on adolescence, provides a convenient index of the ideologies that formed her in postwar America. The work by which Plath is best known to her very large audience is the autobiographical account in *The Bell Jar* of a summer spent as college editor of *Mademoiselle*. (Wagner-Martin says that 80,000 to 100,000 copies of *The Bell Jar* sell annually in the United States.) Later, publication of Plath's college journals and her letters home from England to her mother and brother augmented the novel's callowest tones. But shortly after the pseudonymous publication of *The Bell Jar* Plath committed suicide, at age 30. Then began the slow release of an entirely different level of work:

poetry written from 1961 through early 1963, the last two years of her life. "I am a genius of a writer," she had exulted in a letter home, around the time of her thirtieth birthday. "I am writing the best poems of my life; they will make my name."

Plath's reputation for genius, however, was entirely posthumous. When her first book of poems, *The Colossus,* came out in 1960, notices were favorable but contained the reservation that she had not yet developed a consistent voice. She was then at work on *The Bell Jar* and poems she described as full of "humor and oddnesses." Just attaining professional status as a writer, Plath aspired to reach the same readers as Philip Roth and J. D. Salinger. (p. 656)

Salinger's successful formula was the first-person narrative in which a quintessentially adolescent hero counters the gray-flannel world of benign, deadly grown-ups first with whimsy and then with mental breakdown or suicide. As Wagner-Martin demonstrates, Plath borrowed from Salinger's *The Catcher in the Rye* with surprising frequency in plotting *The Bell Jar*: She "turned to it for structure, and drew on it whenever she ran out of events that seemed to fit [the protagonist] Esther's story."

Humor and oddness were the traits that made stories marketable in Plath's view, and she worked diligently to master a comic tone like Salinger's; she yearned for sales to commercial magazines, and recognized the appeal of adolescent pathos. To her journals Plath could confide, "In the morning light, all is possible; even becoming a god." But her strategies for publication indicate that, for a genius, she set her sights low. "I shall have fulfilled a very long-time ambition if a story of mine ever makes the L[adies] H[ome] J[ournal]," she wrote her mother from England in October 1961.

The apparent contradiction between Plath's grand confidence and her bread-and-butter professional expectations has something to do with the fact that as a woman of her time, she had another project: fulfillment as a wife. At age 24 she had married a mentor, the British poet Ted Hughes, two years her senior. The first four years of marriage were a perpetual private workshop, supported mainly by Plath's grants, teaching and part-time jobs. Hughes was writing full-time, with a sense of vocation she could not approach. For Plath, being Hughes's wife was a vocation in itself. Wagner-Martin characterizes as "almost obsessive" her "need to live the perfect life, love the perfect man, create the perfect household, as a means of proving that she was a success in all areas women were supposed to excel in." Thus while her training as a writer went forward under Hughes's guidance and strong encouragement, her development as an "ideal woman" decelerated under the burdens of chronic financial worries, infant care and, at last, Hughes's infidelities.

Sexual ideologies play a crucial role in the plot of the story Wagner-Martin tells. Plath met Hughes in bohemian Cambridge, at a literary party Plath described in her journal as one of "these sluttish nights" that "make me have a violent nunlike passion to write and sequester myself." Not long after meeting, they began kissing—Hughes ripped off Plath's hairband and earrings; Plath bit him until blood ran down his face. Plath was no longer a virgin, but she had cordoned off her sexuality with a concept: Sex was an instinctual force running through her, driving her toward men who could return her passion and father her children. . . . In her journal she tried out the possibility that her violent sexual feelings might be most useful if sublimated in writing. Once married, she made Hughes the focus of a rather savage will to domesticate them both.

The marriage collapsed just as Plath was gaining recognition in London's literary establishment. This time her violent passions—jealousy, and terror of being abandoned—did get sublimated into writing, having few other outlets. In the mythy poetry Plath wrote during the last bitter months before her suicide, male figures are typically based on an imago of Daddy, beheld with vengeful fascination.

So far Plath represents the late-adolescent female of American culture in the 1950s: a talented young woman deformed by ideologies that segregated masculine and feminine roles while sponsoring ambition. But what about her genius? Wagner-Martin's biography does not help much in illuminating that. Most sorely missing is an analysis of Plath as an artist: Since she is unable to quote at length from the work, Wagner-Martin is able to gesture toward this subject only through paraphrase. Plath became a masterful technician of syllables during her college years, but her genius expressed itself in the extreme condensation of her last poems. No paraphrase can even get close to rendering the layered meanings Plath achieved through juxtaposition and leaps of association in these poems; indeed, paraphrase succeeds only in making them sound banal.

Moreover, Plath's own writing is so autobiographical that any secondary account of it is likely to pale by comparison. Her postcollege journal, like the letters of John Keats, is genius talking to itself. Here, and never in letters home, she stretches toward artistic goals still slightly out of reach; she lets thought snake into metaphors that tell much about the feeling-tone of insights. Only a full publication of Plath's last journals could account for the central mystery of this life at its most interesting: the relationship between the drive for conformity and the drive for originality that Plath negotiated day by day as she neared thirty.

Wagner-Martin has had to confine herself instead to portraying Plath as an exemplar of all that could go wrong or right for a daughter coming of age in the 1950s. This Sylvia Plath lived her life "as though it were some blueprint for a woman's fantasy." But the strength of Wagner-Martin's book is just such sociological consistency. It earns credibility for the insight with which she accounts for Plath's suicide: By February 1963, Plath had come to the end of the fantasy. "Moving to London had not brought her reconciliation with Ted, or professional acclaim, or new friendships," Wagner-Martin observes. "She was becoming depressed, partly with the realization of what faced her: She would live as a single parent, with these two wonderful children, for the rest of her days. Though she did not say it, she would live the life her own mother had led, a life that Sylvia had often criticized for its self-sacrifice and dedication."

Plath's very last poems, written the week of her death, blaze with renunciation not of genius but of ordinary life. Was this choice neurotic? Was it simply pathetic, or was it tragic? The published documents do not agree. For now, it is harder to capture Plath through a biography than to quicken her presence by reading the journals and poems. (pp. 656, 658-59)

Diane Middlebrook, "Forever in Amber," in The Nation, *New York, Vol. 245, No. 18, November 28, 1987, pp. 656, 658-59.*

An Excerpt from *Sylvia Plath: A Biography*

As days passed, time became Sylvia's worst enemy. Each morning brought her closer to her senior year, the year in which she would write her thesis, for which she had no definite topic, and take the extensive comprehensive examinations, for which she felt completely unprepared. Each day also brought her closer to the planned late-summer vacation with Dick, who was coming to Wellesley at the end of August and then returning to Saranac, with Sylvia accompanying him. It would be a repetition of Christmas vacation.

Entries from Sylvia's July journal chart the self-inflicted pain she experienced. Guilt and shame once again blinded her: whatever was wrong with her was *her* fault. She called herself "an Over-grown, Over-protected, Scared, Spoiled Baby," unable to meet real life. In a harsh scolding tone, she addressed herself in second person: "You are so obsessed by your coming necessity to be independent, to face the great huge man-eating world, that you are paralyzed . . . shocked, thrown into a nausea, a stasis." Later she cajoled herself, "I must make choices clearly, honestly, without getting sick so I can't eat." There was no reason, she continued, that she could not be "cheerful and constructive." For a young woman to live the "good" life, the suitable life, especially in the wealthy suburb of Wellesley, she must have the right attitude and wear the proper face, even amid deep depression. Near the end of this July 14 entry, she raged, "Stop thinking selfishly of razors and self-wounds and going out and ending it all. Your room is not your prison. You are."

Mrs. Plath described the horror of the summer in *Letters Home*, recounting the morning in July when she saw gashes on Sylvia's legs. Sylvia admitted that she had tried to kill herself, "'I just wanted to see if I had the guts!'" Then she took Aurelia's hand in her own burning hot ones and cried, "'Oh, Mother, the world is too rotten! I want to die! Let's die together!'"

That morning Aurelia took Sylvia to the bright and sympathetic woman who was the Plath family doctor. She of course referred them to a psychiatrist, a young man who talked with Sylvia and then recommended shock treatments. There was no second opinion. Sylvia received out-patient shock treatments—bipolar, electroconvulsive shock, given with no preparation and no follow-up counseling—at the direction of a doctor she disliked intensely. No sooner were the treatments begun than August came and the supervising doctor went on vacation, referring Sylvia to a colleague of his.

Her experience with shock treatments horrified her. "By the roots of my hair some god got hold of me. / I sizzled in his blue volts" is a description in a late poem. Sylvia felt intense pain. She was frightened beyond the words left to her at this point in her depression. Her mother told her the treatment would make her well, but it was doing nothing of the kind, and her resentment at Aurelia's advice would be a source of later anger.

In reality Aurelia and the Schobers were equally horrified, bearing their anxiety over Sylvia (and their fear of financial ruin from the expense of the therapy) in almost complete secrecy. Characteristically for the time, no one outside the family knew that Sylvia was in therapy or having shock treatments. Nor did Sylvia let on. She dated Gordon on two weekends when he was home from OCS, and as late as August 18, she wrote to Mike Lotz at his

summer baseball camp that she was having a "placid" summer. The word was chosen with her usual wry irony. On August 24, she received a letter from Gordon asking whether he could come over in a few days when he was home on liberty.

But that same day, several days after a shock treatment, Sylvia broke open a cabinet that held sleeping pills and took the nearly full bottle, along with a container of water, to the crawl space under the first-floor bedroom, the entrance to which was usually blocked by a pile of firewood. She was wearing Janet Wagner's green dirndl skirt and white peasant blouse. She left a note for her mother propped plainly on the dining room table: "Have gone for a long walk. Will be home tomorrow." Then she crawled inside the hideaway and took such a quantity of sleeping pills that she lost consciousness for more than two days.

LINDA WAGNER-MARTIN

Ian Hamilton's review of my book *Sylvia Plath: A Biography* [see excerpt above] is somewhat misleading. The book was intended to be about Sylvia Plath. When Mr. Hamilton, a British academic critic and poet, spends most of his space discussing Ted Hughes, the prominent English poet, his skewed perspective becomes clear. Sylvia Plath was not a mirror image of her husband: she could never have written her fine late poems if she were not expressing her own identity.

If Mr. Hamilton finds little that is new in my biography, it is probably because he is looking for the wrong kind of events— perhaps cataclysmic happenings. Plath did not go to war. She did not take lovers and flaunt them in her partner's face. She lived her housewifely life, working also as a writer, more or less quietly. She died the same way, quietly. Given the facts of her life, there are many new details here, and they were the details I was attempting to provide. I have tried to make this biography very "gender specific": it chronicles a *woman's* life, and the details are appropriate.

Plath wrote in her powerful late poem **"The Jailer"** (one of those poems Ted Hughes deleted when he published *Ariel*), "I am myself. That is not enough." My biography insists that Sylvia Plath *was* enough, enough subject for a book that says women's lives must be understood on their own merits—not those of their families or their husbands. While one might not expect Mr. Hamilton to understand the intricacies of Plath's life, one might have thought he would have understood the approach to describing it.

> *Linda Wagner-Martin, in a letter to the editor, in* The New York Times Book Review, *December 13, 1987, p. 46.*

EDWARD BUTSCHER

Although I have no major quarrel with Ian Hamilton's critique of Linda Wagner-Martin's *Sylvia Plath,* I must protest the protracted apologia for Ted Hughes embedded in and often overwhelming his peculiar review [see excerpts above].

Mr. Hamilton's intimate knowledge of the English-American poetry scene makes it seem disingenuous of him to claim that there have been "one or two full-length biographies" of Plath to date. As he should be aware, my controversial *Sylvia Plath: Method and Madness* (1976) was the sole biography to appear before Ms. Wagner-Martin's. More relevant, several other substantial biographies in the works over the last decade never saw print, largely because of the obstructionist tactics of Olwyn Hughes, Mr. Hughes's sister and manager of the Plath estate.

In my own case, Olwyn Hughes was initially cordial, even generous. This situation altered dramatically, however, after she read the galleys and began demanding numerous changes, the bulk of which entailed excising any negative references to the Hughes family and modifying several remarks about Plath's mother. Acute criticisms of Plath herself occasioned no similar objections.

It was evident that Olwyn Hughes intended to protect *her* family name at all costs, threatening to withhold reprint permissions if I did not capitulate. Thanks to the generous "fair use" provision of our copyright law and a shrewd (and expensive) lawyer, I was eventually able to persuade Seabury Press to publish my book without the permissions.

I do not wish to further hector Ted Hughes—several female critics have, in fact, charged me with being too "soft" on him—and regard as disgraceful the many vicious attacks against him by the lunatic fringe of the feminist movement. But his behavior has been equally disgraceful in terms of distorting recent literary history. Not only did he destroy valuable pages in his wife's journals, he also rearranged her poetry manuscripts, the same poetry Mr. Hamilton credits him with so "lovingly" ushering into print. One of the genuine virtues of Ms. Wagner-Martin's biography is its successful efforts to establish Plath's original intentions anent her unpublished works, *Ariel* in particular.

I respect Mr. Hamilton as a biography and editor, but in this instance friendship or some other private need has patently undermined his professional judgment.

> *Edward Butscher, in a letter to the editor, in* The New York Times Book Review, *December 13, 1987, p. 46.*

ELAINE KENDALL

[*In the following excerpt, Kendall briefly summarizes Plath's life and tragic death. She characterizes Wagner-Martin's biography as conscientious but unremittingly bland because it lacks authorial opinions.*]

Although Linda Wagner-Martin was initially promised full cooperation from the executors of Sylvia Plath's estate [for *Sylvia Plath: A Biography*], that approval was withdrawn midway through the project.... Undeterred, she soldiered on, publishing the biography without essential quotations that would have enlarged and expanded the text.

While Wagner-Martin states in her preface that the changes and cuts insisted upon by Ted Hughes and his sister Olwyn would have drastically altered her point of view, her approach to the material available to her is so flatly mater-of-fact that a point of view is barely discernible.

As a writer and editor responsible for two volumes of literary criticism on Plath, one would expect the author to have developed strong opinions about her subject's literary achievement, but there are no value judgments here, either personal or professional. Even with the disputed 15,000 words left in place, this biography seems so blandly unexceptional that

it's hard to imagine anyone taking issue with it. Intractable and unreasonable as they may have been, both Hugheses are treated with the same polite circumspection that characterizes the rest of the book.

The Sylvia Plath who emerges from Wagner-Martin's diligent interviews and conscientious perusal of letters and papers is a precociously talented young woman who considered herself a professional writer by the age of 17.

As an undergraduate at Smith College, she was published in *Harper's* and *The Atlantic* as well as in *Mademoiselle* and *Seventeen*, and by the time she was in her early 20s, the list included *The New Yorker*, *The Nation* and the prestigious literary reviews.

According to her biographer, Plath's childhood "if not idyllic, came close." The first child of highly educated and loving parents, Sylvia also had the attention of her grandparents and an affectionate aunt and uncle; the arrival of a younger brother Warren causing no more than the usual amount of perturbation.

The death of her father when Sylvia was only 8 sadly altered this stability, and despite the best efforts of her extended family, that early loss would remain the central trauma of an otherwise happy girlhood. Though Wagner-Martin emphasizes the perfectionism of Sylvia's mother Aurelia and reiterates Sylvia's own passion to succeed socially and academically, the immediate result was not despair but achievement. No adolescence is entirely tranquil, but there is little in Sylvia Plath's history to presage her mental breakdown and early suicide. As a scholarship student at a highly competitive college, she was often tired and harried, but her efforts were appreciated and rewarded. There were college romances and several satisfying friendships with classmates—every outward sign that Sylvia Plath would not only live up to the rigorous Smith ideal but exceed it.

With so few clues from the poetry and prose written during these years, Plath's first attempt at suicide seems all but inexplicable. Though we're told that Plath was deeply affected by the American political climate in the early '50s, there is little evidence of her anguish except passing references to her disappointment at Adlai Stevenson's defeat and her horror at the Rosenberg execution.

If Sylvia Plath truly believed that "whatever happened anywhere in the word was entirely her fault," demonstrations of her guilt are absent. Ed Cohen, a sensitive young man who had been corresponding with her, was apparently the only person to be fully aware of the depth of her misery. Advising her to seek immediate psychiatric help, he cited "the agitation, the dissatisfaction, the unrest, the annoyance, the lack of co-ordination, the nervous tensions that mark the time that a person approaches the ultimate breaking point," but these signs eluded those closer to her.

Honours and prizes continued to come her way, and her family and friends saw no reason for concern. In spring of 1953, Plath was named to the Mademoiselle College Board, a plummy summer job that not only offered her a month in New York but a chance to write for the magazine. Unfortunately, the senior editor to whom she was assigned proved so capricious and demanding that Plath's mental state worsened. Returning home exhausted and tense, she learned that she had not been accepted into the Harvard summer fiction program for which she'd applied. The triumphs paled, and convinced she was a fraud and a failure, Sylvia became so depressed that she was quite summarily subjected to electro-shock, then thought to be a quick cure for her condition. The therapy only exacerbated her illness, and in late August, she swallowed the contents of a bottle of sleeping pills and crawled under the family house to die, leaving a note saying she'd taken a long walk and would return the next day.

Discovered barely alive two days later, Sylvia was given more effective and appropriate treatment. By February she seemed well enough to return to Smith for her last year. Her well-publicized suicide attempt had turned her into a tragic heroine, and she was the subject of awe, envy and admiration. Suffering lent her natural good looks a particular intensity and her writing acquired increased depth. Upon graduation summa cum laude she was granted a Fulbright fellowship for further study at Cambridge, sailing for England in September 1955.

The rest of her life would be compressed into the next 8 years; her meeting with the extravagantly gifted and handsome poet Ted Hughes, their marriage, the birth of their two children; Plath's uneven but often dazzling new work. With the gradual disintegration of the marriage, the depression she'd suffered in college recurred, culminating in her suicide in 1963. . . . Though Wagner-Martin avoids all but the most rudimentary speculation, she does suggest at several points that Plath was undone by the insurmountable difficulties of reconciling the rigorous discipline of her art with the inexorable demands of her life as wife and mother.

Even more of a perfectionist than her mother, she could not compromise her lofty ideals. "Even now, Plath's reputation as a writer is incomplete. Her later journal and the partial draft of the last novel she was writing have yet to be recovered. Only when all of Plath's work is accessible will the full impact of her art during the last years of her life be felt; only then can the distinction of her work be fully evaluated." For the moment, we have only an inconclusive account of a tragically abbreviated life.

> Elaine Kendall, *"The Foiled Biography of a Fallen Poet,"* in Los Angeles Times Book Review, January 31, 1988, p. 12

ANNE STEVENSON

[*Stevenson is an English-born poet, dramatist, and critic best known for her verse, which evokes a strong sense of place. Her poetry has focused on the people and landscapes of New England, Scotland, Wales, and England. In the following excerpt, she observes that despite exhaustive research, Wagner-Martin's biography is ultimately crippled by its unsubstantiated feminist preconceptions and focus. She further comments that Wagner-Martin's analyses of Plath's poems are inexcusably simplistic.*]

Anyone who attempts a biography of Sylvia Plath has my sympathy. The life and work of this gifted, self-imprisoned poet, who killed herself at 30, is surrounded by such a thorny hedge of rumour and controversy that no champion would approach it if truly conversant with its perils. Linda Wagner-Martin's credentials are those of a sincere but naïve feminist. She believes, with reason, that Plath's life "was shaped by her ambition to be a writer" and that, through feminist ideology, her anger derived (in part) from knowledge that "as a woman writer, her work would be judged by standards different from those used to judge the work of male writers".

Having pre-judged Plath's case in the light of the latter supposition—wholly unsupported by Plath's writing, although this biographer claims to have used "every scrap" of it—Wagner-Martin, [in *Sylvia Plath: A Biography*] tells us everything about Plath her feminist followers want to hear. We learn that she was a feminist "in a broad sense of the term" because "she never undervalued herself or her work"—this about the author of journals which continually debate the question of her being worth anything at all, while at the same time conveying an impression of *over*valuing her achievements in order to prove herself superior. Wagner-Martin perceives the contradiction, but her book does not follow it through.

Nor does it build on the impressive picture of 1950s American culture which emerges, despite clumsy writing, from the first six or seven chapters. An indefatigable, if sometimes inaccurate, researcher and interviewer, Wagner-Martin uses a mass of accumulated information to criticise the conformist society in which Sylvia Plath knew herself to be an outsider, even as she struggled to convince it and herself that she was a model of bright-eyed, stereotyped American girlhood. The picture here presented of the over-protected, idealistic, terrified, self-righteous, not-quite-rich-enough young writer is one that should have helped set the scene in later chapters for Plath's disastrous confrontation with adulthood and, incidentally, England—a country Wagner-Martin appears hardly at all to understand.

It is when Wagner-Martin attempts to analyse Plath's relationships with Cambridge, Ted Hughes, English literary life and, above all, her own complex psyche, that the book lurches helplessly off the rails. Everything is explained according to a simplified theory of "patriarchy". At Cambridge she made friends with men, not women, as "this practice reflected her understanding of the patriarchal world she was moving in". When Hughes's friends criticised her poems, "male jealousy was part of the criticism".

Wagner-Martin's misunderstanding of Cambridge intellectual life, however, is nothing in comparison to the martyr's pillory she makes of Plath's marriage to Hughes. After a too-hasty secret wedding with the "violent Adam" of her imagination, poor Sivvy accompanies her husband to Spain where, says Wagner-Martin, she hated "being asked to keep house in primitive conditions" and "resented having to do the marketing and cooking as well as the housework".

Now, there were aspects of Spain that frightened Sylvia because they presaged as yet undiscovered themes of her late, remarkable poems, but she undoubtedly loved "the marketing and cooking", and in Spain her husband shopped with her. Sylvia was subject to great fluctuations of mood throughout her marriage, as throughout her life. Nowhere does this biography investigate the source of these mood-swings, except to proclaim that they must have been due to her oppressed role in a relationship that gave her husband all the advantages. Only a convinced feminist, blinded by consoling dogma, could conclude from the evidence of Plath's notebooks and letters that her marriage was responsible for her deeply-rooted psychological anguish.

Journals of Plath's Cambridge years, her time as an instructor at Smith and the months of her residence in Boston, are all readily accessible. Wagner-Martin seems to have combed them for references to "fights" between Plath and Hughes (well, yes, Sylvia was a good fighter) while ignoring the fascinating particulars of the psycho-therapy she underwent in Boston. At that time, overwhelmed and completely absorbed by what she saw as her Electra complex, Sylvia was for the first time encouraged to express her furious resentment of her mother (or what her mother represented: authority, gentility, guilt). The other side of this "complex", of course, had to do with her obsessive relationship with her father. With the writing of her Boston poems and her **"Poem for a Birthday,"** Plath began to take measure of the huge psychic wound which again and again drove her to seek renewal and purity through self-destruction. It was principally through a determined exploration of her psyche, aided by images from dreams and what she had read of primitive societies, that she painfully developed the distinctive totems—moons, pools, hospitals, nurse-nuns, mirrors—of her mythology.

The critical limitations of this book are too many to enumerate, but surely anyone who thinks **"Tulips"** is "an imagined dialogue between the woman and the flowers" or that **"Elm"** merely speaks "a woman's wisdom and truth, unflinchingly", or—heaven help us—that the defiant poem, **"Kindness,"** describes "the kind of happy lives Sylvia wished for her children" opens herself to attack on a scale which only a literary innocent would consent to tolerate. Even when Wagner-Martin's generalised thematic readings of the poems show insight—as when she connects the arrow in **"Ariel"** with an image in *The Bell Jar*—her Identikit preconception of Plath as a woman poet does her power as an artist an injustice which amounts to insult.

What, then, can be said for this biography? It would have given me pleasure to review it favourably, since in some respects Wagner-Martin and I are companions in arms. The final chapter, describing Sylvia's desperate last weeks in London, is moving. The book assembles 20 pages of fascinating photographs and there is an impressive but biased bibliography. It unfortunately fails to mention important critical studies by Elizabeth Hardwick and Joyce Carol Oates—two distinguished writers whose critical approach to Plath's Romanticism and dominating psychodrama do much to explain her ultimate despair. There are also lists of books in Plath's library and names of more then 200 people with whom Wagner-Martin conducted interviews. Alas, in Britain, at least, most of Plath's close friends and associates towards the end of her life are missing.

It is probably too soon to ask for a fully-documented, historically objective biography of Sylvia Plath. The principal members of her family are still alive and vulnerable. Another generation will have to assume responsibility where this one, in the nature of the undertaking, cannot. Meanwhile, each biography that appears reveals a different facet of this amazing poet's hold on contemporary imagination. Wagner-Martin's effort is of interest as a revealing document—perhaps even now of a past phase—in the history of literary feminism.

> Anne Stevenson, *"Who Was Sylvia, What Was She?"*
> in The Sunday Times, *London, February 28, 1988,*
> p. G3.

VICTORIA GLENDINNING

Sylvia Plath wanted to be famous. Her suicide ensured that she would be, whatever posterity's judgment was on her poetry; but that was not why she killed herself. Just before Christmas 1962 she came to London with her two small children from the house in Devon where she lived with her husband Ted Hughes, from whom she was separated. Lonely and vulnerable, she found a flat in Fitzroy Road, off Primrose Hill, in the house where Yeats once lived. She was hopeful; in London there would be friends, and professional contacts.

It was the coldest winter for more than a century. She had no telephone, and when she managed to contact people they were mostly busy with their own families over Christmas and put her off. Her American publisher turned down her novel *The Bell Jar.* She and both children were continuously ill with flu. There were power cuts. She stopped cooking and gave up going out. She saw a doctor, and was on anti-depressants. But in the small hours of 11 February 1963, she cups of milk beside her children's beds, wrote a note, and gassed herself in the kitchen. She was 30 years old.

The last chapter of [*Sylvia Plath: A Biography*] is unbearably sad. It is not a conspicuously well-written book, and the critical judgments on Plath's poems—'spellbinding expressions of emotion'—are simple, and sometimes clumsily phrased: 'The magic of Plath's collection occurs because domestic events are transformed by art.' Vast quantities of Plath material—manuscripts, drafts, journals, letters—are deposited in American university libraries, notably at Indiana and at Smith College, and Professor Wagner-Martin had access to most of them. Yet there is relatively little direct quotation. This may be because publication of the papers is 'controlled by Ted Hughes, Plath's husband'. Hughes did not meet the author of this biography, and he is not thanked for anything in the acknowledgements.

Under these circumstances, Wagner-Martin has not done a bad job. She is not a blame-thrower, though her interpretation of Plath's life has a justifiably feminist slant. This involves her in some odd judgments. Noting Plath's tendency to keep as friends the men she had affairs with, she writes that 'this practice reflected her understanding of the patriarchal world she was moving in'. I don't see why. It seems a perfectly normal and pleasant thing to do.

Plath's father has the makings of a great comic character. His doctoral dissertation was on *Bumblebees and their Ways*. In order to show his students that most human reactions are learnt, not innate, he skinned and cooked a rat which he than ate. His unqualified wife did most of his academic work for him, drafting chapters, grading students' papers and correcting graduate theses. But Wagner-Martin is not a humorist, and Otto Plath was not much fun as a father. He was critical and withdrawn, and he died.

Mrs Plath urged her daughter to be ambitious and to excel. Nothing was to be done just for the fun of it. Young Sylvia learned that love and approval depended on achievement. She won all the prizes at school, and was not popular. She was desperate to succeed socially and sexually as well as academically; in the 1950s, being 'feminine' and getting married were the primary goals of most girls, and she was no exception. The bravado of her letters home from Smith College are in pathetic contrast to what she wrote in her private diaries.

Conditioned to have an insatiable hunger for public success and to be emotionally dependent on other people's approval, any setback threw her into panic and despair. She was astonishingly successful as a young writer, having poems and stories published in the best places when she was still an undergraduate. But when she was rejected for a Harvard summer school fiction course, she made her first suicide attempts. She returned to college as an object of interest, 'a dramatic loner'. She did make close friends, but they had to be able to handle her intensity and her demands on them.

In 1955 she won a Fulbright Fellowship to Newnham College, Cambridge. She met Ted Hughes, and they were married within a few months. She wrote that he was 'the strongest man in the world', not only a brilliant poet but 'a large, hulking, healthy Adam.' They loved one another, but there were serpents in their Eden. When they went together to the United States, he was lionised and she was just the wife.

In her first description of Hughes she had noted with delight that he was a wanderer, 'a vagabond who will never stop'. This proved, undelightfully, to be true. But his infidelity was less the issue than her own 'almost obsessive need to live the perfect life, love the perfect man, create the perfect household.' Out of her unhappiness came the last and best poems. Is an imperfect life preferable to an unhappy, curtailed life? That is the unromantic view. But what this interesting imperfect book suggests most strongly is the destructiveness of the success ethic.

Victoria Glendinning, "The Day of Her Death Was a Cold, Dark Day," in The Spectator, *Vol. 260, No. 8330, March 5, 1988, p. 34.*

CLAIRE TOMALIN

The best poems of Sylvia Plath can stop your breath with their spare, intense, thrilling images. They are crafted as carefully as Cellini pieces. They are observant, witty and often—though not always—angry and violent. She was in no sense a Romantic poet, but a professional who cared a great deal about publication and success. During the last years of her short life, working alongside her poet-husband, Ted Hughes, she made sensational advances.

The shape and imagery of many of these poems, once read, become fixed in the mind forever. The moon is 'thin as the skin seaming a scar'. Of a bunch of roses ageing in a vase: 'Their yellow corsets were ready to split'. . . . The loss of such a gift remains heart-breaking. Like many who die young, Sylvia Plath has become almost more famous for her tragedy than for her achievement. And although this is all wrong, the conflicts of her life are woven into her writing, and can't be ignored. . . .

Linda Wagner-Martin's account [in *Sylvia Plath: A Biography*] is respectful but fails to get inside the skin of its subject (Plath's own letters to her mother are admittedly a hard act to follow, and Wagner-Martin's text was cut at the insistence of the Hughes family.) The best chapters are on the Boston girlhood and education. She shouldn't, as an American, be blamed for failing to convey the atmosphere of Cambridge in the 1950s, or the character of its teachers; or for describing Primrose Hill as a working-class area. On the other hand, you would expect the Hughes's trip across the United States, with all the images it offered to a poet, to be detailed; here we are not even told which states they visited.

It is surprising, too, that Wagner-Martin makes nothing of the fact that doctors looking after Sylvia at the time of her death were convinced that she had not intended to kill herself, since a nurse was due to arrive so soon after she swallowed the pills and turned on the gas; but the nurse was delayed, and so she died, instead of being found in time to be saved.

Her death is no less of a tragedy, no less of a waste. She is rightly mourned as 'our missing contemporary' (the phrase Elizabeth Bowen applied to Katherine Mansfield). I have heard her blamed for her ambition (by men) and canonised for her marital suffering (by women); the sex war can't be ignored, but above its fury she is best remembered as a true and conscientious poet.

Claire Tomalin, "Whom the Gods Love . . . ," in The Observer, *March 6, 1988, p. 43.*

VICTORIA RADIN

In 1963, when she was 30 years old, Sylvia Plath committed suicide. All her life she had battled her private monsters of good and evil. "Who will give me a child, that will bring me again to be a member of that race which throws snowballs at me, sensing perhaps the rot at which they strike?" she wrote (with uncharacteristic awkwardness) when she was 23 and a student at Cambridge.

That rotten perception of herself spreads everywhere in her journal; it forms the texture of most of her best poems. Perhaps it was the result of the inevitable failure of her desire to please everyone, to be the all-successful, all-American good girl she nearly was. Or perhaps that desire to please, to be perfect in every way, was the bright paint she threw over the image of her rottenness. While Sylvia elaborated her sense of self-disgust in her diaries (". . . what is tragedy? I am.") she fabulised her life to the outside world, presenting a vivacious, rosy and in all senses winning complexion.

Nowhere is this more apparent than in **Letters Home,** a volume of the effusions written to her mother every few days from the age of 17 when she went away to Smith College until a month before her death. I once saw a theatrical adaptation of these letters which highlighted the bat-squeaks of anger and dependence that lay behind their protestations of radiance. Awards, scholarships, elections, publications, her marriage to Ted Hughes ("the only man in the world who is my match"), even the deliveries of her two children, form a catalogue of successes recounted to the mother under whose roof Sylvia had first attempted, with utmost seriousness, to kill herself when she was 20, and whom a great, secret part of herself deeply hated. "I guess I need somebody to cheer me up by saying I've done all right so far," she wrote in her last letter to Dear Mother. It was an uncommonly direct request for validation. All her life Plath had done a whitewash job on her misgivings.

Self-glorification and the search for success for its own sake, even if it is only to hide rottenness, is not an enlightening activity. But Linda W. Wagner-Martin in **Sylvia Plath: A Biography** grasps it to her bosom and stumbles down the football pitch, shouldering psychological truths out of her way.

Nearly all the life is taken at Sylvia's public estimation of it: Wagner-Martin never questions what Plath thought she was doing all those years writing, along with good poetry, bad stories for the women's magazines whose values she despised; she goes gushingly along with Plath's really rather silly student editorial stint at the glossy *Mademoiselle* ("this honour") while only laconically cataloguing Sylvia's concurrent prizes for poetry at Smith and publication in the excellent *Harpers*. She does not quote from or analyse the poems at all. There are "life choices" and "value judgements" and "role models": dead words, unambiguous and stupendously incurious. When she attempts a rare interpretation, the results show a lack of imaginative sympathy that suggests that (probably for the wrong reasons) she does not like her subject much at all. "Always central in the life of her family, Sylvia expected events to revolve around her," is Wagner-Martin's bizarre explanation of why, on the day Sylvia's father died, the child of eight asked her mother to sign a note saying she would never remarry. But what person who had read, as she says, "every scrap" of Plath's writings, who had interviewed 200 people on her behalf and perhaps (though the evidence is meagre) even read the poems, could write in her Preface: "Plath was a feminist, in the broad sense of the term: she never undervalued herself or her work"? Plath was mistress of undervaluing.

The book gives one less insight and only a few more facts than one could piece together by oneself from Plath's own published letters and diaries, A. Alvarez's perceptive account of her last days in *The Savage God* and, indeed, the verse itself. This last moves so irresistibly towards a total fusion of life and art that Plath's last poem, written a week before her suicide, forsees it with perfect clarity: "The woman is perfected. Her dead/ Body wears the smile of accomplishment . . ."

Even in Wagner-Martin's only partial bibliography there are some 50 studies, anthologies, ruminations, recollections, bashings and gnashings of this poet who has been canonised and cannibalised by "feminists" looking, so illogically, for a victim-saint. Yes, as Wagner-Martin suggests, Plath was caught in her femaleness; but she was scuppered by her pathology. What she sought was control. She was able to construct her own death but couldn't take care of the after-life. (pp. 32-3)

> Victoria Radin, "Desire to Please," in New States-
> man, Vol. 115, No. 2972, March 11, 1988, pp. 32-
> 3.

JEFFREY MEYERS

[*Meyers is an American critic, literary biographer, and professor of English. Among his many books are biographies of Wyndham Lewis, Katherine Mansfield, D. H. Lawrence, and Ernest Hemingway. In the following excerpt, Meyers finds the biography competent but plodding, bereft of any literary insights and stylistically dull.*]

There is a desperate need for a good biography of Sylvia Plath. Plath's *Letters Home* (1975), edited by her mother, Aurelia, present an idealized view of her life; the first biography, by Edward Butscher (1977), is thoroughly inadequate; her *Journals* (1982), edited by Frances McCullough, are heavily censored; and her husband, Ted Hughes, has suppressed or destroyed many of her other works. Hughes, who controls Miss Plath's literary estate, has also used his power to censor works about her; his version of their marriage has never been told. Feminists, who have virtually accused Hughes of murdering Miss Plath, have translated her into a martyr.

Miss Wagner-Martin's life [*Sylvia Plath: A Biography*] does nothing to improve this situation. She has done extensive research at Smith College and Indiana University but—denied access to Hughes and to Plath's psychatric records—has made no significant discoveries. Her competent but pedestrian book is filled with clichés and trivial details, has a sinking style, is more descriptive than interpretive, lacks a dramatic sense, and is imperceptive about Miss Plath's poetry and fiction. The book transforms a fascinating life into a dull one and remakes a tragedy into a soap opera.

Miss Wagner-Martin has also recycled a number of myths. Plath's father, Otto, was born in 1885 in a town between Hamburg and Berlin—not in the Polish Corridor, which was created in 1919. Northwestern College, which he attended, was in Minneapolis—not in Watertown, Wisconsin. Greenwood could not possibly be the maiden name of Miss Plath's maternal grandmother, who was Austrian. Miss Wagner-Martin does not give the date of Otto Plath's first (1915) or second marriage (January 4, 1932), or mention that Yeats was only a

small child when he lived in the house that Miss Plath later rented. And she does not see that Miss Plath's revealing poem about her father's death, **"Electra on Azalea Path,"** is really about Sylvia on Aurelia Plath.

The main events of Miss Plath's life—described in her brilliant novel, *The Bell Jar* . . . are well known. The daughter of a German entomology professor, who died when she was eight, and an Austro-American mother, who moved from Catholicism through Methodism to Unitarianism, Miss Plath grew up in suburban Boston. She was a first-rate student [and] won a scholarship to Smith. . . . Despite her considerable achievements, she became severely depressed and, after disastrous shock treatments, tried to kill herself. She was successfully treated at McLean Hospital and took a therapeutic series of loves (she compared one of them to "a small bug crawling on me" and claimed another had raped her). She returned to Smith, won a Fulbright to Cambridge University, and fell in love with a handsome poet, Ted Hughes. She married him, spent her honeymoon in Spain, taught at Smith, was invited to the writer's colony Yaddo, and returned to live in London and Devon. Her marriage broke up after Hughes's adultery, and she retaliated by burning his papers. After moving back to a fierce winter in London and writing, in a single month, most of the poems in her best book, *Ariel* (1965), she gassed herself.

This biography, which suffers from intellectual poverty, misses nearly every opportunity to illuminate Miss Plath's life. Miss Wagner-Martin solemnly maintains that "the Plaths believed in a natural, healthy existence for their daughter" (did any sane parents ever want an unnatural, unhealthy existence for their children?). She says that Otto's death "made Sylvia heavily dependent on her mother." She dutifully plods with her through the seventh and then the eighth and then the ninth grades. She explains Miss Plath's lifelong habit of hiding unpleasant truths from her mother by stating: "Like a child, Sylvia seemed to believe that pretending would make any situation improve." Instead of probing the nature of Miss Plath's college friendships, she states that "they talked nonstop, giggled, accepted each other's personalities and loved them."

Miss Wagner-Martin does not mention any of the negative criticism of Miss Plath's poetry by George Steiner, Irving Howe, and James Dickey, nor does she comment on the fact that Miss Plath almost always published in middle-brow journals rather than in the more intellectually demanding little magazines. She portrays Miss Plath as downtrodden and oppressed, but does not recognize that if Miss Plath wanted to write and become famous, she should not have had children; if she wanted children, she should not have complained about the time they took from her writing. Though Hughes betrayed her and ruined her life, he also hurt her into the greatest poetry she ever wrote.

Despite Miss Wagner-Martin's book, all the major aspects of Miss Plath's life remain unexplored: her father's background and character; her parents' marriage; the effect of Otto's death on his daughter; her troubled relations with her mother; the radical problems of her childhood; her adult friendships; her connections with other poets; Hughes's parents, background, and character; the failure of Miss Plath's marriage; Hughes's affair with Assia Wevill (who later killed herself and her child by Hughes); the pattern of Miss Plath's suicide attempts; and the factors that led her—with two small children, and at the height of her poetic powers—to take her own life. (pp. 52-4)

> Jeffrey Meyers, "Wreckage," in National Review,
> New York, Vol. XL, No. 5, March 18, 1988, pp.
> 52-4.

BETTY ABEL

Many legends have grown up around the life and early death of the poet Sylvia Plath. Particularly, she has been regarded by many as one who described 'the contemporary predicament'; and latterly as a liberator of women, of oppressed minorities such as Jews and of all who have been tortured or massacred. This greatly exaggerated view of her importance as a poet is not one which the author of [*Sylvia Plath: A Biography*] holds. Rather does she present a clear, straightforward account of the events of Plath's life in America and England, showing her as a sensitive, highly gifted young woman whose talent brought her early success in the literary world of Boston and London. Her later disappointments and final tragic suicide could have been the result of a life passed at too hectic a pace and at too intense a level for so delicate a talent and temperament.

When the author of this volume tries to match the poems and novels Plath wrote with certain periods and events in the poet's life she does so with a depth of insight which precludes any mistakes that could easily have been made in such an attempt. The dates of some poems are indication enough of the happenings to which they refer, as in **"Burning the Letters"**, a long poem describing the bonfire she made when destroying the papers of her husband on discovering his intention of leaving her. But that and other poems are clear pointers to the often disturbed state of her mind when, to most observers, she was at her most contented and balanced. Dr. Linda Wagner-Martin has arrived at an interpretation unclouded by psychological theorising and, at the same time, full of useful pointers to a permanently troubled state of mind.

Sylvia Plath was born in Boston and died in London. At the end of her life, when her marriage to Ted Hughes had broken up, her whole existence became, on its surface, poetry. . . . She had published **The Colossus** in 1960: but it is generally thought to be the poems in the posthumous **Ariel** that are her most significant. It is probably true that all her poetry was written at white heat (one critic calls her 'a minor poet of great intensity') but, far from the subject matter being the ills of the age or of womankind, as feminists tend now to assert, it was entirely concerned with her personal predicament. It could show euphoria as well as depression but it in no way 'defines the age'.

So fashionable criticism has been wrong in emphasising the universal nature of her poems. They do, however, tell us much about herself and the type of illness she suffered. Thus they are a valuable record in a particularly vivid mellifluous form. The author of the book has done full justice to this aspect of Sylvia Plath's work without making the extravagant claims others have sometimes made for what are essentially brilliant minor poems and novels. Her account should be read by all who wish to understand how close to her life Plath's poetry was. (pp. 166-67)

Betty Abel, "The Troubled Life and Verse of Sylvia Plath," in Contemporary Review, *Vol. 252, No. 1466, March, 1988, pp. 166-67.*

MARK FORD

[As related in *Sylvia Plath: A Biography*] Sylvia Plath grew up hoping to be the perfect American girl. Her desire to succeed was awesome. At school and college she scored straight As, and began publishing poems and short stories in prestigious magazines when still only in her teens. With numbing regularity she won prizes and scholarships for her fiction, poetry, journalism, her academic record and her church attendance. At Smith College entries for the annual poetry competition were submitted under pseudonyms. Plath sent in two different groups of poems under different names, and won both first and second prizes. Her competitive instinct was finely honed, and her attitude to rivals healthily up-front. "I keep reading about this damn adrienne cecile rich, only two years older than I, who is a yale younger poet and regularly in all the top mags. . . . Occasionally I retch quietly in the waste basket", she confided in a letter to a friend in 1955.

Plath's compulsion to excellence is often attributed to the fact that her father, a Professor of Entomology at Boston University, died when she was only ten. She felt if she kept her grades up he might come back. Her mother also instilled in her from an early age the virtues of a thrifty Puritan work ethic, to the extent that when the young Sylvia was away at summer camp she would list in letters home everything she ate to show she was being good and getting her money's-worth. Not surprisingly, she approached relationships with the same kind of determination she brought to her school-work, as the self-exhorting diaries of her adolescence often reveal; "I know I am capable of getting good marks; I know I am capable of attracting males", she reassures herself. When she found her boy-friends discouraged by her seriousness she began calling herself Sherry rather than Sylvia, in the hope that this would help her become more go-ahead and fun-loving. She wrote out lists of dates "requested" and dates "gone on in all", and computed her popularity as accurately as possible. When she set out for England on a Fulbright in 1955, she was absolutely determined about one thing. she wrote to her mother that she would not return to America until she was married.

In a radio broadcast she recorded for the BBC shortly before she died, Plath introduced the speaker of **"Lady Lazarus"** as "a woman who has the great and terrible gift of being reborn. The only trouble is, she has to die first. She is the Phoenix, the libertarian spirit, what you will. She is also just a good, plain, very resourceful woman." The remark is revealing, suggesting some of the disorientations her poetry's confusion of myth and reality might be heir to. It is interesting to spy behind the legends of neurotic genius a few glimpses of Plath's steely professionalism, the abilities of a "very resourceful woman". When she married Ted Hughes in 1956 she also became his literary agent and business manager, and attempted to keep at least twenty of his poems and stories out to magazine editors at all times. She promised to place fifteen poems a year for him, and succeeded in doing so. Plath and Hughes both wrote extremely successful poetry during their marriage, but it seems Plath had the greater push in finding markets for it.

It is something of a shock to be reminded that the Hugheses' union lasted over six years; popular imagination tends to characterize it as something out of Strindberg, a single apocalyptic blaze. Obviously there were problems. Linda Wagner-Martin relates that the "huge derrick-striding Ted", as Plath once called him, wouldn't do the washing-up, nor fill in his cheque stubs so she should not know how much money they had left in their account. More damagingly, towards the end of their relationship he used to take off for weeks at a time without telling her where he was going. Plath, naturally, was jealous, and well up to retaliating. When lunch with a female interviewer from the BBC lasted longer than expected, Hughes came home to find that Plath had burnt all the notes and drafts of the project he was working on. Plath commemorated their final split with an even bigger blaze, feeding a bonfire in the back garden of their cottage in Devon not only with Hughes's letters to her, but with his drafts of work in progress, his business papers, and the manuscript of her new novel that was to be about her great love for him. Her famous poem **"Burning the Letters",** collected first in the posthumously published *Ariel* (1965), describes the event.

Wagner-Martin hasn't been helped much by the Plath estate, and large chunks of her biography have had to be excised to avoid court action. Hughes has professed himself baffled by her insensitivity and calls her *Sylvia Plath* a travesty. For her part Wagner-Martin hints darkly in her preface at the reasons behind his secretiveness over Plath's papers, and wonders why he destroyed the journal that covered the last few months of her life, and how exactly the draft of her last novel, *Double Exposure,* "disappeared somewhere around 1970". Hughes needn't worry, though, that this will become the definitive biography. Wagner-Martin's prose is shoddy and execrably dull, and her vision of Plath nauseously sentimental:

> For all her studious bent, Sylvia was more of an outdoor girl than an indoor one. She responded honestly to weather, opening out into the sunlight as if she drew physical nourishment from it.

Who, I wonder, ever responded dishonestly to weather? Plath desperately needs a far more astringent account of her life and work to rescue her from the sentimentalities to which her reputation has been so unjustly prone. Let us hope that Anne Stevenson, whose authorized biography, scheduled for publication later this year, and which has already been rewritten five times to satisfy the pernickety Plath estate, will provide it.

Mark Ford, "A Go-Ahead Genius," in The Times Literary Supplement, *No. 4439, April 29-May 5, 1988, p. 468.*

Appendix

The following is a listing of all sources used in Volume 50 of *Contemporary Literary Criticism*. Included in this list are all copyright and reprint rights and acknowledgments for those essays for which permission was obtained. Every effort has been made to trace copyright, but if omissions have been made, please let us know.

THE EXCERPTS IN CLC, VOLUME 50, WERE REPRINTED FROM THE FOLLOWING BOOKS:

Brown, Edward J. From *Russian Literature Since the Revolution*. Revised edition. Cambridge, Mass: Harvard University Press, 1982. Copyright © 1963, 1969, and 1982 by Edward J. Brown. All rights reserved. Reprinted by permission of the author.

Carlisle, Olga. From *Poets on Street Corners: Portraits of Fifteen Russian Poets*. Random House, 1969. Copyright © 1968 by Random House, Inc. All rights reserved. Reprinted by permission of the publisher.

France, Peter. From *Poets of Modern Russia*. Cambridge University Press, 1982. © Cambridge University Press 1982. Reprinted with permission of the publisher.

Hirsch, Edward. From "In Spite of Everything the Stars," in *Wild Gratitude*. Knopf, 1986. Copyright © 1985 by Edward Hirsch. All rights reserved. Reprinted by permission of Alfred A. Knopf, Inc.

Lee, Dennis. From "The Poetry of Al Purdy: An Afterword," in *The Collected Poems of Al Purdy*. By Al Purdy, edited by Russell Brown. McClelland and Stewart, 1986. © 1986 Dennis Lee. All rights reserved. Used by permission of The Canadian Publishers, McClelland and Stewart Limited, Toronto.

Purdy, Al. From *The Collected Poems of Al Purdy*. Edited by Russell Brown. McClelland and Stewart, 1986. Copyright © 1986 Al Purdy. All rights reserved. Used by permission of The Canadian Publishers, McClelland and Stewart Limited, Toronto.

Appendix

THE EXCERPTS FROM THE AUTHOR'S WORKS IN CLC, VOLUME 50, WERE REPRINTED FROM THE FOLLOWING BOOKS:

Card, Orson Scott. From *Speaker for the Dead*. Tom Doherty Associates, 1986. Copyright © 1986 by Orson Scott Card. All rights reserved.

Cohen-Solal, Annie. From *Sartre: A Life*. Edited by Norman Macafee, translated by Anna Cancogni. Pantheon Books, 1987. Copyright © 1985 by Annie Cohen-Solal. Translation Copyright © 1987 by Random House, Inc. All rights reserved.

Dove, Rita. From *Thomas and Beulah*. Carnegie-Mellon University Press, 1986. Copyright © 1986 by Rita Dove. All rights reserved.

Duffy, Bruce. From *The World as I Found It*. Ticknor & Fields, 1987. Copyright © 1987 by Bruce Duffy. All rights reserved.

Eisenstadt, Jill. From *From Rockaway*. Alfred A. Knopf, 1987. Copyright 1985, 1987 by Jill Eisenstadt. All rights reserved.

Foreman, Richard. From an excerpt from *The Cure*. Ontological-Hysteric Theatre, Inc., 1986.

Foreman, Richard. From an excerpt from "Film Is Evil: Radio Is Good," in *The Drama Review*, Vol. 31, No. 4, Winter, 1987. Copyright, © 1987 New York University and the Massachusetts Institute of Technology.

Francis, Claude, and Fernande Contier. From *Simone DeBeauvoir: A Life...a Love Story*. Translated by Lisa Nesselson. St. Martin's Press, 1987. Translation copyright © 1987 by St. Martin's Press. All rights reserved.

Fraze, Candida. From *Renifleur's Daughter*. Henry Holt and Company, 1987. Copyright © 1987 by Candida Fraze. All rights reserved.

Gibbons, Kaye. From *Ellen Foster*. Algonquin Books of Chapel Hill, 1987. © 1987 by Kaye Gibbons. All rights reserved.

Glendinning, Victoria. From *Rebecca West: A Life*. Alfred A. Knopf, 1987. Copyright © 1987 by Victoria Glendinning. All rights reserved.

Heinemann, Larry. From *Paco's Story*. Farrar, Straus and Giroux, 1986. Copyright © 1979, 1980, 1981, 1984, 1986 by Larry Heinemann. All rights reserved.

Jones, Rod. From *Julia Paradise: A Novel*. Summit Books, 1986. Copyright © 1986 by Rod Jones. All rights reserved.

Kaplan, David Michael. From *Comfort*. Viking, 1987. Copyright © David Michael Kaplan, 1984, 1985, 1986, 1987. All rights reserved.

Laurent, Antoine. From *Cuisine Novella*. Viking, 1987. Copyright © 1987 by Antoine Laurent. All rights reserved.

Lively, Penelope. From *Moon Tiger*. Grove Press, 1987. Copyright © 1987 by Penelope Lively. All rights reserved.

Lynn, Kenneth S. From *Hemingway*. Simon and Schuster, 1987. Copyright © 1987 by Kenneth S. Lynn. All rights reserved.

McCauley, Stephen. From *The Object of My Affection: A Novel*. Simon and Schuster, 1987. Copyright © 1987 by Stephen McCauley. All rights reserved.

McMillan, Terry. From *Mama*. Houghton Mifflin Company, 1987. Copyright © 1987 by Terry McMillan. All rights reserved.

Munro, Alice. From an excerpt in *The Progress of Love*. Alfred A. Knopf, 1986. Copyright © 1985, 1986 by Alice Munro. All rights reserved.

Osborne, Lawrence. From *Ania Malina*. Charles Scribner's Sons, 1987. Copyright © 1986 Lawrence Osborne. All rights reserved.

Pollock, Sharon. From *Doc*. Playwrights Canada, 1986. Copyright © 1984 Sharon Pollock.

Purdy, Al. From *The Collected Poems of Al Purdy*. Edited by Russell Brown. McClelland Stewart, 1986. Copyright © 1986 Al Purdy. All rights reserved. Used by permission of The Canadian Publishers, McClelland and Stewart Limited, Toronto.

Price, Reynolds. From *Kate Vaiden*. Atheneum Publishers, 1986. Copyright © 1986 by Reynolds Price. All rights reserved.

Saint, H. F. From *Memoirs of an Invisible Man*. Atheneum Publishers, 1987. Copyright © 1987 by H. F. Saint. All rights reserved.

Savan, Glenn. From *White Palace*. Bantam Books, 1987. Copyright © 1987 by Glenn Savan. All rights reserved.

Sayers, Valerie. From *Due East*. Doubleday & Company, Inc., 1987. Copyright © 1987 by Valerie Sayers. All rights reserved.

Scott, Joanna. From *Fading, My Parmacheene Belle*. Ticknor & Fields, 1987. Copyright © 1987 by Joanna Scott. All rights reserved.

Taylor, Peter. From *A Summons to Memphis*. Alfred A. Knopf, Inc., 1986. Copyright © 1986 by Peter Taylor. All rights reserved.

Tytell, John. From *Ezra Pound: The Solitary Volcano*. Anchor Press, 1987. Copyright © 1987 by John Tytell. All rights reserved.

Appendix

☐ Contemporary Literary Criticism

Indexes

Literary Criticism Series
  Cumulative Author Index
Cumulative Nationality Index
Title Index, Volume 50

This Index Includes References to Entries in These Gale Series

Contemporary Literary Criticism

Presents excerpts of criticism on the works of novelists, poets, dramatists, short story writers, scriptwriters, and other creative writers who are now living or who have died since 1960. Cumulative indexes to authors and nationalities are included, as well as an index to titles discussed in the individual volume. Volumes 1-50 are in print.

Twentieth-Century Literary Criticism

Contains critical excerpts by the most significant commentators on poets, novelists, short story writers, dramatists, and philosophers who died between 1900 and 1960. Cumulative indexes to authors, nationalities, and titles discussed are included in each new volume. Volumes 1-29 are in print.

Nineteenth-Century Literature Criticism

Offers significant passages from criticism on authors who died between 1800 and 1899. Cumulative indexes to authors, nationalities, and titles discussed are included in each new volume. Volumes 1-19 are in print.

Literature Criticism from 1400 to 1800

Compiles significant passages from the most noteworthy criticism on authors of the fifteenth through eighteenth centuries. Cumulative indexes to authors, nationalities, and titles discussed are included in each new volume. Volumes 1-9 are in print.

Classical and Medieval Literature Criticism

Offers excerpts of criticism on the works of world authors from classical antiquity through the fourteenth century. Cumulative indexes to authors, titles, and critics are included in each volume. Volumes 1-2 are in print.

Short Story Criticism

Compiles excerpts of criticism on short fiction by writers of all eras and nationalities. Cumulative indexes to authors, nationalities, and titles discussed are included in each new volume. Volumes 1-2 are in print.

Children's Literature Review

Includes excerpts from reviews, criticism, and commentary on works of authors and illustrators who create books for children. Cumulative indexes to authors, nationalities, and titles discussed are included in each new volume. Volumes 1-15 are in print.

Contemporary Authors Series

Encompasses five related series. *Contemporary Authors* provides biographical and bibliographical information on more than 90,000 writers of fiction, nonfiction, poetry, journalism, drama, motion pictures, and other fields. Each new volume contains sketches on authors not previously covered in the series. Volumes 1-124 are in print. *Contemporary Authors New Revision Series* provides completely updated information on active authors covered in previously published volumes of *CA*. Only entries requiring significant change are revised for *CA New Revision Series*. Volumes 1-24 are in print. *Contemporary Authors Permanent Series* consists of updated listings for deceased and inactive authors removed from the original volumes 9-36 when these volumes were revised. Volumes 1-2 are in print. *Contemporary Authors Autobiography Series* presents specially commissioned autobiographies by leading contemporary writers. Volumes 1-7 are in print. *Contemporary Authors Bibliographical Series* contains primary and secondary bibliographies as well as analytical bibliographical essays by authorities on major modern authors. Volumes 1-2 are in print.

Dictionary of Literary Biography

Encompasses three related series. *Dictionary of Literary Biography* furnishes illustrated overviews of authors' lives and works and places them in the larger perspective of literary history. Volumes 1-70 are in print. *Dictionary of Literary Biography Documentary Series* illuminates the careers of major figures through a selection of literary documents, including letters, notebook and diary entries, interviews, book reviews, and photographs. Volumes 1-5 are in print. *Dictionary of Literary Biography Yearbook* summarizes the past year's literary activity with articles on genres, major prizes, conferences, and other timely subjects and includes udpated and new entries on individual authors. Yearbooks for 1980-1987 are in print. A cumulative index to authors and articles is included in each new volume.

Concise Dictionary of American Literary Biography

A six-volume series that collects revised and updated sketches on major American authors that were originally presented in *Dictionary of Literary Biography*. Volumes 1-3 are in print.

Something about the Author Series

Encompasses two related series. *Something about the Author* contains heavily illustrated biographical sketches on juvenile and young adult authors and illustrators from all eras. Volumes 1-52 are in print. *Something about the Author Autobiography Series* presents specially commissioned autobiographies by prominent authors and illustrators of books for children and young adults. Volumes 1-6 are in print.

Yesterday's Authors of Books for Children

Contains heavily illustrated entries on children's writers who died before 1961. Complete in two volumes. Volumes 1-2 are in print.

Literary Criticism Series
Cumulative Author Index

This index lists all author entries in the Gale Literary Criticism Series and includes cross-references to other Gale sources. For the convenience of the reader, references to the *Yearbook* in the *Contemporary Literary Criticism* series include the page number (in parentheses) after the volume number. References in the index are identified as follows:

AITN: *Authors in the News*, Volumes 1-2
CAAS: *Contemporary Authors Autobiography Series*, Volumes 1-7
CA: *Contemporary Authors* (original series), Volumes 1-124
CABS: *Contemporary Authors Bibliographical Series*, Volumes 1-2
CANR: *Contemporary Authors New Revision Series*, Volumes 1-24
CAP: *Contemporary Authors Permanent Series*, Volumes 1-2
CA-R: *Contemporary Authors* (revised editions), Volumes 1-44
CDALB: *Concise Dictionary of American Literary Biography*, Volumes 1-3
CLC: *Contemporary Literary Criticism*, Volumes 1-50
CLR: *Children's Literature Review*, Volumes 1-16
CMLC: *Classical and Medieval Literature Criticism*, Volumes 1-2
DLB: *Dictionary of Literary Biography*, Volumes 1-70
DLB-DS: *Dictionary of Literary Biography Documentary Series*, Volumes 1-5
DLB-Y: *Dictionary of Literary Biography Yearbook*, Volumes 1980-1987
LC: *Literature Criticism from 1400 to 1800*, Volumes 1-9
NCLC: *Nineteenth-Century Literature Criticism*, Volumes 1-19
SAAS: *Something about the Author Autobiography Series*, Volumes 1-6
SATA: *Something about the Author*, Volumes 1-52
SSC: *Short Story Criticism*, Volumes 1-2
TCLC: *Twentieth-Century Literary Criticism*, Volumes 1-29
YABC: *Yesterday's Authors of Books for Children*, Volumes 1-2

Andersen, Hans Christian
1805-1875.................. NCLC 7
See also CLR 6
See also YABC 1

Anderson, Jessica (Margaret Queale)
19??-........................CLC 37
See also CANR 4
See also CA 9-12R

Anderson, Jon (Victor) 1940- ....CLC 9
See also CANR 20
See also CA 25-28R

Anderson, Lindsay 1923- ....CLC 20

Anderson, Maxwell 1888-1959 .... TCLC 2
See also CA 105
See also DLB 7

Anderson, Poul (William)
1926-........................CLC 15
See also CAAS 2
See also CANR 2, 15
See also CA 1-4R
See also SATA 39
See also DLB 8

Anderson, Robert (Woodruff)
1917-........................CLC 23
See also CA 21-24R
See also DLB 7
See also AITN 1

Anderson, Roberta Joan 1943-
See Mitchell, Joni

Anderson, Sherwood
1876-1941.............TCLC 1, 10, 24
....................SSC 1
See also CAAS 3
See also CA 104, 121
See also DLB 4, 9
See also DLB-DS 1

Andrade, Carlos Drummond de
1902-........................CLC 18

Andrewes, Lancelot 1555-1626 .... LC 5

Andrews, Cicily Fairfield 1892-1983
See West, Rebecca

Andreyev, Leonid (Nikolaevich)
1871-1919................... TCLC 3
See also CA 104

Andrézel, Pierre 1885-1962
See Dinesen, Isak
See also Blixen, Karen (Christentze
Dinesen)

Andrić, Ivo 1892-1975 ....CLC 8
See also CA 81-84
See also obituary CA 57-60

Angelique, Pierre 1897-1962
See Bataille, Georges

Angell, Roger 1920-...............CLC 26
See also CANR 13
See also CA 57-60

Angelou, Maya 1928- ....CLC 12, 35
See also CANR 19
See also CA 65-68
See also SATA 49
See also DLB 38

Annensky, Innokenty
1856-1909................. TCLC 14
See also CA 110

Anouilh, Jean (Marie Lucien Pierre)
1910-1987........CLC 1, 3, 8, 13, 40,
50 (277)
See also CA 17-20R

Anthony, Florence 1947-
See Ai

Anthony (Jacob), Piers 1934-.......CLC 35
See also Jacob, Piers A(nthony)
D(illingham)
See also DLB 8

Antoninus, Brother 1912-
See Everson, William (Oliver)

Antonioni, Michelangelo 1912- .....CLC 20
See also CA 73-76

Antschel, Paul 1920-1970
See Celan, Paul
See also CA 85-88

Anwar, Chairil 1922-1949 ...... TCLC 22
See also CA 121

Apollinaire, Guillaume
1880-1918................. TCLC 3, 8
See also Kostrowitzki, Wilhelm Apollinaris
de

Appelfeld, Aharon 1932- ...... CLC 23, 47
See also CA 112

Apple, Max (Isaac) 1941-....... CLC 9, 33
See also CANR 19
See also CA 81-84

Aquin, Hubert 1929-1977..........CLC 15
See also CA 105
See also DLB 53

Aragon, Louis 1897-1982....... CLC 3, 22
See also CA 69-72
See also obituary CA 108

Arbuthnot, John 1667-1735.......... LC 1

Archer, Jeffrey (Howard)
1940-........................CLC 28
See also CANR 22
See also CA 77-80

Archer, Jules 1915-................CLC 12
See also CANR 6
Scc also CA 9-12R
See also SATA 4

Arden, John 1930-......... CLC 6, 13, 15
See also CAAS 4
See also CA 13-16R
See also DLB 13

Arenas, Reinaldo 1943-...........CLC 41

Arguedas, José María
1911-1969............... CLC 10, 18
See also CA 89-92

Argueta, Manlio 1936- ....CLC 31

Ariosto, Ludovico 1474-1533........ LC 6

Arlt, Roberto 1900-1942........ TCLC 29
See also CA 123

Armah, Ayi Kwei 1939- .... CLC 5, 33
See also CANR 21
See also CA 61-64

Armatrading, Joan 1950-..........CLC 17
See also CA 114

**Arnim, Achim von (Ludwig Joachim von
Arnim)** 1781-1831.......... NCLC 5

Arnold, Matthew 1822-1888 ...... NCLC 6
See also DLB 32, 57

Arnold, Thomas 1795-1842 ...... NCLC 18
See also DLB 55

Arnow, Harriette (Louisa Simpson)
1908-1986...............CLC 2, 7, 18
See also CANR 14
See also CA 9-12R
See also obituary CA 118
See also SATA 42, 47
See also DLB 6

Arp, Jean 1887-1966...............CLC 5
See also CA 81-84
See also obituary CA 25-28R

Arquette, Lois S(teinmetz) 1934-
See Duncan (Steinmetz Arquette), Lois
See also SATA 1

Arrabal, Fernando 1932- ..... CLC 2, 9, 18
See also CANR 15
See also CA 9-12R

Arrick, Fran 19??-.................CLC 30

Artaud, Antonin 1896-1948 .... TCLC 3
See also CA 104

Arthur, Ruth M(abel)
1905-1979....................CLC 12
See also CANR 4
See also CA 9-12R
See also obituary CA 85-88
See also SATA 7
See also obituary SATA 26

Arundel, Honor (Morfydd)
1919-1973...................CLC 17
See also CAP 2
See also CA 21-22
See also obituary CA 41-44R
See also SATA 4
See also obituary SATA 24

Asch, Sholem 1880-1957.......... TCLC 3
See also CA 105

Ashbery, John (Lawrence)
1927-.....CLC 2, 3, 4, 6, 9, 13, 15, 25,
41
See also CANR 9
See also CA 5-8R
See also DLB 5
See also DLB-Y 81

Ashton-Warner, Sylvia (Constance)
1908-1984...................CLC 19
See also CA 69-72
See also obituary CA 112

Asimov, Isaac
1920-............. CLC 1, 3, 9, 19, 26
See also CLR 12
See also CANR 2, 19
See also CA 1-4R
See also SATA 1, 26
See also DLB 8

Astley, Thea (Beatrice May)
1925-........................CLC 41
See also CANR 11
See also CA 65-68

Aston, James 1906-1964
See White, T(erence) H(anbury)

Asturias, Miguel Ángel
1899-1974............... CLC 3, 8, 13
See also CAP 2
See also CA 25-28
See also obituary CA 49-52

Atheling, William, Jr. 1921-1975
See Blish, James (Benjamin)

Author Index

Gallant, Roy A(rthur) 1924- .... CLC 17
See also CANR 4
See also CA 5-8R
See also SATA 4

Gallico, Paul (William)
1897-1976.....................CLC 2
See also CA 5-8R
See also obituary CA 69-72
See also SATA 13
See also DLB 9
See also AITN 1

Galsworthy, John 1867-1933 ...... TCLC 1
See also CA 104
See also DLB 10, 34

Galt, John 1779-1839 .... NCLC 1

Galvin, James 1951- .... CLC 38
See also CA 108

Gann, Ernest K(ellogg) 1910- ...... CLC 23
See also CANR 1
See also CA 1-4R
See also AITN 1

García Lorca, Federico
1899-1936................. TCLC 1, 7
See also CA 104

García Márquez, Gabriel (José)
1928-.......CLC 2, 3, 8, 10, 15, 27, 47
See also CANR 10
See also CA 33-36R

Gardam, Jane 1928- .... CLC 43
See also CLR 12
See also CANR 2, 18
See also CA 49-52
See also SATA 28, 39
See also DLB 14

Gardner, Herb 1934- .... CLC 44 (208)

Gardner, John (Champlin, Jr.)
1933-1982...... CLC 2, 3, 5, 7, 8, 10,
18, 28, 34 (547)
See also CA 65-68
See also obituary CA 107
See also obituary SATA 31, 40
See also DLB 2
See also DLB-Y 82
See also AITN 1

Gardner, John (Edmund)
1926-........................CLC 30
See also CANR 15
See also CA 103
See also AITN 1

Garfield, Leon 1921-..............CLC 12
See also CA 17-20R
See also SATA 1, 32

Garland, (Hannibal) Hamlin
1860-1940.................... TCLC 3
See also CA 104
See also DLB 12

Garneau, Hector (de) Saint Denys
1912-1943................. TCLC 13
See also CA 111

Garner, Alan 1935-..............CLC 17
See also CANR 15
See also CA 73-76
See also SATA 18

Garner, Hugh 1913-1979 ....CLC 13
See also CA 69-72

Garnett, David 1892-1981 ....CLC 3
See also CANR 17
See also CA 5-8R
See also obituary CA 103
See also DLB 34

Garrett, George (Palmer)
1929-..................... CLC 3, 11
See also CAAS 5
See also CANR 1
See also CA 1-4R
See also DLB 2, 5
See also DLB-Y 83

Garrigue, Jean 1914-1972 .... CLC 2, 8
See also CA 5-8R
See also obituary CA 37-40R

Gary, Romain 1914-1980.........CLC 25
See also Kacew, Romain

Gascar, Pierre 1916-..............CLC 11
See also Fournier, Pierre

Gascoyne, David (Emery)
1916-........................CLC 45
See also CANR 10
See also CA 65-68
See also DLB 20

Gaskell, Elizabeth Cleghorn
1810-1865.................. NCLC 5
See also DLB 21

Gass, William H(oward)
1924-.....CLC 1, 2, 8, 11, 15, 39 (477)
See also CA 17-20R
See also DLB 2

Gautier, Théophile 1811-1872 ..... NCLC 1

Gaye, Marvin (Pentz)
1939-1984....................CLC 26
See also obituary CA 112

Gébler, Carlo (Ernest)
1954-.................. CLC 39 (60)
See also CA 119

Gee, Maurice (Gough) 1931-.......CLC 29
See also CA 97-100
See also SATA 46

Gelbart, Larry (Simon) 1923-......CLC 21
See also CA 73-76

Gelber, Jack 1932- .... CLC 1, 6, 14
See also CANR 2
See also CA 1-4R
See also DLB 7

Gellhorn, Martha (Ellis) 1908- ..... CLC 14
See also CA 77-80
See also DLB-Y 82

Genet, Jean
1910-1986........CLC 1, 2, 5, 10, 14,
44 (385), 46
See also CANR 18
See also CA 13-16R
See also DLB-Y 86

Gent, Peter 1942-.................CLC 29
See also CA 89-92
See also DLB-Y 82
See also AITN 1

George, Jean Craighead 1919- .....CLC 35
See also CLR 1
See also CA 5-8R
See also SATA 2
See also DLB 52

George, Stefan (Anton)
1868-1933................ TCLC 2, 14
See also CA 104

Gerhardi, William (Alexander) 1895-1977
See Gerhardie, William (Alexander)

Gerhardie, William (Alexander)
1895-1977....................CLC 5
See also CANR 18
See also CA 25-28R
See also obituary CA 73-76
See also DLB 36

Gertler, T(rudy) 1946?- ...... CLC 34 (49)
See also CA 116

Gessner, Friedrike Victoria 1910-1980
See Adamson, Joy(-Friederike Victoria)

Ghelderode, Michel de
1898-1962................. CLC 6, 11
See also CA 85-88

Ghiselin, Brewster 1903- ....CLC 23
See also CANR 13
See also CA 13-16R

Ghose, Zulfikar 1935-.............CLC 42
See also CA 65-68

Ghosh, Amitav 1943- .... CLC 44 (44)

Giacosa, Giuseppe 1847-1906 ..... TCLC 7
See also CA 104

Gibbon, Lewis Grassic
1901-1935................... TCLC 4
See also Mitchell, James Leslie

Gibbons, Kaye 1960-........ CLC 50 (46)

Gibran, (Gibran) Kahlil
1883-1931................. TCLC 1, 9
See also CA 104

Gibson, William 1914- ....CLC 23
See also CANR 9
See also CA 9-12R
See also DLB 7

Gibson, William 1948- ...... CLC 39 (139)

Gide, André (Paul Guillaume)
1869-1951................ TCLC 5, 12
See also CA 104

Gifford, Barry (Colby)
1946-................. CLC 34 (457)
See also CANR 9
See also CA 65-68

Gilbert, (Sir) W(illiam) S(chwenck)
1836-1911................... TCLC 3
See also CA 104
See also SATA 36

Gilbreth, Ernestine 1908-
See Carey, Ernestine Gilbreth

Gilbreth, Frank B(unker), Jr. 1911-
See Gilbreth, Frank B(unker), Jr. and
Carey, Ernestine Gilbreth
See also CA 9-12R
See also SATA 2

Gilbreth, Frank B(unker), Jr. 1911- and
Carey, Ernestine Gilbreth
1908-........................CLC 17

Gilchrist, Ellen 1935- .... CLC 34 (164), 48
See also CA 113, 116

Giles, Molly 1942-.......... CLC 39 (64)

Gilliam, Terry (Vance) 1940-
See Monty Python
See also CA 108, 113

Author Index

Author Index

Kesey, Ken (Elton)
1935-............ CLC **1, 3, 6, 11, 46**
See also CANR 22
See also CA 1-4R
See also DLB 2, 16

Kesselring, Joseph (Otto)
1902-1967...................CLC **45**

Kessler, Jascha (Frederick)
1929-.......................CLC **4**
See also CANR 8
See also CA 17-20R

Kettelkamp, Larry 1933-.........CLC **12**
See also CANR 16
See also CA 29-32R
See also SAAS 3
See also SATA 2

Kherdian, David 1931-..........CLC **6, 9**
See also CAAS 2
See also CA 21-24R
See also SATA 16

Khlebnikov, Velimir (Vladimirovich)
1885-1922.................. TCLC **20**
See also CA 117

Khodasevich, Vladislav (Felitsianovich)
1886-1939.................. TCLC **15**
See also CA 115

Kielland, Alexander (Lange)
1849-1906.................. TCLC **5**
See also CA 104

Kiely, Benedict 1919- .... CLC **23, 43**
See also CANR 2
See also CA 1-4R
See also DLB 15

Kienzle, William X(avier)
1928-.......................CLC **25**
See also CAAS 1
See also CANR 9
See also CA 93-96

Killens, John Oliver 1916-.........CLC **10**
See also CAAS 2
See also CA 77-80
See also DLB 33

Killigrew, Anne 1660-1685........... LC **4**

Kincaid, Jamaica 1949?- ....CLC **43**

King, Francis (Henry) 1923- ....CLC **8**
See also CANR 1
See also CA 1-4R
See also DLB 15

King, Stephen (Edwin)
1947-................ CLC **12, 26, 37**
See also CANR 1
See also CA 61-64
See also SATA 9
See also DLB-Y 80

Kingman, (Mary) Lee 1919- ....CLC **17**
See also Natti, (Mary) Lee
See also CA 5-8R
See also SATA 1

Kingsley, Sidney 1906- ...... CLC **44** (229)
See also CA 85-88
See also DLB 7

Kingston, Maxine Hong
1940-................... CLC **12, 19**
See also CANR 13
See also CA 69-72
See also DLB-Y 80

Kinnell, Galway
1927-.......... CLC **1, 2, 3, 5, 13, 29**
See also CANR 10
See also CA 9-12R
See also DLB 5

Kinsella, Thomas 1928- ..... CLC **4, 19, 43**
See also CANR 15
See also CA 17-20R
See also DLB 27

Kinsella, W(illiam) P(atrick)
1935-............. CLC **27, 43**
See also CAAS 7
See also CANR 21
See also CA 97-100

Kipling, (Joseph) Rudyard
1865-1936............... TCLC **8, 17**
See also CA 20, 105
See also YABC 2
See also DLB 19, 34

Kirkup, James 1918-...............CLC **1**
See also CAAS 4
See also CANR 2
See also CA 1-4R
See also SATA 12
See also DLB 27

Kirkwood, James 1930- ....CLC **9**
See also CANR 6
See also CA 1-4R
See also AITN 2

Kizer, Carolyn (Ashley)
1925-............... CLC **15, 39** (168)
See also CAAS 5
See also CA 65-68
See also DLB 5

Klausner, Amos 1939-
See Oz, Amos

Klein, A(braham) M(oses)
1909-1972...................CLC **19**
See also CA 101
See also obituary CA 37-40R

Klein, Norma 1938-...............CLC **30**
See also CLR 2
See also CANR 15
See also CA 41-44R
See also SAAS 1
See also SATA 7

Klein, T.E.D. 19??-.......... CLC **34** (70)
See also CA 119

Kleist, Heinrich von
1777-1811.................. NCLC **2**

Klimentev, Andrei Platonovich 1899-1951
See Platonov, Andrei (Platonovich)
See also CA 108

Klinger, Friedrich Maximilian von
1752-1831................... NCLC **1**

Klopstock, Friedrich Gottlieb
1724-1803................... NCLC **11**

Knebel, Fletcher 1911-............CLC **14**
See also CAAS 3
See also CANR 1
See also CA 1-4R
See also SATA 36
See also AITN 1

Knight, Etheridge 1931-...........CLC **40**
See also CA 21-24R
See also DLB 41

Knight, Sarah Kemble 1666-1727..... LC **7**
See also DLB 24

Knowles, John 1926-......CLC **1, 4, 10, 26**
See also CA 17-20R
See also SATA 8
See also DLB 6

Koch, C(hristopher) J(ohn)
1932-.......................CLC **42**

Koch, Kenneth
1925-...............CLC **5, 8, 44** (239)
See also CANR 6
See also CA 1-4R
See also DLB 5

Kock, Charles Paul de
1794-1871.................. NCLC **16**

Koestler, Arthur
1905-1983....... CLC **1, 3, 6, 8, 15, 33**
See also CANR 1
See also CA 1-4R
See also obituary CA 109
See also DLB-Y 83

Kohout, Pavel 1928- ....CLC **13**
See also CANR 3
See also CA 45-48

Konrád, György 1933- .... CLC **4, 10**
See also CA 85-88

Konwicki, Tadeusz 1926-....... CLC **8, 28**
See also CA 101

Kopit, Arthur (Lee)
1937-.................. CLC **1, 18, 33**
See also CA 81-84
See also DLB 7
See also AITN 1

Kops, Bernard 1926-...............CLC **4**
See also CA 5-8R
See also DLB 13

Kornbluth, C(yril) M.
1923-1958............... TCLC **8**
See also CA 105
See also DLB 8

Korolenko, Vladimir (Galaktionovich)
1853-1921.................. TCLC **22**
See also CA 121

Kosinski, Jerzy (Nikodem)
1933-............ CLC **1, 2, 3, 6, 10, 15**
See also CANR 9
See also CA 17-20R
See also DLB 2
See also DLB-Y 82

Kostelanetz, Richard (Cory)
1940-.......................CLC **28**
See also CA 13-16R

Kostrowitzki, Wilhelm Apollinaris de
1880-1918
See Apollinaire, Guillaume
See also CA 104

Kotlowitz, Robert 1924-............CLC **4**
See also CA 33-36R

Kotzwinkle, William
1938-................ CLC **5, 14, 35**
See also CLR 6
See also CANR 3
See also CA 45-48
See also SATA 24

Kozol, Jonathan 1936- ....CLC **17**
See also CANR 16
See also CA 61-64

Lawrence, D(avid) H(erbert)
1885-1930.............TCLC **2, 9, 16**
See also CA 104
See also DLB 10, 19, 36

Lawrence, T(homas) E(dward)
1888-1935................. TCLC **18**
See also CA 115

Lawson, Henry (Archibald Hertzberg)
1867-1922................. TCLC **27**
See also CA 120

Laxness, Halldór (Kiljan)
1902-......................CLC **25**
See also Gudjonsson, Halldór Kiljan

Laye, Camara 1928-1980...... CLC **4, 38**
See also CA 85-88
See also obituary CA 97-100

Layton, Irving (Peter) 1912- .... CLC **2, 15**
See also CANR 2
See also CA 1-4R

Lazarus, Emma 1849-1887 .... NCLC **8**

Leacock, Stephen (Butler)
1869-1944................... TCLC **2**
See also CA 104

Lear, Edward 1812-1888 .... NCLC **3**
See also CLR 1
See also SATA 18
See also DLB 32

Lear, Norman (Milton) 1922- ......CLC **12**
See also CA 73-76

Leavis, F(rank) R(aymond)
1895-1978...................CLC **24**
See also CA 21-24R
See also obituary CA 77-80

Leavitt, David 1961?- .... CLC **34** (77)
See also CA 116, 122

Lebowitz, Fran(ces Ann)
1951?-................... CLC **11, 36**
See also CANR 14
See also CA 81-84

Le Carré, John
1931-........ CLC **3, 5, 9, 15, 28**
See also Cornwell, David (John Moore)

Le Clézio, J(ean) M(arie) G(ustave)
1940-......................CLC **31**
See also CA 116

Ledwidge, Francis 1887-1917 .... TCLC **23**
See also DLB 20

Leduc, Violette 1907-1972 ....CLC **22**
See also CAP 1
See also CA 13-14
See also obituary CA 33-36R

Lee, Andrea 1953-................CLC **36**

Lee, Andrew 1917-
See Auchincloss, Louis (Stanton)

Lee, Don L. 1942-................CLC **2**
See also Madhubuti, Haki R.
See also CA 73-76

Lee, (Nelle) Harper 1926-.........CLC **12**
See also CA 13-16R
See also SATA 11
See also DLB 6
See also CDALB 1941-1968

Lee, Lawrence 1903-........ CLC **34** (457)
See also CA 25-28R

Lee, Manfred B(ennington) 1905-1971
See Queen, Ellery
See also CANR 2
See also CA 1-4R
See also obituary CA 29-32R

Lee, Stan 1922- ....CLC **17**
See also CA 108, 111

Lee, Tanith 1947- ....CLC **46**
See also CA 37-40R
See also SATA 8

Lee, Vernon 1856-1935........... TCLC **5**
See also Paget, Violet
See also DLB 57

Lee-Hamilton, Eugene (Jacob)
1845-1907.................. TCLC **22**

Leet, Judith 1935-................CLC **11**

Le Fanu, Joseph Sheridan
1814-1873.................. NCLC **9**
See also DLB 21, 70

Leffland, Ella 1931-..............CLC **19**
See also CA 29-32R
See also DLB-Y 84

Léger, (Marie-Rene) Alexis Saint-Léger
1887-1975
See Perse, St.-John
See also CA 13-16R
See also obituary CA 61-64

Le Guin, Ursula K(roeber)
1929-...............CLC **8, 13, 22, 45**
See also CLR 3
See also CANR 9
See also CA 21-24R
See also SATA 4, 52
See also DLB 8, 52
See also AITN 1

Lehmann, Rosamond (Nina)
1901-......................CLC **5**
See also CANR 8
See also CA 77-80
See also DLB 15

Leiber, Fritz (Reuter, Jr.)
1910-......................CLC **25**
See also CANR 2
See also CA 45-48
See also SATA 45
See also DLB 8

Leino, Eino 1878-1926 .... TCLC **24**

Leithauser, Brad 1953-............CLC **27**
See also CA 107

Lelchuk, Alan 1938- ....CLC **5**
See also CANR 1
See also CA 45-48

Lem, Stanislaw 1921- .... CLC **8, 15, 40**
See also CAAS 1
See also CA 105

Lemann, Nancy 1956-........ CLC **39** (75)
See also CA 118

Lemonnier, (Antoine Louis) Camille
1844-1913.................. TCLC **22**

Lenau, Nikolaus 1802-1850 ...... NCLC **16**

L'Engle, Madeleine 1918-..........CLC **12**
See also CLR 1, 14
See also CANR 3, 21
See also CA 1-4R
See also SATA 1, 27
See also DLB 52
See also AITN 2

Lengyel, József 1896-1975 ....CLC **7**
See also CA 85-88
See also obituary CA 57-60

Lennon, John (Ono)
1940-1980....................CLC **35**
See also Lennon, John (Ono) and
McCartney, Paul
See also CA 102

Lennon, John (Ono) 1940-1980 and
McCartney, Paul 1942- ....CLC **12**

Lennon, John Winston 1940-1980
See Lennon, John (Ono)

Lentricchia, Frank (Jr.)
1940-................... CLC **34** (571)
See also CA 25-28R

Lenz, Siegfried 1926- ....CLC **27**
See also CA 89-92

Leonard, Elmore
1925-............... CLC **28, 34** (212)
See also CANR 12
See also CA 81-84
See also AITN 1

Leonard, Hugh 1926- ....CLC **19**
See also Byrne, John Keyes
See also DLB 13

Lerman, Eleanor 1952-............CLC **9**
See also CA 85-88

Lermontov, Mikhail Yuryevich
1814-1841................... NCLC **5**

Leroux, Gaston 1868-1927....... TCLC **25**
See also CA 108

Lesage, Alain-René 1668-1747........ LC **2**

Lessing, Doris (May)
1919-....... CLC **1, 2, 3, 6, 10, 15, 22, 40**
See also CA 9-12R
See also DLB 15
See also DLB-Y 85

Lessing, Gotthold Ephraim
1729-1781................... LC **8**

Lester, Richard 1932-.............CLC **20**

Leverson, Ada 1865-1936....... TCLC **18**
See also CA 117

Levertov, Denise
1923-.........CLC **1, 2, 3, 5, 8, 15, 28**
See also CANR 3
See also CA 1-4R
See also DLB 5

Levi, Peter (Chad Tiger) 1931-.....CLC **41**
See also CA 5-8R
See also DLB 40

Levi, Primo
1919-1987.......... CLC **37, 50** (323)
See also CANR 12
See also CA 13-16R
See also obituary CA 122

Levin, Ira 1929-................ CLC **3, 6**
See also CANR 17
See also CA 21-24R

Levin, Meyer 1905-1981............CLC **7**
See also CANR 15
See also CA 9-12R
See also obituary CA 104
See also SATA 21
See also obituary SATA 27
See also DLB 9, 28
See also DLB-Y 81
See also AITN 1

Author Index

Author Index

Mitchell, Joni 1943-..............CLC 12
See also CA 112

Mitchell (Marsh), Margaret (Munnerlyn)
1900-1949.................. TCLC 11
See also CA 109
See also DLB 9

Mitchell, W(illiam) O(rmond)
1914-.......................CLC 25
See also CANR 15
See also CA 77-80

Mitford, Mary Russell
1787-1855.................. NCLC 4

Mitford, Nancy
1904-1973.............. CLC 44 (482)
See also CA 9-12R

Mo, Timothy 1950-................CLC 46
See also CA 117

Modarressi, Taghi 1931-...... CLC 44 (82)
See also CA 121

Modiano, Patrick (Jean) 1945- .....CLC 18
See also CANR 17
See also CA 85-88

Mofolo, Thomas (Mokopu)
1876-1948.................. TCLC 22
See also CA 121

Mohr, Nicholasa 1935-............CLC 12
See also CANR 1
See also CA 49-52
See also SATA 8

Mojtabai, A(nn) G(race)
1938-.................CLC 5, 9, 15, 29
See also CA 85-88

Molnár, Ferenc 1878-1952...... TCLC 20
See also CA 109

Momaday, N(avarre) Scott
1934-.................... CLC 2, 19
See also CANR 14
See also CA 25-28R
See also SATA 30, 48

Monroe, Harriet 1860-1936...... TCLC 12
See also CA 109
See also DLB 54

Montagu, Elizabeth 1720-1800 .... NCLC 7

Montagu, Lady Mary (Pierrepont) Wortley
1689-1762......................LC 9

Montague, John (Patrick)
1929-.................... CLC 13, 46
See also CANR 9
See also CA 9-12R
See also DLB 40

Montaigne, Michel (Eyquem) de
1533-1592......................LC 8

Montale, Eugenio
1896-1981.............. CLC 7, 9, 18
See also CA 17-20R
See also obituary CA 104

Montgomery, Marion (H., Jr.)
1925-.......................CLC 7
See also CANR 3
See also CA 1-4R
See also DLB 6
See also AITN 1

Montgomery, Robert Bruce 1921-1978
See Crispin, Edmund
See also CA 104

Montherlant, Henri (Milon) de
1896-1972.................. CLC 8, 19
See also CA 85-88
See also obituary CA 37-40R

Montisquieu, Charles-Louis de Secondat
1689-1755......................LC 7

Monty Python ....CLC 21
See also Cleese, John
See also Gilliam, Terry (Vance)
See also Idle, Eric
See also Jones, Terry
See also Palin, Michael

Moodie, Susanna (Strickland)
1803-1885.................. NCLC 14

Mooney, Ted 1951-................CLC 25

Moorcock, Michael (John)
1939-.................... CLC 5, 27
See also CAAS 5
See also CANR 2, 17
See also CA 45-48
See also DLB 14

Moore, Brian
1921-.........CLC 1, 3, 5, 7, 8, 19, 32
See also CANR 1
See also CA 1-4R

Moore, George (Augustus)
1852-1933.................. TCLC 7
See also CA 104
See also DLB 10, 18, 57

Moore, Lorrie 1957- ...... CLC 39 (82), 45
See also Moore, Marie Lorena

Moore, Marianne (Craig)
1887-1972...... CLC 1, 2, 4, 8, 10, 13,
19, 47
See also CANR 3
See also CA 1-4R
See also obituary CA 33-36R
See also DLB 45
See also SATA 20

Moore, Marie Lorena 1957-
See Moore, Lorrie
See also CA 116

Moore, Thomas 1779-1852........ NCLC 6

Morand, Paul 1888-1976 ....CLC 41
See also obituary CA 69-72

Morante, Elsa 1918-1985 .... CLC 8, 47
See also CA 85-88
See also obituary CA 117

Moravia, Alberto
1907-.........CLC 2, 7, 11, 18, 27, 46
See also Pincherle, Alberto

More, Henry 1614-1687 ....LC 9

Moréas, Jean 1856-1910........ TCLC 18

Morgan, Berry 1919- ....CLC 6
See also CA 49-52
See also DLB 6

Morgan, Edwin (George)
1920-.......................CLC 31
See also CANR 3
See also CA 7-8R
See also DLB 27

Morgan, (George) Frederick
1922-.......................CLC 23
See also CANR 21
See also CA 17-20R

Morgan, Janet 1945-........ CLC 39 (436)
See also CA 65-68

Morgan, Robin 1941- ....CLC 2
See also CA 69-72

Morgenstern, Christian (Otto Josef Wolfgang)
1871-1914.................. TCLC 8
See also CA 105

Mori Ōgai 1862-1922 .... TCLC 14
See also Mori Rintaro

Mori Rintaro 1862-1922
See Mori Ōgai
See also CA 110

Mörike, Eduard (Friedrich)
1804-1875.................. NCLC 10

Moritz, Karl Philipp 1756-1793 ......LC 2

Morris, Julian 1916-
See West, Morris L.

Morris, Steveland Judkins 1950-
See Wonder, Stevie
See also CA 111

Morris, William 1834-1896 .... NCLC 4
See also DLB 18, 35, 57

Morris, Wright (Marion)
1910-............. CLC 1, 3, 7, 18, 37
See also CA 9-12R
See also DLB 2
See also DLB-Y 81

Morrison, James Douglas 1943-1971
See Morrison, Jim
See also CA 73-76

Morrison, Jim 1943-1971..........CLC 17
See also Morrison, James Douglas

Morrison, Toni 1931-   CLC 4, 10, 22
See also CA 29-32R
See also DLB 6, 33
See also DLB-Y 81

Morrison, Van 1945-..............CLC 21
See also CA 116

Mortimer, John (Clifford)
1923-.................... CLC 28, 43
See also CANR 21
See also CA 13-16R
See also DLB 13

Mortimer, Penelope (Ruth)
1918-.......................CLC 5
See also CA 57-60

Mosley, Nicholas 1923-............CLC 43
See also CA 69-72
See also DLB 14

Moss, Howard
1922-1987..... CLC 7, 14, 45, 50 (351)
See also CANR 1
See also CA 1-4R
See also DLB 5

Motion, Andrew (Peter) 1952-......CLC 47
See also DLB 40

Motley, Willard (Francis)
1912-1965....................CLC 18
See also obituary CA 106
See also CA 117

Mott, Michael (Charles Alston)
1930-.............. CLC 15, 34 (460)
See also CAAS 7
See also CANR 7
See also CA 5-8R

Mowat, Farley (McGill) 1921-......CLC 26
See also CANR 4
See also CA 1-4R
See also SATA 3

Author Index

Patchen, Kenneth
 1911-1972.............CLC 1, 2, 18
 See also CANR 3
 See also CA 1-4R
 See also obituary CA 33-36R
 See also DLB 16, 48

Pater, Walter (Horatio)
 1839-1894.................NCLC 7
 See also DLB 57

Paterson, Katherine (Womeldorf)
 1932-...................CLC 12, 30
 See also CLR 7
 See also CA 21-24R
 See also SATA 13
 See also DLB 52

Patmore, Coventry Kersey Dighton
 1823-1896..................NCLC 9
 See also DLB 35

Paton, Alan (Stewart)
 1903-.................CLC 4, 10, 25
 See also CAP 1
 See also CANR 22
 See also CA 15-16
 See also SATA 11

Paulding, James Kirke
 1778-1860..................NCLC 2
 See also DLB 3

Paulin, Tom 1949-................CLC 37
 See also DLB 40

Paustovsky, Konstantin (Georgievich)
 1892-1968...................CLC 40
 See also CA 93-96
 See also obituary CA 25-28R

Paustowsky, Konstantin (Georgievich)
 1892-1968
 See Paustovsky, Konstantin (Georgievich)

Pavese, Cesare 1908-1950 .... TCLC 3
 See also CA 104

Payne, Alan 1932-
 See Jakes, John (William)

Paz, Octavio 1914-..... CLC 3, 4, 6, 10, 19
 See also CA 73-76

Peake, Mervyn 1911-1968 ....CLC 7
 See also CANR 3
 See also CA 5-8R
 See also obituary CA 25-28R
 See also SATA 23
 See also DLB 15

Pearce, (Ann) Philippa 1920-.......CLC 21
 See also Christie, (Ann) Philippa
 See also CA 5-8R
 See also SATA 1

Pearl, Eric 1934-
 See Elman, Richard

Pearson, T(homas) R(eid)
 1956-................... CLC 39 (86)
 See also CA 120

Peck, John 1941-.................CLC 3
 See also CANR 3
 See also CA 49-52

Peck, Richard 1934- ....CLC 21
 See also CLR 15
 See also CANR 19
 See also CA 85-88
 See also SAAS 2
 See also SATA 18

Peck, Robert Newton 1928-........CLC 17
 See also CA 81-84
 See also SAAS 1
 See also SATA 21

Peckinpah, (David) Sam(uel)
 1925-1984...................CLC 20
 See also CA 109
 See also obituary CA 114

Pedersen, Knut 1859-1952
 See Hamsun, Knut
 See also CA 104

Péguy, Charles (Pierre)
 1873-1914.................. TCLC 10
 See also CA 107

Percy, Walker
 1916-........CLC 2, 3, 6, 8, 14, 18, 47
 See also CANR 1
 See also CA 1-4R
 See also DLB 2
 See also DLB-Y 80

Pereda, José María de
 1833-1906.................. TCLC 16

Perelman, S(idney) J(oseph)
 1904-1979........CLC 3, 5, 9, 15, 23,
         44 (499), 49
 See also CANR 18
 See also CA 73-76
 See also obituary CA 89-92
 See also DLB 11, 44
 See also AITN 1, 2

Péret, Benjamin 1899-1959 ...... TCLC 20
 See also CA 117

Peretz, Isaac Leib
 1852?-1915................ TCLC 16
 See also CA 109

Pérez, Galdós Benito
 1853-1920................. TCLC 27

Perrault, Charles 1628-1703 .... LC 2
 See also SATA 25

Perse, St.-John
 1887-1975............. CLC 4, 11, 46
 See also Léger, (Marie-Rene) Alexis Saint-
 Léger

Pesetsky, Bette 1932-..............CLC 28

Peshkov, Alexei Maximovich 1868-1936
 See Gorky, Maxim
 See also CA 105

Pessoa, Fernando (António Nogueira)
 1888-1935.................. TCLC 27

Peterkin, Julia (Mood)
 1880-1961...................CLC 31
 See also CA 102
 See also DLB 9

Peters, Joan K. 1945- .... CLC 39 (91)

Peters, Robert L(ouis) 1924- ....CLC 7
 See also CA 13-16R

Petrakis, Harry Mark 1923- ....CLC 3
 See also CANR 4
 See also CA 9-12R

Petrov, Evgeny 1902-1942 and **Ilf, Ilya**
 1897-1937
 See Ilf, Ilya 1897-1937 and Petrov, Evgeny
 1902-1942

Petry, Ann (Lane) 1908-...... CLC 1, 7, 18
 See also CLR 12
 See also CAAS 6
 See also CANR 4
 See also CA 5-8R
 See also SATA 5

Pétursson, Halligrímur 1614-1674 .... LC 8

Phillips, Jayne Anne 1952-..... CLC 15, 33
 See also CA 101
 See also DLB-Y 80

Phillips, Robert (Schaeffer)
 1938-.......................CLC 28
 See also CANR 8
 See also CA 17-20R

Pica, Peter 1925-
 See Aldiss, Brian W(ilson)

Piccolo, Lucio 1901-1969 ....CLC 13
 See also CA 97-100

Pickthall, Marjorie (Lowry Christie)
 1883-1922.................. TCLC 21
 See also CA 107

Piercy, Marge
 1936-............ CLC 3, 6, 14, 18, 27
 See also CAAS 1
 See also CANR 13
 See also CA 21-24R

Pilnyak, Boris 1894-1937? .... TCLC 23

Pincherle, Alberto 1907-
 See Moravia, Alberto
 See also CA 25-28R

Pineda, Cecile 1942- .... CLC 39 (94)
 See also CA 118

Piñero, Miguel (Gomez) 1947?-......CLC 4
 See also CA 61-64

Pinget, Robert 1919-........ CLC 7, 13, 37
 See also CA 85-88

Pink Floyd.......................CLC 35

Pinkwater, D(aniel) M(anus)
 1941-.......................CLC 35
 See also Pinkwater, Manus
 See also CLR 4
 See also CANR 12
 See also CA 29-32R
 See also SAAS 3
 See also SATA 46

Pinkwater, Manus 1941-
 See Pinkwater, D(aniel) M(anus)
 See also SATA 8

Pinsky, Robert 1940-........ CLC 9, 19, 38
 See also CAAS 4
 See also CA 29-32R
 See also DLB-Y 82

Pinter, Harold
 1930-........CLC 1, 3, 6, 9, 11, 15, 27
 See also CA 5-8R
 See also DLB 13

Pirandello, Luigi
 1867-1936................ TCLC 4, 29
 See also CA 104

Pirsig, Robert M(aynard)
 1928-..................... CLC 4, 6
 See also CA 53-56
 See also SATA 39

Pix, Mary (Griffith) 1666-1709 .... LC 8

Plaidy, Jean 1906-
 See Hibbert, Eleanor (Burford)

Author Index

Rogers, Will(iam Penn Adair)
1879-1935 . . . . **TCLC 8**
See also CA 105
See also DLB 11

Rogin, Gilbert 1929- . . . .**CLC 18**
See also CANR 15
See also CA 65-68

Rohan, Kōda 1867-1947 . . . . **TCLC 22**

Rohmer, Eric 1920- . . . .**CLC 16**
See also Scherer, Jean-Marie Maurice

Rohmer, Sax 1883-1959 . . . . **TCLC 28**
See also Ward, Arthur Henry Sarsfield
See also DLB 70

Roiphe, Anne (Richardson)
1935- . . . . **CLC 3, 9**
See also CA 89-92
See also DLB-Y 80

Rolfe, Frederick (William Serafino Austin
Lewis Mary) 1860-1913 . . . . . **TCLC 12**
See also CA 107
See also DLB 34

Rolland, Romain 1866-1944 . . . . . . **TCLC 23**
See also CA 118

Rölvaag, O(le) E(dvart)
1876-1931 . . . . **TCLC 17**
See also CA 117
See also DLB 9

Romains, Jules 1885-1972 . . . .**CLC 7**
See also CA 85-88

Romero, José Rubén
1890-1952 . . . . **TCLC 14**
See also CA 114

Ronsard, Pierre de 1524-1585 . . . .**LC 6**

Rooke, Leon 1934- . . . . **CLC 25, 34** (250)
See also CA 25-28R

Rosa, João Guimarães
1908-1967 . . . .**CLC 23**
See also obituary CA 89-92

Rosen, Richard (Dean)
1949- . . . . **CLC 39** (194)
See also CA 77-80

Rosenberg, Isaac 1890-1918 . . . . . . **TCLC 12**
See also CA 107
See also DLB 20

Rosenblatt, Joe 1933- . . . .**CLC 15**
See also Rosenblatt, Joseph
See also AITN 2

Rosenblatt, Joseph 1933-
See Rosenblatt, Joe
See also CA 89-92

Rosenfeld, Samuel 1896-1963
See Tzara, Tristan
See also obituary CA 89-92

Rosenthal, M(acha) L(ouis)
1917- . . . .**CLC 28**
See also CAAS 6
See also CANR 4
See also CA 1-4R
See also DLB 5

Ross, (James) Sinclair 1908- . . . .**CLC 13**
See also CA 73-76

Rossetti, Christina Georgina
1830-1894 . . . .**NCLC 2**
See also SATA 20
See also DLB 35

Rossetti, Dante Gabriel
1828-1882 . . . .**NCLC 4**
See also DLB 35

Rossetti, Gabriel Charles Dante 1828-1882
See Rossetti, Dante Gabriel

Rossner, Judith (Perelman)
1935- . . . . **CLC 6, 9, 29**
See also CANR 18
See also CA 17-20R
See also DLB 6
See also AITN 2

Rostand, Edmond (Eugène Alexis)
1868-1918 . . . .**TCLC 6**
See also CA 104

Roth, Henry 1906- . . . .**CLC 2, 6, 11**
See also CAP 1
See also CA 11-12
See also DLB 28

Roth, Philip (Milton)
1933- . . . . . .**CLC 1, 2, 3, 4, 6, 9, 15, 22,**
　　　　　　　　　　　　　　　　31, 47
See also CANR 1, 22
See also CA 1-4R
See also DLB 2, 28
See also DLB-Y 82

Rothenberg, Jerome 1931- . . . .**CLC 6**
See also CANR 1
See also CA 45-48
See also DLB 5

Roumain, Jacques 1907-1944 . . . . **TCLC 19**
See also CA 117

Rourke, Constance (Mayfield)
1885-1941 . . . . **TCLC 12**
See also CA 107
See also YABC 1

Rousseau, Jean-Baptiste
1671-1741 . . . .**LC 9**

Roussel, Raymond 1877-1933 . . . . **TCLC 20**
See also CA 117

Rovit, Earl (Herbert) 1927- . . . .**CLC 7**
See also CA 5-8R
See also CANR 12

Rowe, Nicholas 1674-1718 . . . .**LC 8**

Rowson, Susanna Haswell
1762-1824 . . . .**NCLC 5**
See also DLB 37

Roy, Gabrielle 1909-1983 . . . . . . **CLC 10, 14**
See also CANR 5
See also CA 53-56
See also obituary CA 110

Różewicz, Tadeusz 1921- . . . . **CLC 9, 23**
See also CA 108

Ruark, Gibbons 1941- . . . .**CLC 3**
See also CANR 14
See also CA 33-36R

Rubens, Bernice 192?- . . . . **CLC 19, 31**
See also CA 25-28R
See also DLB 14

Rudkin, (James) David 1936- . . . . . .**CLC 14**
See also CA 89-92
See also DLB 13

Rudnik, Raphael 1933- . . . .**CLC 7**
See also CA 29-32R

Ruiz, José Martínez 1874-1967
See Azorín

Rukeyser, Muriel
1913-1980 . . . .**CLC 6, 10, 15, 27**
See also CA 5-8R
See also obituary CA 93-96
See also obituary SATA 22
See also DLB 48

Rule, Jane (Vance) 1931- . . . .**CLC 27**
See also CANR 12
See also CA 25-28R
See also DLB 60

Rulfo, Juan 1918-1986 . . . .**CLC 8**
See also CA 85-88
See also obituary CA 118

Runyon, (Alfred) Damon
1880-1946 . . . . **TCLC 10**
See also CA 107
See also DLB 11

Rush, Norman 1933- . . . . **CLC 44** (91)
See also CA 121

Rushdie, (Ahmed) Salman
1947- . . . . **CLC 23, 31**
See also CA 108, 111

Rushforth, Peter (Scott) 1945- . . . . . .**CLC 19**
See also CA 101

Ruskin, John 1819-1900 . . . . **TCLC 20**
See also CA 114
See also SATA 24
See also DLB 55

Russ, Joanna 1937- . . . .**CLC 15**
See also CANR 11
See also CA 25-28R
See also DLB 8

Russell, George William 1867-1935
See A. E.
See also CA 104

Russell, (Henry) Ken(neth Alfred)
1927- . . . .**CLC 16**
See also CA 105

Rutherford, Mark 1831-1913 . . . . **TCLC 25**
See also DLB 18

Ruyslinck, Ward 1929- . . . .**CLC 14**

Ryan, Cornelius (John)
1920-1974 . . . .**CLC 7**
See also CA 69-72
See also obituary CA 53-56

Rybakov, Anatoli 1911?- . . . .**CLC 23**

Ryder, Jonathan 1927-
See Ludlum, Robert

Ryga, George 1932- . . . .**CLC 14**
See also CA 101
See also DLB 60

Sabato, Ernesto 1911- . . . . **CLC 10, 23**
See also CA 97-100

Sachs, Marilyn (Stickle) 1927- . . . . . .**CLC 35**
See also CLR 2
See also CANR 13
See also CA 17-20R
See also SAAS 2
See also SATA 3, 52

Sachs, Nelly 1891-1970 . . . .**CLC 14**
See also CAP 2
See also CA 17-18
See also obituary CA 25-28R

Schneider, Leonard Alfred 1925-1966
  See Bruce, Lenny
  See also CA 89-92

Schnitzler, Arthur 1862-1931 ..... TCLC 4
  See also CA 104

Schorer, Mark 1908-1977 ....CLC 9
  See also CANR 7
  See also CA 5-8R
  See also obituary CA 73-76

Schrader, Paul (Joseph) 1946-......CLC 26
  See also CA 37-40R
  See also DLB 44

**Schreiner (Cronwright), Olive (Emilie
    Albertina)** 1855-1920 .... TCLC 9
  See also CA 105
  See also DLB 18

Schulberg, Budd (Wilson)
  1914-..................... CLC 7, 48
  See also CANR 19
  See also CA 25-28R
  See also DLB 6, 26, 28
  See also DLB-Y 81

Schulz, Bruno 1892-1942 .... TCLC 5
  See also CA 115

Schulz, Charles M(onroe)
  1922-.......................CLC 12
  See also CANR 6
  See also CA 9-12R
  See also SATA 10

Schuyler, James (Marcus)
  1923-..................... CLC 5, 23
  See also CA 101
  See also DLB 5

Schwartz, Delmore
  1913-1966...........CLC 2, 4, 10, 45
  See also CAP 2
  See also CA 17-18
  See also obituary CA 25-28R
  See also DLB 28, 48

Schwartz, Lynne Sharon 1939-.....CLC 31
  See also CA 103

Schwarz-Bart, André 1928-...... CLC 2, 4
  See also CA 89-92

Schwarz-Bart, Simone 1938-........CLC 7
  See also CA 97-100

Schwob, (Mayer Andre) Marcel
  1867-1905 .... TCLC 20
  See also CA 117

Sciascia, Leonardo 1921- ..... CLC 8, 9, 41
  See also CA 85-88

Scoppettone, Sandra 1936-........CLC 26
  See also CA 5-8R
  See also SATA 9

Scorsese, Martin 1942-............CLC 20
  See also CA 110, 114

Scotland, Jay 1932-
  See Jakes, John (William)

Scott, Duncan Campbell
  1862-1947.................. TCLC 6
  See also CA 104

Scott, Evelyn 1893-1963 ....CLC 43
  See also CA 104
  See also obituary CA 112
  See also DLB 9, 48

Scott, F(rancis) R(eginald)
  1899-1985...................CLC 22
  See also CA 101
  See also obituary CA 114

Scott, Joanna 19??- .... CLC 50 (88)

Scott, Paul (Mark) 1920-1978 ....CLC 9
  See also CA 81-84
  See also obituary CA 77-80
  See also DLB 14

Scott, Sir Walter 1771-1832..... NCLC 15
  See also YABC 2

Scribe, (Augustin) Eugène
  1791-1861.................. NCLC 16

Scudéry, Madeleine de 1607-1701..... LC 2

Seare, Nicholas 1925-
  See Trevanian
  See also Whitaker, Rodney

Sebestyen, Igen 1924-
  See Sebestyen, Ouida

Sebestyen, Ouida 1924-............CLC 30
  See also CA 107
  See also SATA 39

Sedgwick, Catharine Maria
  1789-1867.................. NCLC 19
  See also DLB 1

Seelye, John 1931-.................CLC 7
  See also CA 97-100

Seferiades, Giorgos Stylianou 1900-1971
  See Seferis, George
  See also CANR 5
  See also CA 5-8R
  See also obituary CA 33-36R

Seferis, George 1900-1971 ...... CLC 5, 11
  See also Seferiades, Giorgos Stylianou

Segal, Erich (Wolf) 1937-....... CLC 3, 10
  See also CANR 20
  See also CA 25-28R
  See also DLB-Y 86

Seger, Bob 1945- ....CLC 35

Seger, Robert Clark 1945-
  See Seger, Bob

Seghers, Anna 1900-1983...........CLC 7
  See Radvanyi, Netty Reiling
  See also DLB 69

Seidel, Frederick (Lewis) 1936-.....CLC 18
  See also CANR 8
  See also CA 13-16R
  See also DLB-Y 84

Seifert, Jaroslav
  1901-1986..... CLC 34 (255), 44 (421)

Selby, Hubert, Jr.
  1928-...................CLC 1, 2, 4, 8
  See also CA 13-16R
  See also DLB 2

Sénacour, Étienne Pivert de
  1770-1846 .... NCLC 16

Sender, Ramón (José)
  1902-1982...................CLC 8
  See also CANR 8
  See also CA 5-8R
  See also obituary CA 105

Serling, (Edward) Rod(man)
  1924-1975...................CLC 30
  See also CA 65-68
  See also obituary CA 57-60
  See also DLB 26
  See also AITN 1

Serpières 1907-
  See Guillevic, (Eugène)

Service, Robert W(illiam)
  1874-1958................. TCLC 15
  See also CA 115
  See also SATA 20

Seth, Vikram 1952-...............CLC 43

Seton, Cynthia Propper
  1926-1982...................CLC 27
  See also CANR-7
  See also CA 5-8R
  See also obituary CA 108

Settle, Mary Lee 1918-............CLC 19
  See also CAAS 1
  See also CA 89-92
  See also DLB 6

Sexton, Anne (Harvey)
  1928-1974....... CLC 2, 4, 6, 8, 10, 15
  See also CANR 3
  See also CA 1-4R
  See also obituary CA 53-56
  See also CABS 2
  See also SATA 10
  See also DLB 5
  See also CDALB 1941-1968

Shaara, Michael (Joseph)
  1929-.......................CLC 15
  See also CA 102
  See also DLB-Y 83
  See also AITN 1

Shackleton, C. C. 1925-
  See Aldiss, Brian W(ilson)

Shacochis, Bob 1951- .... CLC 39 (198)
  See also CA 119

Shaffer, Anthony 1926-............CLC 19
  See also CA 110
  See also CA 116
  See also DLB 13

Shaffer, Peter (Levin)
  1926-...............CLC 5, 14, 18, 37
  See also CA 25-28R
  See also DLB 13

Shalamov, Varlam (Tikhonovich)
  1907?-1982...................CLC 18
  See also obituary CA 105

Shamlu, Ahmad 1925- ....CLC 10

Shange, Ntozake 1948-...... CLC 8, 25, 38
  See also CA 85-88
  See also DLB 38

Shapcott, Thomas W(illiam)
  1935-.......................CLC 38
  See also CA 69-72

Shapiro, Karl (Jay) 1913-..... CLC 4, 8, 15
  See also CAAS 6
  See also CANR 1
  See also CA 1-4R
  See also DLB 48

Sharpe, Tom 1928- ....CLC 36
  See also CA 114
  See also DLB 14

Shaw, (George) Bernard
  1856-1950.............TCLC 3, 9, 21
  See also CA 104, 109
  See also DLB 10, 57

Shaw, Henry Wheeler
  1818-1885.................. NCLC 15
  See also DLB 11

Stewart, Mary (Florence Elinor)
1916-..................... CLC 7, 35
See also CANR 1
See also CA 1-4R
See also SATA 12

Stewart, Will 1908-
See Williamson, Jack

Still, James 1906-................CLC 49
See also CANR 10
See also CA 65-68
See also SATA 29
See also DLB 9

Sting 1951-
See The Police

Stitt, Milan 1941-.................CLC 29
See also CA 69-72

Stoker, Bram (Abraham)
1847-1912.................. TCLC 8
See also CA 105
See also SATA 29
See also DLB 36, 70

Stolz, Mary (Slattery) 1920-........CLC 12
See also CANR 13
See also CA 5-8R
See also SAAS 3
See also SATA 10
Sec also AITN 1

Stone, Irving 1903- ....CLC 7
See also CAAS 3
See also CANR 1
See also CA 1-4R
See also SATA 3
See also AITN 1

Stone, Robert (Anthony)
1937?-................. CLC 5, 23, 42
See also CA 85-88

Stoppard, Tom
1937-........ CLC 1, 3, 4, 5, 8, 15, 29,
34 (272)
See also CA 81-84
See also DLB 13
See also DLB-Y 85

Storey, David (Malcolm)
1933-.................CLC 2, 4, 5, 8
See also CA 81-84
See also DLB 13, 14

Storm, Hyemeyohsts 1935-..........CLC 3
See also CA 81-84

Storm, (Hans) Theodor (Woldsen)
1817-1888................... NCLC 1

Storni, Alfonsina 1892-1938....... TCLC 5
See also CA 104

Stout, Rex (Todhunter)
1886-1975.....................CLC 3
See also CA 61-64
See also AITN 2

Stow, (Julian) Randolph
1935-................ CLC 23, 48
See also CA 13-16R

Stowe, Harriet (Elizabeth) Beecher
1811-1896.................. NCLC 3
See also YABC 1
See also DLB 1, 12, 42
See also CDALB 1865-1917

Strachey, (Giles) Lytton
1880-1932.................. TCLC 12
See also CA 110

Strand, Mark 1934-......... CLC 6, 18, 41
See also CA 21-24R
See also SATA 41
See also DLB 5

Straub, Peter (Francis) 1943- ......CLC 28
See also CA 85-88
See also DLB-Y 84

Strauss, Botho 1944-..............CLC 22

Straussler, Tomas 1937-
See Stoppard, Tom

Streatfeild, (Mary) Noel 1897-......CLC 21
See also CA 81-84
See also obituary CA 120
See also SATA 20, 48

Stribling, T(homas) S(igismund)
1881-1965....................CLC 23
See also obituary CA 107
See also DLB 9

Strindberg, (Johan) August
1849-1912..............TCLC 1, 8, 21
See also CA 104

Strugatskii, Arkadii (Natanovich) 1925-
See Strugatskii, Arkadii (Natanovich) and
Strugatskii, Boris (Natanovich)
See also CA 106

Strugatskii, Arkadii (Natanovich) 1925-
and **Strugatskii, Boris**
(Natanovich) 1933-...........CLC 27

Strugatskii, Boris (Natanovich) 1933-
See Strugatskii, Arkadii (Natanovich) and
Strugatskii, Boris (Natanovich)
See also CA 106

Strugatskii, Boris (Natanovich) 1933- and
Strugatskii, Arkadii (Natanovich) 1925-
See Strugatskii, Arkadii (Natanovich) and
Strugatskii, Boris (Natanovich)

Strummer, Joe 1953?-
See The Clash

Stuart, (Hilton) Jesse
1906-1984.......... CLC 1, 8, 11, 14,
34 (372)
See also CA 5-8R
See also obituary CA 112
See also SATA 2
See also obituary SATA 36
See also DLB 9, 48
See also DLB-Y 84

Sturgeon, Theodore (Hamilton)
1918-1985........... CLC 22, 39 (360)
See also CA 81-84
See also obituary CA 116
See also DLB 8
See also DLB-Y 85

Styron, William
1925-............ CLC 1, 3, 5, 11, 15
See also CANR 6
See also CA 5-8R
See also DLB 2
See also DLB-Y 80

Su Man-shu 1884-1918......... TCLC 24

Sudermann, Hermann
1857-1928.................. TCLC 15
See also CA 107

Sue, Eugène 1804-1857.......... NCLC 1

Sukenick, Ronald
1932-.................CLC 3, 4, 6, 48
See also CA 25-28R
See also DLB-Y 81

Suknaski, Andrew 1942-..........CLC 19
See also CA 101
See also DLB 53

Summers, Andrew James 1942-
See The Police

Summers, Andy 1942-
See The Police

Summers, Hollis (Spurgeon, Jr.)
1916-........................CLC 10
See also CANR 3
See also CA 5-8R
See also DLB 6

Summers, (Alphonsus Joseph-Mary Augustus)
Montague 1880-1948 .... TCLC 16

Sumner, Gordon Matthew 1951-
See The Police

Surtees, Robert Smith
1805-1864.................. NCLC 14
See also DLB 21

Susann, Jacqueline 1921-1974......CLC 3
See also CA 65-68
See also obituary CA 53-56
See also AITN 1

Süskind, Patrick 1949-...... CLC 44 (111)

Sutcliff, Rosemary 1920- ....CLC 26
See also CLR 1
See also CA 5-8R
See also SATA 6, 44

Sutro, Alfred 1863-1933.......... TCLC 6
Sec also CA 105
See also DLB 10

Sutton, Henry 1935-
See Slavitt, David (R.)

Svevo, Italo 1861-1928 .... TCLC 2
See also Schmitz, Ettore

Swados, Elizabeth 1951-...........CLC 12
See also CA 97-100

Swados, Harvey 1920-1972 ....CLC 5
See also CANR 6
See also CA 5-8R
See also obituary CA 37-40R
See also DLB 2

Swarthout, Glendon (Fred)
1918-........................CLC 35
See also CANR 1
See also CA 1-4R
See also SATA 26

Swenson, May 1919-........... CLC 4, 14
See also CA 5-8R
See also SATA 15
See also DLB 5

Swift, Graham 1949-..............CLC 41
See also CA 117

Swift, Jonathan 1667-1745.......... LC 1
See also SATA 19
See also DLB 39

Swinburne, Algernon Charles
1837-1909................... TCLC 8
See also CA 105
See also DLB 35, 57

Swinfen, Ann 19??-......... CLC 34 (576)

Swinnerton, Frank (Arthur)
1884-1982....................CLC 31
See also obituary CA 108
See also DLB 34

Wagman, Fredrica 1937- ....CLC 7
See also CA 97-100

Wagner, Richard 1813-1883 ...... NCLC 9

Wagner-Martin, Linda
1936- .... CLC 50 (439)

Wagoner, David (Russell)
1926- .... CLC 3, 5, 15
See also CAAS 3
See also CANR 2
See also CA 1-4R
See also SATA 14
See also DLB 5

Wah, Fred(erick James)
1939- .... CLC 44 (323)
See also CA 107
See also DLB 60

Wahlöö, Per 1926-1975 ....CLC 7
See also CA 61-64

Wahlöö, Peter 1926-1975
See Wahlöö, Per

Wain, John (Barrington)
1925- ....CLC 2, 11, 15, 46
See also CAAS 4
See also CA 5-8R
See also DLB 15, 27

Wajda, Andrzej 1926-............CLC 16
See also CA 102

Wakefield, Dan 1932-..............CLC 7
See also CAAS 7
See also CA 21-24R

Wakoski, Diane
1937-...........CLC 2, 4, 7, 9, 11, 40
See also CAAS 1
See also CANR 9
See also CA 13-16R
See also DLB 5

Walcott, Derek (Alton)
1930-...........CLC 2, 4, 9, 14, 25, 42
See also CA 89-92
See also DLB-Y 81

Waldman, Anne 1945- ....CLC 7
See also CA 37-40R
See also DLB 16

Waldo, Edward Hamilton 1918-
See Sturgeon, Theodore (Hamilton)

Walker, Alice
1944-..........CLC 5, 6, 9, 19, 27, 46
See also CANR 9
See also CA 37-40R
See also SATA 31
See also DLB 6, 33

Walker, David Harry 1911-........CLC 14
See also CANR 1
See also CA 1-4R
See also SATA 8

Walker, Edward Joseph 1934-
See Walker, Ted
See also CANR 12
See also CA 21-24R

Walker, George F. 1947- .... CLC 44 (329)
See also CANR 21
See also CA 103
See also DLB 60

Walker, Joseph A. 1935- ....CLC 19
See also CA 89-92
See also DLB 38

Walker, Margaret (Abigail)
1915-..................... CLC 1, 6
See also CA 73-76

Walker, Ted 1934-................CLC 13
See also Walker, Edward Joseph
See also DLB 40

Wallace, David Foster
1962-.................. CLC 50 (92)

Wallace, Irving 1916- .... CLC 7, 13
See also CAAS 1
See also CANR 1
See also CA 1-4R
See also AITN 1

Wallant, Edward Lewis
1926-1962.............. CLC 5, 10
See also CANR 22
See also CA 1-4R
See also DLB 2, 28

Walpole, Horace 1717-1797.......... LC 2
See also DLB 39

Walpole, (Sir) Hugh (Seymour)
1884-1941.................. TCLC 5
See also CA 104
See also DLB 34

Walser, Martin 1927- ....CLC 27
See also CANR 8
See also CA 57-60

Walser, Robert 1878-1956....... TCLC 18
See also CA 118

Walsh, Gillian Paton 1939-
See Walsh, Jill Paton
See also CA 37-40R
See also SATA 4

Walsh, Jill Paton 1939-............CLC 35
See also CLR 2
See also SAAS 3

Wambaugh, Joseph (Aloysius, Jr.)
1937-..................... CLC 3, 18
See also CA 33-36R
See also DLB 6
See also DLB-Y 83
See also AITN 1

Ward, Arthur Henry Sarsfield 1883-1959
See Rohmer, Sax
See also CA 108

Ward, Douglas Turner 1930-.......CLC 19
See also CA 81-84
See also DLB 7, 38

Warhol, Andy 1928-1987..........CLC 20
See also CA 89-92
See also obituary CA 121

Warner, Francis (Robert le Plastrier)
1937-.......................CLC 14
See also CANR 11
See also CA 53-56

Warner, Rex (Ernest)
1905-1986....................CLC 45
See also CA 89-92
See also obituary CA 119
See also DLB 15

Warner, Sylvia Townsend
1893-1978................ CLC 7, 19
See also CANR 16
See also CA 61-64
See also obituary CA 77-80
See also DLB 34

Warren, Mercy Otis
1728-1814.................. NCLC 13
See also DLB 31

Warren, Robert Penn
1905-....... CLC 1, 4, 6, 8, 10, 13, 18,
39 (254)
See also CANR 10
See also CA 13-16R
See also SATA 46
See also DLB 2, 48
See also DLB-Y 80
See also AITN 1

Washington, Booker T(aliaferro)
1856-1915......... TCLC 10, CLC 34
See also CA 114
See also SATA 28

Wassermann, Jakob
1873-1934.................. TCLC 6
See also CA 104

Wasserstein, Wendy 1950-.........CLC 32
See also CA 121

Waterhouse, Keith (Spencer)
1929-.......................CLC 47
See also CA 5-8R
See also DLB 13, 15

Waters, Roger 1944-
See Pink Floyd

Wa Thiong'o, Ngugi
1938-.............CLC 3, 7, 13, 36
See also Ngugi, James (Thiong'o)
See also Ngugi wa Thiong'o

Watkins, Vernon (Phillips)
1906-1967....................CLC 43
See also CAP 1
See also obituary CA 25-28R
See also CA 9-10
See also DLB 20

Waugh, Auberon (Alexander)
1939-.......................CLC 7
See also CANR 6, 22
See also CA 45-48
See also DLB 14

Waugh, Evelyn (Arthur St. John)
1903-1966..... CLC 1, 3, 8, 13, 19, 27,
44 (520)
See also CANR 22
See also CA 85-88
See also obituary CA 25-28R
See also DLB 15

Waugh, Harriet 1944-..............CLC 6
See also CANR 22
See also CA 85-88

Webb, Beatrice (Potter) 1858-1943
See Webb, Beatrice (Potter) and Webb,
Sidney (James)
See also CA 117

Webb, Beatrice (Potter) 1858-1943 and
Webb, Sidney (James)
1859-1947.................. TCLC 22

Webb, Charles (Richard) 1939-......CLC 7
See also CA 25-28R

Webb, James H(enry), Jr.
1946-.......................CLC 22
See also CA 81-84

Webb, Mary (Gladys Meredith)
1881-1927.................. TCLC 24
See also DLB 34

CLC Cumulative Nationality Index

ALGERIAN
Camus, Albert **1, 2, 4, 9, 11, 14, 32**
Cohen-Solal, Annie **50**

ALSATIAN
Arp, Jean **5**

AMERICAN
Abbey, Edward **36**
Abbott, Lee K., Jr. **48**
Abish, Walter **22**
Abrahams, Peter **4**
Abrams, M. H. **24**
Acker, Kathy **45**
Adams, Alice **6, 13, 46**
Addams, Charles **30**
Adler, C. S. **35**
Adler, Renata **8, 31**
Ai **4, 14**
Aiken, Conrad **1, 3, 5, 10**
Albee, Edward **1, 2, 3, 5, 9, 11, 13, 25**
Alexander, Lloyd **35**
Algren, Nelson **4, 10, 33**
Allen, Woody **16**
Alta **19**
Alter, Robert B. **34**
Alther, Lisa **7, 41**
Altman, Robert **16**
Ammons, A. R. **2, 3, 5, 8, 9, 25**
Anaya, Rudolfo A. **23**
Anderson, Jon **9**
Anderson, Poul **15**
Anderson, Robert **23**
Angell, Roger **26**
Angelou, Maya **12, 35**
Anthony Piers **35**
Apple, Max **9, 33**
Archer, Jules **12**

Arnow, Harriette **2, 7, 18**
Arrick, Fran **30**
Ashbery, John **2, 3, 4, 6, 9, 13, 15, 25, 41**
Asimov, Isaac **1, 3, 9, 19, 26**
Auchincloss, Louis **4, 6, 9, 18, 45**
Auden, W. H. **1, 2, 3, 4, 6, 9, 11, 14, 43**
Auel, Jean M. **31**
Auster, Paul **47**
Bach, Richard **14**
Baker, Elliott **8**
Baker, Russell **31**
Bakshi, Ralph **26**
Baldwin, James **1, 2, 3, 4, 5, 8, 13, 15, 17, 42, 50**
Bambara, Toni Cade **19**
Banks, Russell **37**
Baraka, Imamu Amiri **1, 2, 3, 5, 10, 14, 33**
Barbera, Jack **44**
Barnard, Mary **48**
Barnes, Djuna **3, 4, 8, 11, 29**
Barrett, William **27**
Barth, John **1, 2, 3, 5, 7, 9, 10, 14, 27**
Barthelme, Donald **1, 2, 3, 5, 6, 8, 13, 23, 46**
Barthelme, Frederick **36**
Baumbach, Jonathan **6, 23**
Baxter, Charles **45**
Beagle, Peter S. **7**
Beattie, Ann **8, 13, 18, 40**
Becker, Walter **26**
Beecher, John **6**
Behrman, S. N. **40**
Belitt, Ben **22**
Bell, Madison Smartt **41**
Bell, Marvin **8, 31**
Bellow, Saul **1, 2, 3, 6, 8, 10, 13, 15, 25, 33, 34**

Benary-Isbert, Margot **12**
Benchley, Peter **4, 8**
Benedikt, Michael **4, 14**
Bennett, Hal **5**
Bennett, Jay **35**
Benson, Jackson J. **34**
Benson, Sally **17**
Bentley, Eric **24**
Berger, Melvin **12**
Berger, Thomas **3, 5, 8, 11, 18, 38**
Bergstein, Eleanor **4**
Berrigan, Daniel J. **4**
Berrigan, Ted **37**
Berry, Chuck **17**
Berry, Wendell **4, 6, 8, 27, 46**
Berryman, John **1, 2, 3, 4, 6, 8, 10, 13, 25**
Bessie, Alvah **23**
Betts, Doris **3, 6, 28**
Bidart, Frank **33**
Bishop, Elizabeth **1, 4, 9, 13, 15, 32**
Bishop, John **10**
Blackburn, Paul **9, 43**
Blackmur, R. P. **2, 24**
Blaise, Clark **29**
Blatty, William Peter **2**
Blish, James **14**
Bloch, Robert **33**
Bloom, Harold **24**
Blount, Roy, Jr. **38**
Blume, Judy **12, 30**
Bly, Robert **1, 2, 5, 10, 15, 38**
Bochco, Steven **35**
Bogan, Louise **4, 39, 46**
Bogosian, Eric **45**
Bograd, Larry **35**
Bonham, Frank **12**
Bontemps, Arna **1, 18**

Booth, Philip **23**
Booth, Wayne C. **24**
Bourjaily, Vance **8**
Bova, Ben **45**
Bowers, Edgar **9**
Bowles, Jane **3**
Bowles, Paul **1, 2, 19**
Boyle, Kay **1, 5, 19**
Boyle, T. Coraghessan **36**
Bradbury, Ray **1, 3, 10, 15, 42**
Bradley, David, Jr. **23**
Bradley, Marion Zimmer **30**
Brammer, William **31**
Brancato, Robin F. **35**
Brand, Millen **7**
Branden, Barbara **44**
Branley, Franklyn M. **21**
Brautigan, Richard **1, 3, 5, 9, 12, 34, 42**
Brennan, Maeve **5**
Breslin, Jimmy **4, 43**
Bridgers, Sue Ellen **26**
Brin, David **34**
Brodsky, Joseph **4, 6, 13, 36, 50**
Brodsky, Michael **19**
Bromell, Henry **5**
Broner, E. M. **19**
Bronk, William **10**
Brooks, Cleanth **24**
Brooks, Gwendolyn **1, 2, 4, 5, 15, 49**
Brooks, Mel **12**
Brooks, Peter **34**
Brooks, Van Wyck **29**
Brosman, Catharine Savage **9**
Broughton, T. Alan **19**
Broumas, Olga **10**
Brown, Claude **30**
Brown, Dee **18, 47**

Nationality Index

Nationality Index

CLC-50 Title Index